The Phenomenology of Intelligence-focused Remote Sensing

Volume 1: Electro-optical Remote Sensing

The Phenomenology of Intelligence-focused Remote Sensing is the first-of-its-kind textbook to include phenomenology, sensors, and intelligence applications under one cover. It builds on over three decades of specialized instruction in electro-optical remote sensing technologies and geospatial applications. Authored by Riverside Research's Senior Technical Experts under a Cooperative Research and Development Agreement with the Air Force Institute of Technology, this textbook thoroughly discusses all the necessary elements of spatial, spectral, and temporal signature collection in the visible and infrared, including non-literal imagery interpretation, thermal, reflective, and polarimetric target characterization, radiative transfer, advanced technical intelligence collection systems, and data processing, analysis, and exploitation techniques. This text is a valuable resource for faculty, staff, students, and personnel across the spectrum of academia, government, and industry. This book is scientifically and mathematically correct and rigorous, but it emphasizes conceptual understanding with numerous examples drawn from geospatial intelligence areas of interest.

Howard Evans • James Lange • James Schmitz

Copyright © 2014 Riverside Research

Riverside Research
156 William Street, 9th Floor
New York, NY 10038
Email: textbook@riversideresearch.org
www.riversideresearch.org

Library of Congress Cataloging-in-Publication Data:
Evans, Howard.
The phenomenology of intelligence-focused remote sensing / Howard Evans, James Lange, James Schmitz.
ISBN 978-0-9833620-4-3
2013950153

First Edition, Hardback - published 2015
The Phenomenology of Intelligence-focused Remote Sensing, Pre-release - Copyright © 2014 Riverside Research
ISBN 978-0-9833620-5-0 (First Edition) - ISBN 978-0-9833620-4-3 (Pre-release)
10 9 8 7 6 5 4 3 2 1

All rights reserved. No part of this publication may be reproduced or distributed in any form or by any means without written permission from the publisher. This work was created in the performance of a Cooperative Research and Development Agreement with the Department of the Air Force. The Government of the United States has certain rights to use this work.

Printed in the United States of America

This textbook was reviewed for security concerns. The views expressed in this document are those of the authors and do not reflect the official policy or position of Riverside Research, the Air Force Institute of Technology, the Intelligence Community, the United States Air Force, Department of Defense, or the United States Government.

Managing Editor: Taylor Renner, Riverside Research
Technical Reviewer: Dr. Ronald Tuttle, AFIT Faculty and Former Center Director of the
  AFIT Center for Technical Intelligence Studies and Research
Graphic Designer: Jerome Gantner

CONTENTS

FOREWORD VI
PREFACE VIII
ACKNOWLEDGEMENTS IX
SUPPORT WEBSITE X

1 INTRODUCTION 1
1.1 INTELLIGENCE   2
1.2 ATI MANAGEMENT   6
1.3 ROADMAP   8

2 LIGHT EMITTING TARGETS 11
2.1 LIGHT WAVES AND PARTICLES   12
2.2 IDEAL THERMAL SOURCES   16
2.3 REAL THERMAL SOURCES   22
2.4 SELECTIVE SOURCES I: ATOMS   27
2.5 SELECTIVE SOURCES II: MOLECULES   32
2.6 SELECTIVE SOURCES III: ENSEMBLES   43

3 TARGET REFLECTIVE SIGNATURES 53
3.1 TARGET CHARACTERISTICS   54
3.2 REFLECTION AND POLARIZATION   59

4 RADIOMETRY 73
4.1 RADIOMETRIC QUANTITIES   74
4.2 RADIATIVE TRANSFER   88
4.3 METRICS   99

5 ATMOSPHERIC EFFECTS 109
5.1 THE ATMOSPHERE   110
5.2 BEER'S LAW   118
5.3 PROCESSES   123

6 GATHERING INFORMATION: OPTICS 141
6.1 LENS & MIRROR   142
6.2 OPTICAL TRANSMISSION FACTOR   149
6.3 POINT SPREAD FUNCTION   154

7 PHOTOELECTRIC DETECTORS 159
7.1 RADIATION DETECTION   160
7.2 FOCAL PLANE ARRAYS   165
7.3 PHOTODETECTOR CHARACTERISTICS   171
7.4 PHOTODETECTOR OPERATION   176

8 SPATIAL IMAGING PROPERTIES 181
8.1 SPATIAL RESOLUTION   182
8.2 CALCULATING SPATIAL SAMPLING   186

9 SPECTRAL FILTERS 193
9.1 REQUIREMENTS AND APPROACHES   194
9.2 GENERALIZED INTERFERENCE OF TWO LIGHT WAVES   195
9.3 THIN FILM FILTERS   197

10 SIGNALS AND NOISE 205
- 10.1 END-TO-END EQUATIONS — 206
- 10.2 IMPROVING COLLECTIONS — 213
- 10.3 NOISE SOURCES — 214

11 PLATFORMS AND ORBITS 221
- 11.1 PLATFORMS USED FOR REMOTE SENSING — 222
- 11.2 SATELLITE ORBITS — 224
- 11.3 AIRBORNE VS SPACEBORNE SENSING — 235

12 COLLECTION STRATEGIES 237
- 12.1 COLLECTION CONSIDERATIONS — 238
- 12.2 STARING SENSORS — 240
- 12.3 SCANNING SENSORS — 242
- 12.4 TEMPORAL SAMPLING — 247
- 12.5 SPECTRAL SAMPLING — 250

13 TEMPORAL SENSING: TARGETS & SIGNATURES 253
- 13.1 SENSORS — 254
- 13.2 PERSISTENT EVENTS — 256
- 13.3 TRANSIENT TARGETS — 264

14 INTERPRETING NON-LITERAL FPA DATA 271
- 14.1 PROCESSING — 272
- 14.2 ANALYSIS — 276
- 14.3 EXPLOITATION — 283

15 CLASSICAL MSI IN THE VISIBLE TO SWIR 287
- 15.1 COLLECTION OPTIONS AND ISSUES — 288
- 15.2 LANDSAT — 292
- 15.3 APPLICATIONS AND ALGORITHMS — 297
- 15.4 OTHER MSI SPACEBORNE SENSORS — 317

16 MSI INVOLVING THE THERMAL INFRARED 321
- 16.1 METEOROLOGICAL SATELLITES — 322
- 16.2 SURFACE TEMPERATURE DETERMINATION — 328
- 16.3 MSI FAR OFF-NADIR VIEWING — 343

17 HSI TECHNIQUES 349
- 17.1 HSI SENSOR PERFORMANCE CHARACTERISTICS — 350
- 17.2 PRISMS — 351
- 17.3 DIFFRACTION GRATINGS — 360
- 17.4 THIN FILM INTERFERENCE APPLIED TO SPECTROMETERS — 375
- 17.5 FOURIER TRANSFORM SPECTROMETERS — 380
- 17.6 HSI COLLECTION OPTIONS AND ISSUES — 388

18 HSI IN THE VISIBLE TO SWIR 391
- 18.1 AIRBORNE HSI SYSTEMS — 392
- 18.2 AIRBORNE HSI APPLICATIONS AND DATA ANALYSIS — 393
- 18.3 SPACEBORNE HSI SENSORS — 407

19 HSI IN THE THERMAL INFRARED 409
- 19.1 APPLICATIONS — 410
- 19.2 HSI SENSORS — 413
- 19.3 ALGORITHMS AND APPLICATIONS — 414

20 HSI GAS DETECTION INCLUDING IDENTIFICATION 419
  20.1 AIRBORNE HSI FOR GAS DETECTION — 420
  20.2 GROUND-BASED HSI FOR GAS DETECTION — 423
  20.3 ACTIVE SPECTRAL SENSING FOR GAS AND AEROSOL DETECTION — 426

21 POLARIMETRIC IMAGING 431
  21.1 SPECULAR VERSUS DIFFUSE REFLECTION — 432
  21.2 SOURCES, COLLECTION, AND DETECTION OF LINEARLY POLARIZED LIGHT — 437
  21.3 APPLICATIONS AND COLLECTION GEOMETRIES FOR LINEAR POLARIMETRIC IMAGING — 444

22 THE FUTURE OF REMOTE SENSING 449
  22.1 GROUPING REMOTE SENSING APPLICATIONS — 450
  22.2 APPLICATION CLASSES — 450
  22.3 SPECIFIC INTERESTS — 457
  22.4 SUMMARY — 464

REFERENCES 467

ACRONYMS 474

NOMENCLATURE 478

INDEX 485

ADDITIONAL SOURCES FOR INFORMATION 494

AUTHOR BIOGRAPHIES 498

This textbook was reviewed for security concerns. The views expressed in this document are those of the authors and do not reflect the official policy or position of Riverside Research, the Air Force Institute of Technology, the Intelligence Community, the United States Air Force, Department of Defense, or the United States Government.

FOREWORD

Since its earliest days as the "Air School of Application" in 1919, the Air Force Institute of Technology's (AFIT) mission has been to provide relevant, defense-focused education to its students. In carrying out this mission, AFIT offers numerous programs in key technical research areas related to various defense-related activities, particularly those related to the science, technology, engineering, and mathematics (STEM) areas. Over time, applications of specific AFIT education and research activities were found to support the measurement and signature (MASINT) intelligence discipline in the area of remote sensing phenomenology. As students were learning to apply quantitative and qualitative techniques to analyze the physical attributes of targets and events, a new AFIT center was created to provide defense-focused research at security classification levels which met the Intelligence Community (IC) criteria. This was the catalyst for the creation of AFIT's Center for Measurement and Signature Intelligence Studies and Research (CMSR).

Over a decade ago, beginning in 2002, the CMSR, with sponsorship and support from the US Army Deputy Chief of Staff for Intelligence, developed and offered the MASINT Certificate Program (MCP). The purpose of the MCP was to provide a rigorous academic program, focused on unique MASINT intelligence disciplines, which would serve military, government civilian, government contractors, and other civilians operating in the IC. The curriculum concentrated on the phenomenologies of electro-optical (EO), Infrared (IR), Thermal Infrared (TIR), Synthetic Aperture Radar (SAR), Multi-Spectral Imagery (MSI), and Hyper-Spectral Imagery (HSI).

With the creation of the National Geospatial Intelligence Agency (NGA), and new direction provided by the Director of National Intelligence (DNI), the roles and responsibilities of the IC were further refined and defined. In keeping pace with the dynamic and ever evolving mission of the IC, the CMSR and MCP also evolved: the certificate program transformed into the Advanced Geospatial Intelligence (AGI) IR/SAR Certificate Program (ACP) in 2006 and the CMSR was later renamed as the Center for Technical Intelligence Studies and Research (CTISR). AFIT's efforts to stay in-step with the community's evolution, and its contributions to the IC were formally recognized in 2005 with the first NGA Director's Award for AGI to the MCP team. The award cited the MCP as "the 'education' element guide used for Advanced Geospatial Intelligence training and education."

Since a graduate-level textbook that specifically addressed the content of the ACP curriculum did not exist, the AFIT instructor cadre, consisting of DOD, IC, and commercial industry subject matter experts, created detailed technical notes, presentations, and tailored laboratory exercises for the program. It became apparent over time that a comprehensive, graduate-level textbook was needed. Thus, the idea was born to engage in a collaborative DOD, academia, and industry effort to create such a textbook.

In 2010, AFIT and Riverside Research, the not-for-profit AFIT team member who helped to create the MCP/ACP, signed a Cooperative Research and Development Agreement (CRADA) to create an "Advanced Geospatial Intelligence Textbook," which would not only support the intelligence-related instructional and research missions of AFIT, but could also support the diverse missions and objectives of the numerous IC partners, particularly those in the GEOINT, MASINT, and other STEM-related fields. These IC partners include a large and diverse cadre of technicians, academics, professionals, and leaders located in local, state, and federal government offices and agencies, academic institutions, and commercial and private industrial sectors, all serving to accomplish our nation's homeland security and national defense missions. The fruitful effort of this CRADA is this book, *The Phenomenology of Intelligence-focused Remote Sensing, Volume I: Electro-optical Remote Sensing*.

As a civilian leader of a military academic organization supported by our industry partners, I have the distinct advantage of seeing how important a textbook of this nature is to the DOD, IC, and the nation. Not only will this contribute to the ever growing body of STEM knowledge integral to the DOD and IC, it will also serve as an important tool in the education of future military officers and civilian leaders serving in the arenas of intelligence and remote sensing. AFIT is proud to be a contributor to this effort, and it is our hope that this textbook will not only become a valuable teaching tool for students, but that it will also be a valuable reference tool for our nation's intelligence and remote sensing professionals.

Dr. Todd I. Stewart
Major General, United States Air Force (Retired)
Director and Chancellor
Air Force Institute of Technology

PREFACE

We, the authors, have collectively served the United States for over 100 years as active duty military personnel and contributors to the Intelligence Community (IC). We raised our hands and pledged to "… support and defend the Constitution of the United States against all enemies, foreign and domestic; … bear true faith and allegiance to the same; … take this obligation freely, without any mental reservation or purpose of evasion; and … well and faithfully discharge the office …" and we are still doing this today. This book is a part of our continuing contribution.

This textbook arises from our four-course sequence on remote sensing, with applications from the IC, taught at the Air Force Institute of Technology (AFIT), Wright-Patterson Air Force Base, Ohio from 2002 through 2013. The genesis of these courses was AFIT's Graduate Space Operations Master of Science degree program, which educated officers for the Air Force Space Command and other agencies. As operational requirements for technical intelligence providers and analysts became more critical, particularly in the post-September 11, 2001 environment, the remote sensing portion of this degree was packaged into AFIT's first certificate program, known as the Advanced Geospatial Intelligence Infrared/Synthetic Aperture Radar Certificate Program. This ten-week program provided a fundamental education in remote sensing phenomenology with direct application to IC missions. Each course was three-credit hours (30 contact hours) at the senior undergraduate or introductory graduate level, but was taught in a non-traditional, concentrated two-week block. These courses were also offered as distance learning courses for students unable to attend in residence, supporting students from all operational theaters. In the eleven years of the program, over 400 analysts and managers benefited from this education.

In this book, the term "Advanced Technical Intelligence (ATI)" is used to aid the educational process. As explained in Chapter 1, our use of ATI is broadly defined as the information collected using remote sensors to form images and interpreted using digital signal processing methods. Prior to 2005, most of the material contained in this book fell under the broad discipline known as "Measurement and Signature Intelligence (MASINT)." However, over the years of our service, other terms have since evolved to encompass these activities, to include "Imagery-Derived MASINT," "non-literal Geospatial Intelligence (GEOINT)," "Advanced Geospatial Intelligence (AGI)," and "Full-Spectrum GEOINT."

This text is a valuable resource for faculty, staff, students, and personnel across the spectrum of academia, government, and industry. It is anticipated the typical reader will possess a degree in science, engineering, mathematics, or technology. While this text is mathematically, scientifically, and technically correct, conceptual understanding is emphasized over manipulative sophistication (i.e., no theorems and proofs). In a few chapters, the calculus and physics theories may present a challenge to the casual reader. We assume the typical reader has been exposed to at least some of the physical concepts involved, for example the thin lens formula and the photoelectric effect, but has never had a remote sensing course that ties all these concepts together: target characteristics, propagation, attenuation, collection, detection, processing, analysis, exploitation, and production. Thus, we emphasize advanced technical intelligence as the result of correctly selecting and linking these concepts together with what we call phenomenology. This volume, Volume I: Electro-optical Remote Sensing, is part of a planned technical series to support the transmission of fundamental scientific knowledge to the broader science, technology, engineering, and math (STEM), DOD, and intelligence communities.

As a supplement to this text, additional suggested reading, homework problems and solutions, interactive tools, and other supplemental materials have been compiled on a support website, which is referenced throughout the text. Readers can access these materials by visiting: **www.riversideresearch.org/textbook**

As with any first edition textbook, we are certain that our efforts are incomplete. We welcome any feedback or suggestions to improve the readability and utility of this text. Our greatest hope is you will find it useful in your career.

Howard Evans, James Lange, James Schmitz

ACKNOWLEDGEMENTS

We thank many who provided help and insight in the development and presentation of the technical aspects of this material. Foremost are the faculty of the Air Force Institute of Technology (AFIT) who assisted in the pedagogy with many useful discussions, reviews, and comments: Dr. Steven Fiorino, Dr. Robert Hengehold, the late Dr. Ted Luke, Dr. Michael Marciniak, Dr. Glen P. Perram, Col. Karl Walli, and others who have escaped our memories. Also helpful were AFIT staff members, Mr. J.D. Hailbronner, Ms. Michelle Via, Mr. Joe Sugrue, Mr. Joshua Wilson, and others. We thank Dr. Todd I. Stewart, Dr. Heidi R. Ries, and Dr. Robert A. Calico, Jr., for their support in promoting this work, and we especially appreciate the final review led by Dr. David Bunker. Naturally, we thank all our AFIT students, over 400 during the past ten years, for their comments and feedback on course notes which served as the basis for this text. Without our students, this text would not exist.

Special acknowledgment is due to Dr. Ronald Tuttle for his role in the development of the textbook. Dr. Tuttle's contributions began as the founder and first Director of the AFIT Center for Technical Intelligence Studies and Research (CTISR, originally the Center for MASINT Studies and Research, CMSR). In his role as Center Director, Dr. Tuttle initiated and directed the MASINT Certificate Program, later called the Advanced Geospatial Intelligence IR/SAR Certificate Program. This program was the catalyst for the creation of this textbook to fill the need for a graduate-level technical reference text that fully addressed the certificate program curriculum. In addition to supporting the development of this text from its inception, Dr. Tuttle provided a thorough technical review of all the chapters. His technical comments were essential to the accuracy and clarity of this text.

Several members of the professional staff at Riverside Research supported and contributed to the development of this text. We thank Mr. Richard Annas, Ms. Mary Barefoot-Greiner, Mr. Robin Gibson, Mr. Shawn Kalis, Ms. Jan Long, Mr. Michael D. Nelson, and Mr. Joel Rieman for supporting this endeavor. Special thanks to Ms. Taylor Renner for her long hours spent managing the compilation of this text. Ms. Danielle Righi and Mr. Clinton J. Asbury, III tirelessly obtained the figure permissions. We express our gratitude to Ms. Jamie Howard, Mr. Casey Johnson, Ms. Lisa Williams, Ms. Stacy Burns, and Mr. Jerome Gantner for their graphics support. We appreciate Mr. Larry Benson, Mr. Rondle L. Cole, Mr. Theodore Josue, Dr. Nicholas Scott, and Mr. James F. (Bill) Setchell, Jr. for their technical contributions and support. We also thank Ms. Stephanie LaPlant, Mr. Benjamin Leach, and Mr. Steve Yantko for their contributions.

Additionally, we would like to acknowledge and thank many of our government and industry associates who provided inputs, commentary, and critical assessment of various pieces of material. We also want to recognize the technical expertise and outstanding insights into the science and phenomenology of remote sensing provided by Dr. Joseph Bastian, Ms. Susan Boyd, Mr. Robert Cody, Dr. James Stark Draper, Ms. Kori Elder, Mr. James Engel, Dr. James Grigsby, Mr. Larry Lillard, Mr. John Morris, Dr. David L. Perry, Dr. Martin Pilati, Mr. Nathan E. Setters, and Ms. Sharon Staley. In particular, dedication of this finished work goes to the inspiration provided by the late Dr. Judy King and the late Mr. Ken Miller, whose unparalleled knowledge and efforts greatly contributed to the world of technical intelligence.

SUPPORT WEBSITE

A Support Website has been established as a supplement to this textbook. This Support Website is referenced throughout the textbook and contains additional suggested reading, homework problems and solutions, interactive tools, and other supplemental materials to aid in the understanding of the content. Readers can access this support website by visiting:

www.riversideresearch.org/textbook

1 INTRODUCTION

The emphasis of this text is to provide a technically accurate foundation for understanding remote sensing and its role in supporting the various missions of the Department of Defense and the Intelligence Community. The approach is to first limit the discussion to what can be learned by collecting information in the visible through thermal infrared portion of the electromagnetic spectrum (roughly 0.4–12 µm). Second, the following chapters methodically examine the scientific details of targets (spatial, spectral, and temporal), propagation (radiometry), attenuation (atmospherics), and the technologies of collection (optics), detection (focal plane arrays (FPAs)), and Digital Signal Processing (DSP) (analysis, processing, and exploitation). Selecting the appropriate pieces of science and technology from this list results in a phenomenological solution to answer the fundamental question, "What is out there?"

This chapter shows the need for information and relates the place of visible through thermal infrared remote sensing in providing that information, here called Advanced Technical Intelligence (ATI), to people or agencies who need to know and act on the question's answer. Ultimately, the reports resulting from application of the ATI methods presented in this text will provide those decision makers the means to interpret the content and significance of collection products such as the multispectral image above.

SECTIONS
1.1 INTELLIGENCE
1.2 ADVANCED TECHNICAL INTELLIGENCE MANAGEMENT
1.3 ROADMAP

1.1 INTELLIGENCE

Since the word intelligence is used in the title of this book, its meaning in this context will be explained.

INFORMATION

To make correct decisions affecting international policies, economic strategies, defensive postures, etc., it is imperative to have sufficient information. Therefore, all governments (and many other organizations) establish intelligence agencies to learn about their adversaries. The goal of those agencies, using methods called INTs, is to gather as much of the needed information as possible, often clandestinely, and package it into concise products for their customers.[1] *Judgments, or assessments, (not the information itself) based on those products which establish the opponent's motive, infer intent, or predict behavior are intelligence.* Some of the products, like images of recent battlespace activity, are amenable to immediate judgement by operational customers, while other products require considerable time to process and correlate with additional collected information.

There are three important features of the products generated by the intelligence agencies. First, they are necessarily incomplete because a report cannot *ever* capture 100% of the information about any objective, i.e., an activity or weapon system. That is because it is not possible to make observations from *all* directions at *all* times using *all* relevant methods. Second, (and as a consequence of the first feature) for products to be useful, they *must* clearly state the limitations of their information or their degree of uncertainty. Third, products must be provided to customers on a timely basis. Therefore, the purpose of an intelligence product is to provide *information* and facts to the extent to which they are known, *not* to speculate their significance. Thus, it is strictly inappropriate to call the products "intelligence," because without judgments, inferences, and predictions, they are only *information*. In summary, intelligence is the application of these products to assist Governments in rendering judgments to project economic, political, and military power.

Therefore, intelligence collection is nothing more than information gathering. In this text, *technical* intelligence collection refers to methods that use high-tech electronic devices to gather information. *Advanced* technical intelligence collection means the intelligence agencies must use scientific principles and mathematical algorithms to process gathered information into products for their customers. The sheer volume of information now collected by technical sensors necessitates that increasingly more of the work be relegated to semi-autonomous processing.

INFORMATION GATHERING

There are essentially two ways to gather information: 1) by *direct contact* with the person, object, activity, or event;[2] or 2) by observation from afar. Observing from afar is called *remote sensing*; although the term will be expanded beyond its familiar usage. To most of the non-intelligence world, remote sensing means the use of commercially available multi-spectral, thermal, and radar images for land utilization studies, crop yield predictions, mineral prospecting, and similar activities. Although that is true, the use of the phrase in this text will incorporate *all* information gathering using non-direct contact.

Direct contact information gathering conjures up visions of spying, which is partially true. Human Intelligence (HUMINT), largely the

---

[1] Customers can include government branches, departments, agencies, commissions, or any other office. Military units from major commands to troops in the field can be customers. The customer is both the requester of information and the end user of the products.

[2] What's in a word? Calling a person, an object, an activity, or an event the target of interest should not confuse anyone. However, some would insist that targets are only the objects killed. Merely gathering information does not kill anything directly. However, in this text, objects will be freely and conversationally referred to as targets.

purview of the Central Intelligence Agency (CIA), is about direct contact in one form or another. For this discussion, Open Source Intelligence (OSINT) could be considered direct contact information gathering, as could Foreign Materiel Exploitation (FME). In today's world, Computer-Internet Intelligence (CYBERINT) also falls into this category.

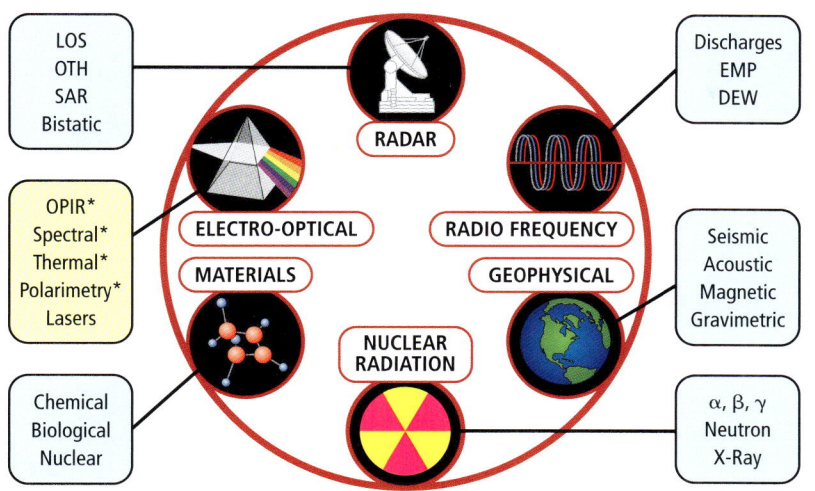

Figure 1-1
The original sub-disciplines of MASINT.

*Discussed in this text.

Remote sensing information gathering is everything else that is *not* collected by direct contact. Originally, it included traditional IMagery INTelligence (IMINT),[3] mostly the responsibility of the National Geospatial-Intelligence Agency (NGA); SIGnals INTelligence (SIGINT),[4] mostly the responsibility of the National Security Agency (NSA); and Measurement and Signature INTelligence (MASINT),[5] mostly the responsibility of the Defense Intelligence Agency (DIA). MASINT initially encompassed six[6] sub-disciplines, tied together by common phenomenology: electro-optics (EO), geophysical, materials, nuclear radiation, radar, and radio frequency (RF) (**Figure 1-1**). More recently, some parts of the electro-optical and radar sub-disciplines were combined together with IMINT into GEOspatial INTelligence (GEOINT) under NGA. The phenomenology discussed in this text is broadly applicable to all six sub-disciplines, but the emphasis is on EO, principally Overhead Persistent InfraRed (OPIR), spectral, thermal, and polarimetric remote sensing. **Figure 1-2** shows the overall schema. (Note, GEOINT includes these areas and Synthetic Aperture Radar (SAR).)

[3] IMINT is imagery taken from aircraft or satellites, and PHOTINT is imagery taken by hand-held cameras.

[4] The primary subdisciplines of SIGINT are Electronic Signals Intelligence (ELINT), Communications Intelligence (COMINT), and Foreign Instrumentation Signals Intelligence (FISINT).

[5] MASINT was conceived as a catch-all for everything that was not HUMINT, IMINT, or SIGINT. But, because of the diversity of its technical information gathering methods, it has been logically divided amongst CIA, NGA, DIA, and some specialized agencies. The word is still used and refers to non-literal (metrics and signature) interpretation of collected data.

[6] Informally, a seventh sub-discipline of MASINT is biometrics, relating to non-traditional means for personal recognition such as body temperature, distinguishing odors, and characteristic gaits.

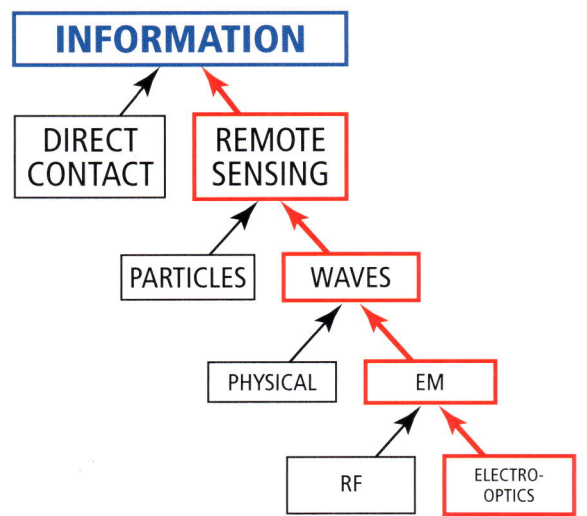

Figure 1-2
The hierarchy of ATI gathering.

TECHNICAL INFORMATION GATHERING

To use remote sensing to learn about targets, *something* must pass between a target and an information gathering device (hereafter called a *remote sensor*) whether the target knows it or not. That carrier of information bears characteristics about the target's identity and nature, called the *signature*, and about the target's location and activity, called the *metrics*. The particular propagator of information can be either a particle or a wave.

Particles are common information carriers, and remote sensors were developed to collect many types of them. Nuclear particles, alphas and betas, escaping the shielding of their containers reveal the exact isotopes from which they originate. Atoms and molecules carried downwind from agricultural or industrial facilities have unique chemical properties identifying their sources. Debris from ash clouds and dust plumes can lead back to the events that created them. Conceivably, even bullets and projectiles can be considered particles, and collecting them provides the size and locations of the weapons from where they originated.

Waves are probably more ubiquitous than particles, and are perhaps more useful because of their longer range. They come in two types. The *first* type is the physical, or mechanical, wave; this wave requires an actual medium between the source and sensor to do the "waving." Examples of mechanical waves[7] are: 1) seismic waves which travel through the Earth, for which there are wide arrays of seismometers to detect and characterize them; 2) sound waves which travel through the oceans, for which SONAR was developed; and 3) acoustic waves which propagate through air and water, for which ACOUSTINT exists. The *second* type of wave is the electromagnetic (EM) wave; one in which the waving is done by electric and magnetic *fields*. The EM wave[8] is unique because it can propagate through a vacuum as well as solids, liquids, and gases. Later discussions will explain how EM waves interact with these media as a function of their wavelengths (or energies). These interactions make the EM wave ideal for remote sensing.

When considering gathering information propagated via EM waves, the focus is on a wave's impinging onto the remote sensor. Lower frequency, f (or longer wavelength, λ), waves spanning electric power transmission ($f \approx 60$ Hz) through millimeter radar ($f \approx 10^{12}$ Hz) are typically gathered by *antennas* connected to radio receivers. But, shorter wavelength (higher frequency) waves from extreme infrared ($\lambda \approx 10^{-4}$ m) through gamma rays ($\lambda \approx 10^{-12}$ m) are collected by *electro-optic* devices. Although there is some overlap in phenomenology between these two regimes, this difference in detection hardware serves as a primary discriminator between them.

This text concentrates on short wavelength (high frequency, high energy) detection and interpretation of EM wave information, called electro-optics.[9,10] The low frequency (long-wavelength, low energy) end of the EM spectrum, called RF,[11,12] involves significantly different sensors and analytical methods that are outside the scope of this text. (See **Figure 7-1** for more details.)

ADVANCED TECHNICAL INFORMATION GATHERING

As will be discussed in the opening chapters, all targets exhibit spectral, spatial, and temporal characteristics that make each class of target unique. These features of a target can be generalized as {TGT}. One goal of an intelligence agency employing remote sensing is to discover

---

[7] Mechanical waves can be either transverse or longitudinal propagating oscillations or disturbances of a medium. Transverse waves move at right angles to the direction of energy propagation, like surface waves on water for example. Longitudinal waves are pressure waves where the medium compresses and expands in the direction of energy propagation. Sound waves through solids, liquids, and gases (atmospheres) are longitudinal.

[8] Like their mechanical counterparts, EM waves can be transverse or longitudinal, depending on the electrical and magnetic properties of the medium they are propagating through. Only the transverse variety that dominates in transparent media (air and vacuum) will be considered.

[9] Hereinafter, the EM waves detected by EO sensors will be generically called light regardless of its wavelength. It is acknowledged that there is no scientific difference between the light and radio ends of the EM spectrum, but the technology is distinctly different.

[10] EO remote sensing is mostly passive, therefore clandestine, deployed sensors that operate in the waiting-for-information mode. The exception would be lidar, which is radar with lasers.

[11] Although these two classifications (EO and RF) are among the six named sub-disciplines of MASINT, the examples show the terms are intended to be much more inclusive of technical information gathering modes that share common methodology. For instance, radar is included in RF because it uses similar collection and signal processing.

[12] RF remote sensing can be both active and passive, but in either case, the phenomenology is the same as for EO sensing with appropriate interpretation.

those particular features of {TGT} that identify it for their customer. Since a remote sensor is not in direct contact with {TGT}, it is necessary for the remote sensor to form a faithful replica of {TGT} that bears all of the spatial, spectral, temporal, and radiometric characteristics of {TGT}. The replica is called an *image*,[13] {IMG}. The study of {IMG} implies the characteristics of {TGT}.

There are two aspects of the {TGT}-replica to be noted. *First*, as an amplification of an earlier statement, the replica is *not* perfect. As previously noted, {IMG} is formed by only one remote sensor looking from one direction at one time using only one small slice of the EM spectrum. Furthermore, some information about {TGT} is always lost before it is input to a remote sensor and the replica can be formed. The physical phenomenology[14] is

$$\{IMG\} \approx \{OPT\} \otimes \{ATTN\} \otimes \{PROP\} \otimes \{TGT\}, \quad (1\text{-}1)$$

where {PROP} is the science of EM energy *propagation*, {ATTN} is the science of atmospheric *attenuation*, and {OPT} is the science of *optics*. The symbol "$\otimes$" represents mathematical operations defined in each of the sections covering {PROP}, {ATTN}, and {OPT}. (See the sidebar **About Mathematics** on the next page.)

Second, the intelligence analyst will receive output from a remote sensor, but must understand that he/she is *not* looking directly at {IMG}. Rather, the analyst sees the result of the sensor's EO technology[15] having converted {IMG} into {DATA}:

$$\{DATA\} \approx \{TIME\} \otimes \{SPECT\} \otimes \{SPACE\} \otimes \{IMG\}, \quad (1\text{-}2)$$

where {SPACE}, {SPECT}, and {TIME} are the sensor's technology's spatial, spectral, and temporal *sampling* operations, respectively. This is a subtle, but crucial detail and is often ignored or perhaps not even recognized. It can make considerable difference when attempting to extract target information from sensor data, and even more so when results are compared among sensors. The origination of {SPACE}, {SPECT}, and {TIME} sampling and the associated strategies that can be used to take advantage of them will be discussed in their respective chapters in this text.

The bottom line is {DATA} *is* an image (a digital image to be sure) because 1) it is formed using a remote sensor's optics, {OPT}, to replicate the characteristics of {TGT}; and 2) it is recorded with a remote sensor's detector to preserve and measure those characteristics. The term 'advanced' as used within this text is an intelligence analyst's understanding and application of the underlying science and mathematics to reverse the physical and EO phenomenologies:

$$\{TGT\} \approx \{PROP\}^{-1}\{ATTN\}^{-1}\{OPT\}^{-1}\{SPACE\}^{-1}\{SPECT\}^{-1}\{TIME\}^{-1}\{DATA\}, \quad (1\text{-}3)$$

where the "-1" notation[16] means to "undo" what the operation "$\otimes$" has done. This task would appear formidable, especially considering the mountains of data streaming from modern sensors, but is generally tractable with modern computers. Indeed, since {DATA} is derived from an *image*, the analysis of remote sensor data falls within the realm of DSP, and is ideal for high-speed computing. The discussion of digital image interpretation will be directed to the extraction of *non-literal* information[17] from these images. Chapters in the last half of this text will explain, in general terms, how to unravel **Equation 1-3**.

---

[13] This is a generalized image, not necessarily a two-dimensional picture of a three-dimensional object that is typically shown in photographs. It is only important that this image has enough spatial, spectral, and temporal characteristics to identify its source target.

[14] The use of phenomenology means the science behind each step in the remote sensing process is independently well-understood, and can be freely chained together as needed to form an end-to-end model, even though there is nothing specific in the science that directs one to do so. It is just the right thing to do. Aside, many students who have used this text material in its original staff notes form have commented that they were familiar with some or all of the science topics, but had never considered them joined together into the remote sensing application. That is phenomenology.

[15] The EO technology primarily discussed in this book is the FPA, a two-dimensional grid of individual detectors called pixels. The word pixel is derived from picture element, and hence the output of a FPA is often associated with an ordinary photographic or video image.

[16] The notation "-1" normally means to use the mathematical reciprocal, but here it is used in a more generalized sense doing the inverse operation. For example, $\theta = \sin^{-1} x$ means to find the angle with a sine of x, not to divide one by sin x.

[17] Non-literal information is that which cannot be perceived by human vision. For example, most objects in a photograph can be recognized as what they are, but every object has a temperature. Temperature cannot be "seen." Nonetheless, with the proper kind of collection, temperature information is present in the image. Assignment of temperatures to objects requires extracting their radiometric properties, which is a particular type of signature.

ABOUT MATHEMATICS

This text is rigorously, scientifically, and mathematically correct. It includes some differential and integral calculus. To ease anxiety, the reader will not be required to actually calculate a derivative or an integral,[*] but rather the reader should understand what a derivative and an integral represent. It is important to know what an integral represents, because that is how remote sensors operate. **Equation 1-2**, in particular, expresses that a remote sensor always integrates (that is, *adds* or *accumulates*) its input over spectrum, space, and time to provide data output. All of this will be explained in later chapters.

Therefore, the reader is required to have some familiarity with basic algebraic operations (solve for the unknown), recollection of the trigonometric functions (sine, cosine, and tangent), knowledge of the exponential function (e^x) and the logarithm ($\ln x$), and a willingness to learn how to perform numerical calculations on a hand-held calculator or a computer. *Conceptual understanding is more important than being able to compute answers.* In fact, readers may be surprised at times at how *inexact* calculations are, hoping for answers that are correct within approximately 20%, because of the vast number of approximations, estimates, and even guesses made. Note, this point is emphasized by writing many equations with an "approximately equal to" sign, "$\approx$," to highlight the inexactness of the measurements.

[*] Advanced students can do analytic derivatives and integrals in some of the more difficult homework problems. Otherwise, just complete some *numerical* calculus using simple approximations. Some examples will be given, and odd-numbered homework problem solutions will also demonstrate the process and solution.

[18] Different agencies may use all or some of TCPED in their managment programs, or they may include other terms like requirements.

The solution of **Equation 1-3** yields two kinds of information depending on the depth of the science and mathematics applied to it: *observable* information and *derivable* information. Observables are exactly as they sound. Some property of {TGT} can be seen or measured directly, such as its size, shape, color, and location relative to its surroundings. For example, in a certain collection, a remote sensor's data is rendered into what looks like a photograph and an object is *observed* to be green and lumpy, visibly appearing to be like its surroundings. If the appropriate science and mathematics are applied to the spatial and spectral data from the sensor's detector, one may *derive* that the object is actually man-made. Both observables and derivables will be discussed when appropriate.

Again, any information about {TGT} learned from the study of {DATA} is incomplete. Thus, *all* intelligence products based on {DATA} are to be considered *estimates*, *not* truth. That is, precise, accurate, and timely intelligence assessments should always be caveated with margins of error associated with {DATA}, i.e., the limitations or uncertainties that are inherent in the products need to be clearly stated.

1.2 ATI MANAGEMENT

If ATI were a computer application, it would function in an operating system like Requirements-Collection-Production. (Some readers may recognize this as an abbreviated form of Tasking, Collecting, Processing, Exploitation, and Dissemination (TCPED[18]). Although this text is concerned with the technical side of remote sensing, some brief words about this management system, whence ATI receives its direction, funding, and support, are appropriate here.

REQUIREMENTS

ATI information gathering and eventual products begin and end with the customer. When customers need to know about an adversary's activities or weapon systems, known as target information, they prepare lists of Essential Elements of Information and submit them to the collection management committees for validation. Because the cost and sophistication of advanced technical collection sensors limits their numbers and specializes their capabilities by time, space, and spectrum, the collection management committees work with the customers to determine exactly what, how, when, and where collections are possible, and whether the collections will satisfy the customers' needs. Requirements that pass this negotiation stage are considered to be validated and are assessed for potential collection.

Just because a requirement has been validated does not justify or guarantee the information will be collected. Again, because advanced technical collection assets (remote sensors) are precious resources, validated requirements submitted by all customers are "racked and stacked" against an agreed-upon list of priority targets according to their mission: support to military operations, homeland defense, etc. As expected, requirements regarding the safety and security of deployed armed forces may have higher priority for collection than, for instance, monitoring the United States' southern border for illegal immigrant crossings. Of course, *everything* is important and the prioritization is controversial. Nonetheless, a prioritized list of candidate collections, reviewed on a frequent basis, is sent to the collecting organizations as a tasking order for collection. The collecting organizations then merge all tasking orders into "target decks" for the collecting platforms (sensors) under their control.

COLLECTION

Depending on the target and the sensors' abilities to collect, there are usually further considerations that determine whether collection against prioritized requirements will occur. Specifically, many remote sensors are on board satellites, some high and some low.[19] The geometry of a satellite's orbit usually cannot be changed to satisfy specific tasking requirements, so the time of day and frequency of revisit of a particular remote sensor to a tasked collection site may preclude success. Furthermore, remote sensors' capabilities may be tailored to collect in space, time, and spectrum for specific missions outside the realm of certain customers' requirements.

Other considerations also factor into collection scenarios. For instance, just like a camera cannot take pictures through fog, clouds, and dust storms, neither can the majority of passive remote sensors. If the target area is cloud-covered, then the tasked collection will almost certainly not take place. The world's dynamic situation can also alter scheduled collections. At any moment, priorities can change. It may become more important to quickly focus a remote sensor in another direction. Regardless, many collections are successful, and their data are turned into products for waiting customers.

PRODUCTION

Data passed from a remote sensor is always in the sensor's native format, so it must be revised into a formatted report acceptable to the customer. A report could be graphs, plots, pictures, narratives, tables, etc., and it is usually the result of considerable computation. Producing reports is variously called processing, analysis, and/or exploitation by the organizations involved, but the result is always a *signature*- and *metric*-based product delivering observed and derived facts about the target to the customer. Generically, two important aspects of these products will be highlighted.

First, there is a definite timeline for production, depending on the urgency of the customer's information needs. The urgency depends on the customer's mission. For example, armed forces engaged in hostilities need knowledge of the enemy's locations and warning of attack within seconds; operational headquarters drawing up deployment plans want battlespace awareness within hours; and counter-threat designers have to assess a potential adversary's weapon development programs within months.

Second, although standard algorithms have been developed for many situations, all products start from zero information; and information content increases with time (**Figure 1-3**). As production begins, the amount of information extracted from the data is insufficient for the customer to make assessments and judgments (intelligence!) from it. At some point, the amount of information reaches a threshold at which adequate information is present to make decisions. Note, on the one hand, it is the nature of remote sensing that complete knowledge can *never* be obtained because of the limitations of spatial, spectral, and temporal sampling built into sensor systems. On the other hand, customers *must* understand that less than 100% knowledge necessitates some *uncertainty* in their decisions based on the product.

[19] The descriptions of high (GEO = geosynchronous and HEO = highly elliptical) and low (LEO = low Earth) orbits will be given in **Chapter 11**.

Figure 1-3
Notional Intelligence product timelines.

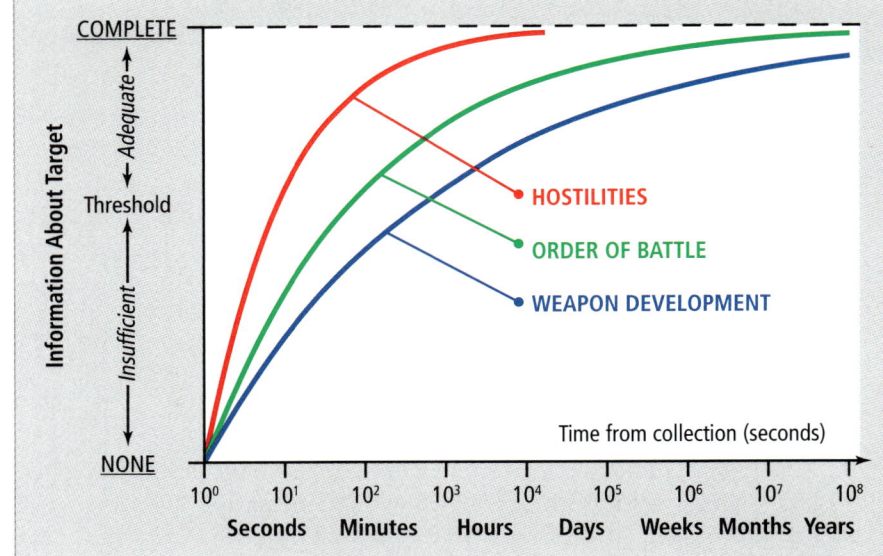

Figure 1-4
In November 1919, Col. Bane helped establish the Air School of Application at Dayton's McCook Field. The Air School was the forerunner of the Air Force Institute of Technology (AFIT). The above image is the composite of Bane's photograph set in copper that hangs at AFIT.

In the end, the goal of production is a satisfied customer. This can be achieved when customers appreciate that the technical side of remote sensing collection, analysis, and production was done correctly. Knowing *why* and *how* products are made helps analysts make them more meaningful, and such knowledge also improves the flow for requirements, collection, and production managers. To emphasize to managers the importance of the technical material in this text, Colonel Thurman Bane (**Figure 1-4**) is cited, "No man can efficiently direct work about which he knows nothing."

1.3 ROADMAP

The following chapters are organized around the concepts and practices of electro-optical remote sensing that are specific to **Equations 1-1, 1-2,** and **1-3**. First, the particulars of how electro-optical ATI sensors work will be explained. Mathematically, this renders **Equation 1-2** as[20]

$$\{DATA\} \approx \sum_{PIX} A/_D \left\{ \int_{\Delta t_{INT}} \int_{\Delta \lambda} \frac{I_\lambda(t)}{R^2} \tau_{ATM}(\lambda,R) A_R \tau_{OPT}(\lambda) \frac{\eta(\lambda) F_{PIX}}{hc/\lambda} d\lambda dt \right\}. \quad (1\text{-}4)$$

This equation, including integrals, sums, and operations, looks extremely intimidating, but it is not! Embedded within this equation are simply all of the phenomenologies of propagation, attenuation, optics, and sampling that were previously introduced. In the following chapters, the physics of each of these will be explained, starting with target characteristics and working methodically through space, time, and spectrum to the optics and electronic back end of an EO ATI sensor.[21] The treatment of each piece of physics will be scientifically sound and mathematically[22] correct, but always remember the intelligence objective of gathering information.

Although **Equation 1-4** is specifically for EO remote sensing, the topic of this book, its phenomenology, is quite general. With appropriate interpretation of the terms, target, propagation, attenuation, collection, and detection, the equation can be modified to apply to remote sensing in the RF portion of the EM spectrum, to remote sensing of mechanical waves, and even to remote sensing of some types of particles.

---

[20] Do not worry about the symbology yet. All of the terms in **Equation 1-4** and **1-5** will be explained in their appropriate chapters.

[21] Interestingly, non-literal ATI may be derived from many electro-optical remote sensors which were not designed to provide such information.

[22] While these discussions show problems that look like calculus, differentials, and integrals, it is not necessary to actually complete calculus. However, an understanding of how the calculus works is required. Case in point is **Equation 1-4**; although this looks like an integral, the sensor does the computation! But to extract information from {DATA}, an understanding of how the sensor did it is needed. The mathematics will be explained as the discussion progresses.

Once the collection **Equation 1-4** is mastered, the method to find target signature and metrics will be developed in **Chapters 13** through **21**. One particular form of a signature, for example, is:

$$\{TGT\} \approx \langle I_\lambda \rangle \approx \mathcal{M} \left(\frac{R^2}{\tau_{ATM}\Delta\lambda} \right) {}^D\!/\!_A \{DATA\}. \tag{1-5}$$

Of course, this is just **Equation 1-3** cast in the symbols of EO. Just as the collection equation was built term-by-term, the phenomenologies of processing, analysis, and exploitation that provide the necessary information (which is why the collection was taken in the first place) will be discussed. In practice, when sensor data streams are measured in terabytes, the procedures were mostly automated. Nonetheless, it is important to have a complete understanding of *why* and *how* the algorithms are impacting the data to ensure the reasonableness of the answers, where reasonableness is the key contribution of trained intelligence analysts. As a result, intelligence products should never be disseminated without human assessment.

After showing how ATI sensors work, generically, and how their data are processed, the focus turns to some particular EO applications. The method in which large-area persistent surveillance programs located far away (high Earth orbit) use the theory developed here will be considered. From relatively near (meaning low Earth orbit and from airborne platforms), the basics of multi/hyperspectral, thermal, and polarimetric sensor programs and their objectives will be discussed. More applications of passive remote sensing are possible than those presented here, but an understanding of the collection and processing phenomenology will enable the ability to develop them.

2 LIGHT EMITTING TARGETS

The first target characteristic to look at in detail is the spectral nature of light emitted targets like the rocket launcher above, but first the relevant characteristics of light waves will be reviewed. To be sure, electromagnetic (EM) radiation obeys a set of differential (or integral) equations collectively known as Maxwell's Equations, but the phenomenological study of advanced technical information collection does not require that much depth. The purpose of understanding phenomenology is to answer the question, "When electromagnetic waves are gathered with remote sensing apparatus, what information is provided about the source of those waves?" With proper spectral analysis, information about a target's temperature and material composition may be derived, from which its function and performance could be inferred. This chapter provides the basis for spectral analysis of light emitting targets.

SECTIONS
- 2.1 LIGHT WAVES AND PARTICLES
- 2.2 IDEAL THERMAL SOURCES
- 2.3 REAL THERMAL SOURCES
- 2.4 SELECTIVE SOURCES I: ATOMS
- 2.5 SELECTIVE SOURCES II: MOLECULES
- 2.6 SELECTIVE SOURCES III: ENSEMBLES

> **INDEX OF REFRACTION**
>
> The speed of light is altered by the medium it propagates through:
>
> $$c_{medium} = \frac{c_{vacuum}}{n_{medium}}$$
>
> where n_{medium} is a material property called *index of refraction*. This could have a significant effect in bathymetry and littoral characterization, e.g., where $n_{water} \approx 1.33$. For usual applications, remote sensing from airborne or spaceborne platforms, the index of refraction of air is $n_{air} \approx 1.0003$ at sea level, and has a negligible influence on the speed with which technical information is gathered.
>
> n is a function of air density and decreases with altitude until $n = 1$ in the vacuum of space. Gradual changes in n near the Earth's surface can slightly bend the path of light traveled from target to sensor, causing mirages or displacement errors. (On the other hand, rapid gradients of n in optical fibers are desirable for confining the optical signal within the fiber.)
>
> Abrupt changes in n from one material to another cause abrupt changes in EM waves' directions, and this is what makes lenses work. This will be used in later chapters. The change of n at surfaces can also cause some problematic reflections, resulting in a loss of information. This will also be discussed later.
>
> Finally, n is also a function of wavelength in most materials, and this is what makes prisms work. Prisms will be discussed as one option for spectral analysis.

2.1 LIGHT WAVES AND PARTICLES

The fundamental energy form collected with advanced technical sensors is EM radiation or *light*. Classical and modern physics treats light both as a particle and as a wave. Which one is it?

WAVE-PARTICLE DUALITY

Figure 1-2 needs further explanation. First, this text concentrates on gaining knowledge of remote objects through the study of *waves*. However, there's more in electro-optics: *wave-particles*. This concept may be familiar; discrete chunks of EM wave energy are treated as particles called *photons*. This topic will be briefly reviewed.

WAVE NATURE OF LIGHT

Early in the study of light, it was understood by Christiaan Huygens (**Figure 2-2**) and others that *light is a wave*, and it is (Maxwell's Equations!). As a wave, EM radiation exhibits all the properties a wave is expected to have, and also one "special" property. Waves have a temporal *frequency*, f; a spatial *wavelength*, λ; and a characteristic propagation *speed in vacuum*, c. These are related by:

$$f\lambda = c \approx 3.00 \times 10^8 \text{ m} \cdot \text{s}^{-1}. \qquad (2\text{-}1)$$

The "special" property of EM waves (besides being the only kind of wave that can propagate in a vacuum) is that "c" is a constant for all observers (as Einstein postulated[1]), meaning remote sensing instruments, regardless of location. (See sidebar on **Index of Refraction**.)

As a wave, light is described as being oscillating (usually sinusoidal) electric ($\vec{E}$) and magnetic ($\vec{B}$) fields, oriented at right angles to one another and both varying perpendicular to the direction of propagation (**Figure 2-1**). The orientation of $\vec{E}$ defines the *polarization* of a light wave, and its progress through its cycle (the sine's angle, or argument) is the wave's *phase*. Both polarization and phase are very important at radio frequencies (waves longer than a millimeter), because they can be readily observed with an antenna and tuned electronic circuit. But, the measurement of either is much more difficult with electro-optic sensors. Traditionally, the wave nature of light is used to easily explain the physical optics phenomena of reflection, refraction, interference, and diffraction (all of which will figure into the study of remote sensing) but there is one more ultimately important feature of light waves.

Figure 2-1
The electric and magnetic fields of a light wave are usually assumed to be sinusoidal.

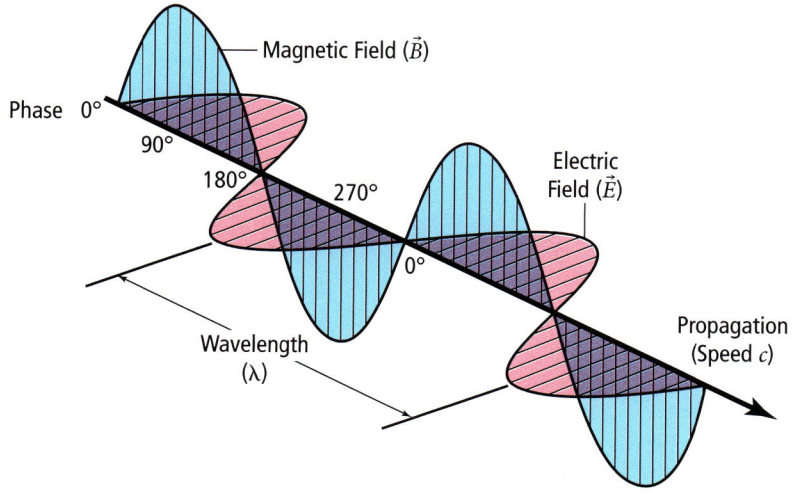

[1] This is strictly true only for observers in relatively moving *inertial* reference frames that are not accelerating. Satellites have to take into account "general" relativistic effects for time-keeping in Earth's gravitational field. However, their motions are so slow compared to the speed of light that relativity can be ignored in these collections.

Christiaan Huygens 1629–1695 **Isaac Newton** 1643–1727 **James C. Maxwell** 1831–1879 **Max Planck** 1858–1947 **Albert Einstein** 1879–1955

Figure 2-2
Notable scientists in the history of electro-optical physics. (Huygens photo courtesy of http://en.wikipedia.org/wiki/File:Christiaan_Huygens.gif; PD-Old. Maxwell photo courtesy of http://commons.wikimedia.org/wiki/File:James_Clerk_Maxwell.png; PD-Old. Einstein photo courtesy of http://commons.wikimedia.org/wiki/File:Einstein1921_by_F_Schmutzer_2.jpg; PD-Old.)

The most important feature of light waves that will be emphasized again and again is that *light carries energy* from its source to a remote sensor, and *energy is information*. Without receiving energy from them, no information about targets is known. For a light wave, the energy is proportional to the square of its average electric or magnetic field, but there will never be an occasion to calculate the fields' values in electro-optics. (Radar is a different story.) For these purposes, just remember the salient aspects of light waves are:

1. They are characterized by their wavelength, λ.
2. They propagate at the speed of light, c.
3. They carry ENERGY; *energy is information*.

PARTICLE NATURE OF LIGHT

Early in the study of light, it was also understood by Isaac Newton and others that *light is a particle*. The particle-like nature of light does not clearly explain refraction, reflection, interference, and diffraction. So, it was more difficult to convince scientists of its existence. Nonetheless, Heinrich Hertz and others demonstrated such particles must exist. Einstein in his *annus mirabilis*, 1905, proposed these light *quanta* as his explanation for the *photoelectric effect*.[2] The existence of light particles was, thus, experimentally and theoretically established, and they were first called photons by G. N. Lewis in 1926.

Therefore, the particle, or photon, nature of light, manifested through its detection with the photoelectric effect,[3] is the basis for writing this text on electro-optical (or *photonic*) remote sensing for advanced technical information gathering. What makes it work, of course, is *light carries energy* and *energy is information*. In particular, the energy of one photon is:

$$E_{photon} = hf = \frac{hc}{\lambda} \ [\text{J}], \qquad (2\text{-}2)$$

where **h** is Planck's constant, $h \approx 6.63 \times 10^{-34}$ J·s, and f and λ are the frequency and wavelength, respectively, of the photon's associated light wave.

As shown in **Example 2-1**, the energy of one photon ($\sim 10^{-19}$ J) is an extremely small amount. A more easily managed unit of energy for photons in the electro-optical regime is the *electron volt* (eV), which is the amount of energy one electron (charge $q \approx 1.60 \times 10^{-19}$ coulombs) acquires when accelerated through one volt. Therefore, the conversion to electron volts from joules is $\{q\} \approx 1.60 \times 10^{-19}$ J · eV^{-1}, and the energy of one photon in this unit is:

$$E_{photon} = \frac{hf}{\{q\}} = \frac{hc}{\{q\}\lambda} \ [\text{eV}]. \qquad (2\text{-}3)$$

---

[2] Albert Einstein is best known for his special and general theories of relativity for which he was cited above. His 1921 Nobel Prize in Physics, however, was awarded "for his services to Theoretical Physics and especially his discovery of the law of the photoelectric effect."

[3] The photoelectric effect will be explained in detail in **Chapter 7**.

TEMPERATURE SCALES

There are three* temperature scales to be familiar with: Fahrenheit, Celsius, and Kelvin. The Fahrenheit scale is commonly used in the United States, whereas the Celsius scale is used throughout the rest of the world. The Kelvin scale is standard for scientific measurements.

Temperature scales are established by assigning values to standardized and repeatable conditions, such as the freezing and boiling of pure water at specified pressures. Between the standardized conditions, increments are marked. The Fahrenheit scale divides the interval into 180 increments, while the Celsius scales (once called centigrade) divides it into 100. The Fahrenheit scale assigns the unusual number 32 to the freezing point of water, but the Celsius scale calls this temperature zero. (Many would denigrate the Fahrenheit scale as amateur, whereas the Celsius scale is more scientific. Nevertheless, zero to one hundred on the Fahrenheit scales makes sense as being a normal human operating range.)

On any temperature scale, objects eventually lose the ability to interact with their surroundings. This does not mean they are out of energy, they just do not have any to share. At such a point, objects reach the zero point. The Celsius scale reaches this condition at $-273.15°C$. The "absolute" or Kelvin scale assigns 0 K to the zero point, and 273.15 K to the freezing point of water. Hence, a change of one kelvin is the same as a change of one degree Celsius. (Note, increments on the Kelvin scale are not called degrees kelvin, just kelvins.)

The figure shows a comparison among the scales for some familiar temperatures, and conversions are

$°F = \frac{9}{5}\{°C\} + 32°F = \frac{9}{5}\{K\} - 459.67°F$

$°C = \frac{5}{9}(\{°F\} - 32°F) = \{K\} - 273.15 K$

$K = \frac{5}{9}(\{°F\} + 459.67°F) = \{°C\} + 273.15°C$

* A fourth scale, the Rankin scale, is used by some engineers and is similar to the Fahrenheit scale.

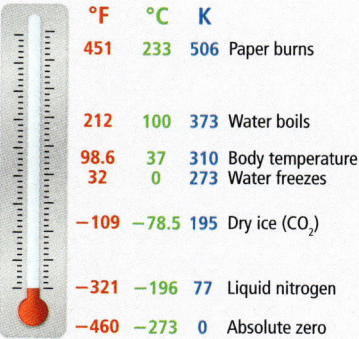

°F	°C	K	
451	233	506	Paper burns
212	100	373	Water boils
98.6	37	310	Body temperature
32	0	273	Water freezes
−109	−78.5	195	Dry ice (CO$_2$)
−321	−196	77	Liquid nitrogen
−460	−273	0	Absolute zero

EXAMPLE 2-1: HOW MANY PHOTONS?

Consider a red laser pointer. Its wavelength is $\lambda_{laser} \approx 0.532$ μm, and it puts out about 1.0 mW.

In one second, this laser emits approximately

$$E_{laser} \approx (1.0\ mW)(1\ s) \approx 10^{-3} J.$$

The energy of each photon is about

$$E_{photon} \approx \frac{(6.63 \times 10^{-34}\ J \cdot s)(3.00 \times 10^8\ m \cdot s^{-1})}{0.532 \times 10^{-6}\ m} \approx 3.74 \times 10^{-19} J.$$

On the average, the laser beam is made up of

$$N = \frac{E_{laser}}{E_{photon}} \approx \frac{10^{-3}\ J}{3.74 \times 10^{-19}\ J} \approx 2.67 \times 10^{15}\ photons.$$

That's a lot of photons!

When using wavelength in units of micrometers (microns (μm)), this becomes:

$$E_{photon} \approx \frac{1.24}{\lambda[in\ \mu m]}\ [eV]. \qquad (2\text{-}4)$$

So, photons in the electro-optic portion of the spectrum have energies ranging from about 0.01 to 10 eV.

Another unit for photon energy sometimes appears, especially in spectroscopy and certain computer codes used to calculate atmospheric transmission (as calculated in later chapters). That unit is the wavenumber, usually measured in units of inverse centimeters, cm^{-1}. Wavenumber is defined as:

$$\upsilon = \frac{1}{\lambda[in\ cm]} = \frac{10{,}000}{\lambda[in\ \mu m]}\ [cm^{-1}]. \qquad (2\text{-}5)$$

Note, the wavenumber is strictly NOT an energy, but has wavelength in its denominator. It is *proportional* to energy (and is customarily *called* energy by those familiar with working with this unit).

SPECTRUM OF LIGHT

Scientists have asked themselves for several centuries, "Is light a wave or a particle?" The answer is, "Yes, it is both, and which nature is used depends on what scientists want to do with it." The wave nature is unequivocally shown when discussing spatial resolution, but it is the particle nature that drives the detectors (focal plane arrays).

The EM spectrum can be represented in terms of wavelength, frequency, or energy. Scales for each are shown in **Figure 2-3**. Wavelength, frequency, and energy are easily converted through the simple **Equations 2-1** and **2-3**.

In the radio frequency end of the spectrum, engineers have internationally agreed upon some band designations.[4] Such is not the case

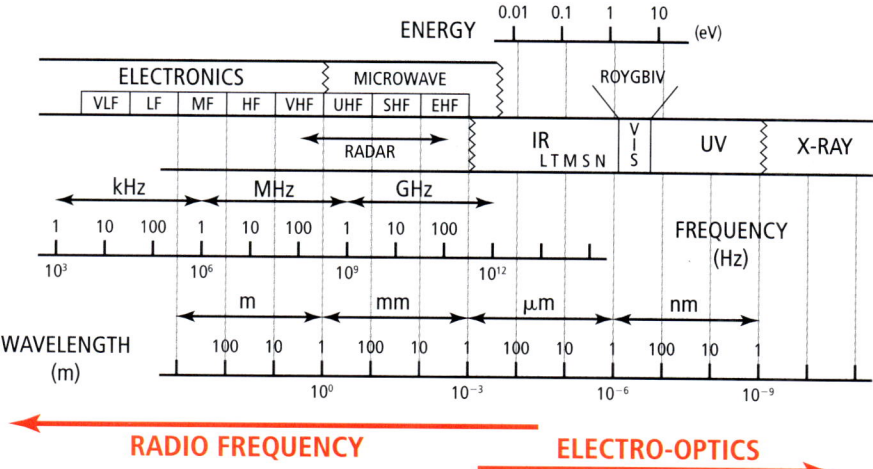

Figure 2-3
The EM spectrum is a continuum, but the technology used to produce and detect light changes from one end to the other. It is only broken up with naming conventions for the convenience of the practitioners of a certain discipline (i.e., radar, electro-optics, nuclear, etc.).

in the electro-optic spectrum. However, several terms are commonly used, but their meanings change slightly depending on application. **Figure 2-3** shows the relative positioning of the following EO bands in increasing wavelength order:

1. VISIBLE (VIS)—Approximately 0.4–0.7 μm, which is defined by the response of the human eye. Colors within the visible spectrum are the well-known ROYGBIV: red, orange, yellow, green, blue, indigo, violet. Different texts give more-or-less exact limits for the different colors, but, conversationally, 0.4 μm means blue[5] and 0.7 μm means red. Targets are typically detected by reflecting sunlight in this band. Although, at extremely high temperatures, emission takes place in this band as well.

2. NEAR INFRARED (NIR)—Approximately 0.7–2.0 μm. Sometimes, the NIR is added to the visible, creating the so-called Vis-NIR. In this case, it typically means the range for which silicon can be used as a photon detector—out to about 1.1 μm. Targets are also generally sunlight reflectors in this band.

3. SHORTWAVE INFRARED (SWIR)—Approximately 2.0–3.5 μm. This band suffers strong attenuation from atmospheric water vapor; yet, it is very useful for detecting very hot targets. So, both sunlight-reflecting and extremely hot self-emitting targets can be seen here.

4. MID-WAVE INFRARED (MWIR)—Approximately 3.5–5.0 μm, although some remote sensing practitioners will skip the SWIR and call the entire 2.0–5.0 μm band MWIR. In its narrower sense, the MWIR is influenced by more strong attenuations, but this time from carbon dioxide. Most targets can be detected from their self-emission in this band.

5. THERMAL INFRARED (TIR)—Approximately 8.0–12.0 μm, yet, sometimes taken to be through 14.0 μm. As its name implies, this is the electro-optic band used to sense heat. Nearly *everything* in the Earth's environment can be sensed in this band from its own energy with minimal interference from reflected sunshine.

6. LONG-WAVE INFRARED (LWIR)—Used by some to mean the thermal band or sometimes meaning wavelengths out to 30 μm or beyond. Because of their low energy (< 0.01 eV), photons at longer wavelengths are more difficult to detect with electro-optic sensors.

[4] For completeness, the RF bands are listed in the following table. There are also two sets of overlapping radar band designations, one old and one new.

Designation		Frequency	Wavelength
ELF	Extremely Low Frequency	3 Hz to 30 Hz	100,000 km to 10,000 km
SLF	Super Low Frequency	30 Hz to 300 Hz	10,000 km to 1,000 km
ULF	Ultra Low Frequency	300 Hz to 3000 Hz	1,000 km to 100 km
VLF	Very Low Frequency	3 kHz to 30 kHz	100 km to 10 km
LF	Low Frequency	30 kHz to 300 kHz	10 km to 1 km
MF	Medium Frequency	300 kHz to 3000 kHz	1 km to 100 m
HF	High Frequency	3 MHz to 30 MHz	100 m to 10 m
VHF	Very High Frequency	30 MHz to 300 MHz	10 m to 1 m
UHF	Ultra High Frequency	300 MHz to 3000 MHz	1 m to 10 cm
SHF	Super High Frequency	3 GHz to 30 GHz	10 cm to 1 cm
EHF	Extremely High Frequency	30 GHz to 300 GHz	1 cm to 1 mm

[5] What happened to indigo and violet? Many people are unsure of those colors and lump them in with purple. Since purple is not part of ROYGBIV, it is ignored (as well as indigo-violet).

Although this text will use the first definitions given for the electro-optic bands, be careful when having casual conversations with others. There needs to be an agreement as to which portion of the spectrum is being discussed. Also, notice there was a hole in the infrared; the 5.0–8.0 μm band was not included. This will be explained in **Chapter 5**.

2.2 IDEAL THERMAL SOURCES

The reason remote sensing works is because energy is received from targets. The energy can either be emitted light or reflected light—or both! If the radiation is emitted, then it must come from some energy source within the target. Light arising from internal energy sources has two possible natures: continuum or selective. A familiar example of continuum radiation is a rainbow in the visible spectrum. All the colors are present from red through blue (or violet, if you wish). On the other hand, selective sources of radiation only emit light at particular wavelengths. The yellow glow of sodium vapor lights, often used in parking lots and garages, is mostly a selective source.

In this section, the most commonly cited continuum source of light will be discussed: the thermal radiator called the blackbody. Although such a thing does not truly exist in nature, *it is one of the most common approximations made in remote sensing*. These theoretical musings will be adjusted with considerations of real materials in the next section. Then, selective radiators will be covered in the following three sections.

CONCEPTS OF TEMPERATURE AND STEADY STATE

All objects have internal energy, and it is a common misconception that *temperature* is a measure of that internal energy. Temperature is actually a measure of an object's ability *to share* or exchange its energy with its neighbors or environment and is *thermodynamic* temperature.[6] High temperature indicates relative ease and propensity to share energy, and low temperature is the opposite. Various temperature scales establish a means to compare the amount of energy objects have to share and are measured relative to repeatable physical conditions, like the freezing and boiling of (pure) water at specified pressures. (See the Sidebar, **Temperature Scales**.)

When two objects share energy, the one with the higher (hotter) temperature will more readily give to the cooler one. Its temperature drops during the process (because, in giving away energy, it has less to share). Meanwhile, the cooler object gains energy and experiences a subsequent increase in its temperature.[7] Eventually, the two objects may come to the same temperature and reach a condition known as *steady state*.[8] But note, at steady state, the exchange of energy has not stopped; the two objects simply have the ability to trade equal amounts of energy with each other and they do. At steady state, the amount of energy given away by the one object is exactly replaced by receiving (absorbing) energy from the other.

In general, there are three ways objects can exchange energy with each other and their surroundings: conduction, convection, and *radiation*. Of these, only the latter will be a concern in remote sensing; the first two require some kind of physical contact. Then, one can surmise that one way to learn about things from a distance is to gather a small portion of the radiation energy they are trying to exchange. Since

---

[6] The temperature most familiar is *physiological* temperature: what is felt with skin. It is proportional to thermodynamic temperature and is usually the same. Other temperatures will be covered in later chapters.

[7] Even though it is cooler, the second object is still transferring energy (because it has a temperature) to the hotter object but not as fast as it is receiving. Hence, a net gain in energy means it has more to share, which is manifested by a rising temperature.

[8] Sometimes the word equilibrium is used, but steady state is a better term. Theoretically, equilibrium implies a condition that will never change and does not allow for internal sources of energy to be expended. That is, many objects have internal energy by virtue of some chemical process or nuclear reaction that eventually comes to an end when the reactants or fuel is gone. Such objects can be in steady state when the processes or reactions proceed at a constant rate while the object exchanges the generated energy with its surroundings. But, it is not strictly equilibrium, because the fuel is not being replaced.

Figure 2-4
The Fifth Solvay Conference of 1927: Electrons and Photons. Twenty-nine luminaries of modern physics (seventeen Nobel Prize winners) discussed the origins of continuum and selective radiation. Standing: A. Piccard, E. Henriot, P. Ehrenfest, Ed. Herzen, Th. DeDonder, E. Schrodinger, J.E. Verschaffelt, W. Pauli, W. Heisenberg, R.H. Fowler, L. Brillouin; Middle: P. Debye, M. Knudsen, W.L. Bragg, H.A. Kramers, P.A.M. Dirac, A.H. Compton, L. DeBroglie, M. Born, N. Bohr; Seated: I. Langmuir, M. Planck, M. Curie, H.A. Lorentz, A. Einstein, P. Langevin, Ch.E. Guye, C.T.R. Wilson, O.W. Richardson.

this radiation's origin[9] is a consequence of objects' temperatures, it is usually called thermal radiation, or emission.

BLACKBODY RADIATION

When an object has a constant temperature (i.e., is in steady state) *and* completely absorbs *all* radiation it receives from its neighbors and environment, that object is said to be a blackbody radiator. It internally processes (thermalizes) all the energy it received and re-emits it (because it's in steady state) in a well-known continuum spectrum. The mathematics of blackbody radiation was developed by German physicist Max Planck (**Figure 2-4**) by assuming the radiation was *quantized* (came in chunks now called photons). The Planck formula for emitted blackbody radiation, $B_\lambda(\lambda,T)$, as a function of wavelength is

$$B_\lambda(\lambda,T) = \frac{2\pi hc^2}{\lambda^5} \frac{1}{(e^{hc/\lambda k_B T} - 1)} \left[\frac{W}{m^2 \mu m}\right], \quad (2\text{-}6)$$

where h is Planck's constant, c is the speed of light, and $\boldsymbol{k_B} \approx 1.38 \times 10^{-23}\,J \cdot K^{-1}$ is Boltzmann's constant. The temperature, T, is expressed in absolute units of kelvins, and wavelength, λ, in meters. Since wavelengths in electro-optics are of micrometer dimension, Planck's formula is more practically written as the following with λ in micrometers:

$$B_\lambda(\lambda,T) \approx \frac{c_1}{\lambda^5 (e^{c_2/\lambda T} - 1)} \left[\frac{W}{m^2 \mu m}\right], \quad (2\text{-}7)$$

where $c_1 = 2\pi hc^2 \approx 3.74 \times 10^8\,W \cdot \mu m^4 m^{-2}$ and $c_2 = \frac{hc}{k_B} \approx 1.44 \times 10^4\,\mu m \cdot K$ are the first and second radiation constants, respectively.

The blackbody function (shown in **Equation 2-6** or **2-7**) requires some explanation:

1. The physical meaning of the Planck function is the power[10] per unit area per unit bandpass exiting the surface (in all directions) of an object at steady state temperature, T. Hence its formal name is spectral exitance, which will be discussed again in the chapters on spatial properties of targets.

---

[9] The physical origin of the radiation is near the *surface* of a target within what is called the "skin depth" of the physical surface, usually only a few wavelengths thick.

[10] Remember POWER = ENERGY PER UNIT TIME | $1\,W = 1\,J \cdot s^{-1}$ | and energy is information.

2. The scientific units of the Planck function are watts per square meter per micrometer, where the area is that of the radiating object and the bandpass,[11] per micrometer, for these purposes, refers to the remote sensing instrument on the energy gathering end of the radiation.

3. Properly, the Planck formula is a *distribution function*. It *does not* provide the exact amount of power per unit area emitted by an object with temperature, *T*, *at* any given wavelength. Rather, it *does* provide how the power is *distributed* within a small bandpass centered on a wavelength of interest; this is the meaning of the per unit bandpass in the definition. Symbolically, that is the meaning of the subscript λ on B_λ. Formally, think of this as:

$$B_\lambda = \frac{dB}{d\lambda}, \tag{2-8}$$

but do not push the calculus notation too far.[12]

Now, see what the Planck function looks like. **Figure 2-5** shows the spectral exitance, B_λ, plotted as a function of wavelength for the temperatures of four somewhat familiar objects. (That is, if they were actually blackbodies, which they are not. But, this will not be corrected until the next section. For now, accept these objects as *approximate* blackbodies.) Note, the figure shows the blackbody function plotted on log-log axes. While correct, this view distorts perception of the comparative shape and amplitude of the curves. This concept is further demonstrated by the interactive spreadsheet, **Appendix 2-1**, on the support website.

Figure 2-5 is restricted to showing only the electro-optic range of blackbody emission, ultraviolet on the left through LWIR on the right, but it is noted that all objects having a steady state temperature emit radiation at *all* wavelengths all the time according to the Planck function (modified as shown in the next section). The minimum value for spectral exitance plotted on the vertical axis is roughly the minimum amount of radiation that can be detected by the human eye at close range from an emitting object (subject to propagation conditions covered in later chapters). Thus, the lab technician pictured with a room temperature skin of about 300 K *is* radiating in the visible spectrum, but not enough to see. The other objects (electric stove burner on high, tungsten light bulb filament, and the sun) are easily visible by virtue of their exitances.[13]

FEATURES OF THE PLANCK FUNCTION

As stated earlier, the blackbody is one of the most useful and common approximations made in advanced technical intelligence remote sensing. The reason is the analyst is not in contact with an energy-emitting target of interest, so the details about its actual emission are not necessarily known. Yet, assuming all emitting targets are approximately blackbodies, some information about them can be gained.

---

[11] This is a point that cannot be emphasized enough, and it will be a recurring theme discussed again in this text: no electro-optic sensor ever measures the energy present at just one wavelength but within a small range of wavelengths called its bandpass.

[12] Mathematical purists would probably insist this pseudo-derivative should be written as a partial derivative, $B_\lambda = \frac{\partial B}{\partial \lambda}$, because the Planck formula is a function of several variables. Since the goal is to accurately *understand* the principles of remote sensing, while using technically correct and rigorously derived results, the equation will be mathematically "sloppy" and will use only single-variable derivative notation so as not to obscure the physics and phenomenology.

[13] The burner on an electric stove emits radiation by virtue of its high temperature. It may reach steady state conditions, but it is not strictly a blackbody. It does not completely absorb all the radiation it receives. Notice, it can still be seen even with the room lights turned off. Its primary energy source is the dissipation of electrical power from the current passing through it pushed by household voltage.

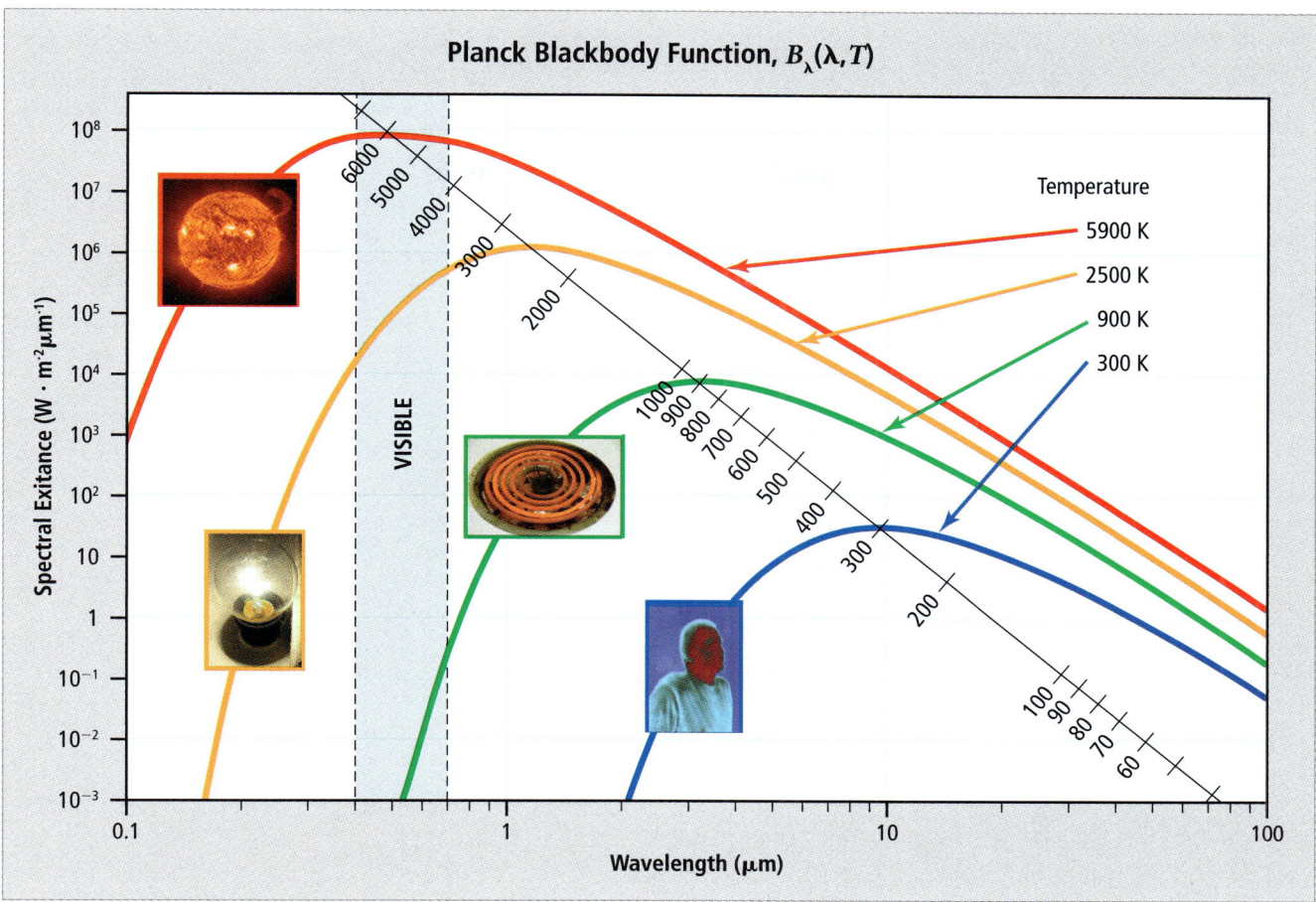

Figure 2-5
The Planck blackbody function plotted on log-log axes. Thumbnails suggest familar objects having the temperatures indicated.

WAVELENGTH MAXIMUM

A feature of **Figure 2-5** that should be noted right away is that, as the temperature increases, the exitance at every wavelength increases; more energy emitted results in more information if collected properly. It is also obvious the peak of the curve moves up and to shorter wavelengths. (Note this feature on the interactive spreadsheet.) In fact, the peak of the curve follows the diagonal line marked on the chart known as Wien's Displacement Law:

$$\lambda_{MAX} \approx \frac{2897.8}{T} [\mu m]. \qquad (2\text{-}9)$$

This inverse relationship gives, for any temperature, T (in kelvins), the wavelength (in μm) at which spectral exitance is maximized for that temperature. As a rule of thumb, the law is often approximated by:

$$\lambda_{MAX} \approx \frac{3000}{T} [\mu m]. \qquad (2\text{-}10)$$

The practical significance of Wien's Displacement Law for remote sensing is to consider selecting an electro-optic sensor that will collect the most information about a target. That is, if a target is known or suspected to be close to a blackbody at a certain temperature, select a sensor capable of collecting in a bandpass that includes λ_{MAX} (**Example 2-2**).

WHAT IS AN INTEGRAL?

Integration is very important because that's what remote sensors do: they *integrate* a target's spectral, spatial, and temporal natures into data.

At its simplest, an integral is a <u>sum</u> or an accumulated effect. For example, the distance a car travels is the effect of its having certain speeds for certain times. Graphically, it is calculating the area under a curve:

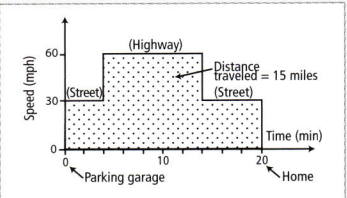

In symbols, the area is represented as approximately

$$\begin{Bmatrix} \text{Distance} \\ \text{traveled} \end{Bmatrix} = \int_{\text{FIRST time}}^{\text{LAST time}} Speed(time)\,d(time),$$

where the integral sign ($\int$) can be thought of as an overgrown S, for sum. The meaning of *d(time)* is to step along in time as the function (*Speed*) changes, accumulating the distance incrementally. In formal calculus, *d(time)* is an infinitesimal step, but in remote sensing it means to go from frame to frame.

When a target's output power changes, and it is recorded over frames by a remote sensor, the target's energy is the integral.

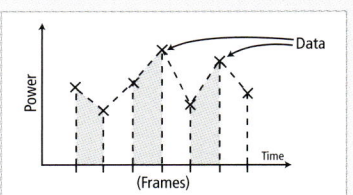

In this case, the integral is found *numerically* by calculating and adding the individual areas between frames. It is an **estimate** of the target's performance.

---

[14] This is consistent with the description of the Planck function as a distribution function (Equation 2-8):

$$\int B_\lambda d\lambda \sim \int \frac{dB}{d\lambda} d\lambda \sim \int dB \sim B$$

EXAMPLE 2-2: USING WIEN'S DISPLACEMENT LAW

A missile is thought to burn a certain type of fuel at about 1500 K. The exhaust plume should therefore be emitting the most power per unit area in a bandpass centered on (rule of thumb) 2.0 μm. Thus, using a sensor with a 1.9–2.1 μm bandpass should collect the most energy. (This is subject to propagation and atmospheric attenuation conditions that will be covered later.)

The converse application of the above is to estimate a target's temperature by measuring the wavelength at which it is emitting its maximum energy. A remote sensor is pointed at the target, but since it is a remote object and no other information is available, assume it is a blackbody. Upon measuring its wavelength of maximum emission, **Equation 2-9** (or **2-10**) can be solved to calculate the target's temperature. Although this procedure sounds simple in theory, it is difficult in practice for a couple of reasons: 1) the remote sensor must be capable of measuring radiation at many different wavelengths to find the peak of the curve; and 2) the sensor must have a bandpass sufficiently narrow to identify the peak when it is shown.

BANDPASS MEASUREMENTS

An inherent feature of *all* radiation-collecting remote sensors is they always collect energy within a finite, designed bandpass—not at any single wavelength. So, beyond using Wien's Displacement Law to help select a sensor, ask how much power a target actually emits within the bandpass of the sensor. This is answered by adding up the Planck function (i.e., integrating the distribution) and is called exitance, symbol **B** for a blackbody:[14]

$$B(T) = \int_{\text{BANDPASS}} B_\lambda(\lambda, T)\,d\lambda \quad \left[\frac{W}{m^2}\right]. \qquad (2\text{-}11)$$

Note, this is a function of temperature alone, so conceivably carefully measuring a target's exitance within a bandpass allows its temperature to be estimated as *if it were a blackbody*. Thus, collecting energy could clearly provide some information about a target.

However, in the algebraic form of the Planck function, the integral **Equation 2-11** can only be computed numerically. **Figure 2-6** shows an example of blackbody spectral exitance integrated within a portion of the SWIR spectrum for temperatures, ~ 300 K (room temperature) to ~ 3,000 K (nearly the evaporation temperature of iron). Note, as the temperature increases, the integrated amount of emitted energy also increases; but, there is no peak in the shape of this curve when λ_{MAX} is within the bandpass. In principle, calculating a curve for the bandpass of a particular remote sensor and entering the vertical axis with a measurement from that sensor allows the temperature of an assumed blackbody to be estimated.

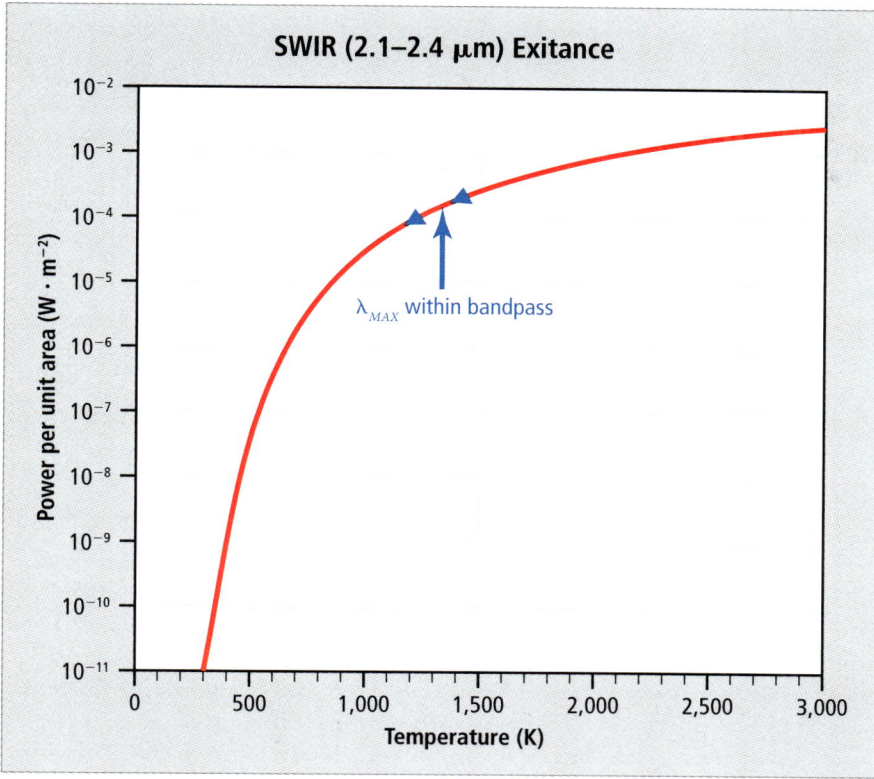

Figure 2-6
Integral of the Planck function in SWIR bandpass.

HISTORICAL NOTES

The analytic form of the Planck function, **Equation 2-7**, requires several sub-calculations and considerable care to calculate by hand. Today, calculation is trivial with electronic computers. Before computers, scientists used tables of logarithms or made mechanical calculators for quick estimates. Other shortcuts used by early practitioners of Planck functions included the Wien and Rayleigh-Jeans (R-J) approximations for wavelengths on the short and long side of the emission peak, respectively:

$$\text{Wien Limit: } B_\lambda \approx \frac{c_1}{\lambda^5} e^{-c_2/\lambda T} \left[W \cdot m^{-2} \mu m^{-1} \right] \text{ when } \lambda \lesssim \lambda_{MAX}, \quad (2\text{-}12)$$

$$\text{R-J Limit: } B_\lambda \approx \frac{c_1 T}{c_2 \lambda^4} \left[W \cdot m^{-2} \mu m^{-1} \right] \text{ when } \lambda \gg \lambda_{MAX}. \quad (2\text{-}13)$$

These simplified forms may be useful today if proper attention is paid to their region of validity. But, the full formula is preferred and easy to implement on a computer. See the interactive spreadsheet, **Appendix 2-1**, on the support website.

Although **Equation 2-11** must be computed numerically, the Planck function can be integrated over all wavelengths (it is often referred to as, "dc to daylight") using a contour integral in the complex plane. The result is the famous Stefan-Boltzmann Law which states a target's total emitted power per unit area is proportional to its temperature raised to the fourth power:

$$B(T) = \int_0^\infty B_\lambda(\lambda, T) d\lambda = \sigma_{SB} T^4 \left[\frac{W}{m^2} \right], \quad (2\text{-}14)$$

where $\sigma_{SB} = \frac{2\pi^5 k_B^4}{15 h^3 c^2} \approx 5.67 \times 10^{-8}$ W·m^{-2}K^{-4} is the Stefan-Boltzmann constant. In spite of the simplicity of this result, it is not completely useful in practice. Because *no single remote sensor can cover the entire EM spectrum*. Yet, sometimes it is a useful approximation.

APPLICATION OF THE PLANCK FUNCTION

A general feature of remote sensing is often analysts do not know exactly what they are looking at. Targets can be temporally transient and do not have time to settle into a thermal steady state. Therefore, they do not meet the requirements for being blackbody radiators. Also, spatial resolution of a remote sensor may preclude literal identification and will spectrally "mix" targets with their surroundings. Furthermore, radiation is not measured at *all* wavelengths, but typically only at a few wider or narrower bandpasses. However, the analysis has to begin somewhere, and one of the standard assumptions, unless there is evidence to the contrary, is to *let all sources of light in the field of view be approximated as blackbodies*. While this is obviously not true (see the next section), in practice, it is usually a good first approximation. The Planck blackbody radiation distribution function thus turns out to be one of the primary analysis workhorses.

2.3 REAL THERMAL SOURCES

According to the Planck function, all objects having a temperature radiate energy at all wavelengths and at all times. However, as hinted in the last section, there is no such thing as an ideal radiator,[15] which would be a blackbody radiator. As a review, to be an ideal blackbody radiator, it would require the source to have a constant, steady-state temperature and to perfectly absorb all radiant energy that falls on it. The latter requirement is obviously not true of any object because everything can be seen by virtue of reflecting some of the energy (in the visible bandpass). Thus, there is a relation between absorption and reflection. This will be explored further in **Chapter 3**.

For now, the question is, "What about the emission (if any) from objects that are not ideal radiators?" An associated question, which will be answered first is, "Why?" The reason why real objects don't radiate like blackbodies is because the substances of which they are made interfere with radiation trying to escape. The details of this obstruction process are in the microscopic and quantum structure of matter, which will be discussed in the next three sections. First, look at the results: a concept called emissivity.

Figure 2-7
Example of common milky quartz.

CONCEPT OF EMISSIVITY—AN EXAMPLE

A common chunk of milky quartz[16] may be a familiar object to most people (**Figure 2-7**). Suppose a piece of it is heated successively to 300 K, 400 K, and 500 K, and its emission is measured as *spectral exitance*,[17] M_λ (which will be formally covered when radiometry phenomenology is studied). The results of the measurements compared to blackbody emission at the same temperatures are shown in **Figure 2-8**. (The data were normalized to present the maximum value for exitance as 1 in each plot to emphasize the features of each curve rather than their sizes. But, note, Wien's Displacement Law is obeyed.)

---

[15] The universe itself is probably the closest thing to an ideal radiator. Its temperature is about 2.725 K, as deduced from the Cosmic Microwave Background radiation. [1]

[16] Quartz is a commonly abundant mineral in the Earth's crust. It is a tetrahedral crystal of SiO_4 with each oxygen sharing between two adjacent tetrahedra giving an overall chemical formula of SiO_2. [2] The most common variety of milky quartz contains minute fluid inclusions that render it unuseful for optical purposes. [3]

[17] Remember the Planck function, B_λ (a distribution function), is the spectral exitance of a blackbody.

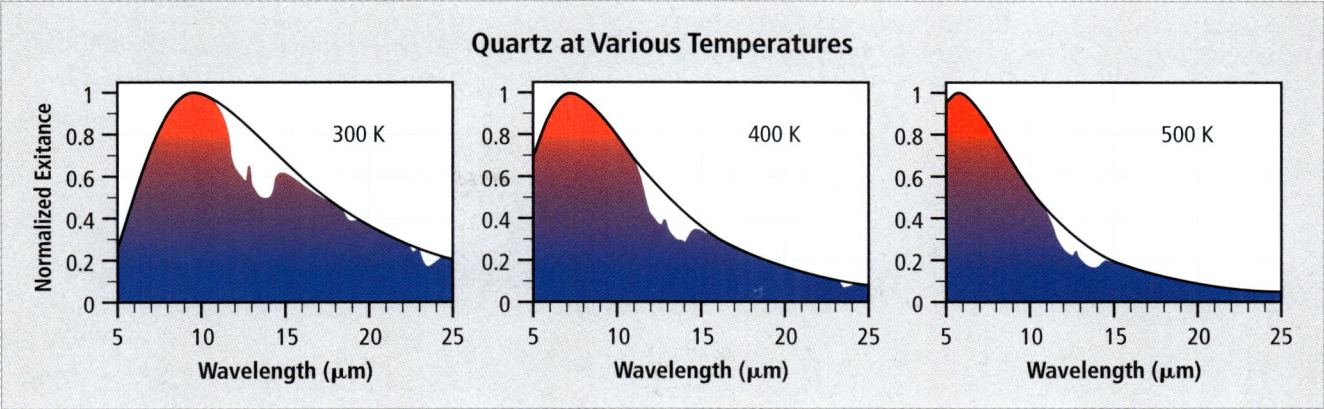

What should first be noted from **Figure 2-8** is the thermal exitance from quartz is *never* more than that from a blackbody at the same temperature at any wavelength. This is a general characteristic of all materials. Also, notice the specific feature that quartz shows a big dip in its exitance between about 12–14 μm at every temperature. There is a second dip showing up around 24 μm. These dips are very specific to quartz but are a general feature of the emission from all materials; every substance will exhibit emission less than that of a blackbody at specific wavelengths characteristic of its type and composition. Importantly, the spectral positions, wavelengths, of emission features are independent of temperature.[18]

In general, the ratio of actual energy emitted by any object at a given wavelength ($M_\lambda(\lambda,T)$, see **Chapter 4**) to that emitted by an ideal blackbody is called the *spectral emissivity* of that object:

$$\epsilon(\lambda) = \frac{M_\lambda(\lambda,T)}{B_\lambda(\lambda,T)}. \tag{2-15}$$

Note, once again, $\epsilon(\lambda)$ is *not* a function of temperature, but emissivity as a function of wavelength is fixed for every material and its surface properties. For milky quartz, the ratio is plotted in **Figure 2-9**, and this is its spectral emission *signature*. Note, $0 < \epsilon(\lambda) \leq 1$.

Figure 2-8
Normalized exitance of quartz (gradient fill) at three different temperatures compared to Planck blackbody exitance (solid line). (These graphs were calculated from the thermal emission spectrometer data shown in **Figure 2-9**.)

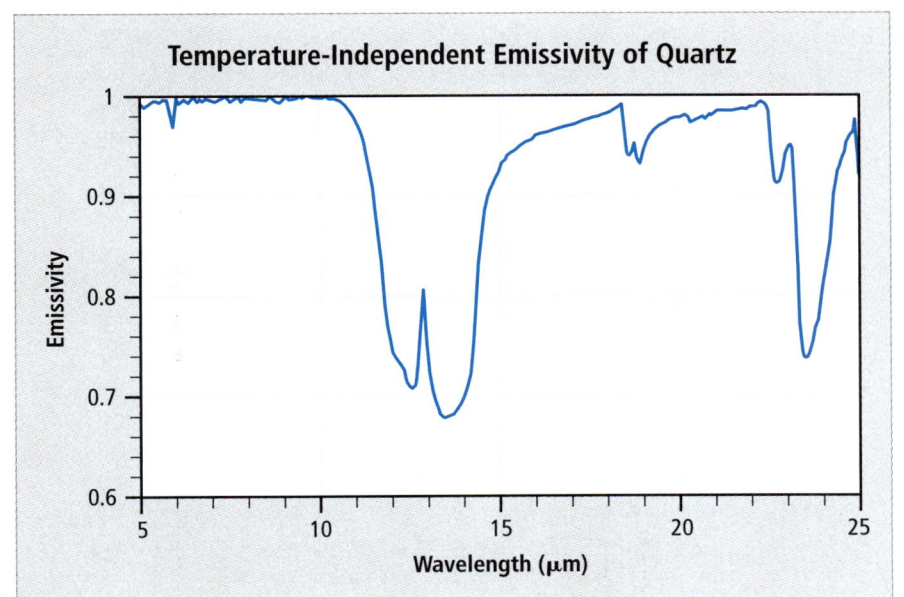

Figure 2-9
Emissivity (emissive signature) of quartz. [4]

[18] This is assuming that as a material is heated, it does not change forms. That is, no melting or boiling is allowed and certainly no chemical reactions. However, some expansion with increasing temperature may be expected to broaden a substance's emission features due to increased access to higher internal energy states. This will be considered later in this chapter.

EMISSIVITIES OF VARIOUS SURFACES

Emissivities of various substances in the visible. All the metals with low emissivities have clean, polished surfaces. [5],[6],[7],[8]

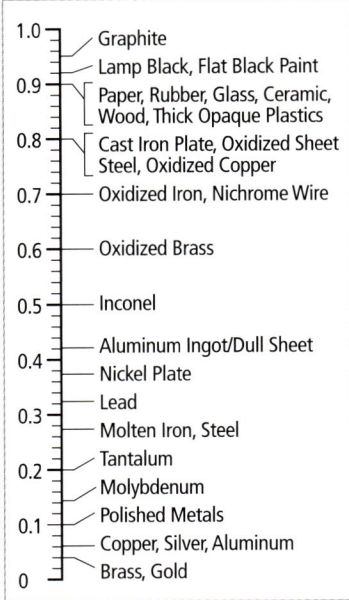

In principle, a spectral emission signature exists for every material, including natural and man-made, and could be used to *identify* objects. This assumes the following capabilities exist and can be completed: perform the measurement, extract the signature from the sensor and collection phenomenology, and compare the results to a signature database (e.g., ground truth). To emphasize one of the main themes of this text, the answer will at best be only an estimate of material identification.

GRAYBODY EMISSIVITY

Another continuing theme of this text is that information collection is always incomplete. In this case, the spectral exitance of any object cannot be measured at *all* wavelengths. What is more, the nature of remote sensing instruments is such that they cannot measure spectral exitance *at* any specific wavelength. (Just as the exact amount of energy emitted *at* a wavelength cannot be described; only its *distribution* can be described. If necessary, review the last section to refresh this point.)

Since a remote sensor has a spectral resolution,[19] what it measures is proportional to the sum of energies a target emits within its bandpass, similar to **Equation 2-11**:

$$M(T) = \int_{\text{BANDPASS}} M_\lambda(\lambda,T)d\lambda \ [\text{W} \cdot \text{m}^2]. \quad (2\text{-}16)$$

Thus, the estimate of spectral emissivity with a particular instrument then becomes:

$$\bar{\epsilon} = \frac{\int_{\text{BANDPASS}} M_\lambda(\lambda,T)d\lambda}{\int_{\text{BANDPASS}} B_\lambda(\lambda,T)d\lambda}. \quad (2\text{-}17)$$

The question then is what to call $\bar{\epsilon}$? Traditionally, $\bar{\epsilon}$ has been called the graybody emissivity, but what is technically meant by that term is $\epsilon(\lambda) = \left\{\begin{array}{l}\text{a constant for } all \\ \text{wavelengths}\end{array}\right\} \equiv \epsilon$. This is certainly not the case, as reference to **Figure 2-9** for quartz shows. Besides, all wavelengths cannot be measured with one instrument. Evidently, $\bar{\epsilon}$ means the *average* or *effective* value of emissivity within a bandpass; although the term graybody is, in fact, customarily used. Again, be cautious when discussing graybody emissivity with colleagues to ensure a mutual definition is being used. Sidebar **Emissivities of Various Surfaces** and **Table 2-1** provide some graybody values for some common materials.

Table 2-1
Graybody emissivities of some common materials measured in the 8–12 μm thermal band. [9]

Material	Emissivity
Granite, typical	0.815
Granite, rough	0.898
Sand, quartz, large-grain	0.914
Asphalt paving	0.959
Concrete walkway	0.966
Water, with thin oil film	0.972
Water, pure	0.993

[19] The definition for the spectral resolution of a remote sensor and how it is determined is logically discussed in the chapters on spectral/thermal/polarimetric remote sensing.

The fact that $\bar{\epsilon}$ is bandpass-dependent leads to an interesting effect. Whereas $\epsilon(\lambda)$ is strictly a function of wavelength and not of temperature, $\bar{\epsilon}$

is a weak function of temperature. As temperature increases, note the peak of the Planck function shifts to shorter wavelengths (Wien's Displacement Law, **Equation 2-9**). As the peak moves through the fixed bandpass of a remote sensor, the shape of the curve shifts from emphasizing exitance on the long-wavelength side of its bandpass to the short wavelength side. This effect is noticeable as the change in slope of **Figure 2-6**. The way a target's exitance depends on its emissivity function and temperature influences its apparent emissivity is shown in **Example 2-3**.

> **EXAMPLE 2-3: GRAYBODY EMISSIVITY**
>
> This example shows that the effective (graybody) emissivity of quartz depends on sensor bandpass, and that it depends on temperature (although a material's emissivity function does not).
>
>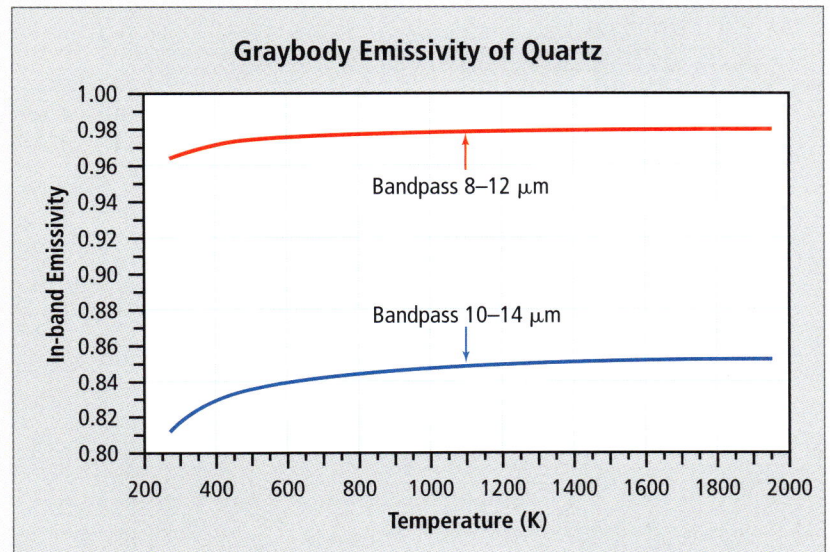
>
> Consider two thermal sensors: one with bandpass 8–12 μm and the other with overlapping bandpass 10–14 μm. Both sensors look at a piece of quartz as it is slowly heated from 250 K to approximately 1950 K (near its melting point). The results of calculating **Equation 2-17** are shown in the plot, where it is clear that effective emissivity indeed depends on the sensor bandpass and is slightly temperature dependent.

CONCEPT OF ABSORPTIVITY

If objects with a temperature (that includes everything) can radiate away energy, then the only way they can maintain their temperature is by absorbing energy from the outside[20] or manufacturing it on the inside.[21] Considering the radiation aspects of the energy alone results in the general steady state condition:

$$\left\{\frac{ENERGY}{TIME}\right\}_{OUT} = \left\{\frac{ENERGY}{TIME}\right\}_{IN}. \quad (2\text{-}18)$$

This follows a fundamental principle of physics, conservation of energy.

Since energy is in terms of a target's emissivity, $\epsilon(\lambda)$, on the left side of the equation, a complementary function called *absorptivity*, $\alpha(\lambda)$, must be defined for the right side.

[20] Outside sources of energy come from conduction, convection, and radiation, as pointed out in the last section. All three processes can come to steady state, but only the radiation will be sensed. In general, conduction and convection are slow, whereas radiation moves at the speed of light. Therefore, ignore conduction and convection and treat the radiation separately; radiant energy in equals radiant energy out, as will be the crux of the discussion in this section.

[21] Internal energy, nuclear/chemical reactions or electrical current resistive power dissipation, occurs below the "skin depth." Skin depth is the first few wavelengths of a target's physical surface. Some of the internal energy percolates to the surface through convection and conduction, but exchanges energy through the surface on a "slow" time scale. Radiation travels at the speed of light, so its origin (emission) and absorption at the surface (i.e., within the skin depth) is the only item of concern here.

To understand absorptivity, consider an experiment of a system consisting of only two objects: one true blackbody and one ordinary object, existing in a closed universe with perfectly reflecting walls.[22] Given enough time, the laws of thermodynamics assert that the two objects will come to the same temperature.[23] Then, **Equation 2-18** must be satisfied for each through the exchange of radiation alone (**Figure 2-10**).

Figure 2-10
Two-object universe.

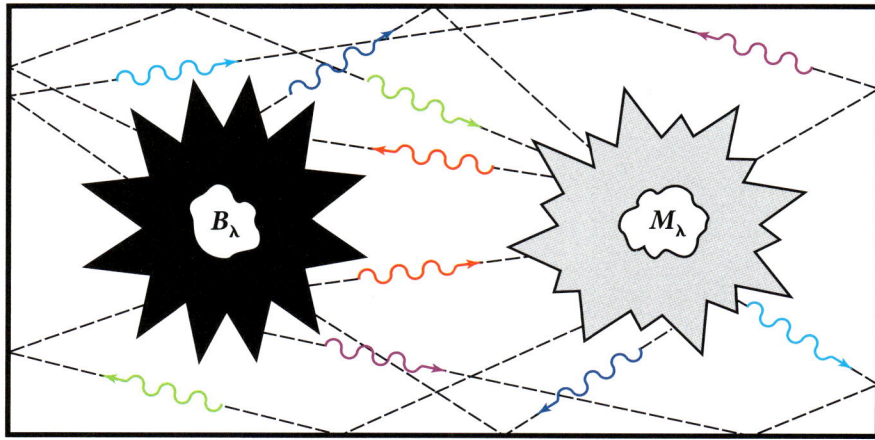

Considering the ordinary object in the box, the left-hand side of **Equation 2-18** must be written[24] from **Equations 2-15** and **2-16** as

$$\left\{\frac{ENERGY}{TIME}\right\}_{OUT} = \int_0^\infty (A_S) M_\lambda(\lambda, T) d\lambda = \int_0^\infty (A_S) \epsilon(\lambda) B_\lambda(\lambda, T) d\lambda, \quad (2\text{-}19)$$

where A_S is the object's surface area, radiating in all directions. Since the blackbody is the only other source of energy in the box, the right-hand side of **Equation 2-18** must be

$$\left\{\frac{ENERGY}{TIME}\right\}_{IN} = \int_0^\infty (A_S) \alpha(\lambda) B_\lambda(T) d\lambda, \quad (2\text{-}20)$$

where $\alpha(\lambda)$ is the emissivity-complementary function (absorptivity) hypothesized above.

At first glance, it is tempting to declare $\alpha(\lambda) = \epsilon(\lambda)$ by comparing **Equations 2-19** and **2-20** and employing the algebraic transitive property. But, this is incorrect! Because **Equations 2-19** and **2-20** are definite integrals (summations) over all energies (associating energy with wavelength through $E = hc/\lambda$), mathematically any functions $\alpha(\lambda)$ and $\epsilon(\lambda)$ could work with appropriate choices of coefficients, exponents, etc. Instead, consider the following:

The blackbody—emitting a blackbody spectrum—is, by definition, required to perfectly absorb all photons (it is opaque). Since it is in steady state, the "gas" of photons surrounding it must therefore be a blackbody spectrum. That "gas" must fill the entire two-body closed-universe system. Meanwhile, the non-ideal object is emitting and absorbing, maintaining its own energy balance (**Equation 2-18**). <u>For the photon gas surrounding the object to have a blackbody spectrum, the object must exactly replace (emit) a photon of the same energy (wavelength) for every one it absorbs.</u> Therefore, the supposition that

$$\alpha(\lambda) = \epsilon(\lambda) \quad (2\text{-}21)$$

---

[22] The concept of reflectivity will be introduced later.

[23] The astute reader will say the first object can't be a blackbody if its temperature changes, because steady state temperature is one of the conditions for a blackbody. As in all thermodynamic thought experiments, it is always *arbitrarily close* to being in steady state, and the experiment could be stopped and put in steady state at any time.

[24] Some *phenomenology* applied here should be obvious:

$$\left\{\frac{ENERGY}{TIME}\right\} = \{POWER\}$$
$$= \left\{\frac{POWER}{AREA}\right\} \times \{AREA\}$$
$$= \{EXITANCE\} \times \{AREA\}$$

is correct, wavelength-by-wavelength. The first glance was correct but for the wrong reason.

The argument just given is usually called detailed balance, and often **Equation 2-21** is spoken of as Kirchhoff's Law of Thermal Radiation or just Kirchhoff's Law. A common rendering of Kirchhoff's Law is *good absorbers are good emitters, while poor absorbers are poor emitters.*[25]

2.4 SELECTIVE SOURCES I: ATOMS

The underlying structure of the world, smaller than the spatial resolution attainable with optical microscopes, is one of atoms and molecules, where the rules of physics are not the same as they appear macroscopically. In particular, things that are typically treated as continuous, mass, energy, momentum, and so forth, are found to be "chunky." This has come to be accepted in modern culture. School children are taught that atoms and molecules are the building blocks for all materials, and they are made of protons, neutrons, and electrons. Today's children may be further taught that these, once thought to be the ultimate elementary particles, are made of even smaller entities: quarks and gluons.

No matter how small, *energy* holds it all together. This is the same energy asserted as the bearer of information to a remote sensor. If energy in its various forms is understood from the splitting of the atom to the movement of tectonic plates, its source can be understood when energy is received. The spectral characteristics of EM energy arising in a heated object as continuum radiation was just discussed,[26] and next the origins of information-transmitting energy from the sub-microscopic, quantum nature of matter will be discussed.

QUANTUM MECHANICS: ATOMS

Late 1800s and early 1900s physics established the model of the atom to be a nucleus of positive protons and neutral neutrons surrounded by a swarm of negative electrons. If the electrons are particles, then the model is like planets orbiting the sun (**Figure 2-11**). But, the consideration that sometimes particles can be waves[27] (conversely to light waves being photon-particles) suggests that the picture is more like a fuzz-ball of interlaced electron-waves. If electrons are waves, then the requirement that they build stable atoms without interfering (in the wave-optical sense) led physicists of a century ago to develop the quantum, or wave mechanics.

[25] Sometimes different values are shown for emissivity and absorptivity quoted for various materials. Caution is necessary when interpreting these values. What is probably meant is that an object has an absorptivity characteristic of its absorption in the visible-NIR infrared (as from sunlight). Whereas, it has an emissivity characteristic of its emission in the thermal band (usually ~ 8–12 μm). There is no requirement for an object to have the same emissivity at every wavelength (unless it is a true graybody).

[26] But remember, treat continuum radiation as being comprised of chunks of EM energy propagating at the speed of light. They are called photons. Planck's derivation of the blackbody distribution function, in fact, depended on the quantum of light hypothesis. This is normally not observable in continuum spectra because the modes are too close together to be told apart. This will be encountered again in Section 2-6.

[27] Suggested in 1924 by Louis de Broglie (Nobel Prize in Physics, 1929, third from right in middle row, Figure 2-4) in his PhD thesis: a particle has a wavelength inversely proportional to its momentum:

$$\lambda = \frac{h}{p} = \frac{h}{mv}\sqrt{1 - \frac{v^2}{c^2}}.$$

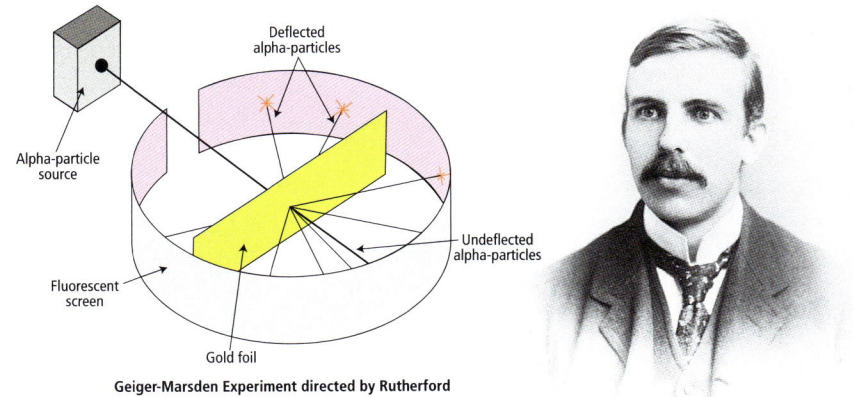

Figure 2-11
Ernest Rutherford (1871–1937), considered to be the father of nuclear physics, received the Nobel Prize in Chemistry in 1908, named the alpha and beta particle emissions from atoms, and discovered the atomic nucleus in 1911, thus establishing the planetary model as an analog to the heliocentric theory of the solar system.

A most provocative prediction of the early wave mechanics is that the energy of an electron whizzing around a nucleus can only be one of a set of allowed values. That is, it is quantized and cannot take on any value in a continuum. The new theory (developed by Niels Bohr, 1885–1962, Nobel Prize in Physics, 1922, right end of middle row in **Figure 2-4**) further predicted that electrons can only quantum leap from one allowed energy state to another, but under the strict universal condition of *conservation of energy*. One way for this to work is to consider a system of an electron (in an atom) and an observable photon such that the sum of their energies is constant.[28] If the electron's energy increases, the photon's decreases, and vice versa. The catch, however, is that the photon's energy comes as one lump and cannot be subdivided; so its energy must be equivalent to the electron's quantum leap between allowed energy states (all or nothing). It is either there, or it is not.

Combining allowed-energy-value-hopping electrons and appearing/disappearing photons with the conservation of energy theorem gives two possibilities (**Figure 2-12**). *Emission* is the process where an electron leaps from a higher energy state (or level) to a lower state, giving its energy difference to a photon. *Absorption* is the reverse process, where a photon invests all its energy in affecting an electron's transition from a lower to a higher state.[29] In either case, the photon's energy is equal to the difference between the electron's energy levels, and its wavelength is:

$$\lambda = \frac{hc}{E_{UPPER} - E_{LOWER}} = \frac{hc}{\Delta E}. \quad (2\text{-}22)$$

Figure 2-12
Conservation of energy in a quantum system.

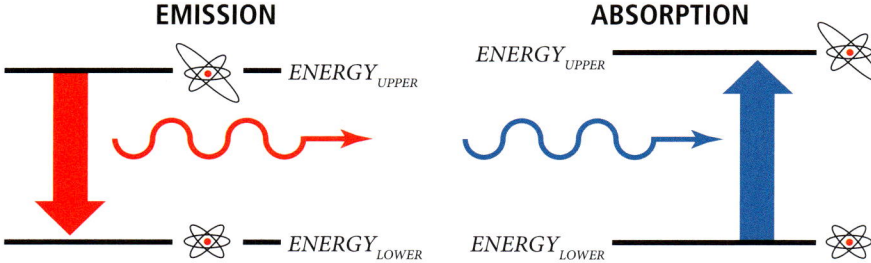

QUANTUM MECHANICS: ATOMS AND PHOTONS

The earliest success of the wave mechanics applied to atoms was calculating the energy levels of hydrogen's electron. The simplistic picture of hydrogen (left side of **Figure 2-13**) is one electron orbiting its single proton in a manner such that its wave function makes 1, 2, 3, … *n* complete oscillations upon returning to its starting point. Such *constructive interference* is required for the atom's stability. In this manner, the hydrogen electron's possible energies are calculated to be:[30]

$$E_{HYDROGEN} \approx \frac{-13.6}{n^2} \text{ [eV]}. \quad (2\text{-}23)$$

Here, *n* is called the principal quantum number and can only take on integer values of 1, 2, 3, … . The lowest energy ($n = 1$ for this electron) is always called the ground state, and all higher energy possibilities are excited states. An electron's energy is customarily given as *negative* when it is *bound* (attached) to its nucleus, like a penny rolling around below the top of a funnel (except the penny loses energy from rolling friction and wind resistance). An electron with

---

[28] Another way for this to work is not observable; two atoms can collide and exchange energy. For example, the electron in one atom jumps to a lower level, while the electron in the other atom jumps to a higher level. The down-jumping energy has to equal the up-jumping energy. Collisional energy exchange is more common in molecular energy modes, which will be studied in the next section.

[29] To be complete, there is a third possibility, *stimulated emission*. Here, a photon with energy equal to the difference between two energy levels tickles a quantum system to leap down to its lower level, emitting a photon with the same energy. Now, there are two photons in lock-step (a property called coherence). This process is the basis for the laser, Light Amplification by the Stimulated Emission of Radiation, but does not naturally occur in the environment.

[30] This formula was actually discovered empirically before it was first derived by Niels Bohr. But, there was no theoretical explanation for it until electrons were hypothesized to be wave-like.

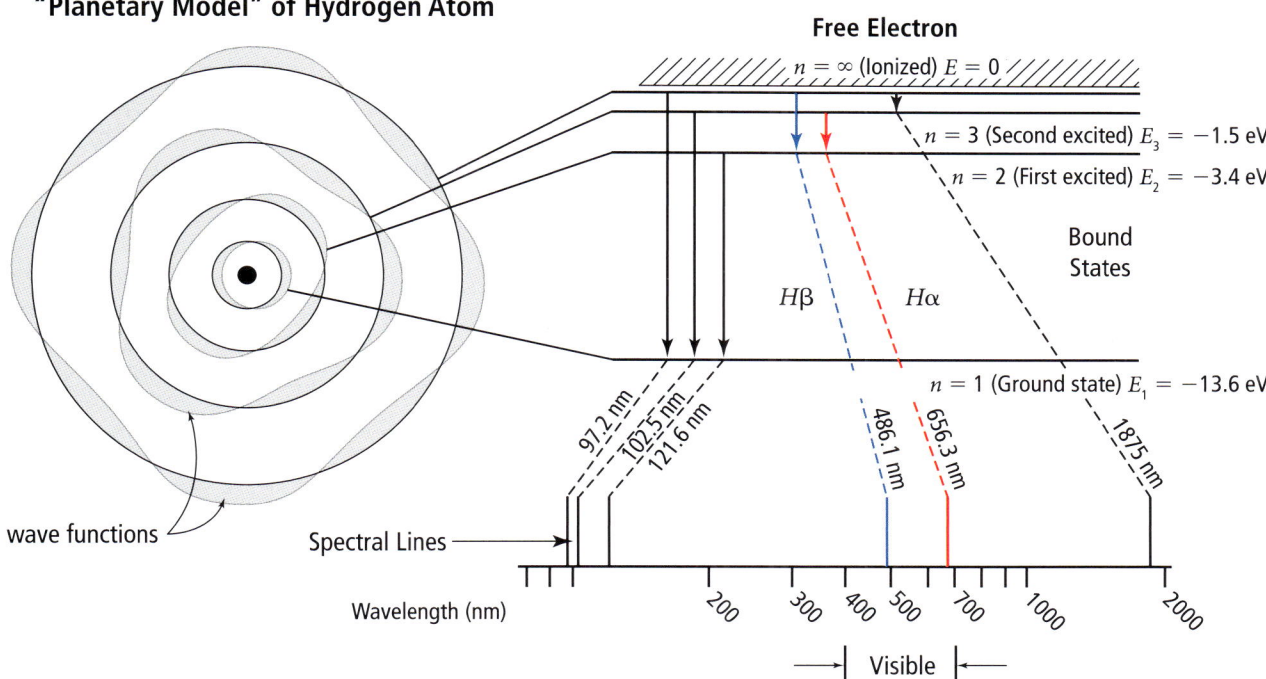

Figure 2-13
Energy levels and spectrum of hydrogen.

positive energy (a penny above the rim of a funnel) in this model is *free* (but, then the atom isn't an atom; it's an ion).

Coupled to the energy levels, the model correctly predicts the wavelengths of photons that can be emitted from hydrogen. The right side of **Figure 2-13** depicts some of them from quantum leaps (transitions, or often called lines) among the first three excited states and the ground state.[31] The importance of knowing the wavelengths of photons that can be emitted (or absorbed[32]) is *the presence of hydrogen from radiation received from a source can be identified.* That is, the particular wavelengths derived from transitions, as shown in **Figure 2-13** using **Equation 2-23,** to calculate the energy levels are the *signature* of hydrogen! Note, only four of hydrogen's lines (**Figure 2-14**) are in the visible spectrum with the brightest red line called H-alpha (Hα). Hα is an extremely important wavelength; the sun is routinely photographed in Hα light by observatories around the world (**Figure 2-15**) and the relative brightness across its surface serves as an indicator of solar storms affecting weather and communications on Earth.

[31] Historically, the wavelengths of photons emitted from hydrogen atoms transitioning to the ground state are known as the Lyman series. The wavelengths of photons emitted from higher energy levels transitioning to the first excited state are known as the Balmer series. Similarly, to the second excited state are the Paschen series; to the third excited state are the Brackett series; and to the fourth excited state are the Pfund series. These are all named for the scientists who first discovered them.

[32] Emitted or absorbed? The preliminary answer is "it depends on temperature," and that question will be addressed in a couple of sections.

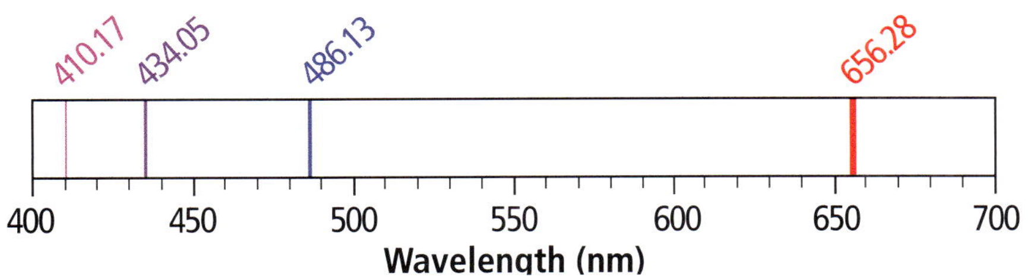

Figure 2-14
The visible signature of hydrogen.

CHAPTER 2 LIGHT EMITTING TARGETS

Figure 2-15
The sun photographed in $H\alpha$ light. One of several solar national observatories, the John W. Evans facility at Sacramento Peak Observatory, Sunspot, New Mexico (inset).

QUANTUM MECHANICS: SIGNATURES

Just as hydrogen can be identified, in principle, so can all of the 90+ chemical elements, their ions, and many molecules from the interaction of their electrons with photons. Beyond hydrogen, however, the calculation of electrons' energy levels becomes significantly more challenging; molecular electron energy states are even more so. For example, **Figure 2-16** shows the energy levels of helium electrons; more quantum numbers come into play, and various rules predict whether an emission or absorption can even take place between particular energy states. Nonetheless, the electronic spectra of many atoms and molecules have been studied extensively and are known.

Figure 2-16
Electronic energy levels of helium. One electron is assumed to remain in its ground state, while the second electron is either spin opposed (parahelium) or spin parallel (orthohelium) to the spin of the first. Spin is a quantum number ($S = 0$ or 1), as are the principal quantum number (labeling the states as $n = 1, 2, 3, 4, \ldots$) and orbital angular momentum quantum number ($\ell = 0, 1, 2, 3, \ldots$, but historically designated as $s, p, d, f, \ldots$).

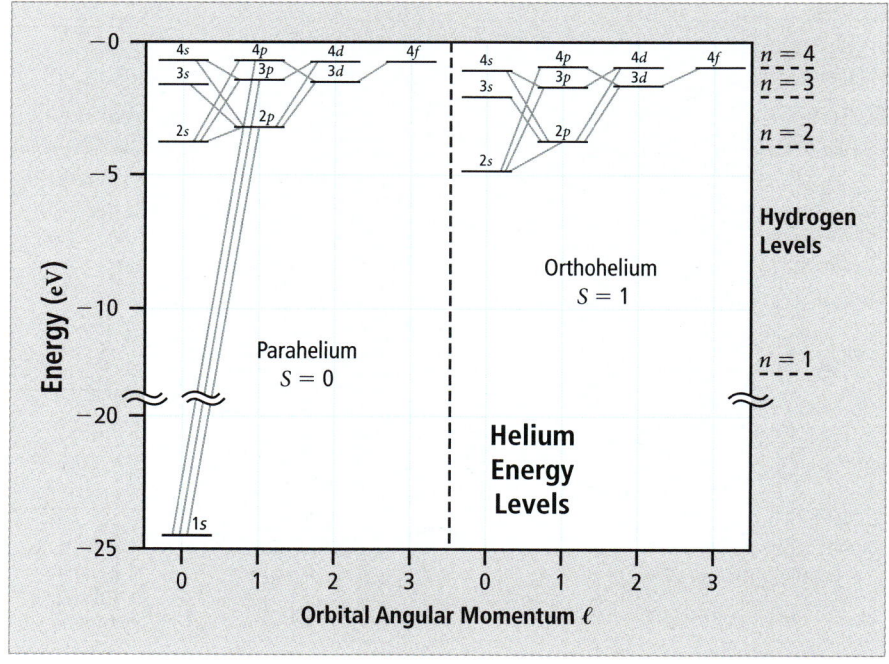

The emission signatures of some elements are shown in **Figure 2-17** and **Example 2-4**. From this figure and **Figures 2-13**, **2-14**, and **2-16** a general rule can be noted: the range of energy jumps for atomic electrons puts their emissions (or absorptions) primarily in the NIR through ultraviolet portions of the EM spectrum. Without proof, the same is generally true for molecules. As atoms and molecules get heavier and more complex, energy binding the electrons to the nuclei increases, and the wavelengths of interacting photons become shorter into the ultraviolet and x-ray spectra. The astute reader will notice, however, the energy levels for large quantum numbers near the top of **Figures 2-13** and **2-16** are close enough together that emissions should be in the infrared (long-wavelengths). This is true, except for the reasons uncovered[33] in Section 2.6 that show these transitions almost never naturally occur in the terrestrial environment.

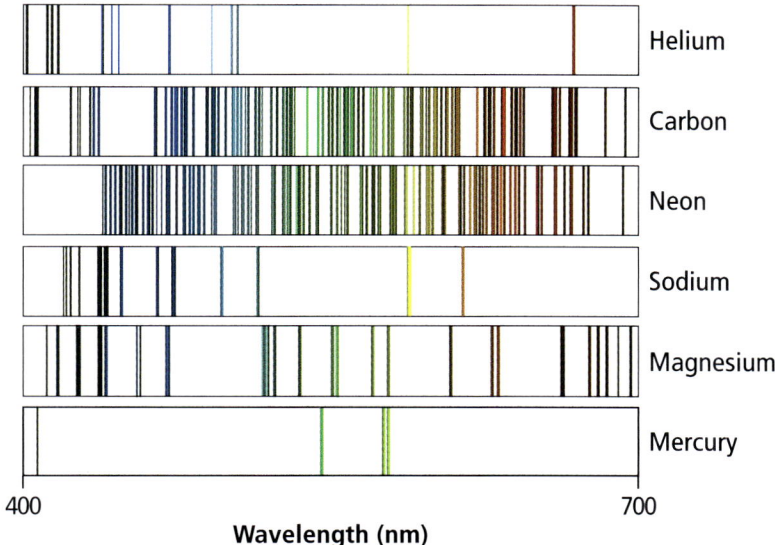

Figure 2-17
Electronic spectra of some abundant elements.

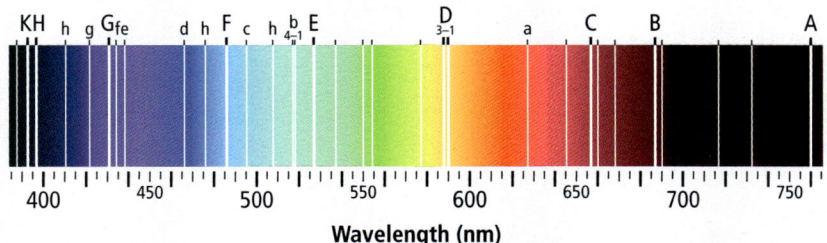

EXAMPLE 2-4: SOLAR SPECTRUM

Identify the chemical elements present in the sun's photosphere.

This classic problem was explored by Fraunhofer in the early 1800's. From the solar spectrum that is often named after him, the elements hydrogen (labeled C, F, G, and h), helium (D_3), sodium (D_1 and D_2), magnesium (b_1, b_2, and b_4), calcium (G), iron (b_3, b_4, c, d, e, and G), and mercury (e) can be identified, as well as singly-ionized calcium (H and K).

The spectra of all stars reveal their compositions. The discovery of the deep violet emissions of technetium, a radioactive element naturally occurring in only miniscule quantities on Earth, from S-type red giants in 1952 boosted the theory of nucleosynthesis; all chemical elements heavier than iron are produced in the interior of stars.

---

[33] To preview the material in Section 2.6, it is about the population of the energy states. If no electrons populate the higher energy states, there can be no emission or absorption. Again, it will be shown that it is all about temperature.

Recognizing materials by their emission (or absorption) of photons between electronic energy states with remote sensors, a topic called spectral identification, is a somewhat more difficult task than one might think. While laboratory measurements can be easily controlled, field measurements are highly dependent on collection geometry, atmospheric attenuation, and background brightness. Again, the goal of information gathering is to collect as much as possible (remember it all cannot be collected). Consequently, many remote sensors will generally not incorporate sufficiently narrow bandpasses to detect and isolate the individual spectral lines necessary for material identification. This will be covered in more detail in the chapters on spectral resolution.

2.5 SELECTIVE SOURCES II: MOLECULES

The next layer of complexity in the structure of the world is the molecule: two or more atoms joined, or bonded, together. The interactions between positive nuclei and negative electrons become complicated, but, somehow the outermost electrons are shared amongst constituent atoms to create a stable[34] configuration. As with the atom, there are discrete energy levels described by electron wave-functions and quantum numbers, and the same rule applies: photons can only be emitted or absorbed between allowed energy states, the electrons quantum leaping between levels to conserve energy and angular momentum. However, in advanced technical intelligence collection practice, analysts rarely look for information transferred by electron transitions in molecules. Instead, efforts are concentrated on looking for two other origins of radiation that will be described in this section: molecular vibration and rotation.

DIATOMIC MOLECULES

To begin the study of molecular vibration and rotation, consider the simplest of molecules: two atoms. The nature of the chemical bond between them is EM with positive nuclei and negative electrons repelling themselves, respectively, yet opposite charges attracting and occupying the space that is the molecule. Thus, there is a concentrated region of electric and magnetic fields arranged according to the way the positive and negative charges are distributed within. If the charge distribution, and hence, the fields are distributed symmetrically when both atoms are the same element, such as N_2 and O_2, a diatomic molecule looks neutral and balanced from the outside. If the two atoms are dissimilar, such as NaCl or CO, then the diatomic molecule is still neutral but asymmetrical. The asymmetric molecule has a dipole moment[35] (**Figure 2-18**).

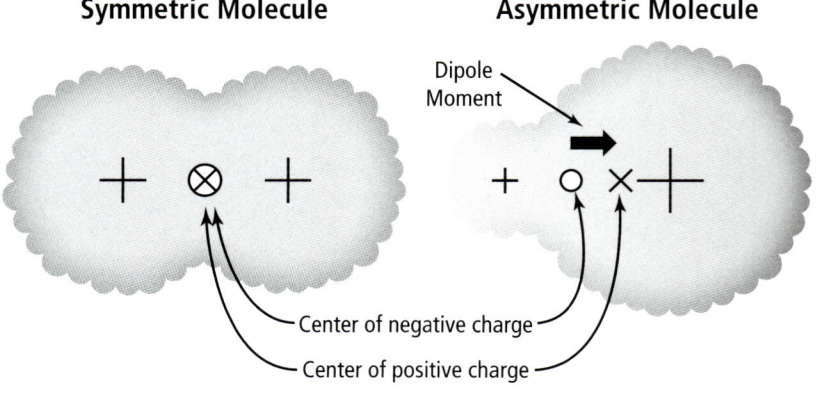

Figure 2-18
Possible diatomic molecule charge distributions: symmetric or asymmetric.

[34] Some molecules are more stable than others. Explosive compounds, for example, are specifically designed to be on the edge of stability so their internal energy can be easily released. Explosives will be considered as advanced technical intelligence targets in support of the warfighter.

[35] Dipole moment is defined as {amount of charge} × {separation distance between centers of charge}, but there is no need to actually calculate it. Only acknowledge it as a feature of molecules having a permanent, or temporary, asymmetrical charge distribution.

The importance of considering molecules' charge distributions is: remember a photon is a packet of EM fields too. For a photon to interact with a molecule through emission or absorption, the molecule *must* have an EM "handle" to interact with the photon's fields. A dipole moment is such a handle. Therefore, photons in the electro-optic spectrum do not interact with symmetric molecules.[36] This convenient physics fact makes remote sensing through the Earth's atmosphere possible,[37] which will be discussed in later chapters.

MOLECULAR VIBRATION

One way to treat the chemical bond is like a spring joining two nuclei (**Figure 2-19**). Classically, the solution to the mass-on-a-spring problem is the harmonic oscillator, which allows the spring to stretch and compress at its natural frequency, but with any amplitude (up to the limit of breaking the spring). The amplitude of oscillation is proportional to the energy of the spring.

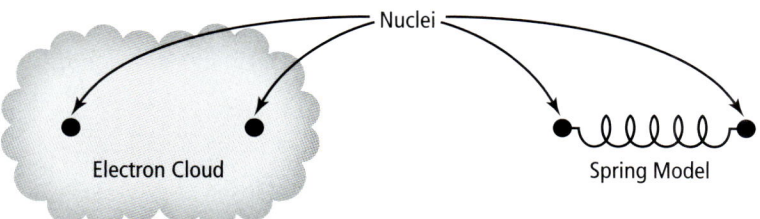

The Chemical Bond

Figure 2-19
The world is really just a bunch of springs.

However, carrying the macroscopic classical solution into the microscopic world of molecules uncovers the peculiar behavior seen before. The quantum spring can only oscillate with discrete, allowed values of energy. Similarly to the atomic electron being represented by a particle-wave making closed laps around its orbit (**Figure 2-13**), the vibrating bond can be envisioned as a wave bouncing constructively within the confines of its spring-bond. (**Figure 2-20** shows the limits of the bond-oscillator to be the potential energy "well" of the spring.) The allowed energies for this vibration are given approximately[38] by

$$E_{VIBRATION} \approx \left(v + \frac{1}{2}\right)E_{v0}, \qquad (2\text{-}24)$$

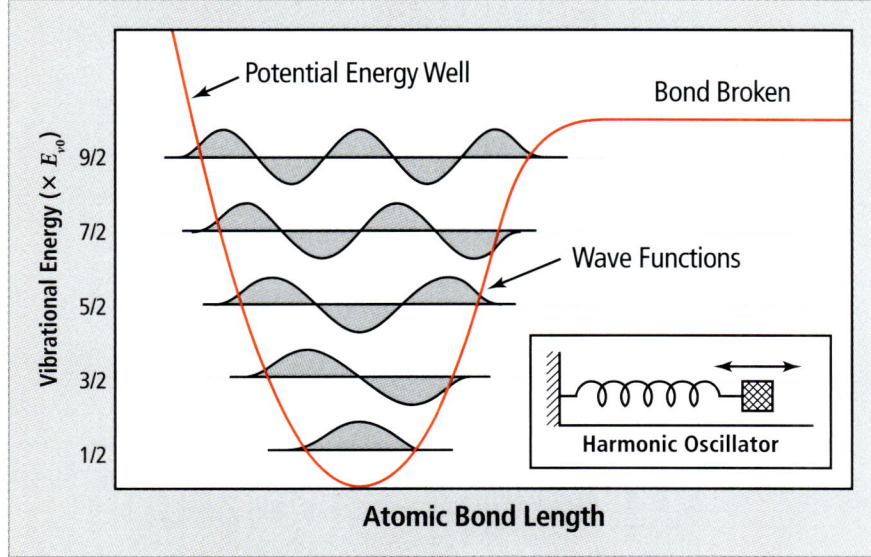

Figure 2-20
Vibrational energy levels and wave functions.

[36] Symmetric molecules may have *magnetic* dipole moments or higher order electric moments (e.g., quadrupole) with which a photon may interact. Such interactions are extremely weak. They are rarely, if ever, seen in advanced technical intelligence collection.

[37] The Earth's atmosphere is 99% symmetric diatomic molecules (nitrogen and oxygen), which have no dipole moments.

[38] The bond's stretchiness becomes slightly non-linear in higher energy states. So, small correction terms are needed. The number of allowed vibrational energy states is usually limited before the bond breaks, as suggested by **Figure 2-20**. For these purposes, corrections are generally not addressed.

where v is the quantum number, and can only have integer values 0, 1, 2, 3, …. For quantum vibration, $v = 0$ is the ground state;[39] $E_{v=0} \approx \frac{1}{2}E_{v0}$ and all other energy levels are excited states.

The constant E_{v0} is specific to each chemical bond in every molecule, depending on the masses of the nuclei, the natural distance between them, and the influence of surrounding bonds. For the common (poisonous) diatomic carbon monoxide molecule, its value is approximately 0.266 eV. **Figure 2-21** depicts the first four energy levels of CO. They are approximately evenly spaced. Identical to the rule for atomic electrons (**Equation 2-21**), only photons with energies equal to the difference between two of its allowed vibrational states may interact with this molecule's bond. For example, the diagram shows that photons of wavelengths 1.55, 2.33, and 4.67 μm could be emitted when excited state CO molecules quantum leap to lower energy states. These wavelengths constitute a *signature* of carbon monoxide.

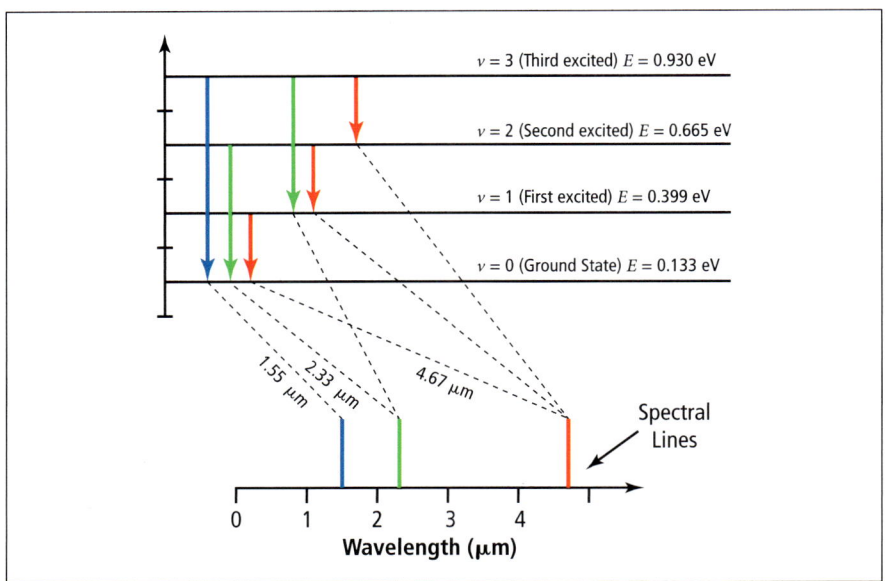

Figure 2-21
Vibrational transitions of carbon monoxide.

The vibrational energies, ~0.1–1.0 eV, calculated for CO in **Figure 2-21** are fairly typical of many chemical bonds. The vibrational transitions of many molecules appear in the SWIR to MWIR portions of the electro-optic spectrum. Their identification through infrared spectroscopy is routine.

MOLECULAR ROTATION

Forsaking the spring model, another way to treat a diatomic molecule in a semi-classical manner is as a rigid rotator or dumbbell (**Figure 2-22**). As with the atomic electron and vibrating bond, when considering the microscopic realm of molecules, the rotational energy is also quantized. This time, the energy of rotation is characterized by a quantum number, J, which can only have integer values 0, 1, 2, 3, …. The energy is approximately:[40]

$$E_{ROTATIONAL} \approx J(J+1)E_{J0}. \qquad (2\text{-}25)$$

Again, as with vibration, the value of E_{J0} is unique to each type of molecule. **Figure 2-23** shows the first few energy levels for the CO molecule, where $E_{J0} \approx 0.0476$ meV. The figure shows the wavelengths of photons that would be emitted from a cloud of CO gas when the molecules quantum leap to lower energy states.[41] This is the *signature* of the molecule.

[39] This energy formula shows it is impossible for a molecule to have zero energy. If a molecule were cooled to absolute zero temperature, its bonds would still be vibrating. But, it would not be able to transfer any of its energy to any other system (which is the meaning of 0 K).

[40] The bond really is not rigid. As well as vibrating, it stretches a little bit as a molecule spins faster and faster, so there are correction terms. But, as with vibration, they are small. Ignore these for advanced technical intelligence collection applications.

[41] How molecules get into excited energy states will be considered in the next section.

Figure 2-22
The world is a bunch of dumbbells.

Rigid Rotator Model

Figure 2-23 requires further explanation. First, the wavelengths shown are typical of rotational energy transitions. They are in the microwave spectrum, ~0.0001–0.001 eV, outside the range of electro-optical sensors. Second, unlike vibration, there is only one transition (emission) shown from each energy state. Are these facts a concern?

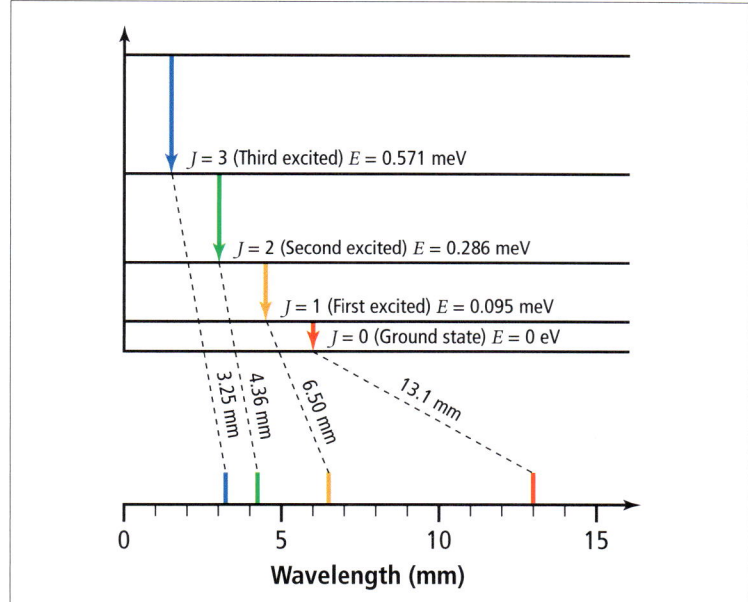

Figure 2-23
Rotational energy levels of carbon monoxide.

The answer is closely tied to the second comment: the astute reader will notice the rotational transitions shown in **Figure 2-23** are only between adjacent energy levels, whereas the vibrational transitions of **Figure 2-21** are between all pairs of levels. The subtle reason is not only do photons carry energy ($E = hf = hc/\lambda$), they also carry one unit of angular momentum,[42] $\ell = h/2\pi = \hbar$ (pronounced "h-bar"). It is quantized like everything else in the microscopic world! A rotating molecule also has angular momentum, as expected, and in fact, has precisely J units. So, another firm rule of physics is *angular momentum must be conserved*. When a rotating molecule quantum leaps to another energy state, emitting or absorbing a photon, it can change only by one unit of angular momentum. Thus, there is a selection rule for rotational transitions:

$$\Delta J = \pm 1. \quad (2\text{-}26)$$

[42] Recall that classically, angular momentum is a property of spinning/rotating bodies. A rotating bicycle wheel, for example, has $\ell = I\omega$ where $I = mr^2$ is the moment of inertia and ω is the angular rotation rate. The mass of the bicycle wheel is m and its radius is r.

VIBROTATION

Admitting that photons carry angular momentum leads to a revisit of previous discussions about electron and vibrational transitions. Apparently electrons encircling their nuclei have an orbital form of angular momentum that can be exchanged with a photon during an emission or absorption quantum leap. So, nothing new can be added to the discussion in **Section 2.4**.[43] There is nothing inherently spinning, turning, or rotating about a harmonic oscillator-like, vibrating chemical bond. So, where does the angular momentum come from that is introduced by the photon?

The answer is a molecule can vibrate *and* rotate at the same time. The two actions are independent of one another up to the point when one of them becomes so violent as to break the bond. So, it makes sense to discuss them separately. Yet in reality, they must always occur together to satisfy both the energy *and* angular momentum conservation requirements. Thus, a mash-up results: *vibrotation*.

Figure 2-24 suggests that a diatomic molecule can have *both* a v and a J. Since rotational energies are typically approximately 10^{-4} eV (while vibrational energies are one hundred or one thousand times that), a molecule's total energy is the sum of the two but dominated by vibration. Quantum leaps between rotational states ($\Delta J = \pm 1$) will still be in the microwave, but vibrational transitions ($\Delta v = $ *any integer*) in the infrared will *always* be accompanied by a simultaneous rotational jump that will change the energy of the photon. This is depicted in **Figure 2-24** (not to scale).

Figure 2-24
Vibrotational energy states and possible transitions (not to scale).

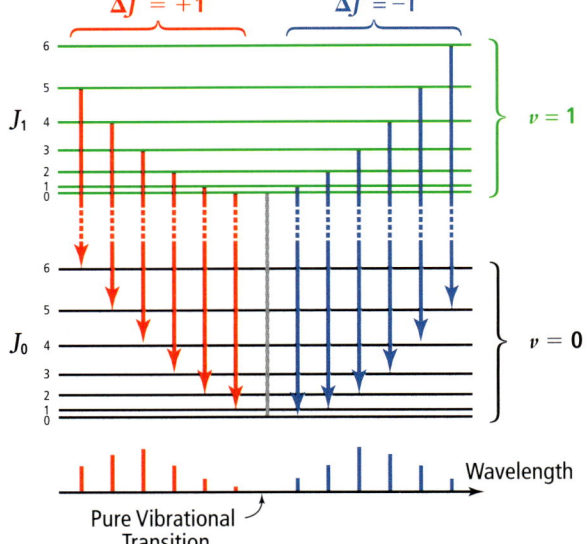

In regards to CO, if its vibrational transitions of **Figure 2-21** and its rotational transitions of **Figure 2-23** are combined, the result is the *vibrotational* infrared spectrum[44] shown in **Figure 2-25**. This is the clear *signature* of a diatomic molecule; the energy is in the infrared range, and all the spikes (lines) are rotational transitions. The shapes of the left and right wings of the signature are due to the populations of the rotational energy states as shown in **Section 2.6**. See **Example 2-5**.

---

[43] This is true for the collection of information needed to support the warfighter. Physics students may solve the Schrodinger wave equation to learn that atomic electrons have a quantum number for orbital angular momentum, for its projection, and for their intrinsic spin. All of these bear on the electrons' energies and have associated selection rules governing transitions.

[44] These data were collected in a controlled laboratory setting with high spectral resolution and are not the typical results expected in a field measurement. Spectral resolution will be discussed in **Chapter 17**.

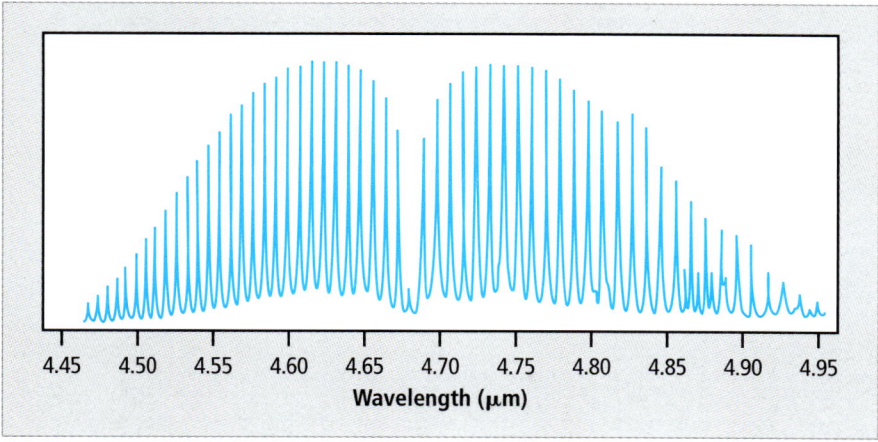

Figure 2-25
Vibrotational spectrum of carbon monoxide (high spectral resolution).

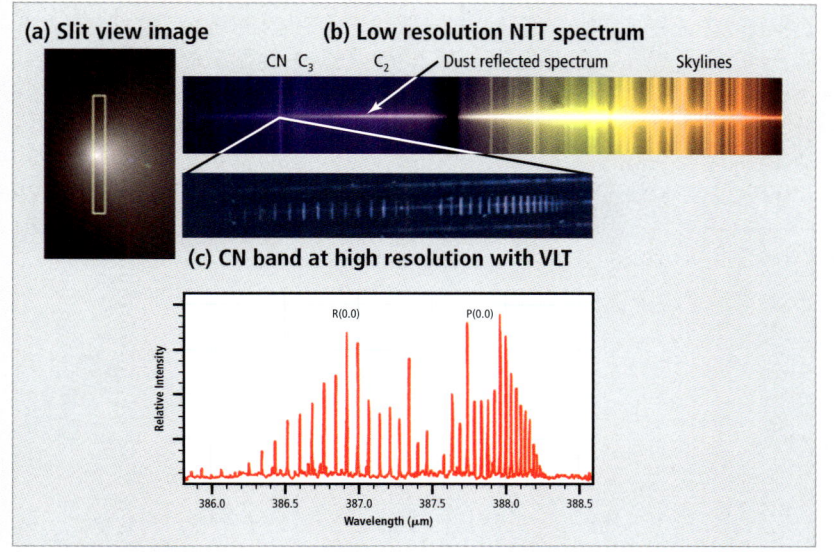

EXAMPLE 2-5: SPACE MOLECULE IDENTIFICATION

Identify an organic compound in the comet Temple I.

On July 4, 2005, the Deep Impact Mission smashed a lander into the head of comet Temple I and recorded the resulting spectrum. The organic radical cyanogen, CN, was identified from its diatomic vibrational emissions in the ultraviolet.

TRIATOMIC MOLECULES

Triatomic molecules represent a significant increase in complexity in nature. But, at least they are linear or planar, and their energy modes are easy to discern. Beyond that, there are many bonds and spatial configurations not so easily visualized.

BENT TRIATOMICS

One of the most important molecules in the environment is an archetypical example of the *bent* triatomic molecule: water. Besides covering three-quarters of the Earth's surface, the lowest few kilometers of the atmosphere is full of it in its gaseous state as water vapor. The molecule's configuration is balanced, but the angle between the hydrogen bonds is approximately 105° to minimize internal potential of the molecule:

$$H\diagup^{\displaystyle O}\diagdown H$$

As a bent molecule, the hydrogen side tends to be slightly positive, as the larger oxygen atom attracts electrons more strongly. Thus, a water molecule has a slight charge asymmetry and consequently, a dipole moment. It therefore interacts with photons through both vibrational and rotational energy modes. All bent triatomics will behave similarly to water.

1. **VIBRATION** Bent triatomics, with two chemical bonds, exhibit three independent vibrational modes: 1) symmetric stretching, 2) bending, and 3) asymmetric stretching. The three modes have separate quantum numbers, v_1, v_2, and v_3, respectively and are illustrated for water in **Figure 2-26**. The figure also gives an energy level diagram for water molecules, indicating their characteristic wavelengths for first excited state to ground state ($v_i = 1 \rightarrow 0$) transitions. That is, these are the wavelengths observed for pure vibrational quantum leaps without any rotational energy change (disregarding conservation of angular momentum): the vibrational *signature* of the water molecule.

Figure 2-26
Vibrational modes of the water molecule.

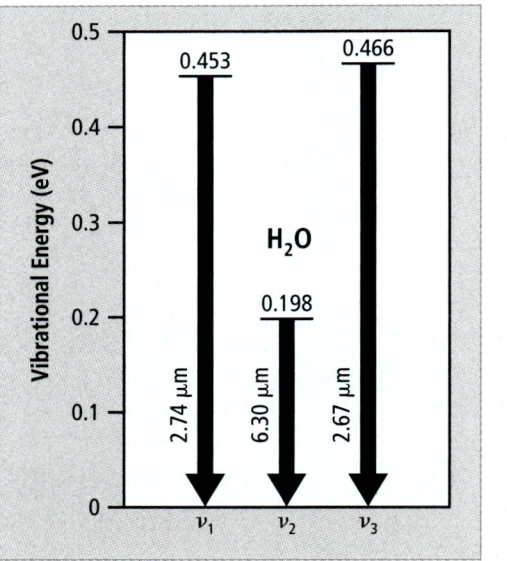
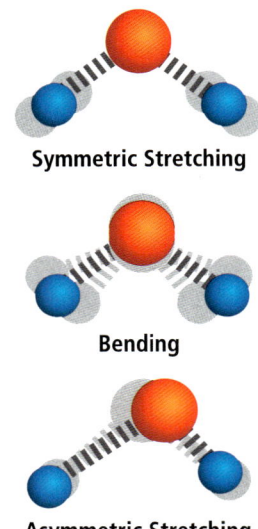

2. **ROTATION** As in classical physics, a bent triatomic molecule, as a three-dimensional rigid structure, can rotate around any of three mutually orthogonal axes. The tinker-toy drawing of **Figure 2-27** shows the three axes for H_2O. Each of the rotations has a characteristic set of energy levels, given by **Equation 2-25**, with quantum numbers J_1, J_2, and J_3, and values of E_{J0} for each axis. Although these rotational energies do not need to be computed for this application, it is important to remember the spinning molecule will have an integral number of units of angular momentum. The effect on the spectral signature of adding rotational energy will be to add vibrational lines on either side of the wavelengths given for vibration alone, similar[45] to **Figures 2-24** and **2-25**.

[45] Refer to the standard textbooks on molecular spectroscopy for more information.

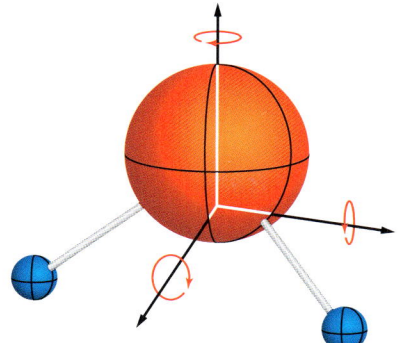

Figure 2-27
Rotating bent triatomic molecule. The origin of coordinates is at the center of mass of the molecule.

LINEAR TRIATOMICS

Another common molecule in the environment is the archetypical example of the *linear* triatomic: carbon dioxide. The configuration of this molecule with two equal bonds is:

$$O = C = O$$

Since this is balanced and charge is symmetric, it would appear this molecule has no dipole moment. So, how can it interact with radiation? This is not true of triatomics in general, of course, because many of them, such as hydrogen cyanide,

$$H - C \equiv N,$$

are inherently asymmetric and do have dipole moments for photons to interact with. But, because CO_2 is such an important molecule, it bears being looked at more closely.

1. **VIBRATION** Like its bent counterpart, a linear triatomic molecule has three possible ways it can vibrate: 1) symmetric stretching, 2) bending, and 3) asymmetric stretching. The CO_2 vibrational modes are shown in **Figure 2-28**, which should be compared to **Figure 2-26**. In its symmetric stretching mode, the two oxygen atoms are always equidistant from the central carbon. So, the molecule will maintain its symmetry and will *not* interact[46] with photons. Notice, no wavelength is associated with the $v_1 = 1 \rightarrow 0$ transition of CO_2 in **Figure 2-28**. However, the other two vibrational modes are quite different.

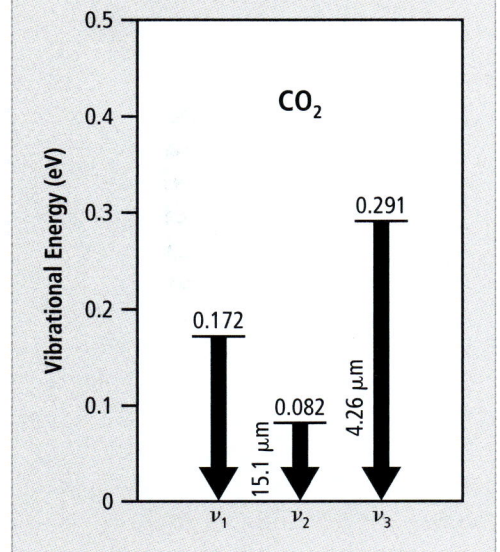

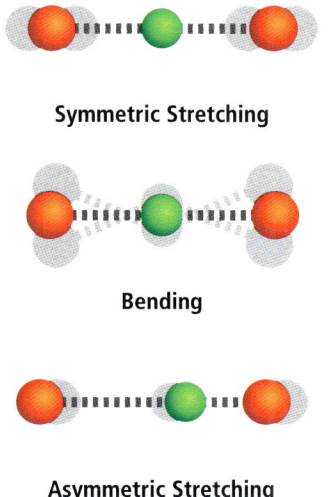

Figure 2-28
Vibrational modes of the linear triatomic carbon dioxide molecule.

[46] At least CO_2 does not have a dipole moment in its symmetric stretch mode, but there could be higher-order moments that are much weaker. These may be observed in a laboratory setting but probably not where field work is being done with advanced technical intelligence collectors.

CHAPTER 2 LIGHT EMITTING TARGETS

In its bending mode, a symmetric linear triatomic molecule like CO_2 will exhibit an oscillating dipole moment. For half its cycle, the oxygen atoms will be "below" the carbon atom, giving the molecule a slight excess of positive charge below the center of negative charge. For the second half of its cycle, the situation is reversed. The oscillating moment is sufficient for emission/absorption of photons, but notice this CO_2 wavelength is well into the LWIR at 15.1 μm.

An interesting feature of the linear molecule's bending mode is that the oscillation could take place in either of two orthogonal planes. For convenience, take these to be horizontal and vertical as illustrated in **Figure 2-29**. Since a CO_2 molecule itself doesn't care which plane it bends in, the vibrational energy is the same for either one.[47] The mode is therefore called degenerate, a concept that will be very important in the next section.

Figure 2-29
Carbon dioxide bending planes.

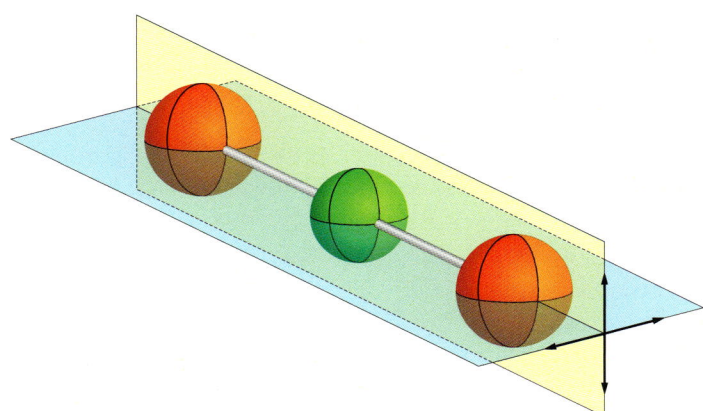

The asymmetric stretching mode, like the bending mode, has an oscillating dipole moment, because the two bonds are vibrating 180° out of phase. For instance, the bottom picture in **Figure 2-28** shows the left O = C bond stretching, while the right C = O bond is compressing. The result is a more positive right end to the molecule and more negative on the left. This situation reverses half a cycle later and so forth. Once again, the oscillating moment is sufficient to allow interaction with the EM fields of a photon. The energy level diagram in **Figure 2-28** shows this emission/absorption occurs in the MWIR, and is the most prominent *signature* of carbon dioxide that will be encountered in remote sensing applications.

2. **ROTATION** For rotation, one would think the linear triatomic could rotate about any of three mutually perpendicular axes like any other three-dimensional structure. In the quantum world, it is not so. Energy is associated with only two of the three possible rotations, as shown in **Figure 2-30**. This is not to say there is no energy associated with a linear triatomic molecule rotating around its bond-axis; it is manifested in the orbital motions of the internal electrons and not the molecule as a whole. Thus, a linear triatomic, like CO_2, will only have a far-infrared or microwave rotational energy spectrum based on the two rotations shown, which are obviously also degenerate. For the sake of conservation of angular momentum, the $\Delta J = \pm 1$ selection rule must apply.

[47] An even more interesting side note: although it makes no practical difference, a CO_2 molecule vibrating with $v_2 = 2$ (two units of bending mode energy) could be simultaneously oscillating in both the horizontal and vertical planes (one unit of energy in each plane). The reader is challenged to visualize what this motion must look like.

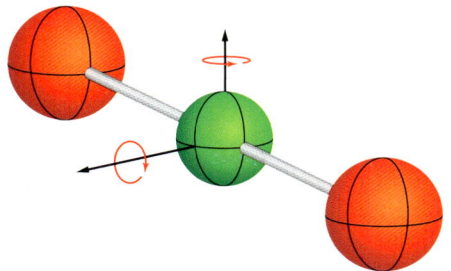

Figure 2-30
Triatomic molecule rotation.

POLYATOMIC MOLECULES

Polyatomic means any molecule with more than one atom (which, by definition, is an element), including the diatomics and triatomics just discussed. A general rule of physics is any polyatomic molecule with N atoms has $3N$ degrees of freedom, or modes, into which it may store energy.

For the diatomics, $N = 2$. So, there are *six* ways they can have energy. As earlier discussed, the bond of a diatomic molecule can vibrate, and the molecule can rotate. Taking the discussion of triatomic rotation backwards, evidently there are two (degenerate) ways a diatomic could rotate (rotation around its bond-axis is otherwise accounted for by orbiting electrons). That makes three (1 vibration + 2 rotation). But, what are the other three? So long as a molecule (any molecule) is free to move (gaseous or perhaps liquid state), the other three energy modes are translation: up⇔down, left⇔right, and back⇔forth. As far as can be discerned, translational energy is not quantized, so photons do not interact with these energy modes.[48]

Regardless of the number of atoms in a molecule, it will never be more than a three-dimensional object. From the discussion of the triatomics, a general rule can be discerned about rotation:

- linear polyatomics can only have rotation energy about two axes, but
- non-linear polyatomics can rotate about any of three axes.

If the reader has been paying attention, the three translational modes for every molecule[49] and either two or three rotational energy modes have been accounted for, depending on whether the molecule is linear or not. What's left are the vibrational energy modes. **Table 2-2** summarizes what has been presented. The rules in the table can be applied to the molecules used as archetypes:

1. CO **linear** 2 atoms × 3 = 6 modes = 3 translation + 2 rotation + 1 vibration
2. H_2O **non-linear** 3 atoms × 3 = 9 modes = 3 translation + 3 rotation + 3 vibration
3. CO_2 **linear** 3 atoms × 3 = 9 modes = 3 translation + 2 rotation + 4 vibration

Molecule	Degrees of Freedom (Energy Modes)		
	Translation	Rotation	Vibration
Linear Polyatomic (N atoms)	3	2	$3N - 5$
Non-linear Polyatomic (N atoms)	3	3	$3N - 6$

Table 2-2
Energy modes of polyatomic molecules.

The photon-molecule interactions that will most likely be seen from these and many other molecules with advanced technical intelligence sensors are their *vibrotational signatures*. Many of them will be in the VIS, SWIR, or MWIR. See **Examples 2-6** and **2-7**.

[48] The translation of molecules *does* influence the wavelengths of photons that can be emitted or absorbed by electronic, vibrational, and/or rotational energy transitions through the famous Doppler shift. But, this does not cause the molecule to quantum leap from one translational energy level to another; there is no such thing. However, classical momentum must be conserved during the interaction.

[49] Even molecules locked into a solid can have translational energy; the solid as a whole can move up ⇔ down, left ⇔ right, and/or back ⇔ forth.

EXAMPLE 2-6: COMBUSTION OF METHANE

Many fuels are simple hydrocarbons. Methane is one carbon atom and four hydrogens arranged in a tetrahedral shape (see next example). When methane is burned (oxidized), the four bonds are broken, and H_2O and CO_2 are formed. (The chemical reaction takes both hydrogen and carbon to their fully oxidized states and is said to be stoichiometric.)

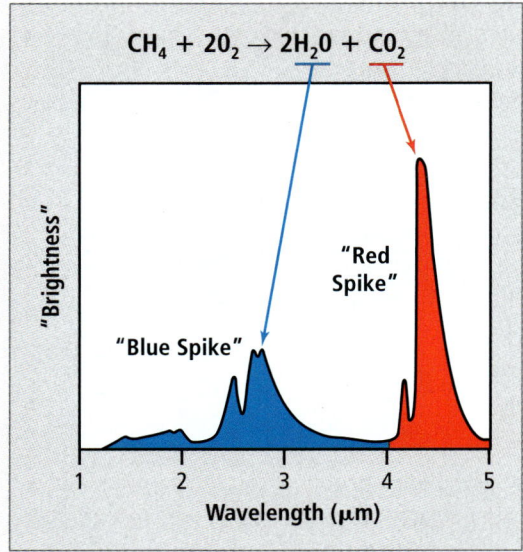

Because the gases are hot, their excited vibrational and rotational energy states are populated (see next section). As the hot molecules relax to lower energy levels, they emit photons. The photons have the characteristic energy of the infrared vibrational transitions shown in **Figures 2-26** and **2-28**, together with rotational transitions shown in **Figure 2-24**. These emissions give the distinctive signatures of water and carbon dioxide shown here (at lower spectral resolution such that the individual rotational lines can't be seen). Their shapes are similar to that of carbon monoxide, shown in **Figure 2-25**, except somewhat more complicated, because these are triatomic molecules. Although these emissions are in the infrared, they may be called the "blue" and "red" spikes for H_2O and CO_2, respectively, because they are "left" and "right" in the SWIR and MWIR just as blue and red are left and right in the visible wavelength spectrum. These radiations are prominent in the exhausts of airplanes, rockets, and motor vehicles burning hydrocarbon fuels.

EXAMPLE 2-7: ENERGY MODES OF METHANE

Methane, CH_4, is a non-linear symmetric top molecule. With five atoms, it will have $3 \times 5 = 15$ energy modes: 3 translational, 3 rotational, and the remaining $15 - 3 - 3 = 9$ vibrational. Many of the vibrational modes will be degenerate and can be studied using the mathematical group theory of objects with mirror and rotational symmetries.

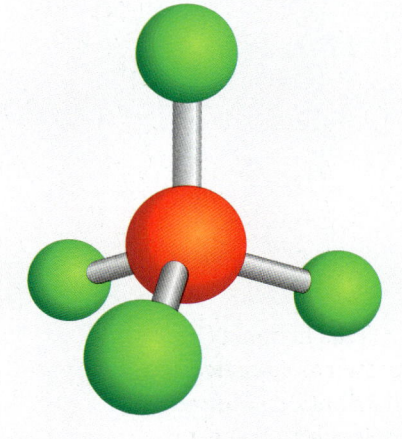

2.6 SELECTIVE SOURCES III: ENSEMBLES

The discussions of radiant energy sources, which carry information, first considered macroscopic thermal sources and then turned to the quantum modes of individual atoms and molecules. Thermal sources are objects, including backgrounds, that glow by virtue of some internal processes related to a property called their temperature, and yet, they are clearly made of atoms and molecules. But, the atoms and molecules are not seen separately. On the other hand, the light from atoms and molecules *can be and is visible in addition to* thermal radiation. However, because advanced technical intelligence sensors have finite spatial collection capabilities,[50] individual atoms and molecules cannot be seen, but large collections of them are visible: clouds of gases, bodies of liquids, and lumps of solids. The nature of radiation received from these collections of atoms and molecules, which are called *ensembles,* will now be examined.

Figure 2-31
Ludwig Boltzmann, 1844–1906. (Photo courtesy of http://commons.wikimedia.org/wiki/File:Boltzmann-Ludwig.jpg; PD-Old.)

GASES

Gases play a prominent role in advanced technical intelligence gathering because nearly all electro-optical remote sensing is done through the atmosphere. The atmosphere, itself, is an object having a temperature, so it emits a characteristic continuum radiation that contributes to background, or at least reduces target contrast. A more interesting behavior, also due to temperature, is selective radiation in the atmosphere and other more-or-less organized[51] gas clouds within or outside of the atmosphere. The cause of this effect (the population of states) will be covered next and then, what is called brightness will be briefly explained.

POPULATION OF STATES

When the concepts of photon emission and absorption between the quantum states of atoms and molecules were introduced in **Figure 2-12**, an important but obvious principle was alluded to: for emission or absorption to happen, the initial energy state (upper or lower, respectively) *must* be occupied. In large ensembles of gas molecules, many moles[52] worth of them, it is hard to conceive that any given starting energy state *wouldn't* be occupied by *some* molecules. But how do they get there? The first answer is they are naturally distributed amongst energy states as a function of temperature, which will now be provided.

Let N_T be the total number of gas molecules in an ensemble. Then the number of molecules, N_i, found to occupy an energy state, "i" (vibrational or rotational), is

$$N_i \approx \frac{N_T}{Z} g_i e^{-\Delta E_i / k_B T}, \quad (2\text{-}27)$$

where g_i is the degeneracy of the ith energy state,

ΔE_i is the ith energy state's energy *above the ground state*[53], and

Z is called the partition function:

$$Z \approx \sum_{All\ states} g_i e^{-\Delta E_i / k_B T}. \quad (2\text{-}28)$$

This formula (**Equation 2-27**) is standard fare for the branch of physics known as statistical mechanics and is often referred to as the Boltzmann distribution (**Figure 2-31**). It gives the steady state[54] distribution of molecules amongst their energy levels, and note it is a strong function of

---

[50] Recall the discussion of target spatial characteristics, {SPACE}, in **Chapter 1**. Remember the remote sensor's spatial sampling capability determines whether a target is to be considered point or extended. This will be highlighted again when discussing sensor optics and focal plane arrays.

[51] Organized gas clouds refers to plumes of gases from chimneys or smokestacks, or the trail of combustion products behind missiles, rockets, and airplanes. These can be treated as ensembles until they dissipate and become diffused with the surrounding air.

[52] A mole is one Avogadro's number of molecules: 6.02×10^{23} of them. In the habitable portion of the atmosphere, sea level to mountain top, one mole occupies a cube roughly 30 cm (1 foot) on a side.

[53] In the case of hydrogen electrons, as in the Sun's atmosphere, the ground state is $n = 1$ ($E_{GROUND} \approx -13.6$ eV), but for vibration and rotation the ground state is $v = 0$ ($E_{GROUND} = \frac{1}{2} E_{v0}$) and $J = 0$ ($E_{GROUND} = 0$), respectively.

[54] This does not mean the ensemble is static in that every molecule in each energy state stays there. "Detailed balance" (**Section 2.3**) shows that for every molecule that quantum leaps to a lower energy state, emitting a photon, another molecule quantum leaps in reverse to the higher energy state, absorbing a photon. This is not necessarily the same photon. In large ensembles of 10^{25} molecules or more, there will be plenty of photons to go around. The natural distribution of photons amongst their energy states can be shown to be the Planck function.

temperature. In this context, temperature means *kinetic* temperature,[55] and is assumed to mean the spread of the molecules across their available energy states (similar to the standard deviation in Gaussian, bell-shaped curve statistics). The more widely distributed molecules are amongst their energy levels (i.e., the higher their temperature), the greater their propensity to share that energy with their neighbors, the environment, etc., which correlates with the thermodynamic temperature discussed in **Section 2.2**.

The degeneracy of an energy state, g_i, was discussed in the last section when a linear triatomic molecule was shown to bend (v_2 oscillation) with equal energy in either of two planes. Such a degeneracy is easy to visualize, because it is semi-classical. But, rotational degeneracy is more difficult. The equations of quantum mechanics for rotating molecules reveal that a molecule rotating in state J can do so in $g_J = 2J + 1$ ways. Although, no one really knows what this must truly look like in the microscopic world because molecules are complex wave-particles, the closest picture (**Figure 2-32**) is like a top precessing g_J different ways. The combination of degeneracies (increasing with increasing J) and exponential terms (decreasing with increasing ΔE_i) in **Equation 2-27** gives a vibrotational emission spectrum its characteristic shape, as shown in **Figure 2-25**.

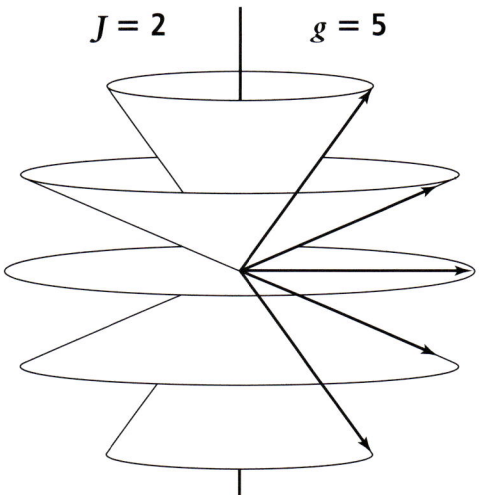

Figure 2-32
Degeneracy of a rotational energy J state envisioned as $2J + 1$ different orientations of precession.

The partition function in the denominator of **Equation 2-27** is a sum of the degeneracy-exponential products over all states. For vibration and rotation, Z is easily calculated because there is only a finite number of energy states possible for a real molecule. As a molecule vibrates and/or rotates with more energy, its bond stretches[56] until it breaks, obviously limiting the number of states. **Figure 2-20** suggested there might be only five allowed vibrational energy states for a particular molecule, for instance. If there was an infinite number of energy states possible (as there theoretically are for the hydrogen electron, **Equation 2-23**, as $n \to \infty$), the partition function goes over into an integral and converges to some definite value.[57]

Example 2-8 illustrates the paucity of molecules that occupy excited states, even at fairly elevated temperatures. (The exhaust plume of a missile may initially be 1,500–1,800 K, as in the example, but cools rapidly in contact with the air as it expands. That is, an exhaust plume is not at steady state.) Thus, highly excited states are typically not occupied,[58]

---

[55] Kinetic temperature is not the same thing as thermodynamic temperature (Section 2.2), but is usually equal to it.

[56] This is the origin of the correction terms noted in Footnote 38 but are ignored.

[57] Stated without proof here. Refer to a calculus textbook.

[58] This is why the vibrational and rotational energy correction terms mentioned in Section 2.5 and Footnote 56 above are neglected.

44 CHAPTER 2 LIGHT EMITTING TARGETS

EXAMPLE 2-8: POPULATION OF ENERGY STATES

Suppose there were only four allowed vibrational energy states for carbon monoxide (**Figure 2-21**). How many molecules would populate those energy levels if the steady state temperature of an ensemble of them is 1500 K?

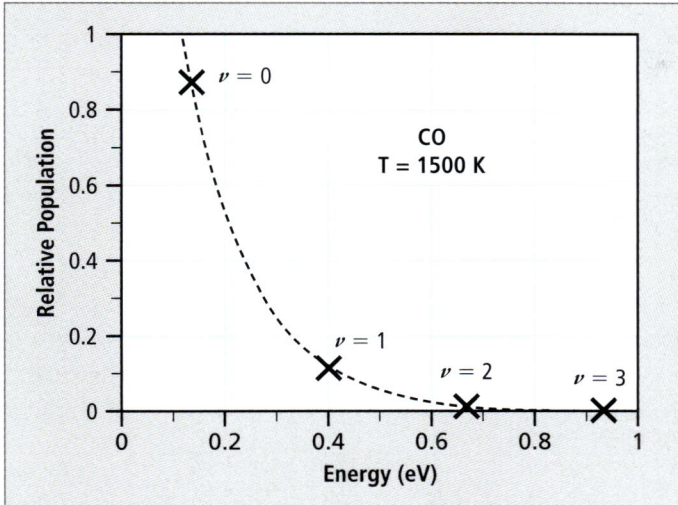

Applying **Equations 2-27** and **2-28** to the energy levels of CO, it can be calculated that there are approximately 87.2%, 11.1%, 1.4%, and 0.2% of the molecules in the $v = 0, 1, 2$, and 3 vibrational energy states, respectively. The calculation is found on the first worksheet of the interactive spreadsheet, **Appendix 2-2**, on the support website. It is instructive to change the temperature therein using the spinner buttons to see that there are almost NO molecules in excited states for normal room temperature (~ 300 K).

and the total energy available to an ensemble of gas molecules will reside mostly in the ground state. The question may still remain: How do molecules attain higher energy states at all?

Molecules in higher energy states are attained through other than steady state processes, such as chemical reactions (propulsion, combustion, or explosion) or optical pumping. **Figure 2-33** is a drawing

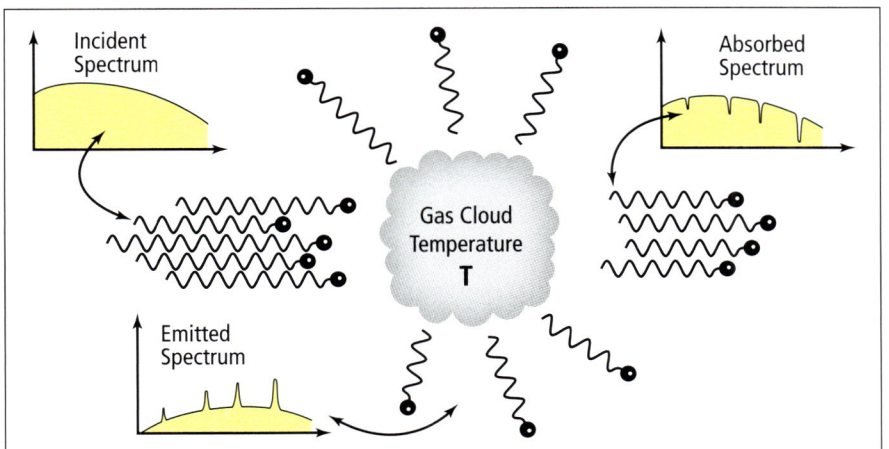

Figure 2-33
Emitted and absorbed spectrum from a gas cloud "pumped" by an incident beam of light.

HOT AND COLD GAS SIGNATURES

The situation discussed in **Figure 2-33** assumed a "cold" gas ensemble. That is, its temperature was low enough that very few, if any, of its molecules were in excited states. In contrast, consider the situation shown here: some industrial process has produced hot waste products that are exhausted through a smokestack. By "hot," it is meant that there is sufficient energy in the process that a significant fraction of the exhausted molecules are in excited states. (Again, carbon monoxide is used in this example because it's a simple molecule, likely to be produced in great quantities in manufacturing requiring combustion of hydrocarbon fuels. (Reference **Section 2.5**)

As the exhaust plume leaves the stack, there are no sources of energy to maintain the hot molecules in their excited states, so many of them will quantum leap to lower levels. Radiating away their energy, molecules will "fill up" lower energy levels in their downward cascade, and a lower temperature will be required in **Equation 2-27** to describe their distribution. The gas has "cooled." Meanwhile, the ensemble will have drifted downwind in the time it takes for this to happen.

An advanced technical intelligence sensor observing this target (the plume) from overhead might see a high level of continuum radiation from the gas near the smokestack. Additionally, it will see emission from the hot CO molecules, vibrational transitions, and the signature will be fairly broad, because there is enough energy (high temperature) to populate large J-valued states. (The signature is shown in the drawing as though it has been collected with a low spectral resolution. The individual vibrational lines cannot be separated.) Looking in this direction, the sensor will also see continuum radiation from the background surrounding the plume. But, it won't be as bright, because it's relatively "cold."

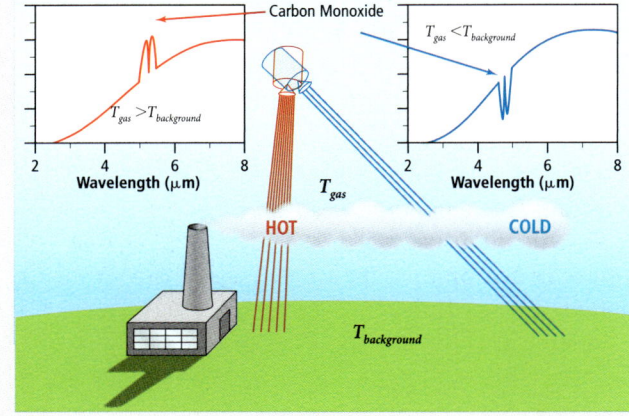

When the sensor turns and looks at the downwind "cold" plume, the situation on the right side of **Figure 2-33** returns. Continuum radiation from the background and plume will be nearly indistinguishable, as they are the same temperature (although their emissivities are different). But, as the plume thins out, CO molecules now in the ground state will absorb photons from the background. Hence, the sensor will be able to detect the *signature* of carbon monoxide in absorption.

In principle, not only could a chemical agent be identified from its hot emissive and cold absorptive signatures, but its concentration could be estimated from radiometric tools developed in later chapters.

---

of the latter; a beam of light enters an ensemble of gas from the left and emerges to the right. The incident beam has any continuum spectrum but includes photons with energies matching differences in energies between quantum states of the gas. The gas is at steady state temperature, T, such that it has a few molecules in its first excited state ($k = 1$[59]), but most are in its ground state ($k = 0$). As the light beam passes through the gas, some of its photons will be absorbed. These photons: 1) will cause some molecules to be "pumped" up to higher excited states ($k = 0 \rightarrow 1, 0 \rightarrow 2, 0 \rightarrow 3, \ldots, 1 \rightarrow 2, 1 \rightarrow 3$, etc.); and 2) will not appear in the output spectrum on the right.

Meanwhile, the gas at temperature, T, will radiate its characteristic steady state (Planck-like) spectrum[60] *and* will emit photons from quantum leaps of its molecules from their pumped states (k = $1 \rightarrow 0, 2 \rightarrow 1, 2 \rightarrow 0, 3 \rightarrow 2, 3 \rightarrow 1, 3 \rightarrow 0$, etc.). Note, this emitted spectrum can be seen by a collection system *anywhere* around the gas, whereas the absorbed spectrum can only be seen by a sensor looking back through the gas toward the source of the incident spectrum.

When the light beam is turned off in **Figure 2-33**, the ensemble will "relax" back to its steady state condition at temperature T. (Assume there is some hidden process that is maintaining its internal energy.[61]) The fact that it will come back is a certainty; further study of quantum mechanics shows that all energy states above the ground state have finite lifetimes.[62] Thus, within a finite time, all of the molecules will have returned[63] to their former condition. (See the **Hot and Cold Gas Signatures** Sidebar for an application.)

LINE STRENGTH

Carrying this example further, **Figure 2-21** shows that the $v = 1 \rightarrow 0$, $2 \rightarrow 1$, and $3 \rightarrow 2$ energy transitions of the vibrating CO molecule are approximately the same. In practice, it cannot be discerned which one of

---

[59] k is used as a generic quantum number; it could represent n, v, J, or any other.

[60] The gas is not a blackbody, because it does not absorb 100% of the radiation falling on it. Obviously, some of the radiation passes through it, but it also absorbs some. Its emissivity is therefore less than one.

[61] Hydrostatic balance in the atmosphere (**Chapter 5**) is such a process, for instance. Gravity and molecular motion combine to keep an air parcel (an ensemble) at a particular altitude where thermodynamic processes keep its temperature constant.

[62] This is the famous Heisenberg uncertainty principle. It is certain that a molecule will relax to a lower energy state, but it is uncertain when it will do so. The principle allows a computation of the average, or expected, time it will take. A lifetime computed by this principle is related to the half-life of a radioactive decay.

[63] The return path to steady state does not need to be through emitting photons. Molecules can collide with one another and exchange their internal excited state for external kinetic energy.

these quantum leaps a 4.67 μm photon[64] came from. Therefore, conclude the line seen at that wavelength is the sum of the photons from the three transitions. Likewise, the line seen at 2.33 μm is the sum of photons emitted from $v = 2 \rightarrow 0$ and $3 \rightarrow 1$ quantum leaps. The 1.55 μm line is shown to be due solely to $v = 3 \rightarrow 0$.

Now, combine this information with the population of states information calculated using **Equation 2-27**. For an ensemble of CO molecules at a temperature of 1,500 K, the results of that computation are shown and discussed in **Example 2-8** (or use the spreadsheet model, **Appendix 2-2**, on the support website). Since $v = 1$ is the most highly populated excited state, it is clear there will be more 4.67 μm photons than any other line. That is, that line will be "brightest" or "strongest." But, what can be said about the brightness of the other lines?

The brightness of spectral lines depends on how well or how poorly the two energy states overlap one another. In the quantum world, remember discrete quantities of energy behave both as particles and waves. The overlap discussed here is like the interference of two light waves. In some sense, when an atom or molecule quantum leaps from one energy state to another, its wave function morphs. Somehow, that morphing will be most successful (if at all) between states that look like one another. **Figure 2-20** visually suggests the wave functions with odd numbers of humps (first, third, and fifth) might match each other fairly well, while the ones with even numbers line-up better. Regardless of trying to make a picture out of it, advanced quantum mechanics pushes through the calculations and derives a number called oscillator strength or transition probability. The higher the number, the more likely, or easier, the quantum leap.

Assuming the oscillator strengths for the CO example and the upper state populations are known, an analyst is close to being able to predict line brightness. But, there is one more detail. Notice that a molecule in state $v = 3$ could quantum leap to state 2, or 1, or 0. Which one does it choose? It does not simply select the highest oscillator strength but decides based on a branching ratio, which compares the oscillator strengths. If their ratio to the $v = 2, 1, 0$ states were 3:2:1, for example, then a $v = 3$ molecule would quantum leap to those states ½, ⅓, and ⅙ of the time, respectively. (Or, out of six molecules, three would go to state 2, two would go to 1, and one would go to 0.)

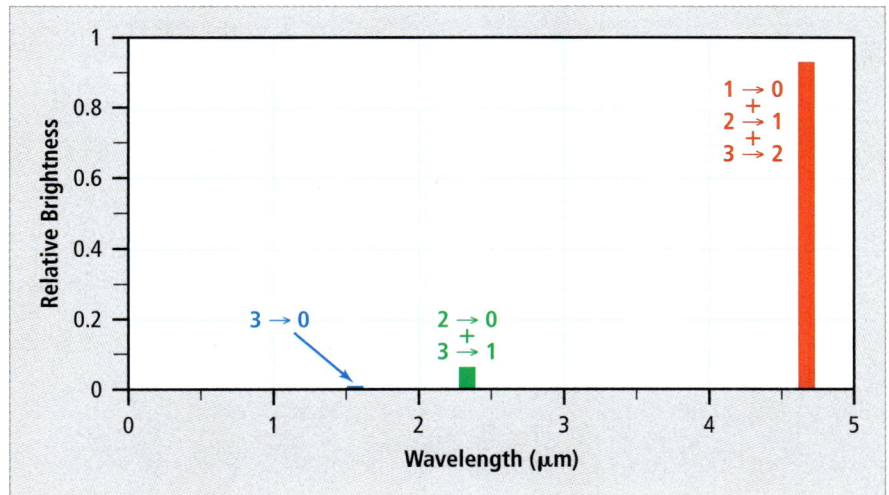

Figure 2-34
Relative strengths of CO emission lines inferred from population of excited states, oscillator strengths, and branching ratios.

[64] The rotational energy part is neglected here, since 4.67 μm is the pure vibrational transition wavelength. The actual photons from all three transitions will be at longer or shorter wavelengths depending on their simultaneous rotational transitions, but the principle will be the same. They will be indistinguishable.

Figure 2-34 shows the estimate of the line strengths for the CO example discussed. The relative heights of the bars take into account the populations of the excited states, the transition probabilities (oscillator strengths), and the branching ratios. As can be seen, the upper state population probably does play the greatest role. (Located on the support website, the worksheet, **Appendix 2-2**, shows the effect of temperature on line brightness, assuming all oscillator strengths and branching ratios are the same.)

All the above is possibly more detail than needed. It would take several years of graduate study in quantum physics to compute. What is necessary to know, however, is that *there is a reason why spectra look the way they do*; they are the result of internal energy states of atoms and molecules, temperature-dependent state populations, and wave function calculations. All these factors taken together constitute the *signatures* of gas molecules as they may be observed within the Field of View of an advanced technical intelligence sensor.

Example 2-9 suggests the combined results of mixing a thermal continuum and molecular emission into a single signature. The origin and phenomenology of this and other signatures, both transient and persistent, will be further developed and discussed in more detail in **Chapter 13**.

CONDENSED MATTER

It is all a matter of energy, and energy is information. If enough energy is present, molecules are separate from one another, and a gas is formed as just studied. If some energy is taken away, the gas cools enough to condense into a liquid. Now, the molecules form into groups that slide past each other. If more energy is taken away, the liquid freezes into a solid where the molecules are locked into place between their neighbors. The reader is familiar with these normal states of matter and has experienced the adding of energy as well; solids melt and liquids boil.[65] While liquids and solids share many properties, the remainder of this chapter's discussion will be confined to solids.

When molecules come together into solids, the forces holding them next to each other are EM in nature. They are similar to the chemical bond within molecules but oriented in multiple directions rather than only along an atom-to-atom axis. Each molecule is tugged into a stable position within the framework of the material. Some materials coalesce into more-or-less haphazard jumbles of molecules as amorphous solids, but others organize into regular crystal lattices. Either way, the near proximity of molecules and the multi-dimensional attractive forces give solids more degrees of freedom, modes for their energy.

Because they are macroscopic conglomerates of many moles of molecules, solids do not follow the rules established at the end of **Section 2.5** for the division of their energy into translational, rotational, and vibrational modes. Translation and rotation of a solid can be treated entirely classically, while vibration must be treated with quantum mechanics (solid state physics). The stretching and bending modes of a solid's inter- and intra-molecular bonds do not lend themselves to the simple photon emission and absorption processes of individual molecules but are more likely to exchange energy with other vibrations.

---

[65] The "fourth" state of matter is with enough energy to dissociate molecules into atoms and strip all the electrons off them: plasma, an ionized gas. Maybe 99% of the visible universe is in the plasma state.

EXAMPLE 2-9: SIGNATURE OF A HYDROCARBON FUEL

What is the SWIR-MWIR spectral *signature* of a burning hydrocarbon-based fuel?

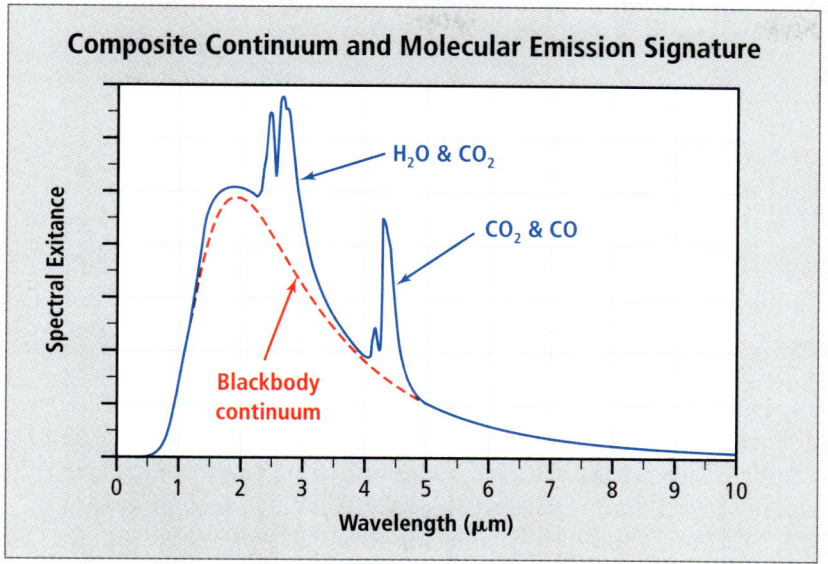

The combustion of a hydrocarbon may be as hot as 1,500 - 2,000 K and the products are mostly water vapor and a combination of carbon dioxide, carbon monoxide, and uncombusted carbon (called soot) depending on the amount of oxidizer present. The hot gas and carbon particles are not completely opaque, but probably have a reasonably high emissivity. Therefore, expect a continuum emission component proportional to a blackbody curve peaking around 2.0 μm (Wien's Law).

The combustion products at ~1,500 K will have a significant fraction (~ 15%) of the H_2O, CO_2, and CO molecules in excited vibrational states, as demonstrated in **Figure 2-33**. Therefore, expect to see line spectrum emission in addition to the continuum radiation. The line spectrum will be similar to the image in **Example 2-6** for methane, where the water vapor emission is a combination of symmetric and asymmetric stretch mode vibrational transitions (**Figure 2-26**) centered around 2.67 and 2.74 μm. The CO_2 and CO will both contribute to MWIR emission between 4.26 μm (**Figure 2-28**) and 4.68 μm (**Figure 2-25**).

Therefore, the interaction of photons with solid matter is most likely to occur with its electronic energy levels. However, within the structure of a solid, the presence of many molecules attracting one another causes the allowed energy levels of their outermost electrons to split into multiple, closely-spaced levels. In fact, these electron energy levels become so numerous that they become like a continuum. **Figure 2-35** sketches this: isolated molecules have discrete energy levels, but solids have *bands* where electrons no longer belong to specific molecules. Rather, some electrons may physically drift throughout a solid, within allowed energy bands, shared by all the molecules. The energy bands are separated by a "gap;" the gap energy being unique to each solid. In principle, a photon could be absorbed in a solid by giving its energy to an electron in a lower band, and the electron would quantum leap to an upper band. The reverse process would emit a photon.

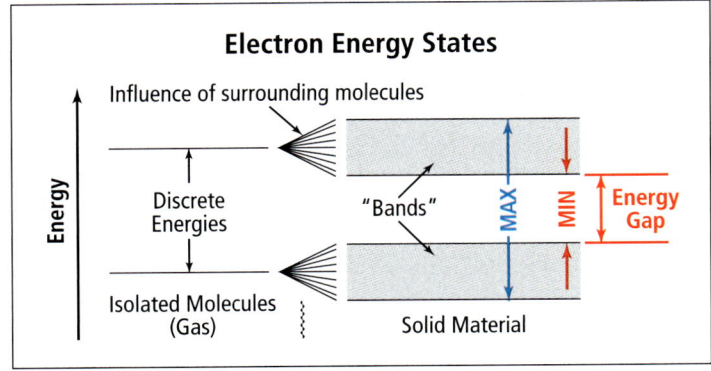

Figure 2-35
Discrete energy levels of molecules split when the molecules move close together. So many energy levels then exist that they are nearly indistinguishable, and are treated as "bands."

Unlike previous studies, the photon in this case could have an energy and corresponding wavelength *anywhere* between the minimum separation of the bands (gap energy) and a maximum, as sketched in **Figure 2-35**.

As before with gas molecules, what governs whether an electron-photon interaction takes place is, dominantly, the population of states. When the electrons in solids become close neighbors, quantum rules require they fill in the available energy states according to what is known as the Fermi-Dirac occupation probability distribution:

$$P(E) = \frac{1}{e^{(E-E_f)/k_B T} + 1}, \qquad (2\text{-}29)$$

where E is an electron's energy above the solid's ground state and E_f is a parameter known as the Fermi energy. E_f is usually a value somewhere in the lower energy band. Importantly, note the distribution is a strong function of temperature. At low temperatures significantly below solids' melting points, the majority of electrons will fill an energy band from the bottom up. An interactive example of the Fermi-Dirac distribution is on the support website as file, **Appendix 2-3**, where the effect of changing E_f and T is shown.

The manner in which electrons occupy a band (by **Equation 2-29**) determines the electrical properties of a solid. Recognize the three classes shown in **Figure 2-36**. First, *metals* are solids having their top-most band only partially filled. Electrons with energies near the top of this band are highly mobile being able to move throughout the volume of a solid. These

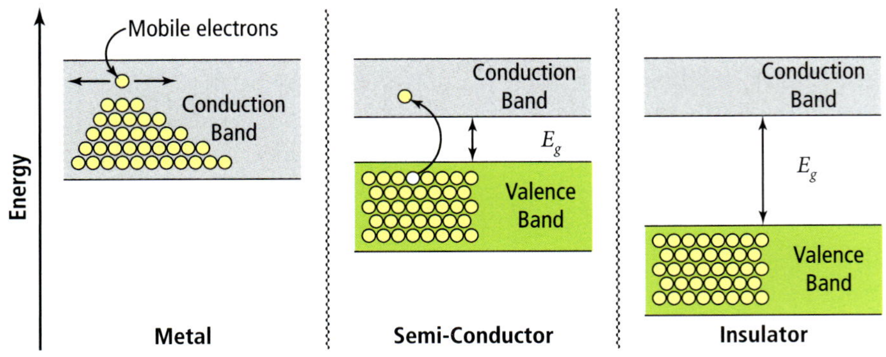

Figure 2-36
Condensed matter energy states and classes of solid-state materials.

electrons, not tied to specific locations, are easily influenced by external electric fields and become the charge carriers of currents moving through electronic circuits. The energy band in which these mobile electrons move through within a metal is called the conduction band.

Second, the combination of Fermi energy and temperature in some materials will completely fill an energy band below the conduction band, called the valence band. Ordinarily, a material of this class would not conduct an electrical current, since the conduction band is normally unoccupied. However, if the energy gap between these bands is small enough, it is possible for a few electrons to be boosted into the conduction band. A material of this class is a *semi-conductor*.

Third, there are materials that are *insulators*. Like the semi-conductors, insulators have a filled valence band. However, the energy gap to the conduction band is so large, it is unreasonable for any electrons to occupy the higher band. The material would probably melt before enough thermal energy would be available to boost any electrons into the conduction band.

Semi-conductors are extremely important to advanced technical intelligence collection. Besides being the basis for modern electronics, semi-conductors are information detectors. As stated in **Chapter 1**, information about a target, {TGT}, can only be found by studying its image, {IMG}. Since the image formed in remote sensing is 100% photons, a device is needed to transform {IMG} into data, {DATA}. That device is a semi-conductor detector, and the way it works is that the photons provide the energy to boost electrons up from the valence to the conduction band. This will be the topic of later chapters.

3 TARGET REFLECTIVE SIGNATURES

*The signature of a target includes the characteristics of the radiation leaving that target. These characteristics include the spatial, spectral, polarimetric, and temporal properties of this radiation as well as the radiometric values associated with each of these properties. These characteristics are further discussed in **Section 3.1**. The source of the radiation given off by a target consists of both thermal self-emission (discussed in detail in **Chapter 2**) and reflection from the target surface of incoming radiation that originated at other sources, both distant and nearby. Examples of distant sources are the sun, moon, and stars. Shown above is a daytime reflective image of New York City with smoke coming from the burning ruins of the Twin Towers shortly after the 9-11 terrorist attack. Examples of nearby sources are man-made lighting, the ground below, and trees and buildings. In **Section 3.2**, the details of specular and diffuse reflection are discussed in detail. Initial discussion of the reflection of the two polarization components of incoming light is given as a prelude to further discussion and application in **Chapter 21**.*

SECTIONS
3.1 TARGET CHARACTERISTICS
3.2 REFLECTION AND POLARIZATION

3.1 TARGET CHARACTERISTICS

As a general rule, customers do not submit requirements for information about completely unknown targets. Most targets are reasonably well known or at least fall into recognized classes. Spectral ({SPECT}), spatial ({SPACE}), and temporal ({TIME}) characteristics[1] of target classes are usually known. A target's *radiometric* characteristic combines certain information about these classes. A target's radiometric characteristics are taken to create a fourth category of knowledge.

To gain knowledge of particular targets in any class, advanced technical intelligence sensors are designed with this science and engineering principle in mind: to achieve maximum information transfer, match the sensor collection capabilities to the information known about the target signatures.[2] Therefore, target signature information must be known or estimated before tasking sensors with specifically designed capabilities.

SPECTRAL CHARACTERISTICS

For *passive* remote sensing in the electro-optics regime, two sources of light need to be considered for the target: 1) emitting targets (e.g., lights, fires, exhausts, etc.); or 2) reflecting targets (external sources of light, e.g., sun, spotlights, etc.). The associated material properties of targets which constitute their non-literal *signatures* are their emissivity, $\epsilon(\lambda)$, or reflectivity,[3] $\rho(\lambda)$, respectively. In general, emissivity and reflectivity are mathematically related and show that targets *both* emit and reflect; which one dominates depends on the bandpass. **Figure 3-1** shows emitting and reflecting targets in the visible spectrum.

Figure 3-1
Emitting (thermal) and reflecting targets.

For *active* EM remote sensing at any wavelength (radar and lidar), targets must reflect some fraction of light energy incident upon them from the remote transmitter. Thus, their spectral response is that of the transmitter, and when reflected back, it is modified by the target's materials, size, shape, and motion. Such reflection is characterized by the radar cross section for macroscopic targets (airplanes, vehicles, the ground, etc.) or by scattering coefficients for microscopic targets (aerosols, clouds, etc.).

In the case of either emitted or reflected light, the *nature* of the light observed by an advanced technical intelligence sensor goes back to its origin from either a *continuum* or *selective* radiator. Continuum radiation is primarily thermal in origin, while selective radiation comes from atoms, molecules, and material structure. These natures will be discussed in depth in later chapters.

---

[1] Targets also have polarimetric characteristics that might be important.

[2] Electrical engineers recognize this principle as *impedance matching*. Mechanical engineers know it as *resonance*.

[3] In this case, the reflectivity is properly the Bidirectional Reflectivity Distribution Function (BRDF). This gives the amount of light reflected *from* a source in a particular direction *to* a remote sensor in another specific direction. The simplifying assumptions that must often be made to deal with this quantity will be discussed at length.

SPATIAL CHARACTERISTICS

All targets occupy some space and are located somewhere. The volume and shape of the space occupied (and sometimes where) is often sufficient to literally identify the target (Imagery Intelligence (IMINT)), although perceived color and surface texture may help. Whether the volume and shape of a target can be observed sufficiently for identification is a matter of *spatial resolution*. Spatially resolving any given target for literal identification is a combination of factors: the size and shape of the target relative to its distance[4] from the remote sensor and the sensor's ability to magnify the image, {IMG}, and capture it on pixels.[5] If the criteria for literal identification are not satisfied, then identification must be accomplished by non-literal means.

Once past the realm of literal identification, targets are spatially classified as either point or extended sources. Point sources are, from the perspective of a remote sensor, targets where their image occupies not more than a few pixels (maybe only one). The image cannot be used for identification because it is too small. Or, conversely, the space sampled by a pixel is too large. See **Example 3-1**. At typical distances for space-based GEOINT sensors, many targets of interest to the Intelligence Community, particularly the military, become point sources. This includes many weapons (rifles, artillery, rockets, etc.) and their delivery systems (tanks, ships, aircraft, and missiles). The fact that some of these are not exactly

---

EXAMPLE 3-1: SPATIAL RESOLUTION OF THE EYE

Suppose one wants to visually identify a modest 20 m high tree. At what distance is literal identification no longer possible?

Human eyes have focal lengths of about 16 mm, and the tree is visualized with cones (pixels) on the retina that are spaced about 10 μm apart. Suppose the criterion to distinguish a tree or building is that the image is about four cones high or a sampling distance of about 5 m.

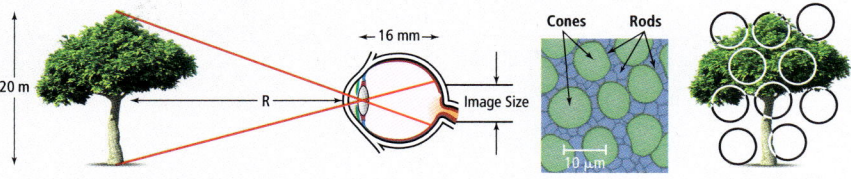

By similar triangles: $\dfrac{\{\text{Image size}\}}{16 \text{ mm}} \approx \dfrac{20 \text{ m}}{R} \Rightarrow R \approx \dfrac{(20 \text{ m})(16 \text{ mm})}{\{\text{Image size}\}}$.

If the image size ≈ 40 μm, then

$$R \approx \dfrac{(20 \text{ m})(16 \text{ mm})\left(\dfrac{1 \text{ m}}{10^3 \text{ mm}}\right)}{(40 \text{ μm})\left(\dfrac{1 \text{ m}}{10^6 \text{ μm}}\right)} \approx 8 \times 10^3 \text{ m} \approx 8 \text{ km} \approx 5 \text{ mi}.$$

Based loosely on the criterion given later in this chapter, this is not unreasonable. But, there is more. Nothing was mentioned about the pupil of the eye, which also matters as will be discussed in **Chapter 8**.

---

[4] Astute image analysts know contrast is also a consideration; how well a target can be discerned against its background and degradation of an image from atmospheric distortion.

[5] Focal plane arrays divided into pixels will be discussed later, but for the moment, do not be confused with the terminology. The technology of digital cameras is well-established in today's culture.

points is obvious, but how to identify many of them by non-literal methods will be shown.

Extended sources are big sources with images across multiple pixels such as fields, deserts, lakes, rivers, clouds, and sometimes roads and runways. However, there is insufficient detail to identify targets literally. Non-literal identification is often possible if material properties such as emissivity or reflectivity can be extracted. Extended sources are often not targets themselves, but are *backgrounds* behind point source targets.

The other component of target spatial characteristics is identifying its *metrics*: *where* is it and *where is it going*? The "where" of a target's position on the Earth's surface is called its *geolocation*, and is given in terms of a coordinate system such as latitude and longitude or Military Grid Reference System (MGRS). For targets on the surface, the third dimension is the terrain elevation at its location. But, for airborne or spaceborne targets, it is an altitude above either the actual terrain or a standard reference model, which must be specified. The "where is it going" is called *trajectory*. The trajectories of many targets are completely determined by the forces of physics (gravity, friction, lift, and drag) and serve to readily identify them as being unique among their particular class of targets. For example, **Figure 3-2** illustrates the powered flight launch trajectory of a missile. Other targets with human input (pilots) do not necessarily have predictable trajectories, but their speeds, turn radii, and climb rates may be indicative of nominal performance.

Figure 3-2
A missile launches into the morning sky. (Image used with permission: Brian Lockett Air-and-Space.com.)

TEMPORAL CHARACTERISTICS

Closely coupled to a target's spatial characteristics is its temporal nature or duration. Targets can be temporally categorized as being either short-lived or long-lived. Short-lived targets are termed *transient*, while long-lived ones are called *persistent*. Persistent targets can include facilities, infrastructure, and weapon delivery systems. Transients are often the weapons themselves (when delivered). The break-point for categorizing a target as transient or persistent is somewhat arbitrary, and depends on the operating characteristics of the particular sensor tasked to collect it. As suggested earlier, a sensor's collection interval should match the lifetime of its target for maximum information transfer. But, it is not always possible.

The interval over which a sensor can collect depends on its sampling rate, time over target, and frequency of visit. Time over target and revisit time are tied to orbital geometry for spaceborne sensors and depend on mission duration and airspace availability for airborne ones. The sampling rate is connected to spatial coverage and data channel bandwidth; that is, virtually all advanced technical intelligence sensors operate in a video-like mode whereby successive images are digitized and downloaded. Demands on sensors' available operational time to collect against tasked prioritized targets must be traded off against the targets' temporal characteristics to determine an appropriate collection strategy. Thus, sensors cannot look at all tasked targets all the time.

For sensors using a *collection strategy* for large areas, targets which endure long enough to be seen on multiple revisits to the same[6] geolocation are persistent. Such long-lived targets are of interest because they can be indicators of pending activity or the aftermath of battle. Otherwise, targets lasting long enough to be seen during one visit, or perhaps not at all, are transient. Since many targets are weapons designed to deliver large amounts of energy in short time intervals, their signatures are short-lived. In either case, the pertinent question is, "Was sufficient data collected to affect an accurate identification and characterization of the target?" This question will be addressed in succeeding chapters when discussing time-intensity signatures.

There is actually a frequently encountered middle-ground between transient and persistent targets. These are called quasi-persistent and are not really single targets, but multiple ones. Quasi-persistent targets are strings of transient events occurring in rapid time sequence. Examples of quasi-persistent targets are carpet bombing (**Figure 3-3**) and lightning storms.

Figure 3-3
A quasi-persistent event in the making.

[6] Or nearby locations in the event of a moving target.

RADIOMETRIC CHARACTERISTICS

The reader has already encountered a target's radiometric characteristic; it is the centerpiece of sensor collection, **Equation 1-4**, and its solution, **Equation 1-5**. The quantity $I_\lambda(t)$ (spectral *intensity*) is one of two radiometric quantities that will be studied extensively; the other is $L_\lambda(t)$ (spectral *radiance*), which is given by a similar equation. These quantities allow all of the above target characteristics to be combined into one and expressed mathematically. Spectrally and polarimetrically, they describe how photons are emitted or reflected from a target and *distributed* across a sensor's bandpass. Spatially, I and L describe a target as a point or extended source. Temporally, they give the time variation of a target's performance. Thus, by solving for the radiometric characteristic of a target, which is essentially the amount of radiant energy received, all possible information that can be collected from remote sensing can be obtained.[7] Before filling in the details of a target's radiometric characteristics in the following chapters, assume for the moment that a target is either "bright" or "dim."

The importance of knowing a target's radiometric characteristics is the information gained about the target's *energy*. For example, does a missile launch have enough energy to reach orbit? Targets require some kind of fuel input to operate: raw materials for factories, petroleum products for vehicles, explosive compounds for weapons, etc. The substances contain *chemical* energy which targets convert and output into other forms, like motion (kinetic energy), mechanical effects (shock waves and shrapnel), and radiation. Radiation is electromagnetic (EM) waves (or particles), and that is what advanced technical intelligence sensors collect. From these EM waves, a target's radiative *signature* can be derived. Also, sensors can observe a target's motion from which a target's *metrics* can be derived. Signature and metrics together allow the total energy to be estimated. This information can prove extremely useful to customers who want to assess the threat value of a particular target.

SUMMARY

Advanced technical intelligence sensors were developed with target characteristics in mind to satisfy customers' requirements. **Table 3-1** summarizes the four target characteristics discussed. Each characteristic has two or three possible descriptions of a target, and every target has one of each. For every combination of characteristics, there is probably a class of target that holds a customer's interest.

Table 3-1 Target characteristics.

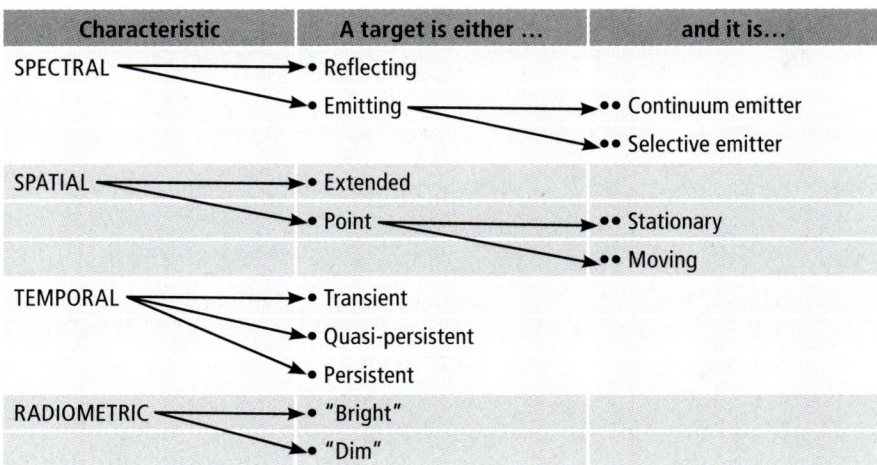

Characteristic	A target is either …	and it is…
SPECTRAL	• Reflecting	
	• Emitting	•• Continuum emitter
		•• Selective emitter
SPATIAL	• Extended	
	• Point	•• Stationary
		•• Moving
TEMPORAL	• Transient	
	• Quasi-persistent	
	• Persistent	
RADIOMETRIC	• "Bright"	
	• "Dim"	

[7] The space-time-spectral sampling imposed by the operation of an advanced technical intelligence sensor, Equation 1-4, places limitations on the fidelity of the knowledge.

3.2 REFLECTION AND POLARIZATION

In the pursuit to understand targets, {TGT}, the previous chapter studied the information they may emit about themselves: continuum and/or selective radiation. In rare circumstances (when the target of interest is a cold gas plume), its presence may be detected from an absorption signature. But, this is a very difficult collection. The emission mode of detection and identification is not the usual case in the visible spectrum where people have the most experience with their normal imaging system (eyes). See **Figure 3-1** for example. Most visible light energy is reflected,[8] and its characteristics will be reviewed next as a means of knowing {TGT}.

CLASSICAL TREATMENT

If the reader previously studied reflection in traditional physics, then the *Law of Specular Reflection* is undoubtedly familiar:

$$\theta_R = \theta_I. \tag{3-1}$$

Likewise, the *Law of Refraction*, also called Snell's Law, is familiar:

$$n_T \sin\theta_T = n_I \sin\theta_I \tag{3-2}$$

In these formulas, the angles subscripted I, R, and T are the angles of incident, reflected, and transmitted radiation, respectively, as illustrated in **Figure 3-4**. Note, they are measured with respect to a "normal" to the surface. The quantity n_I is the index of refraction of the material containing the incident and reflected light, and n_T is the index of refraction for the material receiving the transmitted light. See sidebar in **Chapter 2** for the definition of index of refraction. That is, reflection and refraction can only occur when EM waves encounter an interface between materials having different refractive indices.[9]

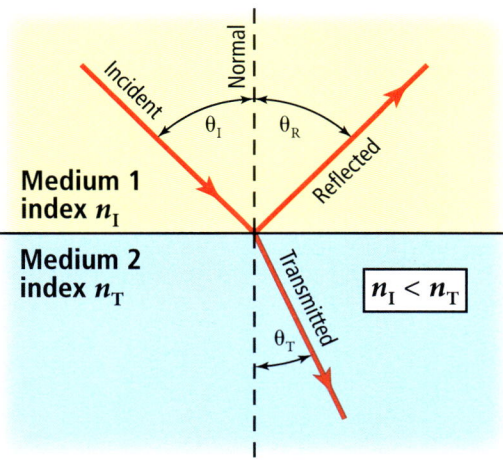

INDEX OF REFRACTION AND REFRACTION

Table 3-2 gives average index of refraction values in the visible bandpass for some common materials. Note n is greater than one for all materials,[10] which causes the situation for refraction as shown in **Figure 3-4**. Light passing into a material with a greater index bends toward the normal,[11] and vice versa. That is, light waves in **Figure 3-4** could follow the refracting path in reverse, in which case the roles of incident and transmitting materials would also be reversed.[12]

---

[8] The issue of when emitted light is visible and when reflected light is visible will be discussed later. It depends first on the bandpass of the sensor and second on the properties of the transmitter's medium.

[9] This is like the familiar demonstration of a glass rod disappearing when it is lowered into a beaker of clear liquid that looks like water. The liquid is actually a solution of sodium metasilicate, Na_2SiO_3, which has the same index of refraction as the glass rod: no difference in index = no reflection or refraction. So, the rod's surface is not visible. The chemical is also known as "water glass" or "liquid glass."

[10] Some exotic materials have been synthesized in laboratories under extraordinary conditions that have an apparent index of refraction less than one. These 'metamaterials' are not likely to be operationally fielded anytime in the foreseeable future.

[11] The index of refraction is a function of wavelength in most materials. So, different colors of light will refract at different angles. This property is called *dispersion* and explains how prisms work and why rainbows appear. This property can be used to separate colors for multi- and hyperspectral advanced technical intelligence sensing (MSI/HSI). The use of prisms and other dispersing elements will be covered in Chapter 17.

[12] For light passing into a material with a smaller index, a condition called Total Internal Reflection occurs at angles of incidence larger than a critical angle:

$$\sin\theta_c = \frac{n_T}{n_I}.$$

Conceivably, this could limit the ability to optically detect and characterize some targets under water, but not in the atmosphere.

Figure 3-4
Classical reflection and refraction at an interface. Note the index of refraction of Medium 2 is greater than that of Medium 1. Hence, the refracted ray bends *toward* the normal. (Snell's Law, **Equation 3-2**, describing this phenomenon is sometimes called the Snell-Descartes Law, but was known earlier. See **Figure 3-15**.)

Table 3-2
Average indices of refraction for some common materials in the visible bandpass. Fused silica, fused quartz, pyrex, crown glass, and flint glass are commonly used in optics. [1], [2], [3], [4]

Index of refraction (n) of some common materials					
Air	1.0003	Fused quartz	1.46	Flint glass	1.62
Beer	1.35	Pyrex	1.47	Sapphire	1.76
Water	1.33	Acrylic	1.49	Cubic zirconium	2.15
Ethanol	1.36	Plexiglas	1.49	Diamond	2.42
Cornea (human eye)	1.31	Sodium chloride	1.50	Gallium arsenide	3.93
Fused silica	1.46	Crown glass	1.54	Silicon	4.01

The index of refraction for air at sea level is about 1.0003 as shown in **Table 3-2**. This value depends on atmospheric temperature and density (or pressure), which will be discussed in **Chapter 5**. So, it must decrease to $n = 1$ (exactly) in the vacuum of space (where there is no material). Even this slight change will cause a bending (i.e., refraction) of upward propagating information from target to sensor (**Figure 3-5**), resulting in a small geolocation error in the metrics of a target.

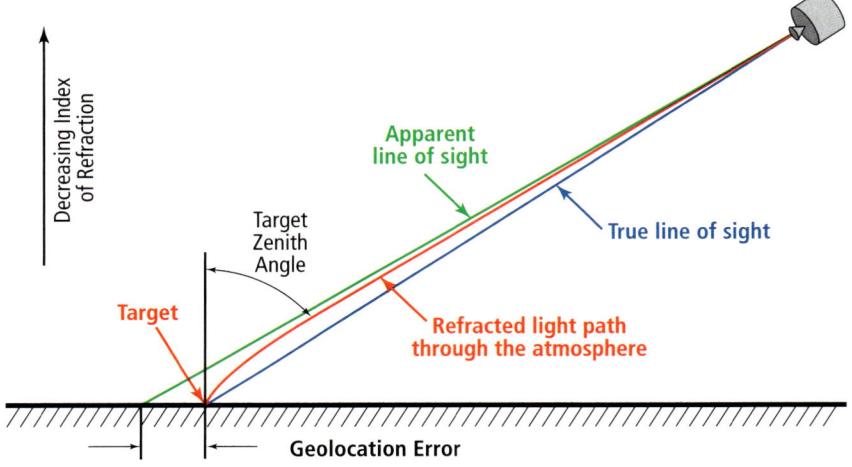

Figure 3-5
Refraction through the atmosphere due to decreasing index of refraction with increasing altitude causing a geolocation error. (Effect exaggerated for illustration.)

REFLECTIVITY

Looking at **Equations 3-1** and **3-2**, traditional classical physics suggests that reflection and refraction are an either/or phenomenon resulting in one or the other. This is not the case, however, as **Figure 3-4** correctly shows that both result. The light energy incident on a material interface is split:

$$E_{INCIDENT} = E_{REFLECTED} + E_{TRANSMITTED}. \qquad (3\text{-}3)$$

This effect can easily be seen (**Example 3-2**).

What becomes of the transmitted component is not a direct concern in remotely sensing the target (but, of course, it is extremely important to the design of sensor components, such as lenses, filters, etc.). If it is transmitted[13] through the material (like a window pane), the analyst is not on the other side to receive it. If it is absorbed, it will contribute to the energy balance of the material. Consequently, the energy may be seen when it is emitted, but it will have the spectrum characteristic of the temperature and emissivity of the material, not necessarily the incident spectrum. Since nearly all targets to be detected by reflected light are macroscopic, opaque objects for all intents and purposes, incident light falling on them that is not reflected is absorbed. Thus, **Equation 3-3** can be modified for solid targets to

$$E_{INCIDENT} = E_{REFLECTED} + E_{ABSORBED}. \qquad (3\text{-}4)$$

---

[13] Light does not generally pass through a material without some absorption. (See **Chapter 6** on Optical Transmission Function). As will be explained in the next section, some reflection will be lost from both surfaces, where the light enters a transparent material and where it exits.

EXAMPLE 3-2: REFLECTION AND REFRACTION OCCUR SIMULTANEOUSLY AT A MATERIAL INTERFACE

Hold any object to the side and look at its reflection in the bathroom cabinet's rear-surfaced mirror. (The reflecting metal film is on the back side of the glass where it is protected.) A dim image of the object will appear on the front of the glass as well as the primary reflection from the back surface.

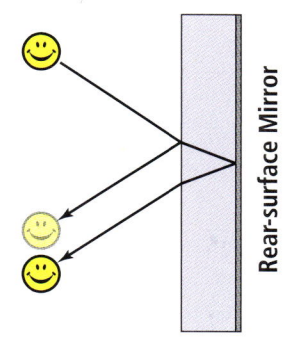

Figure 3-6
Space shuttle Discovery on the launch pad for its final flight, February 2011.

If **Equation 3-4** is divided by $E_{INCIDENT}$, the result is

$$\frac{E_{REFLECTED}}{E_{INCIDENT}} + \frac{E_{ABSORBED}}{E_{INCIDENT}} = 1. \tag{3-5}$$

The second term, recognized as the fraction of light absorbed, was introduced in **Equation 2-21** as the coefficient of absorption, or absorptivity, $\alpha(\lambda)$. The first term, analogously, is the fraction of light energy reflected from the target. This is called the coefficient of reflection, or reflectivity:

$$\rho(\lambda) = \frac{E_{REFLECTED}}{E_{INCIDENT}}. \tag{3-6}$$

Therefore, multiple material *signatures*, emissivity, absorptivity, and reflectivity, exist that are mathematically related. All are functions of wavelength, and if one is known, all are known. The following summarizes **Chapter 2** and the new definition (**Equation 3-6**):

$$\left.\begin{aligned} \epsilon(\lambda) &= \alpha(\lambda) \\ \alpha(\lambda) &= 1 - \rho(\lambda) \\ \rho(\lambda) &= 1 - \epsilon(\lambda) = 1 - \alpha(\lambda) \end{aligned}\right\}. \tag{3-7}$$

The discussion of the specifics of the use of reflective signatures will be discussed in **Chapters 15** and **18** on multi- and hyperspectral sensing, but a suggested application is introduced in **Example 3-3**.

SPECULAR REFLECTION

The most familiar reflection is visible in a smooth surface.[14] The surface can be either metallic (e.g., a mirror) or dielectric (e.g., calm water as in **Figure 3-6**). In any case, the *direction of reflection* is according to the Specular Law, **Equation 3-1**. *The amount of light reflected* is dependent on the reflecting material's index of refraction and the angle of incidence.

Given incident radiation on a smooth surface, recall the wave-nature of light. As stated in **Chapter 2**, the electric and magnetic fields in an EM wave may oscillate in particular planes. **Figure 2-1**, for example, depicts a horizontal electric field by which that wave would be termed horizontally polarized. In the context of reflection, *polarization* is referenced to the plane perpendicular to the reflecting surface containing the incident and reflected wave, as the plane of the page in **Figures 3-4** and **3-7**. For specular reflection, the polarization of the incident wave makes a *huge* difference in the amount reflected.

[14] What is smooth? If an extended surface has vertical or horizontal irregularities (bumps, dips, cracks, etc.) smaller than about one-quarter of one wavelength of the incident light, then it is smooth. Typically, electro-optical photons do not notice non-uniformities smaller than several tens of molecules across.

EXAMPLE 3-3: EFFECT OF MOISTURE ON SOIL SPECTRA [5]

Sandy soil is found almost everywhere in the world. Such soil is quite porous, consisting of many grains of pulverized sand, leaving significant gaps, holes, and fissures between the granules. Such soil can hold a fair amount of water, which influences its stability and suitability to support wheeled vehicle traffic (trafficability). When looking at such soil, reflected light is a spectral combination of the soil itself and the amount of water in the cracks. The following shows the reflected signature (reflectance) of a typical sample of this soil when it has various percentages of moisture.

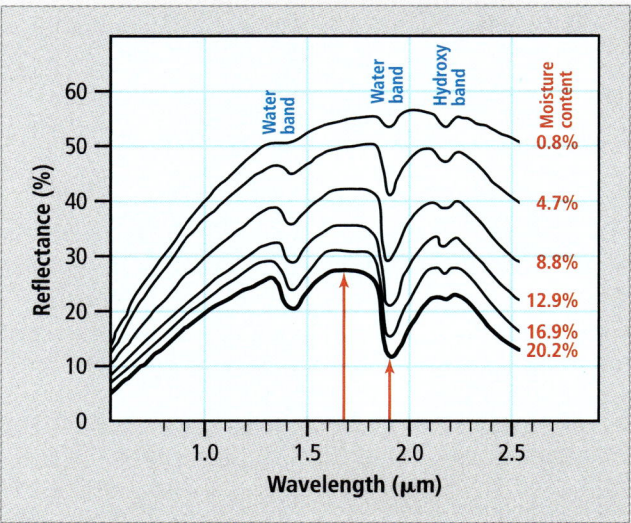

This figure suggests the rate at which the soil's reflectance changes, as a function of water content, is different at various wavelengths. For example, if it was possible to measure the reflectance of the soil at two wavelengths where the rate is different, then a curve like the one below might result. That is, measuring the reflectance in two narrow bandpasses as shown (e.g., $\Delta\lambda \approx 10$ nm) should lead to an estimate of the soil's moisture content, thus allowing military commanders to plan troop mobilization through the area.

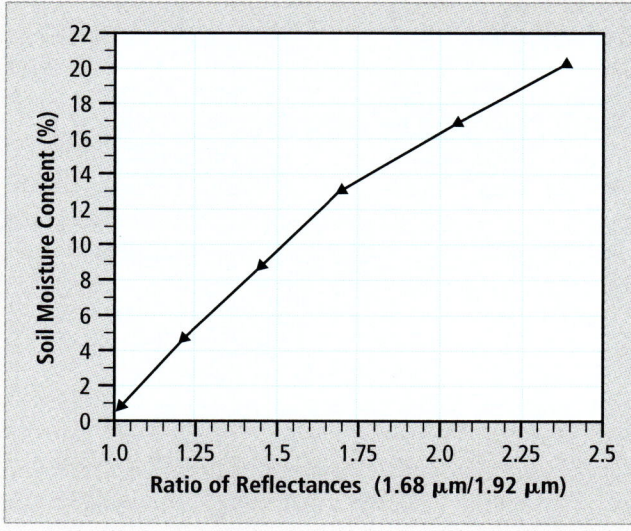

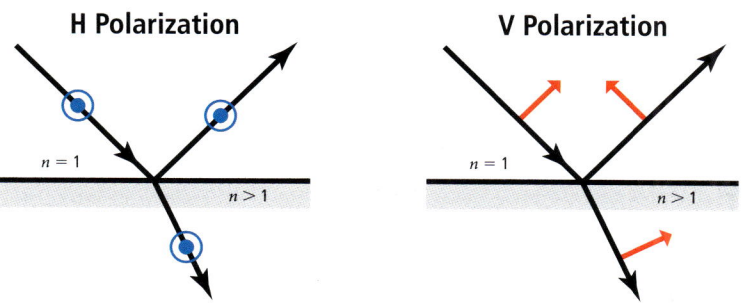

Figure 3-7
Polarization of an incident EM wave with respect to the plane containing that wave and its reflection.

Figure 3-7 illustrates the two extremes of linearly polarized incident light; any other orientation is a combination of the two. The left is called the horizontal, transverse electric, or H polarization. This shows the electric field of the incident and reflected radiation oscillating in and out of the page, horizontal to the reflecting surface. The blue circles represent the tips of the electric field vectors (arrows) pointing out. The right side of **Figure 3-7** shows the other extreme where the electric field (represented by red arrows) is contained within a plane vertical to the reflecting surface. This orientation is called the vertical, transverse magnetic, or V polarization.

The amount of each polarization specularly reflected was calculated by 19th century physicist Augustin-Jean Fresnel (**Figure 3-15**). For smooth dielectric surfaces, the results of his calculations are shown in **Figure 3-8** and are given by the following formulas:

$$\text{H polarization:} \quad \rho_H = \left(\frac{n_I \cos\theta_I - n_T \cos\theta_T}{n_I \cos\theta_I + n_T \cos\theta_T}\right)^2 \quad (3\text{-}8)$$

$$\text{V polarization:} \quad \rho_V = \left(\frac{-n_T \cos\theta_I + n_I \cos\theta_T}{n_T \cos\theta_I + n_I \cos\theta_T}\right)^2. \quad (3\text{-}9)$$

To compute these, the indices of refraction, n_I and n_T, are needed for the medium containing the incident beam and the reflecting material, respectively. Snell's Law (**Equation 3-2**) must be used to compute θ_T for the incident angle, θ_I. For nearly all remote sensing, $n_I \approx 1$ for the atmosphere.

Four important points about **Figure 3-8** are worthy of discussion. *First*, when the angle of incidence is perpendicular (normal) to the surface ($\theta_I = 0°$), note that $\rho_H = \rho_V$. This is because $\theta_T = 0°$ by Snell's law. So, either of Fresnel's formulas reduce to

$$\rho_{NORMAL} = \left(\frac{n_I - n_T}{n_I + n_T}\right)^2. \quad (3\text{-}10)$$

See **Example 3-4** for an application.

Second, there is an angle of incidence for which $\rho_V = 0$. This is called the Polarization Angle, or Brewster's Angle (after Scottish physicist Sir David Brewster, **Figure 3-15**) and is given by

$$\theta_{POLARIZATION} = \tan^{-1}\left(\frac{n_T}{n_I}\right). \quad (3\text{-}11)$$

Third, it is uncommon for natural light sources to emit polarized light. So, ordinary light is considered to be unpolarized or randomly polarized. On average, it is equally horizontally and vertically polarized and will reflect about half *H* and half *V* light from a smooth dielectric surface.

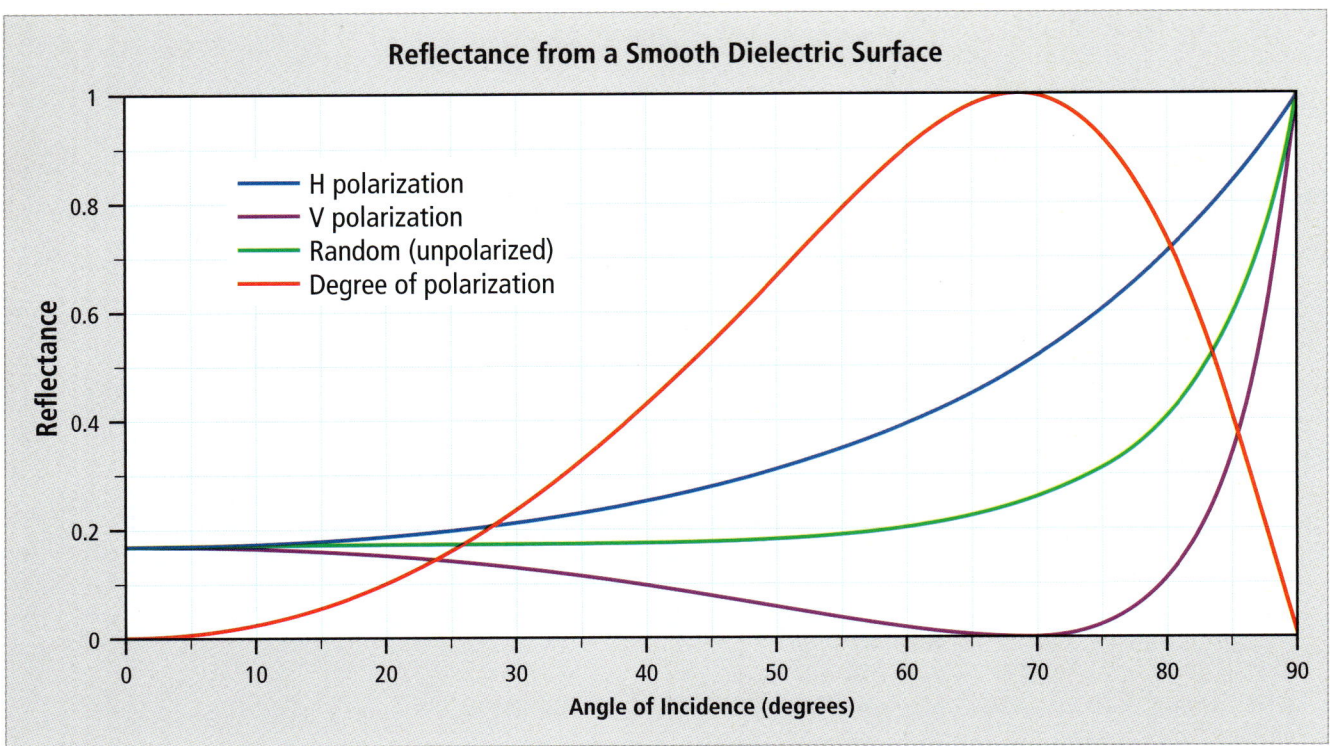

Figure 3-8
Plot of the specular Fresnel coefficients for the two polarizations and their unpolarized, random average. For this example, $n_I = 1.00$ and $n_T = 2.50$.

EXAMPLE 3-4: APPROXIMATELY HOW MUCH VISIBLE LIGHT IS REFLECTED FROM A SILICON SOLAR PANEL AT NORMAL INCIDENCE?

Table 3-2 shows the refractive index of silicon is about $n_T \approx 4.01$ in the visible. Assuming visible sunlight is normally incident on a silicon solar panel through air, $n_I \approx 1$, **Equation 3-10** shows

$$\rho_{NORMAL} = \left(\frac{1 - 4.01}{1 + 4.01}\right)^2 = 0.36.$$

Presumably, this suggests only about 64% of sunshine's visible energy (at most) could penetrate into a silicon solar cell to be absorbed and turned into electricity.

The amount of randomly polarized light reflected is shown as the intermediate line in the figure:

$$\rho_{RANDOM} = \frac{\rho_H + \rho_V}{2}. \quad (3\text{-}12)$$

Fourth, since the TE and TM components of ordinary light reflect with different amplitudes, reflected light is *partially polarized*. The degree of polarization (*DOP*) is shown on the plot and is given by:

$$DOP = \frac{\rho_H - \rho_V}{\rho_H + \rho_V}. \quad (3\text{-}13)$$

This formula affirms that when $\rho_H = \rho_V$ at normal incidence (and at 90°), the reflected light is unpolarized with $DOP = 0$. On the other hand, at Brewster's Angle, $DOP = 100\%$.

Evidence for all of the above is readily apparent upon donning Polaroid™ sunglasses (**Figure 3-9**). Looking toward the sun at shiny objects (or at a wet street when the sun appears after a light rain) and tilting the head will produce a noticeable increase in glare. Manufacturers of these sunglasses specifically orient the lenses (dichroic polarizing filters) to block the *H* polarization. The V polarization is reduced by reflection (**Figure 3-8**).

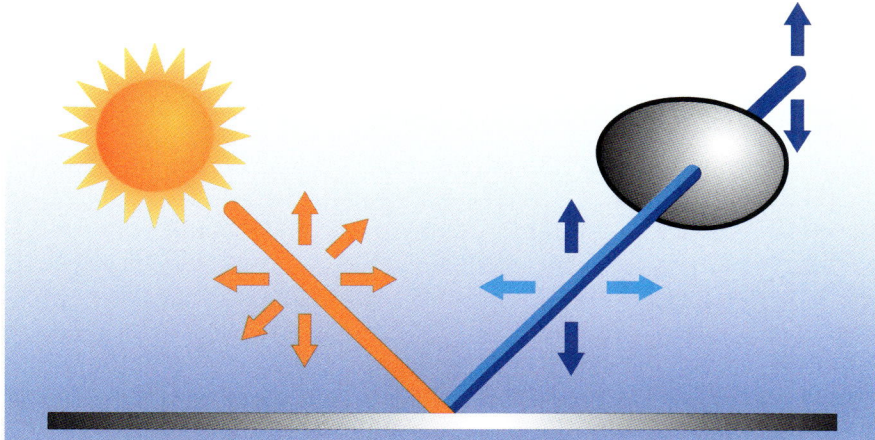

Figure 3-9
Polaroid sunglasses are designed to block the TE polarization.

REALISTIC TREATMENT

Reflection usually studied in school, specular reflection, is the exception and not the rule. If only specular reflection occurs, not much can be seen. Only those objects properly oriented to satisfy $\theta_R = \theta_I$ between the viewer and a light source (natural or artificial) will be visible. Clearly, many more objects can be seen. Why? There are two reasons.

First, many sources of light are diffuse, coming from all directions at once. Skylight[15] is such a source and fills the out-of-doors environment. This is evident by things that can still be seen in shadows out of direct sunlight. Likewise, manufacturers of lighting fixtures design them to be extended and diffuse. Thus, there are light sources everywhere, but the specular condition still has to hold to see objects, regardless of the lights' locations.

Second, if the conditions for specular reflection are not satisfied, yet a target is still visible, there has to be some other feature of a target's surface to make it visible. For example, consider a dark room where a presenter guides viewers' eyes across a slide with a laser pointer. The projector and

[15] The origin of skylight is scattered sunlight from air molecules and suspended aerosols (particles of all kinds and sizes).

laser are definitely not diffuse sources, yet everyone in the auditorium can see them on the screen. The reason is the surface is *not* smooth, as will be investigated now (**Figure 3-10**).

Figure 3-10
A direct beam of light reflects from a non-smooth surface in a **non-specular manner.**

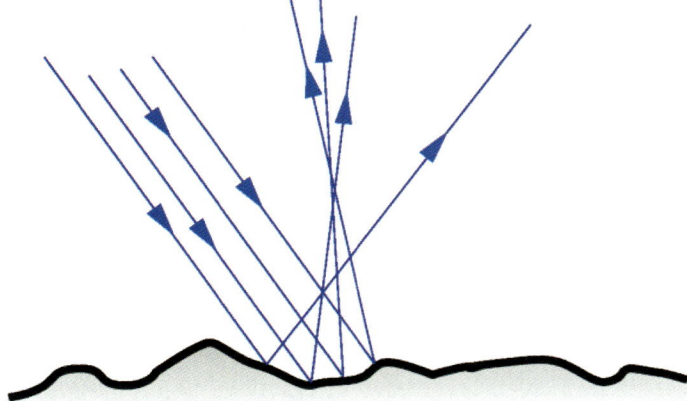

REFLECTIVITY DISTRIBUTION FUNCTIONS

Most surfaces are not smooth, unless they have been carefully polished. There are bumps, pits, cracks, etc. that are larger than one-quarter wavelength, disqualifying ordinary surfaces from specular reflection. Incident photons are "bounced" in many different directions by the irregularities. In fact, one of the prominent features of actual reflection, as opposed to specular reflection, is that reflected light is sent into all directions, not just in the plane of incidence. Real reflection is often characterized as a three-dimensional "bubble" over the point of incidence and is mathematically described as a *reflectivity distribution function*. What is a reasonable form of such functions? A visit to the local paint store will help answer the question. (The selection of paint finish should probably be made by an interior decorator rather than a physicist, but the various surface treatments provide a suitable model for discussing real reflection. The different paint types described here may be familiar, but they probably have not been considered as models for reflection.)

Paint manufacturers supply products with a number of finishes, ranging from near-specular to flat. These finishes are typical of the surfaces of many objects, some of which are painted and some are natural. **Figure 3-11** illustrates some side-views of how light can be reflected, but the real reflection is three-dimensional. Light is also reflected into and out of the plane.

On the left of **Figure 3-11** is a glossy paint finish that dries to a smooth-to-the-touch surface that is nearly specular, reflecting approximately 90% of incident light around a *near*-specular direction. Looking at a glossy wall, the reflection of a lamp can be distinctly seen, but it would not be an in-focus mirror image, just a bright area. Next, a semi-gloss finish still reflects a majority of light around the specular direction, but softens or diffuses it, producing a subtle glare. The specular component is diffused even more in a satin (or eggshell) finish where the majority of light is scattered in all directions. A slightly brighter, but subdued area reflection of a lamp can still be seen on a satin-finish wall. Lastly, on the right, is a dull finish where there is almost no discernible specular component. Matte (or flat) finished walls feel smooth, but not slick to the touch.

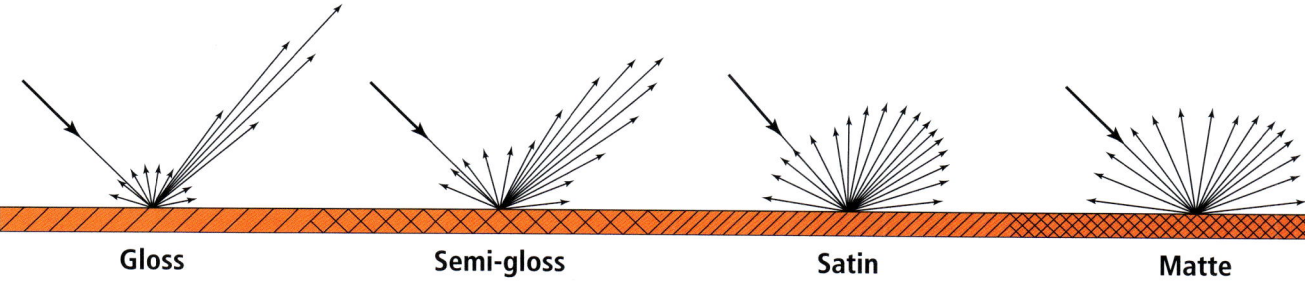

Figure 3-11
Paint finishes reflect light differently.

Less smooth walls are textured wall treatments where decorators use paint mixed with grit. These surfaces are even more diffusely reflecting, simulating rough natural surfaces like stone, sand, or tree bark. Many of these natural substances are composed of micro-surfaces that are individually like the face of one grain of sand (a silicon dioxide crystal). The reflection from each micro-surface may actually be nearly specular, but the random orientations of millions of them result in a completely diffuse distribution. This is the most common type of natural reflection and many man-made materials behave likewise. How are these to be described?

GENERALIZED REFLECTIVITY DISTRIBUTION FUNCTION

Separately, *how much* light is reflected from a surface and *which direction* it is reflected have been discussed. A complete description of reflection must include both; so together they are

$$\rho(\lambda,\Omega_R) = \rho(\lambda)\phi(\Omega_R), \tag{3-14}$$

where a cumbersome[16] notation is now introduced.

$\rho(\lambda)$ is the *how much*, and is the *same* wavelength-dependent reflectivity defined in **Equation 3-6**, and

$\phi(\Omega_R)$ is called the *phase function*, and is the spatial distribution function or *which direction*. Ω_R is a small cone of direction in space,[17] often indicated in three-dimensional coordinates as polar (or co-latitude) and azimuth angles, (θ_R,φ_R), as shown in **Figure 3-12**.

When the *how much* of reflectivity is combined with the *which direction* phase function in **Equation 3-14**, the result is called *reflectance*.[18] Since the amount of light reflected from a target depends on direction, that must also be true of emission and absorption through **Equation 3-7** relations. Thus, emissivity (*how much* is emitted from a surface) combined with *what direction* it is emitted is *emittance* and similarly for *absorptance*.

For classical specular reflection, the reflectivity is given by the Fresnel formulas, **Equations 3-8** and **3-9** (or their combination, **Equation 3-12**, for unpolarized light). Without loss of generality, **Figure 3-12** can be brought into conformity with **Figures 3-4** and **3-7** by letting $\varphi_I = 0°$ and $\varphi_R = 180°$ (or any two angles 180° apart). Thus, specular reflection remains in a plane.

[16] This will be much simpler once assumptions and approximations are made.

[17] Ω will be returned to in **Chapter 4**, where it will be formally defined as *solid angle*. Formally, this gives $\phi(\Omega_R)$ dimensions of per unit direction, and $\rho(\lambda,\Omega_R)$ is reflectivity per unit direction.

[18] In common parlance, reflection, reflectivity, and reflectance may be used interchangeably, but there is a technical difference, whether directionality is included or not. The same applies to the parallel terms for emission and absorption.

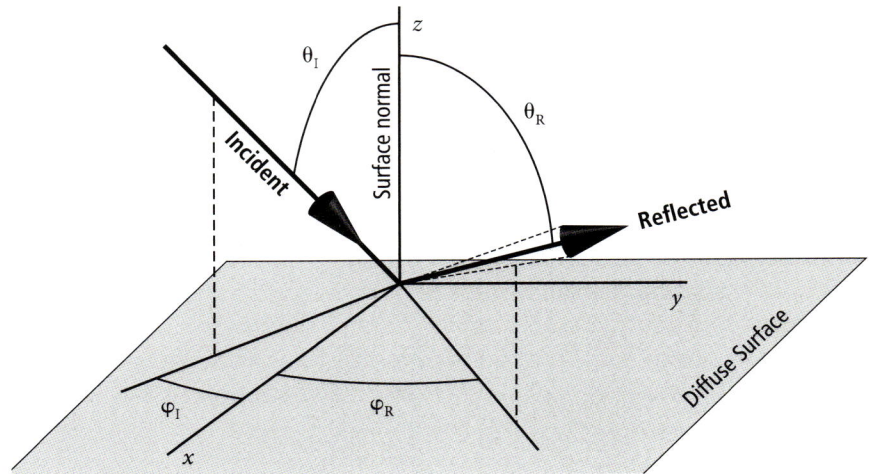

Figure 3-12
Spatial relationships of generalized reflection.

For other than *specular reflection*, reflection from the surfaces discussed in the last section, the most general form of the phase function is formally known as the Bidirectional Reflectivity Distribution Function (BRDF), written in various ways as:

$$\frac{d^2\rho}{d\Omega_I d\Omega_R} = \rho(\lambda)\phi(\theta_I,\varphi_I,\theta_R,\varphi_R). \qquad (3\text{-}15)$$

This notation[19] means the amount of light reflected into a particular direction ($d\Omega_R$ or (θ_R,φ_R)) depends on the direction the light *comes from* ($d\Omega_I$ or (θ_I,φ_I)). This can become cumbersome, but is certainly a natural part of experience; although, it is usually not thought about.

When the field in **Example 3-5** is harrowed (pulverized to dust), the difference in reflection with changing sun direction vanishes, and it looks basically the same regardless of the time of day. This is the situation with many rough but uniform, extended targets: battlefields, runways, parking lots, factory roofs, etc. When this is the case, the BRDF, **Equation 3-15**, reduces to simply a function of reflected direction alone:

$$\phi(\theta_I,\varphi_I,\theta_R,\varphi_R) \Rightarrow \phi(\theta_R,\varphi_R). \qquad (3\text{-}16)$$

APPROXIMATE REFLECTIVITY DISTRIBUTION FUNCTION

Even given the simplification of **Equation 3-16**, it is still difficult to apply reflectivity in advanced technical intelligence collection. The purpose is to gather information about targets by collecting EM energy at a distance, i.e., hundreds to tens of thousands of kilometers away using aerostats, airplanes, or satellites. At those ranges, the exact geometric relationship to the target is often unknown, and there isn't a way to determine it. In particular, when the spatial resolution[20] does not allow the size, shape, texture, and orientation to be discerned, the angles θ_R and φ_R cannot be calculated. How can this be corrected?

The most common estimate made for unknown reflectivity distribution functions is to assume *on average* that reflection is independent of azimuth:

$$\phi(\theta_R,\varphi_R) \Rightarrow \phi(\theta_R). \qquad (3\text{-}17)$$

---

[19] Do not be intimidated by the use of calculus-looking notation. It is just a shorthand way of reminding that what is meant is a "small" cone from the direction of incident light and a "small" cone into the direction of reflected light. Practically, "small" means the smallest increment of anything that can be measured with the rulers, clocks, and scales on hand.

[20] Remember, this will be quantified later.

EXAMPLE 3-5: A COMMON SIGHT WHERE THE AMOUNT OF LIGHT REFLECTED DEPENDS ON THE DIRECTION OF INCIDENT LIGHT

(Copyright Chris Dunlop and licensed for reuse under the Creative Commons License.)

This photograph shows deep furrows in a plowed field illuminated by morning light. When the sun is to the right, as in the picture, the field will appear bright when looking to the left, but dark when looking to the right. Clearly, there is a difference in the amount of reflection depending on direction. In the afternoon, the field will look completely opposite with sunlight coming from the left. So, the appearance also depends on the direction of incidence.

This assumption is usually justified when the remote sensor's Field of View (FOV) (per pixel[21]) is large (larger than target details) or takes in many (millions plus) randomly oriented microsurfaces.

The final step to approximate a real reflectivity distribution is to assume it depends only on the polar angle[22] in some simple way. The simplest choice is one consistent with the accounting (considered in **Chapter 4**) for all the reflected energy received through the sensor's FOV:

$$\phi(\theta_R) = \frac{\cos \theta_R}{\pi}. \qquad (3\text{-}18)$$

Equation 3-18 is known as the Lambertian approximation (**Figure 3-15**), or the fully diffuse model as shown in **Figure 3-13**. (Remember, this is a side view, but a three-dimensional drawing would show this reflectivity distribution function looks like a sphere.) The Lambertian distribution function reflects equal amounts of energy in all directions. *It is one of the most common approximations made in remote sensing.* See Chapter 4 for further discussion.

TECHNICAL NOTES

The next to last sentence, above, may not sit well with readers. The plot of Lambertian reflection, **Figure 3-13**, does not quite agree with the discussion of the drawing for a nearly diffuse matte finish surface in **Figure 3-11**. The former discussion was to qualitatively lead the reader into accepting the concept of diffuse reflection, while the mathematics of **Equation 3-18** and its plot in **Figure 3-13** are *quantitatively* correct. Nonetheless, ask why the Lambertian approximation does not plot as a hemisphere (upside-down bowl) over the point of incidence instead of a sphere.

---

[21] This will be calculated later to show it is correct.

[22] Referred to as the target zenith angle, this is measured from directly overhead of the target (its zenith) to the remote sensor on the receiving end of reflected energy.

Figure 3-13
The Lambertian, fully diffuse reflectivity distribution function.

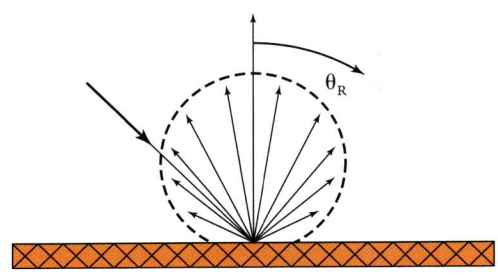

Fully Diffuse (Lambertian) Model

The statement that the Lambertian reflection puts equal energy *in all directions* means into all solid angles for all values of the zenith angle. This can be better understood once the concepts of solid angle and surface radiance are discussed, but the correct picture is **Figure 3-14**. The red, green, and blue bands (top-to-bottom) represent solid angles, centered on the incidence point, at three different reflection angles (i.e., target zenith angles). That is, the red, green, and blue areas on the surface of the hemisphere receive equal amounts of reflected energy.

Figure 3-14
For Lambertian reflectance, equal amounts of power are reflected into equal solid angles at zenith angles θ_R.

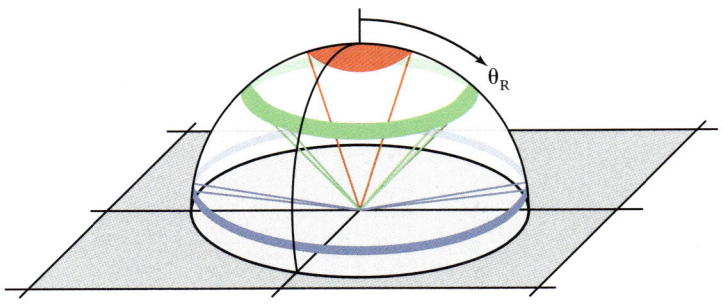

Another important point to re-emphasize is the *conservation of energy*. **Equation 3-7** is essentially just that; all radiant energy must be accounted for in terms of absorption, emission, and reflection. Since reflectance has been greatly simplified through the fully diffuse Lambertian model; energy going every which way from a surface according to zenith angle, but not azimuth, it is necessary to demonstrate that all reflected energy is accounted for. This is done by summing up (integrating) the energy sent in all directions:

Figure 3-15
Luminaries in the field of reflectivity. (Snellius photo courtesy of http://en.wikipedia.org/wiki/File:Willebrord_Snellius.jpg; PD_Old. Lambert photo courtesy of http://en.wikipedia.org/wiki/File:JHLambert.jpg; PD-Old. Brewster photo courtesy of http://en.wikipedia.org/wiki/File:Sir_David_Brewster.jpg; PD-Old.)

$$\underset{\text{All directions}}{\int \rho(\lambda)\phi(\theta_R)d\Omega_R} = \underset{\text{Hemisphere}}{\int \rho(\lambda)\frac{\cos\theta_R}{\pi}d\Omega_R} = \rho(\lambda). \qquad (3\text{-}19)$$

Willebrord Snellius 1580–1626

Johann Heinrich Lambert 1728–1777

Sir David Brewster 1781–1868

Augustin-Jean Fresnel 1799–1827

Thus, the fraction of incident light not absorbed by a target is reflected. The integral is solved in **Appendix 3-1** located on the support website.

Last, another term the reader may encounter is albedo, first used by Lambert. This word means the area-averaged diffuse reflectance of a planet, asteroid, or comet in solar system sciences, or is used in reference to Earth observations from satellites. **Table 3-3** lists some typical values in the visible bandpass.

Surface	Typical albedo
Fresh asphalt	0.04
Worn asphalt	0.12
Coniferous trees	0.08 to 0.15
Deciduous trees	0.15 to 0.18
Bare soil	0.17
Green grass	0.25
Desert sand	0.40
New concrete	0.55
Ocean ice	0.5–0.7
Fresh snow	0.80–0.90
Earth surface (average)	0.35

Table 3-3
Albedos of common materials in the visible bandpass. [6], [7]

4 RADIOMETRY

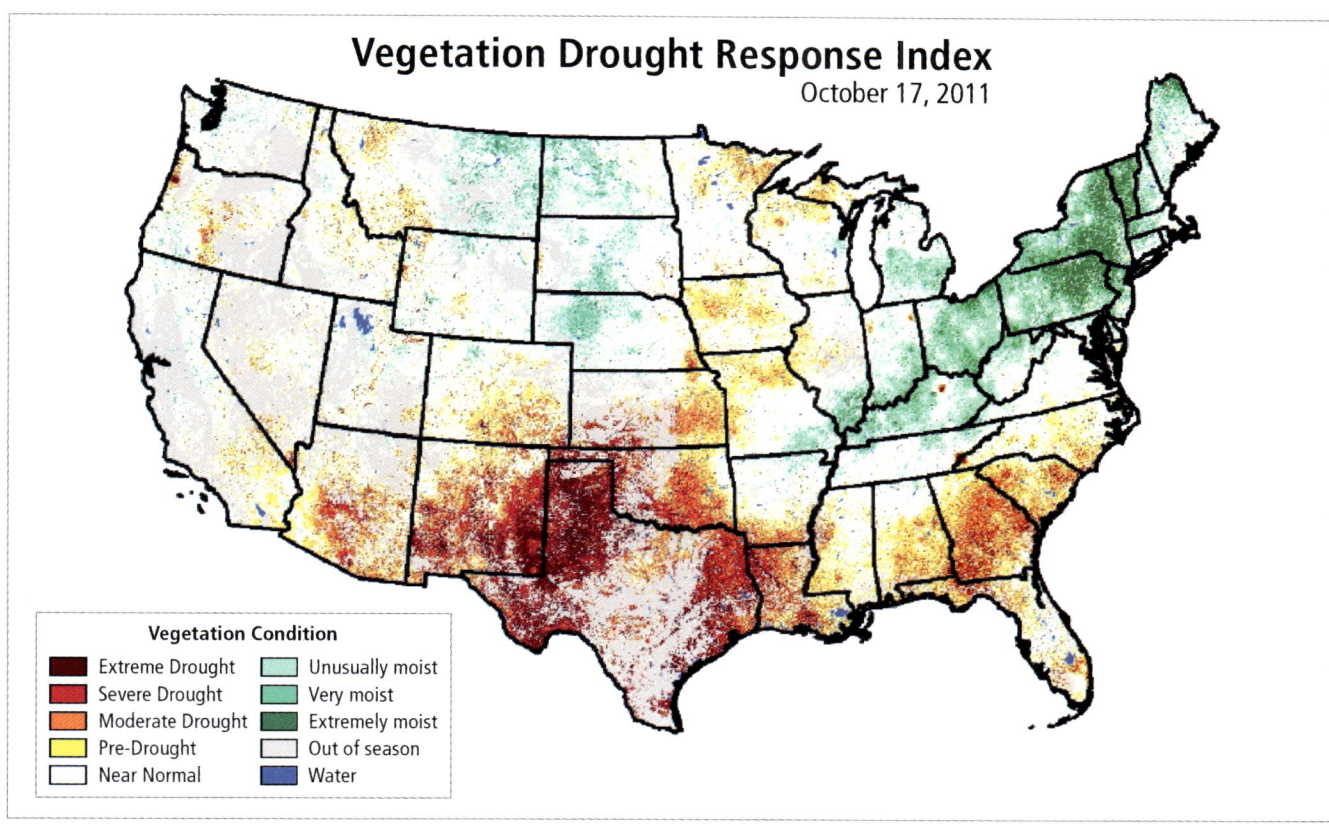

The next topic in this technical information gathering quest is propagation of energy from target to sensor, {PROP}. This science is known as **radiometry**.[1] First, solid angles and the radiometric quantities will be discussed in this chapter, particularly how to use them to characterize what are called **point** and **extended** targets. Then, sources' connections to sensors will be covered. At that point, the question lingering over the previous two chapters will be considered: when are targets seen by virtue of their emitted energy, and when because of reflected energy? This chapter will conclude with a discussion of one aspect of metrics that applies to radiometry: estimating the distance, or range, from target to sensor over which target information propagates.

The diagram above shows an example of radiometric data analysis. Soil and vegetation moisture content has been extracted from reflective and emissive signatures collected by the National Oceanic Atmospheric Administration's Advanced Very High Resolution Radiometer.

SECTIONS
4.1 RADIOMETRIC QUANTITIES
4.2 RADIATIVE TRANSFER
4.3 METRICS

[1] Readers may know of a related subject called *photometry*. As the name suggests, it is commonly encountered in photography and has to do with the amount of light collected on film (or a charged coupled device or complementary metal oxide semiconductor detector in the digital age) in the visible band. This is known as exposure. Photometry includes the response function of the eye to light, but is otherwise mathematically the same as radiometry, but with different quantities and units.

4.1 RADIOMETRIC QUANTITIES

Before jumping into radiometry, the terms and quantities that will be used throughout this chapter will be introduced.

COLLECTION GEOMETRY

A recommended step to solve almost any problem involving physical objects is to draw a picture. In the business of gathering information using advanced technical intelligence sensors, visualization of the target-sensor spatial relationship is essential. First, some fundamental geometric matters will be covered. This topic will be expanded in later chapters when the issues of spatial coverage strategies and orbitology are discussed.

REVIEW: PLANE ANGLES

In two dimensions, recall that an angle is the opening between two lines, joined at a vertex, and formally measured as a ratio (see **Figure 4-1**):

$$\theta = \frac{\text{arc length subtended on a circle}}{\text{radius of circle}} = \frac{s}{r} \text{ [rad]}, \quad (4\text{-}1)$$

where the circle is centered on the vertex, O.

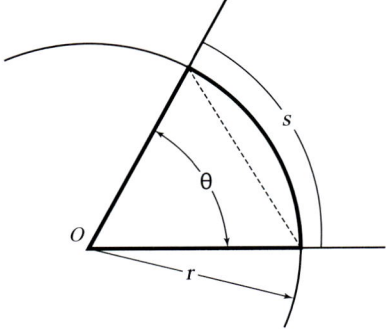

Figure 4-1
Definition of a plane angle.

Since it is a ratio, the measure of a plane angle is $\frac{\text{length}}{\text{length}}$, which has no dimensions,[2] but defines the unit radian (rad). To take this definition to extremes, measure an angle that goes all the way around a circle, and the result is

$$\theta_{CIRCLE} = \frac{\text{circumference}}{\text{radius}} = \frac{2\pi r}{r} = 2\pi \text{ [rad]}. \quad (4\text{-}2)$$

The reader is probably more familiar with angular measure in degrees (°). A circle is customarily divided into 360°. Thus,

$$2\pi \text{ rad} \equiv 360°, \quad (4\text{-}3)$$

where the ≡ means 'is equivalent to' as opposed to 'is equal to'. In order for this equivalence to be correct, the degree (of angular measure) must also be a dimensionless unit.

Figure 4-2
"Small" plane angle approximation.

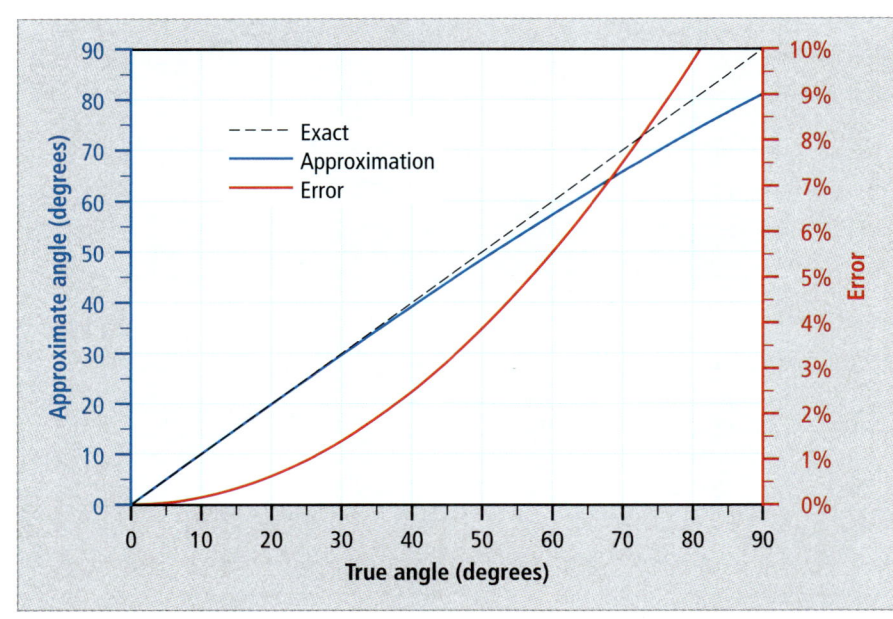

[2] A subtle point in the application of mathematics is that functions taking an argument (e.g., sin(x), exp(y), log(z), etc.) require the argument to be *dimensionless*. Thus, the radian is the ready-made unit for trigonometric functions. The fact that degrees are often used means there is a transparent built-in conversion (Equation 4-3).

For "small" angles, the arc length, **s**, may be replaced by a linear distance (a chord), which is the dashed line in **Figure 4-1**. (From plane geometry, the chord described is perpendicular to the angle bisector.) What constitutes "small" depends on the precision required. **Figure 4-2** shows this approximation has less than 1% error in an angle measuring almost 30°. This substitution of a chord for the arc may be well-known, but note, it is one of many approximations and estimates routinely made in remote sensing metric analysis, as illustrated in **Example 4-1**.

EXAMPLE 4-1: PROJECTED AREAS

Suppose a remote sensor at altitude h looks at a nadir angle θ and sees a linear object (like a runway seen end-on, as in the figure to the right) subtending a small angle, α, in its Field of View (FOV). The runway is at a distance $R \approx h/\cos\theta$ away.

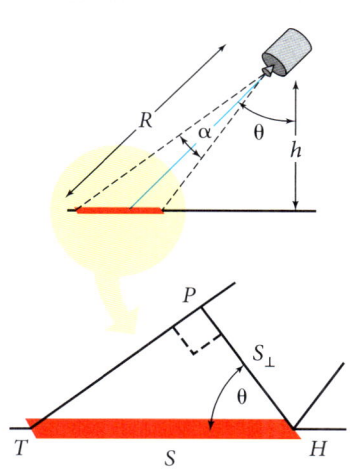

To estimate the length of the runway, S, first invoke the definition of a plane angle and assume α is "small," so $S_\perp \approx R\alpha \approx \frac{h\alpha}{\cos\theta}$ is the projection of the runway in the sensor's Line of Sight (LOS). Next, the lower part of the figure shows $S \approx \frac{S_\perp}{\cos\theta}$ by the definition of the cosine. Therefore,

$$S \approx \frac{h\alpha}{\cos^2\theta}.$$

However, this is just an *estimate*. The reasons are as follows:

1. A flat Earth geometry was assumed.

2. Altitude h and subtended angle α are measured as accurately as possible, but measuring devices with known tolerances were used, having systematic and random errors.

3. It was not specified whether angle θ was measured to the LOS to the near end (H) or far end (T) of the runway, or perhaps to some midpoint. (H refers to the "heel" of the FOV, and T refers to the "toe," as if one were stepping away from the sensor.)

4. The projected length, $S_\perp$, is perpendicular to what? The figure shows it is perpendicular to the LOS to T, so the angle at P is a right angle. But should it be perpendicular to the mid-line of the subtended angle? Well, yes … but then, the angle P would not be quite 90°.

There may be other reasons why the calculation of S is not exact. Once again, the point is to emphasize the information *derived* from the *observations* is only an *estimate*.

One further point about plane angles is every angle of a given measurement looks like every other angle of the same measurement. That is, every 45° angle is similar (in the geometry sense) to every other 45° angle. This may seem simplistic, but this is not so in three dimensions.

SOLID ANGLES

When the spatial dimensions increase by one, a three-dimensional angle can be determined by analogy to the plane angle as:

$$\Omega = \frac{\text{area subtended on surface of a sphere}}{(\text{radius of sphere})^2} = \frac{A}{r^2} \; [\text{sr}], \quad (4\text{-}4)$$

where the area on a sphere's surface is subtended by a cone with its vertex at the center of the sphere (**Figure 4-3**). This is called a solid angle (although it is not solid, it can be seen through). The most familiar solid angle the reader has experienced is looking through the viewfinder of a camera (or at the display screen on modern digital cameras). There, one sees what the camera views looking into the volume of a cone bounded by the optical limits of the lens and detector. Only the view within the sides of the solid angle is visible.

Since the definition of a solid angle is a ratio like the plane angle, it is also dimensionless: $\frac{\text{area}}{\text{length}^2}$, which is a unit known as a steradian (sr).[3] As with the plane angle, this can be taken to extremes; the measure of a solid angle subtending an entire sphere is

$$\Omega_{SPHERE} = \frac{\text{surface area}}{\text{radius}^2} = \frac{4\pi r^2}{r^2} = 4\pi \; [\text{sr}]. \quad (4\text{-}5)$$

Therefore, a hemisphere would be 2π sr. An example of this is the vault of the sky above, assuming the horizon is unobstructed all around.

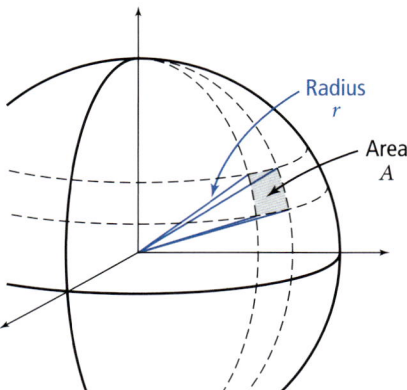

Figure 4-3
A solid angle is a volume bounded by the sides of a cone and the surface of a sphere.

It may now occur to the reader that a solid angle does not have to be rectangular, like the camera's FOV, but could be any shape, as long as there is a continuous area on the surface of a sphere. **Figure 4-4** shows two solid angles that happen to be rectangular in cross-section *but are the same measure in steradians*. So unlike plane angles, not all solid angles of the same measurement are similar to one another. *Therefore, it is necessary to specify the shape (cross-section) of a solid angle as well as its measurement.*

As can be imagined, the two most common solid angle shapes are rectangular (camera viewfinder) and round (ice cream cone). See **Figure 4-5** where the circular solid angle is characterized by a full cone angle, α, and the sides of the rectangular FOV are θ_1 and θ_2. For these configurations, their measure (in steradians) is often approximated by assuming the planar

---

[3] Inappropriately, someone may call the unit of solid angle a ster (or something that sounds like stare). A *ster* is an uncommonly used unit of volume, equal to one cubic meter.

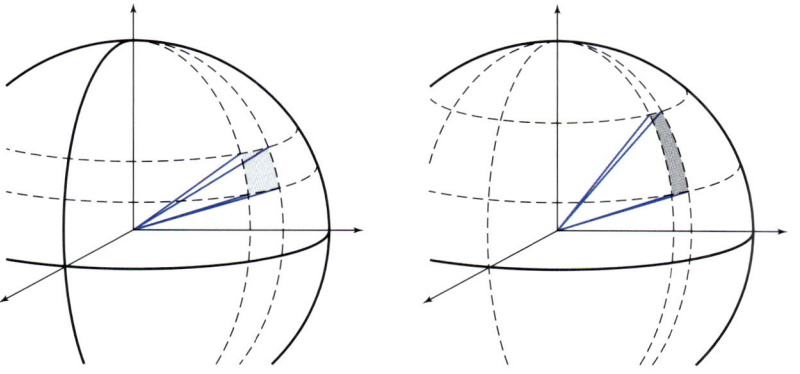

Figure 4-4
Two solid angles, equal in measure, but different in cross-section. If the spheres have radii of 10 units, and if the area on the left sphere's surface measures 2 × 2 while the area on the right measures 1 × 4, then both solid angles are $\Omega = \frac{4 \text{ units}^2}{(10 \text{ units})^2} = 0.04$ sr.

angles are "small," so the curved area subtended on a spherical surface can be replaced by a flat area. For the round cone, its exact measurement is

$$\Omega_{ROUND, \, EXACT} = 2\pi \left(1 - \cos \frac{\alpha}{2}\right) \, [\text{sr}], \qquad (4\text{-}6)$$

which approximates to:

$$\Omega_{ROUND, \, APPROX.} \approx \frac{\pi \alpha^2}{4} \, [\text{sr}] \quad (\text{note: } \alpha \text{ in radians}). \qquad (4\text{-}7)$$

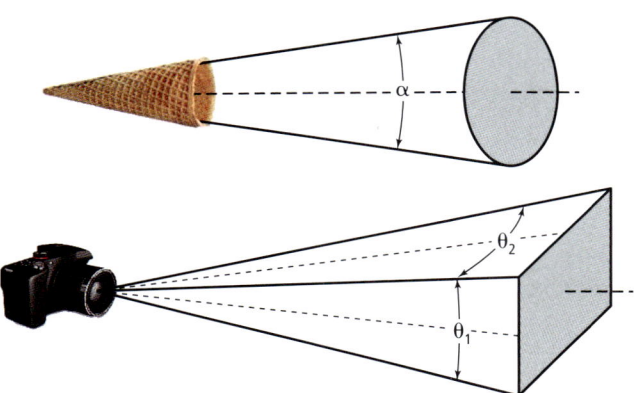

Figure 4-5
Common "small" solid angles.

Like the small plane angle approximation, **Figure 4-6** shows this approximation is also very accurate, having less than 1% error in cone angles measuring to almost 40°.

The small rectangular solid angle in **Figure 4-5** suggests its approximate measure is

$$\Omega_{RECT., \, APPROX} \approx \theta_1 \theta_2 \, [\text{sr}], \qquad (4\text{-}8)$$

where the plane angles are in radians. This formula leads one to believe that a solid angle could be expressed in square degrees if angles θ_1 and θ_2 are given in degrees. This is not completely wrong as astronomers often refer to their starry images covering a number of square degrees of the sky. However, it is not the appropriate computational unit for the remainder of this study of radiometry. *Think steradians!*

Figure 4-6
Small solid angle approximation for a round cone.

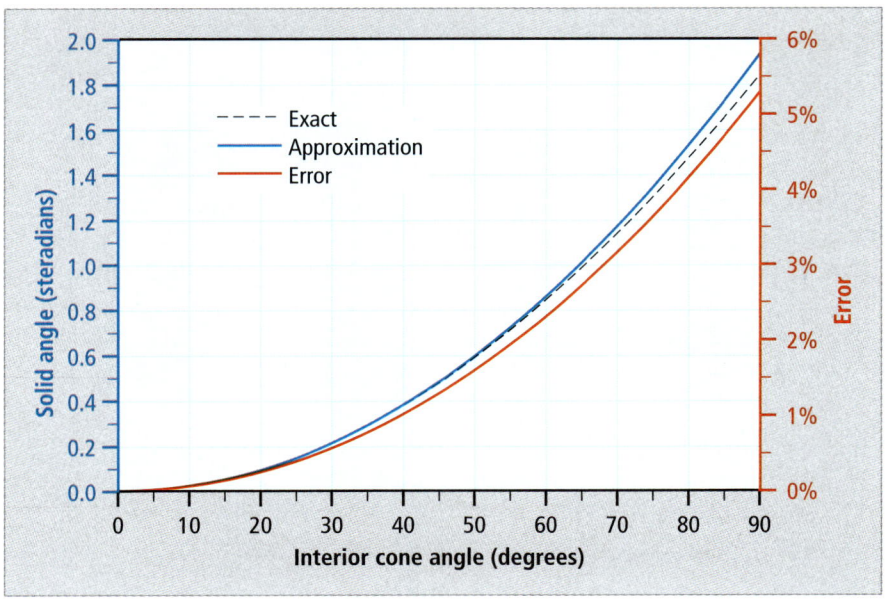

SENDING AND RECEIVING

Finally, a few more solid angle-associated terms are sketched in **Figure 4-7**. The left image shows a sensor receiving information from an element, dA_{SEND}, of a sending (emitting or reflecting) surface. The sensor is at *target zenith angle*, θ_S, with respect to the surface normal, so the sensor receives radiation from the source being sent through the element of solid angle,

$$d\Omega_{RCVR} \approx \frac{dA_{S\perp}}{R^2} \approx \frac{dA_{SEND}\cos\theta_S}{R^2} \quad [\text{sr}]. \quad (4\text{-}9)$$

The total amount of information received from the surface arrives in a solid angle defined by the FOV of the sensor:

$$\Omega_{FOV} \approx \int d\Omega_{RCVR} \approx \int_{SURFACE} \frac{dA_{SEND}\cos\theta_S}{R^2} \quad [\text{sr}], \quad (4\text{-}10)$$

Figure 4-7
Collection geometry terms.

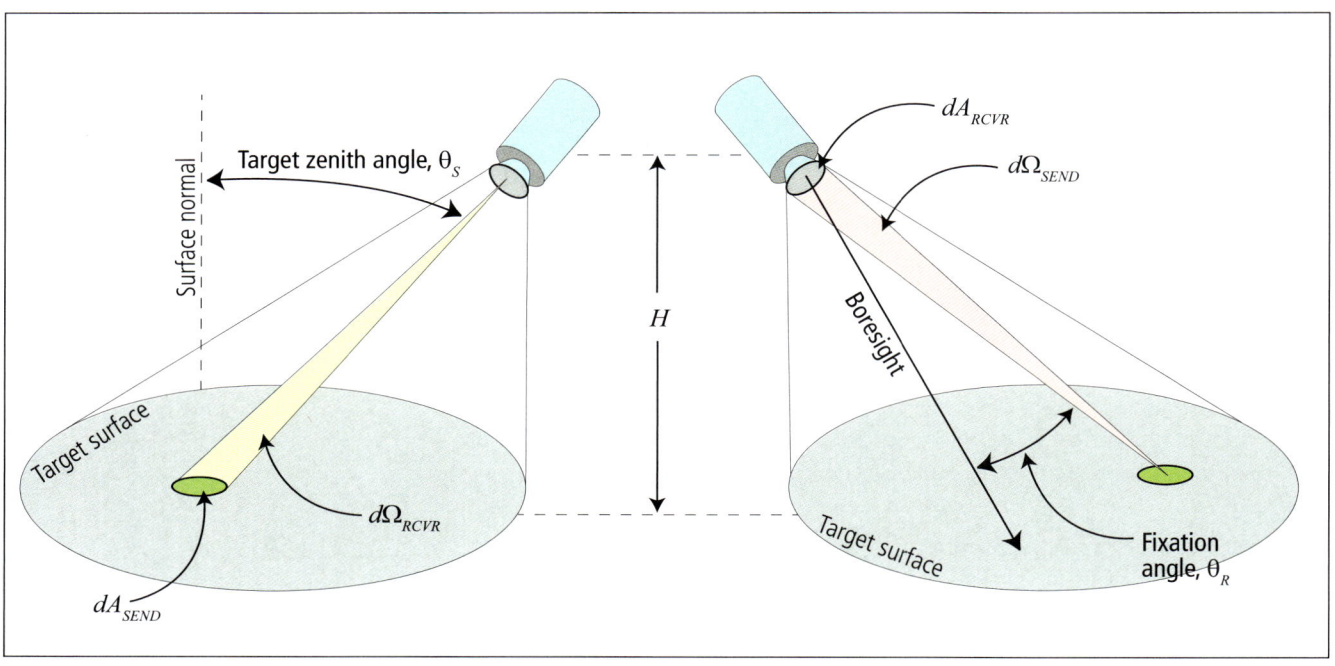

EXAMPLE 4-2: PROJECTED AREAS

In a totally analogous way to the two-dimensional collection, **Example 4-1**, if a sensor looks through its solid angle FOV, Ω, at an area, A, from a distance, R, then an *estimate* for the size of the area is

$$A \approx \frac{R^2 \Omega}{\cos\theta_S},$$

where angle θ_S is the target zenith angle, as shown in **Figure 4-7**. Note, the figure below also defines what is called the sensor's *boresight*: the centerline of its FOV. Alternatively, the boresight is called the sensor's LOS.

As in **Example 4-1**, the calculations for the size of an area visible from a remote sensor are only estimates because of the same reasons provided there.

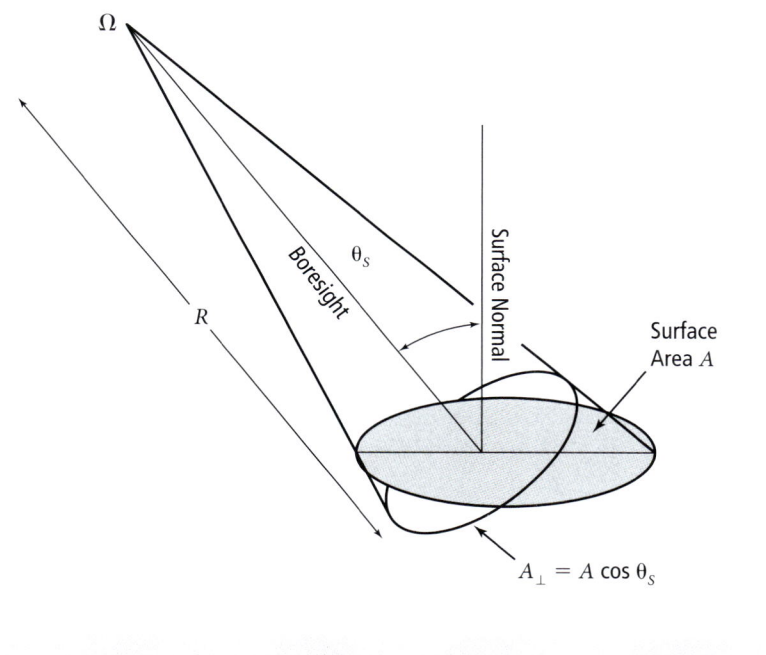

where both θ_S and R vary over the sending surface.[4] In practice, **Equation 4-10** is rarely computed, either because the target of interest occupies only a small portion of the FOV, or the FOV itself is very small. **Example 4-2** shows the way it is usually estimated.

The image on the right in **Figure 4-7** depicts the reverse geometry. The aperture area of the sensor, A_{RCVR}, is receiving information sent from an element of target:

$$d\Omega_{SEND} \approx \frac{dA_{RCVR\perp}}{R^2} \approx \frac{A_{RCVR}\cos\theta_R}{R^2}, \qquad (4\text{-}11)$$

where the receiving angle, θ_R, is called the fixation angle.[5] There is no need to integrate this over the aperture's surface, like **Equation 4-10**, because the aperture area is always very far from the target. (That is, the pseudo-calculus notation is missing from the right hand side of **Equation 4-11**

[4] Distance R is not explicitly shown in Figure 4-7, only the altitude of the sensor, H. The calculation will be shown later.

[5] The terminology comes from the days of jet fighter interceptors going after bomber targets. If the fighter held the bomber at a fixed angle as they approached one another, the two would arrive at the same place in the sky at the same time.

[6] Remember, there is no intent to intimidate anyone with the calculus notation. Although calculus will be used, the manipulations will be straightforward. Remember, something like dt means, in a practical sense, the smallest increment of time that can be measured.

[7] The symbols chosen in this text are not necessarily standardized within the community, but the quantity names, formulas, and units are. The reader is urged to use caution when applying these symbols when studying any other book.

[8] The origin of Q for energy seems to be thermodynamics. Φ for power must come from its being the eff-sounding Greek letter because power is sometimes called flux, the flow of energy. Using M for exitance is mysterious, but I for intensity makes sense. Astronomers talk about luminosity, which is similar to radiance, so that might be where L came from. Using E for irradiance is fairly common, but a script $\mathcal{E}$ will be used to distinguish this quantity from photon energy (e.g., Equation 2-2), atomic or molecular energy level, or electric field (which should be $\vec{E}$).

[9] Remember, power (watts) can always be written as joules/second [J/s]. In fact, that is preferred in unit analysis to help solve the phenomenology of some homework problems.

[10] Exitance was previously introduced when blackbody radiation was discussed. Intensity and radiance are probably words in the reader's vocabulary, but it is important to be pedantic here and strictly adhere to their technical definitions.

because it isn't needed.) $d\Omega_{SEND}$ is only one direction out of all the possible directions the target (point source or extended) could send information.

RADIOMETRY

The phenomenology of radiometry, how energy is transferred from target to sensor, will now be covered. This is also known as the science of radiative transfer. The mathematics will be carefully explained to show how radiometry describes the propagation of information, beginning with selection of quantities to describe the amount of radiation leaving a target or incident on a sensor.

RADIOMETRIC QUANTITIES

The primary entity (that carries information) to remember is *energy*: electromagnetic energy in the form of waves or photons. As previously studied, the origins of that energy from thermal or selective processes, emitted and/or reflected, need to be quantified now: How many photons? From what direction? With what time variation, if any? What are their wavelengths?

To start the quantification process, remember the time variation of energy is called power:

$$POWER = \frac{\Delta ENERGY}{\Delta TIME} = \left\{\begin{array}{c} RATE\ OF \\ EXPENDING \\ ENERGY \end{array}\right\} \left[W\ or\ \frac{J}{s}\right]. \quad (4\text{-}12)$$

Thus, the time-variation of energy is embedded in the concept of power, and some would consider it to be the fundamental propagated quantity of radiometry. However, *energy is information* and is always the answer pursued in analysis of time-sampled data.

In **Table 4-1**,[6] the radiometric quantities, symbols[7,8] and units[9] used throughout this text are defined. The first two quantities, radiant energy and power, are the propagated entities. The next three[10] give spatial substance to the information (energy, or energy per unit time) sent by targets about themselves. Note, as in the Description column of **Table 4-1**, 'sent' can mean either energy emitted or reflected by the target of interest. (In the next section, the conditions to determine which will be discussed.)

Table 4-1 Radiometric quantities.

	Quantity	Symbol	Formula	Units	Description
	Radiant Energy	Q	--	joules	Energy sent*, transferred, or collected
	Power	Φ	$\frac{dQ}{dt}$	watts	Rate of energy sent or received
Sending	Exitance	M	$\frac{d\Phi}{dA_{SEND}}$	watts/m²	Power sent per unit area in all directions
Sending	Intensity	I	$\frac{d\Phi}{d\Omega_{SEND}}$	watts/sr	Power sent per unit direction
Sending	Radiance	L	$\frac{d^2\Phi}{dA_\perp d\Omega} = \frac{d^2\Phi}{dA_{SEND}\cos\theta_S\, d\Omega_{SEND}}$	watts/(m² · sr)	Power sent per unit perpendicular area per unit direction
Receiving	Irradiance	$\mathcal{E}$	$\frac{d\Phi}{dA_{RCVR}}$	watts/m²	Power received per unit area from all directions

* *sent* could mean either emitted or reflected radiation

That leaves the final quantity, irradiance, at the pointy end of the radiometric arrow; it is at the receiving end of information sent by targets. To decipher the formulas for the radiometric quantities given in **Table 4-1**, refer back to **Figure 4-7** that shows the angles, areas, and solid angles.

To better understand the sending and receiving quantities in **Table 4-1**, refer to **Figure 4-8** for visualizations. The first sending quantity, exitance, M, was already discussed in the context of blackbody radiation. In the upper left drawing of **Figure 4-8**, no reference is made to the thermal properties of a surface, only that it sends radiation from all parts of its surface by any process. Furthermore, nothing is said about the *direction* of the radiation leaving the surface; presumably it can go into any, and in fact, ALL directions in any amount it wishes. Exitance is simply tracking how much energy per unit time leaves a unit area of the surface. Clearly, all surfaces have an exitance.

In **Figure 4-8**, the upper right drawing depicts what should be visualized when thinking about the second sending quantity, intensity, I. Again, nothing is said about the nature of radiation being sent, just that it is leaving an object in many different directions. Nothing is said about, nor are any restrictions made on those directions. Whereas exitance is apparently constrained to radiate only into the 2π sr hemisphere external to a surface, presumably this target can radiate anywhere into a 4π sr sphere around itself. Later, specific directions of radiation will be ascertained, so intensity is sometimes spoken of as power (sent) per unit direction, where direction is the measure of a solid angle cone the energy (per unit time) is radiating into. Hence, intensity is watts per steradian.

The third sending quantity, radiance, L, is illustrated in the lower left of **Figure 4-8**. In a way, it is a hybrid of exitance and intensity having both area and direction in its denominator. As can be seen, radiance is like exitance in that power sent from a unit of surface is measured, but this time it matters *in what direction*? The direction is very special. This is because only the information propagated into the direction of a sensor can be received; the rest is outside the FOV.[11] The information sent into the direction of the sensor then appears (looking at the surface

[11] This reaffirms the results of assessing collected information is an *estimate*. It is impossible to collect ALL the information to have complete knowledge of the target.

Figure 4-8
Radiometric quantities visualized.

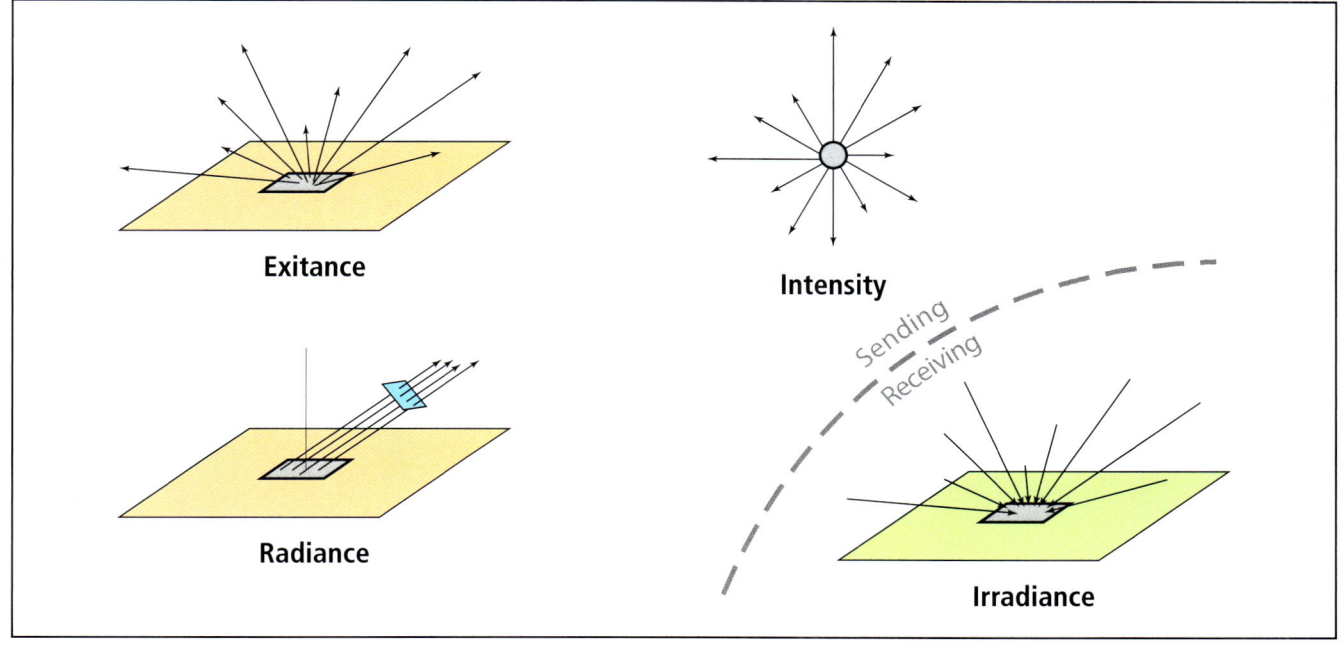

[12] The simplest solutions are often the best solutions.

[13] When might a target have constant exitance? When it is one type of material in steady state and has a constant temperature, then it is a blackbody or a graybody; or, when an external source of light reflecting from the target's surface is a blackbody or graybody.

from the sensor) to come from the *projection* of the area in the sensor's direction. This is the origin of the mysterious cosine that is shown in the denominator of radiance, and is the same cosine discovered in **Example 4-2**.

The lower right drawing in **Figure 4-8** stands apart from the other three as being the only one depicting received radiation. Irradiance, $\mathcal{E}$, is similar to exitance in that it is only concerned with surface area irrespective of incoming direction. In practice, of course, the direction of information propagation is a concern because of the need to see the targets. This focus is achieved through the optics-detector arrangement of the sensors, which will be covered later. Meanwhile, the next section will show how to calculate irradiances from targets.

TARGET QUANTITIES

From the definitions of the target radiometric terms, exitance, intensity, and radiance, the inter-relationship is clear because they all originate at the target. Those relationships will be developed, but first an important remote sensing consideration will be discussed.

1. **CONSTANT TARGETS**

By the nature of this business, information is gathered from afar, and any details about a target's surface or preferred direction for sending information are unknown (and many times cannot be determined). This is particularly true when there is no literal imaging capability due to the limitations of great distance or low spatial resolution. Therefore, it is imperative to make some assumptions about the targets. What are reasonable assumptions? Applying the principle of Occam's Razor:[12] all targets are constant.

  a. If a target's *exitance is constant*[13] over its surface, then estimate the total power sent by the target from its entire surface:

$$M = \frac{d\Phi}{dA_{SEND}} \approx \text{constant} \left[\frac{W}{m^2}\right] \Rightarrow \Phi \approx MA_{SEND} \text{ [W]}. \quad \textbf{(4-13)}$$

  This further assumes the surface area is known, either from a remote measurement (as photogrammetry) or from familiarity with the target class. Details of the calculations for **Equation 4-13** are available on the support website in **Appendix 4-1**.

  b. If a target's *intensity is the same in all directions*, i.e., the target is isotropic, then the total power sent into all directions is

$$I = \frac{d\Phi}{d\Omega_{SEND}} \approx \text{constant} \left[\frac{W}{sr}\right] \Rightarrow \Phi \approx 4\pi I \text{ [W]}. \quad \textbf{(4-14)}$$

  This assumption is very reasonable because very few targets (like a flashlight) send light into a limited direction. When a bright source of radiation is spotted, it is unlikely it is one with a beam pointed at the sensor (it is supposed to be clandestine after all). So presuming the target is emitting or reflecting equally in all directions makes sense. The calculation for **Equation 4-14** is available on the support website in **Appendix 4-1**.

  c. If a target's *radiance is constant* over its surface, then the total amount of power it radiates into the hemisphere above its surface can be estimated by:

$$L = \frac{d^2\Phi}{dA_{SEND}\cos\theta_S d\Omega_{SEND}} \approx \text{constant} \left[\frac{W}{m^2 sr}\right] \Rightarrow \Phi \approx \pi L A_{SEND} [W]. \quad (4\text{-}15)$$

The details of this calculation are available on the support website in **Appendix 4-1**, and notice there is a surprise in the answer which should be explained.

The astute reader will ask "Why is there only a factor of π in the answer, when a hemisphere (over a surface) is 2π sr?" The reason is in carefully stating that constant L means that equal elements of surface area send equal amounts of power into equal solid angles. Further research into the definition of radiance shows the elements of surface are *projected* elements into a sensor's direction, and that direction is only specified at an angle from the surface normal (target zenith angle, θ_S). It is independent of azimuth direction. Therefore, the equal solid angles are precisely the same ones discussed for **Figure 3-16**, which are repeated here as **Figure 4-9** for emphasis. Equal amounts of power are radiated into the onion ring shaped solid angles subtending the red, green, and blue areas in the figure. The conclusion, following **Chapter 3**, is:

Surfaces with constant radiance are Lambertian.

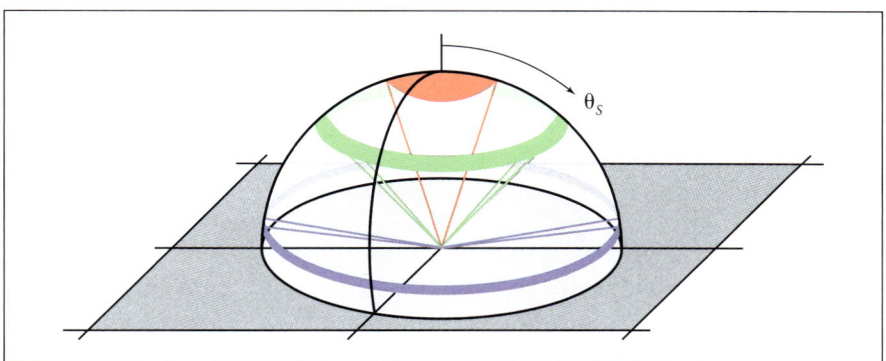

Figure 4-9
For a surface with constant radiance, equal amounts of power are sent into equal solid angles at target zenith angles, represented by the colored areas. (Note, when defining a solid angle, there is no restriction that states a sphere's surface can't have a "hole" in it, like the "onion rings" shown here. The area only needs to be contiguous.)

2. CONNECTED QUANTITIES

Since the three radiometric target quantities are all referenced to surface area, sending direction, or both, it should not be surprising that they are connected. For example, exitance is found contained within radiance:[14]

$$L = \frac{d^2\Phi}{dA_{SEND}\cos\theta_S d\Omega_{SEND}} \quad (4\text{-}16)$$

$$= d\left(\frac{d\Phi}{dA_{SEND}}\right)\frac{1}{\cos\theta_S d\Omega_{SEND}}$$

$$= \frac{dM}{\cos\theta_S d\Omega_{SEND}} \left[\frac{W}{m^2 sr}\right].$$

Assuming a surface's radiance is constant, there is a straightforward connection between its radiance and its exitance:

$$M = \int dM = \int L\cos\theta_S d\Omega_{SEND} = \pi L \left[\frac{W}{m^2}\right]. \quad (4\text{-}17)$$

This calculation closely follows the one for constant L in **Appendix 4-1** on the support website and shows that *surfaces having constant radiance*

[14] Again, ignore the apparent calculus notation if necessary. It is only included to show the derivations are rigorously correct, mathematically. This is done to apply the results to physical collection scenarios.

> **UNITS IN RADIOMETRIC CALCULATIONS**
>
> Look closely at **Equation 4-17** and study the units. It looks simple. Exitance, M, on the left has units of $[W \cdot m^{-2}]$ and radiance, L, on the right has units of $[W \cdot m^{-2} sr^{-1}]$. To make the equation correct in terms of units, the π on the right must therefore have units of $[sr]$. Right? Wrong! Pi is only a numerical factor.
>
> What, then, has become of the steradians?
>
> Recall the definition of solid angle. It is a ratio of an area to a length squared, like $[m^2/m^2]$. Hence, a solid angle is <u>dimensionless</u>, but carries the <u>unit</u> of steradian. A dimensionless unit can appear (or disappear) in an equation as needed without changing any dimensions. Therefore, a $[sr]$ can be included or not included when necessary.
>
> Now refer to **Equation 4-15**, for instance, which says in words
>
> $\{POWER\} = \left\{\begin{array}{c} NUMERICAL \\ FACTOR \end{array}\right\} \times \{RADIANCE\} \times \{AREA\}$
>
> which in units is
>
> $[W] = [nothing] \times \left[\dfrac{W}{m^2 sr}\right] \times [m^2].$
>
> This is perfectly correct because the radiance includes a (dimensionless) solid angle in its definition, but none of the other terms do. Remember this in future problem solving!

also have constant exitance, and vice versa. (See the Sidebar on **Units in Radiometric Calculations** for a short discussion of other functions in this equation.) This is most often stated and will be most useful in later calculations as the Lambertian approximation:

$$L = \frac{M}{\pi} \left[\frac{W}{m^2 sr}\right]. \quad (4\text{-}18)$$

Similarly, intensity can be found embedded within radiance:

$$L = \frac{d^2\Phi}{dA_{SEND}\cos\theta_S d\Omega_{SEND}} = d\left(\frac{d\Phi}{d\Omega_{SEND}}\right)\frac{1}{dA_{SEND}\cos\theta_S} \quad (4\text{-}19)$$

$$= \frac{dI}{dA_{SEND}\cos\theta_S} = \frac{dI}{dA_{SEND\perp}} \left[\frac{W}{m^2\,sr}\right].$$

Again, assuming a target's radiance is constant, its intensity can be derived as

$$I = \int dI = \int L\,dA_{SEND\perp} = L\int dA_{SEND\perp} = LA_{SEND} \left[\frac{W}{sr}\right], \quad (4\text{-}20)$$

where the slight difference from above is the preservation of the directionality of radiation from the radiance. That is, the target will appear as having an intensity arising from its projected area into the LOS from the sensor. **Figure 4-10** illustrates this.

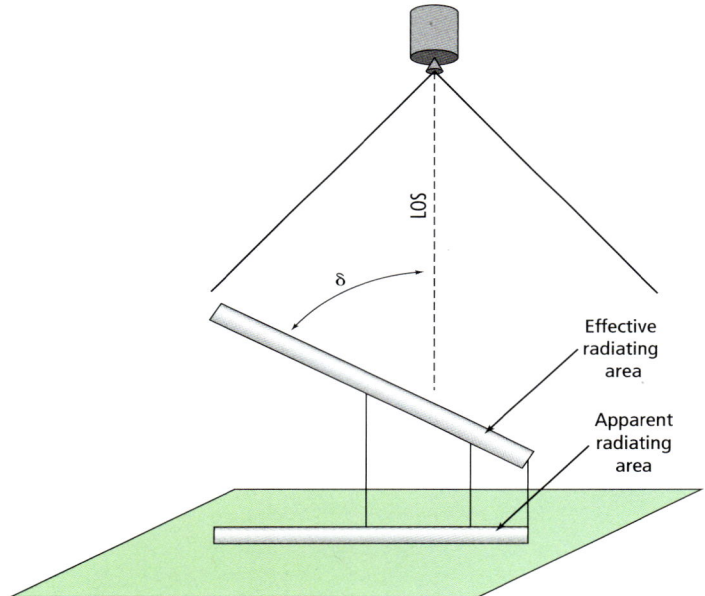

Figure 4-10
A remote sensor sees a cylindrical target as an effective radiating area that is the cross-section of the cylinder projected onto a perpendicular plane.

In this scenario, a sensor views a cylindrical target. Rather than seeing the target as a cylinder, the sensor sees it and receives light from a surface with the effective area of the cross-section of the cylinder, A_{EFF}. Moreover, since the target is not oriented perpendicular to the sensor's LOS, it appears to only have the apparent radiating area of its projection on a horizontal plane, as depicted. In this scenario, the angle, δ, between the cylinder and the sensor's LOS is defined as the *aspect angle*. The intensity of the target is

$$I = LA_{SEND\perp} = LA_{EFF}\sin\delta \left[\frac{W}{sr}\right]. \quad (4\text{-}21)$$

SPATIALLY QUANTIFYING TARGETS

There are now three radiometric quantities (exitance, intensity, and radiance) to characterize targets sending information energy (per unit time). The one to use depends on the spatial nature of the target.

1. POINT SOURCES

Recall from **Chapter 2** that nearly all targets of interest could be spatially categorized as either point or extended targets. There is now a means to radiometrically quantify them, although specific criteria for classifying targets as point or extended will be discussed in later chapters on optics and detectors, covering spatial resolution.

Without too much imagination, the reader can see how the target in **Figure 4-10** could be a point source. In National early warning programs, such as the Defense Support Program[15] and Space-Based Infrared System[16] (SBIRS), the sensors are so far away (~36,000 km in geosynchronous orbits) that almost every target appears to the sensor as only a point of light. When a target has no discernable size, the only startegy that makes sense, radiometrically, is to treat it as having an *intensity*. The quantity of light sent is only a function of direction and not of target surface area.[17] Thus, as a general rule:

Point sources are characterized by intensity.

The direction in which a target may send its information is specific to the target. **Figure 4-11** shows two possibilities: an isotropic point source (like a light bulb) and a beam (like a flashlight). A common way of writing the spatial distribution of light from targets like these is

$$I(\theta) \approx \Phi_{SEND}\phi(\theta) \left[\frac{W}{sr}\right]. \qquad (4\text{-}22)$$

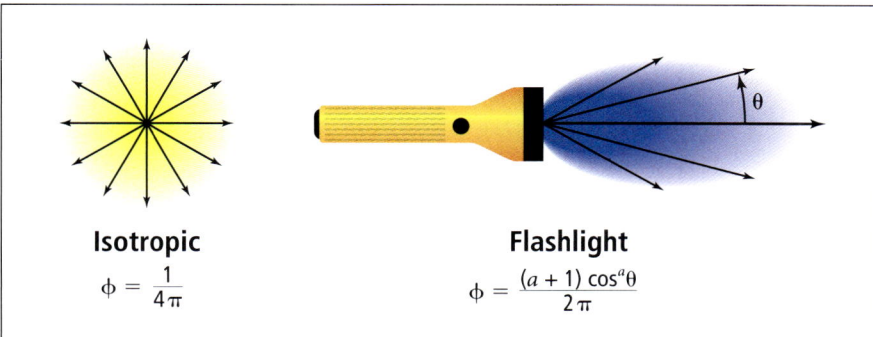

Figure 4-11
Intensity phase functions.

That is, intensity is the product of a power term (like $\Phi_{SEND} \approx MA_{SEND}$, **Equation 4-13**) and a *phase function* (as in the discussion of generalized reflection). The phase functions for the light bulb and flashlight (or an automobile head lamp) are shown in **Figure 4-11**. (The coefficient and exponent "a" is any number[18] larger than 2, depending on design.)

From a remote sensing point of view, when a target appears as a point source, there is no way to discern if it is a light bulb or a flashlight; all that is known is it is a point of light. For emphasis, as discussed earlier in the section regarding targets with constant intensity, *all point source targets are assumed to be isotropic*[19] unless there is knowledge to the contrary.

---

[15] See Section 13.1.

[16] See Section 13.1.

[17] The *origin* of radiation sent from a target is, of course, from some real or effective surface as shown in the last section. However, if that surface cannot be percieved, the only thing left to quantify is direction.

[18] Note, if $a = 0$, $\phi = \frac{1}{2\pi}$ is just half the spatial distribution of an isotropic radiator. The flashlight is shining equally in all directions in front of itself. When $a = 1$, $\phi = \frac{\cos\theta}{\pi}$, which is the Lambertian phase function that applies to Figure 3-14.

[19] An ordinary light bulb (neglecting its base) is isotropic with intensity $I \approx \frac{\Phi_{BULB}}{4\pi}$. The reader is challenged to ask a store clerk for an $I \approx \frac{100\ W}{4\pi} \approx 8\ W \cdot sr^{-1}$ light bulb.

Figure 4-12
Wright Brothers' First Flight Mosaic at the National Museum of the US Air Force, Wright-Patterson Air Force Base, Ohio.

The First Flight Mosaic Mural Tiles	
6,058	Solid Color (lightest tile)
5,648	Side view of the Wright airplane
17,746	Orville Wright
17,889	Wilbur Wright
12,616	The date of the first flight
11,218	Hand tools used by the Wrights

Figure 4-13
A portion of legend for the Wright Brothers' First Flight Mosaic at the National Museum of the US Air Force. The coloring on the individual tiles progresses from none to solid in about 20 steps.

2. EXTENDED SOURCES

The other kind of target, the extended target, can be as large as a forest or as small as the hood of a truck, depending on the particular sensor's spatial resolution. In any case, the object of interest does not have any finer detail than can be seen with the sensor than that it is a surface. Many times, what a sensor looks at is composed of many surface elements with many textures and orientations. "Low" spatial resolution will blend these together to look like a single surface. An illustration of this is shown **Figure 4-12**. The picture of the 1903 Kitty Hawk flight is clear enough, but what are the pixels (tiles in the mosaic)? The picture's legend (**Figure 4-13**) shows the 163,296 tiles that comprise the artwork actually have images varying from 0–100% black-on-white. The camera sees no detail, so the tiles (pixels) are individually "extended" targets for this image.

So, to retrieve information from an extended target, the only interest is the method in which it characteristically sends light from its surface. But it is not possible to capture ALL the radiation. This would require a sensor that completely surrounds the target (and collects energy at all wavelengths). Only the information sent into the particular direction of the sensor can be gathered. The combination of power sent from a surface and into specified directions, therefore, leads to another general rule:

Extended sources are characterized by radiance.

Only knowing that an extended surface is to be characterized by its radiance, how does that radiance originate? The answer is surface radiance is radiation that is either emitted or reflected by the surface or both. In either case, it can only be assumed a surface with details that cannot be seen is Lambertian. Given that, how is radiance calculated?

a. CASE I: **Figure 4-14a** shows if an extended object can be presumed to have a steady state temperature, then it emits thermal radiation. Therefore, an emitting Lambertian surface has radiance:

$$\text{EMITTING SURFACE} \Rightarrow L_{SURFACE} \approx \frac{M_{SURFACE}}{\pi} \approx \frac{\bar{\epsilon} B(T)}{\pi} \left[\frac{W}{m^2 sr} \right] \quad (4\text{-}23)$$

where the surface is further assumed to have an average, or effective, emissivity, $\bar{\epsilon}$.

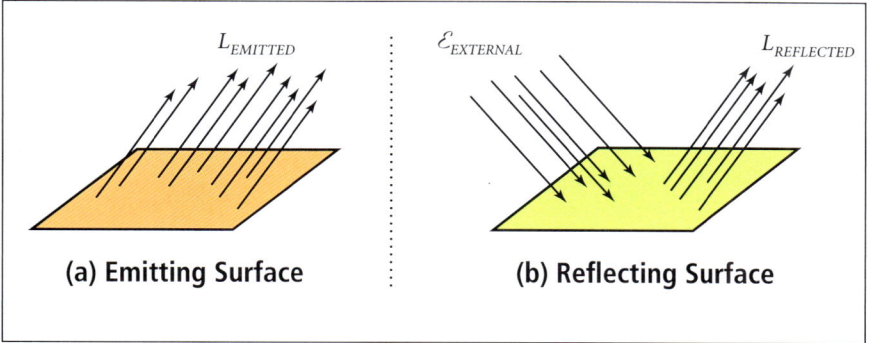

Figure 4-14
Emitted and reflected radiance. A sensor is assumed to be at upper right receiving a) emitted or b) reflected radiation from the surfaces.

b. **CASE II: Figure 4-14b** otherwise shows if an extended surface indeed has an effective emissivity, then it also has an effective reflectivity, $\bar{\rho} \approx 1 - \bar{\epsilon}$. Then, its reflected radiance in terms of some irradiance falling on it from an external source ($\mathcal{E}_{EXTERNAL}$ = sun, sky, clouds, flares, etc.) is

$$\text{REFLECTING SURFACE} \Rightarrow L_{SURFACE} \approx \frac{M_{SURFACE}}{\pi} \approx \frac{\bar{\rho}\mathcal{E}_{EXTERNAL}}{\pi} \left[\frac{W}{m^2 sr}\right]. \quad (4\text{-}24)$$

c. **CASE III:** All *real* surfaces emit and reflect all the time. So which effect should be used, **Equation 4-23 or 4-24**? The answer can be found in which bandpass is chosen, and will be partly answered in the example given in the next section. In general, it is necessary to consider both because one may or may not be larger than the other.

SPECTRALLY QUANTIFYING TARGETS

Once again, note that one topic, except for a couple of passing remarks, has not been discussed in this chapter so far. In **Chapter 2**, it was carefully noted that the blackbody function was a *spectral exitance*; that is, a *distribution function* of wavelength (or frequency). So, it is that *all* radiometric quantities are, properly, distribution functions of wavelength.

Now that the spatial aspect of the target quantities has been thoroughly discussed, it is important to remember their spectral dependence. Remember to append a subscript λ. For instance,

$$L_\lambda = \frac{\text{RADIANCE}}{\text{UNIT WAVELENGTH}} \sim \frac{dL}{d\lambda} = \frac{d^3\Phi}{dA_{SEND}\cos\theta_S d\Omega_{SEND} d\lambda} \left[\frac{W}{m^2 \, sr \cdot \mu m}\right]. \quad (4\text{-}25)$$

Thus, spectral radiance is power per unit projected area per unit sending solid angle per unit wavelength.[20, 21, 22] Therefore, wavelength dependence can be built into every radiometric equation by converting each radiometric quantity with the addition of per unit wavelength:

$$\Phi_\lambda = M_\lambda A_{SEND}, \quad L_\lambda = \frac{M_\lambda}{\pi}, \quad I_\lambda = L_\lambda A_{EFF} \sin\delta, \quad \text{etc.} \quad (4\text{-}26)$$

It is absolutely necessary that wavelength dependence of the radiometric quantities is always remembered *because* it is always necessary to gather information about targets in particular spectral bands or bandpasses. It is an inescapable feature of the remote sensing instruments deployed that they are almost *always* limited to some finite range of wavelengths. Within their bandpasses,[23] they cannot tell the differences among photons' wavelengths, but group them together (i.e., integrate

---

[20] If the definition of power is included, then spectral radiance is radiant energy per unit time per unit projected area per unit sending solid angle per unit wavelength.

[21] Occasionally, one will hear the non-standard unit flick used for spectral radiance. One flick is one watt per square centimeter per steradian per micrometer. In practice, spectral radiance is typically reported in microflicks. [1]

[22] Notice that spectral radiance has three length dimensions in its denominator: an area and a wavelength. If one is not careful to keep the units straight, it is possible this could compute as per unit volume, which is dimensionally the same, but *it is not the same thing*.

[23] Two types of instruments are distinguished which will be described in greater detail: *radiometers* have only *one* bandpass which is fairly broad, and *spectrometers* have *multiple* simultaneous narrow bandpasses. The meaning and applications of broad and narrow will be discussed in later chapters.

them) into a single, effective value. Thus, effectively, an advanced technical remote sensor measures

$$I_{IN\ BAND} = \int_{BANDPASS} \frac{dI}{d\lambda}d\lambda = \int_{BANDPASS} I_\lambda d\lambda \left[\frac{W}{sr}\right] \quad (4\text{-}27)$$

and similarly for the other quantities, as in **Equation 2-11**.

Before concluding this introduction to the radiometric quantities, one more item about their units must be covered. The use of per unit solid angle means per steradian, but it is not uncommon to pronounce it as "per unit direction." Remember, of all possible directions from a target, the target-to-sensor direction is the only one of interest. Likewise, the use of per unit wavelength means per micrometer. Since power can be detected only within the bandpass of the instrument used, this phrase is often rendered "per unit bandpass" to highlight the spectral connection between target and sensor. In this way of speaking, spectral radiance is often heard as power per unit area per unit direction per unit bandpass, and similarly for the other spectral quantities.

4.2 RADIATIVE TRANSFER

Now that radiometric quantities have been introduced, a more complete rendering of the two general rules established in the last section is worth repeating:

1. Point sources are characterized by spectral intensity, I_λ, and
2. Extended sources are characterized by spectral radiance, L_λ.

These rules connect the spatial, {SPACE}, and spectral, {SPECT}, characteristics of targets to their information content: the outward sending or flow of energy, or power, which was the topic of **Chapters 2** and **3**. Although the temporal, {TIME}, characteristic[24] has not been directly included, many point targets are of short duration (transient) while extended targets and backgrounds are of long duration (persistent). (Note, however, target size and duration are not necessarily related.) The propagation, {PROP}, of information from a target to the sensor will now be developed.

IRRADIANCE FROM A POINT SOURCE

At the risk of sounding like a broken record, "What is that light out there? It is too small or too far away to see what it is. All that is known is it appears to be steady." If the light was not steady, one might surmise it is a rotating beacon like a lighthouse. Otherwise, there is no clue of the target's directional characteristics. Therefore, the simplest assumption is that the target is isotropic as argued in the last section:

$$I_\lambda \approx \frac{\Phi_\lambda}{4\pi} \left[\frac{W}{sr \cdot \mu m}\right]. \quad (4\text{-}28)$$

Of all the power radiated by an isotropic point source, only a small fraction, $d\Omega_{SEND}$, goes into the solid angle subtended by the aperture of the sensor, A_{RCVR}, when it is a distance R away. That is, the aperture subtends a small solid angle from the target[25]

$$d\Omega_{SEND} \approx \frac{dA_{RCVR\perp}}{R^2} \approx \frac{dA_{RCVR}\cos\theta_R}{R^2} \ [sr] \quad (4\text{-}29)$$

---

[24] Temporal characteristics will be considered in detail when collection strategies are discussed in later chapters.

[25] Should dA_{RCVR} be used or just A_R? If the sensor is very far away, $R \gg \sqrt{A_R}$, it is really immaterial. Either could be used to make the formulas equate correctly, but to keep the calculus consistent, the differential form will be used. Of course, $A_R = \int dA_{RCVR}$.

as shown in **Figure 4-15**. This receiving cone is only a fraction of the 4π sr surrounding the target, so the power received is

$$d\Phi_R \approx \Phi\left(\frac{d\Omega_{SEND}}{4\pi}\right) \approx \Phi\left(\frac{dA_{RCVR}\cos\theta_R/R^2}{4\pi}\right) \text{ [W]}. \quad (4\text{-}30)$$

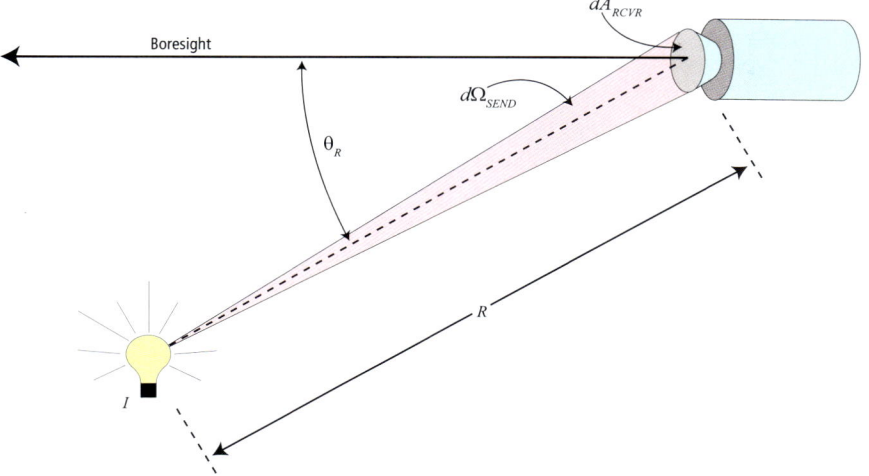

Figure 4-15
Receiving light from a point source.

Dividing both sides of **Equation 4-30** by the aperture area, creates

$$\frac{d\Phi_R}{dA_{RCVR}} \approx \left(\frac{\Phi}{4\pi}\right)\left(\frac{\cos\theta_R}{R^2}\right)\left[\frac{W}{m^2}\right], \quad (4\text{-}31)$$

where the left-hand-side is recognized as received irradiance (**Table 4-1**, bottom row) and the right-hand-side contains the intensity, **Equation 4-28**. Therefore, including the spectral nature of the point source of interest:

$$\mathcal{E}_\lambda \approx \frac{I_\lambda \cos\theta_R}{R^2}\left[\frac{W}{sr \cdot \mu m}\right]. \quad (4\text{-}32)$$

Equation 4-32 is immediately recognizable as the famous one-over-R-squared law, illustrated in **Figure 4-16**. The equation and the figure both emphasize the importance of the units of irradiance: power received *per unit aperture area*. It is independent of the aperture area of the sensor. Tha+t is, at all locations on the receiving plane 3 in the figure, the irradiance is the same.

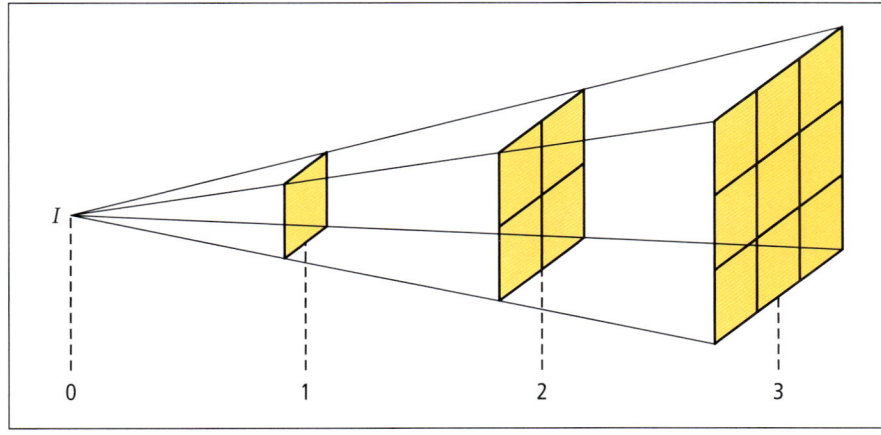

Figure 4-16
The one-over-R-squared law.

Another important feature of the point source equation is the cosine term, which was shown multiple times in the last section. On the receiving end of information, it is evident that the amount of information received from a target can be maximized by minimizing the target's off-boresight angle ($\cos\theta_R \rightarrow 1$, its maximum value). In practice, this is often achieved by limiting a sensor's FOV to only a few degrees as will be fully developed later in this chapter. Some elements of sensor design will be discussed when collection strategies are covered.

IRRADIANCE FROM AN EXTENDED SOURCE

There are many extended sources (e.g., all backgrounds behind point sources). However, sometimes extended objects are targets of interest themselves. It is important to know the information that can be received from them. Assuming that not much can generally be distinguished about the spatial characteristics of extended sources, start by assuming they can be characterized by a constant, Lambertian radiance. At least within some small element of surface area, dA_{SEND}, this can be assumed.

From the definition of radiance in **Table 4-1** and looking at **Figure 4-17**, the element of power sent from an element of surface area into the sensor's direction is the amount of power received, written as:

$$d\Phi_R \approx L dA_{SEND} \cos\theta_S d\Omega_{SEND} \; [W]. \qquad (4\text{-}33)$$

Using **Equation 4-11** and **Figure 4-7**, the sending direction in terms of the sensor's receiving area and the off-boresight, fixation angle can be represented as:

$$d\Phi_R \approx L dA_{RCVR} \cos\theta_S \frac{dA_{RCVR}\cos\theta_R}{R^2} \; [W]. \qquad (4\text{-}34)$$

Performing a mathematical rearrangement and invoking **Equation 4-9**, the power received in terms of the solid angle the sensor sees the sending area element through can be re-written as:

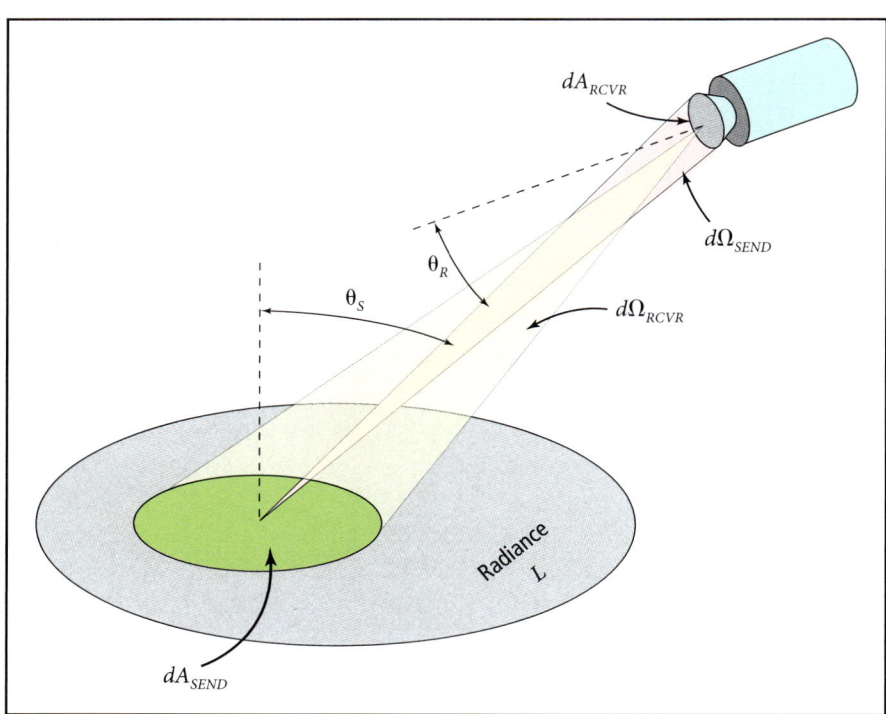

Figure 4-17
Extended source irradiance. Note, both Ω_{SEND} and Ω_{RCVR} from **Figure 4-7** are present and overlapped in this figure.

$$d\Phi_R \approx L\frac{dA_{SEND}\cos\theta_S}{R^2}dA_{RCVR}\cos\theta_R \qquad (4\text{-}35)$$

$$\approx Ld\Omega_{RCVR}dA_{RCVR}\cos\theta_R \ [W].$$

Finally, dividing by the sensor's aperture area, the irradiance it receives is:

$$d\mathcal{E} \approx \frac{d\Phi_R}{dA_{RCVR}} \approx Ld\Omega_{RCVR}\cos\theta_R \left[\frac{W}{m^2}\right]. \qquad (4\text{-}36)$$

The difference between this result and the answer for a point source (**Equation 4-32**) is here only the received irradiance from an element of an extended source is calculated. **Equation 4-32** is for the entire point source. In practice, **Equation 4-36** can be interpreted two ways. First, the interest may be in characterizing only a portion of an extended source. For instance, what is the background behind a point source? In that case, $d\Omega_{RCVR}$ is likely to become[26] Ω_{PIXEL}. That is, a sensor's focal plane array images an entire scene through a receiving cone Ω_{FOV}, but only the portion collected through the receiving cone of one pixel (or a cluster of pixels) is of interest.[27] The pixel is situated on its focal plane so it looks at angle θ_R with respect to the sensor's boresight. So, the collection equation becomes

$$\mathcal{E}_{PIXEL} \approx L\Omega_{PIXEL}\cos\theta_R \left[\frac{W}{m^2}\right]. \qquad (4\text{-}37)$$

Second, sometimes an entire scene is of interest, such as an ocean or an expanse of desert where the radiance is typically considered uniform. Then, the total irradiance is the sum of irradiances received from all of the surface elements:

$$\mathcal{E} \approx \int d\mathcal{E} \approx \int Ld\Omega_{RCVR}\cos\theta_R \approx L\int d\Omega_{RCVR}\cos\theta_R \left[\frac{W}{m^2}\right]. \qquad (4\text{-}38)$$

The difficulty here is the receiving angle for each receiving cone element (which are, in fact, for individual pixels) will be different and must be known. In practice, this is usually circumvented by using sensors with small FOV; θ_R is generally not larger than a few degrees.[28] The cosine term can then be neglected, and irradiance from a uniform extended source fills the FOV and becomes

$$\mathcal{E}_{FOV} \approx L\Omega_{FOV} \left[\frac{W}{m^2}\right]. \qquad (4\text{-}39)$$

Equations 4-37 and **4-39** are simple and measure *power per unit* area at aperture, just like **Equation 4-32** does for point sources. But has the reader noticed something about them? There is no dependence on distance, R, as for a point source in **Equation 4-32**. Nor is there any directional dependence, that is, the location of the sensor relative to the surface of interest (angle θ_S). These effects can be explained by the drawings in **Figure 4-18**. On the left, assume the sensor has a FOV with a "small" cone angle (**Figure 4-5**). By **Equation 4-1**, the diameter of the circle it sees on the ground is approximately $D \approx R\alpha$ from a distance R above the surface. When the distance is halved, the diameter is also halved, but the area decreases by a factor of four. (Area is proportional to diameter squared.) Thus, the closer area is radiating only one-fourth the power toward the sensor (**Equation 4-15**).

---

[26] The pseudo-calculus notation is dropped because Ω_{PIXEL} is the smallest element of solid angle that makes sense.

[27] All of this will become more clear when sensor optics and electro-optic detectors are discussed in later chapters. But as said before, don't expect anyone familiar with digital cameras to be confused.

[28] The reader may be surprised at how large an area of Earth's surface can be seen through even a small cone. With too large a FOV, remote sensing becomes a problem, like looking for a needle in a haystack. Even with θ_R as large as 10°, $\cos\theta_R \approx 0.985$, which is close enough to 1.00 for usual precision.

In **Figure 4-18a**, consider the radiating areas are composed of arrays of point sources that are so closely spaced they cannot be seen separately.[29] The irradiances on the apertures of the sensors are then the superpositions[30] (sums) of the irradiances from all the point sources. For each point source, irradiance on aperture is given by **Equation 4-32**, and is indeed four times greater when the sensor is half as close. (Ignore the cosine because α is small.) Since there are only one-fourth the number of sources at the closer distance, the total irradiance is the same.

Figure 4-18b shows that for sensors at equal distances, but different viewing angles, the area subtended by the FOV increases by the cosine of the angle away from the normal (see the figure in **Example 4-2**). At first glance, this seems to suggest that surfaces should look brighter (provide greater irradiance) at lower viewing angles, until considering the definition of radiance. Radiance contains the angular effect with the cosine term in its denominator. Radiance is *per unit projected area* into a sensor's LOS. So, the apparent increase of viewing area is offset by radiance's definition of being equal power radiated into equal solid angles with respect to viewing direction (angle θ_S in **Figure 4-9**). Thus, the irradiance again remains constant.

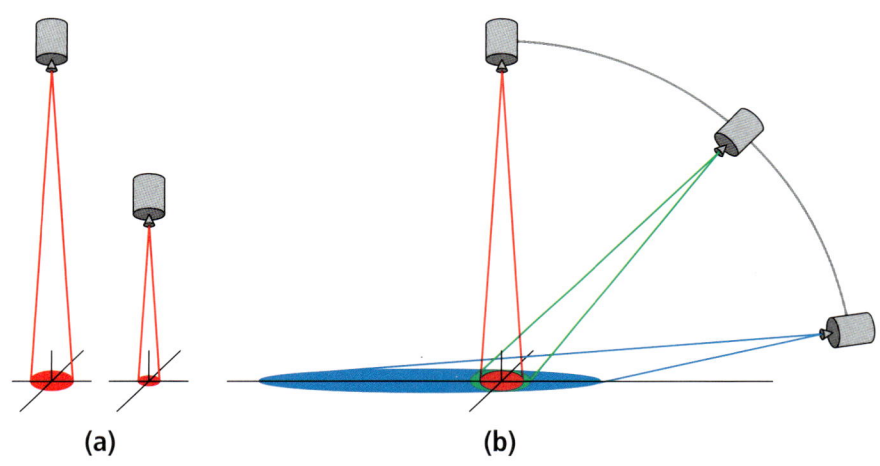

Figure 4-18
Distance and viewing geometry do not influence irradiance from an extended sourcece explained.

[29] In the calculus sense, every surface is an infinite array of zero-dimensional points. In a practical sense, a surface can be considered as an array of points spaced more closely together than a sensor's spatial resolution (to be defined later).

[30] Great importance is placed on the principle of superposition in space, time, and spectrum. If the phenomenology of one entity can be understood, then that of an ensemble of them can also be comprehended.

AN IMPORTANT CALCULATION

The remainder of this section is an elementary calculation of the irradiance on the surface of the Earth from solar radiation, neglecting the atmosphere. It will be calculated three different ways to demonstrate the consistency of radiometry.

The basic geometry is shown in **Figure 4-19**. Approximate values used are $R_{SUN} \approx 6.96 \times 10^8$ m and $R_{ORBIT} \approx 1.50 \times 10^{11}$ m. Since $R_{ORBIT} \gg R_{SUN}$, only consider sunlight rays on the Earth's surface from directly overhead (i.e., noon).

Figure 4-19
Irradiance on the Earth from the Sun.

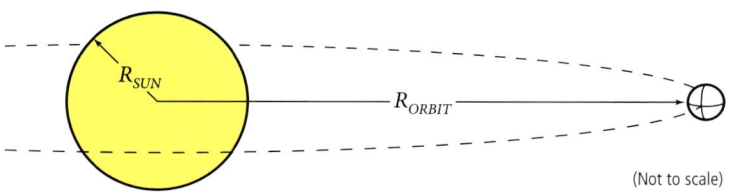

(Not to scale)

ALL WAVELENGTHS

Sunlight streams across space at all wavelengths, but it is generally true that no single sensor can receive it all. Several different detector technologies are usually required. Nevertheless, the total irradiance, summed across all wavelengths will be calculated as a first approximation.

1. FIRST METHOD: SIMPLE REASONING

Assuming the Sun is a blackbody ($T \approx 5900K$), the total power it radiates from its surface is

$$\Phi_{SUN} \approx B_{SUN} A_{SUN} \approx \left(\sigma_{SB} T^4\right) \times \left(4\pi R_{SUN}^2\right) \, [W]. \quad (4\text{-}40)$$

(Since the calculation is for all wavelengths, the Stefan-Boltzmann Law (**Equation 2-14**) was used.) Now, imagine this power propagating outward. At distance R_{ORBIT} away, it passes through an imaginary bubble having a surface area of $4\pi R_{ORBIT}^2$. If the power is uniformly distributed as it passes this surface, its power per unit area is its irradiance on the Earth's surface:

$$\mathcal{E}_{EARTH} \approx \frac{\Phi_{SUN}}{A_{BUBBLE}} \approx \frac{\left(\sigma_{SB} T^4\right) \times \left(4\pi R_{SUN}^2\right)}{4\pi R_{ORBIT}^2} \approx \sigma_{SB} T^4 \left(\frac{R_{SUN}}{R_{ORBIT}}\right)^2 \left[\frac{W}{m^2}\right]. \quad (4\text{-}41)$$

2. SECOND METHOD: THE SUN IS A POINT SOURCE

It is not a good idea to look directly at the Sun, but everyone knows it is not a point source. The Sun subtends about a dime's width at arm's length. Still, pretend the sun is an isotropic point source with intensity,

$$I_{SUN} \approx \frac{\Phi_{SUN}}{4\pi} \approx \frac{\left(\sigma_{SB} T^4\right) \times \left(4\pi R_{SUN}^2\right)}{4\pi} \approx \sigma_{SB} T^4 R_{SUN}^2 \left[\frac{W}{sr}\right], \quad (4\text{-}42)$$

where the same expression for power is used as in the last calculation. Now, apply **Equation 4-32**, but assume $\cos\theta_R \approx 1$, such that

$$\mathcal{E}_{EARTH} \approx \frac{I_{SUN}}{R_{ORBIT}^2} \approx \frac{\sigma_{SB} T^4 R_{SUN}^2}{R_{ORBIT}^2} \approx \sigma_{SB} T^4 \left(\frac{R_{SUN}}{R_{ORBIT}}\right)^2 \left[\frac{W}{sr}\right]. \quad (4\text{-}43)$$

3. THIRD METHOD: THE SUN IS AN EXTENDED SOURCE

From **Equation 4-18**, the Lambertian approximation, it can be argued that the Sun has constant radiance because it has constant exitance:

$$L_{SUN} \approx \frac{B_{SUN}}{\pi} \approx \frac{\sigma_{SB} T^4}{\pi} \left[\frac{W}{m^2 \, sr}\right]. \quad (4\text{-}44)$$

Indeed, the Sun's disk looks like a uniform, flat circle in the sky. Using **Equation 4-39**, the result is:

$$\mathcal{E}_{EARTH} \approx L_{SUN} \Omega \approx \left(\frac{\sigma_{SB} T^4}{\pi}\right) \times \left(\frac{\pi R_{SUN}^2}{R_{ORBIT}^2}\right) \approx \sigma_{SB} T^4 \left(\frac{R_{SUN}}{R_{ORBIT}}\right)^2 \left[\frac{W}{m^2}\right]. \quad (4\text{-}45)$$

Behold! This generates the same answer three different ways, demonstrating the internal consistence of radiometry. Using *any* of these results, the answer is

$$\mathcal{E}_{EARTH} \approx (5.67 \times 10^{-8} \, W \cdot m^{-2} K^{-4})(5900 \, K)^4 \left(\frac{6.96 \times 10^8 \, m}{1.50 \times 10^{11} \, m}\right)^2 \quad (4\text{-}46)$$

$$\approx 1480 \left[\frac{W}{m^2}\right].$$

This value is customarily called insolance, but remember it does not consider the atmosphere. A detailed calculation of insolance using the atmospheric transmission code MODTRAN[31] gives a more realistic answer of 1360 W·m^{-2}, and a NASA high-altitude measurement yields 1353 W·m^{-2}. **Figure 4-20** shows the NASA data.

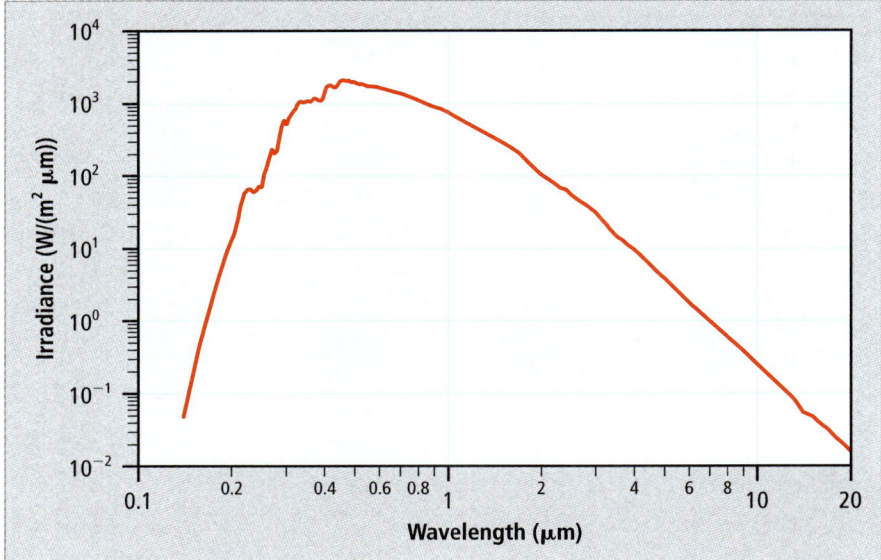

Figure 4-20
NASA solar irradiance data collected at high altitude. [2]

VISIBLE BANDPASS

Since it is impossible to measure total insolance with one instrument, reduce the problem to a familiar bandpass: What is the irradiance on the Earth from solar radiation in the visible, 0.4 μm ≤ λ ≤ 0.7 μm?

This phenomenology is identical to the above three solution methods which all yielded the same answer. The only difference is replacing total solar exitance, $\sigma_{SB}T^4$, in **Equations 4-41, 4-43**, and **4-45** with the Sun's exitance in the visible band. Still assuming the Sun is a blackbody, as learned in **Chapter 2**, **Equation 2-11**:

$$B(T) \approx \int_{BANDPASS} B_\lambda(\lambda,T)d\lambda \left[\frac{W}{m^2}\right]. \quad (4\text{-}47)$$

For the visible bandpass and with T ≈ 5900 K, this integral[32] evaluates to 2.56 × 10^7 W·m^{-2}. This value is computed[33] in **Appendix 4-2** on the support website. Using this value, the answer is:

$$\mathcal{E}_{EARTH} \approx \left(\int B_\lambda d\lambda\right) \times \left(\frac{R_{SUN}}{R_{ORBIT}}\right)^2 \quad (4\text{-}48)$$

$$\approx (2.56 \times 10^7 \text{W·m}^{-2})\left(\frac{6.96 \times 10^8 \text{m}}{1.50 \times 10^{11} \text{m}}\right)^2$$

$$\approx 551 \left[\frac{W}{m^2}\right].$$

Note, this is only about 37% of the total solar irradiance on the Earth, where the Sun is assumed to be an ideal thermal source and atmospheric effects are neglected. Presumably, spacecraft in near-earth orbits would experience the full irradiance on their surfaces, stressing their overall heat management systems.

---

[31] More on MODTRAN in **Chapter 5** on atmospheric attenuation.

[32] Remember, this integral means summing up contributions to solar exitance for all the wavelengths in the bandpass. Visually, it is the area under the plot of solar spectral exitance (Planck function) vs. wavelength. Since the vertical axis has units of [W·m^{-2}μm^{-1}] and the horizontal axis has units of [μm], the area has units of [W·m^{-2}], which is exitance.

[33] A very elementary numerical integration technique was used by assuming the area under the curve can be approximated as a sum of incremental trapezoid areas between data points. More sophisticated algorithms may be found in texts on numerical methods.

SOLAR VS. THERMAL RADIANCE OF THE EARTH

Now the following question can be answered. When looking for targets at or near the Earth's surface, what does the background look like, spectrally? During daylight hours, the Earth is strongly irradiated by sunlight, reflecting a portion of it, and is, itself, a thermal radiating object. At nighttime, the Earth is simply a thermal radiator (neglecting moonshine and starlight).

As an extended source made of many materials of varying shapes and sizes, the Earth's surface must be approximately Lambertian. Reflected solar radiation then gives it a radiance as shown in **Equation 4-24**, which combines the present study of solar irradiance:

$$L_{\lambda, REFLECTED} \approx \frac{\rho(\lambda)\mathcal{E}_{\lambda, EARTH}}{\pi} \approx \frac{\rho(\lambda)}{\pi} B_{\lambda, SUN} \left(\frac{R_{SUN}}{R_{ORBIT}}\right)^2 \left[\frac{W}{m^2 sr \cdot \mu m}\right], \quad (4\text{-}49)$$

where $\rho(\lambda)$ is the reflectivity of the surface. Meanwhile, the Earth as an object having a temperature ($T_{EARTH} \approx 285K$) must have an inherent radiance like **Equation 4-23**:

$$L_{\lambda, EMITTED} \approx \frac{\epsilon(\lambda)}{\pi} B_{\lambda, EARTH} \left[\frac{W}{m^2 sr \cdot \mu m}\right]. \quad (4\text{-}50)$$

Which of these would a remote sensor see when looking at Earth: reflected or emitted radiance? Both. However, the catch is the two sources are related, because

$$\rho(\lambda) + \epsilon(\lambda) \approx 1. \quad (4\text{-}51)$$

Figure 4-21 shows the Earth's reflected (broad daylight) and emitted radiances separately on the left and summed on the right for several values of reflectivity and emissivity. The actual $\rho(\lambda)$ and $\epsilon(\lambda)$ for any location depend on the materials there, of course, but typical values[34] for the Earth's system are about $\bar{\rho} \approx 0.35$ and $\bar{\epsilon} \approx 0.65$. For these values, it is clear, as shown in **Figure 4-21**, that reflected sunlight will dominate the background at wavelengths shorter than about 3.5 μm, while thermally emitted radiation (Earthshine) is more prevalent at wavelengths longer than about 6.0 μm. In between, the scene is about an equal mix of reflected and emitted photons.

This is important in the quest of gathering information about targets using advanced technical sensors. The first clue, at least for thermally emitting targets, is to select a sensor optimized to collect around a wavelength

[34] Recall, an average reflectivity value for a large area containing many materials is its *albedo*. This is the value that astronomers typically use for planets, planetoids, asteroids, and moons.

Figure 4-21
Reflected and emitted radiances from a) the Earth and b) their sum. The legend is the same for both.

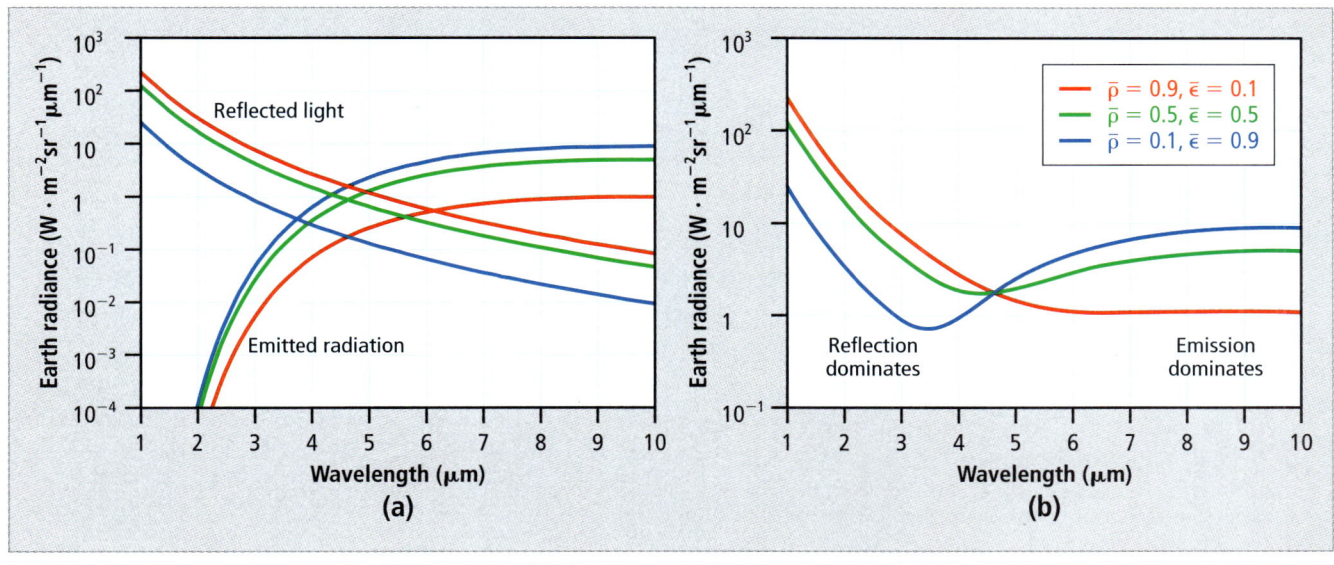

Figure 4-22
Antoine Henri Becquerel, 1852-1908, jointly won the Nobel Prize in Physics in 1903 with Marie and Pierre Curie for the discovery of radioactivity. (Photo courtesy of http://en.wikipedia.org/wiki/File:Portrait_of_Antoine-Henri_Becquerel.jpg; PD-Old.)

[35] That is, maximize the ratio between target and background radiance.

[36] Most materials attenuate information that passes through them, but otherwise does not alter the information. Such materials are termed linear. When the medium resists the flow of energy and modifies it in some way, it is a non-linear medium. An example is an ionized atmosphere (i.e., the ionosphere) where the internal electric and magnetic fields of unattached electrons and ions disperse light waves (at radio frequencies) into a spectrum of waves traveling at different speeds and with different polarizations. Fortunately, significant degradation is not experienced at electro-optical wavelengths and frequencies beyond ordinary attenuation.

[37] Alpha particles are like completely ionized helium nuclei: two protons and two neutrons. They are relatively innocuous and can be stopped by as little as a sheet of paper. Beta particles are like positive or negative electrons ejected from nuclei.

[38] A non-standard unit of activity is the curie (Ci) in honor of Marie Curie, co-discoverer of radioactivity. Although, the unit was originally meant to only measure the activity of the element radium. 1 Ci = 3.7×10^{10} Bq.

[39] Remember, Avogadro's Number is huge: $N_A \approx 6.02 \times 10^{23}$ atoms or molecules per mole. So, just a couple of grams of a radioactive mineral have at least 10^{21} atoms.

where the target is sending the most information about itself; recall Wien's Displacement Law, **Equation 2-9** (or Rule of Thumb **Equation 2-10**), provides those wavelengths. Now, it is necessary to balance collecting the maximum possible energy from the target with collecting as little as possible from its background.[35] **Figure 4-21b** suggests this should be as near to 4.0–4.5 μm as possible (depending on target temperature). Of course, this plot is the worst case when the sun is directly overhead; any other time of day (or night) and shorter wavelengths would become useful. Later chapters will slightly adjust this estimate when considering {ATTN}, the atmosphere.

POSTSCRIPTS ON RADIOMETRY

The phenomenology of propagation of information (energy) through transparent media[36] is universal. Although, the corresponding radiometric terms may need to be redefined, and the relationships among them modified. Below is an example of radioactivity followed by a short discussion of photometry.

RADIOACTIVITY

The isotopes of many chemical elements are radioactive; they spontaneously and randomly emit alpha or beta particles[37] or gamma rays (high energy photons). The energies of these emissions are well-known and constitute *signatures*, just as photons of particular wavelengths are characteristic of the quantum energy level transitions of particular atoms and molecules (**Chapter 3**).

Radioactivity of particular isotopes is measured in terms of their characteristic half-life, $t_{1/2}$, mean lifetime, τ_R, or decay constant, κ_R. These are related by

$$t_{1/2} \approx \frac{0.693}{\kappa_R} \approx 0.693 \tau_R \ [s]. \tag{4-52}$$

The rate of decay of a radioisotope, its activity, A, is then given by

$$A \approx -\frac{dN}{dt} \approx \kappa_R N \ [Bq], \tag{4-53}$$

where N is the number of radioisotopes present. Activity is measured[38] in becquerels (Bq), where 1 Bq = 1 decay per second. (See **Figure 4-22**.) Although N changes with time (radionuclides decay, after all), even small quantities[39] with "long" half-lives appear to have nearly constant activities.

Unless strong external electric or magnetic fields are imposed, particles (or photons) are ejected from radionuclei in a totally random direction.

Thus, the radioactive intensity of a source can be shown as

$$I_R \approx \frac{A}{4\pi} \left[\frac{Bq}{sr} \right]. \tag{4-54}$$

Note, this is the same form as radiative intensity, but A replaces Φ. From a small lump of radioactive material, such as a tiny amount smuggled in a suitcase, an irradiance on aperture of a detector can be measured as

$$\mathcal{E}_R \approx \frac{I_R}{R^2} \cos \theta_R \left[\frac{Bq}{m^2} \right], \tag{4-55}$$

where R and θ_R have their usual meanings. Thus, an exact parallel to radiometry in the remote sensing of particles can be seen. **Example 4-3** shows the information that can be learned from such methods.

EXAMPLE 4-3: THE RADIOACTIVITY OF PLUTONIUM

QUESTION: Plutonium-239, the fissionable material in the August 9, 1945 "Fat Man" bomb (21 kt) dropped on Nagasaki, decays via a 5.157 MeV alpha emission with a half-life of around 24,100 years ($t_{1/2} \approx 7.6 \times 10^{11}$ s). If an airport security detector with a 5 cm² aperture picks up 10^3 of these alphas per second at a distance of 2.0 m from a suitcase, how much plutonium (mass and volume) is in the suitcase? Handbook values for Pu are an atomic weight of 244 and mass density $\rho_m \approx 19.8$ g·cm^{-3}. Assume the abundance of ^{239}Pu in the suitcase was enriched to approximately 1%, and there is no protective shielding.

Mock-up of the FAT MAN atom bomb at the National Museum of the United States Air Force.

SUGGESTED SOLUTION: The irradiance this sensor measures, by definition, is

$$\mathcal{E}_R \approx \frac{10^3 \text{ counts} \cdot \text{s}^{-1}}{5 \times 10^{-4} \text{m}^2} \approx 2 \times 10^6 \text{ Bq} \cdot \text{m}^{-2}.$$

Therefore, from **Equation 4-55**, assuming $\theta_R \approx 0$, the intensity of the sample is

$$I_R \approx \frac{\mathcal{E}_R R^2}{\cos\theta_R} \approx \frac{(2 \times 10^6 \text{ Bq} \cdot \text{m}^{-2})(2 \text{ m})^2}{(1)} \approx 8 \times 10^6 \text{ Bq} \cdot \text{sr}^{-1}.$$

Solving **Equation 4-54** for the sample's activity for alpha emission, results in

$$A \approx 4\pi I_R \approx (4\pi)(8 \times 10^6 \text{ Bq} \cdot \text{sr}^{-1}) \approx 1.0 \times 10^8 \text{ Bq}.$$

Now, combining **Equations 4-52** and **4-53**, the number of ^{239}Pu atoms present can be calculated:

$$N \approx \frac{A}{\kappa_R} \approx \frac{A t_{1/2}}{0.693} \approx \frac{(1.0 \times 10^8 \text{ Bq})(7.6 \times 10^{11} \text{s})}{0.693}$$
$$\approx 1.1 \times 10^{20} \text{ }^{239}\text{Pu atoms}.$$

Since this is only about 1% of the total, there are approximately 1.1×10^{22} plutonium atoms of all isotopes. In terms of number of moles, this is

$$\frac{N}{N_A} \approx \frac{1.1 \times 10^{22} \text{ Pu atoms}}{6.02 \times 10^{23} \text{ mol}^{-1}} \approx 0.018 \text{ moles of Pu}.$$

At an atomic weight of 244 g·mol^{-1}, the mass of Pu in the suitcase is approximately

$$(244 \text{ g} \cdot \text{mol}^{-1})(0.018 \text{ mol}) \approx 4.4 \text{ grams of Pu}.$$

(This is about the mass of four paper clips.) Dividing by the density, the volume of plutonium hidden in the suitcase is only about

$$\frac{4.4 \text{ g}}{19.8 \text{ g} \cdot \text{cm}^{-3}} \approx 0.022 \text{ cm}^3.$$

(This would be a cube measuring approximately six millimeters on each side.)

[40] Oceans vary greatly in temperature and salinity both laterally and depth-wise, so refraction and attenuation (as will be studied in later chapters) are more complicated, but not beyond the reader's appreciation.

[41] Conceivably, photometry could also be concocted to include the response function of some other sensor, electro-optical or biological. But in any case, photometry is bandpass-specific and builds in the response function.

[42] The most common error in radiometric terminology is casually saying illumination, which is a photometric quantity, instead of the correct term, irradiation. This is an easy error, especially when naturally operating in a mode where vision is a primary sensing input.

This application of the principles of radiometry can be extended to many similar physical phenomena. In sonar, for instance, a ping or a submarine's screw constitute point sources of acoustic energy propagating outwards into the water. Because oceans are bounded between the seabed below and the atmosphere above, underwater sources can be characterized as $\frac{1}{4\pi}$ and outward propagation as $\frac{1}{R^2}$ only for distances less than the ocean depth. Beyond that, the equations need to be modified. Otherwise, the idea of calculating acoustic power on a hydrophone's aperture is the same.[40] This is also true for sources of energy (information) underground and in the atmosphere. It's all the same phenomenology.

PHOTOMETRY

The reader may have heard of the science of photometry and has probably used some of its terms (without knowing their technical definitions). In fact, when the study of radiometry was launched in this chapter, many readers may have thought photometry was being discussed. So, there may be some lingering confusion.

Photometry and radiometry are the same in their definitions of quantities relative to sending/receiving surfaces and directions; but, photometry is specific only to the visible bandpass *and* includes the response function of the human eye, $k(\lambda)$.[41] The photometric quantities are given in **Table 4-2**, and the eye's relative response is shown in **Figure 4-23**.

Notice the photometric quantities mirror the radiometric quantities in function. If the human eye was the remote sensor, the following would be expected

$$\Phi_V \approx M_V A_{SEND}, \quad \Phi_V \approx 4\pi I_V \quad \text{and} \quad \Phi_V \approx \pi L_V A_{SEND} \quad (4\text{-}56)$$

for constant targets, with

$$L_V \approx \frac{M_V}{\pi} \quad \text{and} \quad I_V \approx L_V A_{EFF} \sin\delta \quad (4\text{-}57)$$

characterizing targets. Collecting visible light energy from targets is then[42]

$$\mathcal{E}_V \approx \frac{I_V}{R^2} \cos\theta_R \quad \text{and} \quad \mathcal{E}_V \approx L_V \Omega \cos\theta_R. \quad (4\text{-}58)$$

Table 4-2
Photometric quantities.

Quantity	Symbol	Formula	Units	Other Units
Luminous Energy	Q_V	$\int_{0.380}^{0.760} k(\lambda) Q_\lambda d\lambda$	lumen-second	talbot
Luminous Flux	Φ_V	$\frac{dQ_V}{dt}$	lumen	talbot/second
Luminous Exitance	M_V	$\frac{d\Phi_V}{dA}$	lux	lumen/m²
Luminous Intensity	I_V	$\frac{d\Phi_V}{d\Omega}$	candela	lumen/sr
Luminance	L_V	$\frac{d^2\Phi_V}{dA_\perp d\Omega} = \frac{d^2\Phi}{dA\cos\theta\, d\Omega}$	candela/m²	nit
Illuminance	$\mathcal{E}_V$	$\frac{d\Phi_V}{dA}$	lumen/m²	foot candle

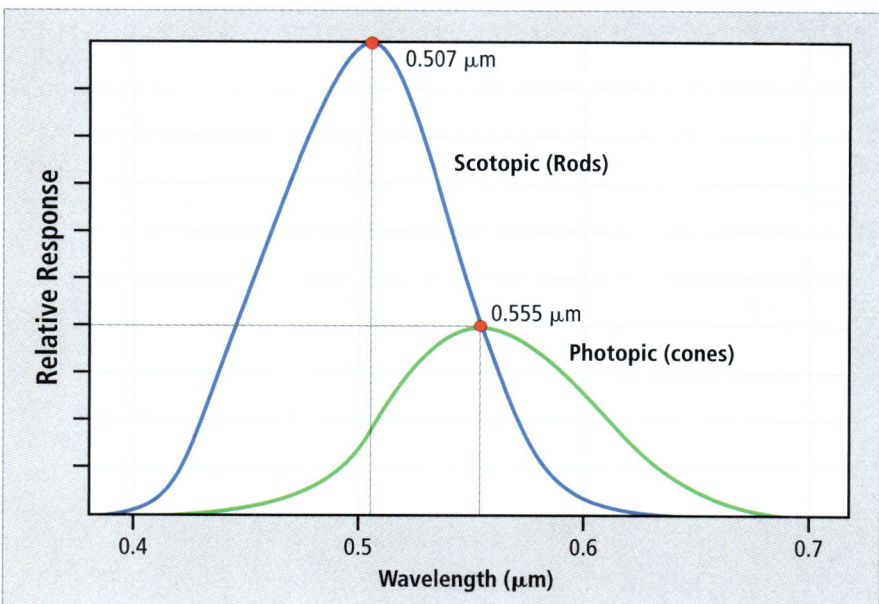

Figure 4-23
Response functions of the human eye. Scotopic vision is response to dim light (nighttime), and photopic vision is for bright light (daytime). There are three types of cones for red, green, and blue vision; only the green response is shown.

The most difficult thing about photometry may be the odd units. While the candela is in fact one of seven non-standard base units, there are several derived units that give the impression they arose from different scientists at different times. Throughout the study of advanced technical information gathering, be careful to use only radiometric quantities and units, especially since they are not restricted to any particular bandpass.

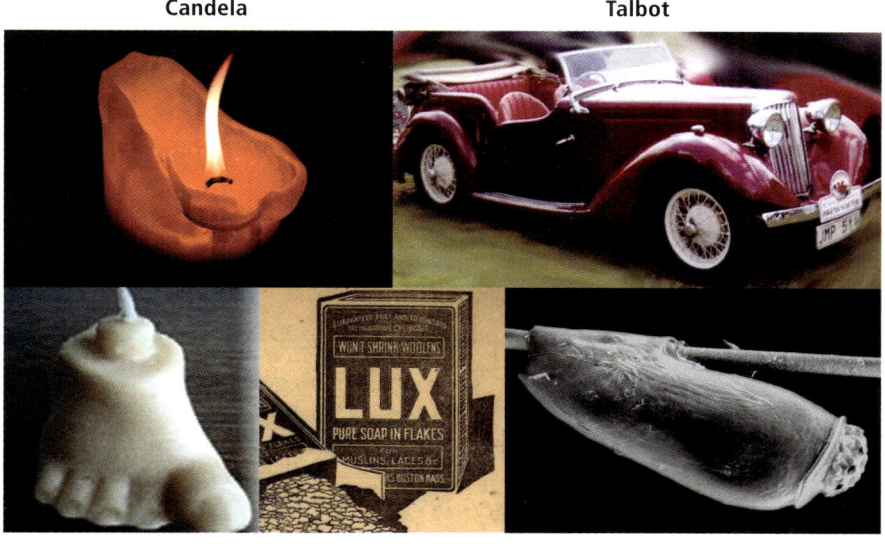

Figure 4-24
Whimsical photometric units. (Candela photo courtesy of Luca Casartelli via http://upload.wikimedia.org/wikipedia/commons/2/2d/Candela_al_buio.jpg; Creative Commons Attribution-Share Alike 3.0 unported. Talbot photo courtesy of Lars-Göran Lindgren Sweden via http://en.wikipedia.org/wiki/File:Talbot_Ten_Tourer_1936.jpg; GNU Free Documentation License Version 1.2 or later & Creative Commons Attribution-Share Alike 3.0 Unported & Creative Commons Share-Alike 2.5 Generic. Foot-candle photo courtesy of http://en.wikipedia.org/wiki/File:Foot_candle.jpg; GNU Free Documentation License, Version 1.2 & Creative Commons Attribution-Share Alike 3.0.)

4.3 METRICS

There is another piece of phenomenology of {PROP} that should logically be discussed here. It will be frequently used in these discussions of remote sensing applications for advanced technical intelligence gathering. This concept was first introduced in **Equation 1-4** when the direction of this text was provided and brings the discussion to **Equation 4-32**. It is the distance R from target to sensor. Knowledge of this dimension was assumed in **Examples 4-1** and **4-2**, but it will now be shown how it is derived.

FLAT EARTH

If those with a contrary view to Christopher Columbus were right, this problem would be much simpler. Within limits, however, it is appropriate to treat the Earth as flat. With this premise, proceed to solve for R and for geolocation, which is part of the *metric* in GEOINT.

Figure 4-25
A flat Earth.

RANGE TO TARGET

If the altitude, H, of a remote sensor (S) (in **Figure 4-26a**) above level terrain is known,[43] then range to target[44] (T) is simply

$$R \approx \frac{H}{\cos\theta_N} \approx H \sec\theta_N \text{ [km]}, \qquad (4\text{-}59)$$

where θ_N is the nadir angle, measured from directly below (toward the middle[45] of the Earth) to the LOS.[46] Directly below the sensor is the nadir, S^*.

Figure 4-26
Range from sensor to target over a flat Earth and over terrain on a flat Earth.

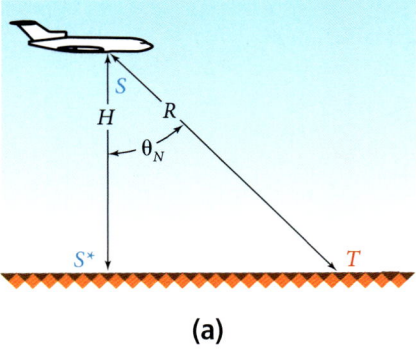 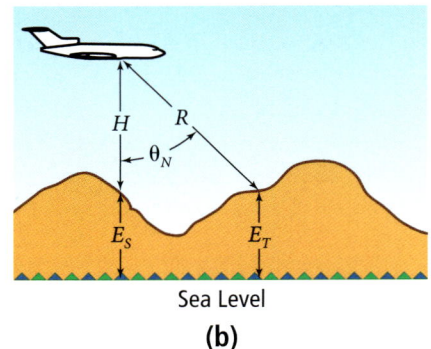

(a)   (b)

[43] Aircraft altimeters measure the ambient air pressure and assume a standard variation in pressure as a function of altitude. This is based on hydrostatic equilibrium which will be covered in **Chapter 5**. Temperature, humidity, and meteorological conditions can cause pressure altitude to be significantly different from actual altitude. More accurate altitudes are measured with radars.

[44] To find distances on the Earth's surface, or between a target and a sensor, often kilometers (km) will be used.

[45] For a flat Earth, there is no "middle;" so what is meant is toward the direction of gravity, where an object would go if it were dropped.

[46] The angle θ_N is easy to measure in principle, but sensor operators on aircraft are more likely to measure the complementary angle between the LOS and the horizontal (artificial horizon). This complement may be called by some the *elevation angle* and can be positive (above the wings) or negative (below the wings).

[47] DTED has six levels of lateral and vertical resolution, depending principally on latitude. Levels 0, 1, and 2 are publically available. [4]

Instead, if the sensor is over uneven terrain, then its altitude over the terrain must be known, as well as the terrain elevation under the sensor, E_S, and the elevation of the target, E_T. The elevations are both with respect to some standard reference plane, like sea-level, as suggested in **Figure 4-26b**. Knowing the altitude and the elevations, the range is given by

$$R \approx \frac{H + E_S - E_T}{\cos\theta_N} \approx (H + E_S - E_T)\sec\theta_N \text{ [km]}. \qquad (4\text{-}60)$$

The catch with **Equation 4-60** is knowing the elevations E_S and E_T. A reliable source for elevations is the Digital Terrain Elevation Data (DTED) provided by the National Geospatial-Intelligence Agency (NGA). [3] If a location on Earth (geolocation) is known, the DTED may be used to look up that elevation at a variety of resolutions[47] depending on the users' needs.

For the flat Earth problem, assume the geolocation of the sensor on the Earth nadir location (G_S in **Figure 4-27**) is known (typically by the Global Positioning System (GPS)). The elevation of the target, and hence range to target, can be determined by some algorithm such as pictured in **Figure 4-27**. In **Figure 4-27a**, the LOS from the sensor, R_1, is allowed to project to sea level (or other standard reference plane). At that geolocation, G_1, the elevation, E_1, is provided by the DTED. Elevation E_1 is then used to adjust the LOS to R_2 in **Figure 4-27b**, where the new elevation, E_2, is provided by the DTED for geolocation, G_2. The process then continues, **Figure 4-27c**, etc., for N steps until some predetermined user criterion declares the Nth values, E_N and R_N, are "close enough." Range $R_N \approx R$ can then be applied in **Equation 4-32**.[48]

Figure 4-27
Range to target estimation algorithm over uneven terrain.

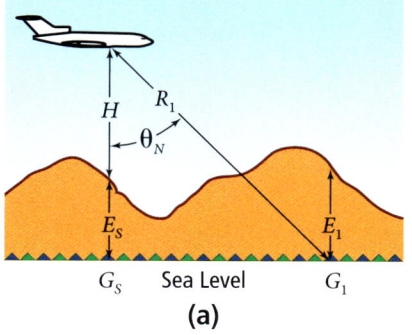
(a)

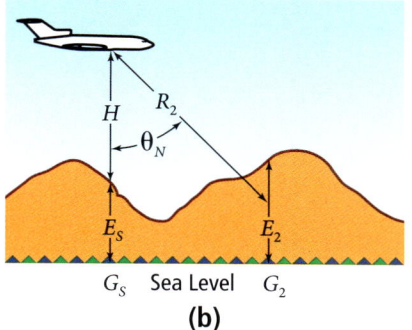
(b)

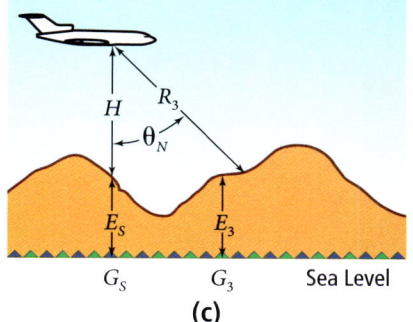
(c)

An additional small geolocation correction may be required when a collection is being taken at extreme nadir angles (θ_N). **Figure 3-6** shows the LOS actually refracts through the atmosphere. For targets on the Earth's surface (below 8 km altitude) and sensors above the atmosphere (> 100 km), **Figure 4-28** quantifies the maximum retractive geolocation error as a function of nadir angle. The error is less than 200 m for nadir angles less than approximately 77°. **Chapter 5** will show that severe atmospheric attenuation makes collections at nadir angles greater than this undesirable. Therefore, atmospheric refraction can nearly always be neglected.

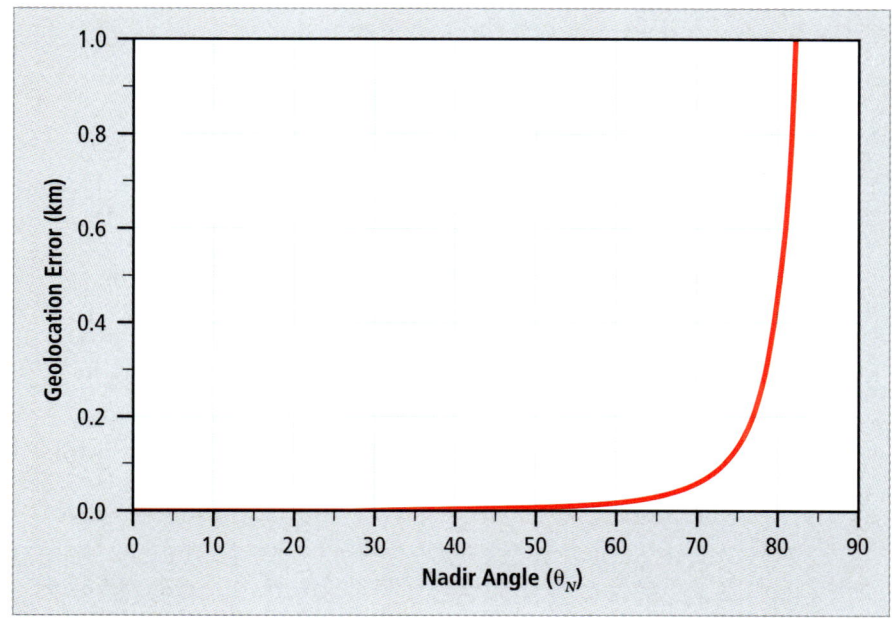

Figure 4-28
Maximum refractive geolocation error when viewing a target within 8.00 km of the Earth's surface from a sensor above 100 km. For lower target and sensor altitudes, the error is negligible.

[48] For now, this will be the application of range to target. In fact, the intelligence objective is to solve **Equation 4-32** for I, which is the target information needed. This is done, in general, by **Equation 1-3** and specifically in **Equation 1-5**. This will be discussed in detail later.

NOTATION
In this section, some standard geometry textbook notation is used as follows: $\overline{S^*T}$ means the distance along a straight line path on a flat Earth from S^* to T, and $\widehat{S^*T}$ means the distance along a curved path, or arc, on a spherical Earth from S^* to T. The curved path is a portion of a "great circle" which is the intersection of the Earth with a plane passing through the center of the Earth and the path's end points.

GEOLOCATION

One piece of information always needed is a target's geolocation, G. How is it determined in the algorithm above? There are a number of ways:

1. Certain types of events are known to take place at known, well mapped locations.

2. Other intelligence methods, such as COMINT or HUMINT, can provide the answer.

3. If the remote sensor has sufficient resolution to use for IMINT, then positioning with respect to other recognized objects in the scene (called fiducials) may suffice.

4. On the other hand, if the remote sensor provides only non-literal GEOINT data, then geospatial analysis of the collection geometry is required.[49] This solution is sketched in **Figure 4-29**.

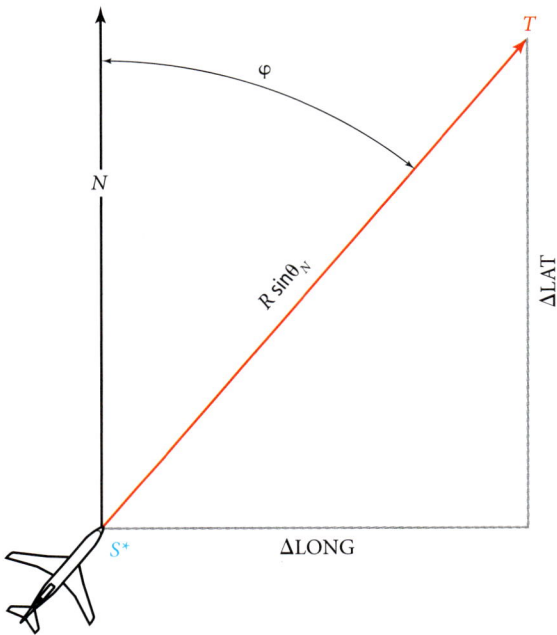

Figure 4-29
Top view of flat Earth geolocation.

Geolocation is given in some set of convenient coordinates on the Earth. The most familiar is latitude and longitude, although other coordinates, such as the Military Grid Reference System (MGRS), are in use. To review, latitude is measured north-south from the equator in degrees. The poles are 90° from the equator. Longitude is measured in degrees east-west from an internationally agreed Prime Meridian passing through the Royal Observatory in Greenwich, England (**Figure 4-30**). Longitude runs to 180° each direction, meeting at the International Date Line in the Pacific.

For the flat Earth geolocation problem, it was previously stated that the sensor's location is known. Then, it is just a matter of locating the end of the sensor-to-target vector. **Figure 4-29** shows a top-down view of the **Figure 4-27** situation where **Equation 4-60** is used to estimate R. Hand-in-hand with that calculation is estimating the *horizontal* distance S^* to T.[50] It is

$$\overline{S^*T} \approx R \sin\theta_N \text{ [km]}. \tag{4-61}$$

---

[49] Assume that methods are in use to estimate the position of the target within the non-literal data. One such method will be described in Chapter 14 on data processing, analysis, and exploitation.

[50] Another assumption/approximation: assume the point on the ground is directly under the sensor, S^*, which is geolocation GS, and the target, T, are level with one another, or at least nearly so.

Figure 4-30
The Royal Observatory in Greenwich, England. (Photo courtesy of Chris O. via http://en.wikipedia.org/wiki/File:Royal_observatory_greenwich.jpg; GNU Free Documentation License Version 1.2 or later.)

In **Figure 4-29**, another part of the observation not yet mentioned is shown. The target is also seen to be at an azimuth angle, φ, as well as at nadir angle, θ_N. The azimuth is measured with respect to a reference direction[51] such as North as shown. Having estimated $\overline{S^*T}$ from the previous estimate of R, components of the geolocation of T, with respect to S^*, can be computed as

$$\Delta\text{LAT} \approx \overline{S^*T}\cos\varphi \text{ [km]} \quad \text{and} \quad \Delta\text{LONG} \approx \overline{S^*T}\sin\varphi \text{ [km]}. \quad \textbf{(4-62)}$$

To go from the geographic coordinates of S^* to those of T using **Equation 4-62** involves two difficulties. First, if R and $\overline{S^*T}$ are estimated in kilometers, then ΔLAT and ΔLONG are in kilometers, whereas they need to be in degrees. Secondly, the flat Earth model is incorrect! Latitude and longitude coordinates do not form an orthonormal grid on the Earth's surface; lines of latitude (meridians) converge at the poles. For distances that are not too large, an approximate solution is[52]

$$\Delta\text{LAT} \approx \frac{\Delta\text{LAT[km]}}{111} \; [°] \quad \textbf{(4-63)}$$

and

$$\Delta\text{LONG} \approx \frac{\Delta\text{LONG[km]}}{111 \times \cos(\text{LAT[°]})} \; [°].$$

Then, with all quantities in degrees,

$$\text{LAT}(T) \approx \text{LAT}(S^*) + \Delta\text{LAT} \; [°] \quad \textbf{(4-64)}$$

and

$$\text{LONG}(T) \approx \text{LONG}(S^*) + \Delta\text{LONG} \; [°].$$

The residual questions in this estimate are, "What is that $\cos(\text{LAT[°]})$ in the denominator of the longitude component conversion, and how large is not too large?" The answer to the first question is: $\cos(\text{LAT[°]})$ takes account of the north-south lines of longitude narrowing closer to the poles. The value of LAT[°] to be used can be the latitude of S^*, the latitude of T, or some value in between, depending on the accuracy required. The accuracy required depends on the answer to the question, which will be explored next.

[51] Depending on the sensor, it may be more logical to measure azimuth with respect to its platform's velocity vector or the axis of the craft, then to convert to an external reference direction. For aircraft, this would entail knowing the True Heading and the sensor's pointing direction relative to the fuselage.

[52] The numerical factor comes from an original definition of the kilometer as 1/10,000, the distance from equator to pole. Meanwhile, mariners measured that distance in nautical miles (NM) with 1 NM corresponding to 1 minute of latitude. Hence, there are

$90° \times 60\frac{\text{minutes}}{\text{degree}} \times 1\frac{\text{NM}}{\text{minute}} = 5,400\,\text{NM} = 10,000\,\text{km}$

from equator to pole.

HOW FLAT IS FLAT?

The fact that the world is not flat may easily be discerned from sounding rocket photos taken from at least 100 km above the surface as shown in **Figure 4-31**. The correct side view of the collection geometry is then as sketched in **Figure 4-32**, where R_E is the radius[53] of the Earth; $R_E \approx 6370$ km. Assuming a flat Earth, a target at T will be calculated to be somewhat closer at T^*, when observed at angle θ_N from altitude H. Target geolocation, at G, will then be wrong too.[54] How big is the difference in R between $\overline{ST^*}$ and $\overline{ST}$ in **Figure 4-32**? (Note, **Figure 4-32** shows the worst case when the nadir angle is at its maximum for a target on the horizon, or limb, of the Earth.)

Figure 4-31
Curvature of the Earth seen from a sounding rocket.

Figure 4-32
Curved Earth collection geometry.

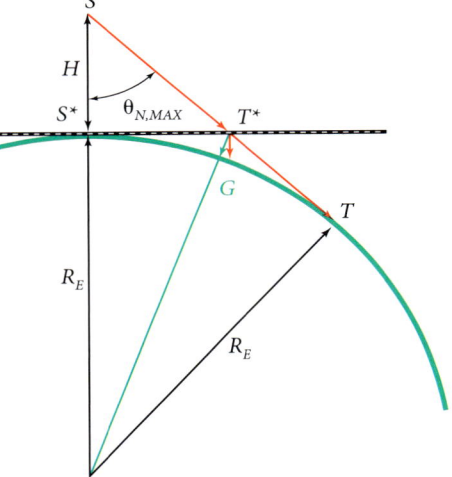

To answer the question, first consider that it depends on the altitude of the sensor. What are appropriate values of H? Altitude depends on the design and performance of a sensor's platform. Air-breathers and lighter-than-air craft rarely fly higher than 30 km ($\approx$ 100,000 ft), but spaceborne craft rarely fly below[55] a few hundred kilometers in their orbits. For the latter, their lifetimes depends on their lowest altitude, where they encounter drag with the atmosphere. **Figure 4-33** shows an approximate relationship between altitude and the expected time before air drag causes re-entry. The chart suggests that in order for an advanced technical intelligence sensor to accomplish its mission, a reasonable space journey is at least a month and requires its minimum service altitude to be greater than 200 km. Thus, there is a "sensor gap" between about 30 and 200 km.

---

[53] The Earth is not a perfect sphere, but it will be assumed so for now. The calculations in this section will show the neglect of the Earth's true shape to be justified for collections from low altitude sensors.

[54] The target geolocation, G, could be wrong in a couple of different ways, as suggested by the figure.

[55] The nearest point in a spacecraft's orbit is its *perigee*. See **Chapter 11** on orbitology.

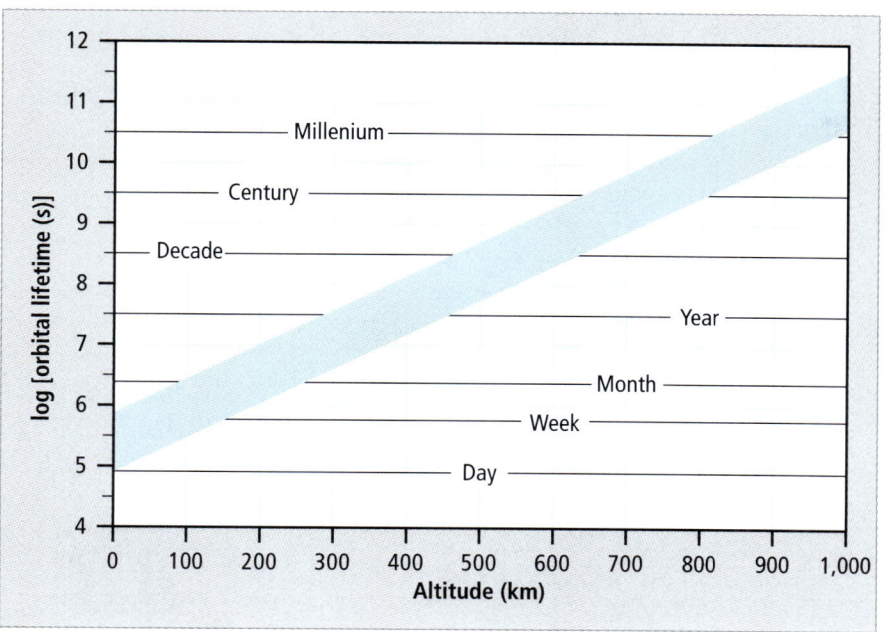

Figure 4-33
Spacecraft expected time in orbit before decaying due to atmospheric drag increases with increasing altitude. There is no exact relationship, but the band in the figure suggests plausible limits based on seasonal atmospheric variations and effects of solar activity.

For the low altitude sensors, manned and unmanned aircraft and aerostats, the geometry of **Figure 4-32** can be used to calculate the error in computing flat Earth range $\overline{ST^*}$ compared to actual range $\overline{ST}$. The formulas involve trigonometry (available on the support website in **Appendix 4-3**) and the results are shown in **Figure 4-34**. Not too surprisingly, the error is less than 1% for all (low) altitudes up to nadir angles of ~70°. (At angles above 70°, the atmospheric attenuation may make collections marginally useful anyway. Furthermore, refraction may complicate geolocation; it certainly will for the high altitude sensors.) Thus, the flat Earth approximation is certainly satisfactory for range estimation and geolocation when collecting with intra-atmospheric sensors.

Figure 4-35 shows the error calculation for high altitude sensors. Contrary to low altitude computations, this error becomes substantial at even modest nadir angles. So, compensation for the curved Earth is required to evaluate R for the propagation equations when taking collections from space.

Figure 4-34
Flat Earth range error for low altitude sensors. (Notional altitudes of typical platforms, past and present, are indicated.)

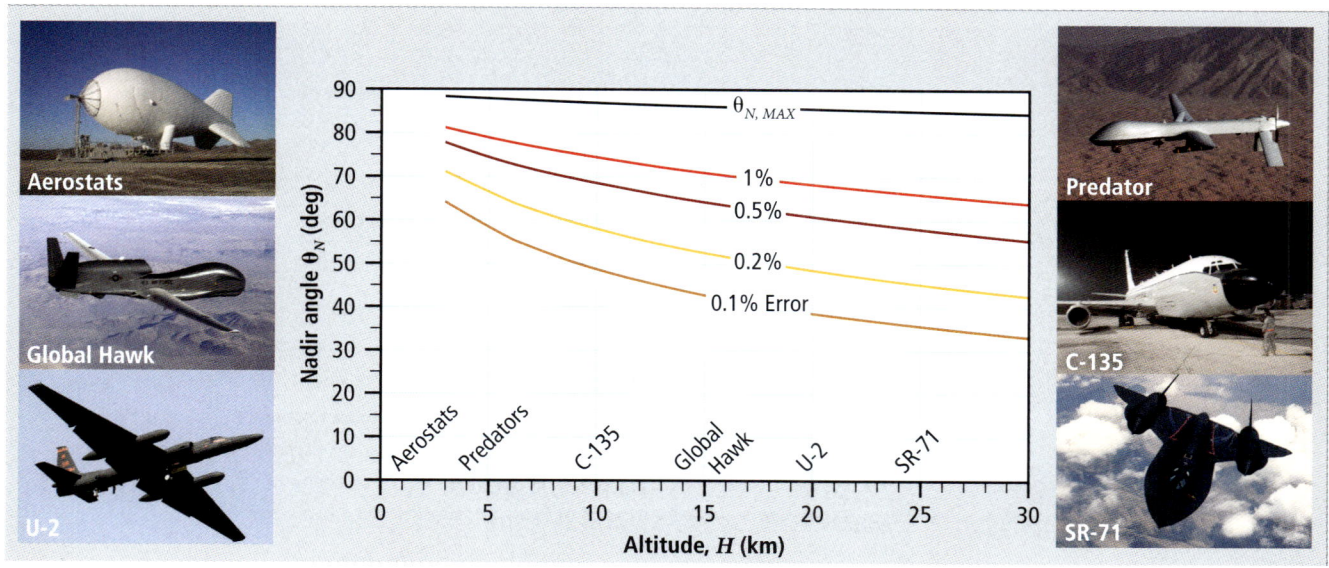

Figure 4-35
Flat Earth range error for altitudes above 400 km.

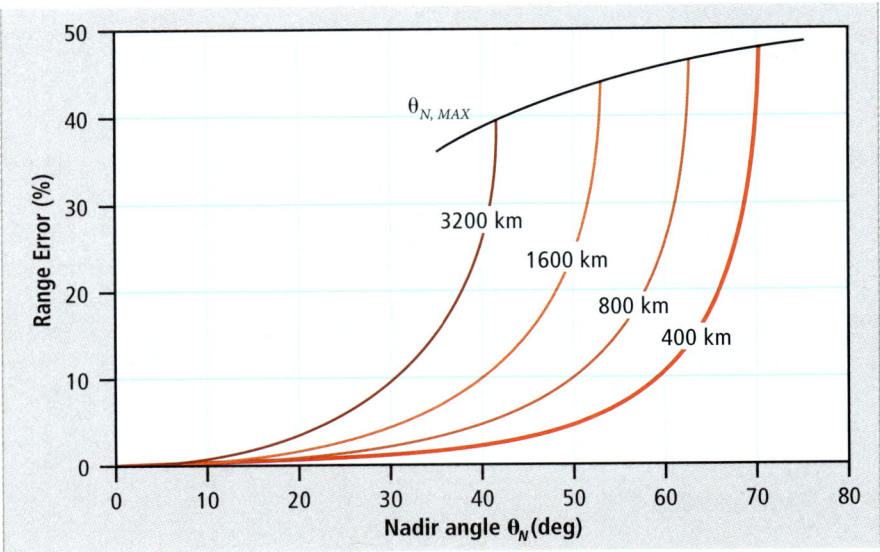

CURVED EARTH

There are two difficulties with estimating range to target from high altitude sensors: 1) the Earth is not a sphere; and 2) visualizing the solution in three dimensions and applying the proper mathematics. Since this is an introductory level text, disregard the fact that the planet is closer to being a bumpy oblate spheroid than a sphere; its departure from "round" is less than 1%. Since concepts and phenomenology are being stressed, simply use a spherical model for now.

RANGE TO TARGET

Figure 4-36 should help visualize high altitude collection geometry. Sensor S is at altitude H above its geolocation, which is its nadir, labeled S^* as in **Figure 4-32**. Again, assume this is known. The latitude and longitude of S^* are shown as blue lines on the globe. Observing at angle θ_N, the sensor spies a target, T, on the Earth. T's latitude and longitude geo-coordinates are marked in red. Notice how the lines of latitude converge at the pole, N, while the lines of longitude are parallel lines encircling the world.

Figure 4-36
High altitude collection geometry.

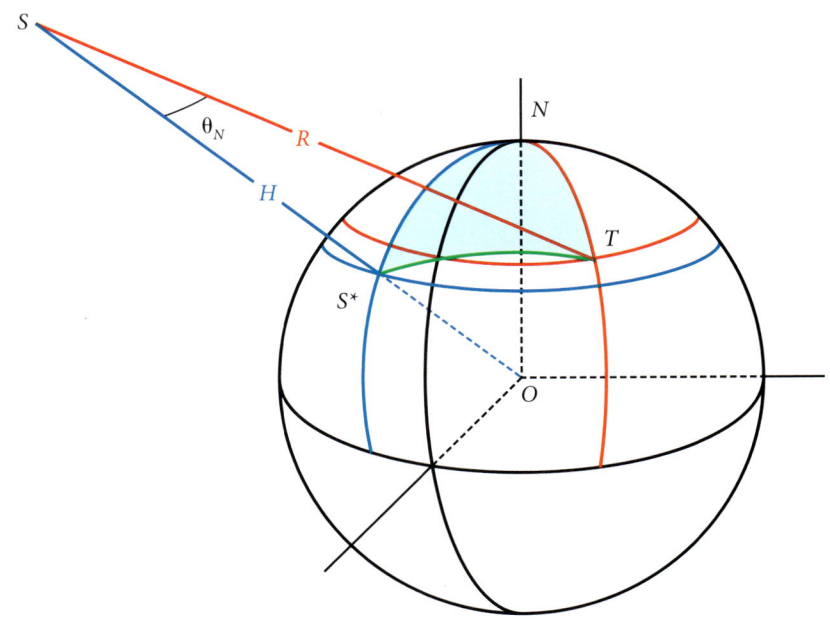

106   CHAPTER 4 RADIOMETRY

Perhaps the most difficult part of this visualization is the green line in the figure. This is the arc $\widehat{S^*T}$ along the Earth's surface as shown inside the view of **Figure 4-32**. In three dimensions, this line is the intersection of the plane defined by points S, S*, and T with the (approximate) sphere of the Earth. The plane just defined also contains the center of the Earth, O. Arc $\widehat{S^*T}$ is a section of what is called a "great circle."[56]

A simplified version of **Figure 4-32** is drawn on the left of **Figure 4-37** to make the view of the plane containing S, T, and O more clear. Of course, the first objective is to calculate $\overline{ST}$, which is R. This was done above for this exact geometry when computing the error for the flat Earth approximation, also available on the support website in **Appendix 4-3**. In that calculation, the Earth's center angle, β, was found. This angle may be used to find the distance along arc $\widehat{S^*T}$, in kilometers, as

$$\widehat{S^*T} \approx R_E \beta \text{ [km]}, \quad (4\text{-}65)$$

where $R_E \approx 6370$ km for the spherical approximation, and β is in radians.

GEOLOCATION

Back to the visualization in **Figure 4-36**, focus on the three-sided shape S*-N-T on the surface of the sphere. It is re-drawn in detail on the right side of **Figure 4-37**. This is a *spherical triangle*; the vertices of which are the geolocation of the sensor, the geolocation of the target, and the pole. As well as the angles at its vertices, the sides of a spherical triangle are expressed in angular measure (degrees or radians); although, they certainly have length along the surface. To see this, for instance, note side $\widehat{S^*N}$ subtends an angle at the center of the Earth, $\angle S^*ON$. The measure of this angle is the measure of side $\widehat{S^*N}$, and likewise for sides $\widehat{S^*T}$ and $\widehat{NT}$ subtending angles $\angle S^*OT$ and $\angle NOT$, respectively.

$\angle S^*OT$ (or side $\widehat{S^*T}$) was already defined as β on the left of **Figure 4-37**. Since S* is a geolocation having a latitude given in degrees from the equator, and because the equator-to-pole angle is 90°, side $\widehat{S^*N}$ is 90° minus the latitude of S*. This is called the co-latitude. Similarly, side $\widehat{NT}$ is the *co-latitude* of the target.

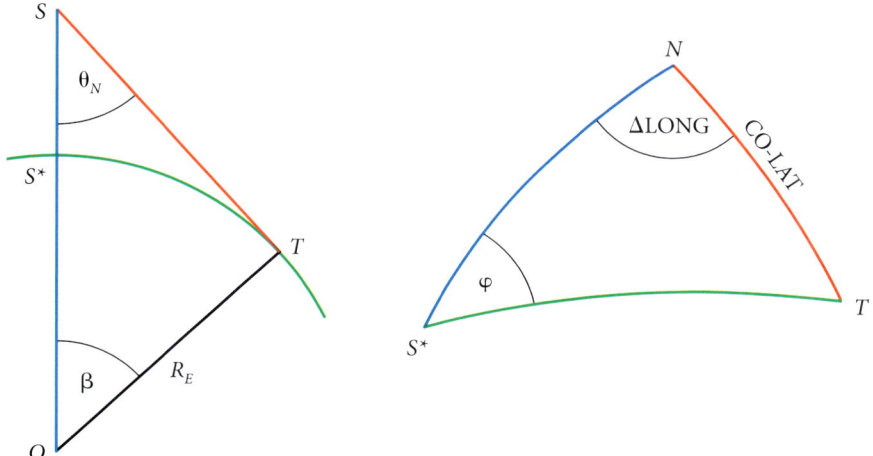

Figure 4-37
Details of the high altitude collection geometry.

At the vertices of the spherical triangle, $\angle NS^*T$ is the same azimuth angle, φ, as defined in **Figure 4-30**, assuming the reference direction is North along a line of latitude. For the angle $\angle S^*NT$, imagine this: standing at N, look along $\widehat{NT^*}$ to the geolocation of S*, then turn to face T along $\widehat{NT}$.

[56] On a sphere, a great circle is a *geodesic*. It is the shortest distance between two points, which can be proven using the calculus of variations. In navigating long distances, one wants to fly (or drive or sail) the great circle route to save time and fuel.

At *N*, one could turn from facing either direction (toward S^* or *T*) to face along the Prime Meridian, which also comes to the pole. Thus, facing either S^* or *T* is turning from the Prime Meridian through an angle which is the longitude of S^* or *T*. Thus, turning from facing S^* to facing *T* is the difference in their longitudes.

To determine the geolocation of *T*,

1. Find its co-latitude, and
2. Determine its difference in longitude from S^*.

This can be accomplished by solving the spherical triangle $\triangle S^*NT$. The mathematical details for this solution are available in **Appendix 4-4** on the support website. The results of the calculation may then be used to find the elevation of *T* from the DTED. If necessary, the iterative procedure of **Figures 4-26** and **4-27** may be applied to improve the estimate of geolocation.

5 ATMOSPHERIC EFFECTS

(Photo courtesy of http://en.wiktionary.org/wiki/File:Cumulus_clouds_in_fair_weather.jpeg; Creative CommonsAttribution-Share Alike 2.0 Generic; Michael Jastremski.)

From the discussions just concluded, it is evident that target information will be gathered through the Earth's atmosphere. Low altitude sensors do not fly on platforms higher than about 30 km, while high altitude sensors are in orbit peering down from above 300–400 km (often well above). Accordingly, because of its importance, this chapter will discuss the air surrounding the Earth and some general features of propagating information through it, the attenuation term {ATTN} of the phenomenological treatment of Advanced Technical Intelligence gathering introduced in **Chapter 1**.

SECTIONS
5.1 THE ATMOSPHERE
5.2 BEER'S LAW
5.3 PROCESSES

5.1 THE ATMOSPHERE

The atmosphere is a complex mixture of gases and particles floating around. (In the visible bandpass, for human eyes, the atmosphere is mostly transparent, but this is not true at other wavelengths as will be discussed later in this chapter.) Only when there are large concentrations of particles, and only for about 1% of the gases, is the propagation of radiation impacted. But what an impact!

GASES

First, look at the composition and distribution of atmospheric gases.

1. COMPOSITION

The standard model used for the atmosphere is the *1976 US Standard Atmosphere* (1976 USSA).[1] A spreadsheet copy of the model is available to the reader in **Appendix 5-1** on the support website. In the model (portion shown in **Figure 5-1**), as a function of altitude (above sea level), standard values for pressure, temperature, and density, and the proportions of 28 different gases can be found. Their proportions are given in "parts per million by volume" (PPMV). That is, if a certain volume contained one million molecules, then how many of them would be that particular species? The 1976 USSA is a good mid-latitude, all-season model.[2]

The number of species of molecules in the atmosphere is probably in the thousands.[3] For most, their proportions are so tiny they make no difference to remote sensing,[4] and they are not listed in the 1976 USSA. But note, the first two gases listed in the model, nitrogen and oxygen, make up 99% of the atmosphere. This is fortuitous; recall the discussion of symmetric diatomic molecules in **Chapter 2**. Symmetric diatomic molecules do not have a dipole moment (internal charge imbalance), so they do not strongly interact with radiation. Therefore, the atmosphere is mostly clear, and targets *should* be easily seen through it.

As for the rest of the gases listed (considered "trace" gases), they don't add up to the remaining 1% of the atmosphere that isn't N_2 or O_2. Where are the missing molecules? The thousands of gases not given in the model probably don't even add up to one molecule out of a million. So, the answer is the missing molecules are atoms of the noble gases. Historically, these were called the "inert" gases because they do not readily enter into chemical reactions, nor do they have electrical handles (**Chapter 2**). If they were listed in the model, their proportions would be about $Ar \approx 9.34 \times 10^3$, $Ne \approx 5.24 \times 10^0$, $He \approx 5.24 \times 10^{-1}$, and Kr, Xe, and Rn would show negligible amounts.

[1] This may seem outdated, but the model provides an estimate and only needs to be locally supplemented to match current conditions.

[2] Note, the U.S. Standard Atmosphere is parenthetically called "Model 6" in the spreadsheet. Five other models are in general use for tropical and arctic latitudes and are fine-tuned for summer or winter conditions. They only list the proportions of the first seven or eight gases; the rest are assumed to be the same as for the Standard Atmosphere. With the exception of water vapor, these models differ so slightly from Model 6 as to make little difference to the remote sensing problem. It is more important, as shown later, to use the correct aerosol (suspended particle) model.

[3] There is often no need to distinguish amongst the species of molecules, so they are generically referred to as "air molecules."

[4] Seemingly insignificant numbers of some species can make a significant contribution to specific applications. For example, sodium atoms are known to exist in a reasonably narrow layer at 90 to 100 km altitude. Although there are miniscule numbers of them, they can be used with a 589 nm laser to create a "guide star" for keeping telescopes in focus using adaptive optics.

Figure 5-1
A portion of the 1976 US Standard Atmosphere spreadsheet. Note the spreadsheet scientific notation: $1.01E + 03$ means 1.01×10^3, etc.

	A	B	C	D	E	F	G	H	I	J	K	L	M	N
1		//// U.S. Standard Atmosphere, 1976 (Model 6)												
2		ALT	PRES	TEMP	DENSITY	N2	O2	H2O	CO2	O3	N2O	CO	CH4	NO	SO2
3		(km)	(mb)	(K)	(cm-3)	(PPMV)	(PPMV)	(PPMV)	(PPMV)	(PPMV)	(PPMV)	(PPMV)	(PPMV)	(PPMV)	(PPMV)
4	0	1.013E+03	288.2	2.548E+19	7.81E+05	2.09E+05	7.75E+03	3.30E+02	2.66E+02	3.20E−01	1.50E−01	1.70E+00	3.00E−04	3.00E−04
5	1	8.988E+02	281.7	2.313E+19	7.81E+05	2.09E+05	6.07E+03	3.30E+02	2.93E+02	3.20E−01	1.45E−01	1.70E+00	3.00E−04	2.74E−04
6	2	7.950E+02	275.2	2.094E+19	7.81E+05	2.09E+05	4.63E+03	3.30E+02	3.24E+02	3.20E−01	1.40E−01	1.70E+00	3.00E−04	2.36E−04
7	3	7.012E+02	268.7	1.891E+19	7.81E+05	2.09E+05	3.18E+03	3.30E+02	3.32E+02	3.20E−01	1.35E−01	1.70E+00	3.00E−04	1.90E−04
8	4	6.166E+02	262.2	1.704E+19	7.81E+05	2.09E+05	2.16E+03	3.30E+02	3.39E+02	3.20E−01	1.31E−01	1.70E+00	3.00E−04	1.46E−04
9	5	5.405E+02	255.7	1.532E+19	7.81E+05	2.09E+05	1.40E+03	3.30E+02	3.77E+02	3.20E−01	1.30E−01	1.70E+00	3.00E−04	1.18E−04
10	6	4.722E+02	249.2	1.373E+19	7.81E+05	2.09E+05	9.25E+02	3.30E+02	4.11E+02	3.20E−01	1.29E−01	1.70E+00	3.00E−04	9.71E−05

The most familiar trace gases are undoubtedly water vapor, H_2O, and carbon dioxide, CO_2, the greenhouse gas. **Figure 5-2** shows 50 years of historical data from a Hawaiian station that clearly tracks about a 20% increase in CO_2 concentration. The future change in its concentration and its contribution to possible global warming is unknown, but it is certain that CO_2 has a major impact on the attenuation of radiation passing through the atmosphere, as will be discussed in this chapter.

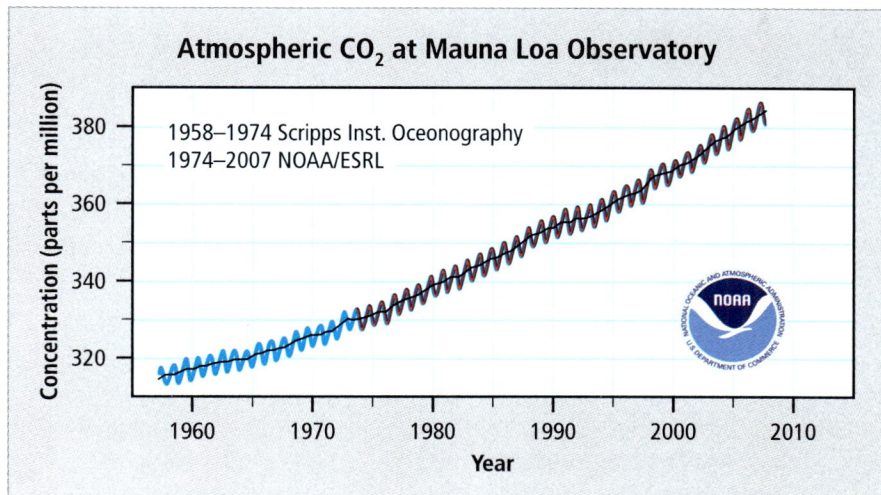

Figure 5-2
Carbon dioxide concentration reported at the Mauna Loa atmospheric observatory.

The presence of water vapor in the atmosphere is called humidity. The amount of H_2O the air can hold depends on temperature and pressure, but is only a few percent at most. Up to the point of saturation, air is considered to be "dry" because water molecules are just another gas. Above saturation, the air is "moist" and water vapor readily condenses into dew, fog, clouds, and precipitation. Some water exists in the atmosphere regardless of local conditions (desert arid or tropical monsoon), and the 1976 USSA shows a nominal amount. More interesting is its distribution.

2. SPATIAL DISTRIBUTION

The most influential atmospheric parameter on the propagation of radiation is the gases' density as a function of altitude, which is in turn influenced by temperature and gravity. Horizontally, the atmosphere is approximately uniform; although, high and low pressure systems and surface types (ocean, desert, forest, etc.) may cause a change of a few percent.

a. NUMBER DENSITY

Figure 5-3 shows the two primary gases are distributed evenly ("well-mixed") from the surface up to about 80 km, with only slight decreases above that. Of the trace gases, different behaviors are apparent. **Figure 5-3** shows carbon dioxide, for instance, to also be well-mixed at altitudes up to about 80 km again. But ozone, O_3, shows increased concentration in broad "layers." (The creation and dissociation of ozone inhibits solar ultraviolet from turning human skin into fried pork rinds; hence, part of the concerns about "ozone holes.") Meanwhile, water vapor decreases in concentration in the lowest 15 km or so, then remains approximately constant for 50 km. This highly variable presence of water vapor in the lower atmosphere has significant consequences for the propagation of light.

Figure 5-3
Proportions of some atmospheric gases. Note, this and other plots of atmospheric properties have the independent variable (altitude) on the vertical axis. This is not customary, but makes sense in visualizing the atmosphere because altitude, *z*, goes up.

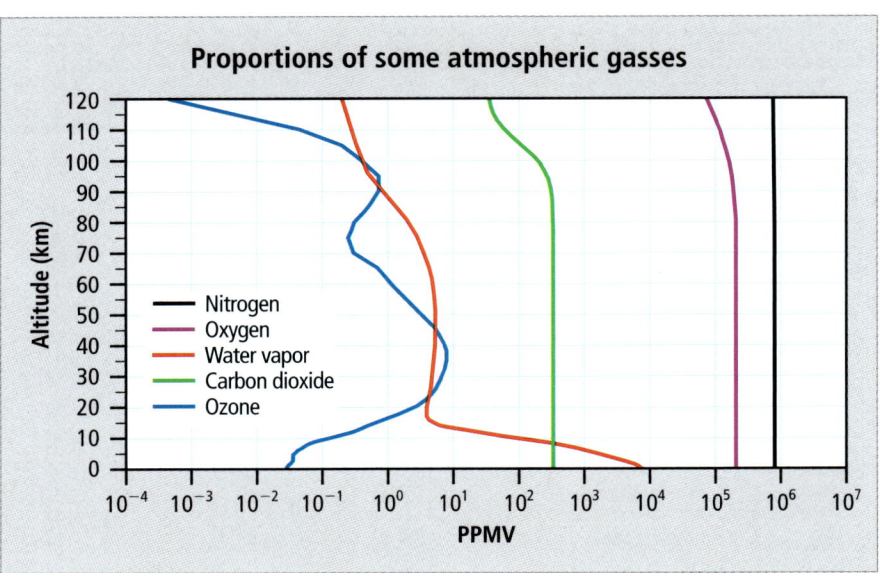

Taken as a whole, the gross properties of the atmosphere are its pressure, temperature, and density. 1976 USSA density (properly, *number density*) and temperature are plotted in **Figure 5-4** as functions of altitude, *z*, above sea level (on the vertical axis). The quantity having the most effect on remote sensing is the density. The proportions of all the gases in the model add up to its number density, *n*. (The model gives this in units of number of molecules per cubic centimeter, but it is plotted in **Figure 5-4** in SI-correct units of per cubic meter.) Inspection of the model shows the number density and pressure are directly related as they should. Under normal conditions, the atmosphere is very nearly an "ideal" gas, obeying the ideal gas law:[5,6]

$$P = nk_B T \text{ [Pa]}, \tag{5-1}$$

where *P* is pressure[7] and *T* is temperature.

Figure 5-4
Number density and temperature of the Standard Atmosphere.

[5] Readers with chemistry or physics in their backgrounds will recall the ideal gas law is a compact expression for the empirical Boyle's and Charles' Laws (inverse relation between pressure and volume, and direct relation between temperature and volume, respectively).

[6] Readers familiar with the ideal gas law may be more familiar with it in the forms $PV = \nu RT$ or $PV = Nk_B T$, where *V* is volume, ν is the number of moles, *N* is the number of molecules, and *R* is the so-called universal gas constant.
This formula makes use of $n = \frac{N}{V}$, $N = \nu N_A$ (N_A is Avogadro's number), and $R = N_A k_B$.

[7] The SI unit for pressure is the pascal (Pa), which is equal to one newton per square meter (N/m²). Inflating tires to a gauge pressure of 32 psi is equivalent to about 220 kPa.

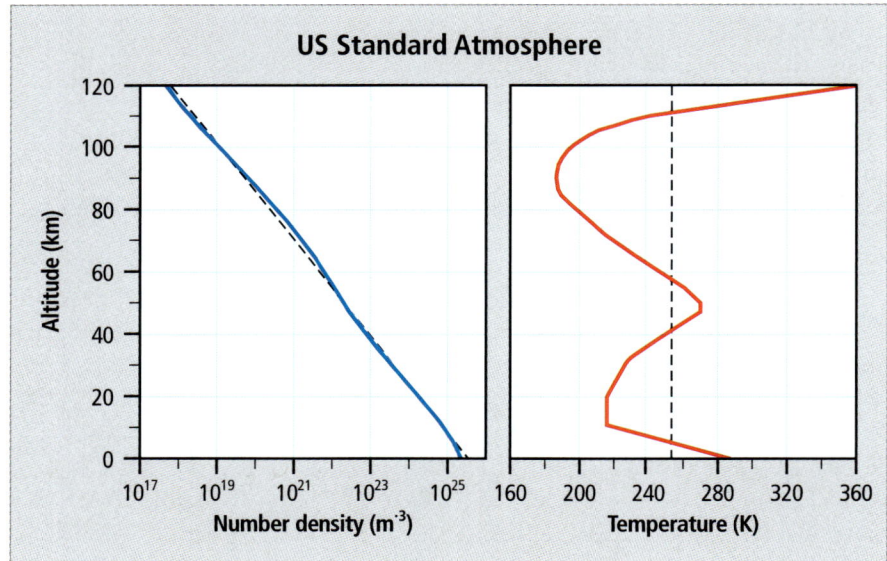

Note, number density is plotted logarithmically on the horizontal axis in **Figure 5-4**. The graph is nearly linear, as suggested by the dashed straight line added to the figure. Data plotting to a straight line in

112 CHAPTER 5 ATMOSPHERIC EFFECTS

semi-log space such as this obeys an exponential dependence.[8] For number density, it is found to be[9]

$$n(z) = n_0 e^{\frac{-\langle m \rangle g z}{k_B T}} = n_0 e^{\frac{-z}{\hat{H}}} \ [m^{-3}], \quad (5\text{-}2)$$

which is called the hydrostatic equation. n_0 is the number density at sea level ($z = 0$) called Loschmidt's number ($\approx 2.69 \times 10^{25} \ m^{-3}$) (**Figure 5-5**). Also, "scale height" is defined as the following grouping of constants:

$$\hat{H} = \frac{k_B T}{\langle m \rangle g} \ [m], \quad (5\text{-}3)$$

where $\langle m \rangle \approx 4.79 \times 10^{-26}$ kg is the mean mass per molecule (very nearly that of nitrogen) and $g \approx 9.81 \ m \cdot s^{-2}$ is the value of gravity near the Earth's surface.

In **Equation 5-2**, the scale height takes on the role of a characteristic length,[10] giving the "e-folding" altitude. That is, when climbing to one scale height, density and pressure decrease to $\frac{1}{e}$ of their sea level values. At two scale heights, these variables decrease to $\frac{1}{e^2}$ of their base values, etc. **Table 5-1** gives values for up to five scale heights. As a general rule of thumb, five characteristic lengths (or times) are a sufficient distance (or time) to have taken in *all* of a phenomenon, such as the decrease in number density to approximately zero. From **Equation 5-3**, scale height is between about[11] 7000–8000 m (depending on temperature). Thus, at some altitude around 35–40 km, one is essentially above 100% of the atmosphere.[12, 13]

Figure 5-5
Johan Josef Loschmidt, 1821–1895. (Photo courtesy of http://commons.wikimedia.org/wiki/File:Haus_Malfatti_Gedenktafel_Loschmidt.jpg; Creative Commons Attribution-Share Alike 3.0 Austria license; Wdvorak.)

[8] See Appendix 5-2 on the support website for a mathematical derivation of the exponential dependence from the plot.

[9] See Appendix 5-3 on the support website for the physical derivation of Equation 5-2.

Table 5-1
The exponential atmosphere.

When one is at altitude _____	One is above _____ of the atmosphere	And only _____ of the atmosphere is above.
$z \approx \hat{H}$	63.2%	36.8%
$z \approx 2\hat{H}$	86.5%	13.5%
$z \approx 3\hat{H}$	95.0%	4.98%
$z \approx 4\hat{H}$	98.2%	1.83%
$z \approx 5\hat{H}$	99.3%	0.674%

The totality of the atmosphere is all of its molecules. Since $\hat{H} \ll R_E$, ignore the curvature of the Earth and use the one-dimensional **Equation 5-2** to account for them all. Phenomenologically, {Number of molecules} ≈ {Molecules per unit volume} × {Volume}, which is[14]

$$N_T = \int n(z) d(Vol) = \int_0^\infty n_0 e^{\frac{-z}{\hat{H}}} A \, dz = n_0 A \hat{H}, \quad (5\text{-}4)$$

where a unit volume was taken as a column dz meters tall over a one-square meter area, A, on the ground. The simple result of **Equation 5-4** provides that if the entire atmosphere was crushed to the point where it had a uniform sea level density, it would be precisely one scale height high. The integral

$$\mathcal{N} = \int_0^\infty n(z) dz = n_0 \hat{H} \ [m^{-2}] \quad (5\text{-}5)$$

is called the *column density*. In number per unit area, it gives how many molecules are in a column over a unit area.

[10] All exponential functions have a characteristic scale factor. In electronics, the characteristic e-folding time for capacitors to charge or discharge is called a circuit's *time constant*. Another characteristic, time in the decay of radioactive substances, was introduced in Equation 4-52. Another characteristic, length, will be covered in Beer's Law later in this chapter.

[11] For reference, the highest mountain in North America is Mt. McKinley (Alaska) at 6,194 m (20,320′) and the world's tallest is Mt. Everest (Nepal) at 8,848 m (29,029′). Hypoxia sets in at 4,302 m (14,115′) on Pike's Peak (Colorado).

[12] The atmosphere being no more than ~ 40 km deep further supports the use of the flat Earth model, even for attenuation to space-borne sensors, as will be argued later in this chapter (but a curved Earth model has to be used to calculate the metrics).

[13] Review the section on "How Flat Is Flat?" in Section 4.3.

[14] The summation only needs to go up to the "top of the atmosphere" which is about 40 km (~ $5\hat{H}$) for these purposes. However, the integral can be taken "to infinity" for convenience to easily include everything.

EXAMPLE 5-1: HOW MANY AIR MOLECULES EXIST?

Over 99% of the atmosphere is probably within $5\hat{H} \approx 40$ km of the Earth's surface. In the study of "How Flat is Flat?" it was concluded to ignore the curvature of the Earth for many purposes. Therefore, using the surface of the Earth as

$$A_E = 4\pi R^2_E \approx (4\pi)(6370 \text{ km})^2 \approx 5.10 \times 10^{14} \text{ m}^2$$

creates from **Equation 5-4**:

$$N_E \approx n_0 A_E \hat{H} \approx (2.69 \times 10^{25} \text{ m}^{-3})(5.10 \times 10^{14} \text{ m}^2)(8 \times 10^3 \text{m})$$
$$\approx 1.10 \times 10^{44} \text{ air molecules.}$$

Perhaps the reader has not lain awake at night worrying that the atmosphere, the air needed to breath, is an unbounded gas bag. There is no lid on it. Molecules seem to be free to float off into space if they want, leaving humans like fish out of water. Apparently, like everything else in this realm, air is held down by gravity. Yet, if gravity alone acted on air molecules, would they all pile up on the floor, and would people have to crawl with their noses on the ground to inhale? Not to worry, neither of these two extremes occurs.

MORE ABOUT TEMPERATURE

The plot of atmospheric temperature as a function of altitude (right side of **Figure 5-4**) shows temperature going "sky-high" (pun intended) above 100 km. Readers may have seen other plots showing temperatures exceeding 1000 K at several hundred kilometers altitude, particularly during times of high solar activity. Do spacecraft at these altitudes (low Earth orbiters and large missiles) burn up? Not at all.

The meaning of "temperature" in a gas is a parameter measuring the distribution of molecular speeds around some average. Gas molecules are in constant motion, but some are moving slowly while others zip along. Maxwell and Boltzmann worked out molecules' speed *distribution* as

$$n_v \approx 4\pi n(z)\left(\frac{\langle m \rangle}{2\pi k_B T}\right)^{3/2} v^2 e^{-\langle m \rangle v^2/2k_B T},$$

which is the number of molecules per unit volume (at altitude z) per unit speed interval, i.e., the number of molecules per unit volume having a certain speed plus-or-minus the amount of resolution that measures the speed with whatever instrument used.

This is a very important point. All instruments used have an *interval* (bandpass) over which they take measurements. Only one exact speed of molecule cannot be measured with any physically realizable instrument. That is the meaning in the formula for the "sub v" on the number density, to serve as a reminder that a number *per unit speed interval* was measured (or is being computed). (This is identically the same as intensity, exitance, radiance, and irradiance being *specular* quantities measured per unit bandpass: the "sub λ" serves as a reminder of this.) To find the actual number of molecules per unit volume in a given speed range, integrate:

$$n \approx \int n_v dv.$$

The Maxwell-Boltzmann speed distribution plots as shown in the figure to the right where there are some slow molecules, some fast molecules, and a lot with medium speed. The "middle" speed can be characterized as the "most probable," "average," or "root-mean-square" speed:

$$v_{mp} \approx \sqrt{\frac{2k_B T}{\langle m \rangle}} \quad \bar{v} \approx \sqrt{\frac{8k_B T}{\pi \langle m \rangle}} \quad v_{rms} \approx \sqrt{\frac{3k_B T}{\langle m \rangle}}$$

In any case, the width of the distribution is dependent on a parameter called T. If T is small, the spread between the slowest and fastest molecules is small and the gas is said to be "cold." Conversely, the spread is large when

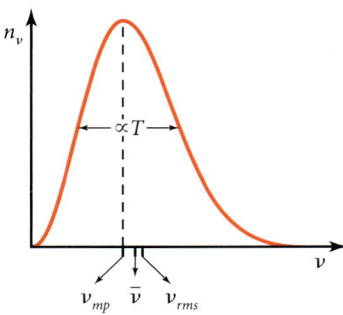

T is big, and the gas is "hot." As the reader may have guessed, this T parameter is called temperature, but it is *kinetic temperature*.

Kinetic temperature is technically different from the thermodynamic temperature discussed in the **Chapter 2 Sidebar Temperature Scales**, and from the molecular energy level temperature of **Equation 2-27**.[*] However, it may be shown (not here) that all of these temperatures are equal to one another under most circumstances. For these purposes, temperature is temperature.

Quickly, back to the question of high temperatures at high altitude. Evidently, these molecules are moving with a great range of speeds, some of them *very* fast. But there are so few of them ($z > 5\hat{H}$), their rate of energy transfer in collisions with a satellite can easily be absorbed, thermalized, and re-emitted as radiation. So, the spacecraft does not burn up.

[*] But wait, there's more! Still another temperature is the *physiological temperature* experienced when sensing moisture evaporating through skin.

The reason is energy balance as can be seen by re-arranging the scale height equation in a more suggestive manner:

$$\langle m \rangle g \hat{H} = k_B T. \tag{5-6}$$

Thus, nature has arranged that molecules' gravitational potential energy, $\langle m \rangle g \hat{H}$ is in steady state with their thermal activity, $k_B T$. Temperature will briefly be discussed next.

b. TEMPERATURE

The vertical hydrostatic density distribution, **Equation 5-2**, is actually based on an assumption that the atmosphere is *isothermal*. (See the physical development of the model in **Appendix 5-3** on the support website for details.) A glance at the right-hand plot in **Figure 5-4** shows it is not. However, weighting 1976 USSA temperatures with corresponding densities to emphasize the importance of greater numbers of molecules, an average temperature for the lower atmosphere ($z < 40$ km) is approximately 253 K. This is shown as the vertical dashed line in **Figure 5-4**, and the 1976 USSA does not vary from this value by more than about 14%. Using 253 K, a nominal scale height is 7.43 km.

The variation in temperature in the lowest atmosphere, below 10 km, is called a lapse, and is directly proportional to air's ability to hold water. Compare the density of water vapor in **Figure 5-3** with temperature in **Figure 5-4**. Interestingly, water-less air is heavier than water-filled air (contrary to what is felt on a hot summer day in "dry heat" as opposed to "wet heat"). This is because water molecules displacing N_2 and O_2 (in PPMV) have a lower molecular weight. Consequently, heavy air on top exerts more pressure and holds water vapor in a solution below. At lower altitudes, the compression "heats up" the water (and other) molecules, causing them to move faster. It is this molecular motion which, in fact, defines temperature (see Sidebar titled **More About Temperature**). As pressure decreases, the opposite effect occurs. On the support website in **Appendix 5-4**, the "lapse rate" for temperature decrease with altitude is calculated.

PARTICLES

The use of "particles" refers to anything that floats around in the atmosphere that isn't a gas; although, air molecules themselves fit the definition. But, generally dust, ash, smoke, fog, and the like are particles (**Figure 5-6**). Particles that form clouds are called suspensions, or aerosols. Clouds move with the wind and may follow thermal gradients, but individual particles are pulled toward the Earth by gravity while being held up by Archimedes's buoyant force, and are meanwhile undergoing Brownian motion from continual molecular pummeling. Two classes of particles are broadly characterized: wet and dry.

Figure 5-6
Clouds of wet and dry particles. The view from space of the volcanic eruption is Iceland's Eyjafjallajokull in April 2010. (Left photo courtesy of http://en.wiktionary.org/wiki/File:Cumulus_clouds_in_fair_weather.jpeg; Creative Commons Attribution-Share Alike 2.0 Generic; Michael Jastremski.)

Table 5-2
Wet aerosol particles.

Particle type	Typical diameter
Fog & clouds	5–50 μm
Mist & drizzle	50–400 μm
Rain & snow	400 μm →
Hail	1000 μm →

1. WET PARTICLES

Wet particles are exactly as they sound: condensed water droplets,[15] sometimes called hydrometeors. When the temperature drops to where the air is saturated (as when ascending to cloud bottom altitude, or when the sun goes down), water vapor cannot remain in solution. Suspended water droplets form and if in sufficient numbers, fog or clouds may be observed. Depending on the amount of water present, droplets can grow large enough to fall as rain, or they can freeze as hail. **Table 5-2** shows the typical size of wet aerosol particles.

Except for snowflakes[16] and cirrus clouds, wet particles accrete water molecules from the air and become spherical droplets.[17] It can be shown (but not here) that a spherical shape, caused by surface tension pulling equally in all directions, has the minimum surface energy. Further suppose that not all droplets in a cloud or mist will be the same size. A standard model for wet particles is to have their sizes distributed exponentially around some nominal value of their radius, r, according to

$$n_r(r) \approx \frac{N_T b^{\alpha+1}}{\alpha!} r^\alpha e^{-br} \quad [m^{-3} \mu m^{-1}], \tag{5-7}$$

where α and b are parameters that depend on the type of condensation process, and N_T is the total number of particles. (This is a *distribution* function, giving the number of droplets per unit volume of size, r, within an interval range of sizes, dr.) **Figure 5-7** gives a log-log plot of this distribution for three models listed in the Air Force Geophysics Lab's *Handbook of Geophysics and the Space Environment*. [1] By elementary differential calculus, it is easy to show the most probable radius, r_{mp}, (peak of the distribution curve) is given by

$$r_{mp} = \frac{\alpha}{b} \quad [\mu m]. \tag{5-8}$$

Figure 5-7
Distribution of wet particle sizes in a fog and two cloud models.

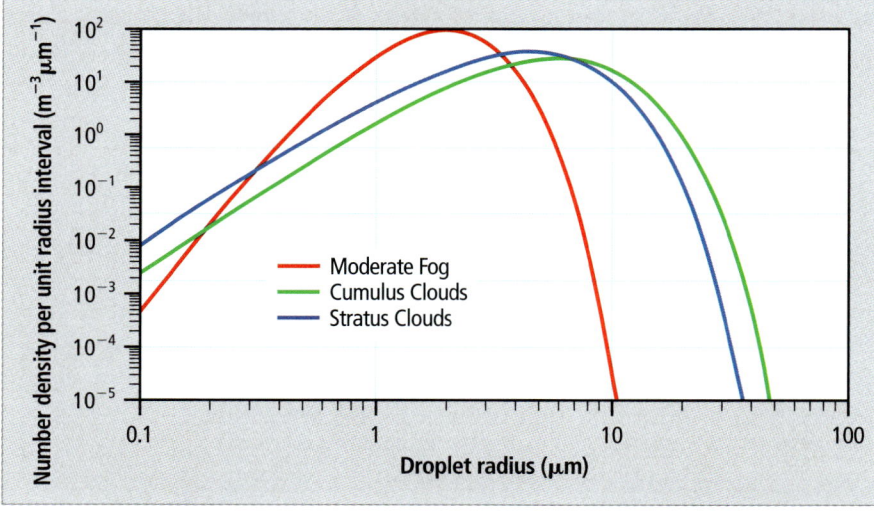

2. DRY PARTICLES

Dry particles differ from wet particles in two obviously different ways: 1) they can be any chemical substance whatsoever; and 2) their shapes are generally not spherical. **Figure 5-8** suggests some of the materials that can compose aerosols of dry particles: dusts, mists, smoke, ash, and the like. The figure shows approximate size ranges for these particles with typical diameters of gas molecules and the wavelength of light in the visible through thermal infrared spectrum shown for comparison.

---

[15] Suspended droplets are rarely made of pure water, but any of the trace gases can be dissolved in them. This often causes precipitation to be "acid rain." Ignore this and treat wet particles as being water.

[16] Snowflakes form on already frozen centers, and preferentially form plate-like crystals.

[17] Hailstones are basically spheres. Up- and downdrafts in clouds throw them about, colliding with water molecules on all sides where they freeze, growing into stones of sometimes gigantic proportions.

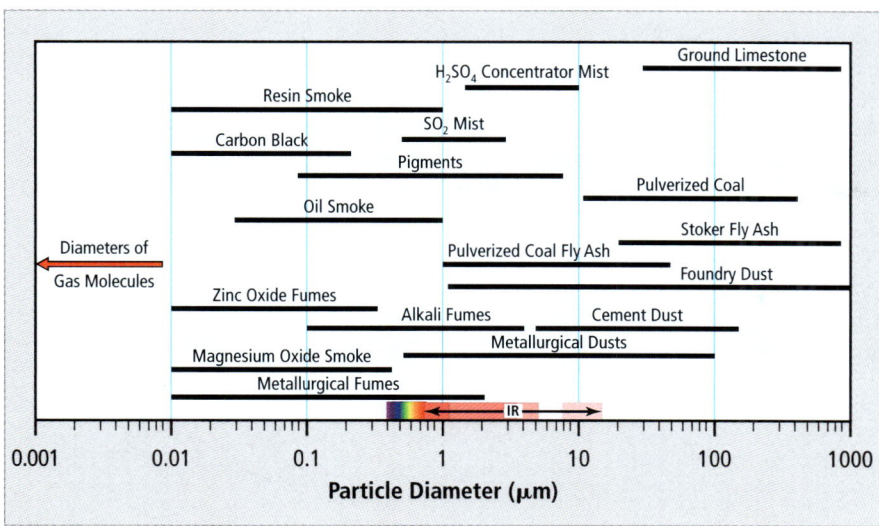

Figure 5-8
Size ranges of some dry aerosol particles.

Many dry aerosols come from pulverizing, fracturing, or grinding processes, and others arise from burning or outgassing.[18] As already mentioned in **Figure 5-8**, dry particles from any given source assume a range of possible sizes and have a variety of irregular shapes, particularly from the breaking-down processes. Because it is necessary in the scattering section of this chapter, some simple characterization of dry particles is required.

The simplest assumption about the shape of dry aerosol particles is, on average, they are spheres. This is obviously not true, because particles will be chunky and lumpy with broken edges and protruding corners. However, to many scientists, making sense of the disarrangement starts with the "spherical cow" assumption.[19] However, take comfort in the "law of large numbers" that states amongst a cloud of many particles, there will be all possible orientations, giving the effect that the average particle can be treated as a sphere with a characteristic radius.

Figure 5-9
The spherical cow is the simplest assumption to make about the shape of dry aerosol particles.

[18] A few dry aerosols, like spores and pollen, come from biological processes. These are reasonably uniform in size and shape and are not considered in this section.

[19] A dairyman was concerned his herd's milk production was decreasing. Through the agricultural extension service, a team of chemists, horticulturists, veterinarians, engineers, etc. arrived from the local university to study the problem. They studied the soil, the barn, the feed, the water, and everything about the farm. Then, they retired to their ivory tower to contemplate, and selected the physicist among their group to summarize their findings. Later, the farmer read the report which began "Consider a spherical cow …" [An urban legend]

CHAPTER 5 ATMOSPHERIC EFFECTS

> **NOTATION**
>
> Several standard mathematical notations are used in this text. As a reminder, they are
>
> $\exp\{X\}$ means e^X
>
> $\sum_i X_i$ means $X_1 + X_2 + X_3 + \ldots$
>
> $\prod_i X_i$ means $X_1 \times X_2 \times X_3 \times \ldots$
>
> The index, i, in the last two notations is sometimes specified and sometimes not. When specified, it means to start with $i = a$ and end on $i = b$, where a and b are the first and last members of the sum or product, respectively.

Recall the observation that many dry aerosols come from crushing processes, where boulders become gravel,...gravel becomes sand,... sand becomes dust, the total volume is constant (barring chemical reactions). Assuming dry particles are spheres, a model that fits the size distribution of such a process is the lognormal distribution:

$$n_r(r) \approx \frac{N_T}{\sqrt{2\pi}\sigma_r r} \exp\left\{-\frac{(\ln r - \ln r_0)^2}{2\sigma_r^2}\right\} \ [\text{m}^{-3}\mu\text{m}^{-1}], \quad (5\text{-}9)$$

where r_0 is a characteristic particle radius and σ_r is a size-spread parameter, like a standard deviation. (Once again, note this is a *distribution* function.) **Figure 5-10** shows log-log plots of three typical dry particle lognormal aerosols from different environments. The urban model is actually a composite of two different sizes and concentrations of particles, as evidenced by the hump on its right side. As before, calculus allows the most probable particle radius to be calculated as

$$r_{mp} \approx \exp\{-\sigma_r^2/2\}r_0 \ [\mu\text{m}]. \quad (5\text{-}10)$$

Figure 5-10
Distribution of dry particle sizes in rural, urban, and maritime environments.

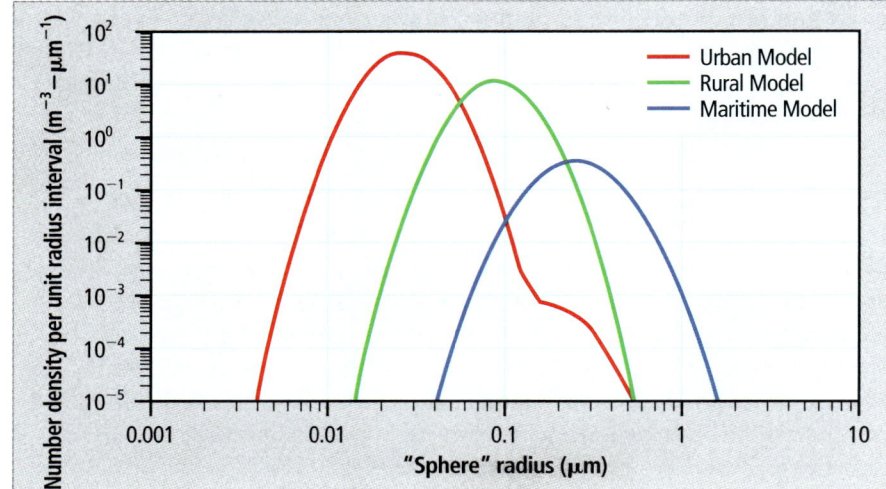

3. SPATIAL DISTRIBUTION

Both wet and dry particle spatial distributions are highly variable, horizontally and vertically. The lowest portion of the atmosphere, up to about 2 km above the surface, is typically termed the "boundary layer," characterized by air flows (winds) and surface heating. For given local meteorological conditions, particles within the boundary layer are generally well-mixed and have a constant number density independent of altitude. Because of the standard temperature lapse rate in the lower atmosphere (see the plot on the right in **Figure 5-4**), wet particles, however, will condense to form clouds when they have cooled to the dew point temperature (when the air has reached saturation, or 100% relative humidity). Above the boundary layer, the concentrations of dry particles are influenced by stratospheric winds, and they may organize into diffuse layers balanced by their sizes (gravity acting on their masses) and their absorption of thermal energy (expanding and becoming buoyant).

5.2 BEER'S LAW

With 10^{26} gas molecules per cubic meter of air and untold numbers of wet and dry aerosol particles floating around, it is easy to imagine some of them may block the information propagating from a target to a sensor. First,

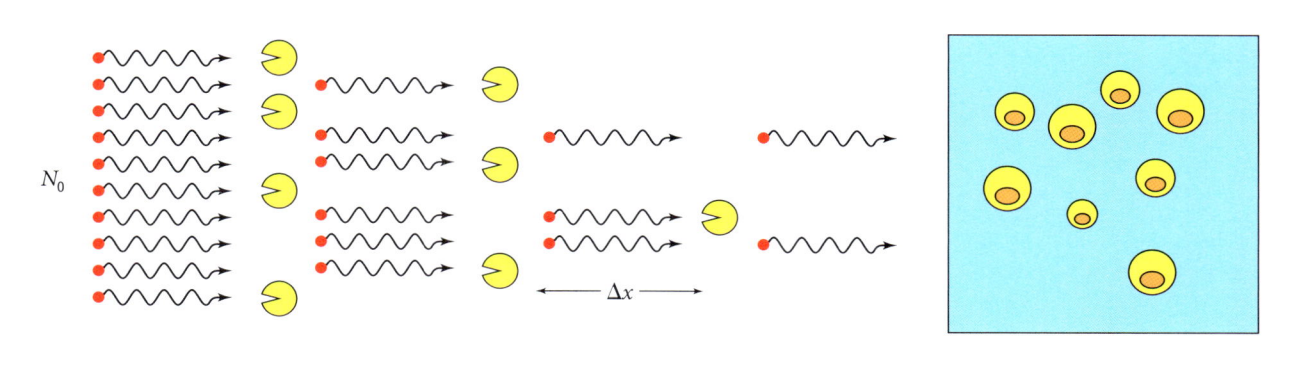

Figure 5-11
Generalized attenuation. Left: A "side-view" of photons negotiating through a cloud of attenuators (Pac-Man) that gobble up some of them. Right: A "front view" of what the photons see as they approach the cloud.

consider the general method used to estimate the amount of attenuation and then examine some specifics in the next section.

ATTENUATION, OR EXTINCTION

The problem of attenuation is easily visualized as shown in **Figure 5-11**. Photons from a target enter the atmosphere from the left, and some never make it to the sensor because of some process. Following the initial N_0 photons, the quantity decreases as they travel. The number of photons lost, ΔN, in passing through a thickness of air, Δx, can be expressed as:

$$\Delta N \approx -Nk\Delta x, \tag{5-11}$$

where N photons start out, and $N - |\Delta N|$ remain after travelling a distance of Δx. (Note, ΔN is negative because it is a *loss* in the number of photons.) The *attenuation coefficient* (or *extinction coefficient*), k,[20] is the *fractional loss per unit length* (m^{-1}) of photons and is specific to the particular attenuation process (next section). This can be seen by rearranging **Equation 5-11** to look like a differential equation:[21]

$$\frac{\Delta N}{N} \approx -k\, \Delta x \;\Rightarrow\; \frac{dN}{N} \approx -k\, dx. \tag{5-12}$$

The solution to the differential equation, assuming it starts with N_0 photons, is

$$N \approx N_0 e^{-kx}, \tag{5-13}$$

where k is also assumed to be constant along the path.[22] Also, embedded in the solution in **Equation 5-13** is the assumption that the processes responsible for the attenuation are linear. This means, as in the right side of **Figure 5-11**, attenuating molecules or particles are not so abundant as to overlap one another.

Equation 5-13 is customarily called Beer's Law, after German physicist August Beer (1825–1863). It is also associated with the names of Pierre Bouguer (1698–1758) and Johann Heinrich Lambert (1728–1777). Readers may explore the effect of varying the attenuation coefficient in Beer's Law in the interactive spreadsheet, **Appendix 5-5**, on the support website.

Depending on the application, the equation is sometimes seen as

$$N \approx N_0 e^{-n\sigma x} \tag{5-14}$$

(which will be explained and used in the atmosphere), or as

$$N \approx N_0 e^{-x/x_{OD}}. \tag{5-15}$$

[20] The attenuation coefficient is also called β instead of k.

[21] Do not worry about the mathematical formality. The point is the units of k are "per unit length." So, the equation is dimensionally correct.

[22] There is a subtle mathematical point here. Equation 5-12 expresses the change in the number of photons in going from N_0 of them (at x_0) to some fewer number of them, N, at some specified location downstream, which is called x. Hence, the equation takes $N_0 \to N$ as moving from $x_0 \to x$. Presumably, one knows where x_0 is (at the origin of photons, or the target) so the attenuation occurs over a path $x - x_0 = \Delta x$ through the medium. All subsequent instances of Equation 5-13 (and its variations) henceforth will use Δx in the exponent to highlight that it is a path length, and not just a coordinate. (Readers familiar with calculus will recognize this as the result of having performed definite integration on Equation 5-12 between limits.)

In this latter formulation, x_{OD} (= $1/k$) is called the *optical depth*, and takes on the same role as $\hat{H}$ in **Equation 5-2**. In any case, the exponential term can be interpreted as being the fraction (of information, of energy, of photons ...) that is transmitted through an attenuating linear medium with constant extinction coefficient:

$$\tau \approx \frac{N}{N_0} \approx e^{-kx}. \qquad (5\text{-}16)$$

This will be simply referred to as the transmission and shown in several forms.

Example 5-2 shows that x_{OD} has the same role in Beer's Law as $\hat{H}$ does in the hydrostatic atmosphere equation. The general rule of thumb that five *e*-folding distances (scale heights) essentially takes in all of the sensible atmosphere and similarly that an information path should not exceed $5x_{OD}$ infers the following is needed: $x_{OD} \geq \hat{H}$, or $k \leq 1/\hat{H}$. If this condition is satisfied, the atmosphere can be considered linear.[23] Remember this when attenuation processes are discussed in the next section.

EXAMPLE 5-2: BEER'S LAW

An example of how the transmission term works is supplied in **Appendix 5-5** on the support website. Using the slider, the reader can change the attenuation coefficient from 0.01 to 1, and can visually see its effect. Setting $k = 0.1$, for example, the spreadsheet shows that out of an initial $N_0 = 10^6$ photons, only 904,837 pass through the first unit of distance (from target toward the sensor, hopefully). That is, the transmission is

$$\tau = e^{-(0.1)(1)} \approx 904{,}837/1{,}000{,}000 \approx 0.905.$$

This will be the same for each increment of distance the photons travel. For instance, from $x = 3$ to $x = 4$ (path length $\Delta x = 4 - 3 = 1$), the result is

$$N_4 \approx N_3 e^{-(0.1)(1)} \approx 670{,}320/740{,}810 = 0.905 N_3.$$

Note, from this example, how the equation works in going from x_0 to $x = 4$ ($\Delta x = 4 - 0 = 4$):

$$N_4 = N_3 e^{-(0.1)(1)} = \left(N_2 e^{-(0.1)(1)}\right) e^{-(0.1)(1)}$$
$$= \left([N_1 e^{-(0.1)(1)}] e^{-(0.1)(1)}\right) e^{-(0.1)(1)}$$
$$= N_0 \left(e^{-(0.1)(1)}\right)^4 = N_0 e^{-(0.1)(4)} = (0.905)^4 N_0 \approx 0.670 N_0$$
$$= \frac{904{,}837}{1{,}000{,}000} \times \frac{818{,}730}{904{,}837} \times \frac{740{,}818}{818{,}730} \times \frac{670{,}320}{740{,}818} N_0 \approx 0.670 N_0.$$

Finally, for this example, notice if $k = 0.1$, $x_{OD} = 10$. So, for one optical depth of path length, the transmission is

$$\tau = e^{-(0.1)(10)} = 1/e \approx 0.378,$$

which is the same e-folding distance behavior as discussed with scale height. Parallel to the observation there, five optical depths reduce the transmission to approximately zero.

---

[23] Astronomers frequently encounter non-linear planetary or stellar "atmospheres" and huge attenuating, nebulous volumes of gases, ions, and space dust. The rate of attenuation through them is called the "curve of growth," and reveals information about their compositions and sizes.

APPLICATIONS TO REMOTE SENSING

As long as the information path from target to sensor passes through the atmosphere, some form of Beer's Law will always be applied. Thus, **Equations 4-32 and 4-39** become:

$$\mathcal{E}_\lambda \approx \frac{I_\lambda \cos\theta_R}{R^2}\tau_{ATM} \text{ and } \mathcal{E}_{FOV} = L\Omega_{FOV}\tau_{ATM} \qquad (5\text{-}17)$$

for point and extended sources, respectively.

1. HORIZONTAL VIEWING: METEOROLOGICAL RANGE

For horizontal paths,[24] sight distance is limited by atmospheric conditions. In the visible and infrared, this is most notably due to condensed water vapor or fog. **Table 5-3** shows, for a range of typical conditions listed in the first column, the distance at which a large black object in daylight or a diffuse bright light at night can be barely discerned, which is often called the meteorological range (MR). The criterion is that mathematically only 2% of the light reflected or emitted from the object can be detected. The meteorological range associated with the conditions is given in the second column.[25]

Condition	MR (km)	k (km^{-1})	x_{OD} (km)	$5x_{OD}$ (km)
Dense fog	< 0.1	> 39	< 0.026	< 0.13
Moderate fog	0.1–0.5	39–7.8	0.026–0.13	0.13–0.64
Light fog	0.5–1.0	7.8–3.9	0.13–0.26	0.64–1.3
Thin fog	1.0–2.0	3.9–2.0	0.26–0.51	1.3–2.6
Haze	2.0–4.0	2.0–0.98	0.51–1.0	2.6–5.1
Light haze	4.0–10	0.98–0.39	1.0–2.6	5.1–13
Clear	10–20	0.39–0.20	2.6–5.1	13–26
Very clear	20–50	0.20–0.078	5.1–13	26–64
"Standard"	23*	0.17	5.9	29

* This may be the distance from crow's nest to horizon on a calm sea.

Table 5-3
MR attenuation coefficient, and optical depth for various low visibility atmospheric conditions. Five times the optical depth is about the maximum distance at which targets can be discerned.

In the third column of **Table 5-3**, using Beer's Law as

$$\tau_{ATM} \approx 0.02 \approx e^{-k\Delta x_{MR}}, \qquad (5\text{-}18)$$

the ranges for the extinction coefficient, k, that correspond to the various visibility conditions are calculated. The fourth column shows the e-folding optical depth and five times that, which is the distance beyond where presumably no information could be received under the various conditions. Thus, the horizontal transmission of information is indeed limited; in battlespace, it is expected that terrain and the commotion of activity will restrict it even more.

2. SLANT VIEWING FROM AIR OR SPACE

Under some circumstances and assumptions, it is straight forward to calculate Beer's Law transmission, τ_0, along a vertical path through the atmosphere,

$$\tau_0 \approx e^{-k\Delta z} \approx e^{-k(z_2 - z_1)} \qquad (5\text{-}19)$$

for the path between altitudes z_1 (target) and z_2 (sensor) along which k is constant. Often using $z_1 = 0$ and $z_2 > 5\hat{H}$ may further simplify the calculation of τ_0.

---

[24] The Earth's curvature plays a role here. Again, "How flat is flat?" in that a truly straight line of sight will vary in altitude above the Earth's surface. Except for the note about visibility on a calm sea at the bottom of **Table 5-3**, ignore the shape of the Earth for the distances shown in the Table (< 1% R_E).

[25] It is not known exactly why 23 km is considered to be "standard" horizontal visibility, but it is thought to be nautical in nature.

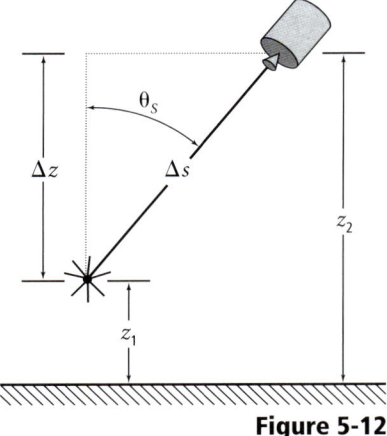

Figure 5-12
Slant path viewing.

Viewing from a position directly over a target is highly unusual, particularly in a surveillance role when the locations of targets are initially unknown. Hence, the situation is more likely to be as sketched in **Figure 5-12**. The information path is slanted at a target zenith angle θ_S with respect to the vertical. In this instance, the slant path distance, along which attenuation will occur, bears the relationship

$$\Delta s \approx \Delta z \sec \theta_S \; [\text{m}] \tag{5-20}$$

to the vertical path. Transmission on this slanted path is then

$$\tau(\theta_S) \approx e^{-k\Delta s} \approx e^{-k\Delta z \sec \theta_S} \approx (\tau_0)^{\sec \theta_S}. \tag{5-21}$$

The exponent $\sec\theta_s \approx 1/\cos\theta_s$ is known as the equivalent number of atmospheres light must pass through, with the vertical path being one atmosphere. This is exaggerated in the inset in **Figure 5-13** where one atmosphere is considered to be about five scale heights ($5\hat{H} \approx 40$ km or so). Since $5\hat{H} \ll R_E$, the flat Earth assumption apparently applies to many remote sensing situations. **Figure 5-13** shows a comparison between the flat Earth, secant-of-the-target-zenith-angle approximation and a more exact calculation. The plot shows that less than a 5% error will be experienced for viewing angles up to almost 70°. However, it is quite possible to reach $\Delta s \approx 5x_{OD}$ before the viewing angle becomes too oblique.

Figure 5-13
Slant path versus zenith angle.

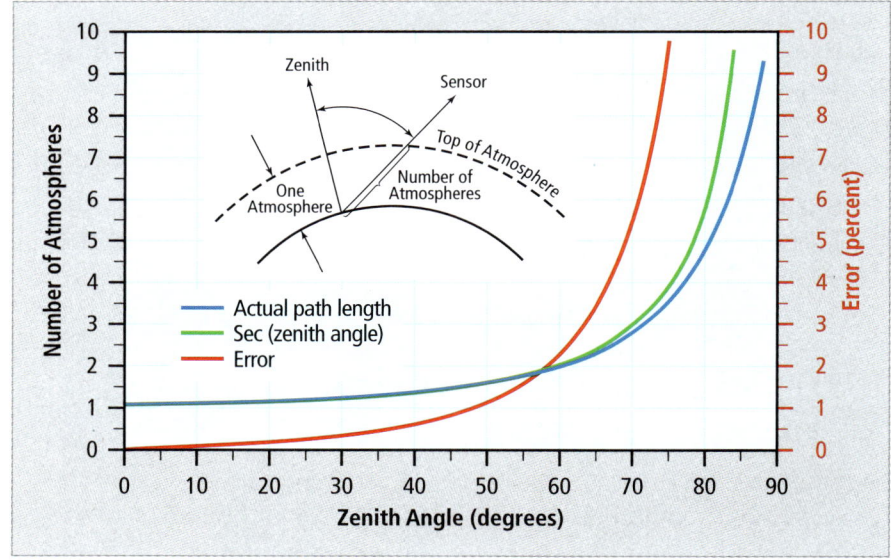

Another situation that could possibly occur when tracking high altitude targets is shown in **Figure 5-14**. The target is still within the atmosphere ($z_1 < 5\hat{H}$), and the sensor sees it above the limb of the earth. Attenuation on the so-called "long path" initially comes from the line of sight, getting closer to the Earth down to the tangent point, N, and then going farther away. The atmospheric transmission function in this case is the product of those two pieces of the path. Such collections should be avoided until the target can be seen above the top of the atmosphere. While the target is within the atmosphere, viewing at such an extreme angle may also have some refractive error.

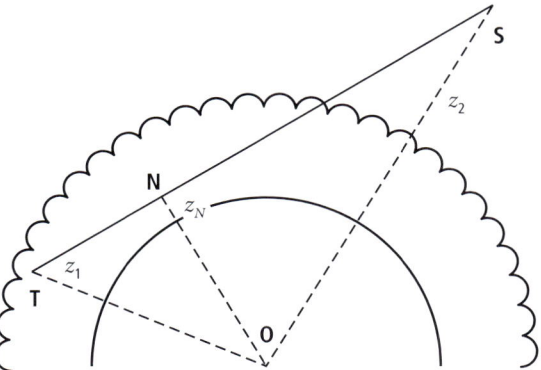

Figure 5-14
Long path slant viewing.

3. REMOTE SENSING IN REVERSE

The simplicity of Beer's Law sometimes provides information about the atmosphere. Everything the atmosphere does to attenuate radiation, some of which will be discussed in the next section, is embodied in the extinction coefficient, k. It can easily be solved for:

$$k \approx \frac{-\ln \tau_{ATM}}{\Delta s} \;\; [\text{m}^{-1}], \qquad (5\text{-}22)$$

where a generic path length, Δs, is used. Calculating k depends on knowledge of Δs, of course, and on $\tau_{ATM} \approx \frac{\Phi_{RECEIVED}}{\Phi_{SENT}}$. That is, the characteristics of the source, Φ_{SENT}, must be known, but $\Phi_{RECEIVED}$ is the result of the measurement. However, note no spatial information can be gained about atmospheric conditions, other than the attenuation occurs *somewhere* along the path.

When a target or source is well-characterized such as a forest fire or explosion, the measurement of its apparent at-sensor intensity could suggest the amount of particulate concentrate present in the atmosphere. Measurements at multiple wavelengths could conceivably assist in chemical analysis of concentrations of attenuating molecules and particles.

Scientists in many other disciplines apply this technique, knowingly or unknowingly. For example, medical doctors specifically trained as radiologists interpret X-rays (**Figure 5-15**) and other diagnostic imagery where the brightness of the source (an X-ray tube) is compared to its exposure on a film[26] to reveal the extent of its absorption in living organisms. Knowing the expected thickness (Δs) of bones and organs, the radiologist interprets the observed attenuation as healthy tissues or tumors. As another example, astronomers point their telescopes at "standard candles" in the sky, stars of well-known spectral classes and temperatures, and at reasonably well-estimated distances. The amount of light received reveals the amount of gases or dust that will fill the intervening space.

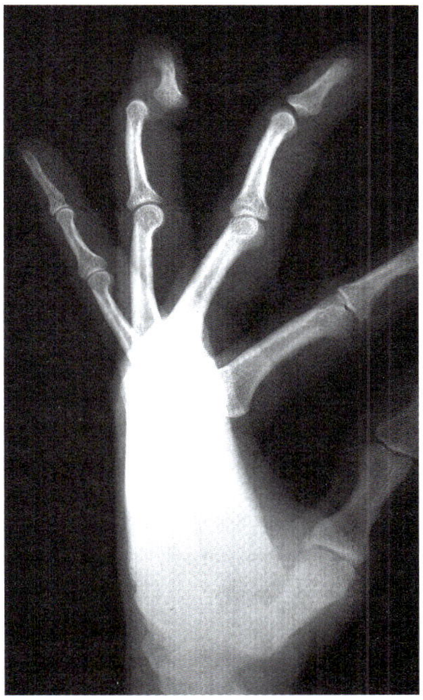

5.3 PROCESSES

Two classes of processes take place in the atmosphere affecting the transfer of information from target to sensor: attenuation processes and image degradation processes. (See **Figure 5-16**.) Absorption and scattering are the first class, which reduce the amount of information passed from target to sensor, and are explained by Beer's Law as described in the last section. These processes impact any collection where all or any part of

Figure 5-15
An application of Beer's Law. The exposure of an x-ray depends on the density and composition of tissues, bones, and organs and their thickness. (Note, the broken ring finger.)

[26] Modern medical diagnostics have advanced to solid-state detectors for X-rays, MRIs, CAT scans, etc.

the optical path from the target to sensor passes through the atmosphere. Scintillation, atmospheric emission, and in-scattering are in the second class. Scintillation potentially distorts the image of point sources, while the other two reduce the contrast of extended sources. (Contrast is defined below.)

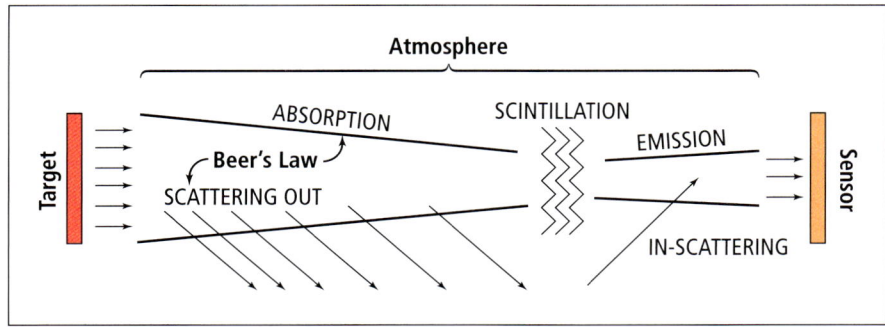

Figure 5-16
Atmospheric attenuation and contrast reduction processes.

ATTENUATION PROCESSES

In this section, Beer's Law, **Equation 5-16**, will be applied to the absorption and scattering processes. The science behind the mathematics is interpretation of the extinction coefficient, k, in terms of physical parameters associated with the processes.

ABSORPTION

Recall the goal in advanced technical intelligence is to use remote sensors to collect information about targets. The medium of choice is electromagnetic waves, or photons, because they propagate through the vacuum of space. Now, those photons spending part (or all) of their trip in the atmosphere are of concern. Further, recall molecules in the atmosphere have quantized energy levels (**Chapter 2**). Because of their energy structures, quantum leaps, and interactions with the electromagnetic fields of photons are possible. Review **Figure 2-12**.

1. SCIENCE OF THE ABSORPTION COEFFICIENT

The basic physics principle of concern here is the right side of **Figure 2-12**: the conversion of a photon's energy, $E \approx hc/\lambda$, into the excited state of a molecule. This amounts to the disappearance of a photon with subsequent loss of information.[27] What are the conditions when this happens?

First, it is necessary for molecules to be present. Since it stands to reason that the more molecules present, the more absorption will occur. Absorption must depend on density, molecules per unit volume, n. The spatial distribution could be according to the hydrostatic distribution, **Equation 5-2**, or any other distribution as long as they are on the photons' path. This is the same as the argument for developing Beer's Law, **Figure 5-11**.

Next, the absorbing molecule must possess a pair of allowed energy states with a difference equal to the energy of the photon. The lower energy state must be populated, awaiting the arrival of the photon. And, the molecule must have an "electrical handle" such as a dipole moment. (Recall the concept of a dipole moment was illustrated in **Figure 2-18**.) This last requirement eliminates 99% of the Earth's atmosphere as photon absorbers, because it is composed of symmetric diatomic molecules, nitrogen, and oxygen.

All the conditions in the last paragraph are consolidated in a number called the cross-section for absorption, σ_{ABS}. It is given in units of area (like m^2), but is not necessarily a real area. A cross-section, in this sense,

[27] Readers may ask, "What about the left side of **Figure 2-12**? Are absorbed photons re-emitted, so the information is recovered?" The answer is generally "No." In the first place, a molecule may lose the photon's energy through some other process, like a collision or another quantum leap to some other level. Second, a re-emitted photon will be delayed in time, so it is not the same information. Third, there is a very slim chance a re-emitted photon would be directed exactly along the previous path when there are many other directions to choose. There may be other reasons, but that is the general idea.

can be thought of as a measure of the *probability* that all the conditions were met for absorption to occur. Quantum mechanical calculation of absorption cross-sections is beyond the scope of this text, as it involves things like correlating the overlap of energy state wave functions, like those sketched in **Figure 2-20**, and other considerations.[28]

Together, molecular number densities and absorption cross-sections give a factor describing the rate of photon absorption per unit distance passing through a cloud of molecules:

$$k_{ABS} \approx n\sigma_{ABS} \quad [\text{m}^{-1}]. \tag{5-23}$$

Yes, this is the attenuation coefficient for absorption, which renders Beer's Law as[29]

$$\tau_{ABS} \approx e^{-n\sigma_{ABS}\Delta s}. \tag{5-24}$$

2. COMPUTING ABSORPTION

Computing **Equation 5-24** is straightforward, given n, σ_{ABS}, and Δs. The path length from target to sensor, Δs, is the same R discussed in **Chapter 4**. But the density of molecules, n, can vary in almost any manner spatially along the information path. Although the result does not depend on *how* molecules are distributed along R, the proper treatment to take them into account is to integrate over the path:

$$\tau_{ABS} \approx \exp\left\{-\int_R n(s)\sigma_{ABS}\,ds\right\}. \tag{5-25}$$

For example, an isothermal vertical distribution was considered in **Equation 5-2**. So, if the variation of molecular density is only in the vertical,

$$\tau_{ABS}\left[\substack{\text{vertical}\\ \text{path}}\right] \approx \exp\left\{-\int_{z_1}^{z_2} n_0 e^{-z/\hat{H}} \sigma_{ABS}\,dz\right\} \approx \exp\left\{-n_0\sigma_{ABS}\hat{H}\left(e^{-z_1/\hat{H}} - e^{-z_2/\hat{H}}\right)\right\}, \tag{5-26}$$

where $R = z_2 - z_1$ as shown in **Figure 5-17**. If the sensor is above five scale heights in altitude, effectively take $z_2 \to \infty$, and **Equation 5-26** becomes

$$\tau_{ABS} \approx \exp\left\{-n_0\sigma_{ABS}\hat{H}e^{-z_1/\hat{H}}\right\}, \tag{5-27}$$

where z_1 is the target's altitude. If that should happen to be on the ground ($z \approx 0$), then the transmission to space along a vertical path is simply

$$\tau_{ABS} \approx e^{-n_0\sigma_{ABS}\hat{H}}. \tag{5-28}$$

Any correction for slant path viewing in either **Equations 5-26**, **5-27**, or **5-28** is made by including the secant of the target zenith angle in the calculation: **Equation 5-21**.

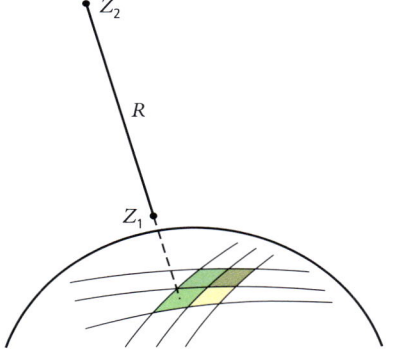

Figure 5-17
Vertical path between two altitudes.

[28] Readers interested in further researching this topic will find molecular cross-sections are connected to what is called oscillator strength and to transition rates known as the Einstein coefficients. (Yes, *that* Einstein.)

[29] A comment on computing with Beer's Law in this form is needed. The exponent, $n\sigma_{ABS}\Delta s$, must be dimensionless. If n is in m^{-3}, then σ_{ABS} should be in m^2 and Δs in m.

The cross-sections, σ_{ABS}, for 39 atmospheric molecules were compiled in the HITRAN 2008 database for 2,713,968 of their possible quantum leap absorptions. This formidable task began in the 1960s by the Air Force Cambridge Research Laboratories and is now under the purview of the Atomic and Molecular Physics Division of the Harvard-Smithsonian Center for Astrophysics.[30,31]

Obviously, calculating **Equation 5-25** (or its variants) wavelength-by-wavelength would be extremely tedious by hand. Fortunately, there is a computer program, that uses the HITRAN database, designed to model transmission for 0.2 < λ < 200 μm called MODTRAN.[32] **Figure 5-18** is a plot of MODTRAN output for four particular molecules and for total transmission through a standard atmosphere from the Earth's surface to space along a vertical path (**Equation 5-28**). The plots for carbon dioxide and water vapor clearly show absorption by their vibrotational energy modes. Note, in particular, the total absorption of light by water vapor in the 5-8 μm region, which explains the missing infrared band discussed in **Chapter 2**.

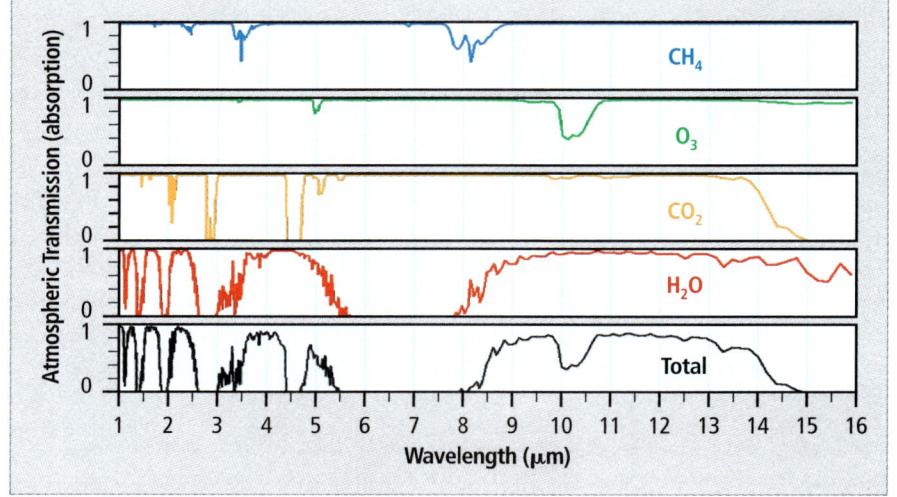

Figure 5-18
Vertical transmission to space calculated by MODTRAN 4.

[30] For an in-depth description of HITRAN see Reference [2].

[31] HITRAN 2012 is available now. [3]

[32] The most recent release of MODTRAN (**MOD**erate resolution atmospheric **TRAN**smission) is version 5. Some aspects of MODTRAN are patented by Spectral Sciences, Inc. and the US Air Force, who have shared development responsibility since 1987. The acronym MODTRAN was registered as a trademark of the US Government, represented by the Air Force, in 2008. All MODTRAN code development and maintenance is currently performed by Spectral Sciences, while the Air Force handles code validation and verification. Software sublicenses are issued by Spectral Sciences, while single-user licenses are administered through Spectral Sciences' distributor, Ontar Corporation. Third parties, including Ontar, developed graphical user interfaces to MODTRAN to facilitate user interaction and ease of use. [4]

[33] For particular collection objectives, plot the atmospheric transmission to include local variations to the standard atmospheric profile, any and all wet and dry particles, and the collection geometry (target zenith angle, if known, for application of **Equation 5-21**). MODTRAN allows all these changes and more.

The total transmission, bottom plot in **Figure 5-18**, is the product of the transmissions through atmospheric concentrations of all 39 molecules in the HITRAN database. If an atmosphere can be considered "linear," meaning photons can only interact with one type of molecule along their information path, the situation is as shown in **Figure 5-19**. Mathematically, multiplication of transmissions is equivalent to adding the molecules' extinction coefficients:

$$\tau_{ATM} = \tau_A \tau_B \tau_C = \prod_i \tau_i = e^{-n_A \sigma_A \Delta s} e^{-n_B \sigma_B \Delta s} e^{-n_C \sigma_C \Delta s} \quad (5\text{-}29)$$
$$= e^{-(n_A \sigma_A + n_B \sigma_B + n_C \sigma_C)\Delta s} = e^{-(k_A + k_B + k_C)\Delta s} = e^{-\sum_i k_i \Delta s}.$$

The appearance of atmospheric transmission plots[33] like **Figure 5-18** is *one of the most important guiding principles in conducting advanced technical intelligence collections*. Depending on wavelength, it is clear the amount of information propagated through the atmosphere may be severely limited. For surveillance or reconnaissance of low altitude targets, sensors need to be designed to see through atmospheric "windows" such as 1.5–1.8 μm (NIR), 2.0–2.5 μm (SWIR), 3–5 μm (MWIR), or 8–13 μm (LWIR). For high altitude targets, on the other hand, there is good reason to select a seemingly opaque band such as 2.5–2.8 μm or 4.2–4.5 μm.

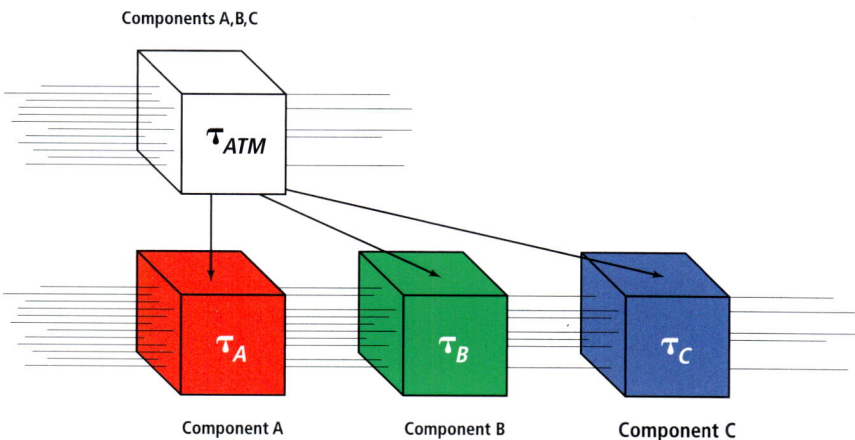

Figure 5-19
Transmission through a multi-component atmosphere.

These bands naturally suppress radiation from the background while allowing at-altitude targets to be seen. For example, **Figure 5-20** plots transmission along a vertical path to space for the 2.53–2.86 μm water absorption band as a function of target altitude. Atmospheric water vapor has a significant effect on transmission for paths starting below 10 km altitude.

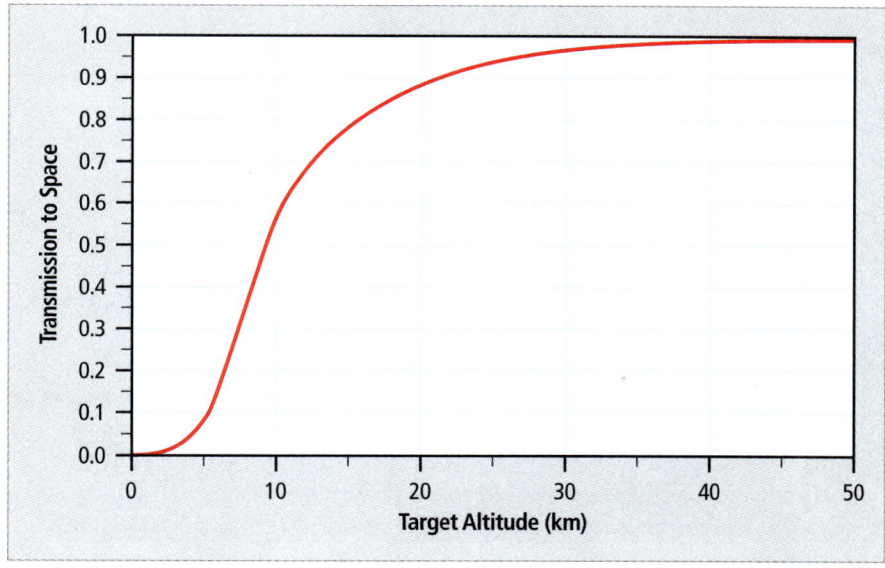

Figure 5-20
Transmission data calculated with MODTRAN for a standard atmosphere in the water absorption band, 2.53–2.86 μm.

SCATTERING

The similarities of scattering to absorption are: 1) both processes are described by Beer's Law; and 2) photons propagating from target to sensor are lost from the information path. Of course, the difference is absorption completely removes photons by quantum interactions with molecules, whereas scattering simply redirects them through "collisions" with particles. The application of Beer's Law is the same in many respects as for absorption. It depends on 1) the number of scattering particles, represented by their number density, n per unit volume; 2) the length and direction of the path, given by Δs and θ_s; and 3) the wavelengths of the photons, manifested in the scattering cross-section, σ_{SCAT}.

Rather than depending on the internal quantum nature of molecules, the wavelength dependence of scattering is determined by particles' physical characteristics: composition, shape, and size. For this discussion, assume all particles suspended in the atmosphere are non-conductive dielectric materials with the specifications discussed above. To summarize, take any given type of particle to be spherical on the average and of a single characteristic size. Beer's Law for scattering then becomes

$$\tau_{SCAT} \approx e^{-n\sigma_{SCAT}\Delta s}, \qquad (5\text{-}30)$$

where the scattering cross-section needs to be explored.

Like the absorption cross-section, the scattering cross-section is not necessarily a real area, but an effective zone of interaction. **Figure 5-21**, for instance, suggests a "target" particle presents a larger-than-life cross-section to a "bullet" particle. The center of the bullet only has to pass within the area demarcated by the sum of the two particles' radii for a collision-like interaction to occur. (A counter-example is **Figure 5-22** where trees apparently have infinite cross-sections.) **Appendix 5-6** on the support website shows the calculation for "hard sphere" scattering cross-section.

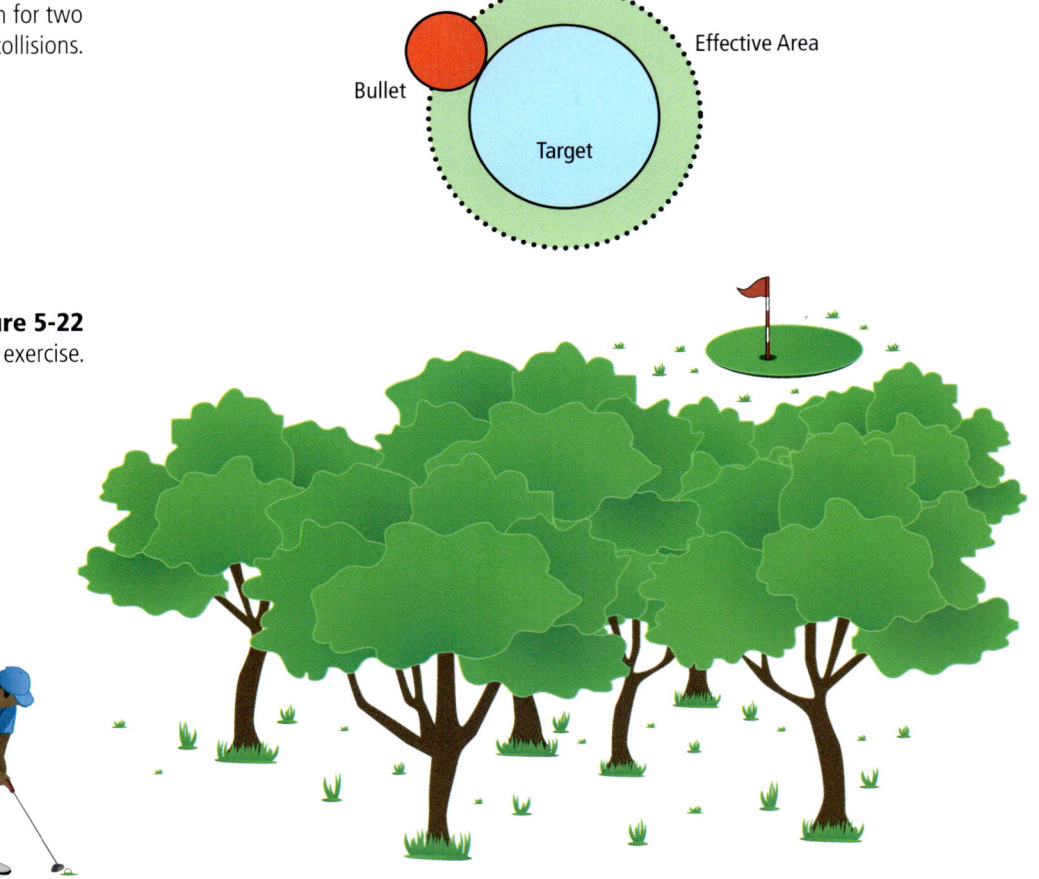

Figure 5-21
Effective cross-section for two particle collisions.

Figure 5-22
A scattering exercise.

Since photons are electromagnetic quanta and particles are ultimately made of electrically charged sub-atomic particles, the interaction is exceedingly complex. Three different scattering behaviors are studied and depend on the relative sizes of particles compared to photons' wavelengths:

1. Rayleigh scattering, for wavelengths long compared to the circumferences of particles, $\lambda > 2\pi r_0$ (where r_0 = particle radius), can be imagined like bowling balls running into marbles. Rayleigh scattering becomes weaker with increasing wavelength and decreasing characteristic radius. Mathematically, it is λ^{-4} and is the dominant mechanism for scattering visible light from air molecules.

2. Mie scattering, for wavelengths about the same as the circumferences of particles, $\lambda \approx 2\pi r_0$, is a resonance phenomenon. It can be envisioned as a photon wrapping its wavelength around a particle and constructively or destructively interfering with itself when it overlaps on the backside.

3. Optical, or non-selective scattering, for wavelengths short compared to the circumferences of particles, $\lambda < 2\pi r_0$, is like marbles running into bowling balls and is effectively the same for all interactions when the wavelength-size criterion is met. This is the dominant process for visible photons scattering within clouds or fog (water droplets).

"Normalized" cross-sections for the three scattering regimes are plotted in **Figure 5-23**. **Example 5-3** shows how to interpret the chart. Although it is mentioned in the example, the units of cross-section must be appropriate for calculation in Beer's Law (**Footnote 29**).

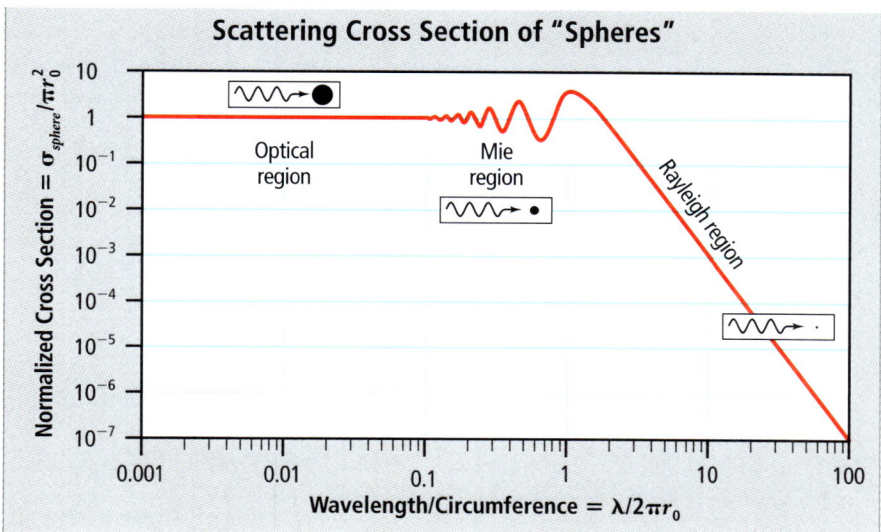

Figure 5-23
Effective scattering cross-section of spheres. (Note, to readers familiar with RF phenomenology, this chart is usually plotted with frequency on the horizontal axis for radar scattering from clouds, swarms of insects, etc. Thus, it is reversed left-and-right.)

The scattering just introduced, Rayleigh, Mie, and optical, are considered to be *elastic* scattering. That is, a scattered photon has approximately the same energy after as before its scatter, although it will propagate in a new direction. For completeness, there is an extremely rare form of *inelastic* scattering, called Raman scattering, that is a hybrid of quantum absorption-emission with scattering. Rare or not, the result of this interaction is the same in advanced technical intelligence collections as any other: loss of information. **Figure 5-24** shows a diagram of the quantum aspect of Raman scattering. **Figure 5-25** pictures its discoverer as well as Lord Rayleigh and Gustav Mie.

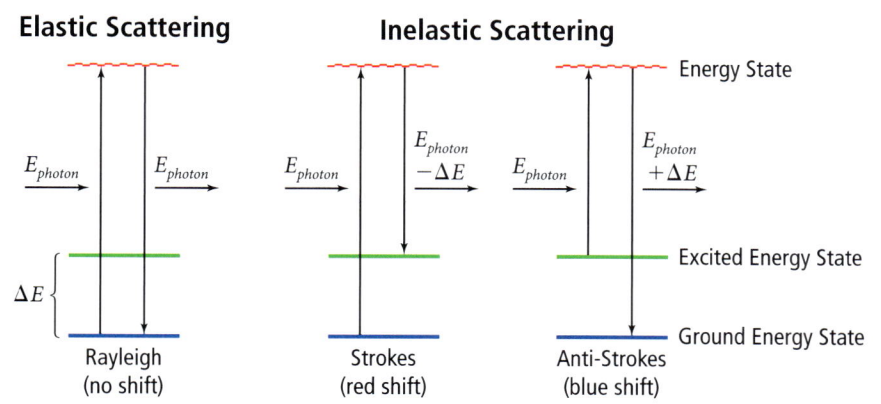

Figure 5-24
Elastic (normal, Rayleigh) scattering and inelastic (rare, Raman) scattering.

EXAMPLE 5-3: ESTIMATING SCATTERING CROSS-SECTION

What is the effective scattering cross-section for 5.00 μm light encountering a cloud of (spherical) dielectric particles with a characteristic size ("radius") of 0.0796 μm?

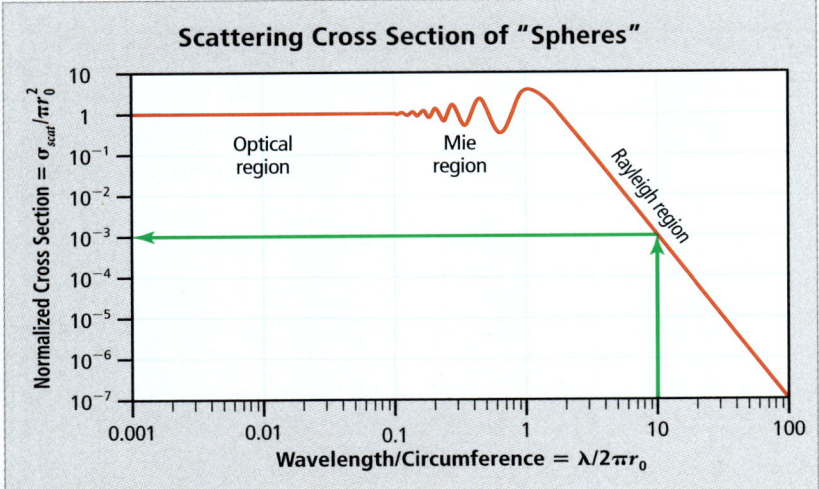

First, calculate the wavelength to circumference ratio

$$\frac{\lambda}{2\pi r_0} \approx \frac{5.00\ \mu m}{(2\pi)(0.0796\ \mu m)} \approx 10.$$

Second, enter the chart at 10 on the x-axis, reflect off the scattering cross-section curve, and read across to $\approx 10^{-3}$ on the y-axis. This is the value of the "normalized" cross-section, $\frac{\sigma_{SCAT}}{\pi r_0^2}$.

Third, calculate the effective scattering cross-section

$$\sigma_{SCAT} \approx 10^{-3} \times \pi r_0^2 \approx 10^{-3} \times \pi(0.0796\ \mu m)^2$$
$$\approx 2 \times 10^{-5}\ \mu m^2 \approx 2 \times 10^{-17}\ m^2.$$

Note, the units must be appropriate for use in Beer's Law.

Figure 5-25
Physicists instrumental in developing the scattering theory. (Mie photo courtesy of http://en.wikipedia.org/wiki/File:GustavMie.gif; Creative Commons Attribution-Share Alike 3.0 unported: ThomasHB4.)

John William Strutt (Lord Rayleigh) 1842–1919

Gustav Mie 1868–1957

Chandresekhara Venkata Raman 1888–1970

As just mentioned, the unfortunate fact of scattering is photons are lost from the information path. *Where* photons are scattered is usually not a concern, just that they are scattered. However, in at least one GEOINT application, it is important where photons are scattered. In monostatic, active sensing systems where a transmitter (irradiator) and sensor are co-located as a radio frequency (RF) radar or laser radar (LIDAR), it is important to see that photons are scattered (or reflected) directly back. A generalized treatment of scattering treats both the amount of scattering and its direction, called the "phase function," in a "differential scattering cross-section," $\frac{d\sigma}{d\Omega}$. For Rayleigh scattering, this is (**Figure 5-26**):

$$\left.\frac{d\sigma}{d\Omega}\right|_{RAYLEIGH} \approx \frac{3\sigma_0}{16\pi}(1 + \cos^2\theta) \ [m^2 sr^{-1}]. \quad (5\text{-}31)$$

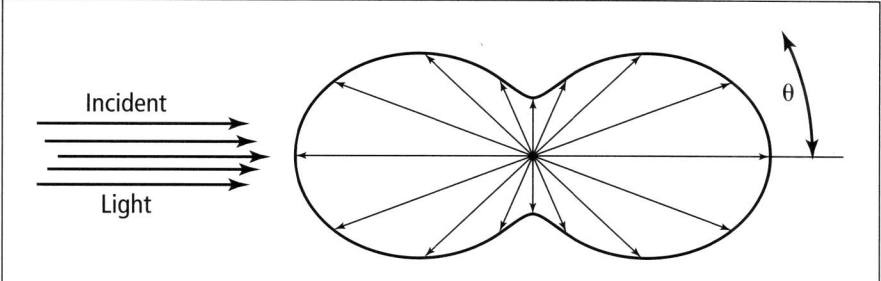

Figure 5-26
Rayleigh scattering phase function.

The back-scattering cross-section for Rayleigh scattering is

$$\sigma_{BACK\text{-}SCATTER} \sim \left.\frac{d\sigma}{d\Omega}\right|_{RAYLEIGH}(\theta = \pi) \approx \frac{3\sigma_0}{8\pi} \ [m^2 sr^{-1}]. \quad (5\text{-}32)$$

The transmission plot in **Example 5-4**, calculated with MODTRAN, assumed a hydrostatic atmosphere with Rayleigh scattering from air molecules as the dominant attenuation mechanism at visible wavelengths. Real atmospheres, of course, may also have significant numbers of aerosol particles. In fact, standard models of atmospheric particle distributions may be added to transmission codes, such as MODTRAN, as well as user-defined distributions. The left plot in **Figure 5-27** shows some of the standard models for northern mid-latitudes. The plot indicates there is an ever-present background of particles aloft, known as the stratospheric background model, that has some seasonal variation. If information warrants, aerosols of volcanic origin can be added as shown in the figure.

EXAMPLE 5-4: WHY IS THE SKY BLUE?

Molecules are Rayleigh particles. From **Figure 5-8**, if $r_0 \approx 0.0063$ μm is chosen as a characteristic size, then for "blue" and "red" photons,

$$\frac{\lambda_{BLUE}}{2\pi r_0} \approx \frac{0.4 \ \mu m}{(2\pi)(0.0063 \ \mu m)} \approx 10.1$$

and

$$\frac{\lambda_{RED}}{2\pi r_0} \approx \frac{0.7 \ \mu m}{(2\pi)(0.0063 \ \mu m)} \approx 17.7.$$

By entering the scattering cross-section chart, **Figure 5-28**, with these arguments, values of 10^{-3} and 10^{-4} are found for blue and red,

Continued on next page

respectively. Thus, the scattering cross-section for blue photons is ten times larger than for red ones. The transmission ratio is therefore

$$\frac{\tau_{BLUE}}{\tau_{RED}} \approx \frac{e^{-n\sigma_{BLUE}\Delta s}}{e^{-n\sigma_{RED}\Delta s}} \approx \frac{e^{-n10\sigma_{RED}\Delta s}}{e^{-n\sigma_{RED}\Delta s}} \approx (\tau_{RED})^9.$$

From a MODTRAN calculation for vertical transmission in the visible band through a standard atmosphere, shown in the following figure, find $\tau_{RED} \approx 0.96$ and calculate

$$\frac{\tau_{BLUE}}{\tau_{RED}} \approx (0.96)^9 \approx 0.69.$$

This is confirmed by the chart where $\tau_{BLUE} \approx 0.66$.

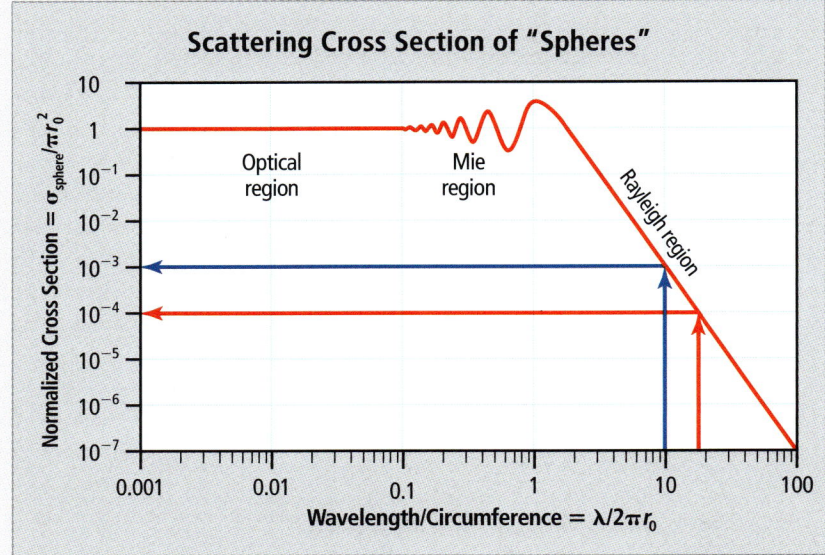

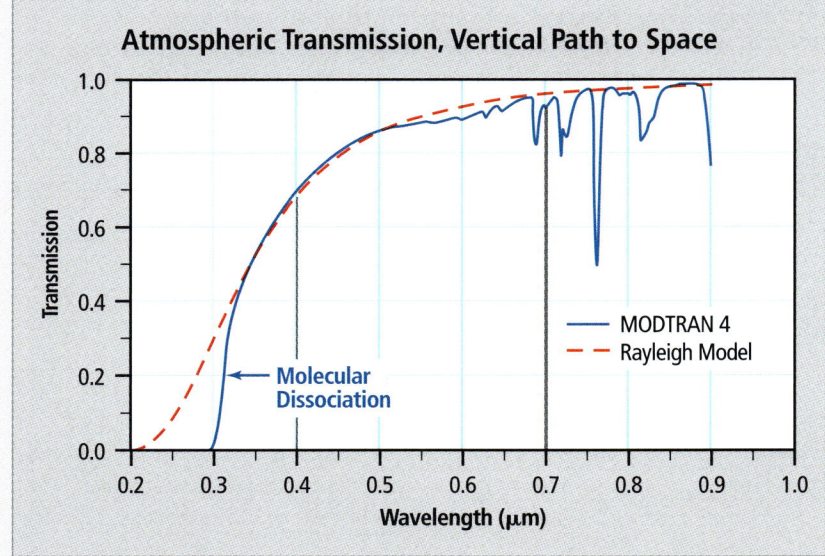

Therefore, the calculations suggest that: 1) looking in any direction in a sunlit sky, it is more likely to see blue photons Rayleigh scattered than red; and 2) looking toward the sun, it is more likely to see red photons *not* scattered than blue ones. Experience confirms this last remark when the sun is distinctly orange-red in appearance when rising and setting.

Continued on next page

The above figure also affirms that molecular scattering is the dominant source of attenuation in the visible spectrum. The red dashed line plots pure Rayleigh scattering with its theoretical λ^{-4} dependence. Note, however, that another photon loss mechanism takes over in the ultraviolet. For wavelengths shorter than ~0.3 μm, photons have sufficient energy to be absorbed by and dissociate molecular bonds, principally oxygen in the upper atmosphere. This is the source of oxygen atoms to combine with O_2 to form ozone, O_3. Ozone then further absorbs UV photons to help protect humans from sunburns. However, it has been shown to be heavily attacked by other trace gases, primarily long lasting chlorofluorocarbons.

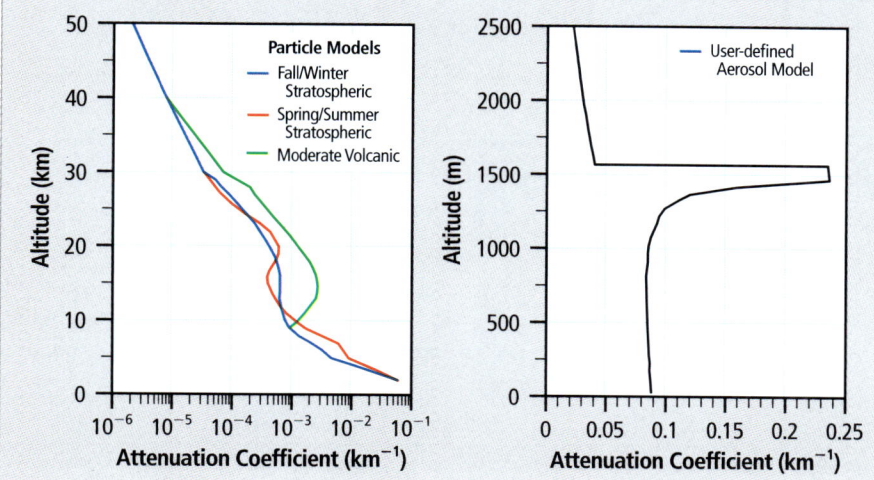

Figure 5-27
Standard models for atmospheric aerosols (left) and a particular user-defined particle concentration model in the boundary layer (right). The attenuation coefficients are appropriate for calculating transmission of 0.55 μm light through the atmosphere.

The plot shows attenuation coefficient, k, plotted as a function of altitude. Assuming background or volcanic particles are roughly of uniform size, their cross-sections are approximately constant as a function of altitude. Since $k \approx n\sigma$, particle number density, n, is directly proportional to the attenuation coefficient. This is probably not strictly true since larger particles may be expected to preferentially settle to lower altitudes.

On the right side of **Figure 5-27**, a plot shows a particular user-defined model for particles in the lowest boundary layer of the atmosphere. This type of model can realistically vary the relative humidity in the boundary layer and allow a user-defined aerosol definition at the surface to vary in size and extinction with altitude. The particular model shown here has a significant extinction maximum just below 1500 m altitude, and was created by the Air Force Institute of Technology's *Laser Environmental Effects Definition and Reference* (LEEDR) software program that can calculate electromagnetic energy propagation through the atmosphere. Again, the attenuation coefficient on the horizontal axis may be taken to be proportional to the aerosol concentration or number density.

IMAGE DEGRADATION I: POINT SOURCES

Although the atmosphere is in continuous motion, it is usually ignored in advanced technical intelligence collection. It is justified to ignore atmospheric changes because the passage of photons through it, at the speed of light, is faster than any change can occur. However, as shown when sensor temporal sampling is discussed, information is sometimes collected from targets during intervals long enough for changes to have an effect.

Not only is the atmosphere in motion, its motion is turbulent. A typical treatment of turbulent air is to break it into irregular "turbules," packets or parcels of air that jumble and smoosh about one another in a semi-organized flow. (Think of beans or corn pouring out of a bag.) Turbules have temperatures and pressures (or densities) that do not vary much from their neighbors, and range from a few millimeters to approximately ten centimeters in size. **Figure 5-28** suggests what turbules might be like.

Figure 5-28
The turbulent atmosphere.

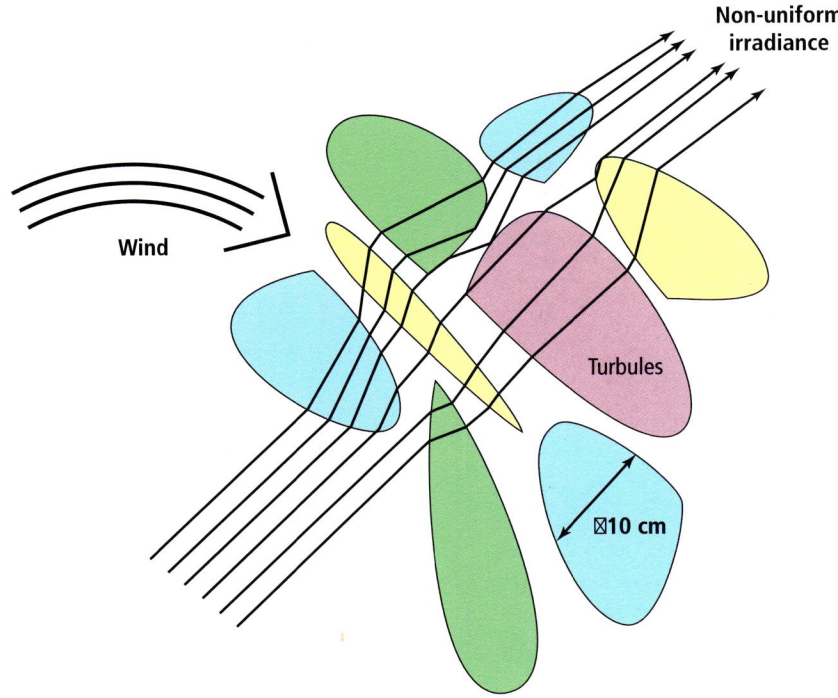

For optical purposes, each turbule with a slightly different density also has a slightly different index of refraction. Therefore, light passing from one to the next slightly refracts (Snell's Law). Admittedly, one refraction barely makes a difference, but upon propagating through 40 km ≈ 10^6 turbules, it could make an impact. The gross effect is similar to that sketched in **Figure 5-28**, or in radiometric terms, a point source target's intensity becomes a non-uniform irradiance at a sensor's aperture, and it is continuously changing. This disturbance is called *scintillation*, or "twinkling."

There are two features of scintillation that limit its concern in advanced technical information gathering: spatial and temporal. First, spatially, if the cone of light (solid angle) from target to sensor is not smaller (in cross-section) than several turbules, scintillation will be averaged out. This is commonly called "aperture averaging," and is illustrated in **Figure 5-29** where the cross-section of the receiving cone, Ω_{RCVR} (**Figure 4-7**), within the atmosphere is typically larger than many turbules.[34]

Secondly, the gross motion of turbules with the wind will carry them through the Field of View (FOV). A typical wind speed might be between a gentle surface breeze (10 km/hr) and a stratospheric jet stream (200 km/hr) or approximately 50 km/hr. With typical sensor "shutter speeds" (integration times) of 0.1–1.0 s to collect sufficient energy, turbules will be swept between 15–150 cm across the FOV, which is larger than an individual turbule. As the turbules move, the

---

[34] Note, **Figure 5-28** illustrates a target larger than a sensor's aperture. This is generally true; point targets are not really points. They only appear as points because of their great distance away, *R*. So, the situation shown in the figure is correct considering the scintillation effect. A "point source" will be more formally defined in a later chapter when its geometric image is considered to be smaller than a resolution cell (pixel) on the sensor's focal plane.

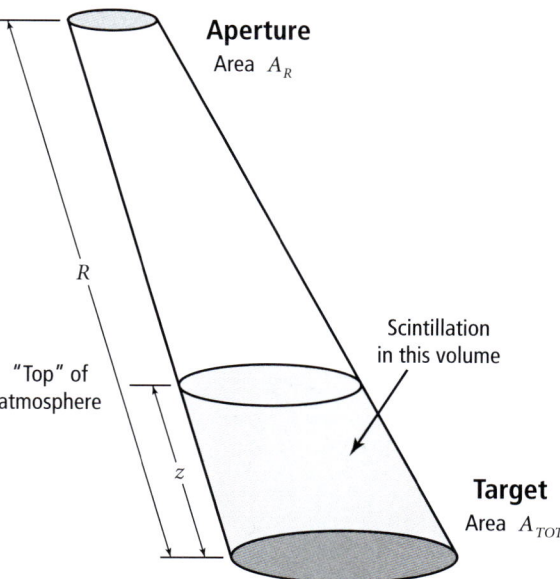

Figure 5-29
Scintillation geometry.

> **WHY DO STARS "TWINKLE" BUT PLANETS DON'T?**
>
> Both stars and planets have large circular cross-sections, but appear as dots. When looking at a star, its cone of light through the atmosphere is not larger than the diameter of the pupil of a human eye, about five to seven millimeters. This pencil of light is sufficiently narrow. So, currents of different temperature and density turbules can refract it and cause the star's image to dance on the retina, which is called twinkling.
>
> When looking at a planet, the cone of light expands from the pupil to the planet's size. Because of a planet's immense size and it is much closer than even the nearest star, the light cone is several meters in diameter only a few kilometers above, passing through the turbulent atmosphere. Since it is dozens to hundreds of turbules in diameter, refraction averages across the cone, giving a spatially stable image on the retina. No twinkling.
>
> **Example calculation:** Saturn is around 116,000 km in diameter and orbits about 1.4×10^9 km from the sun. At opposition (on the other side of the sun), it is nearly 1.55×10^9 km away. The apparent size of its disk at 40 km altitude is approximately
>
> $$\frac{(40 \text{ km})(116{,}000 \text{ km})}{1.55 \times 10^9 \text{ km}} \times \frac{1000 \text{ m}}{\text{km}} \approx 3.0 \text{ m.}$$

irradiance on aperture dances to their motion, but is temporally averaged. Therefore, cross scintillation is generally not a concern.

For an astronomical, but non-GEOINT example, see the **Sidebar Why do Stars "Twinkle" but Planets don't?** that explains another common observation.

IMAGE DEGRADATION II: EXTENDED SOURCES

Contrast is defined as the difference between the brightest and darkest[35] pixels[36] in a scene compared to the average. For example, **Figure 5-30** shows high and low contrast images of tree branches. Suppose the brightness of a pixel is proportional to at-aperture irradiance, then familiarly contrast is

$$C \approx \frac{\mathcal{E}_{MAX} - \mathcal{E}_{MIN}}{\mathcal{E}_{MAX} + \mathcal{E}_{MIN}} \approx \frac{L_{MAX}\Omega_{PIX}\tau_{ATM} - L_{MIN}\Omega_{PIX}\tau_{ATM}}{L_{MAX}\Omega_{PIX}\tau_{ATM} + L_{MIN}\Omega_{PIX}\tau_{ATM}} = \frac{L_{MAX} - L_{MIN}}{L_{MAX} + L_{MIN}}. \quad (5\text{-}33)$$

Figure 5-30
High and low contrast images.

Note atmospheric transmission, if assumed to be uniform across a sensor's FOV, does not play a role in contrast. (This is often a good assumption because sensors' FOVs are typically small.) Evidently, the cause of low contrast is not the multiplicative τ_{ATM} factor, but must be something else. Assume an additive term:

---

[35] "Bright" and "dark" are non-technical descriptors and will do for now until the actual meaning is quantified in later chapters. For now, use an intuitive notion of these terms.

[36] It is expected that most know what a pixel is.

$$C \to \frac{(L_{MAX} + L^*) - (L_{MIN} + L^*)}{(L_{MAX} + L^*) + (L_{MIN} + L^*)} \approx \frac{L_{MAX} - L_{MIN}}{L_{MAX} + L_{MIN} + 2L^*}. \quad (5\text{-}34)$$

What is this additive term, L^*? It is radiation from the intervening atmosphere itself.

ATMOSPHERIC SELF-RADIANCE

The atmosphere is, after all, an object with a temperature. Like all other objects with a temperature, it radiates (**Chapter 2**). Since photons move at the speed of light, the atmosphere cannot change in the length of time a photon passes through it. So, consider atmospheric self-emission to be a static process.

The atmosphere is not isothermal as **Figure 5-4** shows. However, it was considered to be approximately so in the lowest $5\hat{H}$ so the hydrostatic equation could be derived. Yet atmospheric temperature is approximately constant at any given altitude. For temperatures to remain constant, the emission of photons must be balanced by absorption; thermal processes of molecular motions and collisions are too slow compared to photon speed. Therefore, a small volume of air must have an exitance from its "surface," like any other body, of

$$dM_{\lambda, AIR} \approx \epsilon(\lambda)_{AIR} dB_\lambda(\lambda, T(z)) \quad [\text{W} \cdot \text{m}^{-2} - \mu\text{m}^{-1}], \quad (5\text{-}35)$$

where temperature only changes with altitude. The introduction of a calculus notation in this last expression serves as a reminder that this deals with a portion of the whole atmosphere. In fact, only the part contained within the FOV of a sensor is of interest, as this is the part contributing to loss of contrast.

What about the emissivity of the atmosphere, $\epsilon(\lambda)_{AIR}$? The first part of this section was about absorption, and an earlier discussion showed emissivity and absorptivity are equal by the principle of detailed balance. The concept of absorption was already used, through the extinction coefficient, to establish atmospheric transmission in Beer's Law. So, if photons do not pass through a volume of air, they are absorbed:

$$\alpha(\lambda)_{AIR} \approx 1 - \tau(\lambda, z)_{AIR} \approx 1 - e^{-n(z)\sigma_{ABS}\Delta s} \equiv \epsilon(\lambda)_{AIR}, \quad (5\text{-}36)$$

where the path length through a volume is at a particular altitude.

For a short increment of path ($\Delta s < \hat{H}$), the amount of absorption is small. So, **Equation 5-36** can be approximated as

$$\epsilon(\lambda)_{AIR} \approx 1 - (1 - n(z)\sigma_{ABS}\Delta s) \approx n(z)\sigma_{ABS}\Delta s. \quad (5\text{-}37)$$

For this expression, assume the absorption cross-section, σ_{ABS}, depends only on wavelength and not on altitude because the mix of molecules along the path remains constant. In the beginning of this chapter, the seven or eight most abundant gases were shown to be reasonably well-mixed throughout the atmosphere ($z \leq 5\hat{H}$); although, some trace gases may be found more predominantly at preferred altitudes. (Regardless, this variation is obvious when only seeing the combined result of Beer's Law interacting with everything along a path from target to sensor.) Thus, MODTRAN can be used to calculate the transmission along a vertical path, $\tau(0°)$, and ignore the distribution of molecules along the path. This combined with the theoretical result (**Equation 5-22**) estimates:

$$\sigma_{ABS} \approx \frac{-\ln(\tau(0°))}{n_0 \hat{H}}. \qquad (5\text{-}38)$$

Substituting **Equation 5-38** into **Equation 5-37** results in

$$\epsilon(\lambda)_{AIR} \approx (n_0 e^{-z/\hat{H}}) \left(\frac{-\ln(\tau(0°))}{n_0 \hat{H}} \right) \Delta s \approx \frac{-\ln(\tau(0°))}{\hat{H}} e^{-z/\hat{H}} \Delta s. \qquad (5\text{-}39)$$

Finally, if the "surface" of a small body of air is considered to be a fully diffuse (Lambertian) radiator, as it must be, its radiance is

$$dL_{\lambda, AIR} \approx \frac{dM_{\lambda, AIR}}{\pi} \approx \frac{-\ln(\tau(0°))}{\pi \hat{H}} e^{-z/\hat{H}} dB_\lambda(\lambda, T(z)) \Delta s \quad [\text{W} \cdot \text{m}^{-2} \cdot \text{sr}^{-1}\ \mu\text{m}^{-1}]. \qquad (5\text{-}40)$$

Thus, to find the radiance of the atmosphere contributing to contrast reduction, integrate **Equation 5-40** along the path from target to sensor. Fortunately, this calculation is included in MODTRAN. **Figure 5-31** shows the results of a calculation for a vertical path. Where the atmosphere transmission is low (as between 5 and 8 μm), it is heavily absorbing and thus exhibits significant self-radiance.

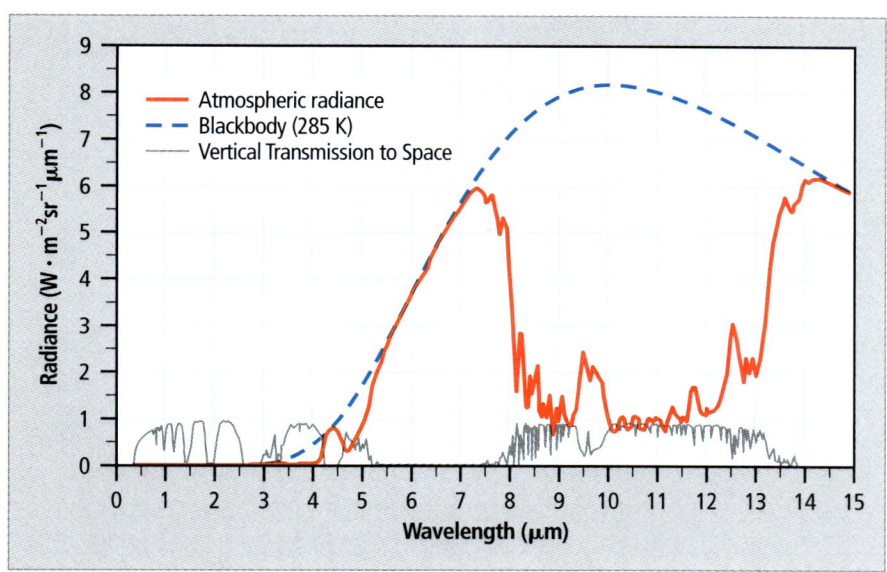

Figure 5-31
Atmospheric radiance and transmission.

IN-SCATTERING

Just as photons propagating from target to sensor can be scattered out of the line of sight, it is possible that photons from some other source can be scattered *into* the line of sight. So, rather than coming from the target, the in-scattered photons come from the Sun, sky,[37] or Earth. Their importance, of course, is the new photons appearing on the path bear no information about the target; they reduce the contrast.

To quantify scattering, a model similar to **Equation 5-40** could be developed. The differences would be replacing absorption cross-sections with scattering ones, and using an incident irradiance of photons onto the scattering volume from external sources. External sources, conceivably, could include original target photons that were scattered out. In a linear atmosphere, the probability of such a multiple scattering is small. (Multiple scattering of *any* photon is possible as it depends on path length from source to collection. Compared to all possible paths through the atmosphere, the path from target to sensor is the shortest.)

[37] Photons from the sky can be either emitted by the atmosphere itself, or multiply scattered, originating from the Sun or Earth. The following discussion will make it clear which is which, depending on wavelength.

> **MODTRAN UNITS**
>
> The units of atmospheric radiance calculated by MODTRAN are watts per centimeter squared per steradian per wave-number
>
> $$\left(L_{\bar{\nu}} = \left[\frac{W}{cm^2 sr \cdot cm^{-1}}\right]\right).$$
>
> "Per wavenumber" refers to a bandpass in reciprocal wavelength which is proportional to a photon's energy. To convert MODTRAN radiance into units as introduced in **Chapter 4**, remember spectral radiance is a distribution function. Units like $L_\lambda = L_{\bar{\nu}}$, cannot simply be converted but instead
>
> $$L_\lambda d\lambda = L_{\bar{\nu}} d\bar{\nu} \Rightarrow L_\lambda = L_{\bar{\nu}} \frac{d\bar{\nu}}{d\lambda}.$$
>
> The link is **Equation 2-5** where
>
> $$\bar{\nu} = \frac{1}{\lambda} \Rightarrow d\bar{\nu} = \frac{1}{\lambda^2} d\lambda \Rightarrow \frac{d\bar{\nu}}{d\lambda} = \frac{1}{\lambda^2},$$
>
> where λ <u>must</u> be in centimeters.
>
> The <u>numerical</u> conversion is therefore
>
> $$L_\lambda = L_{\bar{\nu}} \left(\frac{1}{\lambda^2}\right) \quad [\lambda \text{ in cm!}],$$
>
> where the units are
>
> $$\left[\frac{W}{cm^2 sr \cdot cm^{-1}}\right] \times \left[\frac{1}{cm^2}\right] = \left[\frac{W}{cm^2 sr \cdot cm}\right].$$
>
> The <u>units</u> conversion to engineering units is then
>
> $$\left[\frac{W}{cm^2 sr \cdot cm}\right] \times \left[\frac{10^4 cm^2}{m^2}\right] \times \left[\frac{1 \, cm}{10^4 \, \mu m}\right] = \left[\frac{W}{m^2 sr \cdot \mu m}\right].$$
>
> That is, the numerical conversion (with wavelength in centimeters) also handles the unit conversion.

Figure 5-32
Paths for non-target photons calculated by MODTRAN. Surface thermal emission (I), atmospheric radiance (II), and solar reflection (VI) are the largest components. Paths III, IV, and VII are single scatters, while V and VIII are multiple scatters and/or reflections.

[38] A commonly used value in the visible obtained by averaging across basic different surface types. [5]

The phenomenology of single and multiple scattering is fortunately incorporated into the MODTRAN program. **Figure 5-32** shows some of the possible paths for non-target photons originating from external to a sensor's FOV (labeled "solar"; although the moon, stars, or artificial lights could contribute) from surface thermal emission (labeled "s"), and from the atmosphere (labeled "A") as just discussed. In general downward-propagating photons from all sources are called "down-welling" radiation, and all upward-propagating photons from surface emissions, reflections, and scattering are termed "up-welling" radiation. The balance of down-welling and up-welling absorption, re-emission, and scattering maintains the vertical thermal structure of the atmosphere. The MODTRAN program provides wavelength-tabulated output for the light paths shown in the figure.

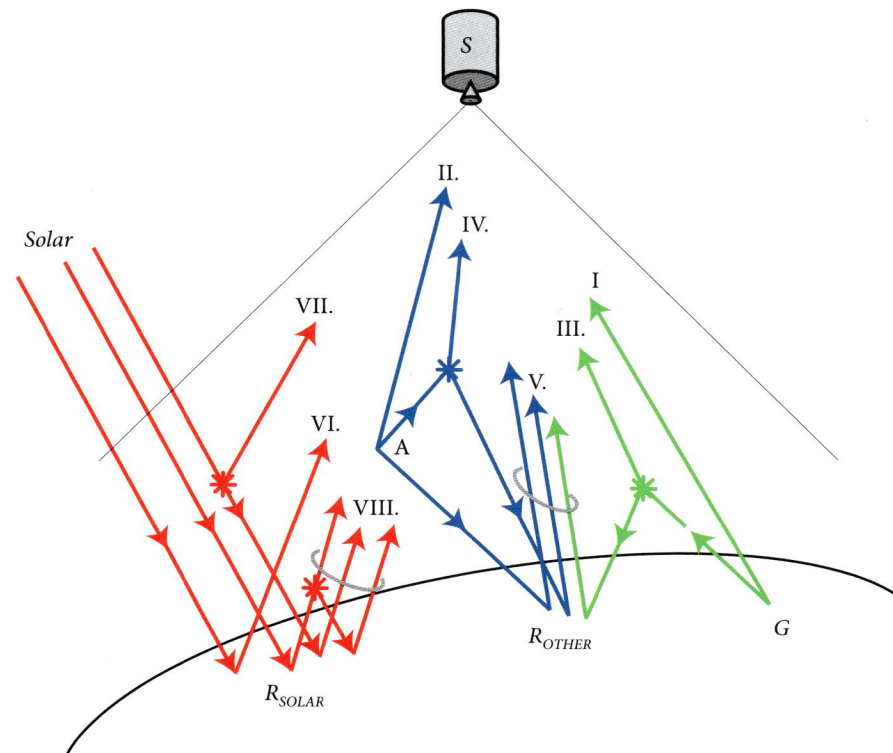

THE SUM OF IT ALL

When a remote sensor is pointed toward the Earth, the radiation collected is the sum of the target and background (and noise, which will be discussed in **Chapter 10**). **Chapters 2** and **3** introduced some of their particular spectral features with regard to emission and reflection, respectively. **Chapter 4** then added a spatial dimension: most targets are point sources characterized by *intensity*, while backgrounds, such as the Earth, are clearly extended sources characterized by *radiance*. **Chapter 4** explained the science of radiometry: how light energy (information) propagates from source to sensor. Included in the discussion was a calculation of the expected radiance of the Earth, which is shown in **Figure 4-20**.

Figure 4-20 can now be adjusted for atmospheric attenuation, scattering, and self-emission. **Figure 5-33** shows this total radiance seen by a sensor looking down at the sunlit Earth as calculated by MODTRAN. The plot is for an average reflectivity,[38] or albedo, of 0.3 (emissivity of 0.7) and Earth surface temperature of 285 K. At short wavelengths, **Figure 5-34** shows background radiance is clearly dominated by reflected and scattered solar radiation (the sum of MODTRAN paths VI, VII, and VIII in **Figure 5-32**).

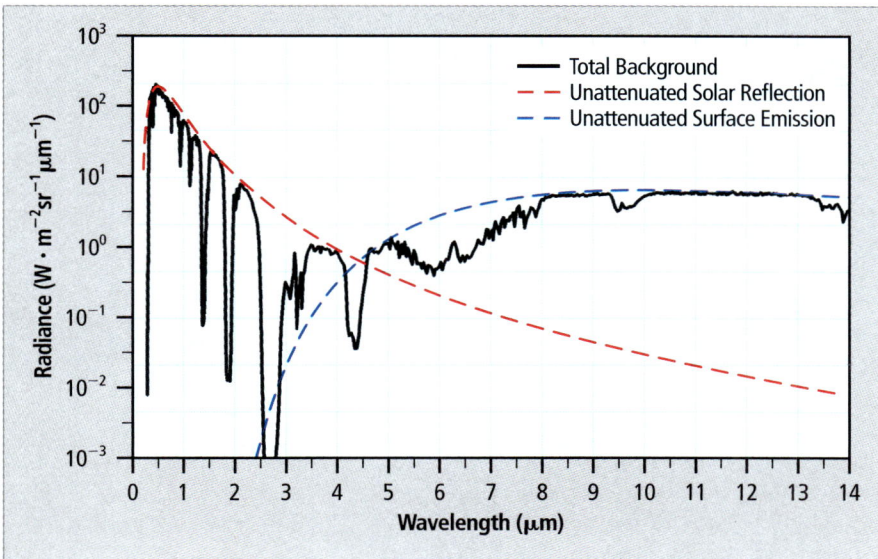

Figure 5-33
Radiance of the Earth as seen by a remote sensor looking down at the sunlit Earth.

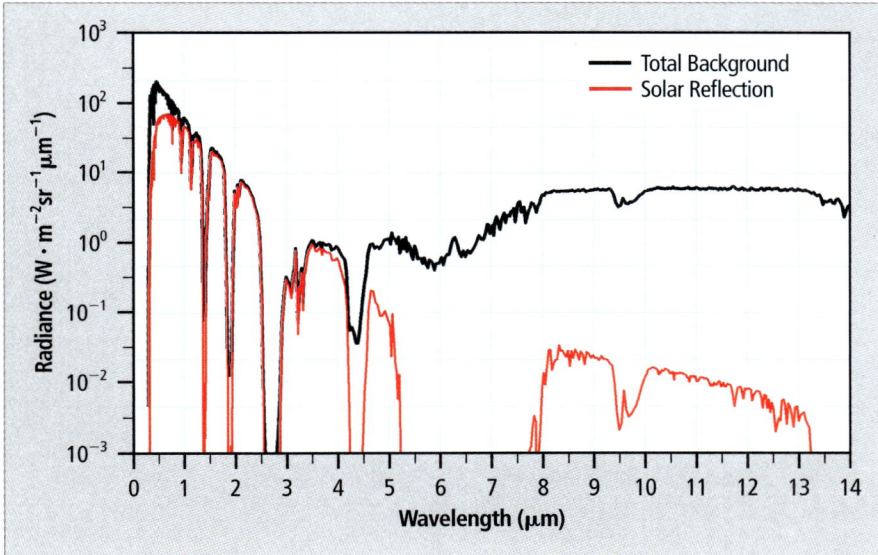

Figure 5-34
Short wavelength background radiance is dominated by solar reflection, single, and multiple scattering.

At long wavelengths, the Earth's background radiance is a combination of surface emission and atmospheric radiance. **Figure 5-35** shows these two terms separately. The surface emission curve is the sum of paths I and II, while the atmospheric radiance is the sum of paths II and IV. The multiple scatter/reflection term (Path V) is not shown. **Figure 5-35** emphasizes the previous statement that the surface emission and scattering component are negligible in wavebands where the atmosphere is strongly absorbing (as in the 5-8 μm band). Atmospheric self-emission and scattering create the entire background at such wavelengths. Of course, the sum of terms shown in **Figure 5-35** will be complete background on a moonless night when there are no external radiation sources.

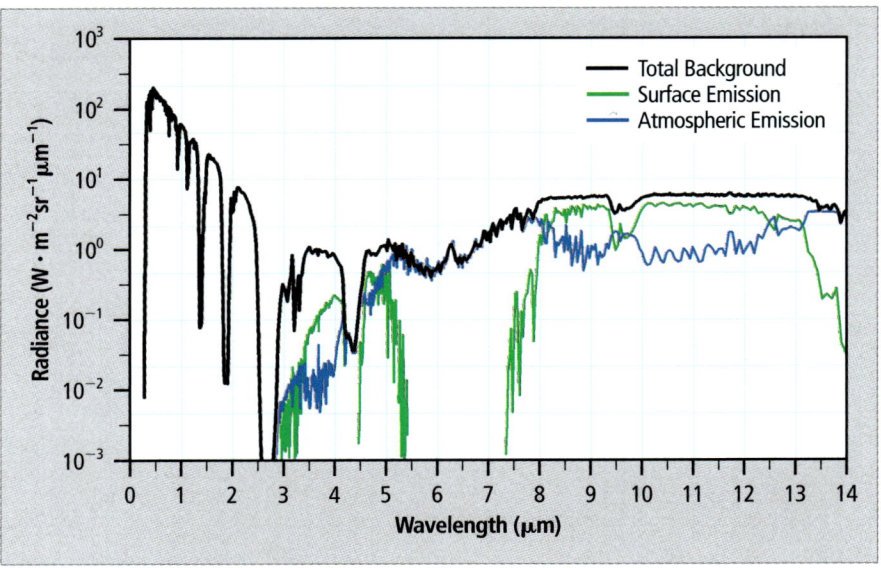

Figure 5-35
Long wavelength Earth background is dominated by thermal radiation from the Earth's surface and the atmosphere.

6 GATHERING INFORMATION: OPTICS

The last four chapters discussed some of the phenomenology of targets, such as emitting and reflecting, as well as propagation and attenuation. That is, the electromagnetic origins of information from targets were considered, including their spatial and spectral characteristics (temporal will come later) that make up their detectable and identifiable signatures and metrics. Then, the science of radiometry was covered to derive some rules about how information in the form of wave energy is transferred from target to sensor. Next, some natural mechanisms (absorption, scattering, and atmospheric radiance) that cause loss of energy and reduction of information were considered.

Now, the information has arrived at a sensor, which is essentially a camera. The camera must be capable of gathering target energy and converting it into exploitable data. In terms of hardware, this is done with a front-end component called optics and a back-end transducer known as a detector. This chapter will discuss the front-end component, and **Chapter 7** will cover how the back-end works.

The picture above shows two examples of contemporary optics. On the left is the Hubble Space Telescope, and on the right is the largest steerable radio telescope in the world at Green Bank, West Virginia.

SECTIONS
- 6.1 LENS & MIRROR
- 6.2 OPTICAL TRANSMISSION FACTOR
- 6.3 POINT SPREAD FUNCTION

[1] *f*-stop is sometimes written as *f*/# but it is only one number. For example, a human eye has focal length of about $f \approx 16$ mm and a typical pupil diameter of $D \approx 2$ mm when outdoors. Thus, $f/\# \approx 16$ mm/2 mm $\approx f/8$ for a normal eye.

[2] This is strictly for parallel rays of incoming light from a target at infinity. Nonetheless, focal length is a property of every lens and is used for targets at any location. Furthermore, light can pass through a lens in either direction, so the focal length could be on either side.

6.1 LENS & MIRROR

In all intelligence collection scenarios, information must be gathered from a target. The device used to gather information is the optics or collector subsystem of a remote sensor. The two primary functions of the collector subsystem are to 1) gather as much energy from an object or event as possible through its *aperture;* and 2) organize the gathered energy on a detector subsystem in a manner that preserves its spatial, spectral, and temporal features, i.e., the collector must form an *image* of the object or event. The ability of a collector to gather information and form an image are typically characterized by the optics' diameter, D, and focal length, f, respectively. The ratio of focal length to diameter is commonly called the *f*-stop.[1]

Even a non-literal sensor must form an image that provides a one-to-one correspondence between a target and its representation on a sensor's detector. This image may not be interpretable in the same manner that a human interprets a photograph for two reasons:

1. Gathered light will never form a perfect image because of diffraction and system misalignments and imperfections. This is the Point Spread Function (PSF) that is a part of *spatial resolution*.

2. Photoelectric detectors' pixels are generally too sparse (i.e., not as many of them as rods and cones on the human retina or film grains on a sheet of film), or the sensor is too far away.

LENS

A short review of the geometric theory of how a lens works will now be presented. A transmissive material which refracts light can, for particular surface shapes, cause rays of light to converge to a point. A refracting material with two curved surfaces is called a lens, and the distance from the lens to the convergence point is its focal length.[2] If the curved surfaces are close enough together that the distance between them can be neglected, it is referred to as a "thin" lens. A thin lens can be either a converging or a diverging type. A converging lens brings rays of light together to a focus, forming an image; while a diverging lens enables the separation of rays of light. **Figure 6-1** illustrates the parameters typically associated with a thin converging lens and the resulting image.

Figure 6-1
Parameters associated with a "thin" lens and the resulting image.

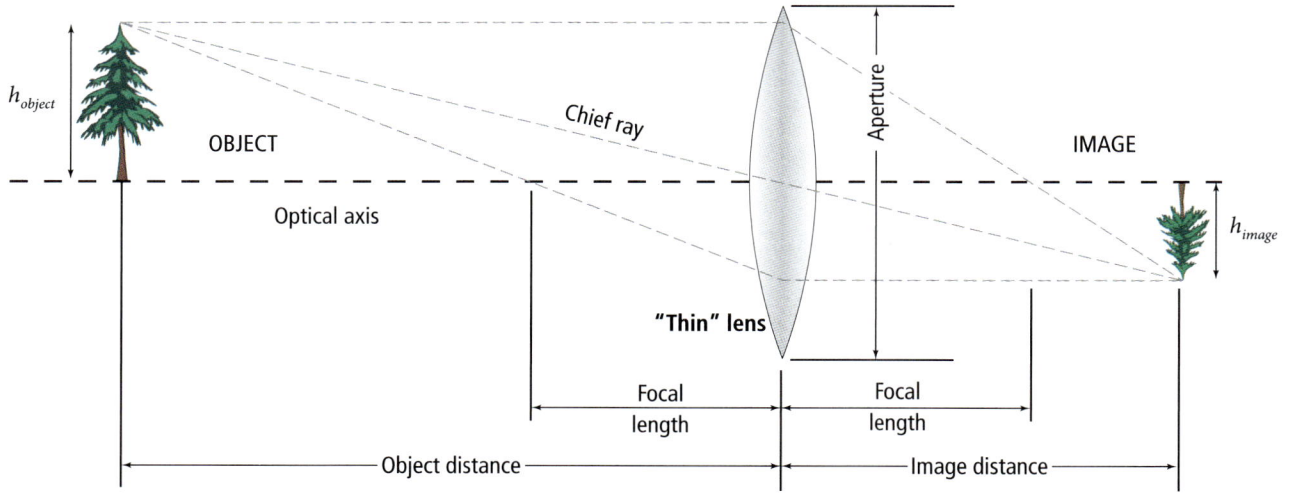

The image formed by a thin lens can be easily located using geometric optics, which describes light propagation in terms of rays. Given an object in front of a lens (at a distance greater than the lens' focal length), a "chief ray" from the object will pass through the center of the lens undeviated. A ray from the object parallel to the optic axis in **Figure 6-1** will be refracted through the lens to pass through its back focal point, and a ray passing through the front focal point will emerge from the lens parallel to the optical axis. The point at which these rays (and others) intersect is the location of the image. This is called the paraxial approximation[3] which operates in the limit of small ray angles and distances from the optical axis.

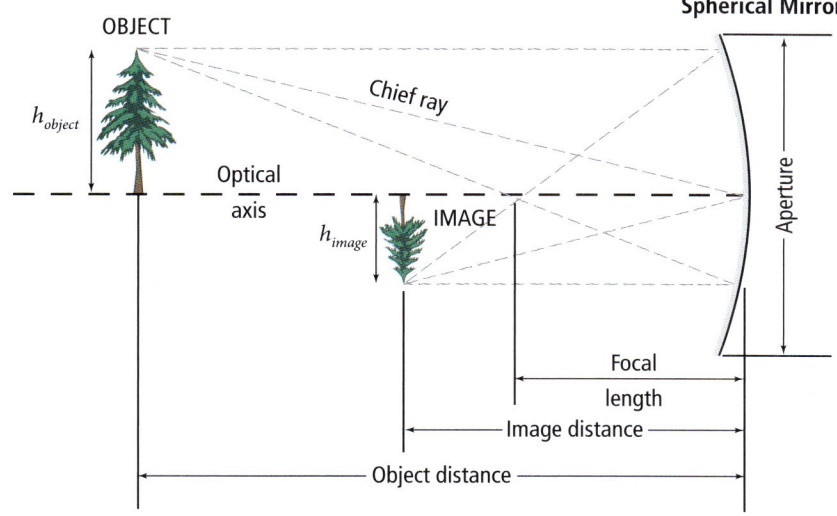

Figure 6-2
Parameters associated with a spherical mirror and the resulting image.

MIRROR

A spherical mirror forms an image using reflection in the same way a lens uses refraction, but the aperture dimension must be small compared to the radius of curvature and all other dimensions and distances to satisfy the paraxial approximation. As with the thin lens, an image's location can be determined using geometric optics. **Figure 6-2** shows the parameters associated with a mirror and the resulting image. The image located in front of the mirror presents an obvious difficulty: how to view the image without blocking the light forming the image. This problem is solved by using optics designed with multiple mirrors and lenses, as will be discussed later.

MATHEMATICS

Mathematically, lenses and mirrors are similar. Their light gathering power is proportional to their aperture area, $A_R = \pi D^2/4$, where D is the diameter of the aperture. The object and image distances illustrated in **Figures 6-1** and **6-2** are related to the focal length by:

$$\frac{1}{d_{OBJECT}} + \frac{1}{d_{IMAGE}} = \frac{1}{f} \quad \text{(Gauss' formula), or} \quad (6\text{-}1)$$

$$(d_{OBJECT} - f)(d_{IMAGE} - f) = f^2 \quad \text{(Newton's formula).} \quad (6\text{-}2)$$

Also, image size is related to object size through magnification, M, which is defined as

$$M = \left|\frac{d_{IMAGE}}{d_{OBJECT}}\right| = \left|\frac{h_{IMAGE}}{h_{OBJECT}}\right|. \quad (6\text{-}3)$$

[3] The paraxial approximation is usually accurate to within 0.5% when the angles are less than 10° and $\sin\theta \approx \theta$ (in radians).

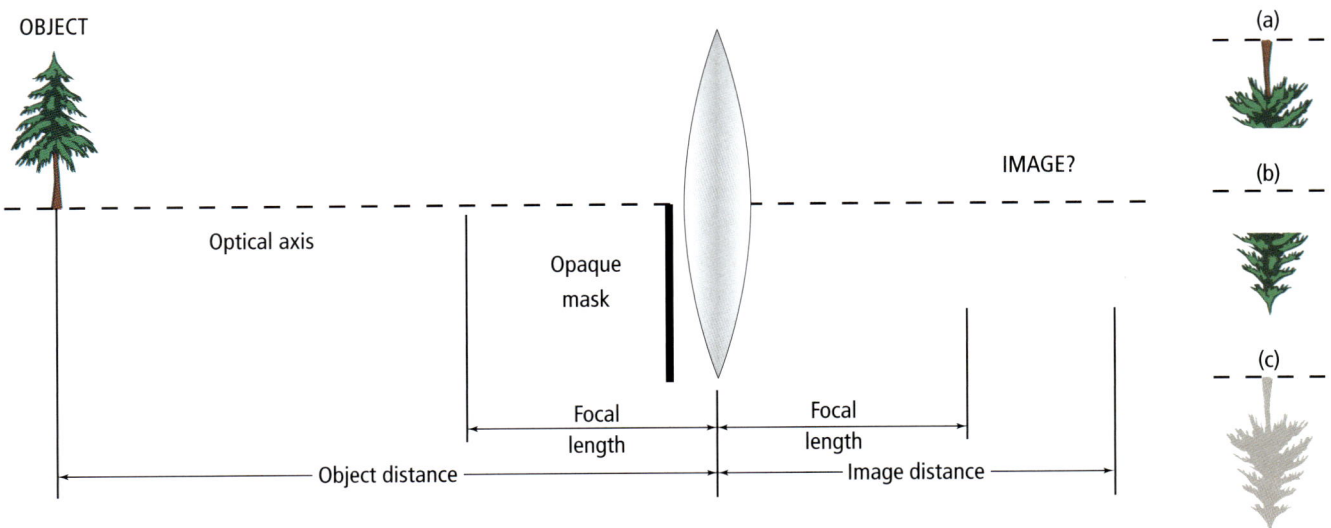

Figure 6-3
How does covering half of a lens affect the image? a) Only the bottom half of the image appears. b) Only the top half of the image appears. c) The whole image appears but it is only half as bright.

APPLICATIONS

Now, suppose half of the aperture of a sensor's collector was blocked as in **Figure 6-3**. What will the resulting image look like? Answer: The image can still be seen, *but it is not as bright* (choice c). Remember, the light gathering power of a lens or mirror is a function of its aperture, and in radiometric terms, only half the power has been collected. In fact, only a small piece of a lens or mirror is needed to form an image as suggested in **Figure 6-4a**, **b**, and **c**. As illustrated in **Figure 6-4d**, several lens segments can be simultaneously used to enhance the image by gathering additional light. The brightness of the composite image will equal the sum of the images formed by the individual segments.

The three "joined" segments in **Figure 6-4** can be modeled as having an effective aperture that, in **Section 6.3**, is related to the spatial resolution of the image. This is the starting concept for interferometry which makes use of the principle of superposition to combine separate waves in a way that will result in their combination having some meaningful property. Using a few segments (or individual

Figure 6-4
Any segment of a lens will form a complete image.

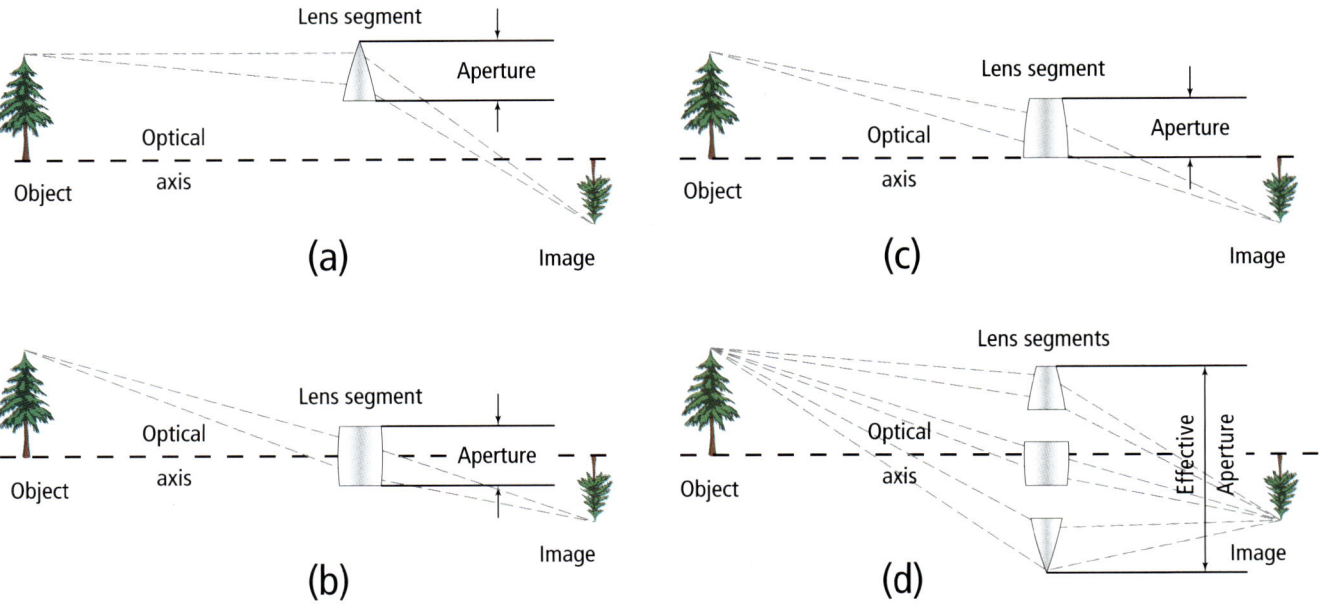

144 CHAPTER 6 OPTICS

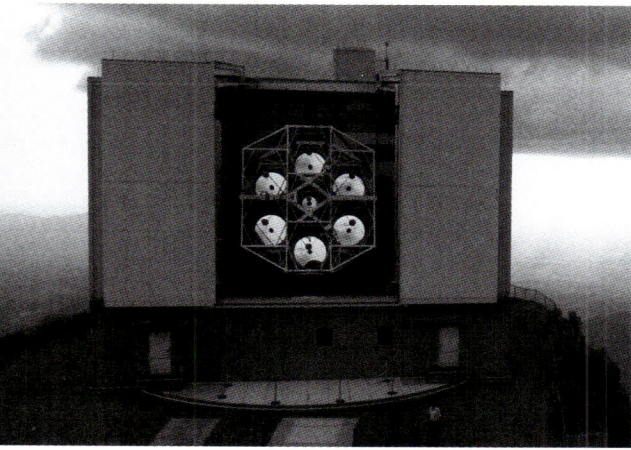

telescopes) to gather light is called a sparse array. A sparse array has the same light gathering power as the sum of the individual actual apertures, but has the spatial resolution[4] of a single aperture as large as the farthest spacing between the segments. Two famous examples are the Very Large Array (VLA) of radio telescopes in Socorro, NM, and the Multiple Mirror Telescope (MMT) formerly[5] at Mt. Hopkins, AZ, shown in **Figure 6-5**.

Instead of using multiple lenses, or lens segments, at one time to collect light to form an image, it is possible to use one lens at multiple locations. This concept is called a synthetic aperture and is used by certain radar systems, hence Synthetic Aperture Radar (SAR). The light gathering ability at any one time is equal to the light gathered by a single lens, but the spatial resolution benefits from the length of the path covered by the collection system. The concept of an optical synthetic aperture collection system is illustrated in **Figure 6-6**. **Figure 6-7** illustrates the basic concept of a SAR system. SAR is usually implemented by mounting a single beam-forming antenna from which a target scene is repeatedly irradiated with radar pulses from a moving platform such as an aircraft or spacecraft. The many radar waveforms successively received at the different antenna positions are processed together to resolve objects in the image.

Figure 6-5
Photos of the VLA at Socorro, NM and the MMT at Mt. Hopkins, AZ. (Images courtesy of NRAO/AUI.)

[4] Spatial resolution will be defined in Section 6.3 of this chapter.

[5] The MMT was a proof of concept experiment (1979–1998) and was replaced with a more advanced system.

Figure 6-6
An optical synthetic aperture system. Note, the lens is moved over the entire length of the effective aperture.

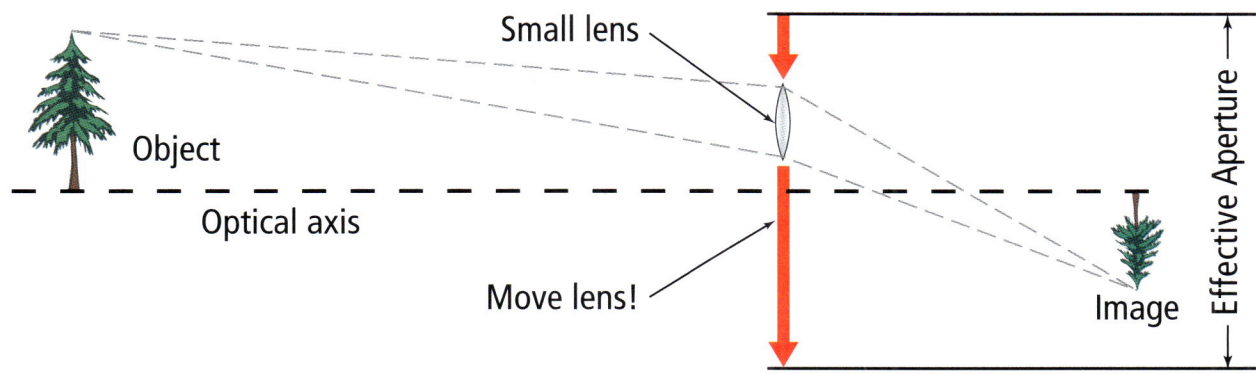

Figure 6-7
A synthetic aperture utilizing a radar system. Note, the antenna elements are "moved" over the entire length of the effective aperture.

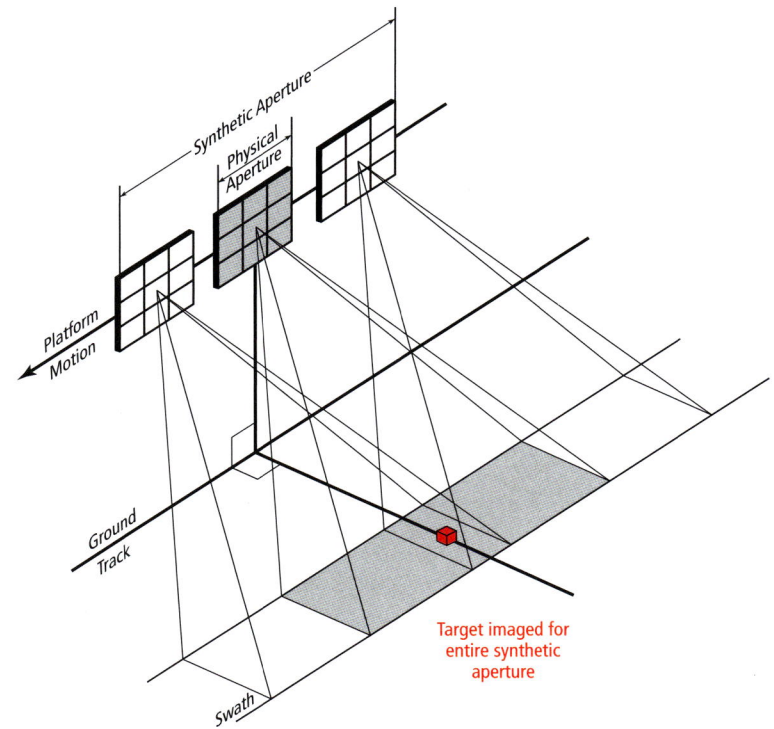

In the previously noted Gauss' formula, **Equation 6-1**, the majority of collections in remote sensing have $d_{OBJECT} \gg f$ so $\frac{1}{d_{OBJECT}} \to 0$. Therefore, Gauss' equation can be rewritten as

$$\frac{1}{d_{IMAGE}} \approx \frac{1}{f} \text{ or } d_{IMAGE} \approx f, \qquad (6\text{-}4)$$

and the sensor's detector can be placed at the focus of the collection system. The magnification (M) then becomes $M = \frac{f}{d_{OBJECT}}$. This approximation for M is sufficient for the majority of electro-optical sensors; therefore, d_{OBJECT} is substituted with the range to the target denoted R.

The reader is probably aware that multiple lenses and mirrors can be used in tandem in an optical collection system to form an image. This concept is illustrated in **Figure 6-8**. Most cameras have lenses comprised of multiple elements rather than a simple single lens.

Figure 6-8
An optical collection system using two lenses in tandem.

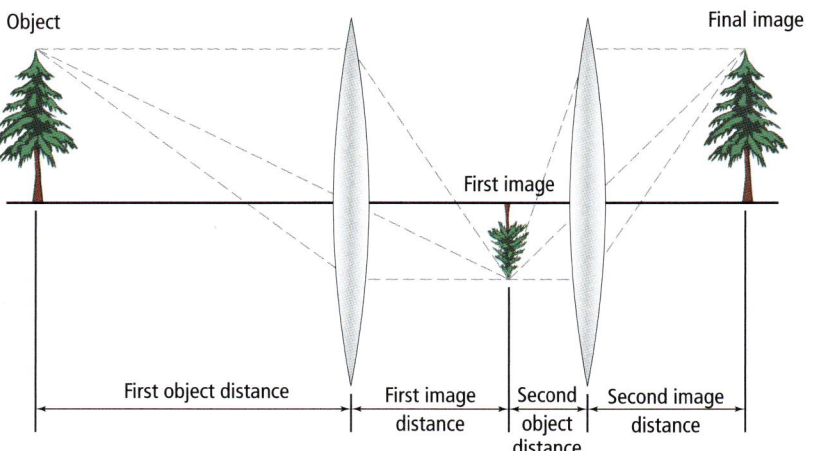

EXAMPLE 6-1: ONE LENS REPLACES TWO

In **Figure 6-8**, assume the first lens has a focal length $f_1 = 13.3$ cm and the second lens has a focal length $f_2 = 6.67$ cm. The distance between them is $d = 30.0$ cm. Now, suppose an object is placed $d_{O1} = 40$ cm in front of the first lens. Where is the image located, and what is its magnification?

Using Gauss' formula, the location of the image formed by the first lens, d_{I1}, is

$$\frac{1}{d_{O1}} + \frac{1}{d_{I1}} = \frac{1}{f_1} \Rightarrow d_{I1} = \frac{f_1 d_{O1}}{d_{O1} - f_1} = \frac{(13.3 \text{ cm})(40 \text{ cm})}{40 \text{ cm} - 13.3 \text{ cm}} = 20 \text{ cm},$$

and its magnification is $M_1 = \frac{d_{I1}}{d_{O1}} = \frac{20 \text{ cm}}{40 \text{ cm}} = 0.50$. That is, the intermediate image is 20 cm to the right of f_1 and half the size of the object.

With the intermediate image 20 cm to the right of the left lens, that places it $d_{O2} = d - d_{I1} = 10$ cm to the left of the second lens. The intermediate image becomes the object for the second lens, and a second application of Gauss' formula gives the location of the image formed by the second lens, d_{I2}, as

$$\frac{1}{d_{O2}} + \frac{1}{d_{I2}} = \frac{1}{f_2} \Rightarrow d_{I2} = \frac{f_2 d_{O2}}{d_{O2} - f_2} = \frac{(6.67 \text{ cm})(10 \text{ cm})}{10 \text{ cm} - 6.67 \text{ cm}} = 20 \text{ cm},$$

and its magnification is $M_2 = \frac{d_{I2}}{d_{O2}} = \frac{20 \text{ cm}}{10 \text{ cm}} = 2.0$. That is, the second and final image is 20 cm to the right of f_2, and it is twice as large as the intermediate object. Overall, this gives a total magnification of the image of $M = M_1 M_2 = (0.50)(2.0) = 1.0$.

Next, could the two lenses be replaced with one, such that the original object and its image are in the same locations AND the magnification is the same? To answer this question, note $d_{O1} + d + d_{I2} = 90$ cm. Then, proceed to find the object and image distances, d_{O3} and d_{I3}, and the focal length, f_3, of the hypothetical single lens with the following three simultaneous equations:

$$d_{O3} + d_{I3} = 90 \text{ cm}, \quad M_3 = \frac{d_{I3}}{d_{O3}} = 1.0, \text{ and } \frac{1}{d_{O3}} + \frac{1}{d_{I3}} = \frac{1}{f_3}.$$

Without boring the reader with the algebra, the solutions are

$$d_{O3} = 45 \text{ cm}, d_{I3} = 45 \text{ cm}, \text{ and } f_3 = 22.5 \text{ cm}.$$

Perhaps, this solution seemed obvious because of the unity magnification, but nonetheless the calculation shows that two lenses can be replaced by one. More often than not, optical design goes the other way and replaces one lens with a combination of others. Good reasons for this include correcting for focusing errors and building a more compact unit.

Lastly, **Equation 6-5** does not give the effective focal length of the two lenses in this example *because* the original object is not at infinity.

Multiple lenses can always be treated as if they were a single optical element with an effective focal length, f_{eff}, which results in the same final image location and magnification. For two lenses in **Figure 6-9**, an object at infinity is focused at f_1. This becomes the object at u for f_2 which focuses it at v. The projection (dashed lines) to intersect the aperture, D, gives the effective focal length, f_{eff}, of the two lenses acting together. Using the lens equation and similar triangles show:[6]

$$f_{eff} = \frac{f_1 f_2}{d - (f_1 + f_2)}. \qquad (6\text{-}5)$$

Figure 6-9
Illustration used to determine effective focal length, f_{eff}, of a two lens system.

Figure 6-10 sketches a Cassegrain telescope system, one of the most common configurations used as a collector. The Cassegrain telescope is a combination of a primary concave mirror and a secondary convex mirror. In a symmetrical Cassegrain system, both mirrors are aligned about the optical axis, and the primary mirror has an opening in the center permitting the light to propagate to a detector. The Cassegrain reflector is named after a published reflecting telescope design that appeared in the April 25, 1672 *Journal des sçavans* which was attributed to Laurent Cassegrain (**Figure 6-11**). Note, the Cassegrain secondary mirror reduces the available clear aperture. Some typical parameters are:

- Space-based sensor: $D = 30$ cm, $f_{eff} = 3.5$ m, $f/\# = 11$
- Ground-based sensor: $D = 60$ cm, $f_{eff} = 3.36$ m, $f/\# = 5.6$
- Hubble space telescope: $D = 240$ cm, $f_{eff} = 57.6$ m, $f/\# = 24$

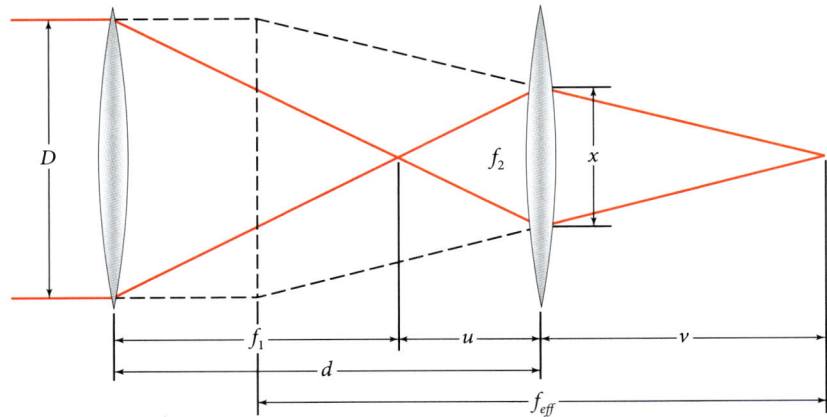

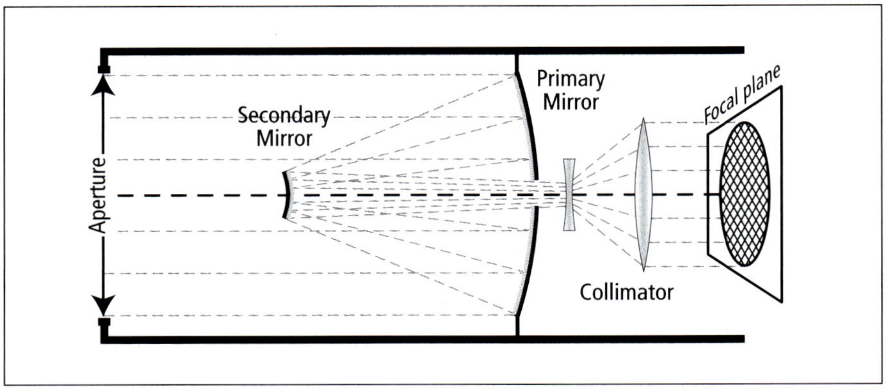

Figure 6-10
The Cassegrain telescope. For simplicity, only two lenses are shown behind the primary mirror directing light energy to a detector. Many Cassegrains will have more mirrors and lenses arranged to allow the telescope to be pointed in different directions while maintaining the focal plane fixed.

[6] Equation 6-5 is only valid when $d_{OBJ} \to \infty$ and $d > f_1 + f_2$. Related formulas for when $d = f_1 + f_2$ and $d < f_1 + f_2$ are exercises for the reader.

6.2 OPTICAL TRANSMISSION FACTOR

The amount of energy passed through a collection system to the detector depends on the number of optical elements and their characteristics. The system's optical transmission and reflection characteristics determine the sensor system's bandpass. Examples of optical elements and their desired characteristics are as follows:

- Windows–highly transmissive at all wavelengths, low reflection[7]
- Lenses–highly transmissive at all wavelengths, low reflection
- Mirrors
  - Beam splitters } high reflection at all wavelengths, low absorption
- Bandpass limiting filters
  - Interference filters } highly transmissive within bandpass, no transmission outside of bandpass
  - Dye filters
- Spectral dispersing elements
  - Prisms } high transmission or reflection in multiple designed bandpasses
  - Diffraction gratings
  - Etalons (interferometer)

Figure 6-11
Astronomer and optical instrument maker Laurent Cassegrain (1629–1693) is memorialized at his birthplace, Chartres, France, as having been the premier telescope maker in the world. (Image courtesy of http://commons.wikimedia.org/wiki/File:James_Gregory.jpg; PD_Old.)

TRANSMISSION THROUGH LENSES

Figure 6-12 shows the optical transmission, τ_{OPT}, of zinc sulfide, a possible infrared (IR) lens material. At the short wavelength cutoff to the left of the curve, high energy photons interact with the electrical structure of the material and are probably reflected. At the long wavelength cutoff to the right of the curve, low energy photons are most likely absorbed by interaction with the material's molecular structure. An acceptable transmission in some wavelength band is denoted by the region contained under the curve between the high and low cutoff wavelengths. If this material was used in a sensor, its bandpass may determine the bandpass of the sensor as a whole. Presumably, the in-band optical transmission of a material such as this may be given by a Beer's Law type of formula,

$$\tau_{OPT} = e^{-\beta \Delta x}, \qquad (6\text{-}6)$$

where β is the material's extinction coefficient and Δx its thickness. The goal of good optical design is to choose materials to make this as large as possible within the bandpass.

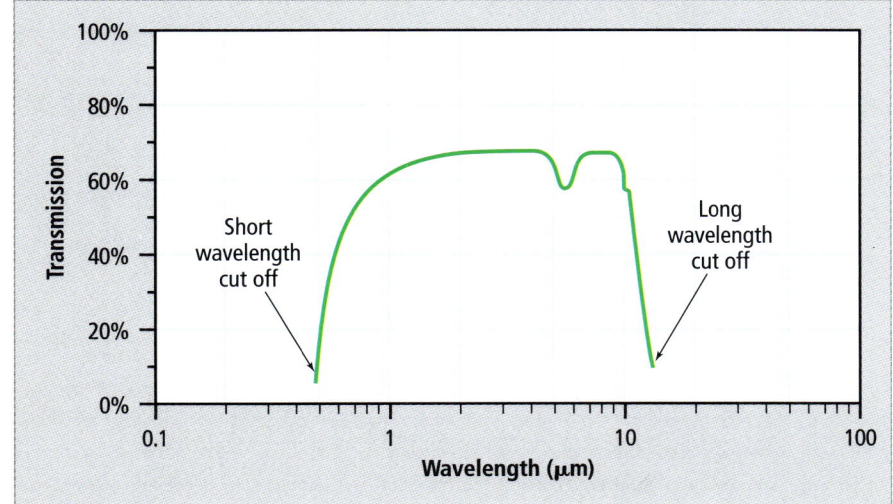

Figure 6-12
Typical transmission of a 5 mm thick window of zinc sulfide (ZnS), showing a usable bandpass between 0.5 and 15 μm. Note the absorption feature at 6 μm due to the material's electronic band energy structure.

---

[7] Sensors on aircraft (in particular) require a clear, non-refracting window to isolate them from turbulent air flow and atmospheric moisture and particles. Ground-based or space-based sensors may also look through windows for protection.

Figure **6-13** shows the transmission of some common optical materials (adapted from *The Infrared Handbook*, The Infrared Information and Analysis Center, Environmental Research Institute of Michigan, 1978). The ends of the bars are approximately the 10% transmission points. Note, in particular, the materials sapphire and germanium. Their transmission curves are shown in **Figure 6-14** as functions of wavelength. **Figure 6-15** shows a person holding samples of germanium and sapphire photographed in the visible and thermal IR regions. (Note, the color in the IR photograph is used to portray hotter and cooler areas, as will be discussed in **Chapter 16**.)

Figure 6-13
Typical bandpasses of some optical materials as a function of wavelength. Sodium chloride (in yellow) is ordinary table salt prepared as a single pure crystal.

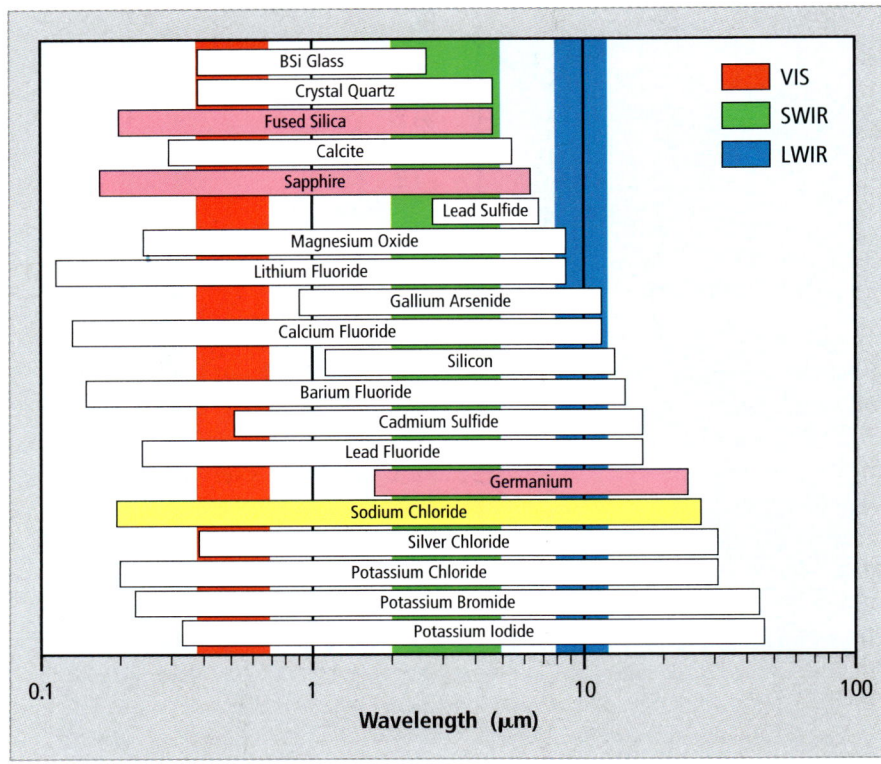

Figure 6-14
Transmission of germanium and sapphire as a function of wavelength. (The thickness of the tested samples is unknown.)

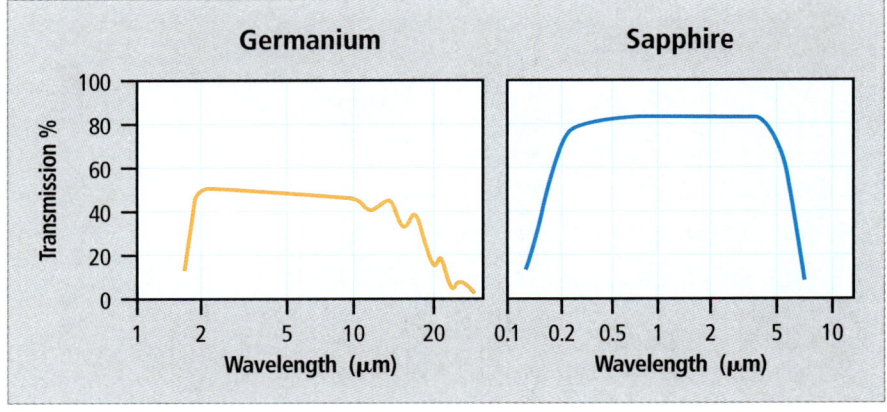

Some light also reflects from the surfaces of all optical elements. The amount of reflection depends on the angle of incidence, polarization of the incident light (if any), and the element's index of refraction; it can be calculated using the Fresnel formulas (**Equations 3-8, 3-9, 3-10,** and/or **3-12**). **Figure 6-16** illustrates that a material with an index of refraction of 1.5 (typical of

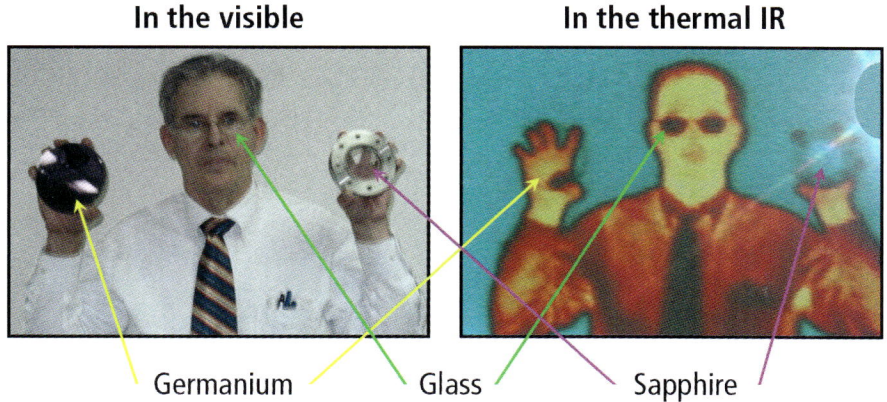

Figure 6-15
Response of germanium, sapphire, and glass in the visible and thermal IR regions. Also, note the eye glasses (most like fused silica in **Figure 6-13**) transmit in the visible, but not in the IR.

glass) reflects about 4% of normally incident unpolarized light. The use of an anti-reflection coating can reduce the reflection from frequently used optical materials. **Figure 6-17** illustrates the use of a material thickness of a quarter-wavelength to decrease the surface reflectance of a material at normal incidence by a factor of two or three depending on the index of refraction. (The physics of reflection and transmission of thin films are discussed in **Chapter 9**.)

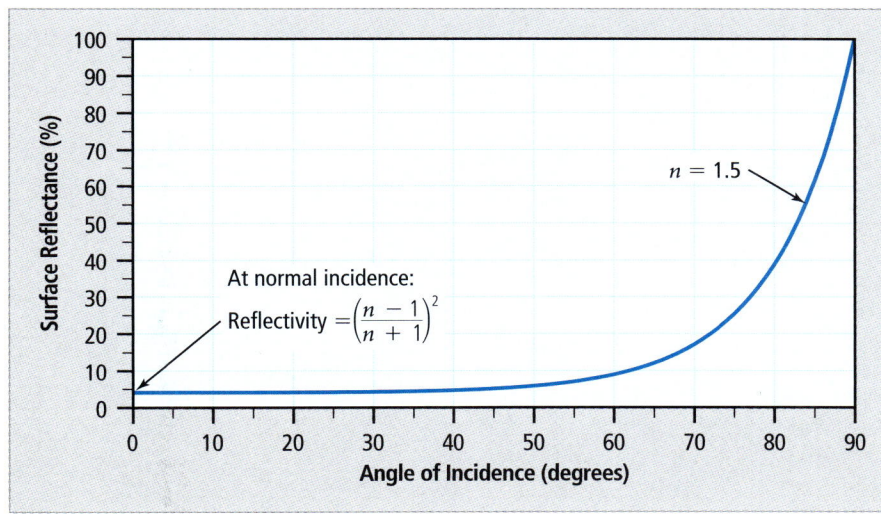

Figure 6-16
Typical surface reflectance as a function of incidence angle for unpolarized light.

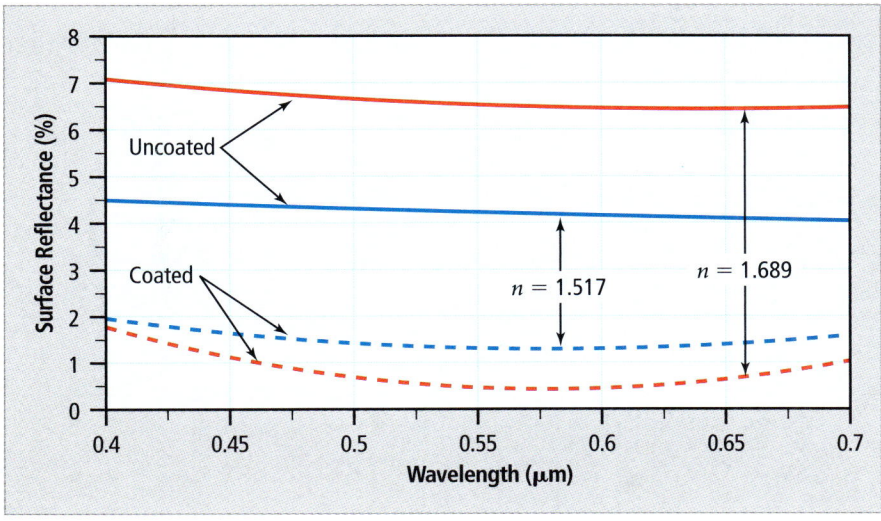

Figure 6-17
Example of the ability of anti-reflection coatings to change the surface reflection of typical optical materials. The effect of adding one-quarter wavelength thickness of magnesium fluoride (MgF_2) to the surface of some glasses is shown here.

CHAPTER 6 OPTICS

REFLECTION FROM MIRRORS

The transmission of an optical system also depends on the reflectivity of any mirrors. **Figure 6-18** and **Figure 6-19** show the reflectivity of some polished metal surfaces. The shapes of the curves in the first figure explain why new dimes look white (silvery), new gold dollars look yellow, and new pennies look red.

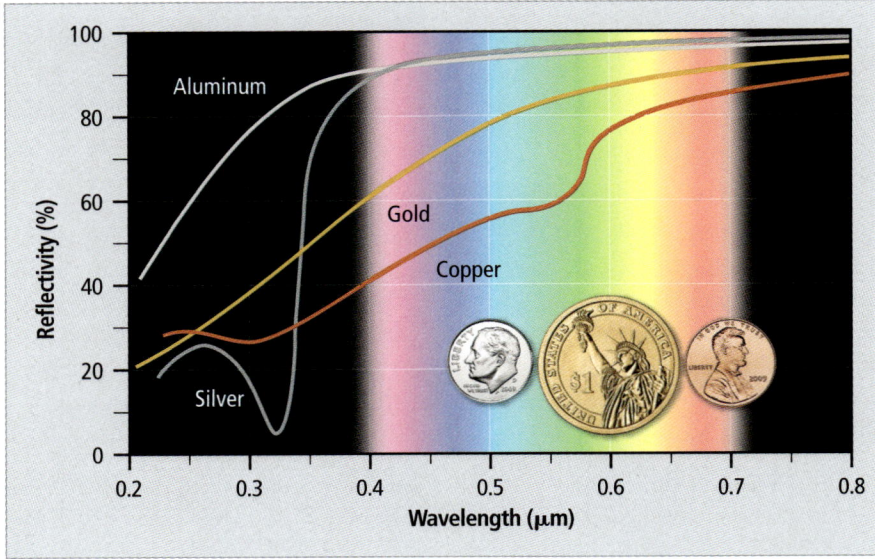

Figure 6-18
Typical materials used to coat mirrors in visible bandpass optical collection systems to enhance the efficiency of the optical system.

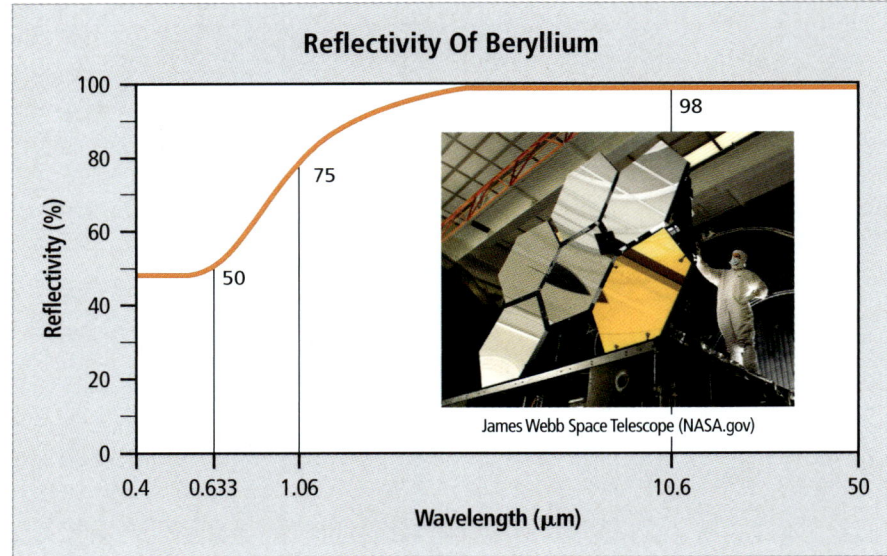

Figure 6-19
Beryllium is a toxic metal but is highly useful for high reflectivity coatings in the IR because of its light weight. (Laser wavelengths are noted: 0.633 = He:Ne, 1.06 = Nd:YAG, and 10.6 = CO_2.) The inset shows the first five segments of the James Webb Space Telescope mounted in place.

BANDPASS LIMITING

In addition to the normal bandpasses of optical materials used to fabricate lenses, windows, and mirrors in an optical collector system, other elements, like filters, may be utilized to specifically limit the total light throughput to an even narrower bandpass. The purpose of a bandpass filter is to restrict the amount of light to a spectral region or feature that is useful for emissive or reflective signature studies. Two common types of bandpass filters are chemical dye and thin film interference filters. Chemical dye or gelatin filters rely upon the absorption of light by the specific chemicals in the filter. Interference filters are made with multiple layers of thin films on a glass substrate. The thin films are typically one-quarter wavelength thick and work on the principle of interference due to multiple internal reflections within the thin layers. These filters are further discussed in **Chapter 9**.

A remote sensor used to record light in multiple bands is a spectrometer. Each individual band of the spectrometer is characterized by bandpass, cutoffs, center frequency, and peak transmissions. For spectrometers, multi-band instruments typically respond over less than ten bands, multispectral instruments typically respond over tens of bands, hyperspectral instruments typically respond over hundreds of bands, and ultraspectral instruments typically respond over thousands of bands. These are broad categories and

EXAMPLE 6-2: TRANSMISSION OF A SIMPLE REMOTE SENSOR

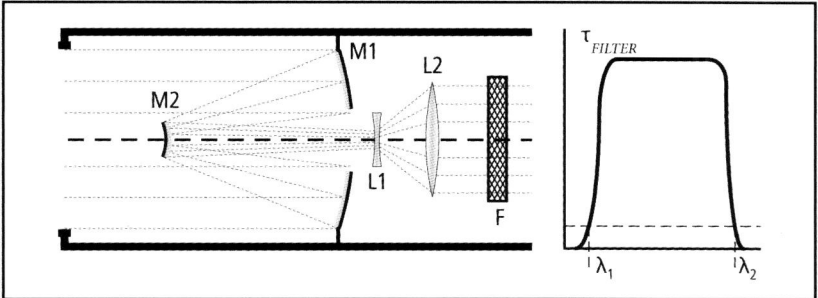

As an example, suppose a remote sensing system's collector consists of two mirrors, two lenses, and a filter as illustrated in the figure above with the following parameters:

- Mirror 1 (M1) is front-surface metal coated with reflectivity $\rho_{M1} = 0.95$
- Mirror 2 (M2) is front-surface metal coated with reflectivity $\rho_{M2} = 0.90$
- Lens 1 (L1) has an average transmission of $\tau_{L1} = 0.93$
- Lens 2 (L2) has an average transmission of $\tau_{L2} = 0.88$
- Both lenses are made of glass with index of refraction $n = 1.5$ (uncoated)
- Filter (F) has peak transmission $\tau_{FILTER} = 0.85$ (includes surfaces)

Additionally, there is a reflective loss at each lens surface, roughly 4%, which must be accounted. This makes the transmission past each surface about $\tau_{SURF} \approx 96\%$.

Now, find the total transmission through the system at the peak wavelength by following the collected light through each element in succession:

$$\tau_{OPT} \approx \rho_{M1} \times \rho_{M2} \times (\tau_{SURF} \times \tau_{L1} \times \tau_{SURF}) \times (\tau_{SURF} \times \tau_{L2} \times \tau_{SURF}) \times \tau_{FILTER}$$
$$\approx 0.95 \times 0.90 \times (0.96 \times 0.93 \times 0.96) \times (0.96 \times 0.88 \times 0.96) \times 0.85$$
$$\approx 0.51.$$

This is a significant loss, especially for a dim target! The use of anti-reflection coating on the surfaces of the lenses can improve the transmission for this collector system to approximately 59%. In general, the optical transmission factor is a function of wavelength as one moves across the bandpass.

are subject to a different interpretation by the various communities. The spectrometer's collection system will include one or more optical elements whose function is to spectrally disperse the light. These optical elements are typically prisms, diffraction gratings and interferometers, and will be considered in more depth in **Chapters 15** through **20**.

6.3 POINT SPREAD FUNCTION

When light passes through any aperture or past an edge, physical optics (treating light as a wave) predict it will bend. That is, it diffracts. Thus, light rays arriving at a focal plane from different parts of an aperture interfere. The resulting distribution of the light from a point source is known as a diffraction pattern by physicists, an impulse response by electrical engineers, a Green's function by mathematicians, and a PSF by remote sensor designers and operators. This last term will be most frequently used in this text. **Figure 6-21** illustrates the concept of a PSF and its resulting image.

Figure 6-20
Sir George Biddel Airy, Mathematician and Astronomer, 1801–1892. (Image courtesy of http://en.wikipedia.org/wiki/File:PSM_V03_D008_George_Biddell_Airy.jpg; PD_Old.)

ELECTRO-OPTIC SYSTEMS

The distribution of irradiance from a distant point source on a focal plane after passing through a circular aperture and being focused by an optical system is called an Airy function after Sir George Biddell Airy (**Figure 6-20**). The central spot of the Airy function, right side of **Figure 6-21**, is referred to as an Airy disk or blur circle[8] and contains 84% of the power in the image. An Airy function is plotted in the middle of **Figure 6-22**. The central peak is clearly dominant while the diffraction rings are small.

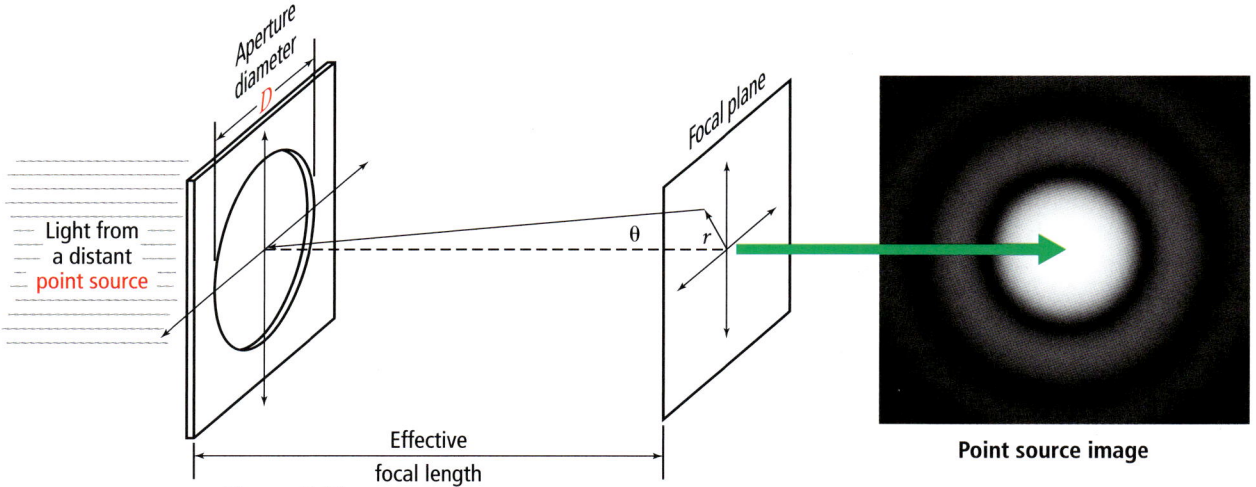

Figure 6-21
The image of a point source is a PSF. The photograph was overexposed so the rings surrounding the central spot can be seen.

Mathematically, the irradiance on the focal plane from a point source is the Airy function which is given as:

$$\mathcal{E}_{FPA}(r) \approx \mathcal{E}_0 \left[\frac{2J_1\left(\frac{\pi D}{f\lambda}r\right)}{\left(\frac{\pi D}{f\lambda}r\right)} \right]^2 = \mathcal{E}_0 Airy(r), \qquad (6\text{-}7)$$

where $\mathcal{E}_0$ is the maximum (peak) irradiance, r is the distance from the center of the PSF, and J_1 is a Bessel function of the first kind.[9] The first zero of the Bessel function is $\frac{\pi D}{f\lambda}r \approx 3.832$, from which the radius of an Airy disk on the focal plane is given as:

---

[8] This does not mean the image is out of focus. Diffraction cannot be avoided by a remote sensor having a finite aperture.

[9] A Bessel function (named for mathematician Friedrich Bessel, 1784–1846) is like a sine or cosine function, but in cylindrical or polar coordinates.

$$r_A \approx \frac{3.832 f \lambda}{\pi D} \approx \frac{1.22 f \lambda}{D}. \qquad (6\text{-}8)$$

Importantly, this says the larger the aperture diameter, the smaller the PSF.[10]

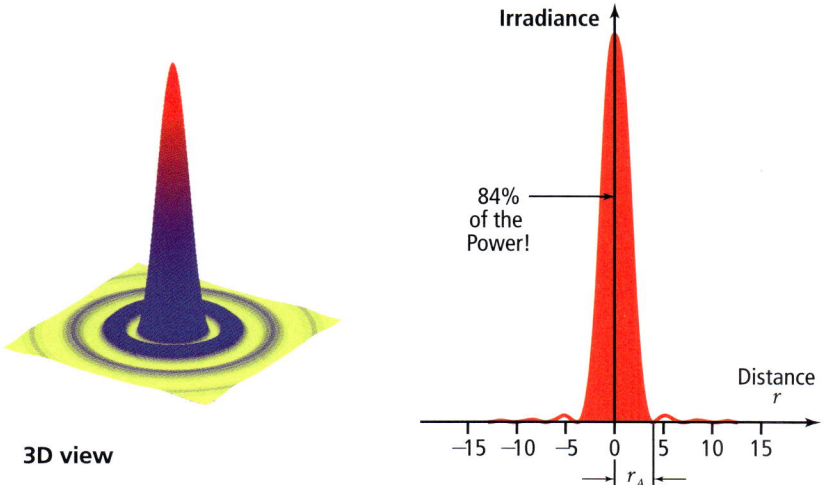

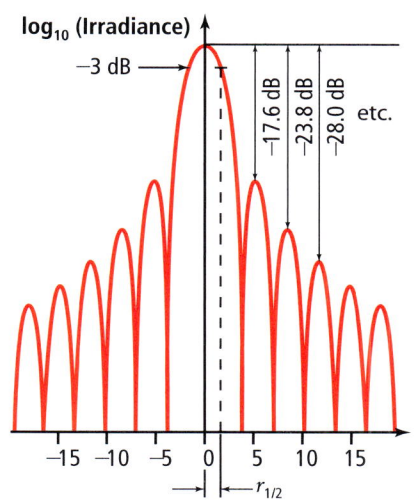

Figure 6-22
The Airy function. Three-dimensional rendering (left) and two-dimensional plots on a rectilinear scale (center) and a logarithmic scale (right).

As just stated, the Airy pattern is a Bessel function of the first kind (J_1). From its mathematical properties, the amplitudes of the diffraction rings, or sidelobes, can be calculated. They are plotted on a log scale on the right side of **Figure 6-22**. This becomes extremely important when accounting for all of the energy collected from a point target.[11]

The calculation of the Airy function is based upon the assumption of diffraction limited, i.e., perfect optics. Actual remote sensing systems generally do not have diffraction-limited optics as a result of imperfect design,[12] mechanical misalignment, temperature changes, vibration, and motion. The actual energy distribution on the focal plane from a point source is more likely to resemble a Gaussian distribution. The Gaussian distribution is usually broader than a theoretical Airy pattern by a factor of two or more, but all energy is contained within a central distribution as illustrated in **Figure 6-23**.

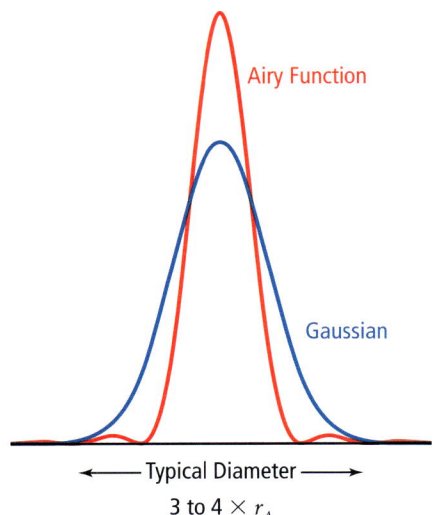

Figure 6-23
Comparison of a theoretically perfect diffraction limited Airy function with a Gaussian distribution. Both functions have the same power, but the standard deviation of the Gaussian blur circle is twice the radius of the Airy disk.

[10] That is, a larger aperture collects more information, and more information forms a better image with sharper features.

[11] In radar, the Airy function is proportional to the radar cross-section (RCS) of a circular metal target. The amplitudes of the sidelobes are crucial to making the identification.

[12] Recall the difficulties with the Hubble Space Telescope. Faulty construction of a mirror caused the PSF to exceed its design specifications. Correcting optics were designed and installed by astronauts on space shuttle servicing missions.

DECIBELS

A decibel (dB) is not a unit, but is a base-10 logarithmic expression of the value of some quantity relative to a reference value. If the maximum irradiance of an Airy function, $\mathcal{E}_0$, is taken to be the reference value, then any other irradiance can be expressed as

$$10 \log \frac{\mathcal{E}}{\mathcal{E}_0} [dB].$$

When the logarithm is negative, the usual phrase is a quantity is so many "*dB down*" (from the reference value).

For example, when irradiance is one-half the peak value,

$$10 \log \frac{\frac{1}{2}\mathcal{E}_0}{\mathcal{E}_0} = -3dB,\ \text{i.e., "three } dB \text{ down."}$$

It is commonly recognized that a factor of two is 3 *dB*, while a factor of ½ is −3 *dB*.

Often if the reference value is not stated, it is taken to be 1 m², 1 W, 1 V, etc., and is assumed.

COMPARISON TO RADAR

As stated previously, the central disk of the Airy function holds 84% of the energy passing through the aperture. Although, it is more common in engineering to note the half-power (3dB) radius, which is approximately

$$r_{\frac{1}{2}} = \frac{0.514 f \lambda}{D}, \qquad (6\text{-}9)$$

holding approximately 50% of the collected power. Another way to look at the PSF is from the center of the aperture, as in **Figure 6-24**, which plots the Airy pattern as a function of an angle, θ, defined in **Figure 6-21**. Note, the Airy disk subtends an angle $\theta_A = \frac{2r_A}{f}$ and a solid angle $\Omega_A \approx \frac{\pi \theta_A^2}{4} \approx \frac{\pi r_A^2}{f_{eff}^2} \approx 4.67 \frac{\lambda^2}{D^2}$. The half-power solid angle could also be defined as

$$\Omega_{\frac{1}{2}} \approx \frac{\pi \theta_{\frac{1}{2}}^2}{4} \approx \frac{\pi r_{\frac{1}{2}}^2}{f^2} \approx 0.83 \frac{\lambda^2}{D^2}. \qquad (6\text{-}10)$$

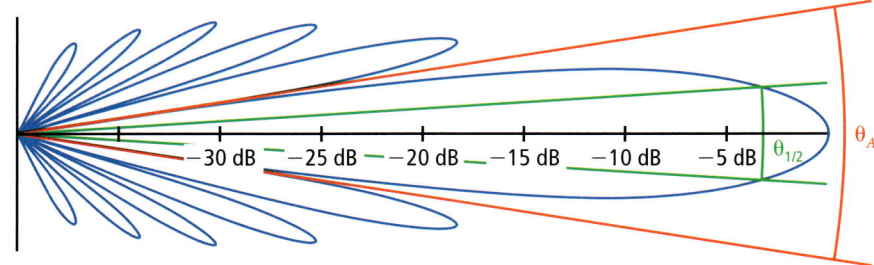

Figure 6-24
Plot of the Airy function in polar coordinates.

The polar plot is reminiscent of the transmit and receive gain patterns of a circular aperture radar antenna (diameter *D*) as illustrated in the sidebar, **Optics is like Radar, but with a Much Larger $\frac{D}{\lambda}$**. Although it is not customary, the sidebar develops an optical analog to radar antenna gain for point sources.

OPTICS IS LIKE RADAR, BUT WITH A MUCH LARGER $\frac{D}{\lambda}$

Radar antenna gain is defined as $G_{ANT} \approx F_{ANT} \frac{4\pi}{\Omega_{\frac{1}{2}}}$, where F_{ANT} is an adjustment factor to account for the shape, material, environmental, and electrical characteristics of a particular antenna. Assuming a radar antenna's beam is like the optical diffraction pattern (Airy function), its gain is

$$G_{ANT} \approx \frac{4\pi F_{ANT}}{\left(0.83 \frac{\lambda^2}{D^2}\right)} \approx 15.1 \left(\frac{D}{\lambda}\right)^2 F_{ANT} \approx \frac{19.3 A_R}{\lambda^2} F_{ANT}.$$

The power passing through a collector's aperture $\left(A_R = \frac{\pi D^2}{4}\right)$, arriving at the image (neglecting losses) is $\Phi_{IMAGE} = \mathcal{E}_{APERTURE} A_R$.

For a point source, this power is distributed over the PSF, which is approximately 84% of the power within the area of the Airy Disk. This gives *irradiance* on the focal plane as approximately

$$\mathcal{E}_{IMAGE} \approx \frac{0.84 \Phi_{IMAGE}}{A_{Airy\ Disk}} \approx 0.84 \mathcal{E}_{APERTURE} \frac{A_R}{\pi r_A^2}.$$

Thus, the optical gain by analogy to radar is defined as:

$$G_{OPT} \approx \frac{\mathcal{E}_{IMAGE}}{\mathcal{E}_{APERTURE}} \approx 0.84 \frac{A_R}{\pi r_A^2} \approx 0.18 \frac{A_R}{(f/\#)^2 \lambda^2} \approx \frac{0.14}{(f/\#)^2} \left(\frac{D}{\lambda}\right)^2.$$

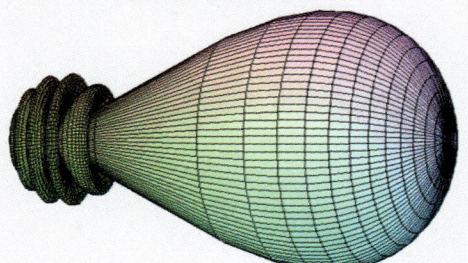

EXTENDED SOURCES

Finally, what about extended sources in the field of view? In theory, an extended source (radiance, L) can be imagined as an infinite array of point sources. Each imaginary point source provides an irradiance on a sensor's aperture and subsequently forms an Airy function on the focal plane. The sum of the infinite number of PSFs must be the irradiance on the focal plane. Thus, if an extended target (or background) has a uniform radiance, the irradiance of its image will also be uniform.

Conventionally, focal planes are comprised of multiple picture elements or *pixels*. Each pixel is an individual detector (**Chapter** 7). If the portion of an extended source which is "imaged" onto a pixel is uniformly radiant, the irradiance on that pixel will be uniform also. From the portion of a source that irradiates a pixel, the irradiance on a sensor's aperture, from **Chapters 4** and **5**, is

$$\mathcal{E}_{APERTURE} \approx L\Omega_{PIX}\tau_{ATM}, \qquad (6\text{-}11)$$

and the power transmitted to the pixel is

$$\Phi_{PIXEL} \approx \mathcal{E}_{APERTURE} A_R \tau_{OPT}. \qquad (6\text{-}12)$$

The irradiance on the pixel is therefore

$$\mathcal{E}_{PIXEL} \approx \frac{\Phi_{PIXEL}}{A_{PIXEL}} \approx \mathcal{E}_{APERTURE}\left(\frac{A_R}{A_{PIXEL}}\right)\tau_{OPT}. \qquad (6\text{-}13)$$

Again, although it is not customary, but being consistent with identifying an optical gain for point sources (in the sidebar), **Equation 6-13** contains a term which could be identified as a gain for extended sources:

$$G_{OPT,EXTENDED} \approx \frac{A_R}{A_{PIXEL}}. \qquad (6\text{-}14)$$

EXAMPLE 6-3: TYPICAL COLLECTIONS FROM A SATELLITE-BASED COLLECTION SYSTEM

For a large area early warning/surveillance mission, suppose it is necessary to image a Ground Sample Distance of 500 × 500 m onto 10 × 10 μm pixels at λ = 2.5 μm (1200 K target). Then, a (diffraction limited) sensor's dimensions may be approximately:

$$D \approx 30 \text{ cm} \Rightarrow A_R \approx 0.071 \text{ m}^2,$$
$$f \approx 3.5 \text{ m} \Rightarrow f/\# \approx 11.7, \text{ and}$$
$$A_{PIX} \approx 10 \times 10 \text{ μm} \approx 10^{-10} \text{ m}^2.$$

Thus, the optical gains for target and background are approximately:

$$G_{TGT} \approx \frac{(0.14)(0.071 \text{ m}^2)}{(11.7)^2(2.5 \times 10^{-6} \text{ m})^2} \approx 1.2 \times 10^7$$

and

$$G_{BKG} \approx \frac{0.071 \text{ m}^2}{(10^{-5} \text{ m})^2} \approx 7.1 \times 10^8.$$

Since the gain is greater for background than for target, it is neccessary that target intensity be greater than background radiance for the target to be visible. (See **Chapters 13** and **14**.)

7 PHOTOELECTRIC DETECTORS

To reiterate, the purpose of advanced technical intelligence is to collect physical information about targets: what they are, where they are, and what they are doing. This text is restricted to the information that can be collected using electromagnetic (EM) waves (light) in the visible and infrared portions of the spectrum. The waves have been characterized as carrying information in packets (quanta or photons) having measurable energy, depending on wavelength or frequency, polarization, and phase.

Traditionally, collected light is formed by optical systems into images (**Chapter 6**), and the images are viewed by an analyst to literally find and identify targets. As stressed several times, detection, identification, and characterization of targets does not necessarily have to be done visually; targets have many other signatures (and metrics). Nonetheless, to get maximum information about a target from a remote location, an image of the target needs to be formed that faithfully reproduces its spatial, spectral, and temporal natures. Those characteristics are then captured with a detector. Detectors transform the optical input signal (the image) into an electrical output signal. Arrays of many detectors are commonly used in man-made sensors as well as many sensors found in nature, such as the eyes of people, animals, and insects (as shown above). This process and associated operating characteristics will be described in this chapter.

SECTIONS
7.1 RADIATION DETECTION
7.2 FOCAL PLANE ARRAYS
7.3 PHOTODETECTOR CHARACTERISTICS
7.4 PHOTODETECTOR OPERATION

7.1 RADIATION DETECTION

Depending on a light wave's energy, there are three basic ways to detect it. For completeness, **Figure 7-1** repeats the electromagnetic spectrum of **Figure 2-3** and shows the three regimes, which are not exclusive but overlap considerably.

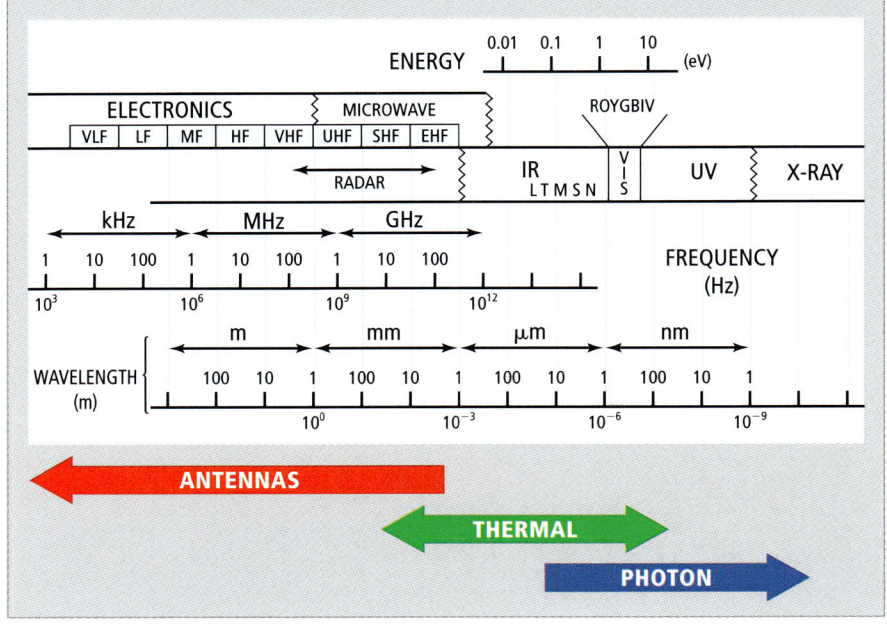

Figure 7-1
Three classes of radiation detectors across the EM spectrum.

LONG WAVELENGTH DETECTORS

In the radio frequency (RF) portion of the spectrum, *antennas*[1] are used. Antennas detect the oscillating electric and magnetic fields in an incident wave, $\vec{E}$ and $\vec{B}$. The fields exert forces on electric charges in the antenna, causing the electrons to move: an electric current. The current is conducted from the antenna by a feed line to a device, fundamentally a radio, which subsequently detects and analyzes the current. **Figure 7-2** sketches a dipole antenna and radio and shows a typical antenna as used by an amateur radio operator and other radio services. A dipole is the basic design for many other complex antennas.

Most metals make excellent antennas[2] since some of their electrons are relatively free to move through their quantum energy bands (**Chapter 2**).

---

[1] It may not be clear that the input to an antenna is an image. It is indeed since it carries spatial, spectral, and temporal information about targets. The difference between what is thought of as optics and antennas is the aperture-to-wavelength ratio. In the visible, it is often 10^6 or more. While in the RF, it is only one to a hundred or so. A telescope's point spread function (PSF) is small, while an antenna's equivalent gain pattern is broad. Thus, a long wavelength image is not literally discernible until a significant amount of signal processing correlates the energy received by an antenna with a geolocation.

[2] Indeed, every wire is an antenna, and all electronic devices can inadvertently receive or transmit unwanted RF signals. Part 15 of the United States Federal Communications Commission regulations stipulates that many devices, like a wireless computer keyboard, may not cause harmful interference [by radiating] and must accept interference received. This is a part of SIGINT on one hand, and computer security on the other.

Figure 7-2
Antennas.

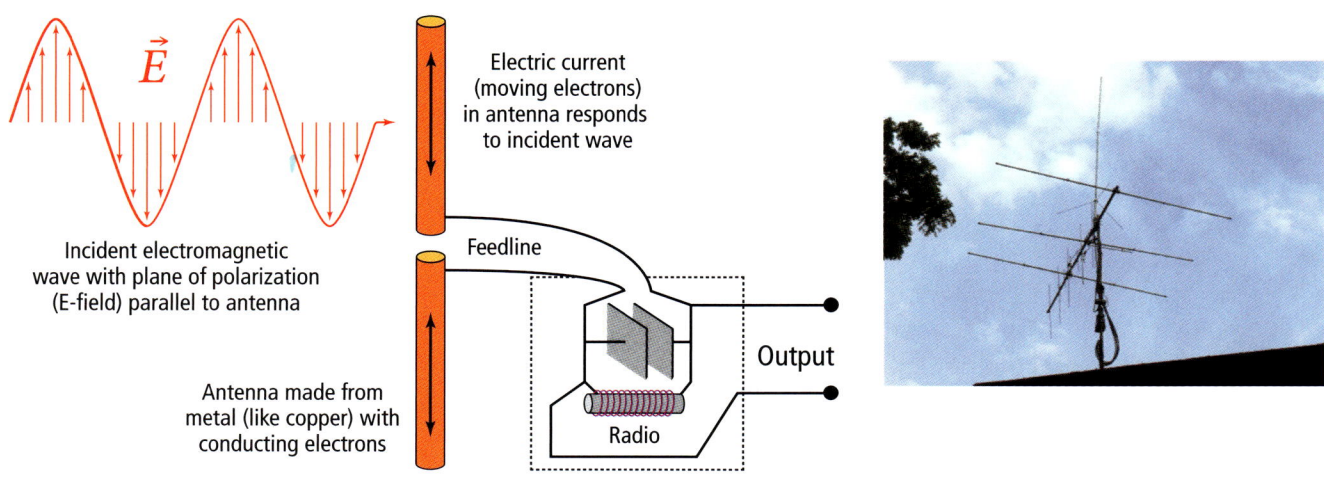

As small as electrons are, their inertia ($m_e = 9.11 \times 10^{-31}$ kg) eventually becomes too great for them to respond to electric and magnetic field oscillations faster than a few hundred gigahertz (~10^{11} Hz).[3] Hence, antennas are limited to the detection of EM waves with wavelengths longer than a few millimeters.

THERMAL DETECTORS

Light waves at any wavelength can be sensed with thermal detectors. Although, this type of sensor is most commonly used to detect micron through millimeter waves. These devices absorb within their volumes absorb the power of an incident EM wave, expressed in terms of the square of the amplitudes of a wave's electric and magnetic fields:

$$U = \frac{\epsilon_0 |\vec{E}|^2}{2} + \frac{|\vec{B}|^2}{2\mu_0} \left[\frac{W}{m^3}\right], \qquad (7\text{-}1)$$

where ϵ_0 and μ_0 are EM constants. The wave's energy is absorbed within the detector per unit time, and the detector responds with some change of its physical or electrical properties. The change could be almost anything: mechanical expansion of a solid or liquid, chemical reactions, induced electrical voltage, or something else. Most importantly, the amount of change can be measured (using a ruler, a scale, a voltmeter, etc.) to determine the causal radiation input. These devices can be quite compact and sensitive, but their obvious disadvantage is energy management. They cannot continue to absorb energy indefinitely, but must be "dumped" and reset. Unless reset against some standard, the utility of a thermal detector is in measuring relative energy inputs rather than absolute ones. **Figure 7-4** sketches a rudimentary thermal detector.

Figure 7-3
Roy J. Glauber, Mallickrodt Professor of Physics, Harvard University, received the 2005 Nobel Prize in Physics for his contributions to the quantum theory of optical coherence: "I don't know anything about photons, but I know one when I see one—a photon is what a photo detector detects."

[3] Terahertz antennas have been recently manufactured. Practical applications in remote sensing outside the laboratory may be developed soon.

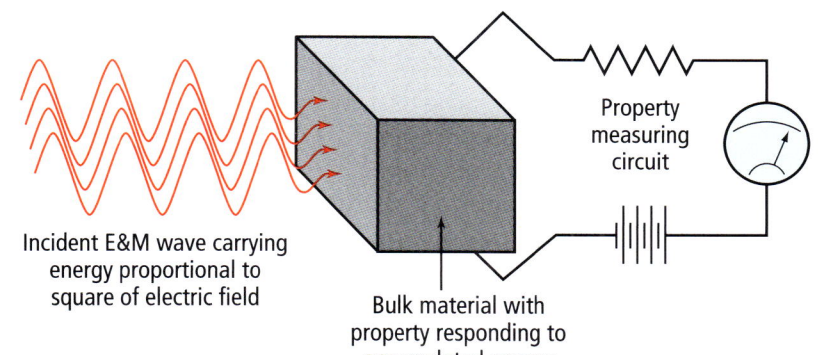

Incident E&M wave carrying energy proportional to square of electric field

Property measuring circuit

Bulk material with property responding to accumulated energy

SHORT WAVELENGTH DETECTORS

At short wavelengths (infrared and visible), the photon properties of light become important (**Figure 7-3**). The process is like absorption, except a photon's energy is converted into the kinetic energy of an electron,[4] rather than putting it into a higher energy state.

1. PHOTOELECTRIC EFFECT

In the basic photoelectric effect, incident photons liberate electrons from a metal, which are collected externally (**Figure 7-5**). Such a device is termed *photoemissive*, and its resulting electrical current is analyzed to deduce the input which created it. However, there is a specific requirement on the input before any output will appear. Incident photons *must* have a minimum amount of energy, called the work function, ϕ, of the detector. **Figure 7-6** is a modification of the left part of **Figure 2-36**, showing the upper energy structure of a metal. Above the conduction band, where electrons can move relatively easily within metal, is the surface potential. With energy above the

Figure 7-4
Thermal detectors. The highway expansion joint on the left responds to thermal input to prevent a section of a bridge from bulging. The fish tank thermometer on the right responds to thermal input by changing colors. (Left photo courtesy of CC-BY-SA-3.0/Matt H. Wade at Wikipedia http://en.wikipedia.org/wiki/User:UpstateNYer.)

[4] It is this conversion of photons to electrical currents that gives the coined word photonics. Photonic devices are the result of merging photoelectric effect detectors with solid state electronics, and may actually convert signals back and forth between electrical currents and beams of photons (using light emitting diodes (LEDs) to propagate information via low-loss optical fiber instead of through wires.

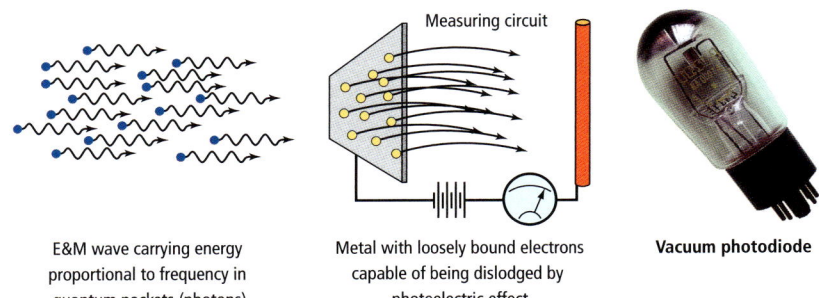

Figure 7-5
Basic photoelectric effect. (Vacuum photodiode picture courtesy of http://commons.wikimedia.org/wiki/File:RA0007A.jpg; Creative Commons Attribution-Share Alike 3.0 Unported; RJB1.)

surface potential, electrons become completely free and are no longer bound to stay within. That is, if an electron in a metal's conduction band absorbs an incident photon with minimum energy, ϕ, it will become free. When the metal is negatively biased (becoming a *photocathode*), free electrons (*photoelectrons*) will become a photocurrent attracted to a positive electrode (anode). Any excess photon energy over and above the work function becomes the kinetic energy of the electron.

Figure 7-6
The work function energy in metals.

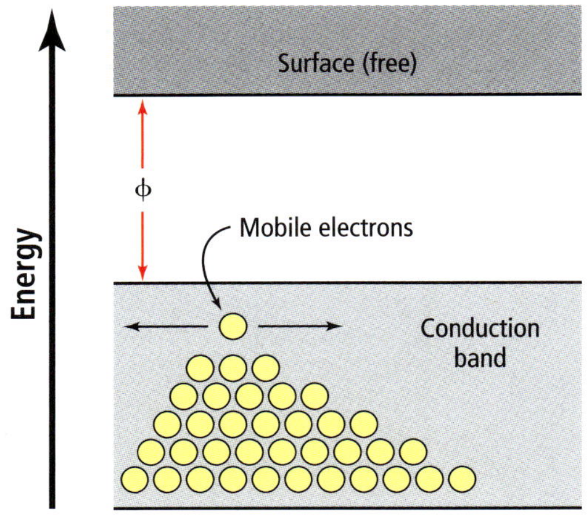

[5] The alkali metals (first column of the periodic table) have lower work functions, but they are highly reactive and difficult to work with. Combinations of alkalis are commonly used as coatings on the photocathodes of vacuum tube devices called *photomultipiers* which can provide visible imagery. They rely on the excess kinetic energy of photoelectrons to subsequently crash into other electrodes within the tube (*dynodes*) to create a shower or cascade of electrons. Thus, photomultipliers provide an internally amplified signal of approximately 10^6 electrons for every incident photon. These tubes are very sensitive, but typically require high voltages (100–1,000 V) to operate.

Since incident photons must have a minimum energy to activate the photoelectric effect, there is a longest detectable wavelength:

$$\lambda_{LONGEST} \approx \frac{hc}{\phi} \approx \frac{1.24}{\phi[eV]} \; [\mu m]. \tag{7-2}$$

Table 7-1 lists the work functions and longest wavelengths for some metallic elements.[5] Note, all but aluminum require a light input in the ultraviolet, in agreement with Heinrich Hertz' observations discussed in the sidebar, **Some History of the Photoelectric Effect**. The necessity for such high photon energies places a severe limitation on taking advantage of the effect for advanced technical intelligence collection without modification. Nonetheless, the discussion will be restricted to applications of photoelectric effect detectors, as they are the most ubiquitous devices in deployed sensors.

Table 7-1
Photoelectric work functions and longest photon wavelengths for some metallic elements.

Work Functions of Some Atomic Elements							
Element		ϕ(eV)	λ(μm)	Element		ϕ(eV)	λ(μm)
Silver	Ag	3.67	0.338	Iron	Fe	3.91	0.317
Aluminum	Al	2.98	0.417	Mercury	Hg	4.50	0.275
Gold	Au	4.73	0.263	Platinum	Pt	4.09	0.303
Beryllium	Be	3.17	0.391	Antimony	Sb	4.01	0.308
Cadmium	Cd	3.68	0.337	Tellurium	Te	4.04	0.307

SOME HISTORY OF THE PHOTOELECTRIC EFFECT

Becquerel | Hertz | Thomson | Tesla | Lenard | Einstein | Millikan

(Becquerel photo courtesy of http://en.wikipedia.org/wiki/File:Portrait_of_Antoine-Henri_Becquerel.jpg; PD_Old. Hertz photo courtesy of http://en.wikipedia.org/wiki/File:Heinrich_Rudolf_Hertz.jpg; PD-Old. Thomson photo courtesy of https://en.wikipedia.org/wiki/File:J.J._Thomson.jpg; PD-Old.)

Discoveries in physics generally do not happen overnight, but are built along wandering paths of investigation. If any scientist is credited with a new development, it is because of seeing farther by "standing on the shoulders of giants." The photoelectric effect is one such example of nearly a century of community effort. Here is a partial history.

In 1839, A. E. Becquerel (1820–1891) noted what is now called the photovoltaic effect. In 1873, W. Smith (1828–1891) observed a related phenomenon in selenium that is now recognized as photoconductivity. Not long after, in 1877, H. Hertz (1857–1894) fiddled around in his lab to find that he could cause a spark to jump across a gap between two metal spheres (held at a voltage difference) by shining a UV light on them. He didn't know why any other light wouldn't work.

In 1899, J. J. Thomson (1856–1940) deduced that Hertz' spark consisted of negatively charged particles (electrons!). Ever the inventor, Serbian-American physicist N. Tesla (1856–1943) ran with this discovery to patent his idea, in 1901, that it would be possible to charge condensers (capacitors) by shining light on them. Crucially, P. Lenard (1862–1947) conducted further experiments in 1903 to show that the discharge effect, which was then thought to be related to cathode rays, depended on the color (wavelength) of light, but not on its irradiance on a metal surface. At that time, there was no explanation for the Hertzian phenomenon.

In his *annus mirabilis* of 1905, A. Einstein (1879–1955) provided the explanation for the photoelectric effect used today by assuming the existence of light quanta first proposed by M. Planck in 1900. Although R. A. Millikan (1868–1953) provided quantitative experimental verification in 1915, and Einstein himself was awarded the 1921 Nobel Prize for his explanation (not for relativity!), he later said "All the fifty years of conscious brooding have brought me no closer to the answer to the question: What are light quanta?"

2. EXTENDING SPECTRAL RANGE

A major research thrust in electro-optics was to develop devices capable of detecting longer wavelength photons. This requires a lower work function, but the list of metals is quickly exhausted. Further surface material research has only been able to push the longest photon wavelengths for the photoelectric effect slightly past 1.0 micrometer. Therefore, research turned to the semiconductor. **Figure 7-7** (taken from the middle of **Figure 2-36**) suggests a photon with minimum energy equal to the band gap, E_g, could promote an electron to a semiconductor's conduction band. With an applied voltage, or bias, to the device, photoelectrons then become internal current, rather than external. In principle, the current is directly proportional to the input of photons, which will be discussed below, and the device is said to be *photoconductive*. **Table 7-2** provides a short list of some semiconductor elements and compounds that have been developed into light detectors.

Table 7-2

Semiconductor materials for detecting photons.

Semiconductors		
Material	Band Gap (ev)	λ(μm)
InSb	0.18	5.54
Ge	0.67	1.85
Si	1.11	1.12
GaAs	1.43	0.87

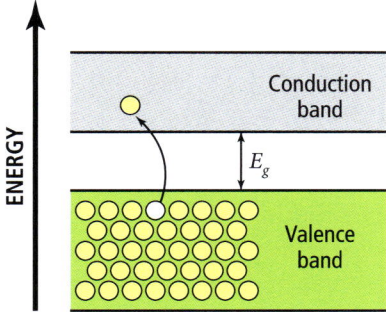

Figure 7-7

Semiconductor material energy levels make them appropriate for use as longer-wavelength photon detectors.

The semiconductor elements listed in **Table 7-2**, silicon and germanium, are from the fourth column of the periodic table. As such, they have four electrons in their outer shells and easily bond together so each atom has eight shared electrons in complete outer shells. The two compounds are III-V compounds, having one element from the third column (Ga and In) and one from the fifth (As and Sb). As with Si and Ge, these elements readily share electrons to become stable materials with effectively complete outer electron shells. Details of their bonding, which are beyond the scope of this text, give the band gaps listed. Note, they are capable of detecting infrared photons.

Other infrared detecting materials can be manufactured by "doping" silicon or germanium with column III or V elements. In the former case, the shell structure is one electron short of being filled, so the vacancy, or hole,[6] acts like a positive charge; and the material is p-type. In the latter case, the opposite is true with an excess negative electron; and the material is n-type. Implantation of these atoms into the structure creates an additional discrete electron energy level *within* the band gap that can either accept or donate electrons to or from the conduction band. The importance of the new energy level is it is closer in energy to the material's conduction band. Lower energy photons can now activate photoelectrons. With these types of materials, longer wavelengths can be detected. For example, the mercury doped germanium in **Figure 7-8** has long wavelength limits far beyond the 1.85 μm listed for pure germanium in **Table 7-2**.

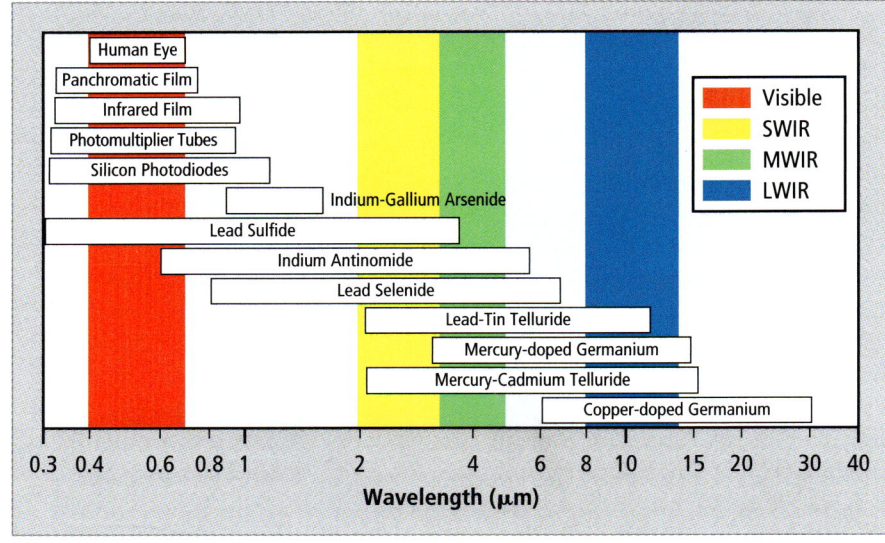

Figure 7-8
Some semiconductor detector materials compared with the human eye, photographic film, and photomultiplier tubes (which use the photoelectric effect).

Another development in photonics is the solid state photodiode. This device is an abutted p-type and n-type semiconductor such that their proximity creates a very small effective bandgap in the narrow transition zone. (Or perhaps, the acceptor levels of one joins with the donor levels of the other.) With proper engineering, these devices may also be sensitive to LWIR.

Figure 7-8 shows the spectral ranges of some popular semiconductor detectors compared to the human eye and infrared film. Notable in the figure are lead sulfide (PbS), a IV-VI standard infrared detector in many older systems, and indium antimonide (InSb), a very commonly used material. Also notable is the mercury-cadmium-telluride amalgam. The band gap in this material can be tuned by changing the Hg:Cd ratio as shown in **Figure 7-9**.

---

[6] Technically, an electric current is defined as the flow of *positive* charge through a wire (or space). Since *negative* electrons are usually the mobile charge carriers, they flow opposite to the current. Most of the time this detail is ignored until it becomes important to determine what is really happening in a semiconductor device. Incident photons (with sufficient energy, of course) create electron-hole pairs by kicking the electron to a higher energy state or the hole to a lower energy state. A hole is actually a void of negative charge. So, it is effectively positive. The electron is attracted to a positive voltage (potential or bias) while the hole is attracted to a negative voltage. The motion of holes is the actual current.

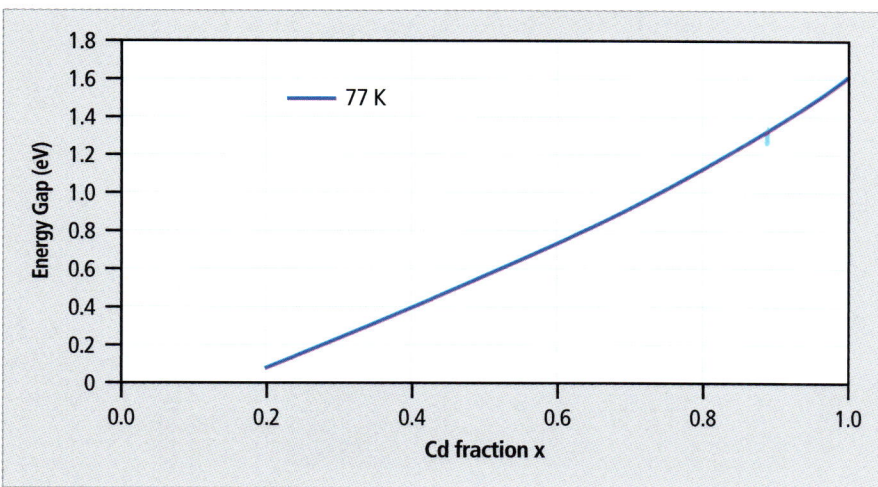

Figure 7-9
Band gap energy of $Hg_{1-x}Cd_xTe$ as a function of the cadmium fraction, x. [1]

7.2 FOCAL PLANE ARRAYS

The *de facto* detector on advanced technical intelligence sensors is an electro-optical device consisting of not just one but hundreds to millions of detectors. They are arranged in a regular array to systematically convert the optical image into an electrical one; this array of detectors is commonly termed a Focal Plane Array (FPA).

DESCRIPTION

A FPA is a rectangular grid of detector elements with each one having a row-column address; numbering is from one corner of the array. Each element is called a pixel (for *picture element*); it is important to remember that *every pixel is an individual detector*. As an individual detector, pixel sizes are on the order of 5–10 μm on a side,[7] and entire focal planes may be no larger than a postage stamp. **Figure 7-10** shows a modern digital single lens reflex (DSLR) camera. Behind the lens is a $3872 \times 2592 \approx 10^7$ pixel FPA measuring only 23.6×15.8 mm. Its pitch is approximately 6.1 μm. (Such a camera would be advertised as a 10-megapixel camera.) **Figure 7-11** shows a primitive, easy to conceptualize example.

Figure 7-10
FPA in a modern digital camera.

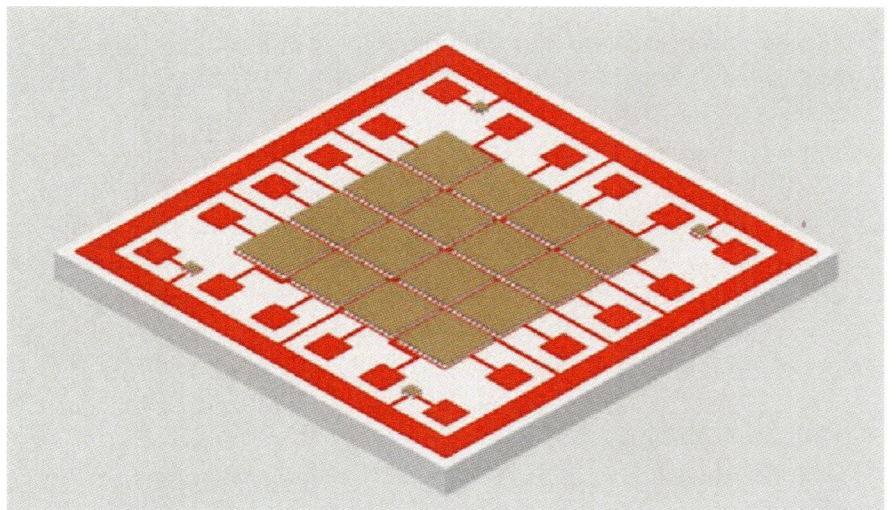

Figure 7-11
A simple FPA of sixteen elements. (Courtesy SPIE Newsroom.) [2]

Modern FPAs are ingenious combinations of photodetectors and their controlling solid state electronics built into a single integrated circuit chip.

---

[7] The spacing between pixels, center to center, is called the pitch. The physical size of a pixel may be slightly smaller to electrically isolate them. See **Figure 7-19**. This difference will generally be ignored in this text.

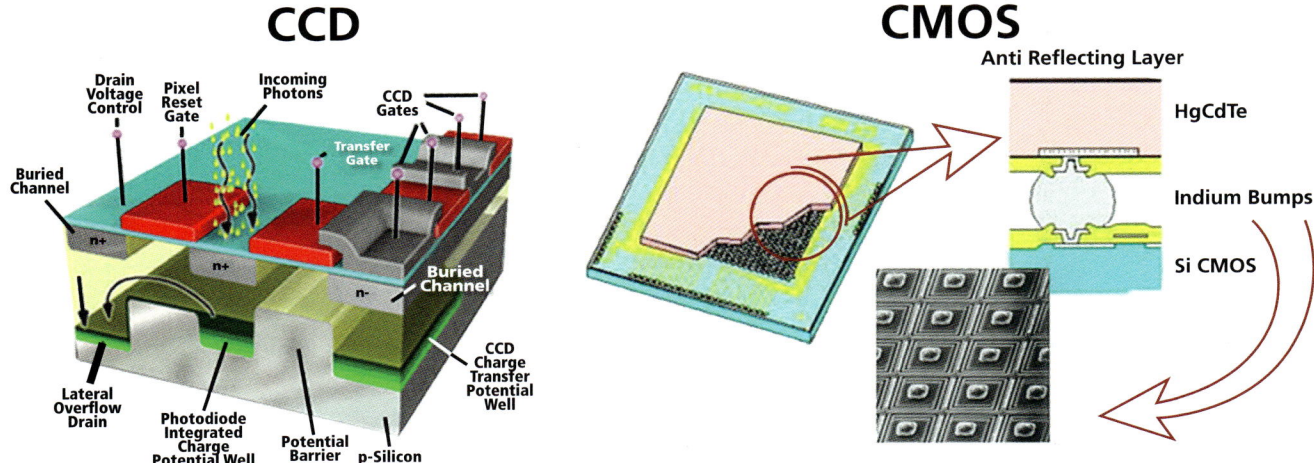

Figure 7-12
CCD and CMOS photodetectors.

Typically, a photosensitive material is joined to a photoelectron collection electrode and its associated read-out circuit in one of two ways:

1. Charge Coupled Devices (CCD) are photodetectors divided into pixels by an overlaying grid of electrodes with implanted regions of p-type and n-type silicon underneath. See the left side of **Figure 7-12**. The collection electrodes are solid-state wells, which store[8] photoelectrons until they are read out. (Electronically speaking, the storage wells are like capacitors.) By changing voltages on the wells, each pixel's collection can be moved along its row or column to the neighboring well, and so on, in a bucket brigade fashion to the edge of the focal plane. At the edge of the focal plane, a well's content (stored electrons) is converted into a voltage. The voltage is digitized, and this is considered to be output data from the pixel. See **Example 7-1** concerning well depth.

2. Complimentary Metal-Oxide Semiconductor (CMOS) detectors are somewhat different from CCDs, but accomplish the same purpose. The term CMOS refers to the integrated solid-state storage, read-out, and conversion electronics (one set per pixel) on the underside of an array. On top, a wafer of photosensitive material is "bump bonded" through dots of indium metal to the CMOS circuits underneath. See the right side of **Figure 7-12**. Electric potentials on the CMOS electrodes collect photoelectrons for controlled intervals of time, and then are periodically converted to voltages directly at each pixel. The voltages are then digitized and read out in a sequential manner to become digitized data.

Either type of FPA is acceptable for advanced technical intelligence collections. There may be particular advantages to one over the other for certain applications and sensors, but both are relatively low noise (defined later) and temporally responsive to rapidly changing input signals.

SPATIAL SAMPLING

Spatially, the purpose of a FPA is to *sample* a target's image in a regular order. The sequence of digitized voltages from the pixels is thus encoded with image information where each pixel's output is proportional to *all* of the target photons that fell on its surface. That is, a single pixel has no way of discriminating *where* on its surface a photon

---

[8] Operationally, pixels are kept "on" to accumulate input for some interval of time before they are turned "off" and their stored output is read out. This is analogous to the shutter on a camera remaining open for a finite interval of time, like 1/100 s, when a picture is taken. Details of this temporal sampling are discussed below.

EXAMPLE 7-1: HOW DEEP IS THE WELL?

Imagining a photoelectron storage well is like an electrical capacitor, a simple calculation can be made to estimate the amount of electrons one well could store.

The definition of capacitance is the amount of charge stored per unit volt induced by the stored charges [1 farad (F) = 1 coulomb (C) per 1 volt (V)]. An elementary model of a capacitor is just two parallel plates of surface area A_{CAP} held apart from one another a distance ℓ by an insulating material with dielectric constant κ. Thus, when the well is filled to capacity:

$$C = \left[\frac{\text{coulomb}}{\text{volt}}\right] \approx \frac{N_{WELL} q_e}{V_{MAX}} \approx \frac{\kappa \varepsilon_0 A_{CAP}}{\ell}.$$

Here, N_{WELL} is the number of electrons in the well,

$q_e \approx 1.60 \times 10^{-19}$ C/electron is the charge on one electron,

$V_{MAX} \approx 6$ V is the maximum output voltage for typical solid-state electronics,

$\kappa \approx 11.6$ is the dielectric constant of silicon (the insulator),

$\varepsilon_0 \approx 8.85 \times 10^{-12}$ F/m is the permittivity of free space (an EM constant),

$A_{CAP} \approx (7 \ \mu\text{m})^2$ is the area of a typical pixel, and

$\ell \approx 1 \ \mu\text{m}$ is about the thickness of a silicon layer.

Solving for well depth and substituting these numbers, results in

$$N_{WELL} \approx \frac{\kappa \varepsilon_0 A_{CAP} V_{MAX}}{\ell \ q_e}$$

$$N_{WELL} \approx \frac{(11.6)(8.85 \times 10^{-12} \ \text{F/m})(7 \times 10^{-6} \ \text{m})^2 (6\text{V})}{(10^{-6} \ \text{m})(1.6 \times 10^{-19} \ \text{C/electron})}$$

$$\approx 1.9 \times 10^5 \text{ electrons.}$$

arrives. In principle, the perfectly focused image of a line falling across a focal plane, as in **Figure 7-13a** for example, would result in an output like that in **Figure 7-13b**. Here the shading of each pixel is intended to represent the fraction of each pixel covered by the line's image.[9] The resulting data of the coarseness of this sampling suggests the line is wider than it really is, or at least has soft edges rather than the actual image's hard edges in **Figure 7-13a**.

[9] Mathematically, Figure 7-13 illustrates the operation of convolution: the spatial function of the image was integrated over the spatial function of the FPA, and Figure 7-13(b) is the result. Ideally, the exact image of the target could be recovered from the data, but the process of de-convolution may be too difficult to accomplish.

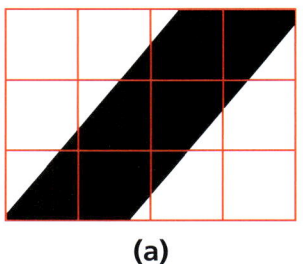
(a)

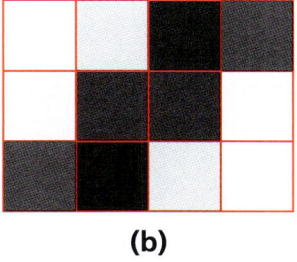
(b)

Figure 7-13
a) A perfect image of a line falls across a FPA. Each pixel's output is proportional to the amount of light received, regardless of where photons fall on its surface. b) Shading represents the output of each pixel.

A complication to spatial sampling ignored in **Figure 7-13** is the physical optics reality of *the point spread function* (PSF) (**Chapter 6**). The image of only a single point is depicted in **Figure 7-14** (assuming only the central disk of the Airy function needs to be accounted for, see **Example 7-2**). Rather than a FPA's output from a point source target being only from a single pixel, a FPA will sample it as shown in the figure, and *all* pixels with any energy in the PSF must be found to understand the target. Any pixel within the PSF, like the one shown, has only a fraction of the total energy, F_{PIX}, and is defined as:

$$F_{PIX} = \frac{\Phi_{PIX}}{\Phi_{PSF}}, \qquad (7\text{-}3)$$

where Φ_{PIX} is the power actually measured by a pixel and Φ_{PSF} is $0.84 \times \tau_{OPT}$ of the at-aperture power from the point source. In theory, Φ_{PIX} could be calculated from the Airy function if the proper set of coordinates on the focal plane[10] is used. Total energy in the image is then found to be the sum of outputs of all pixels within the PSF. So, evidently $\sum_{PIXELS} F_{PIX} \approx 1$.

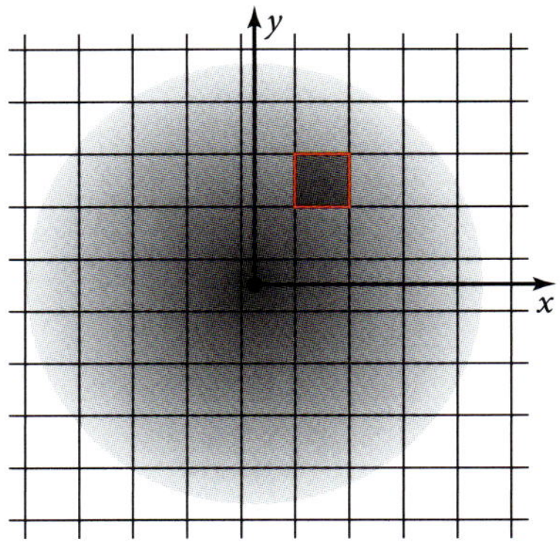

Figure 7-14
The image of a point spans many pixels. Any pixel within a PSF only reports the fraction of light received. The power measured by the pixel outlined in red is Φ_{PIX}.

EXAMPLE 7-2: HOW BIG IS A POINT SPREAD FUNCTION COMPARED TO PIXEL SIZE?

DSLR cameras, like the one shown in **Figure 7-12**, typically have lenses with *f*-stops ranging from 2.8 to 16 (or more if the photographer can afford it). Suppose such a camera is equipped with a silicon FPA, sensitive to visible through near-infrared light, 0.4–1.1 μm (see **Table 7-2**) and has a nominal 7.5 μm pitch. Taking the *diameter* of a PSF to be ~2.44(*f*/#)λ, the PSF sizes in micrometers and number of pixels are shown below.

f/#	Wavelength	
	0.4 μm	1.1 μm
2.8	2.7 μm ≈ 0.4 pixels	7.5 μm ≈ 1 pixels
16	15.6 μm ≈ 2 pixels	43 μm ≈ 6 pixels

Therefore, expect that images of point sources will occupy areas on a focal plane from less than 1 to about 30 pixels, depending on wavelength and aperture setting. However, at these wavelengths and on this focal plane, two adjacent point sources may not be resolved according to the Rayleigh and Nyquist criteria (discussed in **Chapter 8**). Does this mean the camera cannot be used to resolve objects? (No, just a different resolution criterion must be used.)

---

[10] **Chapter 14** will describe how to find the center of a PSF on the focal plane. The origin of the *x-y* coordinates in **Figure 7-14** are shown located at the center of the PSF.

Since targets can be considered as spatial superpositions of point sources, their images are superpositions of PSFs. Thus, the image of the line in **Figure 7-13** becomes a line spread function and is much wider, as in **Figure 7-15a**. The FPA sampling of the diffracted line is then as suggested by the right side of the figure. Note, it is indeed wider than shown in the previous figure, and analysis of the image will require accounting for its energy from multiple pixels.

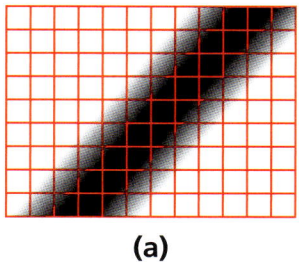
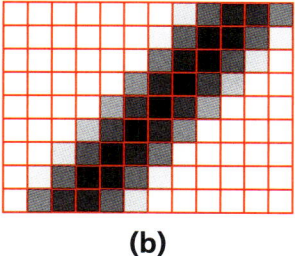
(a)   (b)

Figure 7-15
Image of a line showing its PSF. The pixels are the same size as in the previous figure, but the image is wider, and hence sampled by many more pixels.

Moreover, the PSF also implies every pixel will sample energy from multiple points on a target. What does this mean in terms of resolution? On one hand, as will be discussed in **Chapter 8**, spatial resolution of two adjacent point sources requires both Rayleigh and Nyquist criteria to be satisfied. This necessitates the PSF to be as large as about six pixels in diameter.[11] This is not always the case, particularly in visible-near infrared photography as **Example 7-2** calculates. The calculations in the example suggest the situation depicted in **Figure 7-13a** shows an image with a PSF much smaller than a pixel.

Figure 7-16
Close up of Lincoln's hairline, showing pixelation.

Now, look at the image of a famous American President in **Figure 7-17**. On the left, the original 300 row × 200 column picture is clearly, or literally, discernible to the eye. (Although this is a digital scan of a photograph taken with older technology, it can still be used as an example.) If Lincoln's hairline on the left side of his forehead is examined in **Figure 7-16**, the same effect as in **Figure 7-15** is shown. This is often called pixelation, but here it is attributed to spatial sampling of an image where the PSF is smaller than a pixel. Successive images in **Figure 7-17** were re-sampled to simulate larger pixels (or a smaller image) by a factor of two at each step. At what point is the image of a face no longer resolvable?

Figure 7-17
Spatial resolution.

The fourth image is somewhat recognizable but the fifth image is on the edge of literal identification. Can the sixth image be identified? Identifying a particular person does not seem likely, but there is some resemblance to a human face. The clue is possibly the eyes: two dark pixels staring forward. This leads to another criterion for spatial resolution: *If* two objects are imaged such that their PSFs are smaller than a pixel, *and* there is one pixel between the two images that has little or no energy from the objects, *then* those two images

[11] Recall worst case alignment along a diagonal on the focal plane PSF separation needs to be a minimum of $2\sqrt{2}$ Airy disk radii between centers.

are *literally* resolved (although they may not be identifiable, except perhaps from the context of their surroundings). (An interactive file, **Appendix 7-1**, is available on the support website. This shockwave file should open in a browser window, like Internet Explorer, and allow one to move the images of two objects with no discernible PSF around on a focal plane. Pushing the images closer together with the slider bar will allow one to investigate how much separation is necessary for literal resolution.)

The resolution criterion just discussed is the usual way to specify the resolution of IMINT systems and ordinary cameras. A test target like **Figure 7-18** is imaged and examined to determine the smallest set of line pairs that can be discerned with the eye. A line pair is an alternating set of light and dark bars on the chart.

Figure 7-18 Resolution target.

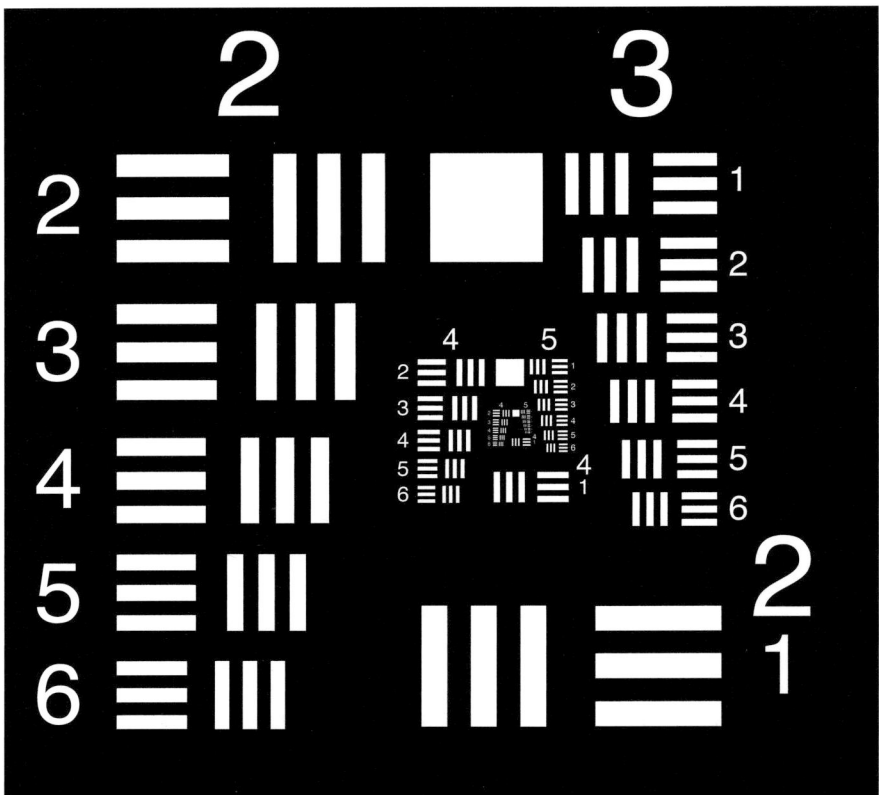

USAF 1951 STANDARD TARGET

One more feature of spatial sampling must be mentioned. Although a FPA may receive all the photons passing through a collector's optics, it may not be able to respond to them, spatially speaking. For instance, the left side of **Figure 7-12** shows some of the photosensitive material of a CCD is overlaid with electrical contacts, which presumably, are not transparent. Therefore, only a fraction of the surface may receive photons, and the input is reduced by an additional geometric factor called F^*_{PIX}:

$$F^*_{PIX} = \frac{\text{Photosensitive pixel area}}{\text{Physical pixel area}}, \quad (7\text{-}4)$$

where the difference between the size of a photosensitive and physical pixel is often referred to as the gap between pixels. This may be approximately known from the manufacturing process and should be the same for every pixel. It is different from the PSF sampling fraction introduced above.

For CMOS photodetectors, the entire surface of the topmost photosensitive wafer is exposed to photons. Pixels are defined by the electro-attracting potentials of the underlying electronics; there are no physical barriers. **Figure 7-19** shows a top view where the dashed lines represent the photoelectrons' attracting voltages and the plot below indicates its value moving along the center of a row of pixels. Photoelectrons (small dots) produced within the conduction bands near boundaries may have enough excess kinetic energy to pass over to a neighboring pixel (indicated by arrows). The amount of this effect is unknown, but assume it will average out during analysis.

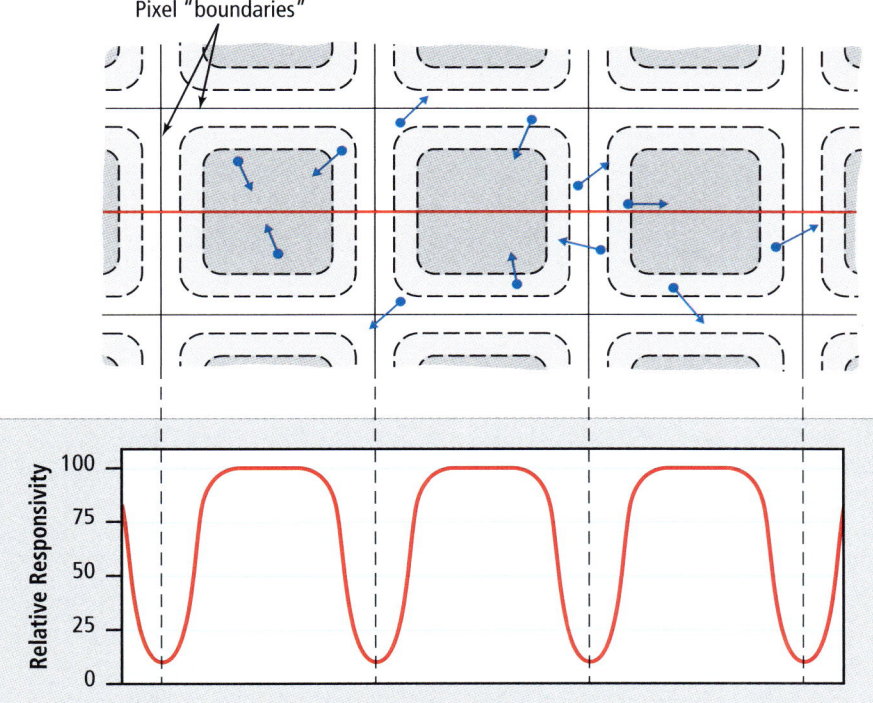

Figure 7-19
CMOS pixel gaps are defined by variation in electron-attracting voltage. Relative responsivity is defined in Equation 7-5.

7.3 PHOTODETECTOR CHARACTERISTICS

Now that photons falling on pixels and the photoelectric effect have been discussed, the focus will turn to a detector's output. A photodetector's output is desired to be directly proportional to its input, so information about the targets can be generated. It is for the most part, but a detector's responsivity and its quirks need to be examined to know the accuracy of its output.

QUANTUM EFFICIENCY

There are several measures of performance (figures of merit) for photodetectors; all of which describe their sensitivity:
- Quantum efficiency (η) is the ratio of output per unit input in units of photoelectrons per photon,
- Responsivity (R) is the ratio of induced current output per unit incident radiant power in units of amperes per watt, and
- Detectivity (D) is a measure of sensitivity equal to the reciprocal of Noise Equivalent Power (NEP) in units of per watt.

In the previous list, NEP is the radiant power input to a detector such that its signal-to-noise output ratio is one. Signal-to-noise is exactly what it sounds like, and inherent detector noise will be discussed below.

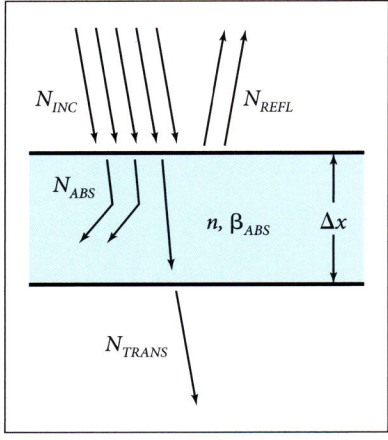

Figure 7-20
Of all the photons incident, N_{INC}, on a material with index of refraction n and absorption coefficient β_{ABS}, some are reflected, N_{REFL}, and a few may be transmitted, N_{TRANS}. Of interest are the remainder that are absorbed, N_{ABS}, of which a fraction creates electron-hole pairs with *quantum efficiency*, η.

Of the various measures, responsivity is straightforward, but quantum efficiency will be used more often because it is intuitive. How many electrons does a device generate for the number of input photons? Mathematically, the two quantities are related by

$$R \approx \frac{q_e \lambda}{hc} \eta \left[\frac{A}{W}\right], \quad (7\text{-}5)$$

where $q_e \approx 1.60 \times 10^{-19}$ coulombs is the charge per electron.

The quantum efficiency of an individual detector depends on its material and construction. To begin the consideration of quantum efficiency, typical photosensitive semiconductor materials have optical indices of refraction (**Table 3-2**) in the range of 3.50–4.50 at visible to infrared wavelengths. By Fresnel's formula for near-normal incident radiation (**Equation 3-10**), these materials therefore reflect 30–40% of photons incident on their surfaces. This can be reduced by an application of anti-reflection coatings.

Next, consider most materials are not entirely opaque, but some light may pass through them at particular wavelengths. (Recall the picture of germanium, **Figure 6-15**.) If the absorption coefficient for the material is known (β_{ABS} = fraction absorbed per unit of distance), use Beer's Law to estimate the fraction of photons absorbed as:

$$\frac{N_{ABS}}{N_{INC} - N_{REFL}} \approx 1 - e^{-\beta_{ABS}\Delta x}, \quad (7\text{-}6)$$

where Δx is the thickness of the photosensitive material (**Figure 7-20**). Of the radiation that is neither reflected nor transmitted, the photons absorbed, if sufficiently energetic, may generate photoelectrons in the conduction band. This absorption-conversion process is not 100% efficient because many of the electrons will immediately collide with atoms in the *material*, lose energy, and recombine[12] into the valence band before they can be removed to a storage well by an external potential (CCD or CMOS) and be counted. The measurement of counting the number of photoelectrons actually collected compared to the number of photons absorbed is the device's *internal quantum efficiency*.

The value quoted for a photodetector's performance, as delivered by its manufacturer, should account for reflection and transmission losses (if any) and is its *external quantum efficiency*. For example, **Figure 7-21** shows the quantum efficiency of an InSb detector, where its high values suggest its designers took great care to eliminate reflection and transmission losses to take maximum advantage of photons originating from a hot exhaust plume. Note, this curve shows a characteristic long-wave cutoff, indicating the band gap energy of the photodetector material (**Table 7-2**).

Figure 7-21
Quantum efficiency of a particular InSb detector. [3]

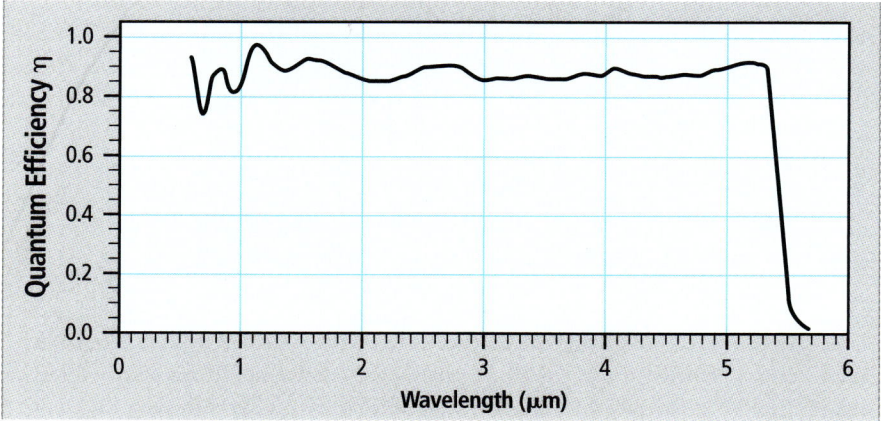

---

[12] Of course, it is not certain that recombination will occur. So, this process is described in statistical terms and is considered to be a component of detector *noise*. It is part of a larger process called generation-recombination (g-r) noise.

Once a detector's quantum efficiency is determined, the application is to discern the number of photons arriving from a target based on the pixel's output. This may be done using the device's operating curve, shown in **Figure 7-22**. Ideally, a detector's output is directly proportional to the input:

$$\{OUTPUT\} \approx \{QUANTUM\ EFFICIENCY\} \times \{INPUT\} \quad (7\text{-}7)$$

as shown by the dotted line in **Figure 7-22**. However, real photodetectors have a response more like that shown by the solid line which differs from the ideal in two significant ways.

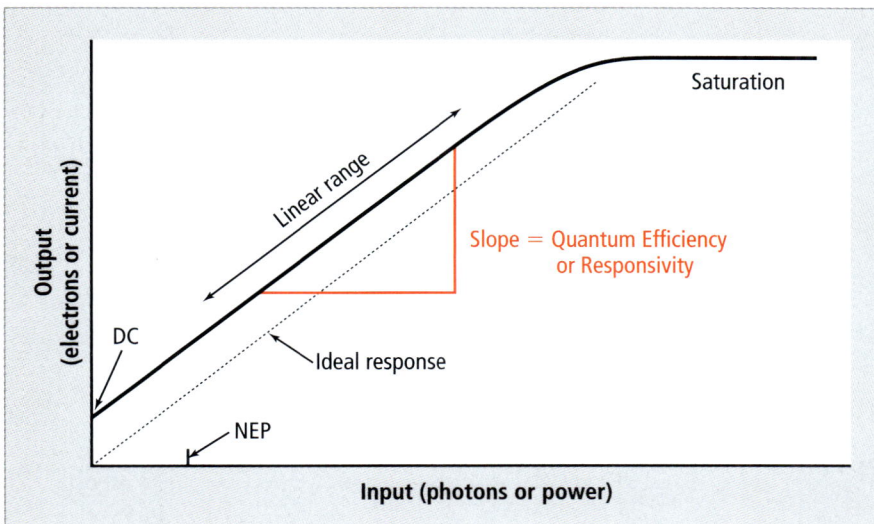

Figure 7-22
A photodetector's input-output response curve.

DETECTOR COOLING TECHNOLOGY

There are several different technologies available for cooling airborne and spaceborne detectors (and hence reduce their DC values). One approach is to keep the detectors in contact with cryogens, which are very cold liquid or solid materials. Commonly used cryogens are liquid nitrogen (77 K boiling point), liquid helium (4 K boiling point), and solid methane (93 K melting point). A second approach is to keep the detectors in a cryocooler, a miniature refrigerator that can achieve very low temperatures in a very small volume. These devices, pioneered by the DOD, operate similarly to their larger commercial counterparts in that input power is required for thermodynamic cooling processes. A third approach, usable only on spacecraft, is radiative cooling. The detectors are kept in contact with a portion of the spacecraft that can be kept at a very low temperature (for example, 85 K for the Landsat Thematic Mapper sensor as discussed in **Chapter 15**). This portion of the spacecraft has a large surface area (cooling fins, in some cases) with high Long-Wave Infrared (LWIR) emissivity to promote strong radiative cooling, and of course, it is never pointed at the sun or the Earth. As a final note, research advances with thermal detectors may provide infrared imaging sensors with high performance that do not require cooling.

First, the curve does not start at zero. Even with *no* input, most photodetectors will show a noisy output. This is called dark current (DC) or dark noise and is a combination of internal noisy processes that are mostly thermal in nature. At any finite temperature, the statistical energy distribution of electrons within a semi-conductor will place a few of them in the conduction band where they will be collected and counted. This DC can be reduced by cooling the detector. For these purposes, treat DC as a non-zero constant added to each pixel's output.

Second, because pixels are physical devices of finite size, they have a limited supply of electrons that can be advanced to the conduction band and stored in the well. Thus, solid-state devices will typically show a saturation effect for high inputs.[13]

With these limitations, the operation of a photodetector is simply the linear expression

$$\{OUTPUT\} \approx \eta \times \{INPUT\} + DC. \quad (7\text{-}8)$$

In many instances, the linear behavior of a detector spans two or three orders of magnitude, and the DC offset, or intercept, can be ignored. For low input levels, however, there is a minimum meaningful input, the NEP (or number of photons). When that is recognized,

$$\{OUTPUT\} \approx \{SIGNAL\} + \{NOISE\} \quad (7\text{-}9)$$

and DC is treated as the noise, then a signal-to-noise ratio of unity provides

[13] For detectors utilized for lights on/lights off indicators, operation in the saturation region is fine. To automatically turn porch lights on and off, for instance: sun up = saturation, but sun down = minimum output, where the saturation current holds the switch open.

$$\frac{\{SIGNAL\}}{\{NOISE\}} \approx \frac{\{OUTPUT\}_{MIN} - \{NOISE\}}{\{NOISE\}} \approx \frac{\{\eta \times NEP + DC\} - DC}{DC} \approx 1 \Rightarrow NEP \approx \frac{DC}{\eta}. \quad (7\text{-}10)$$

This level of input can rarely be detected without specialized data processing and is not to be considered as detection threshold.[14] As discussed in later chapters, the minimum signal usually considered to be reliably detectable (rule of thumb) is for a signal-to-noise ratio of three.

PIXEL CALIBRATION

Processing FPA data is as straightforward as doing the best possible job of solving **Equation 7-8** for the input number of photons, and then relating that input through the sensor's optics through the atmosphere to the target. Therefore, the two key parameters to know are the DC and quantum efficiency (assuming all other sources of noise are negligible). Remembering that every pixel is an independent detector, it is hard to conceive that every one on an array of perhaps millions were manufactured identically, physically and electrically.[15] Variations in DC output and/or quantum efficiency of a pixel may be expected and result in operating curves (for the linear portion, before saturation) as in **Figure 7-23**. The process to determine the slope (η) and intercept (DC) for a pixel is called *calibration*.

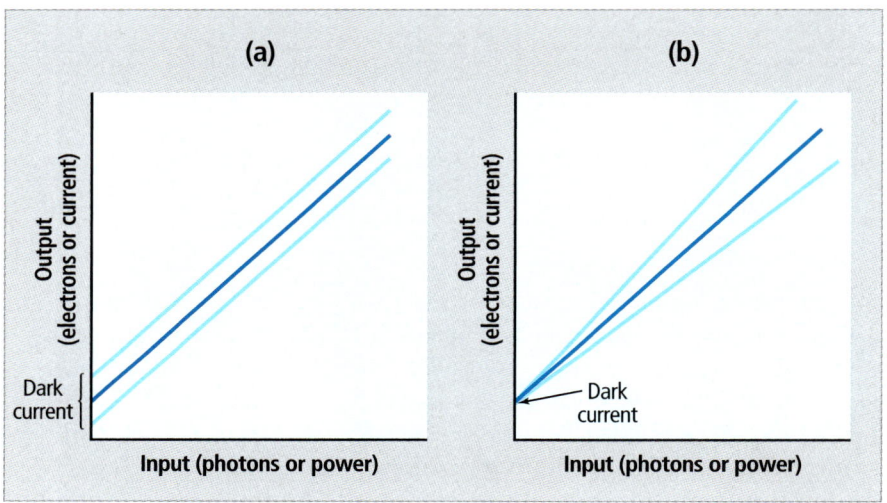

Figure 7-23
Pixel response curves showing a) variation in DC and b) variation in quantum efficiency.

In principle, every pixel on an array would be easy calibrated by alternately providing two known inputs, numbers of photons, N_1 and N_2, and measuring the number of electron outputs, O_1 and O_2. This results in

$$\eta \approx \frac{O_1 - O_2}{N_1 - N_2} \quad \text{and} \quad \text{DC} \approx \frac{N_1 O_2 - N_2 O_1}{N_1 - N_2}. \quad (7\text{-}11)$$

This procedure would be perfectly valid for laboratory-use in monitored surroundings, but unfortunately, deployed sensors, particularly on space platforms, are subject to a variety of uncontrolled circumstances. Thermal stresses from direct sunlight or shadow, depending on orbit and orientation, and voltage (bias) changes from batteries charging and discharging can influence a pixel's performance. Also, solid-state electronics are subject to aging as their materials become brittle; micrometeorite and cosmic ray hits as well as static discharges can also dramatically alter components. All of the above can invalidate a calibration such as **Equation 7-11** and render an absolute conversion of sensor output into questionable target information.

Experience with sensors shows re-calibration of FPAs needs to be conducted as frequently as possible because of the reasons cited above.

---

[14] Indeed, low signal-to-noise detection is very relevant to astronomy and when remote sensors are turned up to look for overhead targets. It is typically not relevant when looking for objects against the Earth's background.

[15] In fact, there are always pixels on the FPA that are defective. One type is "dead detectors" which do not provide any output, no matter the input. A second type is "happy detectors" which provide saturated output, no matter the input. The implications of "happy" and "dead" detectors are there are regions on the ground that will not be covered during a collection, and hence some information about the scene may not be collected.

One method is to carry along calibration sources capable of providing the inputs needed to affect **Equation 7-11**. The obvious difficulty to this method is assuring the calibration sources themselves are calibrated. After all, they are additional pieces of equipment subject to the same environment. Therefore, a more reasonable choice is an external method of calibration.

Attacking the problem directly, **Figure 7-22** and **Equation 7-8** suggest that *without* input to a pixel, its DC could be measured directly. Taking this approach of providing a mechanical shutter[16] to restrict external photons allows a FPA to be exposed as a dark frame, providing a no-input output for every pixel. Again, assuming no other noise source is as large as DC, it can be read directly from the dark frame and *subtracted* from the output of each pixel, leaving only a direct relationship between input and output for each pixel. This is suggested in **Figure 7-24**.

[16] The objection to a mechanical device aboard a spacecraft is the risk of failure. There have been some catastrophic failures of antennas not deploying, attitude control devices freezing up, and so forth, but most telescopes in space do have movable covers to protect their optics. The Hubble Space Telescope is the premier example. The alternate procedure is to point a sensor toward deep space, a portion of the night sky where no (or few) stars can be seen.

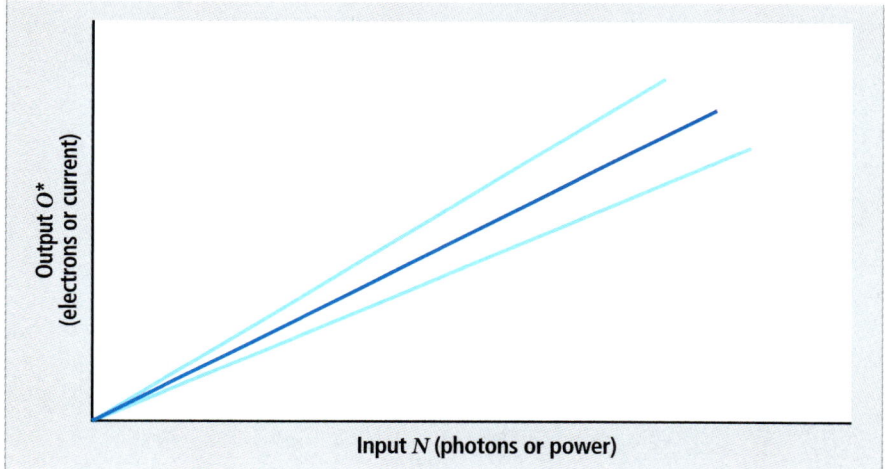

Figure 7-24
Pixel input-output relation after subtraction of DC.

Thus, the calibration problem reduces to providing *one* standard input. Subtraction of the dark frame renders $N_1 = O_1^* = 0$ in **Equation 7-11** (where $O_1^* = O_1 - DC$), leaving only

$$\eta \approx \frac{O_2^*}{N_2}, \qquad (7\text{-}12)$$

where $O_2^* = O_2 - DC$.

Rather than provide an on-board calibration source for this calculation, an appropriate external source is a uniformly radiant scene. This could be the broad ocean, an expanse of desert, or an extended ice sheet (**Figure 7-25**). In any case, the number of photons input to a pixel in a time interval Δt_{INT} is

$$N_2 \approx \int_{BANDPASS} \frac{L_\lambda \Omega_{PIX} \tau_{ATM} A_R \tau_{OPT} \eta}{hc/\lambda} d\lambda \Delta t_{INT}, \qquad (7\text{-}13)$$

where the bandpass is that of the sensor's optics. The disadvantages of this method are estimating the atmospheric transmission function and knowing precisely the spectral radiance, emitted and/or reflected, of the surface.

Figure 7-25
Uniformly radiant extended sources for calibration. (Left photo courtesy of http://commons.wikimedia.org/wiki/File:Morocco_Africa_Flickr_Rosino_December_2005_84527212.jpg; Creative Commons Attribution-Share Alike 2.0 Generic; Rosino. Middle photo courtesy of http://commons.wikimedia.org/wiki/File:44_SAM_2663_(4842337880).jpg; Creative Commons Attribution 2.0 Generic; Victor Grigas. Right photo courtesy of http://commons.wikimedia.org/wiki/File:Polar_Bear_-_Alaska.jpg; Creative Commons Attribution-Share Alike 3.0 Unported; Alan Wilson.)

An alternative method to pointing a sensor down at a uniform earthly source is to look up into space at calibration stars. Catalogs of star spectra (color temperatures) and brightnesses (magnitudes) allow the calculation of their expected irradiances on-aperture. In which case, the number of photons supplied to the focal plane is

$$N_2 \approx \int_{BANDPASS} \frac{\mathcal{E}_\lambda(star) A_R \tau_{OPT} \eta}{hc/\lambda} d\lambda \Delta t_{INT}. \qquad (7\text{-}14)$$

The clear advantage is not accounting for the atmosphere. However, the disadvantage is the (calculated) number of photons is distributed only within a PSF and does not allow calibration of all pixels at once. In addition, the filling factor of **Equation 7-3** comes into play.

7.4 PHOTODETECTOR OPERATION

As the heart of an advanced technical intelligence sensor, the output of a photoelectric detector is data. The detector has spatially sampled a target's image by collecting target photons on its photosensitive surface, and the electronics behind the detector will temporally sample each detector' output. Next, the different possible temporal sampling modes will be discussed. In the applications chapters, spatial sampling will be covered again to consider scanning and staring coverage strategies.

DIRECT (ANALOG) SAMPLING

Since each pixel on a FPA is an independent detector, it is possible to continuously monitor a pixel's output. This is generally not done with modern devices, which are constructed as CCD or CMOS photosensors, but older sensors have used this method. Larger pixels, perhaps measuring several millimeters, were more likely called cells than pixels and were connected in simple circuits like the one in **Figure 7-26**. Radiation power (energy per unit time) falling on the cell creates a continuous output of photoelectrons flowing in the circuit as a current, *i* (electrical charge per unit time), drawn through a load resistor, R_L, by a bias voltage (a battery). By Ohm's Law of elementary circuit theory, the photocurrent generates a voltage across the load resistor:

$$V_{OUTPUT} \approx iR_L \approx \mathcal{R}\Phi R_L \approx \frac{q_e \Phi}{hc/\lambda} \eta R_L \quad [V] \qquad (7\text{-}15)$$

by **Equation 7-5**. This direct relationship between radiant input and electrical output is called *DC-coupled*. If the electrical response of the circuit is fast enough, changes in the input will be seen immediately in the output, and a steady input gives a steady output, of course.

The right side of **Figure 7-26** shows a hypothetical time-varying input to a DC-coupled detector. Supposing a responsivity as drawn in the inset, the output is shown to be directly proportional to the input. Notice the output never goes to zero, but does reach its maximum value, briefly, when the input drives the detector to saturation around the ten second mark. (This is not common, but is shown for the sake of illustration.)

The hypothetical input in **Figure 7-26** is intended to be a pair of small transient events followed by a large persistent event. Noise exists, as can be seen by the jagged nature of the curve. If the sensor was designed to detect these time signatures, then it may have succeeded. The output certainly

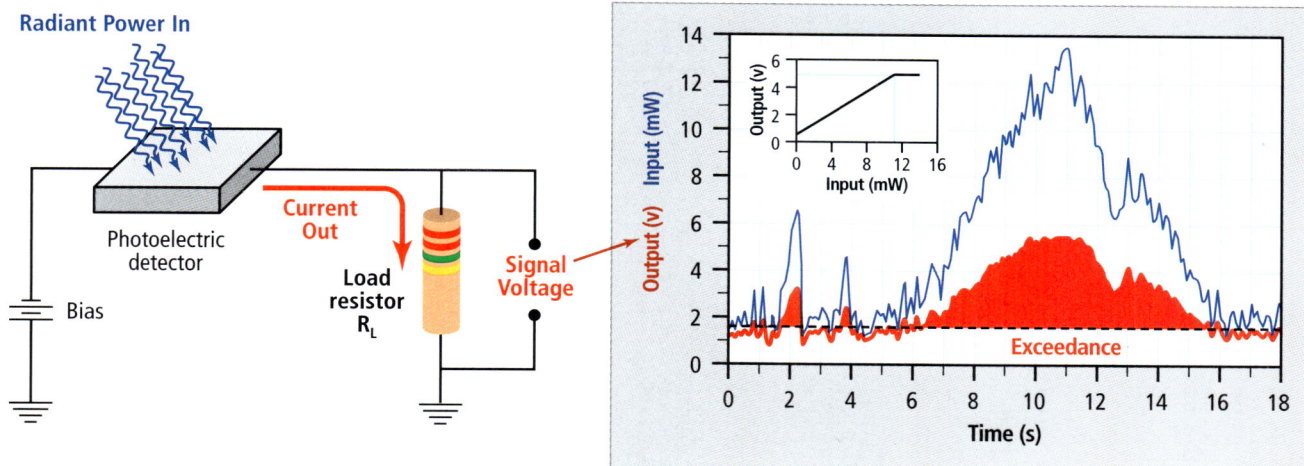

Figure 7-26
A photodetector operated in the continuous, DC-coupled mode.

follows the input, noise and all, but adds additional noise of its own. At the least, the DC offset caused by the dark current of the detector suggests that any apparent signal less than the NEP (**Equation 7-10**) may not be a real signal, but noise. Therefore, in operation of this sensor, a minimum value called exceedance is often set, and sensor output must exceed this value before it will be considered for analysis.

In practice, if multiple DC-coupled detectors were operated simultaneously in a FPA, all their outputs would need to be transmitted (or stored) at once to have spatial information at the same time as temporal information. This would require a high-bandwidth transmitter (or recorder). This difficulty is side-stepped by sampling the amplitudes of the detectors' outputs and multiplexing them together. Sampling rates could be anywhere from a few hertz to many kilohertz, depending on the number of cells and the anticipated time scale of likely events. With modern computational capabilities, the multiplexed signal is digitally encoded.

A problem not yet addressed when considering the output of the photodetector is: there is more to the world than just targets. A detector will dutifully convert some fraction of incident photons, regardless of their origin, into photoelectrons. Often the *background* signal is as strong or stronger than the target. This difficulty will be discussed in more detail later in the application chapters, but for now, a simple electronic solution will be presented.

The right side of **Figure 7-27** shows a target's time-signature riding on a constant background that is several times larger than the signal to be detected. What differentiates the signal in this case is it is changing, whereas the background is not. The circuit diagram on the left shows how to eliminate the constant portion of the input by inserting a *high-pass filter*. A high-pass filter is a combination of electrical components that tells the following parts of a circuit there is a change in the photocurrent. When the current is increasing, the filter's output is positive, and when the current is decreasing, it is negative.[17] The filter's output is shown below the input, and this is termed *ac-coupling*. Note, output voltage of a transient event (two in the first five seconds) is characteristically a double spike, first positive, then negative. The gradual increases and decreases of persistent events will register sustained periods of positive and then negative output.

[17] Readers with a calculus background will see the output of the high-pass filter is essentially the derivative of the photocurrent. Therefore, recovering the original signal is only a matter of integrating the output. Recall that when working with an integral, there is an undetermined constant of integration; that's the constant background level that can be set to zero, leaving only target signal.

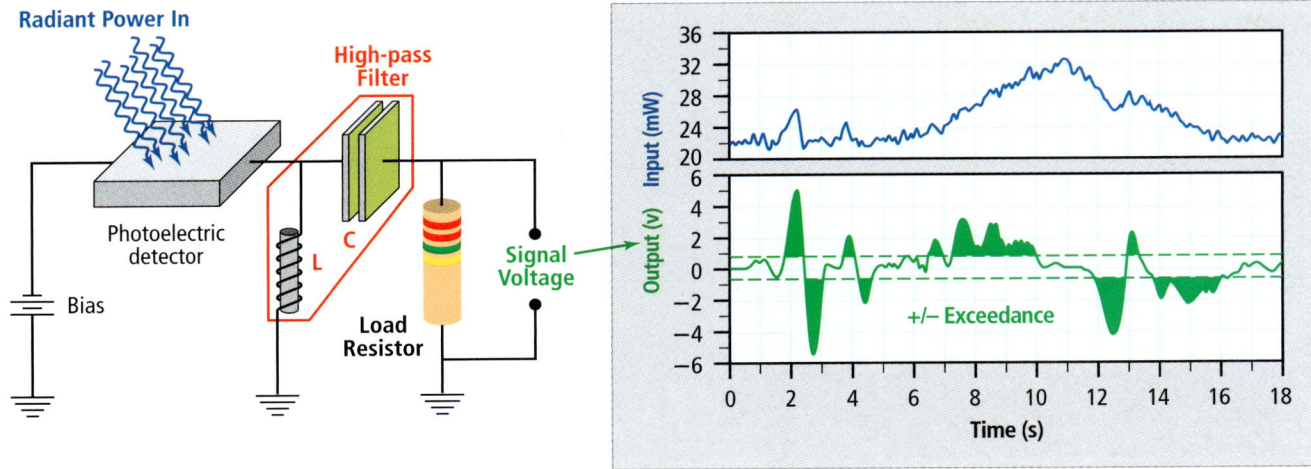

Figure 7-27
A photodetector operated in continuous, AC-coupled mode. The input signal from targets is the same as in **Figure 7-26**, but it rides on a constant background of about 20 mW.

As with DC-coupling some noise is expected, but it typically fluctuates up and down more rapidly than most signatures. It is recognized as a high-frequency ripple in the output. A second filter, this time a *low-pass filter,* could be fitted in the circuit behind the first to eliminate the fast variation of noise. Or as suggested here, positive and negative exceedances can be set. The comments about collecting the output of multiple detectors, as on a FPA, are the same for AC-coupled sensors as for DC-coupled.

INTEGRATED (VIDEO) SAMPLING

The standard CCD and CMOS FPAs introduced earlier work somewhat differently than the directly-reading configurations just discussed. As explained, the modern photodetector and its integrated electronics store photoelectrons in wells for later readout. (See **Example 7-2**.) However, the path to storage could be either AC- or DC-coupled as above.

Figure 7-28 shows a notional circuit for a single pixel operating in a storage mode. The device at the top right of the circuit is a solid-state switch operated by a control pulse from an external timer. When the switch is open, photoelectrons flow from the photosensitive part of the pixel into the storage part. When the switch is closed, stored electrons flow from the well through the load resistor, creating an output signal voltage. Operation of the circuit, as described, depends on the switch positions, storage, and readout having the appropriate time constants.[18]

[18] Time constant is the time required for $\frac{1}{e} \approx 37\%$ of the charge to fill or drain from a capacitor. After a time interval equal to five time constants, the capacitor is considered to be fully charged or completely empty. Physical analogies of time constants already encountered are the atmospheric scale height in the hydrostatic balance equation and the optical absorption depth of Beer's Law.

Figure 7-28
A pixel operating in a store and readout mode and its notional output.

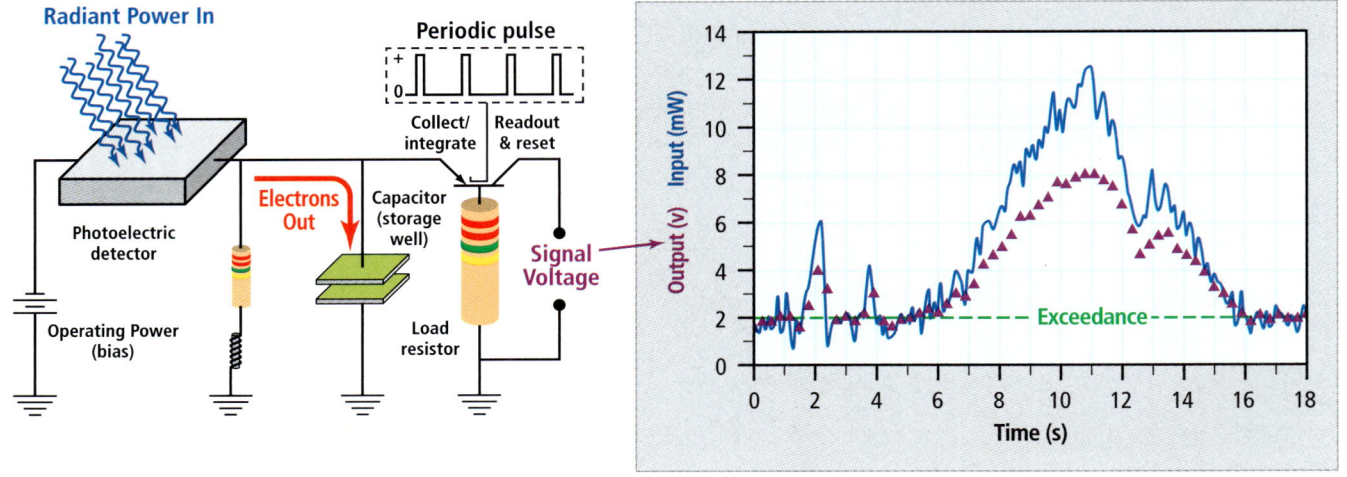

While the switch is open, the circuit needs to accumulate photoelectrons without significant leakage. The switch closed position must completely convert the stored charge into output.

The right side of **Figure 7-28** shows the output of a pixel being proportional to the radiant input (as hoped). While the switch is open, the storage well has accumulated photoelectrons without regard to *when* they were collected during the interval. That is, the pixel has *integrated* its input during an *integration time*, Δt_{INT}, into a single value of stored charge. Integration time of cameras using film is called shutter speed. That is, tripping the shutter on an old film camera (opening the iris or dropping the curtain) exposed the film for a finite and *not* instantaneous time. Shutter speed may have been very fast, only a second or less, but nonetheless film received and processed *all* the photons through the lens during $\Delta t_{SHUTTER}$. Such an exposure is called a frame.

Digital cameras work in the same way as the remote sensors discussed here. There is no physical shutter, but light is electronically integrated for an interval of time. The difference is the camera usually only takes a single picture at a time, whereas the sensor operates in a continuous video-like mode. The rate at which sensors frame depends on their missions and the temporal nature of their intended targets. For transient targets, it could be argued that the Nyquist sampling criterion applies (to be discussed in **Chapter 8**). Another consideration is the apparent brightness of the target; enough photons must be collected to attain meaningful target information above background and noise. This topic will be further considered in the application chapters.

After temporally sampling or integrating an image, the switch in **Figure 7-28** is closed to allow stored photoelectrons to pass through the readout circuit. Normally, the readout circuit has a very short time constant, and the readout is accomplished very quickly so as not to miss any incoming photons. The ratio of integration time to frame time is called the *duty cycle*:

$$\left\{ \begin{array}{c} Duty \\ Cycle \end{array} \right\} \approx \frac{\text{Integration time}}{\text{Frame time}}. \quad (7\text{-}16)$$

With typical readout times of a few microseconds, FPAs can have duty cycles near 100% (**Figure 7-29**).

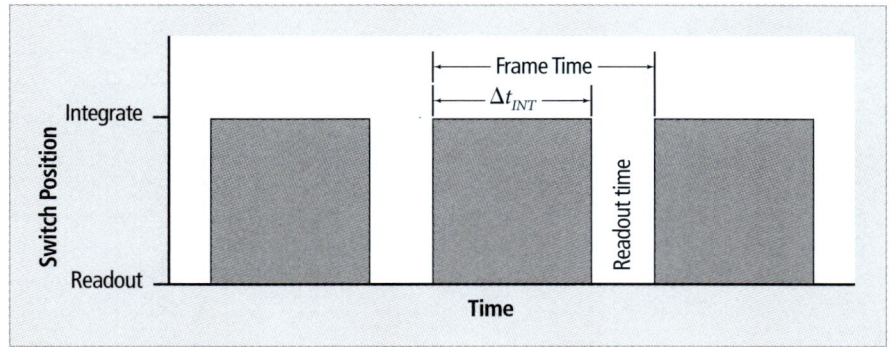

Figure 7-29
Duty cycle.

Finally, data output from FPAs are digitized pixel-by-pixel for transmission from its remote sensor to a processing facility. Each pixel's value is transformed from its output signal voltage (from 0 to V_{MAX} where $V_{MAX} \approx 5$ V for solid state devices[19]) to a binary format of 0 to 2^n bits.[20] The bit depth can be from n = 8 (256 values) to n = 16 (65,536 values) depending on the desired

[19] Ignore the fact that a pixel's minimum output may not be zero because of its DC.

[20] See the sidebar Binary (Digital) Numbers in Chapter 10 for a refresher on converting ordinary decimal (base 10) and binary (base 2) numbers.

radiometric resolution. That is, the digital value is going to ultimately be tracked back to the original intensity or radiance of the target of interest. Also, depending on a sensor's mission, the transformation from pixel output to a binary number is not necessarily linear. For instance, **Figure 7-30** suggests a logarithmic transformation enhances the difference between voltages for dimmer targets,[21] while exponential scaling magnifies the difference between voltages on the higher end of the scale.

Figure 7-30
Digital scaling.

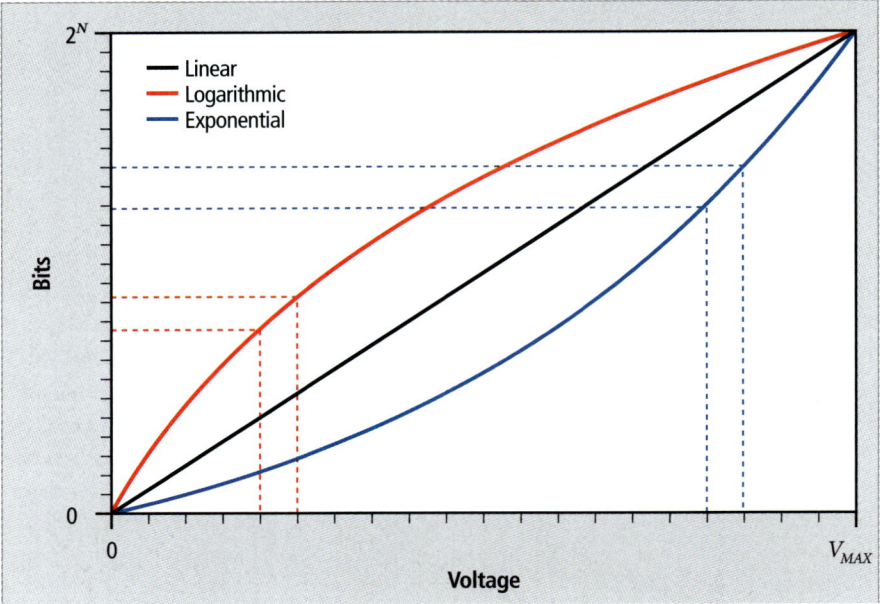

A concern associated with the binary output from a pixel is a form of inverse digitization error. **Figure 7-31** shows an instance of linear scaling at a bit depth of 4 (16 digital values), where the maximum voltage is 4 V. A transmitted value for a particular pixel is shown to be 1001 (decimal 9), but this value could arise from any output signal voltage between 2.25 and 2.50 V. There is a 0.25 V ambiguity that traces back to a corresponding range of target intensities. With greater bit depth,[22] this problem is minimized, but analysts need to be aware it exists.

Figure 7-31
Inverse digitization error.

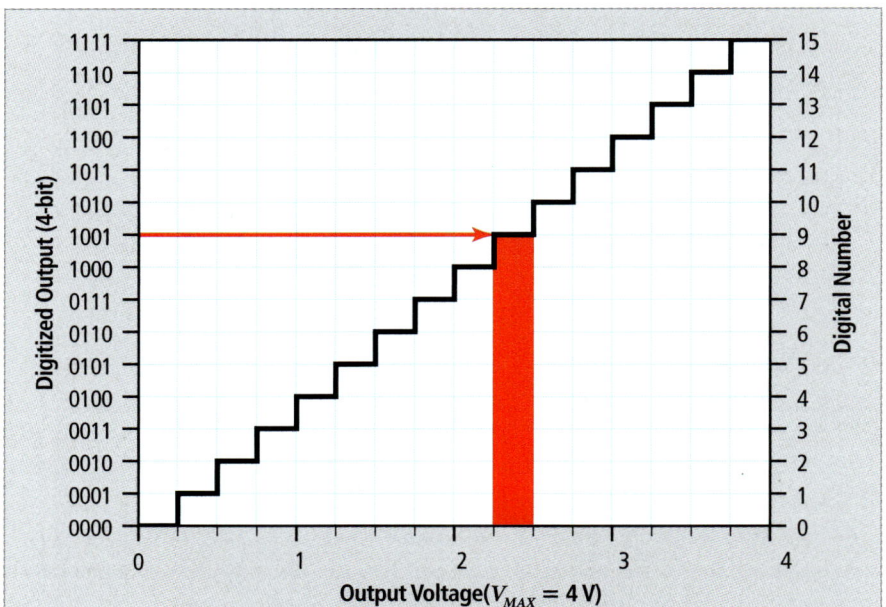

[21] The reader may unknowingly be familiar with this. Human hearing and vision are more logarithmic than linear.

[22] Of course, increased bit depth will increase the fidelity of the inverse digitization, but the cost is increased data rate.

8 SPATIAL IMAGING PROPERTIES

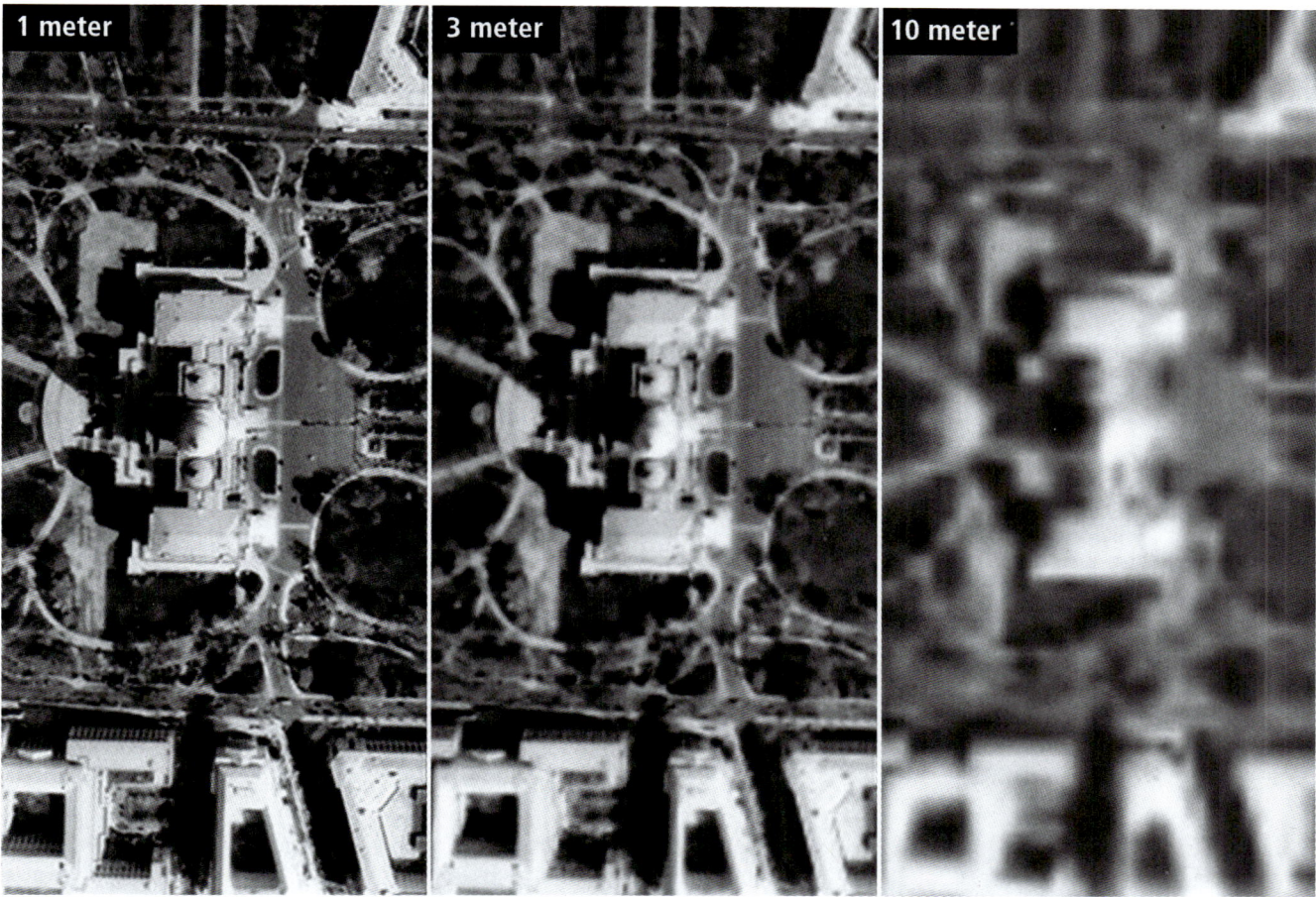

This chapter returns to the question, "What is imaging?" The imagery above of the US Capitol in Washington DC clearly varies in what objects can be recognized. To develop an answer, the criteria required for spatial resolution will be explored, that is, discernment of adjacent sources by separation of their respective images on a sensor's focal plane. The definition of separation depends on whether the targets of interest are point sources or macroscopic objects. Then, this chapter will show how to calculate the physical separation of objects on the ground based on a sensor's optical and detector dimensions.

SECTIONS

8.1 SPATIAL RESOLUTION
8.2 CALCULATING SPATIAL SAMPLING

8.1 SPATIAL RESOLUTION

POINT SOURCE RESOLUTION

The spatial resolution of an optical sensor system is of utmost importance to the ability of the analyst to resolve or distinguish targets that are closely spaced. If two point sources are separated by a distance of X and are far away, $R \gg f_{eff}$, then their resulting Airy disks will be separated on the focal plane by a distance x_A given by

$$x_A \approx f_{eff}\theta \approx f_{eff}\frac{X}{R} \quad [\text{m}], \tag{8-1}$$

where the effective focal length, f_{eff}, angular separation, θ, distance, R, and lateral separation, X, are illustrated in **Figure 8-1**. **Equation 8-1** is valid for angles θ that are small, that is $\theta < 0.5$ radian.

Figure 8-1
Distance parameters associated with the response of an optical system seeing two point sources in the Field of View (FOV). The optical system is treated as having an effective focal length, f_{eff}.

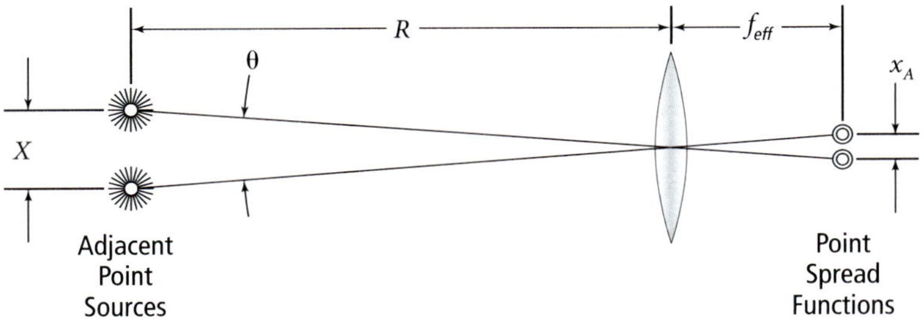

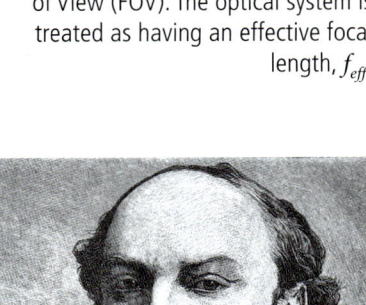

Figure 8-2
John William Strutt, 3rd Baron Rayleigh (1842–1919). (Photo courtesy of http://commons.wikimedia.org/wiki/File:PSM_V25_D738_John_William_Strutt_Lord_Rayleigh.jpg; PD_Old.)

The input is two point sources separated by an angle θ which results in a response with two images that may or may not be resolvable as two separate point sources. The two point sources are considered resolved when their blur circles or point spread functions[1] (PSF) overlap such that the maximum of one rests exactly over the minimum of its neighbor on the focal plane. That is, $x_A \approx r_A$, where r_A is defined as the radius of the blur circle or PSF (**Equation 6-8**). This criterion is called the Rayleigh criterion after Lord Rayleigh (**Figure 8-2**). The minimum angular separation required between two point sources to meet the Rayleigh criteria is thus

$$\theta_{MIN} \approx 1.22\frac{\lambda}{D} \quad [\text{rad}], \tag{8-2}$$

where D is the aperture or lens diameter, and λ is the wavelength. **Figure 8-3** illustrates the response of three different point source inputs where the middle pane demonstrates the Rayleigh criteria (the two signals are separated by r_A which is the radius of the optical blur circle or PSF). The left and right panes illustrate the two point sources being easily resolved and not resolved, respectively. **Figure 8-4** is similar to **Figure 8-3** except the Rayleigh criteria is illustrated with two-dimensional images instead of one-dimensional signals.

Figure 8-3
Adjacent point source images are resolved or not depending on their separation.

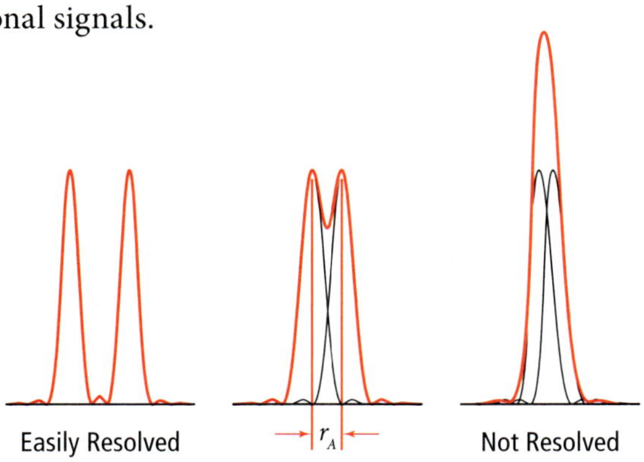

[1] Optical systems which form perfect PSFs are considered to be diffraction limited. In this discussion, assume such perfect optics.

Figure 8-4
Images of adjacent point sources. The middle situation is considered to be resolvable according to the Rayleigh criterion.

Now, how can one determine if the two point sources are resolvable on a Focal Plane Array (FPA)? Not only must the spatial separation criteria be met, but also think in terms of a sampling criteria. The Nyquist-Shannon (**Figure 8-5**) sampling theory[2] requires samples to be taken at a minimum of twice the highest frequency of a signal to recover the original signal. This concept will be explained using the illustration in **Figure 8-6**. **Figure 8-6a** illustrates where the Rayleigh criteria is satisfied by an optical system. But, since all of the energy from two point sources' PSFs is contained within one pixel on the FPA, it is impossible to resolve them. The illustration in **Figure 8-6b** shows the energy falling on four pixels. However, the overlap between the two signals prevents the resolution of the two signals. Once again, **Figure 8-6c** illustrates the energy from the two signals falling on eight pixels, but still the two input signals cannot be resolved. In **Figure 8-6d**, the energy falls on twenty-four pixels where centers of the PSFs are separated by two pixels. This example meets the Nyquist-Shannon sampling requirement where the separation *between the centers* of the two signals or PSFs are *two* pixels. ($r_A = 2$ pixels.)

Figure 8-5
Harry Nyquist (1889–1976). (Used with permission: AIP Emilio Segrè Visual Archives.)

EXAMPLE 8-1: MINIMUM SEPARATION BETWEEN TWO POINT SOURCES

Suppose a sensor's optical system has a collection aperture of $D \approx 30$ cm, an effective focal length $f_{eff} \approx 1.2$ m, and is flown at an altitude of $h \approx 20$ km (where the U-2 aircraft and the Global Hawk UAV commonly fly).

According to the Rayleigh criterion, at a wavelength $\lambda \approx 0.50$ μm in the visible, the minimum resolvable angular separation between two point sources in the Field of View (FOV) would be

$$\theta_{MIN} \approx 1.22 \frac{\lambda}{D} \approx \frac{(1.22)(5.0 \times 10^{-7} \text{ m})}{(0.30 \text{ m})} \approx 2.0 \times 10^{-6} \text{ rad}.$$

On the sensor's FPA, the separation between the centers of the sources' PSFs would then be

$$x_A \approx f_{eff} \theta_{MIN} \approx (1.2 \text{ m})(2.0 \times 10^{-6} \text{ rad}) \approx 2.4 \times 10^{-6} \text{ m or } 2.4 \text{ μm}.$$

If the sensor were pointing straight down, the minimum distance between the (centers of) two point sources on the ground would be

$$X_{MIN} \approx h\theta_{MIN} \approx (2.0 \times 10^{4})(2.0 \times 10^{-6} \text{ rad}) \approx 0.040 \text{ m or } 4.0 \text{ cm}.$$

Suppose the above sensor optics could also image at $\lambda \approx 10$ μm in the Long-Wave Infrared (LWIR). Since $\theta_{MIN} \approx 1.22\lambda/D$, θ_{MIN} at 10 μm will be (10/0.5) 20 times that at 0.5 μm, and the above values for x_A and X_{MIN} will be 20 times larger.

---

[2] The sampling theorem is variously attributed to Harry Nyquist, Claude Shannon, A. T. Whitaker, or Vladimir Kotelnikov.

Figure 8-6e and **Figure 8-6f** illustrate the most stressing case where the orientation of two point sources is at 45° relative to FPAs' rows and columns. **Figure 8-6f** meets the Nyquist-Shannon sampling criterion as there is a two pixel diagonal separation between the centers of the two PSFs. Note, the PSF itself diagonally spans approximately five and one-half pixels.

Figure 8-6
Assuming the Rayleigh criterion has been satisfied, adjacent point images must be spatially sampled.

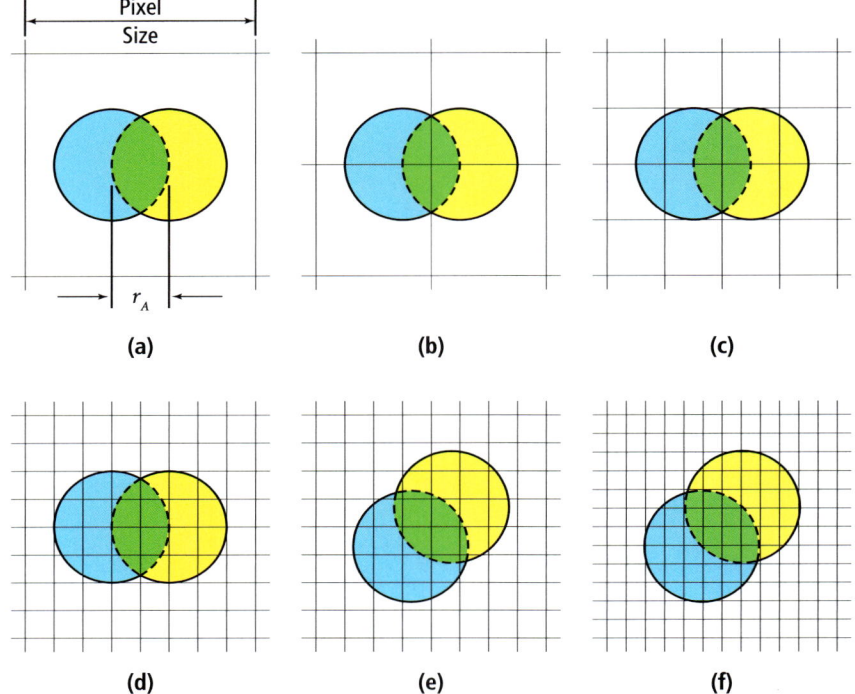

Figure 8-7 shows the relationship between the Rayleigh and Nyquist-Shannon criteria for the spatial resolution of point sources. The horizontal axis represents the Rayleigh criterion and the vertical axis represents the Nyquist-Shannon criterion. The white block in the upper right illustrates where both the Rayleigh and Nyquist-Shannon criteria are met; therefore, two point targets can be resolved. The chart in **Figure 8-7** assumes a perfect optical system and nadir viewing of point sources aligned with the FPA. Other collection geometry and target alignment would complicate the problem and may require modifications of the criteria.

Figure 8-7
Combining the Rayleigh and Nyquist-Shannon criteria for spatial resolution of adjacent point source images on a FPA. Note, the figure is appropriate for the optimum alignment of the source images relative to the FPAs' rows and columns.

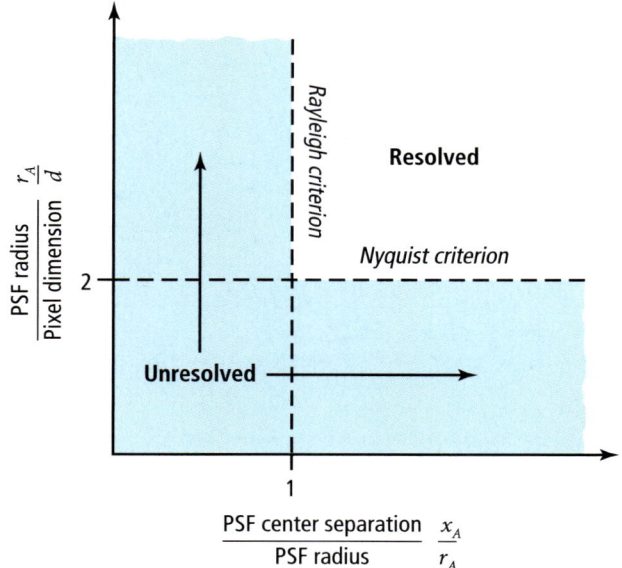

184 CHAPTER 8 SPATIAL IMAGING PROPERTIES

OBJECT RESOLUTION

Note the requirement for two pixel separation is based on the assumption of point source images (PSFs) on the focal plane. Most imaging sensors (e.g., commercial cameras) are designed to image macroscopic targets and a PSF on their focal planes may be smaller than a pixel, as in **Figure 8-6a**, by virtue of their large apertures (**Equation 6-8**). In such systems, the criterion for resolving two adjacent targets is that one pixel between their images must contain significantly less energy than from neighboring panels. In physical terms, the two targets on the ground should be separated by at least one Ground Sample Distance (GSD). GSD is the "footprint" of a pixel on the ground and is a linear dimension equal to the projection's size. Such images are most often taken at or near nadir. The images at the beginning of this chapter and **Figure 8-8** illustrate this concept.

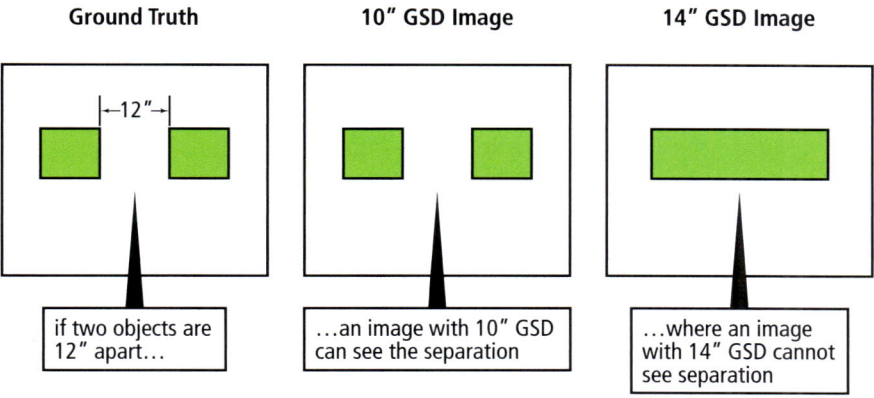

Figure 8-8
GSD used to resolve macroscopic targets.

Figure 8-9 shows the use of Line Spread Functions (LSF) instead of PSF to define resolution and target separability. From varying distances, a person or sensor can resolve the LSF, i.e., where the three white lines are distinguishable from each other.[3] This enables the sensor designer and analyst to understand the capability of the system being designed and the size of targets that can be resolved in the resulting image or video displays.

Figure 8-9
Test target painted on an inactive runway at Wright-Patterson Air Force Base, Area B, Dayton, Ohio. (The visual resolution of line groups in this image depends on the printing process for this text as well as the photography systems that collected the image.) (Courtesy of Google.)

---

[3] The Rayleigh criterion for resolving adjacent line sources is similar to point sources. For imagery, it is often referred to as contrast. For example, the middle of **Figure 8-4** illustrates a contrast effect that shows there are two images.

CHAPTER 8 SPATIAL IMAGING PROPERTIES

8.2 CALCULATING SPATIAL SAMPLING

To begin this section, some terms must be defined (**Table 8-1**).

Table 8-1 Key terms and definitions.

Term	Definition
Field of Regard (FOR)	All the possible locations or directions that a remote sensor could see from its location, but not all at the same time of course. (As an example, a sensor in Geosynchronous Orbit (GEO) could easily have a FOR of nearly an entire hemisphere of the Earth.)
FOV	The solid angle of a remote sensor through which it collects energy: a property of the sensor itself regardless of the direction it is pointing.[4]
Boresight	The centerline of a sensor's FOV.
Instantaneous Field of View (IFOV)	The actual area (on the ground) that a remote sensor sees at a particular time. The IFOV may be given in units of linear dimensions (as 400 km x 600 km) or area (as 240,000 km²), but the collection geometry must also be specified to include: sensor altitude, or range from the sensor to the ground along boresight; direction the boresight is pointing, usually with respect to either zenith or nadir and flight path direction; and orientation of the FOV, usually with respect to a vertical plane including the sensor's flight path.
GSD	The IFOV of one pixel given as a linear dimension both along-track and cross-track. This is approximately the same as the distance from the center of one pixel's IFOV to its neighbor's, but the location of the pixel must be specified within the sensor's FOV.
Zenith and Nadir	Directions directly above and below the sensor, respectively, with respect to the center of the Earth.
Along-Track and Cross-Track	Directions respectively oriented in the direction the sensor is traveling and perpendicular to it.

Starting with a FPA of dimension x by y and a collection system with effective focal length, f_{eff}, the dimensions of the FPA subtended angles are

$$\theta_x \approx \frac{x}{f_{eff}} \text{ and } \theta_y \approx \frac{y}{f_{eff}} \text{ [rad]}. \qquad (8\text{-}3)$$

Figure 8-10 illustrates these angles and their relationship to the optics and FPA.

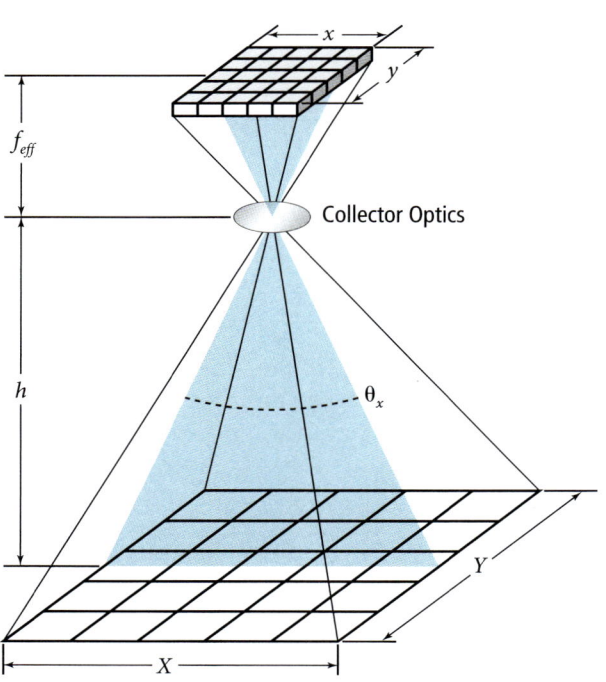

Figure 8-10 Relationship of FPA dimensions to IFOV dimensions for nadir viewing. Note, θ_Y is not shown to keep the figure uncluttered.

---
[4] When discussing spatial sampling *strategies* in Chapter 12, the definition of FOV will be expanded for staring and scanning systems.

The solid angle FOV is

$$\Omega_{FOV} \approx \theta_x \theta_y \approx \frac{xy}{f_{eff}^2} \text{ [sr]}. \quad (8\text{-}4)$$

Assuming a remote sensor is at an altitude h and has the rectangular FOV above, the resulting dimensions of its IFOV are

$$X \approx h\theta_x \approx \frac{hx}{f_{eff}} \quad \text{and} \quad Y \approx h\theta_y \approx \frac{hy}{f_{eff}} \text{ [km]}, \quad (8\text{-}5)$$

and the area is

$$A_{FOV} \approx XY \approx h^2\theta_x\theta_y \approx h^2\Omega_{FOV} \text{ [km}^2\text{]} \quad (8\text{-}6)$$

as shown in **Figure 8-10**. Note, all the calculations are approximate because the small angle approximation was used, and the curvature of the Earth's surface was ignored.

Now, suppose the sensor is not looking at nadir but along some slant path. This is a more difficult problem to solve as illustrated in **Figure 8-11**. Suppose a sensor at altitude h looks away from nadir at an angle θ_N. The rectangular FOV of the sensor is shown in **Figure 8-11** intersecting a trapezoidal-like area on the ground.

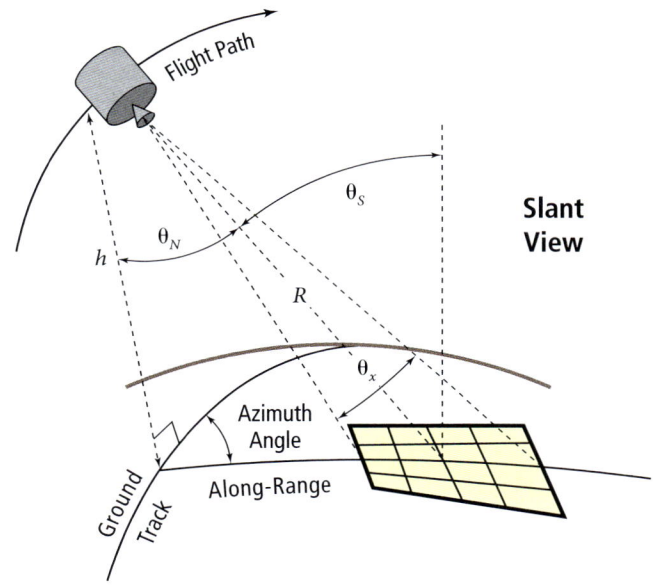

Figure 8-11
Illustration of sensor IFOV and area along the slant path of a sensor.

If the Earth were flat, the boresight range would be calculated first as

$$R \approx \frac{h}{\cos\theta_N} \text{ [km]}, \quad (8\text{-}7)$$

and note, $\theta_S = \theta_N$. Assuming θ_x is "small," then

$$X \approx \frac{R\theta_x}{\cos\theta_N} \approx \frac{h\theta_x}{\cos^2\theta_N} \text{ [km], and} \quad (8\text{-}8)$$

$$Y \approx R\theta_Y \approx \frac{h\theta_Y}{\cos\theta_N} \text{ [km]}.$$

Therefore, at boresight, the area is

$$A_{FOV} \approx XY \approx \frac{R^2\theta_x\theta_y}{\cos\theta_N} \approx \frac{R^2\Omega}{\cos\theta_N} \approx \frac{h^2\Omega}{\cos^3\theta_N} \text{ [km}^2\text{]}. \quad (8\text{-}9)$$

To be more precise, correct for the near- and far-side ranges[5] (**Figure 8-12**):

$$R' \approx \frac{h}{\cos\left(\theta_N - \frac{\theta_x}{2}\right)} \quad \text{and} \quad R'' \approx \frac{h}{\cos\left(\theta_N + \frac{\theta_x}{2}\right)} \quad \text{[km]}. \quad \textbf{(8-10)}$$

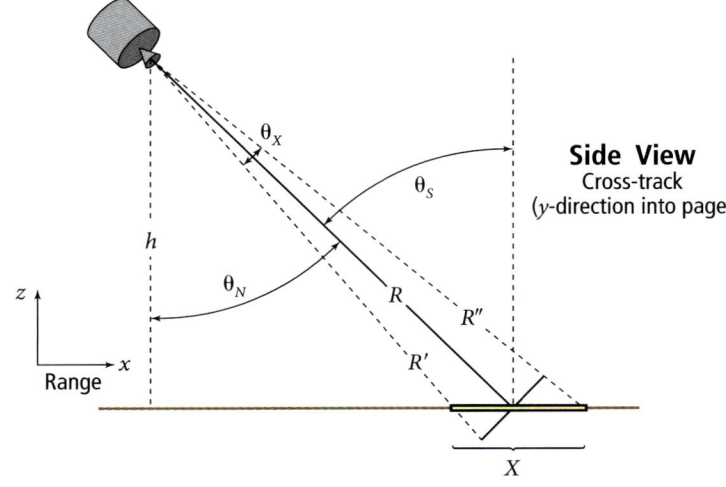

Figure 8-12
Illustration for derivation of parameters for a sensor at a slant path. Note, for flat-Earth geometry, the nadir viewing angle θ_N equals the target zenith angle θ_s.

Then, the near- and far-side along-track dimensions of the IFOV are

$$Y' \approx R'\theta_y \quad \text{and} \quad Y'' \approx R''\theta_y \quad \text{[km]}, \quad \textbf{(8-11)}$$

giving an approximate area of:

$$A_{FOV} \approx \frac{X(Y' + Y'')}{2} \approx \frac{R\theta_x(R'\theta_y + R''\theta_y)}{2 \cos \theta_N} \approx \frac{R\Omega(R' + R'')}{2 \cos \theta_N} \quad \text{[km}^2\text{]}. \quad \textbf{(8-12)}$$

These approximations are reasonable for low-altitude sensors, as depicted in **Figure 8-13**, when $h \ll R_E = 6370$ km, the radius of the Earth.

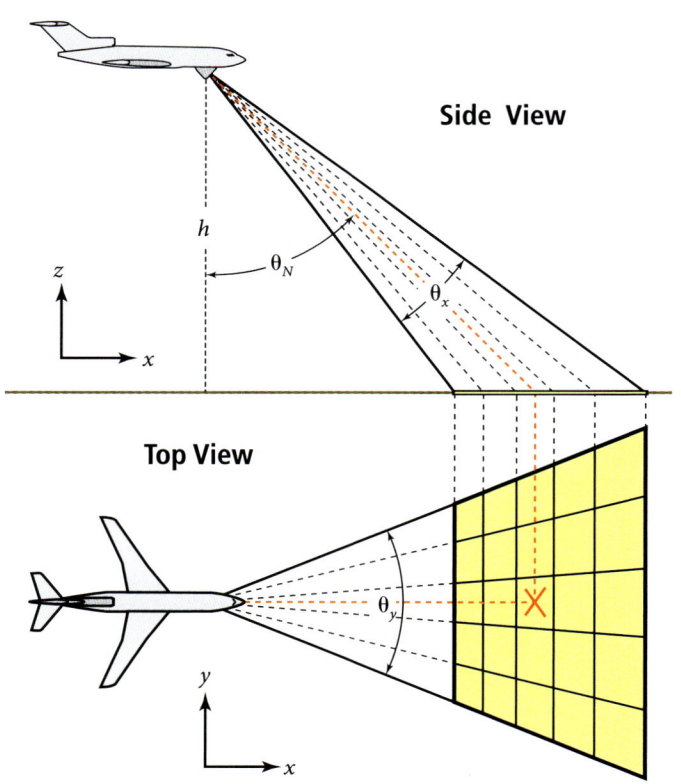

Figure 8-13
Illustration of sensor IFOV and area along the slant path of a sensor for $h \ll R_E$.

[5] As drawn in **Figure 8-12**, the near-side of the IFOV footprint is the "heel" and the far-side is the "toe."

Since the Earth is not flat, for high-altitude remote sensing, the correct range from sensor to Earth must be solved using some trigonometry. In triangle STO illustrated in **Figure 8-14** (where point **O** is the center of the Earth), the sine law can be used to solve for angle θ_G, where

$$\frac{\sin\theta_G}{R_E + h} = \frac{\sin\theta_N}{R_E} \quad [\text{km}^{-1}]. \tag{8-13}$$

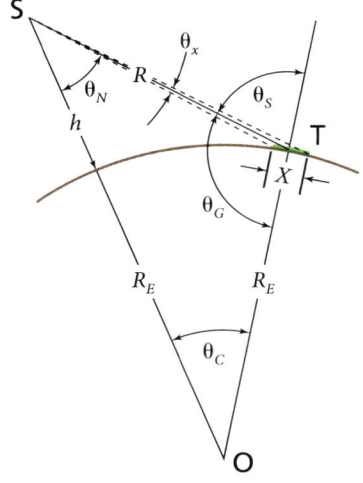

Figure 8-14
Side view of collection geometry when the curvature of the Earth cannot be ignored. Note, for this geometry, the viewing angle θ_N is usually significantly smaller than the target zenith angle θ_s.

Now, calculate $\theta_S = \pi - \theta_G$ and $\theta_C = \pi - \theta_N - \theta_G$. Next, use the sine law again to calculate R:

$$\frac{R}{\sin\theta_C} = \frac{R_E}{\sin\theta_N} \quad [\text{km}]. \tag{8-14}$$

Assuming θ_x and θ_y are small, **Equation 8-8** can be used again as a close approximation,

$$X \approx \frac{R\theta_x}{\cos\theta_S} \quad \text{and} \quad Y \approx R\theta_y \quad [\text{km}]. \tag{8-15}$$

The approximate area is

$$A_{FOV} \approx XY \approx \frac{R^2\Omega}{\cos\theta_S} \quad [\text{km}^2]. \tag{8-16}$$

Figure 8-15 illustrates the change of the IFOVs with viewing angle of the sensor for a high altitude sensor. Note, as the sensor elevation and azimuth angles change, the size, shape, and *orientation* of the IFOVs also change.

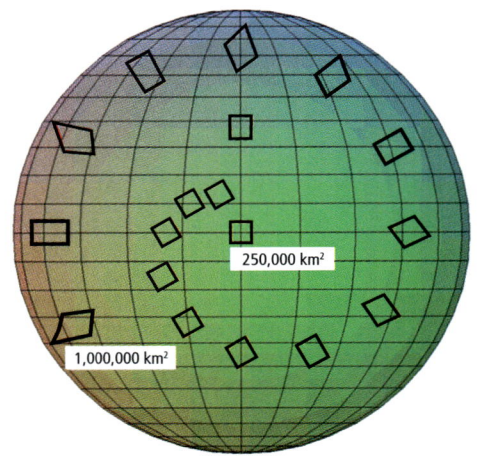

Typical Numbers:
FPA: 1000 by 1000 pixels
Pixel: 20 by 20 µm
Focal Length: 1.4 m
Aperture: 30 cm
Altitude: 35,000 km
IFOV: 500 by 500 km
GSD: 500m

Figure 8-15
Change in sensor IFOV resulting from the optical system at a high altitude at various look angles and orientations. Sensor remains at the equator.

As illustrated in **Figure 8-16**, a focal plane is typically divided into pixels, m rows by n columns, where the pixel dimensions are

$$x_{PIX} \approx \frac{x}{m} \quad \text{and} \quad y_{PIX} \approx \frac{y}{n} \quad [\mu m], \tag{8-17}$$

and the angles subtended by a pixel are

$$\theta_{PIX,x} \approx \frac{x_{PIX}}{f_{eff}} \approx \frac{\theta_x}{m} \quad \text{and} \quad \theta_{PIX,y} \approx \frac{y_{PIX}}{f_{eff}} \approx \frac{\theta_y}{n} \quad [\text{rad}]. \tag{8-18}$$

Therefore, the FOV of an individual pixel is

$$\Omega_{PIX} \approx \theta_{PIX,x} \theta_{PIX,y} \approx \frac{x_{PIX} y_{PIX}}{f_{eff}^2} \approx \frac{\Omega_{FOV}}{mn} \quad [\text{sr}]. \tag{8-19}$$

The IFOV of an individual pixel at nadir then becomes:

$$IFOV_{PIX} \approx \frac{A_{FOV}}{mn} \approx (GSD_x)(GSD_y) \quad [\text{km}^2], \tag{8-20}$$

where

$$GSD_x \approx h\theta_{PIX,x} \approx \frac{X}{m} \quad \text{and} \quad GSD_y \approx h\theta_{PIX,y} \approx \frac{Y}{n} \quad [\text{km}]. \tag{8-21}$$

The above calculations are based on nadir viewing, as suggested by **Figure 8-16**, and assume θ_x and θ_y are small. Viewing at any slant angle requires corrections for the target zenith angle, θ_S, and computation of actual range from sensor to target.

Figure 8-16
Ground pixel dimensions resulting from the optical system.

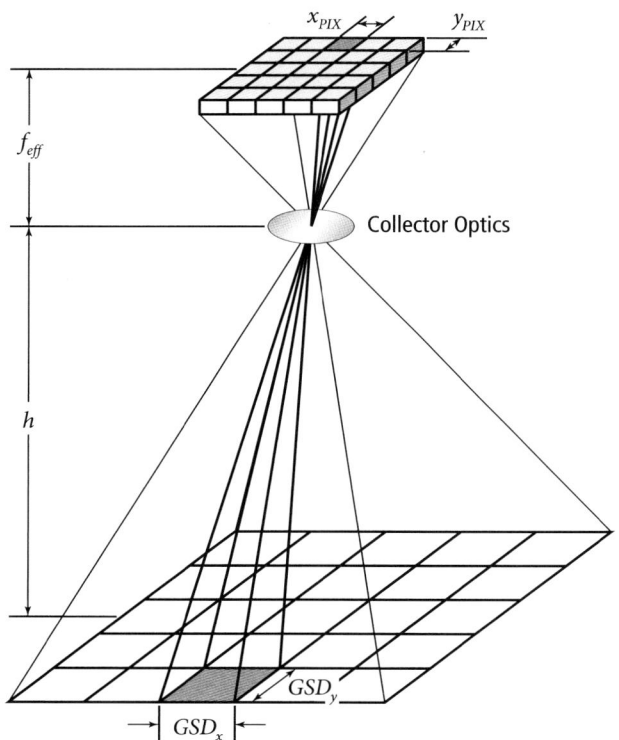

Remember, the values for GSD calculated here are not necessarily the separation between two resolved point sources (as discussed previously).

EXAMPLE 8-2: SIZE OF GROUND PIXELS

Imagine a sensor optical system where the pixel angles $\theta_{PIX,x} \approx \theta_{PIX,y} \approx 5.0 \times 10^{-6}$ rad. At an altitude of $h \approx 700$ km, typical for a Low-Earth Orbit (LEO) satellite, the size of a ground pixel at nadir is given by

$$GSD_x \approx GSD_y \approx h\theta_{PIX,x} \approx h\theta_{PIX,y}$$
$$\approx (7.0 \times 10^5 \text{ m})(5.0 \times 10^{-6} \text{ rad}) \approx 3.5 \text{ m}.$$

For a viewing geometry characterized by a nadir angle $\theta_N \approx \theta_S \approx 40°$ (where the flat-Earth approximation is appropriate because $h \ll R_E \approx 6370$ km and $\theta_N < 80°$), **Figure 8-12** shows that

$$GSD_y \approx R\theta_{PIX,y} \approx \left(\frac{h}{\cos\theta_N}\right)\theta_{PIX,y} \approx \frac{3.5 \text{ m}}{\cos 40°} \approx 4.6 \text{ m} \text{ and}$$

$$GSD_x \approx \frac{R\theta_{PIX,x}}{\cos\theta_S} \approx \left(\frac{h}{\cos\theta_N}\right)\left(\frac{\theta_{PIX,x}}{\cos\theta_S}\right) \approx \frac{3.5 \text{ m}}{(\cos 40°)^2} \approx 6.0 \text{ m}.$$

Note, as $\theta_N (\approx \theta_S)$ increases, the square ground pixel at nadir becomes approximately an elongated rectangle.

At a higher satellite altitude, $h \approx 35{,}780$ km $\approx 5.6 R_E$, typical of a GEO, the curved Earth geometry (**Figure 8-14**) must be used even for relatively small values of θ_N. The size of a ground pixel at nadir is given by

$$GSD_x \approx GSD_y \approx h\theta_{PIX,x} \approx h\theta_{PIX,y}$$
$$\approx (3.578 \times 10^7 \text{ m})(5.0 \times 10^{-6} \text{ rad}) \approx 180 \text{ m}.$$

Off nadir as θ_N increases, θ_S increases more rapidly. For viewing near the limb at a nadir angle of $\theta_N \approx 8.0°$, the solution of triangle **STO** in **Figure 8-14** using **Equations 8-13** and **8-14** gives

$$\theta_G \approx 112.9°, \theta_S \approx 67.1°, \theta_C \approx 59.1°, \text{ and } R \approx 39{,}300 \text{ km}.$$

Finally, the size of a ground pixel at this viewing angle from this altitude is

$$GSD_y \approx R\theta_{PIX,y} \approx (3.93 \times 10^7 \text{ m})(5.0 \times 10^{-6} \text{ rad}) \approx 200 \text{ m} \text{ and}$$
$$GSD_x \approx \frac{R\theta_{PIX,x}}{\cos\theta_S} \approx \frac{200 \text{ m}}{\cos(67.1°)} \approx 500 \text{ m}.$$

Again, as θ_N increases, the square ground pixel at nadir becomes an elongated rectangle. Note, the largest value for θ_N, at which the sensor's line of sight is tangent to the Earth's surface, is about $8.69°$. For that value, $\theta_G = \theta_S$, $\theta_C \approx 81.3°$, and $R \approx 41{,}700$ km.

9 SPECTRAL FILTERS

(Photo courtesy of http://en.wikipedia.org/wiki/File:Soap_Bubble_-_foliage_background_-_iridescent_colours_-_Traquair_040801.jpg; Creative Commons Attribution-Share Alike 3.0 Unported license & GNU Free Documentation License 1.2 or later: Tagishsimon.)

In the operation of a sensor, it is often useful to limit the number of wavelengths that can pass through the sensor to the detector: the spectral bandpass. As will be discussed in later chapters, this can be extremely important when viewing a target, which emits or reflects light over a narrow range of wavelengths against a background that includes many additional wavelengths. The detector response, the transmission (or reflection) of the various optical elements (lenses and mirrors), and atmospheric transmission may limit the number of wavelengths that can be detected. Sometimes, however, a narrower spectral bandpass is required. To accomplish this, a spectral filter may be inserted into the sensor, often just in front of the detector. One type of spectral filter frequently employed uses thin films of varying thickness and dielectric materials. The soap bubbles shown above act as such a filter for reflected sunlight.

SECTIONS
9.1 REQUIREMENTS AND APPROACHES
9.2 GENERALIZED INTERFERENCE OF TWO LIGHT WAVES
9.3 THIN FILM FILTERS

9.1 REQUIREMENTS AND APPROACHES

In defining a spectral bandpass between λ_1 and λ_2, as seen in **Figure 9-1a** below, the ideal optical transmission, $\tau(\lambda)$, of a spectral filter is 100% between λ_1 and λ_2 and zero at all other wavelengths. These properties are often difficult to achieve, as seen in **Figure 9-1b**, especially the drop-off in transmission at wavelengths λ_1 and λ_2 and the near zero values at all other wavelengths (the so-called out-of-band rejection). Spectral filter design is further complicated by the desired spectral response to be independent of temperature and slight misalignment within the sensor.

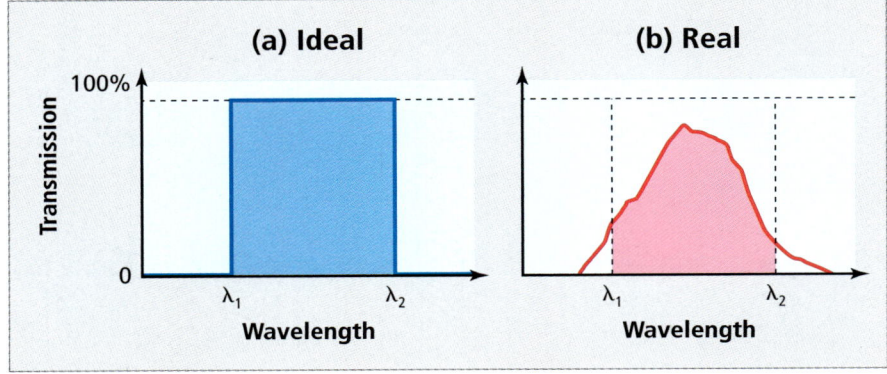

Figure 9-1
a) The ideal filter transmits 100% of the light within a bandpass ($\lambda_1 - \lambda_2$) and no light outside of the bandpass.
b) A real filter transmits less than 100% in the band and also passes some light outside of the desired limits.

There are two types of spectral filters in common use: selective absorption filters and interference filters. Selective absorption filters are a product of older, less-expensive technologies. At least two dyes of desired absorption properties are used to define the desired spectral bandpass of the filter. The use of these two dyes is illustrated in **Figure 9-2**. One dye with an absorption feature at wavelengths just short of λ_1 was chosen, and the second just beyond λ_2. The transmission of the combination, a layer of one dye atop a layer of the other, is the result shown in **Figure 9-2**. This type of real filter does not have the ideal characteristics, of course, and additional optical elements may be needed to eliminate[1] any transmission "wings" at shorter and longer wavelengths.

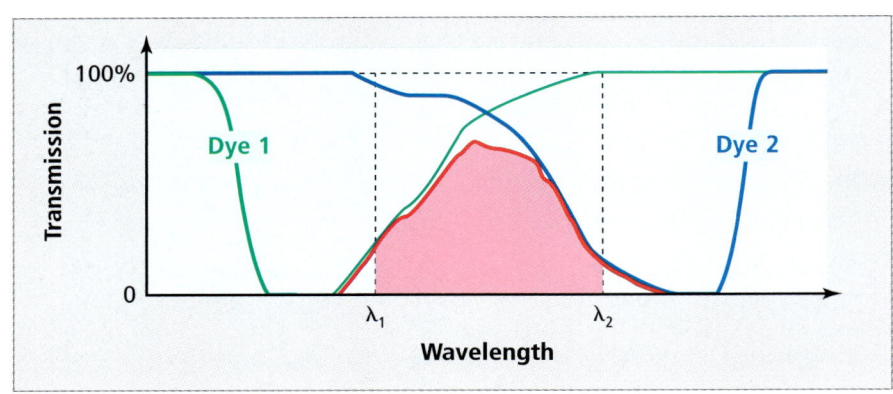

Figure 9-2
Two dyes with strong absorption features at wavelengths shorter and longer than a desired bandpass can be combined to approximate the required transmission.

One of the challenges of this approach is finding dyes with the appropriate absorption features, both in terms of wavelength location as well as shape (for sharp cut-off and out-of-band rejection). Today, this approach is rarely used in the design and manufacture of remote sensors. It is, however, used in photographic film, digital cameras, and the human eye.

The second type of filter, the interference filter, utilizes thin-film interference. Before discussing in more detail, some details about the interference of two light waves will be presented. These details will be helpful in the spectral filter problem as well as later topics, such as diffraction gratings in **Chapter 17**.

[1] Remember, atmospheric transmission and detector responsivity may also contribute to defining a sensor's bandpass.

9.2 GENERALIZED INTERFERENCE OF TWO LIGHT WAVES

Consider the overlap of two transverse electromagnetic (EM) waves with the same frequency, f (Hz), same direction of propagation, same speed of propagation, c (m/s), and same plane of oscillation (i.e., the same polarization). The instantaneous electric fields (at time t) of these two waves can be represented mathematically by the expressions

$$E_1 = A_1 \sin(2\pi ft + \phi_1) \left[\frac{V}{M}\right] \text{ and} \quad (9\text{-}1)$$

$$E_2 = A_2 \sin(2\pi ft + \phi_2) \left[\frac{V}{M}\right],$$

where A_1 and A_2 are the maximum amplitudes, and ϕ_1 and ϕ_2 are phase angles. (Recall from **Chapter 2** the period of oscillation, $P = 1/f$, and wavelength, $\lambda = c/f$.)

There are three ways to add these two waves: 1) graphically; 2) algebraically; and 3) phasors (vectors). In the process, the amplitude and phase of the resulting combined wave are determined.

1. With the graphical approach, each wave is plotted on the same set of axes for all times, for the same location, and the two are added on a point-by-point basis.
2. With the algebraic approach, the following expression results:

$$E = E_1 + E_2 = A_1 \sin(2\pi ft + \phi_1) + A_2 \sin(2\pi ft + \phi_2) \left[\frac{V}{M}\right]. \quad (9\text{-}2)$$

With some trigonometric identities, this can be consolidated to

$$E = A \sin(2\pi ft + \psi) \left[\frac{V}{M}\right], \quad (9\text{-}3)$$

where $A^2 = A_1^2 + A_2^2 + 2A_1A_2 (\cos \phi_1 - \phi_2)$ and

$$\tan\psi = \frac{A_1 \sin\phi_1 + A_2 \sin\phi_2}{A_1 \cos\phi_1 + A_2 \cos\phi_2}.$$

In the special case of two waves with the same amplitude but different phases,[2] $A_1 = A_2 \equiv A_0$, and $\phi_1 = 0$ and $\phi_2 = \phi_0$. Then,

$$E = A \sin\left(2\pi ft + \frac{\phi_0}{2}\right) \left[\frac{V}{M}\right], \quad (9\text{-}4)$$

where $A = A_0\sqrt{2(1 + \cos \phi_0)}$.

If $\phi_0 = 0$, the two waves are exactly in phase, $A = 2A_0$, and *constructive interference* occurs. On the other hand, if $\phi_0 = 180°$, the two waves are exactly out of phase, $A = 0$, and *destructive interference* occurs.

3. With the phasor addition approach, vector[3] addition of E_1 and E_2 is used. A snapshot in time of E_1 and E_2 is shown in **Figure 9-3** when the term $2\pi ft$ is equal to a multiple of 360° (relative to a horizontal reference axis). The amplitudes of the phasors, A_1 and A_2, are represented by the lengths of the arrows, and their phases, ϕ_1 and ϕ_2, are indicated by an angle measured counter-clockwise from the reference axis.

---

[2] Only the *difference* in phase between the two waves is important. Hence ϕ_1 can always be chosen to be zero, while ϕ_2 represents the difference, called ϕ_0 here.

[3] Technically, E_1 and E_2 are not static vectors, but are termed phasors because they are vectors that rotate with frequency f.

Figure 9-3
Representation of the maximum amplitude of the EM waves, E_1 and E_2, as phasors.

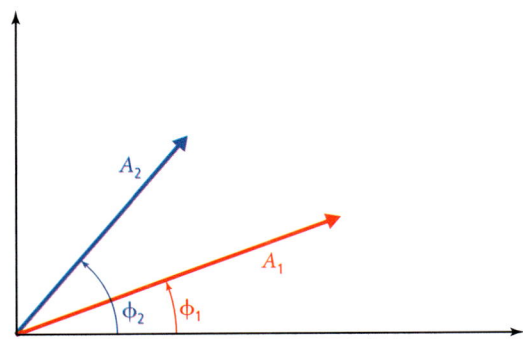

The addition of the two phasors is like vector addition: the tail of E_2 is translated to the head of E_1 (or *vice versa*), and the resultant is drawn from the tail of E_1 to the head of E_2 (or *vice versa*). **Figure 9-4** shows this, where the resultant is also the diagonal of a parallelogram with opposite sides of length A_1 and A_2. The resultant phasor, E, has maximum amplitude, A, and phase angle, ψ, as shown. It rotates in the same sense as the two waves and at the same rate.

Figure 9-4
Phasor (vector) addition of two EM waves.

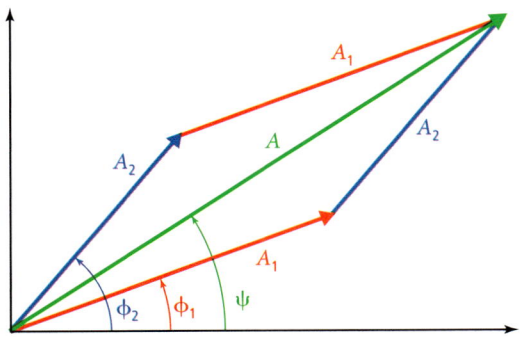

Figure 9-4 considerably simplifies the special case discussed above, namely when the amplitudes are equal, $A_1 = A_2 \equiv A_0$, and when the phases are set to $\phi_1 = 0$ and $\phi_2 = \phi_0$. Furthermore, selecting $\phi_0 = 0$ results in the situation shown in **Figure 9-5a** where the two phasors line up. (The resultant phasor is shown offset for clarity.) The amplitude is clearly seen to be $A = 2A_0$ for *constructive interference*. But if $\phi_0 = 180°$, then *destructive interference* occurs, as shown in **Figure 9-5b**, because the two phasors cancel out. (Again, the phasors are shown offset for clarity.)

Figure 9-5
a) Constructive and b) destructive interference of two equal-amplitude phasors.

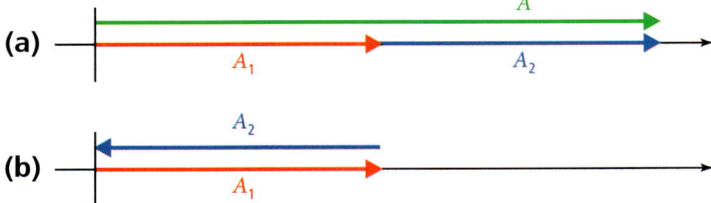

While the above discussion may seem excessive for the simple cases of constructive and destructive interference, this phasor (vector) addition approach proves quite useful in the discussion of interference filters in the next section and later when discussing diffraction gratings.

One additional point involves the measurement of the EM wave that has an amplitude equal to the sum of two other EM waves, overlapping in space and time. While microwave and radio frequency detectors (antennas) directly measure the *amplitudes* of electric and magnetic field components of EM waves, electro-optic detectors measure arriving *energy* (averaged over time because frequencies are quite large). This energy arrival rate is the incident irradiance, $\mathcal{E}(t)$, in units of W/m² and this power (energy per unit time) is proportional to the square of the EM wave amplitude. Hence, for the special case of equal-amplitude waves, $A_1^2 = A_2^2 \equiv A_0^2$, giving $\mathcal{E}_1 = \mathcal{E}_2 \equiv \mathcal{E}_0$. Combining the phasors,

$$A^2 = \left[A_0\sqrt{2(1+\cos\phi_0)}\right]^2 = 2A_0^2(1+\cos\phi_0) \quad \left[\frac{V^2}{m^2}\right] \quad (9\text{-}5)$$

which gives

$$\mathcal{E} = 2\mathcal{E}_0(1+\cos\phi_0) \quad \left[\frac{W}{m^2}\right]. \quad (9\text{-}6)$$

Therefore, for constructive interference, $\mathcal{E} = 4\mathcal{E}_0$ when $\phi_0 = 0°$, and for destructive interference, $\mathcal{E} = 0$ when $\phi_0 = 180°$.

9.3 THIN FILM FILTERS

Consider a "thin" film of material[4] with thickness d and index of refraction n as shown in **Figure 9-6**. This thin film's surfaces are flat and smooth compared to a wavelength of incident radiation, and it can act as either a mirror or a window. To center the discussion on the optical properties of the thin film, assume it is immersed in air as shown.

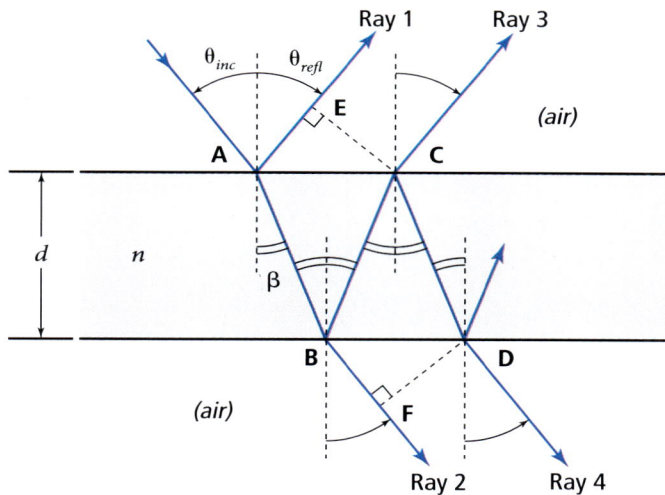

Figure 9-6
A ray of light incident on a thin film may be partially reflected and partially transmitted depending on the thickness of the film, its index of refraction, and the wavelength of light.

A light ray[5] incident at point **A** at an angle θ_{inc} will be split: part will be specularly reflected ($\theta_{refl} = \theta_{inc}$, Ray 1), and part will be refracted and internally transmitted to point **B**. At **B**, part of the light will be refracted (Ray 2) and part will be internally reflected to point **C**. At **C**, reflection and refraction (Ray 3) will again take place.[6]

Now, the question to address is how do the reflected Ray 1 and the transmitted-reflected-transmitted Ray 3 combine to produce a single, effective, reflected ray? To answer this question, calculate the difference in path length Ray 1 traveled from **A** to **E** compared to the path length Ray 3 traveled from **A** to **B** to **C** (which is abreast of **E**). However, this calculation is not in terms of physical distance, but in terms of optical path length counted in units of wavelengths the rays travel. This optical path length, Γ, relates to $\phi = \phi_3 - \phi_1$, the phase difference between Rays 1 and 3.

[4] What is "thin?" It may be less than one wavelength of light as shown in **Example 9-1**. Normally, thin films are supported on some smooth substrate, like a lens or a mirror, but this discussion will only center on the optical properties of the thin film itself.

[5] Light rays are constructions showing the direction of propagation of an EM wave. The wave itself has a wavefront, a surface with the same phase, perpendicular to the ray that extends sufficiently far in all sideward directions to overlap its own reflections and transmissions. (The wavefronts of Rays 1 and 3 overlap in space so as to interfere with one another, for example.)

[6] What happens to the light ray beyond **D** is considered in the discussion of **Figure 9-9**.

[7] In **Figure 9-6**, all external angles marked with a single arrow arc are equal to θ_{inc}, and all internal angles marked with a double arc are equal to β.

[8] This 180° phase shift only occurs when a ray passes into a medium with a larger index of refraction. For this situation, the index for air is approximately one, and that of the thin film could be anything larger.

$$\frac{\Gamma}{\lambda} = \frac{\phi}{2\pi}. \qquad (9\text{-}7)$$

Its calculation depends on the following details:
1. Snell's Law of refraction[7] at **A**, $n \sin \beta = \sin \theta_{inc}$, and at **C**, $\sin \theta_{ref} = n \sin \beta$
2. Light travels at a reduced speed c/n within the film; and
3. Ray 1 has a 180° phase shift[8] (equivalent to one-half wavelength of optical path length) from its reflection at point **A**.

The result of the calculation is

$$\Gamma = 2nd \cos \beta + \frac{\lambda}{2} \quad [\mu m]. \qquad (9\text{-}8)$$

Two special cases exist in this result. *First*, if the optical path length is an integral number of wavelengths, $\Gamma = m\lambda$ for $m = 1, 2, 3, \ldots$, the condition for *constructive interference* is

$$2nd \cos \beta = \left(m - \frac{1}{2}\right)\lambda \quad [\mu m]. \qquad (9\text{-}9)$$

Second, if the optical path length is an integral plus a half number of wavelengths, $\Gamma = \left(m + \frac{1}{2}\right)\lambda$ for $m = 1, 2, 3, \ldots$, the condition for *destructive interference* is

$$2nd \cos \beta = m\lambda \quad [\mu m]. \qquad (9\text{-}10)$$

Any condition between $\Gamma = m\lambda$ and $\Gamma = \left(m + \frac{1}{2}\right)\lambda$ results in a condition somewhere between full constructive and full destructive interference as shown later.

The next question is how the overlap of transmitted Rays 2 and 4 combine to produce a single effective transmitted ray? This time, the calculation involves the difference in optical path length from **B** to **F** versus from **B** to **C** to **D** (which is abreast of **F**). Again, calling the difference in optical path lengths Γ, the answer is

$$\Gamma = 2nd \cos \beta \quad [\mu m]. \qquad (9\text{-}11)$$

The difference (from **Equation 9-8**) is there is no 180° phase shift at **B**, **C**, or **D**.

As before, two special cases exist in **Equation 9-11**. *First*, if the optical path length is an integral number of wavelengths, $\Gamma = m\lambda$ for $m = 1, 2, 3, \ldots$, the condition for *constructive interference* is

$$2nd \cos \beta = m\lambda \quad [\mu m]. \qquad (9\text{-}12)$$

Second, if the optical path length is an integral plus a half number of wavelengths, $\Gamma = \left(m + \frac{1}{2}\right)\lambda$ for $m = 1, 2, 3, \ldots$, the condition for *destructive interference* is

$$2nd \cos \beta = \left(m - \frac{1}{2}\right)\lambda \quad [\mu m]. \qquad (9\text{-}13)$$

The results are summarized in **Table 9-1**:

	Reflection	Transmission
Constructive interference	$2nd \cos \beta = (m - 0.5)\lambda$	$2nd \cos \beta = m\lambda$
Destructive interference	$2nd \cos \beta = m\lambda$	$2nd \cos \beta = (m - 0.5)\lambda$

Table 9-1
Summary of formulas for constructive and destructive interference for reflection and transmission by a thin film.

Note the reversal of formulas between transmission and reflection cases; wavelengths with good transmission are those with poor reflection and *vice versa*. This is simply understood as conservation of energy: the sum of reflected plus transmitted energy must equal the incident energy (assuming no absorption in the thin film).

EXAMPLE 9-1: HOW THIN IS THIN?

What is the minimum thickness of a layer of cryolite ($n \approx 1.35$) to transmit 0.589 μm light at normal incidence? (This is the bright yellow sodium D_2 line in the solar spectrum.)

For constructive interference (transmission), **Table 9-1** shows

$$2nd \cos \beta = m\lambda$$

is necessary. For normal incidence, $\theta_{inc} = 0°$, and Snell's Law (**Chapter 2**) also gives $\beta = 0°$. Thus, solving for the film's thickness:

$$d = \frac{m\lambda}{2n} = \frac{(m)(0.589 \text{ μm})}{(2)(1.35)} = 0.218 \, m \, [\text{μm}].$$

The smallest value of d results when $m = 1$. Hence, $d = 0.218$ μm. By contrast, a human hair has a diameter of about 100 μm, and a 1 mil Mylar trash bag is 25.4 μm thick. Approximately 390 NaCl (salt) molecules could be stacked in this distance.

EXAMPLE 9-2: THE TILTED FILTER

From **Example 9-1**, how would the transmission peak shift if the filter (thickness 0.218 μm) was tilted by 10° with respect to the incident light?

From Snell's Law, first use $\theta_{inc} = 10°$ to calculate:

$$n \sin \beta = \sin \theta_{inc} \Rightarrow \beta = \sin^{-1}\left(\frac{\sin \theta_{inc}}{n}\right) \approx 7.39°.$$

Next, compute:

$$\lambda = \frac{2nd \cos \beta}{m} = \frac{(2)(1.35)(0.218 \text{ μm})(\cos 7.39°)}{1} \approx 0.584 \text{ μm}.$$

Thus, tilting the filter by only 10° shifts the wavelength it transmits by 0.589 μm − 0.584 μm ≈ 0.005 μm = 5 nm. Although this shift may seem small, it is significant. It is large enough that the filter will no longer transmit the sodium D_2 spectral line.

Some examples of thin film wavelength selection from everyday life are shown in **Figure 9-7** and the introduction photograph at the beginning of this chapter. The introduction figure shows simple children's soap bubbles and **Figure 9-7** is highly complex. In either case, the coloring is based on the thickness of the soap film at various locations of the bubble.

Figure 9-7
Soap film takes on a shape and thickness that minimizes it's surface energy. (Image courtesy of Paul Nylander; http://www.bugman123.com/MinimalSurfaces/index.html.)

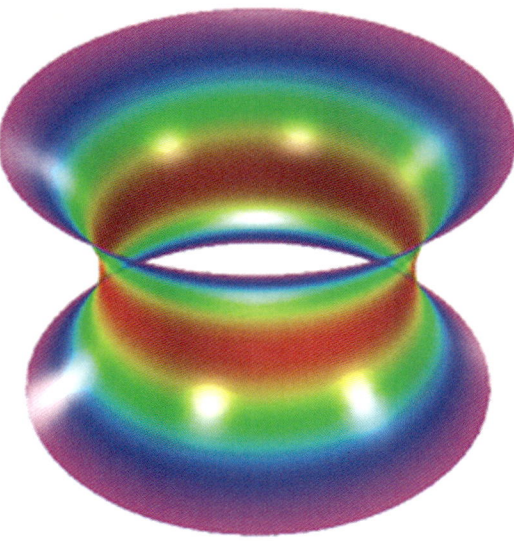

Another familiar example is a thin film of oil (or radiator fluid) on a garage floor as shown in **Figure 9-8**. The coloring of this film is based on the film thickness at various locations across the film. This may result from irregularities in terms of smoothness and flatness of the support structure behind the film, such as a cement floor of a garage.

Figure 9-8
A thin film of oil on a seemingly smooth floor. (Photo courtesy of http://en.wikipedia.org/wiki/File:Dieselrainbow.jpg; Creative Commons Attribution-Share Alike 2.5 Generic: John.)

Referring back to **Figure 9-6** from which the conditions for the electric field of a wave were derived to constructively or destructively interfere in one or two reflections, now ask what becomes of a light ray as it continues to reflect and transmit (to the right in the figure). That is, consider the total transmission $\tau_o(\lambda)$ of a single layer thin film. Think of an incident ray at near-normal incidence and multiple subsequent rays as shown in **Figure 9-9** (spread out for clarity) with no significant absorption within the film or at either boundary.

At each boundary or interface, the reflected portion of the electric field is r times the incident field, and the transmitted portion is t times the incident field. At any interface between two materials, the power (or

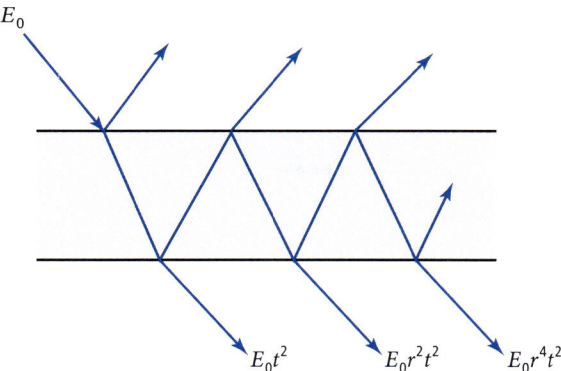

Figure 9-9
A light ray reflects multiple times within a thin film. A portion of the ray is transmitted at each reflection.

energy per unit time) reflected from the interface is the square of the reflected field:[9] $\rho = r^2$. The power transmitted is $\tau = t^2$. (Conservation of energy requires $\rho + \tau = 1$, or $r^2 + t^2 = 1$.)

Summing the electric fields associated with all the transmitted rays at a single λ gives Airy's formula,[10]

$$\tau_0(\lambda,\rho) = \frac{\mathcal{E}_{Trans}}{\mathcal{E}_0} = \frac{1}{1 + \frac{4\rho}{[1-\rho]^2}\sin^2\frac{\varphi}{2}}, \quad (9\text{-}14)$$

$$\text{where } \varphi = \frac{4\pi n d}{\lambda}\cos\beta.$$

This formula is the basis for a device known as an etalon that will be introduced as a hyperspectral dispersing element in **Chapter 17**, and it is plotted in **Figure 9-10** as a function of φ (increasing to the right) and λ ("normalized" by $2nd\cos\beta$ and increasing to the left) for three values of ρ.[11]

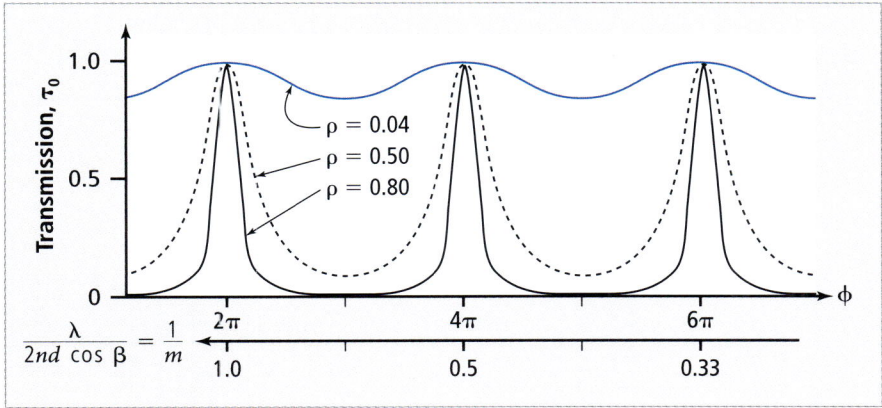

Figure 9-10
The Airy formula plotted for increasing wavelength to the left.

Note, the transmission peaks are located based on constructive interference conditions (and the value of m). The width of these peaks, $\Delta\lambda$, is a strong function of the reflectance values, ρ, at the boundary between the thin film and air or other materials. An expression for the relative width can be derived directly from Airy's formula above and given as:

$$\frac{\Delta\lambda}{\lambda} = \frac{1-\rho}{m\pi\sqrt{\rho}}, \quad (9\text{-}15)$$

$$\text{where } m = \frac{2nd}{\lambda}\cos\beta.$$

This ratio is related to the resolving power of spectral sensors discussed in later chapters.

---

[9] This is the *how much* of the reflectivity function introduced in **Chapter 3**, **Equation 3-12** for example.

[10] This is not the same as the Airy pattern of **Equation 6-7** for the point spread function. Details of the infinite sum to derive this formula are left to advanced optics textbooks.

[11] According to **Equation 3-10** and **Table 3-2**, the highest values for ρ for dielectric materials might be approximately 0.36 for light at normal incidence. Higher values of ρ may be achieved with partially mirrored (i.e., metalized) surfaces, or possibly multiple layers of thin dielectric films. These technologies introduce complications that will be ignored here.

For the initial design of a spectral filter using thin-film interference phenomenology and technology, selection of the values of *n* and *d* for the thin-film will determine the location of the various transmitted wavelengths (assuming normal incidence and β = 0). Further selection of the reflectivity value, ρ, at the boundary surfaces[12] of the thin film (along with its *n* and *d* values) will determine the width of the various wavelength transmission peaks, $\Delta\lambda/\lambda$.

Additional design issues remain. The desired filter spectral response was shown at the beginning of this chapter (**Figure 9-1a**). A good uniform response near τ = 1.0 in band helps in the analysis of collected data, especially when the spectral bandpass is large and the wavelength behavior of the target is poorly known. Having a good out-of-band rejection (τ as close to zero as possible) avoids collecting unwanted background. Both design considerations are important in transforming the collected data to derived characteristics of the target (such as reflectivity or temperature). Poorly designed filters can lead to large uncertainties in these derived characteristics. These issues will be further discussed in later chapters.

For multiple adjacent narrow spectral bands, some of these issues may become less severe, but they are not necessarily negligible. Consider the two adjacent spectral bands shown in **Figure 9-11** with two possible spectral response curve shapes: the ideal square-top and a triangular shape. As plotted, the two bands with the ideal square-top spectral response are not close enough together; they leave a narrow gap in spectral coverage. The two bands with the triangular shape allow for considerable "cross-talk" between adjacent spectral bands; that is, some wavelengths are covered by both spectral bands. Also plotted is a possible target with strong wavelength variation. The ratio of measured sensor outputs between the two spectral bands, for either filter shape, is not an accurate value of what is characteristic of the source. (Interestingly, the physiological absorption filters of the human eye have spectral response curves shaped more like the triangle than the ideal box-top. But, the human eye is not a calibrated

Figure 9-11
Possible filter shapes (as functions of wavelength) and hypothetical spectral characteristics of a target.

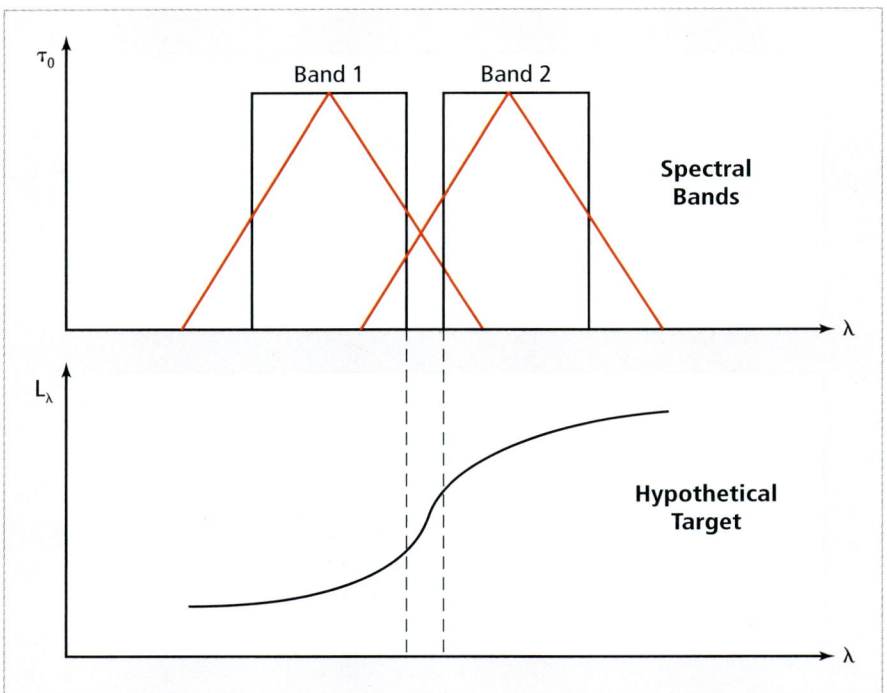

[12] See Footnote 11.

system used to determine the reflectivity of any source. It just discerns relative differences in reflectivity quite well.)

Another design issue is the elimination of the multiple transmission peaks (wavelengths) to which a desired detector could respond. Recall from **Table 9-1** and **Figure 9-10**, for any given choice of n, d, and β, a single layer thin film will pass multiple wavelengths, λ, given by the expression:

$$\lambda = \frac{2nd}{m}\cos\beta \ [\mu m], \quad (9\text{-}16)$$

where m can be any positive integer. Hence, this thin film's spectral response is as shown in **Figure 9-12**, where wavelength was normalized by the factor $2nd\cos\beta$.

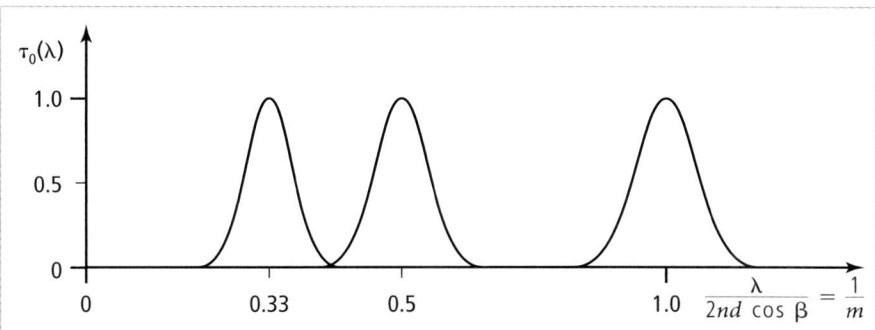

Figure 9-12
Thin film transmission as a function of normalized wavelength.

One possible solution to this design issue is the use of multiple layers of thin film with different values of the product nd. A simple example is shown in **Figure 9-13**. To facilitate the drawing, transmission peaks are drawn as if they have no width. In **Figure 9-13a**, the location of transmitted wavelengths is shown for some selected value of n_1d_1. Suppose only the wavelength indicated by the dotted line is desired and other nearby wavelengths are not. The selection of a second thin film with a selected value $n_2d_2 = 0.5n_1d_1$ provides transmitted wavelengths shown in **Figure 9-13b**. The desired wavelength is still transmitted, but the nearest undesired transmitted wavelengths of the first film are not. Two options are now possible: use the second thin-film instead of the first thin-film, or use the second thin-film on top of the first. In the latter case, which may be preferable for other reasons, the combined response would be the transmission of the first times that of the second as shown in **Figure 9-13c**.

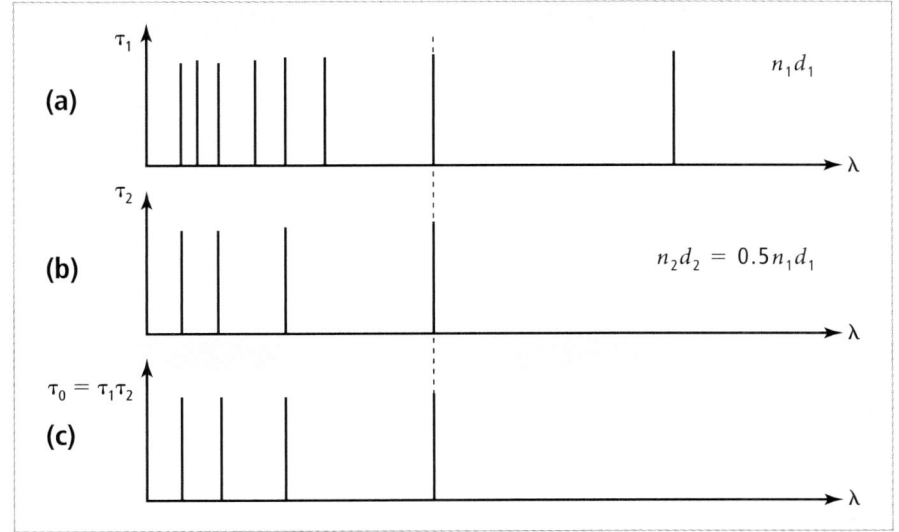

Figure 9-13
Two interference films stacked together (only the maximum transmissions are shown).

Combining the results previously discussed with those in **Chapter 6** (optics) and **Chapter 7** (detectors), the spectral bandpass of an advanced technical remote sensor is determined. If a spectral filter is used, generally, it is the optical element which sets the spectral bandpass. The total optical transmission, τ_{OPT}, is generally determined by the combination of the transmission values of the spectral filter, the optics and the detectors.

EXAMPLE 9-3: WHAT IS THE BANDPASS?

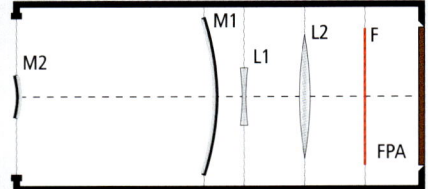

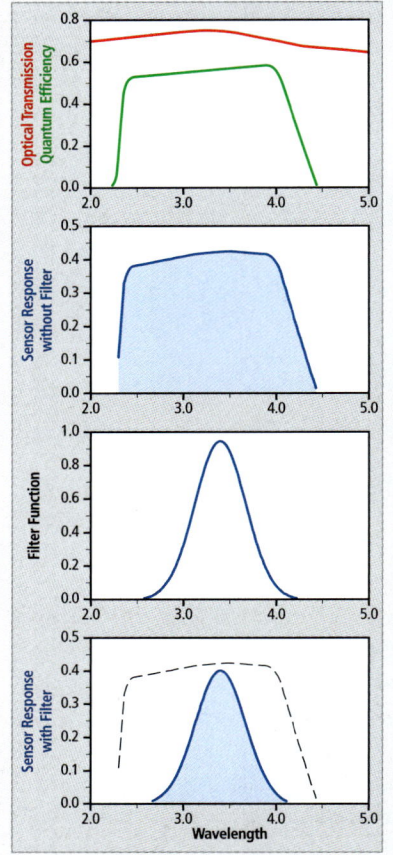

An advanced technical intelligence remote sensor has a Cassegrain telescope configuration, similar to **Figure 6-10**. The optics' transmission function and the detector's quantum efficiency are as shown in the top plot. Without any filter, these two terms determine the bandpass of the sensor. Multiplying them gives a sensor response function as shown in the second plot, which indicates the sensor is sensitive to light of wavelengths between about 2.30–4.43 μm. The short- and long-wavelength cutoffs of the detector's quantum efficiency appear to be responsible for these limits.

Introducing a filter, whose transmission function is as shown in the third plot, narrows the sensor's bandpass significantly. Multiplying the unfiltered response function by the filter's transmission results in the last, bottom plot. The sensor's bandpass is now approximately 2.67–4.12 μm.

10 SIGNALS AND NOISE

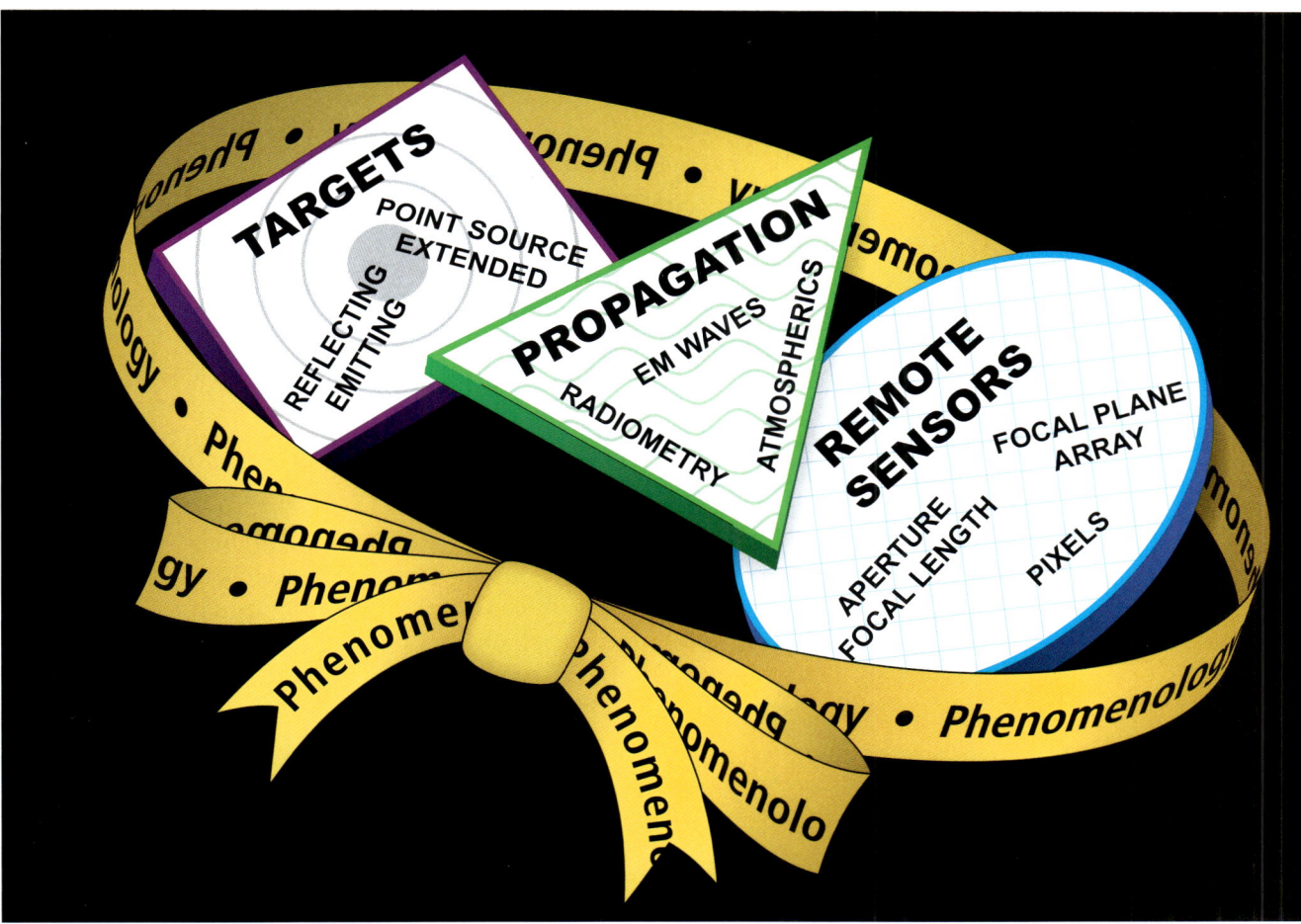

Now that all of the phenomenology of electro-optical remote sensing collection has been covered, it is time to put the pieces together. Although electromagnetic (EM) radiation (light) was emphasized, the phenomenology applies equally well to collecting any kind of energy (particles or waves) emitted by or reflected from a target. Now, two grand equations, one for point sources and one for extended sources, will be written to bring everything together. Specific applications of the grand equations will be covered in the chapters on large area surveillance and multi- and hyperspectral techniques.

This chapter also introduces the unavoidable consequence of doing advanced technical intelligence collection in the real world with physical technology affected by noise.

SECTIONS
10.1 END-TO-END EQUATIONS
10.2 IMPROVING COLLECTIONS
10.3 NOISE SOURCES

10.1 END-TO-END EQUATIONS

Up to this point, this text reviewed several independent subjects that are components of remote sensing: the sciences of materials emissivity and reflectivity, radiometric propagation, the atmosphere, optical devices, and photoelectric detection. There are no rules or laws that tell how these sciences should be put together, and not every problem in remote sensing necessarily uses all the pieces. It is basically the phenomenology of "following the photons" that tells how to select appropriate parts of the sciences.

THE PHENOMENOLOGY

Consider a point source in a sensor's Field of View (FOV), as illustrated in **Figure 10-1**. In the radiometry of **Chapter 4**, the point source was characterized by its emitted (**Chapter 2**) or reflected (**Chapter 3**) spectral intensity, I_λ [W · sr^{-1}µm^{-1}], which provides an unattenuated irradiance at the sensor's aperture, $\mathcal{E}_\lambda = I_\lambda/R^2$ [W · m^{-2}µm^{-1}]. When an atmosphere is present (**Chapter 5**), irradiance at the sensor is modified to $\mathcal{E}_\lambda = I_\lambda \tau_{ATM}/R^2$ [W · m^{-2}µm^{-1}] where the transmission function is a form of Beer's Law taking into account the number and types of absorbing and/or scattering molecules and/or particles and the path length through them. Only a certain amount of arriving power then passes through the projected[1] aperture area, $A_R \cos\theta_R$ [m^2], and is further attenuated by the sensor's optical transmission function, τ_{OPT}, as discussed in **Chapter 6**. The power arriving at the sensor's focal plane is now $\Phi_\lambda \approx \mathcal{E}_\lambda A_R \cos\theta \mathcal{E}$ [W · µm^{-1}], where τ_{OPT} includes a possible bandpass-limiting filter as covered in **Chapter 9**. The power is spatially distributed within a Point Spread Function (PSF) (**Chapter 6**), and appears on a sensor's Focal Plane Array (FPA) as in **Figure 7-14**, but this and the inclusion of the fraction F_{PIX} will be discussed in the application chapters.

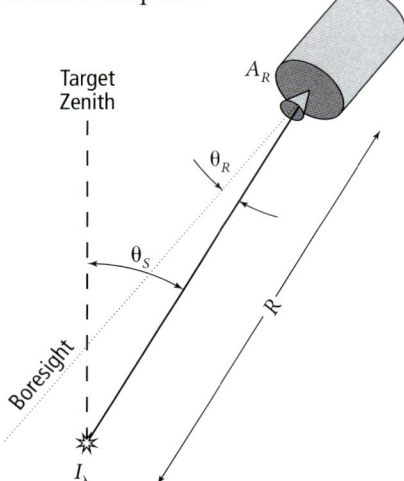

Figure 10-1
A remote sensor collecting energy from a point source.

Since modern solid-state detectors work on the photoelectric effect (**Chapter 7**), **Chapter 2** suggests the power can be written in terms of the number of photons, N_{PHOT}, arriving at the sensor's focal plane by dividing by the energy per photon, $E_{PHOT} \approx hc/\lambda$ [J (per photon)], as[2]

$$\frac{\Delta N_{\lambda, PHOT}}{\Delta t} \approx \Phi_\lambda/E_{PHOT}$$

[photons · s^{-1}µm^{-1}]. The photons falling on the focal plane (**Chapter 8**) are the *optical* image. It is the purpose of the detector (**Chapter 7**) to convert this into an *electronic* image called "data" using its quantum efficiency, η [electrons · photons^{-1}]. The output signal is now

---

[1] The fixation angle θ_R is often small, so the cosine term may frequently be neglected.

[2] The delta notation is introduced here as a reminder that photons are arriving from the target at a particular *rate*, photons per unit time. In calculus, this would be a derivative. Here, the "per unit time" will be integration time, Δt_{INT}.

206 CHAPTER 10 SIGNALS AND NOISE

$$\frac{\Delta N_{\lambda,e}}{\Delta t} = \frac{\Delta N_{\lambda,PHOT}}{\Delta t} \eta \ [\text{electrons} \cdot \text{s}^{-1} \mu\text{m}^{-1}].$$ **Chapter 7** further discussed that the common detector operation is to sum (i.e., integrate) over an interval of time, Δt_{INT} [s (per frame)], and **Chapters 7** and **9** show that a sensor responds only within a specific bandpass, $\Delta\lambda$ [μm]. Putting all the above phenomenology together and summing (integrating) over bandpass and integration time[3] gives sensor output for one frame of data as an *end-to-end equation* incorporating all the above as

$$\Delta N_e \approx \int_{\Delta\lambda} \frac{I_\lambda \tau_{ATM} A_R \cos\theta_R \tau_{OPT} \eta}{R^2 (hc/\lambda)} d\lambda \Delta t_{INT} \ [\text{electrons (per frame)}]. \quad (10\text{-}1)$$

For transmission from the remote sensor to its control center, the output of **Equation 10-1** is commonly digitized, and data appears at an analyst's desk as

$$\tilde{N}_{TGT} \approx {}^A\!/\!_D\{\Delta N_e\} \ [\text{DU (per frame)}], \quad (10\text{-}2)$$

where the notation ${}^A\!/\!_D\{...\}$ means analog-to-digital conversion,[4] and the units, DU, stand for non-dimensional Digital Units (DU), referred to as counts. Because this collection is on a FPA, the data will actually appear at the analyst's desk as digitized values *per pixel*. The sum of all the pixels' values within a target's PSF will be the total given by **Equation 10-2**. The per pixel numbers are customarily arranged in some formatted order to correspond to the rows and columns of pixels on the sensor's focal plane, so they can be reassembled into a display on the analyst's computer screen. The numbers themselves range from zero (no output) to $2^m - 1$ (maximum output), where m is called the bit depth, dividing a pixel's output into 2^m digital levels, as in **Figure 7-31**. (See the Sidebar, **Binary Numbers**.) Often the 2^m levels are color coded either on a gray or colored scale. (See **Chapter 16** where thermal images are rendered in color, for example.)

Now, consider an extended source or background filling a sensor's FOV, or a portion thereof, as illustrated in **Figure 10-2**. Using the same chain of phenomenology as above, except $\mathcal{E}_\lambda = L_\lambda \tau_{ATM} \Omega$ [W $\cdot$ m^{-2}μm^{-1}], where L_λ may include both surface (**Chapter 2** or **3**) and path (**Chapter 5**) radiance, the digitized output from a remote sensor is another *end-to-end equation*,

$$\tilde{N}_{BKG} \approx {}^A\!/\!_D \left\{ \int_{\Delta\lambda} \frac{L_\lambda \tau_{ATM} \Omega A_R \cos\theta_R \tau_{OPT} \eta}{hc/\lambda} d\lambda \Delta t_{INT} \right\} \ [\text{DU (per frame)}]. \quad (10\text{-}3)$$

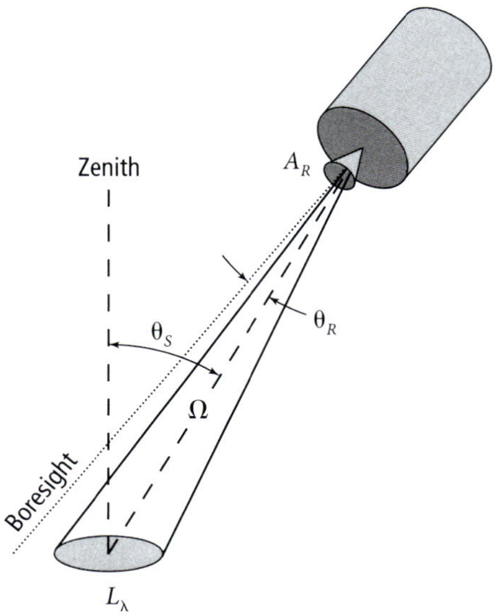

[3] Why does Equation 10-1 show the mathematical operation of integration over wavelength (bandpass), but not over time (integration time)? Because, the only time-varying quantity in the phenomenological equation is the target intensity, and it is presumed that *how* it varies in time is unknown. (This will be discussed further in Chapters 12 and 13.) Therefore, since a sensor's output per frame is representative of the accumulation of target photons over the integration time, it is what it is, and there is no need to mathematically integrate. On the other hand, a target's *spectral* characteristics may also be mostly unknown, but the wavelength variation of the atmospheric transmission (from MODTRAN), the optical transmission function (including any possible filter), and the quantum efficiency of the detector are known. Therefore, the mathematical operation of integrating combines these with the target's variation, and is necessary. If the bandpass is sufficiently small, the integral is easily approximated.

[4] Technically, this really isn't analog-to-digital conversion since the number being converted is not a continuous (analog) value, but a countable number of electrons. More properly, it is a re-scaling from the maximum number of electrons (the well depth) to the maximum of some other number, which is conventionally chosen to be a power of two for binary representation. See Figure 7-31 for example.

Figure 10-2
A remote sensor collecting energy from an extended source or background.

> **BINARY (DIGITAL) NUMBERS**
>
> In base 2, or binary, only the digits 0 and 1 are used. Each place in a binary number, starting from the right, represents a power of 2. For example, with a bit depth of 8 (meaning eight binary digits), the number
>
> | 1 | 0 | 1 | 1 | 0 | 0 | 1 | 0 |
> |---|---|---|---|---|---|---|---|
> | 2^7 | 2^6 | 2^5 | 2^4 | 2^3 | 2^2 | 2^1 | 2^0 |
>
> represents the customary base-10 number
>
> $$\begin{aligned} 1 \times 2^7 &= 128 \\ +0 \times 2^6 &= 0 \\ +1 \times 2^5 &= 32 \\ +1 \times 2^4 &= 16 \\ +0 \times 2^3 &= 0 \\ +0 \times 2^2 &= 0 \\ +1 \times 2^1 &= 2 \\ +0 \times 2^0 &= 0 \\ \hline &178 \end{aligned}$$
>
> Conversion from base 10 to binary, which is the meaning of the A/D {...} notation, follows the reverse path: find the largest power of 2, then the next largest, etc., and write the answer down from left to right. For example, to convert 117 to 8-bit binary,
>
> $$\begin{aligned} &117 \\ &\underline{-64} \ (=2^6) \\ &53 \\ &\underline{-32} \ (=2^5) \\ &21 \\ &\underline{-16} \ (=2^4) \\ &5 \\ &\underline{-4} \ (=2^2) \\ &1 \\ &\underline{-1} \ (=2^0) \\ &0 \end{aligned}$$
>
> The answer is 01110101.

On one hand, if radiance and the atmosphere are uniform, then **Chapters 2**, **3**, **4**, **5**, and **8** argue that **Equation 10-3** will be the same output for each and every pixel, where $\Omega = \Omega_{PIX}$. As for the cosine term, if the FOV is small, then even this can be neglected. One of the prime assumptions of advanced technical information gathering for large area surveillance (to be further discussed in **Chapters 13** and **14**) is that pixels give a nearly uniform background output. On the other hand, the objective of multi- and hyperspectral remote sensing (**Chapters 15 – 20**) is to combine the spectral variability of surface radiance with spatial resolution and imaging (**Chapters 6**, **8**, and **12**) to use the pixel-to-pixel differences of **Equation 10-3** as indicators of the spectral nature of objects for their identification and characterization.

Some additional notes on the end-to-end equations are as follows:

1. The *bandpass*, $\lambda_1 \rightarrow \lambda_2$, is generally determined by an optical filter, although source characteristics, atmospheric transmission, or detector responsivity, could contribute. The integral over the bandpass is a reminder that detectors convert *any* photon received within the bandpass to an electron (according to their quantum efficiencies).

2. *Source terms,* intensity or radiance, depend on the physical size of the source and whether it is emitting or reflecting energy.
   a. If the geometric image of a target is smaller than one pixel on the FPA, then the source must be considered a point source.
   b. Sources with a geometric image that spans many pixels may still be treated as point sources, particularly if the ground sample distance (**Chapter 8**) is smaller than the source-to-sensor distance, R. Backgrounds are usually considered to be extended sources.

3. The *geometry* of a particular collection will determine the *range to source*, R (**Section 4.3**), the *source sending direction*, θ_S, and the *fixation angle*, θ_R.

4. The *FOV* of the sensor, Ω, or of a pixel, Ω_{PIX}, is determined by the size of its focal plane, or pixel, and its optics' effective focal length (**Chapter 8**).

5. The *atmospheric transmission factor*, τ_{ATM}, was discussed in **Chapter 5** for absorption and scattering and calculated with Beer's Law. As a matter of practice, a computer program like MODTRAN is used to calculate this term.

6. The sensor's *optical transmission factor*, τ_{OPT}, and its *clear aperture area*, A_R, were discussed in **Chapter 6**. The end-to-end equations assume all the energy passing through the aperture and the optics arrives at the detector, but this may not be true for real optical systems.

7. Even a perfect optical system does not put all the energy into a perfect image on a *FPA* because of physical (wave) optics considerations. Therefore, the energy from all pixels within a PSF must be summed to account for everything.

8. The detector's *quantum efficiency*, η, assumes a sensor in the visible or infrared portion of the spectrum where a photon detector is appropriate. In that case, the term in the denominator, hc/λ, converts the incident radiation's energy into photons.

9. *Integration time,* Δt_{INT}, introduced in **Chapter 7**, suggests a detector collects energy for a finite interval of time, then reports a single number without regard to when it was received during the interval.

10. Not all of the energy collected comes from a target and its background; there is also noise. Noise will be discussed in the last section of this chapter.

11. To reiterate, the end-to-end equations give only summed (integrated) sensor outputs because of the finite bandpass (Note 1), finite pixel size (Notes 7 and 8), and finite integration time (Note 9). Thus, some spectral, spatial, and temporal fidelity is automatically lost in the sampling process.

12. Finally, although the grand end-to-end **Equations 10-1** and **10-3** were developed in this text for collection of EM waves (light) in the electro-optic spectrum, the phenomenology is perfectly general. With appropriate definitions of target (or background) energy emission and/or reflection, spatial propagation and attenuation processes, and energy collection and detection technologies, similar equations could be developed for any sub-discipline of Geospatial Intelligence. **Example 10-1** exercises the equations.

EXAMPLE 10-1: PREDICT SENSOR OUTPUT SIGNALS

Predict (i.e., estimate) the output signals of a remote sensor collecting on a $I_\lambda \approx 10^4$ W·sr^{-1}μm^{-1} point source against a uniform daytime background from $R \approx 35{,}780$ km overhead (geosynchronous orbit, see **Chapter 11**) in the MWIR 3.70 – 3.90 μm "window" band. Surface albedo is $\bar{\rho} \approx 0.30$. The sensor has a $D \approx 0.60$ m diameter aperture and a $f/4.0$ optical system with a $\tau_{OPT} \approx 0.50$ transmission factor (including a bandpass-limiting filter). The detector is a 2.00 cm square 16.8 megapixel (4096×4096) FPA with quantum efficiency $\eta \approx 0.35$, operated at eight frames per second. Output is linearly digitized to 16 bits with a well depth of 250,000 electrons per pixel.

First, assuming the bandpass is sufficiently narrow and all the terms in **Equation 10-3** are approximately constant over the bandpass, the phenomenology of the background reduces to an output per pixel of

$$\Delta N_{BKG} \approx \frac{\overline{L_\lambda} \Omega_{PIX} \overline{\tau_{ATM}} A_R \tau_{OPT} \overline{\lambda} \eta \Delta\lambda \Delta t_{INT}}{hc} \text{ [electrons (per pixel per frame)]}.$$

Preliminary calculations for evaluating this formula are:

- From **Figure 5-34**, surface (both reflected and thermal) and atmospheric radiance combined is about 1.0 W·m^{-2}sr^{-1}μm^{-1}, but this value includes $\overline{\tau_{ATM}}$, as that figure was plotted. Thus, $\overline{L_\lambda \tau_{ATM}} \approx 1.0$ W·m^{-2}sr^{-1} μm^{-1}.

- From the optics and detector specifications, $f_{eff} \approx (f/\#)(D) \approx (4.0)(0.60 \text{ m}) \approx 2.40$ m, and $x_{PIX} \approx \frac{2.00 \text{ cm}}{4096 \text{ pixels}} \approx 4.88 \times 10^{-6}$ m (called the pitch, which will be taken to be the detector size). Hence, $\Omega_{PIX} \approx \frac{(4.88 \times 10^{-6} \text{ m})^2}{(2.40 \text{ m})^2} \approx 4.13 \times 10^{-12}$ sr.

- $A_R \approx \frac{\pi D^2}{4} \approx \frac{(\pi)(0.60)^2}{4} \approx 0.283$ m^2. Assume $\theta_R \approx 0$ so, $\cos\theta_R \approx 1$.

Continued on next page

- Assuming a near-100% duty cycle, $\Delta t_{INT} \approx \frac{1}{\{\text{Frame Rate}\}} \approx \frac{1}{8 \text{ s}^{-1}} \approx 0.125$ s.

Then, substituting known values and being careful with the units,

$$\Delta N_{BKG} \approx \frac{\left(1.0 \frac{W}{m^2 \text{sr} \cdot \mu m}\right)(4.13 \times 10^{-12} \text{sr})(0.283 \text{ m}^2)(0.50)(3.80 \times 10^{-6} \text{m})(0.35)(0.20 \text{ }\mu m)(0.125 \text{ s})}{(6.63 \times 10^{-34} \text{ J} \cdot \text{s})(3 \times 10^8 \text{ m} \cdot \text{s}^{-1})}$$

$\approx 9.77 \times 10^4$ electrons (per pixel per frame).

Since a full well of 250,000 electrons would be represented by a digital value of $2^{16} = 65{,}536$ DU, the background signal will be

$$\tilde{N}_{BKG} \approx \left(\frac{65{,}536 \text{ DU}}{250{,}000 \text{ electrons}}\right)(97{,}700 \text{ electrons})$$

$\approx 26{,}611$ DU (per pixel per frame)

Second, assuming the target is a constant function of wavelength, **Equation 10-1** can be approximated as

$$\Delta N_{TGT} \approx \frac{\overline{I_\lambda} \, \overline{\tau_{ATM}} A_R \tau_{OPT} \overline{\lambda} \eta \Delta \lambda \Delta t_{ATM}}{hcR^2}.$$

The preliminary calculation needed for this formula, in addition to the above, is to run MODTRAN to estimate $\overline{\tau_{ATM}} \approx 0.86$ for the 3.70 – 3.90 μm band. Thus, being careful of the units again,

$$\Delta N_{TGT} \approx \frac{\left(10^4 \frac{W}{\text{sr} \cdot \mu m}\right)(0.86)(0.283 \text{ m}^2)(0.50)(3.80 \times 10^{-6} \text{m})(0.35)(0.20 \text{ }\mu m)(0.125 \text{ s})}{(6.63 \times 10^{-34} \text{ J} \cdot \text{s})(3 \times 10^8 \text{ m} \cdot \text{s}^{-1})(3.58 \times 10^7 \text{ m})^2}$$

$\approx 1.59 \times 10^5$ electrons (per frame).

Converted to a digital output, this is

$$\tilde{N}_{TGT} \approx \left(\frac{65{,}536 \text{ DU}}{250{,}000 \text{ electrons}}\right)(1.59 \times 10^5 \text{ electrons})$$

$\approx 41{,}681$ DU (per frame).

This second answer is for the *entire point source image*, and is calculated as though *all* photons through the aperture are converted to electrons (with quantum efficiency η), but the background output is for a single pixel. To compare, consider the following:

- The image of a point target is a PSF (**Chapter 6**), and possibly only the central spot (airy disk for perfectly aligned optics) of 84% of the photons passing through the aperture is detectable.
- The PSF has a size of approximately $\pi r_A^2 \approx \pi \left(\frac{1.22 f \overline{\lambda}}{D}\right)^2 \approx \pi \left(\frac{(1.22)(2.4 \text{ m})(3.8 \text{ }\mu m)}{0.60 \text{ m}}\right)^2 \approx 1080 \text{ }\mu m^2$. This covers approximately $\frac{\pi r_A^2}{(x_{PIX})^2} \approx \frac{1080 \text{ }\mu m^2}{(4.88 \text{ }\mu m)^2} \approx 45$ pixels.
- Hence, within the PSF, the *average* pixel output (ignoring the shape of the Airy pattern) will be about $\Delta \overline{N}_{TGT} \approx \frac{(0.84)(1.59 \times 10^5 \text{ electrons})}{45 \text{ pixels}} \approx 2970$ electrons (per pixel per frame), which is $\tilde{N}_{TGT} \approx \left(\frac{65{,}536 \text{ DU}}{250{,}000 \text{ electrons}}\right)(2979 \text{ electrons}) \approx 778$ DU (per pixel per frame).

Continued on next page

Therefore,
- The predicted sensor output is 25,611 DU per pixel *outside* the target's PSF, and
- Approximately 25,611 + 778 ≈ 26,389 DU *within* the target's PSF.
- The *total* counts an analyst might expect to find for the target would be about (45 pixels)(778 DU) ≈ 35,010 DU.
- Note, the *signal-to-background* ratio for the portion of the FPA covered by the PSF is only $\frac{\text{Signal}}{\text{Background}} \approx \frac{35{,}010 \text{ DU}}{(45 \text{ pixels})(25{,}611 \text{ DU})} \approx 0.03$.

THE SOLUTIONS

Now that the end-to-end **Equations 10-1** and **10-3** were developed phenomenologically, it is important to understand they are *not* the answer. That is, the syntax of an equation reads like a sentence in noun-verb-object order where most of the emphasis lies on "equal." This implies that if values are provided for all the "known" variables on the right side (after the equal sign) and the mathematical operations are carried out, then the value of the "unknown" variable on the left side (before the equal sign) is generated. But, this is incorrect because the values of the signals are known! They are the numerical data outputs of the sensor. *The actual unknowns are the spectral intensity or radiance of the sources of interest.* These values are buried under the integral, where the integral represents the response of the sensor within its bandpass and integration time. In general, a function under an integral cannot be solved, as it is not unique. See **Example 10-2**.

EXAMPLE 10-2: FIND THE FUNCTION

Simplistically, an integral can be represented by an area under a curve. Suppose the value of a certain integral is known to be 1 on the interval $0 \leq x \leq 1$; what is the curve?

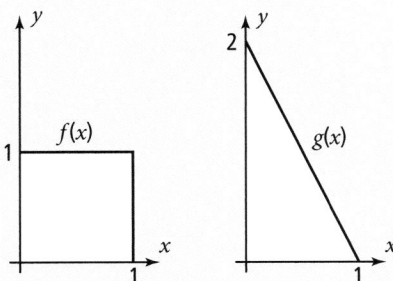

The figure suggests two possibilities. On the left, $f(x) = 1$ and the area under the curve is a square: $1 \times 1 = 1$.

On the right, $g(x) = -2x + 2$ and the area is a triangle: $\frac{1}{2} \times 1 \times 2 = 1$.

These are just two of an infinite range of possibilities, so it is impossible to know exactly what is the correct curve.

The effort to solve for a function of interest under an integral is further complicated by another generality; the integral of a product of functions is not equal to the product of the integrals of the functions. Examples of this are the integrals in **Equations 10-1** and **10-3** over several functions of wavelength: $I_\lambda(\lambda,t)$ or $L_\lambda(\lambda,t)$, $\tau(\lambda,\theta_S)_{ATM}$, $\tau(\lambda)_{OPT}$, $\eta(\lambda)$, and λ itself.

Nevertheless, if the bandpass is sufficiently narrow so all these functions are approximately constant over that bandpass, the integral in **Equations 10-1** and **10-2** can be approximated as:

$$\tilde{N}_{TGT} \approx {}^{A}\!/\!_{D}\left\{\left(\frac{\cos\theta_R A_R \Delta t_{INT}}{hcR^2}\right)\int I_\lambda \tau_{ATM}\tau_{OPT}\eta\lambda d\lambda\right\} \quad (10\text{-}4)$$

$$\approx {}^{A}\!/\!_{D}\left\{\left(\frac{\cos\theta_R A_R \Delta t_{INT}}{hcR^2}\right)\langle I_\lambda\rangle \overline{\tau_{ATM}}\,\overline{\tau_{OPT}}\,\overline{\eta}\,\overline{\lambda}\Delta\lambda\right\},$$

where the overbar notation indicates the most representative values of those terms within the bandpass were chosen. The angle brackets, $\langle\,\rangle$, on the unknown spectral intensity indicate that its most likely value, or "expectation value," will satisfy the equation.

Now, **Equation 10-4** can be solved algebraically, and the estimate for the spectral intensity is

$$\langle I_\lambda\rangle \approx \frac{{}^{D}\!/\!_{A}\{\tilde{N}\}}{\left(\dfrac{\cos\theta_R A_R \Delta t_{INT}}{hcR^2}\right)\overline{\tau_{ATM}}\,\overline{\tau_{OPT}}\,\overline{\eta}\,\overline{\lambda}\Delta\lambda}, \quad (10\text{-}5)$$

where the notation "D/A{…}" means an inverse, digital-to-analog rendering of the sensor output into "engineering units." (See **Figure 7-31** again.)

EXAMPLE 10-3: ESTIMATING INTENSITY

An intelligence analyst has suppressed background (see **Chapter 14**) and isolated a point target on the FPA of a sensor with characteristics similar to that in **Example 10-1** but in a low Earth orbit, like the Space Shuttle (see **Chapter 11**). The analyst finds a *total* signal of 1,000,000 DU when the collection was taken from $h \approx 250$ km altitude at $\theta_N \approx 30°$ nadir angle. (The sensor was pointing directly at the target, so $\theta_R \approx 0°$.) It is important and necessary to estimate the spectral intensity of the target.

First, the analyst does the following sidework:

- 1,000,000 is the sum of approximately 45 pixels' output, so counts per pixel is approximately $\frac{1{,}000{,}000 \text{ DU}}{45 \text{ pixels}} \approx 22{,}222$ DU per pixel, which resulted from ${}^{D}\!/\!_{A}\{22{,}222 \text{ DU}\} \approx (22{,}222 \text{ DU})\left(\frac{250{,}000 \text{ electrons}}{65{,}536 \text{ DU}}\right) \approx 84{,}800$ electrons. This is a total of $(45 \text{ pixels})(84{,}800 \text{ electrons}) \approx 3.82\times 10^6$ electrons.
- Distance to target $R \approx \frac{h}{\cos\theta_N} \approx \frac{h}{\cos 30°} \approx 289$ km since the sensor's orbit is low enough so the Earth can be considered flat (**Section 4.3**).
- Atmospheric transmission in-band at 30° is $\tau(30°) \approx [\tau(30°)]^{\sec\theta_N} \approx (0.86)^{\sec 30°} \approx 0.84$.

Second, the analyst applies **Equation 10-5**:

$$\langle I_\lambda\rangle \approx \frac{(3.82\times 10^6 \text{ electrons})(6.63\times 10^{-34}\text{ J}\cdot\text{s})(3\times 10^8 \text{ m}\cdot\text{s}^{-1})(2.89\times 10^5 \text{ m})^2}{(0.283 \text{ m}^2)(0.125 \text{ s})(0.84)(0.50)(0.35)(3.78\times 10^{-6}\text{ m})(0.2\ \mu\text{m})}$$

$$\approx 16.1 \text{ W}\cdot\text{sr}^{-1}\mu\text{m}^{-1}.$$

Remember, "engineering units" means expressing the value of a quantity in proper standard units. The engineering units of spectral intensity are, of course, watts per steradian per micrometer (W · sr^{-1}μm^{-1}), and similarly for spectral radiance (W · m^{-2} sr^{-1}μm^{-1}).

Since many targets of national interest are point sources, particularly in large area surveillance, remote sensing intelligence analysts have many occasions to use **Equation 10-5**. A difficulty is that sensor output is from *all* incident sources, so a target is seen against the Earth or space background which necessitates solving **Equation 10-3** in like manner.[5] And then, there is noise. However, what often distinguishes many point targets is they are dynamic, changing in both signature and metrics. And finally, successful target detection, identification, and characterization ultimately depend on sensor calibration. **Example 10-3** gives an application for $\langle I_\lambda \rangle$ without background present.

10.2 IMPROVING COLLECTIONS

Notice the end-to-end equations contain terms that depend on the Source, Geometry and Sensor parameters, grouped in that order in **Equations 10-6** and **10-7**, where there is some overlap in the terms.

$$\tilde{N}_{TGT} \approx {^A\!/_D} \left\{ \int_{\Delta\lambda} \frac{1}{hc}(I_\lambda) \left(\frac{\tau_{ATM} \cos\theta_R}{R^2} \right) (A_R \tau_{OPT} \eta \lambda \, d\lambda \, \Delta t_{INT}) \right\} \quad (10\text{-}6)$$

$$\tilde{N} \approx {^A\!/_D} \left\{ \int_{\Delta\lambda} \frac{1}{hc}(L_\lambda)(\tau_{ATM} \cos\theta_R)(\Omega A_R \tau_{OPT} \eta \lambda \, d\lambda \, \Delta t_{INT}) \right\} \quad (10\text{-}7)$$

For the sensor designer and the collection manager, it is important to consider how to take advantage of the various terms in the equations to achieve the best possible collection.

Recall, the analyst becomes aware of a target by receiving energy from it. Energy is either emitted or reflected by the source and demonstrates spatial, spectral, and temporal characteristics of its origin. The question to ask is "Is the selected sensor adequate to collect and detect the appropriate type of energy?" From the information known about a target, should a sensor collect particles or waves, and therefore is it operating in the mechanical or EM domain? Is there the proper spatial, spectral, and temporal resolution to distinguish a target or event from others and background to correctly identify and characterize the source and to adequately evaluate its threat potential?

Some geometry and sensor considerations are delineated in **Tables 10-1** and **10-2**, presenting general improvements and limitations of the parameters used in the end-to-end equations.

Table 10-1
Geometry considerations for the development of a sensor system.

Scenario Factor	For Improved Collections...	Possible Limitations
R	Reduce range for greater irradiance, but increase range for survivability	Greater range makes pointing control and accuracy more difficult
θ_R	Center target/event in FOV if possible, avoid edge of FPA	Probable unknown target location; focal plane registration
τ_{ATM}	Reduce range through atmosphere (nadir viewing if possible) and select appropriate transmission band	Atmosphere is somewhat unpredictable

[5] Solving **Equation 10-3** for $\langle L_\lambda \rangle$ is left as an exercise for the reader.

Table 10-2
Sensor parameter considerations for the development of a sensor system.

Design Factor	For Improved Collections...	Possible Limitations
Ω_R	Larger FOV for extended targets, but smaller for less background	FPA size, enhanced background, and noise
A_R	Larger for greater throughput and better spatial resolution	Cost, size, and weight of larger optics; aberrations
τ_{OPT}	Minimize number of surfaces and use anti-reflection coatings	Cost and materials availability; larger sensor; $\tau_{OPT} \leq 1.0$
η	Select highest possible responsivity	Lifetime of sensor cooling equipment; $\eta \leq 1.0$
$\Delta\lambda$	Match bandpass to target and atmospheric transmission	Trade-off throughput and spectral resolution
Δt_{INT}	Synchronize timing with event energy output	Too slow for fast events or too fast for dim targets

Resolution is an important factor in whether the sensor system can fulfill the intelligence or mission requirements. Spectral resolution (**Chapters 17-20**) is the ability to distinguish and measure the energy of incident information from a source. It depends on the wavelength and/or frequency of radiation (photons) or mechanical waves and kinetic energy of particles. Spatial resolution (**Chapters 6**, **8**, and **12**) is the ability to distinguish between separate, simultaneous events or possibly to discern the size of an object. It is an interplay between PSF and Nyquist criterion applied to FPA design. Temporal resolution (**Chapters 12** and **13**) is the ability to distinguish the time history of an event. Once again, the Nyquist criterion determines the interplay between energy (brightness) evolution of an event and time sampling (integration) by a remote sensor.

The interpretation and exploitation of a remote sensor's output in all dimensions (spatial, temporal, spectral, and radiometric) are critically dependent on understanding its performance. Spatial calibration pertains to issues like the location of the sensor, knowledge of where the sensor is pointing, and the size of the sensor FOV. Temporal calibration pertains to issues like time of data collection which provides the time stamped on the data, the time of the event, or the time the energy arrived at the sensor. Spectral calibration pertains to the sensor's throughput and response as a function of wavelength. Finally, radiometric calibration pertains to the determination of the amount of energy received as a function of when, where, and wavelength.

10.3 NOISE SOURCES

Noise is an unwanted and unpredictable fluctuation that obscures and distorts the energy received from a target of interest and hence complicates the ability to detect, identify, and characterize it. Noise may enter the sensor system from the outside or may be generated within the components of a remote sensor system. Noise generally limits the useful range of a sensor's response and places requirements on the sensor putput necessary to ensure good signal analysis. Energy typically cannot be distinguished from real sources through general analysis of the sensor output. Noise requires a threshold to be set for the energy that is important to the desired information; energy below the threshold is considered to be noise and is discarded. Noise obscures and degrades the ability to completely evaluate the intelligence content of collected energy above the threshold; that is, some energy from every source is lost in the noise. For example, recall only about 84% of collected energy appears in the central image region of a point source; the other 16% would probably be below threshold and "lost" in the energy extraction process.

Signal is compared to noise in the Signal-to-Noise Ratio (SNR), which is the ratio of a sensor's output arising from a target in the FOV to the undesirable noise present. *Note, SNR is not the same as the signal-to-background ratio.* A common rule of thumb, based on statistical distributions, is the SNR must be approximately three or greater for reliable target detection.

Noise is a continuously changing signal, but its average effect can be estimated. If a sensor were operated in continuous mode, its output would be a continuously changing signal, $N(t)$. (See **Figure 10-3**.) On average, over some time interval, Δt, the signal would be

$$\overline{N} \approx \frac{1}{\Delta t} \int N(t) dt, \tag{10-8}$$

but would randomly fluctuate above and below this value. A measure of the fluctuation, or noise, is the Root-Mean-Square (RMS) value defined as[6]

$$\mathcal{N}_{RMS} \approx \sqrt{\frac{1}{\Delta t} \int [N(t) - \overline{N}]^2 dt}. \tag{10-9}$$

The usual case, though, is to operate in a time-sampling mode where a sensor's output signal is a discrete series of data, N_i, as in **Figure 7-28**. These are shown as the red triangles in **Figure 10-3** where the jagged line suggests a continuously operating sensor's signal. In the discrete case, the average sensor output for M samples is

$$\overline{N} \approx \frac{1}{M} \sum_i N_i. \tag{10-10}$$

Similarly to the continuous mode, a RMS value of the noise can be estimated as

$$\mathcal{N}_{RMS} \approx \sqrt{\frac{1}{M} \sum_i (N_i - \overline{N})^2}. \tag{10-11}$$

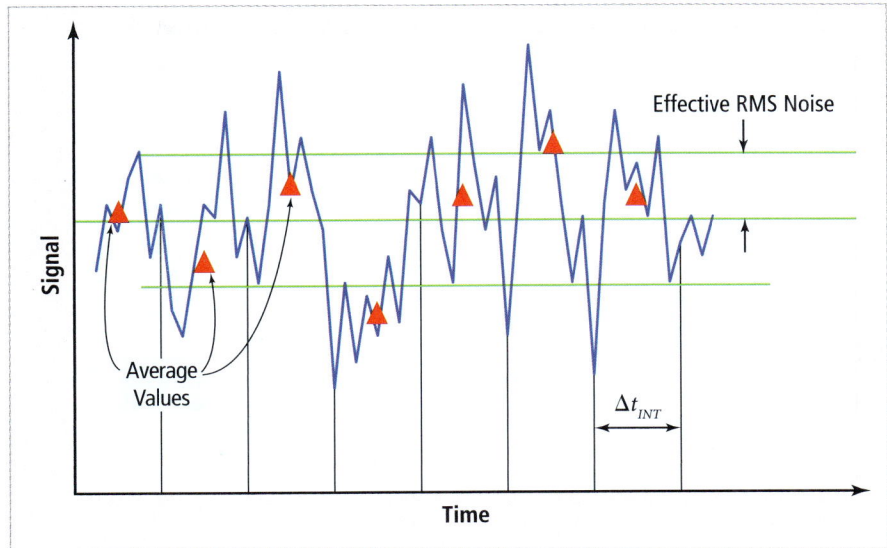

Figure 10-3
A noisy signal as a function of time and the resulting average and RMS values.

[6] This section suffers from a notational difficulty not present in any other part of this text. A Times Roman capital "N" can refer to either a number of photons (emitted from a target, passing through an aperture, arriving at a detector, etc.) or a number of electrons (from the photoelectric effect, stored in a pixel's well, etc.) A script "$\mathcal{N}$" refers to the variation in the number of those photons or electrons, which is taken to be the random, uncontrollable noise in those numbers.

From the point of view of a detector, everything that provides photons could be an external source of noise. That is, the detector responds to photons regardless of their source and converts the photons into electrons with some quantum efficiency. Some sources of photons are: 1) background and the target; 2) atmospheric radiance; 3) the warm structure of the sensor system (lens, mirrors, filters, and physical structure) including any parts of its platform that may be in the FOV; and 4) stray light (photons from outside a sensor's FOV that scatter through the telescope). See **Figure 10-4**.

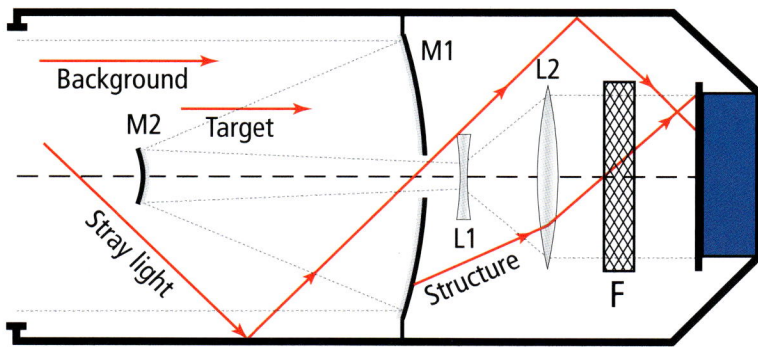

Figure 10-4
A simple remote sensor with two mirrors, two lens, a filter (F), and a detector (blue). Red arrows are sources of noise photons from outside the telescope and from the warm components within the system.

Photons from all these sources arrive at random rates. Dark current (**Chapter 7**) is also randomly generated by detectors and contributes to photon noise. In principle, a steady arrival rate could be subtracted, so really only the variations contribute to noise. This noise is called "photon noise" and the RMS number of photons incident on a detector, in one integration time, attributable to this randomness from any source can be estimated by[7]

$$n_{PHOTON\ NOISE} \approx \sqrt{N_{SOURCE}} \quad \text{where} \quad N_{SOURCE} \approx \frac{\Phi_{SOURCE}\Delta t_{INT}}{hc/\lambda}, \quad (10\text{-}12)$$

where Φ_{SOURCE} is the power received by the detector.

EXAMPLE 10-4: PHOTON NOISE ANALOGY

Popcorn provides an analogy for photon noise (called shot noise in electronic circuits). Suppose many identical bags of popcorn, where a bag represents one frame of collection, were "nuked" for identical times in identical microwave ovens (about three minutes depending on oven power). All the kernels in all of the bags would not pop, and there would be different numbers of popped kernels in each bag. Taking the average, suppose 1,000 kernels are popped per bag. The RMS variation of the number of kernels popped would be the measure of the "noise." If popcorn kernels obeyed the same statistics as emitted photons, the "popcorn noise" would be

$$n_{POPCORN} \approx \sqrt{1{,}000} \approx 32 \text{ kernels}.$$

---

[7] Since the creation of a noise photon at a source is a "rare" event, its creation rate is governed by Poisson statistics. The square root is the "standard deviation" of the creation distribution.

Internal noise sources are processes which add or remove electrons from a detector's output. Data processing does not distinguish between "real" electrons and internally generated ones. Common internal noise sources are: 1) thermal (or Johnson or resistive) noise; 2) low frequency (or 1/*f*) noise; and 3) generation-recombination (G-R) noise. The noise source that dominates depends on a number of operating parameters. **Figure 10-5** illustrates their behavior as a function of the sampling rate. Refer to other texts on electronics, sampling theory, and detector technology for more complete information.

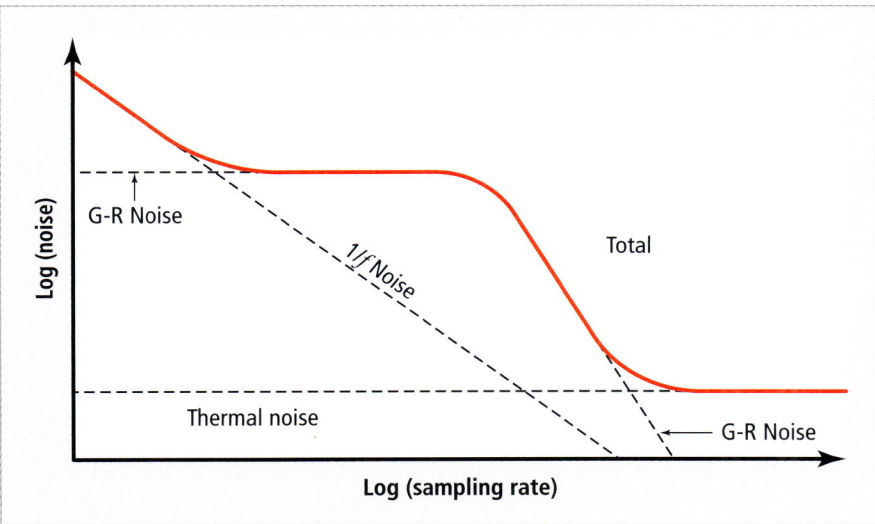

Figure 10-5
A typical noise spectrum and the variation of the 1/*f*, G-R, and thermal noise variations as a function of sampling rate.

When multiple noise sources are present, the usual assumption is the sources are unrelated or uncorrelated. Therefore, the total noise is not the simple sum of the independent noises, but is calculated in quadrature: the square root of the sum of squares of separate noises. The total noise can be calculated using the RMS values of multiple noise sources and expressed as

$$n_{TOTAL \atop NOISE} = \sqrt{n_1^2 + n_2^2 + n_3^2 + \ldots}. \qquad (10\text{-}13)$$

The dominant source of noise is often a result of the background fluctuation. The background is the largest source of input to the detector. So, naturally, it contributes the most noise. A detector operating under these conditions is said to be background limited, and sometimes the acronym BLIP, for Background Limited Infrared Photodetection, is used.

The result of **Example 10-5** displays an important point in remote sensor signal processing: target signals are often small compared to background. Recall from **Chapters 4** and **5**, at wavelengths shorter than about four micrometers, the reflected sunlight from the Earth and clouds is the dominant background (during daylight hours, but not at night). At longer wavelengths, the emitted thermal radiation from the Earth's surface is the background. These reflected or emitted radiations may be minimized by the appropriate choice of bandpass in an "absorption" band where transmission through the atmosphere reduces or eliminates reflected or emitted surface light. The background then becomes the re-emitting and scattering atmosphere itself. Thus, the target-to-background ratio is largely determined by bandpass and the time of day a collection is taken.

EXAMPLE 10-5: ESTIMATING SNR

Calculate (estimate) the SNR for the collection described in **Example 10-1**. Assume the sensor consists of only a collecting lens, a bandpass filter, and a detector. Include the sensor's lens ($T_{LENS} \approx 300$ K) as a source of photon noise, but assume all other components of the optical/mechanical structure, including the filter and the detector, are sufficiently cooled so they are not significant contributors of photons.

First, the phenomenology of the lens providing an input to the detector is as follows, calculating the number of photons delivered on the average to each pixel ~

$$\left\{ \begin{array}{c} \text{Irradiance} \\ \text{of lens} \\ \text{on a pixel} \end{array} \right\} \approx \left\{ \begin{array}{c} \text{Radiance} \\ \text{of lens} \end{array} \right\} \left\{ \begin{array}{c} \text{Solid angle} \\ \text{subtended} \\ \text{by lens} \end{array} \right\} \left\{ \begin{array}{c} \text{Optical} \\ \text{transmission} \\ \text{factor} \end{array} \right\}$$

$$\left\{ \begin{array}{c} \text{Power} \\ \text{on pixel} \end{array} \right\} \approx \left\{ \begin{array}{c} \text{Irradiance} \\ \text{of lens} \\ \text{on a pixel} \end{array} \right\} \left\{ \begin{array}{c} \text{Pixel} \\ \text{area} \end{array} \right\}$$

$$\left\{ \begin{array}{c} \text{Energy} \\ \text{on pixel} \end{array} \right\} \approx \left\{ \begin{array}{c} \text{Power} \\ \text{on pixel} \end{array} \right\} \left\{ \begin{array}{c} \text{Integration} \\ \text{time} \end{array} \right\}$$

$$\left\{ \begin{array}{c} \text{Photons} \\ \text{on pixel} \end{array} \right\} \approx \left\{ \begin{array}{c} \text{Energy} \\ \text{on pixel} \end{array} \right\} \Big/ \left\{ \begin{array}{c} \text{Energy} \\ \text{per photon} \end{array} \right\}.$$

Together this chain of reasoning becomes (in symbols):

$$N_{PIX \atop LENS} \approx \left(\frac{(\epsilon_{LENS}) \overline{B_\lambda}(T_{LENS}) \Delta\lambda}{\pi} \right) \left(\frac{\pi D^2}{4 f^2} \right) (\tau_{FILTER})(x_{PIX})^2 (\Delta t_{INT}) \left(\frac{\overline{\lambda}}{hc} \right).$$

Assuming the transmission of the lens is approximately 0.96 (4% absorbing), $\tau_{OPT} \approx \tau_{LENS}\tau_{FILTER}$ gives $\tau_{FILTER} \approx \frac{\tau_{OPT}}{\tau_{LENS}} \approx \frac{0.50}{0.96} \approx 0.52$.

The average in-band blackbody exitance is $B_\lambda(300 \text{ K}) \approx 1.58$ W·m$^{-2}\mu$m^{-1}.

Substituting all the appropriate values into the formula gives,

$$N_{PIX \atop LENS} \approx \frac{(0.04)\left(1.58 \frac{W}{m^2 \mu m}\right)(0.2 \text{ }\mu\text{m})(0.6 \text{ m})^2 (0.52)(4.88 \times 10^{-6} \text{ m})^2 (0.125 \text{ s})(3.8 \times 10^{-6} \text{ m})}{(4)(2.4 \text{ m})^2 (6.63 \times 10^{-34} \text{ J·s})(3 \times 10^8 \text{ m·s}^{-1})}$$

$$\approx 5{,}840 \text{ photons (per pixel per frame)}.$$

The noise associated with this number of photons is

$$\eta_{PIX \atop LENS} \approx \sqrt{N_{PIX \atop LENS}} \approx \sqrt{5{,}840 \text{ photons}} \approx 76 \text{ photons (per pixel per frame)}.$$

Assuming this photon noise is uncorrelated from pixel to pixel, and there are approximately 45 pixels within the target PSF, the total RMS noise due to the lens is $\eta_{LENS} \approx \sqrt{45 \times 76^2} \approx 510$ photons (per frame).

Now going back to **Example 10-1** and extracting the same information for the background and target, the phenomenology is summarized in the following table. (Numbers of photons for target and background are calculated by dividing the number of electrons collected in the previous example by the quantum efficiency.)

Continued on next page

	# Photons per pixel per frame	# Noise photons per pixel per frame	Total photons within PSF per frame	Total noise photons within PSF per frame
Lens	5,840	76	2.63×10^5	510
Target	8,490	92	3.82×10^5	618
Background	2.79×10^5	528	1.26×10^7	3,540

The total photon noise can now be calculated as
$$n_{TOTAL} \approx \sqrt{510^2 + 618^2 + 3540^2} = 3630 \text{ photons (per frame).}$$

The SNR can now be calculated as
$$\left(\frac{S}{N}\right) \approx \frac{3.82 \times 10^5 \text{ photons}}{3,630 \text{ photons}} \approx 105.$$

Therefore, from an optical point of view, this target is easily detectable in this bandpass, even though it is only 3% of a daytime background (assuming background can be suppressed, as in **Chapter 14**). Note, the final calculation was in terms of target and noise photons, but since $\tilde{N}$ is directly proportional to N_e, calculating in terms of digital units gives the same answer.

Thus, an objective of remote sensing is to have the most benign background possible, but it is not necessarily small. For example, **Figure 10-6** suggests a sensor's output is large but nearly constant (with some noise) where looking at background. A target passes through the sensor's FOV, raising the output by only about 10%; thus, the signal-to-background ratio is much less than one. However, the target must be larger than the noise to be seen. In **Figure 10-6**, the maximum target signal is drawn to be about twice the level of noise, but again this is not always the case. Some signal processing issues, background suppression, and artifact correction will be discussed in later chapters that will allow finding dim targets amidst large noisy backgrounds.

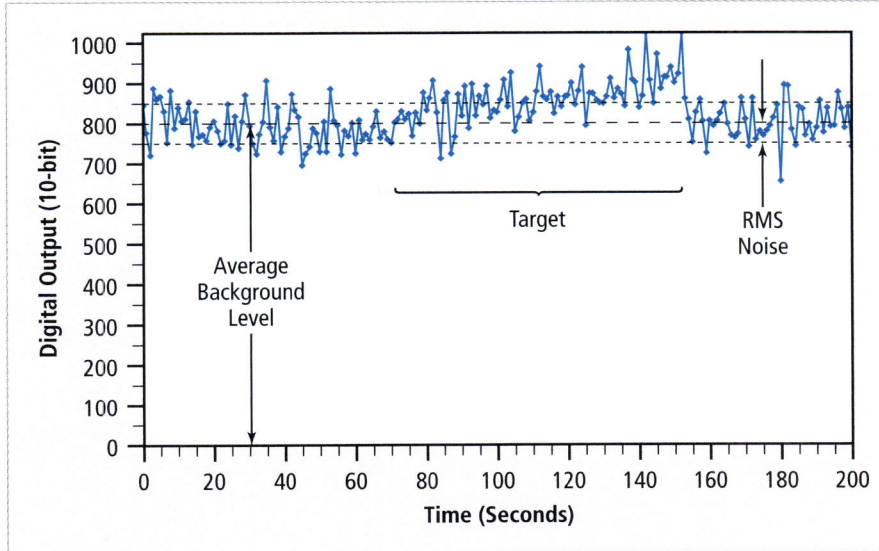

Figure 10-6
Target signals are often smaller than the background.

Some of the success of signal processing also depends on the proper choice of detectors, primarily their sensitivity to respond to small signal changes. Some common figures of merit, in addition to quantum efficiency discussed in **Section 7.3**, that relate to detector's sensitivity are:

- Noise Equivalent Irradiance (NEI) is defined as the incident irradiance necessary for a remote sensor to produce a signal output equal to its output from noise alone; the input irradiance for which SNR $\approx$ 1.
- Noise Equivalent Power (NEP) is defined as the radiant power that produces a SNR $\approx$ 1 at the output of a detector at a given sampling rate, wavelength, and effective bandwidth.
- Detectivity (D) is defined as the reciprocal of the NEP; 1/NEP (W^{-1}).

11 PLATFORMS AND ORBITS

The utility of any given sensor is often dependent upon the host platform. As discussed later in this chapter, the choice of platform often can determine the size of ground pixels, the signal-to-noise ratio for a particular object of interest, as well as the time and frequency of collection of data for that object. As shown by the soldier-launched Raven above and figures throughout the chapter, these platforms come a variety of shapes and sizes. These characteristics will be discussed for the various platforms, including satellites. This chapter will also provide a more detailed discussion of the various satellite orbits that are important to remote sensing.

SECTIONS

11.1 PLATFORMS USED FOR REMOTE SENSING
11.2 SATELLITE ORBITS
11.3 AIRBORNE VS SPACEBORNE SENSING

11.1 PLATFORMS USED FOR REMOTE SENSING

A basic list of platforms includes ground-based, airborne, or spaceborne platforms. Ground-based platforms include towers, ground vehicles, and ships. Airborne platforms include not only traditional manned aircraft, but also unmanned aerial vehicles (UAVs). UAVs range in size from those as large as a commercial passenger aircraft such as a B-737 to those that can be handheld and launched by a single person. **Figure 11-1** shows a Predator in flight. **Figure 11-2** shows an Army Raven being launched by a soldier in Afghanistan. The Goodyear blimp in **Figure 11-3** is a commercial example of an airship, the military term for a blimp or dirigible.

Figure 11-1
A Predator on a mission controlled by a pilot and sensor operator half a world away.

Figure 11-2
The Raven carries color-visible and infrared nighttime cameras, and is controlled from an operator's laptop within visual range.

Figure 11-3
Airships can carry a more extensive suite of electro-optic sensors. They may be operated either in a tethered mode over a battlespace or in free flight.

Some of the flight characteristics of historical and modern airborne platforms are shown below in **Table 11-1**.

Table 11-1
Airborne platforms that host (or have hosted) electro-optic remote sensors.

System		Altitude	Speed	Range/endurance
U-2 [1]		> 21,000 m	> 180 m/s	> 11,000 km
SR-71 [2], [3] (no longer in service)		> 26,000 m	> 900 m/s	> 4,600 km without refueling
KC-135 [4]		> 15,000 m	> 230 m/s	~ 17,300 km
Predator [5]		> 7,600 m	< 60 m/s	> 24 hr
Global Hawk [6]		> 18,000 m	~ 160 m/s	~ 28 hr

CHAPTER 11 PLATFORMS AND ORBITS

Using any airborne or spaceborne platform,[1] there are two possible collection geometries: direct overflight and long-range stand-off. These are shown in **Figure 11-4**. Using either geometry, sensor scanning or staring modes can be used for collection. These are the topics of the next chapter.

Satellite orbits for remote sensing are often classified in terms of altitude above the ground using two general categories:[2] 1) Low-Earth Orbits (LEO), which include polar (circular or elliptical) and sun-synchronous (circular or elliptical); and 2) high-Earth orbits, which include Geosynchronous Orbits (GEO) or Geostationary and Molniya (Highly Elliptical Orbits referred to as HEO). Listed under these categories are some special orbits that have proven most useful for remote sensing. Before pursuing a discussion of sensing capabilities from various platforms, it is important to understand why satellites orbit and the role of these special orbits.

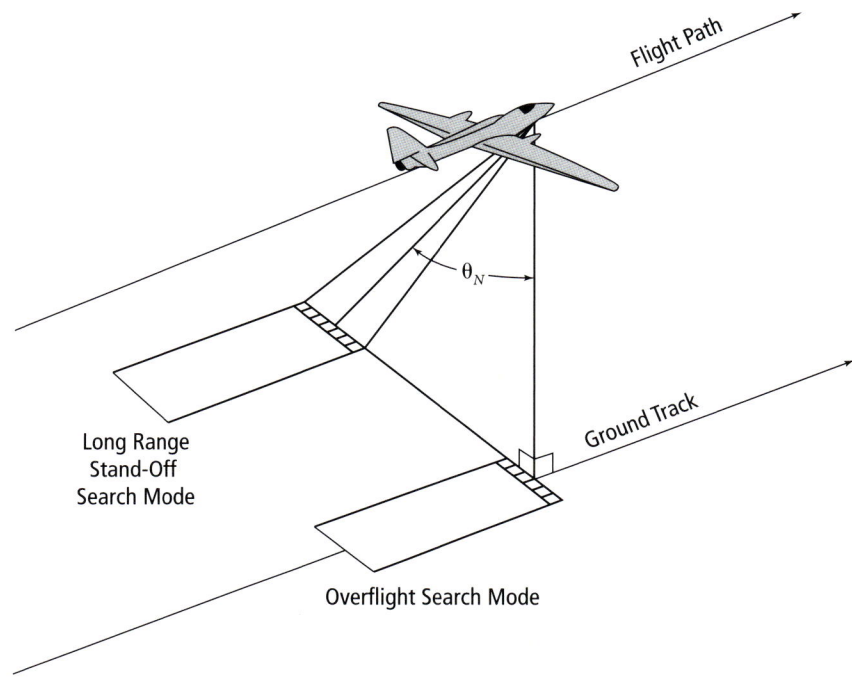

Figure 11-4
Direct overflight and long-range stand-off collection geometries.

[1] As with airborne systems, spaceborne platforms can be either unmanned or manned, like the Space Shuttle or a space station. Remote sensing from other celestial bodies, like the moon, is not out of the question.

[2] A third altitude class is the Medium Earth Orbit (MEO), at which the Earth's Van Allen belts provide the highest amount of high energy electrons that can interact with sensor FPAs and electronics. Thus, they are typically not used for remote sensing. The most familiar example of MEO satellites is the GPS constellation.

[3] Because the Earth's mass is huge compared to the satellite's, assume the Earth to be fixed and ignore the reaction force the satellite exerts on the Earth (Newton's Third Law), because it is too small to move the Earth.

11.2 SATELLITE ORBITS

ORBITAL MECHANICS

The physical law that holds satellites in their orbits is the "Universal Law of Gravitation," developed by Sir Isaac Newton, shown in **Figure 11-5**. The law states "two bodies attract one another with a force in direct proportion to the product of their masses and inversely as the square of the distance between them." For a satellite (mass m_{SAT}) in orbit around the Earth (mass $M_E \approx 5.979 \times 10^{24}$ kg), the gravitational force on the satellite[3] (**Figure 11-6**) is

$$F_{SAT} = \frac{G_N M_E m_{SAT}}{r^2} \quad [N], \tag{11-1}$$

where r is the distance between the Earth's and satellite's centers of mass, and $G_N \approx 6.673 \times 10^{-11}$ N·m²·kg⁻² is Newton's Constant.

Figure 11-5
Sir Isaac Newton (1642–1727) developed "Newton's Universal Law of Gravitation."

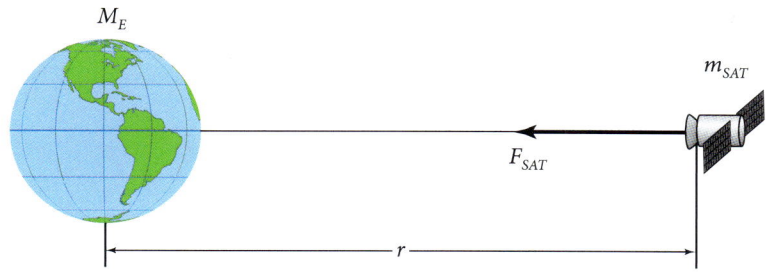

Figure 11-6
Terms in Newton's "Universal Law of Gravitation."

A few observations about Newton's Law follow:

1. It is this (incredibly weak) force that appears to hold the universe together! Astronomical observations confirm that Newton's Law describes the motion of planets, stars, and galaxies.

2. When two objects are far apart ($r \gg$ the objects' dimensions), their internal distributions of mass can be ignored and the *centers of mass* can be used to measure r as stated above.

3. When close to the Earth or near the surface, the force of gravity is referred to as *weight*. Weight (**Figure 11-7**) is the Earth's force on an object or person of mass, m:

$$F \approx \frac{G_N M_E m}{R_E^2} \equiv mg \quad [\text{N}], \quad (11\text{-}2)$$

where $R_E \approx 6370$ km is the mean radius of the Earth, and g is the gravity *field* or *acceleration of gravity* given by

$$g = \frac{G_N M_E}{R_E^2} = \frac{\mu_E}{R_E^2} \cong 9.81 \text{ m} \cdot \text{s}^{-2}. \quad (11\text{-}3)$$

(The combination $G_N M_E \approx 3.99 \times 10^5 \text{ km}^3 \cdot \text{s}^{-2}$ occurs frequently enough in orbital mechanics to be given the symbol μ_E.) Note, for a satellite at altitude h above the Earth's surface, the gravity field is decreased to:

$$g = \frac{\mu_E}{(R_E + h)^2} \quad [\text{m} \cdot \text{s}^{-2}]. \quad (11\text{-}4)$$

4. Near a large body (like the Earth), the distribution of mass on the large body can and does make a difference. Large accumulations of rocky material (continents) attract low altitude satellites more, and depressions filled with water (oceans) attract less. The orbits of low altitude satellites are "perturbed" by variations in the gravity field, which is given by a model describing the "lumpiness" of the Earth's shape. The usual model, WGS-84,[4] is used extensively by commercial and defense agencies who keep track of the locations of satellites.

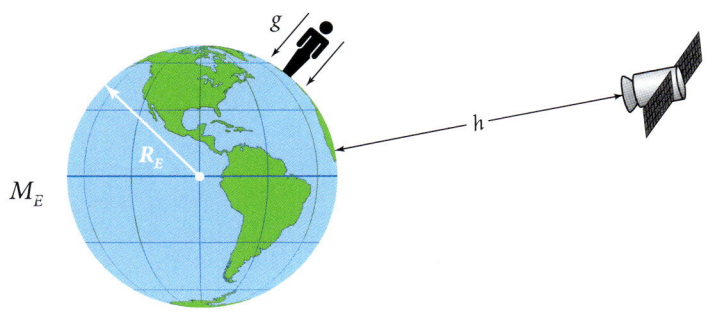

Figure 11-7
"Weight" of a near-surface object.

[4] NGA is the custodian for WGS-84 and its improvements. [7]

5. Gravitational potential energy is defined as:

$$U_E = \int F dr = -\frac{\mu_E M_{SAT}}{r} \quad [J]. \tag{11-5}$$

Note, the gravitational potential (**Figure 11-8**) is plotted as negative implying there are gravity "wells" around massive objects (actually in three dimensions, but difficult to visualize). Objects (satellites) *in* the well are gravitationally *bound* (in orbits) while objects above the well are *free* (have escaped). The other important consideration is satellites have energy of motion (kinetic energy) that keeps them up on the side of the well. (That is, they do not just fall in; their motion is in a direction not directly toward or away from the attracting object.)

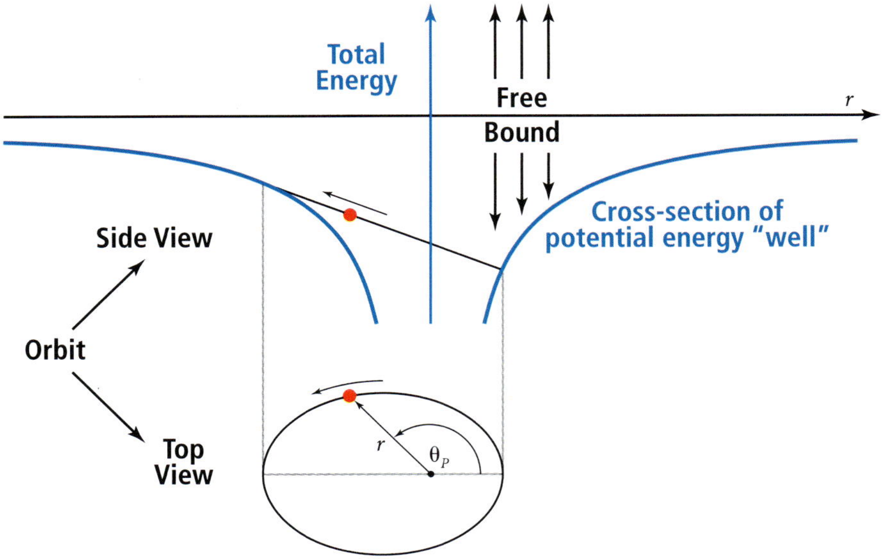

Figure 11-8
Potential energy acts like a "well." An orbit is similar to the trajectory of a coin rolling on the inside of a funnel (except there is no friction).

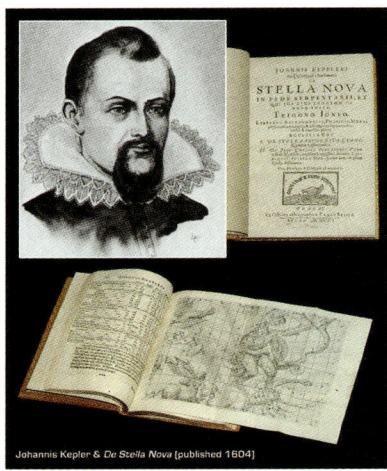

Figure 11-9
Johannes Kepler (1571–1630) developed "Kepler's Laws."

The motion of satellites in their orbits is described by Kepler's Laws[5] (**Figure 11-9**) where "satellite" may be substituted for "planet," and "Earth" for "Sun":

1. First Law: The planets orbit the sun on elliptical paths with the sun at one focus. (Assumption, $M_{sun} \approx \infty$.)

2. Second Law: A line joining a planet to the sun sweeps out equal areas in equal times (conservation of angular momentum).

3. Third Law: The square of a planet's orbital period is proportional to the cube of its mean distance from the sun.

Any ellipse (used in Kepler's first law) is defined as a curve in a plane such that the sum of distances from any point on the curve to two fixed points, F_1 and F_2, called foci, is constant. Nomenclature associated with the dimensions of an ellipse includes the following (**Figure 11-10**):

1. a = semi-major axis.
2. b = semi-minor axis.
3. c = focal distance.
4. A quantity *eccentricity* is defined as $\hat{e} = \frac{c}{a}$, where[6] $0 \le \hat{e} < 1$ for closed (bound) orbits. Note, $\hat{e}$ is dimensionless.

[5] Kepler derived his laws of motion by hand calculating (before computers) the meticulous observations of Tycho Brahe (1546–1601). Kepler's Laws are fully compatible with Newton's Laws of Motion.

[6] An ellipse is one of several possible curves created by slicing a cone with a plane. The "conic sections" have eccentricities and orbits according to the following table:

Eccentricity	Curve	Orbit
0	Circle	Closed-Bound
$0 < \hat{e} < 1$	Ellipse	Closed-Bound
1	Parabola	Open-Free
>1	Hyperbola	Open-Free

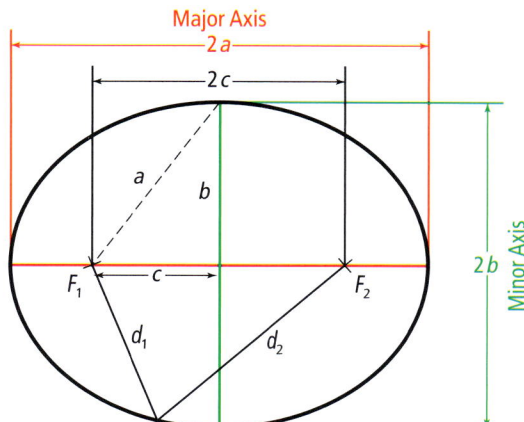

Figure 11-10
Parameters associated with an ellipse.

Note, the following relations among the dimensions:

$$d_1 + d_2 = 2a \text{ and} \quad (11\text{-}6)$$
$$b^2 + c^2 = a^2. \quad (11\text{-}7)$$

With the Earth at the attracting focus, a satellite follows its elliptical path through space. At any moment, its position is a distance r from the center of the Earth, and at a polar angle,[7] θ_P, as shown in **Figures 11-8** and **11-11** Given any two ellipse features (from among a, b, c, and e) that define the size and shape of a satellite's orbit, its location is

$$r(\theta_P) = \frac{a(1 - \hat{e}^2)}{1 + \hat{e} \cos \theta_P}. \quad (11\text{-}8)$$

Note, when $\theta_P = 0°$, the satellite is at its closest distance to the Earth, the perigee,

$$r_P = a(1 - \hat{e}) \text{ [km]}, \quad (11\text{-}9)$$

and when $\theta_P = 180°$, the satellite is at its greatest distance from the Earth, the apogee,

$$r_a = a(1 + \hat{e}) \text{ [km]}. \quad (11\text{-}10)$$

Useful relations involving perigee and apogee[8] are

$$r_a + r_p = 2a \text{ [km] and } \hat{e} = \frac{r_a - r_p}{r_a + r_p}. \quad (11\text{-}11)$$

Kepler's Second Law provides constant specific angular momentum, ℓ_{sp}, (i.e., angular momentum per unit mass) for a satellite of

$$\ell_{sp} = rv \cos \varphi \text{ [km}^2 \cdot \text{s}^{-1}\text{]}, \quad (11\text{-}12)$$

where r is the distance defined in **Equation 11-8**,

v is the satellite's speed (usually kilometers per second), and

φ is the "flight path angle" defined relative to a local horizontal direction as shown in **Figure 11-11**.

Examining **Figure 11-11** shows that when a satellite is at either perigee or apogee, the local horizontal is perpendicular to the orbit's major axis, and $\varphi = 0°$. Thus, when at perigee or apogee,

$$\ell_{sp} = r_p v_p = r_a v_a \text{ [km}^2 \cdot \text{s}^{-1}\text{]}, \quad (11\text{-}13)$$

[7] The polar angle is formally called the *true anomaly*. Deeper study of orbital mechanics will also bring in related angles called the *mean* anomaly and the *eccentric* anomaly.

[8] Note, perigee and apogee are *distances* from the center of the Earth, but sometimes *altitudes* are meant. This is usually clear from the context. For example, an apogee of 800 km has to be an altitude because the Earth's radius is over 6,000 km.

where v_p and v_a are the respective speeds. Importantly, this relation shows that for minimum distance (perigee), a satellite is traveling at its maximum speed; and when at maximum distance (apogee), it is moving at its minimum speed.

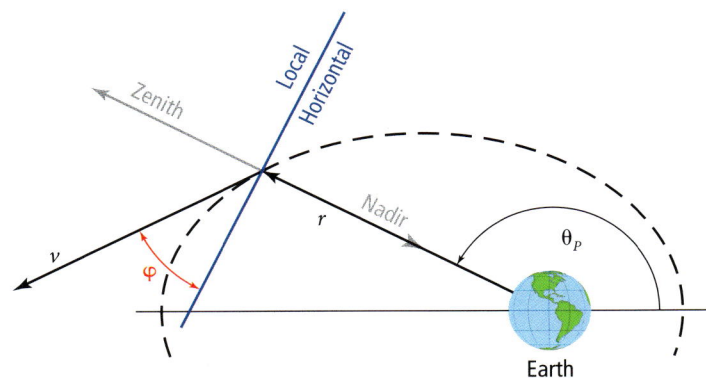

Figure 11-11
Definition of satellite's local horizontal and flight path angle.

Yet another important relation between a satellite's distance and speed is its total energy (sum of kinetic and potential) is constant. This is expressed for specific energy (energy per unit mass) as[9]

$$E_{sp} = \frac{v^2}{2} - \frac{\mu_E}{r} = -\frac{\mu_E}{2a} \quad [\text{J} \cdot \text{kg}^{-1}], \quad (11\text{-}14)$$

where a is the semi-major axis distance.

Finally, Kepler's Third Law expressed in symbols is

$$P^2 = \frac{4\pi^2}{\mu_E} a^3 \quad [\text{s}^2], \quad (11\text{-}15)$$

where P is a satellite's orbital period, and a is its semi-major axis dimension.[10] (When $\frac{4\pi^2}{\mu_E} \cong 9.895 \times 10^{-5} \text{s}^2 \cdot \text{km}^{-3}$, P is in seconds when a is in kilometers.)

SATELLITES IN THREE DIMENSIONS

Now that satellites' orbits have been discussed as ellipses, consider the problem of locating a satellite in three-dimensional space, which is called its *ephemeris* (plural *ephemerides*). The next requirement for this is to refer to a known set of axes or coordinates. Latitude-longitude-altitude is such a set of coordinates, for example, but is generally not used; fixed to the Earth, latitude-longitude-altitude is continuously changing directions because the Earth rotates. This is unsatisfactory because the plane of a satellite's ellipse remains fixed[11] relative to a larger, *inertial* frame of reference stationary to the stars.

To establish a satellite's ephemeris, choose a set of "inertial" coordinates fixed to the center of the Earth: the Earth-Centered Inertial (ECI) coordinate system. See **Figure 11-12**. In ECI coordinates, the X-axis is chosen to point at the location in the sky where the sun's apparent path (its *ecliptic*) crosses the projection of the Earth's equator from south to north. This point in the sky is variously known as the Vernal Equinox, the "first day of Spring"[12] or the "First Point of Aries."[13] See **Figure 11-13**. The Z-axis is chosen to point towards the Earth's North Pole (presently near the star Polaris, but see **Footnote 13** regarding precession). The Y-axis is then taken to form a right-handed orthogonal coordinate system.

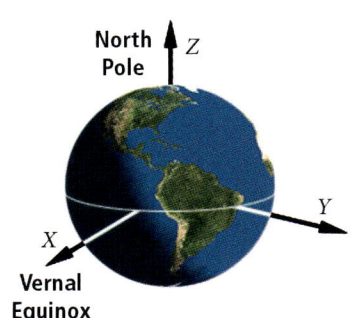

Earth rotates while coordinates maintain fixed pointing directions.

Figure 11-12
The ECI coordinate system.

---

[9] The last part of **Equation 11-14** is a consequence of the "virial theorem" which will not be proven; the total energy of an ensemble of interacting particles is the average of their potential energies.

[10] It can be shown (but not here) that a satellite's "mean distance from [its attracting focus]" is just the semi-major axis by doing the elliptic integral $\frac{1}{2\pi}\int_0^{2\pi} r(\theta_P) d\theta_P$.

[11] Except for perturbations by the near-Earth gravity field. These are not large enough to drag a satellite's orbit plane at the same rate of the Earth's rotation. However, see the important discussion of the sun-synchronous orbit later in this section.

[12] In the Northern Hemisphere.

[13] Today, the Vernal Equinox is in the constellation Pisces, not Aries. It moves along the ecliptic because the Earth's axis, tilted at about 23.5°, precesses like a top in about 22,000 years. The equinox is now approaching Aquarius, and people living in AD 16,000 will again see it in Aries. About every ten years the ECI coordinates are "locked in" to what is called an "epoch." Ephemerides are then calculated in that epoch until the next update.

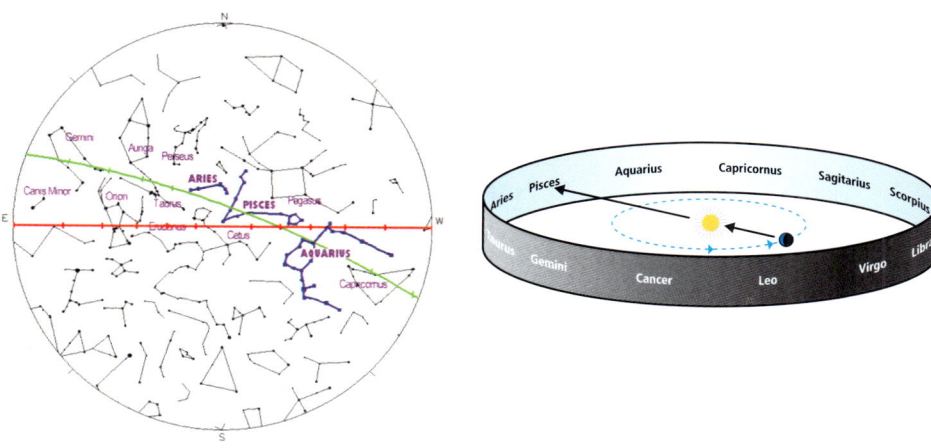

Figure 11-13
The Vernal Equinox occurs when the Sun appears to cross the equator from south to north in the constellation Pisces.

Considering now that a two-body problem (Earth and satellite) exists in three-dimensional space, six coordinates are needed to locate them. In ECI coordinates, the Earth is automatically at the origin, (0, 0, 0) while the satellite is at its ephemeris (x, y, z), which is a function of time. To calculate (x, y, z), use the following six pieces of information about the satellites's motion, which are called its *orbital elements* (illustrated in **Figure 11-14**):

1. a semi-major axis } size and shape of the orbit[14]
2. $\hat{e}$ eccentricity
3. i inclination[15]
4. Ω longitude of ascending node } orientation of the orbit[16]
5. ω argument of perigee
6. T_p time of perigee passage. } where the satellite is on the orbit[17]

The orbital elements for orbit plane orientation are illustrated in **Figure 11-14**.

[14] Any two ellipse size-shape dimensions from among a, b, c, $\hat{e}$, r_a, and r_p will suffice. The others can be calculated from the chosen two.

[15] Inclination can be from 0° to 180° with 90° being a polar orbit. Inclinations greater than 90° are termed retrograde.

[16] For students of classical mechanics, these orientation angles are also known as Euler angles after Swiss mathematician Leonhard Euler (1707–1783).

[17] If the time of perigee passage is known, then the interval of time since then, ΔT_p, is related to the true anomaly, θ_p, from which the distance from the Earth's center can be found through **Equation 11-8**. (The relation between ΔT_p and θ_p is complicated and is not given here.)

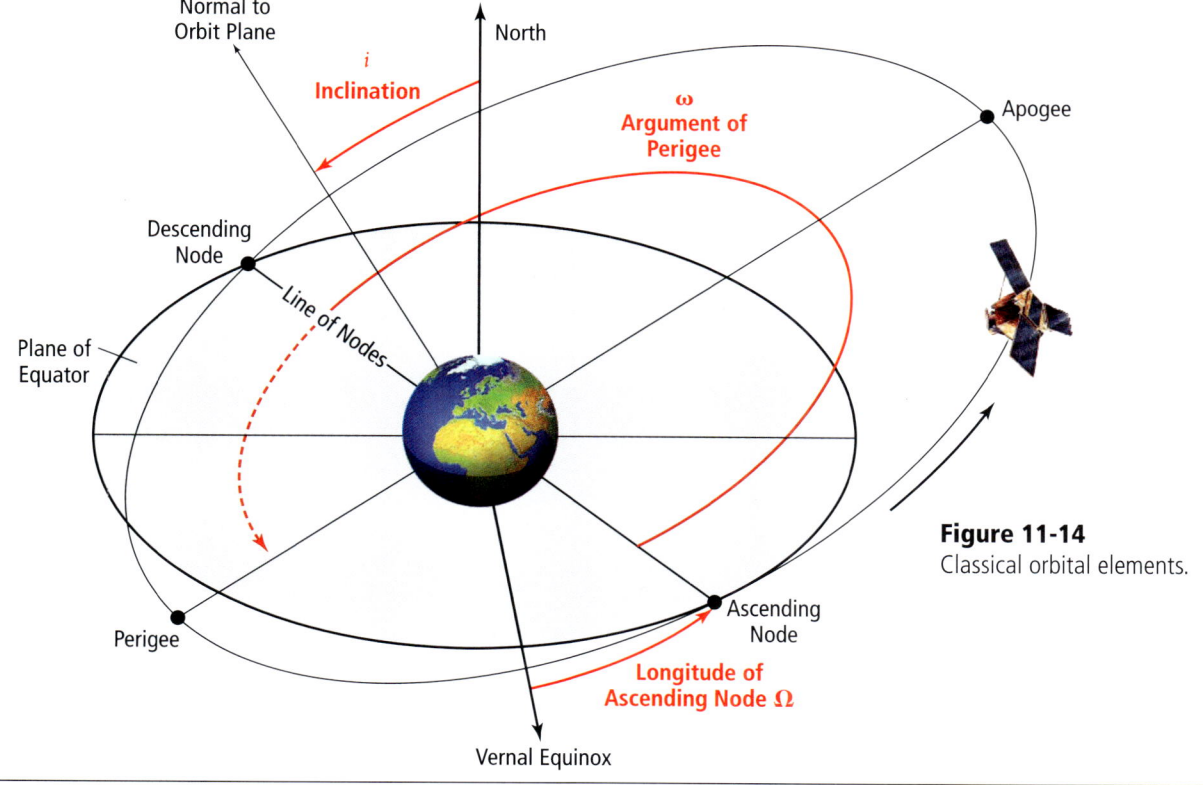

Figure 11-14
Classical orbital elements.

The derivation of (x, y, z) from the orbital elements is a straightforward exercise in rotational mechanics (linear algebra), but will not be given here. Commercial and defense agencies that are responsible for tracking satellites maintain databases of the orbital elements (called Two-Line Element sets (TLEs)) for thousands of space objects and routinely compute their ephemerides. The TLEs are frequently updated through geodesic methods such as laser range finding. [8]

COMMON ORBITS FOR REMOTE SENSING

A remote sensor's mission will determine the choice of its platform's orbit. Since reconnaissance sensors generally require high spatial resolution, they are typically flown on low-altitude (LEO) satellites. If the required spatial coverage includes collecting data from high latitudes and if consistent target solar irradiation is desired, then the LEO will most likely be put into a nearly polar, sun-synchronous orbit. On the other hand, large area surveillance sensors require platforms in high-altitude GEO and HEO orbits. Each of these orbit types will be briefly discussed.

LEO encompasses the altitudes from approximately 160 to 1400 km. Below 160 km, drag on the satellite caused by atmospheric density is significant. As a result, the satellite cannot stay in orbit for more than a few orbits unless its on-orbit velocity is continually boosted. (See the discussion on "Range to Target" in **Chapter 4** and **Figure 4-31**.) Above 1400 km, the high-energy electrons of the Earth's Van Allen belts provide a generally unfavorable environment for most satellite sensors. LEOs are typically near-circular and the majority of satellites in this orbit make an entire orbit around the Earth in approximately 90 to 100 minutes. Since there is more atmosphere at lower altitudes, satellites in LEO tend to have a shorter life span than satellites in higher orbits. The LEO is illustrated in **Figure 11-15**. Although the ground track appears to move west with each orbit, it is actually the Earth rotating to the east underneath the satellite. LEO satellites are used for reconnaissance, atmospheric characterization, Space Shuttle missions, and other NASA unmanned missions (e.g., Landsat). Polar orbits (inclination of 90°) can provide frequent coverage of the whole Earth.

Sun-synchronous orbits are near polar-orbiting LEOs which are excellent for weather and remote sensing satellites that require the sun-angle (and hence solar irradiance) at a ground location to remain as constant as possible from one data collection to the next. In a sun-synchronous orbit, the orbit plane maintains its orientation relative to

Figure 11-15
Illustration of LEO (left) and ground tracks for a LEO satellite in a high inclination orbit (right). Results were generated with Systems Tool Kit (STK) (developed and marketed by Analytic Graphics Inc., a widely-used software for visualizing collection scenarios, especially those involving satellites. [9]

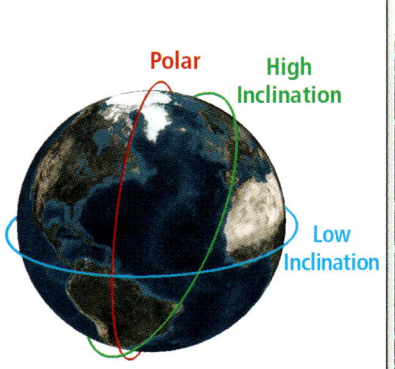
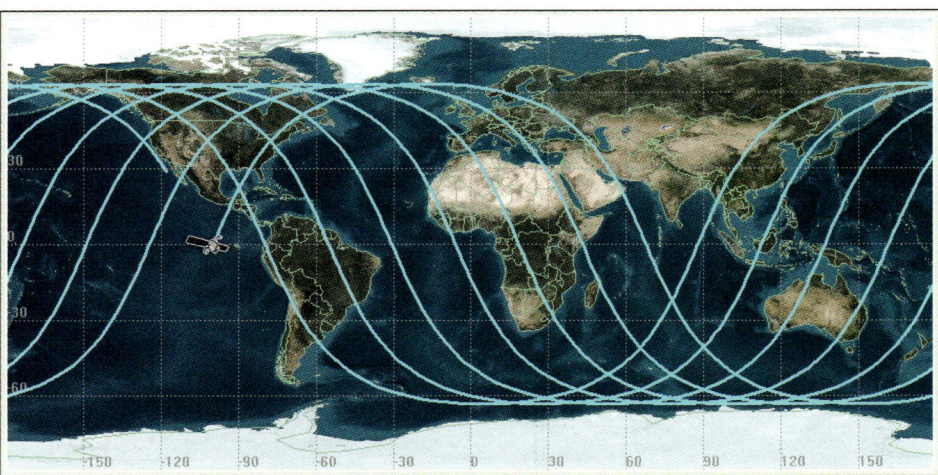

the sun throughout the year. Since the Earth is not a perfect sphere, it has more mass at the equator than the poles. This additional mass at the equator causes a gravitational attraction on the satellite that is directed out of the orbital plane toward the equator. This force results in a rotation in the orbital plane. The effect of this gravitational attraction caused by the additional mass at the equator is dependent on the satellite's altitude and inclination. These factors can be combined to create an orbit plane which is fixed relative to the sun throughout the year with minimal effort required to keep the satellite in this orbit.

The non-spherical Earth can be modeled as a sphere with a "weight belt" around its equator that produces the torque to rotate a satellite's orbit plane (**Figure 11-16**). If the torque is sufficient to regress (move eastward) the orbit by $\approx \frac{360°}{365.25} \approx 0.987°$/day, the result is a sun-synchronous orbit. **Figure 11-16** plots the amount of an orbit's daily regression as a function of altitude and inclination. Typical sun-synchronous satellites are in retrograde orbit with inclinations of 96°–104° at altitudes of less than 1,000 km.

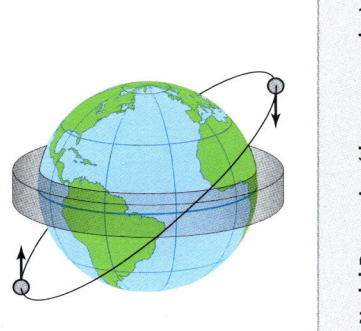

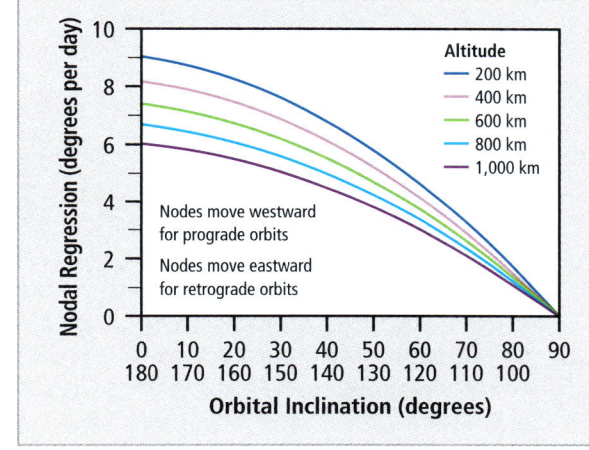

Figure 11-16
Orbital regression rates for various satellite altitudes and orbital inclinations.

SIDEREAL TIME

A detail about high-altitude orbits that is not so obvious from LEOs is time-keeping. Because orbital planes have fixed orientation in space and do not rotate in Earth time, they use what is called sidereal time. As anyone who subscribes to satellite TV knows, the 1,000+ channel satellite has to stay where the antenna on the roof is pointing. But look at the image to the right. From noon to noon, which is 24 hours on the clock, an antenna has moved from pointing at the satellite in the sunward direction to pointing at the satellite while being carried by the Earth through an angle greater than 360°. Meanwhile, to maintain its position in the antenna beam, evidently the TV satellite completed one orbit (360° in one orbital period) in less than 24 hours. The correct orbital period for the TV satellite is one sidereal day, which in solar (clock) time is about 23 hours, 56 minutes, 4.09 seconds (or 86,164.09 seconds, compared with 86,400 seconds in a 24 hour day).

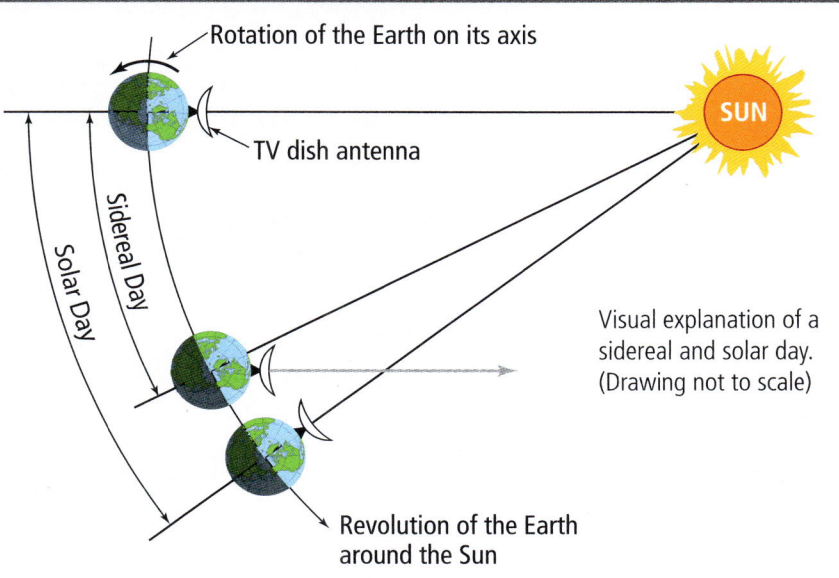

Visual explanation of a sidereal and solar day. (Drawing not to scale)

EXAMPLE 11-1: SIDEREAL TIME-KEEPING

An important lesson and application of sidereal time-keeping is shown in the figure below. Suppose a satellite has a period of $23^h56^m4.09^s$ (h-hours, m-minutes, s-seconds), and it just happens to be seen directly overhead when it is at apogee at noon on the first day of December. What time will the satellite be directly overhead (at apogee) on the first of March? (This is the same as asking: when will it appear to be in the same position against the starry background?) The answer is the satellite will return to the same point in the sky $24^h - 23^h56^m4.09^s = 3^m55.91^s$ *earlier* each day. Thus, after 90 days (1 December to 1 March in a non-leap year), it will reach apogee approximately $90 \times 3^m55.91^s = 5^h53^m51.90^s$ *earlier*. This is about 6 AM. The figure shows the progression throughout the year.

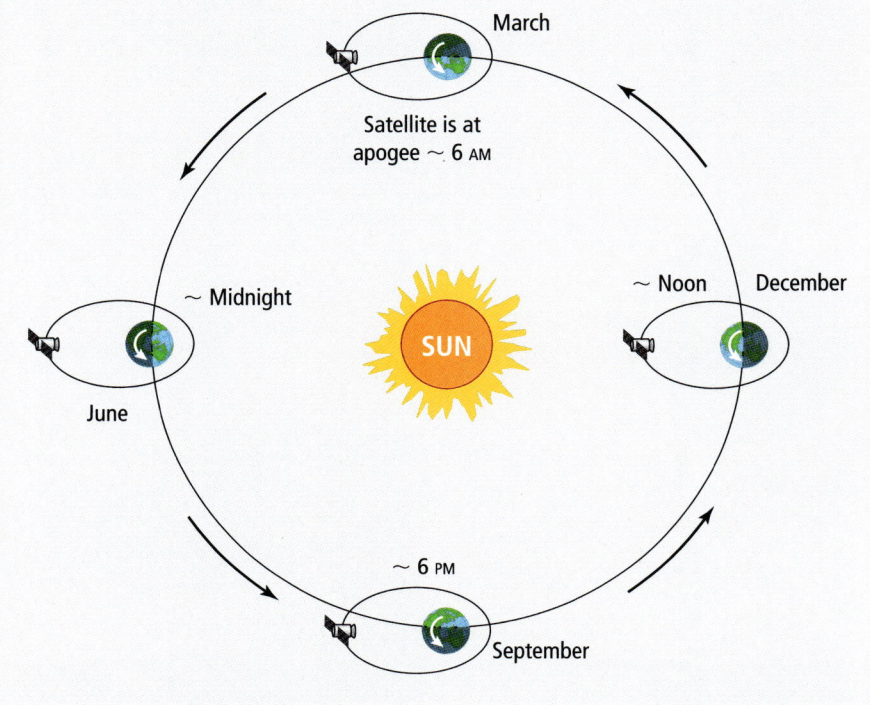

Above 30,000 km are the high Earth orbits. The two most commonly used such orbits are the GEO and the HEO of which the Molniya is the prime example (discussed later in this chapter).

GEO, therefore, refers to any orbit with a period of one sidereal day at an altitude of approximately 35,780 km. A GEO may be slightly inclined, producing a figure-eight ground track. A special type of GEO is a geostationary orbit which has an inclination of zero degrees. A satellite in this orbit remains stationary with respect to the rotating Earth and therefore appears over the same spot on the Earth's equator, although achieving these exact orbital elements is very difficult (and hence expensive). The majority of communication satellites exist in a near-geostationary orbit. **Figure 11-17** illustrates the ground tracks of GEO satellites with different inclinations, and **Figure 11-18** shows the near-hemispherical field of regard. Some sensors may be able to view a near-hemispherical field of regard.

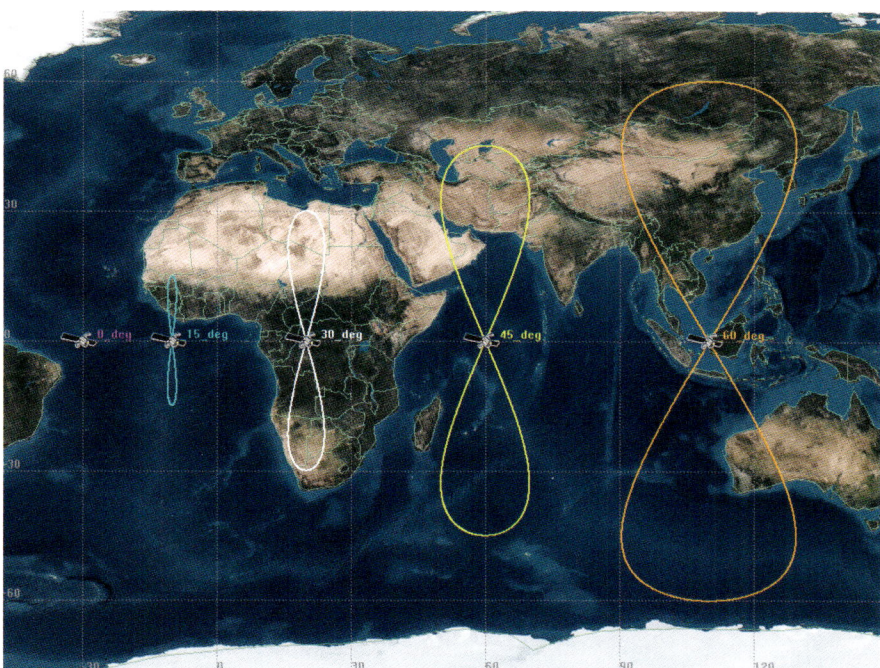

Figure 11-17
Ground tracks of GEO satellites with different inclinations. (Results generated with STK.)

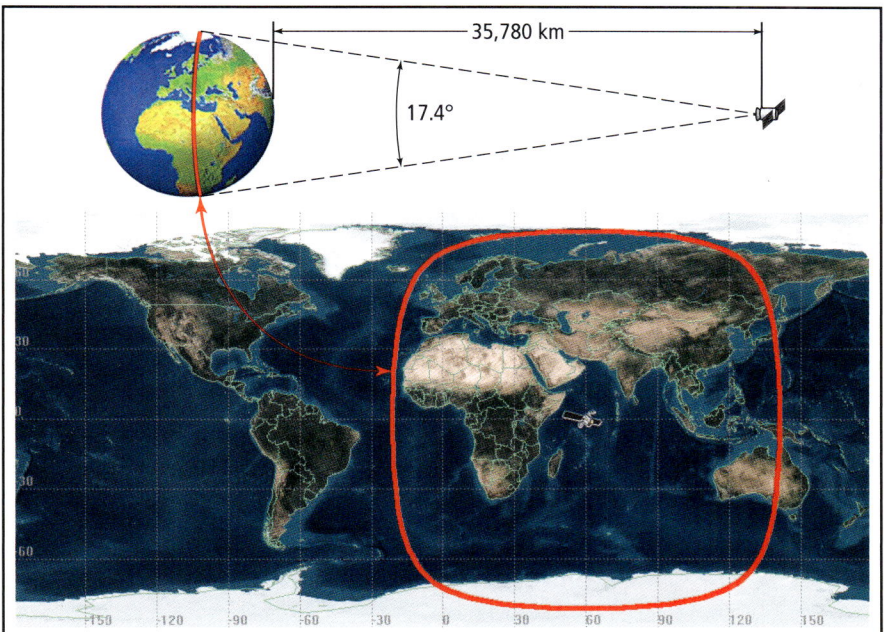

Figure 11-18
Field of Regard of a GEO satellite when over the equator. The tangent circle shown on the globe is also plotted on the map below.

Figure 11-19
Russian postage stamp honoring the invention of the Molniya communications satellite.

HEO refers to an orbit with a high degree of eccentricity. One possible type of HEO is the Molniya[18] orbit named for a class of Russian communication satellites (**Figure 11-19**) that were the first to extensively use it. Molniya orbits are both highly elliptical and highly inclined at approximately 63.4°. Satellites in Molniya orbits have periods of one-half a sidereal day ($11^h 58^m 2.05^s$), giving them repeating ground tracks after two orbits ("revs"). This results in the appearance of "hanging," spending the majority of their period near apogee (in accordance with Kepler's second law). The fact that the majority of their orbit is spent near apogee makes a satellite in a Molniya orbit ideal for coverage of the area surrounding the North Pole. **Figure 11-20** shows a satellite in HEO and its corresponding orbit track (in blue).

[18] Molniya means "lightning" in Russian. Since Russia (the former Soviet Union) is a huge country spanning ten time zones, a reliable communications system was needed for eastern districts to keep in touch with their western headquarters. Unfortunately, geostationary satellites will not work because much of the country lies above 60°N. Therefore, the Molniya orbit was invented. A constellation of two Molniyas in appropriate orbits solves the telecommunications problem.

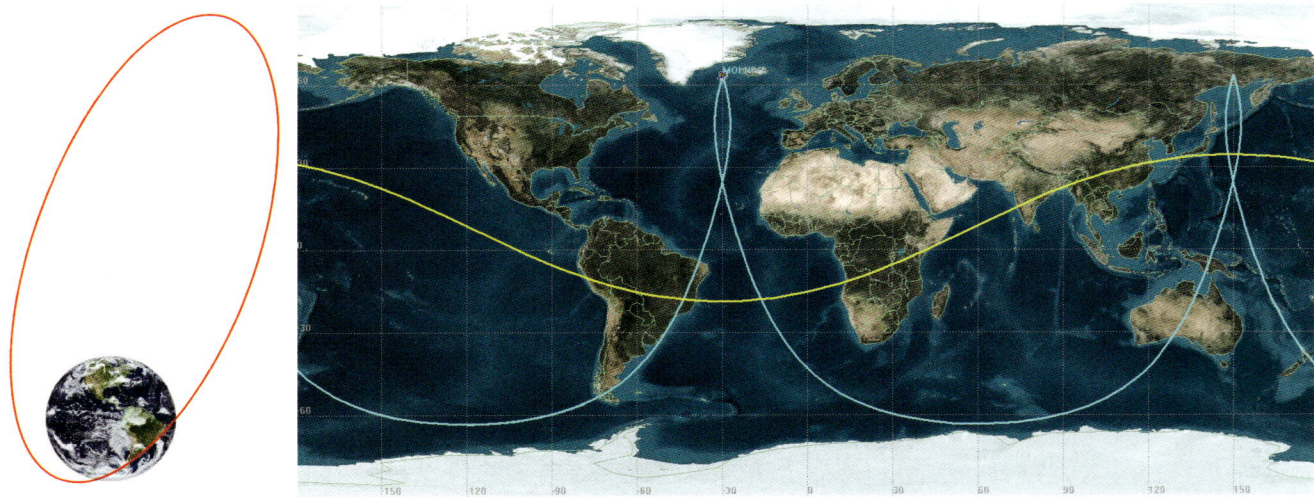

Figure 11-20
The repeating ground track of a HEO satellite making two revs per day. The yellow line is the southern edge of the satellite's field of regard form its apogee over the North Atlantic.

To emphasize the hanging effect, **Figure 11-21** shows the hourly position of a HEO from perigee. It spends less than two of approximately 12 hours on every rev below the equator. But, its field of regard includes the north polar region for over ten hours. Also, importantly, a Molniya satellite looks *over* the pole, giving it more coverage of some areas.

Figure 11-21
Hourly motion of HEO satellite from perigee.

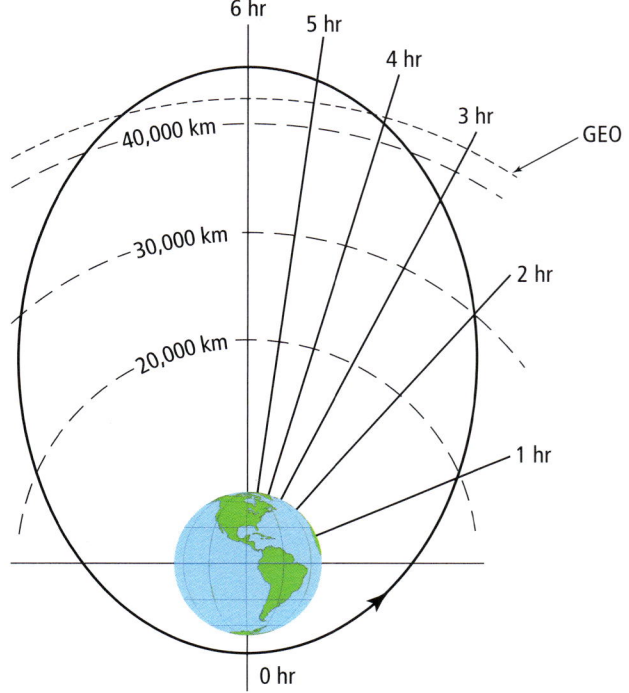

EXAMPLE 11-2: HOW LONG CAN A HEO SENSOR SEE BAGHDAD?

Baghdad is located at 33.32N, 44.39E. If a Molniya satellite was put into an orbit having an apogee at 10° west longitude, and one rev later an apogee over 170E, then on its Atlantic orbit, a sensor could see Baghdad for 11.1 hours. And, on its Pacific orbit, looking over the pole, it could view Baghdad for 5.9 hours. That is a total of 17 hours per day.

234 CHAPTER 11 PLATFORMS AND ORBITS

In summary, **Table 11-2** presents typical values for orbit parameters in the LEO, HEO, and GEO orbits for common commercial satellites.

Orbit	LEO (Sun-Synchronous)	HEO (Molniya)	GEO
Typical Satellite	Landsat	Russian communications	Satellite TV
Altitude: Apogee	703 km	39,850 km	35,809 km
Altitude: Perigee	701 km	500 km	35,766 km
Distance: Apogee	7,081 km	46,228 km	42,187 km
Distance: Perigee	7,079 km	6,878 km	42,144 km
Semi-major axis	7,080 km	26,553 km	42,166 km
Period (Solar Time)	98.8 minutes	11.96 hr	23.94 hr
Inclination	98.21°	63.4°	2.97°
Eccentricity	0.00010760	0.741	0.000510
Rev/Day	14.5711	2.00643	1.0027

Table 11-2
Orbit comparison. Values were calculated using STK.

11.3 AIRBORNE VS SPACEBORNE SENSING

Table 11-3 shows a comparison among two airborne collection modes (down-looking and stand-off) and two satellite orbits (LEO and HEO). Highlighted in yellow are those properties where one or more of the collection modes have a distinct advantage over the others. For example, satellite sensors can cover far more area in a single pass than the same sensor on an aircraft. Both airborne and spaceborne sensors have their advantages and disadvantages. No single collection mode is best for every type of application. In general, aircraft have the advantage of flexibility of collection. Satellites have the advantage of covering any part of the Earth within a few days. Aircraft and satellite access may be intrusive or non-intrusive. Presumably, if an aircraft intrudes within a country's airspace (including the area above their proclaimed off-shore limits), that country can attempt to shoot down the aircraft. An example of intrusion and shoot-down occurred with a US U-2 aircraft that was shot down over the then USSR in 1960. Satellite passes over a country are generally

Table 11-3
Comparison of some airborne and spaceborne sensor systems.

Property	Down-looking airborne	Stand-off airborne	LEO satellite	High earth orbit satellite
Altitude	Low to moderately high (100 m–20 km)	Moderately high (10–20 km)	Very high (160–1,400 km)	Extremely high (30,000 km plus)
Area coverage	Narrow – many strips to cover large area	Can be narrow or wide	Wide—single strip can cover large area	Very wide—can cover a hemisphere
Spatial resolution	Can be varied to suit requirements	Can be varied to suit requirements	Fixed by orbit, more difficult to achieve	Fixed by orbit, extremely difficult to achieve
Detector output	Very high	Somewhat lower	Generally low	Extremely low
Flight path	Variable – user defined	Variable – user defined	Fixed by orbit and launch time	Fixed by orbit and launch time
Viewing geometry	Flexible	Flexible	Fixed by orbit	Fixed by orbit
New site visit	Must be deployed to region	Must be deployed to region	Automatic coverage within a few days	Can be within a few hours (HEO)
Same site revisit	Frequent and flexible (minutes)	Frequent and flexible (minutes)	Fixed by orbit (100 minutes to 12 hours)	Can be continuous (GEO)
Access	Intrusive	Can be non-intrusive	Non-intrusive	Non-intrusive
Worldwide capable	Yes	Only if intrusive	Yes, at latitudes less than inclination	Yes, limited to northern hemisphere (or southern hemisphere)

not considered intrusive. However, measures may be taken to shoot down a satellite or blind its sensors. In recent years, only the US, Russia, and China have demonstrated the capability to shoot down LEO satellites.

For a particular sensor type, there tends to be fewer satellite systems than aircraft sensors. This conclusion results from three different causes. First, satellite sensor fabrication and integration times often are longer. Second, satellite sensor programs have much larger up-front costs. Finally, satellite sensor system-related failures are often not correctable. The more well-funded satellite sensor systems may have redundancy in some areas (power, telemetry, computers, etc). The Space Shuttle capabilities for retrieval and/or astronaut space-walk repair of sick or failed satellites were demonstrated several times for LEO satellites. The most extensive effort involved on-orbit repair of the NASA Hubble Space Telescope. These repair activities are expensive and require a modular design of the sensor and spacecraft.

12 COLLECTION STRATEGIES

Following the discussion of airborne and spaceborne platforms in **Chapter 11**, the focus now turns to how the sensors collect information. First, some general considerations for all sensors will be discussed. Then, the spatial, temporal, and spectral strategies used to collect sensor data based on a pre-defined set of intelligence requirements will be covered. Spatially, sensors operate in either a staring or scanning mode with several possibilities of how to scan. Temporally, all sensors operate on a duty cycle of collection-and-readout to satisfy their spatial coverage and data rate requirements. Spectrally, either a broadband or multiple narrow band operation is chosen, depending on the sensor's mission.

SECTIONS

12.1 COLLECTION CONSIDERATIONS
12.2 STARING SENSORS
12.3 SCANNING SENSORS
12.4 TEMPORAL SAMPLING
12.5 SPECTRAL SAMPLING

12.1 COLLECTION CONSIDERATIONS

There are several factors to consider when deploying or selecting sensors to collect information on targets of interest. Whereas airborne collection platforms have the ability to fly over a target at will (in a permissive environment), satellites are constrained to their orbits. The amount of target area seen by a sensor on a spaceborne platform is called the Field of Regard (FOR)[1] and is purely a function of the satellite's altitude. **Figure 12-1** shows the Earth's surface area within the FOR is given by:

$$A_{FOR} \approx 2\pi R_E^2 (1 - \sin \theta_{N,MAX}) \ [\text{km}^2], \qquad (12\text{-}1)$$

where $\theta_{N,MAX}$ is the maximum nadir viewing angle at a Line of Sight (LOS) tangent to the Earth (called the limb of the Earth), and $R_E \approx 6{,}371$ km is the radius of the Earth. $\theta_{N,MAX}$ is given by:

$$\theta_{N,MAX} \approx \sin^{-1}\left(\frac{R_E}{R_E + h}\right). \qquad (12\text{-}2)$$

Figure 12-2 plots both the FOR area and $\theta_{N,MAX}$ as a function of satellite altitude, h, where typical altitudes for Low-Earth Orbits (LEO) and geosynchronous orbits (GEO) platforms are annotated.

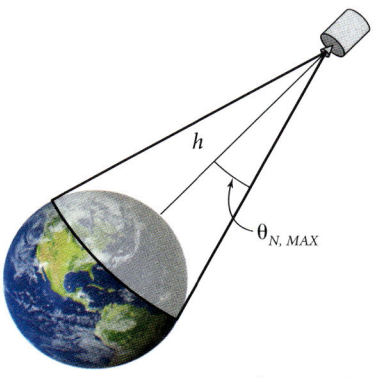

Figure 12-1
FOR and maximum nadir angle.

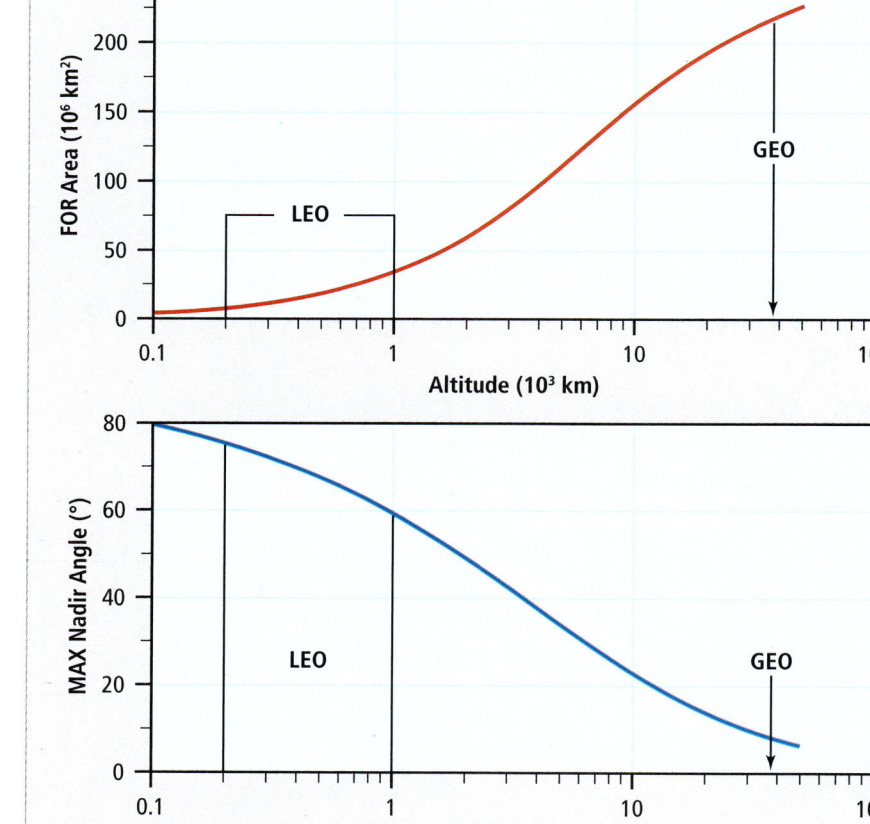

Figure 12-2
FOR area (top) at maximum nadir angle to the Earth's limb (bottom).

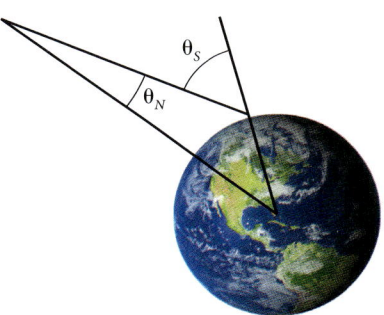

Figure 12-3
Sensor viewing at a larger nadir angle makes the LOS pass through more atmosphere.

Although the maximum nadir viewing angle was calculated and plotted, this is not necessarily the maximum *usable* angle. This is due to atmospheric attenuation (**Chapter 5**). **Figure 12-3** serves as a reminder that as the viewing angle increases from nadir, the sensor is looking

---

[1] The amount of area actually seen within the FOR is a sensor's Field of View (FOV). This is the topic of the next two sections.

through more and more atmosphere.[2] Along a longer path, at nadir angle θ_N, **Equation 5-21** shows the atmospheric transmission is

$$\tau(\theta_N) \approx \tau_0^{\sec \theta_S}, \quad (12\text{-}3)$$

where θ_S is the target zenith angle, given by **Equation 8-14**,

$$\theta_S \approx \pi - \sin^{-1}\left(\frac{R_E + h}{R_E} \sin \theta_N\right). \quad (12\text{-}4)$$

The exponent in **Equation 12-3**, $\sec \theta_S = 1/\cos \theta_S$, is sometimes called the "number of atmospheres" the LOS effectively passes through.[3] For example, **Figure 12-4** shows a view of the Earth from a GEO satellite with multiple atmospheres indicated.

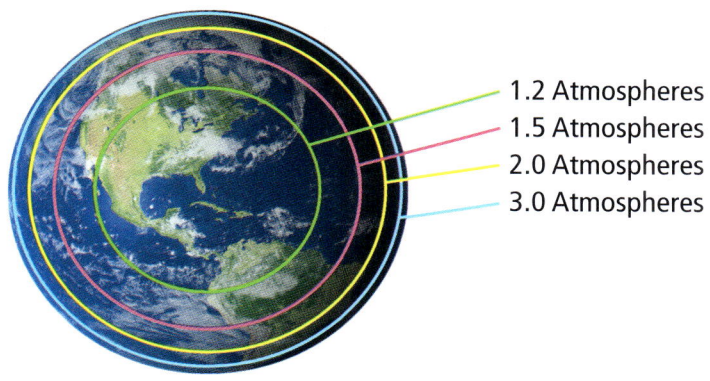

Figure 12-4
The number of atmospheres that a GEO sensor must look through to view a target at the Earth's surface.

EXAMPLE 12-1: HOW MANY ATMOSPHERES?

Suppose the atmospheric transmission to a surface target at nadir is $\tau_0 \approx 0.100$, but processing and analysis methods (to be discussed in later chapters) make it possible to extract useful target information from data with only $1/100$th as much energy. What is the maximum nadir viewing angle to this target?

Assuming atmospheric attenuation is the only cause of energy loss, $1/100$th as much energy means $\tau(\theta_N) \approx \tau_0/100 \approx 0.001 = (0.100)^3$. Therefore, the maximum number of atmospheres that can be tolerated is three. The figure plots the maximum usable nadir viewing angle as a function of sensor altitude.

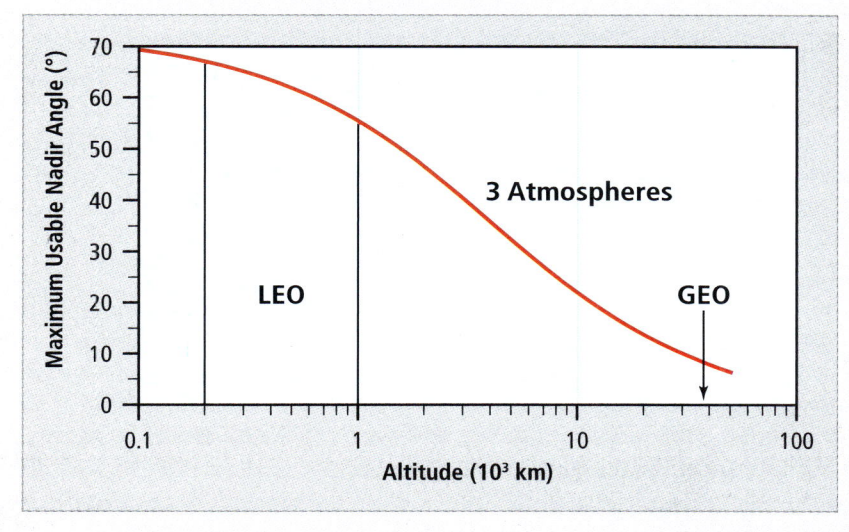

[2] An important but rare exception is looking *above* the limb of the Earth. An airborne target, a satellite, or a missile launch visible above the limb could be either nearer or farther than the tangent point ("short path" or "long path" in MODTRAN calculations, for example). In such cases, the atmospheric transmission is greater than or less than that predicted by **Equation 12-3**.

[3] **Equation 12-3** predicts zero transmission at the limb, but only because it was derived for a flat Earth. Nonetheless, the equation is accurate within 10% for the spherical Earth up to a target zenith angle of 75°, at which point the LOS is passing through about 10 atmospheres.

Another important consideration in selecting sensors to collect against targets is the amount of time to view the target. As suggested at the beginning of this chapter, airborne sensors often have the luxury of indefinite loiter time over target (TOT), at least in a non-threatening battlespace (air superiority assumed). Alternatively, if persistent surveillance of a target in a hostile environment or "denied area" is required, satellites must be used. In general, TOT is a function of a satellite's altitude and its orbital inclination. **Figure 12-5** illustrates a sensor acquiring a surface target, tracking it, and passing out of view when the viewing angle exceeds its maximum usable value. The accompanying plot shows the available collection time intervals[4] for sensors in circular orbits as a function of their altitude. These time intervals are based on the time the satellite is above the horizon as seen from a point on the Earth. (For highly elliptical orbit (HEO) sensors, see **Figure 11-21** and **Example 11-2**.)

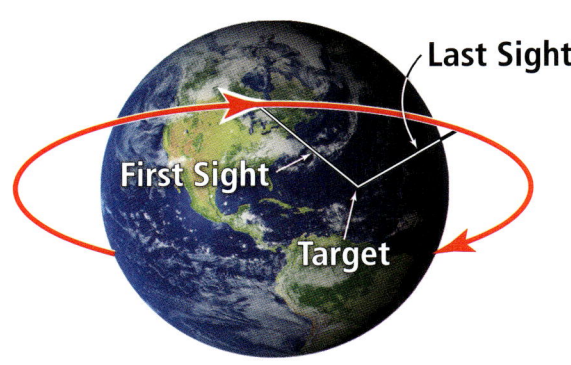
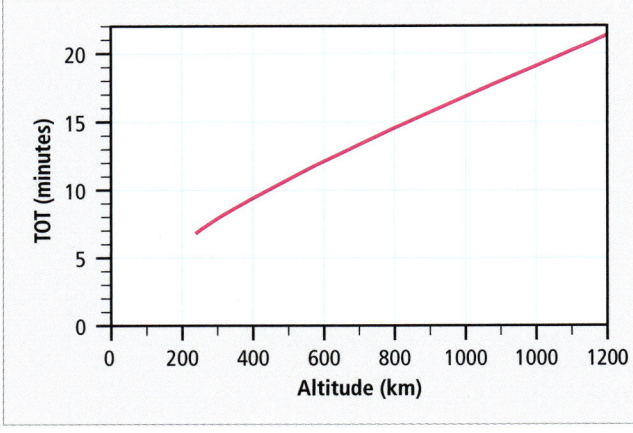

Figure 12-5
TOT as a function of altitude. The image on the left depicts the situation for a LEO sensor.

When discussing TOT, the concept of revisit rate is also an important consideration. The revisit period of a satellite-based sensor can vary from hours to days. Because of some overlap in the FORs of successive orbits, the increase in this overlap with escalating latitude will allow revisit to some areas of the Earth more frequently. Also, some satellite systems are able to point their sensors to collect the same area on successive satellite passes.

The ability to collect target information of the same area of the Earth's surface at different periods of time is one of the most important elements of remote sensing. Spatial and spectral characteristics of objects of interest may change over time, and these changes can be detected by collecting and comparing multi-temporal information. For example, during the growing season, vegetation can be in a continual state of change, and the ability to monitor those subtle changes using remote sensing is dependent on when and how frequently information is collected. By collecting on a recurring basis at regular intervals, the changes of the Earth's surface, caused by either natural occurrence (e.g., plant growth, floods, or some type of disaster) or by human intervention, can be quantified.

12.2 STARING SENSORS

The spatial collection strategy to visualize most easily is the staring mode[5] as shown in **Figures 12-6** and **12-7**. The optics focus energy on a square or rectangular Focal Plane Array (FPA) that continuously looks at a particular area, detecting changes in the incoming radiation over time. All of the detectors in the FPA are simultaneously exposed to the information sensed from the target or area of interest and therefore can produce output in parallel or nearly simultaneously. Because of long stare time requirements, this collection strategy is appropriate for GEO and HEO sensors.

---

[4] The general solution for TOT and revisit interval is more complicated because of the Earth's rotation. A sophisticated computer program such as Systems Tool Kit (STK) by Analytic Graphics Inc can be useful. [1]

[5] In radar, the staring mode is often called "spotlight" mode.

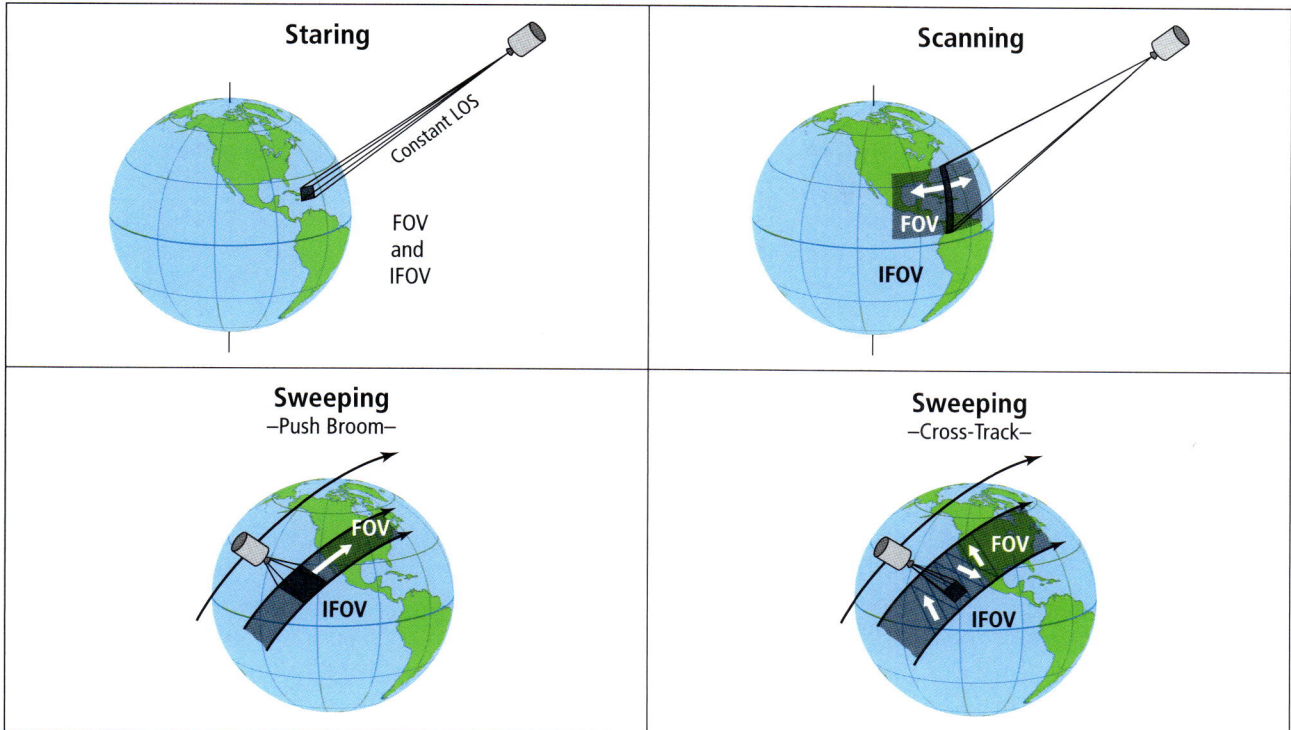

Figure 12-6
Possible spatial collection modes.
(FOV = Field of View;
IFOV = Instantaneous Field of View)

In this mode, a two-dimensional FPA of detectors is used, and each detector accepts radiation from its own ground pixel.[6] As discussed in **Chapter 8**, the size of each detector, x_{PIX} by y_{PIX}, and the effective focal length, f_{eff}, define the location and size of a ground pixel with dimensions of GSD_x and GSD_y. They also define the pixel's, or detector's, Field of View (FOV) designated by θ_{PIX}. The size of the FPA, designated by x and y, determines the area coverage, or footprint, of the sensor shown in **Figure 12-7** as X and Y.

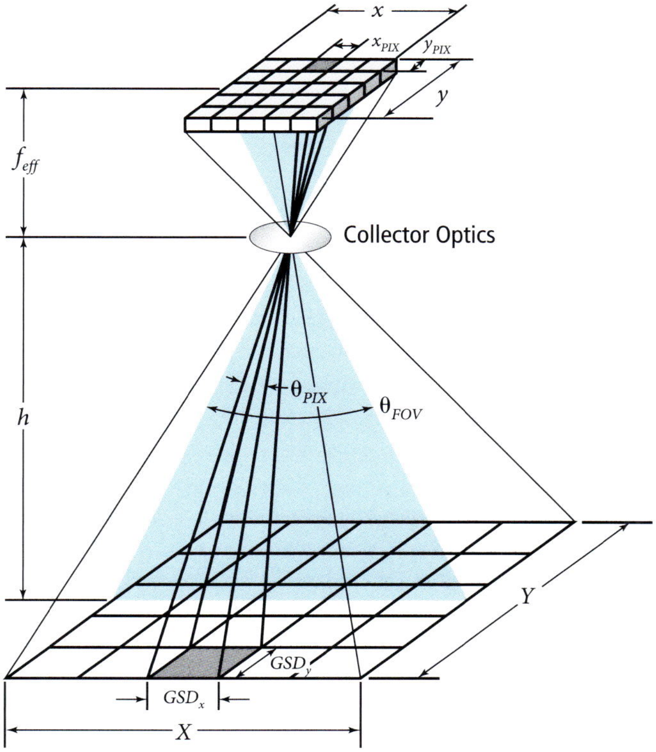

Figure 12-7
Simplified staring collection mode.

[6] Each detector actually accepts energy from within adjacent Point Spread Functions.

CHAPTER 12 COLLECTION STRATEGIES

The output of the FPA detecting elements is computed once to create a complete image or frame. For example, in standard video, each frame is composed of a specified period of time, typically one-thirtieth of a second. The frame rate is the frequency at which the frame, or all the elements in the FPA, is computed. Therefore, in standard video the frame rate would be 30 Hz. The frame rate limits the amount of time each element of the image is incident upon the detecting elements, and is typically known as the dwell time or integration time. (See **Chapter 7**.) In a staring sensor, the dwell time can be nearly as long as the duration of the frame, or the reciprocal of the frame rate. Generally, the longer the dwell time, the more sensitive the detector is to dim objects of interest. Additionally, longer dwell time increases the signal-to-noise ratio associated with each FPA read out. (See **Chapter 13**.)

The advantage of a staring sensor is its capability to "stare" or watch an area of interest within its FOR and detect small, quick changes in incident radiation irradiance values. FPA parameters such as quantum efficiency and well depth determine its sensitivity and response time. The drawback to a staring FPA is it must be quite large to cover a significant area. Because of the limited capability to manufacture quality, large FPAs (except in the visible), the footprints of staring sensors are relatively small unless large ground pixels are used. For example, a large infrared FPA of 2096 by 2096 detectors could cover a footprint that ranges in size from 2096 by 2096 km (or larger) with ground pixels sized 1 km by 1 km (or larger) down to just 2 km by 2 km (or smaller) with ground pixels sized 1 m by 1 m (or smaller).

In principle, staring sensors should be quite sensitive because they can integrate for a long time; each detector is dedicated to receiving radiation from its ground pixel during the entire integration time. In practice, for a moving sensor platform (and/or possibly a moving object of interest on the ground or in the air), integration times of any length require sophisticated pointing, tracking, and stabilization (PTS) systems to perform forward motion compensation. That is, each detector must remain pointed at the same point on the ground during the entire integration time. Without adequate stabilization, images will be blurred. (PTS issues are further discussed in **Chapter 15**.)

12.3 SCANNING SENSORS

A second collection strategy is to use a smaller array of detectors, perhaps a single row, and scan their footprints over the ground for a larger coverage area. This technique is particularly useful for large area surveillance missions where the number of pixels required to stare at an area of interest is prohibitive. The obvious disadvantage to scanning in this manner is the entire area is not seen simultaneously nor continuously. Therefore, small, rapid changes in target signature may be missed. Nonetheless, scanning is a widely used strategy when targets are not expected to change or move significantly over short time intervals.

Figure 12-8 suggests some high-altitude scanning methods suitable for GEO or HEO sensors. In each case, a small set of pixels is caused to move over the ground in some regular motion, usually circularly or linearly, using a mechanical arrangement on-board the host platform. The entirety of where a sensor of this sort is programmed to see in one complete cycle constitutes its FOV, which is likely to be a sub-set of its FOR. At any instant, the area which a sensor sees is termed its Instantaneous Field of View (IFOV). In any complete cycle, it may be possible to reconstruct a composite image scene by spatially arranging all of the IFOV samples into a mosaic. Such a scene would not represent a simultaneous collection of the entire area, of course.

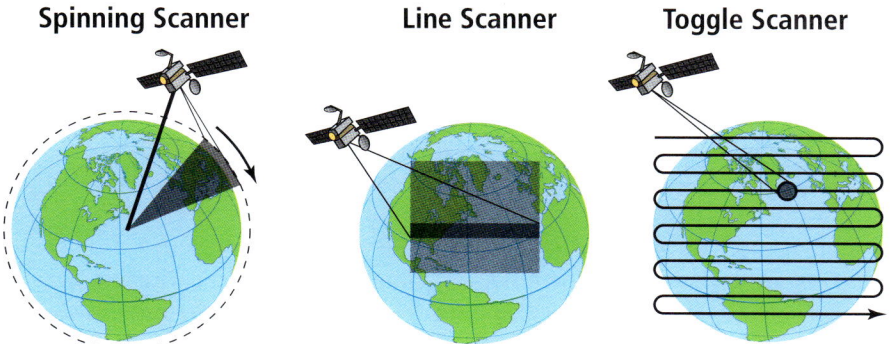

Figure 12-8
Some high-altitude scanning methods.

For low-altitude scanning, the simplest arrangement is to allow the motion of a sensor's platform to provide area coverage. A row of detectors is mounted perpendicular to the flight path or orbit, and their footprints (IFOVs) are "pushed" along the ground track, covering a swath (FOV). A common name for this type of system is a "pushbroom scanner," as the motion of the detector array is analogous to the bristles of a broom being pushed along a floor. Each individual detector measures the energy for a single ground resolution cell. The linear array of detectors scans a row of ground pixels across a region to compose a picture of the entire scene.

Figure 12-9 shows pushbroom collection geometries, where the pixel movement is produced by the forward motion of the platform. (Note the distortion of pixel footprint with increasing distance from the platform for standoff collection.) These scanners collect data in a series of lines (rows of ground pixels). The lines are oriented perpendicular to the direction of motion of the sensor platform. If the motion of the platform is in a straight

Figure 12-9
Pushbroom collection geometries.

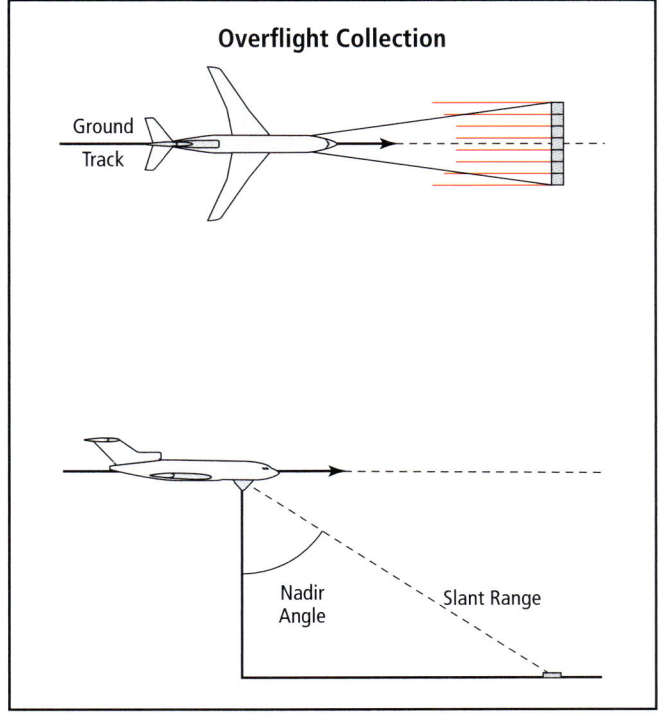
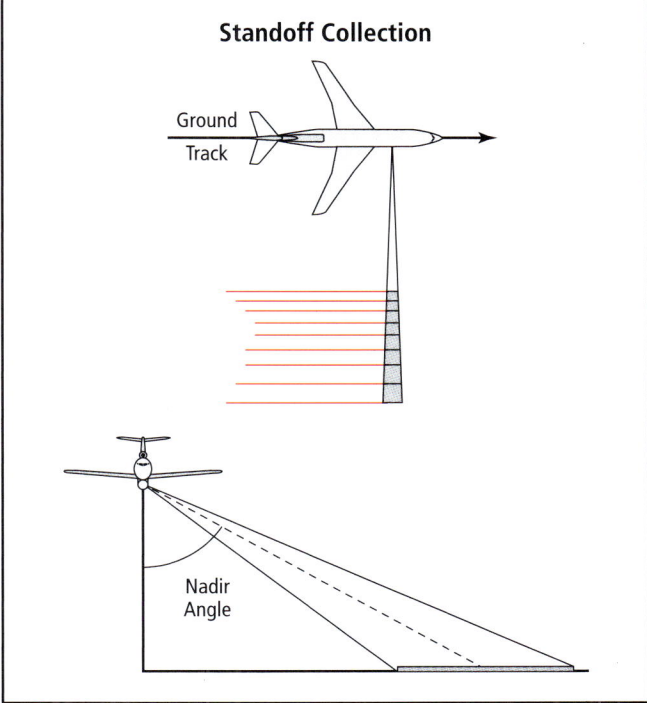

CHAPTER 12 COLLECTION STRATEGIES

line, the coverage area is a long, straight swath with a well-defined swath width equal in number of ground pixels to the number of detectors. With proper sensor design, the length of this swath can be varied and controlled by the sensor operators. For example, a scanning sensor with a 10,000 detector linear FPA (or one-dimensional FPA) can provide a swath that is 10,000 ground pixels wide, but of variable length. Such an array is easier to manufacture than a 10,000 by 10,000 detector FPA, which if used in staring mode has a footprint limited to 10,000 by 10,000 ground pixels.

Another common form of scanning is the cross-track "whiskbroom" scan, illustrated in **Figure 12-10**. In whiskbroom scanning, a mirror is used to move a row of ground pixels back and forth across the direction of flight (in the cross-track direction). A second mirror is also needed to compensate for the forward motion of the platform and maintain the sweep perpendicular to the track. As the sensor platform moves forward, successive scans create a two-dimensional image of the area. The size of the angular sweep of the row of ground pixels determines the width of the imaged area. Satellite based scanners sweep fairly small angles (10-20°) to cover a broad region because of the higher altitude. Since the distance from the sensor to the area of interest increases towards the edges of the sweep, the pixel size also becomes larger and therefore introduces geometric distortions to the resulting images. This is illustrated in **Figure 12-10**. A detailed calculation of the size of these ground pixels was introduced in **Chapter 8** and will be continued in **Chapter 16**.

Figure 12-10
Whiskbroom scanning geometry.

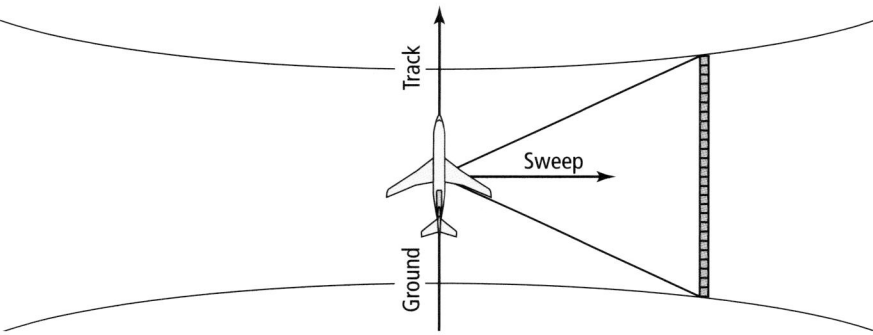

In either the pushbroom or the whiskbroom scanner, some PTS capability is required because of platform motion that deviates from a perfectly straight level flight at constant speed. Without this stabilization, collected images will be distorted. Objects of interest will appear distorted in size and shape, and there may be gaps in coverage. (See **Chapter 15** for examples.)

Platform motion (primarily airborne) is considered in the discussion below for a pushbroom scanner in terms of the characteristic aircraft motions of roll, pitch, and yaw.

1. Aircraft roll is defined as rotational motion of the aircraft about the axis of its fuselage. The coverage produced by aircraft roll effects is shown in **Figure 12-11** with the swath of area on the ground that is intended to be covered (dashed lines). Each rectangle represents a row of pixels at a given instant of time. The time interval between adjacent rows of pixels is the same. It represents the location of a row at the time of a collection, assuming the sample time is short compared to the collection time. As the aircraft rolls back and forth, the shaded areas indicate gaps in coverage for this swath. In addition to gaps in coverage, roll produces image distortion. The simplest example is a straight street running parallel to the ground track. In the imagery, it will appear crooked.

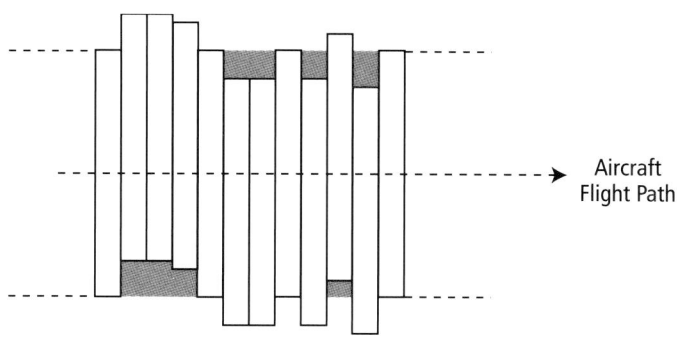

Figure 12-11
Gaps in ground coverage produced by platform roll.

2. Aircraft pitch is defined as motion of the nose up or down relative to horizontal. The resulting motion is undulating, like a children's roller coaster at an amusement park. The shaded areas in **Figure 12-12** are the gaps in coverage. Interestingly, there are also strips of land where there are overlapping rows of ground pixels, and hence oversampling of the image. In those locations, objects will appear longer in the dimension along the ground track than they really are.

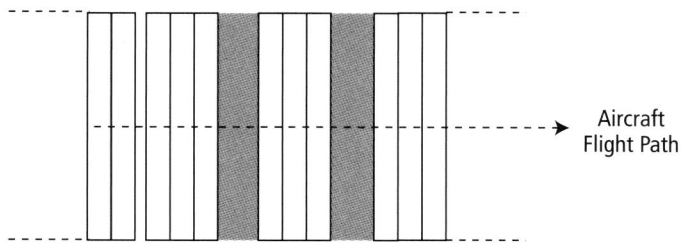

Figure 12-12
Gaps in ground coverage produced by platform pitch.

3. Aircraft yaw is defined as a shift of the nose left or right in the horizontal plane. The resulting motion, shown in **Figure 12-13**, produces regions at the edge of the swath that are oversampled or undersampled (producing gaps in coverage). Again, objects in oversampled regions will appear larger than they really are in the dimension parallel to the ground track.

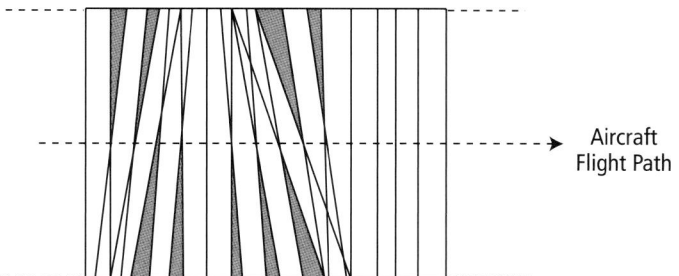

Figure 12-13
Gaps in ground coverage produced by platform yaw.

Whiskbroom scans, resulting from the use of a scanning mirror, can either be in-track (i.e., parallel to the ground track) or cross-track (i.e., perpendicular) to the ground track. The latter case is illustrated in **Figure 12-14**.

There are a few consequences of a moving platform on a cross-track scanner. The use of such a scan is usually to collect data over a swath wider than that defined by the number of detectors in a row. The longer (in time) the scan, the wider the swath and the more area covered. The length of the scan may require a fast scan to prevent coverage gaps and hence, lower detector output for every collection along a row of ground pixels. These scans may produce a swath in which there is variability in pixel shape and size between the near edge and the far edge of the swath. If gaps in coverage should not exist at the near edge, then significant over-sampling and image distortion may occur at the far edge. Roll, pitch, and yaw produce effects to the swath similar to those just discussed for the pushbroom scan.

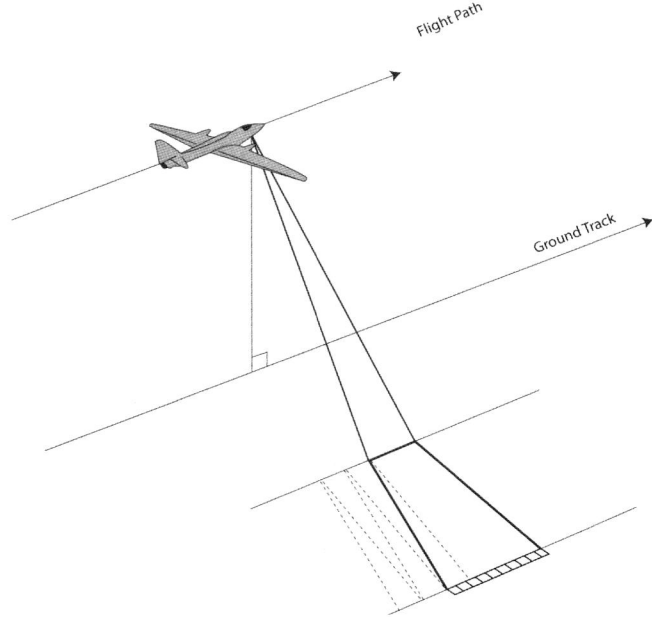

Figure 12-14
Wide swath produced by cross-track scanning.

An additional trade-off between spatial resolution and footprint (or area coverage) is suggested. To improve spatial resolution by decreasing the size of the ground pixels, FPAs must be manufactured with smaller, more closely spaced detectors and/or longer focal length optics must be used. But, in either case, to maintain wide area coverage, there are three possible options: 1) increase the number of detectors in each of the detector rows; 2) for a pushbroom scanner, change to a cross-track scanner (detector output may suffer); or 3) for a cross-track-scanner, increase the scan speed and hence the width of the swath (detector output may suffer).

Figure 12-15 summarizes the different collection modes all of which can be used with imaging sensors.

Figure 12-15
Summary of data collection modes. Note, all FOV and FOR are not included in order to not complicate the figure.

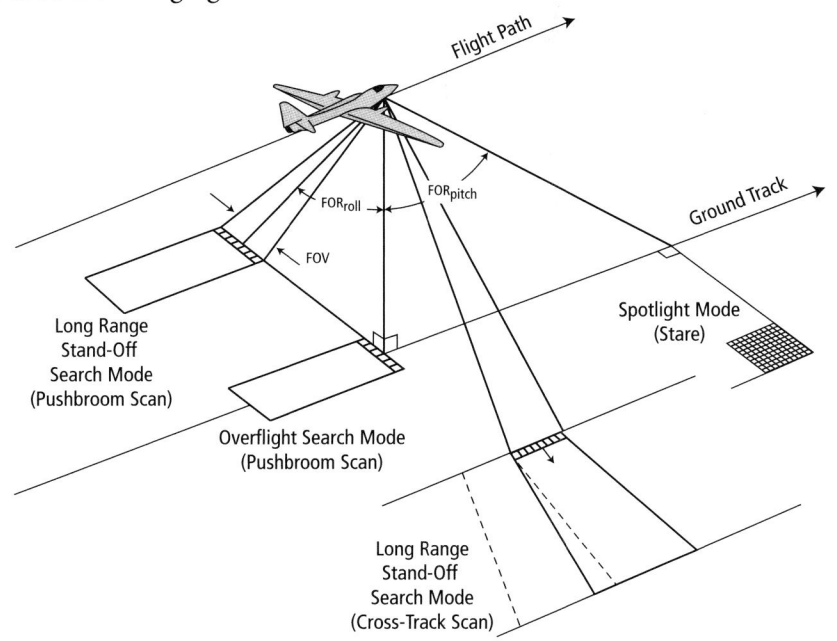

246 CHAPTER 12 COLLECTION STRATEGIES

The properties of the collection modes are summarized in **Table 12-1**.

Table 12-1
Comparison of common collection strategies.

	Imaging Type		
	Staring	**Pushbroom Scanner**	**Cross-track Scanner**
PTS System Required for High Quality Imagery	Extensive	Much less than staring	Much less than staring
Type FPA Required	2-D	Linear	Short linear
Coverage Capabilities	Limited by 2-D FPA size	Can be large using long linear FPAs	Can be large using long scans
Necessary Moving Parts	None	None	Scanning mechanism (reliability/possible failure issues)
Integration Time Possible	Can be long	Short, limited by platform motion	Shortest, often limited by swath width and platform motion
Sensor Usage	Few systems	Commonly used	Some systems

As the manufacturing of larger FPAs has progressed, the use of cross-track scanners has declined in favor of push-broom scanners. Eventually, the use of push-broom scanners may decline in favor of staring sensors.

12.4 TEMPORAL SAMPLING

Today, most sensor output signals are temporally sampled and digitized. **Figure 12-16** is a simple high-level block diagram of an electro-optical (EO) sensor system. The photons are detected and their accumulation is converted to a charge on a capacitor (the storage well). At specified times, the capacitor results are read and the resulting voltage is converted to a digital signal through an analog-to-digital (A/D) converter for transmission to the satellite ground station or for on-board recording.

Figure 12-16
Block diagram of EO sensor system.

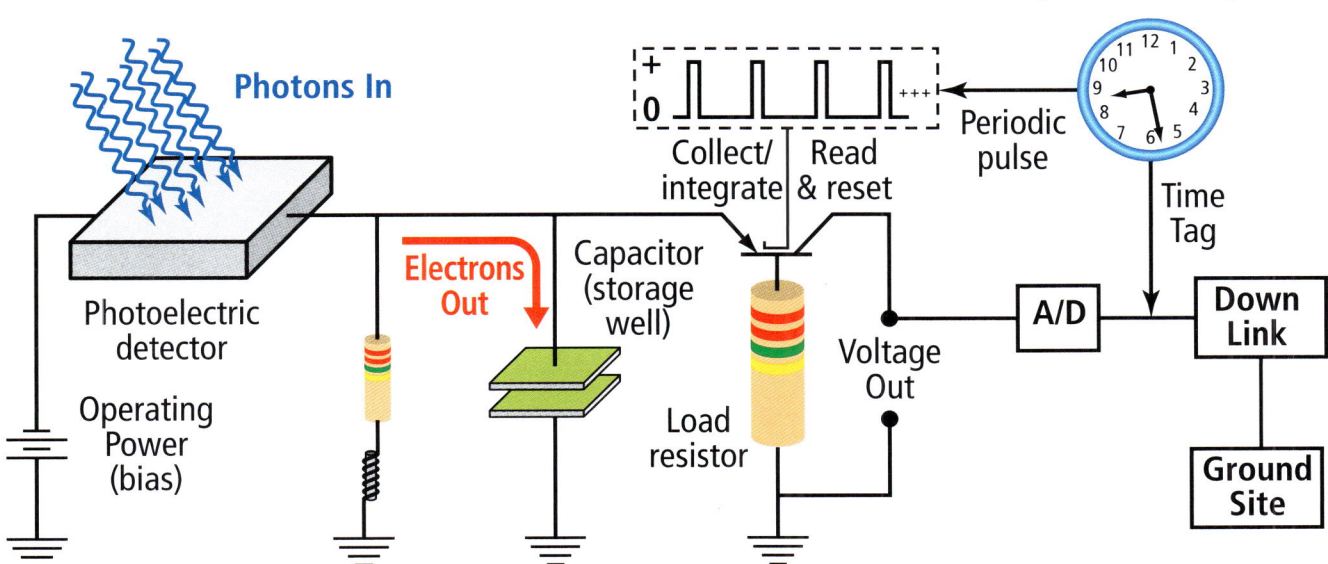

The concepts of duty cycle and integration time are repeated from **Chapter 7** and illustrated in **Figure 12-17** where duty cycle is defined as integration time, Δt_{INT}, divided by frame time, and frame rate is then defined as the reciprocal of frame time. These concepts are used to determine the number of photons, or amount of energy, the sensor must collect before an object of interest can be detected.

Figure 12-17
Sensor integration time and duty cycle.

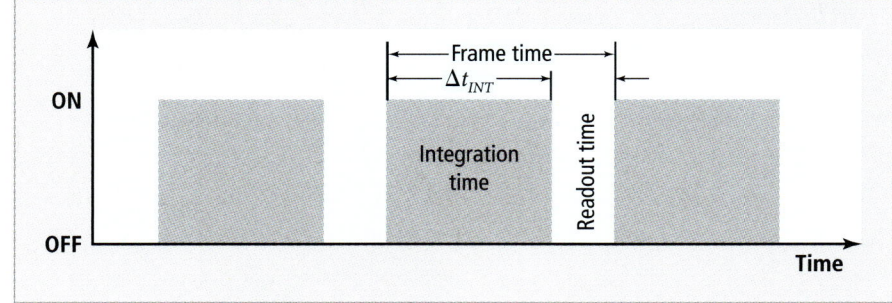

Most sensor systems are downlink restricted or limited. This is especially true of satellite based sensor systems. Of utmost importance to the majority of sensors is the amount of information they create that must be transferred to the processing systems. The data downlink or recording rate for the sensor system is defined as:

$$\left\{\begin{array}{c} \text{Data} \\ \text{Rate} \\ \text{(bits/s)} \end{array}\right\} \approx \left\{\begin{array}{c} \text{Number} \\ \text{of} \\ \text{Pixels} \end{array}\right\} \times \left\{\begin{array}{c} \text{Sampling} \\ \text{Rate} \\ \text{(frames/s)} \end{array}\right\} \times \left\{\begin{array}{c} \text{A/D Bit} \\ \text{Depth} \\ \text{(bits/pixel)} \end{array}\right\} \quad (12\text{-}5)$$

In effect, time sampling "smooths" a time-varying signal. The shortest event that can be unambiguously identified is one that fills one time sample. For signatures with temporally varying components, the most rapid component can only be distinguished at one-half the sample rate as defined by the Nyquist criterion. **Figure 12-18** shows the effects of sampling a time varying signal at discrete times with the resulting output.

Figure 12-18
Discrete sampling of a time varying signal.

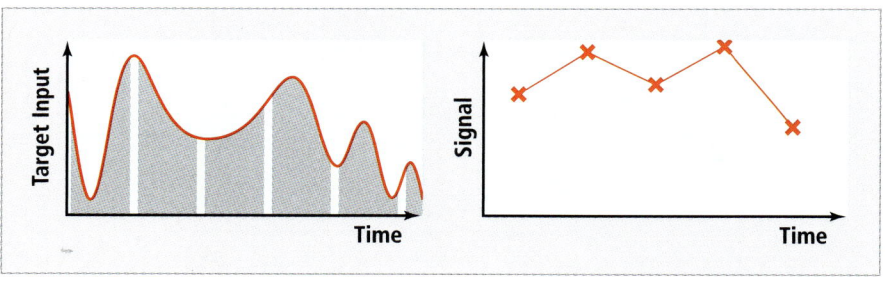

Temporal sampling time affects the coverage capabilities of both scanning and staring sensors. As long as the object of interest is in view of the staring sensor, it can "continuously" collect on the object of interest subject to the sensor design and downlink bandwidth considerations. In contrast, a scanning sensor only collects information regarding an object of interest when it is in the active pixel or cell. This affects both the along-track and cross-track sampling of the sensor.

EXAMPLE 12-2: WHAT IS THE DWELL TIME FOR THE SeaWiFS?

The Sea-viewing Wide Field of view Sensor (SeaWiFS) was an ocean color measuring sensor on the SeaStar platform and was active from August 1, 1997 to December 11, 2010. From a $h \approx 705$ km circular orbit, SeaWiFS was a cross-track scanner with $GSD_x \approx 1.13$ km ground pixel at nadir. It would scan a line $\theta_{FOV} \approx 116.6°$ wide (from 58.3° on one side to 58.3° on the other), then repeat. (See image below.)

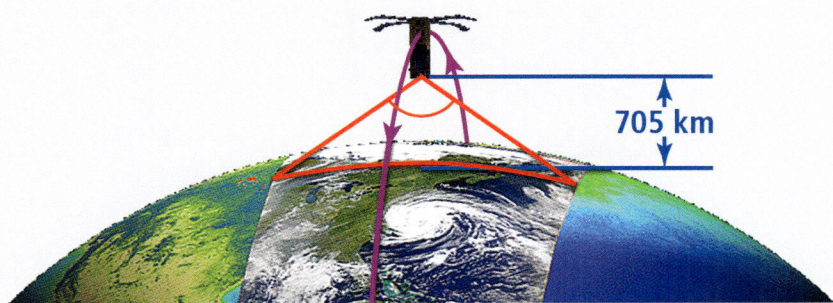

First, use Kepler's Third Law (**Equation 11-15**) to calculate SeaWiFS' orbital period to be

$$P \approx \sqrt{\frac{4\pi^2}{\mu_E}a^3} \approx \sqrt{(9.895 \times 10^{-5} \text{s}^2 \cdot \text{km}^{-3})(6370 \text{ km} + 705 \text{ km})^3}$$

$$\approx 5920 \text{ s, or } 98.7 \text{ min.}$$

Next, since the FOV goes around the circumference of the Earth once each orbit, its along-track speed is

$$v_{ALONG \atop TRACK} \approx \frac{2\pi R_E}{P} \approx \frac{(2\pi)(6370 \text{ km})}{5920 \text{ s}} \approx 6.76 \text{ km} \cdot \text{s}^{-1}.$$

The time to move forward one ground pixel (the time to complete one cross-track scan) is then

$$\Delta t_{SCAN} \approx \frac{GSD_x}{v_{ALONG \atop TRACK}} \approx \frac{1.13 \text{ km}}{6.76 \text{ km} \cdot \text{s}^{-1}} \approx 0.167 \text{ s.}$$

With a 1.13 km ground pixel at nadir, the pixel's angular FOV is approximately

$$\theta_{PIX} \approx \frac{GSD_x}{h} \approx \frac{1.13 \text{ km}}{705 \text{ km}} \approx 1.60 \times 10^{-3} \text{ rad} \approx 0.0918°.$$

Completing one scan, the number of samples SeaWiFS collects per scan without overlap is

$$N \approx \frac{\theta_{FOV}}{\theta_{PIX}} \approx \frac{116.6°}{0.0918°} \approx 1{,}270 \text{ samples.}$$

Finally, the dwell time (time to collect one sample) is thus about

$$\Delta t_{DWELL} \approx \frac{\Delta t_{SCAN}}{N} \approx \frac{0.167 \text{ s}}{1270} \approx 1.31 \times 10^{-4} \text{ s.}$$

Actual sensor operation may have less dwell time than the calculation here to allow for some overlap between frames, read-out time, and scan reversal.

12.5 SPECTRAL SAMPLING

The final but equally important requirement for sensor designers to address is the spectral phenomenology associated with the object or set of objects of interest to a user community. To appreciate the complexities of spectral sampling, it is important to review the electromagnetic (EM) spectrum as illustrated in **Figure 12-19**. Recall the discussion is about EO remote sensing applications that typically include wavelengths from the ultraviolet (UV) to the Long-Wave Infrared (LWIR). Application areas typically include reconnaissance, surveillance, target acquisition, weapon delivery, navigation, threat warning, meteorology, and countermeasures. General sensor performance measures encompass metrics such as maximum useful range, sensitivity, and spatial resolution.

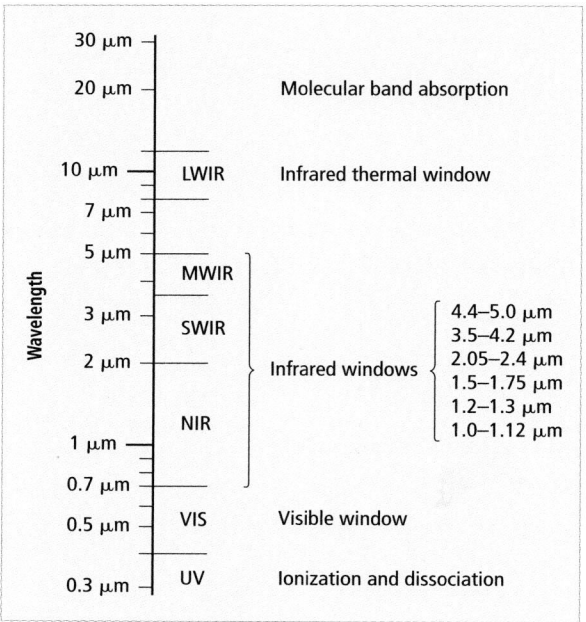

Figure 12-19
The EM spectrum from UV through LWIR.

Spectral sampling determines the various techniques used to collect spectral information. If storage of data is not a concern, the choice may be to sample the entire spectral curve of interest with numerous narrow spectral bands. Sometimes the decision is made to perform more coarse sampling over a spectral region that includes numerous wavelengths. The obvious question is, "Which method of sampling in the spectral domain is better for the mission?" Obviously, the use of a finer resolution sampling method can detect more types of phenomenology. Also unmistakable is the fact that finer spectral resolution provides additional spectral information. Instruments commonly used to detect and measure the spectrum of an object of interest include: 1) monochromer, for a single wavelength (or more realistically, a very narrow spectral bandpass, or range of wavelengths); 2) broadband for all wavelengths integrated together or those in a wide spectral bandpass; and 3) spectrometer, which is used to detect and measure EM waves independently at multiple wavelengths.

Ultimately, the sensor's mission and spectral fidelity determine the cost of the instrument. **Figure 12-20** illustrates atmospheric transmission as a function of wavelength. Based on MODTRAN calculations, curves are presented for transmission from various altitudes to space. The molecular or thermal emission of the objects of interest determines the wavelengths over which the sensor is optimized.

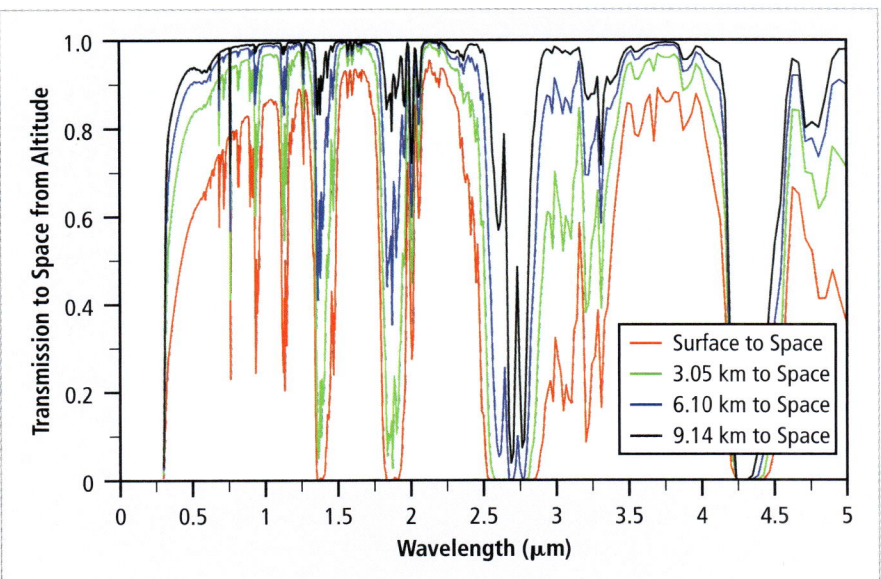

Figure 12-20
Transmission on a vertical path to space from altitudes given in kilometers is in the legend. A surface visibility of 23 km and the rural haze model in MODTRAN were used. [2]

For example, to conduct meaningful analysis, it is important to know the thermal spectrum of a typical hydrocarbon flame. The figure in **Example 2-6** shows an infrared emission spectrum of a natural gas flame (methane, CH_4). This spectrum shows strong emission bands between 2 and 3 μm and between 4 and 5 μm where the emission is dominated by the combustion products of the hydrocarbon, namely the H_2O and CO_2, respectively. The low spectral resolution sketch in **Figure 12-21** shows strong emission bands corresponding to the CO_2 emission peak at 4.3 μm wavelength and that of H_2O at 2.7 μm.

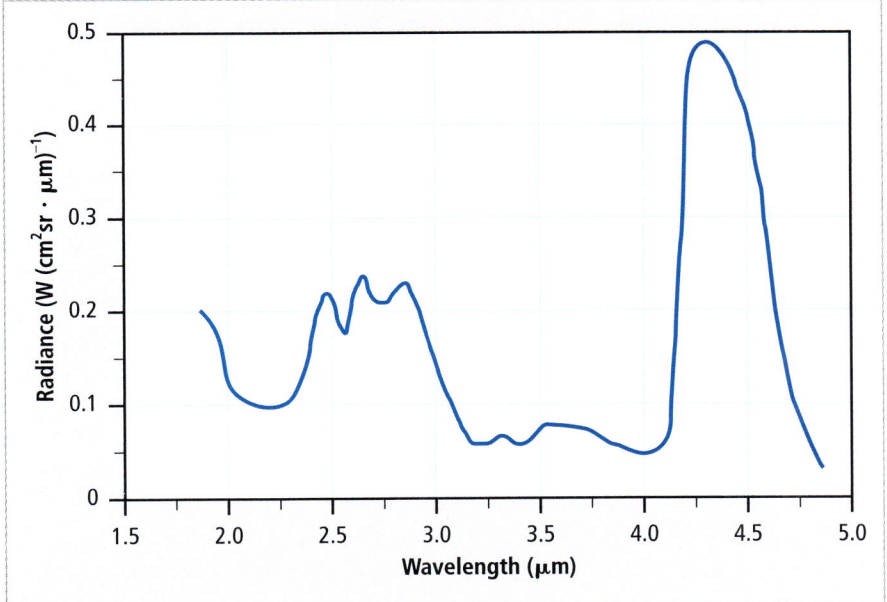

Figure 12-21
Low resolution infrared emissions of hydrocarbon fuel. Note, the H_2O "blue spike" between 2.4-3.0 μm and the CO_2 "red spike" between 4.2-4.7 μm as in **Example 2-6**. [3]

If the sensor is designed to measure the change in vegetation or areas not covered with vegetation, different bands would be chosen than for rocket engines. **Figure 12-22**, for instance, illustrates the spectral bands selected for the Landsat Thematic Mapper (TM) bands. The Landsat TM sensor was designed to achieve higher image resolution, sharper spectral separation, improved geometric fidelity, and greater radiometric accuracy and resolution than earlier sensors. The Landsat TM sensor has 7 bands that simultaneously record reflected or emitted radiation from the Earth's surface in the blue-green (band 1), green (band 2), red (band 3), near-infrared (band 4), shortwave infrared (SWIR) (bands 5 and 7), and the LWIR (band 6, not shown in **Figure 12-22**) portions of the EM spectrum. TM band 2 can detect green reflectance from healthy vegetation, and band 3 is designed for detecting chlorophyll absorption in vegetation. TM band 4 is ideal for near-infrared reflectance peaks in healthy green vegetation and for detecting water-land interfaces. TM band 1 can penetrate water for bathymetric (water depth) mapping along coastal areas and is useful for soil-vegetation differentiation and distinguishing forest types. The two SWIR bands on TM are useful for vegetation and soil moisture studies and discriminating between rock and mineral types. The LWIR band on TM is designed to assist in thermal mapping and for soil moisture and vegetation studies.

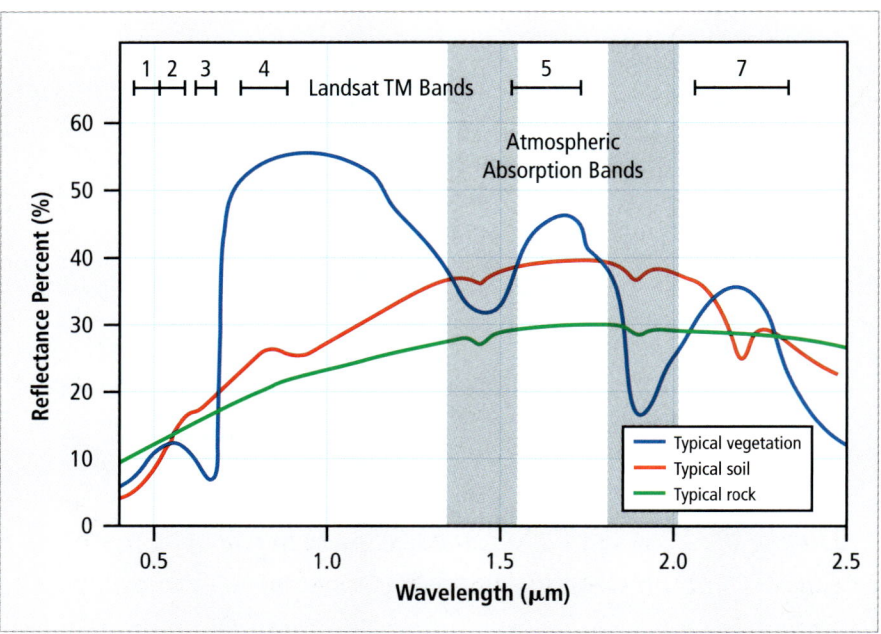

Figure 12-22
The spectral bands associated with the Landsat TM sensor. [4]

Table 12-2 presents the spectral bands used on the sensors on the following weather satellites: DMSP, NOAA, NOAA GOES, GMS, and METEOSAT. (See **Chapter 16** for more details.) As the legend denotes, some bands were chosen for discriminating snow and ice from clouds as well as mid- and upper-level moisture contents. It is of extreme importance to correlate the phenomenology of the objects of interest with the spectral bands chosen for the sensor. Spectral sampling and applications will be discussed further in **Chapters 15** to **21**.

Table 12-2
Different spectral bands can be utilized for differentiating between snow and ice from clouds as well as mid- and upper-level moisture content.

	DMSP	NOAA	NOAA GOES	GMS	METEOSAT
Visible	0.4–1.1 μm	0.55–0.68 μm 0.725–1.1 μm	0.55–0.75 μm	0.55–0.75 μm	0.55–0.75 μm
IR	10.2–12.8 μm	3.33–3.93 μm* 10.5–11.5 μm 11.5–12.5 μm	3 bands around 7 μm** 10.5–12.5 μm	10.5–12.6 μm	5.7–7.1 μm** 10.5–12.5 μm

* This mid-infrared channel is useful for differentiating snow and ice from clouds.
** These "water vapor" channels are used to display the mid- and upper-level moisture content and wind patterns at three levels.

The foregoing discussion about the broadband and narrow band spectral sensors illustrates the absolute necessity for the sensor designers to know the types of targets of interest to the sensor's mission. Understanding the phenomenology associated with a target or set of targets will guide sensor designers in selecting the appropriate spectral bands.

13 TEMPORAL SENSING: TARGETS & SIGNATURES

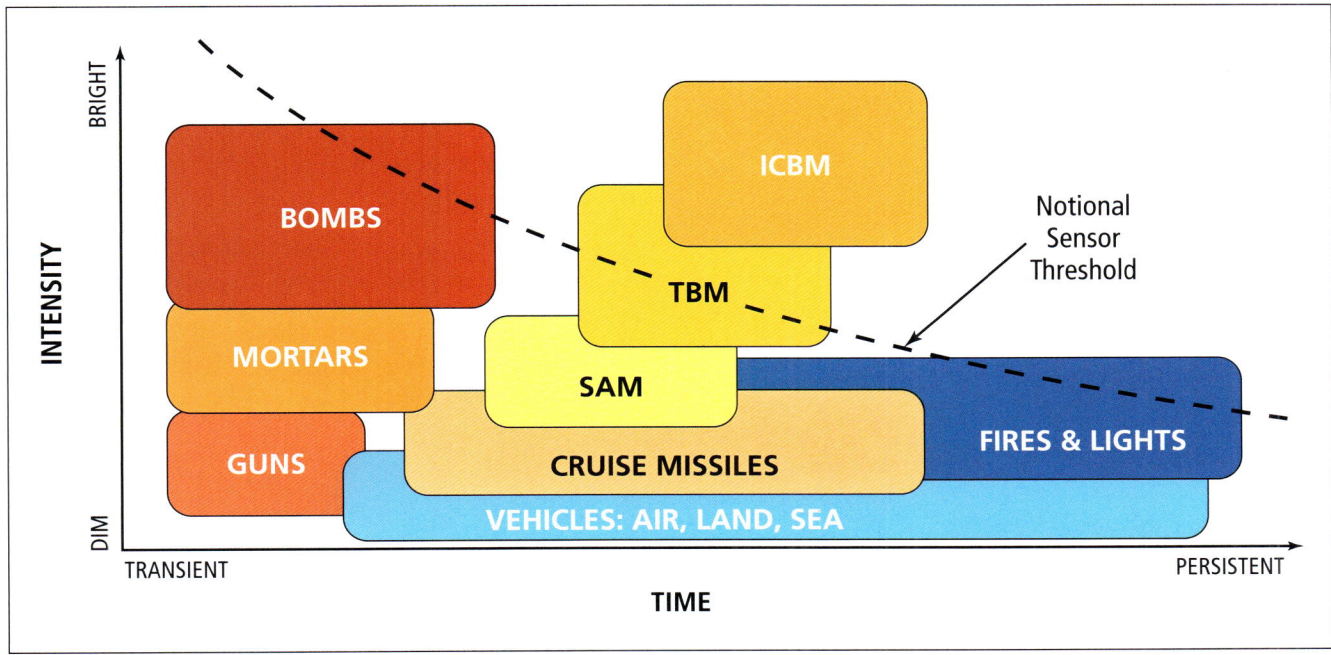

During the Cold War, it became necessary to gather Technical Intelligence (TI) on weapons and delivery systems developed behind the Iron Curtain, and to provide Early Warning (EW) of hostile strategic missile launches. The latter was only possible on a near-real time basis by deploying overhead assets with large area surveillance of "denied areas" and long time-over-target capabilities. Starting in 1955, studies determined satellite-based infrared (IR) sensors could provide the necessary warning and collect the required TI on missile and warhead testing. Operational systems were then deployed beginning in the 1970s and continue through today. [1], [2]

With the demise of the Soviet Union in the 1990s, the long-range missile threat and the ominous overcast of global nuclear war diminished (under treaties), but the proliferation of regional-size conflicts using smaller, tactical weapons increased. This shift from global to regional threats in no way reduced the necessity for large area surveillance, but pushed the envelope to obtain characterization of smaller weapons and their deployment. With improved 21st century technology, a hallmark of the continuing large area surveillance systems is their increasing ability to detect the smaller weapons. [3], [4]

SECTIONS
13.1 SENSORS
13.2 PERSISTENT EVENTS
13.3 TRANSIENT TARGETS

13.1 SENSORS

A distinguishing feature of advanced technical intelligence is identifying targets, not by their literal (visual) images, but by other distinguishing, non-literal characteristics: *signatures and metrics*. That could not be more true than in the topics explored in this chapter. Here, the *time-intensity history* of targets and their *space-time trajectories* that make them unique and identifiable will be considered. The need to rely on signatures for identification and characterization of targets is driven by requirements for nearly real-time surveillance and analysis over long intervals of time, often over large areas.[1] The last two chapters clearly pointed the way for this application: sensors aboard high-altitude platforms (Geosynchronous Earth Orbit (GEO) and Highly Elliptical Orbit (HEO)) with either scanning or staring collection strategies are required. Consequently, traditional imaging is prohibitive and the signature is depended on.

As pointed out in the introduction of this chapter, the earliest large area surveillance challenge was the EW mission. To meet this challenge and to augment knowledge of foreign weapon systems through TI evaluation, the US was particularly successful in developing large-area-viewing sensors to provide persistent surveillance. The first such sensor program was the venerable Defense Support Program (DSP), a hemisphere-scanning sensor shown in **Figure 13-1**, which has been the backbone of North American defense for over 40 years. However, the last DSP sensor was launched and the program is phasing out by attrition. It is being replaced by the Space-Based InfraRed System (SBIRS).

A history of DSP, summarized from Air Force Fact Sheets and Northrop Grumman [5], [6] follows:

Figure 13-1
The venerable DSP large area surveillance sensor, the backbone of the US' Cold War ballistic missile defense.

> DSP satellites use IR sensors to detect heat from missile and booster plumes against the Earth's background. The satellites orbit the Earth approximately 35,780 kilometers over the equator...
>
> The DSP grew out of the successful 1960s space-based IR Missile Defense Alarm System known as MIDAS....Between 1960 and 1966, twelve MIDAS launches deployed four different types of increasingly sophisticated sensors, leading the way to the development, launch, and use of DSP.
>
> In response to evolving threats, DSP underwent five major upgrades, allowing it to provide more accurate and reliable data to the warfighter. For example, the addition of a mid-wave IR capability provided enhanced missile warning mission utility. This upgrade marked the first space sensor application of mercury cadmium telluride IR sensors, the material of choice for today's IR sensors...
>
> On November 6, 1970, the US Air Force launched ... the first of many DSP satellites to be launched over the next [37] years. DSP has a history of launching atop Titan III and IV family of launch vehicles ... with one exception to date. DSP-16 was launched aboard NASA's Space Shuttle Atlantis in November 1991...
>
> The 23rd and final DSP satellite launched in December 2007.... In recent years, scientists developed methods to use DSP's IR sensor as part of an EW system for natural disasters like volcanic eruptions and forest fires.

---

[1] Indeed, most information collected by large-area surveillance sensors is unprocessed because it does not include targets; the sensor is simply turned on and monitors for rare events to occur at not necessarily known places and times. This is in distinct contrast to other sensors' tasking, where all gathered information is scrutinized because it has specifically tasked collections on targets at known places and times.

After the Cold War, and particularly after Desert Storm, sights were set on deploying more sensitive large-area surveillance systems with warfighter support capabilities to adequately provide overhead coverage for Missile Warning (MW), Missile Defense (MD), and Battlespace Awareness (BA), as well as TI. The program developed to replace DSP in the 21st century is the SBIRS. A short description of the present SBIRS suite of sensors from the Air Force's website follows, and a conceptual image of the GEO sensors is shown in **Figure 13-2**. [7], [8], [9]

Figure 13-2
Conceptual rendering of the SBIRS GEO sensors, replacement for DSP.

The SBIRS constellation will consist of IR payloads on host satellites in HEO and two IR sensors each on dedicated SBIRS satellites in GEO. The GEO scanning sensor is designed to perform the Strategic MW mission, the Global TI, as well as the initial phase of the Strategic MD mission. It provides a shorter revisit time and greater sensitivity than the DSP sensor over its full Field of View (FOV). The GEO staring sensor is designed to perform the Theater MW and Theater MD missions, the BA mission, the TI mission in focus areas, and the final phase of the Strategic MD mission. It provides step-stare or dedicated stare operations over smaller regions than the scanning sensor.

The Department of Defense recognized the need to replace the venerable DSP system in a summer study completed in September 1994. SBIRS achieved Increment 1 Initial Operation Capability on December 18, 2001 when the [Mission Control Station] consolidated command and control and data processing elements from legacy [DSP] systems into a modern peacetime facility, processing all Air Force and other IR data in a fused manner.... SBIRS Increment 2 is the designation of the full deployment of the new SBIRS constellation of satellites and sensors, along with the new Ground Segment hardware and software.

Thus, as the world becomes more dangerous, the original two missions for large-area surveillance (EW and TI) have expanded into four (MW, MD, BA, and TI), and the targets of interest have generally become smaller. However, the larger targets have not completely gone away. Additionally, the conclusion of the DSP Fact Sheet (above) suggests yet another mission: civil applications for natural disaster monitoring insofar as there are IR signatures for forest fires, volcanoes, and the like.

The primary factor determining whether any target can be collected by these or any other sensor is the interplay between the target's radiant time history and the collection strategy and duty cycle used by the sensor. The SBIRS HEO sensor employs a scanning strategy, whereas SBIRS GEO has both a staring and a scanning capability in companion sensors on the same platform. [8], [9] Thus, if the duration of a target's radiant output is sufficiently long such that one of the scanners has a reasonable expectation of collecting it, then the target is considered to be "persistent." Otherwise, it is "transient." A general rule of thumb, although arbitrary, is targets with durations shorter than about five seconds are considered transient.

The introductory figure shows the classification of several types of targets as being of either transient or persistent duration. The chart assumes all targets emit (or reflect) radiation in a sensor's bandpass, and also places them in an unquantified relative order of their radiant intensities: dim to bright. As discussed in **Chapter 4**, remember intensity is the radiometric quantity used for point sources, which is certainly true for the targets on the figure when viewed from GEO or HEO. The units of intensity (integrated within a bandpass) are watts per steradian, which is energy per unit time per unit direction.

To decide if any target can be collected by a sensor, consider whether that target emits (or reflects) sufficient energy in the sensor's spectral bandpass. That is, the sensitivity of every sensor is designed to detect a minimum level of energy, or threshold. Therefore, a notional sensor threshold was plotted in the introduction figure, which is a line of constant energy:[2,3,4]

$$\{INTENSITY\} \times \{DURATION\} \approx \{ENERGY\}. \quad (13\text{-}1)$$

That is, a bright but short duration target will deliver as much energy (number of photons) as a dim, long duration target. Since energy is information, it is critical that sensors are designed with a threshold as low as possible to collect the targets of interest.[5]

13.2 PERSISTENT EVENTS

The introductory figure shows that persistent events span the entire range from bright to dim. Discriminators of classifying targets as bright or dim are their target-to-background ratio and Signal-to-Noise Ratio (SNR), considered in **Chapter 10**. Bright persistent targets with large ratios are typically missile launch events, which will be considered first in this section, and dim persistent targets are considered next. How can the ratios be improved for better detection? Amongst the dim targets, vehicles are often the subject of thermal imagery, which will be covered in **Chapter 16**.

MISSILES AS BRIGHT PERSISTENT EVENTS

One of the most prominent persistent targets for large area surveillance sensors is the Intercontinental Ballistic Missile (ICBM). **Figure 13-3** shows the phases of a typical surface-to-surface missile's trajectory: boost, midcourse, and re-entry. Of the three phases, the midcourse segment has the least IR signature; it is generally too dim to be visible against the Earth's background (but may be seen by ground-based or airborne sensors looking up). In addition to detecting missile launches, an immediate goal

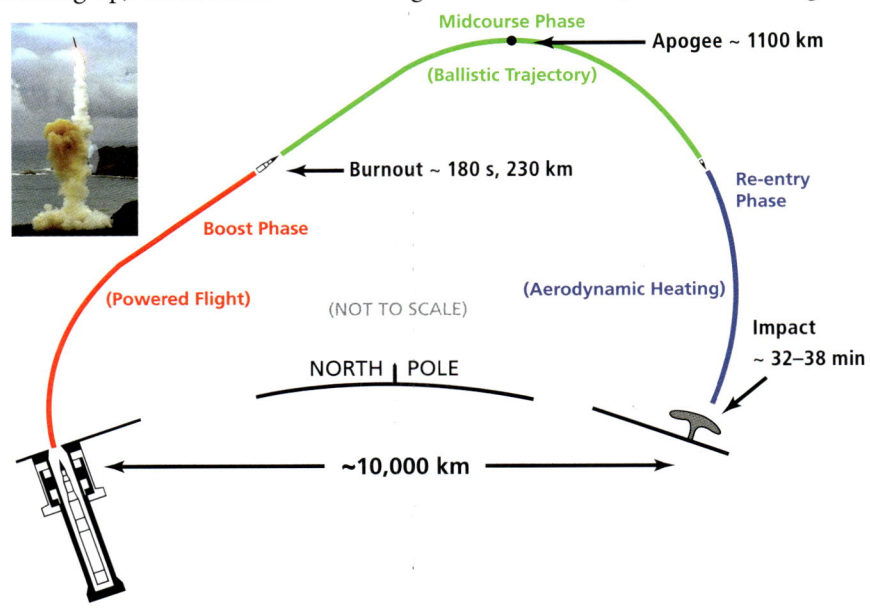

Figure 13-3
The three phases of a missile's flight from launch to impact (not to scale). Inset shows a test launch of a Minuteman. [10]

[2] What happened to the steradians? Refer to the sidebar "Units in Radiometric Calculations" in Chapter 4.

[3] Photographers know this line as constant *exposure*. A wide open aperture with a fast shutter speed will give the same picture as a small aperture and a slow shutter speed. There are specific reasons other than just exposure (such as motion of the camera or subject) for selecting aperture size and shutter speed.

[4] Mathematically, the threshold line is a hyperbola.

[5] This does not guarantee a successful collection. Data processing has a significant impact. See Chapter 14.

of sensor signal analysis is to obtain metrics, i.e., to measure the position, velocity, and acceleration of the vehicle to know its launch point and to predict its impact. Both the signatures and metrics of missiles will be discussed later in this chapter.

Starting with the basics, **Figure 13-4** illustrates the observables of a rocket engine: plume intensity and motion. Recall Newton's third law which states that for every action there is an equal, but opposite reaction. The *action* in this case is expelling hot gas out the bottom end of the engine and the *reaction* is the missile experiencing upward force and motion. The upward force is the rate at which momentum is transferred to the rocket by the escaping gases:

$$F_M = \frac{\Delta m}{\Delta t} v_e \ [\text{N}], \qquad (13\text{-}2)$$

where $\frac{\Delta m}{\Delta t}$ is the mass burn (ejection) rate (kg · s^{-1}), and v_e is the gas escape speed (m·s^{-1}). The gas escape speed is a characteristic of the rocket engine's geometry (**Figure 13-5**) and the rocket fuel's chemistry.

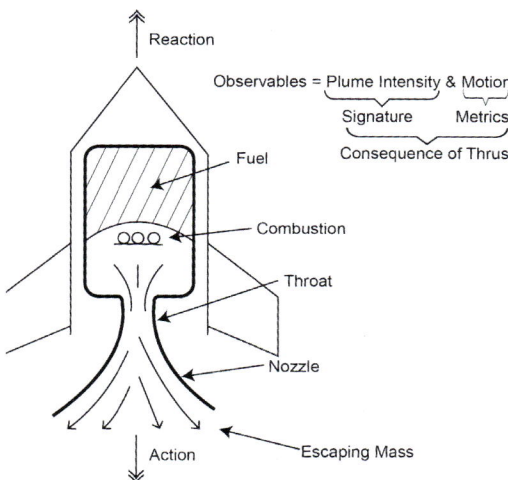

Figure 13-4
Observables of a rocket engine.

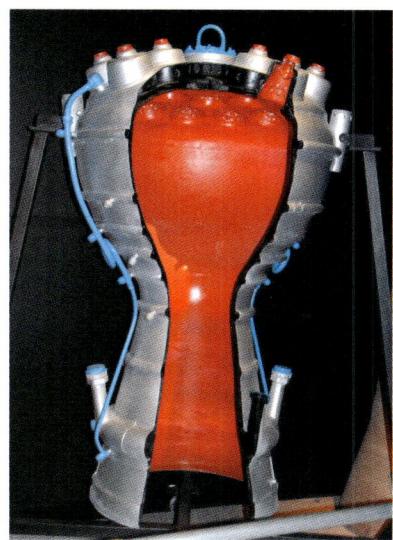

Figure 13-5
Cut-away model of a rocket engine combustion chamber, throat, and nozzle.

Mass burn rate, $\frac{\Delta m}{\Delta t}$, is not necessarily constant. There are two basic types of chemical fuel-burning missiles, liquid and solid, each having their own means of controlling burn rate. Liquid fueled missiles can easily open and close valves to allow more or less fuel to burn per unit time and can quench the flow altogether to save fuel for later burns. Solid fuel rockets generally cannot stop combustion until the burn has completed, but forward thrust may be terminated by redirecting the exhaust. Also, the rate of burn can be varied by the manner in which solid fuel is shaped inside the rocket body, as shown in **Figure 13-6**.

Looking straight up into the cylinder of a rocket body, the left drawing in **Figure 13-6** shows solid fuel like a hollow tube. Fuel burning occurs on its inner surface. So as the tube burns, its surface gets larger. This increases the mass flow rate and hence the thrust. The plot suggests this, and the thrust is termed "progressive." The center drawing depicts a rod of fuel inside and separate from the tube. Here, combustion occurs on both an outside and an inside surface; the one becomes larger while the other becomes smaller. The result is an approximately "neutral" thrust history. The drawing on the right suggests a "regressive" burn, where a rod of fuel burns inward.

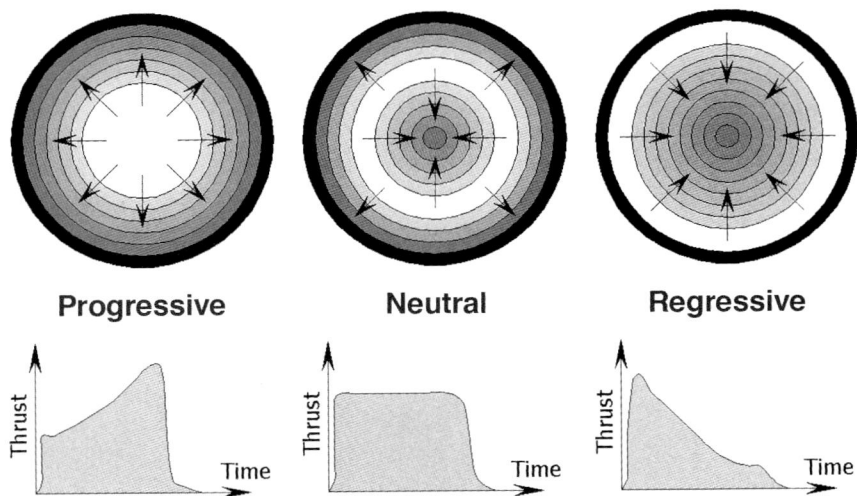

Figure 13-6
Top drawings are looking into a solid fuel rocket body. Arrows show direction of burn on the fuel's surface. Lower drawings suggest the resulting thrust. Increasing, unchanging, and decreasing thrust are called progressive, neutral, and regressive burns, respectively.

A common feature of these burns is a small thrust tail. Whereas liquid fuel rockets can have clean thrust termination by shutting off the valves (or running out of fuel), solid fuel rockets do not have such control. Non-uniformities in solid fuels make them sputter at the end in unpredictable ways, resulting in a small uncertainty in their total thrust.

As a consequence of nozzle shape and escape gas speed, the combustion products expelled from a rocket have a certain designed exit pressure, P_{NOZ} [N·m^{-2}]. This pressure can be greater than, equal to, or less than ambient atmospheric pressure, P_{ATM}. The difference in pressure inside and outside the nozzle acts on the effective cross-sectional exit area of the nozzle, A_{NOZ}, to add a force component on the rocket,

$$F_P = (P_{NOZ} - P_{ATM}) A_{NOZ} \quad [N], \quad (13\text{-}3)$$

which is upwards if $P_{NOZ} > P_{ATM}$. Otherwise, it is downwards. As a missile climbs, P_{ATM} decreases with increasing altitude (like **Equation 5-2** for number density), eventually becoming approximately zero in space (above five scale heights). Therefore, rocket engines will be designed to push a missile upwards above a critical altitude where $P_{NOZ} = P_{ATM}$.

Taken together, **Equations 13-2** and **13-3** give an upward force on a missile, called its *thrust*: [11]

$$\text{Thrust} \approx F_M + F_P \approx \frac{\Delta m}{\Delta t} v_e + (P_{NOZ} - P_{ATM}) A_{NOZ} \quad [N]. \quad (13\text{-}4)$$

Intuitively, the amount of radiation (the radiant intensity) of a rocket plume might be expected to be related to the thrust. After all, the more mass a rocket consumes, the larger its plume. A plume is characterized as a hot volume of gases. From far away, a large area surveillance sensor sees the projection of the plume's volume in its direction, an effective radiating area (see **Figure 4-10**). The apparent intensity is therefore proportional to a cross-sectional area of the plume (**Equation 4-20**). Suppose there is a representative dimension of the plume, S, such that its volume is S^3 and its cross-section is S^2. Then, it can be argued that

$$\text{Thrust} \sim \text{Volume} \sim S^3 \text{ and Intensity} \sim \text{Area} \sim S^2 \quad (13\text{-}5)$$

or

$$S \sim (\text{Thrust})^{1/3} \text{ while } S \sim (\text{Intensity})^{1/2}. \quad (13\text{-}6)$$

Combining these relations results in the phenomenological association between thrust and intensity:

$$\text{Thrust} \sim (\text{Intensity})^{3/2}. \qquad (13\text{-}7)$$

Equation 13-7, though only an intuitive proportionality at best, nonetheless gives intelligence analysts one means of typing the collected signatures of missiles approximately according to their size. [12]

Another measure of a rocket engine's performance is called specific impulse, or impulse per unit mass, I_{sp}. Formally, the physics definition is

$$I_{SP} = \frac{\text{Impulse}}{\text{Mass}} = \frac{\int F dt}{\Delta m} \left[\frac{\text{N·s}}{\text{kg}}\right], \qquad (13\text{-}8)$$

where F is the force causing the impulse (or change in momentum), which is thrust, and m is the mass of the body acted upon by the force.

Suppose thrust is approximately constant over an interval of time, Δt, **Equation 13-8** becomes

$$I_{SP} \approx \frac{F \Delta t}{\Delta m} = \frac{F}{\Delta m \frac{1}{\Delta t}} \approx \frac{F}{\frac{\Delta m}{\Delta t}} \left[\frac{\text{N}}{\text{kg·s}^{-1}}\right]. \qquad (13\text{-}9)$$

Although, a definition of specific impulse has now been provided, the historical definition[6] used by rocket scientists includes a factor of g, the gravity field (9.807 m·s^{-2}), to make the denominator the rate of weight (mg) flow:

$$I_{sp} = \frac{F}{\frac{\Delta(mg)}{\Delta t}} \quad [\text{s}], \qquad (13\text{-}10)$$

where the unit of specific impulse (thus defined) is just "seconds."

Specific impulse is an important missile parameter and is a function of fuel type. Fuels with higher I_{sp} values provide greater thrust (acceleration), as do fuels with higher bulk densities, and hence have greater range. **Tables 13-1** and **13-2** provide the I_{sp} values for some liquid and solid fuel combinations. Liquid fuels generally have higher values, but require more handling precautions.

Table 13-1
Specific impulses of some liquid fuels and oxidizer combinations given in units of seconds. [13], [14]

Oxidizer	Ammonia (NH_3)	RP-1*	UDMH**	50% UDMH and 50% Hydrazine	Hydrazine (N_2H_4)	Hydrogen
Liquid oxygen	294	300	310	312	313	391
Chlorine trifluoride	275	258	280	287	294	318
95% Hydrogen peroxide and 5% water	262	273	278	279	282	314
Red fuming nitric acid (15% NO_2)	260	268	276	278	283	326
Nitrogen tetroxide	269	276	285	288	292	341
Liquid fluorine	357	326	343	n/a	363	410

* Rocket Propellant-1 (RP-1) is a mixture of hydrocarbons with an effective chemical formula $CH_{1.97}$
** Unsymmetrical dimethyl hydrazine, chemical formula $(CH_3)_2N\text{-}NH_2$

[6] Perhaps because early rocket experimenters used the English system where there has always been confusion whether to treat the "pound" as a unit of mass or weight (force).

Table 13-2
Specific impulses of some solid fuel and oxidizer combinations. Typically, fuel and oxidizers are mixed with an inert binder. [13], [14]

Fuel Base	Oxidizer	I_{sp} (seconds)
Asphalt (bitumen)	Perchlorate	200
Nitrocellulose and nitroglycerine	(Self-oxidizing)	240
Polyurethane	Perchlorate	245
Carboxy-terminated polybutadiene (CTPB)	Perchlorate	260
Hydroxy-terminated polybutadiene (HTPB)	Perchlorate	260
Cross-linked double base	(Self-oxidizing)	270
Boron	Perchlorate	270
Metallic hydride	Fluoride	300

Note, many of the rocket fuels in **Tables 13-1** and **13-2** are nitrogen-hydrogen-carbon compounds. When oxidized (i.e., burned in the combustion chamber), the reaction products will be molecular nitrogen (N_2), water vapor (H_2O), and carbon dioxide (CO_2) (and, of course, many other environmentally unfriendly chemicals). The mixture of gases expelled out of the nozzle will be at a high temperature, typically 1,500–3,000 K depending on the fuel to oxidizer ratio. Therefore, thermal (near-blackbody) radiation may be expected to be seen from the bulk of the plume, together with selective radiation from the hot molecules. (See **Chapter 2**.) Since N_2 is a symmetric diatomic molecule, the line radiation will be dominated by H_2O, CO_2, and CO emission, resulting in a spectral signature like **Figure 13-7**. See **Example 2-9**.

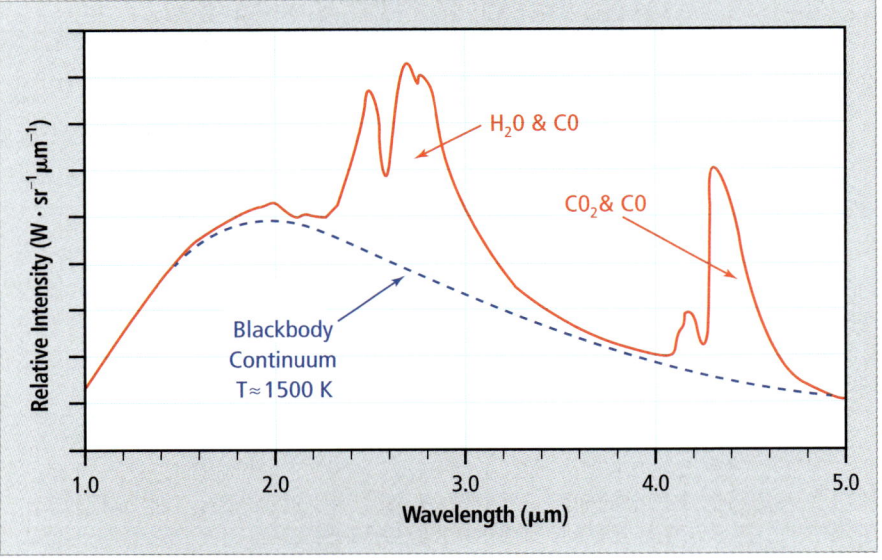

Figure 13-7
Simulated IR signature of an exhaust plume combining a thermal continuum with the emission of a burning hydrocarbon (as in **Example 2-6**).

The signature of **Figure 13-7** is what would be seen near the target without atmospheric attenuation. From far away, the signature will appear quite different, primarily because of H_2O and CO_2 molecules in the atmosphere. (See **Chapter 5** and **Figure 5-18**, in particular.) Therefore, selecting the appropriate bandpass to see this target depends on both its signature and atmospheric transmission.

Unfortunately, the IR wavelengths, where the signature is the strongest, are also the wavelengths where the atmosphere absorbs the most. But, there is one important difference. The signature emanates from *hot* molecules, whereas the atmosphere consists of *cold* molecules. For example, the top plot in **Figure 13-8** shows the IR vibrational spectrum of a hot diatomic combustion product molecule. It is "broad" (in terms of wavelength) because its high temperature populates its higher energy vibrational quantum states. (See **Chapter 2**.) The middle plot in **Figure 13-8** shows the detailed atmospheric transmission at the same wavelengths. It is inverted from the top plot because the same molecules in the atmosphere as in the signature are absorbing photons, and it is not as "broad." This is because the atmosphere's lower temperature does not allow the molecules' higher energy vibrational energy states to be populated. The result, shown in the bottom plot of **Figure 13-8**, is most of the central portion of the signature will be absorbed while the "hot wings" will pass through the atmosphere unabsorbed.

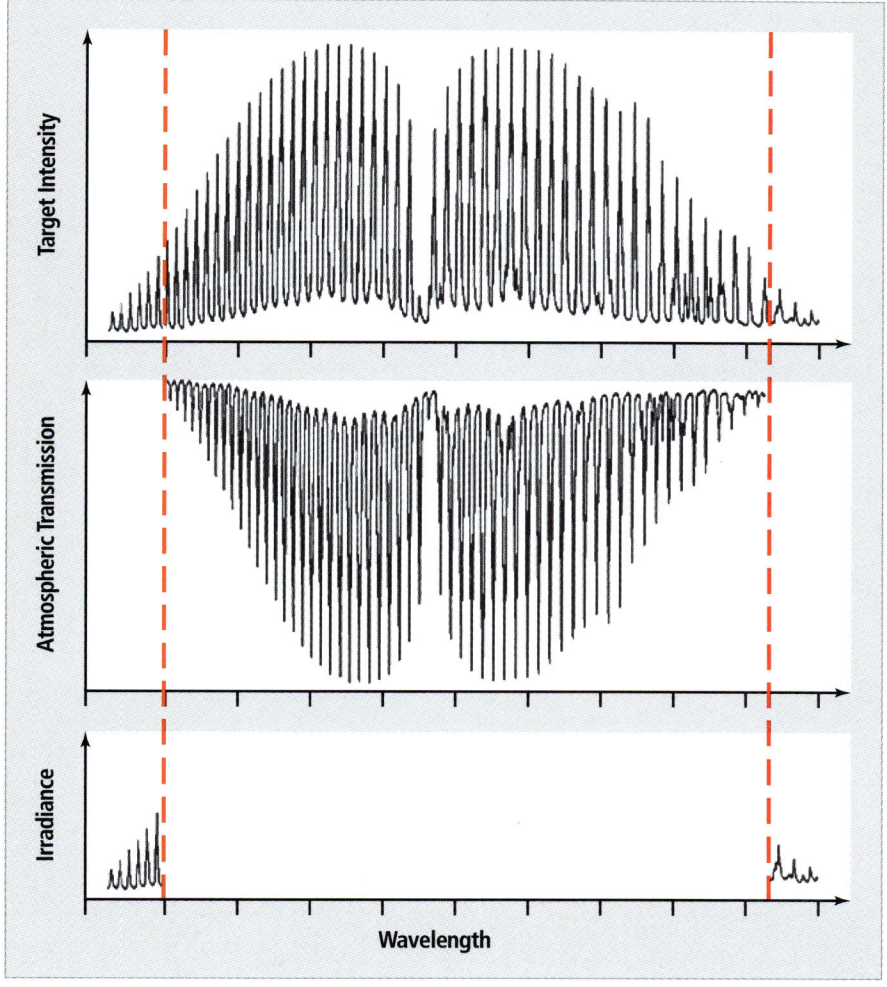

Figure 13-8
Concept of "hot wings." *Cold* molecules in the atmosphere absorb radiation emitted by the same *hot* molecules in an exhaust plume except for photons originating from high energy states.

Therefore, the greatest chance to observe a signature like **Figure 13-7** through the atmosphere is to look in the edges of the molecular emission bands. Using this strategy, extrapolations [7] suggest targets with spectral intensities on the order of 10^4 - 10^8 W · sr^{-1} μm^{-1} in the long-wavelength hot wing of the H_2O/CO emission band, about 2.9 - 3.1 μm. **Example 13-1** provides such a calculation.

When a target is on the ground, its signature will appear the weakest because of the greatest atmospheric attenuation. As the target climbs, the amount of atmosphere between itself and a remote sensor will decrease, thus the signature will increase. **Figure 13-9** plots the atmospheric transmission (for a vertical path through a standard atmosphere) as a function of target altitude, integrated in 2.9-3.1 μm band. The plot shows both a MODTRAN calculation and a Beer's Law approximation

[7] See Reference [15] for more information, where data given on page 268 (**Figure 14.4**) suggest a Delta-class mid-sized ICBM main engine has a measured spectral intensity of about 5×10^5 W · sr^{-1} μm^{-1}. The reference's page 131 (**Figure 6.1**) shows results of a calculation for a Titan II to be approximately 3×10^6 W · sr^{-1} μm^{-1}.

EXAMPLE 13-1: CAN A HOT TARGET BE DETECTED?

Can a remote electro-optic sensor (similar to that in **Example 10-1**) detect a hot target in the long-wavelength hot wing of the water band (2.9–3.1 μm) during the daytime (i.e., worst case)? Consider this prototype calculation. As deduced from **Chapter 10**, the electron output of a sensor viewing a point target (summed over the 45 pixels of its PSF), integrated over the bandpass is approximately

$$N_{TGT} \approx \frac{(0.84)\langle I_\lambda \rangle \overline{\tau_{ATM}} A_R \overline{\tau_{OPT}} \eta \overline{\lambda} \Delta\lambda \Delta t_{INT}}{R^2 \; hc} \quad \text{[electrons(per frame)]},$$

and the electron output from background (for the same detectors) is

$$N_{BKG} \approx \frac{\langle L_\lambda \rangle (0.84)(GSD)^2 \overline{\tau_{ATM}} A_R \overline{\tau_{OPT}} \eta \overline{\lambda} \Delta\lambda \Delta t_{INT}}{R^2 \; hc} \quad \text{[electrons(per frame)]},$$

(To approximate the integrals, the values of τ_{ATM} and τ_{OPT} have been assumed constant over the bandpass, and the off-boresight cosine term has been ignored.)

Suppose in-band intensities, $\langle I_\lambda \rangle$, run from 10^4 to 10^8 W·sr^{-1}μm^{-1}, and **Figure 5-33** shows the background radiance, $\langle L_\lambda \rangle$, is in the range of 0.15–0.45 W·m^{-2}sr^{-1}μm^{-1} for a standard Earth albedo of 0.30. Suppose the sensor has a large 8192 × 8192 pixel staring Focal Plane Array (FPA) that spans the entire Earth. At nadir, Ground Sample Distance (GSD) is approximately 1.56 × 1.56 km.

Since many of the terms in the two phenomenology equations above are common, the target-to-background ratio is simply

$$\frac{N_{TGT}}{N_{BKG}} \approx \frac{(0.84)\langle I_\lambda \rangle}{\langle L_\lambda \rangle (45)(GSD)^2}$$

and has the following values for the ranges of background radiance and target intensities expected.

		Target spectral intensity (W·sr^{-1}μm^{-1})				
		10^4	10^5	10^6	10^7	10^8
Background solar radiance (W·m^{-2}sr^{-1}μm^{-1})	0.15	3.8×10^{-4}	3.8×10^{-3}	3.8×10^{-2}	0.38	3.8
	0.45	1.3×10^{-4}	1.3×10^{-3}	1.3×10^{-2}	0.13	1.3

For all but the greatest intensity, the target signal is less than the background, apparently establishing the smallest target this sensor can detect during the daytime. If instead, the SNR is computed (as advised in **Chapter 10**), a different story emerges. Assuming photon noise to be the dominant noise source, divide the above phenomenological sensor electron output equations by quantum efficiency to find the expected numbers of photons. Then calculate the photon noise as in **Chapter 10**, and find the following.

		Target spectral intensity (W·sr^{-1}μm^{-1})				
		10^4	10^5	10^6	10^7	10^8
Background solar radiance (W·m^{-2}sr^{-1}μm^{-1})	0.15	4.2	42	410	3400	17000
	0.45	2.4	24	240	2300	15000

Thus, all but the smallest suggested target can be detected by this remote sensor when considering signal-to-noise instead of signal-to-background. This requires proper signal processing, which will be discussed in the next chapter.

(**Equation 5-27**). The inset in **Figure 13-9** plots the effect of the atmospheric transmission increase on apparent target intensity seen by a sensor. Suppose a target uniformly accelerates (boosts) from launch to 40 km altitude in 25 seconds and has a smooth progressive burn (black "source" line). The target's *apparent* intensity, after passing through the atmosphere, then increases as shown by the red *apparent* line.

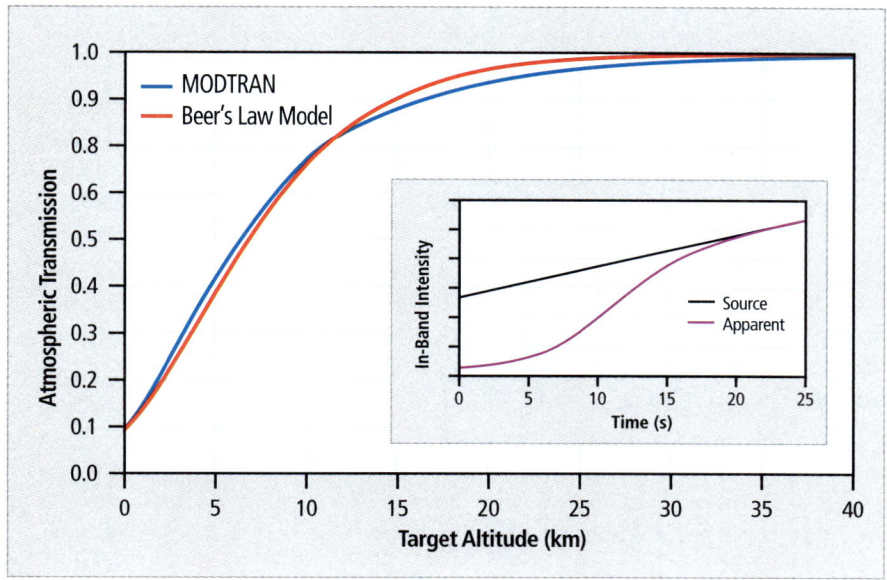

Figure 13-9
The transmission from a target increases as the target increases in altitude. The inset figure suggests how the apparent time-intensity signature is affected by the transmission.

OTHER PERSISTENT EVENTS

There are many other types of persistent targets, some that produce significant amounts of radiant intensity, that may be of interest:

- Large power generators
- Factories with smokestacks and/or heat exchangers
- Ore smelting and petroleum refining facilities
- Forest fires, volcanic eruptions, and lava flows
- Residential, industrial, and sports arena lighting
- Commercial and business districts (e.g., Times Square)

Typically, the SNR for these types of targets is fairly small, often less than one. Increasing integration time collects more photons from a source, but background increases at the same rate. So, little or no advantage is gained with an increase in integration time alone. (Furthermore, increased integration time exacerbates the pointing-tracking-stabilization problem if the target-sensor geometry changes during the collection.) With multiple stacked frames, however, signal strength co-adds to increase effective output proportional to the number of frames.[8,9] If noise is random and uncorrelated (background-driven photon noise), then total effective noise is the square root of the sum of squares of noise. That is, noise increases as the square root of the number of co-added frames. Thus, the enhanced SNR for M co-added frames is

$$(SNR)_{M \text{ FRAMES}} \approx \frac{M \times \text{Signal}}{\sqrt{M} \times \text{Noise}} \approx \sqrt{M}\,(SNR)_{1 \text{ FRAME}}, \quad (13\text{-}11)$$

which is an effectively increased sensitivity. [16], [17]

[8] Stacking (co-adding) frames requires analysis software that can align (register) the frames and adjust their magnifications if the geometry changed during the collection.

[9] Astronomers have used this technique in astrophotography for a long time. Most images of deep-sky objects are not single pictures of long exposure, but are multiple stacked pictures of short exposure. (To an astronomer, "long" means hours and "short" means minutes.)

13.3 TRANSIENT TARGETS

As stated previously, the working definition for a *transient* target is one with a response or signal that persists for five seconds or less. Man-made and natural types of targets of interest include nuclear detonations (initial phase) and lightning bolts.

Note, the temporal superposition of multiple, successive transient events may render their composite signature to look like persistent events. This phenomenon will be discussed at the end of this section.

NUCLEAR DETONATIONS

Since the dawn of the atomic age in 1945, monitoring for nuclear detonations has always been of great concern for evaluating the state of weapon development in "denied areas," for treaty monitoring, and for detecting the proliferation of nuclear technology into the third world. [18] The unmistakable signatures of above-ground (surface, atmospheric, or near-space) detonations of nuclear devices are easily detectable electromagnetic disturbances produced by bursts of gamma rays and x-rays, and pulses of ultraviolet through visible light. Subsequent interaction with the atmosphere extends the radiative signature into the radio and electrical power generation spectrum through a phenomenon called electromagnetic pulse. All of these initial radiations are transients, but their after-effects are persistent.

Programs to detect the transient radiative signatures of nuclear bursts began during the Cold War in the 1940s and continue today. First were the Vela series of satellites with non-imaging electro-optic silicon photodiode sensors called *bhangmeters* which could detect the characteristic double-humped signature of an initial millisecond-long flash followed by a second optical energy release lasting up to several seconds. The Vela satellites were replaced by similar bhangmeter sensors on board the DSP satellites, which were subsequently augmented by the Integrated Operational Nuclear Detection System on the Navstar GPS. [19], [20]

LIGHTNING BOLTS

Lightning is certainly a transient event. Literature describes a lightning bolt as an electric discharge, forging a current channel between cloud and ground, or cloud and cloud at a rate of ~ 10^8 m·s^{-1}. The duration of a single bolt may be only a few microseconds, depending on the length of the channel; although often multiple return strokes occurring in the same channel can boost the duration to several milliseconds. The persistence of human vision makes lightning bolts appear to last much longer.

Because lightning bolts are truly transient events, they are strictly non-steady state, so they do not have time to emit anything close to thermal radiation. Instead, the high energy of the passage of a large electrical current through the atmosphere dissociates all molecules and ionizes all atoms in the channel, leaving them in highly excited energy states (**Chapter 2**) and giving the particles (ions and electrons) high kinetic energy. Subsequently, ions and electrons strongly interact through the Coulomb force, producing "free-free" transitions between their non-quantized kinetic energy states. This results in a bright continuum of radiation called *bremsstrahlung*, or "braking radiation," in the microwave through ultraviolet. Meanwhile, excited oxygen, nitrogen, hydrogen, and other ions and atoms produce additional line radiation at their respective energies as they relax to lower energy states. Again, this characteristic radiation adds to the microwave through ultraviolet spectrum of the flash.

Perhaps as many as 50 lightning flashes occur worldwide every second, with the majority above the clouds, i.e., cloud-to-cloud. Hence, there is a high likelihood that lightning should be detectable looking down from space. In 1970, a Defense Meteorological Support Program satellite was equipped with a simple non-imaging broad area (700 × 700 km) silicon photodiode sensor, and thousands of lightning flashes were observed with estimated radiative power (in the 0.3 – 1.1 μm silicon band) between 10^8 and 10^{10} W, with 10^9 W being the median and a few significantly more powerful. [21] Indeed, rare lightning "superbolts" with estimated (in-band) radiative powers of $10^{11} - 10^{13}$ W were detected by the Vela satellite sensors. [22]

Lightning may thus serve as a prototype for detection of other transient events of interest. **Example 13-2** gives examples of calculations for signal-to-background and signal-to-noise that demonstrate the sensor parameters required to detect a transient event such as lightning.

EXAMPLE 13-2: DETECTING LIGHTNING

For a prototype detector to investigate whether lightning bolts can be detected from space, consider the simplified device shown here. A silicon photodiode is exposed directly to photons through an open collimator tube; there are no focusing optics.

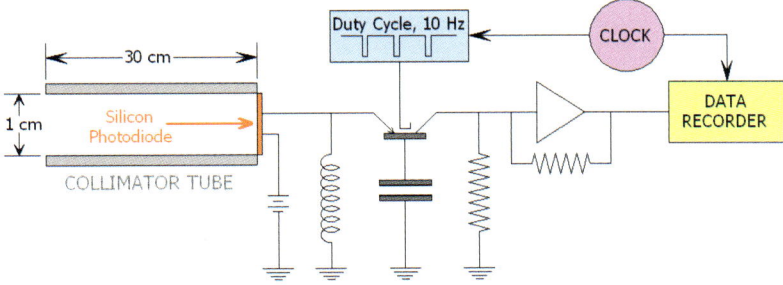

This detector is intended to be hand-held by an astronaut on a space station, perhaps 250 km above the Earth. The FOV is approximately

$$\Omega \approx \pi \frac{(1 \text{ cm})^2}{4(30 \text{ cm})^2} \approx 8.73 \times 10^{-4} \text{ sr},$$ which allows an astronaut the ability

Continued on next page

to sample a 55 km² area (8.3 km across), which should be big enough to take in several thunderstorm cells where lightning might be expected.

If the detector is set to time-sample with a near-100% duty cycle at a frequency of 10 Hz, then expect to collect one or two (at most) data points per bolt. With the silicon photodiode having roughly 50% quantum efficiency in the 0.3–1.1 μm band, and atmospheric losses negligible for cloud-top lightning, the detector's output is approximately

$$N_{BOLT} \approx \frac{\Phi}{4\pi R^2} A_R \frac{\eta \Delta t_{INT}}{hc/\overline{\lambda}} \approx 17.6\Phi \text{ [electrons]}.$$

Meanwhile, the background the astronaut might expect to collect is at most direct sunlight reflecting off cloud tops at approximately $L \approx 390$ W·m⁻²sr⁻¹ in the bandpass. The maximum reflected background at night would be under a full moon, which amounts to about $L \approx 9.8 \times 10^{-4}$ W·m⁻²sr⁻¹. The output from the simple detector due to background is then

$$N_{BKG} \approx L\Omega A_R \frac{\eta \Delta t_{INT}}{hc/\overline{\lambda}} \approx 1.21 \times 10^{10} L \text{ [electrons]}.$$

Comparing a lightning signal to background, the following is calculated, where lightning bolts of all sizes are larger than the background at night, but not during the day.

		Lightning bolt power (W)					
		10^8	10^9	10^{10}	10^{11}	10^{12}	10^{13}
Reflected Radiance (W·m⁻²sr⁻¹)	(Daytime) 390	3.7×10^{-4}	3.7×10^{-3}	3.7×10^{-2}	0.37	3.7	37
	(Nighttime) 0.00098	15	150	1500	1.5×10^4	1.5×10^5	1.5×10^6

Can lightning bolts be detected during the day? Refer to **Example 13-1** to discover that calculating the SNR instead of signal-to-background reveals that detection should be possible. Assuming photon noise is the dominant noise source in this example as well, the calculation can be mimicked in the previous example to show the following values for SNR:

		Lightning bolt power (W)					
		10^8	10^9	10^{10}	10^{11}	10^{12}	10^{13}
Reflected Radiance (W·m⁻²sr⁻¹)	(Daytime) 390	1200	1.1×10^4	1.1×10^5	9.8×10^5	5.3×10^6	1.9×10^7
	(Nighttime) 0.00098	5.7×10^4	1.9×10^5	5.9×10^5	1.9×10^6	5.9×10^6	1.9×10^7

This example shows it should be possible to detect some transient events from space. More sophisticated and sensitive sensors should be able to push the envelope to smaller and more distant targets.

CHEMICAL EXPLOSIONS

Most transient events are chemical explosions; the physics and chemistry of a conventional air-delivered bomb can be described as a typical transient target. Examples of these bombs are shown in **Figure 13-10**. Bombs are usually about 50% explosive material[10] and 50% cast iron casings.[11] **Figure 13-11** illustrates the typical components of a generic bomb. A blasting cap in the fuse initiates a detonation wave in the explosive material which completes the chemical reaction in microseconds.[12]

Figure 13-10
MK-82, 83, 84 general purpose 500, 1000, 2000 pound bombs.

Figure 13-11
Illustration of the general make-up of a bomb.

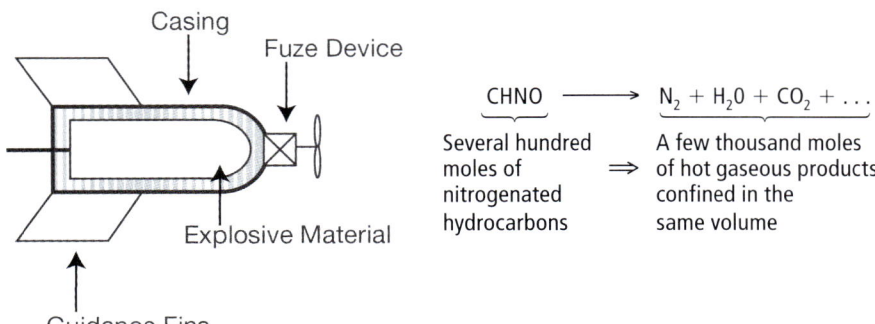

The chemical reaction is "self oxidizing" in that there is an internal rearrangement of atoms into a state of lower chemical potential. The excess energy between that initially stored in the explosive compound and that of its products makes the reaction exothermic and contributes to the heat and kinetic energy of the explosion. The order in which reaction products are normally created is N_2 first, then H_2O, followed by carbon oxides, and finally O_2 if any remains. The creation of carbon oxides is important. The reaction wants to burn the carbon to its lowest energy state, CO_2, but if there is not enough oxygen, the reaction will stop at CO. If there is not enough oxygen to form CO, then the explosion will yield just C, which is soot. Hot CO and C from an incomplete reaction are likely to produce a secondary extended "afterburn" when combining with ambient air. **Figure 13-12** shows the reactions of one mole of three typical explosive compounds.[13] **Table 13-3** lists other typical explosives, their make-up, and TNT equivalent. [23]

[10] The amount of explosive materials in a bomb is measured in moles. Recall a mole is one Avagadro's number of molecules: 6.02×10^{23} molecules. Typically, one mole of an explosive compound (**Table 13-3**) has a mass of about 220 g and occupies a volume of about a tea cup.

Figure 13-12
Some explosive compounds and their reaction products.

[11] The cast iron used in general purpose bombs is deliberately **not** uniform in density. It has intentional cracks, fissures, and impurities to facilitate its breaking into lethal pieces of flying shrapnel. Some special purpose bombs (and artillery shells) have hardened shells to direct the explosion in propelling the blast forward (as in a tank penetrator weapon).

[12] The chemical reaction completed in microseconds is a "detonation" and occurs on a time scale too fast to be detected as such by large area surveillance sensors. The subsequent expansion of hot reaction products and its aftermath is an "explosion" lasting fractions of seconds to seconds—long enough to be detected.

[13] These compounds are explosive (unstable) because of the delicate electrical balance of the N^+–O^- bonds.

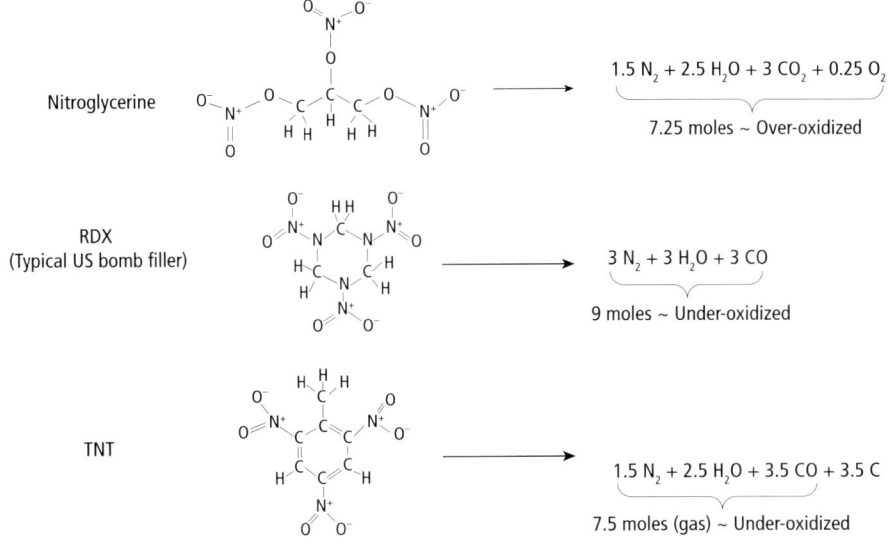

CHAPTER 13 TEMPORAL SENSING: TARGETS & SIGNATURES

Table 13-3
Common explosive compounds used in manufacturing weapons and their typical TNT equivalent values [24], [25].

Name	Composition	TNT Equivalent*
Ammonium Nitrate	(Fertilizer)	0.56
Black Powder	74% Potassium nitrate, 10% sulfur, 15% charcoal	0.50
C-4	91% RDX, 9% Plasticizer	1.30
Dynamite	75% RDX, 15% TNT, 5% Starch, 5% Oil	1.22
Nitroglycerine	(See **Figure 13-12**)	1.40
Propellant, Gun (5 in)	Nitroglycerine/Nitrocellulose + Stabilizer	1.00
RDX	(See **Figure 13-12**)	1.50
TNT	(See **Figure 13-12**)	1.00
Tritonal	80% TNT, 20% Al	1.24

*1kg TNT $\approx 4.184 \times 10^6$ J released

The chronology and physics phenomenology of a typical general purpose bomb explosion after its detonation are as follows: [26]

- Thousands of moles of hot gases are initially confined within the volume of the bomb casing and have pressures of thousands of atmospheres and temperatures of tens of thousands of degrees Kelvin;
- Expansion of the gases fractures the iron casing, propelling shrapnel at speeds up to Mach 1;
- About 60–80% of the chemical energy goes into kinetic energy of the shell casing, 10–30% into expansion of the gases (shock wave and work on surrounding air), and 5–10% into thermal radiation;[14]
- The fireball expands to 10–40 m radius in approximately 10 ms (faster than one video frame at 30 Hz) until pressure more or less equilibrates with the atmosphere, and cools rapidly to temperatures of 500–1,000 K;
- The complete explosion takes only 0.5 to 1.0 seconds, depending on the size of bomb, target interaction, details of weapon delivery, meteorological conditions, etc.; and finally
- Any un-combusted particles (C, Al as an additive, etc.) or incomplete reactions (CO) may burn to completion (CO_2, Al_2O_3) very rapidly in the collapsing fireball ("afterburning") when mixing with ambient air. The temperature of afterburning may reach 800 to 1,200 K.

Field tests and experience have demonstrated that numerous types of isolated explosive events have similar time-intensity signatures, sketched in **Figure 13-13**. Although explosions are transient and non-equilibrium in human terms, they are sufficiently steady-state in physics terms (photon transient time across a fireball) and opaque to be considered as thermal radiators, albeit rapidly cooling. Signatures of explosions are therefore

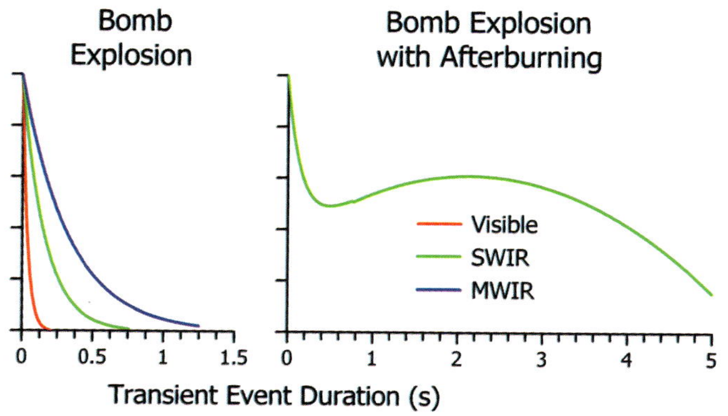

Figure 13-13
Notional transient event time-history radiation signatures. (Only the SWIR signature is sketched for an after burning event. Its shape depends on target materials and uncombusted chemicals.)

[14] The purpose of a bomb blast and shock are not necessarily to produce radiation. Nevertheless, the generation of thermal through visible light is a notable side effect that allows an electro-optic sensor to detect it.

necessarily more persistent at longer wavelengths. The Nyquist Sampling Theorem suggests that a framing rate (assuming staring sensor) of about 10 Hz is required to collect this type of signature. Faster rates would be acceptable, but the resulting shorter sampling time decreases sensitivity to low intensity signals while (unnecessarily) increasing the data rate to be processed, analyzed, and potentially archived. [27]

Successful collection of transient events by framing sensors is problematic because of their duty cycles. For example, **Figure 13-14** serves as a reminder that periodic integration (accumulation) of a signature provides a discrete time signal that does not show details that happen faster than the duty cycle (Nyquist's Theorem).

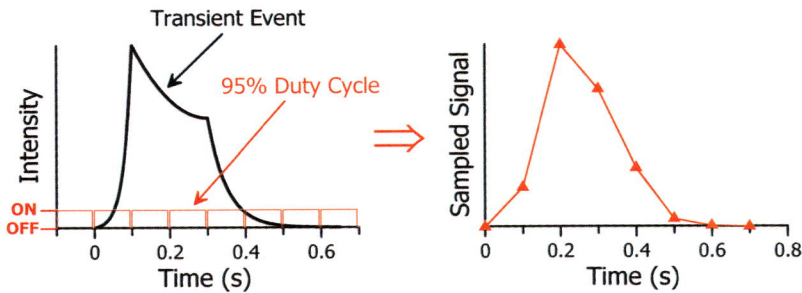

Figure 13-14
Temporal sampling of a hypothetical transient event's signature.

Furthermore, a peculiar difficulty with sampling transient events is they are not synchronized with a sensor's duty cycle, but may begin anytime during an integration time. The timing offset, or phasing, will cause a sensor's temporal output signal to have vastly different appearances. **Figure 13-15** shows what one event may look like if sampled by three different sensors (or three identical events sampled by one sensor).

Figure 13-15
Multiple samples of an event by non-synchronized sensors (or sampling of multiple identical events) yield different apparent time histories depending on the phasing between when the event starts and the sensor's duty cycle.

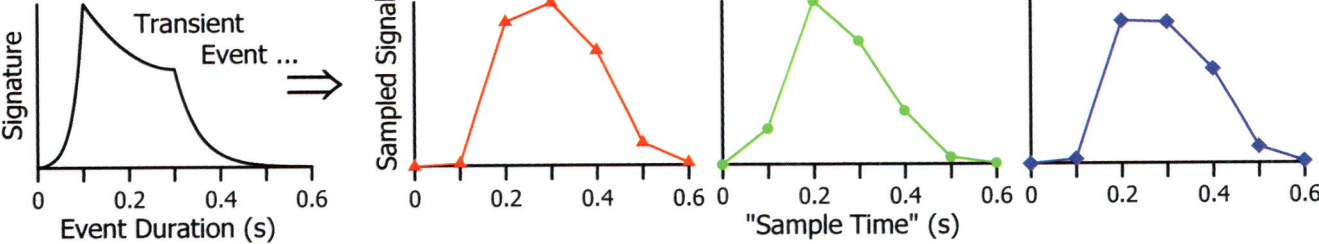

SUPERPOSITION OF EVENTS

An intermediate temporal class of targets is the "quasi-persistent" event. This is actually a superposition of transient events overlapping so as to appear like a single persistent event. Examples are weapons that are fired in salvos, like the Multiple Launch Rocket Systems (MLRS) (pictured in **Figure 13-16**) and carpet bombing (**Figure 13-17**). Some area and anti-personnel weapons like cluster bombs have also extended temporal signatures when hundreds of individual two to five pound "bomblets" strike the ground. Each bomblet may have a transient signature no longer than about 0.2 seconds, but together the composite signature may last for several seconds.

Figure 13-16
A truck-mounted MLRS and a MLRS canister at the White Sands Missile Range Museum, New Mexico.

Figure 13-17
A B-52 bomber drops a load of conventional bombs; a quasi-persistent signature in the making.

14 INTERPRETING NON-LITERAL FPA DATA

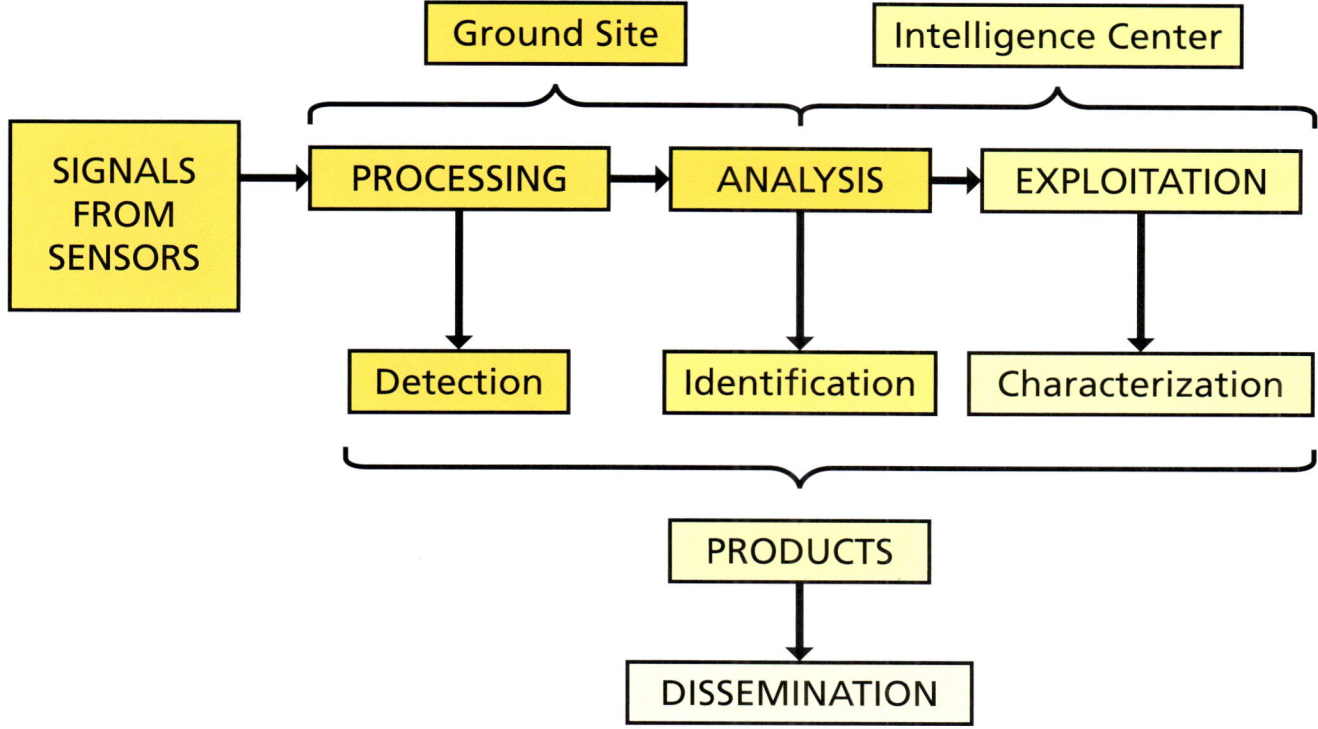

The objective of advanced technical intelligence collection is to obtain literal (visual or photographic) and non-literal (signature and metric) information about targets of interest, mostly foreign weapon systems and other potential threats. Sensors have become increasingly sensitive and sophisticated to accomplish this mission, but remember their output signals are target information as sampled by the sensor's spatial, temporal, and spectral collection strategies. Output signals also contain as much (or more) of a target's background and noise, which must be separated from the target. Therefore, it is necessary to understand the sampling schemes, background, and noise, which were the subjects of previous chapters, and remove them, which is the subject of this chapter. While target information extraction from sensor signals may be generally called data processing, or digital signal processing, this chapter categorizes it into three phases, processing, analysis, and exploitation, which can be generic to any scanning or staring sensor's data stream. [1] Remember, the use of the word "target" refers to the object of interest.

SECTIONS
14.1 PROCESSING
14.2 ANALYSIS
14.3 EXPLOITATION

The general flow of information-bearing signals from remote sensors is to one or several ground sites where it may be processed or distributed to other intelligence centers. Data collected for reconnaissance purposes are mostly from low-orbiting platforms or aircraft. Often, all collected data is scrutinized because it is for specifically tasked collections against known or suspected targets and activities. In contrast, signals from large area surveillance sensors in Geosynchronous Orbits (GEO) or Highly Elliptical Orbits (HEO) are nearly devoid of target information; events of interest are relatively few and far between, and the times and places of their occurrence are not known in advance.

Therefore, data flow for large area surveillance sensors follows a scheme like **Figure 14-1**. At a sensor's ground site, its signal goes straight to storage. On its way, the data stream is watched by computer algorithms that are programmed to recognize the time-intensity signatures of some transient, quasi-persistent, and persistent events. The signals may also be displayed in near real time and watched by trained human operators who can correlate possible events with their geographic locations, match them with priority lists of targets of interest, and put them into context of the world situation. With the computer's assisted event recognition, human operators copy segments of sensors' data streams into data packages containing suspected targets. [2]

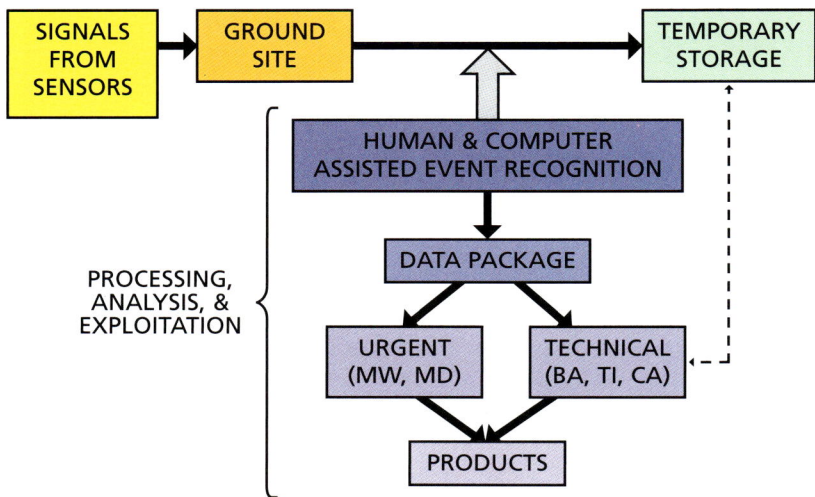

Figure 14-1
Data flow for large area surveillance sensors. Data in temporary storage may be recalled later for processing, but cannot be kept indefinitely. Missions cited as "urgent" are Missile Warning (MW) and Missile Defense (MD). Missions noted as "technical" include Battlespace Awareness (BA), Technical Intelligence (TI), and Civil Applications (CA).

Depending on a sensor's mission (see **Section 13.1**), end users may or may not require information immediately from collections (as discussed in **Chapter 1**, see **Figure 1-3** in particular). If urgent processing is needed, the products for detection and identification are required within minutes and are most logically prepared as close to the sensor's ground site as feasible. Otherwise, data packages may be turned over to off-site intelligence centers for in-depth product development over longer time scales. In either case, there is a commonality of steps in processing sensor data which will now be discussed.

14.1 PROCESSING

The first goal in signal processing is to determine if targets are present. High intensity targets, such as intercontinental ballistic missiles, with large signal-to-background ratios should be easy to detect, but perhaps not low-intensity targets. An issue with target detection is ascertaining that a sensor is providing appropriate output responses to inputs, as studied in **Chapter 10**. Sensors with many detectors, either in rows for scanning or in a grid-like array for staring, unfortunately sometimes deliver false signals due to erratic operation or manufacturing defects. Such failures are generally termed "artifacts" in the data. [3]

Sensor artifacts are independent of input and can be caused by manufacturing issues: contamination, variations in quality control, or faulty electrical connections. Artifacts may not be constant, but can vary as a result of sensor operating conditions (like fluctuating bias voltage as batteries charge and discharge), temperature changes (primarily from diurnal and seasonal solar loading), and aging. Every sensor has its own unique and peculiar artifacts which must be studied and documented to understand and mitigate their effects on output signals.

BAD PIXELS

Inappropriate detector response, known as "bad pixels" on a focal plane, is one sensor artifact that impacts data. **Figure 14-2** shows a manufacturing defect and a consequential result of a defective detector in an image. Anecdotally, less than 1% of detectors in arrays are noted to give an erratic response that is not proportional to photon input. [4] These defects can usually be mitigated by applying "masks" to the data stream for the purpose of "blanking out" these pixels. Obviously, the information contained in these pixels is lost for radiometric and spectral exploitation, as well as some potential loss of spatial coverage.

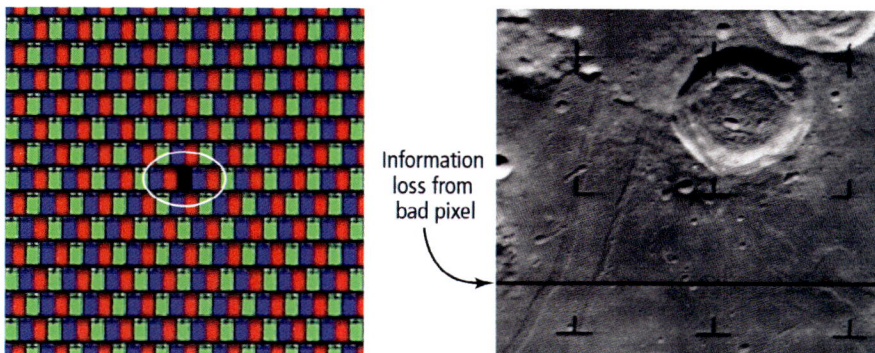

Figure 14-2
A defective cell on a LCD television screen (left), and the unmistakable track of a bad detector in a lunar probe's scanner (right).

The response of defective detectors can be over-, under-, or non-responding, or a mixture thereof. Various terms are used to describe these types of detectors. "Happy" or "hot" pixel describes a detector that is always saturated, delivering maximum output regardless of input. At the other extreme, "dead" pixel describes a detector that gives zero output. There are also recognized "noisy" pixels that have a Root Mean Square (RMS) noise exceeding the mean of the entire focal plane. Terms such as "slightly," "moderately," or "extremely" are applied to noisy detectors depending on the value of their RMS noise. These designations do not necessarily mean the information from a defective detector is unusable, but it must be used with caution or only in some of the data processing steps.

If the ultimate goal is to solve for spectral intensity of a point target (**Equation 10-4**), it is necessary to have a correct value of output from every detector within the target's Point Spread Function (PSF). How is this possible if there are bad pixels within an image (the PSF)? These inappropriate outputs must be replaced with appropriate ones. [5]

[1] The "median filter" method uses the nine values of eight surrounding detectors plus the "bad" value, so there will be an odd number of values. This is not necessary. One could use eight values and take an average of the middle two or any other reasonable method. The logic in using nine values is to use integer arithmetic, which is computationally faster than floating point arithmetic.

Numerous methods have been designed and implemented to recover the information from inappropriately responding detectors. For example, **Figure 14-3** shows the replacement of a single "bad" detector's output with the median value of the eight surrounding detectors.[1] Obviously, if there are groups or clusters of "bad" detectors, more sophisticated methods are required to replace them with accurate and useful information. [6] In any case, remember the value(s) used to replace faulty values are only estimates. The correct values are unknown, but analysts must select reliable methods that they hold in high confidence. In cases where the locations of "bad" detectors are known from previous experience, the correction algorithm can run in the background before further processing.

Figure 14-3
Example of median replacement for a "bad" detector. (Values represent detector output digitized to 12 bits.) The 4095 value within a PSF is a "happy" pixel and is clearly incorrect. The replacement value of 2314 is likely incorrect as well, but it is closer to being correct.

FOCAL PLANE ARRAY CORRECTIONS

Two other phenomena appearing in the output of photodetectors that could be considered artifacts affecting all the pixels on a focal plane array (FPA) were already mentioned in **Chapter 7**: 1) dark current; and 2) variations in quantum efficiency from detector to detector. **Figures 7-23** and **7-24** explain that dark current is a detector's output as a consequence of being turned on, and variations in quantum efficiency cause each detector to have a higher or lower output when seeing the same input. Again, because of the goal for radiometric accuracy, these artifacts must be mitigated. [7]

The correction for dark current is fairly simple. Record the output for every detector when there is no input (a "dark frame") and subtract these values from data frames. Here, assume dark current values thus obtained are noise–free and will remain reasonably consistent. Since the physical origin of dark current is probably associated with both solid-state energy level thermal populations and bias voltage, these assumptions are not necessarily valid in the long run. Ideally, a dark frame should accompany every collection. Practically, this is usually not possible, but should be accomplished frequently. **Figure 14-4a** shows what a dark frame could look like with detectors on the right side of a FPA having somewhat more dark current than those on the left.

Figure 14-4
a) Example of a possible dark frame from a staring FPA. b) Example of a possible flat frame from a staring FPA. (Right photo courtesy of http://commons.wikimedia.org/wiki/File:CCD_Flat_Field.jpg; GNU Free Documentation License, Version 1.2 or later: H. Raab (User:Vesta), Johannes-Kepler-Observatory, Linz, Austria (http://www.sternwarte.at).)

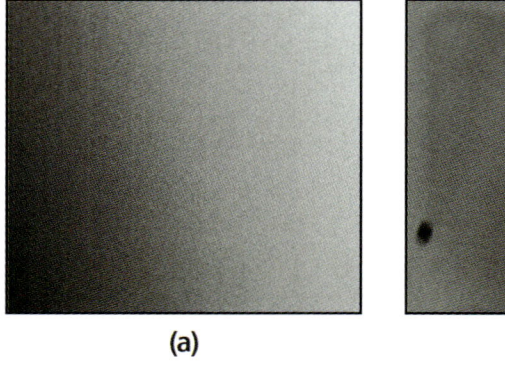
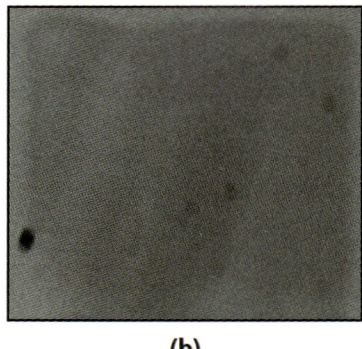

(a)   (b)

274 CHAPTER 14 INTERPRETING NON-LITERAL FPA DATA

Practically, how does a remote sensor in space accomplish a dark frame? A mechanical shutter over a telescope's aperture or a smaller opaque filter that can be inserted into the optical system are options. Although such devices are possible; unserviceable moving parts on spacecraft are generally avoided because of their potential for mission-ending failure.[2] The alternative is to turn the sensor around and collect data of "deep space" where there are no (or few) emitting or reflecting light sources.

As suggested in **Chapter 7**, the solution to the second full-frame artifact, variations in quantum efficiency, is to collect a "flat frame" from a uniform external or internal calibration source: flood the focal plane with equal input to every detector. The right side of **Figure 14-4b** shows how such a frame could look. It is apparent there is considerable variation with three regions of lower response (dark areas), two sections of higher response (upper left and more-or-less diagonally), and some obvious anomalies. There are also small groupings and individual light-colored detectors that may be defective detectors. The four brightest areas on top and bottom edges may be where mechanical or electrical attachments to the FPA are perturbing the collection. In principle, the output values of all appropriately responding pixels in a flat frame can be averaged to find the FPA's expected response. A scaling factor can then be determined for every pixel to "level" its output to the average. As with the dark frame, a flat frame should accompany every collection, but this is impractical to take time from a busy observing schedule.

As with the dark frame, on-board solutions for accomplishing a flat frame are impractical. Moving parts (at least a mirror needed to re-direct a sensor's Field of View (FOV)) and a stable, reliable source are required. A better solution is a broad, uniform external source (as in **Figure 7-25**). Such a source is further discussed as one for radiometric calibration in **Section 14.3**.

OTHER ARTIFACTS

Since advanced technical intelligence collectors are developed and fielded as very costly long-term programs, the sensors themselves are not carbon copies, but each one is unique. Therefore, to discover and understand individual artifacts, each sensor must be turned on and operated in extensive pre-launch testing. Even then, the space environment will inevitably induce changes in sensors' operation. Analysts will certainly notice, in particular, the electronic performances of a charge-coupled device and complimentary metal oxide semiconductor detector arrays will display temperature, voltage, and age artifacts. Streaks, shadows, and blooming are common in a FPA response, like persistence on the retina of the eye when looking at bright lights. For instance, **Figures 7-27**, **7-28**, **12-11**, and **Example 13-4** all suggest sensor electronics include capacitance (C), inductance (L), and resistance (R). Such circuitry always operates on specific *time constants* related to the combinations RC and L/R. The duty cycle and read-out of each detector's well cannot happen faster than a circuit's natural time constant, $\sqrt{LC}$.

As artifacts associated with a sensor's electronics are discovered, methods and techniques must be developed to compensate for them. However, because artifacts will change with conditions, it is impossible to always correct for them, leaving some uncertainty in later results based on detector output signals. At best, understanding artifacts may

[2] The Hubble Space Telescope has a commandable shutter for protection from micrometeorites and intense solar activity. By design, the Hubble was serviced by visiting astronauts who could presumably repair any problems with the mechanism.

lead to statistical expectations of their influence on detection, identification, and characterization products, which emphasize the assertion that such information products are estimates.

14.2 ANALYSIS

Once artifacts are cleaned from a data stream as much as possible, the second goal of processing, here called "analysis," is to separate a target's signal from noise and background. This is often called extraction and prepares it for metric and signature exploitation.

If the signal-to-noise ratio is large, noise mitigation is primarily a matter of statistically characterizing the fluctuations. The characterization could be completed detector-by-detector or taken as a spatial average over the range of detectors covering the target. In either case, the procedure is straightforward:

1. Select data frames that do <u>not</u> contain the target, either before or after the target's duration, or both.
2. Find the mean value of the output for these frames/detectors using **Equation 10-10**.
3. Calculate the effective values of the RMS noise using **Equation 10-11**.
4. Assume the RMS noise will remain constant for the duration of the event, and
5. Subtract it from the target frames/detectors.

If the RMS noise is thought to drift, or if the target moves across a field of detectors, then estimation schemes using temporal and/or spatial averaging may be developed.

Alternatively, if signal-to-noise is small, as suggested in **Figure 14-5**, the method of co-addition discussed at the end of **Section 13.2** may be applicable.

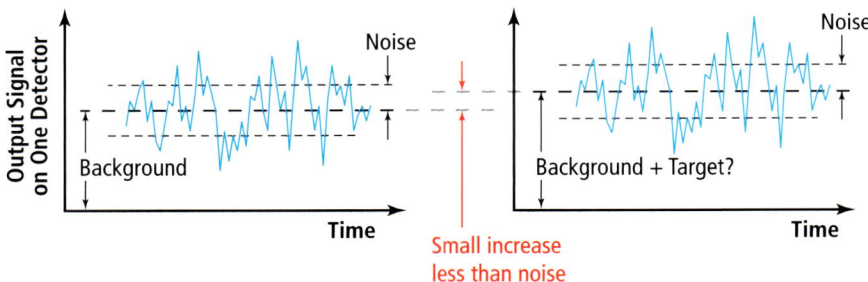

Figure 14-5
A small increase in detector output due to the appearance of a target may require alternative algorithms.

BACKGROUND SUPPRESSION

As for background, if it were temporally constant, although spatially varying, it would be simple to remove through subtraction of an initial frame without a target from all subsequent frames containing a target. But unfortunately, the background continuously changes due to effects such as sensor and platform motion, temporal variation of the scene within the sensor FOV, and sensor pointing inaccuracies and instabilities (jitter). Anecdotal experience with hand-held video cameras, for instance, shows that jitter often dominates the change in background on short time scales to produce what is typically called "clutter." **Figure 14-6** gives a simplified example.

Figure 14-6
Four different spatial samples of a scene as a sensor's line of sight jitters. The line of sight is in continuous motion, so the pixel placements represent their average positions during their respective frames.

For urgent processing and when signal-to-noise is expected to be high, a moving average (or "fading memory") clutter suppression technique can help remove background and isolate targets. This method is shown in **Figure 14-7** for the output of a single detector or a group of detectors. Since targets of interest rarely pass through the FOV of a particular detector (pixel), most frames (or scans) are assumed to contain only cluttered background plus noise. The effect of clutter and noise in a given frame can be reduced by taking an average (detector by detector) of several previous frames and subtracting it from the present frame. Averaging "smooths" the signal and the subtraction results (the "residual") should ideally show zero, or at least nothing larger than the RMS noise, which can be set as a detection threshold. [8]

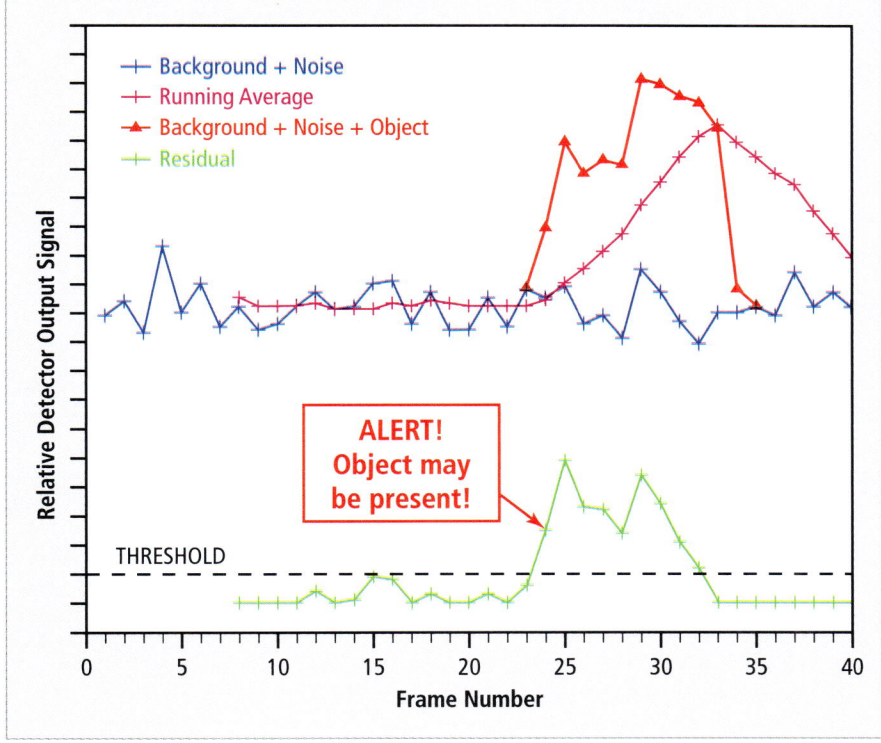

Figure 14-7
An example of how moving average background clutter and noise suppression might assist in detecting a target.

When an object appears in the FOV, the output signal will rise, of course, and so will the average, but only after a delay of a few frames. As **Figure 14-7** shows, the residual rises above threshold, and an assisting computer target recognition algorithm, or a human operator, will be alerted that an object may have been detected. At this time (not shown in the figure), the moving average clutter and noise suppression would be turned off, and the last and best-known background value would be taken and subtracted from the signal through the duration of the object's presence. In practice, this technique should remove sufficient background to allow signature identification, but is not adequate for accurate radiometric intensity calculation (**Equation 10-4**).

To achieve greater radiometric accuracy, more computer- and time-intensive methods are available for background/clutter/noise suppression and signature extraction. These methods can be applied after the fact to already processed urgent mission requirement collection (recalled from temporary storage as the dashed line in **Figure 14-1**), or applied to new collections for non-time-critical missions. Such technical analysis thus occurs off-line.

A proven reliable technique for handling and removing background is the multi-variate statistical method called Principal Components (PC). (See Sidebar **Principal Components** and **Example 14-1**.) PC is fundamentally like a two-dimensional spatial Fourier transform,[3] but is very matrix algebra-intensive. (It will show up again in the analysis of multi-spectral data beginning in **Chapter 15**.) The computer algorithms implemented for PC are known as singular value or proper orthogonal decompositions and are variations developed in the Karhunen-Loeve and the Hotelling transformations (**Figure 14-8**). [9]

Figure 14-8
Joseph Fourier (1768–1830) and Michel Loeve (1907–1979) who collaborated on the Karhunen-Loeve and Hotelling transformations. (Photo of Michel Loeve courtesy of http://en.wikipedia.org/wiki/File:Michel_Lo%C3%A8ve.jpg; GNU Free Documentation License, Version 1.2 or later: George M. Bergman.)

As a transform, PC calculates an approximation of the background a sensor has seen behind a target. With M frames of a $M \times M$-pixel section of a FPA, PC could, in theory, calculate up to M^2 PCs and assemble them together to synthesize what the average background looks like in each frame. For collections with significant motion and jitter, experience with Fourier signals analysis shows that perhaps only the first 10% of the components are necessary to adequately characterize a background. **Figure 14-9** shows an artistic license of what the first three PCs may look like to characterize the scene sampled in **Figure 14-6**. After a background

[3] See Sidebar **Fourier Analysis** in Chapter 17.

PRINCIPAL COMPONENTS

Data sets are usually collected in a format that is convenient to the instrument designed and used to take the collection. For instance, the data frames in **Figure 14-6** are represented by arrays of pixel values, one for each frame. Because of platform motion and jitter, the background does not look the same in every frame. The method of PCs finds the most likely appearance of the background by transforming what has been seen by the sensor to a representation of how the background presents itself. That is, PC finds the background in its own coordinate system rather than the sensor's. The following is an example.

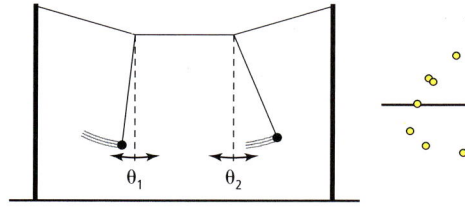

Two weakly coupled pendulums are measured in a lab as having positions θ_1 and θ_2. An experimenter takes 10 "frames" of data and wants to make sense of the observed motion. Applying the method of PC finds that the pendulums prefer to be measured in terms of two PCs of their motion (mathematically called "characteristics," "eigenvectors," or "basis functions" in the language of Fourier transforms). These are simply $\theta_1 = \theta_2$ and $\theta_1 = -\theta_2$ (often called the symmetric and antisymmetric modes). By transforming and replotting the data in terms of their natural, or PCs, the researcher finds the motion can be represented by an ellipse in the new coordinates.

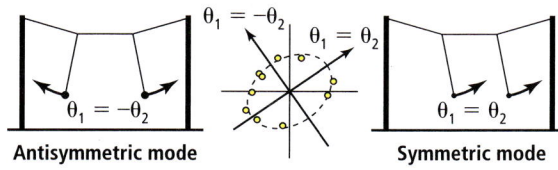

Antisymmetric mode   Symmetric mode

In this example, the 10 frames of two-pendulum data represent 10 frames collected before a target (a new coupler perhaps) appeared in the apparatus. If the target-to-background ratio were small, then departure of the collection from only background might not be noticed. After characterizing background (the ellipse) and suppressing it, the presence of the target should be observed as falling well inside or outside the expected background. **Example 14-1** shows this further.

EXAMPLE 14-1: PRINCIPAL COMPONENTS

Can PCs help detect a target?

Imagine a very simple experiment: periodically recording the position of a marble rolling around in a two-dimensional box. Its position is recorded as **X**, **Y** where the coordinates have been normalized to a scale $0 \to 1$. (This may be a model for locating an ion held in an electrostatic trap.) The marble is believed to be moved by a conventional force with a nominal energy potential, but it may sometimes hop to an "excited state" for a short time. (This is an analogy for an electron in a valence band being thermally excited to a conduction band, but its lifetime there is short according to the Heisenberg Uncertainty Principle.) Does the marble change energy states?

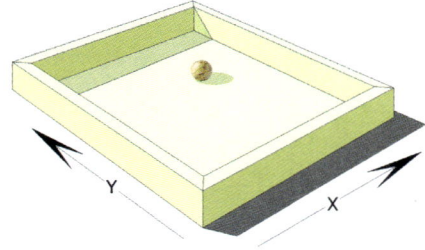

Repeated measurements of the marble's position give **X**, **Y** values, some are shown in the table. Inspection of the data reveals nothing unusual; the **X** values fall predominately within the range 0.2–0.8, as do the **Y** values. Any excursions outside these ranges are minor, not enough to arouse suspicions of a new energy level.

If the marble's expected energy is treated as a background against which an excited state may appear (a target!), a PC transformation can be performed. (The mathematics of PC analysis can be found in textbooks on multi-variable statistics.) Since there are only two coordinates, **X** and **Y**, the transformation reveals the two basis functions to be their sum and difference: **X** + **Y** and **X** − **Y**. Plotting the recorded position data in terms of these new coordinates gives the chart shown here. Visually, it is now obvious the marble did indeed hop out of its normal energy state once. This is the same type of result to be expected when applying PC to remote sensor data.

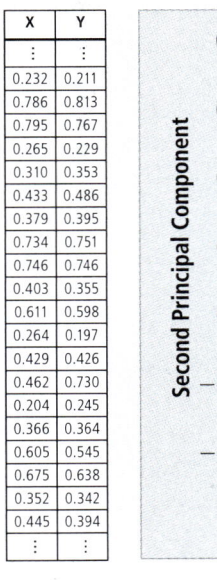

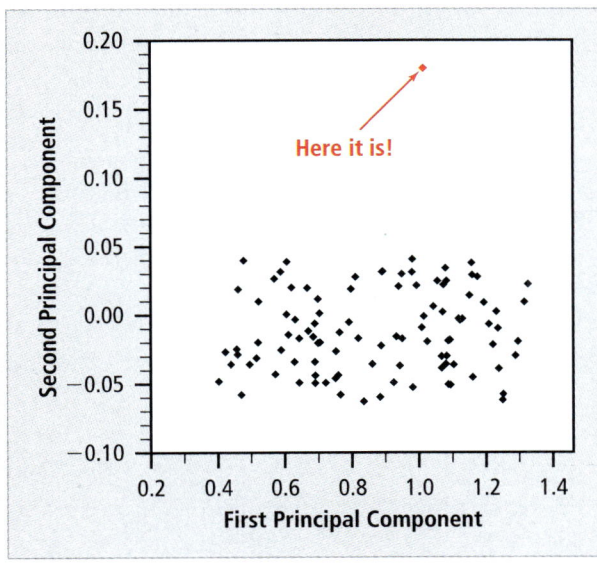

is thus approximated, it may be subtracted from data frames containing a target. This process will not completely remove background from the data, but will adequately *suppress* it to reveal the target.

Figure 14-9
Hypothetical PCs may look like various size checker boards with different colors and shades. Correctly added together, they can approximate a background scene.

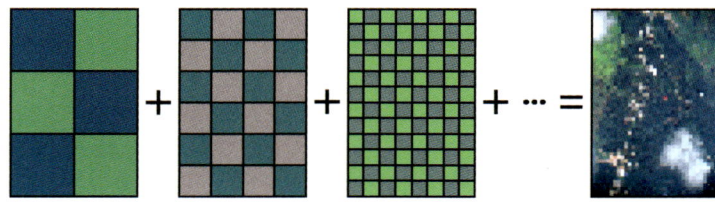

TIMING ISSUES

With background/clutter/noise suppressed in technical analysis, an extracted signature should reveal a target's apparent time-intensity history. This signature could look like a missile time history or any of the other transient signatures in **Chapter 13**. A subtle feature of these signatures is placing them in time. For example, **Figure 12-16** suggests that every frame of data is driven by a clock which does two things: 1) establishes the duty cycle and frame rate; and 2) marks each frame with a time tag. The time tag is necessarily a time *at the sensor* associated with the collection process and *not the time the event happens*. At a distance R from the sensor (**Section 4.3**), an event actually occurs at a time

$$\Delta t \approx \frac{R}{c} \ [\text{s}] \quad (14\text{-}1)$$

before its photons arrive at the sensor. For sensors in GEO with a typical $R \approx 36{,}000$ km, this time delay is about 0.12 s. Additionally, there may be internal delays associated with on-board buffering, formatting, and transmission before a time tag is assigned to any frame of data. This time difference may seem small and probably is insignificant for most events, at least for single sensor collections, but needs to be understood to correctly know the absolute time of an event.

When two or more sensors are involved in a collection, as in triangulation and trajectory reconstruction (**Figures 13-12** and **13-14**), timing becomes critical. Even when accounting for internal delays, the relationship between the time tag and the duty cycle must be known. **Figure 14-10** shows the possibilities. Again, the uncertainty in the time interval may seem insignificant, but it is not. If the missile in **Figure 13-14** has attained about half of its burn-out speed, approximately 3,000 m·s^{-1}, and the collecting sensors frame at 5 Hz ($\Delta t_{INT} \approx 0.2$ s with ~100% duty cycle), then the missile moves approximately 600 m during the collection. Obviously, this could make a difference, especially since a goal

Figure 14-10
A time tag could be associated with any absolute time within a sensor's duty cycle.

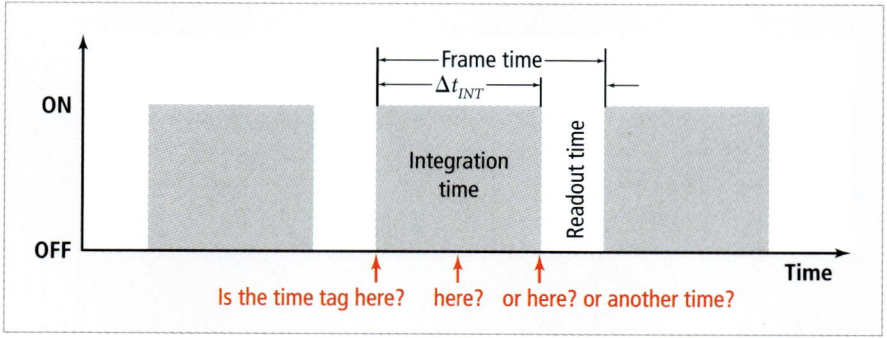

of trajectory reconstruction is estimating the burn-out state vector, which determines impact location.

PSF LOCATION

Having isolated a target on a focal plane by suppressing background, clutter, and noise, the next analysis step is to position the target on the focal plane. That is, determine the location of the image in terms of the rows and columns of the detector array. For point targets, recall the image is a PSF spanning several detectors (first discussed in **Chapter 6**). This may seem counter-productive, but it is an advantage in the following sense. A "point" target having a true point image cannot be accurately located within a detector's Instantaneous Field of View (IFOV) (which could be as large as several square kilometers), but the center of an extended PSF can be calculated fairly precisely. The row and column can be found where a PSF's center lies to a fraction of a detector.

Figure 14-11 suggests that real PSFs are probably not ideal Airy patterns as studied in **Chapter 6**, but are most likely to be spread out by their passage through the atmosphere and a sensor's optical transfer function. Also, platform motion and sensor pointing errors induce continuous small jitter, although feedback and control circuitry and motion compensation should hold this to a minimum. Nonetheless, a PSF integrated over the detectors' duty cycle will result in a more realistic PSF shown in **Figure 14-11**. Just as temporal integration gives a "smoothed" time history signature, jitter and motion will give a "smoothed" spatial function, and a PSF's *average* position on a focal plane can be located for each frame.

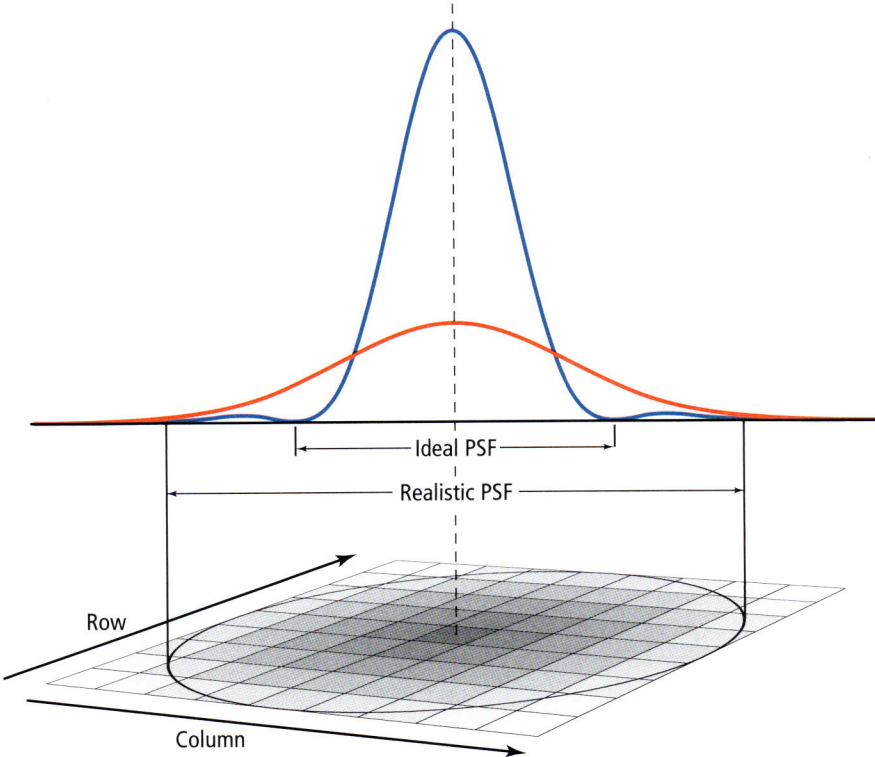

Figure 14-11
Motion, jitter, atmospherics, misaligned optics, and thermal stresses can contribute to a PSF appearing less than ideal on a FPA. Nonetheless, the *average* center of the distribution (for one frame) can be calculated.

EXAMPLE 14-2: FINDING THE CENTER OF A PSF

The image below shows one frame of digitized detector outputs on a portion of a FPA where a target was extracted. All artifacts were removed (the yellow and pink detectors are bad pixel replacements (**Figure 14-3**)) and background, clutter, and noise was suppressed, leaving only target counts. Note, the PSF appears irregular in shape, perhaps suggesting that spatial averaging is not uniform (jitter is presumed random) or some target counts were inadvertently removed with artifact and background clean-up procedures.

Row										Row Counts	Weighted Row Counts	
91	0	0	0	0	0	0	0	0	0			
91	0	0	155	491	587	336	0	0	0	1,569	142,779	
90	0	124	814	1805	2057	1349	387	18	0	6,554	589,860	
89	0	293	1514	3007	3425	2314	797	47	0	11,397	1,014,333	Average Row
88	0	281	1457	2926	2314	2237	750	50	0	10,015	881,320	
87	0	102	733	1654	1904	1214	342	0	0	5,949	517,563	
86	0	9	102	401	492	261	29	0	0	1,294	111,284	
85	0	0	0	0	12	0	0	0	0	12	1,020	
⋮	0	0	0	0	0	0	0	0	0	36,790	3,258,159	

The method for finding the apparent center of the PSF follows:

First, add the signal outputs across each row (1,569; 6,554; …) and add them together (36,790 counts).

Second, multiply the row counts by the row numbers (rows 85 through 91 in this example) to get weighted row counts (142,779, 589,860, …). Add the weighted row counts together (3,258,159).

Third, divide the total weighted row counts by the total of the unweighted row counts,

$$\frac{3{,}258{,}159}{36{,}790} \approx 88.6$$

Fourth, locate this position on the focal plane (horizontal red line). Half the detector output values lie above and half below.

Fifth, repeat the procedure for the columns. (Calculation not shown, but results are represented by the vertical red line.)

Two comments about the interpretation of the center of a PSF are required. First, numbering of the rows (as row 85, row 86, …) presumably shows where the output of a detector is imagined to be, namely its middle since it receives photons over all of its surface. Then, where is "row 88.6?" Row 88.5 is halfway between the middle of rows 88 and 89 in the gap between them. Row 88.6 is then 60% of the way from the middle of row 88 to the middle of row 89, which actually places it on the 89th row of detectors, as shown in the figure.

Second, the division step above could theoretically give a PSF center location of 88.56099…, but such precision is unwarranted as each frame is actually an average of jitter during a sensor's integration time. The jitter of each sensor must be characterized to determine its influence on the center-weighting method. So, in practice, the accuracy may be found to be some larger fraction of a detector.

Figure 14-11 also suggests how the center of a PSF can be located. Note, the shading on the detectors is proportional to the amount of energy (number of photons) received by each detector during an integration time. Of course, the distribution of energy is greatest in the center and the method of finding its center is mathematically equivalent to finding the center of mass (or center of gravity).[4] **Example 14-2** on the previous page illustrates this calculation, but there are limitations to the method. [10], [11] In the event that some defective detector output signals may have been replaced (as in the example) and other artifact corrections may have changed some detector values, the center of a PSF's distribution may also be altered.

14.3 EXPLOITATION

RADIOMETRIC CALIBRATION

Crucial to the exploitation of extracted target signatures is radiometric calibration of a sensor's output signal. This is necessary for absolute knowledge of a target's intensity and for comparison with other sensors. In **Chapters 2, 4, 5, 6, 7**, and **10**, considerable effort was exerted to develop the phenomenology of remote sensing to arrive at an understanding of detector output. Except for "bad" pixel replacement, assuming artifacts have been removed and background has been suppressed, the output of one detector within the PSF of a target's image (assuming $\cos \theta_R \approx 1$) is

$$\tilde{N}_{PIX}^{TGT} \approx {}^A\!/_D \left\{ \int \frac{I_\lambda}{R^2} \tau_{ATM} A_R \tau_{OPT} \frac{\eta F_{PIX}}{hc/\lambda} \Delta t_{INT} d\lambda \right\} \quad [\text{DU}]. \quad (14\text{-}2)$$

This end-to-end equation was then approximately solved for the unknown (target spectral intensity) with a host of assumptions as

$$\langle I_\lambda \rangle_{PIX} \approx \frac{{}^D\!/_A \{\tilde{N}_{PIX}^{TGT}\}}{\frac{A_R F_{PIX} \Delta t_{INT}}{hcR^2} \bar{\tau}_{ATM} \bar{\tau}_{OPT} \bar{\eta} \bar{\lambda} \Delta\lambda} \quad \left[\frac{W}{sr \cdot \mu m}\right]. \quad (14\text{-}3)$$

Of course, **Equation 14-3** is just for one detector, so for the entire target signal within its PSF, the spectral intensity is

$$\langle I_\lambda \rangle \approx \sum_{PIXELS} \langle I_\lambda \rangle_{PIX} \quad \left[\frac{W}{sr \cdot \mu m}\right]. \quad (14\text{-}4)$$

Now, combining **Equation 14-3** with **Equation 14-4** creates nothing more than

$$\langle I_\lambda \rangle \approx K \sum_{PIXELS} {}^D\!/_A \{\tilde{N}_{PIX}^{TGT}\} \quad \left[\frac{W}{sr \cdot \mu m}\right], \quad (14\text{-}5)$$

where K represents all the values and approximations in the denominator of **Equation 14-3** combined together. In practice, **Equation 14-5** includes the values for "bad" pixel replacements within the target's PSF.

The natural question arising at this point is, "Is this correct?" After all, as just pointed out, there were a lot of assumptions, approximations, and maybe even some guesses included. The answer is radiometric calibration.

Radiometric calibration means obtaining a sensor output *from a known input source* to compare to the output from an unknown source (a target). Known sources could either be internal or external. Internal calibration

[4] Another method is to assume the PSF has a two-dimensional bell-shape (Gaussian), the product of two one-dimensional normal distributions along the row and column axes. A least-squares routine then finds the mean row and column values and their standard deviations for a best fit.

sources could be, for example, near-blackbody "hot wire" filaments that heat up quickly to ~2,000 K (to simulate a missile plume's temperature). The objections to such internal sources are: 1) some mechanical flip-mirror device is needed to introduce their radiation to the detectors; and 2) their temperatures must be controlled in the spacecraft environment. As thermal sources, hot wires suffer aging from what is called thermionic emission that contaminates their surroundings with metal ions[5] and changes their physical and electrical properties. Hence, such filaments degrade with time and their temperatures become uncertain.

External calibration sources could be either ground- or space-based. Ground-based sources should be relatively accessible and supportable, but have to be large, at least the size of a detector's IFOV ($10^4 - 10^6$ m² or more) and held at high temperature. Supplying sufficient power to heat such a source to incandescence may be problematic (or prohibitively costly), and temperature control has to deal with conduction and convection (wind). Seeing such a source from a remote sensor is the same as looking at other near-surface targets in dealing with atmospheric transmission, which is one of the assumed pseudo-constants in **Equation 14-3**.

Other possible external sources are readily available and do not require special support; they are literally out of this world: namely *stars*. The nearest star is Sol, the sun, and has been extensively studied with its radiative properties well-documented in NASA Technical Report TR-R-351 and other papers. However, it is not recommended to turn a remote sensor to look directly at the sun without putting appropriate filters in place because of the expected ~1,350 W·m^{-2} irradiance. (Hence, the recurring argument against having more possible mechanical failures on orbit.) Therefore, other stars are candidates for calibration and many of them have been studied and cataloged by ground-, aircraft-, and space-based observatories. [12], [13]

Assuming the spectral irradiance of a selected calibration star, $\mathcal{E}_\lambda^{STAR}$, is known from astrophysical measurements, an equation similar to **Equation 14-2** for the star is

$$\tilde{N}_{PIX}^{STAR} \approx {}^A\!/\!_D \left\{ \int \mathcal{E}_\lambda^{STAR} A_R \tau_{OPT} \frac{\eta F_{PIX}}{hc/\lambda} \Delta t_{INT} d\lambda \right\} \; [\text{DU}], \quad (14\text{-}6)$$

where the background (empty space) presumably does not have to be suppressed, but artifact correction is necessary. Treating this expression as if a star's irradiance were the unknown, it can be solved in a manner similar to **Equation 14-5** to obtain

$$\mathcal{E}_\lambda^{STAR} \approx \sum_{PIXELS} \left(\mathcal{E}_\lambda^{STAR}\right)_{PIX} \approx \frac{\sum_{PIXELS} {}^D\!/\!_A\left\{\tilde{N}_{PIX}^{STAR}\right\}}{\frac{A_R F_{PIX} \Delta t_{INT}}{hc} \bar{\tau}_{OPT} \bar{\eta} \bar{\lambda} \Delta\lambda} \quad (14\text{-}7)$$

$$\approx \mathcal{M} \sum_{PIXELS} {}^D\!/\!_A\left\{\tilde{N}_{PIX}^{STAR}\right\} \; \left[\frac{W}{m^2 \mu m}\right],$$

where $\mathcal{M}$ contains all the values and approximations from the denominator.

Since a star is selected for this measurement and its irradiance, $\mathcal{E}_\lambda^{STAR}$, is known and the detector output signals, $\tilde{N}_{PIX}^{STAR}$, are measured, the proportionality $\mathcal{M}$ can easily be evaluated and *is the calibration constant*.

---

[5] This is essentially why incandescent light bulb filaments eventually burn out.

Although there is no particular magic to this, $\mathcal{M}$ is customarily called the "magic number."

Comparing **Equations 14-5** and **14-7** shows the calculation of source intensity is correct when

$$K = \frac{\mathcal{M}}{\tau_{ATM}/R^2} \left[\frac{W}{sr \cdot \mu m \cdot DU}\right]. \qquad (14\text{-}8)$$

That is, the knowledge of all sensor parameters can be embodied in one calibration number, and the only remaining uncertainty is in the geometry of a particular collection. **Chapter 4** discussed the method to obtain an estimate for range to target, R, and that the viewing direction for a collection determines inputs to an atmospheric transmission calculation. (See **Chapter 5**.)

CHARACTERIZING POINT TARGETS

An early discussion in beginning the study of "point" targets was their spatial extent cannot be perceived (because the target is so far away), and it is unknown if they radiate preferentially in any particular direction. For instance, from a remote sensor, an analyst cannot discern if a sensor is looking at a bare light bulb or a flashlight. There is no way to tell without being able to move and collect from other locations. Therefore, without other specific information, it is necessary to assume all point targets emitting power Φ are isotropic, giving them an intensity:

$$I \approx \frac{\Phi}{4\pi} \left[\frac{W}{sr}\right]. \qquad (14\text{-}9)$$

This assumption is probably reasonable for targets aloft but might not hold up for surface targets having strong interaction with the ground (i.e., surface explosions have strong interactions with their targets). Nonetheless, the amount of energy a target emits (per frame) within a sensor's bandpass can be estimated assuming an isotropic target with calibrated radiometric intensity:

$$E_{FRAME} \approx \int \Phi \, dt \approx \int 4\pi I \, dt \approx 4\pi \langle I_\lambda \rangle \Delta\lambda \Delta t_{INT} \quad [J], \qquad (14\text{-}10)$$

The total *energy* emitted by a target is just

$$E_{TGT} \approx \sum_{FRAMES} E_{FRAME} \quad [J]. \qquad (14\text{-}11)$$

CHARACTERIZING TARGET ENERGY

To exploit a target's energy, it much be well understood. Advanced technical intelligence sensors collect both signature and metric components of energy. The energy of most targets of interest (the transient and persistent events discussed in the last chapter) starts as chemical energy (heat of formation) of either explosive compounds or fuels. The transformation of chemical energy is either uncontrolled (most transients) or controlled (persistent), but in any case is exothermic, meaning the energy becomes available for other uses. For explosives, it is a blast; while for fuels, it is propulsion.

In uncontrolled energy releases, shown in **Figure 14-12**, only a small fraction of the energy is observable by remote sensors: a radiation characteristic of a rapidly cooling thermal source, probably a graybody in the visible through mid-wave infrared. The duration of radiant energy received provides a rough indication of the type of blast. However, there is considerable ambiguity without an extensive study of possible weapon signatures:

$\Delta t \approx 0.1$–0.2 s $\Rightarrow$ possible artillery or mortar fire or air bursts,

$\Delta t \approx 0.5$–2.0 s $\Rightarrow$ probably general purpose bombs or rockets,

$\Delta t > 5.0$ s $\Rightarrow$ secondary effects from bombs, rockets, and shell impacts.

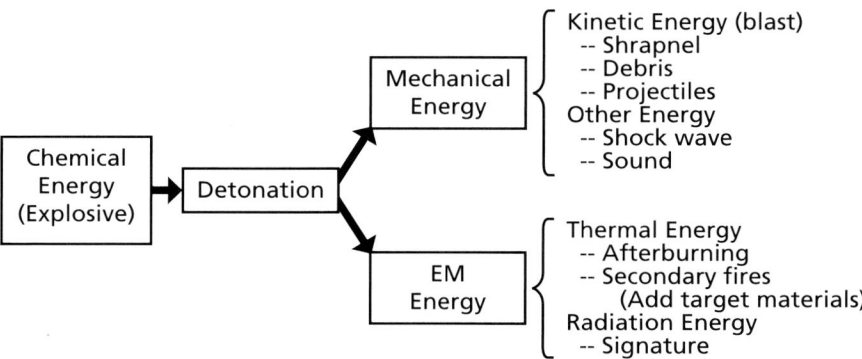

Figure 14-12
The energetics of an uncontrolled (transient) energy conversion.

The amount of energy received (area under the extracted signature, **Equation 14-10**) is highly dependent on weapon-target interaction (soft/wet soil, hard/rocky soil, vegetation, buildings, etc.). It is not a reliable indicator of the weapon type. For all these events, the metrics consist of a single geolocation. Tied to other geospatial intelligence, an observed event location may provide answers as to the intended targets of the weapons observed.

Controlled energy releases, shown in **Figure 14-13**, provide considerably more opportunity for exploitation. Features of the time-history signature provide characteristic and identifiable stages in an event. Integration of the estimated trajectory metrics gives specific kinetic energy (proportional to the square of the speed), while the altitude is potential energy. Integration of speed then gives the net acceleration, a result of thrust (proportional to $I^{1/2}$), gravity, and drag (dependent on air density and speed squared). These factors were discussed in **Section 13.3**.

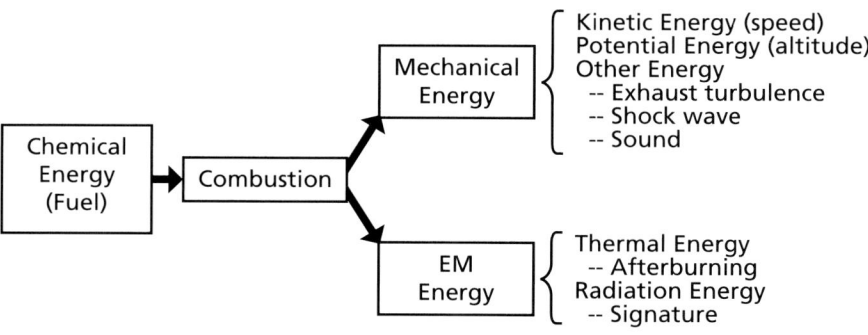

Figure 14-13
The energetics of a controlled (persistent) energy conversion.

15 CLASSICAL MSI IN THE VISIBLE TO SWIR

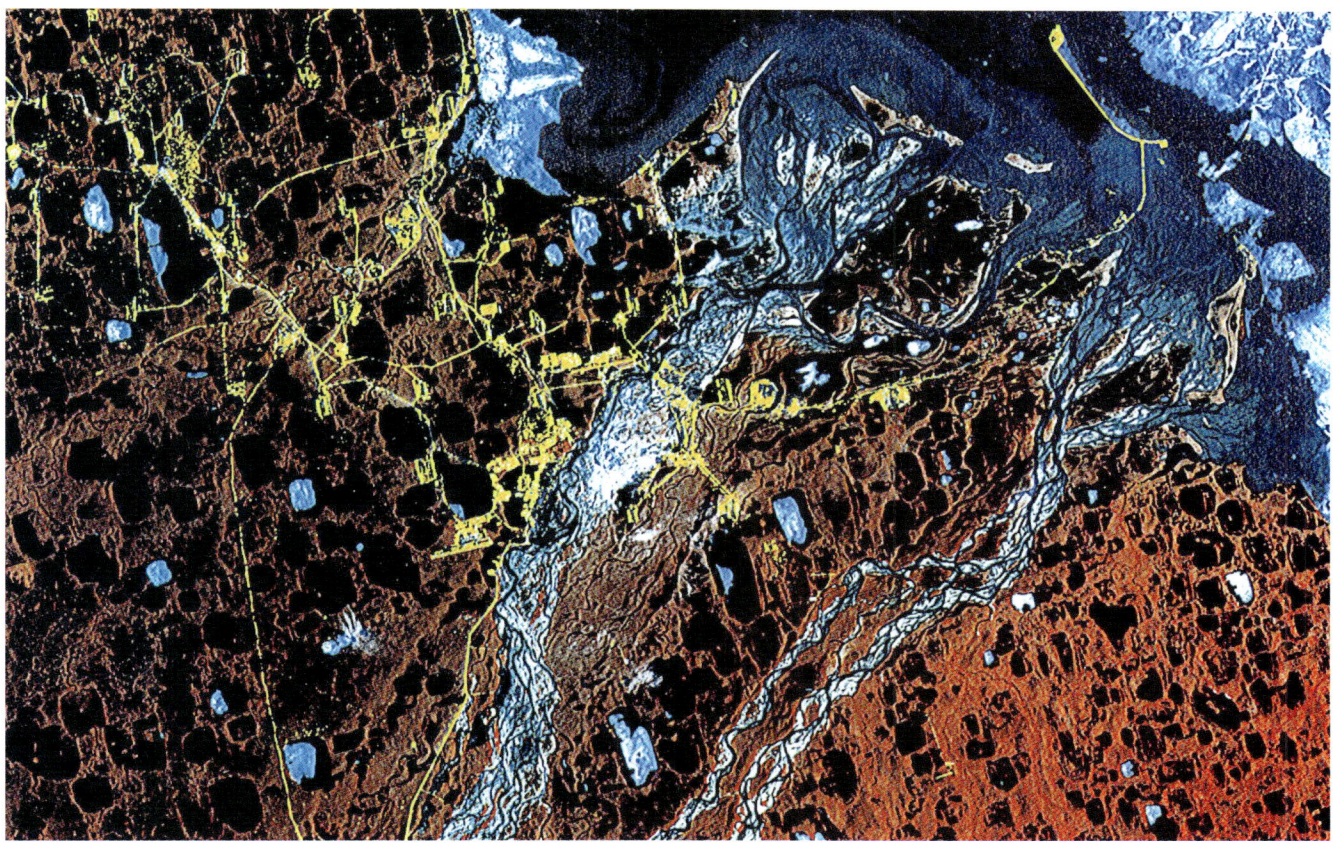

Multispectral imaging (MSI) involves the collection of images in two or more spectral bandpasses (commonly shortened to "bands"). Classical MSI involves spectral bands in the visible to the shortwave infrared (SWIR) portion of the electromagnetic spectrum because detectors for these spectral regions have existed for many years (i.e., long before practical thermal infrared sensors began to be used). Active airborne MSI collection programs date back to the 1950s, leading to the launch of the first National Aeronautics and Space Administration (NASA) Landsat satellite in 1972.

SECTIONS

15.1 COLLECTION OPTIONS AND ISSUES
15.2 LANDSAT
15.3 APPLICATIONS AND ALGORITHMS
15.4 OTHER MSI SPACEBORNE SENSORS

15.1 COLLECTION OPTIONS AND ISSUES

To collect MSI data, the collection strategies introduced in **Chapter 12** for imagery in a single spectral bandpass become more complicated. The two basic types of collection, staring and scanning, can be used. In either case, different filters must be used to define each of the spectral bands. Each detector of a Focal Plane Array (FPA) is assigned a particular spectral band, and an appropriate filter must be put in front of it.

MSI STARING COLLECTORS

For staring sensors, there are two approaches. For systems such as the human eye, color photographic film, and digital cameras, detectors for each spectral band are placed in close proximity to each other for a particular ground pixel. This enables all the spectral information for a given ground pixel to be gained at the same time. The detectors in the FPA in the human eye (three types of cones on the retina) and those in photographic film (grains of silver chloride with three different dyes for coatings) are positioned somewhat randomly. By contrast, the silicon detectors with three different types of coatings in the FPA of a digital camera are manufactured in systematic rows and columns giving the checkerboard pattern shown in **Figure 15-1**. This approach becomes more complicated when more than four spectral bands are desired. It is difficult to imagine manufacturing such a checkerboard of detectors with different filters for a system with ten or more spectral bands.

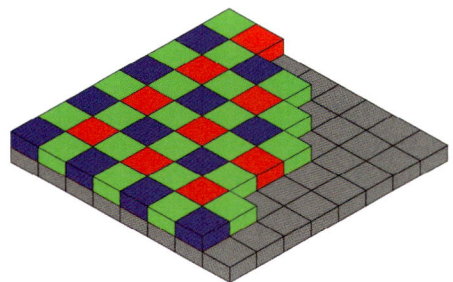

Figure 15-1
Filter arrangement on a FPA of a digital camera using spectral bands of red, blue, and green. (Photo courtesy of https://en.wikipedia.org/wiki/File:Bayer_pattern_on_sensor.svg; GNU Free Documentation License Version 1.2 and Creative Commons Attribution-Share Alike 3.0 unported.)

Another approach for staring sensors with moderate success over the last 20 years uses one or more filter wheels. As shown in **Figure 15-2**, each filter wheel has up to 10 or 12 filters arranged in a circle. As the wheel is precisely rotated, each of the filters is in front of the staring FPA for a designated amount of time. Hence, the images in the various spectral bands are collected sequentially. For more spectral bands, two or more filter wheels may be used. One of the filters on each of the filter wheels must be sufficiently broad to cover all the desired spectral bands. In fact, instead of such a filter, an open cutout would allow all wavelengths through that particular filter wheel.

Figure 15-2
Filter wheel used with a staring FPA.

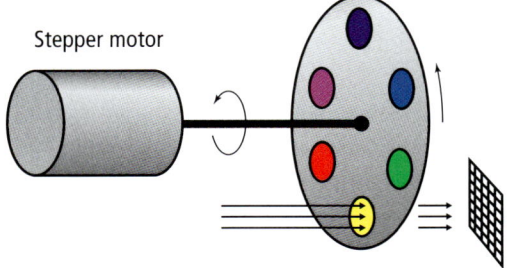

One drawback of the filter wheel concept is the fact the stepper motor used to rotate the filter wheel can fail. In 1966, the NASA Orbiting Astronomical Observatory experienced a filter wheel motor failure three days after launch. The sensor designers put a calibration source in one of the filter positions of the wheel assembly. As Murphy's Law would predict, this source was in front of the FPA when the filter motor wheel failed. So, data collection of stellar images was impossible, and NASA turned off the satellite. At the other extreme, some satellite sensor systems have now flown for several years, and their filter wheels continue to operate flawlessly.

A variation of the filter wheel is the continuously variable filter (CVF) in which the whole filter wheel acts as a thin-film filter instead of having a series of discrete filters. As shown in **Figure 15-3**, this filter has continuously varying thickness around its circumference. Like the filter wheel, the imagery in the various spectral bands is collected sequentially, but unlike the filter wheel, the spectral bandpass of the FPA at any instant in time varies somewhat across the FPA. The spectral bandpass for any particular detector is changing as the CVF is spun at a uniform rotational rate.

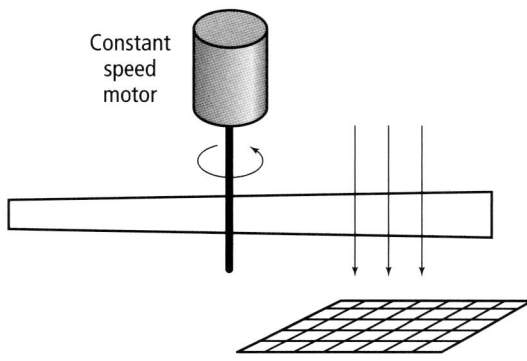

Figure 15-3
CVF used with staring FPA.

In addition to the FPA consisting of a two dimensional array of detectors, staring sensors on a moving platform, such as an airplane or satellite, must remain accurately pointed at the same point on the ground during the time necessary to collect a complete spectrum (**Figure 15-4**). Otherwise, the collected images will be smeared, resulting in a loss of spatial resolution. Also, the spectrum of any one pixel may be smeared across several of its neighboring ground pixels and vice versa. To maintain this accurate sensor pointing, a pointing, tracking, and stabilization (PTS) system is required. (PTS is sometimes referred to as forward motion compensation.)

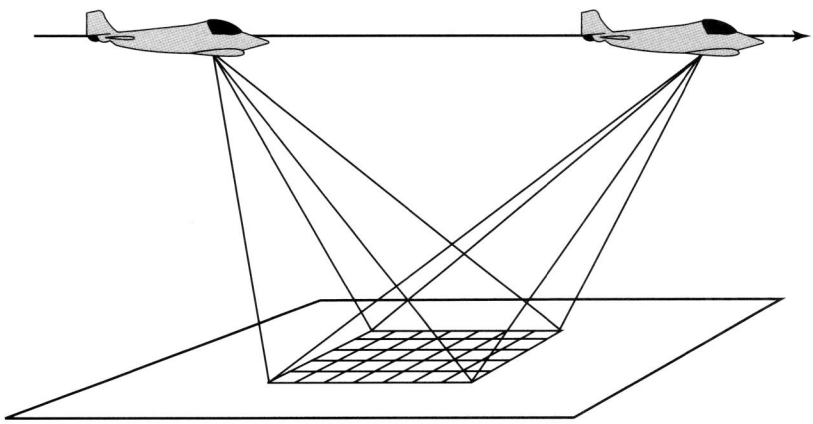

Figure 15-4
Need for a PTS when a staring sensor is used in collection.

This collection scenario suggests a trade-off between detector output, spectral and spatial resolution capabilities, and the sophistication (and hence price) of the PTS system. For example, for more spectral bands or longer collection times for each spectral band, the filter wheel must turn more slowly, and a longer total collection time is required. To achieve the required pointing stabilization over longer periods of time, PTS systems with enhanced capabilities are required.

An additional trade-off between spatial resolution and footprint (or area coverage) is suggested. To improve spatial resolution by decreasing the size of the ground pixels, FPAs must be manufactured with smaller, more closely spaced detectors, and/or longer focal length optics must be used (**Chapter 8**). In either case, unless the total number of detectors in the FPA is increased, the total sensor Field-of-View (FOV) decreases and the area of coverage decreases. Collections with these staring sensors are sometimes termed "soda straw" collections, that is, similar to viewing a scene through a soda straw.

MSI SCANNING COLLECTIONS

The other approach to data collection is scanning rather than staring. In this approach, a series of linear arrays of detectors are used; each array typically has its own filter. Then, the rows of ground pixels from the rows of detectors are swept across the ground in sequential fashion; the first row at λ_1, the next row at λ_2, the next row at λ_3, ..., the last row at λ_N. Hence, **N**, the number of detector rows, equals the number of spectral bands. Several techniques have been used to scan these ground pixels across a scene. These include using the forward motion of the platform (referred to as a pushbroom scanner) illustrated in **Figure 15-5**, a scanning mirror in front of the optics (often referred to as a whiskbroom scanner or in some cases a cross-track scanner), and a combination of forward motion of the platform and a scanning mirror.

Figure 15-5
Pushbroom scan data collection.

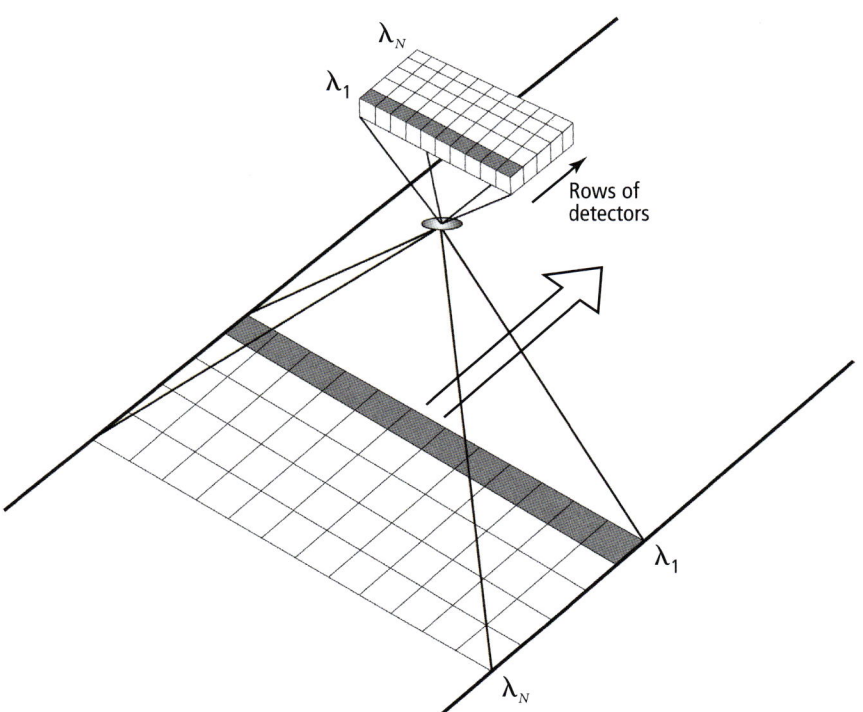

With a pushbroom scanner, as shown in **Figure 15-5**, the motion of the platform and the long rows of ground pixels generate a collection area that is a long swath with a width in ground pixels equal to the number of detectors in one of the rows of detectors. The length of the swath in the direction of flight is determined by the length of time the sensor is designed to collect data. Because all of the spectral data from an object on the ground is not collected at exactly the same time, there are some requirements for a PTS system, although not as many as that for a staring sensor system. Without sufficient sensor stabilization, artifacts will occur in the imagery, such as size and shape distortion of objects and possible gaps in the coverage. Also, the spectrum of any one ground pixel may be smeared across several of its neighboring pixels and vice versa.

The need for large FPAs (as discussed in **Chapter 12**) to obtain both high spatial resolution as well as large area coverage is further increased for the collection of MSI (and Hyperspectral Imaging (HSI)). **Table 15-1** summarizes the current state-of-the-art of FPA technology as compiled by the authors based on their experience.

SPECTRAL REGION	VIS-NIR	SWIR-MWIR	LWIR
MATERIAL TYPE	Si, HgCdTe	InSb, HgCdTe	HgCdTe, Si:Ga
SCANNING FPA SIZES	16,384 × 1 12,000 × 64	2,500 × 12	1,500 × 8
STARING FPA SIZES	9,000 × 13,000	2,084 × 2,084	2,084 × 2,084

Table 15-1
FPA availability. (NIR = Near-visible Infrared; MWIR = Mid-Wave Infrared; LWIR = Long-Wave Infrared)

Normal silicon detectors have a long wavelength cut-off of about 1.1 μm. To operate at longer wavelengths in the Long-Wave Infrared (LWIR), the silicon used for the detectors must be "doped" with a controlled amount of impurity, such as gallium or arsenic (**Section 7.1**). This impurity dramatically changes the energy levels within the silicon detector and facilitates detection far beyond 1.1 μm. These detectors usually have to be cooled to 4 K (around the liquid helium boiling point) for optimum performance. HgCdTe is a metallurgical mix of HgTe and CdTe. The relative mix of these two compounds determines in which spectral bandpass the detectors will best operate (**Figure 7-9**). For example, a single mix does not exist so the detectors would work well in both the Mid-Wave Infrared (MWIR) and the LWIR. These detectors must be cooled to 77 K (around the liquid nitrogen boiling point) for optimum performance.

Several conclusions are readily apparent from **Table 15-1**. Visible to Near-Infrared (NIR) FPA technology is the furthest advanced, while LWIR FPA technology is the least developed. (LWIR FPA technology is approximately 20 to 30 years behind visible-NIR FPA technology.) This should not be a surprise. Commercial contractors have invested millions of dollars in silicon detector and FPA manufacturing because of the strong demand for commercial digital cameras and camcorders. This huge commercial investment is especially true for staring sensor FPAs. LWIR detector and FPA manufacturing have been of interest to the military and intelligence communities only in recent years. In the past, long linear FPAs for scanning sensors in the MWIR and LWIR were easier to manufacture than staring sensor FPAs. This is true because long linear arrays are often fabricated by the use of smaller linear sub-arrays positioned in a staggered pattern, as shown below in **Figure 15-6**.

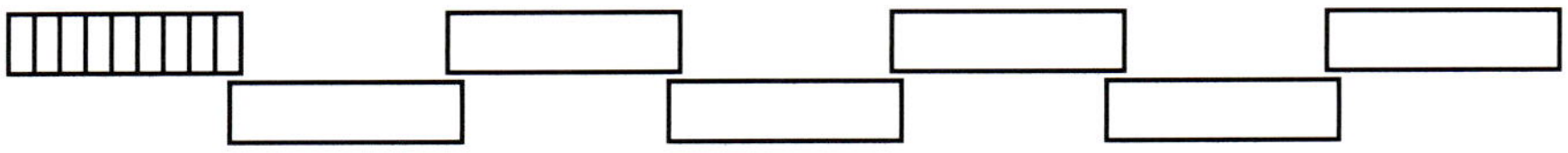

Figure 15-6
Long linear array resulting from the use of smaller linear sub-arrays.

Table 15-2 summarizes the spectral imaging collection modes: staring, linear pushbroom scanner, and cross-track scanner by comparing them in a number of previously discussed categories. (See **Table 12-1** for similar comparison of single band imagers.)

Table 15-2
Comparison of staring, linear pushbroom, and cross-track scanner spectral imaging.

Issues	Data Collection Modes		
	Staring	Linear Pushbroom Scanner	Cross-track Scanner
PTS System Required for High Quality Imagery	Extensive	Much less than staring	Much less than staring
Possible Imagery Artifacts	One "bad" pixel for every uncorrected "bad" detector	One streak for every uncorrected "bad" detector; also, possible band effects	One streak in every scan for every uncorrected "bad" detector
Possible Spectral Artifacts	No spectrum for each "bad" pixel	Erroneous info in one spectral band for all pixels in streak	Erroneous info in one spectral band for all pixels in streak
Coverage Capabilities	Limited by 2-D FPA size	Can be large using long linear FPAs	Can be large using long scans
Spectral Sensor Required Components	Filter wheel or CVF	In-place spectral filter on each detector	In-place spectral filter for each detector
Reliability/Possible Failure Issues	Filter or CVF motor	No mechanical failure modes	Scanning mirror or other mechanism
Current Spectral Sensor Usage	Few systems	Commonly used	Some systems

15.2 LANDSAT [1]

Landsat 1 was the first major MSI collection platform. From the initial launch in 1972, Landsat satellites have provided an enormous archive of spectral imagery taken worldwide. **Table 15-3** lists the eight Landsat launches to date. With the exception of Landsat 6, NASA was responsible for the sensor fabrication and launch of all Landsat sensors. Landsat 6 was a joint program between NASA and the US Air Force. All launches were successful except for Landsat 6, which splashed into the Pacific Ocean off the coast from its launch site at Vandenberg Air Force Base, California. Landsat 5 completed over 29 years of successful collection until it was decommissioned on June 5, 2013 after a spacecraft gyroscope failure.

Table 15-3
Landsat missions.

	Launch Date	Status	Data Availability
1	Jul 1972	Turned off	USGS or CSIL archive
2	Jan 1975	Turned off	USGS or CSIL archive
3	Mar 1978	Turned off	USGS or CSIL archive
4	Jul 1982	Turned off	USGS or CSIL archive
5	Mar 1984	Over 29 years of successful data collection until decommissioned on June 5, 2013	EOSAT initially (expensive) or CSIL archive USGS now (inexpensive) or CSIL archive
6	Oct 1993	Failed to orbit	N/A
7	Apr 1999	Good data until May 2003; Degraded data since then	USGS or CSIL archive
8	Feb 2013	Good data currently	USGS or CSIL archive

Landsat 7 continues to collect despite a sensor malfunction in 2003 that has resulted in degraded imagery since then. Landsat 8 was recently launched in 2013.

Data archive and distribution has been accomplished primarily by US Geological Survey (USGS) from their facility, Earth Resources Observation and Science (EROS) Center, in Sioux Falls, South Dakota. The Commercial Satellite Imagery Library (CSIL), now part of the National Geospatial-Intelligence Agency (NGA) Unclassified National Imagery Library (UNIL), has served as data archive and distribution center for sharing all imagery acquired by any Department of Defense (DOD) agency. In the 1980s, Congress decided to organize a private company to process and distribute data. This company, EOSAT, was allowed to charge customers prices based on their costs instead of the government subsidized-price charged by USGS. The difference in prices discouraged many customers. For example, the EOSAT price for a single Landsat 5 image taken of an overseas location and processed at an overseas ground station was expensive. A Landsat 7 image acquired from USGS for the same location was significantly cheaper. In 2009, USGS began free data downloads from their Internet site (landsat.usgs.gov/Landsat_Search_and_Download.php).

The orbits of all of the Landsat satellites have been similar. Current Landsats are located in a 700 km altitude, sun-synchronous orbit with a 98.8 minute period. This orbit, which is nearly polar, provides coverage of all locations on the Earth. It also provides for passage over a given location at the same local time. (At the equator, the time is 10:00 AM for Landsat 7.) Because of this property of sun-synchronous orbits, the sun angle will remain nearly the same for weeks at a time. Thus, the solar illumination onto a given location from collection to collection has been made as constant as possible. The altitude of 700 km is sufficiently high to ensure precise orbit timing and stability against orbit decay. Hence, satellite location and collections can be predicted months in advance, and collection coverage swaths remain the same, year after year.

The coverage swaths are illustrated in **Figure 15-7**. The sensor is hard-mounted to the satellite and is always pointed towards the nadir. The sensor coverage for every orbit is a 185 km wide swath. Because of the 98.8 minute

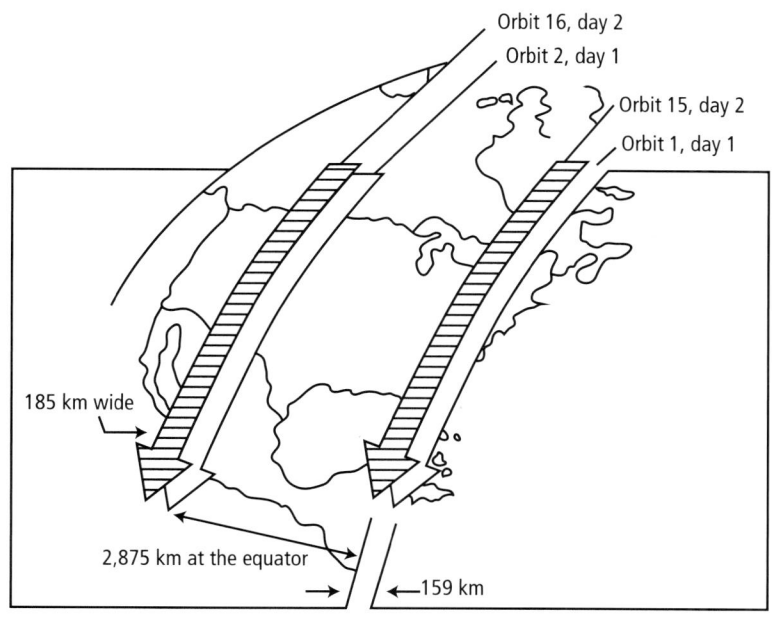

Figure 15-7
Landsat ground coverage. [1]

orbital period, the distance between two successive orbits is 2,875 km to the west at the equator. Because of the precision timing of the orbit, the swaths produced by the satellite on successive days are shifted from the previous day by 159 km to the west at the equator. Therefore, there is a small overlap between swaths covered on successive days. It takes the satellite 16 days to cover the whole Earth. On the seventeenth day, the swaths are identical to those on the first day. While such a long time for total Earth coverage is excessive for many applications, including those of the DOD and intelligence communities, it is totally acceptable for NASA and land use applications, such as inventorying crop acreage.

The spectral bands and the ground pixel size are shown in **Table 15-4** for the Landsat 5 Thematic Mapper (TM) and the Landsat 7 Enhanced Thematic Mapper Plus (ETM+). The traditional 6 MSI bands covering the visible through the SWIR continue to have 30 m ground pixels. The LWIR band, which started at 120 m on Landsat 5, was reduced to 60 m on Landsat 7. The visible-NIR broadband PAN (panchromatic) band made its initial appearance on Landsat 7 with 15 m ground pixels.[1] Landsat 8 (**Table 15-5**) has two additional bands in the visible-SWIR: coastal aerosol at 0.433–0.435 and cirrus cloud 1.360–1.390 μm. In the LWIR, two bands, 10.3–11.2 and 11.5–12.5 μm, replace the previous

Table 15-4 Landsat 5 and 7 sensor parameters. [1]

Sensor Nomenclature			Ground pixel size	
Spectral bands[1]			Landsat 5 TM	Landsat 7 ETM+
B	1	0.45 – 0.52 μm	30 × 30 m	30 × 30 m
G	2	0.52 – 0.60 μm		
R	3	0.63 – 0.69 μm		
NIR	4	0.76 – 0.90 μm		
SWIR	5	1.55 – 1.75 μm		
SWIR	7	2.08 – 2.35 μm		
LWIR	6	10.4 – 12.5 μm	120 × 120 m	60 × 60 m
PAN	8	0.52 – 0.90 μm	None	15 × 15 m

Table 15-5 Landsat 8 sensor parameters. [2]

Spectral Bands			Ground Pixel Size
			Landsat 8 OLI (Operational Land Imager)
Coastal Aerosol	1	0.433 – 0.435 μm	30 × 30 m
B	2	0.450 – 0.515 μm	
G	3	0.525 – 0.600 μm	
R	4	0.630 – 0.680 μm	
NIR	5	0.845 – 0.885 μm	
SWIR 1	6	1.560 – 1.660 μm	
SWIR 2	7	2.100 – 2.300 μm	
Panchromatic	8	0.500 – 0.680 μm	15 × 15 m
Cirrus	9	1.360 – 1.390 μm	30 × 30 m
Thermal IR 1	10	10.3 – 11.2 μm	100 × 100 m
Thermal IR 2	11	11.5 – 12.5 μm	100 × 100 m

[1] Through Landsat 7, the band numbering remained the same. Initially with Landsat 1, only one SWIR band was planned, and so the planned bands were numbered 1 through 6, starting with the blue and going through to the LWIR. When a second SWIR band was added, the existing numbering was not changed, and the second SWIR band became band 7 and the LWIR band remained band 6.

single 10.4–12.5 μm band, and the pixel size increased to 100 m, but they are resampled to 30 m in delivered data product. Also, the traditional band numbering system is revised.

The 185 km wide swath of coverage is produced by the Landsat sensors using a scanning mirror to produce a cross-track scan as shown in **Figure 15-8**. This coverage is performed using just 16 detectors per spectral band for all the bands except the LWIR and the PAN. Interestingly, in order to produce the same swath width and ground pixel size using a pushbroom scan, over 6,000 (185 km/30 m) detectors would be required.

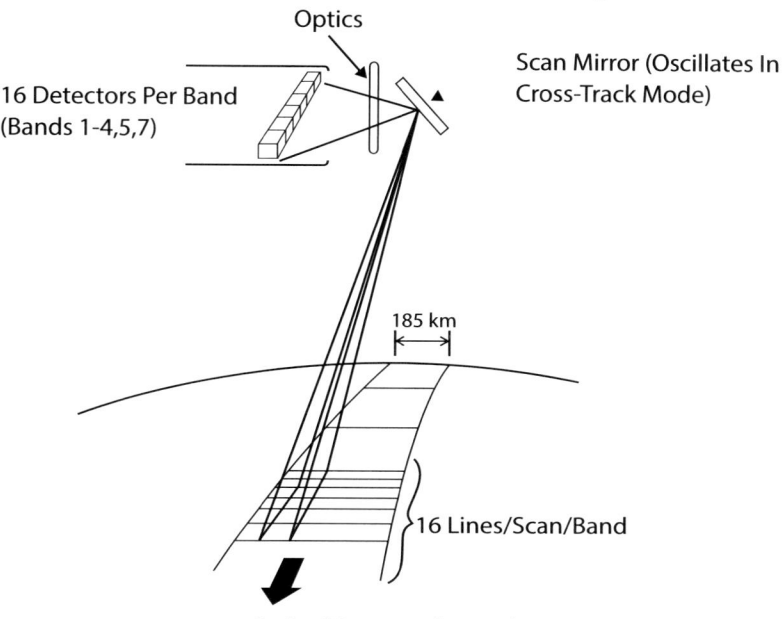

Figure 15-8
Landsat cross-track scan. [1]

The optical system for the Landsat 5 TM is shown in **Figure 15-9**. Note, the collected energy is split into two paths with each path leading to a different FPA. One path leads to an un-cooled FPA of silicon detectors for bands 1, 2, 3, and 4, and the other to a cooled FPA of indium-antimonide (InSb) for bands 5 and 6 and mercury-cadmium-telluride (HgCdTe) detectors for band 7.

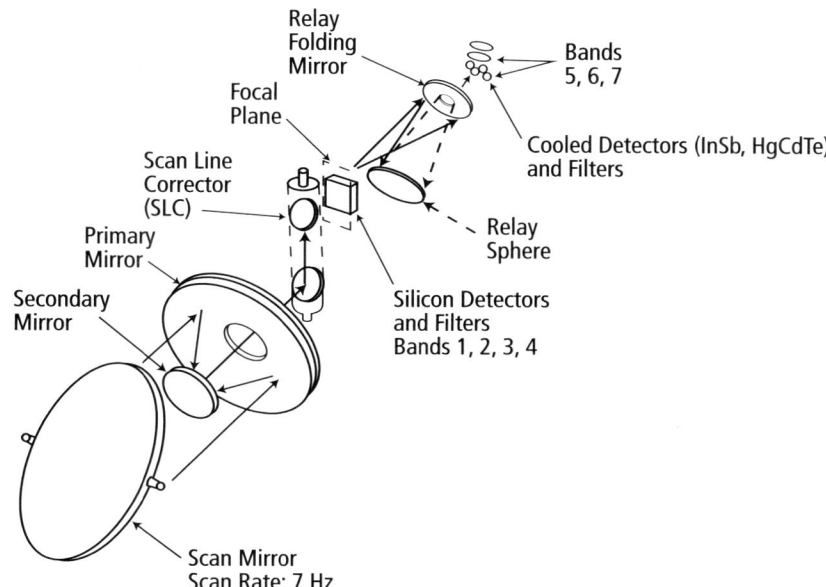

Figure 15-9
Schematic of Landsat optical layout. [1]

The actual detector layout and relative size of the two FPAs for the Landsat 7 ETM+ are shown in **Figure 15-10**. Note, the PAN and LWIR bands, having smaller and larger ground pixels than 30 m for all the other bands, must have smaller and larger detector sizes, respectively. To have the same size cross-track scan width, the PAN band with its smaller detectors must have more of them in the row. Similarly, the LWIR band with its larger detectors must have fewer of them.

Figure 15-10
Schematic layout of Landsat 7 FPAs. [1]

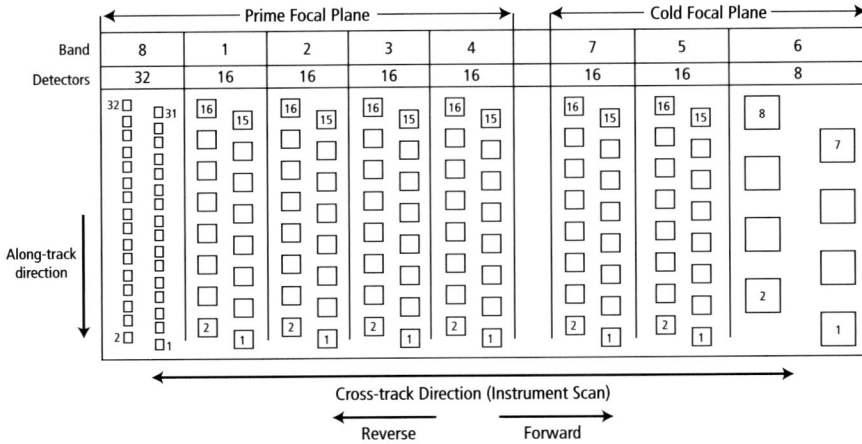

The role of another oscillating mirror, the scan line corrector (SLC) in **Figure 15-9** for forward motion compensation, is illustrated in **Figure 15-11**. In Landsat 7, the motor driving the SLC failed on May 31, 2003. Its failure produced image artifacts in the data swaths. NASA removed some of the artifacts by data re-sampling.

Figure 15-11
Pixel path during Landsat scan. [1]

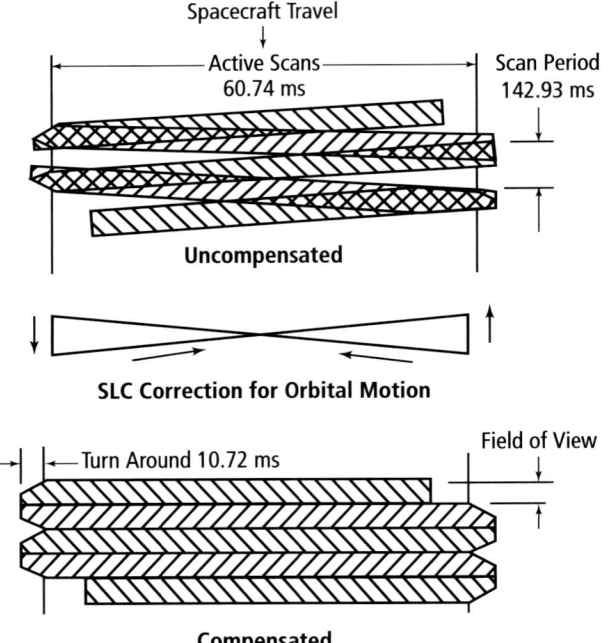

Landsat strengths include:
- Collected imagery is high quality imagery with few artifacts.
- Collected imagery is well-calibrated using on-board sources and a bit depth of 8 (256 levels).
- Large data archive exists with over 20 years of consistent collections.

- Sensor is nearly always on and collecting; advanced tasking is not required.
- Landsat MSI is both inexpensive and easily acquired.
- Spectral analysis procedures for Landsat data are well-developed.
- Landsat swath coverage areas is relatively large compared to many sensors.

Landsat weaknesses and possible solutions are listed in **Table 15-6**.

WEAKNESS	POSSIBLE SOLUTION
Slow site revisit	Use another sensor system with off-nadir look capability OR A constellation size > 1
Slow overseas ground site processing and distribution	Eagle Vision deployed to within about 2,000 km of collection site
No real time MSI available (even with CONUS ground sites)	Eagle Vision
Large pixels	Subpixel analysis algorithms OR SPOT 4, SPOT 5, Ikonos, Quick Bird (all with less spectral capability than Landsat)[2]

Table 15-6
Landsat weaknesses and possible solutions. (SPOT=Satellite Pour l'Observation de la Terre)

The Eagle Vision solution mentioned in **Table 15-6** is a DOD program that built and deployed five systems (**Figure 15-12**). Each system contains an antenna to download data directly from Landsat and other satellites, as well as computers to perform the initial processing of the data to form spectral images.

Figure 15-12
Eagle Vision van. (Courtesy of ERIM.)

15.3 APPLICATIONS AND ALGORITHMS

Many MSI applications and algorithms were developed using Landsat data because of the large amounts of MSI collected starting in 1972. Some of the applications and MSI products are very simple; others are significantly more complex. The discussion here will proceed from the simplest to the more complex. The following spectral analysis algorithms and tools will be discussed:

- True-color images
- Band-sharpened spectral images with and without terrain elevation information
- Full scene characterization
- Target spectral matching
- Principal component analysis (PCA)
- Sub-pixel analysis
- Change detection
- Bathymetry

[2] Characteristics for these sensors will be given later in this chapter (Table 15-9).

TRUE COLOR IMAGES

The simplest of MSI products is the true color map or image of a region of interest. A true color image, or 321 image, involves Landsat bands in the red (band 3), green (band 2), and blue (band 1), and can either stand alone or be combined with a map of the area. There are few technical challenges except when the region of interest is not solely contained in one Landsat imagery swath. Then, portions of two adjacent Landsat imagery swaths must be combined together. While there is always overlap between any two Landsat data swaths, there are still technical challenges to overcome. To overlay the two imagery swaths, objects visible in both images, called tie points, have to be found and used. In Landsat imagery with its 30 m ground pixels, finding tie-points can sometimes be a problem. This is especially true in areas distant from cities where there are few objects that can be tie-points. The intersection of roads can be used, but even these may be sparse in the scenes of desert and forest regions. When using two adjacent Landsat imagery swaths, another potential challenge exists because the swaths are collected on different days. Hence, atmospheric conditions can be different, especially in terms of the presence of aerosols. So, one imagery swath may appear overall lighter or darker than the other. Color normalization procedures have been developed to make the two imagery swaths appear the same in overall brightness.

A variation of this product is merging a Landsat true color image onto a map. To accomplish this merging, the image must be shifted and perhaps stretched to make the objects in the image overlay on their locations designated on the map. These objects are called control points. The quality of the product increases with the number of control points that can be found and used in the image. The quality of the product is also enhanced if the location of these points is spaced across the image, rather than concentrated all in one portion of the image.

Another application of a Landsat image is ingress-egress panoramic views (or movies). In these, Landsat true color images are "draped" onto digital terrain elevation data (DTED) to provide color imagery with a three-dimensional appearance for use by aircraft pilots, crews of ships, and ground forces for mission planning and general orientation. For example, aircraft pilots may use these images as part of an aircraft simulator exercise for landing on an unfamiliar runway in mountainous terrain. **Figure 15-13** provides an example of a three-dimensional appearing image in the French Alps. The inset photo shows the Alps without any terrain information included.

Figure 15-13
Landsat image merged with terrain information. (Courtesy of ERIM.)

BAND-SHARPENED IMAGES

Another application of Landsat true color imagery is to merge it with higher spatial resolution panchromatic imagery. This is often called pan sharpened MSI. **Figure 15-14** provides an example, in which the highway interchange of I-70 and I-495 west of Baltimore is shown first as an non-pan-sharpened false color image using SWIR (band 7), NIR (band 4), and red (band 3), and then as pan sharpened using the higher spatial resolution (15 m) Satellite Pour l'Observation de la Terre (SPOT) panchromatic imagery. Notice the additional detail in the pan sharpened spectral image.

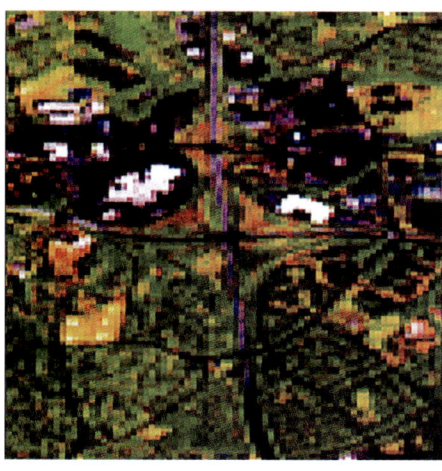

Figure 15-14
Pan sharpened Landsat imagery. (Courtesy of ERIM.)

FULL-SCENE CHARACTERIZATION

More sophisticated spectral imagery products require spectral analysis. Full scene characterization, or terrain categorization (tercat for short), is a product which has been used extensively for a number of years. The objective of full scene characterization is to identify every pixel in the scene, or region of interest, in terms of several categories (e.g., grass, forest, crop land, bare soil, gravel, rock, and water). The results of this analysis are portrayed as an image or map, and these results are often merged with DTED to provide ground force commanders with information for trafficability (ease of force movement) or planning of artillery salvos. To provide this terrain analysis, the US Army Corps of Engineers has detachments at locations worldwide (mostly located at the headquarters of DOD unified commands and US Army commands).

The spectral analysis technique used involves computer-generated scatter plots. Consider MSI data involving N spectral bands. The data used in the analysis can either be irradiance values for each pixel (level 1, which has no atmospheric correction) or reflectivity values (level 2, in which irradiance values have been atmospherically corrected). Usually, irradiance values are used because MSI data cubes are difficult to atmospherically correct given the small number of spectral bands. The spectrum of each ground pixel in the scene can be represented by N irradiances $\mathcal{E}_1, \mathcal{E}_2, \ldots, \mathcal{E}_N$ as an N-dimensional spectral vector

$$\mathcal{E} = \mathcal{E}_1 \boldsymbol{x}_1 + \mathcal{E}_2 \boldsymbol{x}_2 + \ldots + \mathcal{E}_N \boldsymbol{x}_N \left[\frac{\text{W}}{\text{m}^2}\right], \qquad (15\text{-}1)$$

where $\boldsymbol{x}_1, \boldsymbol{x}_2, \ldots, \boldsymbol{x}_N$ are unit vectors, one for each spectral band.

The N numbers for each pixel can be used as the coordinates to locate a point in an N-dimensional scatter plot representing the spectrum of each pixel. Alternatively, the tip of each vector will locate the point representing the spectrum of each pixel in an *N*-dimensional vector space. This plot of data is then observed for data clustering with each cluster representing pixels of different material types. In two dimensions, the plot might look like **Figure 15-15**. In this example, there are two distinct clusters representing the spectra of pixels of two different material types, for example, vegetation and water, that appear to make up the entire scene.

Figure 15-15
Two dimensional representation of pixel spectra across the scene.

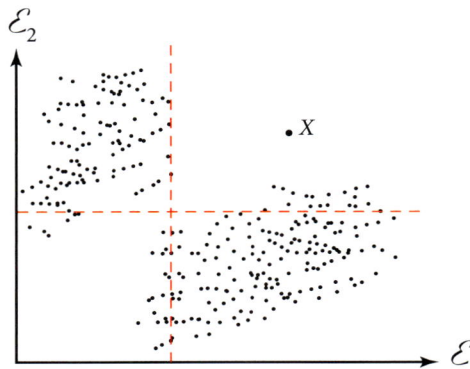

Note the power of spectral clustering even when using only two spectral bands. In the example, there are pixels with values in band 1 (**Figure 15-15**) that are such that the analyst is not sure which material type is in the pixel, similarly for the values of band 2. But, the values for bands 1 and 2 together allow the analyst to determine the material type with the exception of point X.

If all the pixels in a cluster are the same material type, why are the values in bands 1 and 2 different, and hence, should the cluster of points really be just one point? The answer is many MSI sensors, such as Landsat, have large ground pixels (30 by 30 m) and few pixels are pure (i.e., contain only one material). So, the variation in values in bands 1 and 2 within the cluster represents pixels having varying amounts of other materials present (e.g., a road passing through a grassy meadow). Also, all of the pixels of a given material type in the scene do not have the same irradiation because of shadowing produced by broken clouds, low sun angles, and tall objects.

So what about pixel X? Which material type is it, or is it the one pixel in the scene having a material that is not one of the two types that comprise most of the scene? Several methods are available to compare the spectrum represented by point X with the spectra of other pixels in the scene. Some are totally automated, and the analyst merely accepts the result of the computer implemented algorithms. This analysis is termed unsupervised. Others require analyst involvement throughout the process. This analysis is termed supervised.

Once all (or most) the pixels have been assigned to one of the several clusters in a scatter plot, the material identification for each cluster must be made. Generally, the analyst does this by some combination of image context and comparison with reference spectra. Image context can provide a variety of insight. For example, long straight objects in a scene are more apt to be roads than rivers. Cars are usually not found in the middle of lakes. Reference spectra used for identification can be found in two places: 1) known pixels in the scene using level 1 or 2 data; or 2) archived lab or field measurements, usually provided as reflectance (level 2 data).

To compare spectra between pixels or between pixels and references, a methodology must be designed and followed. Suppose two spectra are given by

$$\left.\begin{array}{l} \textbf{A}: \{\lambda_j, a_j\}, \text{ and} \\ \textbf{B}: \{\lambda_j, b_j\} \end{array}\right\} \quad (15\text{-}2)$$

where for each spectral band λ_j (where $j = 1,2,\ldots,N$), spectrum **A** has irradiances a_j, and spectrum **B** has irradiances of b_j.

These two spectra are plotted in **Figure 15-16**.

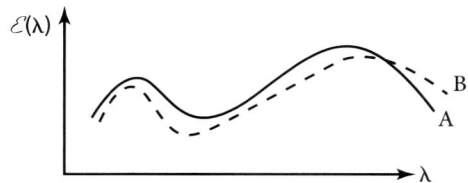

Figure 15-16
Two spectra to be compared.

Several basic algorithm types have been used. One algorithm type involves least squares from statistics:

1. Document the differences between the two spectrum, band by band, by calculating $\Sigma[a_j - b_j]^2 = [a_1 - b_1]^2 + [a_2 - b_2]^2 + \ldots + [a_N - b_N]^2$.
2. Select a threshold, d_T.
3. Apply the following test:

    If $\Sigma[a_j - b_j]^2 < d_T$, then the spectra A and B are the *same*.

    If $\Sigma[a_j - b_j]^2 > d_T$, then the spectra A and B are *different*.

The method to select an appropriate value for the threshold, d_T, will be considered in **Chapter 18**.

A second approach involves vector algebra, or equivalently plane geometry, applied to the scatter diagrams. The following discussion describes vector algebra, but the same results can be obtained using plane geometry. The two spectra **A** and **B** to be compared can be represented as two vectors.

$$\left.\begin{array}{l} \mathbf{A} = \sum_{i=1}^{N} a_i \mathbf{x}_i = a_1 \mathbf{x}_1 + a_2 \mathbf{x}_2 + \ldots + a_N \mathbf{x}_N. \\ \mathbf{B} = \sum_{i=1}^{N} b_i \mathbf{x}_i = b_1 \mathbf{x}_1 + b_2 \mathbf{x}_2 + \ldots + b_N \mathbf{x}_N. \end{array}\right\} \quad (15\text{-}3)$$

One useful vector algebra calculation is the magnitude of the vector difference $|\mathbf{A} - \mathbf{B}|$. This difference is illustrated in **Figure 15-17**, which shows spectra **A** and **B** in $\mathcal{E}_1, \mathcal{E}_2$ space. This difference is sometimes referred to as the "spectral distance d." In the N-dimensional vector space,

$$d^2 = |\mathbf{A} - \mathbf{B}|^2 = \sum_{i=1}^{N} [a_i - b_i]^2 = [a_1 - b_1]^2 + [a_2 - b_2]^2 + \ldots + [a_N - b_N]^2. \quad (15\text{-}4)$$

A second useful vector algebra calculation is the angle ξ between the two vectors, which is shown in **Figure 15-17** for two bands. This angle is sometimes referred to as the "spectral angle."

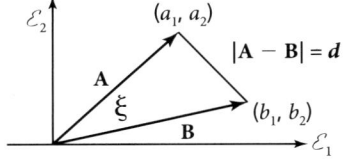

Figure 15-17
Spectral distance and spectral angle between two spectra.

In the N-dimensional vector space,

$$\cos \xi = \frac{1}{|\mathbf{A}||\mathbf{B}|}\sum_{i=1}^{N} a_i b_i = \frac{1}{|\mathbf{A}||\mathbf{B}|}[a_1 b_1 + a_2 b_2 + \ldots + a_N b_N], \quad (15\text{-}5)$$

where the magnitudes of A and B are given by

$$\left.\begin{array}{l}|\mathbf{A}| = \sqrt{\sum_{i=1}^{N} a_i^2} = \sqrt{a_1^2 + a_2^2 + \ldots + a_N^2} \\ |\mathbf{B}| = \sqrt{\sum_{i=1}^{N} b_i^2} = \sqrt{b_1^2 + b_2^2 + \ldots + b_N^2}.\end{array}\right\} \quad (15\text{-}6)$$

Once this angle is calculated, a threshold angle ξ_T is chosen, and the following test is performed.

If $\xi < \xi_T$, spectra **A** and **B** are the same.

If $\xi > \xi_T$, spectra **A** and **B** are different.

EXAMPLES OF FULL-SCENE CHARACTERIZATION

Now that some of the details about the comparison of spectra necessary for full scene characterization have been discussed as well as other MSI analysis, some examples of scene characterization will be presented.

The Landsat MSI image product in **Figure 15-18** shows a 90 × 160 km region containing the US Navy's Chocolate Mountain Training Area in Southern California located about 200 km inland from San Diego and about 50 km north of the Mexican border. Also included to the west of the Chocolate Mountains are the Salton Sea and the Imperial Valley with its irrigated cropland. Each pixel has been characterized by comparing its spectrum with a reference spectrum for each of the following categories: urban (portrayed as red), healthy vegetation (green), rangeland (gold), sparse vegetation (yellow), water (blue), light soils (grey), medium soils (brown), dark soils (dark brown), basalt flow (orange), and salt flat (white). The category colors are suggestive of the material they represent: blue

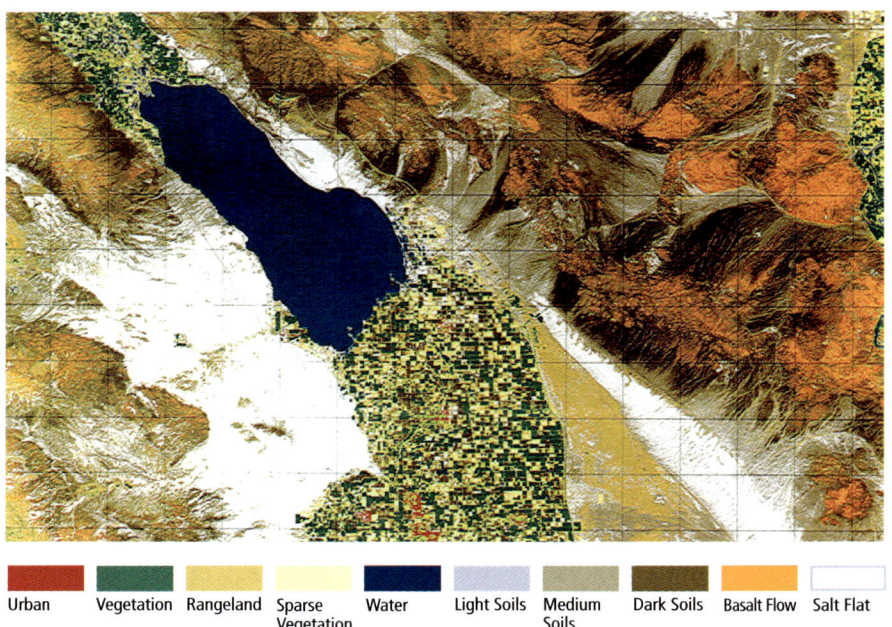

Figure 15-18
Scene characterization of inland southern California. (Courtesy of ERIM.)

for water, white for salt flats, etc. It is tempting to think of this spectral product as merely a color image of the scene. But it is more than that. The water pixels could have been portrayed as orange and those of basalt flats as purple.

In **Figures 15-19** and **15-20**, spectrally processed Landsat imagery of the Eglin Air Force Base area on the Florida panhandle is shown. This area is primarily low vegetation with cleared areas for roads, airfields, and training areas. **Figure 15-19** shows the scene categories, and **Figure 15-20** shows trafficability, or mobility assessment. It is not surprising that cleared areas correspond to low impedance (to travel) areas, while heavy vegetation and swampy areas correspond to high impedance areas.

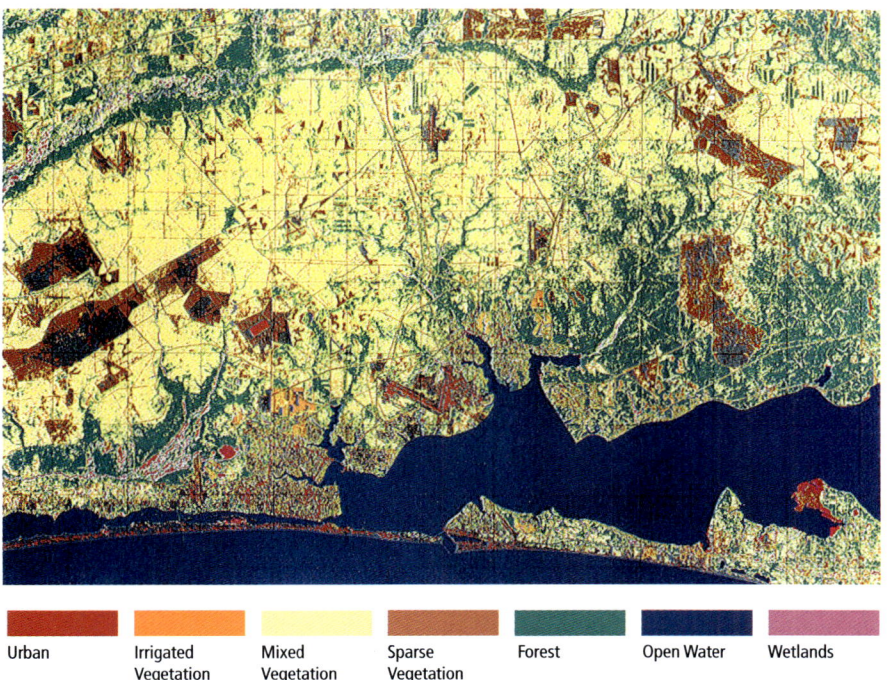

Figure 15-19
Scene characterization of Eglin Air Force Base, Florida area. (Courtesy of ERIM.)

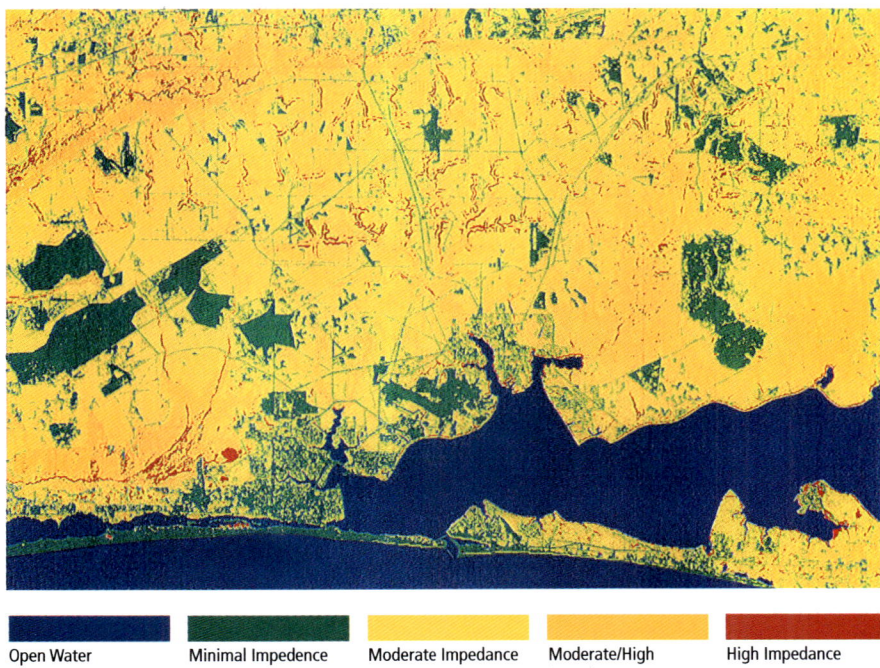

Figure 15-20
Trafficability maps of Eglin Air Force Base, Florida area. (Courtesy of ERIM.)

In **Figure 15-21**, a completely different type of scene is characterized. Ice classification is shown in the Saginaw Bay of Lake Huron. The Michigan land areas are portrayed as black.

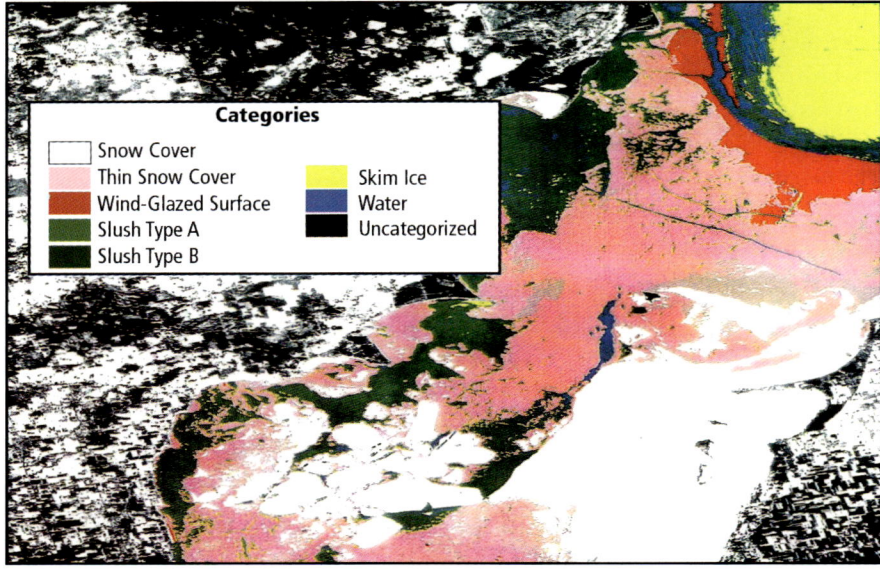

Figure 15-21
Scene classification of Michigan ice. (Courtesy of ERIM.)

Another example of scene characterization involves a man-made complex, shown in **Figure 15-22**, where the construction materials of a facility are identified. The enhanced spatial resolution (1 m) imagery was taken by ERIM's airborne M-7 MSI scanner.

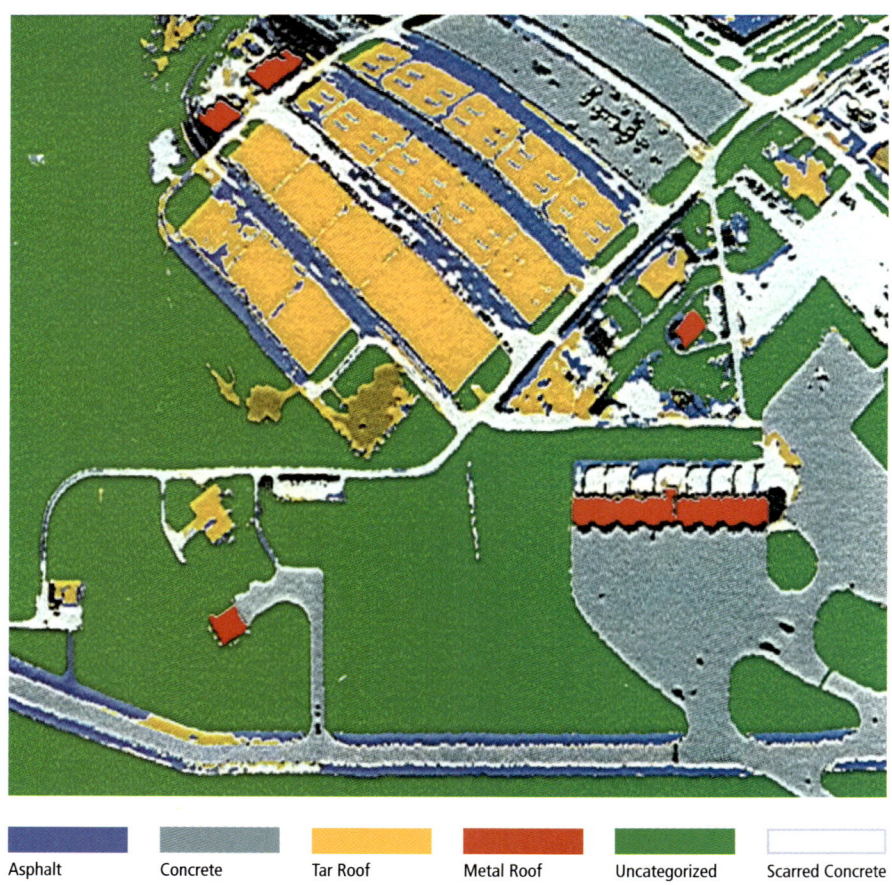

Figure 15-22
Scene characterization of building material. (Courtesy of ERIM.)

304 CHAPTER 15 CLASSICAL MSI IN THE VISIBLE TO SWIR

A final example of scene classification involves a Landsat image of the water off the shore of Kuwait during Desert Storm as shown in **Figure 15-23**.

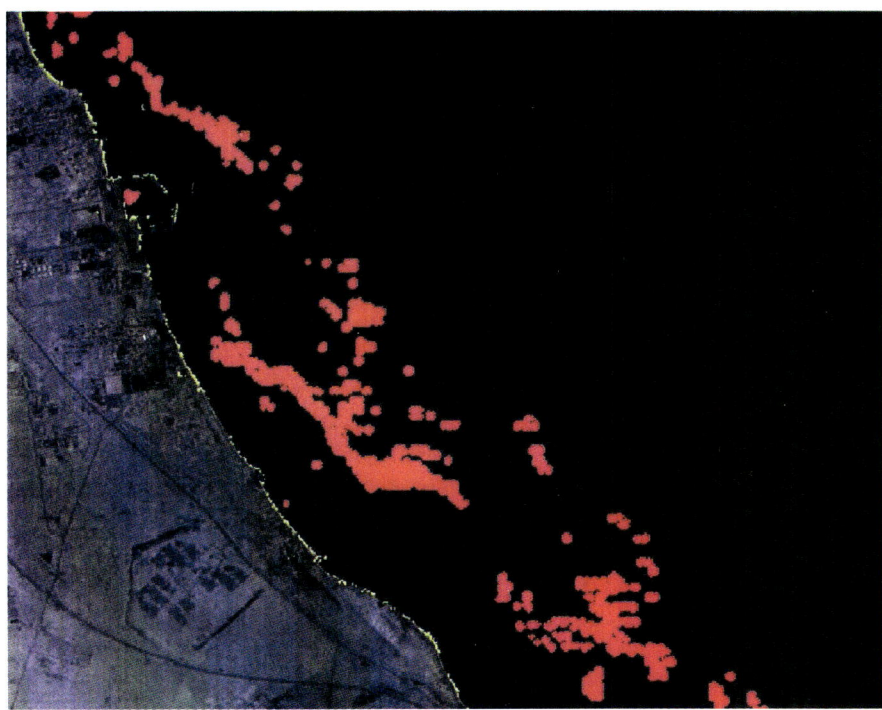

Figure 15-23
Scene characterization of water offshore from Kuwait. [3]

TARGET SPECTRAL MATCHING

Another form of MSI analysis is termed "target spectral matching." This analysis can be used to locate all the pixels in the scene of a particular material type. Approaches can utilize either irradiance MSI (level 1 data) or reflectance MSI (level 2 data). For scene irradiance data, one or more ground pixels that were identified as the material of interest using some other means are used to provide a "scene specific" reference signature. Then, the spectra of all other pixels in the scene are compared one at a time with this reference spectrum. To obtain scene reflectance data, the MSI irradiance data must be corrected for the atmosphere (convert level 1 data to level 2 data.) Historically, this has been done with in-scene pixels of known reflectance. Any number of reference spectra can be chosen from libraries of measured material reflectance data. Then, the spectra from each ground pixel in the scene can be compared with any of the chosen reference spectra from the libraries. For processing either level 1 or 2 MSI data, spectra comparisons can be done using either spectral angle or spectral distance.

A simplified and more popular approach is the false-color-composite display. In this approach, three bands or features (combinations of bands) are chosen to display the data, so the spectral differences between the object of interest and background are emphasized in imagery seen by an analyst. This is illustrated in **Figure 15-24**.

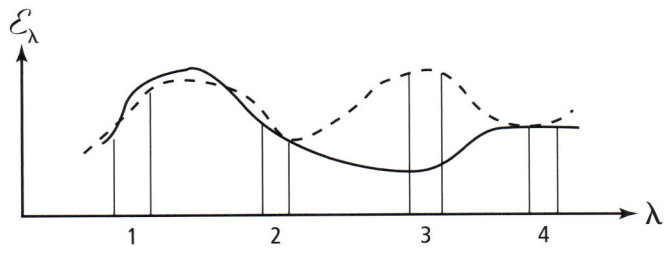

Figure 15-24
Illustration of band sampling of spectra of the object of interest and background.

The advantages of this approach are its simplicity and ease of application. (It is a primitive form of a spectral matched filter.) The disadvantages are it works well only when backgrounds are spectrally homogenous and target-background differences are large in at least one band (or feature); it is not automatic; and it does benefit from the involvement of an analyst.

Figure 15-25, using Landsat MSI from the Wright-Patterson Air Force Base, Ohio area, illustrates both the development and utility of false-color composite imagery. In the 321 true color composite, city structure is visible but with little information of the material types present. In the 432 false color composite involving the NIR, ground pixels containing mostly healthy vegetation appear as red. This results because the spectra of healthy vegetation show very strong reflectance in the NIR (**Chapter 3**). In the 753 false color composite involving both SWIR bands, ground pixels containing healthy vegetation appear as dark green, and those with concrete in the city appear as light purple, or lavender. Again, in the spectra of healthy vegetation, the reflectance in band 5 (SWIR1) portrayed as green is considerably larger than in band 3 (red) portrayed as blue or band 7 (SWIR2) portrayed as red. In the spectrum of concrete, the reflectance in band 7 (SWIR2) portrayed as red and in band 3 (red) portrayed as blue are considerably larger than in band 5 (SWIR1) portrayed as green. Hence, concrete in the city is portrayed as lavender, which is a mix of red and blue.

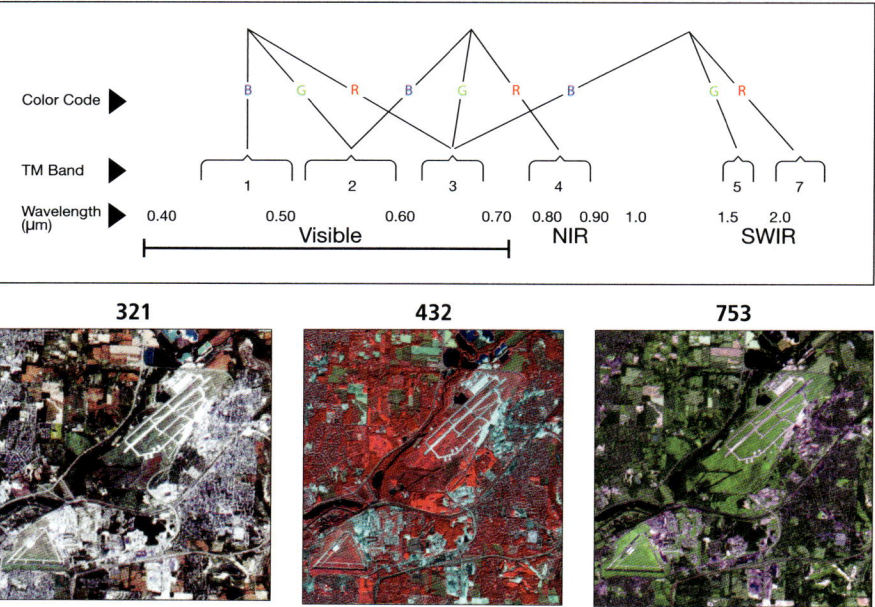

Figure 15-25
Introduction of false-color composite images.

Another example is shown in **Figures 15-26**, **15-27**, and **15-28**. These images, a quarter of a full Landsat image, show the north coast of Germany on the North Sea, including the port cities of Bremerhaven and Wilhelmshaven, in 321 true-color composite, 432 false-color composite involving the NIR, and a 753 false-color composite involving the SWIR, respectively. Clearly visible in the true color composite as well as the other composites are the remnants of two jet contrails, a puff of a cirrus cloud, the North Sea, inlets for ports, a river, and considerable urban and coastal structure.

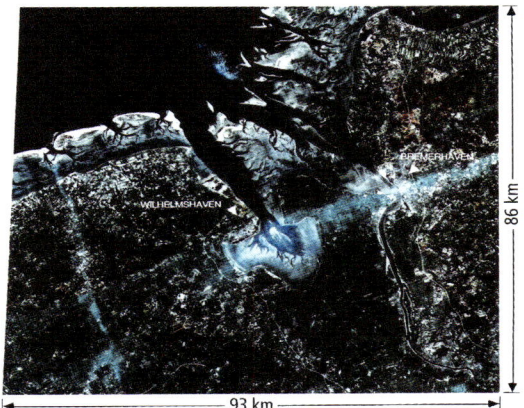

Figure 15-26
True-color composite (321) image of north German coast.

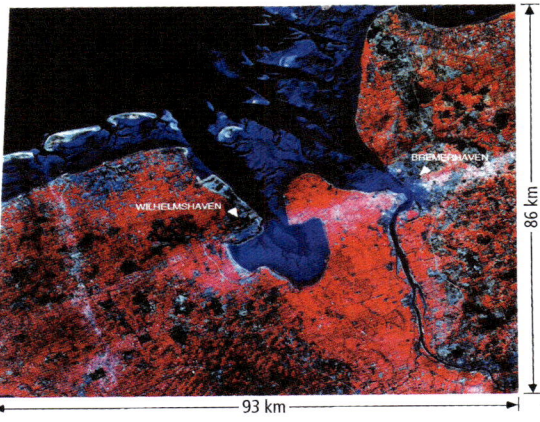

Figure 15-27
False color composite (432) involving the NIR of the north German coast.

In the 432 false-color composite involving the NIR, the presence of vegetation (in red) is clearly indicated, while the coastal and port structure appears more subdued.

Figure 15-28
False color composite (753) involving the SWIR of the north German coast.

In the false-color composite involving the SWIR, vegetation is still clearly indicated (in green), while much of the coastal structure has completely disappeared with the exception of some long narrow barrier islands. This results from the property of water that does not reflect and transmit almost any light in the SWIR compared with shorter wavelengths in the visible. So, much of the coastal and port structure shown in the visible image is below the surface of the water. The depths are quite shallow between the coastline and the barrier islands. This shallow coastline is part of the German Wattenmeer National Park and extends into the Netherlands as well.

PRINCIPAL COMPONENT ANALYSIS

PCA can be applied in several ways to spectral data. One result is background suppression[3] in MSI. **Figure 15-29** illustrates this result in two dimensions. Starting with the original scatter plot shown earlier with two clusters visible in bands 1 and 2, a change in bands may be useful to detect one material type by suppressing the other.

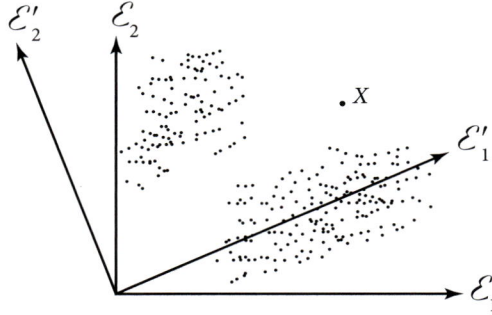

Figure 15-29
Results of PCA in two dimensions (two spectral bands).

This may be accomplished by defining a new feature space with two new bands in which the pixel values are just some linear combination of those in the original bands. See below:

$$\mathcal{E}'_1 = x_{11}\mathcal{E}_1 + x_{12}\mathcal{E}_2 \tag{15-7}$$
$$\mathcal{E}'_2 = x_{22}\mathcal{E}_1 + x_{22}\mathcal{E}_2$$

These equations just represent a linear transformation of the pixel values, and in this case, a rotation of coordinate axes from one set of bands to the new set. In the new bands, one of the materials now has very low pixel values of $\mathcal{E}_2$ than it originally had. Thus, the pixels of the other material will stand out in contrast to the pixels in this spectral band.

Another result from PCA, especially useful for HSI, describes the features (combinations of bands) in which the pixel values have the largest variability (first few principal components) and the least variability (all higher components). In doing so, any number of spectral bands may be identified as having little or no effect on some spectral analyses, and hence data in those bands does not require processing.

An example of the use of PCA for background suppression in Landsat MSI imagery is shown in **Figure 15-30**. The spectral image of a desert scene before and after PCA was applied is shown. In the original true-color composite, only a few roads are seen in the mottled desert background of sand and sagebrush. After PCA, this desert background is suppressed, and the roads as well as a matrix of small objects (only a few pixels in size) within the red box are more clearly seen.

Figure 15-30
PCA applied for background suppression in MSI. [3]

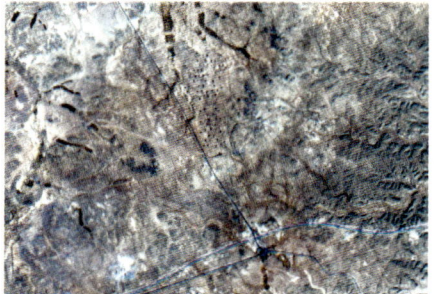 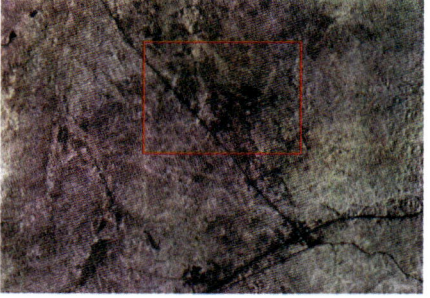

[3] Recall PCA was also used to suppress the background in large area surveillance. See Section 14.2, Example 14-1, and Sidebar **Principal Components** (located in **Section 14.2**).

SUB-PIXEL ANALYSIS

Another valuable tool that can often be used with spectral analysis on data with large ground pixels such as Landsat is sub-pixel purification. Because Landsat ground pixels are large (30 m) compared with many objects of interest, or because multi-pixel objects may be composed of several material types, both of these objects can be a challenge to conventional spectral analysis. The use of spectral purification of individual ground pixels before comparison with reference spectra can produce impressive results. The basic idea of spectral pixel purification, as illustrated in **Figure 15-31**, is to characterize the spectrum of the nearby background pixels and subtract the correct amount of background spectra from the spectrum of the pixel in question.

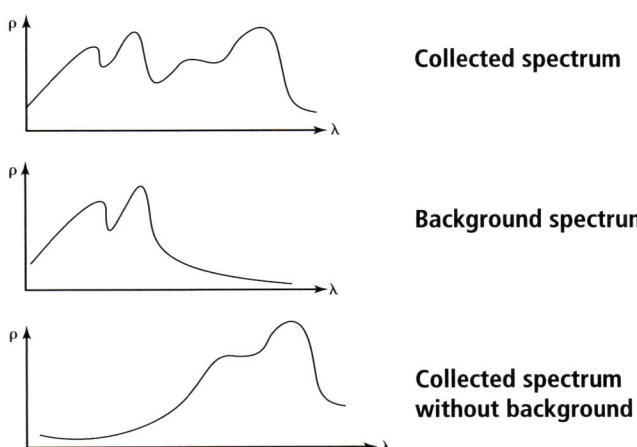

Figure 15-31
Pixel purification concept for sub-pixel detection.

In **Figure 15-31**, this procedure appears to be quite easy, because it was drawn so the spectrum of the average background is concentrated at the lower wavelengths and that of the possible object of interest is concentrated at the higher wavelengths. This is rarely the case. So, the amount of background to be removed from a pixel depends on two factors: knowledge of the dimensions of the possible object of interest and the skill and experience of the analyst.

CHANGE DETECTION

Change detection involves two MSI images of the same area. Products of change detection flag pixels where a change has occurred between collections. These changes are then used to cue other sensors. The area searched can be as extensive as a full Landsat scene (185 by 185 km) or localized to a known, but complex area. It has also been used to document the extent of known changes of interest in a large scene. Some general steps involved in change detection include the following:

1. Acquire two Landsat MSI images of the same area at the same time of year. Otherwise, growing season changes could be overwhelming in number.
2. Register the two MSI images spatially, so they accurately overlay one-another within a fraction of a ground pixel. With the large pixels of Landsat, finding control points are again a problem, especially in rural desert or wooded scenes.

More detailed steps in a change detection spectral analysis technique are listed below for the Pisces technique developed by ERIM and implemented in COSMEC (discussed later in the chapter):

1. Screen out unwanted objects (that will produce unwanted changes) from both scenes (such as clouds and their shadows).
2. Select spectral features to help identify the desired change type (e.g., clearing greenery before construction, melting ice to open bodies of water.
3. Normalize both scenes for possible irradiation differences.
4. Subtract the two MSI images portrayed in the desired spectral feature.
5. Annotate the changes for further investigation.

An example of a change detection analysis using Landsat images of the Nizhnyaya–Tavda area in Russia is shown in the following figures. **Figures 15-32** and **15-33** show two full-scene Landsat SWIR composite images collected three years apart. The change image is shown in **Figure 15-34**, documenting many changes. The white pixels represent the presence of clouds in either of the two images. The black pixels represent pixels where no change occurred between the two images. Red pixels represent pixels brighter in the second image caused in many cases by vegetation removal. Cyan pixels represent pixels brighter in the first image caused by the presence of vegetation.

Figure 15-32
Full Landsat scene on first day (July 2, 1984). (Courtesy of ERIM.)

Figure 15-33
Full Landsat scene on second day (June 25, 1987). (Courtesy of ERIM.)

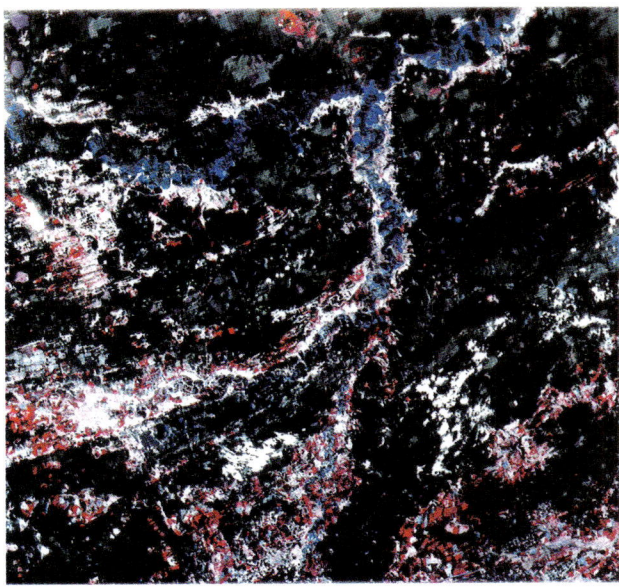

Figure 15-34
Change detection product.
(Courtesy of ERIM.)

Within this large Landsat scene is an industrial facility. Images of this area (15 by 15 km in size) for the two dates are shown side-by-side in **Figure 15-35**. The changes in this simple object are readily apparent: construction of many additional buildings in the north half of the facility as well as a new wider entry road from the main highway to the South. These changes are confirmed in the change image shown in **Figure 15-36**. While change detection image generation was not necessary for such a simple object of interest, it illustrates the utility the analysis might have for a more complex facility, such as a large military base or chemical plant.

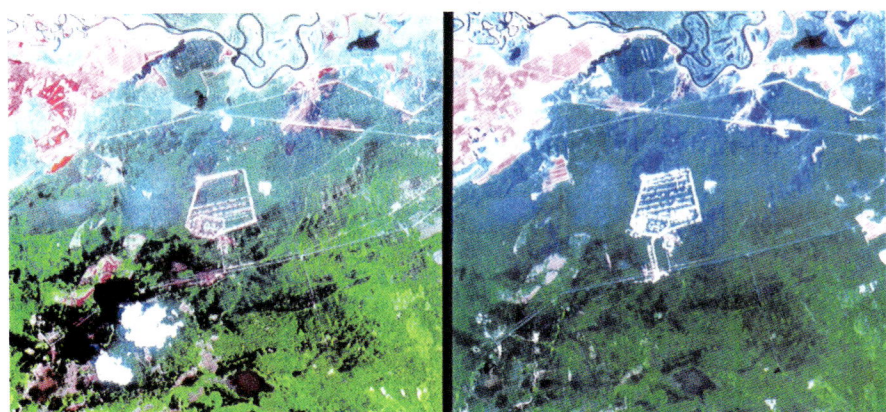

Figure 15-35
Known facility day 1 and day 2.

Figure 15-36
Known facility spectral change detection product. (Courtesy of ERIM.)

The final two examples of Landsat change images, **Figures 15-37** and **15-38**, are not designed to find new objects but rather to document the extent of known changes. **Figure 15-37** documents the extent of a portion of the Alaskan pipeline around the north slope Prudhow Bay oil fields (colored in yellow). **Figure 15-38** documents the extent of a large flood of the Mississippi River in the St. Louis area where the Missouri and Illinois Rivers empty into the Mississippi River. Light blue denotes the normal extent of these rivers, while dark blue denotes the extent of the 1993 flood.

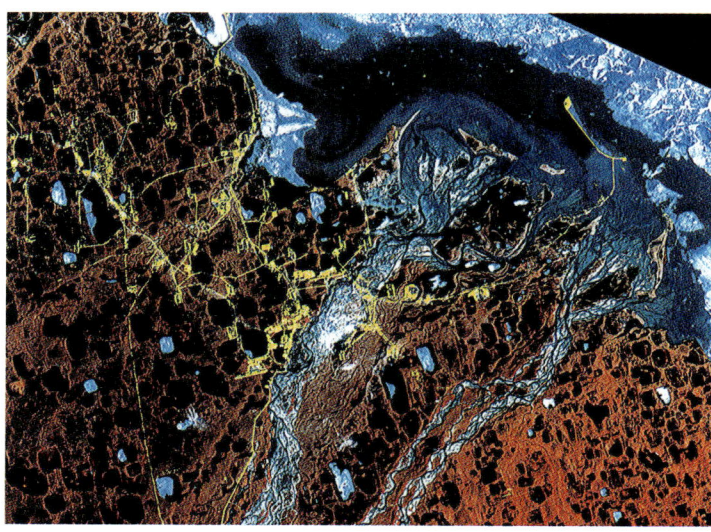

Figure 15-37
Documenting the extent of known large area change: Alaska north shore oil pipeline. (Courtesy of ERIM.)

Figure 15-38
Documenting the extent of known large area change: flooding in Missouri. (Courtesy of ERIM.)

BATHYMETRY

Bathymetry[4] products may result from the most interesting of all MSI processing. These products are generally maps of coastal (or littoral) regions with the water depths (and perhaps bottom type) indicated at each location. Bathymetry is a very different MSI application. Most electromagnetic radiation does not penetrate water very well. Within the visible region of the spectrum, blue and green are the best. Outside of the visible, NIR, SWIR, MWIR, and LWIR wavelengths are readily absorbed by the surface layer of water; hence, reflection from the surface as well as transmission through the water are very low. Additional complications result from water turbidity (amount of water-suspended sediment), scum or algae on the water surface, and sea state (wave height).

[4] Bathymetry is the study of the underwater depth of bodies of water (lakes and oceans). Bathymetric charts are produced to support safety of surface or sub-surface navigation.

To estimate water depth, a complex propagation/transmission problem must be solved for each location. This is illustrated in **Figure 15-39**. Of the irradiance incident from the sun onto the surface, some radiation is reflected at the air-sea boundary, and some is transmitted. As the portion which is transmitted propagates through the water, some is absorbed or scattered by the water and any sediment that might be present. Some radiation reaches the bottom, where some is absorbed, and some is diffusely reflected. Of the reflected portion in the direction of the sensor, some finally reaches the surface and is transmitted back to the air where it is collected. Different irradiances will arrive at the sensor depending on the wavelengths involved. This whole water transmission problem is similar to the atmospheric transmission problem for which computer codes such as MODTRAN are routinely used. A water transmission code is HydroLight developed by Sequoya Scientific in Bellevue, Washington.

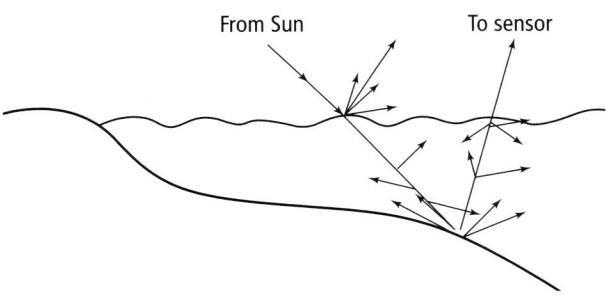

Figure 15-39
Bathymetry viewing geometry.

The simplest scenario for bathymetry analysis involves low turbidity, often found in Hawaii, the Bahamas, and other locations where there is minimal run-off and storms (to stir up the bottom material) rarely occur. Known bottom type, and hence reflectivity, greatly simplify the analysis. For these simple scenes, Landsat imagery can be used, and the ratio of the received irradiance in blue and green can be used to estimate depth. Examples of these bathymetry products are seen **Figures 15-40** to **15-43**.

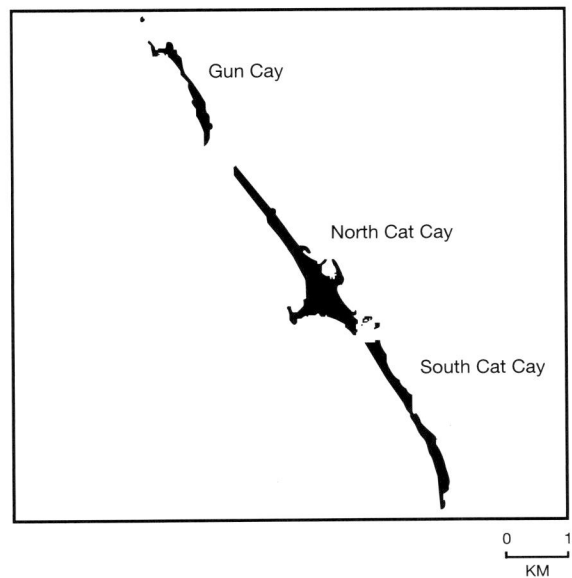

Figure 15-40
Map of Gun, North Cat, and South Cat Cays in the Bahamas.

Figure 15-41
MSI Bathymetry Product of the Cat Cay area in Bahamas. (Courtesy of ERIM.)

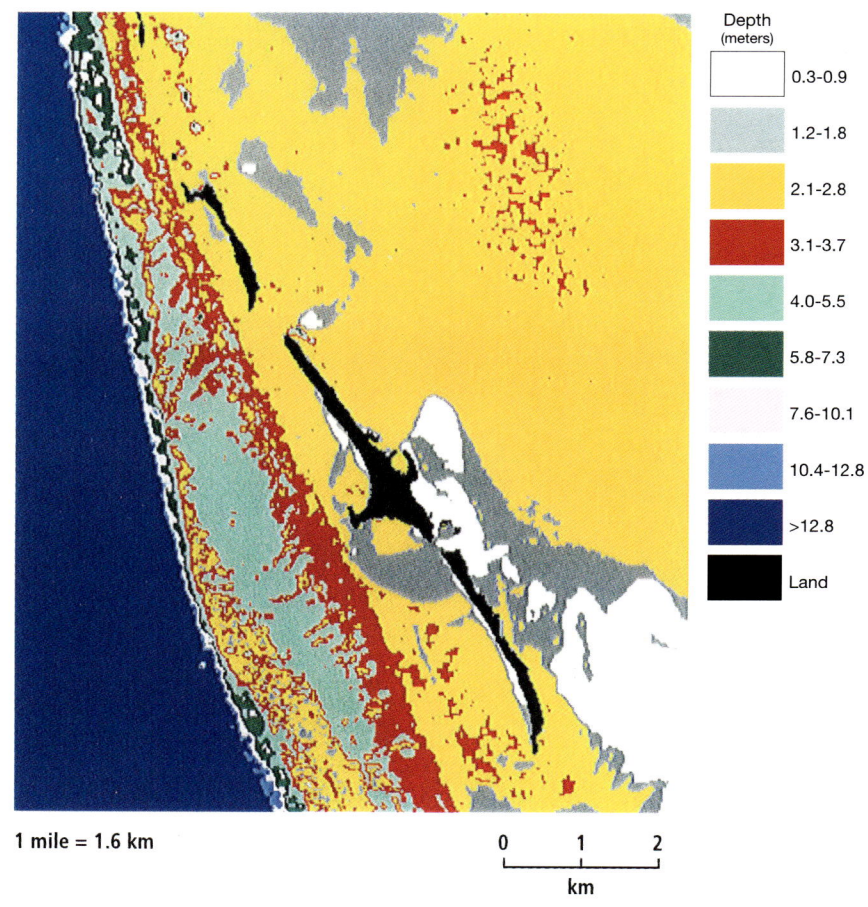

The scene in **Figures 15-40** and **15-41** shows the area around North Cat Cay, a long narrow island in the Bahamas, first as an area map and then a bathymetry product with depth color coded. In the bathymetry product, it is interesting to note the relatively slow increase in depth northeast of the island, but the rapid fall-off in depth southwest of the island. Beyond 12.8 m depths, insufficient light is reflected off the bottom for the Landsat measurement.

Figure 15-42 shows a bathymetry product for the waters northwest of the nation of Qatar, located on a peninsula sticking out into the Persian Gulf from Saudi Arabia. In this image, the black area in the lower right quadrant of the scene is a land area that is part of Qatar. **Figure 15-43** shows a bathymetry product for the waters on all sides of the small island nation of Bahrain, that is northwest of Qatar. In both products, there are regions that stretch several kilometers from the coast where the water remains quite shallow. Such regions of slightly submerged sandbars prove hazardous to large vessels entering or exiting the nearby harbors.

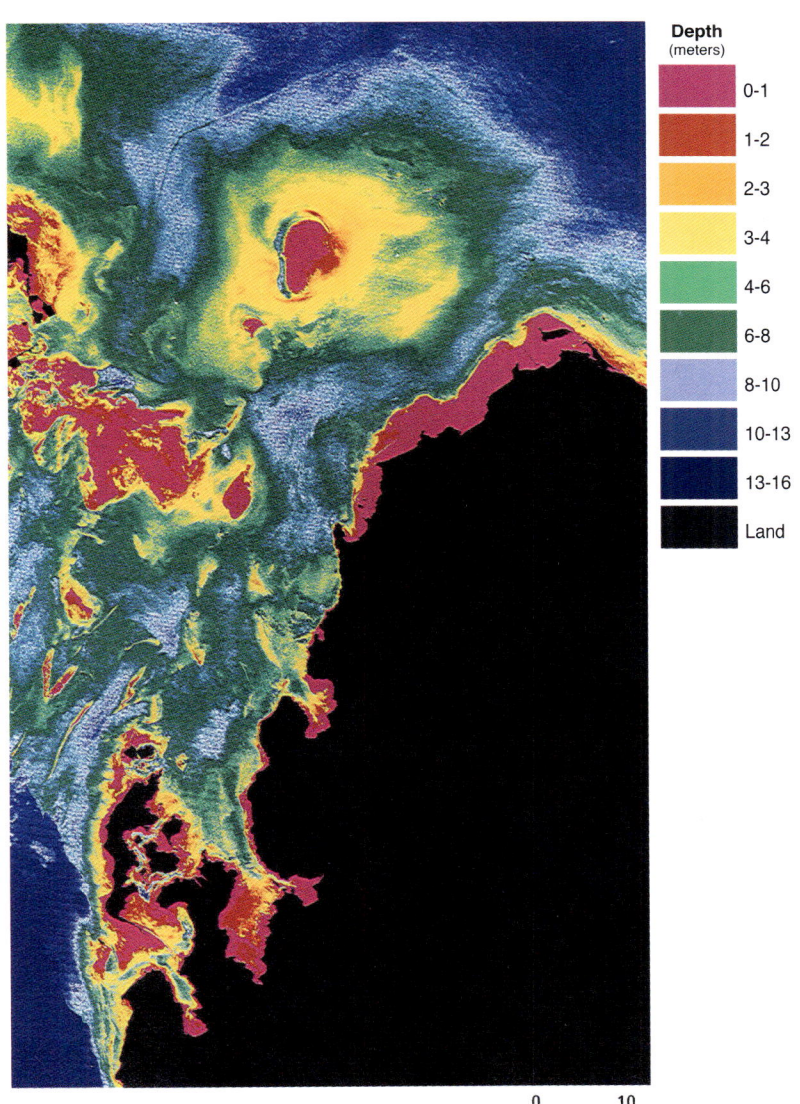

Figure 15-42
MSI bathymetry product of area northwest of Qatar. (Courtesy of ERIM.)

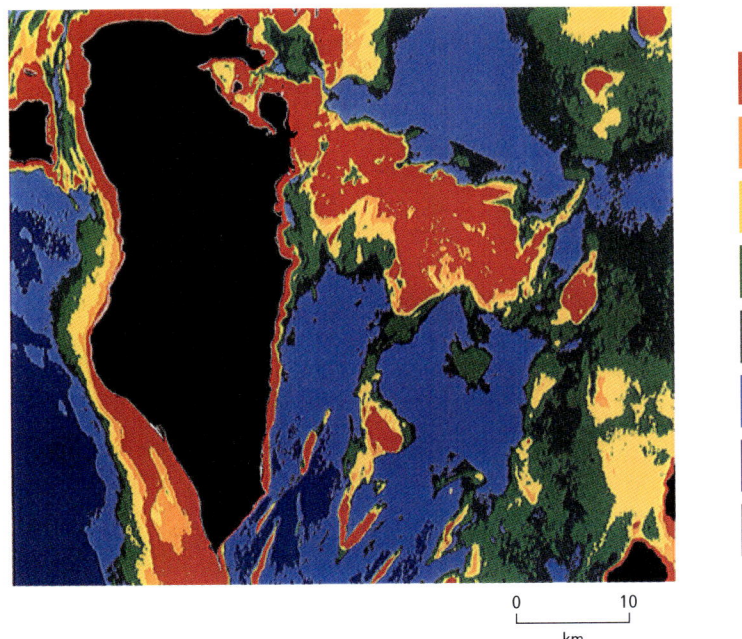

Figure 15-43
MSI bathymetry product area around Bahrain. (Courtesy of ERIM.)

CHAPTER 15 CLASSICAL MSI IN THE VISIBLE TO SWIR

More complex scenes, involving higher turbidity and/or unknown bottom types, require advanced bathymetry analysis and usually more spectral bands. Techniques are still under development. Satellite MSI is not the only bathymetry technique. Other techniques can sometimes be applied using satellite Synthetic Aperture Radar (SAR), airborne Light Detection and Ranging (LIDAR), and ship sonar. **Table 15-7** summarizes and compares these techniques.

Table 15-7 Comparison of the bathymetry techniques.

Technique	Platform Operating Areas	Coverage Area	Mapping Accuracy	Maximum Depth	Limitations
Satellite MSI	Friendly or hostile waters	Global	Can be difficult	18.3 m	Surface films or water turbidity
Satellite SAR[5]	Friendly or hostile waters	Local or global	Depends on location	Depends on water wave wavelength	Observations require water waves
Airborne LIDAR	Friendly waters only	Local	Precision	Depends on power of lasers used	Surface films or water turbidity
Ship Sonar	Friendly waters only	Local	Better capability in deep waters	Depends on power of sonar source	Thermal gradients or salinity

As spectral applications and analysis techniques have developed over the years, several toolboxes of spectral exploitation algorithms have been developed and are currently available to analysts. The three most commonly used include:

1. Intergraph (formerly ERDAS) IMAGINE,
2. RSI's (now Exelis Visual Information Solutions) ENVI (Environment for Visualizing Images), and
3. DOD's COMET[6]

These three spectral exploitation toolboxes are described and compared in **Table 15-8**. The general trend of all three toolboxes has been to add algorithms and diversify from initial strengths to capabilities in many areas.

Table 15-8 Comparison of spectral analysis toolboxes.

General Information	IMAGINE	ENVI	COMET
Developer	Intergraph (ERDAS)	RSI (Kodak, Exelis)	Ball Aerospace (and General Dynamics)
Time frame of Initial Release	1970s	1980s	2000
Gov't Sponsor of Development	None	None	DOD
Distributor	Intergraph (License fee)	Exelis (License fee)	NASIC (free to US government and contractors)
Initial Data Set Inputs	MSI	HSI	MSI and HSI
Initial Applications	Civilian	Civilian	Military
Initial User Background	Spectral Scientist	Spectral Scientist	High school graduate
Initial Software language	Unix	IDL	C++
DODIIS[7] Certified	Yes	No	Yes

[5] Wavelength and motion of surface water waves are used to estimate water depth.

[6] The spectral analysis portion of COMET is available as Opticks from a dedicated website set up by developer Ball Aerospace in Fairborn, Ohio (www.opticks.org).

[7] Department of Defense Intelligence Information System (DODIIS).

15.4 OTHER MSI SPACEBORNE SENSORS

Since the first Landsat launched in 1972, many other satellites have launched with MSI sensors. These satellites have ranged from fully government-sponsored to fully commercial. Some have collected extensive amounts of data worldwide and became MSI data providers for customers worldwide. The satellite families that fill this role are organized in two categories:

1. Lower quality spatial resolution but initially *more* spectral bands
   - Landsat,
   - SPOT from France
   - Indian Remote Sensing (IRS) and Resourcesat from India
2. Improved spatial resolution but initially *fewer* spectral bands
   - Initial competing US systems and teams
     - Ikonos—Space Imaging (Lockheed Martin, Raytheon, and Kodak)
     - Quick Bird—Digital Globe (formerly Earth Watch) (Ball Aerospace and Kodak)
     - Orbview—Orbimage (Orbital Sciences Corp, Northrop-Grumman)
   - Next competing systems and teams following recent mergers
     - WorldView—Digital Globe (Ball Aerospace, Exelis using recently acquired Kodak)
       - WorldView 1—panchromatic only, launched September 2007
       - WorldView 2—launched October 2009
     - Geoeye–DigitalGlobe (merged to form Digital Globe; Orbimage bought Space Imaging; General Dynamics using recently acquired Spectrum-Astro; Exelis using recently acquired Kodak Aerospace)
       - Geoeye 1—launched September 2008
   - Current single system and team
     - WorldView 3—launched August 2014
     - Digital Globe

Characteristics of collection and sensor performance for all these sensors are shown in **Table 15-9**. The first five rows are those in the category of "poorer spatial resolution but initially *more* spectral bands." The next three rows are the *initial* systems in the category of "improved spatial resolution but *fewer* spectral bands." The next two systems are the next systems in the category of "improved spatial resolution but *fewer* spectral bands." The final system is the most current system.

Some interesting comparisons are visible in **Table 15-9**. All the satellites except for Landsat and IRS 1C and 1D have the capability to look off-nadir to collect images. This capability allows for more rapid acquisition of data of a particular location as well as faster revisit times. This is illustrated in **Figure 15-44** that shows the average revisit times for the Ikonos MSI sensor for various locations and desired spatial resolution. Clearly, the further off-nadir the sensor collects, the more frequently it collects a particular location but with poorer spatial resolution.

There are other interesting sensor trade-offs among the sensors listed in **Table 15-9**. Those in higher, more stable orbits (680 km altitude and above) require a sensor design that is more difficult to achieve adequate spatial resolution and sensitivity. For example, Ikonos 2 has a 70 cm diameter collecting mirror, and Geoeye 1 has a 1.1 m diameter collecting mirror.

Table 15-9
Commercial MSI sensor performance and collection characteristics. [4], [5], [6]

	Altitude (km)	Off-nadir FOR	MSI Bands	MSI Pixel Size (m)	Pan Pixel Size (m)	MSI Swath Width (km)
Landsat 7	705	0	B, G, R, NIR, SWIR (2) LWIR	30 60	15	185
IRS 1C, 1D	800	0	G, R, NIR, SWIR	23.5 (20)	5.8	141
Resourcesat1	817	+/– 26	R, G, NIR	5.8	5.8	23.9
SPOT 1, 2, 3	822	+/– 30	R, G, NIR	20	10	60
SPOT 4	822	+/– 30	R, G, NIR, SWIR	20	10	60
SPOT 5	822	+/– 30	R, G, NIR, SWIR	10 (20)	2.5 or 5	60
Ikonos 2	680	+/– 40	B, G, R, NIR	3.2	0.8	11
QuickBird 2	450	+/– 30	B, G, R, NIR	2.5	0.6	16.5
OrbView 3	470	+/– 30	B, G, R, NIR	1.65	1.0	8.0
GeoEye 1	684	+/– 60	B, G, R, NIR	1.8	0.41	15.2
WorldView 2	770	+/– 45	B (2), G, Y, R, NIR (3)	1.8	0.46	16.4
WorldView 3	617	+/– 20	Vis-NIR (8), SWIR (8), Other (12)	1.2-30	0.31	13.1

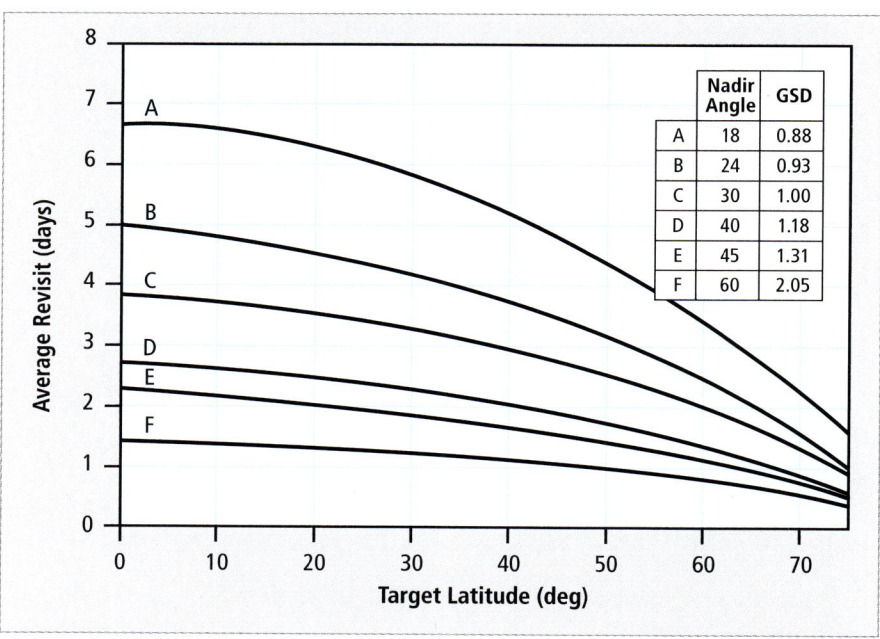

Figure 15-44
Ikonos revisit time.

Spectral products from these MSI sensors other than Landsat are a work in progress partially because they are relatively new and partially because they provide better spatial resolution imagery but in fewer spectral bands than Landsat. So, some spectral products developed with Landsat data have been produced by SPOT and some of the other spectral sensors. These include true color maps, ingress-egress panoramic imagery and movies, band sharpened versions of the above, full scene characterization, target spectral matching, and change detection cueing. Less spectral information can degrade these products. Merging (in optimal manner) the better spatial resolution with the spectral information is still a work in progress. So far, each application and object of interest seem to require varying amounts of spatial and spectral information. For example, for man-made vehicles of known multi-pixel extent, isolated single detected pixels have less importance than those that cluster at a particular location with a cluster size of about the dimensions of the vehicle.

16 MSI INVOLVING THE THERMAL INFRARED

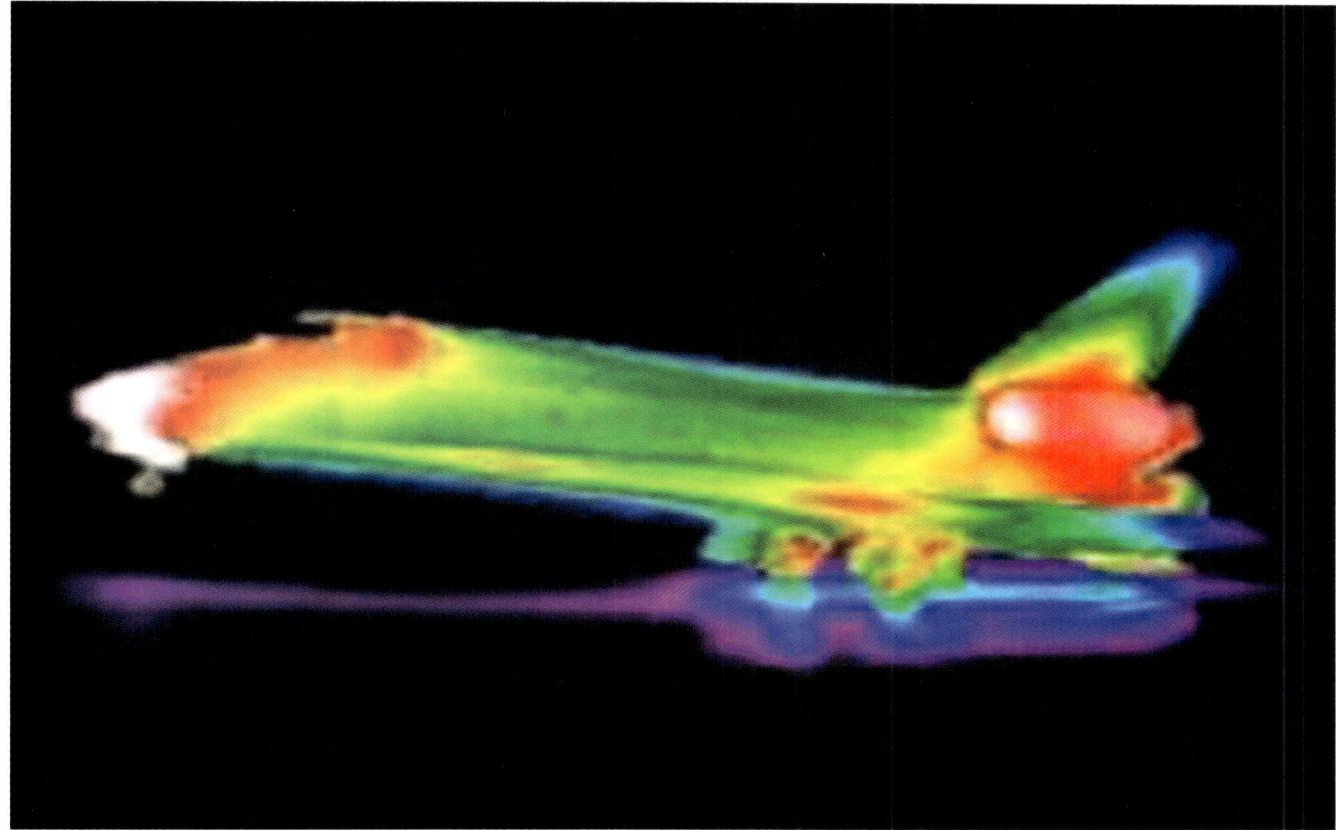

Multispectral imaging (MSI) can involve one or more spectral bands in the thermal infrared (Mid-Wave Infrared (MWIR) and Long-Wave Infrared (LWIR)) portion of the electromagnetic spectrum. The earliest such systems are found on meteorological satellites (metsats), and that is a logical place to begin this discussion. MSI in the thermal infrared has many other applications involving objects of interest on the Earth's surface. Intertwined with these systems and applications is the inherent capability to determine surface temperature from the data. Finally, MSI with spectral bands in the visible through thermal infrared can be collected not only with near-nadir viewing but also with viewing far off-nadir to almost horizontal viewing.

SECTIONS

16.1 METEOROLOGICAL SATELLITES

16.2 SURFACE TEMPERATURE DETERMINATION

16.3 MSI FAR OFF-NADIR VIEWING

16.1 METEOROLOGICAL SATELLITES

Metsats generally have two types of spectral sensors involving infrared spectral bands. The simpler, and by far the most familiar because of its use for TV weather programs, is the cloud imager. This will be the starting point for discussion, followed by the other sensor type, the atmospheric sounder.

CLOUD IMAGERS

The requirements for metsat cloud imagers are simple: to detect, identify, and map the full range of clouds from ground fog through high-altitude cirrus. To accomplish this, it is necessary to distinguish clouds from the background snow and ice and regions of light colored soil or sand.

There are several sensor/platform families. In low-altitude sun-synchronous orbits, the Department of Defense (DOD) Defense Meteorological Support Program (DMSP) and National Oceanic and Atmospheric Administration (NOAA) metsats cover every point on the Earth at least twice per day. Improved sensing capabilities are currently under development by the DOD and NOAA's advanced weather satellite programs.

In geosynchronous orbits, several families of sensors operate with each satellite continuously covering nearly a whole hemisphere. These include the NOAA Geostationary Operational Environmental Satellite (GOES) as well as the European Space Agency's (ESA) Meteorology Satellite (METEOSAT), Japan's Multi-functional Transport Satellite (MTSAT), India's Indian National Satellite (INSAT), Russia's Geostationary Operational Meteorological Satellite (GOMS), and China's Feng Yun 2. These satellites are distributed around the Earth's equator such that all areas of the world are covered with the exception of the polar regions. Intergovernmental cooperation enables any nation to obtain information beyond the access areas of particular satellite(s).

Some sensor parameters of the metsat cloud imagers aboard DMSP, NOAA-N, and NOAA GOES are listed in **Table 16-1**.

Table 16-1
Sensor parameters of the metsat cloud imagers aboard DMSP, NOAA-N, and NOAA GOES. [1], [2], [3]
(Vis = Visible; NIR = Near Infrared)

	DMSP	NOAA-N	GOES
Orbit type	Sun-synchronous	Sun-synchronous	Geosynchronous
Altitude (km)	780–890	830–870	35,800
Imaging mode	Cross-track scan	Cross-track scan	2-axis scan
Swath width (km)	3000	2900	N/A
Spectral dispersion technique	Interference filters	Interference filters	Interference filters
Spectral bands – best nadir pixel size (km)	1 Vis – 0.55 (day) 1 Vis – 2.7 (night) 1 LWIR – 0.55	1 Vis – 1.1 2 LWIR – 1.1 1 NIR – 1.1 1 MWIR – 1.1	1 Vis – 1 2 LWIR – 4 1 SWIR – 4 1 H_2O (6.7 μm) – 8

It is important to note all three sensors use interference filters (**Chapter 9**) to define their spectral bands. All use some sort of scan to provide sufficiently large coverage. To cover the whole Earth at least twice per day. with DMSP or NOAA-N, teh swaths must be much larger than that of Landsat Recall from the Landsat discussion in the last chapter that the Earth rotates nearly 3,000 km at the equator during the 100 minutes between successive equator passes by a low-altitude satellite. DMSP uses a cross-track scan of a single detector. Instead of a scanning mirror, the whole sensor telescope swings back and forth like a pendulum as the satellite moves in its near-polar orbit.

Figure 16-1
GOES visible band image in the western United States.

Figure 16-2
GOES LWIR band image in the western United States. (Image taken simultaneous as **Figure 16-1**.)

This movement poses a large challenge to maintain satellite stability. For such a wide swath, special provisions must be made to maintain both constant ground pixel size and measured pixel radiance across the swath.

The three sensors in **Table 16-1** have large ground pixels (greater than 500 m on a side) and at least one spectral band in both the visible and the LWIR. These two bands provide a capability to detect all clouds types at both high and low altitude. Cloud images collected by NOAA GOES sensors are shown in **Figures 16-1** through **16-4**. For both scenes (**Figure** pairs **16-1**, **16-2** and **16-3**, **16-4**), the visible image is positioned above the LWIR image. The LWIR images show differences in temperature, as will be explained in the next section.

In **Figure 16-2**, the infrared image is portrayed with the brighter objects representing areas with lowest temperatures. The low altitude clouds over the Pacific Ocean appear in the visible because of the difference in reflectivity between clouds and water. They do not appear in the infrared because the cloud temperature is nearly the same as the nearby water surface temperature. However, the high-altitude cirrus clouds over Kansas appear in the infrared images, while they are not very reflective in the visible.

CHAPTER 16 MSI INVOLVING THE THERMAL INFRARED

Figure 16-3
Metsat visible image of the United States. (Image provided by The Weather Channel.)

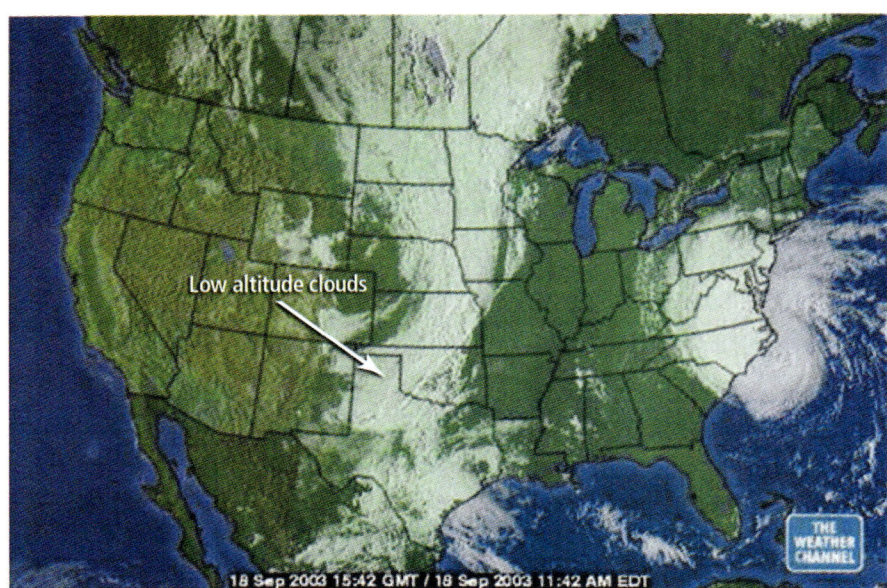

Figure 16-4
Metsat infrared image of the United States. (Image provided by The Weather Channel.)

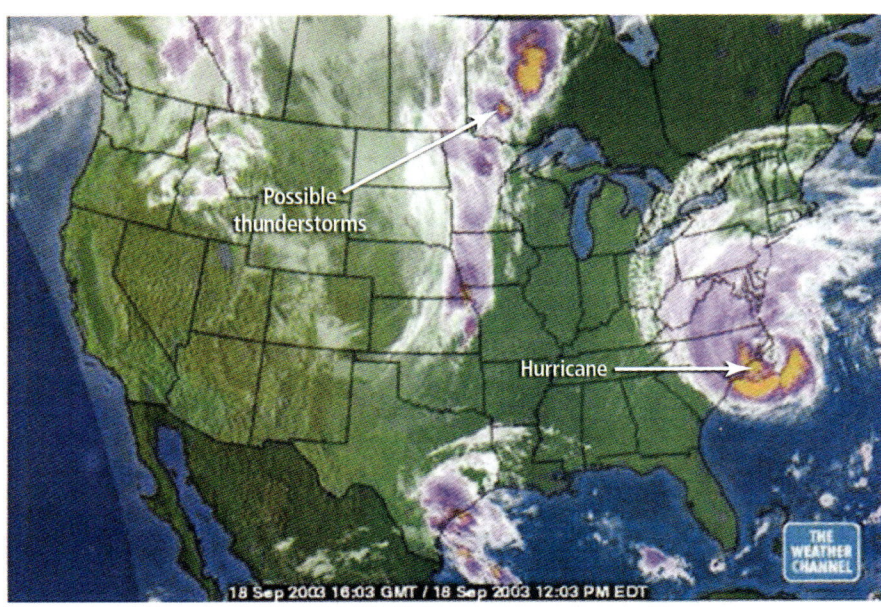

In **Figure 16-3**, the low altitude clouds over Oklahoma and northern Texas appear in the visible because of the difference in reflectivity between clouds and water. They do not appear in the infrared in **Figure 16-4** because the cloud temperature is nearly the same as the nearby land surface temperature. On the other hand, the infrared images show the high-altitude cloud tops as part of the hurricane off the coast of North Carolina and possible thunderstorms in western Ontario, Canada while they are just as reflective as nearby clouds in the visible. Note, the infrared image is color coded to show cloud tops with the highest and coldest areas in the brightest colors.

DMSP is famous for its nighttime and daytime cloud mapping capabilities. During clear conditions, bright objects on the ground, such as street lights, can also be seen. For example, in **Figures 16-5** and **16-6**, the extent of the infamous electrical black-out of August 2003 can be seen across Ohio, Pennsylvania, and New York.

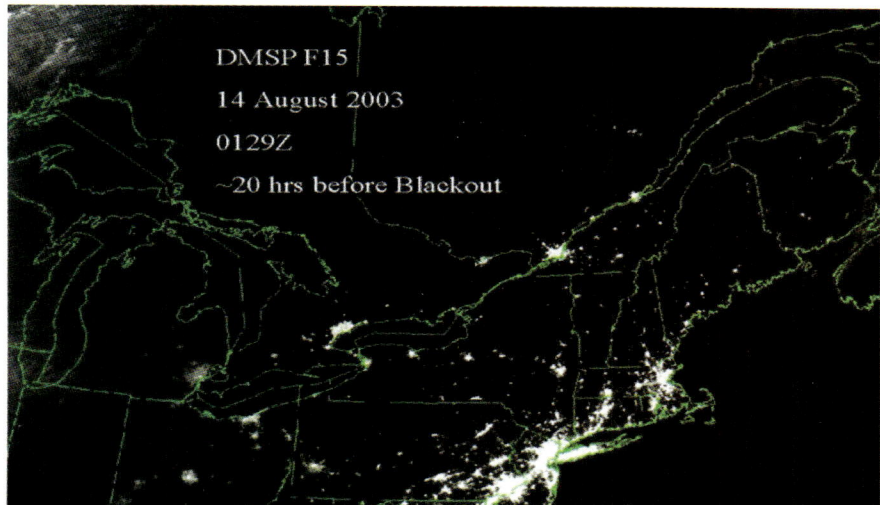

Figure 16-5
DMSP visible image of northeastern United States on the night of August 14, 2003. Lights on. (Image courtesy of NOAA DMSP.)

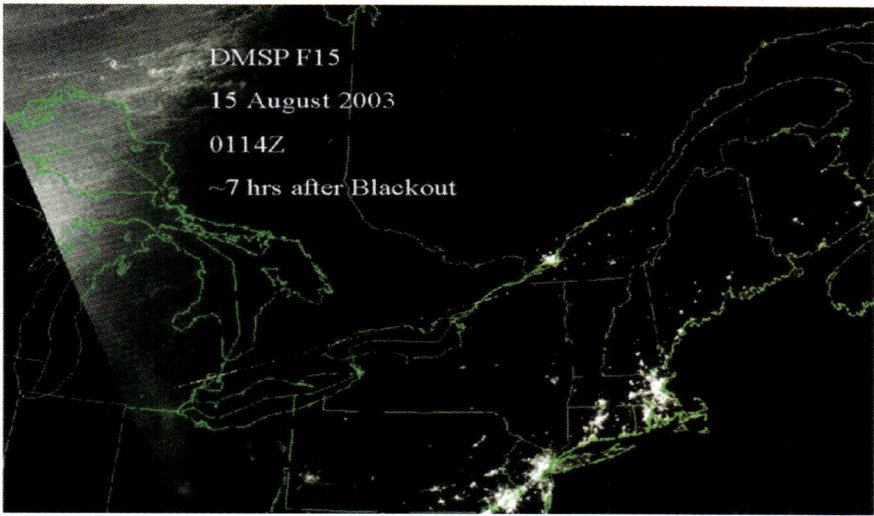

Figure 16-6
DMSP visible image of northeastern United States on the night of August 15, 2003. Lights off during black-out. (Image courtesy of NOAA DMSP.)

ATMOSPHERIC SOUNDERS

The less familiar spectral sensor aboard most metsats is the atmospheric sounder. It provides forecasters with atmospheric profiles at a grid of points around the world. These profiles consist primarily of temperature, $T(z)$, pressure, $P(z)$, and to a lesser extent water vapor concentration (mass density in units of $g \cdot cm^{-3}$), $\rho(z)_{H_2O}$, and potentially carbon dioxide concentration (density), $\rho(z)_{CO_2}$, all as functions of altitude, z. While this information is useful for weather forecasting computer models, it is particularly useful to spectral analysts for atmospheric correction of spectral data cubes in processing sensor irradiance (Level 1) into spectral reflectivity on the ground (Level 2). Of the information obtained, water vapor and carbon dioxide concentration profiles are the most useful to the spectral analyst.

The spectral regions and numbers of spectral bands used by several of these sensors are shown in **Table 16-2**. Note, LWIR+ denotes a spectral region slightly broader than the traditional 8–13 μm LWIR that is defined by the extent of the atmospheric "window" there. While earlier atmospheric sounders utilized the LWIR, more recent sounders utilize passive sensors in the microwave region of the spectrum where radiation can penetrate clouds.

Operator/User	Sensor/Satellite	Past	Present	Recent launch
Air Force (operational) DOD	DMSP	16 bands LWIR+	6-8 bands microwave	To be determined
NOAA (operational) Civilian	NOAA-N	Various LWIR	17 bands MWIR-LWIR+ 4 bands microwave	CrIS: 159 bands SWIR, 433 bands MWIR, 713 bands LWIR ATMS: 22 bands microwave
	NOAA GOES	Various LWIR	18 bands MWIR-LWIR+ and 1 visible	Same as present
NASA (Research and Development)	MODIS on EOS – Terra and Aqua	N/A	2 bands MWIR (temperature) 3 bands NIR (water density)	N/A
	AIRS on EOS – Aqua	N/A	2378 bands MWIR-LWIR	N/A

Table 16-2
Spectral regions and spectral bands of several metsat sounders.
CrIS = Cross-track Infrared Sounder; ATMS = Advanced Technology Microwave Sounder; MODIS = MODerate resolution Imaging Spectrometer; EOS = Earth Observing System; AIRS = Atmospheric InfraRed Sounder [4], [5], [6]

Sounders aboard the NOAA GOES satellites provide data across the Earth at a grid of points spaced 10 km apart, and the size of the ground pixel at each point is 8.5 km. To collect this data in 19 spectral bands from geosynchronous orbit, a two-axis scanning mirror is used along with interference filters mounted on a filter wheel. **Table 16-3** gives the location and width of its various spectral bands in terms of wavelength and wave number. Notice, only bands 7, 8, 17, and 18 are within traditional atmospheric windows and can be used to see to the ground and potentially provide data for temperature determination of objects on the ground. The remaining bands are within ozone, water vapor, and carbon dioxide absorption bands. The locations of the first twelve bands are shown in **Figure 16-7** along with a measured spectrum of the radiation received from the Earth.

Table 16-3
Location and width of spectral bands for GOES sounder. [6], [7]

Band Number	Band Center Wavelength (μm)	Band Center Wavenumber (cm^{-1})	Spectral Bandpass (μm)	Spectral Bandpass (cm^{-1})	Purpose
1	14.71	680	0.28	13	Temperature Sounding
2	14.37	696	0.27	13	Temperature Sounding
3	14.06	711	0.26	13	Temperature Sounding
4	13.64	733	0.3	16	Temperature Sounding
5	13.37	748	0.29	16	Temperature Sounding
6	12.66	790	0.8	50	Temperature Sounding
7	12.02	832	0.72	50	Surface Temperature
8	11.03	907	0.61	50	Surface Temperature
9	9.71	1030	0.24	25	Total Ozone
10	7.43	1346	0.3	55	Water Vapor Sounding
11	7.02	1425	0.39	80	Water Vapor Sounding
12	6.51	1536	0.25	60	Water Vapor Sounding
13	4.57	2188	0.048	23	Temperature Sounding
14	4.52	2212	0.047	23	Temperature Sounding
15	4.45	2247	0.046	23	Temperature Sounding
16	4.13	2421	0.068	40	Temperature Sounding
17	3.98	2513	0.063	40	Surface Temperature
18	3.74	2674	0.14	100	Surface Temperature
19	0.94	14367	0.4	9,000	Clouds

The radiation shown in this spectrum within the 8–13 μm LWIR atmospheric window originates on the ground and is compared with blackbody spectra for various temperatures. The measured data is consistent with a 290 K blackbody. Outside the atmospheric windows, the radiation originates in the atmosphere and is characteristic of the temperatures at the various layers within the atmosphere. (See **Figure 5-31**).

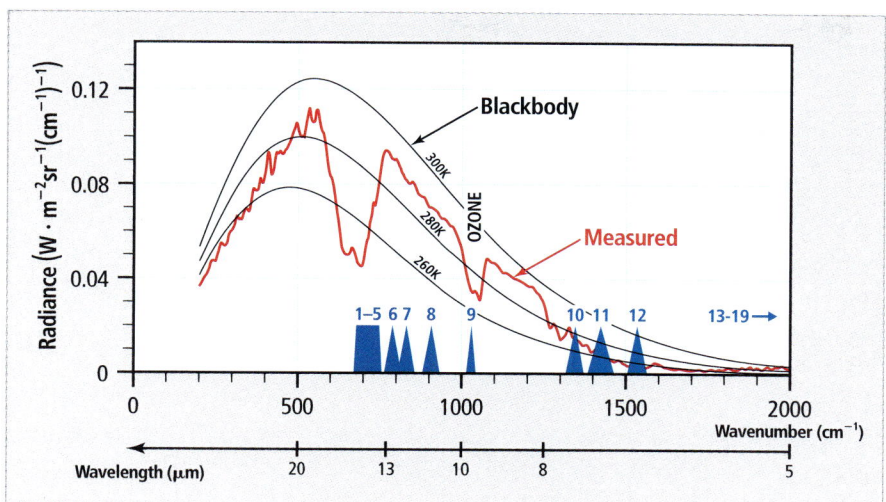

Figure 16-7
Location of GOES sounder spectral bands relative to atmospheric transmission features.

Analysis of sounder data has been refined over the past 30 years. In the early years, analysts started by assuming reasonable values of the ground temperature and the atmospheric profiles of temperature, pressure, and absolute humidity. Then, the radiance was calculated at the top of the atmosphere within each of the sounder bands using an atmospheric transport code such as MODTRAN. Comparison of these calculated predicted values with the actual sounder measured values led to analyst revision of the initial values of ground temperatures and atmospheric profiles. New atmospheric radiances were calculated and compared with the actual data. This process was iterated until agreement was achieved between the calculated and the measured radiance values. At this point, the model ground temperature and atmospheric profiles were accepted as actual values.

After years of experience, spectral band locations and widths on recent sensors were optimally selected to simplify and expedite the data analysis process. The accuracy of this process is shown in **Table 16-4**. Note, the stated accuracy at 22 altitude levels was determined by comparing sounder temperatures with those measured in situ with thermometers on weather balloons. These latter values also have some degree of uncertainty.

	Altitude levels z_i		Measurement Accuracy
	Number	Separation	
Temperature	22	0.2-1.5 km	± 1–3° K
Water Vapor Density	22	0.2-1.5 km	± 20–30%

Table 16-4
GOES sounder accuracies. [8]

Currently, sounders provide the atmospheric temperature and pressure profile grid that are adequate for input into today's worldwide weather forecasting computer models. Improved sounders, such as the recently launched Cross-track Infrared Sounder (CrIS) with 1305 bands, are necessary for future improved three-day forecasts. These require the following atmospheric inputs:

- Temperatures accurate to < 1.0 K.
- Pressures accurate to $< 1.0\%$.
- Relative humidity accurate to $< 10\%$.
- Vertical resolution of 1 km. [9], [10]

Currently, sounders provide relatively poor H_2O and CO_2 density profiles ($\rho(z)_{H_2O}$ and $\rho(z)_{CO_2}$) for spectral atmospheric correction. Future solutions include the use of HSI in the LWIR. This will be obtained from CrIS observations[1] or a LWIR HSI collection system incorporated into a satellite spectral sensor. The latter is, in effect, a "carry your own sounder" concept in which those number of spectral bands in the atmospheric absorption regions provide atmospheric inputs to the data correction of all the other "see to the ground" bands.

16.2 SURFACE TEMPERATURE DETERMINATION

Thermal imaging of objects of interest on the Earth has many interesting applications. All such images can be converted to surface temperatures to some degree of accuracy. Some of the applications require more or less accuracy in that determination. Before focusing on thermal imagery applications, a variety of thermal images will be presented to push the reader towards "thinking infrared."

CONCEPTS OF OBJECT INFRARED RADIATION

Two important concepts must be continually kept in mind.

1. In the shorter wavelengths, visible through SWIR, relatively few sources of radiation have a high enough temperature to irradiate everything else in the scene (e.g., the sun, moon, stars, man-made lights, etc.). In the thermal infrared, MWIR, and LWIR, every surface with a temperature is a source of emitted radiation. This includes trees, people, vehicles, buildings, and even the atmosphere to name only a few.

2. In the thermal infrared, the amount of radiation an object of interest emits is driven, first and foremost, by the temperature of its surfaces but also by its emissivity, ϵ, (absorptivity, α) and reflectivity, ρ.[2] Emissivity, in addition to temperature, determines the amount of radiation thermally emitted by a surface. Reflectivity determines the amount of radiation a surface will reflect that originated at all other sources within sight of the surface.

Two images of a cup of coffee are shown in **Figure 16-8**. The image at left is in the visible, while the image at right is in the thermal infrared. In the infrared image, received energy levels were converted to temperature values, assuming $\epsilon = 1.0$. These temperatures are portrayed as various colors on a scale with the hottest as red, orange, and yellow, and the cooler temperatures as green, blue, purple, and violet. (The choice of colors for such a temperature representation is arbitrary.)

The visible image suggests a dark liquid, but it does not indicate whether the liquid is hot or cold. Unlike the visible imagery, the thermal infrared image provides evidence that the cup is filled with a hot liquid. Interestingly, also note the thermal image of the spoon. Despite the large value of thermal conductivity for metal objects, such as a spoon, there is

---

[1] CrIS has begun operations. Visit http://npp.gsfc.nasa.gov/cris.html for more information.

[2] Recall emissivity and reflectivity are related: $\epsilon(\lambda) = \alpha(\lambda) = 1 - \rho(\lambda)$.

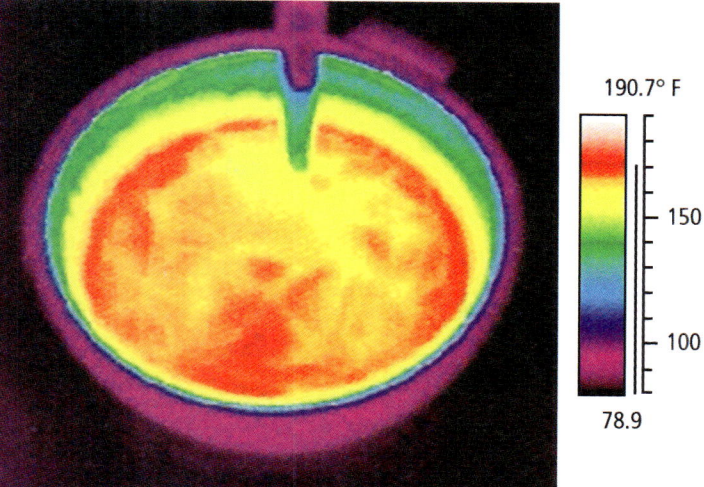

still evidence of a large difference in temperature between the end of the spoon closest to the coffee and that furthest away. Perhaps the spoon is plastic with a lower value of thermal conductivity.

A series of images involving two plastic drinking cups is shown in **Figure 16-9**. The two visible images on the left show that the cups have liquid inside, but they do not reveal anything further about the liquid. The two images to the right show one cup contains hot liquid and the other cold liquid. In addition, the fill levels in both cups are evident. Note, infrared photons usually cannot penetrate materials. So, the infrared images show differences in temperature along the surface of the cup because part of the cup wall is in direct contact with the liquid and part is *not* in direct contact.

Figure 16-8
Comparison of visible and thermal infrared images of a cup of coffee. [11]

Figure 16-9
Comparison of visible and thermal infrared images of plastic cups containing hot and cold liquid. [11]

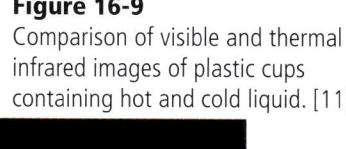

CHAPTER 16 MSI INVOLVING THE THERMAL INFRARED

A person is featured in the next pair of images in **Figure 16-10**. The exposed skin of the man is evident, namely his face and neck. The man is wearing glasses, which are opaque to thermal radiation emitted by the face behind them and are cooler than the face. The hair, beard, and mustache are also cooler than the exposed skin.

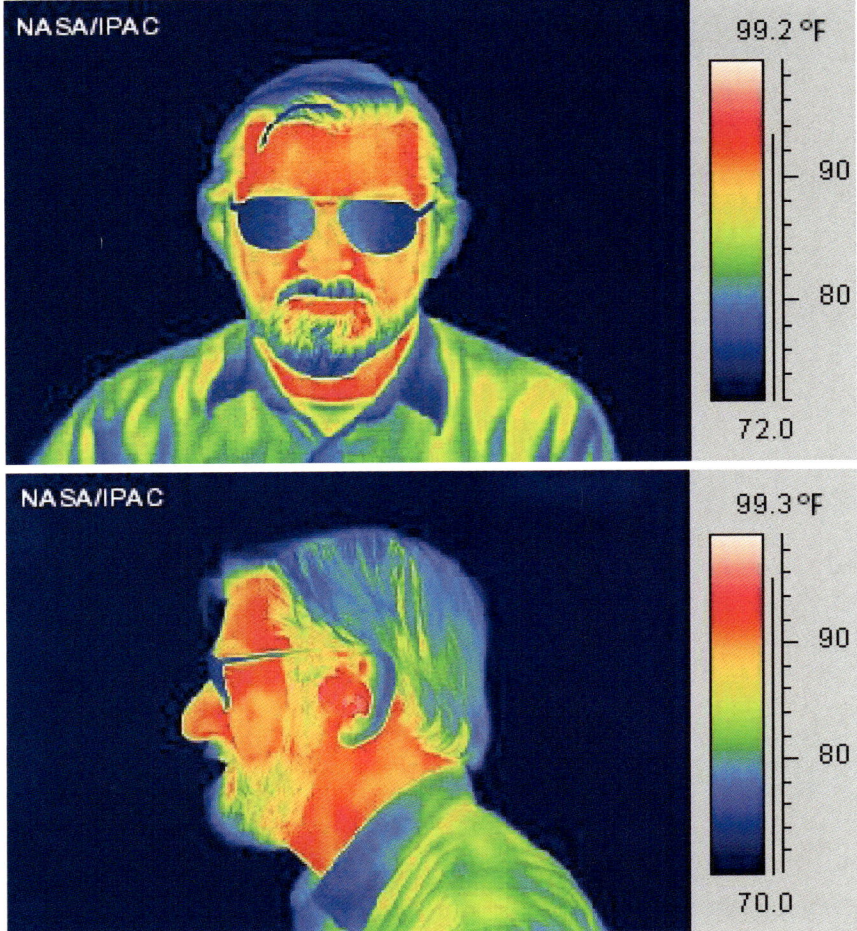

Figure 16-10
Thermal infrared image of a man. [11]

The sensitivity of thermal infrared is illustrated in **Figure 16-11**. The infrared image clearly shows that a barefoot person (or in stocking feet) recently crossed the floor. Images such as this one suggest the degree of sensitivity of infrared sensing. Some common thermal imagers can easily distinguish temperature differences of less than 0.1 K (0.2° F) between two adjacent pixels. Of course, these capabilities are best when there is one bright pixel against a uniform background of cooler pixels.

Figure 16-11
Comparison of visible and thermal images of a floor recently crossed by a person. [11]

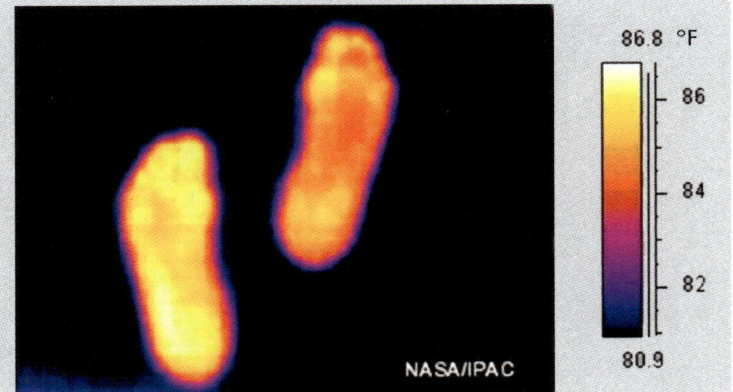

The eruption of steam from the Old Faithful Geyser at Yellowstone National Park is shown in **Figure 16-12**. In the visible image, the spatial extent of the steam cloud is evident. However, the infrared image shows where the hot gas source is located and the direction of the wind and subsequent "blow-off."

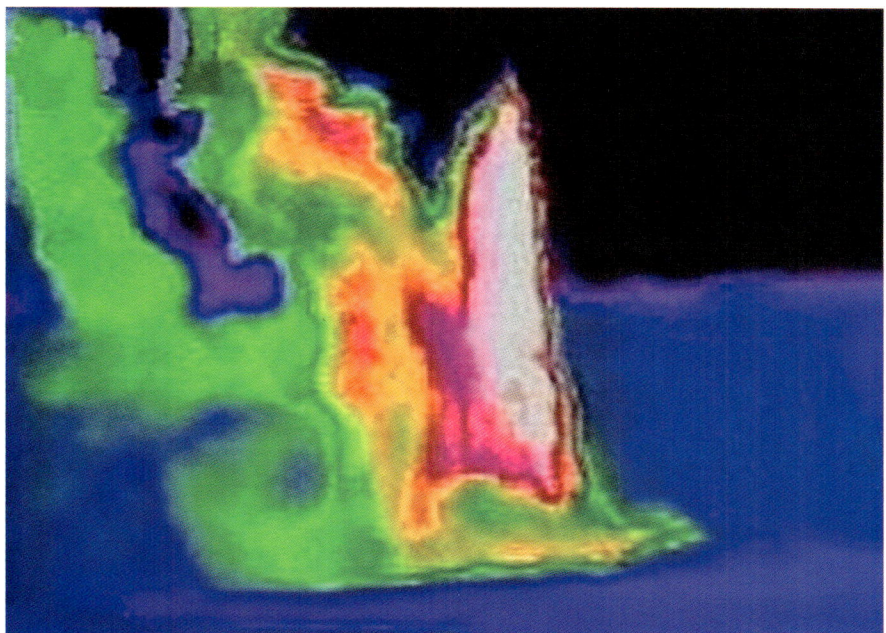

Figure 16-12
Old Faithful Geyser eruption in the visible and thermal infrared. [11]

Two widely used civilian applications of thermal imaging are shown in **Figures 16-13** and **16-14**. In **Figure 16-13**, a thermal infrared medical image of a patient's legs shows some internal injuries to an ankle and some increased circulation in the other leg as the patient shifts his weight to compensate for the ankle injury. Remember the images only portray skin temperature differences, *not* radiation originating below the surface. Infrared radiation generally does not sufficiently transmit through materials, especially those with high water content, such as living tissue.

Figure 16-13
Medical application of thermal infrared imagery. (Image courtesy of Meditherm.)

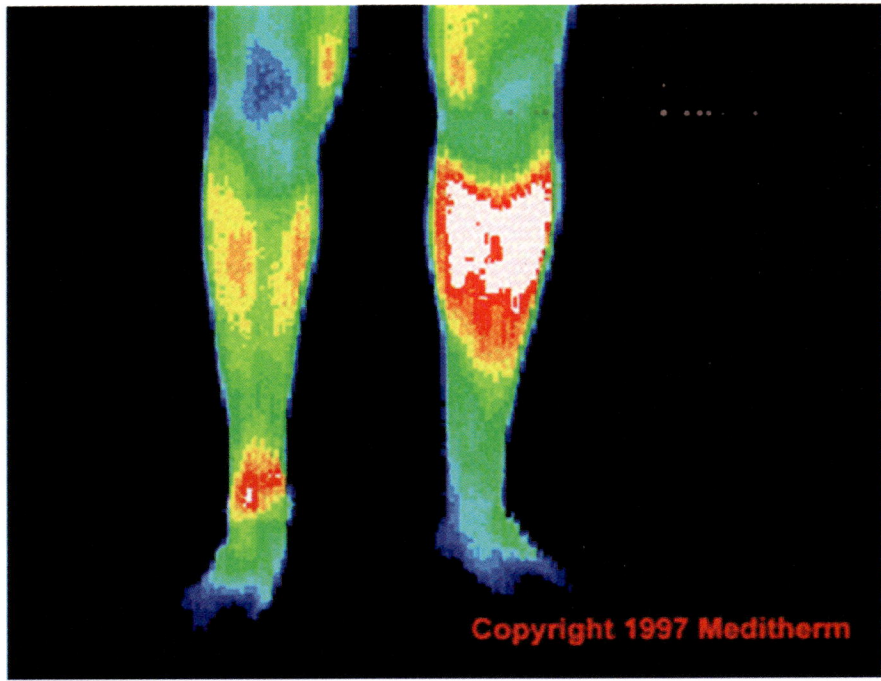

A thermal image of the exterior of a home is shown in **Figure 16-14**. This image was taken during the months when the air conditioning is on inside the home. The escape of cool air evident on the outer surface of the home gives the locations on walls where there is relatively less insulation than the rest of the wall. In this case, the windows and roof overhang are losing cool air. Many companies provide this sort of information as part of a home energy audit in an attempt to save utility costs.

Figure 16-14
Building construction application of thermal infrared imagery. [11]

Thermal imaging allows nighttime monitoring of activities for police work as well as military surveillance. An outdoor infrared nighttime scene of a boat is shown in **Figure 16-15**. The Boston Marathon bomber is hiding in the boat. The warm body is visible against a relatively cold boat.

332 CHAPTER 16 MSI INVOLVING THE THERMAL INFRARED

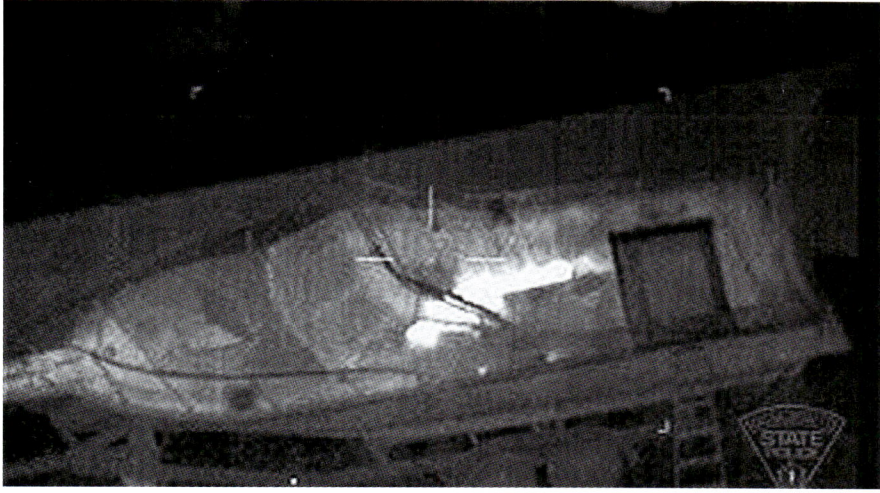

Figure 16-15
Thermal infrared imagery of nighttime activity.

Another interesting thermal image, the Space Shuttle landing, is shown in **Figure 16-16.** The hot portions of the vehicle nose and leading edges are evident because of atmospheric re-entry heating. The concrete beneath the shuttle is evident because of the reflected radiation from the Shuttle.

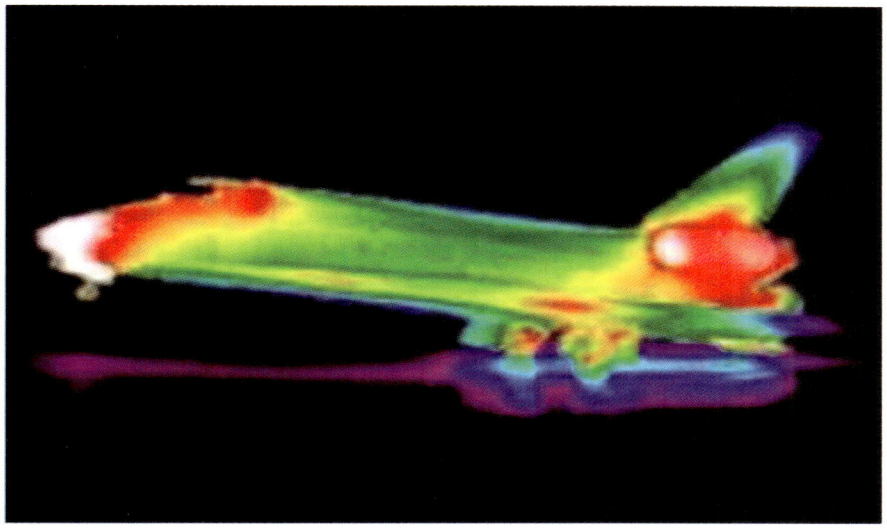

Figure 16-16
Thermal infrared imagery of the Space Shuttle landing. [11]

POSSIBLE THERMAL IMAGING APPLICATIONS

A partial list of possible thermal imaging applications include:
- Weather forecasting, which includes surface atmospheric layer temperature; cloud top temperature; and ocean surface temperature
- Coastal (littoral) sea surface temperature identification
- Oil spill detection and characterization
- Volcano surveillance
- Forest fire surveillance
- Medical diagnostics
- Abnormality detection in electrical circuitry

Each application will be briefly discussed below.

Weather forecasting: The use of thermal imagery for cloud detection was presented earlier, but cloud top temperatures for cumulus type clouds can also play a significant role in weather forecasting. Experience shows the colder the cloud top, the higher in altitude the cloud top, and the more likely such a cumulonimbus cloud will be associated with tornados and

Figure 16-17
Thermal image of the southwestern United States. High altitude cloud tops are portrayed as white or bright. Inset shows an intense thunderstorm.

hail. A Landsat thermal infrared (band 6) image of the southwestern United States in **Figure 16-17** shows several intense thunderstorms, including one in southwestern New Mexico over the Elephant Butte Reservoir. (Remember, in contrast to other thermal infrared images, those in meteorology portray cold (rather than warm) temperature objects (clouds) as white or bright.)

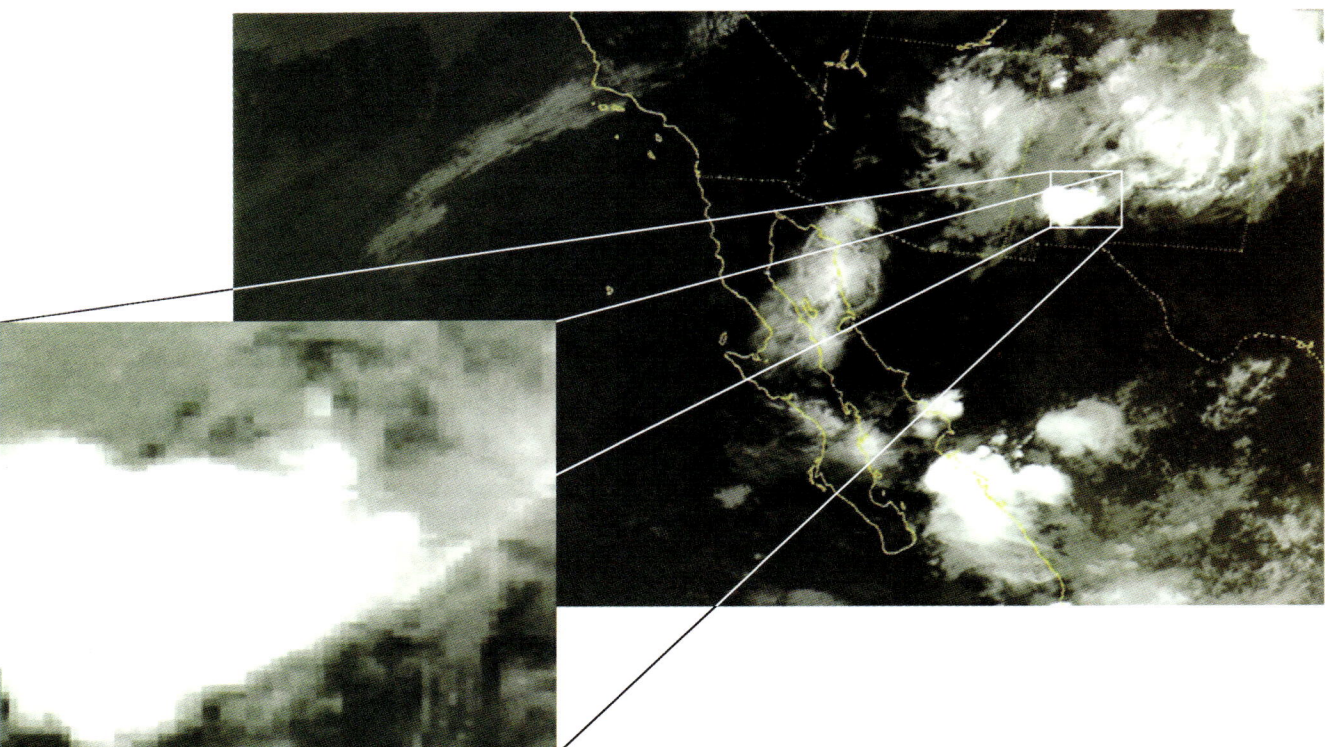

Coastal (littoral) sea surface temperature: Important for oceanography and Navy and Marine battlespace preparations, coastal sea surface temperature maps can be readily obtained from overhead thermal images. Such a product is shown in **Figure 16-18** for the waters off the southern coast of New Jersey. As will be discussed later in this chapter, water temperatures are easier to determine than land temperatures. Also shown in this figure, on the left, are the temperatures at various depths along the line AB in the main part of the figure.

Oil spill detection and characterization: Oil spills appear quite distinctly in the infrared because the absorptivity of oil differs considerably from that of water in the visible and the Near Infrared (NIR) (**Figure 15-28**). Hence, temperatures will differ. LWIR emissivities differ between oil and water as well. Oil film thickness can also be determined using models of heating and cooling thin slabs of material.

Volcano surveillance: Volcano surveillance in the thermal infrared provides more accurate predictions of an eruption. Daily temperature determination of the floor of the crater provides this prediction when there is a sudden temperature rise.

Forest fire surveillance: Forest fire surveillance and mapping in the infrared provides firefighters as well as military ground forces in the region indications of the most intense portions of the fire and a sense of the fire's direction.

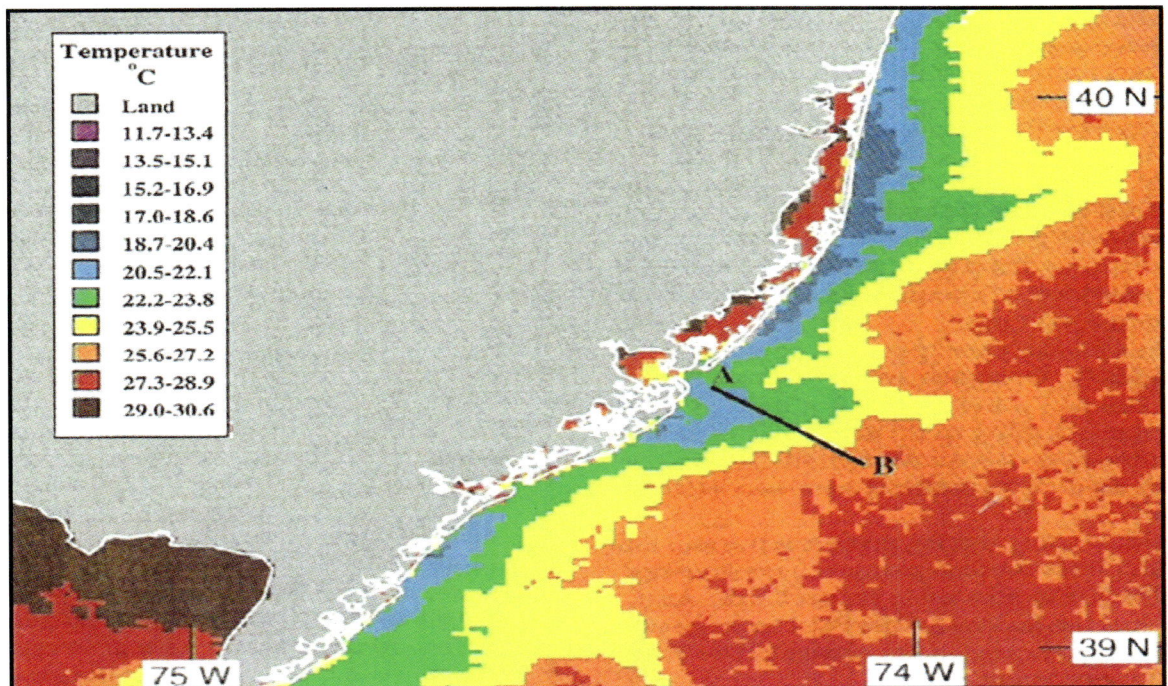

Figure 16-18
Sea surface temperatures off the coast of New Jersey. ("Underwater observatory captures coastal upwelling events off New Jersey," Eos, Transactions American Geophysical Union Journal, Volume 77, Issue 25, 1996 (pages 233-236). Copyright 1996, John Wiley & Sons, Inc. This material is reproduced with permission of John Wiley & Sons, Inc.)

Medical diagnostics: Thermal images of the human body with various abnormalities (**Figure 16-13**) can be used along with other diagnostic testing, such as x-rays, CAT-scans, ultrasounds, etc., to remotely (non-invasive) visualize and quantify abnormalities within the body and monitor the healing process. To develop this capability to its current state of utility, extensive studies were performed over the past 20 plus years on human anatomy to obtain the range of normal values and correlate these images with other types of diagnostic testing. Again, thermal and other models as well as composites of thermal images were utilized.

Abnormality detection in electrical circuitry: These range in sophistication and size from semi-conductor components to fuse boxes to transformers within the power grid. Again, thermal images, collected or modeled, are necessary for reference regarding normal operation.

These applications highlight some common elements. All require the use of thermal imagery, sometimes just one image and sometimes repeated imagery over selected intervals of time. All require some amount of temperature determination. At one extreme, an analyst visually sees a difference in brightness in the image that may correspond to several degrees difference in temperature; at the other extreme, an accurate determination is made with a desired accuracy of less than one degree. All require some sort of model to use the temperature measurements to produce information about the object of interest. In some cases, this model is rudimentary (i.e., vehicles with engines running are much hotter than those not running). In other cases, this model may involve considerable computer computations regarding the heating and cooling processes across the geometry of the object of interest.

ESTIMATING SURFACE TEMPERATURES

What are the challenges of determining the temperature of an object of interest from thermal infrared imagery? To answer this question, the discussion will first consider the use of imagery from a single band in the thermal infrared and then the improvements offered with the use of multiple spectral bands. Recall the remote sensing geometry and the associated radiometric quantities previously discussed in **Chapter 4**.

As discussed in **Chapter 10**, radiation is followed from the object of interest, through the atmosphere, and into a sensor, where detectors convert photons of radiation to electrons, and electrons are counted and given as a digital number. To determine temperature, analysts must work in reverse taking the measured numbers of electrons and work back through the sensor, atmosphere, and object of interest to its temperature. The difficulty of this effort depends on the width of the single spectral band, as will be discussed below. Also important is the spatial resolution of the imaging sensor. If the ground pixels are sufficiently small so the object of interest subtends several ground pixels, then several independent determinations of temperature may be possible. If the ground pixel is so large that it fully contains the object of interest and some background, then there is the additional complication of attributing the "average" temperature determined for the ground pixel to that of the object of interest.

Proceeding with the approach used for a single broadband sensor, the previously discussed end-to-end **Equations 10-3** is expanded to include target emitted *and* reflected radiation. Assuming a pixel is filled with a target,

$$\tilde{N}_{TGT} \approx {}^{A}\!/_{D} \left\{ \int_{\Delta\lambda} \frac{\mathcal{E}_\lambda(\lambda)_{TGT}}{hc/\lambda} A_R \tau(\lambda)_{OPT} \eta(\lambda) \Delta t_{INT} d\lambda \right\} \text{ [DU]}, \quad (16\text{-}1)$$

where $\mathcal{E}_\lambda(\lambda)_{TGT} \approx [L_\lambda(\lambda)_{TGT} \tau(\lambda)_{ATM} + L_\lambda(\lambda)_{ATM}] \Omega_{PIX}$,

$$L_\lambda(\lambda)_{TGT} \approx \frac{1}{\pi}[(\epsilon(\lambda)_{TGT} B_\lambda(\lambda, T_S)_{TGT} + \rho(\lambda)_{TGT} \mathcal{E}_\lambda(\lambda)_{EXT})],$$

and $\mathcal{E}_\lambda(\lambda)_{EXT}$ is the sum of all external irradiances incident on the target.

Careful sensor design, fabrication, and calibration provide measured values of sensor parameters Ω_{PIX}, A_R, as well as $\tau(\lambda)_{OPT}$, $\eta(\lambda)$, $\Delta\lambda$, and Δt_{INT}. The use of MODTRAN with suitable atmospheric inputs gives values for atmospheric transport, $\tau(\lambda)_{ATM}$, $L(\lambda)_{ATM}$, and the downwelling sky irradiance $\mathcal{E}_\lambda(\lambda)_{EXT}$. If these quantities and the emissivity (and reflectivity) of the object of interest are relatively constant across the sensor spectral bandpass, approximate values can be used in place of the integral as calculated in **Chapter 10**. The more narrow the spectral bandpass, the more likely this situation. If any of the above quantities significantly vary across the spectral bandpass, an iterative process is required. This is accomplished as follows: first, estimate the temperature of the object of interest; then, numerically integrate the end-to-end equation; compare predicted results with sensor measurements; adjust the temperature estimate; and iterate.

For some objects of interest, such as foliage, water, and grass, where $\epsilon(\lambda) \approx 1.0$ and $\rho(\lambda) \approx 0$ in the MWIR and LWIR, determining temperature is relatively easy. Routine weather satellite results are often as accurate as ± 3 K absolute or ±1 K relative. [12]

Most other objects of interest present more complex problems. Objects such as bare soils, rocks and minerals, vehicles, and buildings generally have

$\epsilon(\lambda) < 1.0$, and hence $\rho(\lambda) > 0.0$ in the MWIR and LWIR. To determine temperature in these cases, the specific type of surface material of the object must be known, and its $\epsilon(\lambda)$ must be input in the calculations. Often, this is unknown. Typically, the general category of material (e.g., asphalt, concrete, tank paint, roofing material, water, etc.) can be determined from image context if there is enough spatial resolution to provide multiple ground pixels across the object of interest. If available, spectral imagery of the object in the visible through SWIR might also help identify these surface materials. Once the specific material type or the general category of material type is identified, the appropriate $\epsilon(\lambda)$ can often be obtained from one of the comprehensive spectral libraries such as the Advanced Spaceborne Thermal Emission and Reflection Radiometer (ASTER) spectral library. [13]

Unfortunately, within any particular general category of material types (e.g., soil, asphalt, concrete, paint, etc.), there can be variability between the various specific material types and/or individual samples of the same material type. For example, **Figure 16-19** shows the spectra of two different mineral samples. [14] Some of this variability also involves the age of a material type. This is particularly true for the categories of asphalts, concrete, and paints. Consider concrete and asphalt roads in the visible. When they are freshly poured, concrete is a bright, highly reflective white, and asphalt is a dark, highly absorbing black. In time, the concrete slowly darkens partially because of vehicles depositing minute amounts of rubber from their tires, and the asphalt slowly lightens. In fact, after many years, the eye may not be able to discern if a road is concrete or asphalt from a distance.

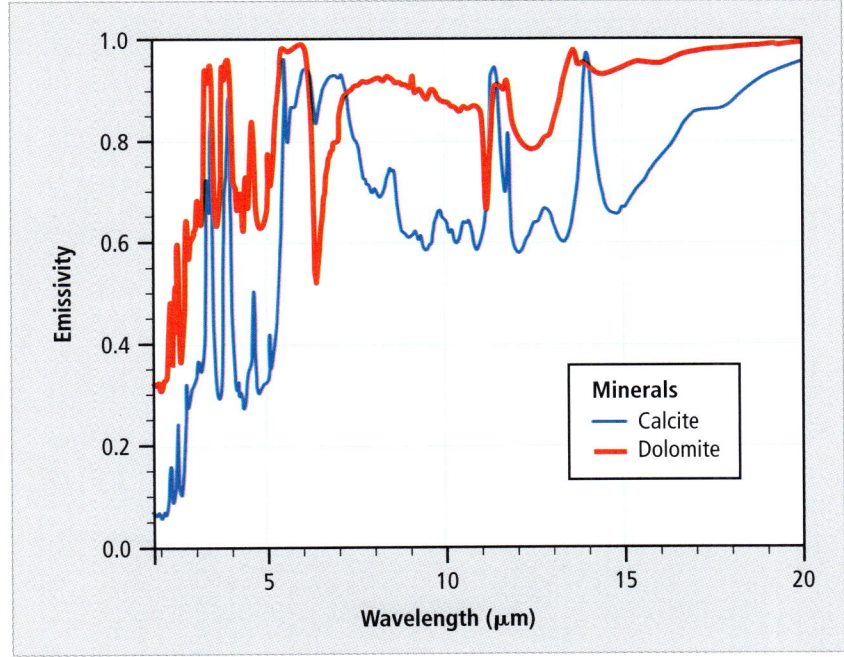

Figure 16-19
Emissivity values for two different mineral types. [14]

Thus, the accuracy of surface temperature determination is only as accurate as the appropriateness of the input $\epsilon(\lambda)$ for the surface material type. Including the possible uncertainties produced by the atmospheric inputs into MODTRAN calculations for a particular location, the total uncertainty may be as large as ± 10 K for some objects. Objects smaller than or comparable in size to a ground pixel provide additional challenges. (See **Chapter 15**.)

MULTIBAND TEMPERATURE ESTIMATION

Multiband images in the thermal infrared offer the possibility of improved temperature determination of objects. For a N-band MSI sensor, there will be N measured DU values, each for a different spectral band. If these spectral bands are sufficiently narrow, $\rho(\lambda)$ and $\epsilon(\lambda)$ are approximately constant in each spectral band.

If $\epsilon(\lambda)$ is well known, the N radiance measurements can yield N independent determinations of the object of interest's surface temperature within any given ground pixel. In this case, an average of these values should improve the accuracy of the determined object surface temperature.

If $\epsilon(\lambda)$ is poorly known, the analyst should calculate the temperature from the radiance value in each spectral band, assuming $\epsilon(\lambda) = 1.0$. Then, the largest value of temperature should be selected as the best estimate of object surface temperature, because in the band producing the largest temperature value, $\epsilon(\lambda)$ is closest to 1.0. But, if $\epsilon(\lambda)$ in this band is not equal to 1.0, the estimated surface temperature value will be lower than actual.

THERMAL IMAGING SENSORS

Single broad-band thermal imaging sensors are in use on a variety of platforms, listed in **Table 16-5**.

Table 16-5
Single broad-band thermal imaging sensors. [15], [16], 17], [18]

Sensor Family	Number and Location of Bands	Smallest Ground Pixel Size	Calibration
Typical cloud Metsat sensors	1-2 bands LWIR	550 m	On-board
Landsat 7	1 band LWIR	60 m	On-board and in-scene
Landsat 8	2 bands LWIR	100 m	On-board and in-scene
Airborne Imager	1 band MWIR	Varies with altitude	On-board or in-scene

Landsat imagery is shown in **Figure 16-20** in which the T_S was determined across the Elephant Butte Reservoir on the Rio Grande River in southwestern New Mexico and compared with ground truth measurements. DAF1 and DAF2 in the figure denote locations where ground-truth measurements were made from small boats.

Figure 16-20
The middle image is Landsat LWIR (Band 6) image of Elephant Butte Reservation, New Mexico collected on October 23, 1994. The left image is a natural color composite (321) collected on October 21, 1993. (Courtesy of ERIM.)

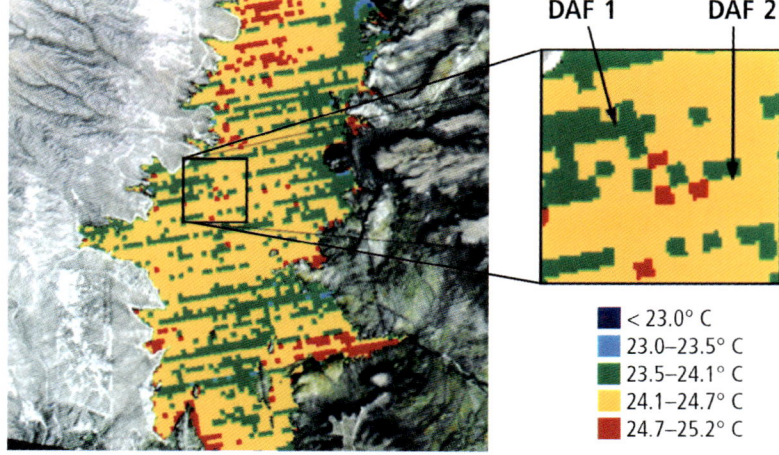

USE OF TARGET THERMAL MODELING

Some applications only require coarse T_S determination and models. The appearance of relatively hot and cold objects in an image can provide useful information about some objects of interest. For example, determining whether the engine of a vehicle, such as a car parked along the side of the highway, is currently or was recently running.

More accurate T_S determination and models are necessary to provide detailed information about some complex objects of interest. For example,

- Land vehicles using the Multi-Service Electro-optic Signature (MuSES) model developed under Army Tank-automotive and Armaments Command (TACOM) sponsorship. [19]
- Aircraft from thermal images of the aircraft in flight using the Spectral and In-band Radiometric Imaging of Targets and Scenes (SPIRITS) (including both aerodynamic heating and plume emission). [20]
- Thermal models of electrical components in operation.

These models do not run in reverse, that is, converting collected images and T_S determinations to input parameters. They must be used in an iterative fashion; estimate necessary input values, calculate predicted T_S, compare predicted with measured T_S values, revise the inputs, and continue the process until predicted and measured T_S values agree. Ground pixel size is important in this process. Many small ground pixels across the object provide more detail but also decrease the problem of uncertainty where these pixels are located relative to the object.

HEATING AND COOLING RATES

To further explain these models, some basic heating and cooling physical concepts and a simple (in terms of geometry) example will be discussed.

If a target is in steady-state, its temperature, $T = T_{SS}$, is a constant, and the amount of energy gained during time interval Δt equals the amount of energy lost during Δt. If a target is *not* in steady state, its temperature, T, changes by an amount ΔT which is proportional to the net energy gained or lost during Δt. This relationship is expressed in more detail by the formula,

$$C_M M \Delta T \cong [\Phi_{ABS} - \Phi_{RAD} - \Phi_{COND} - \Phi_{CONV}]\Delta t \; [J], \quad (16\text{-}2)$$

where

C_M = Mass specific heat of the material making up the object, defined as the amount of energy necessary to increase T by one degree for one unit of mass. Typical units are joules per kilogram per Kelvin ($J \cdot kg^{-1} K^{-1}$).

M = Mass of object in kg.

Φ = Power, or energy per unit time, (in W) gained or lost from the following processes: Absorption (*ABS*), Radiation (*RAD*), Conduction (*COND*), and Convection (*CONV*).

An additional assumption is the targets considered are so small and thermally conductive that there are no temperature gradients across the object. That is, the temperature of the object can be described by a single value.

Often radiative emission, Φ_{RAD}, is the most important of the three loss mechanisms.

$$\Phi_{RAD} = A_s \int_0^\infty \epsilon(\lambda) B_\lambda(\lambda, T) d\lambda \; [W], \quad (16\text{-}3)$$

where

$\epsilon(\lambda)$ = emissivity of the surface,
A_S = total surface area of object, and
$B_\lambda(\lambda, T)$ = the familiar Planck blackbody function.

If $\epsilon(\lambda)$ is approximately constant in the LWIR, where most objects ($T < 400K$) radiate, the majority of their energy, then, as shown in **Chapter 2**:

$$\Phi_{RAD} \approx \epsilon_{LW} A_S \sigma_{SB} T^4 \; [W]. \tag{16-4}$$

During the day, Φ_{ABS} results primarily from the sun (on a clear day) and the thermal radiation from the Earth's atmospheric layers (downwelling radiance). Therefore,

$$\Phi_{ABS} \approx A_{SUN} \int_0^\infty \alpha(\lambda) \mathcal{E}_\lambda(\lambda)_{SUN} d\lambda + A_{SKY} \int_0^\infty \alpha(\lambda) \mathcal{E}_\lambda(\lambda)_{SKY} d\lambda \; [W], \tag{16-5}$$

where A_{SUN}, A_{SKY} = surface area of the target projected in the direction of sun and sky, respectively, with $A_{SUN}, A_{SKY} < A_S$, and $\alpha(\lambda)$ = absorptivity of the surface.

If $\alpha(\lambda)$ is nearly a constant α_{VIS} in the visible where most solar radiation occurs, and if $\alpha(\lambda)$ is nearly a constant α_{LW} in the LWIR where most thermal radiation occurs, **Equation 16-5** becomes

$$\Phi_{ABS} \approx \alpha_{VIS} A_{SUN} \mathcal{E}_{SUN} + \alpha_{LW} A_{SKY} \mathcal{E}_{SKY} \; [W] \tag{16-6}$$

to close approximation. The incident solar irradiance, $\mathcal{E}_{SUN}$, is termed the solar insolation (not insulation, which is used in buildings), and it is a tabulated quantity based on the location, day of year, and time of day. The incident thermal irradiance, $\mathcal{E}_{SKY}$, from the Earth's atmospheric layers can be calculated using an atmospheric transport code such as MODTRAN with suitable atmospheric inputs for the location, day of year, and time of day.

Now, the original heat gain/heat loss equation (ignoring conduction and convection effects) becomes

$$C_M M \frac{\Delta T}{\Delta t} \approx \alpha_{VIS} A_{SUN} \mathcal{E}_{SUN} + \alpha_{LW} A_{SKY} \mathcal{E}_{SKY} - \epsilon_{LW} A_s \sigma T^4 \; [W] \tag{16-7}$$

to reasonable approximation. **Equation 16-7** suggests that $T(t)$ depends on the following parameters:

- Size and shape of the target, A_S, A_{SUN}, A_{SKY},
- Material coatings on surface of object with properties $\alpha_{VIS}, \alpha_{LW} = \epsilon_{LW}$,
- Materials inside the target which have properties M, C_M, and
- Initial conditions $T(t_0) = T_0$.

In steady state, T is not changing, and $\frac{\Delta T}{\Delta t} = 0$. Assuming $\mathcal{E}_{SUN}$ is a constant during daylight hours,

$$0 \approx \alpha_{VIS} A_{SUN} \mathcal{E}_{SUN} + \alpha_{LW} A_{SKY} \mathcal{E}_{SKY} - \epsilon_{LW} A_s \sigma T_{ss}^4 \; [W] \tag{16-8}$$

and thus, the steady-state temperature, T_{ss}, is approximated by

$$T_{ss} \approx \left(\frac{\alpha_{VIS} A_{SUN} \mathcal{E}_{SUN} + \alpha_{LW} A_{SKY} \mathcal{E}_{SKY}}{\epsilon_{LW} A_s \sigma_{SB}} \right)^{1/4} \; [K]. \tag{16-9}$$

If $T(t_0) = T_0 < T_{SS}$, where t_0 refers to some reference time (such as sunrise), the notional behavior of $T(t)$ is shown in **Figure 16-21**. After significant time, $T(t)$ will reach its steady state value, T_{SS}.

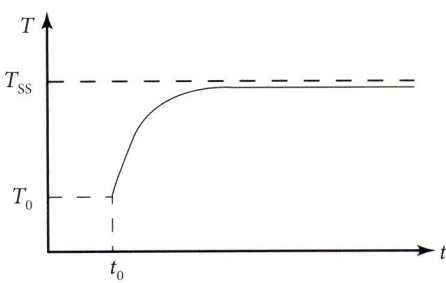

Figure 16-21
Notional behavior of $T(t)$.

An example of the impact on steady-state temperature of the absorptivity in visible wavelengths is shown in **Figure 16-22**. In the top image (visible) is a placard with words of different colors sitting in the sun. The visible reflectivity of the colors increases from top to bottom (and the visible absorptivity decreases). The two infrared images below the top visible image show that as the colors go from black to red, the measured

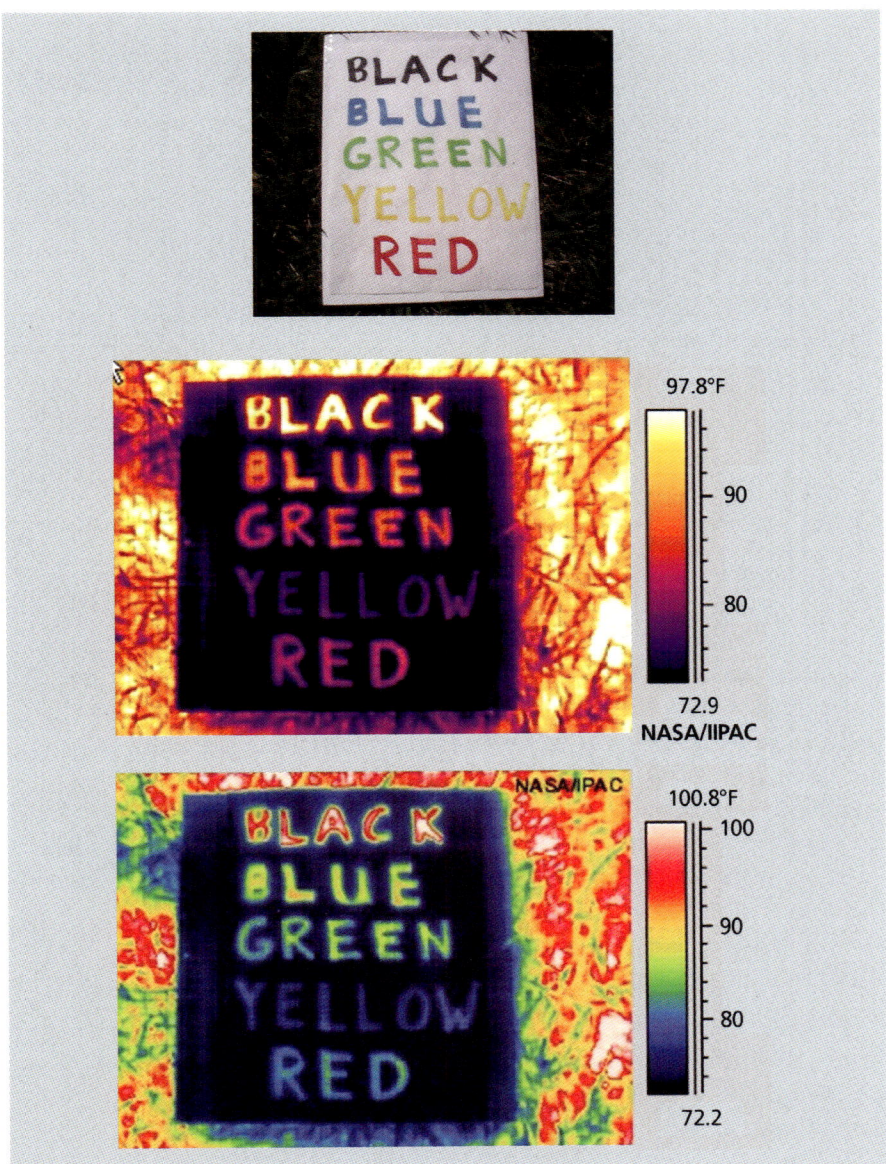

Figure 16-22
Visible and thermal infrared images of various colored printing. (Top visible image collected when the placard was placed on the grass at noon. Middle infrared image taken about 10 minutes later, and bottom image about 30 minutes later.) [11]

temperatures transition from relatively warmer to colder. A similar example may be observed in a parking lot on a sunny summer afternoon. Black or dark colored cars are too hot to touch, while white or silver colored cars are much cooler.

Returning to **Equation 16-7**, if ΔT and Δt become infinitely small, then $\frac{\Delta T}{\Delta t}$ becomes the derivative $\frac{dT}{dt}$, and **Equation 16-7** becomes a differential equation for $T(t)$,

$$C_M M \frac{dT}{dt} \approx \alpha_{VIS} A_{SUN} \mathcal{E}_{SUN} + \alpha_{LW} A_{SKY} \mathcal{E}_{SKY} - \epsilon_{LW} A_s \sigma_{SB} T^4 \quad [\text{W}]. \quad (16\text{-}10)$$

This differential equation may be solved numerically for $T(t)$. However, in its present form, it provides an expression for the instantaneous heating rate, $\frac{dT}{dt}$,

$$\frac{dT}{dt} \approx \frac{\alpha_{VIS} A_{SUN} \mathcal{E}_{SUN} + \alpha_{LW} A_{SKY} \mathcal{E}_{SKY} - \epsilon_{LW} A_s \sigma_{SB} T^4}{C_M M} \left(\frac{\text{K}}{\text{s}}\right). \quad (16\text{-}11)$$

Under certain circumstances, for example, t_0 after sunrise and observations shortly thereafter,

$$\alpha_{VIS} A_{SUN} \mathcal{E}_{SUN} + \alpha_{LW} A_{SKY} \mathcal{E}_{SKY} \gg \epsilon_{LW} A_s \sigma_{SB} T^4, \quad (16\text{-}12)$$

or equivalently

$$\left(\frac{T}{T_{ss}}\right)^4 \ll 1. \quad (16\text{-}13)$$

the instantaneous rate becomes approximately

$$\frac{dT}{dt} \simeq \frac{\alpha_{VIS} A_{SUN} \mathcal{E}_{SUN} + \alpha_{LW} A_{SKY} \mathcal{E}_{SKY}}{C_M M} \left(\frac{\text{K}}{\text{s}}\right). \quad (16\text{-}14)$$

For short intervals of time Δt, **Equation 16-14** can be approximated as

$$\frac{\Delta T}{\Delta t} \simeq \frac{dT}{dt} \left(\frac{\text{K}}{\text{s}}\right), \quad (16\text{-}15)$$

and the corresponding increase in temperature ΔT can be estimated.

An important conclusion of this approximate result is the temperature of massive objects with little surface area increases slowly; in fact, they may never reach steady state. The time required to reach steady state may be greater than the time from sunrise to sunset. The classic example of such a massive object is the Earth itself. The temperature of the outer layers increase during the day and decrease during the night. A few meters below the surface, the temperature remains the same during day and night, summer and winter. This temperature is roughly 13° C (55°F) as commonly found in caves and caverns. This property is used by some home builders to dramatically reduce heating and cooling bills by building the home with most of the structure below the surface of the Earth, or installing geothermal heating using the heat exchange between the Earth and the fluids in buried pipes.

Frequent collections and the use of the heating rate formula tend to reduce the effects that produce uncertainties (caused by errors in sensor calibration and/or atmospheric correction) of surface temperature determination.

16.3 MSI FAR OFF-NADIR VIEWING

Up to this point, all the spectral imaging, both in the visible through SWIR and in the MWIR-LWIR, involved sensors that look primarily near nadir from their various platforms, either airborne or spaceborne. However, there are a few sensors, such as Senior Year Electro-optical Reconnaissance Sensor (SYERS)-2 (which will be discussed at the end of this chapter), designed to look far off-nadir.

COLLECTION ADVANTAGES

There are some advantages of far off-nadir viewing. Airborne platform collection in long-range standoff against hostile nations can be accomplished by flying either on the friendly side of the border and peering into unfriendly territory or flying along the coast of a country just beyond their declared off-shore limit. As a result, the platform is significantly less vulnerable to hostile anti-aircraft fire. Another advantage for airborne sensors occurs when their collection occurs in controlled airspace against covert activities. An airborne platform collecting off-nadir is less conspicuous to those involved on the ground than if it were to fly directly overhead. Therefore, there is less chance of the platform deterring the activities of interest.

Sensors that pushbroom scan from either airborne or satellite platforms can cover a much wider swath when they collect far off-nadir as shown in **Figure 16-23**.

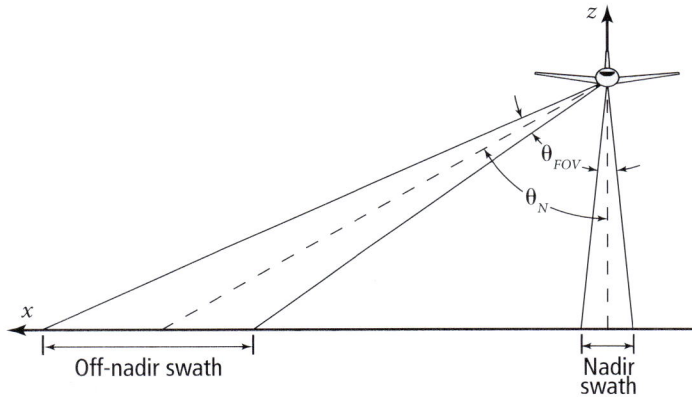

Figure 16-23
Pushbroom scanner flying off the page toward the reader (defined as y-axis).

When viewing some horizontal man-made objects at grazing angles (large nadir angles), specular reflections may result with higher reflectivity values as well as higher degrees of horizontal polarization. This is due to far off-nadir collection (especially at times of low-sun angles) (Review **Section 3.2**. Polarization will be discussed in detail in **Chapter 21**.)

COLLECTION DISADVANTAGES

There are several disadvantages of far off-nadir viewing. These are long slant range and oblique viewing effects. Increased slant paths through the atmosphere from sensor to object of interest can produce significantly decreased atmospheric transmission τ_{ATM}.

Recall the "secant" transmission law, **Equation 5-21**

$$\tau_{ATM}(\lambda,\theta_N) = [\tau(\lambda,\theta_N = 0°)_{ATM}]^{\sec\theta_N}. \quad (16\text{-}16)$$

Also, atmospheric path radiances increase to some extent because longer slant range allows more atoms, molecules, and particles to scatter and/or emit background radiation.

Off-nadir viewing and its long slant ranges provide significant increases in ground pixel size as briefly discussed in **Chapters 8** and **12**. Consider the geometry shown in **Figure 16-23** and in more detail in **Figure 16-24**. Using trigonometry relations and the small angle approximation,

$$\tan \theta_{PIX} \simeq \sin \theta_{PIX} \simeq \theta_{PIX} \text{(radians) for } \theta_{PIX} \text{ small.} \quad (16\text{-}17)$$

The size of the ground pixels at nadir, $GSD(0°)_x$ and $GSD(0°)_y$, are calculated in **Equation 16-18** for a square pixel at nadir as:

$$GSD(0°)_x = GSD(0°)_y = 2h \tan(0.5\theta_{PIX}) \simeq h\theta_{PIX} \quad (16\text{-}18)$$

to close approximation.

When viewing off-nadir, the size of the ground pixels, $GSD(\theta_N)_x$ and $GSD(\theta_N)_y$, are larger as shown in **Table 16-6**. A "vertical ground pixel distance, $GSD(\theta_N)_z$," can also be defined, as shown in **Figure 16-24**. The sizes of these sampling distances are calculated as

$$\left.\begin{array}{l}GSD(\theta_N)_x \simeq \dfrac{r\,\theta_{PIX}}{\cos \theta_N} \simeq \dfrac{h\theta_{PIX}}{\cos^2\theta_N} \simeq \dfrac{GSD(0°)_x}{\cos^2\theta_N} \text{ [m]};\\[1em] GSD(\theta_N)_y \simeq r\,\theta_{PIX} \simeq \dfrac{h\theta_{PIX}}{\cos \theta_N} \simeq \dfrac{GSD(0°)_y}{\cos \theta_N} \text{ [m]; and}\\[1em] GSD(\theta_N)_z \simeq \dfrac{r\,\theta_{PIX}}{\sin \theta_N} \simeq \dfrac{h\theta_{PIX}}{\sin \theta_N \cos \theta_N} \simeq \dfrac{GSD(0°)_y}{\sin \theta_N \cos \theta_N} \text{ [m].}\end{array}\right\} \quad (16\text{-}9)$$

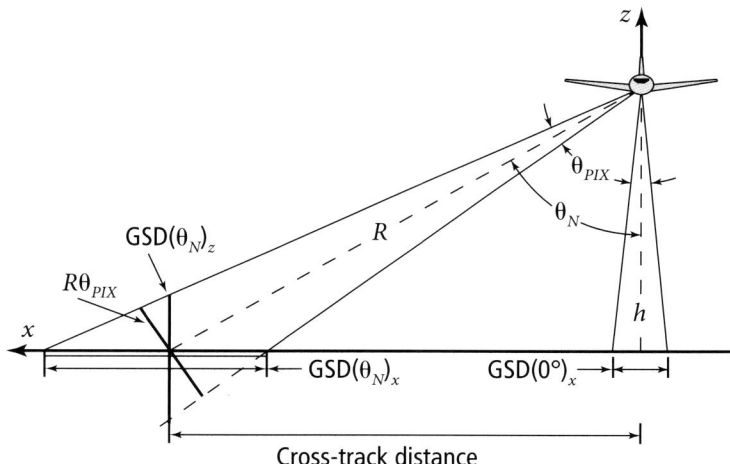

Figure 16-24
Ground pixels of pushbroom scanner flying off the page toward the reader.

This large pixel size will be illustrated later with a numerical example with the results shown in **Table 16-6**.

Another long slant range disadvantage involves the reduction of spectral irradiance received at the sensor. This reduction is strictly a radiometry effect independent of atmospheric attenuation. If either the object of interest is smaller than a ground pixel, or if it is larger than a pixel but with dimensions much less than the slant range, the point source approximation is valid. The received spectral irradiance is given by the expression:

$$\mathcal{E}_\lambda(\lambda) = \frac{I_\lambda(\lambda)}{r^2} \left[\frac{W}{m^2 \mu m}\right], \qquad (16\text{-}20)$$

where $I_\lambda(\lambda)$ is the point source spectral intensity ($W \cdot sr^{-1} \mu m^{-1}$) of the object of interest.

A consequence of the off-nadir dimensions of ground pixels is that on the near edge of the swath, pixels are smaller and more nearly square in shape than those on the far side of the swath (**Figure 16-25**). This results from the variation in the size of the slant range from one edge to the other. The wider the swath width, the larger the effect.

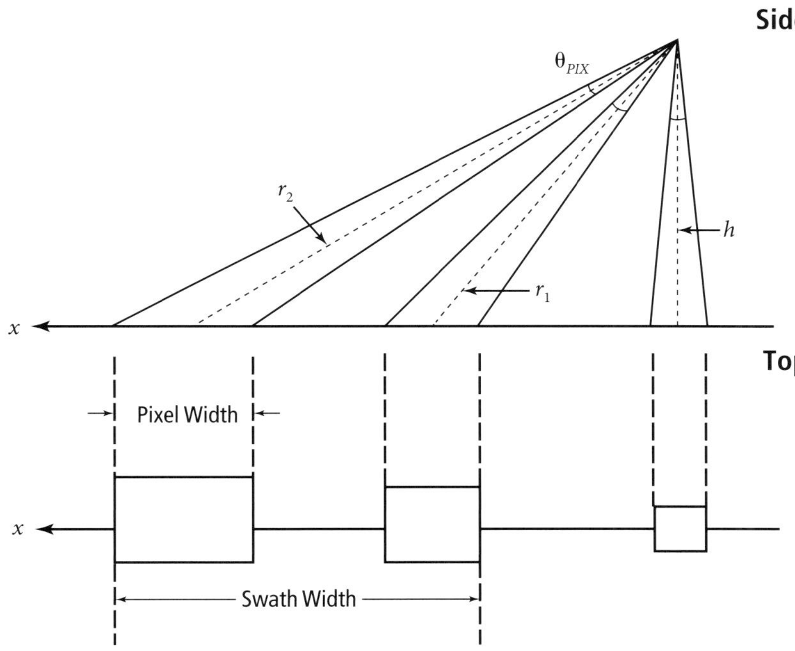

Figure 16-25
Ground pixel size variation across the collected swath located far off-nadir.

This size variation of ground pixels is associated with another effect, which distorts the sizes of objects of interest, especially those near the far edge of the swath. In the top view of the swath shown in **Figure 16-26**, if data is collected rapidly so there are no gaps in coverage along the near edge A*B* of the swath where ground pixels are smaller, there is overlapping of ground pixels near the far-edge AB of the swath. This results in oversampling that portion of the scene. Hence, for a sub-pixel size object of interest located in the cross-hatched area denoting the overlap between two adjacent pixels, the object will be reported in both pixels. Therefore, in the collected image, it will appear to be significantly larger than reality.

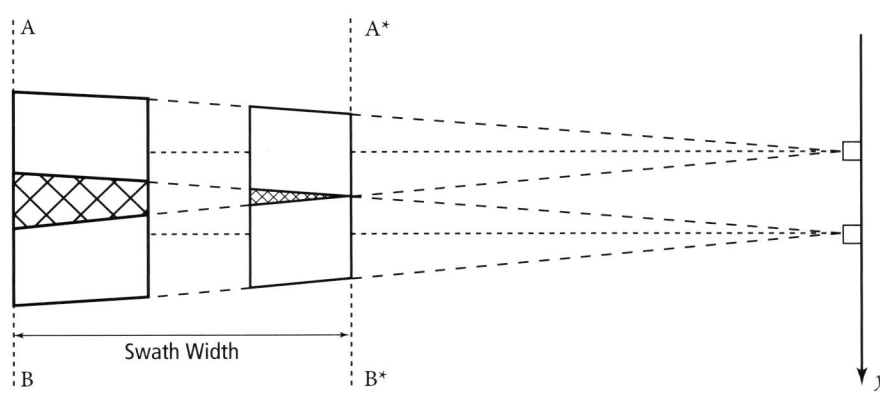

Figure 16-26
Top view of round pixel overlap towards the far edge of the collected swath located far off-nadir.

Also, when considering oblique viewing effects, another important effect occurs when an object of interest is shielded by a larger object in front of it. This is illustrated in **Figure 16-27**.

Figure 16-27
Shadowing effects for long-range stand-off viewing.

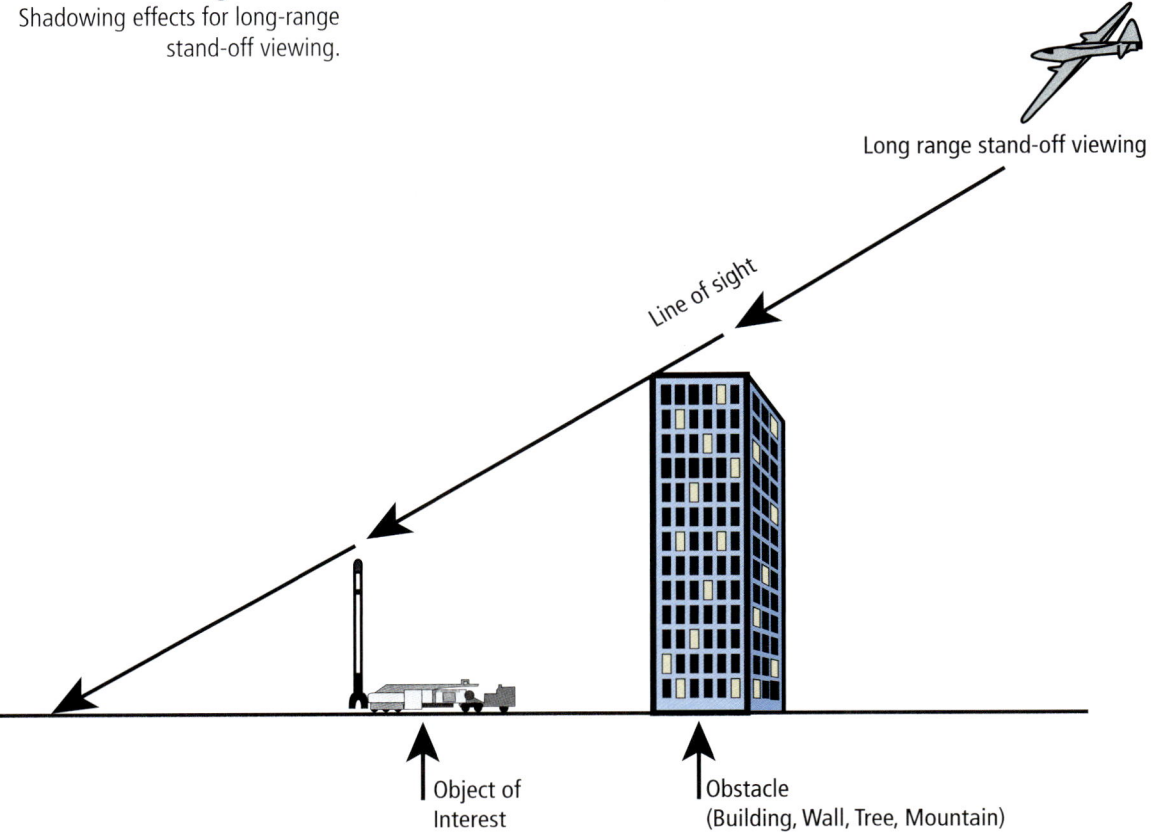

One mitigating factor with the large ground pixels occurs when a three-dimensional object of interest is viewed far off-nadir. As the slant range, r, and the stand-off range, x, both increase with sensor viewing angle θ_N. With altitude, h, remaining constant, as θ_N becomes larger and approaches 90°, and $(90° - \theta_N)$ decreases and approaches 0 (**Figure 16-28**), then, to close approximation,

$$r = \frac{h}{\cos\theta_N} \quad \text{and} \quad x = h \tan \theta_N. \tag{16-21}$$

Therefore, a three-dimensional object will be viewed more side-on than overhead, and $GSD(\theta_N)_z \simeq GSD(\theta_N)_y$ is a more relevant pixel size than $GSD(\theta_N)_x$ which is $1/\cos\theta$ times larger.

Figure 16-28
Slant range and stand-off range increases with nadir angle increases.

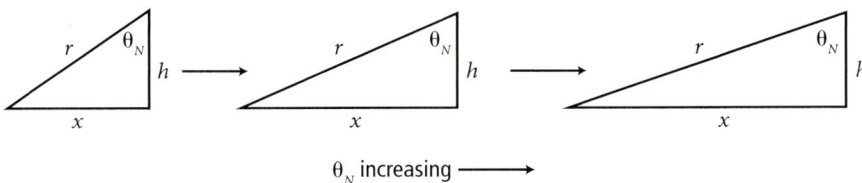

An example showing the magnitude of some of these effects is summarized in **Table 16-6**. Listed in the first columns are the viewing angle, θ_N, measured from nadir, and $1/\cos\theta$ of that angle. Based on those values and **Equation 16-19**, the ground pixel sizes are listed for $GSD(0°_N)_y$, $GSD(0°_N)_z$, and $GSD(0°_N)_x$ in columns 3, 4, and 5, assuming

θ_N	$\frac{1}{\cos\theta_N}$	Ground pixel relative size			Atmospheric transmission for $\tau(\theta_N)$			Slant range r (km)		Stand-off range x (km)	
		$GSD(\theta_N)_y$	$GSD(\theta_N)_z$	$GSD(\theta_N)_x$	0.9	0.8	0.7	$\frac{h}{\cos\theta}$	SE	$h\tan\theta$	SE
0°	1.0	1.0	n/a	1.0	0.9	0.8	0.7	20	20	0	0
45°	1.4	1.4	0.70	2.0	0.86	0.73	0.60	28.3	28.3	20	20
60°	2.0	2.0	2.3	4.0	0.81	0.64	0.49	40	40	34.6	34.6
70°	2.9	2.9	3.1	8.5	0.74	0.52	0.35	58.5	58.5	54.9	54.9
75°	3.9	3.9	4.0	14.9	0.67	0.42	0.25	77.3	77.3	74.6	74.6
77.5°	4.6	4.6	4.7	21.3	0.62	0.36	0.19	92.4	92.4	90.2	90.2
80°	5.8	5.8	5.9	33.2	0.55	0.28	0.13	115.2	**119.0**	113.4	**117.2**

Table 16-6
Pixel size and viewing geometries as the nadir angle increases. (SE = Spherical Earth.) Sensor altitude is 20 km.

$GSD(0°)_y = GSD(0°)_x = 1$. Atmospheric transmission values along the line of sight are given in columns 6, 7, and 8 based on the values 0.9, 0.8, and 0.7, respectively, for the vertical, or nadir, line of sight from sensor to object on the ground.

To better visualize the viewing geometries considered, the last four columns give both the slant range, r, and the stand-off range, x, for each of the nadir angles θ_N, based on a sensor altitude $h = 20$ km (or 65,000 feet). For most values of nadir angle, θ_N, ranging from zero up to almost 80 degrees, the flat-Earth model is adequate, and the values of r and x (AC and BC, respectively, in **Figure 16-29**) result from simple trigonometry. Beyond 80°, the Earth's surface curvature must be considered. (Also, see **Figure 4-32**.)

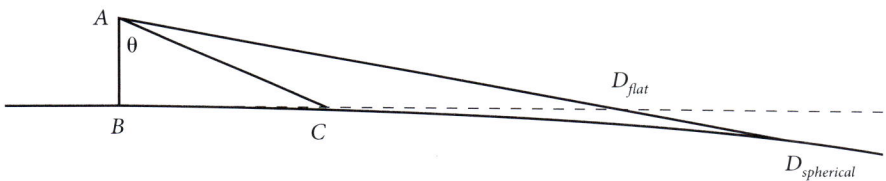

Figure 16-29
Complexities of spherical Earth to slant range and stand-off range.

For these larger angles, the slant range is considerably longer, $AD_{spherical}$ versus AD_{flat}. This is similar for the stand-off range, $BD_{spherical}$, versus BD_{flat}. The values for slant range, r, and the stand-off range, x, are listed in columns 10 and 12 of **Table 16-6**, respectively, based on the spherical Earth (SE) geometry and more complex trigonometry calculations. The blue, bolded values indicate those that diverge from the flat-Earth model and simple trigonometry.

OFF-NADIR COLLECTIONS

An interesting sensor specifically designed to gather data in the long range stand-off mode is the SYERS-2 which is flown on U-2 aircraft (hence, the reference to Senior Year in its name). To facilitate far off-nadir viewing, SYERS-2 is mounted in a special nose for the aircraft. When installed on U-2 aircraft, the sensor can be rolled from nadir to point at objects of interest. [17]

The original U-2A first flew in August 1955. Recently, the U-2 provided intelligence during operations in Korea, The Balkans, Afghanistan, and Iraq. When requested, the U-2 has provided peacetime reconnaissance in support of disaster relief from floods, earthquakes, and forest fires as well as search and rescue missions. [20]

17 HSI TECHNIQUES

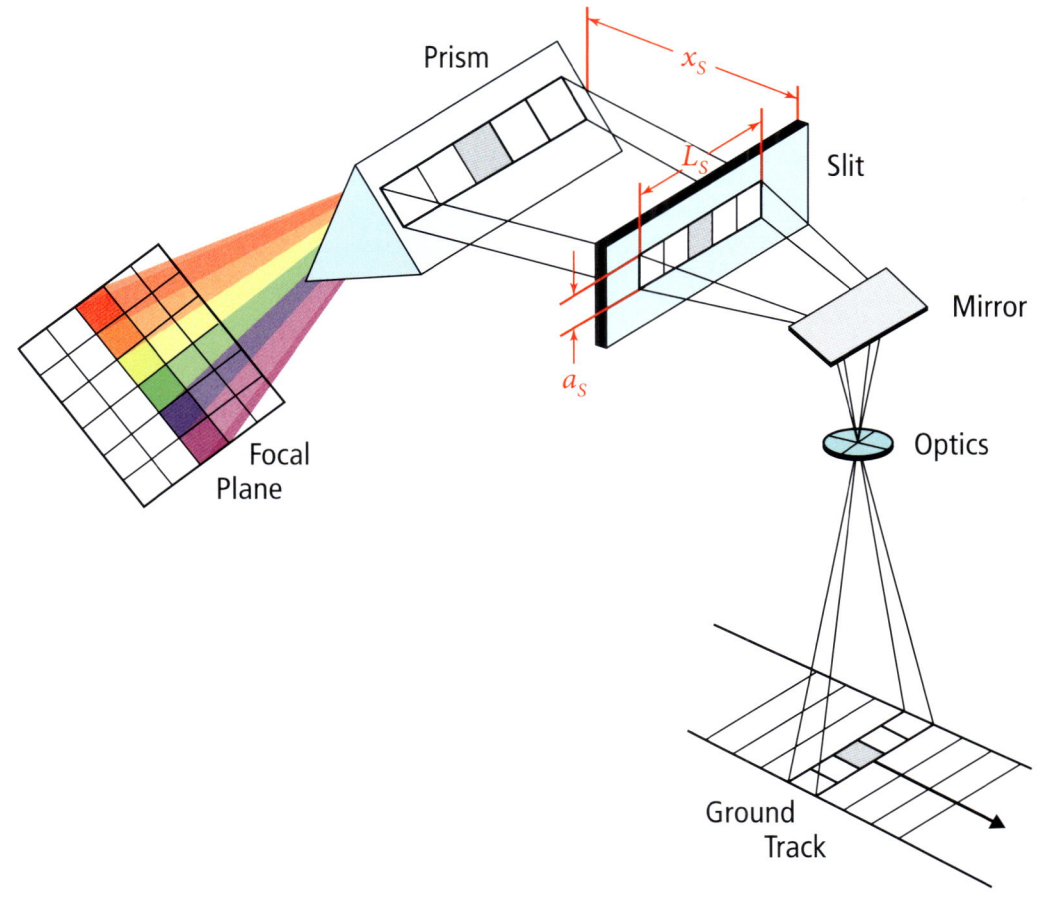

Hyperspectral Imaging (HSI) sensors generally utilize one of four common approaches: prisms, gratings, Fabry-Perot etalons, or Michelson interferometers with Fourier-transform data processing. This chapter will start with some common performance characteristics that will be considered for each of the four optical approaches. These performance characteristics will provide the basis for comparison of the four different approaches. Following the introduction of performance characteristics, each HSI approach will be discussed beginning with the oldest (prisms dating back to Sir Isaac Newton in 1666) and progressing to the newest (imaging Fourier-Transform Spectrometers (FTS) developed in the 1950s). Following this discussion, HSI collection options will be explored as well as the challenges and consequences of high data rate collections and techniques to lessen this challenge.

SECTIONS

17.1 HSI SENSOR PERFORMANCE CHARACTERISTICS

17.2 PRISMS

17.3 DIFFRACTION GRATINGS

17.4 THIN FILM INTERFERENCE APPLIED TO SPECTROMETERS

17.5 FOURIER TRANSFORM SPECTROMETERS

17.6 HSI COLLECTION OPTIONS AND ISSUES

17.1 HSI SENSOR PERFORMANCE CHARACTERISTICS

MSI VS. HSI

One of the differences between Multispectral Imaging (MSI) and HSI data is the number of spectral bands (or correspondingly the width of spectral bands). Although, no two authors agree at what number of spectral bands MSI data becomes HSI data. In terms of sensor hardware, MSI systems can have as many spectral bands as the number of different filters that are used, and these bands can be adjoining in wavelength or not. Also, they can be spread across several spectral regions (for example, the three bands in the visible-Near Infrared (vis-NIR), two in the Shortwave Infrared (SWIR), and one in the Mid-Wave Infrared (MWIR) for Senior Year Electro-optical Reconnaissance System (SYERS), as discussed in **Chapter 16**). HSI sensors, as discussed in this chapter, always have large numbers of adjoining bands, usually within one spectral region. Often, some of these bands may not be useful, because they are located in an atmospheric absorption band.

To begin, consider the spectrum of a point source. In this geometry, incoming radiation arrives from only one direction. The first characteristic of performance is *spectral dispersion*, which can be a function of wavelength. Spectral dispersion describes the degree to which different incoming wavelengths are separated from one another. Depending on the HSI technique used, dispersion can be measured in terms of angle, voltage relating to physical separation, or time relating to location. An important consideration relates to whether the spectral dispersion is linear with respect to wavelength or not. Sensors with spectral dispersion constant across a spectral bandpass are much easier to calibrate spectrally than those that are not.

Another HSI sensor performance characteristic is the Free Spectral Range (FSR), which is the effective spectral bandpass limited by the dispersal technique.

A more common characteristic is the spectral resolution, $\Delta\lambda_{MIN}$. Spectral resolution is the minimum separation in wavelength between two infinitely narrow spectral lines of incoming radiation that can be resolved as two lines after they have been dispersed by the spectrometer. This concept is illustrated in **Figure 17-1**. As defined, improved spectral resolution is characterized by a smaller value of $\Delta\lambda_{MIN}$.

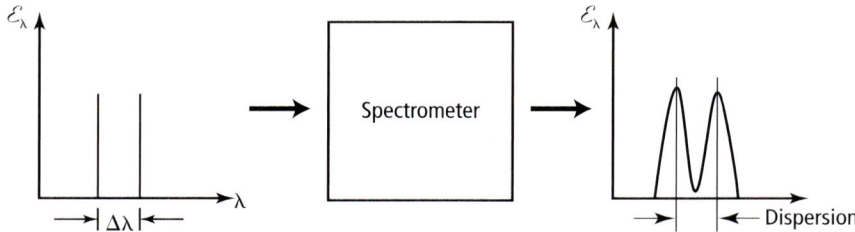

Figure 17-1
Spectral sampling by a HSI instrument broadens spectral lines.

Another characteristic related to the spectral resolution is the resolving power, $\overline{RP}$, given by the formula:

$$\overline{RP} = \frac{\lambda}{\Delta\lambda_{MIN}}. \tag{17-1}$$

Improved spectral resolution is characterized by a larger value of $\overline{RP}$. A variation of the resolving power sometimes used is the finesse, F, which will be discussed later in this chapter.

To determine a value for $\Delta\lambda_{MIN}$, the Rayleigh criterion is used, as shown in **Figure 17-2**, to determine the wavelength spacing necessary to

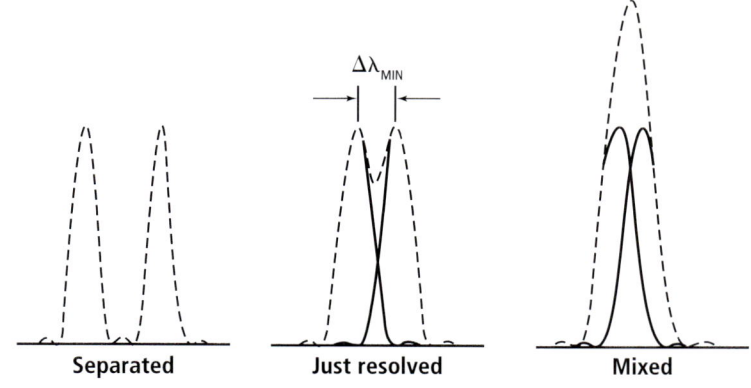

Figure 17-2
Spectral resolution Rayleigh criterion is identical to that for spatial resolution. The dispersion associated with $\Delta\lambda_{MIN}$ is one-half the width of a dispersed spectral line.

resolve the two peaks as separate peaks after they have been dispersed. This is the same criteria used in **Chapter 8** to determine how closely two point sources of radiation can be spaced and still appear as two sources in the image. An important trade-off involving spectral resolution is apparent. As the spectral resolution increases, the signal-to-noise ratio decreases. This can be immediately understood given the fact that sources of radiation emit a fixed amount of power. As spectral bands become narrower, spectral resolution improves; but the drawback is less energy is available per band.

Important additional characteristics can be defined when spectrally imaging an extended source. All the radiation from a source is not incident at the sensor from exactly the same direction. There is a range of values for the angle of incidence, θ_{inc}. Although it is not obvious at this point, this will produce additional spread in angular dispersion for all wavelengths. The range of values for the angle of incidence relates to a solid angle, Ω_{PIX}, and the energy collection capability (light gathering power or *throughput*) of the sensor. One measure of the sensor throughput, U, is the collection area-pixel solid angle product,

$$U = A_R \Omega_{PIX} \left[\frac{cm^2}{sr} \right], \qquad (17\text{-}2)$$

where A_R is the sensor's receiving aperture area and Ω_{PIX} is measured in steradians. Recall the two quantities that create the throughput are found in the end-to-end equation discussed in **Chapter 10**. Another commonly used name for the throughput is the French word *etendue*.

There is a trade-off for each type of HSI sensor, shown in the equation

$$(\overline{RP})U = \text{constant} \left[\frac{cm^2}{sr} \right], \qquad (17\text{-}3)$$

where the value of the constant depends upon the HSI sensor type. Consequences include: 1) increased throughput, U, produces decreased resolving power, $\overline{RP}$, and increased spectral resolution, $\Delta\lambda_{MIN}$; and 2) decreased throughput, U, can produce larger resolving power and smaller spectral resolution, $\Delta\lambda_{MIN}$, values.

17.2 PRISMS

A prism is a triangular shaped piece of glass with two polished faces (**Figure 17-3**). The standard dimensions of a prism are the apex angle α, a plane angle between the two polished faces, and the base width b as shown in **Figure 17-4**.

Figure 17-3
An ordinary prism with the apex being the leading edge and the base being the rear side.

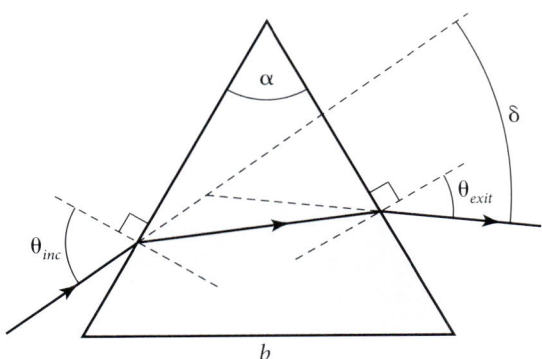

Figure 17-4
A light ray incident on one face of a prism is twice refracted and exits the second face after being redirected, or deviated, by an angle δ.

Consider radiation of a single wavelength that is incident onto one of the prism faces at angle θ_{INC} as shown in **Figure 17-4**. When Snell's Law (**Equation 3-2**) is applied to the two polished prism faces which separate the surrounding medium (usually air, with index of refraction n_a) from the prism (usually glass with index of refraction n_p), the resulting deviation angle, δ, is given by the expression,

$$\delta = \theta_{inc} - \alpha + \sin^{-1}\left(\sin\alpha\sqrt{\left(\frac{n_p}{n_a}\right)^2 - \sin^2\theta_{inc}} - \cos\alpha\sin\theta_{inc}\right) \quad [\text{rad}]. \quad (17\text{-}4)$$

Note, this result depends on the angle of incidence θ_{inc}, but not the location of the incident ray on the prism face. For a given prism (n_p, n_a, and α), the resulting function $\delta(\theta_{inc})$ is plotted in **Figure 17-5**.

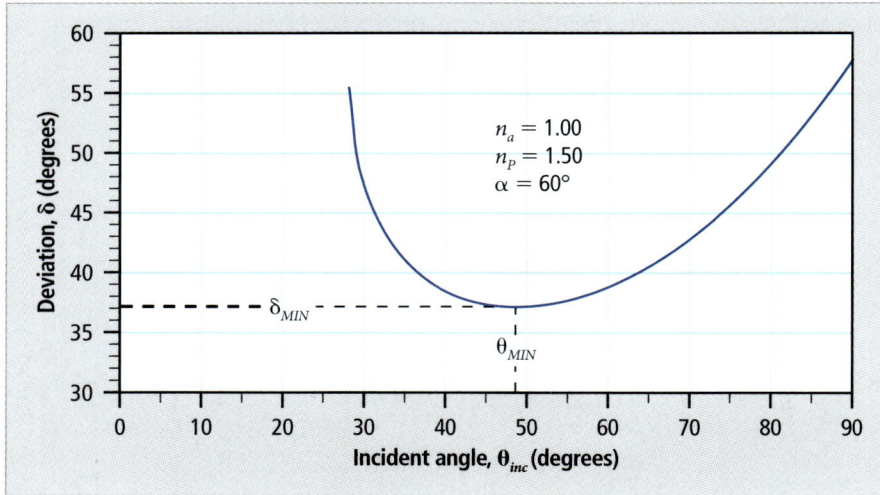

Figure 17-5
Deviation angle as a function of incident angle. θ_{MIN} is the incident angle for which δ is minimized.

For general ease of optical alignment, a prism is generally used so the angle of incident radiation is near the minimum of $\delta(\theta_{inc})$. To find the location of this minimum, θ_{MIN}, the standard method of calculus is to set the derivative of **Equation 17-4** equal to zero:

$$\frac{d\delta}{d\theta_{inc}} = 0. \quad (17\text{-}5)$$

The solution of **Equation 17-5** is often written as the "Prism Equation:"

$$\frac{n_p}{n_a} = \frac{\sin\left(\frac{1}{2}(\delta + \alpha)\right)}{\sin\left(\frac{1}{2}\alpha\right)}. \quad (17\text{-}6)$$

The result of using a prism at minimum deviation is shown in **Figure 17-6**, where the incident ray is refracted parallel to the base:

$$\theta_{inc} = \theta_{exit} = \sin^{-1}\left(\frac{n_p}{n_a}\sin\frac{\alpha}{2}\right) \quad [\text{rad}]. \quad (17\text{-}7)$$

Hereafter, assume light is incident at this angle.

For many types of glass, $n_p = n(\lambda)$, so $\delta = \delta(\lambda)$. *This is the basis for obtaining spectra.* In **Figure 17-7**, $n(\lambda)$ is plotted for several different types of glass. These curves of measured data are often fit to a Cauchy series expansion (**Equation 17-8**), where λ_0 is a wavelength in the middle of the bandpass of interest.

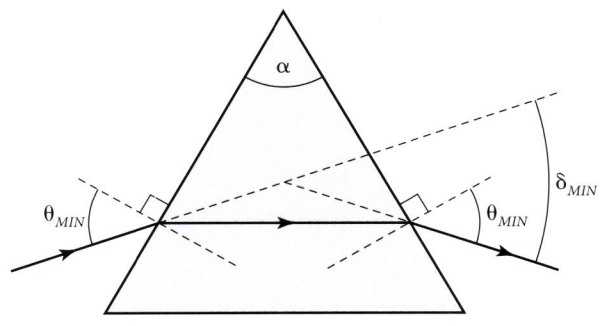

Figure 17-6
Light passing through a prism at the minimum deviation angle presents symmetric incident and exit angles.

$$n(\lambda) = n_0 + n_2\left[\frac{\lambda_0}{\lambda}\right]^2 + n_4\left[\frac{\lambda_0}{\lambda}\right]^4 + \ldots \quad (17\text{-}8)$$

The curve-fit coefficients, $n_0, n_2, n_4, \ldots$ are often used when ordering optical glasses from catalogs.

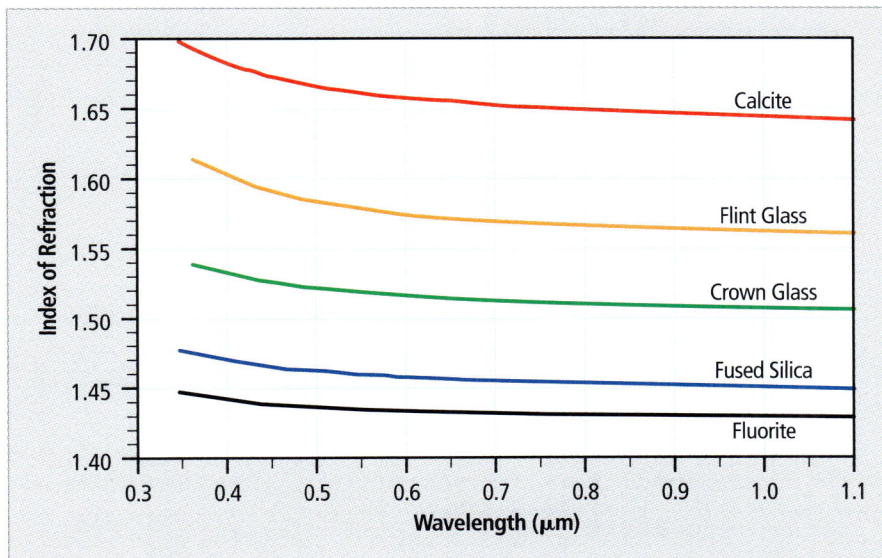

Figure 17-7
Index of refraction for various glasses as a function of wavelength.

The derivative of the deviation angle with respect to wavelength is called *dispersion*, $\delta_\lambda(\lambda)$. Dispersion is the familiar separation of color in a sunbeam, often thought to be first quantitatively studied by Newton (**Figure 17-8**).

$$\delta_\lambda = \frac{d\delta}{d\lambda} = \left(\frac{d\delta}{dn_p}\right)\left(\frac{dn_p}{d\lambda}\right) \quad \left[\frac{\text{rad}}{\mu\text{m}}\right]. \quad (17\text{-}9)$$

To determine the dispersion, use the prism equation above and an approximation for the index of refraction:

$$n(\lambda) \approx n_0 + n_2\left[\frac{\lambda_0}{\lambda}\right]^2. \quad (17\text{-}10)$$

Figure 17-8
Dispersion of visible light through a prism due to variation of the index of refraction with wavelength.

Thus, the derivatives are:

$$\frac{d\delta}{dn_p} = \frac{2\sin\left(\tfrac{1}{2}\alpha\right)}{\sqrt{n_a^2 - n_p^2 \sin^2\left(\tfrac{1}{2}\alpha\right)}} \quad [\text{rad}] \quad \text{and} \quad (17\text{-}11)$$

$$\frac{dn_p}{d\lambda} = -2\frac{n_2}{\lambda}\left[\frac{\lambda_0}{\lambda}\right]^2 \quad [\mu\text{m}^{-1}].$$

Substituting these two expression into **Equation 17-9** gives the dispersion:

$$\frac{d\delta}{d\lambda} \approx -4\frac{n_2}{\lambda}\left(\frac{\lambda_0}{\lambda}\right)^2 \sin\frac{\alpha}{2}\left[n_a^2 - \left(n_0 + n_2\left(\frac{\lambda_0}{\lambda}\right)^2\right)^2 \sin^2\frac{\alpha}{2}\right]^{-1/2} \left[\frac{\text{rad}}{\mu m}\right]. \quad (17\text{-}12)$$

Inspection of **Equation 17-12** indicates the dispersion δ_λ of a prism is not constant. Hence, prism spectrometers are difficult to spectrally calibrate.

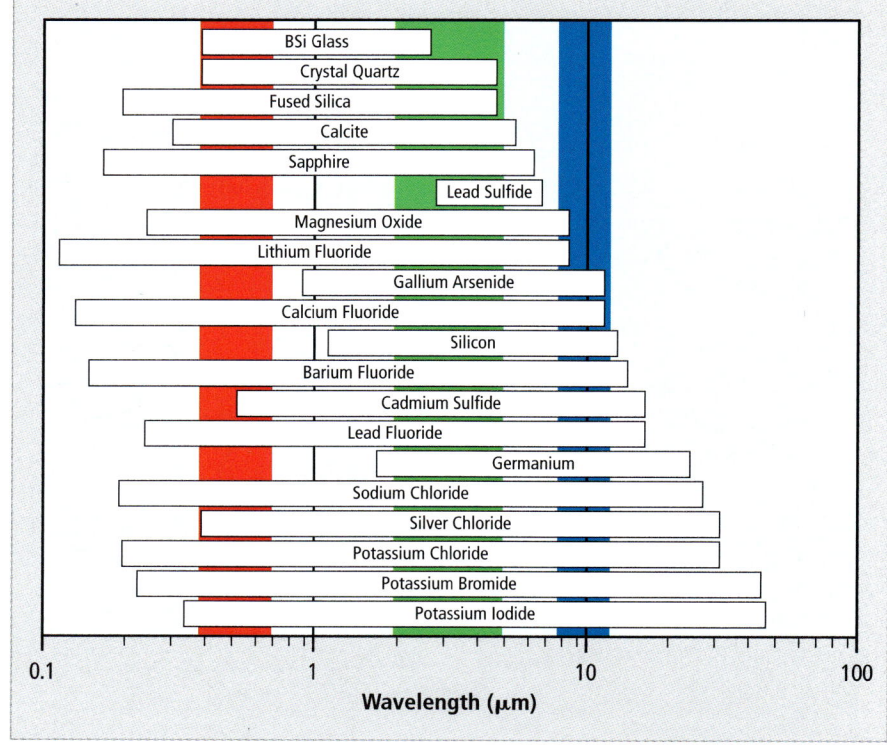

Figure 17-9
Approximate wavelengths of greater than 10% transmission through some optical materials. The red vertical stripe is the visible bandpass; the green is the SWIR-MWIR; and the blue is the LWIR. (Compare to **Figure 6-13**.) (Adapted from the Infrared Handbook, Wolfe and Zissis, eds, 1978.)

In choosing prism materials, the first step is to find optical materials that transmit light in the spectral region of interest. **Figure 17-9** shows the transmission properties of some common optical materials. In each case, the bars show the approximate 10% transmission cut-off points. Note, many of the optical materials that transmit in the visible do not transmit in the Long-Wave Infrared (LWIR). This is illustrated in the introductory figure of this chapter and in **Figure 17-10**. The black mylar trash bag does not transmit light in the visible, but does transmit light in the LWIR. The man's glasses transmit light in the visible, but do not transmit in the LWIR. Also note many of the optical materials that transmit in the LWIR are salts (chloride, fluoride, and bromide compounds). These materials tend to crumble when machined. Consider what happens when standard "salt" pellets (NaCl) are dropped on concrete; many of them fracture. Also, many of these salts are hygroscopic; they strongly attract water vapor molecules from the air. For example, if a bag of ice-melt salt is not used in the same season as it was purchased, the salt particles fuse, and a small puddle of water may appear under the bag, even though it was never opened.

In choosing a material for a prism, it must transmit across the desired spectral bandpass, and its $n(\lambda)$ must vary with wavelength across this bandpass. With proper materials chosen for a prism, its inclusion in a sensor's optics will not affect the desired spectral bandpass of the sensor. Hence, FSR issues rarely occur with a prism.

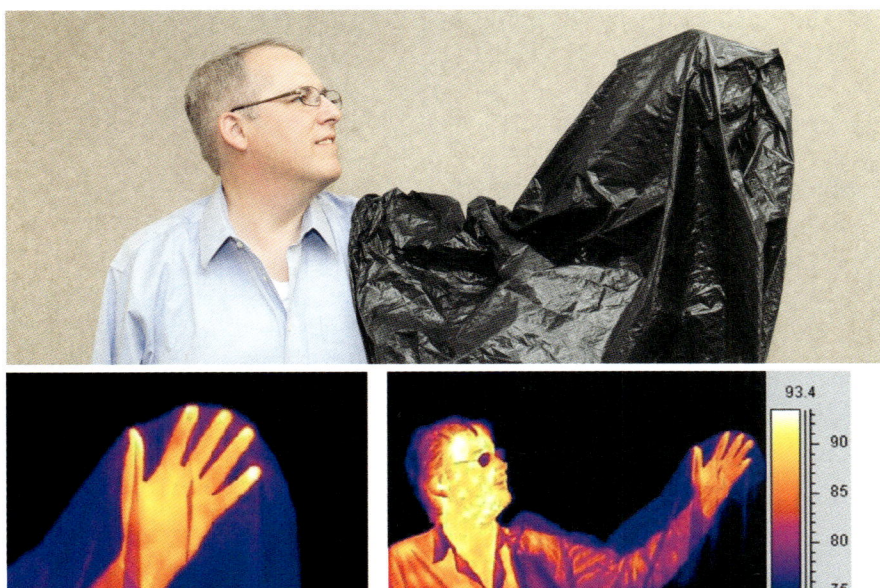

Figure 17-10
Materials that do and do not transmit visible light (spectacle glass and trash bag) reverse roles in LWIR. Temperature scales are Fahrenheit. (Compare to Figure 6-15.)

The spectral resolution of a prism spectrometer results from considering how close two input spectral lines (λ_o and $\lambda_o + \Delta\lambda$) can still be resolved as two peaks in dispersion rather than one. The finite dimensions of a prism's face will slightly disperse even a perfectly collimated input beam containing a single wavelength. This is similar to the spread, or diffraction, of a perfectly collimated input beam caused by a single finite circular or square aperture as in **Chapter 6**, **Figure 6-21**. If δ_λ becomes so small that the corresponding dispersion becomes smaller than the diffraction, the two wavelengths cannot be resolved. As a result, formulas expressing spectral resolution and resolving power of a prism spectrometer are

$$\Delta\lambda_{MIN} = \frac{\lambda}{b\frac{dn_p}{d\lambda}} \text{ and } \overline{RP} = \frac{\lambda}{\Delta\lambda_{MIN}} = b\frac{dn_p}{d\lambda}, \quad (17\text{-}13)$$

respectively, where $\frac{dn_p}{d\lambda} \approx \frac{\Delta n_p}{\Delta\lambda}$ to close approximation. See **Example 17-1** regarding prism deviation and resolution values.

The final aspect of prisms considered deals with the observation of extended sources and their resulting range of angles of incidence onto a prism. Consider such a range of angles of incidence, $\Delta\theta_{inc}$, as seen in **Figure 17-11** for a single wavelength.

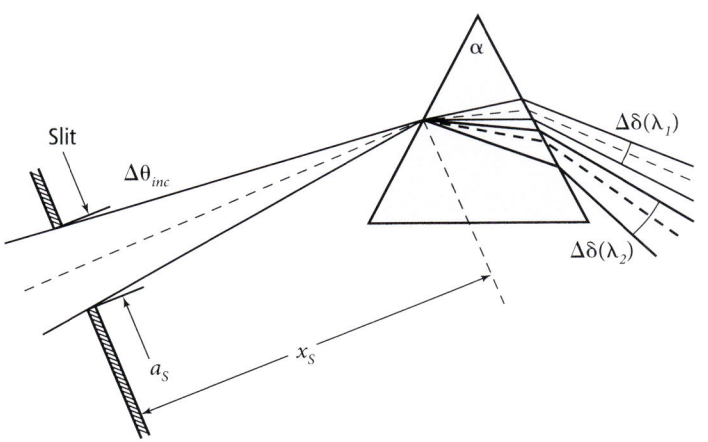

Figure 17-11
Light of two wavelengths within a range of incidence angles will be dispersed into a range of deviation angles.

EXAMPLE 17-1: CHARACTERIZING A PRISM

Calculate the angular dispersion between blue (0.48 μm) and red (0.65 μm) light passing through a 60° prism with $n_{blue} \approx 1.652$, $n_{red} \approx 1.618$, and base $b \approx 5$ cm. Calculate the prism's spectral resolution and resolving power. Assume $n_a = 1.00$ and a beam of white light is incident at θ_{MIN}.

There are two approaches to calculate the dispersion. In the first, calculate the deviation for blue and red separately, then subtract. This is accomplished by first solving the prism **Equation 17-6** for deviation:

$$\delta = 2 \sin^{-1}\left(\frac{n_p}{n_a} \sin\left(\frac{\alpha}{2}\right)\right) - \alpha.$$

Then, calculating for a ray of blue light,

$$\delta_{blue} = 2 \sin^{-1}\left(\frac{1.652}{1.00} \sin(30°)\right) - 60° \approx 51.38°.$$

For a ray of red light,

$$\delta_{red} = 2 \sin^{-1}\left(\frac{1.618}{1.00} \sin(30°)\right) - 60° \approx 48.00°;$$

and taking the difference to find how much the two colors are dispersed,

$$\Delta\delta \approx \delta_{blue} - \delta_{red} \approx 3.38°.$$

The second approach is to approximate the **Equation 17-11** expression for $\frac{d\delta}{dn_p}$ as

$$\Delta\delta_\lambda \approx \frac{2 \sin\left(\frac{\alpha}{2}\right)}{\sqrt{n_a^2 - \overline{n}_p^2 \sin^2\left(\frac{\alpha}{2}\right)}} \Delta n_p,$$

where $\Delta n_p = n_{blue} - n_{red} \approx 0.034$ and $\overline{n}_p = \frac{1}{2}(n_{blue} + n_{red}) \approx 1.635$. Computing,

$$\Delta\delta_\lambda \approx \frac{2 \sin 30°}{\sqrt{1^2 - (1.635)^2 \sin^2 30°}}(0.034) \approx 0.0590 \text{ rad} \approx 3.38°.$$

Note, this answer must be converted from radians to degrees and is the same, of course.

To calculate spectral resolution, **Equation 17-13**, first approximate

$$\frac{\Delta n_p}{\Delta\lambda} \approx \frac{0.034}{(0.65 \text{ μm} - 0.48 \text{ μm})} \approx 0.2 \text{ μm}^{-1}$$

and use an average wavelength in the middle of the bandpass, $\overline{\lambda} = \frac{1}{2}(0.65 \text{ μm} + 0.48 \text{ μm}) \approx 0.565 \text{ μm}$ to estimate

$$\Delta\lambda_{MIN} \approx \frac{\overline{\lambda}}{b\frac{\Delta n_p}{\Delta\lambda}} \approx \frac{0.565 \text{ μm}}{\left(5 \text{ cm} \times \frac{10^4 \text{ μm}}{1 \text{ cm}}\right)(0.2 \text{ μm}^{-1})} \approx 5.65 \times 10^{-5} \text{ μm} \approx 0.0565 \text{ nm}.$$

The resolving power (**Equation 17-13**) is then

$$\overline{RP} \approx \frac{\overline{\lambda}}{\Delta\lambda_{MIN}} \approx \frac{0.565 \text{ μm}}{5.65 \times 10^{-5} \text{ μm}} \approx 10^4.$$

Assuming diffraction effects are small, a range of incident angles will produce a range in deviation angles for one of the wavelengths, $\Delta\delta(\lambda_1)$, as shown in **Figure 17-11**. This would also be true for a second incident wavelength. However, if $\Delta\theta_{inc}$ were to become too large, the widths of the two deviations would become so wide that they would overlap such that an observer could not distinguish between λ_1 and λ_2. Hence, to achieve desired spectral resolution, it is necessary to limit $\Delta\theta_{inc}$. This is done by putting a narrow slit in the optics with an effective width a_s at a distance x_s from the point of incidence on the prism. The long dimension of the slit, L_s, is into and out of the page in **Figure 17-11**.

The use of a slit has two important consequences. The first deals with data collection and the second with spectrometer throughput. In **Figure 17-12**, the slit defines a row of ground pixels. The width of the row is determined by the number of columns of detectors in each row on a two-dimensional Focal Plane Array (FPA) as shown. The prism takes the light from each ground pixel and spectrally disperses it across the appropriate detector in each column. The number of detectors in each column defines the number of spectral bands. A two-dimensional spectral image (or swath) can be built by scanning the row of ground pixels across the scene. This is most easily accomplished, as shown in **Figure 17-12**, using the forward motion of the platform (pushbroom collection). Moving parts are not required within the sensor except for a scanning mirror (not shown) acting as a motion compensator. Alternatively, other scanning directions can be achieved with the use of a scanning mirror. A combination of both approaches can also be used.

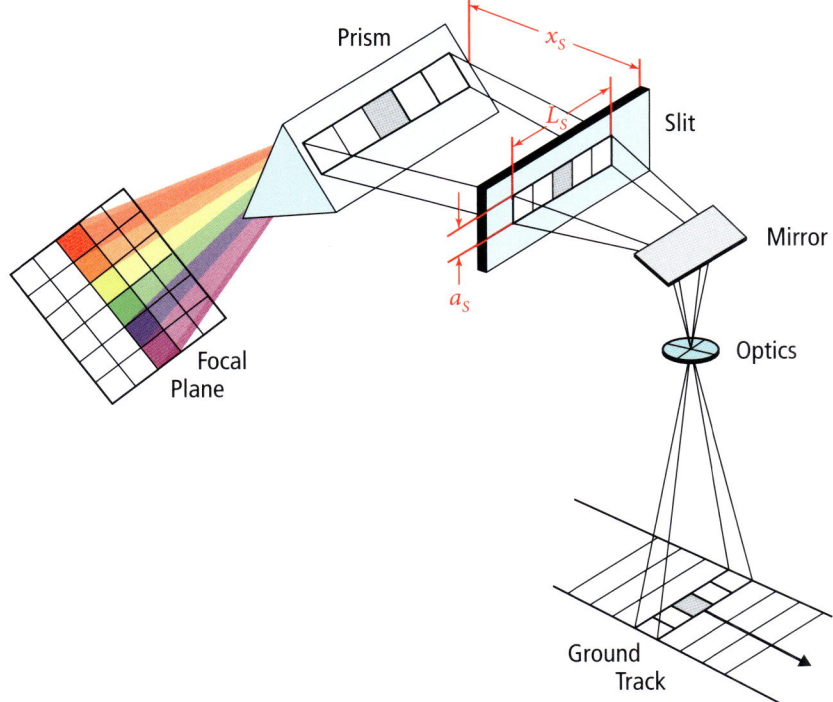

Figure 17-12
Schematic of a pushbroom prism spectrometer.

The second consequence of using a slit to maintain spectral resolution is its limitation on spectrometer throughput, or etendue U, which is the $A_R\Omega_{PIX}$ product. In **Figure 17-12**, Ω_{PIX} is the solid angle subtended by the slit vertically and by one of the detectors composing a column in the FPA horizontally. From **Figures 17-11** and **17-12**, if there are N columns of detectors, then,

$$\Omega_{PIX} \approx \left(\frac{a_s}{x_s}\right)\left(\frac{L_s/N}{x_s}\right) \approx \frac{a_s L_s}{N x_s^2}. \qquad (17\text{-}14)$$

If square ground pixels are desired, $N = \frac{L_s}{a_s}$ and

$$\Omega_{PIX} \approx \frac{a_s^2}{x_s^2}. \qquad (17\text{-}15)$$

How large can $\Delta\theta_{inc}$ be without significantly reducing spectral resolution? Mathematically, $\Delta\delta_\theta$ caused by a variation in θ_{inc} for one wavelength is much less than $\Delta\delta_\lambda$ caused by a variation in wavelength for one θ_{inc}. To demonstrate this, expressions for $\Delta\delta_\theta/\Delta\theta$ and $\Delta\delta_\lambda/\Delta\lambda$ are required. First, apply differential calculus to the general equation for $\delta(\lambda,\theta_{inc})$ shown earlier (**Equation 17-4**),

$$\Delta\delta_\theta \approx \left(1 - \frac{\sin\alpha \sin\theta_{inc} \cos\theta_{inc}}{W\sqrt{1-V^2}} - \frac{\sin\alpha \cos\theta_{inc}}{\sqrt{1-V^2}}\right)\Delta\theta_{inc}, \quad (17\text{-}16)$$

where $V = W\sin\alpha - \cos\alpha \sin\theta_{inc}$ and $W = \sqrt{n_p^2 - \sin^2\theta_{inc}}$.

Second, let $n_a = 1$, $n_p = n$, and ignore the variation of n with wavelength (**Equations 17-8** and **17-10**). **Equations 17-9** and **17-11** can be approximated as

$$\Delta\delta_\lambda \approx \frac{2\left(\frac{\Delta n}{\Delta\lambda}\right)\sin\left(\frac{\alpha}{2}\right)}{\sqrt{1 - n^2\sin^2\left(\frac{\alpha}{2}\right)}} \Delta\lambda. \qquad (17\text{-}17)$$

These derivatives are compared in **Example 17-2**.

EXAMPLE 17-2: FURTHER CHARACTERIZATION OF A PRISM SPECTROMETER

For the prism in **Example 17-1**, calculate $\Delta\delta_\theta$ for mid-band wavelength $\overline{\lambda} \approx 0.565$ µm and compare it to $\Delta\delta_\lambda \approx 0.0015°$, which corresponds to the $\overline{RP} = 10^4$ value calculated there. Also, estimate the prism's throughput when $\Delta\theta_{inc} \approx \frac{a_s}{x_s} \approx \frac{10 \text{ µm}}{1 \text{ cm}} \approx 10^{-4}$ rad, assuming square pixels.

First, for minimum deviation at λ, assume $n_p \approx \overline{n} \approx 1.635$. Then, using **Equation 17-7**:

$$\theta_{inc} \approx \sin^{-1}(1.635 \sin 30°) \approx 54.84°.$$

Now before using **Equation 17-17**, calculate

$$W \approx ((1.635)^2 - \sin^2 54.84°)^{1/2} \approx 1.416,$$

$$V \approx (1.416)\sin 60° - \cos 60° \sin 54.84° \approx 0.8175, \text{ and}$$

$$\sqrt{1-V^2} \approx \sqrt{1 - 0.8175^2} \approx 0.5759.$$

Continued on next page

Then,

$$\Delta\delta_\theta \approx \left(1 - \frac{\sin 60° \sin 54.84° \cos 54.84°}{(1.416)(0.5759)} - \frac{\cos 60° \cos 54.84°}{0.5759}\right)(10^{-4})$$

$$\approx 5.476 \times 10^{-9} \text{rad} \approx 3.14 \times 10^{-7} \text{ degrees}.$$

As advertised, $\Delta\delta_\theta \ll \Delta\delta_\lambda$.

As for the throughput,

$$U \approx A_R \Omega_{PIX} \approx A_R (\Delta\theta_{inc})^2 \approx A_R (10^{-4} \text{rad})^2 \approx 10^{-8} A_R,$$

where A_R is the optical system's receiving aperture area.

For good measure, the resolving power-etendue product is

$$\overline{(RP)}U \approx (10^4)(10^{-8} A_R) \approx 10^{-4} A_R,$$

where the resolving power was calculated in the previous example.

To summarize the performance of a prism spectrometer and begin the comparison with other types of spectrometers, see **Table 17-1**. More information will be added at the end of the discussion of each of the other three types of spectrometers.

	Prism
Spectral dispersion variation	Non-linear with λ
FSR	Large, limited only by prism material properties
Possible spectral sampling	All λ at once for one row of spatial pixels
2-D scene coverage	Slit required so sequential rows of pixels scanned over time
Resolving power etendue product	Low

Table 17-1
Performance characteristics of a prism spectrometer.

Finally, some examples of nature's "prisms" are shown in **Figure 17-13**. The rainbow and glory result from sunlight dispersing through multiple total internal reflections in spherical water droplets, while the halo and sundogs are from flat hexagonal ice crystals.

Figure 17-13
Although diffraction plays some part in creating these phenomena, the colors in a) the rainbow, b) a solar halo, c) sundogs, and d) a glory are from prismatic effects. (Rainbow image courtesy of http://en.wikipedia.org/wiki/File:Double-alaskan-rainbow.jpg; Creative Commons Attribution-Share Alike 2.5 Generic: Eric Rolph at English Wikipedia. Glory image courtesy of http://en.wikipedia.org/wiki/File:IMG_7474_solar_glory.JPG; GNU Free Documentation License Version 1.2; Creative Commons Attribution-Share Alike 3.0 Unported - Brocken Inaglory.)

17.3 DIFFRACTION GRATINGS

The traditional starting point for the discussion of gratings is Young's double slit interference. The experimental layout in **Figure 17-14** shows the two slits, S_1 and S_2, and an opaque screen with an observer at point P located by the coordinates x and y. The two slits are separated by a distance d, and the width of each slit is a. The observer's location is far from the slits, so that $x \gg d$. The observer is also located near the axis of the experiment, so $x \gg y$. The initial consideration is for light characterized by a single wavelength incident along the x-axis.

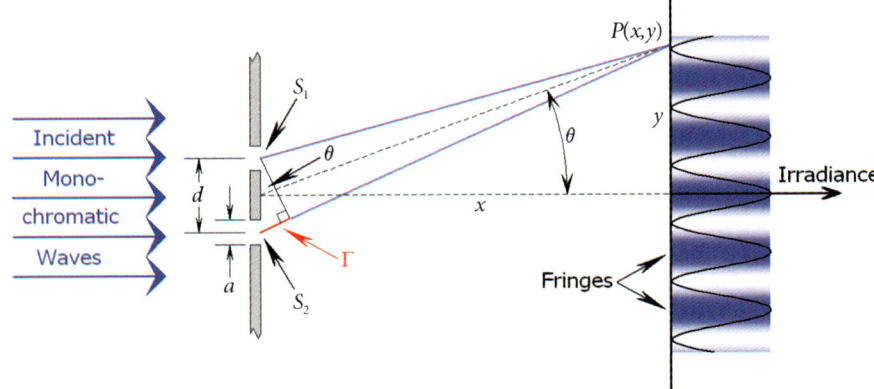

Figure 17-14
Young's double slit experiment (not to scale).

Annotated in **Figure 17-14** is the difference in path traveled, Γ, between S_1P and S_2P. It is shown as approximately one of the legs of a right triangle, so

$$\Gamma \simeq d\sin\theta \quad [\mu m]. \qquad (17\text{-}18)$$

(Careful geometric calculations of Γ give the same result to close approximation.) The corresponding phase[1] *difference*, ϕ, between the two waves arriving at P is given by

$$\phi = 2\pi\frac{\Gamma}{\lambda} \cong \frac{2\pi d\sin\theta}{\lambda} \quad [\text{rad}]. \qquad (17\text{-}19)$$

Two special cases must be considered:

1. *Constructive Interference*. If the two waves from S_1 and S_2 arrive at point P such that

$$\Gamma = d\sin\theta = m\lambda \quad [\mu m], \qquad (17\text{-}20)$$

where $m = 0, \pm 1, \pm 2, \ldots$ then $\phi = 2\pi m$, and they arrive exactly in phase and produce a "fringe". (Irradiance is plotted along the observer's screen in **Figure 17-14**. Some of the fringes are marked.) The integer "m" is called the order of constructive interference.

2. *Destructive Interference*. If the two waves from S_1 and S_2 arrive at point P such that

$$\Gamma = d\sin\theta = \left(m + \frac{1}{2}\right)\lambda \quad [\mu m], \qquad (17\text{-}21)$$

where $m = 0, \pm 1, \pm 2, \ldots$ then $\phi = 2\pi(m + \frac{1}{2})$, and they arrive exactly out of phase and produce no irradiance. (See **Figure 17-14**.)

---

[1] Assuming EM waves are sinusoidal, phase is the argument of the sine function representing the electric field. (See **Figure 2-1**.)

In general, the irradiance, $\mathcal{E}$, which is proportional to the square of the electric field, arriving at point P is given in various forms as:

$$\mathcal{E}(\phi) = \mathcal{E}_0 \frac{\sin^2 \phi}{\sin^2\left(\frac{\phi}{2}\right)} = 4\mathcal{E}_0 \cos^2\left(\frac{\phi}{2}\right) \left[\frac{W}{m^2}\right], \text{ or}$$

$$\mathcal{E}(\Gamma) = \mathcal{E}_0 \frac{\sin^2\left(\frac{2\pi\Gamma}{\lambda}\right)}{\sin^2\left(\frac{\pi\Gamma}{\lambda}\right)} = 4\mathcal{E}_0 \cos^2\left(\frac{\pi\Gamma}{\lambda}\right) \left[\frac{W}{m^2}\right], \text{ or} \qquad (17\text{-}22)$$

$$\mathcal{E}(\theta) = \mathcal{E}_0 \frac{\sin^2\left(\frac{2\pi d \sin\theta}{\lambda}\right)}{\sin^2\left(\frac{\pi d \sin\theta}{\lambda}\right)} = 4\mathcal{E}_0 \cos^2\left(\frac{\pi d \sin\theta}{\lambda}\right) \left[\frac{W}{m^2}\right],$$

where $\mathcal{E}_0$ is the irradiance received on the observer's screen if there was only one slit.[2]

Note, from any of **Equations 17-22**, the irradiance of a fringe, where waves from two slits overlap, will be *four* times the irradiance of one wave. But also, the irradiance midway between fringes will be zero. Thus, *on average*, the irradiance is twice the irradiance of one, which is expected if the wave-nature of light was not taken into account. The consideration of how electric fields add together makes the difference with the wave-nature. This is often envisioned by the addition of "phasors" as explained in the sidebar below.

[2] This ignores diffraction which will now be covered.

PHASORS

The overlapping *electric fields* of EM waves produce interference. A typical construct to represent the electric field is the *phasor*. A phasor is depicted as an arrow positioned at an angle representing the phase of a sinusoidal wave as the following diagram shows. (The standard convention is a positive angle is rotated counter-clockwise from horizontal, whereas a negative angle is a clockwise rotation.)

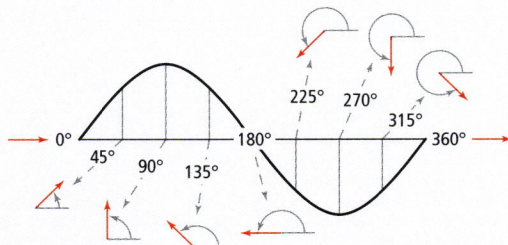

In Young's double-slit experiment, when two waves arrive at an observer *in phase*, the phasors add for constructive interference. (The sum is shown offset for clarity in the drawing.)

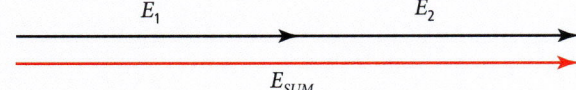

When the two waves arrive at the observer 180° *out of phase*, the phasors *add*, but their sum is zero for destructive interference. (In the following drawing, the E_1 phasor is fixed horizontally and the E_2 phasor has rotated 180° around E_1's tip, but is shown offset for clarity.)

$E_{SUM} = 0$

As the E_2 phasor rotates, its alternating alignment and anti-alignment explain the alternating fringes and zeros.

For a three-slit experiment, the next figure shows what happens as the phase difference of arrival at an observer increases. The second phasor rotates around the tip of the first, and the third phasor rotates around the tip of the second. The resultant sum then goes from the origin of the first phasor to the tip of the third, and this length is the amplitude of the resulting overlapped electric field. (The 0° and 180° cases are again shown offset for clarity.)

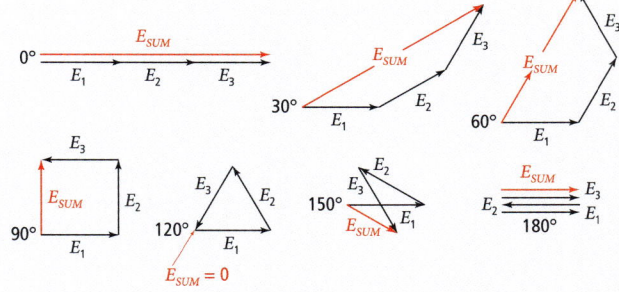

The extension of the phasor concept to 4, 5, 6, ..., N phasors should be obvious. The important features to note are listed below.

(1) The maximum electric field only occurs when the phasors are in alignment for $\phi = 0°, \pm 360°, \pm 720°, \ldots$

(2) Except as noted in (1), the electric field will always be less than its maximum.

(3) There are instances when the electric field amplitude is *zero*.

The next logical step in the discussion is to expand the results from two slits to that for N slits. Consider the case with N evenly spaced slits that have the same width and spacing, so $\phi_1 = \phi_2 = \phi_3 = \ldots = \phi_N$. This geometric layout is shown in **Figure 17-15**. Constructive interference occurs when $\phi = 2\pi$ and $\Gamma = m\lambda$, and the N phasors are aligned.

Figure 17-15
The light from N equally spaced slits will arrive at a distant observer with equal phase shift.

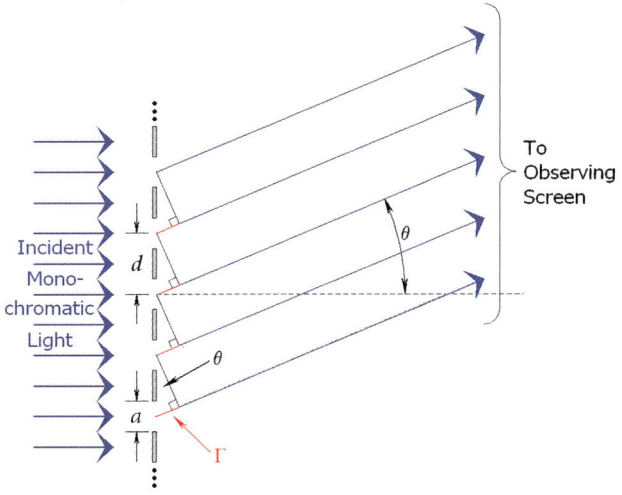

In this case, peak amplitude occurs, and $E_{MAX} = NE_0$ where E_0 is the electric field associated with a single slit. Maximum irradiance is $\mathcal{E}_{MAX} = N^2 \mathcal{E}_0$, where $\mathcal{E}_0$ is the irradiance from a single slit. Destructive interference happens when $\Gamma = (m + \frac{1}{2})\lambda$ and the phasors form a closed polygon as suggested in the sidebar, titled **Phasors**, and **Figure 17-16**.

Figure 17-16
Phasor addition for destructive interference.

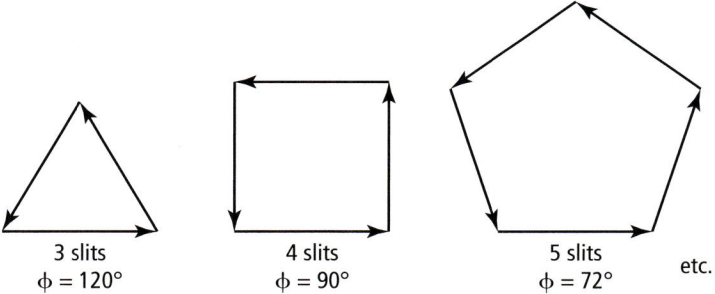

The irradiance pattern for N-slit interference is plotted in **Figure 17-17** for 3, 6, and 20 slits. Note, the irradiance values have been scaled by ⅑, ¹⁄₃₆, and ¹⁄₄₀₀, respectively, to "normalize" their maximum amplitudes to unity. This way the maxima of the three curves are the same height. (In fact, as the number of slits increases and the width of the constructive interference maxima narrows, their height increases rapidly as the square of the number of slits. This is necessary to preserve the area under the curve (its integral) which is proportional to the power of passing through the slits.) **Figure 17-17** was plotted from a generalization of **Equation 17-22** (derived in optics textbooks) to the case for N slits:

$$\frac{\mathcal{E}(\theta)}{\mathcal{E}_0} = \frac{\sin^2\left(\frac{N\phi}{2}\right)}{\sin^2\left(\frac{\phi}{2}\right)} = \frac{\sin^2\left(\frac{N\pi\Gamma}{\lambda}\right)}{\sin^2\left(\frac{\pi\Gamma}{\lambda}\right)} = \frac{\sin^2\left(\frac{N\pi d \sin\theta}{\lambda}\right)}{\sin^2\left(\frac{\pi d \sin\theta}{\lambda}\right)}. \quad (17\text{-}23)$$

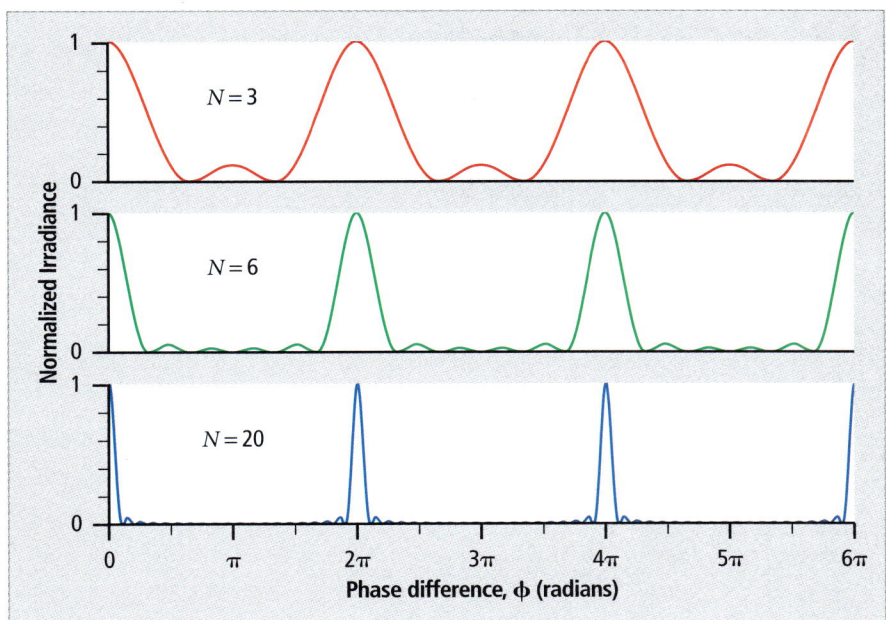

Figure 17-17
Normalized irradiance for N-slit interference.

Inspection of **Figure 17-17** and **Equation 17-23** reveals the following characteristics of N-slit interference:

1. Primary constructive interference maxima occur[3] at $\phi = 0, \pm 2\pi, \pm 4\pi, \ldots$

2. The width of a primary maximum decreases as N increases.

3. There are $N - 1$ destructive interference zeros between primary maxima, spaced at intervals of $\Delta\phi = \frac{2\pi}{N}$.

4. There are $N - 2$ smaller maxima between the primaries, decreasing in amplitude as N increases.

The second characteristic is particularly important. The half-width of the central constructive interference maximum ($m = 0$) is measured from its center ($\phi = 0$ and $\theta = 0$) to the first minimum, where the numerator of **Equation 17-23** is zero. The arguments at the first zero are $\frac{N\phi}{2} = \pi$ and $\frac{Nd\sin\theta}{\lambda} = 1$. When constructing grating interference spectrometers, the half-width is usually needed in terms of the physical angle:

$$\theta_{\frac{1}{2}} = \sin^{-1}\left(\frac{\lambda}{Nd}\right). \tag{17-24}$$

Since this discussion of interference began with specifications that $x \gg y$, (i.e., only interference close to an instruments' axis is considered), an acceptable approximation is $\sin\theta \approx \tan\theta \approx \theta \approx \frac{y}{x}$. Thus, the half-width of a constructive interference maximum is

$$\theta_{\frac{1}{2}} \approx \frac{\lambda}{Nd}. \tag{17-25}$$

Looking ahead, the fact that these constructive interference peaks narrow with increasing number of slits will be useful in providing improved spectral resolution for grating spectrometers.

The multi-slit interference pattern of fringes discussed above is the basis for the so-called "diffraction grating" in that different values of wavelength will narrow or widen this pattern slightly. But, in addition to the interference pattern, there is also, as the name diffraction grating suggests, single slit diffraction effects.

---

[3] Note, when $\phi = 2m\pi$ (m an integer), Equation 17-23 equates to $\frac{0}{0}$, but division by zero is not allowed. Fortunately, L'Hospital's Rule of calculus allows this impossible fraction to be evaluated as 1. The use of L'Hospital's rule is further discussed in the development of **Equations** 17-32 and 17-33.

To understand single slit diffraction, an experimental layout similar to Young's double slit experiment is necessary and is shown in **Figure 17-18**. The slit has width a, and the observer is located at point P at coordinates x and y, where $x \gg a$ and $x \gg y$. Again, monochromatic (single wavelength) incoming light along the x axis is considered. When a is large compared with the wavelength of the incoming light, $\mathcal{E}(\lambda)$ follows experience, as shown on the right of **Figure 17-18**.

Figure 17-18
Single slit diffraction experimental arrangement.

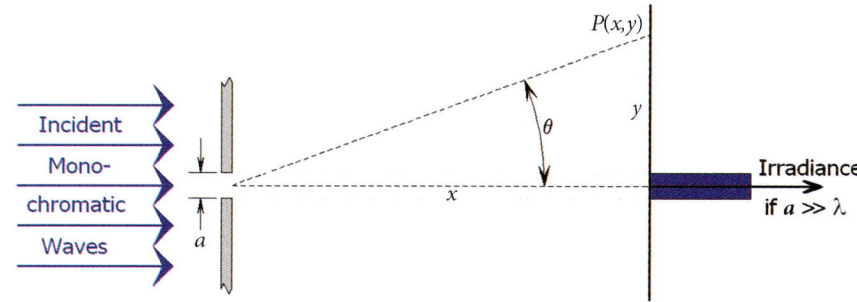

When a is comparable, or smaller than λ in size, Fraunhofer diffraction occurs (**Figure 17-20**). To obtain some insight into Fraunhofer diffraction effects for a narrow slit, the approach is to divide the single slit into N virtual sub-slits, each with width a/N. Center-to-center distance between adjacent sub-slits is also a/N and associated with each is electric field E_0/N. With this layout, as shown in **Figure 17-19**, the result of multi-slit interference may be applied.

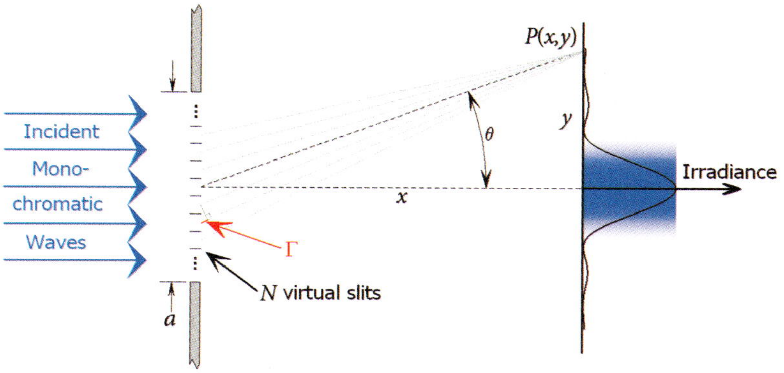

Figure 17-19
Single slit diffraction is the result of multiple sub-slit interference.

Figure 17-20
Joseph von Fraunhofer (1787–1826). (Image courtesy of http://en.wikipedia.org/wiki/File:Fraunhofer_2.jpg; PD_Old.)

To quickly develop how diffraction modifies interference, consider interference between two adjacent sub-slits. The difference in path traveled, Γ, and the corresponding difference in phase, ϕ, are related

$$\Gamma = \frac{a}{N}\sin\theta \ [\mu m] \quad \text{and} \quad \phi = 2\pi\frac{\Gamma}{\lambda} = \frac{2\pi a}{N\lambda}\sin\theta \ [\text{rad}]. \quad (17\text{-}26)$$

Now, the effects of all N sub-slits must be considered. For $\phi = 0$, the phasor diagram is shown in **Figure 17-21** and a central maximum occurs. The electric field, E_{TOT}, and the irradiance $\mathcal{E}$ associated with this central maximum are

$$E_{TOT} = \sum_{k}^{N} E_k = N\left[\frac{E_0}{N}\right] = E_0 \quad \text{and} \quad \mathcal{E} = \mathcal{E}_0. \quad (17\text{-}27)$$

Figure 17-21
Constructive interference of the electric fields of N sub-slits.

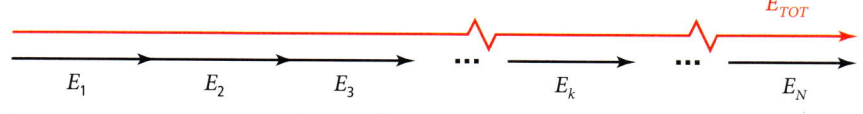

As φ slowly increases, the total electric field, E_{TOT}, decreases and will eventually reach zero. The phasor diagram for very large N is shown in **Figure 17-22**. In the limit of an infinite number of sub-slits, the total phase difference becomes

$$\phi_{TOT} = \frac{2\pi a}{\lambda} \sin\theta. \qquad (17\text{-}28)$$

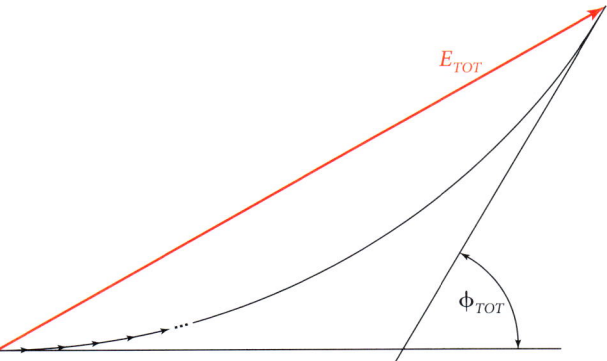

Figure 17-22
Total electric field from N sub-slits decreases as total phase angle increases.

Using this last result for ϕ_{TOT}, the location in phase difference for destructive interference (zeroes) can be obtained when $\phi_{TOT} = \pm 2\pi, \pm 4\pi, \ldots$. From these phase difference values, the location of the observer P can be determined using the angle θ. The phasor diagrams in **Figure 17-23** shows the first, second, and third zeroes along with the corresponding values of total phase difference and the corresponding values of θ. From the pattern for the angle θ shown in the figure, the generalization for the kth zero is

$$\sin\theta = \frac{k a}{\lambda}. \qquad (17\text{-}29)$$

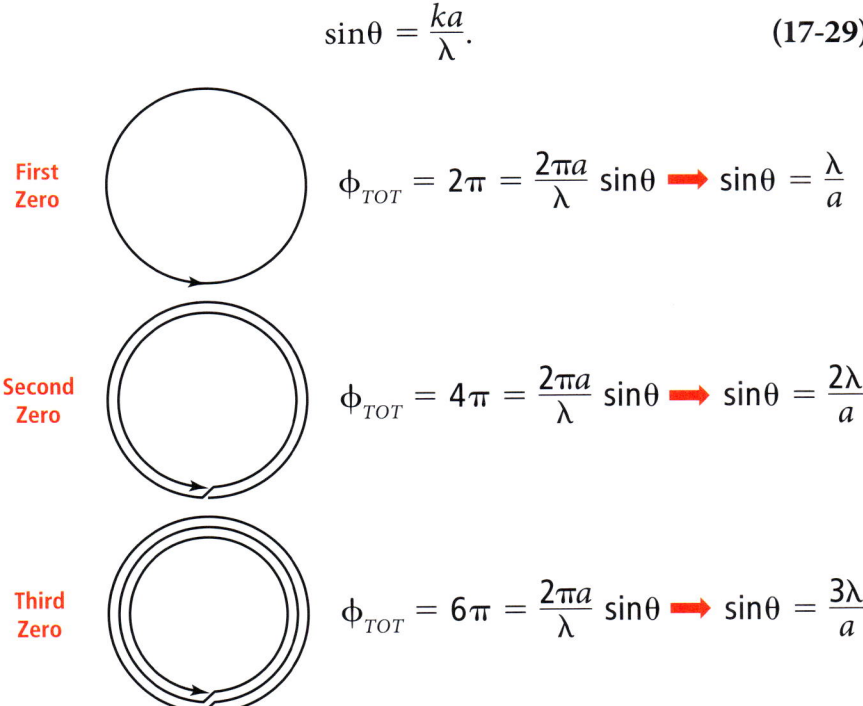

Figure 17-23
Zeroes for single-slit diffraction. The phasor diagrams for the second and third zero are drawn offset for clarity.

Locating the secondary maxima and their amplitudes is slightly more complex. As shown in the phasor diagrams in **Figure 17-24**, secondary maxima appear to occur approximately when E_{TOT} lies along a diameter of the circle representing the contributions of all the sub-slits. The phasor diagram shows the first, second, and third secondary maxima (following the first, second, and third zeroes) with the corresponding values total phase difference, ϕ_{TOT}, and the corresponding value of the peak electric field, E_{TOT}, and the irradiance, $\mathcal{E}$.

Figure 17-24
Secondary maxima are located approximately midway between the zeroes. The phasor diagrams are drawn offset for clarity.

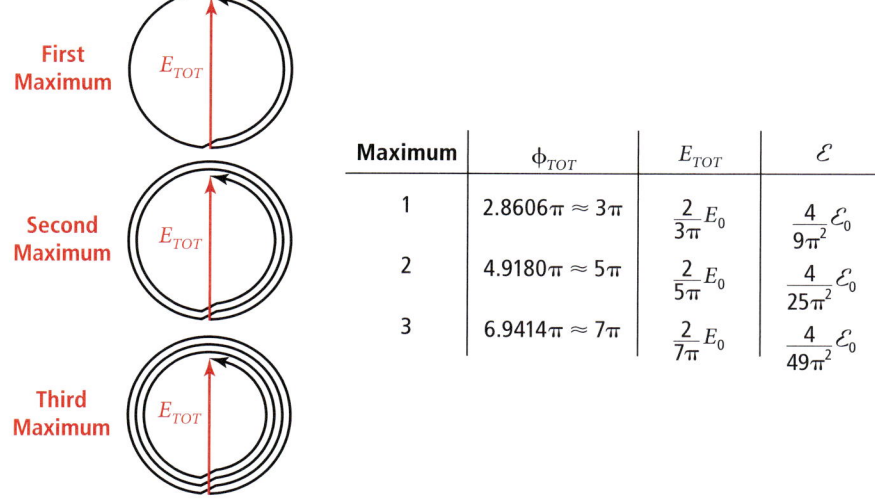

Maximum	ϕ_{TOT}	E_{TOT}	$\mathcal{E}$
1	$2.8606\pi \approx 3\pi$	$\frac{2}{3\pi}E_0$	$\frac{4}{9\pi^2}\mathcal{E}_0$
2	$4.9180\pi \approx 5\pi$	$\frac{2}{5\pi}E_0$	$\frac{4}{25\pi^2}\mathcal{E}_0$
3	$6.9414\pi \approx 7\pi$	$\frac{2}{7\pi}E_0$	$\frac{4}{49\pi^2}\mathcal{E}_0$

The farther a secondary maximum is from the central peak, the closer its total phase difference approaches $(2k+1)\pi$. Similarly, the peak irradiance of a secondary maximum becomes nearly $\frac{4}{(2k+1)^2\pi^2}\mathcal{E}_0$. Integrating the irradiance in the first secondary maximum shows that it contains approximately 4.5% of the total power passing through the slit (9.0% for the first secondary maxima on both sides of the central maximum). The secondary maximum holds approximately 1.6% (3.2%) of the power, and the third has 0.8% (1.6%). The central maximum represents about 86% of the total power. This is easily seen on the right of **Figure 17-26**.

For θ in general, the multi-slit interference result with $d = a/N$ and $E = E_0/N$ is given by

$$E(\theta) = \frac{E_0}{N}\frac{\sin\left(\frac{N\pi d}{\lambda}\sin\theta\right)}{\sin\left(\frac{\pi d}{\lambda}\sin\theta\right)} = \frac{E_0}{N}\frac{\sin\left(\frac{\pi a}{\lambda}\sin\theta\right)}{\sin\left(\frac{\pi a}{N\lambda}\sin\theta\right)}. \quad (17\text{-}30)$$

For infinite sub-slits, this expression initially does not appear to be well-defined,

$$\lim_{N\to\infty} E(\theta) = \frac{0}{0}. \quad (17\text{-}31)$$

Figure 17-25
Guillaume de L'Hospital (1661–1704). (Image courtesy of http://en.wikipedia.org/wiki/File:Guillaume_de_l%27H%C3%B4pital.jpg; PD_Old.)

But, using L'Hospital's rule (**Figure 17-25**) from calculus, this limit can be evaluated and gives

$$E(\theta) = \lim_{N\to\infty}\frac{\frac{-E_0}{N^2}\sin\left(\frac{\pi a}{\lambda}\sin\theta\right)}{\cos\left(\frac{\pi a}{N\lambda}\sin\theta\right)\left(\frac{-\pi a}{N^2\lambda}\sin\theta\right)} = \frac{E_0\sin\left(\frac{\pi a}{\lambda}\sin\theta\right)}{\frac{\pi a}{\lambda}\sin\theta}. \quad (17\text{-}32)$$

The corresponding value of irradiance is given by the expression,

$$\mathcal{E}(\theta) = \mathcal{E}_0\frac{\sin^2\left(\frac{\pi a}{\lambda}\sin\theta\right)}{\left[\frac{\pi a}{\lambda}\sin\theta\right]^2}\left[\frac{W}{m^2}\right] \quad (17\text{-}33)$$

which is plotted on the right side of **Figure 17-26**.[4]

---

[4] The single-slit diffraction pattern is similar to the Point Spread Function in **Chapter 6**, where the aperture was assumed to be round. (See **Equation 6-7**.)

Why is the single slit diffraction expression so different than the multi-slit interference expression (**Equation 17-23**) which was used to derive the single slit diffraction expression? The answer involves the total energy transmitted. With N-slit interference, more energy is transmitted with each additional slit. But, when N-slit interference is applied to a single slit, the total transmitted energy is constant.

Finally, combining the irradiance expressions for multi-slit interference and slit diffraction, irradiance on an observer's screen behind a multiple slit diffraction grating is

$$\mathcal{E}(\theta) = \mathcal{E}_0 \frac{\sin^2\left(\frac{\pi a}{\lambda}\sin\theta\right) \sin^2\left(\frac{N\pi d}{\lambda}\sin\theta\right)}{\left(\frac{\pi a}{\lambda}\sin\theta\right)^2 \sin^2\left(\frac{\pi d}{\lambda}\sin\theta\right)} \left[\frac{W}{m^2}\right]. \quad (17\text{-}34)$$

This expression is plotted in **Figure 17-26** for two slits using $d = 4a$, i.e., the separation between adjacent slits is four times the width of any single slit. In this example, because $d = 4a$, the diffraction envelope eliminates the $m = 4$ constructive interference peak. Higher order peaks are also effectively eliminated because the secondary maxima of the diffraction pattern is so small compared to the central peak. Hence, only the constructive interference peaks for $m = 0, 1, 2,$ and 3 have sizeable amplitudes. Thus, these are the only orders useful in obtaining spectra.

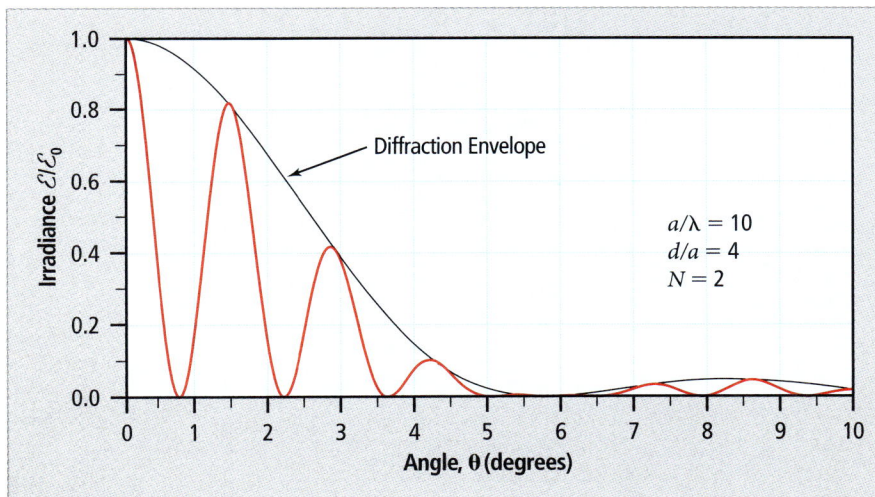

Figure 17-26
Two-slit interference with diffraction.

A photograph of these effects is shown in **Figure 17-27**. In the top image, a single-slit diffraction pattern is shown with its central and secondary peaks spaced in angle based on its width, a. In the middle image, the combined diffraction-interference pattern is shown for two slits with width a separated by a distance, d. The d/a ratio is not given, but measurements of the image are about 7. Appropriately, 13 interference peaks ($m = 0, \pm1$ to 6) are visible under the central diffraction peak. Finally, in the bottom image, the slits are narrower, but the spacing, d, between them remains the same. In the resulting combined diffraction-interference pattern, the central diffraction peak is significantly broader, and there are many more interference peaks visible under this peak. The spacing of the interference peaks remains the same as that in the middle image, because the spacing between slits has not changed.

Figure 17-27
Photograph of a) single slit diffraction, b) double slit interference-diffraction with same slit width as (a), and c) double slit interference-diffraction with narrower slits.

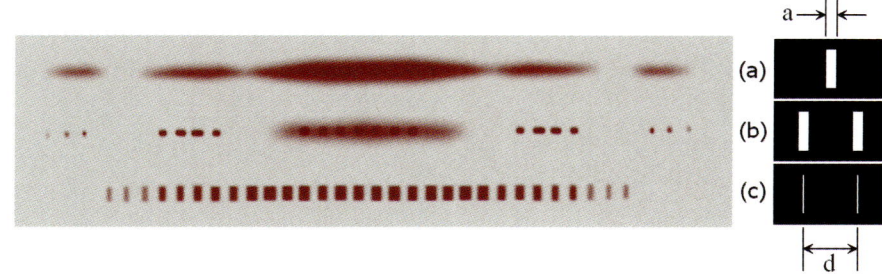

All the results discussed above result from an opaque screen with multiple narrow slits that transmit incoming light. Such an arrangement is, in effect, a primitive diffraction grating. A more traditional grating is a slab of glass with multiple grooves carefully machined on its surface. Two types of such a grating exist. If only the grooves transmit, the grating is termed "amplitude transmission" type. If the non-grooves also transmit, but retard the phase of the incident light, the grating is termed "phase transmission" type. Nevertheless, the results discussed above are applicable.

Modern day gratings are reflective and are blazed with saw-tooth grooves as shown in **Figure 17-28**. These grooves are shown in a thin metallic layer that is uniform in thickness and deposited on a glass substrate. The blaze angle is defined as shown in the figure. With today's technology, gratings are available with as many as 5,000 lines (or grooves)/mm etched on a 1 cm by 1 cm surface or with a lesser number of grooves/mm on a surface as large as 50 cm by 75 cm.

Figure 17-28
A reflection grating consists of angled grooves in a metal layer on a glass substrate.

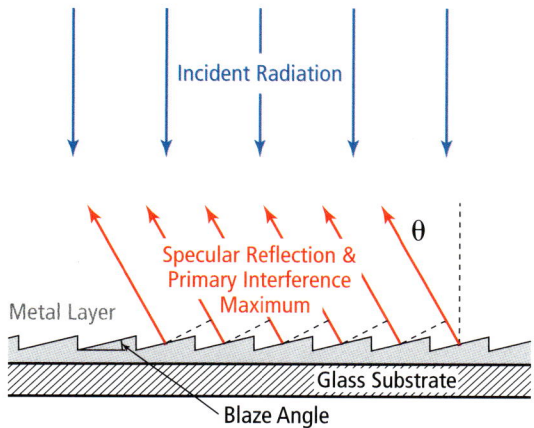

The previous discussion examined "how gratings work" when light with a single wavelength was incident. The effects of multiple incident wavelengths will be discussed next as well as the standard performance parameters associated with a grating spectrometer.

If light with two closely spaced spectral features centered at λ and $\lambda + \Delta\lambda$ is incident on a grating, there is a difference in angular location, $\Delta\theta$, or dispersion angle between the maxima corresponding to λ and $\lambda + \Delta\lambda$. These angular differences are illustrated in **Figure 17-29** for orders $m = 0, 1, 2,$ and 3. Note, there is no $\Delta\theta$ for $m = 0$.

From the grating equation, $\Gamma = d \sin\theta = m\lambda$, the following expression can be obtained:

$$\Delta(d \sin\theta) = d \cos\theta \, \Delta\theta = m\Delta\lambda \qquad (17\text{-}35)$$
$$\frac{\Delta\theta}{\Delta\lambda} = \frac{m}{d \cos\theta} \cong \frac{m}{d} \quad \text{for } \theta \ll 1 \text{ radian.}$$

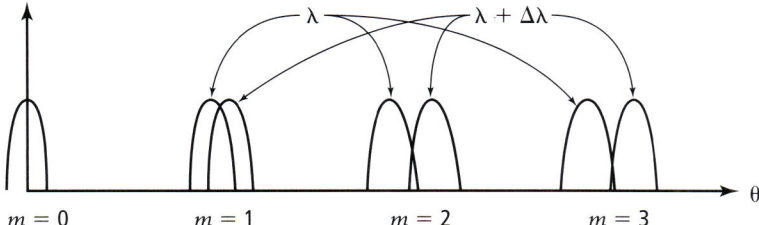

Figure 17-29
Angular dispersion between two spectral lines.

Since $\Delta\theta/\Delta\lambda$ is independent of λ, the dispersion, $s(\lambda)$, is nearly constant. Also, for a given $\Delta\lambda$, $\Delta\theta$ increases with increasing values of m as shown in **Figure 17-29**. A photograph of the spectra of a mercury lamp taken by a grating spectrograph shows some of these effects in **Figure 17-30**. Here the "primary spectrum" is associated with $m = 1$, the "secondary spectrum" with $m = 2$, while the "slit" is $m = 0$. The mercury lamp spectral features are clearly dispersed more in second order than they are in first order. Also, the linearity of the system can be verified, using the noted wavelengths of the spectral features and performing rough measurements of the distances between the locations of the features and the slit.

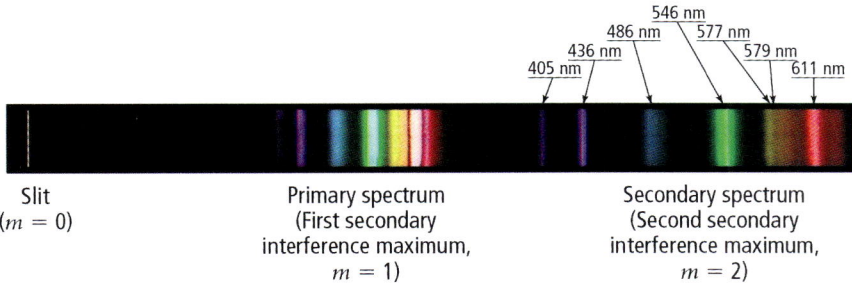

Figure 17-30
Light from a mercury vapor lamp reflected from a diffraction grating. (Image by Simon Quellen Field via scitoys.com.)

To determine spectral resolution, the question "How small can $\Delta\lambda_{MIN}$ be to resolve the two peaks in dispersion using the Rayleigh criterion?" must be answered. Re-arranging **Equation 17-35**,

$$\Delta\lambda_{MIN} = \frac{d\cos\theta}{m}\Delta\theta_{MIN}. \qquad (17\text{-}36)$$

But, since half the width[5] of a constructive interference peak (**Equation 17-25**) is $\theta_{\frac{1}{2}} = \frac{\lambda}{Nd}$, where N is the *total* number of slits and d is the distance between any two adjacent slits,

$$\Delta\lambda_{MIN} = \frac{d\cos\theta}{m}\Delta\theta_{\frac{1}{2}} = \frac{\lambda}{Nm} \;\;[\mu m] \text{ for } \theta \ll 1 \text{ radian and} \qquad (17\text{-}37)$$

$$\overline{RP} = \frac{\lambda}{\Delta\lambda_{MIN}} = Nm. \qquad (17\text{-}38)$$

These results for spatial resolution and resolving power suggest some interesting systems trade-offs involving grating spectrometers:

Slit size, $a\sim$
- Smaller a values imply increased possible m values, which imply increased spectral resolution but less transmitted light.
- Larger a values (keeping a always less than d) imply more throughput, but only small possible m values and poorer spectral resolution.

[5] The use of an interference peak's half-width is analogous and justified, similar to **Chapter 8**, where the Rayleigh resolution criterion used the radius (one-half the diameter).

Total number of slits, N~
- More slits imply increased spectral resolution and more energy transmission, both of which imply a more difficult grating to manufacture and an associated higher cost.

Slit spacing, d~
- Wider spacing (larger d) implies narrower interference peaks but also narrower orders for all wavelengths. Hence, there is no gain in spectral resolution.

There are FSR problems with gratings. To start the discussion, consider the example of a desired spectral bandpass of the visible (0.4 to 0.7 μm) and a grating with 100 lines/mm. For this example, $d = 1$ mm/100 $= 0.01$ mm $= 10$ μm. Next, the locations of the interference peaks are calculated for the shortest and longest wavelengths of the desired spectral bandpass for a number of values of m, using the grating equation, $d \sin\theta = m\lambda$. **Table 17-2** lists the results, and **Figure 17-31** presents a graphical display.

Table 17-2
Location of mth interference peaks for two wavelengths that describe desired spectral bandpass.

m	θ ($\lambda = 0.4$ μm)	θ ($\lambda = 0.7$ μm)	FSR
0	0.00 rad	0.00 rad	No λ dispersion
1	0.04	0.07	Unrestricted
2	0.08	0.14	High λ restricted
3	0.12	0.21	Low, high λ restricted
4	0.16	0.28	Low, high λ restricted
5	0.20	0.35	Low, high λ restricted
6	0.24	0.42	Low, high λ restricted

Figure 17-31
FSRs of the first interference maxima have significant overlap.

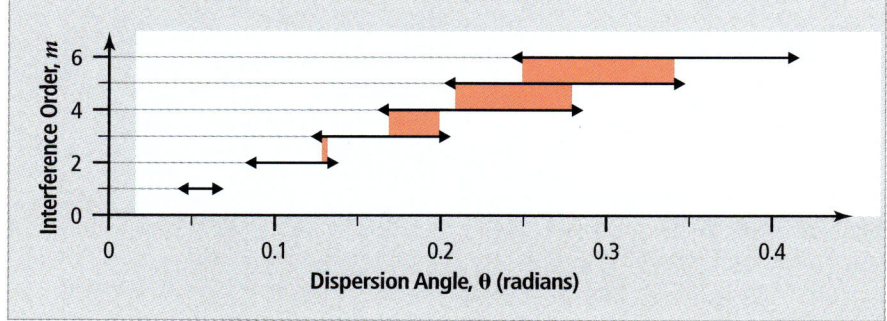

From either **Table 17-2** or **Figure 17-31**, it is clear the peak locations in order $m = 1$ do not overlap those of $m = 2$. But, those of order $m = 2$ overlap those of $m = 3$. Thus, when a detector is placed at $\theta = 0.13$ radians, the analyst has no idea whether the incident light was all red wavelengths in second order, all blue wavelengths in third order, or some unknown combination of the two wavelengths and orders. Beyond order $m = 2$ (larger values of m), the overlap of adjacent orders becomes worse and worse. To operate in one of these higher orders, the spectral bandpass must be reduced significantly from the desired spectral bandpass. This new bandpass is the FSR. It is the spectral bandpass dictated by the particular grating to be used.

From the above example, simple, general formulas can be derived for the FSR. Consider the angular locations of the interference peaks corresponding to λ_{MIN} and λ_{MAX} for two orders, m and $m + 1$.

For order m,

$$\theta_{m,MAX} = \frac{m\lambda_{MAX}}{d} \quad [\text{rad}], \tag{17-39}$$

and for order $m+1$,

$$\theta_{m+1,MIN} = \frac{(m+1)\lambda_{MIN}}{d} \quad [\text{rad}]. \tag{17-40}$$

For no overlap between adjacent orders,

$$\theta_{m,MAX} \leqq \theta_{m+1,MIN} \quad [\text{rad}]. \tag{17-41}$$

Hence, for a given value of λ_{MIN},

$$\lambda_{MAX} \leqq \frac{(m+1)\lambda_{MIN}}{m} \quad [\mu m], \tag{17-42}$$

or, for a given value of λ_{MAX},

$$\lambda_{MIN} \geqq \frac{m\lambda_{MAX}}{m+1} \quad [\mu m]. \tag{17-43}$$

Therefore, the resulting FSR based on the above equations is

$$\text{FSR} = \lambda_{MAX} - \lambda_{MIN} \leqq \frac{(m+1)\lambda_{MIN}}{m} - \lambda_{MIN} = \frac{\lambda_{MIN}}{m} \quad [\mu m]$$
$$\leqq \lambda_{MAX} - \frac{m\lambda_{MAX}}{m+1} = \frac{\lambda_{MAX}}{m+1} \quad [\mu m]. \tag{17-44}$$

The consequences of grating FSR include the following:
- Use only very low orders where FSR is largest.
- Use higher orders, but accept a possibly less than desired spectral bandpass, the FSR. (Recall the use of higher orders is limited by the width of the slits and hence the width of the diffraction central maximum.)
- Work beyond the limits of FSR by using filters on some of the detector rows to block one of the overlapping orders.

To evaluate the etendue, U (throughput), off-axis incidence must be considered as shown in **Figure 17-32**. Thus, the difference in path traveled, Γ, has two components:

$$\Gamma = \Gamma_1 + \Gamma_2 = d(\sin\theta_{inc} + \sin\theta) \quad [\mu m]. \tag{17-45}$$

The corresponding phase difference is still $\phi = 2\pi\Gamma/\lambda$. There are several different cases:

When $\theta_{inc} = 0$, Γ is the on-axis result previously discussed.

When $\theta_{inc} > 0$, Γ is larger than the previous result.

When $\theta_{inc} < 0$, Γ is smaller than the previous result (and vanishes when $\theta_{inc} = -\theta$).

These results can be applied to the consideration of light incident from an extended source. Consider such a range of angles of incidence, $\Delta\theta_{inc}$, shown in **Figure 17-33** for a single wavelength. Assuming that diffraction effects are small, the range of incident angle will produce a range in dispersion angles, $\Delta\theta(\lambda_1)$, as shown in the figure. This would also be true

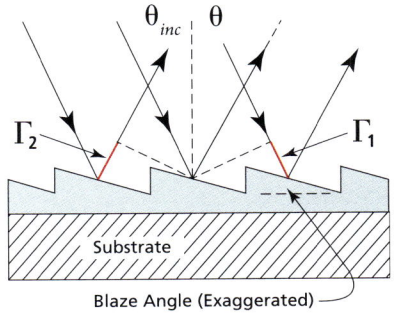

Figure 17-32
Both incident and reflected path length differences contribute to interference.

for a second incident wavelength. However, if $\Delta\theta_{inc}$ was to become too large, the width of the two dispersion peaks would become so wide the observer could not distinguish between λ_1 and λ_2 in dispersion. Hence, to achieve desired spectral resolution, it is necessary to limit $\Delta\theta_{inc}$. This is accomplished by putting a narrow slit in the optical path with an effective width a_s and a distance x_s from the point of incidence on the prism. The long dimension L_s of the slit is off of the page.

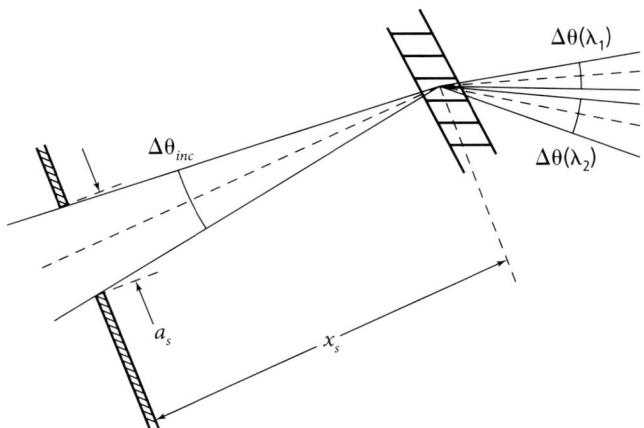

Figure 17-33
Light of two wavelengths within a range of incidence angles broadens the interference peaks.

The use of this slit has two important consequences: the first deals with data collection and the second with spectrometer throughput. In **Figure 17-34**, the slit defines a row of ground pixels. The length of the row is determined by the number of detectors in each row of the two-dimensional FPA shown. The grating takes the light from each ground pixel and spectrally disperses it across the appropriate detectors in each of the FPA rows shown. The number of rows defines the number of spectral bands. The two-dimensional spectral image (or swath) is built by scanning the row of ground pixels across the scene. This can be achieved most easily using the forward motion of the platform. No moving parts are required within the sensor. Alternatively, other scanning directions can be achieved with the use of a scanning mirror. Some combination of both approaches can also be used.

The second consequence of using a slit to maintain spectral resolution is the limitation on spectrometer throughput, or etendue, U, which is the $A_R \Omega_{PIX}$ product, where A_R is the effective area of the collecting optics, and Ω_{PIX} is the solid angle subtended by the slit and one of the N detectors making up a row in the FPA. From **Figures 17-33** and **17-34**,

$$\Omega_{PIX} \approx \left(\frac{a_s}{x_s}\right)\left(\frac{L_s/N}{x_s}\right) \approx \frac{a_s L_s}{N x_s^2} \text{ [sr]}. \quad (17\text{-}46)$$

If square ground pixels are desired, $N = \dfrac{L_s}{a_s}$, and

$$\Omega_{PIX} = \frac{a_s^2}{x_s^2} \text{ [sr]}. \quad (17\text{-}47)$$

How big can $\Delta\theta_{inc}$ be without significantly reducing spectral resolution? Mathematically, $\Delta\theta_\theta$ caused by $\Delta\theta_{inc}$ (for one wavelength) is much less than $\Delta\theta_\lambda$ caused by $\Delta\lambda$ (for one θ_{inc}). To estimate $\Delta\theta_\theta$, the extended grating equation, **Equation 17-45**, is differentiated to give

$$\cos\theta \, \Delta\theta + \cos\theta_{inc}\Delta\theta_{inc} \cong 0 \text{ [rad]}. \quad (17\text{-}48)$$

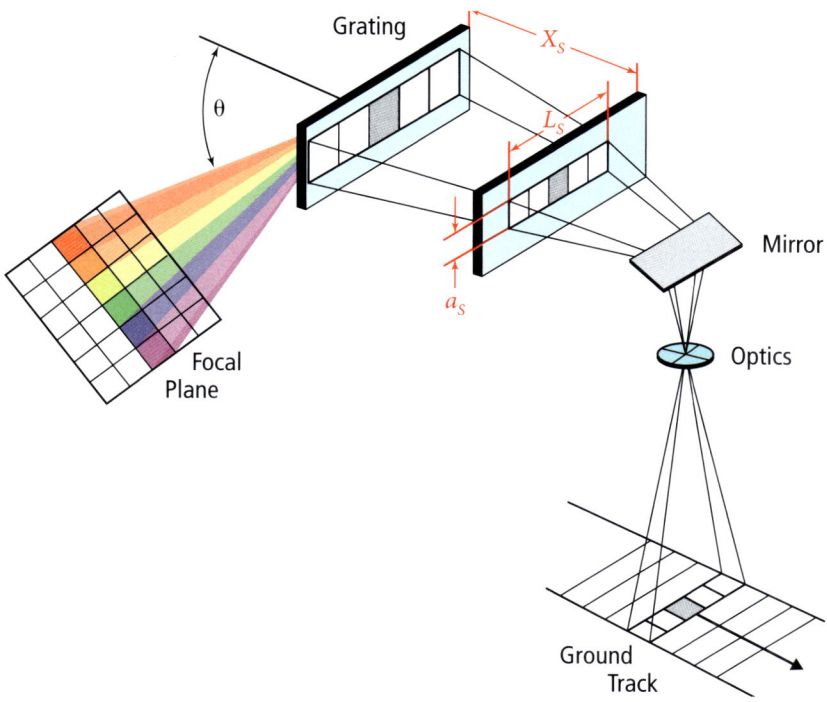

Figure 17-34
Transmission grating spectrometer flown in a pushbroom collection mode.

If θ and θ_{inc} are small (much less than one radian), then $\cos\theta \approx \cos\theta_{inc} \approx 1$, so

$$\Delta\theta_\theta \cong |\Delta\theta_{inc}| \quad [\text{rad}]. \tag{17-49}$$

To estimate $\Delta\theta_\lambda$, recall the interference peak half-width $\Delta\theta_{\frac{1}{2}} = \lambda/Nd$, and hence the minimum separation $\Delta\theta_{MIN}$ corresponding to minimum resolvable $\Delta\lambda_{MIN}$ (within the same order.) Thus,

$$\Delta\theta_\lambda = \frac{\lambda}{Nd} \quad [\text{rad}]. \tag{17-50}$$

For no loss in spectral resolution,

$$\Delta\theta_{inc} \ll \Delta\theta_\lambda \quad [\text{rad}]. \tag{17-51}$$

A summary of the grating spectrograph performance characteristics and comparison of them with those of a prism spectrograph are shown in **Table 17-3**.

	Prism	Grating
Spectral dispersion variation	Non-linear with λ	Nearly constant with respect to λ
FSR	Large, but limited by prism material properties	Possibly limited by adjacent orders
Possible spectral sampling	All λ at once for one row of spatial pixels	All λ at once for one row of spatial pixels
2-D scene coverage	Slit required so sequential rows of pixels scanned over time	Slit required so sequential rows of pixels scanned over time
Resolving power-etendue product	Low	Low

Table 17-3
Second comparison of hyperspectral sensing techniques.

As discussed, the use of a grating or prism spectrometer without a slit usually does not make sense. One notable exception occurs when there is a single dominant point source object of interest in the sensor Field of View (FOV) that is subtended by the FPA. This means the object of interest must be smaller in size than a pixel, here defined by the detector size and the effective optical focal length of the spectrometer. Also, this object of interest must dominate the contributions of irradiance from all other nearby pixels, especially those in the scene along a line perpendicular to the lines or grooves of the grating. Historically, applications for such a slit-less spectrograph have been limited to astronomy and the spectra of bright stars in faint background regions of the night sky. Slit-less spectrometers could be used to obtain spectra of both missile plumes and re-entry vehicles when viewed against the night sky or in spectral regions of low earth background (nighttime visible to Mid-Wave Infrared (MWIR)). See **Example 17-3**.

EXAMPLE 17-3: A GRATING SPECTROMETER

Compute the limits of spectral resolution for $\lambda \approx 0.5$ μm light through an instrument with a 1 cm $\times$ 1 cm grating with 1000 lines/mm. Calculate the resolving power and etendue.

First, calculate

$$d \approx \frac{1 \text{ mm}}{1000 \text{ lines}} \approx 10^{-3} \text{ mm and}$$

$$N \approx \frac{1000 \text{ lines}}{1 \text{ mm}} \times 1 \text{ cm} \times \frac{10 \text{ mm}}{1 \text{ cm}} \approx 10^4 \text{ lines.}$$

Then,

$$\Delta\theta_\lambda \approx \frac{\lambda}{Nd} \approx \frac{0.5 \times 10^{-6} \text{ m}}{(10^4 \text{ lines})(10^{-3} \text{mm})} \times \frac{10^3 \text{ mm}}{1 \text{ m}} \approx 5 \times 10^{-5} \text{rad} \approx 0.0029°.$$

Thus, if $\Delta\theta_{INC} \ll \Delta\theta_\lambda \approx 5 \times 10^{-5}$ rad, no spectral resolution is lost. Otherwise, there is no benefit to use a grating with 1000 lines/mm. A less expensive grating could be used.

The consequences of restricting $\Delta\theta_{INC}$ to less than 5×10^{-5} rad could be as follows. For an airborne spectrometer flying at $h \approx 6{,}000$ m, the pixel size at nadir would be

$$\Delta x \approx h\Delta\theta_{INC} \approx (6{,}000 \text{ m})(5 \times 10^{-5} \text{rad}) \approx 30 \text{ cm};$$

although other pixel sizes are possible through the use of front-end optics that do not affect spectrometer throughput.

The resolving power (**Equation 17-38**) is easily calculated as

$$\overline{RP} \approx Nm \approx 10^4 m,$$

where m is the order of interference.

The etendue (for square pixels) is simply

$$U \approx A_R \Omega_{PIX} \approx A_R (5 \times 10^{-5} \text{rad})^2 \approx 2.5 \times 10^{-9} A_R,$$

where A_R is the spectrometer's collecting aperture area.

For good measure, the resolving power-etendue product is

$$(\overline{RP})(U) \approx (10^4 m)(2.5 \times 10^{-9} A_R) \approx 2.5 \times 10^{-5} m A_R$$

which is quite small compared to the FTS.

17.4 THIN FILM INTERFERENCE APPLIED TO SPECTROMETERS

When considering possible approaches to gathering HSI data, it is tempting to consider approaches that work for collecting MSI data and extend them to HSI data. Recall the two MSI approaches discussed in **Chapter 15**: 1) pushbroom or whiskbroom scanners with multiple rows of detectors, each row with a different interference filter (the number of rows = the number of spectral bands); and 2) staring sensors with a full two-dimensional FPA and a filter wheel or continuously variable filter (the number of positions on the filter wheel(s) = the number of spectral bands).

Extending the pushbroom approach involves more rows of detectors each with its own filter. Some of the manufacturing difficulties of this approach can be resolved by using a single wedge filter. Extending the staring approach involves replacing the mechanical filter wheel with a single rapidly-tunable filter (called a Fabry-Perot etalon), which is described below. A version of the wedge imaging spectrometer is shown in **Figure 17-35**.

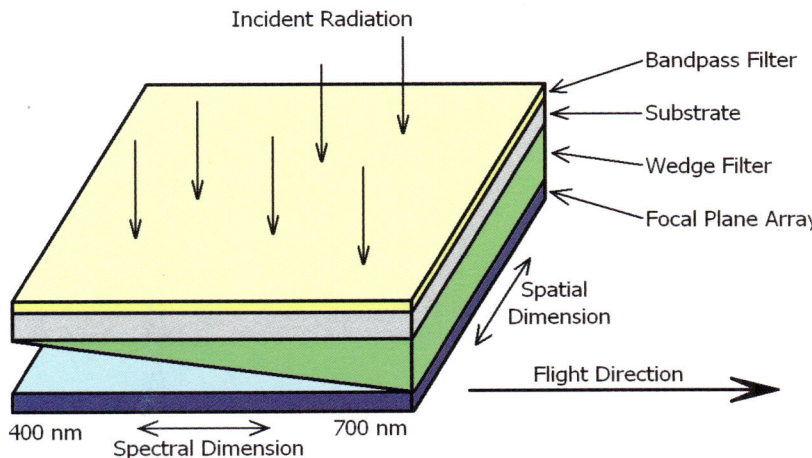

Figure 17-35
Model of a wedge filter for the visible bandpass.

The manufacture and use of a wedge shaped filter represents a new technology developed in the late 1990s by Hughes Santa Barbara Research Center (now part of Raytheon). As the wedge varies in thickness, it varies in transmitted wavelengths of incoming light. Each row of detectors detect light at a different wavelength. Used as a pushbroom scanner, each row of detectors must be scanned past a source before a complete spectrum for that source is collected. To date, several versions of the wedge spectrometer have been built in each of the spectral regions: vis-Near Infrared (Vis-NIR), SWIR, MWIR, and LWIR. They have been lab-tested and flight-tested aboard low-altitude airborne platforms. A drawback to the wedge is platform motion during the relatively long period of time to fly all rows of detectors past an object on the ground. This creates a band-to-band registration problem and potentially is a strong requirement for a Pointing, Tracking, and Stabilization (PTS) system.

A Fabry-Perot imaging etalon is equivalent to a scanning interference filter and is sketched in **Figure 17-36**. This technology is well-proven for laboratory use. The etalon is simply two parallel glass plates that are very closely spaced with a medium of gas or other material in between with an index of refraction, n. Interference between the plates selects the wavelength(s) transmitted to the FPA as discussed in **Chapter 9**.

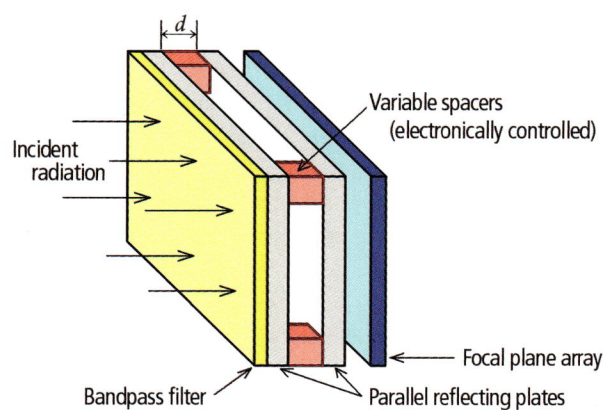

Figure 17-36
Model of a Fabry-Perot etalon using electronically controlled spacers.

For a given n and d, the Fabry-Perot etalon transmits a series of wavelengths, just as an interference filter does. To scan or select other wavelengths, the index of refraction of the material between the plates and/or the distance of separation between the plates is changed in a precisely controlled manner. In the lab, this has been accomplished by heating the medium and inserting more gas; this is a slow process, suited for the lab but not for a moving platform. Newer technology for moving platforms involves applying either a high voltage to certain materials such as $BaTiO_3$, which have a large piezoelectric effect, or low radio frequency (RF) voltage to materials, such as Te_2O, that have a large acousto-optical effect. Both approaches are used to vary the separation between the glass plates in a precisely controlled manner.

Accomplishments to date with the tunable Fabry-Perot etalon have been successful on the ground (in the lab, observatory, or field). Airborne systems have been or will soon be demonstrated on a variety of platforms, but the Fabry-Perot etalon is still considered a high-risk approach. While it has the advantage of no moving parts that pose a risk for multispectral staring sensors with filter wheels or continuously variable filters, the disadvantage and high-risk involve the use of high voltage applied across a narrow gap, especially on spacecraft or high altitude aircraft, or low RF voltage applied in the vicinity of other sensitive electrical components.

Fabry-Perot spectrometer performance can be characterized beginning with the thin-film formula (**Equation 9-12**):

$$2nd \cos\beta = m\lambda, \qquad (17\text{-}52)$$

where β is the light's refracted angle in the medium (by Snell's Law).

Dispersion by Fabry-Perot interferometers occurs in n and/or d, which is often scanned by varying the applied voltage. Thus,

$$\frac{\Delta(nd)}{\Delta\lambda} = \frac{m}{2\cos\beta} = \text{constant} \quad \text{for any given order } m. \qquad (17\text{-}53)$$

Hence, dispersion of Fabry-Perot interferometers is constant, and they are easier to calibrate.

Spectral resolution, $\Delta\lambda_{MIN}$, is limited by the width of the transmission interference peaks:

$$\Delta\lambda = \frac{\lambda(1-\rho)}{m\pi\sqrt{\rho}} \; [\mu m], \qquad (17\text{-}54)$$

which is a result of Airy's formula. (See **Chapter 9**, **Equation 9-15**, where ρ is the reflectivity of the etalon's plates.) To determine how close in wavelength two spectral lines can be spaced and still be resolved by a Fabry-Perot interferometer, the Rayleigh criterion is again used as illustrated in **Figure 17-37**, where

$$n_1 d_1 = \frac{m\lambda_1}{2\cos\beta} \quad \text{and} \quad n_2 d_2 = \frac{m\lambda_2}{2\cos\beta} \quad [\mu m]. \quad (17\text{-}55)$$

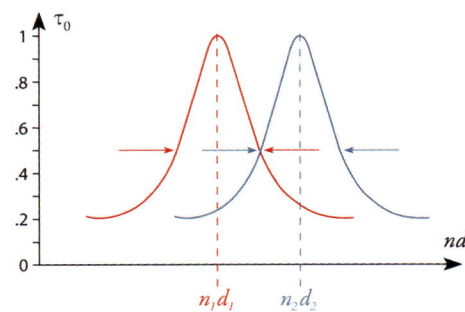

Figure 17-37
Notional transmission of radiation interference peaks through an etalon.

The peaks for λ_1 and λ_2 are resolvable when $\Delta\lambda$ is equal to the half-width of either peak. Hence,

$$\Delta\lambda_{MIN} \approx \Delta\lambda \quad [\mu m], \quad (17\text{-}56)$$

and the resolving power, $\overline{RP}$, is given by the expression,

$$\overline{RP} = \frac{\lambda}{\Delta\lambda_{MIN}} = \frac{m\pi\sqrt{\rho}}{1-\rho}, \quad \text{where} \quad m = \frac{2nd\cos\beta}{\lambda}. \quad (17\text{-}57)$$

An alternate figure of merit for spectral resolution, used primarily for Fabry-Perot interferometers, is the finesse, F, which is defined to be the resolving power/order. An expression for the finesse is:

$$F = \frac{\overline{RP}}{m} = \frac{\pi\sqrt{\rho}}{1-\rho}. \quad (17\text{-}58)$$

Figure 17-38 plots the finesse of a parallel-plate etalon as a function of the plate's reflectivity.

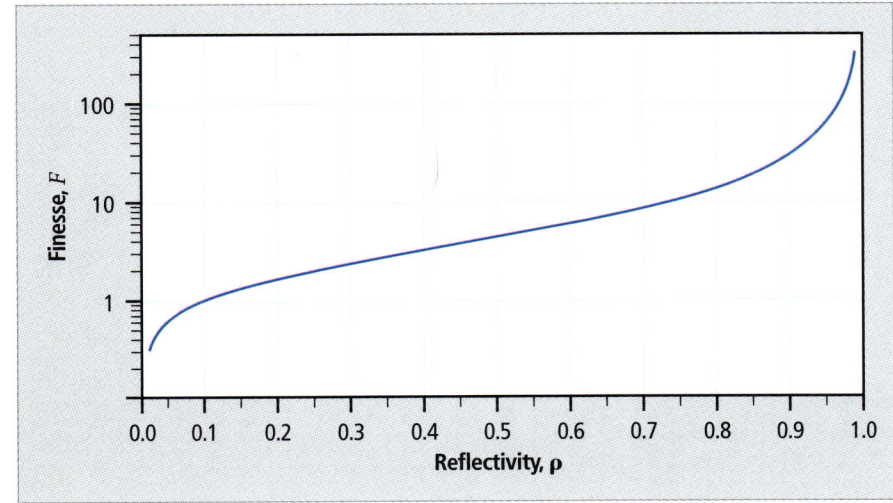

Figure 17-38
Finesse as a function of an etalon's reflectivity.

m	$d(\lambda = 0.4\ \mu m)$	$d(\lambda = 0.7\ \mu m)$
1	0.20 μm	0.35 μm
2	0.40 μm	0.70 μm
3	0.60 μm	1.05 μm
4	0.80 μm	1.40 μm
5	1.00 μm	1.75 μm
6	1.20 μm	2.10 μm

Table 17-4
Location of the mth interference peaks for two wavelengths that describe desired spectral bandpass.

Fabry-Perot interferometers have limited FSRs based on the fact that a single thin-film interference selects more than one wavelength to transmit. If the interferometer is scanned in n and/or d, the range of wavelengths detected in a given order, m, is limited by possible overlap with those in adjacent orders. The conclusions of limited FSRs are a trade-off between RP and FSR as m is increased or decreased. Increased FSR is possible using multiple etalons in succession (similar to using multiple layers in the design of a thin film interference filter).

A numerical example, similar to that used to introduce grating FSR problems, is considered below. Suppose light normally incident onto a Fabry-Perot interferometer, $n = 1.0$ (air) for the media between the two plates of the etalon, and the desired spectral band-pass is 0.4 to 0.7 μm. The thin-film interference transmission formula $2nd \cos\beta = m\lambda$ becomes simply $d = 0.5\ m\lambda$. The thickness values for the smallest and the largest wavelengths are calculated for various orders in **Table 17-4** and are shown in **Figure 17-39**. The results are similar to that of the grating discussed earlier. The $m = 1$ and the $m = 2$ orders do not overlap. However, for $m = 2$ and beyond, there is significant overlap between adjacent orders. As m increases, the amount of overlap also increases.

Figure 17-39
FSRs of the etalon's interference maxima shows significant overlap.

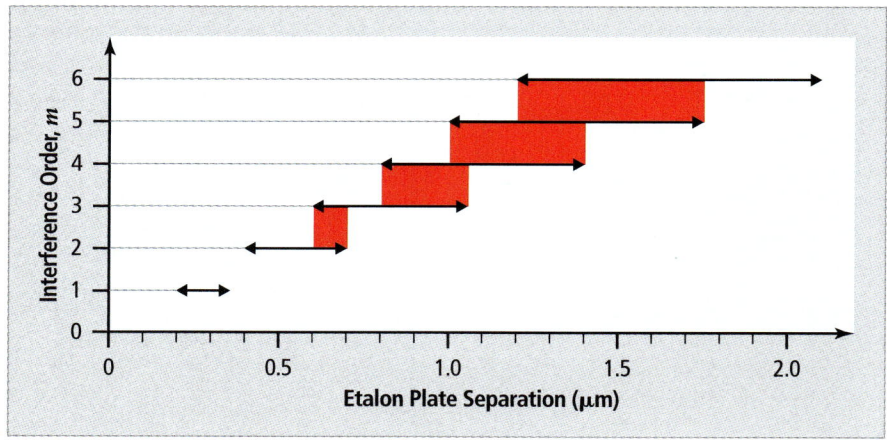

The final characteristic of performance, which involves extended sources and off-axis incidence onto the Fabry-Perot etalon, is the etendue U (throughput). The size and spacing of detectors on the two-dimensional FPA and its distance from the collecting optics of the etalon (usually the focal length) determine a pixel FOV as well as a range of values for θ_{INC}, as illustrated in **Figure 17-40**. Because $\theta_{PIX} = \Delta\theta_{inc}$, light is accepted by an individual detector only over a range of incident angles $\Delta\theta_{inc}$.

Figure 17-40
Extended source collection geometry for a Fabry-Perot spectrometer.

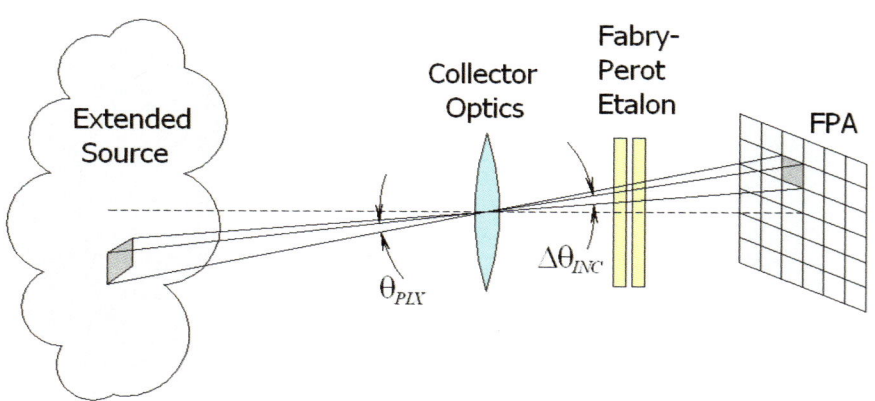

To determine how large $\Delta\theta_{inc}$ can be without significantly reducing spectral resolution, the thin-film interference transmission formula $2nd\cos\beta = m\lambda$ must be used along with Snell's law, $\sin\theta_{inc} = n\sin\beta$. When θ_{INC} and β are small (much less than one radian), Snell's law is approximately $\theta_{INC} \approx n\beta$, and therefore, $\Delta\theta_{INC} \approx n\Delta\beta$. Thus, for a single wavelength,

$$\Delta[2nd\cos\beta] = 2\Delta(nd)\cos\beta - 2nd\sin\beta\,\Delta\beta = 0. \quad (17\text{-}59)$$

Therefore,

$$\frac{\Delta(nd)}{\Delta\beta} = nd\frac{\sin\beta}{\cos\beta} = nd\tan\beta \approx nd\beta. \quad (17\text{-}60)$$

For a given β, the spread in $\Delta\lambda$ corresponds to a spread in $\Delta(nd)$, resulting in

$$2\Delta(nd)\cos\beta = m\Delta\lambda, \quad (17\text{-}61)$$

which yields

$$\frac{\Delta(nd)}{\Delta\lambda} = \frac{m}{2\cos\beta} = \frac{nd}{\lambda}. \quad (17\text{-}62)$$

Recall the Fabry-Perot system spectral resolution for point source radiation incident at θ_{inc},

$$\Delta\lambda_{MIN} = \frac{\lambda(1-\rho)}{m\pi\sqrt{\rho}}, \text{ where } m = \frac{2nd}{\lambda}\cos\beta. \quad (17\text{-}63)$$

Example 17-4 considers the resolving power etendue product for a Fabry-Perot spectrometer.

EXAMPLE 17-4: A FABRY-PEROT SPECTROMETER

Suppose it is desired to have a spectral resolution of $\Delta\lambda_{MIN} \approx 0.5$ nm at a wavelength of $\lambda \approx 633$ nm when using a Fabry-Perot spectrometer with $n = 1.00$ and $d \approx 2.85$ μm. The radiation is collected in ninth order ($m = 9$) on a FPA at an off-axis angle of $\beta \approx 0.1$ rad $\approx 5.73°$.

First, calculating $\Delta(nd)$ from **Equation 17-62**,

$$\Delta(nd) \approx \frac{m\Delta\lambda}{2\cos\beta} \approx \frac{(9)(0.5 \text{ nm})}{2\cos(0.1)} \approx \frac{(9)(0.5 \text{ nm})}{(2)(0.995)} \approx 2.26 \text{ nm}.$$

Second, calculating $\Delta\beta$ for a value of $\Delta(nd) \approx 0.226$ nm, which is 0.1 of the value just calculated that corresponds to $\Delta\lambda_{MIN} \approx 0.5$ nm, from **Equation 17-60**,

$$\Delta\beta \approx \frac{\Delta(nd)}{nd\beta} \approx \frac{0.226 \text{ nm}}{(1)(2.85 \text{ μm})(0.1)} \times \frac{1 \text{ μm}}{10^3 \text{ nm}} \approx 0.000793 \text{ rad} \approx 0.0454°.$$

$\Delta\theta_{INC}$ may be larger than β depending on the value of n for the medium. In this example, $n = 1.00$; hence $\Delta\theta_{INC} = \Delta\beta$.

Continuing, the etendue (or throughput) and resolving power are

$$U \approx A_R\Omega_{PIX} \approx A_R(\Delta\theta_{INC})^2 \approx A_R(7.9 \times 10^{-4}\text{rad})^2 \approx 6.2 \times 10^{-7} A_R$$

$$\overline{RP} \approx \frac{\lambda}{\Delta\lambda_{MIN}} \approx \frac{633 \text{ nm}}{0.5 \text{ nm}} \approx 1270.$$

Finally, the resolving power-etendue product is then

$$(\overline{RP})(U) \approx (1270)(6.2 \times 10^{-7} A_R) \approx 7.9 \times 10^{-4} A_R,$$

which is again small compared to a FTS.

If Δβ increases, the throughput also increases. If the Δ(nd) caused by Δβ becomes comparable in magnitude with the Δ(nd) produced by the width of a single transmission peak, the spectral resolution will be compromised.

A summary of the performance characteristics of a Fabry-Perot interferometer as well as a comparison with previously discussed grating and prism spectrometers is given in **Table 17-5**.

Table 17-5 Third comparison of hyperspectral sensing techniques.

	Prism	Grating	Fabry-Perot
Spectral dispersion variation	Non-linear with λ	Nearly constant with respect to λ	Constant with respect to λ
FSR	Large, but limited by prism material properties	Possibly limited by adjacent orders	Possibly limited by adjacent orders
Possible spectral sampling	All λ at once for one row of spatial pixels	All λ at once for one row of spatial pixels	λ collected sequentially in time over the 2-D scene
2-D scene coverage	Slit required so sequential rows of pixels scanned over time	Slit required so sequential rows of pixels scanned over time	Continuous stare at an entire 2-D scene
Resolving power-etendue product	Low	Low	Low

17.5 FOURIER TRANSFORM SPECTROMETERS

A discussion of FTSs usually begins with the Michelson interferometer. The optical layout is illustrated in **Figure 17-41**. (Michelson, Fabry, and Perot are shown in **Figure 17-42**.)

Light incident from a source strikes a beam splitter, where it is split in half, with half going on the path leading to mirror M_1 and half going on the path leading to mirror M_2. The simplest of all beam splitters is a normal glass surface coated with silver, but only to the extent that half the incident light is reflected and the other half transmitted. The two beams of light are completely reflected by mirrors M_1 and M_2 back to the beam splitter, where each is again split. Of the light reflected by mirror M_1, half will be reflected back towards the source, and half will be transmitted to a detector. Of the light reflected by mirror M_2, half will be reflected toward the detector, and half will be transmitted towards the source.

Figure 17-41 Schematic of a typical Michelson interferometer.

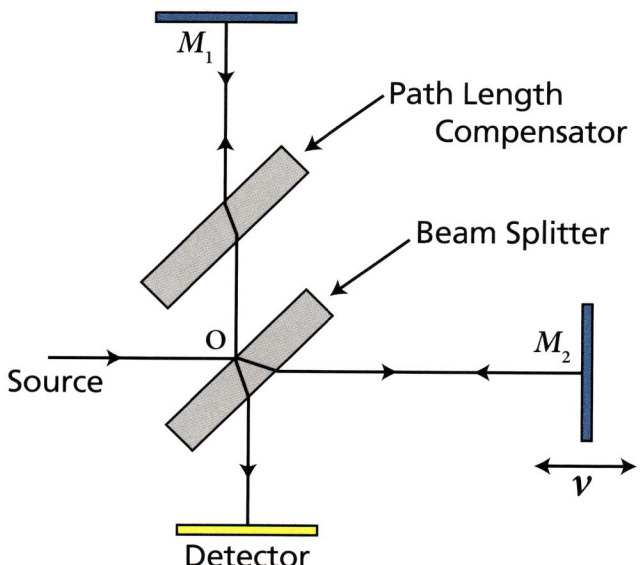

The distance[6] from point O to mirror M_1 and back to point O is designated by d_1; the distance from point O to mirror M_2 and back to point O is designated by d_2. Interference conditions involve the difference in distance traveled, $\Gamma = |d_1 - d_2|$.

If $|d_1 - d_2| = m\lambda$, where $m = 0, 1, 2, \ldots$, constructive interference occurs on axis.

If $|d_1 - d_2| = (m + \tfrac{1}{2})\lambda$, where $m = 0, 1, 2, \ldots$, destructive interference occurs on axis.

Michelson interferometers have been used to make precise measurements of distances and indices of refraction in the laboratory and in the field.

Suppose one of the two mirrors, M_1 or M_2, can be moved in a very precise way with speed v over very small distances so $|d_1 - d_2|$ changes value in amounts comparable to a single wavelength of incident light in time $\Delta t = t_2 - t_1$. This mirror movement will produce alternating bright and dark irradiance values at an on-axis detector (on the center-line of the optical system). The output current, i (in Amperes, A), from the detector depends on this mirror motion and wavelength,

$$i(\lambda,t) = i(\lambda)_{MAX} \sin^2\left(2\pi \frac{vt}{\lambda}\right) \quad [\text{A}], \qquad (17\text{-}64)$$

where $i(\lambda)_{MAX}$ = maximum value of $i(\lambda,t)$, and v = constant velocity of moving mirror, so vt represents the distance traveled since time $t = 0$. That is,

$$\Delta\Gamma = 2vt \quad [\mu\text{m}] \qquad (17\text{-}65)$$

is the change in optical path length difference over a time t when the mirror is moving at speed v. The factor of 2 arises from the light reflected back along the same shortened (or lengthened) path.

Using $\sin^2 x = \tfrac{1}{2}(1 - \cos 2x)$, **Equation 17-65** may be written as

$$i(\lambda,t) = \frac{i(\lambda)_{MAX}}{2}\left[1 - \cos\left(4\pi\frac{vt}{\lambda}\right)\right] \quad [\text{A}]. \qquad (17\text{-}66)$$

A plot of $i(\lambda,t)$ versus t is called an *interferogram*; and in general the maximum, $i(\lambda)_{MAX}$, is the value sought, having the information about the amount of wavelength, λ, present in the input.

If many wavelengths are present, each produces an output current with a different frequency and magnitude.

If N discrete wavelengths are present:

$$i(t) = \sum_{k=1}^{N} i_k(\lambda_k, t) \quad [\text{A}]. \qquad (17\text{-}67)$$

If a continuous distribution of wavelengths is present between λ_1 and λ_2:

$$i(t) = \frac{1}{\Delta\lambda}\int_{\lambda_1}^{\lambda_2} i(\lambda,t)\,d\lambda \qquad (17\text{-}68)$$

$$= \frac{1}{2\Delta\lambda}\int_{\lambda_1}^{\lambda_2} i(\lambda)_{MAX}\left[1 - \cos\left(4\pi\frac{vt}{\lambda}\right)\right]d\lambda$$

$$= \frac{1}{2\Delta\lambda}\int_{\lambda_1}^{\lambda_2} i(\lambda)_{MAX}\,d\lambda - \frac{1}{2\Delta\lambda}\int_{\lambda_1}^{\lambda_2} i(\lambda)_{MAX}\left[\cos\left(4\pi\frac{vt}{\lambda}\right)\right]d\lambda \quad [\text{A}],$$

Charles Fabry
1867–1945

Alfred Perot
1863–1925

Albert Michelson
1852–1931

Figure 17-42
Physicists for whom interferometers are named. (Photo of A. Perot courtesy of http://commons.wikimedia.org/wiki/File:Alfred_Perot.jpg; PD_Old.)

[6] The path length compensator is a piece of glass identical to the beam splitter. Its purpose is to ensure the *optical* path traveled by the light beam to and from M_1 is the same as the path to and from M_2. Both beams pass through three thicknesses of glass to arrive at the detector.

where $\Delta\lambda = \lambda_2 - \lambda_1$. In the first term, $\frac{1}{\Delta\lambda}\int_{\lambda_1}^{\lambda_2} i(\lambda)_{MAX}d\lambda$ is just the average value of $i(\lambda)_{MAX}$ across the interval $\Delta\lambda$.

Remember $i(t)$ is measured, but the spectrum $i(\lambda)_{MAX}$ is what the analyst desires. In general, it is difficult to uniquely determine a function, $f(x)$, when only its integral is known. For example, if

$$\int_0^1 f(x)dx = 1.0, \tag{17-69}$$

then $f(x)$ could be one of many possible functions. (See **Example 10-2** for instance.) For the detector output from the Michelson interferometer, there can be many measured values of $i(t)$ taken at different times. Fortunately, the integral form of $i(t)$ has the right form so $i(\lambda)_{MAX}$ can be retrieved using the Fourier Transform theory (see sidebar, **Fourier Analysis**, on the next page). The finite Fourier cosine transform (FT) of $i(\lambda)_{MAX}$ is given by the expression,

$$i(t) = \frac{1}{2\Delta\lambda}\int_{\lambda_1}^{\lambda_2} i(\lambda)_{MAX}\cos\left(4\pi\frac{vt}{\lambda}\right)d\lambda \quad [A]. \tag{17-70}$$

Applying the "inverse" finite Fourier cosine transform, FT^{-1}, of $i(t)$ retrieves $i(\lambda)_{MAX}$ as shown in the following equation:

$$i(\lambda)_{MAX} = \frac{1}{\pi\Delta t}\int_{t_1}^{t_2} i(t)\cos\left(4\pi\frac{vt}{\lambda}\right)dt \quad [A]. \tag{17-71}$$

Obtaining the interferogram, $i(t)$, and applying Fourier analysis introduced new technology, methods, and terminology into remote sensing:

- Accurately maintaining a mirror's velocity, v, is difficult. It is easier to oscillate (or vibrate) the mirror at some frequency. Fortunately, FT^{-1} can still recover $i(\lambda)_{MAX}$. Michelson interferometers (and others similar in optical layout) when operated in a spectral scanning mode are referred to as FTSs.
- Michelson interferometers are easier to construct and align in the infrared where λ values are larger (> 1 μm). A FTS operating in the infrared is referred to as a Fourier Transform Infrared spectrometer.
- Applying inverse Fourier transforms to the measured interferogram for each pixel on a FPA must be done numerically. To accomplish this task, large computers and efficient (accurate and rapid) algorithms are required. Hence, a whole mathematical discipline, Fast Fourier Transforms (FFT), has been developed.

Now that the basis for FTSs has been discussed, performance characteristics will be discussed, beginning with the possible linearity of the dispersion of $i(\lambda,t)$. The interferogram equation (**Equation 17-66**) and other such equations often involve $1/\lambda$. It is often convenient to use wavenumbers, υ, instead of wavelengths, λ. (Recall the definition, $\upsilon \equiv 1/\lambda$ with most commonly used units of reciprocal centimeters, or cm^{-1}. See sidebar **On Wavenumbers**.) Hence, the interferogram becomes

$$i(\upsilon,t) = \frac{i(\upsilon)_{MAX}}{2}(1 - \cos(4\pi\upsilon vt)) \quad [A]. \tag{17-72}$$

FOURIER ANALYSIS

Fourier analysis finds that any well-behaved (not infinite) signal can be represented by an appropriate combination of simple "basis functions" like sines and cosines. If the signal is discrete, like time-sampled data, the combination is a sum, but if it is similar to a continuous detector output, the combination is expressed as an integral.

Take a square wave as a discrete example, having period $2T$:

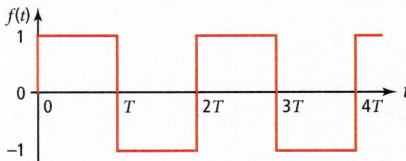

Fourier analysis shows that $f(t) = \frac{4}{\pi}\sum_{n=1}^{\infty}\frac{1}{2n-1}\sin\left(\frac{(2n-1)\pi t}{T}\right)$, which is a sum of sine waves having frequencies $f = \frac{2n-1}{2T}$ (where n is a non-zero positive integer). The first four terms of this series are shown below on the left, and their successive sums are shown on the right. It is evident that as more terms are added, the sum will more closely approximate the square wave.

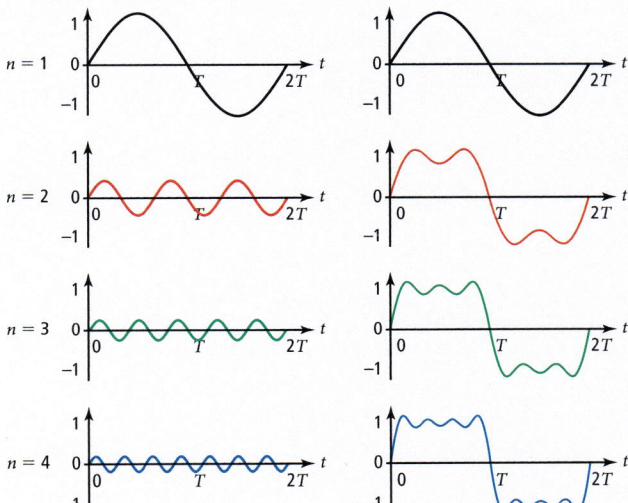

Notice the amplitudes of the terms decrease with increasing n. Properly, the amplitudes are called the *Fourier Transform* of $f(t)$ and may be written as $\text{FT}[f(t)] = F(n)$. *It is the goal and purpose of Fourier analysis to find $F(n)$.* A common computer code for computing the FT is the FFT, using the Cooley-Tukey algorithm (after James W. Cooley, born 1926, and John W. Tukey, 1915–2000).

Graphically, for the square wave example: $F(n) = \frac{4}{\pi(2n-1)}$.

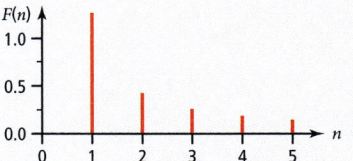

The Fourier Transform is sometimes called the *spectrum* of $f(t)$ because it tells how much of which frequencies of basis functions to use. The *Inverse Fourier Transform* of $F(n)$ is $f(t)$, written as $\text{FT}^{-1}[F(n)] = f(t)$, which is the square wave in this example. *$F(n)$ and $f(t)$ are fully equivalent ways to express a signal.*

For a continuous example, the Fourier Transform of

$$f(t) = e^{-|t|} = \begin{cases} e^{-t} & \text{for } t \geq 0 \\ e^{t} & \text{for } t < 0 \end{cases} \text{ is}$$

$$\text{FT}[f(t)] = 2\int_0^\infty e^{-t}\cos(\omega t)dt = \frac{2}{1+\omega^2}.$$

Of course, the Inverse Fourier Transform is

$$\text{FT}^{-1}\left[\frac{2}{1+\omega^2}\right] = \frac{1}{\pi}\int_0^\infty \frac{2}{1+\omega^2}\cos(\omega t)dt = e^{-t}.$$

(The left half of $f(t)$ is recovered by arguing that the inverse transform must be symmetric about $t = 0$ because the transform is symmetric about $\omega = 0$.) The function and its transform plot as:

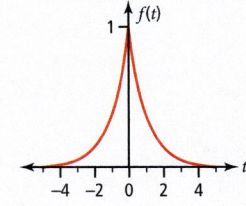 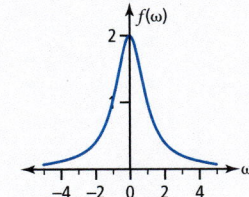

For two closely spaced spectral lines, $\lambda_0, \lambda_0 + \Delta\lambda$ (or $\upsilon_0 = \frac{1}{\lambda_0}$ and $\upsilon_0 + \Delta\upsilon$, where $\Delta\upsilon = \frac{1}{\lambda^2}\Delta\lambda$)

$$\Delta i(\lambda) = \frac{i(\lambda)_{MAX}}{2}\sin\left(\frac{4\pi vt}{\lambda}\right)\left(\frac{-4\pi vt}{\lambda^2}\right)\Delta\lambda \qquad (17\text{-}73)$$

$$= -i(\lambda)_{MAX}\frac{2\pi vt}{\lambda^2}\sin\left(\frac{4\pi vt}{\lambda}\right)\Delta\lambda \text{ [A] or}$$

$$\Delta i(\upsilon) = \frac{i(\upsilon)_{MAX}}{2}\sin(4\pi\upsilon vt)(4\pi vt)\Delta\upsilon \qquad (17\text{-}74)$$

$$= i(\upsilon)_{MAX}(2\pi vt)\sin(4\pi\upsilon vt)\Delta\upsilon \text{ [A]}.$$

Hence, the detectable Δi corresponding to $\Delta\lambda$ varies strongly with λ^2, *but* the detectable Δi corresponding to $\Delta\upsilon$ is nearly *constant* with υ across the bandpass. For this and the ease of notation, FTS performance and data are usually discussed in terms of wave number.

ON WAVENUMBERS

Starting with the definition of wavenumber, $v = 1/\lambda$, a numerical equation relating to $v(cm^{-1})$ to $\lambda(\mu m)$ is

$$v(cm^{-1}) = \frac{1}{\lambda(\mu m)} \times \frac{10^4 \, \mu m}{1 \, cm} = \frac{10{,}000}{\lambda(\mu m)}.$$

As an example, wavenumbers corresponding to the LWIR bandpass are

$\lambda(\mu m)$	$v(cm^{-1})$
8	1250
9	1110
10	1000
11	909
12	833

Within a wavelength bandpass, $\Delta\lambda$, the amount of power received by a remote sensor is contained within the equivalent wavenumber bandpass, Δv. Thus,

$$\Delta v = v_2 - v_1 = \frac{1}{\lambda_2} - \frac{1}{\lambda_1}$$

$$= \frac{\lambda_1 - \lambda_2}{\lambda_1 \lambda_2} = \frac{-\Delta\lambda}{\lambda_1 \lambda_2}.$$

If the bandpass is small, this may be approximated as

$$\Delta v = \frac{-\Delta\lambda}{\lambda^2} = -v^2 \Delta\lambda = -\frac{v}{\lambda}\Delta\lambda.$$

(The significance of the minus sign is that an increase in wavelength is a decrease in wavenumber, and vice versa. This is usually ignored and absolute values are used.) This last expression can be rearranged to show that a proportional change in wavenumber is equal to a proportional change in wavelength:

$$\frac{\Delta v}{v} = \frac{|\Delta\lambda|}{\lambda}.$$

For example, a 1% change in wavenumber at 1000 cm^{-1} is a 1% change in wavelength at $\lambda = 10 \, \mu m$, which is $\Delta\lambda = 0.1 \, \mu m$ or 100 nm.

To discuss FTS spectral resolution and other performance characteristics, consider a source with two wavelengths, λ_1 and λ_2, or two wavenumbers, $v_2 = 1/\lambda_2$ and $v_1 = 1/\lambda_1$, of equal strength. They produce two oscillating currents

$$i_1(v,t) = 0.5 \, i_{MAX}[1 - \cos(2\pi f_1 t)] \text{ and} \quad (17\text{-}75)$$

$$i_2(v,t) = 0.5 \, i_{MAX}[1 - \cos(2\pi f_2 t)] \, [A],$$

where f_1 and f_2 are the frequencies of current oscillation, defined as:

$$f_1 = 2v/\lambda_1 = 2v_1 v \text{ and } f_2 = 2v/\lambda_2 = 2v_2 v \, [Hz]. \quad (17\text{-}76)$$

The corresponding periods of current oscillation, t_{p1} and t_{p2}, are

$$p_1 = \frac{1}{f_1} = \frac{\lambda_1}{2v} \text{ and } p_2 = \frac{1}{f_2} = \frac{\lambda_2}{2v} \, [S]. \quad (17\text{-}77)$$

The measured current $i(t)$, from the two inputs combined is

$$i(t) = i_1(t) + i_2(t) = i_{MAX} - 0.5 \, i_{MAX}[\cos(2\pi f_1 t) + \cos(2\pi f_2 t)] \, [A]. \quad (17\text{-}78)$$

After the use of a trigonometric identity,

$$i(t) = i_{MAX} - i_{MAX} \cos\left(2\pi\left[\frac{f_1 + f_2}{2}\right]t\right)\cos\left(2\pi\left[\frac{f_1 - f_2}{2}\right]t\right) \, [A]. \quad (17\text{-}79)$$

where $\frac{f_2 + f_1}{2}$ is the average frequency and $\frac{f_2 - f_1}{2} = \Delta f_B$ is the modulation frequency.

When $\Delta f_B = \frac{|f_2 - f_1|}{2} \ll f_2 \text{ or } f_1$, the modulation frequency is sometimes referred to as the beat frequency. This terminology refers to low frequency modulation frequencies produced by two nearly equal frequency low frequency sound waves, as demonstrated by two tuning forks in beginning physics classes or riding in an old MD-80 commercial jetliner with two engines strapped on either side of the fuselage. Graphically, the combination of two waves for $10P_1 = 9P_2$ and, hence, $9f_1 = 10f_2$ is shown in **Figure 17-43**. The comparison of the beat patterns when two waves of equal amplitudes are added versus unequal amplitudes is shown.

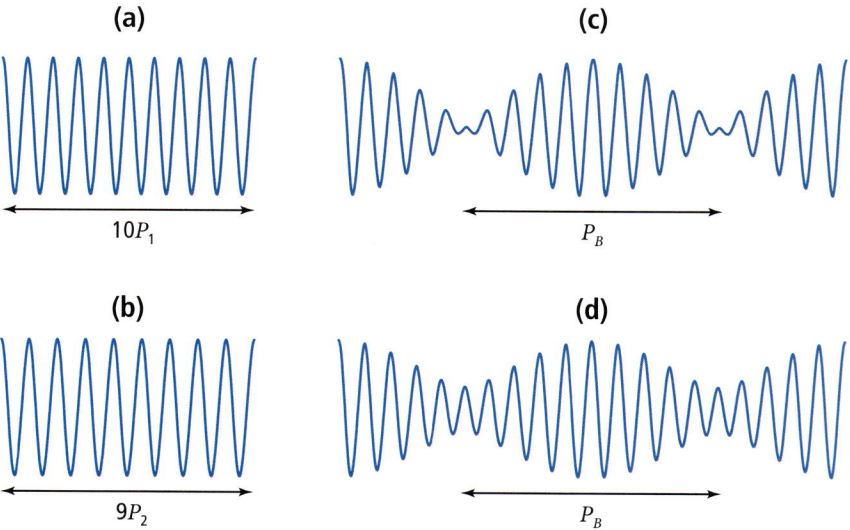

Figure 17-43
A comparison of two waves of nearly the same frequency. a) The higher frequency wave. b) The lower frequency wave, oscillating nine times in the same time the higher frequency wage oscillates ten times. c) Their sum when they have equal amplitudes. d) Their sum when the higher frequency wave has twice the amplitude of the lower frequency wave.

To resolve two closely spaced spectral lines, a FTS must measure the beat frequency, Δf_B, of the beat pattern of $i(t)$. Hence, data must be collected and the mirror moved for a time, t, that is at least as long as the period P_B of the beat pattern:

$$t = P_B = \frac{1}{\Delta f_B} \quad [S]. \tag{17-80}$$

Since f is related to the wavelength (or wavenumber) of the incoming radiation, **Equation 17-76**,

$$\Delta v = \frac{\Delta f_B}{2v} = \left[\frac{1}{t}\right]\left[\frac{1}{2v}\right] = \frac{1}{2vt} \quad [cm^{-1}] \quad \text{and} \tag{17-81}$$

$$\Delta v_{MIN} = \frac{1}{2(vt)_{MAX}} \quad [cm^{-1}]. \tag{17-82}$$

This result[7] for the spectral resolution in wave number is amazing. In principle, if the mirror could travel an infinite distance, $\Delta v_{MIN} \to 0$. There are no theoretical limits. Of course, practically, there are limits. Larger distances (and usually long travel times) become increasingly difficult especially on moving platforms. Typically, vt can vary from 0.25 mm to 5 cm. Continuous sampling is also required if $i(t)$ is sampled, more data must be numerically processed in the inverse FT to recover the source spectrum.

To better understand the FTS spectral resolution result, the Fourier series (and also Fourier integral or transform) representation of $i(t)$ in terms of sines (and/or cosines) of varying frequency should be considered. The larger the number of frequencies used, the better the representation of $i(t)$. This was previously illustrated for the square wave function as part of the **Sidebar, Fourier Analysis**.

For a FTS, the spectrum of $i(t)$ in wavelength is its Fourier transform,

$$i(\lambda) = \frac{1}{\pi \Delta t} \int_{t_1}^{t_2} i(t) \cos\left(4\pi \frac{vt}{\lambda}\right) dt \quad [A], \tag{17-83}$$

where the frequencies of the cosines are just $\frac{2vt}{\lambda}$. So, the higher frequencies are directly related to larger distances traveled by the mirror.

The final characteristic of performance, which involves extended sources and off-axis incidence onto the FTS, is the etendue, U (throughput). The size and spacing of detectors in the two-dimensional FPA and its distance from the collecting optics of the interferometer (usually the focal length) determine a pixel FOV as well as a range of values for θ_{inc} as suggested by **Figure 17-44**.

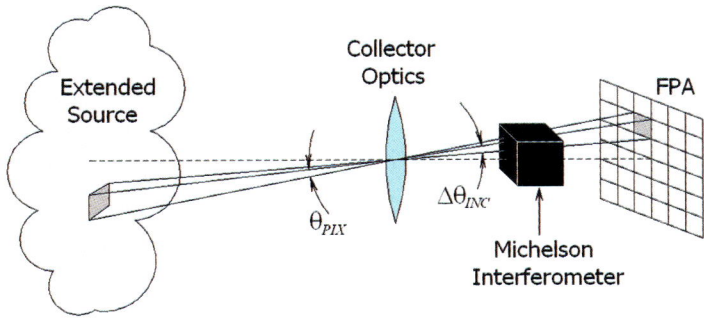

Figure 17-44
Schematic of a FTS with the interferometer represented as a "black box" whose internal operation is as depicted in **Figure 17-41**.

[7] More sophisticated analysis produce results without the factor of 2.

Because $\theta_{PIX} = \Delta\theta_{inc}$, light is accepted by an individual detector only over a range of incident angles, $\Delta\theta_{inc}$. To determine how large $\Delta\theta_{inc}$ can be, consider the behavior of the FTS to off-axis incident light as shown in **Figure 17-45**. The difference in path traveled for light incident normal and traveling on-axis is denoted by $\Gamma(\theta_{inc} = 0) = \Gamma_0 = |d_1 - d_2|$. At incidence angle θ_{inc}, $\Gamma(\theta_{inc}) = \Gamma_0/\cos\theta_{inc}$. The difference in Γ between radiation incident at $\theta_{inc} = 0$ and $\theta_{inc} \geq 0$ is given by the expression,

$$\Delta\Gamma = \frac{\Gamma_0}{\cos\theta_{inc}} - \Gamma_0 = \Gamma_0\left[\frac{1 - \cos\theta_{inc}}{\cos\theta_{inc}}\right] \; [\mu m]. \qquad (17\text{-}84)$$

Figure 17-45
Off-axis incidence into an interferometer increases the light's optical path length.

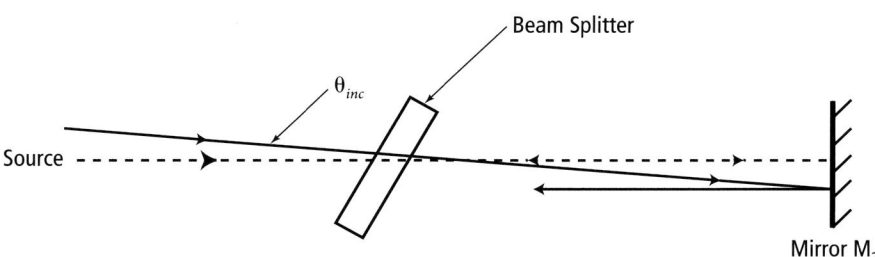

For $\theta_{inc} \ll 1$, the power series expansion of $\cos\theta_{inc}$ gives, to very close approximation, $\cos\theta_{inc} \approx 1 - \tfrac{1}{2}\theta_{inc}^2$. Hence,

$$\Delta\Gamma \approx \frac{\Gamma_0 \theta_{inc}^2}{2} \; [\mu m]. \qquad (17\text{-}85)$$

As θ_{inc} increases, the extreme ray $(\theta_{inc})_{MAX}$ can be out of phase with the central ray $(\theta_{inc} = 0)$ for the first time when $\Delta\Gamma = 0.5\lambda = 1/(2\upsilon)$. Using **Equations 17-65** and **17-85**,

$$\upsilon t (\theta_{inc})^2_{MAX} \leq \frac{1}{2\upsilon} \; [\mu m], \qquad (17\text{-}86)$$

and since $\Delta\upsilon_{MIN} = \dfrac{1}{2(\upsilon t)_{MAX}}$ (**Equation 17-82**),

$$(\theta_{inc})^2 \approx \Omega_{MAX} \leq \frac{\Delta\upsilon_{MIN}}{\upsilon} \; [sr]. \qquad (17\text{-}87)$$

This result shows the degree that etendue $(A_c \Omega_{MAX})$ and spectral resolution $(\Delta\upsilon_{MIN})$ are interrelated. Calculation of the etendue (throughput), resolving power, and the product of the resolving power and etendue are:

Etendue:

$$U = A_R \Omega_{MAX} = A_R \frac{\Delta\upsilon_{MIN}}{\upsilon} \; [cm^2 sr]. \qquad (17\text{-}88)$$

Resolving power:

$$\overline{RP} = \frac{\lambda}{\Delta\lambda_{MIN}} = \frac{\frac{1}{\upsilon}}{\frac{1}{\upsilon^2}\Delta\upsilon_{MIN}} = \frac{\upsilon}{\Delta\upsilon_{MIN}}. \qquad (17\text{-}89)$$

Resolving power-etendue product:

$$\overline{(RP)}(U) = \left(\frac{\upsilon}{\Delta\upsilon_{MIN}}\right)\left(A_R \frac{\Delta\upsilon_{MIN}}{\upsilon}\right) = A_R \; [cm^2 sr], \qquad (17\text{-}90)$$

which is usually large compared to that of prism, grating, or Fabry-Perot systems. This is often called the "Jacquinot Advantage" of a FTS after a more general analysis performed by Pierre Jacquinot (1910–2002) in the 1950s.

A summary of the performance characteristics of a FTS and a comparison of these with those of prism spectrometers, grating spectrometers, and Fabry-Perot interferometers is listed in **Table 17-6**.

	Prism	Grating	Fabry-Perot	FTS
Spectral dispersion variation	Non-linear with λ	Nearly constant with respect to λ	Constant with respect to λ	Nearly constant with respect to υ
FSR	Large, but limited by prism material properties	Possibly limited by adjacent orders	Possibly limited by adjacent orders	Large, but limited by FPA response
Possible spectral sampling	All λ at once for one row of spatial pixels	All λ at once for one row of spatial pixels	λ collected sequentially in time over the 2-D scene	All λ collected over time for 2-D scene (Fellgett's Advantage)
2-D scene coverage	Slit required so sequential rows of pixels scanned over time	Slit required so sequential rows of pixels scanned over time	Continuous stare at entire 2-D scene	Continuous stare at entire 2-D scene
Resolving power-etendue product	Low	Low	Low	High (Jacquinot Advantage)

Table 17-6
Fourth comparison of hyperspectral sensing techniques.

A short review of Fellgett's Advantage (named for P. B. Fellgett, 1922–2008) (listed in **Table 17-6**), specifically how the various spectrometers collect a HSI data cube, will now be provided. Consider a HSI data cube collected in a time interval t_{CUBE}, consisting of N_X by N_Y spatial pixels and N_λ spectral bands. This data cube is illustrated in **Figure 17-46**.

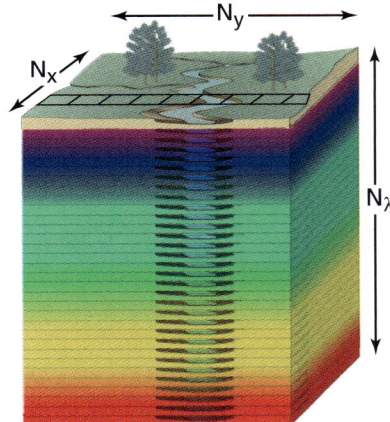

Figure 17-46
A notional hyperspectral data cube.

The amount of time spent collecting an element of data from each pixel and each spectral band will be compared for the four spectrometer types. For prism and grating spectrometers (pushbroom scanners moving in the y-direction), N_X by N_λ "pixels" can be sampled during a time interval, t_{CUBE}/N_Y. For a Fabry-Perot interferometer (staring system), N_X by N_Y pixels can be sampled during a time interval, t_{CUBE}/N_λ. For a FTS, N_X by N_Y pixels can be sampled for a time interval, t_{CUBE}, for each λ. Although during t_{CUBE}, at times there are many photons and at other times, there are few photons as the mirror moves through constructive interference peaks and destructive interference zeroes for each wavelength. Hence, the effective integration or dwell time for the current collected from each pixel in the HSI cube is much larger for the FTS. This is the Fellgett Advantage.

Although it has many advantages, the FTS also has some disadvantages. Data processing is much more complex. All the other (non FTS) spectral systems provide data, each element of which, when the calibration factors are applied, becomes an element of the data cube. The FTS provides a two-dimensional array of interferograms to each of which the inverse FT must be applied to produce the spectrum of each pixel. Since the FTS can provide very high spectral resolution data at reasonable detector outputs, FTS data cubes can be enormous. In addition, more values of $i(t)$ must be measured and processed during the extended collection times. Also, there is the possibility of motion of some objects during this long time required to sample the interferogram, $i(t)$.

17.6 HSI COLLECTION OPTIONS AND ISSUES

HSI data collections with staring FTS and Fabry-Perot interferometer systems require full two-dimensional FPAs, where every detector provides the spectrum of a pixel in the scene. The collection geometry of such systems are shown in **Figure 15-4**.

These sensors must be accurately pointed so they are "staring" at the same point on the ground during the time period necessary to obtain a complete spectrum. (This collection mode is sometimes referred to as "spotlight" mode.) Otherwise, spectra of one pixel may be smeared across several of its neighboring pixels and vice versa. Hence, a detector output/spectral resolution/PTS trade-off is often necessary.

HSI data collections with scanning prism and grating spectrometer systems also require full two-dimensional FPAs. The slit of the system defines a row of ground pixels. Each row of detectors is collecting a different spectral band from the row of ground pixels. Examples of this type of HSI data collection geometry are illustrated in **Figures 17-12** and **17-34**. The full 2-D spectral image (or swath) is created by scanning the row of ground pixels across the scene. Several possible scanning mechanisms include forward motion of platform using a pushbroom scan (shown above), a scanning mirror in front of the collecting optics, or a combination of both. The use of a PTS is required, but not as sophisticated as that for a staring HSI sensor system.

No matter which HSI spectrometer and collection approach is used, desired performance improvements include higher spatial resolution, higher spectral resolution, larger area coverage, and larger detector output. While some of these desired improvements can be accomplished, there are potential consequences for the analyst, sensor designer, or both. Analysts may have to process significantly more data resulting from larger data cubes that are acquired at fast data rates. The sensor designers may have to use larger, heavier, more expensive components, such as larger collecting optics and larger FPAs. Both the analysts and the sensor designers may have to consider higher data recording/data telemetry capabilities, data compression, or some on-board data processing capability. These will now be discussed in some detail.

Spectral and spatial resolution dramatically impacts the size of a HSI data cube. Consider the airborne or spaceborne example shown in **Table 17-7**. The MSI sensor is patterned after Landsat in terms of number of its spectral bands and size of the footprint (area covered per collection). The HSI sensor is patterned after the largest airborne systems so far deployed.

Table 17-7
Examples of collected spectral data cube size, assuming a square-shaped scene.

	Number of bands	×	(Swath width)^2 (pixels)^2	=	Data cube size (elements)
MSI	7	×	6,000 pixels	=	2.5×10^8
HSI	210	×	1,000 pixels	=	2.1×10^8

Spectral and spatial resolution impacts the rate of collected data. Consider the airborne example shown in **Table 17-8**. Both sensors are flown on a medium speed airborne platform. The Predator and Global Hawk Unmanned Aerial Vehicles (UAVs) fly somewhat slower; fighter jets such as the F-15 and F-16 fly faster.

Table 17-8
Examples of spectral data collection rate.

	Number of bands	×	Swath width (pixels)	×	Aircraft speed (m/sec)	÷	Ground pixel size (m)	=	Data rate (elements / sec)
MSI	7	×	6,000	×	200	÷	1.0	=	0.84×10^7
HSI	210	×	1,000	×	200	÷	1.0	=	4.2×10^7

The size of a single spectral data cube is not that overwhelming, especially if the sensor only collects a few times per day. The spectral data collection rate is also not intimidating if the sensor mission is only a few hours. But, high endurance platforms allow SYERS-2 on the U-2 aircraft to fly 8-hour missions and the Global Hawk UAV can fly over 24-hour missions. The massive amounts of data collected on a single mission must now be discussed in terms of terabytes of hard drive storage.

A few types of techniques continue to be discussed (and to some extent analyzed and implemented) to help the storage or telemetry problems faced with such huge data collections. Hyperspectral image data cubes can be collected, compressed for storage or telemetry, and decompressed in the hands of the analyst. Several compression techniques exist that were designed for panchromatic imagery. After decompression, imagery is preserved with only slight added noise or reduced information content. Also, spectral algorithms are thought to have decreased performance on compressed-decompressed hyperspectral images than on original uncompressed hyperspectral images. More research and development is necessary before any valid conclusion can be reached.

With on-board processing of data, either in real-time or later (before landing of airborne systems), interim results can be downlinked either immediately or later. Many analysts feel that such an operation is acceptable for HSI data collected in a "standard" manner against a "standard" object of interest; however, the processing results of some "non-standard" hyperspectral image cubes are questioned by some analysts, who prefer to process the data themselves.

18 HSI IN THE VISIBLE TO SWIR

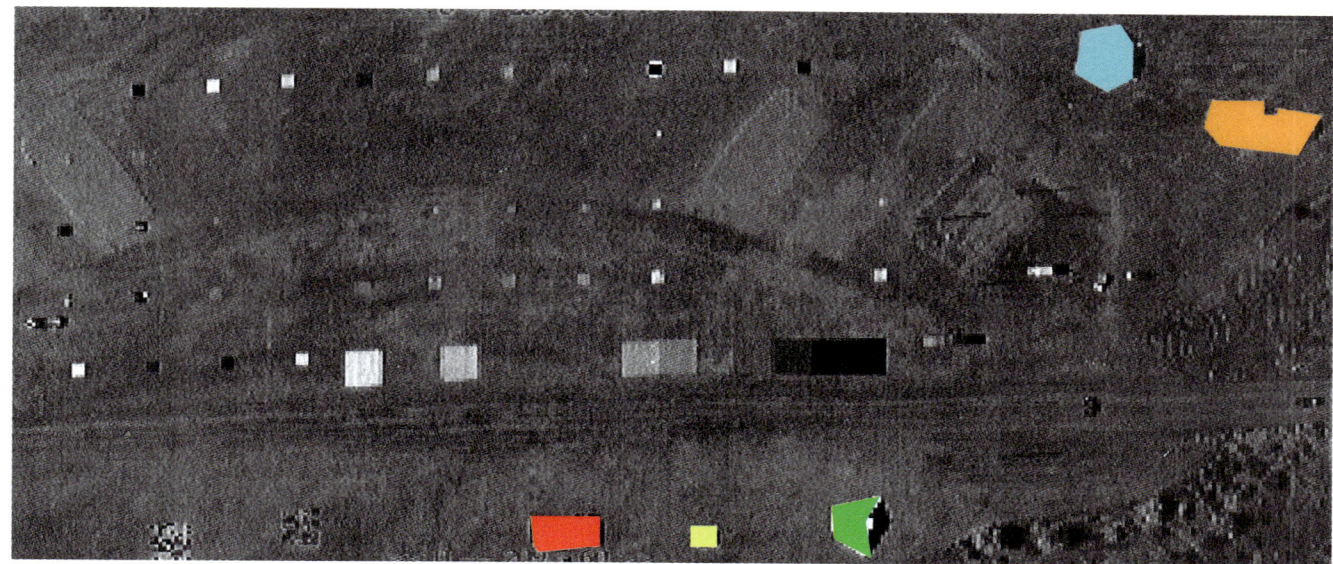

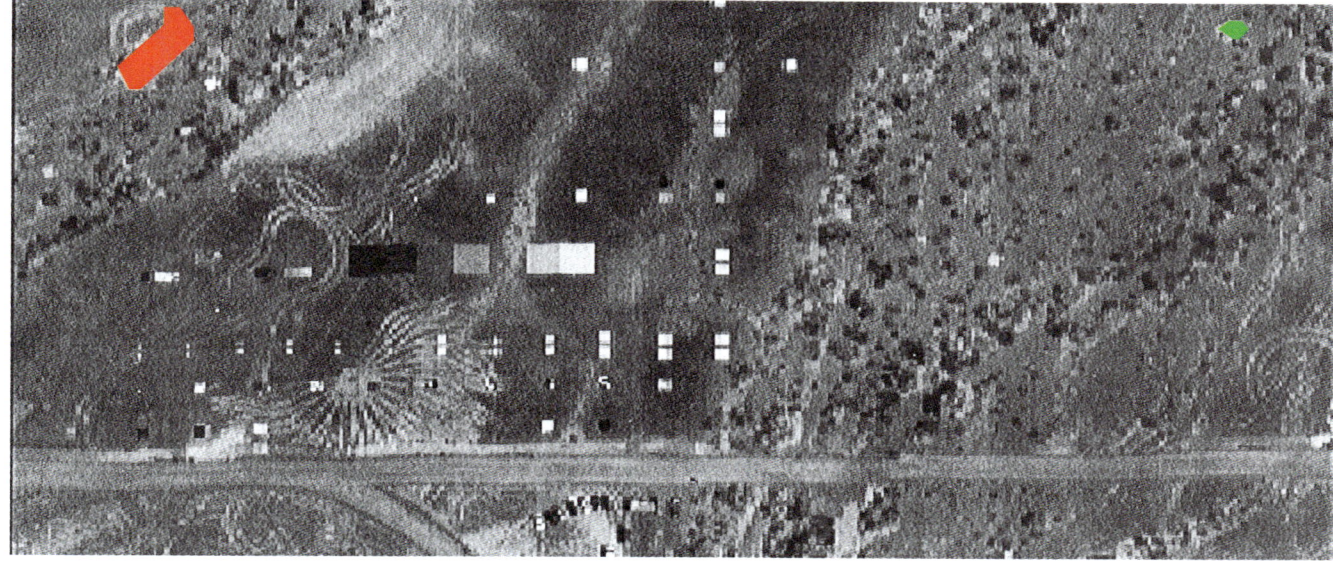

The discussion of specific Hyperspectral Imaging (HSI) sensors, applications, and algorithms begins in the visible to Shortwave Infrared (SWIR), where far more data collection and analysis has occured than in the thermal infrared. Considerable HSI efforts have been made in the last 20 years within the civilian, military, and intelligence communities. Several airborne HSI sensors have emerged in various operational roles, and the applications for HSI data continue to grow.

SECTIONS

18.1 AIRBORNE HSI SYSTEMS
18.2 AIRBORNE HSI APPLICATIONS AND DATA ANALYSIS
18.3 SPACEBORNE HSI SENSORS

18.1 AIRBORNE HSI SYSTEMS

There are a sizable number of airborne HSI sensors in the visible to SWIR, both commercial and military. Each of these two categories can be further divided into sensors that are used operationally and sensors built for research and development (R&D). This text only considers those sponsored by the Department of Defense (DOD) that are operational or at least quasi-operational. These HSI sensors fall into three different sensor families: 1) Night Vision Imaging Spectrometer (NVIS); 2) Littoral Airborne Sensor (Hyperspectral) (LASH); and 3) Tactical Real-time Image Processing Spectrometer (TRIPS), now called Aurora.

The above types of spectrometers use gratings and a pushbroom scan. It is compact in design and requires no moving parts (hence, low cost). To date, it is the most commonly used airborne and spaceborne spectrometer. Of course, a grating spectrometer presents the issue of free-spectral range (FSR). For the airborne spectrometers, small two-dimensional Focal Plane Arrays (FPAs) have been used, which limit the number of spectral bands and the swath width. The detector type as well as the FSR issues limit the spectral coverage. For the two Navy systems, LASH and TRIPS, spectral coverage limited to the visible is provided by silicon detectors and a single grating. This coverage is adequate for most naval interests, especially bathymetry. (Recall, only the blue, green, and, to some extent, red wavelengths propagate through water.)

For NVIS, originally sponsored by Defense Advanced Research Projects Agency (DARPA), Army Night-Vision and Electro-optical Systems Division (NVESD), and later the Air Force, extending spectral coverage into the SWIR was initially accomplished with two FPAs (silicon and InSb) and two gratings. More recent versions, COMPact Airborne Spectral Sensor (COMPASS) and Hyperspectral Collection and Analysis System (HYCAS), accomplish spectral coverage from the visible through the SWIR with a single FPA (HgCdTe), representing a recent FPA breakthrough. Also, in versions of COMPASS and HYCAS, a cross-track scan was introduced to extend the swath width beyond the FPA size limitations. Ground pixel size for most airborne systems ranges from 0.5 to 3.0 m, depending on the flight altitude and sensor collecting optics. [1], [2], [3], [4]

Some of the sensor parameters for the initial sensors of the NVIS, TRIPS, and LASH families are compared in **Table 18-1** with each other and those of another earlier R&D system, HYperspectral Digital Imagery Collection Experiment (HYDICE), that was built and operated by the Naval Research Laboratory (NRL).

Table 18-1 Comparison of some airborne HSI systems. [1], [3], [4], [5]

	HYDICE	NVIS	LASH	Aurora TRIPS
Spectral Regions	Visible-SWIR	Visible-SWIR	Visible	Visible
Number of Bands	210	384	48 or 96	64 or 128
Swath Width (pixels)	320	256	770	600 or 1024
Status on Existing Platform	R & D Retired	Operational in some versions	Operational in some versions	Operational in some versions
Design Special Features	Well calibrated	Well calibrated	Gimbaled, can track a point on the Earth's surface	Small, simple, blue enhanced response

Currently, there are two data processing options for collected airborne HSI data: data recorded for later analysis and data downloaded as collected to provide battlefield commanders with near-real time information. Both options are stressed by the large size and the number of HSI data cubes collected during a mission. If the data is recorded onboard the aircraft with download and analysis performed after completion of the aircraft mission, huge data storage capabilities are required, usually in terms of a number of hard-drives of data. In the future, these requirements may be lessened using data compression techniques that do not result in a loss of information.

If the data is downloaded as it is collected for near-real time analysis, a high data-rate downlink is required as well as large dedicated computers using accurate but fast-running algorithms and ground stations in locations that can remain in direct radio contact with the aircraft during collection. In the future, these radio data downlink requirements can be lessened with automated near real-time, on-board data processing.

Members of the NVIS, LASH, and TRIPS sensor families have flown on a number of different platforms with a wide variety of government-sponsorship. Some of these efforts have been more successful than others.

18.2 AIRBORNE HSI APPLICATIONS AND DATA ANALYSIS

Applications and algorithms developed by the DOD and its contractors using the sensors discussed earlier as well as some R&D sensors will now be discussed. Some of the data and results collected and analyzed by the DOD and its contractors will also be presented and discussed.

COMPARISON OF SPECTRA

As the case for Multispectral Imaging (MSI) analysis, spectra of ground pixels must often be compared with reference spectra in HSI analysis. This problem is illustrated in **Figure 18-1** where the two spectra to be compared can be represented as

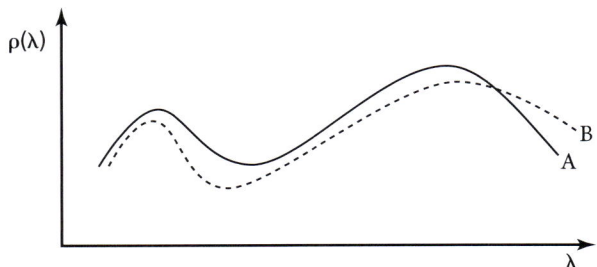

Figure 18-1
Two spectra to be compared.

$$\left. \begin{array}{l} A: \{\lambda_j, a_j\} \text{ for } j = 1, 2, \ldots, N \text{ spectral bands, and} \\ B: \{\lambda_j, b_j\} \text{ for } j = 1, 2, \ldots, N \text{ spectral bands,} \end{array} \right\} \quad (18\text{-}1)$$

where for each spectral band, λ_j, spectrum A has a reflectivity value of a_j, and spectrum B has a reflectivity value of b_j.

With more spectral bands, there is another technique to perform this comparison in addition to those previously discussed in **Chapter 15**: 1) least squares, 2) spectral distance, and 3) spectral angle. This discussion is repeated below for completeness.

1. One algorithm type involves least squares from statistics:

   Determine the differences between the two spectra, band-by-band, by calculating

   $$\Sigma[a_j - b_j]^2 = [a_1 - b_1]^2 + [a_2 - b_2]^2 + \ldots + [a_N - b_N]^2. \quad (18\text{-}2)$$

   Select a threshold, d_T.

   Apply the following test:

   $$\left.\begin{array}{l} \text{If } \Sigma[a_j - b_j]^2 < d_T, \text{ then the spectra A and B are the } same. \\ \text{If } \Sigma[a_j - b_j]^2 > d_T, \text{ then the spectra A and B are } different. \end{array}\right\} \quad (18\text{-}3)$$

   Selecting an appropriate value for the threshold d_T will be considered later in this chapter.

   Another approach involves vector algebra or, equivalently, plane geometry applied to the scatter diagrams. The two spectra, A and B, to be compared can be represented as two vectors:

   $$\left.\begin{array}{l} \mathbf{A} = \sum_{i=1}^{N} a_i \hat{x}_i = a_1 \hat{x}_1 + a_2 \hat{x}_2 + \ldots + a_N \hat{x}_N, \text{ and} \\ \mathbf{B} = \sum_{i=1}^{N} b_i \hat{x}_i = b_1 \hat{x}_1 + b_2 \hat{x}_2 + \ldots + b_N \hat{x}_N, \end{array}\right\} \quad (18\text{-}4)$$

   where $\hat{x}_i$ are unit vectors.

2. One useful vector algebra calculation is the magnitude of the vector difference $|\mathbf{A} - \mathbf{B}|$. This difference is illustrated in **Figure 18-2** which shows spectra A and B in ρ_1, ρ_2 space. This difference is sometimes referred to as the spectral distance.

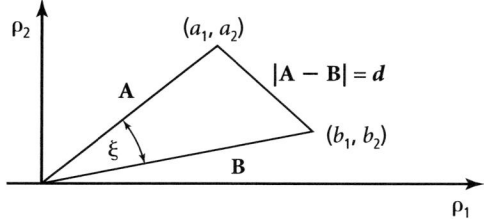

Figure 18-2
Spectral distance and spectral angle between two spectra.

   In the N-dimensional vector space,

   $$d^2 = |\mathbf{A} - \mathbf{B}|^2 = \sum_{i=1}^{N} [a_i - b_i]^2 = [a_1 - b_1]^2 + [a_2 - b_2]^2 + \ldots + [a_N - b_N]^2. \quad (18\text{-}5)$$

   This is the same result as that obtained from least squares considerations.

3. A second useful vector algebra calculation is the angle ξ between the two vectors, shown in **Figure 18-2**. This angle is sometimes referred to as the spectral angle.

   In the N-dimensional vector space,

   $$\cos\xi = \frac{1}{|\mathbf{A}||\mathbf{B}|} \sum_{i=1}^{N} a_i b_i = \frac{1}{|\mathbf{A}||\mathbf{B}|} [a_1 b_1 + a_2 b_2 + \ldots + a_N b_N], \quad (18\text{-}6)$$

   where the magnitudes of A and B are given by

$$\left.\begin{array}{l}|A| = \sqrt{\sum_{i=1}^{N} a_i^2} = \sqrt{a_1^2 + a_2^2 + \ldots + a_N^2}, \text{ and} \\ |B| = \sqrt{\sum_{i=1}^{N} b_i^2} = \sqrt{b_1^2 + b_2^2 + \ldots + b_N^2}.\end{array}\right\} \quad (18\text{-}7)$$

Once this angle is calculated, a threshold angle ξ_T is chosen and the following test is performed.

$$\left.\begin{array}{l}\text{If } \xi < \xi_T, \text{ spectra A and B are the } \textit{same.} \\ \text{If } \xi > \xi_T, \text{ spectra A and B are } \textit{different.}\end{array}\right\} \quad (18\text{-}8)$$

These three comparison techniques all involve the general shape of the spectra, including the data from all the bands.

With a large number of bands, another comparison technique is possible. In this technique, rather than compare the overall shapes of spectra, specific features in the two spectra are identified and their locations in wavelength are compared. This approach is illustrated in **Figure 18-3**.

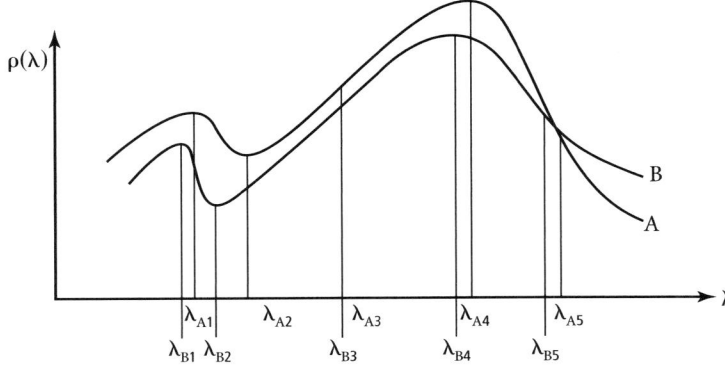

Figure 18-3
Location of features in two spectra (maxima, minima, and points of inflection).

The specific procedure for the feature location comparison techniques is the following:

Smooth both spectra to the point of removing all noise.

Locate the wavelength position of all features (primarily maxima, minima, points of inflection,…) in both spectra, λ_{Aj}, for $j = 1, 2, \ldots$, and λ_{Bj}, where $j = 1, 2, \ldots$

Select threshold $\Delta\lambda_T$.

Apply test:

$$\left.\begin{array}{l}\text{If } [\lambda_{Aj} - \lambda_{Bj}] < \Delta\lambda_T \text{ for some number of } j \text{ features,} \\ \text{the spectra are the } \textit{same.} \\ \text{If } [\lambda_{Aj} - \lambda_{Bj}] > \Delta\lambda_T \text{ for some number of } j \text{ features,} \\ \text{the spectra are } \textit{different.}\end{array}\right\} \quad (18\text{-}9)$$

To date, most analyses have concentrated on using only the locations of maxima for the comparison. This comparison technique is frequently used for laboratory spectra comparison to identify unknown compounds and gases.

Throughout the discussion of all these methods, one single question remains: How does the analyst select threshold values? This depends on the application and the selected algorithm approach. This topic is discussed later in this chapter.

ANOMALY DETECTION

Three types of HSI applications and algorithms include:
- Anomaly detection (search the scene for pixels that are different from the background);
- Signature based detection (search the scene for a specific type of object of interest); and
- Signature based identification for entire scene (e.g., terrain classification by mineral type) and known object characterization (e.g., roofing material identification).

Anomaly detection can be the simplest of spectral algorithms. Its objective is to find all the pixels in a scene that contain material different from the background. Intelligence problems addressed with this algorithm include cueing for targeting or other intelligence sensors, or for signature based detection. In either case, anomaly detection finds a limited number of pixels in the scene that warrant further attention in terms of a particular application. HSI data input to an anomaly detection algorithm can be either atmospherically corrected or *not*, but as a minimum, HSI data must be flat-field corrected. For further details see **Appendix 18-1** on the support website. For some approaches, the results of an initial scene characterization are used as an input to the anomaly detector. Output results from anomaly detection algorithms are presented as annotated locations on an image. In addition, these anomalies can be organized into various classes based on spectral similarity among some of the anomalies found in the scene. Some anomaly detection approaches produce this automatically; others produce it as a separate step.

The limitation of the use of anomaly detection algorithms is there are many valid anomalies in even the simplest scenes. Most of these anomalies have no military interest. As an example, consider a rural scene composed of forests and farm land. Valid spectral anomalies could be clearings in the forest, farm equipment in the fields, sheds, abandoned vehicles, a lone tree adjacent to a field, and many other possibilities. Certainly, the number of anomalies grows substantially in an urban versus a rural scene. In the latter, for example, every car in a partially filled parking lot could be a detected anomaly.

Verification and validation of various anomaly detection algorithms often involves collection of HSI data over a known scene with a number of added objects of interest. Metrics of algorithm performance usually involve probability of detection versus the number of false alarms based on the results of analyzing the scene. These metrics will be defined later in the chapter. The problem still remains regarding the possibly large number of naturally occurring anomalies within the scene. The entire scene must be adequately "ground truthed," so all existing anomalies are known and their locations are documented. Based on the size of the scene over which HSI data was collected, the "ground truth" effort may be extensive.

Table 18-2 lists a number of existing anomaly detection algorithms and the government agencies, companies, or universities that developed them. While this list is far from complete, it gives some insight into the developers for such algorithms.

Algorithm	Developer(s)
Reed, Xu (RX)	NRL, Space Computer Corp. (SCC) (Now part of ITT Exelis)
Gauss-Markov Random Field (GMRF)	Science Applications International Corp. (SAIC) and Carnegie Mellon
ASIT Anomaly Detection Tool	Applied Signal and Image Technology (ASIT)
END-member FINDeR (N-FINDR)	Technical Research Associates
Optical Real-time Adaptive Spectral Identification System-Advanced Spectral Identification System (ORASIS-ASPIS)	NRL and Advanced Power Technologies Inc. (APTI)
Stochastic Expectation Maximization (SEM)	Space and Naval Warfare Systems Command (SPAWAR), SCC

Table 18-2
Anomaly detection algorithms and associated developers.

Figure 18-4 presents three general anomaly detection approaches.

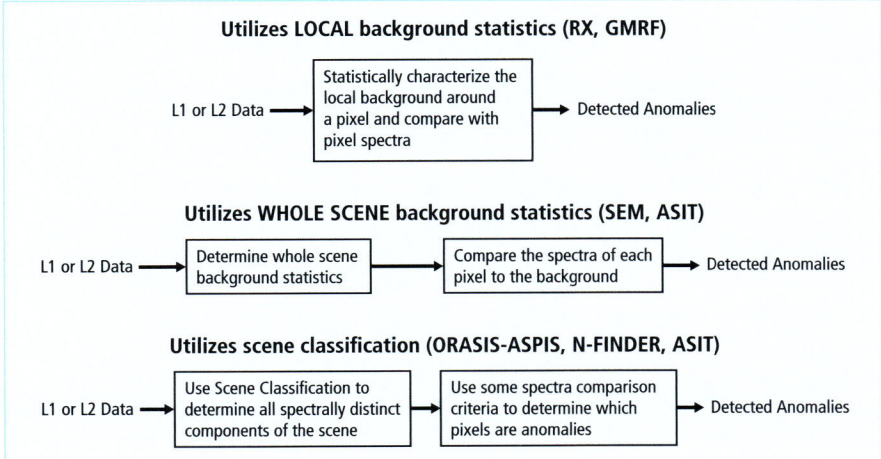

Figure 18-4
Three approaches to spectral anomaly detection. L1 HSI data have not been atmospherically corrected, while L2 data have.

For each approach above, several algorithms are listed that use that approach. The use of local background statistics implies that the spectrum of every pixel is compared with the average spectrum of its nearest neighbor pixels. There are several ways to statistically characterize the whole scene. Scene classification with HSI data is similar to that which uses MSI data. Possible cluster diagrams, illustrated in **Figure 18-5**, are used to determine independent spectra for scene classification.

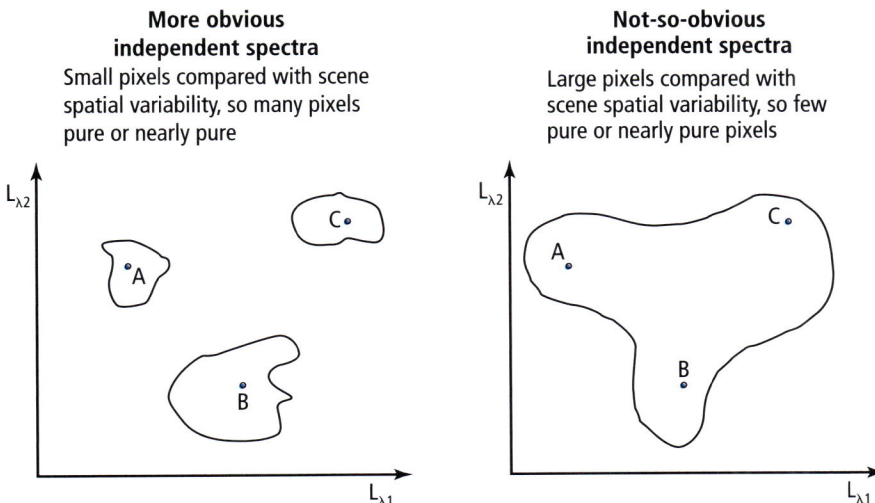

Figure 18-5
Spectral cluster diagrams for two ground pixel sizes.

There is some terminology used to describe this process. "End-member" is another name for the independent spectra in the scene, each of which represents a spectrally distinct material type. "Linear unmixing" is another name for scene characterization to determine the independent spectra or "end-members" in the scene. The basic assumption of this analysis is the spectral radiance of every pixel in the scene is a linear sum of scene end-members; that is, the radiation from one type of material in a pixel does not significantly affect that of another material in the scene.

More sophisticated anomaly detection schemes have been developed using combinations of one or more of the previously named algorithms. One example, developed by ASIT, is shown in **Figure 18-6**. In two steps, it first finds the exposed anomalies, and then the concealed and shadowed anomalies. Details of the exact steps of this scheme are proprietary to ASIT, a common property of algorithms developed by small companies.

Figure 18-6
Examples of combination algorithms for anomaly detection.

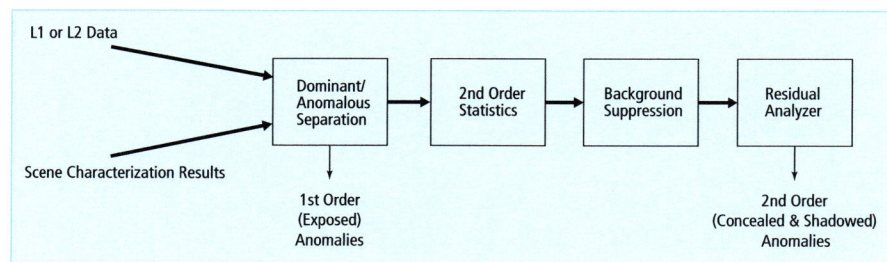

Another example of a simple combination algorithm is shown in **Figure 18-7**. It is a two-step process to find anomalies first in the open and then in the shadow. To accomplish the first step, a scene characterization type anomaly detection algorithm is used. To accomplish the second step, RX (a local background anomaly detection algorithm named after its developers) is applied to the shadow regions identified by the scene characterization algorithm in the first step.

Figure 18-7
An anomaly detection and classification algorithm. [6]

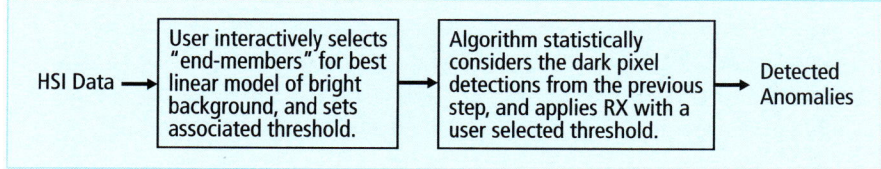

Interesting demonstrations of HSI collection and anomaly detection cueing for other sensors were conducted. HSI and panchromatic visible imagery were collected from a low-flying Twin-Otter aircraft over the forested areas of Ft. A. P. Hill, Virginia. The HSI data was processed in real-time with RX, Stochastic Expectation Maximization (SEM), and Optical Real-time Adaptive Spectral Identification System (ORASIS) anomaly detection algorithms from each of the three different approaches. The locations of anomaly detections were used to trigger a snap-shot of visible imagery of the area for a ground-based imagery analyst to assess whether the anomaly had any military significance (for example, a tank versus a clearing in the woods). Despite the rural background, low collection platform speeds, and small sensor swath width, about one anomaly was detected per second, which was thought to be the maximum work rate for ten imagery analysts. Follow-up activities to decrease the anomaly detection rate were two-fold. First, a declared anomaly resulted only if all three algorithms found it to be an anomaly. This approach appeared flawed because different anomaly detection approaches do not perform the same on all types of scenes and under all viewing conditions. So, even though one of the three detected an anomaly, it could be an actual anomaly. Second, a simple fast-running signature-based detection algorithm using spectral angle was employed on the anomalies to detect specific objects of interest, such as camouflage painted tanks and other vehicles. As imagined, this greatly reduced the "relevant" anomaly detection rate.

NRL performed a continuing series of airborne collections (Warhorse, Dark Horse, etc.) using versions of the TRIPS hyperspectral spectrometer along with a visible panchromatic imager aboard Navy P-3 aircraft and other airborne platforms. The collected HSI data were used to support in-house NRL and contractor algorithm development efforts.

SIGNATURE-BASED DETECTION

More sophisticated spectral analysis than anomaly detection is signature-based detection, where the objective is to find all pixels in a scene that have spectra that match the spectrum of an object of interest. Inputs to this type of algorithm are the HSI data cube and a reference spectrum in a compatible form. Two possibilities include: 1)HSI data cube (*not* atmospherically corrected) with *only* in-scene reference spectra. 2)HSI data cube (atmospherically corrected to reflectance) with most library spectra collected at other times, locations, and viewing conditions (that is also atmospherically corrected to reflectance). For further details, see **Appendix 18-1** on the support website.

Other possible data inputs could include the results of an initial scene classification or anomaly detection analysis. Output results from signature-based detection are usually displayed in an image or on a map showing the location of the pixels having the spectra of the desired object of interest.

Limitations of signature-based detection include the availability of a reference spectral signature for the object of interest and the quality of the atmospheric correction. Verification and validation of signature-based detection algorithms involve data collections in a well ground-truthed scene where all the locations of all objects of interest are known and documented.

Table 18-3 provides an incomplete list of signature-based detection algorithms and their developers.

Algorithm	Developer
Constrained Energy Minimization (CEM)	ASIT
Spectral Angle Mapper (SAM)	Many developers
Advanced Spectral Identification System–Bloodhound (ASPIS)	APTI
Bands	Applied Analysis Inc.
Pair-wise Adaptive Linear Matched filter algorithm (PALM)	Veridian, now a part of MDA Information Systems
ASIT Signature Based Detection Tool	ASIT

Table 18-3
Signature-based algorithms and associated developers.

Figure 18-8 shows two general approaches to signature-based detection.

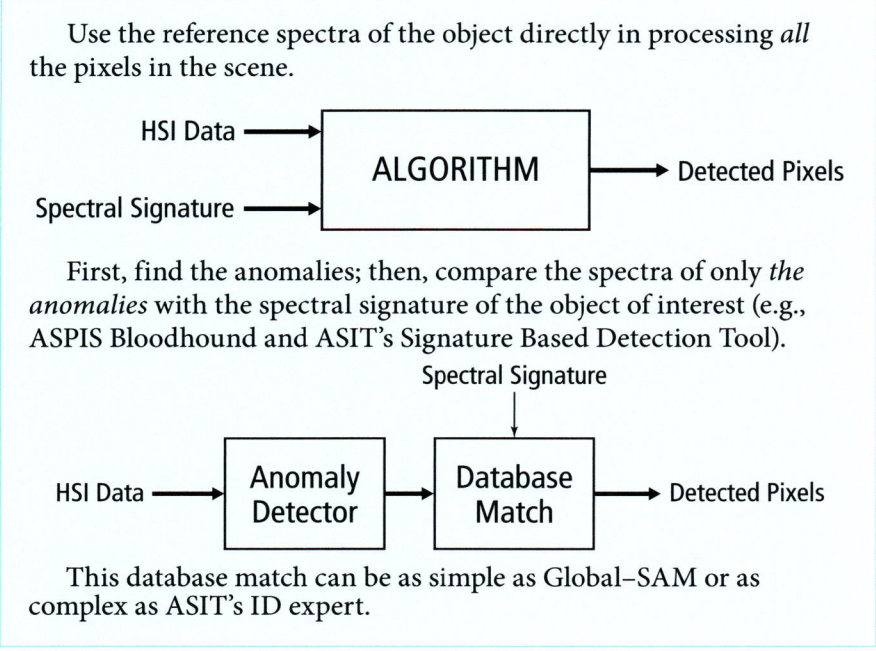

Figure 18-8
Two approaches to signature-based detection.

In one basic type of algorithm, the overall shape of the two spectra (each pixel and reference) are compared using the values in all the spectral bands. SAM places equal emphasis among the spectral bands. Other algorithms, such spectral matched filters (SMF), CEM, and PALM, place more emphasis on some bands over others. In another basic type of algorithm, such as Bands, the location in wavelength of the various features in the two spectra are compared.

While the basic ideas of SAM and spectral feature location (used by Bands) were previously discussed, the ideas behind SMF will be introduced next by comparing it with SAM and as shown in **Figure 18-9**.

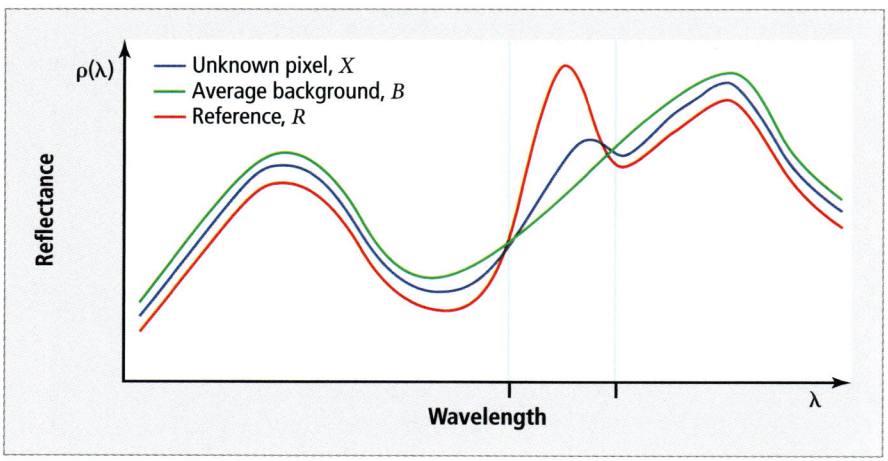

Figure 18-9
Spectra to illustrate differences between SAM and a simple SMF.

With both SMF and SAM, the spectrum X of each unknown pixel is compared with the reference spectrum, R, using all the spectral bands in a computation of the spectral angle between each X and R. For SAM, no one spectral band is emphasized over any other. For the simplest of SMFs where the scene background is characterized by one average spectrum, those spectral bands, where the reference spectrum, R, is different than the background spectrum, are emphasized. This is illustrated in **Figure 18-10**.

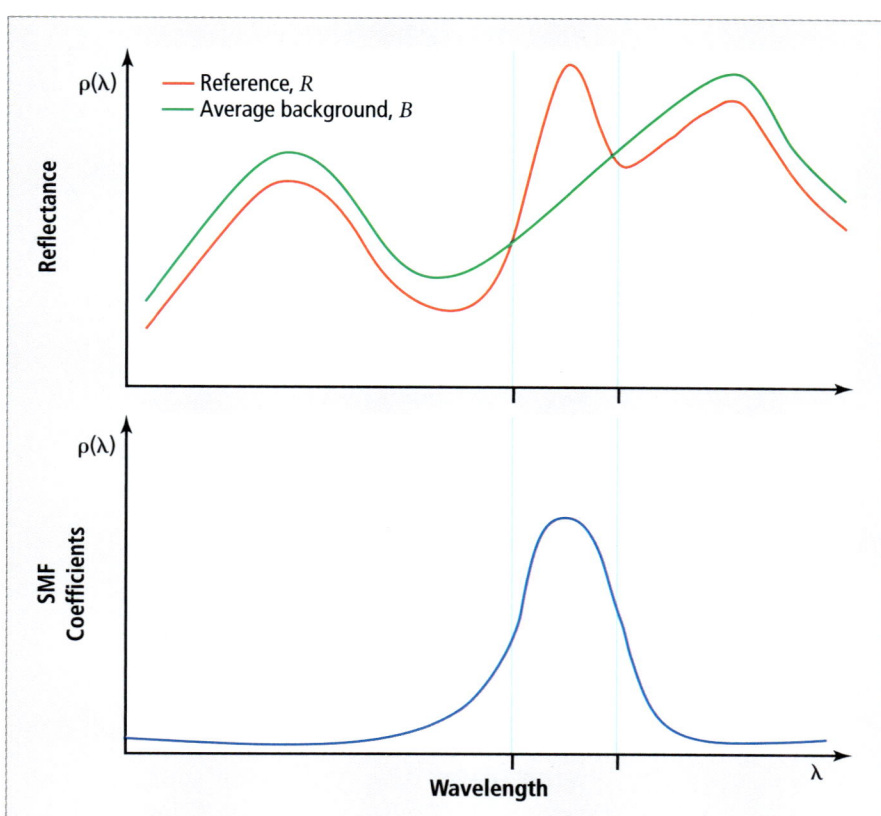

Figure 18-10
Approach to a simple SMF.

Signature-based detection techniques can utilize a combination of several algorithms. The simplest of these combined techniques involves first using anomaly detection with database matching to obtain a possible list of pixels with possible objects of interest and then using a signature-based detection algorithm on the anomalies. This approach is illustrated in **Figure 18-11**.

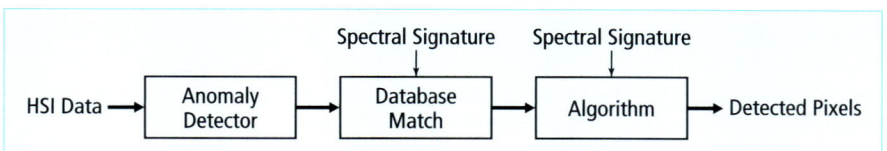

Figure 18-11
Two-step algorithm for signature-based detection.

A more sophisticated combined approach is ASIT's signature-based detection tool illustrated in **Figure 18-12**.

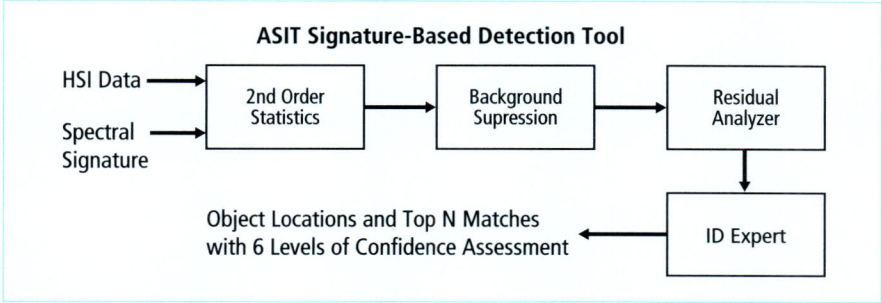

Figure 18-12
Example of a combination algorithm for signature-based detection.

Another combined approach is illustrated in **Figure 18-13**.

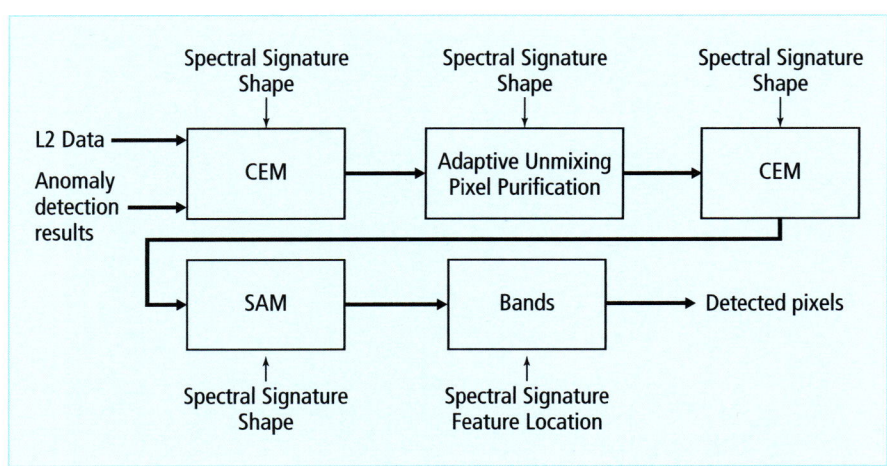

Figure 18-13
A signature-based detection algorithm. [7]

In the empirically developed approach in **Figure 18-13**, several signature-based detection algorithms are used in series to process the HSI data. The philosophy of this approach is to take advantage of each algorithm's strengths and minimize their weaknesses. Each stage takes the results of the previous stage and provides those pixels that may be objects of interest. The final stage, consisting of the Bands algorithm, is the most calculation intensive and provides the final location of pixels that may be objects of interest. In the first stage, the SMF CEM is ran with a rather loose threshold, and a few hundred pixels may be "detected." Then, these pixels are ran through a pixel purification process followed by running CEM with a tighter threshold. The output pixels are then ran through SAM before going through Bands.

ROC CURVES AND THRESHOLDS

After discussing these detection algorithms and spectra comparisons in terms of thresholds, it is time to discuss which values to use. To do this, algorithm performance is discussed in terms of a somewhat standard concept, the Receiver Operating Characteristics (ROC) curve, which is borrowed from the radar community. For a given object type data type (sensor, platform, and collection geometry), algorithm, and choice of thresholds), the number of correctly detected objects and incorrectly detected objects are counted. The probability of detection (Pd) is the ratio of the number of correctly detected objects of interest to the total number of objects in the scene. The probability of false alarms (Pfa) is the ratio of the number of incorrectly detected objects of interest to the total area of the scene. This pair of Pd and Pfa values is a single point on the ROC curve. Such a curve is illustrated in **Figure 18-14**.

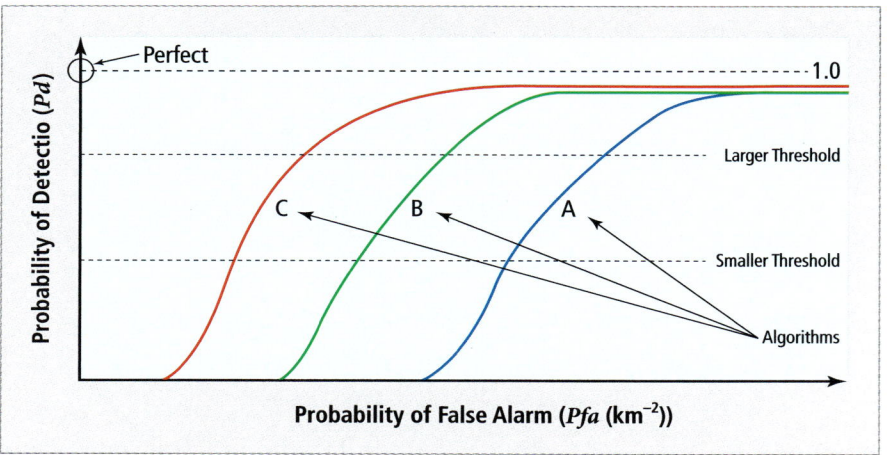

Figure 18-14
ROC curves displaying spectral analysis results.

Now, the thresholds can be varied and the entire process just described can be repeated. Each repetition provides another point on the ROC curve. Clearly, the larger the threshold value, the more detections and false alarms will occur; and conversely, the smaller the threshold value, the fewer detections and false alarms will occur.

The challenge is to find algorithms and thresholds to maximize Pd (values closer to 1.0 are desired) and minimize Pfa (values closer to zero are desired). In **Figure 18-14,** algorithm B applied to the same HSI data set clearly outperforms algorithm A, and algorithm C outperforms algorithm B.

So, for a given data set and analysis approach, which thresholds should be selected and used? In part, the answer reflects the analyst's experience with the data set and algorithm. A larger (loose) threshold provides high Pd, but also increase Pfa. A threshold that is too small (tight) will lower Pd and also Pfa. The application may also play a role in the selection. Suppose aircraft are looking for targets to bomb, such as tanks, and they do not have as many weapons as there are tanks. In this case, a small (tight) threshold provides adequate numbers of targets without many false alarms. In this case, not all the tanks are expected to be found, and if they are, destroyed. Expensive weapons would not be used on false alarms.

There are several issues with the use of ROC curves to characterize algorithm performance on a particular set of data. One such issue is how to score the detection of objects of interest that are large enough to be detected in multiple adjacent pixels. The question is how many of these pixels must be detected in order to declare the object detected. For example, for an object roughly 6 pixels by 4 pixels in size, would detection of five of these pixels constitute detection of the object? Perhaps, or perhaps not. Certainly, methodology must be stated which includes the answer to this question, and this methodology must be applied uniformly throughout the scene. And, this methodology must be documented and reported along with the ROC curve.

Another important issue is the characterization and documentation of the background of the scene. Simple backgrounds can make an algorithm appear ideal, while complex backgrounds using the same objects of interest can make an algorithm appear inadequate. In order to characterize the difficulty of a background, adequate metrics must be used. For sub-pixel objects of interest, simple statistics (such as mean and variance) can be used to characterize the background. For larger multiple pixel objects of interest, a simple statistical description of the background is not adequate. More likely, spatial frequency distributions should be used to characterize the background.

Another more difficult issue is describing the deployment of objects of interest. Tanks parked in the middle of a grassy area are easy to detect using almost any algorithm. But, if these tanks are moved near a forest treeline or into the forest, their detection is more difficult. For reporting ROC curve results, how can the difficulty of target deployment be described or qualified?

There are other critical parameters that can affect algorithm performance:
- The size of an object relative to the size of a pixel.

- The degree of similarity within a group of objects of interest used in a data collection. For example, a group of T-72 tanks found at a particular location may or may not have the same paint, even if they appear the same to the eye.
- Viewing conditions, involving levels of incident radiation and atmospheric effects along the line of sight between the object of interest and the sensor.

Some examples of successful signature detection results are shown in **Figure 18-15** using HSI data in the visible-SWIR collected by the HYDICE sensor in 1993. This collection occurred at the Yuma Proving Grounds, Arizona during a HSI data collection exercise named Desert Radiance. [6] The basic idea of the collection was to lay panels of various material types in three different sizes on the ground in a structured way on the first day. After collection, analysts were told the location of all the panels and used the data to derive in-scene reference spectra for all the materials present. Two days later, HSI data were collected from the same scene, but all the panels were moved and re-arranged in the scene. The analyst's challenge was to use the in-scene reference spectra derived two days earlier to find the various panels in the scene. The detection results for the various material types are shown in **Figure 18-15**. The top image shows the panels on the first day when in-scene "reference" spectra were acquired. The bottom image shows the detected panels on the second day after they were relocated for the algorithm "test."

Figure 18-15
Spectral detection of various materials. [6]

- Desert BDU (light)
- Desert BDU (heavy)
- Cotton BDU (green)
- Nylon BDU (woodland)
- Cotton/nylon BDU (woodland)
- Tan vinyl
- Rust plastic
- Fiberglass (dark brown)
- Foam rubber
- Tan plastic

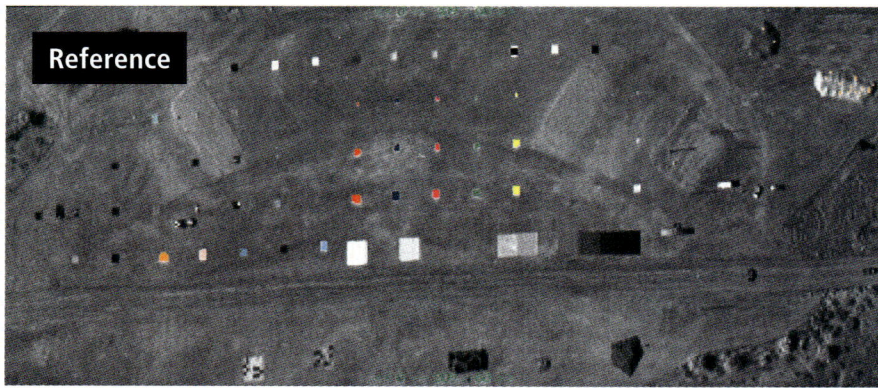

SPECTRAL LIBRARIES

Libraries of reference spectra play a vital role for spectral analysis. Sources of reference spectra are numerous and varied. Spectral irradiance of identified pixels in a scene can be used without further processing as a reference spectrum within the same (or similar) scenes. Usually, these scene spectral measurements along with similar ground (field) and laboratory measurements used as reference spectra have been corrected to reflectivity (or emissivity) as a function of wavelength. To obtain these spectra, the irradiance data must be processed with the sensor calibration factors as well as atmospheric correction. These reference reflectance (or emissivity) spectra can then be used in the analysis of any other collected spectral data regardless of the sensor and viewing geometry as long as this data have also been converted to reflectance.

Over the past 30 years, many spectral measurements have been made involving a wide variety of people, techniques, instruments, and collection conditions. Many measurements lack complete documentation. They range from a single curve of reflectivity versus wavelength and the words "camouflage net" to well-documented digital data complete with a chemical analysis of the sample measured. Yet, even in the latter case, the documentation suffers from the "big picture" of what it and related spectra represent. For example, **Figure 18-16** plots the infrared spectra of two samples of minerals with different chemical composition.

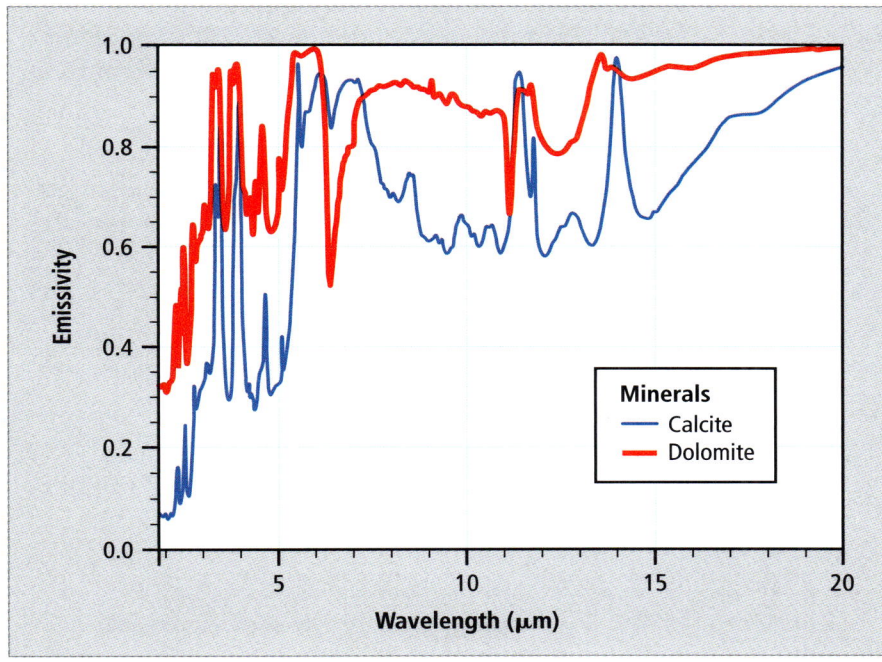

Figure 18-16
Spectra of two mineral types.

Chemical analyses and location of each of these two samples are documented, as well as the measurement instrumentation and techniques. However, the samples lack information regarding the applicability of a particular sample and spectrum from a specific location (usually in the US) to that in another part of the world.

Aging asphalt, paints, and other materials can produce very large spectral variations at wavelengths from 1.5–2.5 μm. (This is not surprising. Recall in the visible, newly paved asphalt looks dark and it lightens to a grey after several years.) So which spectrum should an analyst use when looking at asphalt in foreign countries? One opinion suggests trying to select the most appropriate spectrum based on the limited information known about that country. Another opinion suggests using all the spectra in the library for asphalt and consider the amount of variation in results from spectral analysis for each choice of asphalt spectrum.

Another issue is the wide variety of existing spectral databases. Some are searchable and some are not. Some exist in soft copy and others only in hard copy. Some are available at no cost and some charge a fee for access. Some are classified, but many others are not.

There are additional issues in the use of a spectral library. While spectra in most databases represent a single material type, many objects of interest are composed of multiple material types (camouflage nets, trucks, crops, etc.). The pixel size of most measurements is sufficiently large to allow one or more materials in many of the pixels covering the object of interest.

Another issue is dealing with multiple spectra of the same reported object or material made on different samples at different times, locations, and viewing geometries. For example, there may be up to 40 different documented measurements of the paint on a T-72 tank. One solution is to develop an "exemplar," a composite of all the existing spectra of the object in which all the instrumental effects from each measurement have been removed. [6] While early successes have been demonstrated for some objects, more need to be considered.

The analyst must address another issue when a known reference spectrum for the object of interest does not exist. Currently, two possible approaches are: 1) use several reference spectra for objects "similar" to the object of interest; or 2) use a "generic" spectrum indicative of the object of interest.

While the results of spectral analysis can sometimes completely solve intelligence problems, typically they are used in combination with other forms of sensing data or their products. The recipe for combining the various forms of data and their products varies with the type of application as well as the situation within each type. Listed below are examples of such combinations of data and products.

- Spectral anomaly detection results and broadband visible imagery:
  - For a large number of detected pixels clustered on an object in an open field, hyperspectral anomaly detection cues visible imagery analysts.
  - For several pixels on an object in thin foliage, hyperspectral anomaly detections can receive improved confidence of the presence of an object from visible imagery.
  - For one pixel on an object in thick foliage, hyperspectral detections receive minimal help from visible imagery.
- Spectral signature-based detection and radar imagery:
  - Spectral can only detect the type of paint used on objects, not the presence of the object itself. For example, spectral can only detect a camouflage net and maybe the paint underneath it.
  - Coincident spectral and radar detection improves the confidence of each.
    - For spectral detection, radar adds that the possible object is metallic with approximate shape or size information.
    - For radar detection, spectral adds that the possible object has appropriate military paint.
- Spectral detection combined with other detection phenomenology:
  - Spectral signature-based detection can identify the outer layer of an object and thermal imagery can provide some indication of material type or sources of heat inside the object.

18.3 SPACEBORNE HSI SENSORS

Four satellite HSI sensors discussed include the following: 1) Hyperion on National Aeronautics and Space Administration (NASA) EO-1; 2) Warfighter on Orbview 4; 3) Advanced Responsive Tactically Effective Military Imaging Spectrometer (ARTEMIS) on Air Force TacSat 3; and 4) Coastal Ocean Imaging Spectrometer (COIS) on Naval Earth Map Observer (NEMO).

Hyperion on NASA EO-1 was launched on November 12, 2000 and collection operations continue today. This sensor was built by TRW, Inc. as a descendent of the airborne NVIS sensor and the NASA Lewis satellite which failed on-orbit soon after launch. Warfighter on the Orbview 4 satellite was launched on September 21, 2001, failed to orbit, and dropped into the Pacific Ocean near Vandenberg Air Force Base. Warfighter was co-sponsored by the Air Force Research Laboratory (AFRL) at Kirtland Air Force Base, New Mexico and Orbital Sciences Corporation. ARTEMIS was launched in May 2009 aboard the Air Force TacSat 3 satellite. Collection operations ceased on February 15, 2012, and the satellite decayed in the Earth's atmosphere on April 30, 2012. It was another Warfighter-like effort sponsored by AFRL. COIS was built, but the satellite never launched due to lack of funding. It was co-sponsored by NRL, Office of Naval Research (ONR), DARPA, and an industrial consortium. [8], [9], [10], [11]

All four spectrometers used gratings and collected HSI data in pushbroom mode. In all cases, small two-dimensional FPAs were used. The advantage of these spectrometers was their compact design with no moving parts (hence, low cost). The disadvantages were their FPA size (limited swath width and number of spectral bands) and FSR issues.

Each of the spectrometers had varying spectral bandpasses achieved by one or more gratings and FPAs. In particular, Hyperion and COIS had two gratings and two FPAs (silicon for the visible-Near Infrared (vis-NIR) and HgCdTe for the SWIR). Warfighter had three gratings and three FPAs (silicon for the vis-NIR, HgCdTe for the SWIR, and HgCdTe to overlap the two previous). ARTEMIS had one grating and one FPA (HgCdTe for the visible through the SWIR). More specific details about spectral coverage of each of these spectrometers is listed in **Table 18-4**.

System	Spectral region (μm)	Number of bands	Average width of each band (nm)
Hyperion	Vis-NIR (0.40–1.0)	60	10
	SWIR (0.9–2.5)	160	10
Warfighter	VIS (0.45–0.905)	40	11.4
	NIR (0.83–1.74)	80	11.4
	SWIR (1.58–2.49)	80	11.4
	*MWIR (3.00–5.00)	80	25.0
ARTEMIS	VIS-SWIR (0.4–2.5)	400	5
COIS/NEMO	Vis-NIR (0.4–1.0)	60	10
	SWIR (1.0–2.5)	150	10

* Abandoned before launch

Table 18-4
Sensor characteristics of satellite-borne HSI systems. [8], [9], [10], [11]

Pixel size for these systems is driven by the sponsor's mission. NASA's Hyperion has 30 m pixels because of its R&D mission for worldwide surveys of land use. The NASA EO-1 satellite has an advanced Landsat sensor prototype as its primary sensor and flies formation with Landsat 7. The DOD's interest in Hyperion for terrain categorization increased after the launch failure of the Orbview 4 satellite which carried Warfighter. Warfighter had a pixel size of 8 m driven by Army and Air Force interest primarily in the demonstration of the detection of large mobile military vehicles, such as missile transporter erector launchers(TELs), tanks, and high-mobility multipurpose wheeled vehicles (HMMWVs). The Navy NEMO sensor aboard their COIS satellite had a pixel size of 30 or 60 m because of their interest in worldwide littoral mapping, including bathymetry and shoreline terrain classification.

There are two consequences of such large pixels. First, most pixels are mixed; hence, algorithm performance is degraded even for terrain classification. End-member selection is more difficult. There are fewer pixels on target for false alarm reduction in signature-based detection. Also, there is a basic trade-off between cost (driven by FPA size in terms of numbers of detectors), ground pixel size, and area coverage. Values for the swath width, which are driven by ground pixel size and FPA size, are given in **Table 18-5** for each of the spectrometers.

Table 18-5 Values for swath width. [8], [9], [10], [11]

System	Pixel size (m)	Swath Width	
		Pixels	km
Hyperion	30	256	7.5
Warfighter	8	640	5.1
COIS/NEMO	30	1000	30

19 HSI IN THE THERMAL INFRARED

Continuing from the last chapter, the discussion of specific Hyperspectral Imaging (HSI) sensors, applications, and algorithms continues into the thermal infrared where exploitation and research and development (R&D) activities have been less than that in the visible to Shortwave Infrared (SWIR). This is a result of the emphasis and investment by the commercial market for silicon Focal Plane Arrays (FPAs) and the requirement (until very recently) for detectors operating in the thermal infrared to be cooled to cryogen temperatures to ensure low dark current and optimum performance.

SECTIONS

19.1 APPLICATIONS
19.2 HSI SENSORS
19.3 ALGORITHMS AND APPLICATIONS

19.1 APPLICATIONS

The use of HSI in the thermal infrared (Mid-Wave Infrared (MWIR) and Long-Wave Infrared (LWIR)) provides some unique contributions to military and intelligence community problems as well as civilian applications. These are listed below.

- Atmospheric sounding (see **Chapter 16**)
- Ground objects
    - Surface temperature determination (improved accuracy over a single broadband sensor) (see **Chapter 16**)
    - Day and night object detection (and identification)
    - Some contributions to scene classification (see **Chapter 15**)
        □ Soil/mineral identification
        □ Soil moisture
    - Disturbed soil
- Gas detection (and identification) (see **Chapter 20**)
    - Chemical, biological, and nuclear agent use on the battlefield
    - Facility exhaust plumes

A major military thermal sensing problem involves nighttime object detection and identification. Currently, many military weapon delivery systems (aircraft, tanks, and helicopters) use broadband imagers in the LWIR, and more recently in the MWIR, to find targets to attack. Such systems are often referred to as Forward Looking InfraRed sensors (FLIRs). The basis for the problem is shown in **Figure 19-1** where the spectral radiances (and temperatures) are compared for a tank (with camouflage paint) in direct sunlight, grass in direct sunlight, and the tank and grass in shade. In this comparison, assume both the tank and the nearby grass have the same temperature at sun-up and their surface emissivities across the spectral bandpass are both equal to unity.

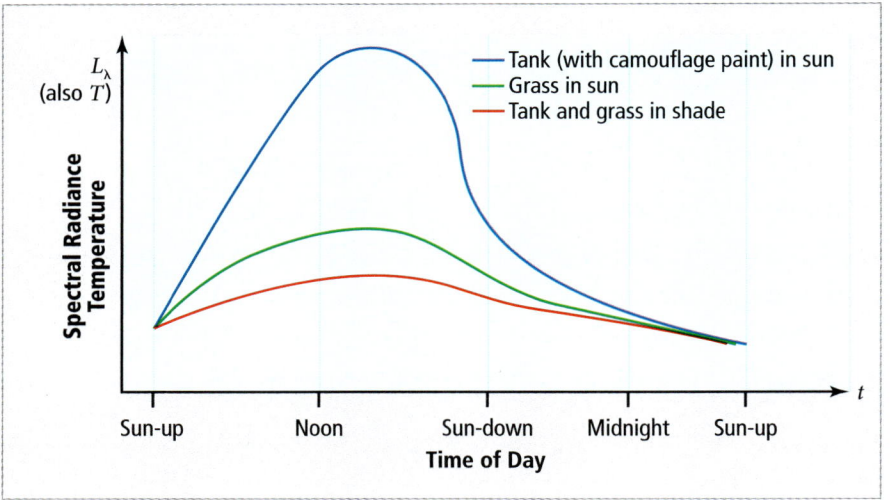

Figure 19-1
Heating and cooling of various objects throughout the day assuming they all have the same temperature at sun-up.

First, consider the tank and the nearby grass that are both in direct sunlight. After sun-up, the temperature of tank surface increases more rapidly than the grass, because although the tank is massive, it is not as massive as the Earth to which the grass is attached. In the afternoon, there can be as much as a 20 to 30 K difference between the surface of the tank and the grass. Around sunset in the evening, both the tank and the grass start to cool, and the difference between their temperatures becomes smaller and smaller. A few hours before dawn, this temperature difference becomes less than a few degrees. While such a temperature difference is detectable, finding the tank may be more difficult amid other objects (other camouflage-painted vehicles, rocks, patches of bare earth, etc.) that are also slightly warmer than the grass.

If the tank and the grass are in the shade, the temperature increase is not as significant during the day, and there is minimal temperature difference throughout the day and night. It may not be obvious that a tank and grass nearby could be in shade all day. But consider as an example, these objects positioned on the north side of a tall building or grove of trees somewhere in the Northern Hemisphere at latitudes above 23 degrees N. Throughout the day and the various seasons, the sun is never directly overhead.

A more complicated comparison is shown in **Figure 19-2**. Again, the same objects are compared as before with their surface emissivities both equal to unity. But now, at sun-up, assume the grass is slightly warmer than the tank.

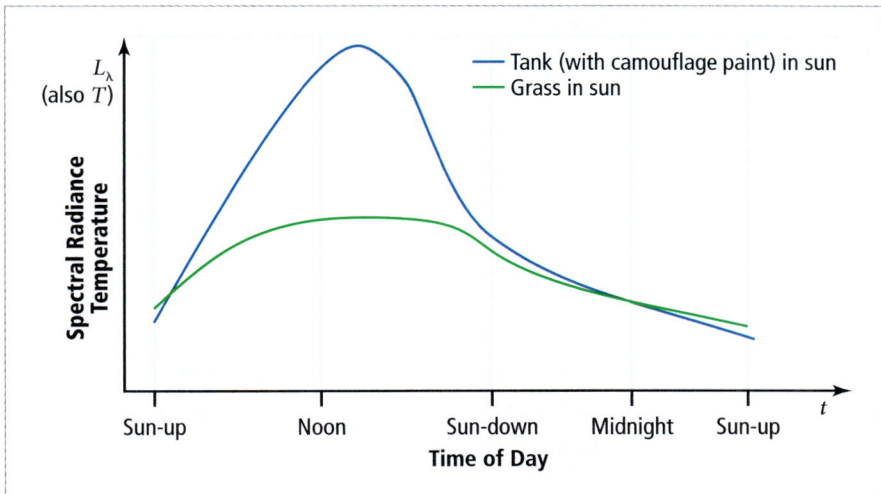

Figure 19-2
Heating and cooling of the tank in grass throughout the day if the tank is slightly cooler at sun-up than the grass.

Thus, shortly after sun-up, the rapid warming of the tank causes its temperature to surpass that of the grass. Then long after sunset, the tank temperature drops below that of the grass. At sun-up, the tank is very detectable (although in negative contrast with the background grass). But at the two times when their temperatures are the same, referred to as thermal cross-over, detection of the tank is impossible.

Another application is the identification of minerals, which contributes to terrain categorization as well as other agricultural and resource assessment applications. An example of the spectrum of sandy soil is shown in **Figure 19-3**.

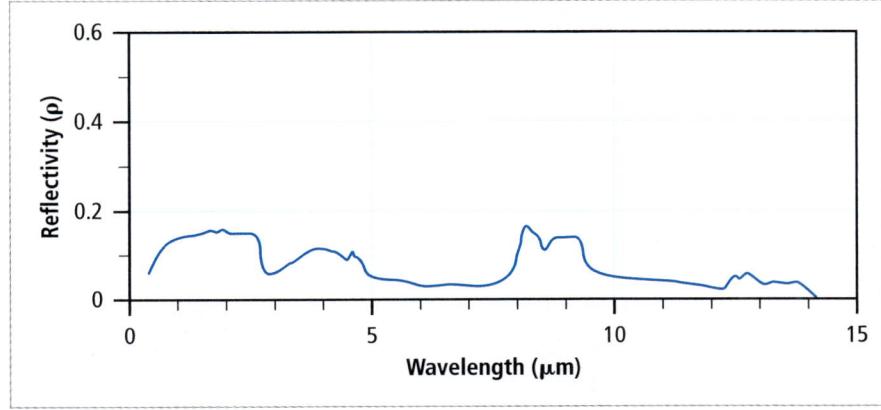

Figure 19-3
Spectrum of sandy soil in the infrared. [1]

In this example, the strong quartz component of the soil is evident from a quartz characteristic spectral feature occurring between 8 and 9.5 μm.

These spectral features in the LWIR afford the capability to detect disturbed earth. The basis for this capability is shown in **Figure 19-4** for sandy soil. [1]

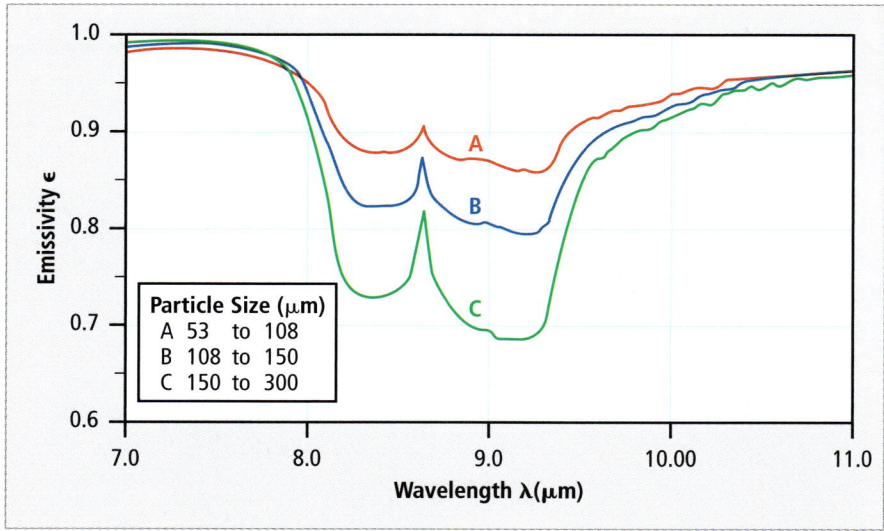

Figure 19-4
LWIR emissivity of quartz particles of various sizes. [1]

The spectra for quartz particles of various sizes are shown. The cause for the differences in the size of the quartz feature (shown in emissivity rather than reflectance in **Figure 19-3**) is illustrated in **Figure 19-5**. [2]

Figure 19-5
Illustration of how particle size affects reflectivity (and hence emissivity). [2]

Light at LWIR wavelengths incident on a surface larger than the wavelength tends to reflect specularly if the surface is smooth. For larger soil particles, incident light has a chance to reflect back to the sensor after reflecting off one or two soil particles. For smaller soil particles, some of the incident light may reflect off several particles on its way to the sensor. With each reflection off a particle, there is some absorption. So, more reflections result in less light reflected overall and a higher apparent emissivity. Disturbed soil generally has more small, or fine, soil particles at the surface compared to undisturbed soil. This results from the fact that on undisturbed soil surfaces, wind tends to blow away these fine particles, and rain tends to wash them away or carry them down beneath the surface. In some arid areas, this surface effect has been detectable with HSI in the LWIR at some locations for over six months after the surface was disturbed.

19.2 HSI SENSORS

Two airborne R&D/demonstration families of HSI sensors that were funded and flown by the American and Canadian defense communities are considered: Spatially Enhanced Broadband Array Spectrograph System (SEBASS) and Hyper-Cam, respectively.

These families of thermal infrared HSI sensors are dramatically different: SEBASS is a pushbroom (sometimes called a whiskbroom) scanner designed for nighttime target detection with emphasis on high signal-to-noise. Hyper-Cam is a staring Fourier Transform Spectrometer (FTS) designed with the emphasis on high spectral resolution. A further comparison of these two sensors is shown in **Table 19-1**.

Table 19-1
Comparison of SEBASS and Hyper-Cam sensor parameters. [3], [4], [5], [6]

	SEBASS	Hyper-Cam
Spectral region	MWIR and LWIR	MWIR and LWIR
Spectral bands	128 each region	Up to 1600
Dispersive device	Prism	FTIR
Selectable spectral resolution	Fixed	Variable
Spectral resolution	25 and 50 nm	$0.25–150\ cm^{-1}$
FPA type	Si:As	InSb and HgCdTe
FPA size	128 × 128 each region	320 × 256
FPA operating temperature	10 K	70 K
Pixel FOV	1.0 mrad	0.35 mrad

Two striking differences between the two sensors are the smaller pixel Field of View (FOV) and enhanced spectral resolution for Hyper-Cam. This is understandable because of the unique characteristics of a FTS: good spectral resolution along with large throughput.

The SEBASS family of sensors involves prisms and primarily pushbroom scans. When originally designed, gratings for the LWIR did not perform as well as they do today. Originally fielded by Aerospace Corp., El Segundo, California, aboard their own Twin-Otter aircraft, this sensor has found residence on several other platforms collecting against various vehicles and gaseous objects of interest. [3], [4]

Since Hyper-Cam is a staring system, significant forward motion compensation is required so each ground pixel remains fixed during a collection. To accomplish this as well as sensor pointing stabilization against aircraft vibration, a rather elaborate pointing, tracking, and stabilization system was required and built with demonstrated pointing stability of 0.79 pixels. Developed and built by Telops Inc., Quebec, Canada, Hyper-Cam has provided airborne HSI of experimental targets set up by Defence R&D Canada-Valcartier as well as gas releases at industrial sites. [5], [6]

A satellite-borne HSI sensor in the MWIR and LWIR as well as SWIR is the advanced atmospheric sounder Cross-track Infrared Sounder (CrIS) which was launched in October 2011 on the National Polar-orbiting Partnership satellite. This is a R&D/demonstration effort for possible new sensors on future meteorological satellites. CrIS was initially mentioned in **Chapter 16** in terms of the improvements it would provide to the atmospheric sounding capability now provided by Multispectral Imaging (MSI) in the MWIR and LWIR. Here, CrIS, a form of FTS, is compared with Hyper-Cam in **Table 19-2**. [5], [6], [7], [8]

Table 19-2 CrIS and Hyper-Cam sensor parameters.

	CrIS	Hyper-Cam
Spectral region	SWIR, MWIR, LWIR	MWIR and LWIR
Spectral bands	159, 433, 713	Up to 1600
Dispersive device	FTIR	FTIR
Selectable resolution	Fixed	Variable
Spectral resolution	2.5, 1.25, 0.625 cm^{-1}	0.25–150 cm^{-1}
FPA type	HgCdTe	InSb and HgCdTe
FPA size (detectors)	3 × 3 each region	320 × 256
FPA operating temperature	98 K, 98 K, 81 K	70 K
Pixel FOV	16.8 mrad	0.35 mrad

19.3 ALGORITHMS AND APPLICATIONS

HSI data in the MWIR-LWIR is very different than in the visible-SWIR. Recall the radiation coming from any object of interest can always be a combination of thermal emission and reflectance of the radiation coming from some other source (**Figure 19-6**).

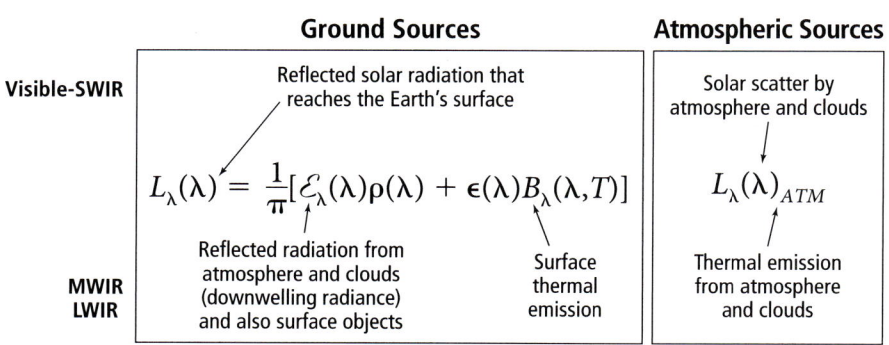

Figure 19-6 Sources of radiation received by the sensor.

In addition, unlike the visible where the sun is the dominant source of radiation for objects to reflect, the thermal emission of every object in the scene and the atmosphere becomes potential sources of radiation for objects to reflect. The resulting scene differences between the visible-SWIR and MWIR-LWIR are summarized in **Table 19-3**.

Table 19-3 Scene differences between the visible-SWIR and MWIR-LWIR.

	Visible-SWIR	MWIR-LWIR
Radiation source	Sun primarily	All objects
Radiation processes	Reflective	Thermal emissive and reflective
Scene content		
Spatial structure	Segmented	Homogenous mixture
Components	Major segment types: Sunlit and shadow backgrounds	Object types: Natural—mostly emissive Man-made—part emissive, part reflective Any object may vary in temperature across the scene
Algorithm challenge	Identify segments Treat each type separately Identify by spectral reflectance differences (often large)	Remove temperature effects in scene Identify by spectral emissivity differences (often small)

In visible-SWIR imagery, there are often large areas (segments) that appear as different materials because of the large inherent differences in reflectance between materials. Additional segments may also be shadowed areas. In the MWIR-LWIR, these segments may appear nearly the same because of similar emissivities (e.g., grass lands and nearby lakes). The dominant cause of variability within the scene may be temperature variability within a particular material type. For example, small patches of sparse grass might have pixels that include larger amounts of soil. While these pixels will have slightly different emissivities than areas of thick grass, they will appear different in the MWIR-LWIR primarily because of their higher temperature, a result of the large differences of reflectance at wavelengths in the visible-SWIR. So, the challenge for HSI data analysts is to remove (or suppress) the temperature effects in the scene, so material emissivity differences are apparent and allow for material identification.

First, the HSI data in the MWIR-LWIR must be converted to spectral radiance using either atmospheric correction or in-scene calibration techniques (as discussed in **Appendix 18-1** on the support website). Then, to reduce the data to a scene emissivity map, scene temperature effects must be removed or suppressed, or temperature and emissivity effects must be separated.

One approach to separate temperature and emissivity is emissivity normalization. For each ground pixel, the Planck function (assuming emissivity is equal to one) is used to determine a possible pixel temperature from each of the measured spectral radiance values. The largest value is used under the assumption that the emissivity in that spectral band is closest to one. This may not be true. Thus, the temperature determined may be a lower bound to the actual pixel temperature. (Note, the above procedure was discussed in **Chapter 16** for determining pixel temperature from MSI data.) From the ground pixel temperature values, the emissivity function values can be calculated for each spectral band from the measured spectral radiance values for that pixel.

One approach to scene temperature removal (or suppression) utilizes spectral band correlation when spectral radiance differences between pixels in a region of the scene are dominated by temperature differences (rather than emissivity differences). Spectral radiance values dominated by thermal emission are given by the formula below,

$$L_\lambda(\lambda) = \frac{1}{\pi}[\epsilon(\lambda)B_\lambda(\lambda,T)] \left[\frac{W}{m^2 sr \cdot \mu m}\right]. \qquad (19\text{-}1)$$

The Planck function is certainly not linear with temperature, T, over significant ranges in value of T, but over smaller variations of T, it is approximately linear with T. Hence, the scatter plot using the images in two adjacent spectral bands of a scene containing two background materials A and B might appear as shown in **Figure 19-7**.

Rather than the pixel values for materials A and B forming roughly circular blobs as they would with sufficiently small ground pixel sizes and HSI data in the visible-SWIR, they are more cigar-shaped, exhibiting the temperature variation of pixels of material types A and B. Now, if the HSI data are portrayed in an image in a feature space defined by $L_\lambda(\lambda_2) - L_\lambda(\lambda_1)$,

Figure 19-7
Scatterplot of scene pixels for two spectral bands in the LWIR (compare with **Figure 15-15** for a scene in the visible-SWIR.).

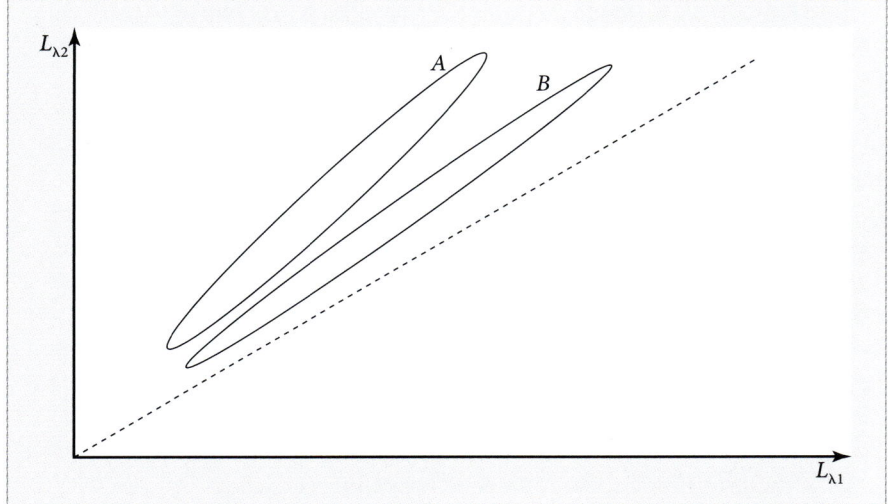

the pixel radiation in the scene composed of materials A and B would often be suppressed. Objects that are not made of materials A or B may remain bright in the scene. If materials A and B constitute the background in the scene, the remaining bright objects may be of interest to the analyst.

Once the image has been converted to an emissivity map or the background has been suppressed, some sort of signature based detection algorithm can be applied. An example is the spectral matched filter (Environmental Research Institute of Michigan (ERIM) in Michigan (acquired by MDA Information Systems) and Aerospace Corporation in El Segundo, California).

A signature based detection algorithm, introduced in **Chapter 18**, is shown again in **Figure 19-8**.

Figure 19-8
A signature based detection algorithm applied in the LWIR (first shown as **Figure 18-13**). (CEM = Constrained Energy Minimization. SAM = Spectral Angle Mapper.)

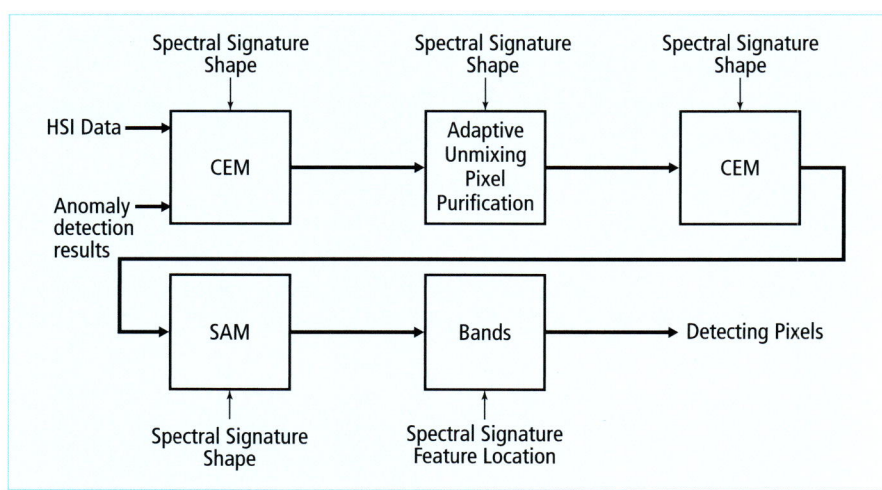

While this algorithm was developed for analysis of HSI data in the visible-SWIR, it was used on HSI data in the MWIR-LWIR with moderate success. In the pixel purification step, the complication of background interaction with the object of interest can sometimes be more severe in the MWIR-LWIR than in the visible-SWIR. This effect is illustrated in **Figure 19-9**.

416 CHAPTER 19 HSI IN THE THERMAL INFRARED

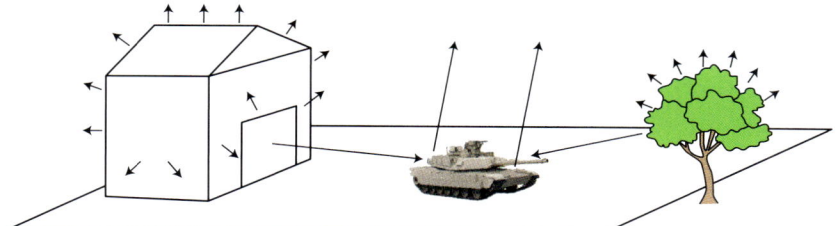

Figure 19-9
Interaction of the object of interest with nearby background.

In the visible-SWIR, the effect results from solar irradiance onto background objects near the object of interest with some of the radiation reflected by the background onto the object of interest and then in the direction of the sensor line of sight. In the MWIR-LWIR, the effect results from background objects near the object of interest thermally emitting radiation with some of it reflected by the object of interest in the direction of the sensor line of sight. In either case, this interaction of the background with the object of interest makes it more difficult to remove the appropriate amount of background in the pixel purification process.

20 HSI GAS DETECTION INCLUDING IDENTIFICATION

Hyperspectral Imaging (HSI) for gas detection was initiated by the Environmental Protection Agency (EPA) to help monitor industrial pollution of gases and aerosols. In the past 20 years, the remote sensing community has became interested in this capability to detect and identify discharges of these gases and aerosols to help identify the production processes occurring at various industrial facilities.

Ground-based HSI for chemical agent gas detection on the battlefield has been available to the US Army for over 20 years. Improvements in this sensing capability have continued to provide greater detection range and battlefield mapping capabilities.

Active ground-based spectral sensing using lasers has been investigated for over 20 years with the goal of longer-range detection of chemical agents as well as biological agents on the battlefield.

SECTIONS

20.1 AIRBORNE HSI FOR GAS DETECTION

20.2 GROUND-BASED HSI FOR GAS DETECTION

20.3 ACTIVE SPECTRAL SENSING FOR GAS AND AEROSOL DETECTION

20.1 AIRBORNE HSI FOR GAS DETECTION

The viewing geometry and some generic spectra for such an airborne HSI system are illustrated in **Figure 20-1**, as might be applied against the smokestack plumes in the introductory picture.

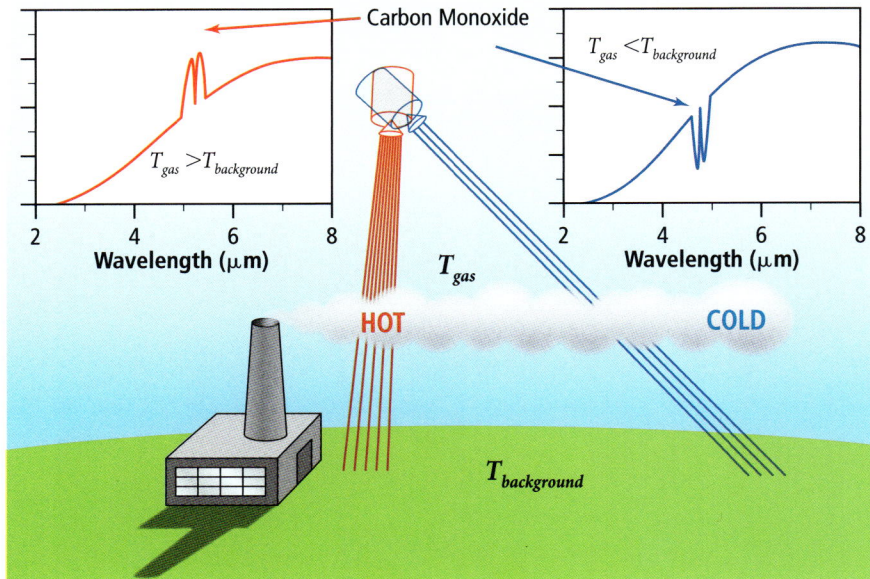

Figure 20-1
Viewing geometry and generic spectra for spectral collection from industrial facilities.

In this viewing scenario, the background is characterized by a surface temperature, T_{BACK}, and a constant emissivity, $\epsilon = 1.0$. Initially, the gas exhausted from the smokestack may be higher in temperature than that of the background. In this case, the received spectral irradiance will have two components: blackbody radiation from the background and small gas *emission* features with location and magnitude that are characteristic of the gas or gases that are exhausted. After release, the gas cloud will expand and cool to air temperature, which may be lower than the background. In this case, the received spectral irradiance will again have two different components: blackbody radiation from the background and small gas *absorption* features with location and magnitude that are characteristic of the gas or gases exhausted. An example of a collection from a test release is shown in **Figure 20-2**, where the background has been subtracted. The collected spectra show the presence of three gases, SF_6, CH_3Cl, and SO_2, where SF_6 is a commonly released test gas because it has a very strong spectral feature in the Long-Wave Infrared (LWIR).

The previous discussion describes the simplest ($\epsilon_{BACK} = 1.0$) of the possible scenarios, because in reality the emissivity of the background may be a constant less than one, or it may vary across the wavelength region considered. All three cases will now be discussed and compared. To assist this discussion, the spectral radiance of a gas cloud and the background are considered in **Equation 20-1**, in which the spectral radiance from the background is *modified by its transmission through* the gas cloud.

$$L_\lambda(\lambda) \approx L_\lambda(\lambda)_{BKG}\,\tau(\lambda)_{GAS} + L_\lambda(\lambda)_{GAS} \left[\frac{W}{m^2 sr \cdot \mu m}\right]. \quad (20\text{-}1)$$

After inserting the appropriate Planck functions and emissivities for the spectral radiances of the background and the gas cloud, **Equation 20-1** becomes:

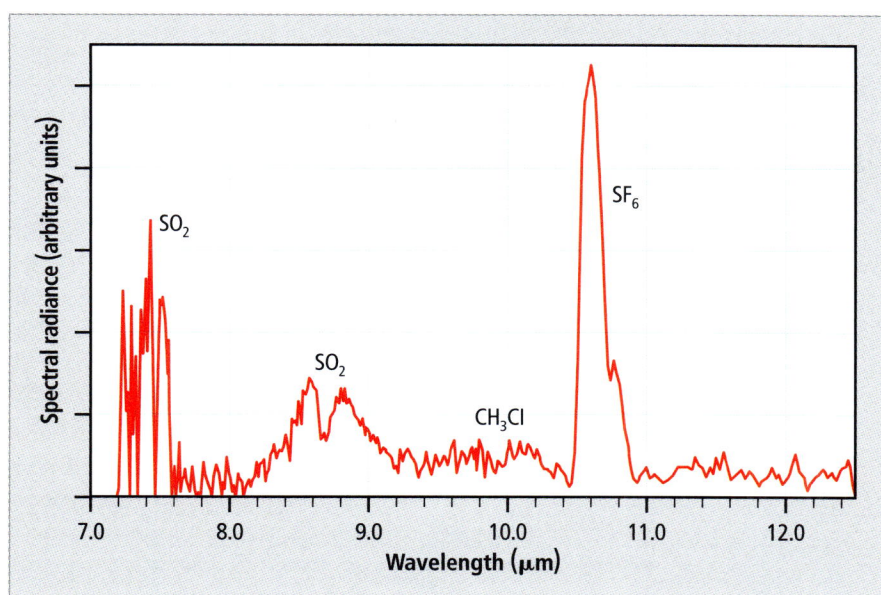

Figure 20-2
Example of the spectrum of test release of gases showing emissions from sulfur dioxide (SO_2), methyl chloride (CH_3Cl), and sulfur hexafluoride (SF_6).

$$\pi L_\lambda(\lambda) \approx \epsilon(\lambda)_{BKG} B_\lambda(\lambda, T_{BKG})\left[1 - \epsilon(\lambda)_{GAS}\right] + \epsilon(\lambda)_{GAS} B_\lambda(\lambda, T_{GAS}) \quad \left[\frac{W}{m^2 \mu m}\right]. \tag{20-2}$$

After re-arranging the various terms, **Equation 20-2** becomes:

$$\pi L_\lambda(\lambda) \approx \epsilon(\lambda)_{BKG} B_\lambda(\lambda, T_{BKG}) + \epsilon(\lambda)_{GAS}\left[B_\lambda(\lambda, T_{GAS}) - \epsilon(\lambda)_{BKG} B_\lambda(\lambda, T_{BKG})\right] \quad \left[\frac{W}{m^2 \mu m}\right]. \tag{20-3}$$

Of special interest in **Equation 20-3** is the difference in the square brackets. It explains the results for the three cases listed in **Table 20-1**.

Case	$\epsilon(\lambda)_{BACK}$	Condition	Result
Case 1	$\epsilon(\lambda)_{BACK} = 1.0$	$T_{GAS} > T_{BACK}$	Gas emission
		$T_{GAS} < T_{BACK}$	Gas absorption
Case 2	$\epsilon(\lambda)_{BACK} < 1.0$ but constant	$T_{GAS} > T_{BACK}$	Gas emission
		$T_{GAS} < T_{BACK}$	Gas emission or absorption depending on value of $\epsilon(\lambda)_{BACK}$
Case 3	$\epsilon(\lambda)_{BACK} < 1.0$ not constant		Spectral features introduced and the results of Cases 1 and 2 must be applied on a wavelength by wavelength basis.

Table 20-1
Three cases for gas conditions after release from an industrial facility.

Equation 20-3 shows both the background contribution to the spectral radiance as well as the gas cloud contribution. In Case 1, because the background emissivity $\epsilon = 1.0$, the difference in the square brackets is a straight comparison of the temperatures of the gas cloud and the background. So, when the gas is warmer than the background, the difference is positive (gas emission), and when the gas is cooler than the background, the difference is negative (gas absorption).

In Case 2, the background emissivity is a constant with a value less than one. Again, if the gas is warmer than the background, the difference is positive (gas emission). But, if the gas is cooler than the background, the difference depends on the numerical value of the background emissivity (gas emission or gas absorption). In fact, if the background is not spatially uniform (the situation in most industrial facilities), the gas cloud far from the smokestack may appear as emission in some locations and absorption in others.

The most difficult case is Case 3, in which the background emissivity is a function of wavelength. However, the gas emission can shift back and forth between emission and absorption at a given location as the emissivity varies with wavelength.

Early analysis developmental work involved controlled gas releases and airborne HSI collections following the work of the EPA. Most of these were performed at the Department of Energy (DOE) Nonproliferation Test and Evaluation Complex, located within the DOE Nevada Test Site (NTS). This facility consists of a single, tall smoke stack, where one to four gases may be released, each at a constant rate. About fifty possible gases could be released with the EPA's approval. In addition, ground truth and analysis support data (meteorology, release rates, and ground-based spectral measurements) were readily available. [1]

In most of these releases and spectral data collections, gases with relatively strong spectral bands in the LWIR were detected and identified. A few crude attempts were made to quantify the relative abundance of the released gases.

In addition to several years of success at NTS, spectral data collections have been made at existing facilities within the US, such as oil refineries. [2] The complexity of these scenarios presents challenges for the spectral data analysts. Unlike a single smokestack at a known location with a uniform background, actual chemical facilities, like the one shown in this chapter's introductory picture, present several complexities. Actual chemical production facilities have multiple ongoing production processes and multiple gas release points. These may not be only smokestacks, but also roof vents and plumbing leaks. The backgrounds around a release point in a chemical production plant are spatially complex with various materials present.[1] Often, there are not any pixels near a plume that do not contain the gases and have the same background as those pixels under the plume. Many production processes do not release gases at a constant rate. Ground truth and analysis support data are usually not available within a chemical plant. Often wind and temperature patterns and fluctuations are poorly known within the plant and do not relate well to those prevailing outside the plant. Release rates of many exhaust gases are unknown to plant managers unless these gases are on the EPA's toxic release inventory of harmful gases. Because of these complexities, gas cloud detection and identification algorithms have undergone dramatic modifications with a limited degree of success.

Two early approaches were successful on the spectral data from the early NTS gas releases. One approach was basically the same approach used to detect and identify objects on the ground. (See **Section 18-3**.) This approach included the following steps:

1. Correct the pixel spectra for atmosphere (remove water vapor).
2. Detect plume pixels with Constrained Energy Minimization (CEM) (a form of spectral matched filter) using a small library of reference spectra of the approved (≈ 50) gases.
3. Identify each gas in the plume by comparison of the location of spectral features in the data with those of various gases in a spectral library. [3]

An alternate approach used by some researchers included the following steps:

1. Detect plume pixels with spectral matched filter using a small library of reference spectra of the approved (≈ 50) gases.

---

[1] This "high thermal clutter" was anticipated by S. J. Young [2].

2. Confirm plume detection with videos of successive detections. Motion of suspected gas blobs will move in the same direction.
3. Average the spectra of the detected pixels of each plume.
4. Using least squares, compare each plume spectrum with a computer-generated spectrum of possible plume gases and atmospheric gases using a spectral library of gases. Iterate with the amounts of suspected gases. [3]

To cope with the complexities of actual chemical production facilities, the following approach was revised to include additional steps. These additions are italicized below.

1. Correct the pixel spectra for atmosphere (remove water vapor).
2. Detect plume pixels with CEM (a form of spectral matched filter) using the small library of reference spectra of approved gases. *For each detected plume, find nearby background pixels (those with no plume).*
3. *For the N strongest detection plume pixels, subtract the spectra of the background pixels. N typically ranges in value from 4 to 30.*
4. *Average the N resulting difference spectra to obtain a residual spectrum of each plume.*
5. Identify the gas or gases in each plume by comparing features in residual spectra with those in a much more comprehensive (9000 gases) spectral library.
6. *Perform an accuracy check with the chemistry:*
   - *Physical properties: Does the material have a melting point and a boiling point that make it possible for a significant amount to be present in the vapor phase at the collection site?*
   - *Industrial chemical processes: Does the combination of detected gas plumes make any sense from an industrial process standpoint?*
   - *Further iteration: Do known plant processes suggest further gases to again search for?* [3]

20.2 GROUND-BASED HSI FOR GAS DETECTION

Another important application of gas detection is described by the following two objectives:

1. Detect, identify, and locate clouds of Chemical, Biological, Radiological, Nuclear, and Explosive (CBRNE) agents present on the battlefield at a distance of at least a few kilometers.
2. Monitor large areas of the battlefield for the presence of these agents.

Gaseous chemical warfare agent detection, identification, and location are by far the most advanced in terms of capability compared with biological and nuclear agent detection. Two current operational systems are the M-21, or Remote Sensing Chemical Agent Alarm (RSCAAL), and the Joint Service Lightweight Standoff Chemical Agent Detector (JSLSCAD). Both were developed by the US Army Edgewood Chemical Biological Center (ECBC). Both of these HSI systems utilize Fourier Transform InfraRed (FTIR) spectrometers (see **Chapter 17**). Improved HSI sensor performance is in development for future operational deployment. One such effort is Adaptive InfraRed Imaging Spectrometer (AIRIS), which will provide enhanced gas cloud location using an imaging Fabry-Perot interferometer (see **Chapter 17**). Another effort is Artemis,[2]

[2] Not to be confused with the ARTEMIS satellite HSI system described in **Chapter 18**.

formerly Joint Service Warning and Identification LIDAR [3] Detector (JSWILD), which provides increased detection range, better range resolution, and limited biological agent aerosol detection.

The current detection and identification capability is limited for biological agent/aerosol clouds, and this capability is confined to the use of LIDAR. Nuclear agent clouds, fallout, and production effluent probably offer concentrations that are too low to be detected remotely by HSI, either passively or actively.

Detecting clouds of CBRNE agents dispersed on the battlefield with ground-based sensors has some similarities and differences compared to detecting a facility effluent with airborne sensors. Two obvious differences are the viewing geometries just mentioned and the number of possible gases. There are less than 100 known chemical warfare agents, while there are over 9,000 industrial gases. The similarities are more subtle. Both have thermal background, although from slightly different sources. The Earth's surface provides thermal background in airborne sensing; the long, nearly horizontal path through the lowest layer of the Earth's atmosphere is a source of thermal radiation in ground-based sensing. Both have possible large amounts of spatially varying background (clutter). In airborne sensing of an industrial facility, this is provided by the maze of buildings, pipes, reactors, concrete pads, and roads. In ground-based sensing of clouds of chemical agent on the battlefield, this is provided by clouds of dust generated by explosives and heavy vehicle traffic, vehicle exhaust pollutants, and fuel vapors.

Both must sense clouds of gas that may be hotter (emission spectral features) or colder (absorption spectral features) than the background. Both industrial exhaust and chemical agent clouds can be hotter than the background when they are first released.

Two operational HSI sensors that can detect and identify clouds of chemical agent on the battlefield, the M-21 (also known as RSCAAL) and the follow-on JSLSCAD, are compared in **Table 20-2**.

The differences between the initial M-21 and the JSLSCAD follow-on are their weight, size, and power, rather than their sensor design and detection capability. The follow-on JSLSCAD is more mobile and versatile. It can be hand-held and operated while moving. The Fox, referred to in **Table 20-2** is a CBRNE reconnaissance vehicle and is shown in **Figure 20-3**.

Figure 20-3
Fox M93 NBC reconnaissance vehicle.

[3] LIght Detection and Ranging (LIDAR) is explained and discussed in the next section of this chapter on active HSI sensing of gases.

	M-21 (RSCAAL)	JSLSCAD
Sensor type	FTIR Spectrometer	FTIR Spectrometer
Spectral range	LWIR	LWIR
Spectral resolution	4 or 16 cm^{-1}	4 or 16 cm^{-1}
FOV	1.5 × 1.5 degrees	1.5 × 1.5 degrees
FOR (auto scan mode)	60 degree arc	60 degree cone airborne, 360 × 23 degrees on ground
Spectral scan rate	18 or 72 Hz	18 or 72 Hz
Spatial scan rate	0.44 Hz on ground	0.44 Hz on ground
Aperture	6.4 cm in diameter	6.4 cm in diameter
Detector type	HgCdTe	HgCdTe
Detector operating temperature	80 K	80 K
Stand-off range	2 km	2 km best case
Weight	50 kg	30 kg
Size	1.4 ft^3	0.9 ft^3
Power	120 W	28 W
Operation	Stationary	Stationary, on the move
Status	Operational mid 1990s	Operational 2000
Current deployment	Tripod, Fox CBRNE recce vehicle	Tripod, handheld, Fox, and Stryker CBRNE recce vehicles
Proposed future deployment	None	Various ground vehicles, helicopters, ships, Air Force C-130s, and UAVs of the armed forces

Table 20-2
Characteristics of two remote spectral sensors used to detect chemical agent on the battlefield. [4], [13]

A possible future operational chemical agent cloud detection system is AIRIS, an imaging Fabry-Perot spectrometer. AIRIS provides better geolocation because of its higher spatial resolution imaging capability. Some of its characteristics are shown in **Table 20-3**.

Spectral range	8.0–9.8 μm, m = 2 9.9–10.9 μm, m = 3
Spectral resolution	40 spectral bands (7 – 9 cm^{-1})
Sensor FOV	32 × 32 degrees
Pixel FOV	2.1 × 2.1 mrad
Spectral scan rate	114.9 Hz
Aperture	5.1 cm
Detector type	HgCdTe
FPA size	256 × 256
Detector operating temperature	77 K
Sensitivity	1 μW · cm^{-2}sr^{-1}μm^{-1}
CW agent surrogate gases detected	DMMP, SF$_6$
BW aerosol surrogate detected	*Bacillus globigii (BW)*
Typical detection range	2–5 km ground-based or airborne on UH-1 at 1,000 ft altitude
Sensor system size and weight	1 ft^3, 26 kg

Table 20-3
Characteristics of AIRIS, a recently developed chemical agent cloud detection system. (DMMP = DiMethyl MethylPhosphonate) [5], [6]

[4] Nd:YAG is a neodynium-doped yttrium-aluminum-garnet crystal that lases at 1.06 μm. It is the Air Force's primarliy used laser for laser-designated smart bombs and is often frequency doubled to 0.532 μm (green) as in this application

20.3 ACTIVE SPECTRAL SENSING FOR GAS AND AEROSOL DETECTION

So far in the discussion of spectral remote sensing, only passive techniques have been considered. Passive sensing implies the use of any light source nature provides, primarily the Sun or thermal radiation from other objects. By contrast, active remote sensing implies bringing an additional light source, usually a laser chosen specifically for the application. When a laser source is incorporated into a sensor, that sensor is often referred to as a LIDAR. This terminology is most often used; however, another term sometimes used is Laser Detection And Ranging (LADAR). LADAR is directly comparable to its microwave counterpart Radio. Detection And Ranging (RADAR), or radar, has become an accepted everyday word instead of an acronym. Interestingly enough, laser has now achieved the same status as radar. Few people remember that laser came from the acronym LASER, short for Light Amplification by Stimulated Emission of Radiation. While the study of laser characteristics could be extensive, this discussion will be limited to only those laser properties used in spectral sensing applications. Such characteristics include nearly monochromatic beams, hence extremely narrow spectral bandwidth; some ability to tune the wavelength of the output beam; a highly directional source; and a source of continuous or pulsed radiation over time.

As a result of the previous characteristics, a laser can provide far more energy (and photons) in a narrow spectral bandpass than can either the Sun or a 300 K blackbody. As a numerical example, consider the visible where the average solar insolation is 550 $W \cdot m^{-2}$ across the spectral bandpass of 0.4–0.7 μm. This is approximately 0.9 $W \cdot m^{-2}$ across a 0.5 nm bandpass, the linewidth of some lasers, such as Nd:YAG. Nd:YAG Laser technology provides laser outputs of 200 mJ across a 7 ns pulse at 0.532 μm with the above linewidth. Hence, the power during this pulse is 30 MW. At 10 km, with a beam divergence of 1.5 mrad, the illuminated ground area is 15 by 15 m with the irradiance as large as 160,000 $W \cdot m^{-2}$. In this case, the laser does not emit energy at nearby wavelengths that are not of interest (for example, gas detection) and would merely add to the background in most sensors.

To fully understand the two LIDAR options for gas detection, the various interactions of light with individual atoms or molecules will be reviewed. 1) Elastic scattering is the most common interaction. When photons are elastically scattered, they may be redirected, but do not lose energy. Photons of different wavelengths (and hence energy) are thus dispersed in direction by elastic Rayleigh scattering from atmospheric atoms and molecules. This is the cause of commonly observed blue skies and red sunsets (**Chapter 5**). The actual identity of the individual atoms and molecules in the atmosphere does not greatly affect the Rayleigh scattering process, since all are generally small in size compared with the wavelength of visible or infrared light.

2) Inelastic scattering involves energy loss of the incoming photons to the atoms and molecules comprising the gas. Because of their electronic and molecular structure, these atoms and molecules can only absorb specific values of energy. If the incoming photons have energies exactly equal to one of these atomic or molecular absorption values, they may be completely absorbed (**Chapter 3**). The absorption process is referred to as resonant excitation, and the electrons of the atom or molecule go into an

excited state, or the molecules go into an excited vibrational or rotational state. The energy can then be used to increase the kinetic energy of the atom or molecule within the gas, and hence heat the gas through collisions and kinetic energy sharing with other nearby atoms and molecules. Under some circumstances, as is illustrated in **Figure 20-4**, the atom or molecule in an excited state may radiate enough energy to drop to a lower state.

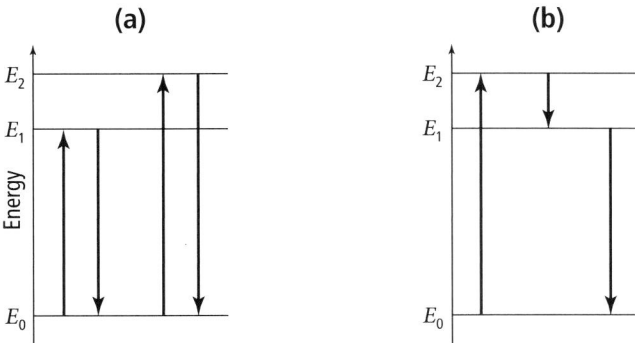

Figure 20-4
Atomic energy levels and transitions for a) resonance and b) fluorescence.

If the atom or molecule was initially in its lowest possible energy level, E_0, or ground state, then was excited to a higher level such as E_1 and E_2, and then radiates a single photon back to the ground state, the process is referred to as resonant radiation (**Figure 20-4a**). If the radiation occurs in two steps (two photons radiated), the process is referred to as fluorescence (**Figure 20-4b**).

Because lasers provide a huge number of photons in a concentrated beam, another rare, one in ten million type of scattering can reveal the presence of gases. That is the inelastic scattering effect called Raman scattering and is illustrated in **Figure 20-5**. Conservation of energy gives **Equation 20-4**:

$$E_{IN} = E_{SCAT} + [E_1 - E_0] = E_{SCAT} + E_{EMIT} \text{ [J]}. \quad (20\text{-}4)$$

Hence, the inequality,

$$E_{IN} \geq E_{EMIT} \text{ [J]}. \quad (20\text{-}5)$$

Since the energy per photon E is related to its wavelength by the expression,

$$E = \frac{hc}{\lambda} \text{ [J]}, \quad (20\text{-}6)$$

the inequality (**Equation 20-5**) becomes

$$\lambda_{IN} \leq \lambda_{EMIT} \text{ [}\mu\text{m]}. \quad (20\text{-}7)$$

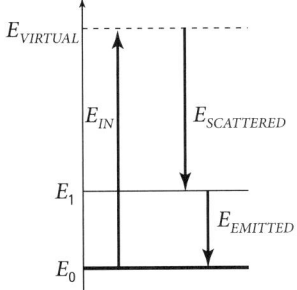

Figure 20-5
Raman scattering. Because a laser beam is so strong, it overpowers some (one in ten million) atoms or molecules, forcing them to absorb a laser photon into a virtual energy state from which a "scattered" photon immediately emerges, leaving the atom or molecule in an excited state. A second photon may then be emitted from the excited state.

In this process, the energy of the incident photon does not have to match that of a transition between energy levels of an atom or molecule. As long as the incident photon has ample energy for the transition, the atom or molecule absorbs the energy for the transition and the remaining energy is emitted as a photon of lower energy.

Since both resonant excitation and Raman scattering are processes that may result in laser detection and identification of various atoms or molecules comprising a gas cloud, it is important to compare them, examine their strengths and weaknesses, and provide possible solutions to their weaknesses. This comparison is provided in **Table 20-4**.

Table 20-4 Comparison of resonant excitation and Raman scattering laser detection of a chemical agent.

	Resonant excitation		Raman scattering	
Choice of laser wavelength	Must exactly match a transition from the ground state of an atom or molecule		Can use ANY WAVELENGTH LESS than the transition from the ground state to lowest excited state	
	Shortcoming	Solution to shortcoming	Shortcoming	Solution to shortcoming
Detection of multiple gas types	Requires a different laser for every type	Frequency agile lasers (FALs) in some cases	ONE laser line can be used for a large number of atom or molecule types	None required
Relative probability of occurrence	High	None required	Very low	High energy lasers
Unwanted contributions in laser return pulse	Elastic scattering from all atoms and molecule types present	Differential Absorption LIDAR (DIAL) systems	Very low	None required

A single laser can be used to detect several different types of atoms or molecules using Raman scattering, while resonant excitation requires a different laser wavelength for each atom or molecule to be detected and identified. This advantage for Raman scattering sensing over resonant excitation sensing is somewhat mitigated with the use of lasers that emit multiple wavelengths that can be utilized in an organized way. Such a laser system is the Frequency Agile Laser (FAL) using the CO_2 laser system developed by ECBC. (More details will follow.) In terms of relative probability of occurrence, resonant scattering ranks much higher than Raman scattering. Raman scattering systems can mitigate this with the use of a very high energy laser. This is limited by the choice of platform and the power available. In terms of contributions to the return pulse, Raman systems only measure photons generated by atoms and molecules of interest. With resonant excitation systems, the photons in the return pulse can originate either as resonant radiation from the atoms or molecules of interest as well as elastic scattering by atoms or molecules of all other types. To mitigate this shortcoming, resonant excitation systems are Differential Absorption LIDAR (DIAL) systems. (More details will follow.)

One example of a FAL utilizes the CO_2 laser and was built by Hughes Aircraft (now part of Raytheon), located in El Segundo, California, under the sponsorship of ECBC. Characteristics of this device are listed in **Table 20-5**.

The CO_2 laser radiates 55 different wavelengths in the LWIR near 10 μm (actually 9.2-10.7 μm). Instead of irradiating a gas cloud with all 55 wavelengths at once, a fixed grating and scanning mirror are utilized to send laser pulses, one wavelength at a time. With a pulse rate of 200 Hz, all 55 wavelengths are sent four times in a time interval slightly longer

Table 20-5 Characteristics of a FAL used for chemical agent detection. [7].

Pulse output	Greater than 100 mJ in all wavelengths
Pulse rate	200 Hz
Wavelength shift rate	200 Hz
Number of wavelengths	55
Spectral bands	9.2–10.7 μm
Wavelength shifter	Fixed grating and scanning mirror
Beam size	3 by 3 cm
Beam divergence	3 mrad
Size, weight	4 ft^3, 100 pounds

than a second. Fortunately, the CO_2 laser output occurs at the correct wavelength region where many gases have spectral features.

DIAL systems use two lasers: one at λ_1 and one at λ_2, where λ_1 and λ_2 are closely spaced, but λ_2 is readily absorbed by atoms or molecules of type X, while λ_1 is not (**Figure 20-6**).

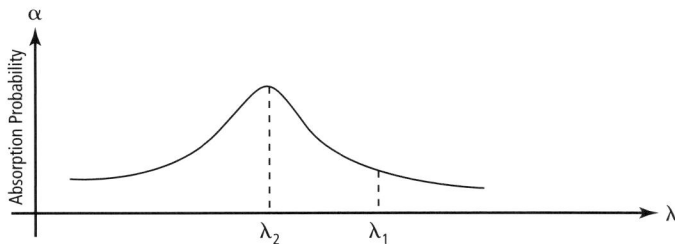

Figure 20-6
Absorption probability of an atom or molecules as a function of wavelength.

To process the data, the return at λ_2 is subtracted from the return in λ_1 in order to obtain the return from only type X molecules that are present. If the lasers are used in continuous wave mode, only the column density (number or mass per unit area) can be obtained. If the lasers are used in pulse mode, analysis of the return pulses in λ_1 and λ_2 as a function of time give the density (number or mass per unit volume) at all points along the line of sight (**Figure 20-7**).

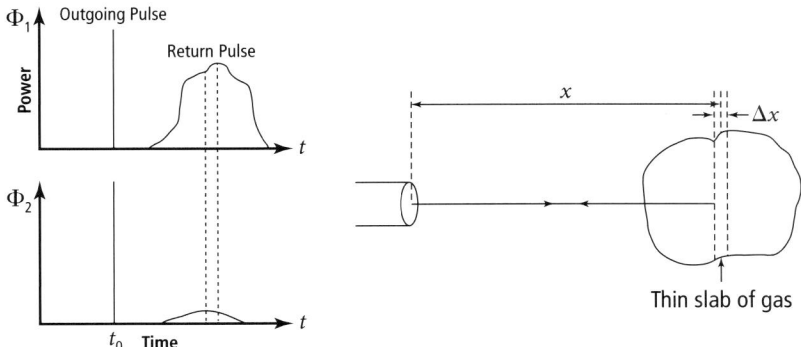

Figure 20-7
The use of DIAL for gas cloud detection and location.

The challenge is to fine-tune the laser output wavelengths to the correct values.

Numerous ground-based DIAL and Raman LIDAR systems have been built and deployed as either fixed site or minivan mobile by universities, the National Aeronautics and Space Administration (NASA), and the EPA. Numerous collections and demonstrations have been made against most of the common atmospheric gas types (methane, hydrogen chloride, carbon dioxide, ozone, ethylene, oxygen, chloroethylene, ammonia, nitrous oxide, carbon monoxide, water vapor, sulfur dioxide, nitric oxide, and freon). Several airborne DIAL and Raman LIDAR systems have been built and flown on low-altitude, low-performance aircraft by research institutes, NASA, and the EPA. Again, many collections and demonstrations have been made against most of the common atmospheric gas types. NASA's plans for a DIAL LIDAR aboard a satellite have not been realized to date.

There have been a few active spectral atmospheric sensing efforts by the DOD and DOE. One such effort was the Chemical Analysis by Laser Interrogation of Proliferation Effluents (CALIOPE), sponsored by the DOE. The effluents considered were characteristic of various production processes leading to nuclear weapons. This research and development exploratory effort in the 1990s was executed across most of the DOE labs: Lawrence Livermore National Laboratory, Los Alamos National Laboratory, Sandia National Laboratory, Brookhaven National Laboratory, and Pacific Northwest National Laboratory. Data collections and demonstrations were conducted using various LIDAR and laser types over several years. [8]

To perform longer-range chemical agent detection on the battlefield, ECBC conducted two programs. The first program, Frequency Agile Laser Standoff Chemical Agent Detection (FALSCAD), was an advanced development effort utilizing the CO_2 FAL. Against chemical agent surrogates deployed on the battlefield, FALSCAD successfully demonstrated longer-range detection capabilities than the currently fielded JSLSCAD. The Army never made FALSCAD operational because of several deployment issues: higher cost than JSLSCAD because of FAL; appropriate for fixed mounting sites but not moving platforms; and high maintenance costs since the FAL optical components degrade with use. A second effort, Artemis (formerly JSWILD), a follow-on to FALSCAD, is currently in development. Its performance goals are 20 km detection range and 360 degree coverage. [9], [10]

To perform the initial and improved biological agent detection on the battlefield, ECBC has performed a series of efforts. These biological agents are frequently dispersed as aerosols (spores mixed into water droplets). Classical detection approaches involve Nd:YAG lasers at 1.06 μm, which produce enough elastic backscatter to detect clouds of aerosols on the battlefield. Classical identification approaches involve ultraviolet lasers, which induce enough molecular fluorescence to discriminate between cloud types: biological agent aerosols versus other aerosols. The sequence of some of the deployed systems is listed below:

1. First Long Range Biological Standoff Detection System (LR-BSDS) deployed in 1993 for cloud detection only

2. XM-94 LR-BSDS for cloud detection only

3. Short Range Biological Standoff Detection System (SR-BSDS) for cloud detection and discrimination

4. Joint Biological Point Detection System (JBPDS) currently deployed

5. Joint Biological Standoff Detection System (JBSDS) future deployment

Current capabilities are cloud detection at ranges of 3–10 km and cloud discrimination at ranges of 1–3 km. New technologies under consideration are improved LWIR FALs, improved sensitivity LWIR FTIRs, and depolarization LIDAR. [9], [10], [11], [12], [13]

21 POLARIMETRIC IMAGING

In **Chapters 15** through **20**, spectral imaging sensors, data collection, and analysis were discussed. This chapter begins by considering a topic not previously discussed in these chapters, namely the effect of specular versus diffuse (or Lambertian) reflection from the surfaces of objects of interest. Interestingly, this topic is strongly related to linear polarimetric effects and Polarimetric Imaging (PI). After discussing the data collection, applications, and analysis of PI, similarities and differences of PI with Multispectral Imaging (MSI) and Hyperspectral Imaging (HSI) will be summarized.

SECTIONS

21.1 SPECULAR VERSUS DIFFUSE REFLECTION

21.2 SOURCES, COLLECTION, AND DETECTION OF LINEARLY POLARIZED LIGHT

21.3 APPLICATIONS AND COLLECTION GEOMETRIES FOR LINEAR POLARIMETRIC IMAGING

21.1 SPECULAR VERSUS DIFFUSE REFLECTION

Consider a source of a single wavelength incident onto a surface from a single direction, that is, a point source (or close approximation to one), such as the Sun. There are two extreme cases: specular and diffuse reflection. (See initial discussion in **Chapter 3**.) A rough surface is composed of many tiny, randomly oriented facets that produce a surface in which the size of irregularities on the surface is large compared to a wavelength. An edge-on view of a rough surface is illustrated in **Figure 21-1**.

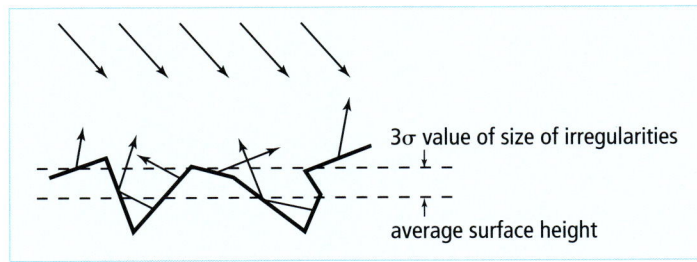

Figure 21-1
Light incident on a rough surface.

For short wavelengths, such as those in the visible through thermal infrared, the surfaces of most objects are rough. For much longer wavelengths, such as those in the microwave and radio, many surfaces are smooth. (The surface irregularities are small compared to a wavelength.) For the rough surface, reflectance is usually considered to be perfectly diffuse, or Lambertian. The radiance from such a surface is the same for all observer locations, as is illustrated in **Figure 21-2**.

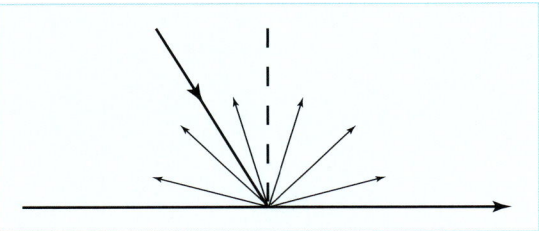

Figure 21-2
Light incident and reflected by a rough surface.

Few surfaces are smooth in the visible through thermal infrared. Some naturally occurring smooth surfaces are still water (small ponds or swamps with little or no prevailing winds), ice, and packed or smooth bare earth. Some examples of man-made smooth surfaces are glossy painted surfaces or well-sanded and polished metallic surfaces. In contrast, many surfaces are smooth in the microwave and radio regions. For these smooth surfaces, reflection is specular. Hence, the angle of reflection, θ_{ref}, equals the angle of incidence, θ_{inc}, and all the incident radiation is reflected in one direction, as illustrated in **Figure 21-3**.

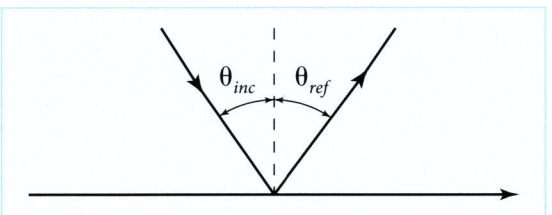

Figure 21-3
Light incident and reflected by a smooth surface.

For all cases in between the two extremes, perfectly rough or perfectly smooth, the reflection of radiation from a surface is described by the directional reflectance, ρ_Ω (λ, θ_{obs}, ϕ_{obs}, θ_{inc}, ϕ_{inc}), commonly called the Bidirectional Reflectivity Distribution Function (BRDF). The geometry describing the direction of the incoming light (θ_{inc}, ϕ_{inc}) and the location of the observer (θ_{obs}, ϕ_{obs}) are illustrated in **Figure 21-4**.

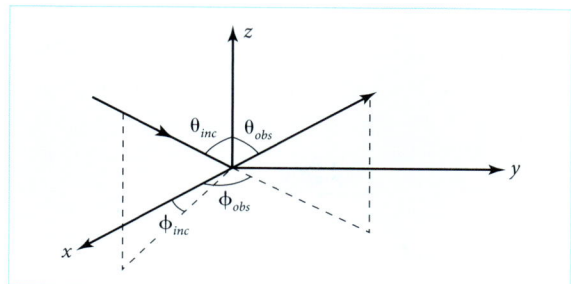

Figure 21-4
Viewing geometry for BRDF.

When integrated over the entire upper hemisphere,

$$\rho(\lambda) = \int_0^{2\pi} \rho_\Omega(\lambda) d\Omega \qquad (21\text{-}1)$$

is sometimes referred to as the "diffuse hemispheric reflectance," where

$$\rho_\Omega(\lambda) = \frac{\rho(\lambda)\cos\theta_{obs}}{\pi} \text{ for perfectly diffuse, and}$$

$$\rho_\Omega(\lambda) = \begin{cases} \rho(\lambda) \text{ for } \theta_{obs} = \theta_{inc} \text{ and } \phi_{obs} = \phi_{inc} \\ 0 \text{ for all other } \theta_{obs} \text{ and } \phi_{obs} \end{cases} \text{ for specular.}$$

This reflectivity was used throughout the preceding MSI and HSI discussions.

The reflected radiation distribution is shown in the polar plots (**Figures 21-5, 21-6,** and **21-7**) for incident light in the x-z plane and the reflecting surface (the x-y plane) that is smooth, somewhere between smooth and rough, and rough, respectively. For the smooth case and specular reflection, the reflected energy distribution is confined to a very narrow lobe centered on the direction such that $\theta_{ref} \simeq \theta_{inc}$.

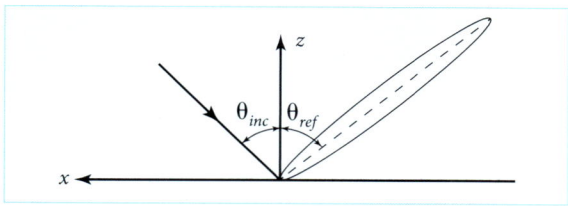

Figure 21-5
Light incident and reflected by a smooth surface.

For the general case, between the extremes of perfectly smooth or perfectly rough, two of the three components of BRDF are shown (namely a widened specular lobe plus a small diffuse hemisphere).

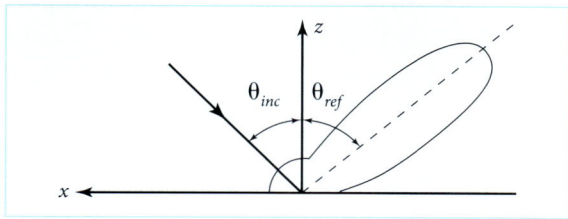

Figure 21-6
Light incident and reflected by a surface that is neither smooth nor totally rough.

For the perfectly rough case and diffuse reflection, equal amounts of radiation are reflected in all directions as shown below.

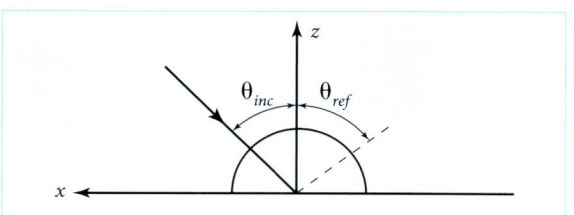

Figure 21-7
Light incident and reflected by a rough surface.

The previous results can have significant effects in the analysis of MSI and HSI as well as broadband thermal imagery. Unless there is some knowledge to the contrary, perfect diffuse reflection is assumed when correcting collected pixel values to reflectivity (or emissivity) using **Equation 21-2**.

$$L_\lambda(\lambda) = \frac{M_\lambda(\lambda)}{\pi} = \frac{\rho(\lambda)\mathcal{E}_\lambda(\lambda) + \epsilon(\lambda)B_\lambda(\lambda,T)}{\pi} \left[\frac{W}{m^2 sr \cdot \mu m}\right]. \quad (21\text{-}2)$$

If a surface is known to be smooth (mostly man-made objects), spectral library reference signatures should be used that have appropriate angular dependence for the solar and viewing geometry involved. For the same material type and viewing geometry, the degree of surface smoothness can produce large spectral reflectance variations (e.g., flat versus glossy paint of the same color applied to the same surface). BRDF effects can significantly alter derived temperatures for smooth surfaces, although the uncertainty in the type of material composing an object's surface and the atmospheric correction can also produce large uncertainties in temperature determination.

There are many diffuse reflectivity databases. In these databases, surface reflection is assumed to be perfectly diffuse, or Lambertian, and diffuse hemispheric reflectivity is reported. Only one angle of incidence is used in measurements. So, results in any database can be somewhat dependent on the degree of surface smoothness and the size of the sample measured.

There are some BRDF databases with limited numbers of BRDF measured samples, partially because of the additional efforts required to make the measurements. One such database, developed by Mitsubishi Electric Research Laboratories, contains the measurements of 100 material samples (metals, plastics, painted surfaces, and fabrics). [1] The utility of any such database critically depends on degree of surface smoothness of the sample measured.

At this point, it is of interest to consider the reflection of polarized light of both a perfectly smooth and a perfectly rough surface. In the wave description of light involving an oscillating electric (and magnetic) field, polarization is one parameter necessary to describe a single electromagnetic (EM) wave. For the case where the wave is linearly polarized, as shown in **Figure 21-8**, the wave is characterized by a wavelength λ (or frequency f) of oscillation, maximum amplitude of oscillation A, and polarization. The latter can be characterized by either the plane of polarization which is the plane of oscillation of the electric field (x-z plane) or the direction of polarization which is a line parallel to the direction of the oscillation (x-axis).

Figure 21-8
Propagation of an EM wave.

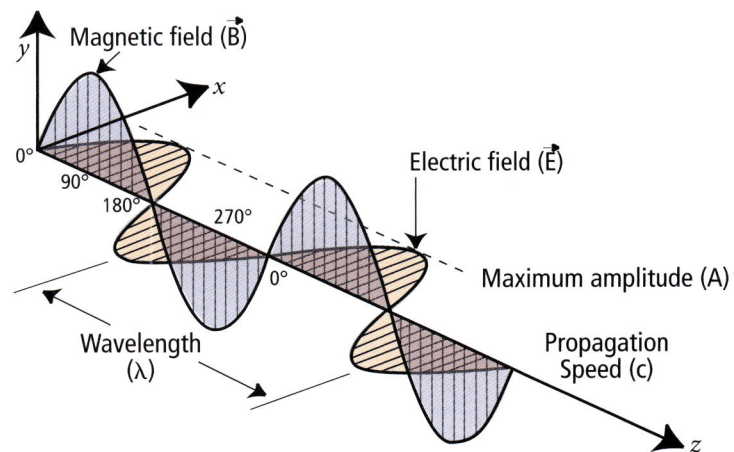

The line of polarization is often designated relative to the plane of incidence onto a horizontal surface (such as the Earth) or relative to this surface itself. As illustrated in **Figure 21-9**, if the line of polarization is parallel to the horizontal surface, it is referred to as E_H. If it is perpendicular to E_H, it is referred to as E_V. At large angles of incidence, E_V becomes nearly vertical and perpendicular to the horizontal surface. This terminology is commonly used in remote sensing, in the visible through thermal infrared as well as in the radar wavelengths.

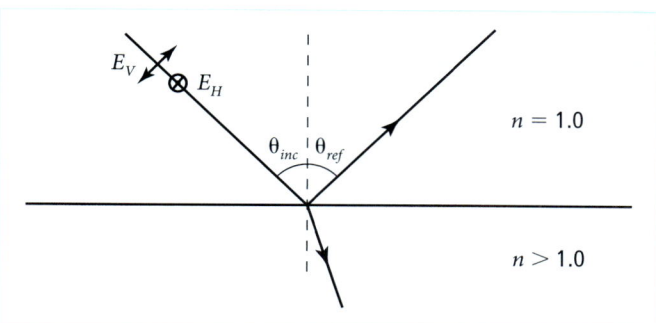

Figure 21-9
Polarization components of light incident onto a smooth surface of a material with index of refraction n.

Unfortunately, this terminology is not universally used. Many physics and electrical engineering textbooks use other terminology. Some of that terminology is shown along with E_H and E_V in **Table 21-1**.

E oscillation relative to a horizontal surface	Commonly used notation	E oscillation relative to plane of incident and reflective rays	Other notation in use
Horizontal, or parallel	E_H	Perpendicular	$E_\perp$, E_S, E_σ, TE
Vertical, or perpendicular (at large θ_{inc})	E_V	In plane, or parallel	$E_\parallel$, E_P, E_π, TM

Table 21-1
Notation for polarization components relative to a horizontal surface.

If Maxwell's equations are used to describe the oscillating E and B field of the EM wave in regions slightly above and below the surface, the results are the Fresnel equations (**Equations 3-8** and **3-9**) which give ρ_H, ρ_V, τ_H, and τ_V in terms of θ_{inc} and n. As an example, the results for $n = 2.5$ (the typical value for many paints) are shown in **Figure 21-10**. (Compare to **Figure 3-9**.)

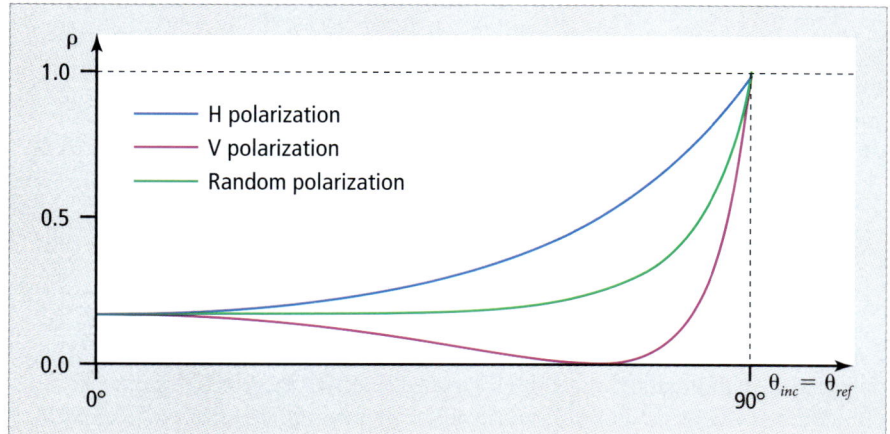

Figure 21-10
Reflectivity of the polarization components by a smooth surface.

These results can be easily understood in physical terms to some extent. Both the reflected and transmitted EM waves originate from oscillating electrons near the surface. At normal incidence ($\theta_{inc} = 0$), both E_V and E_H are parallel to the surface, so there should not be a difference in their reflectance values.

As the angle of incidence increases, both types of wave encounter more surface electrons to set-up the reflected waves than they would at smaller angles of incidence. The horizontal component steadily increases, but $\rho_H > \rho_V$. The electron oscillations are more restricted by the location of the surface if this motion is aligned vertically rather than horizontally. So, as the angle of incidence increases, the reflectance of the vertical component initially decreases because of this limitation on electron oscillation, but eventually increases because of the vertical EM wave encountering more surface electrons.

As the surface becomes less smooth and more rough compared to the wavelength of incident light, the differences between ρ_H and ρ_V become smaller. The results for directional reflectance (**Figures 21-5, 21-6,** and **21-7**) are combined with the polarimetric reflectance values previously discussed and summarized in **Figures 21-11, 21-12,** and **21-13** for the case where the incident and specular rays are in the x-z plane.

For the smooth specular reflection case, the reflected energy distribution is confined to a very narrow lobe centered on the direction, so $\theta_{ref} = \theta_{inc}$.

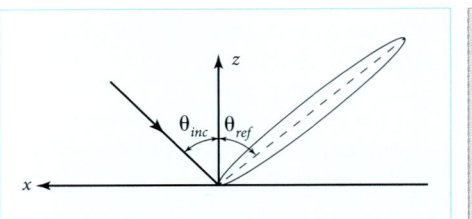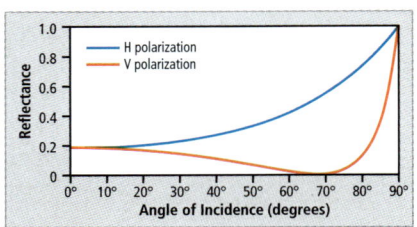

Figure 21-11
Reflective properties of a smooth surface.

Typically, most surfaces are between the extremes of perfectly smooth or perfectly rough. A simple example of a mixed BRDF is shown in **Figure 21-12** (namely a widened specular lobe plus a small diffuse hemisphere).

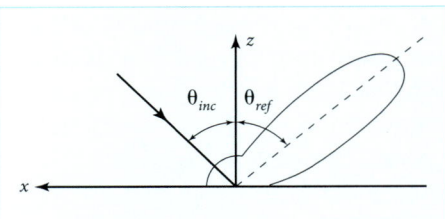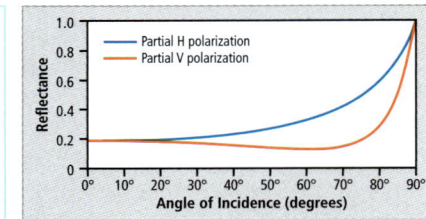

Figure 21-12
Reflective properties of a surface that is neither smooth nor rough.

For the perfectly rough case and diffuse reflection, equal amounts or radiation are reflected in all directions as shown in **Figure 21-13**.

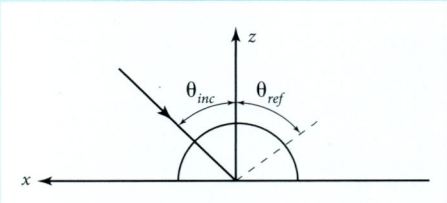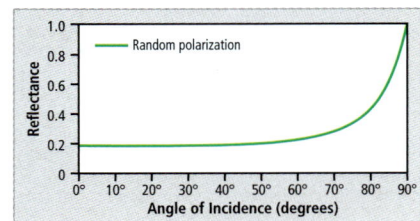

Figure 21-13
Reflective properties of a rough surface.

Basic applications can be developed if images could be collected in two polarizations, such as vertical and horizontal. Smooth surfaces will reflect more radiation in the horizontal state than in the vertical state. Thus, these surfaces will stand out in the polarimetric imagery compared to rough surfaces (that are more diffuse reflectors). Hence, smooth objects (often man-made) in the scene could be easily detected and located, prompting analysts to use BRDF for processing spectral and thermal data from these objects.

21.2 SOURCES, COLLECTION, AND DETECTION OF LINEARLY POLARIZED LIGHT

Before addressing applications, the sources, collection, and detection of linear polarization will be discussed. Most naturally occurring sources of EM radiation are randomly polarized, or sometimes termed "non-polarized." Because of the random motion of individual atoms and molecules and their orbiting electrons, the generated radiation is a mixture of all planes of polarization. Thus, the radiation observed at some location at a distance from the source, such as the sun, man-made lamps, and thermal radiation, is a mixture of all planes of polarization. There are some notable exceptions: randomly polarized light after it is reflected by a smooth surface; solar scatter off the individual molecules in the atmosphere when appropriately viewed; thermal radiation from smooth surfaces; radar; and some lasers.

Radar transmitter outputs are inherently polarized. For example, consider the simplest transmitter, the linear dipole antenna. This geometry and an imposed alternating voltage force the electrons to oscillate in a non-random way (i.e., back and forth along the wire antenna). Therefore, the electrons produce radiation with plane of polarization that is parallel to the dipole.

As previously discussed, smooth surfaces produce large differences in the reflectance of the polarimetric components of incident randomly polarized light. These differences are the largest for a single bounce off a large (multi-pixel) surface (e.g., a tin roof). A strong specular reflection, or glint, occurs when the viewing geometry is such that the sensor line-of-sight (LOS) coincides with the direction of the specular reflection. (Recall, angle of reflection equals angle of incidence.) Thus, at the surface, sun zenith angle equals observer zenith angle, and the sun, surface normal, and the observer must lie in the same plane. Lesser polarimetric differences occur when a pixel contains multiple small, smooth surfaces, such as the leaves on some trees. If there are many different surface orientations within a ground pixel, there will be some difference in the polarization of the reflected radiance for all values of the Sun and observer zenith and azimuth angles. Smaller polarimetric differences also occur when there is multiple bounce reflection from various smooth surfaces within a ground pixel. In the limit of many reflections, the ground pixel approximates a single rough surface which produces diffuse reflection without preferential polarization.

Polarization differences can occur in the thermal emission from a surface. Since $\epsilon = 1 - \rho$, then $\epsilon_V = 1 - \rho_V$ and $\epsilon_H = 1 - \rho_H$. If ρ_H and ρ_V are non-zero and differ significantly, then ϵ_V and ϵ_H will also differ significantly, and the thermal emission will be polarized and directional. The difference in polarization components is given by **Equation 21-3**,

$$L_H - L_V = \frac{1}{2}(\epsilon_H - \epsilon_V)(L_{EMISSION} - L_{SKY}) \left[\frac{W}{m^2 sr}\right]. \quad (21\text{-}3)$$

Another source of partially polarized light involves the scattering of randomly polarized light from gas molecules. Since EM radiation is a transverse wave (oscillating E and B fields always perpendicular to the direction of propagation), orientation of the induced electron oscillations within each molecule, or individual dipole, will also be perpendicular to the direction of propagation, as illustrated in **Figure 21-14**.

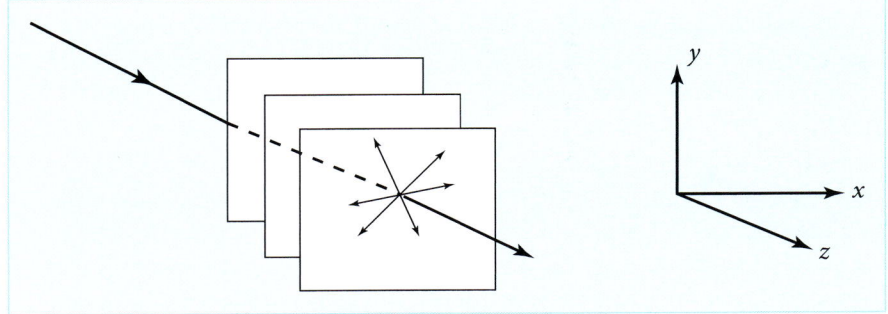

Figure 21-14
Geometry of randomly polarized light traversing the atmosphere. Only three such oscillations are shown.

There are two extreme cases of viewing geometry:

1. In the first case, the observer is looking directly at a randomly polarized source (along the negative z-axis). If the dipole is oriented along the x-axis, radiation will not occur along the x-axis. If the dipole is oriented along the y-axis, radiation will not occur along the y-axis. The combined scatter from many molecules will be randomly polarized.

2. In the second case, the observer's LOS is confined to the x-y plane (or a plane parallel to it). The combined scatter from many molecules will be linearly polarized with the polarization direction in that plane and perpendicular to the LOS. The combined scatter from many molecules will be linearly polarized.

As an example, consider an observer on the ground looking up at the sunlit sky on a clear day when the sun is located at 60° zenith angle (or 30° elevation angle) relative to the observer. The fraction of the light received by the observer that is linearly polarized is shown in **Figure 21-15** as a function of the observer's viewing direction, as given by a zenith angle within the vertical plane of the observer's LOS and the LOS to the sun.

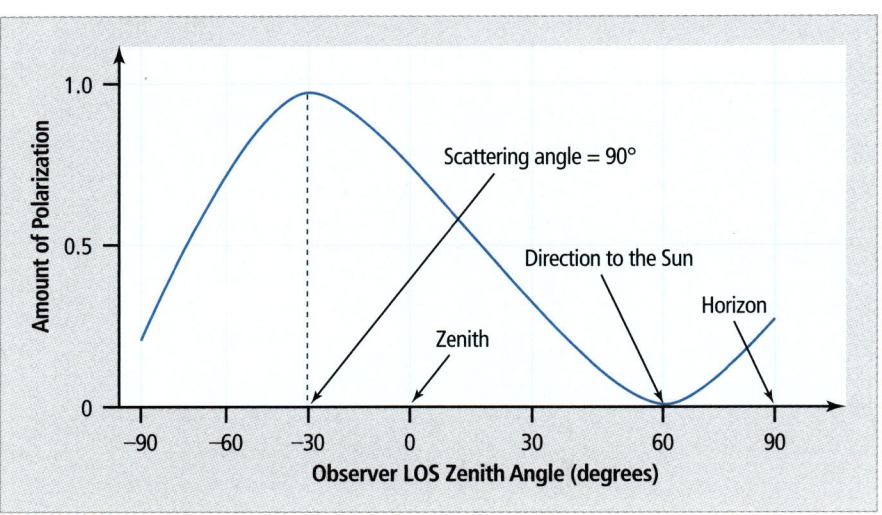

Figure 21-15
Amount of polarization in the radiation originating at various sky locations.

Note, the maximum amount of observed polarization occurs at a zenith angle that is 90° relative to the direction of the sun. (The presence of aerosols tends to reduce the amount of observed polarization because of multiple scattering.) Such concentrations of aerosols can significantly impact the battlefield.

Extending the previous example to the entire sky gives the results shown in **Figure 21-16**. This figure only gives the direction of the linearly polarized light, not the amount seen by the observer as shown in **Figure 21-15**.

While the previous example involves single scattering of incident randomly-polarized sunlight by the ambient atmospheric molecules, similar localized effects can be caused by gas clouds and plumes where gas densities and composition may be different than ambient. Also, these exhausts may have higher than ambient aerosols. Therefore, industrial exhaust plumes may sometimes be detected because of differences in polarization in the received radiation.

From sources of polarized light, the discussion turns to detecting various polarization directions of linearly polarized light. Radio wave detectors can use various antennas, such as the linear dipole, to detect polarized radio waves of the appropriate polarization direction. Visible and infrared detectors are sensitive to photons of energy, not the polarization of an EM wave. Thus, thin film filters are used to separate incoming light into various polarization directions. There are two approaches. In the first approach, traditional thin films of materials with birefringent crystal structure can be used. Hence, the material index of refraction, n, varies with polarization direction relative to the crystal. Some common examples are quartz, calcium carbonate (calcite), and sodium chlorite. Index of refraction, n, and thickness, d, are chosen so one polarization direction is transmitted, and the one perpendicular to it is not.

In the second approach, since linear dipole antennas can be used to detect polarized radio waves of the appropriate polarization direction as well as transmit them, tiny parallel metal wires can be inserted in a thin film to define the polarization direction that will be preferentially transmitted. Such a film is a form of dichroic filter. Another form, developed in the late 1920s, is a Polaroid sheet which contains millions of microscopic crystals that are needle-shaped.

Transmission, $\tau(\theta)_{opt}$, of such films for incident light is described by Malus' Law (**Equation 21-4**) below:

$$\tau(\theta)_{opt} = \frac{\mathcal{E}(\theta)}{\mathcal{E}_0} = \cos^2\theta, \qquad (21\text{-}4)$$

where θ is the angle between the polarization direction of an incoming EM wave with irradiance $\mathcal{E}_0$, $\mathcal{E}(\theta)$ is the transmitted irradiance, and the preferred polarization direction (in the x-y plane below) designed into the filter (**Figure 21-17**). When $\theta = 0$, all the incident radiation is transmitted; when $\theta = 90°$, all the incident radiation is absorbed.

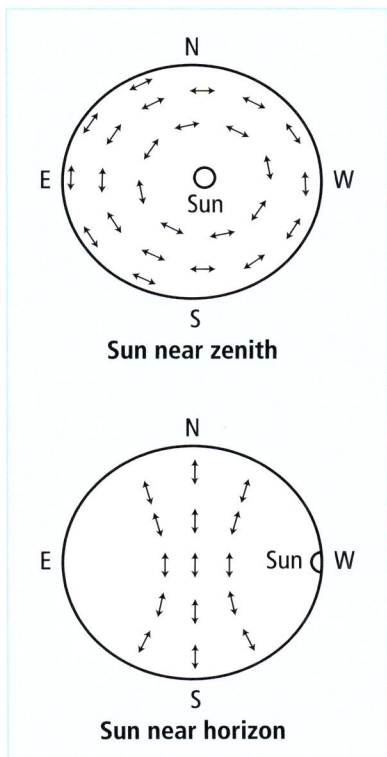

Figure 21-16
Direction of polarization in the radiation originating at various locations across the sky.

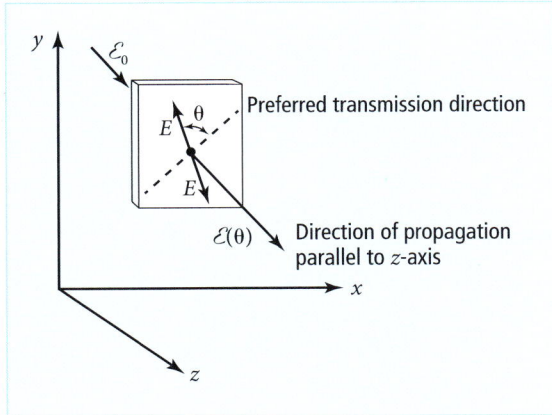

Figure 21-17
Geometry of transmission of linearly polarized light through a filter.

Many sunglasses have lenses that are linear polarization filters. The transmitted polarization is perpendicular to horizontal surfaces. These glasses provide improved vision for boating and driving especially during the "glare" conditions when looking into the sun at sunrise or before sunset. An example of sunglasses removing the glare from water surfaces is shown in **Figure 21-18**.

Figure 21-18
Strong reflected image blocked by polarimetric filters.

In the first image, the water surface strongly reflects the pole of a street light. In the second image, polarimetric filters used in sunglasses block the strong reflection of the street light.

Polarizing filters are used in photography to reduce any glare in the scene and also to enhance "blue sky" backgrounds. **Figure 21-19** shows the sky with and without a polarimetric camera filter.

Figure 21-19
Image of scene without (left) and with (right) "blue sky" enhancement using a polarizing filter.

A less obvious, but very important use of polarization filters is in Liquid Crystal Displays (LCDs) used in various calculators, instruments, and some flat-screen television screens. Actually, a sizeable number of these filters are used in each display. The preferred direction of each filter is slightly different than ones nearby, and they are arranged so vertically polarized light is bent 90 degrees to become horizontally polarized light. See **Figure 21-20**.

An internal source produces light incident on the LCD that would normally pass through the LCD to the observer. If an electric field is applied across one or more of the pixels in the LCD, the normal orientation of the various filter layers becomes randomized, and none of the incident light is transmitted. Thus, the black pixels are formed that create the displayed information. The transmitted light is normally all horizontally polarized, which can be quickly verified by observing the display with polarized sunglasses.

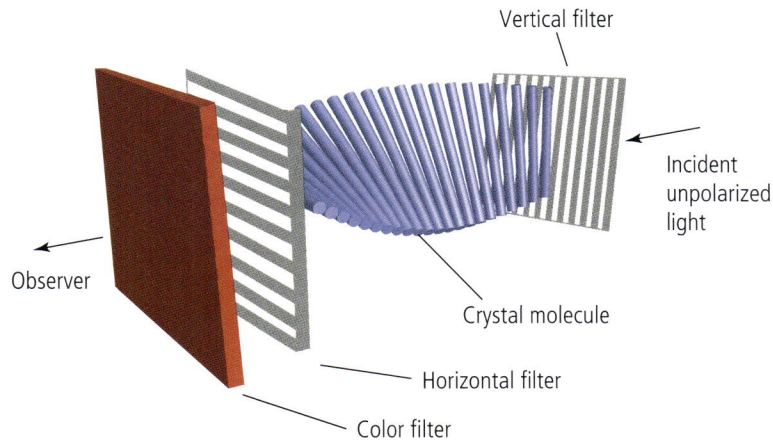

Figure 21-20
Use of polarization filters in a LCD.

Table 21-2
One possible set of four filters for complete polarization collection.[1]

Received power in PI band	Preferred direction relative to that of the first band
Φ_0	0 degrees
Φ_{45}	45 degrees
Φ_{90}	90 degrees
Φ_{135}	135 degrees

Collecting linear polarimetric imagery that is useful for remote sensing applications can be easily accomplished with a pushbroom scanner as illustrated in **Figure 21-21**. For spectral imagery collections, each row of detectors has a different spectral filter and defines a row of ground pixels, each covering a different spectral band. For polarimetric imagery collections, linear polarization filters are used instead of spectral filters. Each polarization filter has a different preferred polarization direction. One possible set of four filters is given in **Table 21-2**.

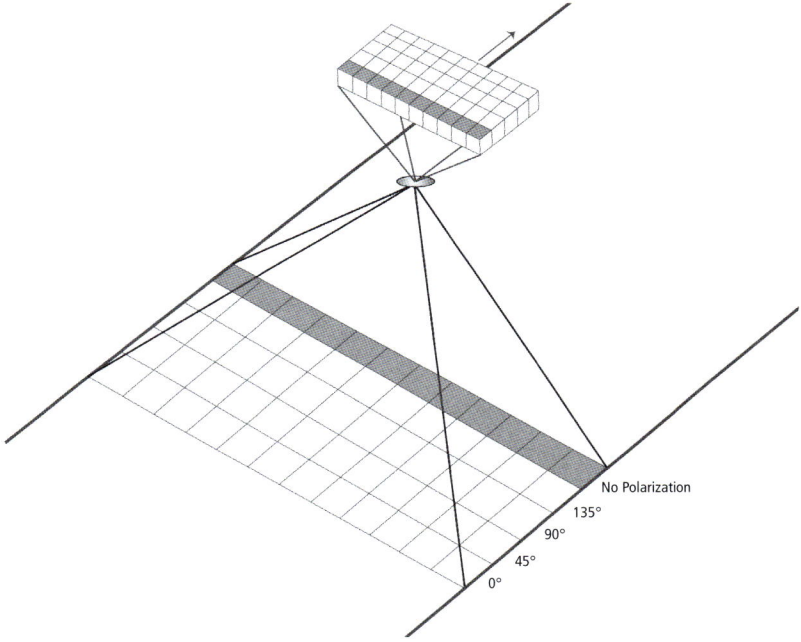

Figure 21-21
Example of pushbroom sensor to collect a complete polarization image.

Sensor outputs can provide four images, each of the received radiation in its particular preferred polarization direction. The images are more commonly provided in terms of Stokes parameter bands. The definitions of the Stokes parameters in terms of the power measured in the PI bands are given below.

$$S0 = \Phi_0 + \Phi_{90} = \Phi_{45} + \Phi_{135} = 0.5\,(\Phi_0 + \Phi_{45} + \Phi_{90} + \Phi_{135}).$$
   This is the total received energy.

$S1 = \Phi_0 - \Phi_{90}$, emphasizes flat, smooth horizontal or vertical surfaces.

$S2 = \Phi_{45} - \Phi_{135}$, emphasizes flat, smooth surfaces which are neither vertical nor horizontal.

S3 is used only for circularly or elliptically polarized light (non linearly polarized) and is not applicable for passive remotely sensed imagery.

(21-5)

[1] The French space agency, CNES, used a staring array with a filter wheel in their POLarization and Directionality of the Earth's Reflections (POLDER) sensors launched by the Japanese space agency JAXA first on the ADvanced Earth Observation Satellite 1 (ADEOS-1) on August 17, 1996, and then on ADEOS-2 on December 14, 2002. An upgrade of POLDER was later launched by CNES on the French Polarization and Anisotropy of Reflectances for Atmospheric Science coupled with Observations from LIDAR (PARASOL) satellite on December 18, 2004. The pushbroom scan approach is shown because linear scanners have generally replaced the staring/filter wheel approach for spectral remote sensing. See Section 15-1 for a discussion of these collection modes.

Since all the Φ values are positive numbers, S0 is always positive, and S1 and S2 can be either positive or negative. The use of Stokes parameters provides a standard reference system for characterizing polarized light, and imagery in bands defined by Stokes parameters accentuates various surface orientations. Stokes parameters are more useful when circularly polarized light is present (generally laboratory produced).

Examples of linear polarization signatures from various surfaces are listed in **Table 21-3**.

Table 21-3
Collected polarization filter values for common surface orientation.

Surface Orientation	Orientation Angle θ (between normal to the surface and vertical)	S0	S1	S2
Horizontal	0°	Positive	Positive	0
Vertical	90°	Positive	Negative	0
Tilted	45°	Positive	0	Positive
Tilted	135°	Positive	0	Negative

The orientation of the plane of polarization,

$$\tan(2\theta) = \left(\frac{S2}{S1}\right), \tag{21-6}$$

determines the orientation of a surface in the pixel that shows strong linear polarization.

Additional possible PI bands have proven useful at times. These include the following that involve the amount of linear polarization and emphasize pixels showing strong linear polarization independent of surface orientation.

Total Linear Polarization (ToLP) = $[(S1)^2 + (S2)^2]^{0.5}$

Linear Polarized Radiance (LPR) = ToLP

Total Polarization (TPoL) = ToLP when S3 = 0

Degree of Linear Polarization (DoLP) = $\frac{[(S1)^2 + (S2)^2]^{0.5}}{S_0}$

Degree of UnPolarization (DoUP) = 1 − DoLP

Yet another band that combines the magnitude of linear polarization as well as surface orientation is Target Polarization Signature = ABS(S2) − S1, where ABS(S2) is the absolute value of S2.

A common image flow is shown in **Figure 21-22**.

Figure 21-22
Common image flow from collection to analysis.

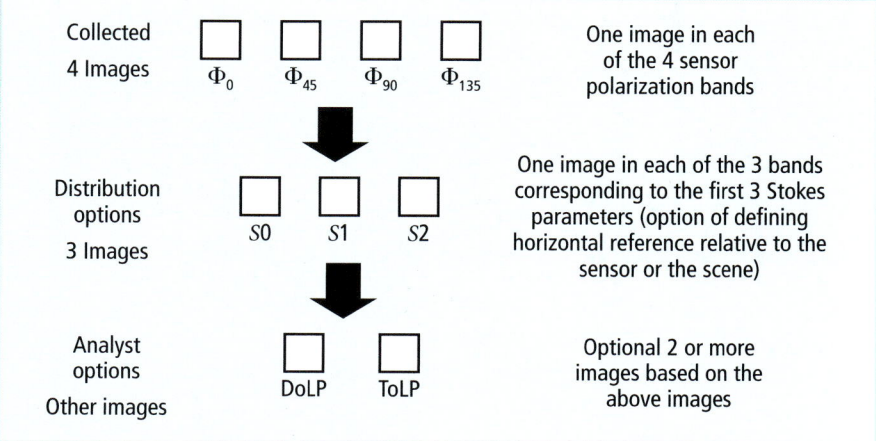

In **Figures 21-23** and **21-24**, polarimetric images of various objects are shown in a variety of polarization bands. Note, the smooth, flat surfaces are prominent in S1, but not in S0.

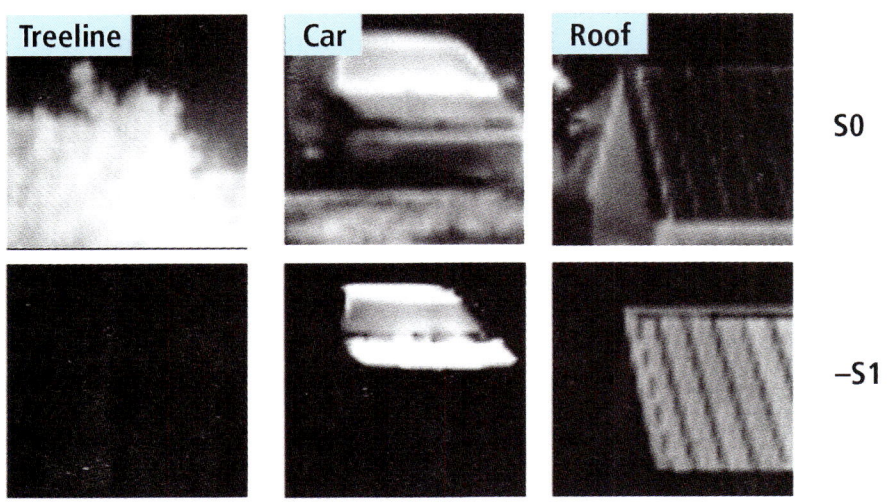

Figure 21-23
Common objects seen in the Mid-Wave Infrared (MWIR) broad-band (top row) and MWIR S1 (bottom row). (Courtesy of ERIM, now part of General Dynamics Advanced Information Systems)

Figure 21-24 shows a vehicle-panel scene in the visible (top) and in the Long-Wave Infrared (LWIR) PI (bottom). Note, some of the objects are clearly visible in the LWIR DoLP that are difficult to see in the LWIR S0.

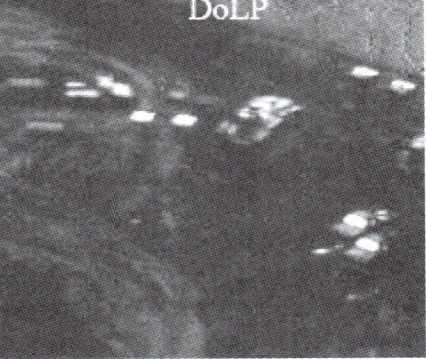

Figure 21-24
Images taken of a military equipment scene with the top image in the visible, the bottom left in the broadband LWIR, and the bottom right using LWIR polarimetry. (Images courtesy of the US Army.) [2]

CHAPTER 21 POLARIMETRIC IMAGING **443**

21.3 APPLICATIONS AND COLLECTION GEOMETRIES FOR LINEAR POLARIMETRIC IMAGING

In the preceding discussion of sources, detection, and data collection of linear PI, several applications were identified and possibly illustrated. Differences in material surface properties (in particular smoothness) provide the basis of all these applications. These differences are identified by detecting differences in collected radiation in terms of polarization direction (e.g., V versus H). This radiation can be reflected (primarily in the visible to Shortwave Infrared (SWIR) or thermally emitted (primarily in the MWIR and LWIR).

As previously discussed, single flat surfaces (multipixel or subpixel in spatial extent) that differ in smoothness from the background can be readily identified. Often these surfaces are smoother than vegetation background. These surfaces can be man-made, such as vehicles, metal rooftops, storage tanks, etc; and some can be naturally occurring, such as still water in puddles, ponds, or swamps, ice, packed soil, etc. Some object surfaces of interest can be more rough than a background of bare earth, such as disturbed earth.

Multiple surfaces in a variety of spatial orientations, each of which differs from that of the background, can be identified. Examples include some forms of broadleaf vegetation amid conifer forests. In addition to identifying flat surfaces with smoothness different than the surfaces of the background, the orientation, or aspect, of the surface can often be determined. For a single surface larger than a pixel with an orientation angle θ relative to a horizontal surface, see **Equation 21-6**. For multi-surface objects greater than one pixel in size, surface orientation and size give a general idea of shape. Several studies have provided successful analysis, including that of G. A. Atkinson and E. R. Hancock. [3]

Gas plume detection is possible because of differences in the polarization of solar scattering by gases and aerosols in the plume versus the ambient atmosphere. Such gas plumes can be observed within industrial facilities as well as amid vegetation. Another interesting capability of PI is detection in shadows. Examples of this capability are shown in **Figures 21-25** to **21-27**. The top color image in **Figure 21-25** is taken in the visible, while the bottom two involve visible PI. At the top of the lower right image, two cars appear amid the shadows of the trees (circled in red).

Figure 21-25
Detection of cars parked in shadows using PI. (Courtesy of US Army Research Lab, Adelphi, MD.) [4]

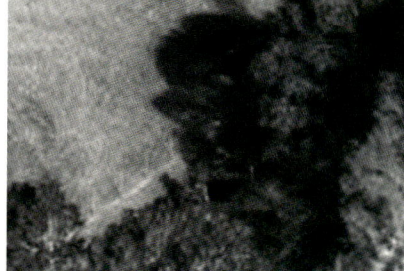
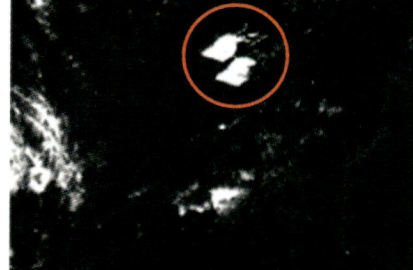

In **Figure 21-26**, the top row of images displays broadband visible on the left and broadband thermal on the right. In the bottom row of images, PI imagery results on the left and superimposed on the broadband thermal on the right. Both of these images show a possible vehicle parked along the treeline.

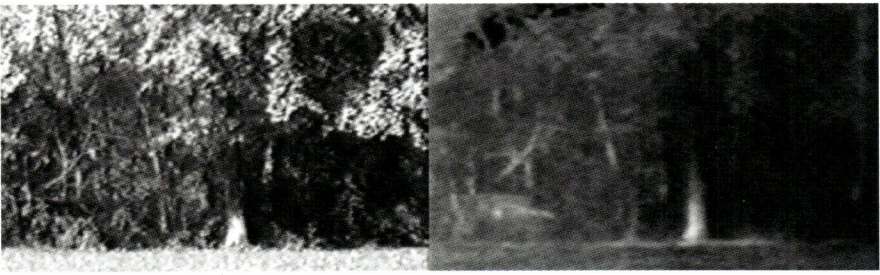

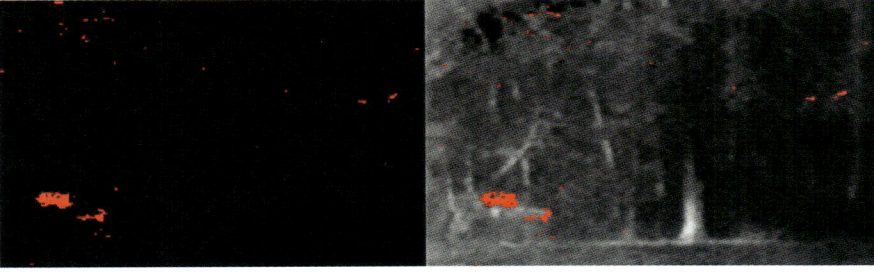

Figure 21-26
Detection of vehicles parked in shadows of a treeline using PI. [5]

In **Figure 21-27**, the broadband visible image (top) shows three parked aircraft. In the visible PI (bottom), the aircraft visible as well as details of the walls and ceiling of the hanger.

Figure 21-27
Details of the inside of a hanger using PI. [6]

As described in the previous discussion, PI provides many of the same possible capabilities as spectral imagery. Both sensing modalities have demonstrated anomaly detection and terrain categorization, including swamps and disturbed earth, to some extent (varying from application to application).

In considering preliminary conclusions regarding PI, sufficient evidence does not exist to decide whether PI or spectral imagery provides a better capability in any of the applications. Probably neither one is better under all conditions. If both types of data can be collected in the same scene (this will be discussed later in this section), the difference in phenomenology between the two could produce increased confidence versus collecting only one type of data. Certainly both sensing modalities provide some advantageous capabilities. Unique to spectral sensing is the chemical identification of solid, liquid, and gas materials that compose the objects of interest.

Characteristic of polarimetric sensing is object surface orientation or aspect determination and crude material categorization by surface smoothness. These are summarized in **Figure 21-28**, as well as the relation of PI to MSI, HSI, and single broadband imagery. Of course, the latter integrates the most spectral and polarimetric properties of the imaged scene.

Figure 21-28
Relationships of panchromatic, spectral, and polarimetric imagery.

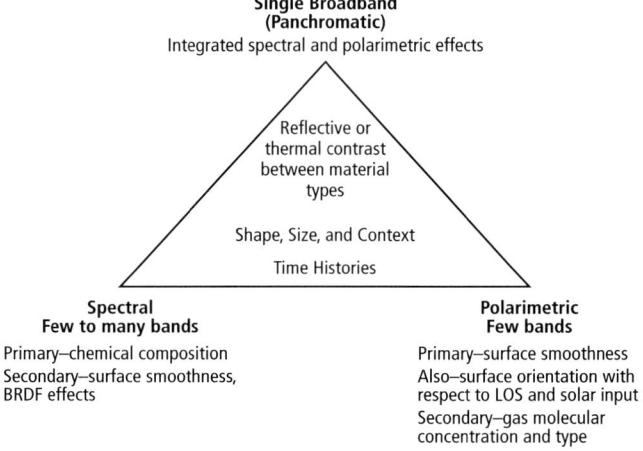

Spectral imagery and polarimetric imagery in the visible-SWIR can be further compared regarding the optimum data collection geometries. **Table 21-4** shows this comparison in terms of sun location versus sensor location for the collection.

Table 21-4
Comparison of the collection of spectral data with that of visible linear polarimetric data.

	Spectral	Polarimetric
Sun location Elevation angle	Most experience to date is near mid-day to maximize received irradiance	Larger nadir angles promote larger ρ_H, ρ_V, and $(\rho_H - \rho_V)$ values; hence low sun elevation angles desired (up to a point) for horizontal surfaces
Sensor location Nadir angle	Most experience to date is near nadir to maximize received irradiance and minimize atmospheric transmission effects	Larger nadir angles promote larger ρ_H, ρ_V, and $(\rho_H - \rho_V)$ values; hence far off nadir viewing desired for horizontal surfaces**
Sun/Sensor location Azimuthal angle	Sensors avoid looking anywhere near sun	Sensors need to look toward (but not directly at) the sun to maximize received irradiance

** Recall that off-nadir viewing increases ground pixel size

While spectral imagery collection prefers the sun high in the sky and sensors looking generally downward, PI collection in the visible-SWIR prefers the sun lower in the sky with sensors looking in the general direction of the sun. This latter requirement comes from the strong differences in reflection between the H and V components at angles far from nadir viewing. As discussed below, fewer constraints exist for collecting PI in the MWIR and LWIR, especially at night.

Recall the enlarged ground pixels from off-nadir viewing. The size of this effect is shown in **Figure 21-29** (and **Table 21-5**), initially presented in **Chapter 16**, where the y-axis lies along the nadir path of the platform (off of the page), and the z-axis is perpendicular to the Earth's surface.

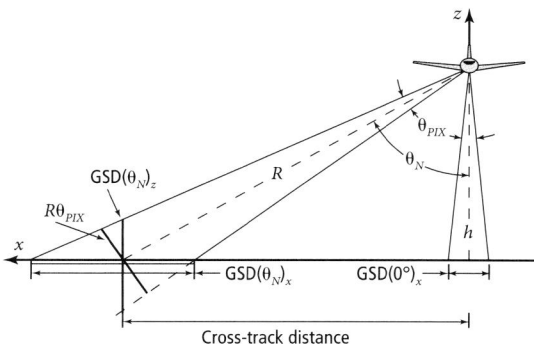

Figure 21-29
Geometry of off-nadir imaging.

Based on the above discussion, together spectral and polarimetric sensing in the visible-SWIR can expand the coverage capabilities of either one if used by itself. When viewing the horizontal surfaces of a given target at a given location relative to the sensor, spectral is best for targets near to nadir of the sensor, while PI is best for targets far-off nadir of the sensor. (When viewing the other surfaces of a target, other conclusions may result.)

For spectral and polarimetric measurements taken of a target from the same platform, either one or the other (or possibly both) will not produce the highest quality imagery in terms of detected objects of interest and overall received irradiance.

Multiple polarimetric imagery collections of the same scene may only show some objects when the viewing conditions are nearly optimum. This may provide possible increased confidence of detection of flat smooth objects that are specularly reflecting. Objects that appear in imagery taken over a variety of viewing conditions are likely not flat, smooth specular reflectors.

Collection of PI is considerably different in the thermal emission dominated MWIR-LWIR than in the solar reflective dominated visible-SWIR. Because of very little reflected sunlight in the MWIR-LWIR for most objects, there is little consideration of sun-sensor viewing geometry necessary for specular reflections. Thermal emission involves emissivities that are often close to one in value. Based on the previously discussed specular reflection curves for smooth surfaces, **Figure 21-30** shows the corresponding polarimetric reflectivity and emissivity curves. Based on these curves, the difference in radiance in the MWIR-LWIR from a smooth surface is given by **Equation 21-3**.

Table 21-5
Increase of ground pixel size with increasing nadir angle.

θ_N	$\dfrac{(GSD)_Y}{(GSD(0))_Y}$	$\dfrac{(GSD)_Z}{(GSD(0))_Y}$	$\dfrac{(GSD)_X}{(GSD(0))_X}$
0	1.0	N/A	1.0
45	1.4	0.7	2.0
60	2.0	2.3	4.0
70	2.9	3.1	8.5
75	3.9	4.0	14.9
80	5.8	5.9	33.2

Figure 21-30
Reflectivity, ρ, (top) and emissivity, ϵ, (bottom).

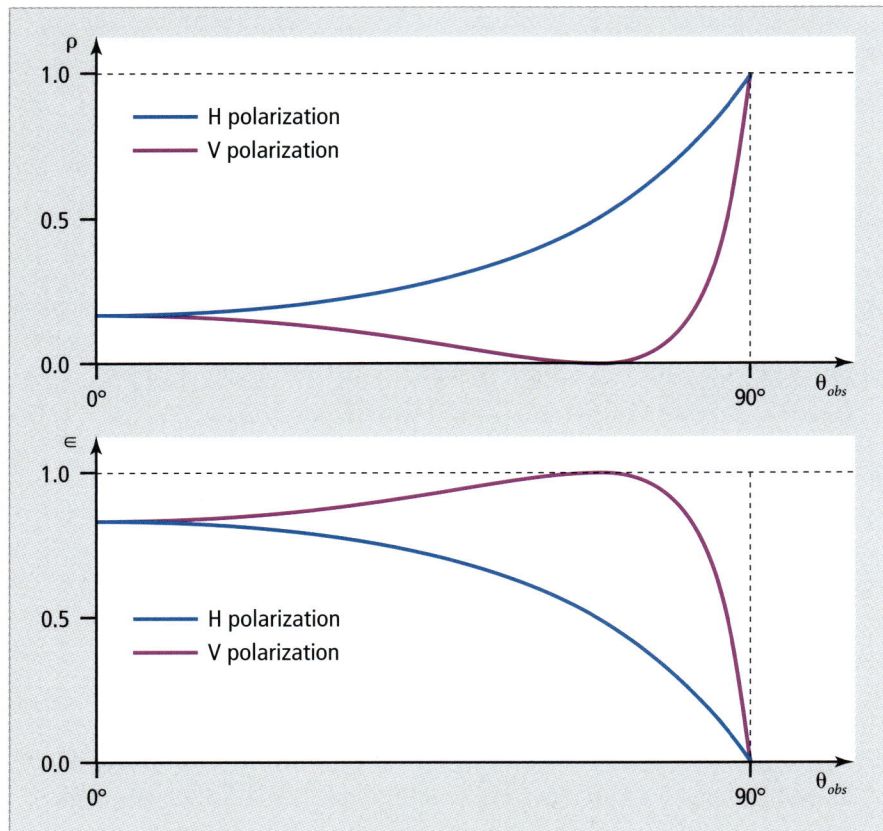

The collection strategies for PI in the MWIR-LWIR are slightly different than in the visible-SWIR. Although nadir viewing provides larger emissivity values, there is no difference between L_H and L_V. The largest values of $L_H - L_V$ occur at similar off-nadir angle values in the thermal infrared as in the visible-SWIR. One important difference is the specular sun-sensor viewing geometry does not need to be maintained, only the large nadir angle (independent of sun location in the sky).

22 THE FUTURE OF REMOTE SENSING

*In **Chapters 12** to **21**, several remote sensing applications were discussed in the illustration of various sensors and analysis techniques. In fact, the remote sensing community has spent considerable effort demonstrating many of these applications because of their potential to provide answers to some of the Department of Defense (DOD) and the Intelligence Community's (IC) most pressing intelligence applications that only remote sensing can answer.*

This chapter surveys a broad range of interests for which remote sensing has significant potential to provide useful information to the all-source analyst. Some additional applications will be introduced for the first time; these may have been considered by the remote sensing community but not yet demonstrated.

SECTIONS

- 22.1 GROUPING REMOTE SENSING APPLICATIONS
- 22.2 APPLICATION CLASSES
- 22.3 SPECIFIC INTERESTS
- 22.4 SUMMARY

22.1 GROUPING REMOTE SENSING APPLICATIONS

There are several approaches for grouping remote sensing applications. One approach divides them into three groups of applications: military, civilian, or intelligence. As illustrated in **Figure 22-1**, these three groups considerably overlap in that two or three of these communities may be involved with the same sort of application in various parts of the world for different reasons. Or, they may be collaborating to solve a problem of interest to all of them. Examples of this will be described in the following discussion.

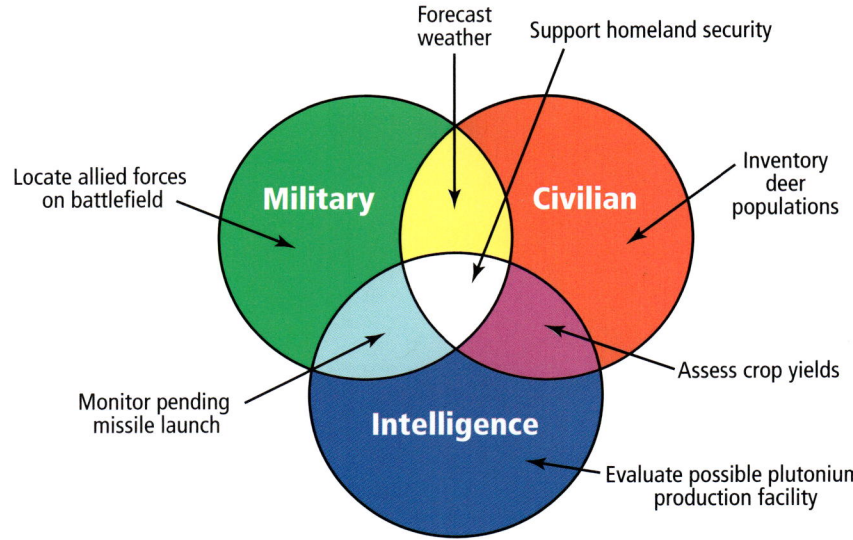

Figure 22-1
Interconnection of groups of remote sensing applications and some specific and overlapping examples. Security classification and communication limitations often reduce the amount of overlap that can be achieved.

Another approach to grouping application types is in terms of two common functions: reconnaissance (wide area survey) and surveillance (monitoring). Reconnaissance involves the infrequent observation of a wide area to identify (and locate) significant objects or events of interest. While all the remote sensing communities perform this function, the targets may vary considerably. The military may be interested in potential objects of interest such as surface-to-air missile batteries and the civilian community is interested in targets such as forests.

On the other hand, surveillance involves repeated observation of a specific area for changes of known targets or the appearance of new targets as a function of time. Again, while all the sensing communities perform this kind of function, the objects of interest may vary considerably. The military may be interested in potential targets such as aircraft parked at a foreign air base; the IC may focus on foreign power plants; and the civilian community may be interested in nighttime criminal activity at a given location. Some applications could be classified as either of the two functions. For example, the application of missile launch detection involves repeatedly searching a large area.

22.2 APPLICATION CLASSES

Within the application groups are a number of classes. These classes of specific applications are quite similar in nature.

SUPPORT TO MILITARY OPERATIONS

The first application class is Support to Military Operations (SMO). Because this is such a broad applications class, it can be divided into the following six sub-classes:

- Intelligence Preparation of the Battlespace (IPB)
- Indications and Warnings (I&W)
- Situational Awareness (SA)
- Special Operations (SO)
- Targeting support
- Deployment and employment of forces

Closely allied to the SMO class of remote sensing applications is Scientific and Technical Intelligence (S&TI), providing military planners and battlefield commanders with information on the capabilities and performance of an enemy's weapon systems.

The first three sub-classes of SMO are similar in function, although they vary over the time frame they are performed. The first, IPB, occurs throughout the world before there is even a hint of possible military activities involving a particular country. The goal is to obtain all possible information about every country, including its military capabilities, economic capabilities, and political characteristics. This information becomes part of a larger schema, the Joint Intelligence Preparation of the Operational Environment, as described in Joint Publication 2-01.3, 16 June 2009. [1], [2] This is retained for future use. The Central Intelligence Agency (CIA) also supports this activity and maintains all the information in their "World Fact Book," an unclassified version that can be accessed on their unclassified website. [3]

The second sub-class, I&W, focuses on specific parts of the world where there is evidence for future hostilities. Specific locations are watched for significant changes.

The third SMO sub-class, SA, or threat assessment, occurs during the "heat of battle." For example, a pilot flying an aircraft over a foreign country wants to know who else is in the air nearby, the location of enemy planes, the direction they are flying, and the type of armament they are carrying. And, the pilot wants all this information from battlespace surveillance sensors immediately, or as close to "real time" as possible. This information channel is sometimes known as sensor-to-shooter. [4]

For SO, all three activities previously described are accomplished, but on a significantly finer scale over a substantially smaller local area. Instead of needing a street map of a large city to observe the movement of large numbers of troops and vehicles, a small SO team would require a map of the alleyways and pedestrian paths within a two block area of the city.

The above discussion focuses on the capabilities, activities, and threats on land involving various foreign countries. In addition, the US Navy conducts maritime domain analysis, which includes global maritime SA and threat analysis for naval operations as well as civilian commercial shipping.

Targeting support, the fifth sub-class, provides aircraft pilots the capability to find desired targets and assist in putting "bombs on targets." Post-strike follow-up activities use intelligence sensors for battle damage assessment to ascertain mission effectiveness and determine the need for re-strike or further operations.

Lastly, deployment of forces involves locating and tracking ground vehicles, ships, submarines, aircraft, and troops (**Figure 22-2**). Employment of forces includes detecting missile launches, geolocating, and detecting their impact (bomb explosions).

Figure 22-2
Troops deploying for battle action.

S&TI is critical to SMO. An important aspect of S&TI is the "all-source" analyst who is the US expert for some system or facility of interest. He/she uses information from all sources of intelligence (including the results from remote sensing). Depending on the system or facility, the location of the all-source analyst varies. For foreign aircraft, long-range missiles, satellites, and their supporting equipment and facilities, the Air Force's National Air and Space Intelligence Center (NASIC) has the all-source responsibility. [5] For foreign ground vehicles of all kinds, the Army's National Ground Intelligence Center (NGIC) has the lead. [6] For all foreign ships and ocean activity, the Navy's Office of Naval Intelligence (ONI) is the leading responsible organization. Intelligence for expeditionary missions in littoral areas is the purview of the Marine Corps Intelligence Activity (MCIA). [7], [8] Finally, for short-range missiles, DIA's Missile and Space Intelligence Center (MSIC) has the lead. [9]

FOREIGN RELATIONS

Another application class is Arms Control/Treaty Monitoring with associated sub-classes of weapons proliferation, trade, and economic security. Generally, the US government does not become a signatory to any treaty or agreement unless sufficient sensor capability is present to ensure all other signatory countries are abiding by the terms of the treaty or agreement. Three examples of such treaties or agreements are listed below.

- Nuclear, Biological, Chemical (NBC) weapons conventions, or the more recent term Chemical, Biological, Radiological, Nuclear, Explosives (CBRNE): Nuclear or other radioactive material can be detected with radioactivity monitoring sensors if it is moved illegally. These sensors could be deployed at strategic locations, such as points of entry on the border between two countries; seaport, airport, or cargo areas; or major public events. [10]

- Treaty on Open Skies: First suggested by President Eisenhower in 1955, 34 nations now agree to allow aircraft carrying video, optical panoramic, and framing cameras; infrared line scanners; and synthetic aperture radars over other nation's territories. Observation flights may only be restricted for reasons of flight safety, not national security. Imagery resolution may not be better than 30 centimeters, sufficient to distinguish between tanks and trucks. [11]
- Limited Nuclear Test Ban Treaty: Nuclear detonation detection sensors, called bhangmeters, which are similar in design to the lightning detection sensor discussed in **Chapter 14**, are deployed on the constellation of Global Positioning System (GPS) satellites. [12]

The first treaty involves manufacturing, storage, and the use of weapons involving NBC, or CBRNE, agents. The second treaty, enacted in 2002, specifies the number and types of sensors that signatory nations may fly over each other's sovreign territories. The third was initiated earlier (1963) and limits testing nuclear weapons in the atmosphere or space.

Associated with arms control is weapons proliferation. After the recent years of search across Iraq (**Figure 22-3**), this term immediately brings to mind weapons of mass destruction (WMD). Most commentators think of a WMD as a large amount of chemical, biological, or radioactive material. But, there is more to it. A WMD includes the means to deliver and distribute the WMD agent. For example, a sealed 55-gallon drum of the nerve gas sarin at a location is not a WMD even though it contains enough lethality to likely kill everyone in a large city. A way to deliver this sarin to a desired location and spread it over a large area is also required.

Figure 22-3
Part of a weapons stockpile discovered south of Baghdad.

Conventional weapon proliferation is also challenging. Many countries export various military equipment, such as fighter aircraft and ballistic missiles, to other countries with whom they are allied, or for profit, or both. Unfortunately, this equipment may be re-sold to other governments or organizations. Tracking the equipment a particular country or organization possesses is a real challenge. Further compounding this problem is the business activity that upgrades certain equipment as it passes from one owner to the next. For example, the Soviet Union built thousands of MiG-21 fighter aircraft beginning in the 1970s. While the aircraft as it was initially built does not pose a significant threat by today's standards, industry in various countries has retrofitted and upgraded certain sub-systems of the aircraft, such as engines, avionics, munitions, etc. Therefore, images of MiG-21s on a country's airfields do not provide much information about that country's air capability.

Also closely associated with monitoring a nation's weapons is realizing all possible remote sensing assets to track their trade and economic activities. Trade and Economic Security, monitoring energy, raw materials, and agricultural production, makes this application seem extremely civilian oriented. Many findings are posted in the previously mentioned CIA World Fact Book.

HOMELAND SECURITY

An important class of remote sensing applications is homeland security: detecting and locating transnational organized crime, primarily illegal drug trafficking; assisting in anti- and counter-terrorism activities; protecting the borders; and law enforcement in general. Of course, any reconnaissance or surveillance completed within the US or directed toward any US person or entity by any DOD/IC asset must have the proper permission from the appropriate oversight authority.

Counterdrug operations include the discovery, location, and characterization of crops, processing sites, and distribution methods. This application class suggests a civilian focus and employment through such agencies as the Drug Enforcement Administration and Department of Homeland Security (DHS). However, the DOD and IC play an important role as well. One of the major DOD unified commands, US Southern Command, whose area of responsibility is the entire Western Hemisphere south of the US-Mexican border, has counterdrug as its primary mission.

Finding drug crops, such as coca bushes, opium poppies, or marijuana plants, is frequently touted as an easy application of spectral sensing. This is not totally true; it sometimes requires knowledge of the growing season as well as other crops which may also be purposely growing amid the drug crops. Some of these challenges are illustrated in **Figure 22-4** for the opium poppy. When poppy plants are filled with red flowers or white capsules, spectral detection becomes much easier than when the plants look very similar to other green plants.

Figure 22-4
Opium poppy properties.

Mature Capsule Mature Plant with Flowers Poppy Flower Poppy Field

(Mature capsule photo courtesy of http://en.wikipedia.org/wiki/File:Papaver_somniferum_%27Opium_poppy%27_(Papaveraceae)_seed_pod.JPG; Creative Commons Attribution-Share Alike 3.0 Unported, 2.5 Generic, 2.0 Generic and 1.0 Generic: Magnus Manske. Mature plant photo courtesy of http://en.wikipedia.org/wiki/File:Papaver_somniferum_%27Opium_poppy%27_(Papaveraceae)_plant.JPG; Creative Commons Attribution-Share Alike 3.0 Unported, 2.5 Generic, 2.0 Generic and 1.0 Generic: Magnus Manske. Poppy flower photo courtesy of http://en.wikipedia.org/wiki/File:Oriental_poppies_gone_wild_-_geograph.org.uk_-_1397319.jpg; Creative Commons Attribution-Share Alike 2.0 Generic: Evelyn Simak. Poppy field photo courtesy of http://en.wikipedia.org/wiki/File:Field_of_opium_poppies_and_gallop_-_geograph.org.uk_-_496807.jpg; Creative Commons Attribution-Share Alike 2.0 Generic: Hugh Chevallier.)

Processing sites where the appropriate harvested plant parts are processed into powder (e.g., coca bush leaves into white powder that will eventually be sold as cocaine) are usually not far from the growing fields. But, often this processing activity does not require significant facilities or equipment. In the case of coca bush leaf processing in Columbia, open metallic roof shelters house the processing that consists of microwave cookers, diesel generators, large reactor vessels, and large amounts of common chemicals. Authorities often find such a facility after processing activities have stopped and moved to a new location.

Detection of the distribution of the drugs to market, primarily to the US and Europe, is more difficult. Clever approaches are in place. For example, moving cocaine from Columbia and other Southern American countries has involved miniature submarines following the Central American coastline to the US and transnational organized crime owned jet aircraft flying to West Africa on its way to European markets or even those in the US. Also, large foreign cargo ships can be used. Once near the coastlines of the market area, the large ship loaded with drugs is met by smaller high speed boats that transport the product to market. Of course, if any of these "pleasure boats" come in sight of the Coast Guard, the contraband can easily be thrown overboard. [13], [14]

Counter-terrorism and anti-terrorism have become very important from almost every government agency's perspective. Unfortunately, it is not always well-defined because of the large differences worldwide regarding terrorist organizations and operations.

Border defense is another important application class that utilizes the DOD and IC's sensing technology. While DHS is in charge of border monitoring, Predator unmanned aerial vehicles have routinely flown the US-Mexican border for a number of years, and they now patrol the US-Canadian border. Infrastructure protection within the US is performed by the DHS and contractor personnel associated with the particular site involved. [15] Again, DOD and IC sensing equipment is utilized. Overseas, US government infrastructure protection is the responsibility of the DOD and IC.

Law enforcement is an application class that is seems completely civilian. Certainly within the US this may be true, but consider the military campaigns involving US troops overseas in the last 20 years: Somali, Grenada, Bosnia, Kosovo, Afghanistan, and Iraq. In each, US personnel performed "law enforcement" duties because the local police forces were either insufficient or non-existent.

EARTH ENVIRONMENT

Remote sensors have been successfully used for decades to help understand the Earth's environment. Observations of the atmosphere, the oceans, and the land have led to many important applications.

Weather forecasting is a well-defined application of strong interest to both the civilian community and the DOD and IC. Interestingly, since the 1960s, both parties have maintained their own weather satellites. These satellite sensors include two spectral sensing applications: cloud mapping and determining temperature, pressure, and humidity profiles around the world (**Figure 22-5**).

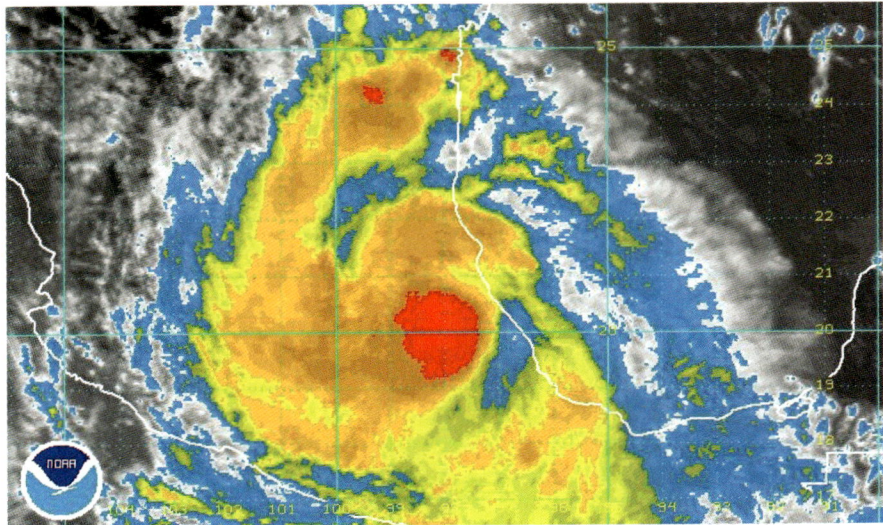

Figure 22-5
Satellite image of Hurricane Dean over Mexico on August 22, 2007 charting wind speed and rainfall.

Oceanography is another well-defined application of strong interest to both the civilian community and the DOD and IC. Both are interested in sea state (wave height, etc.) in the broad ocean areas as well as sea-state and bathymetry in the littoral (shoreline) regions.

Land-use analysis is important to civilian planners as well, because they provide indications of an expanded capability of a particular country. Environmental applications, traditionally the purview of the civilian community, have been of increasing interest to the DOD and IC. The US Army cannot conduct a mock tank battle in the remote area of one of their installations, such as Ft. A. P. Hill, Virginia, without first filing an environmental impact statement as well as a remediation plan. Spectral and other remote sensing is necessary to support these activities. Likewise, this sensing can be used for site clean-up where various types of industrial waste were buried in the past.

LOOKING UP

Astronomical sciences and astrophysics is an important application for the National Aeronautics and Space Administration (NASA) and multiple universities. But, sometimes the DOD and IC have led the way. An idea generated over 40 years ago within the DOD is tracking satellites and missiles in the post-boost portion of their flight using sensors in the Long-Wave Infrared (LWIR). The satellite or missile should be warmer than the effective temperature of the cold space background. It was quickly recognized that this background has some warm objects such as stars. So, the DOD and IC approached NASA and the civilian universities in search of infrared star catalogs. To their initial amazement, few of these catalogs existed because the DOD was at the forefront of infrared detector technology. So, the DOD and IC started measurements for the first infrared star catalogs, building infrared observatories (e.g., Mt. Haleakala, Hawaii), providing detectors, and funding measurement campaigns. Visible star images do not always spatially correlate with those in the infrared, as shown in **Figure 22-6**. [16], [17], [18]

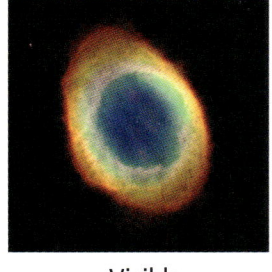

Figure 22-6
Visible and infrared imagery compared for various astronomical objects. (M-29 Star Cluster Visible photo used with permission from Kopernik Observatory & Science Center. M-29 Star Cluster SWIR and M-57 Ring Nebula SWIR photos: Atlas Image obtained as part of the Two Micron All Sky Survey (2MASS), a joint project of the University of Massachusetts and the Infrared Processing and Analysis Center/California Institute of Technology, funded by the National Aeronautics and Space Administration and the National Science Foundation. M-57 Ring Nebula MWIR photo courtesy of NASA/JPL-Caltech.)

22.3 SPECIFIC INTERESTS

Various specific challenges will now be discussed. Each of these is included in one or more of the application classes discussed in **Section 22.2**.

LAND, SEA, AND SHORE INTERESTS

Thorough knowledge of the littoral regions is an essential specific application for the conduct of maritime operations. Both bathymetry and underwater obstacle maps are required. Bathymetry involves knowing the water depth and is dependent on the ocean floor (e.g., sand, coral, vegetation, etc.) to some extent at any given location. Some examples of the results of multispectral imagery bathymetry were shown in **Chapter 15**.

Broad ocean and harbor navigation are further complicated by ice at high latitudes during winter months. Solid ice sheets and icebergs pose challenges for naval operations and civilian commercial shipping. The condition of ice sheets must be carefully monitored and mapped throughout the winter. (See **Figure 15-21**.)

Mine detection has continued to be a critical specific application since the 1940s. It is difficult because of the wide variety of mines (shape and size) deployed in the water (on or below the surface) and on land (on or below the surface). This difficulty is further emphasized by the continuing reports of civilian injuries from detonation of previously undetected land mines that have remained in place for long periods of time, dating back to World War II in some cases.

MILITARY INTERESTS

The first specific challenge involves the terrain categorization (tercat) and trafficability products shown in **Chapter 15**. The Army requires safe, rapid movement of troops and vehicles between two points, either over roads or cross-country. Just because a road exists does not necessarily mean it will support the weight of heavy vehicles. A road that will support the heavy weight involved may suffice for one trip. But, this first trip may sufficiently damage the road, making it impassable for any follow-on trips. Cross-country travel raises other risks, primarily marsh and swamps. If vehicles get mired in a swampy area, their movement is significantly slowed; they become more vulnerable to the enemy, and excessive efforts are required to free them. A related application is to use the tercat information for a given region with elevation data to provide images for mission training movies for force commanders. These may become part of simulator exercises (e.g., an aircraft pilot landing at an airport with nearby mountains, such as Denver Colorado, or a ship captain sailing to a complex harbor, such as New York City). Additional simulated missions could involve aircraft departures and aircraft drop-zones.

Tracking the movement of single or multiple vehicles across land or sea is an important requirement for the conduct of military operations. When a large number of vehicles are involved, the job is easier. Tracking single vehicles is more difficult, especially if it is desired for the tracking to be completed in a stealthy manner. Again, the spectral tagging discussed in **Chapter 18** is relevant.

Counter camouflage, concealment, and deception for threat detection and target location are a very important set of specific challenges. Countries do not want the location of their valuable military equipment or facilities known by their enemies. The use of camouflage netting is widespread. Small camouflage nets may be used to hide vehicles, and circus tent-size camouflage nets may be used to hide the specifics of on-going activities. Camouflage nets were initially designed to have similar spectra to that of nearby vegetation, primarily across the visible and near-visible infrared. An older type of this camouflage also provides a textured "leafy" look to further blend into nearby vegetation. Such netting is shown **Figure 22-7**, first close-up, and then deployed amid prevailing vegetation. This type of camouflage netting is difficult to deploy because it tends to snag easily. Hence, more recent camouflage nets are flat sheets with a pattern of holes to make them lighter in weight.

Figure 22-7
Left: Close-up view of a camouflage net with a textured look.
Right: View of a camouflage net with a textured look deployed amid vegetation. (Photos Copyright: Saab Barracuda.)

Camouflage technology and production have significantly expanded. There is now a camouflage net for every location and season, as shown in **Figure 22-8**. To alleviate the necessity of continually covering and

Figure 22-8
Images of camouflage nets deployed for all seasons and locations.
Top: desert
Bottom: winter woodland
(Photos Copyright: Saab Barracuda.)

uncovering mobile vehicles, either appropriate camouflage paint or custom camouflage netting may be used, as shown in **Figure 22-9**. Camouflage paint can be used to reduce the LWIR signature of a vehicle, and hence make it more difficult to detect.

Figure 22-9
Customized camouflage for a tank. (Image courtesy of http://en.wikipedia.org/wiki/File:Marder_1A5_Mobile_Camouflage_System_Barracuda.jpg; Creative Commons Attribution 3.0 Unported: Sonaz.)

Decoys are surrogate look-alikes for the real objects. Often these decoys are located where overhead sensors cannot miss them. Decoys range in expense and degree of fidelity from crude, but effective construction made of existing materials in the field to an actual outer shell of the real object coupled with a few heaters inside to provide a thermal signature. An intriguing approach to decoys is "inflatables." These are specially designed balloons that, when inflated, have the correct size, shape, and color. Examples of such decoys are shown in **Figures 22-10** and **22-11**. Barely visible in these photos at close range are the stakes and guide wires necessary to keep these decoys from blowing away from their desired location. To a pilot rapidly flying above, this decoy looks like the "real thing."

Figure 22-10
Inflated decoys.
(Courtesy of buzzmuseum.com) [19], [20]

Figure 22-11
Inflated decoys.
(Courtesy of buzzmuseum.com) [19], [20]

Another important specific interest, battle damage assessment (formerly known as bomb damage assessment), has existed for a number of years. Since the first bombing of targets from airborne platforms, the question to every pilot after the mission is, "Did you destroy, or put out of business, your assigned target?" If not, further missions may need to be conducted against the same target. Visible imagery of the target, both before and after the bomb arrived, is often used as a basis for answering this question. Unfortunately, such imagery often does not answer the question. Consider some kind of production facility. Obviously, a bomb on target may leave a large hole in the roof of the building. But, the real question is "Did the bomb stop the production activities within the facility?," or "Did the bomb simply damage the storage area?"

Nuclear testing, either in the lower or upper levels of the atmosphere or with shallow buried devices, can provide indications of the design of the nuclear device. This could include the types of materials used in a warhead as well as the energies of the various nuclear particles released by the detonation, such as gamma rays and high energy electrons.

Field testing or battlefield use of chemical and biological agents are of immense interest to the US Army and other ground forces. Providing ground forces with the earliest possible alert of the presence of these agents at a distance can enable them the opportunity to don protective gear. [21]

Underground facilities (UGFs), or their more recent nomenclature, Hard Deeply Buried Targets (HDBTs), are a long-time interest (**Figure 22-12**). In the US, there is Cheyenne Mountain near Colorado Springs, Colorado, which was built to house the command post for combating the Soviet bomber and ICBM threat during the Cold War. UGFs are used worldwide for multiple purposes, from common uses such as command posts and ammunition storage to submarine docks and aircraft storage. The UGF interest is not just to detect them, but also to characterize them in terms of status, ongoing or potential use, and physical structure. [23], [24], [25]

Figure 22-12
The challenge of UGFs. [22]

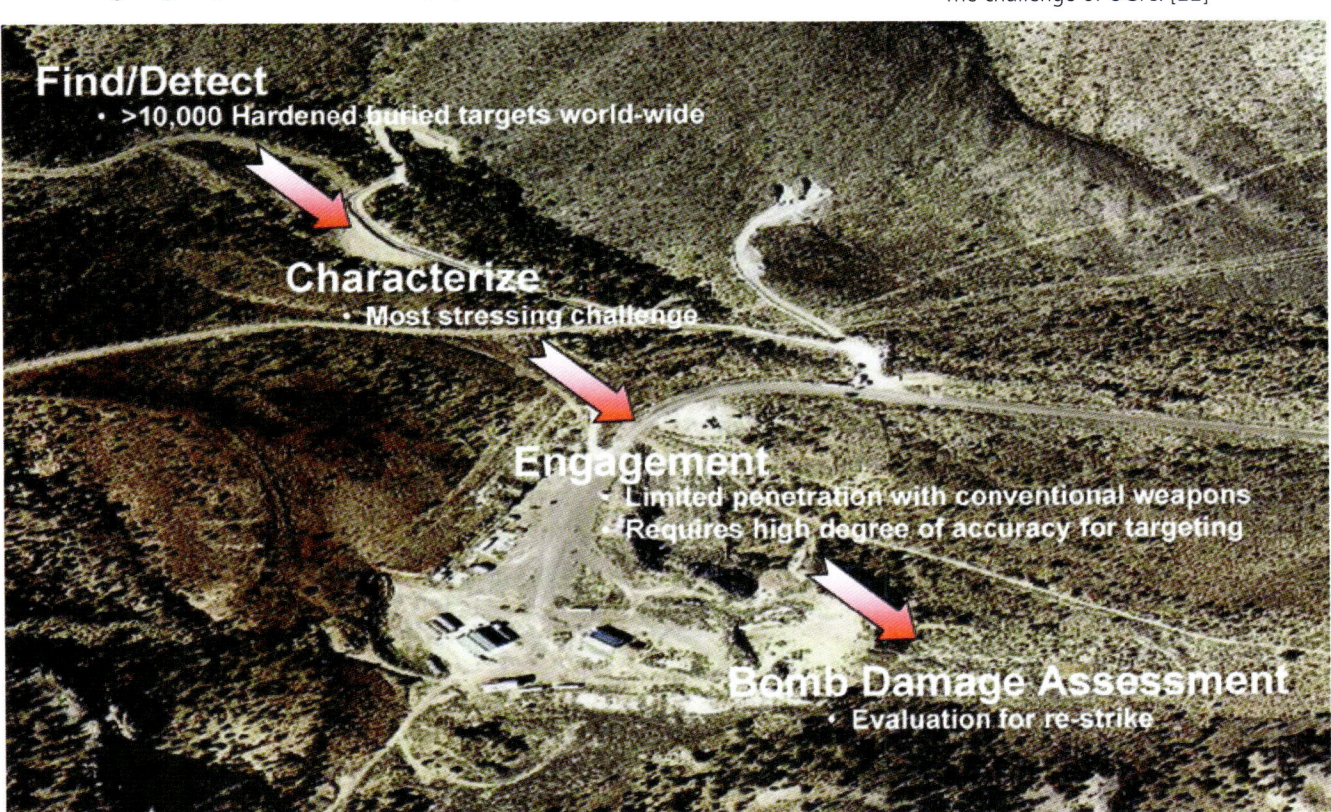

CIVIL AND ENVIRONMENTAL INTERESTS

Identification of new construction can be indicative of a nation's infrastructure development. For remote sites, there can be an extremely large area to cover on a routine basis. For urban sites, the degree of complexity across the image may be equally challenging to easily find a small change. On a large scale, the pattern of urban development can also provide information about the future infrastructure of a nation. Change detection, using a large-scale coverage sensor such as Landsat (discussed in **Chapter 15**), can assist in this application.

Facility effluent detection and identification can provide information regarding the processes occurring within the facility. This effluent can take the form of gas releases or waste liquid or solid dumping into nearby bodies of water or even onto the ground. Remember, most nations do not have the same pollution regulations as the US. Hyperspectral imaging detection and identification of atmospheric gas clouds were discussed in **Chapter 20**. Detection and identification of gases near a known volcano crater can be indicative of future eruption. Further discussion of the prediction of a volcanic eruption is below.

Crop identification and characterization is another interest that is not as simple as sometimes advertised. Crop identification was discussed earlier in the context of drug crops. Characterization in terms of crop yield or plant health can vary in difficulty, depending upon the crop type. For some crops, such as those in which the plant leaves are harvested, crop yields can be based on the measured spectral values of the plant material contained in a pixel. For other crops, such as corn or beans, the amount of healthy vegetation per pixel may or may not correlate with the number of ears of corn or beans present. Finding crops in poor health because of drought, fungus, disease, or insects is certainly an important need within the civilian community so farmers may attempt to rectify the situation. Assessing crop health is also important within the IC to accurately estimate a country's economic strength. Spectral measurements can certainly locate areas of stressed crops within a larger area of healthy crops, but determining causes other than drought can be difficult.

Temperature determination of air, ground, and objects of interest is important for a variety of reasons. Air temperatures for all altitudes and locations provide weather forecasters with inputs to weather forecasts to support both civilian activities and military operations. All weather satellites have sounders to measure these temperatures using spectral sensors, either in the infrared, microwave, or both. (See **Chapter 16**.) Ground temperatures can be useful to the Army and Navy trafficability problem. For the Army, ground temperatures below freezing for prolonged periods of time provide more options for the movement of forces over soil that may not ordinarily support vehicle weight. For the Navy, prolonged periods of surface temperature below freezing may provide a significant ice barrier to Navy vessels.

Forest fire patrol for the detection and characterization of fire threats is routinely provided in the US by the United States Forest Service, and US ground force operations oversea also require similar capabilities. Characterization includes the type of fire (what is burning) and the direction and speed of movement.

Disaster evaluation is important to any multi-agency relief operation. Within the US, DOD forces often lead the civilian agencies in performing initial and continuing search and rescue. Spectral applications, as well as other sensors, have been deployed to help assess the situation and search for survivors. Disaster evaluation overseas is equally important. Small countries, such as those in the Central and South America (the US Southern Command area of interest), depend on the US military for these capabilities. Often the stability of these countries is reliant on effectively helping them through crisis situations.

Volcanic activity detection, characterization, and prediction are the responsibility of the US Geologic Survey. Volcano prediction is a complex technical challenge. Volcanos can create tremors, expel ash, ooze gas for days, and then, nothing else happens. Or, they can start a major eruption with little or no warning. To complicate matters, people tend to establish homes around volcanoes, because the soils are often more fertile from previous eruptions and associated lava flows. These tendencies result in evacuation commitments to Third World countries and protection of our overseas assets and bases. For example, for nearly 93 years, Clark Air Force Base (AFB) in the Philippines was a major hub for supplies and aircraft in and out of the Pacific theater. Then, Mt. Pinatubo (**Figure 22-13**) erupted in 1991. While lava did not flow across Clark AFB, it was severely damaged by the earthquakes, extensive ash deposits from the volcano, and wind and rain from Typhoon Yunya. Aircraft operations in the region were at risk because ash in the air could stall engines, threatening both civil and military air operations. The US decided to abandon Clark AFB and redeploy assets elsewhere.

Figure 22-13
Mt. Pinatubo was the second largest volcano eruption of the 20th century on June 15, 1991.

AIR AND SPACE INTERESTS

Missile launch detection and warning has been performed by satellite sensors for years. Worldwide coverage is important because of the continuing increase in number, range, and countries holding these missiles. These increases can accentuate regional conflicts.

Space satellites are routinely tracked by the US using ground based radars and optical sensors. Characterizing foreign satellites in terms of status, mission, and structure is more difficult. Those satellites in low-earth orbit (altitudes of 185 to 1200 km) can be imaged in the visible, infrared, and microwave, using ground-based telescopes owned and operated by the DOD and IC (e.g., those at the peak of Mt. Haleakala in Hawaii). Higher-earth orbit satellites, such as those in geosynchronous orbits (altitudes of 35,700 km), cannot be imaged. (See **Section 6.3** on the Point Spread Function and its relation to spatial resolution in **Section 8.1**.) In either case, spectrometers can provide valuable information about the reflectivity of the surface materials used, which give some indication of the heating and cooling of the satellite. [16] (See **Chapter 6**.)

22.4 SUMMARY

The objective of advanced technical intelligence remote sensing is to provide information to customers about their targets of interest. Scientifically, as presented in this text, information is embodied in the amount of target energy (or energy per unit time: power) that can be collected. That energy is in the form of electromagnetic (EM) radiation (light waves or photons), and the emphasis in this chapter was on the electro-optical portion of the spectrum (visible and infrared). Collecting EM radiation is important because it is associated with *all* targets, can pass through "windows" in the atmosphere (to a limited extent), and has the unique property of being able to pass energy through the vacuum of space to remote sensors onboard satellites.

EM radiation arises as either continuum (thermal) radiation linked to the temperature of a target, or as selective radiation (atomic and molecular electronic, vibrational, and/or rotational quantum leaps) which is also linked to a target's temperature as the populations of its energy states. Thus, targets are seen as the emitters themselves or as reflectors, and rarely as absorbers. In any event, a target's spectral nature (emitting or reflecting, usually dependent on the bandpass of interest) is the target's *signature* for identification.

A target's radiation energy then propagates toward its interaction with and collection by an advanced technical intelligence remote sensor. Depending somewhat on collection geometry (principally distance), targets are viewed as either point sources (no discernible size or shape) or extended sources. But, backgrounds behind and surrounding targets are always seen as extended, albeit usually cluttered. The science of radiometry provides the mathematical link between target (or background) and the amount of energy (information) collected by a sensor.

Since intelligence collections are typically accomplished at long distances (to be stealthy and/or secure) and at visible through microwave wavelengths, significant atmospheric target energy loss mechanisms (absorption and scattering) must be understood and taken into account. Furthermore, the Earth's atmosphere interjects its own energy as a component of background and contrast reduction by virtue of its temperature and scattering properties. Particles of many sizes and materials (wet and dry) also "cloud" the issue as very mobile obscuring and radiating masses. However, knowing the composition, temperature, and distribution of atmospheric gases and suspended aerosols allows their influence on the remote sensing problem to be adequately compensated through proper application and interpretation of the attenuation law. This is often accomplished through sophisticated computer applications such as MODTRAN or LEEDR.

Energy from targets is therefore collected and detected, but not all remote sensors have the capability to see targets from all directions, in all bandpasses, or at all times. The amount of information to obtain is necessarily incomplete, and there will always be an amount of uncertainty as to the importance and significance of the information that could not be collected. Furthermore, the information obtained is not exactly from the target itself, but from studying the *image* of the target *within* a remote sensor. That is, a sensor's optics (collector) form a replica of a target that reproduces as accurately as possible the space-time-spectrum characteristics of a target, but on a two-dimensional array of detectors (whereas targets are three-dimensional objects). The detectors then *sample* the image.

Embedded within the formation of an image as a representation of a target is the fact that the image will be blurred by physical wave-optics considerations (the point spread function), target-sensor motion and jitter, and background/atmosphere obscuration. Additionally, the sampling process introduces limitations on the target energy acquired by imposing finite pixel size spatial sampling, limited duty cycle temporal integration, and continuous spectral dispersion. And there is noise: photon noise externally from the random production of energy from sources, thermal noise internally from warm sensor components, and quantum noise electronically from the conversion of an optical image into electrical digital data. All of these considerations determine the spatial, temporal, and spectral resolution limits with which information about a target may be discerned.

At the output end of the target-propagation-atmosphere-collection-detection chain of phenomenology (**Figure 22-14**), remote sensor data must proceed through more: processing, analysis, and exploitation. This is because of the facts previously stated, and here re-emphasized, that an image, although containing target information (energy), is *not* the target, but is the target as *sampled by* the sensor: spatially, spectrally, and temporally. Any information to be gained about a target's size, temperature, materials, geolocation, and motion must be extracted from a sensor's data by "reverse engineering" the image's formation through the sampling, collection, and propagation of target energy. This includes understanding the performance and calibration of the sensor.

Figure 22-14
The remote sensor phenomenology chain.

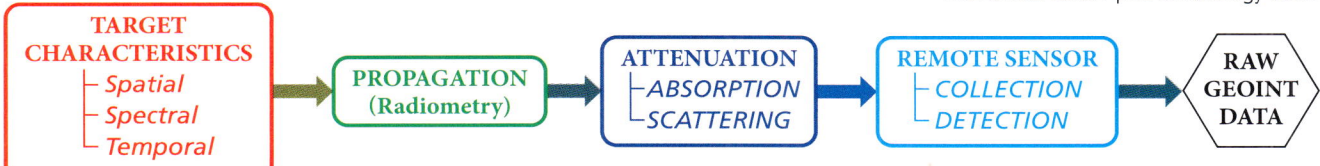

As presented in this text, processing is an act of removing artifacts from sensor data that are not related to a target (or background) and were introduced by manufacturing defects, operation conditions, or the environment. Processing ensures the correctness of data in an image through focal plane detector array calibration for radiometric accuracy. The next step, analysis, isolates energy associated with a target's image by several background removal or suppression algorithms. Analysis thus discovers the time-intensity or spectral-spatial signature, allowing possible identification of targets by comparison to ground truth (or previous collections). Finally, exploitation is the step that characterizes a target's metrics: its geolocation, relationship to the background, and trajectory (if moving).

Ultimately, the goal of advanced technical intelligence collection is to generate a *product* for a customer, providing as much information about a target of interest as can be inferred from remote sensing data. However, it is crucial to recognize that *all products are estimates* and will never have full and complete information about a target. This is because, as previously discussed, a target's energy output (information) has only been *sampled* by remote sensing methods. The time scale driving the requirement for a product may determine the completeness of processing-analysis-exploitation accomplished, but in all circumstances, intelligence products must state their degree of uncertainty.

Many intelligence collections have become routine over the years as sensor technology has matured and computer processing power has increased. This text was written to discuss the science and phenomenology practiced in advanced technical remote sensing today. The interests discussed in this chapter are open for investigation and development by those who have come this far and are looking into the future.

CHAPTER 2

[1] Fixsen, D. J., The Temperature of the Cosmic Microwave Background," The Astrophysical Journal, 707 (2): 916-920, December 2009.

[2] Anthony, J. W., R. A. Bideaux, K. W. Bladh, and M. C. Nichols (eds.), Handbook of Minerology III (Halides, Hydroxides, Oxides), Mineralogical Society of America, Chantilly, VA, 2001.

[3] The Quartz Page. Milky Quartz. http://www.quartzpage.de/milky.html (accessed 6 November 2013).

[4] TES and Spectral Emissivity Curves: Quartz, Feldspar, & Hornblende. http://spectralemissivity.com/what-is-tes-and-spectral-emissivity-curves-quartz-feldspar-hornblende/ (accessed 6 November 2013).

[5] The Engineering Tool Box: Emissivity Coefficients of some common materials. http://www.engineeringtoolbox.com/emissivity-coefficients-d_447.html (accessed 4 March 2014).

[6] Emissivity values of common materials. http://www.frigidn.com/resources/emissivitytable.pdf (accessed 4 March 2014).

[7] Emissivity of Common Materials. http://www.omega.com/literature/transactions/volume1/emissivitya.html (accessed 4 March 2014).

[8] Emissivity Values for Common Materials. http://www.infrared-thermography.com/material.htm (accessed 4 March 2014).

[9] Hudson, R. D., "Infrared System Engineering," John Wiley & Sons, New York, NY, 1969.

CHAPTER 3

[1] The Engineering Tool Box: Refractive Index of some common Liquids, Solids and Gases. http://www.engineeringtoolbox.com/refractive-index-d_1264.html (accessed 4 March 2014).

[2] Filmetrics: Refractive Index Database. http://www.filmetrics.com/refractive-index-database (accessed 4 March 2014).

[3] Index of Refraction. http://hyperphysics.phy-astr.gsu.edu/hbase/tables/indrf.html (accessed 4 March 2014).

[4] IOR—Index of Refraction Values. http://www.pixelandpoly.com/ior.html (accessed 4 March 2014).

[5] Remote Sensing and Soils. http://www.ucalgary.ca/GEOG/Virtual/Remote%20Sensing/rssoils.html (accessed 4 March 2014).

[6] The Encyclopedia of the Earth: Albedo. http://www.eoearth.org/view/article/149954/ (accessed 4 March 2014).

[7] Climate Data Information. http://www.climatedata.info/Forcing/Forcing/albedo.html (accessed 4 March 2014).

CHAPTER 4

[1] University of North Carolina at Chapel Hill. A dictionary of units of measurement. http://www.unc.edu/~rowlett/units/dictF.html (accessed 24 September 2010).

[2] Thekaekara, Matthew P. "The Solar Constant and the Solar Spectrum Measured from a Research Aircraft." NASA Technical Report, National Aeronautics and Space Administration, October 1970.

[3] National Geospatial-Intelligence Agency. NGA Raster Roam. http://geoengine.nga.mil/geospatial/SW_TOOLS/NIMAMUSE/webinter/rast_roam.html (accessed 30 September 2010).

[4] United States Geological Survey. Performance Specification: Digital Terrain Elevation Data (DTED). http://dds.cr.usgs.gov/srtm/version2_1/Documentation/MIL-PDF-89020B.pdf (accessed 30 September 2010).

CHAPTER 5

[1] Jursa, Adolph S. (Ed.), Handbook of Geophysics and the Space Environment, Air Force Geophysics Laboratory, Air Force Systems Command, United States Air Force, 1985.

[2] Rothman, L.S., et al., "The HITRAN 2008 Molecular Database," J. Quant. Spect. and Rad, Trans., 110:533-572 (2009).

[3] *HITRAN 2012*. Version 2012, Harvard University. Computer software. Harvard University, Cambridge, MA, 2012.

[4] Wikipedia. MODTRAN. http://en.wikipedia.org/wiki/MODTRAN (accessed 6 December 2011).

[5] Zissis, George J. (ed.). The Infrared Electro-Optical Systems Handbook, Volume I, Sources of Radiation. Infrared Information Analysis Center, SPIE Engineering Press, pp. 213-219, 1993.

CHAPTER 7

[1] Norton, P. "HgCdTe Infrared Detectors," Opto-Electronics Review, 10(3):159-174 (2002).

[2] Liddiard, Kevin, "Developing the next generation of passive infrared security sensors," SPIE Newsroom (11 May 2008). http://spie.org/x24481.xml?pf=true&ArticleID=x2 (accessed 18 November 2010).

[3] Flexible Efficient & Practical, System Efficiency. http://astro.berkeley.edu/~jrg/ngst/multispectral/practical.html (accessed 4 March 2014).

CHAPTER 11

[1] US Air Force Fact Sheet: U-2S/TU-2S. http://www.af.mil/AboutUs/FactSheets/Display/tabid/224/Article/104560/u-2stu-2s.aspx (accessed 20 May 2014).

[2] National Museum of the U.S. Air Force: Lockheed SR-71A. http://www.nationalmuseum.af.mil/factsheets/factsheet.asp?id=395 (accessed 24 January 2011).

[3] National Museum of the U.S. Air Force: Lockheed B-71 (SR-71). http://www.nationalmuseum.af.mil/factsheets/factsheet.asp?id=2699 (accessed 24 January 2011).

[4] US Air Force Fact Sheet: KC-135 Stratotanker. http://www.af.mil/AboutUs/FactSheets/Display/tabid/224/Article/104524/kc-135-stratotanker.aspx (accessed 20 May 2014).

[5] US Air Force Fact Sheet: MQ-1B Predator. http://www.af.mil/AboutUs/FactSheets/Display/tabid/224/Article/104469/mq-1b-predator.aspx (accessed 20 May 2014).

[6] US Air Force Fact Sheet: RQ-4 Global Hawk. http://www.af.mil/AboutUs/FactSheets/Display/tabid/224/Article/104516/rq-4-global-hawk.aspx (accessed 20 May 2014).

[7] National Geospatial-Intelligence Agency. WGS Earth Gravitational Model. http://earth-info.nga.mil/GandG/wgs84/gravitymod/ (accessed 18 March 2011).

[8] National Aeronautics and Space Administration. Definition of Two-Line Element Set Coordinate System. http://spaceflight.nasa.gov/realdata/sightings/SSapplications/Post/JavaSSOP/SSOP_Help/tle_def.html (accessed 15 April 2011).

[9] Analytic Graphics Inc. (AGI). Space Missions. http://www.agi.com/solutions/space-missions/default.aspx (accessed 30 June 2011).

CHAPTER 12

[1] Analytic Graphics Inc. (AGI). Space Missions. http://www.agi.com/solutions/main.aspx/id/space-missions/ (accessed 30 June 2011).

[2] Berk, A., G.P. Anderson, P.K. Acharya, and E.P. Shettle. MODTRAN 5.2.1 Users Manual. Spectral Sciences, Inc., Burlington, MA, and Air Force Research Laboratory, Space Vehicles Directorate, Air Force Materiel Command, Hanscom AFB, MA (May 2011).

[3] Muhulikar, S., H.R. Sonawane, and G.A. Rao. "Infrared signature studies of aerospace vehicles," Progress in Aerospace Sciences, 43(7-8):218-245 (October-November 2007). (Abstract available at http://www.sciencedirect.com/science/article/pii/S0376042107000504.)

[4] National Aeronautics and Space Administration. Landsat 7 Science Data Users Handbook. http://landsathandbook.gsfc.nasa.gov/ (accessed 13 July 2011).

CHAPTER 13

[1] Hall, R.C., Missile Defense Alarm: The Genesis of Space-Based Infrared Early Warning. National Reconnaissance Office, Washington, D.C. (July 1988). [Approved for release: http://www.nro.gov/foia/docs/foia-mda.pdf (accessed 26 August 2013)].

[2] RAND Corporation. Infrared Techniques Applied to the Detection and Interception of Intercontinental Ballistic Missiles. http://www.rand.org/pubs/research_memoranda/RM1572.html (accessed 20 February 2014).

[3] Lockheed Martin. Space Based Infrared Systems: The Next Generation in Global Persistent IR Surveillance. http://www.lockheedmartin.com/content/dam/lockheed/data/space/documents/sbirs/SBIRS%204Fold.pdf (accessed 26 August 2013).

[4] NRO History - Missile Defense Alarm: The Genesis of Space-Based Infrared Early Warning. http://www.nro.gov/foia/docs/foia-mda.pdf (accessed 20 February 2014).

[5] U.S. Air Force. Defense Support Program Satellites. http://www.af.mil/AboutUs/FactSheets/Display/tabid/224/Article/104611/defense-support-program-satellites.aspx (accessed 26 August 2013).

[6] Northrop Grumman. Defense Support Program (DSP) Overview. http://www.Northropgrumman.com/Capabilities/DefenseSupportProgram/Documents/DSP_Fact_Sheet_082080.pdf (accessed 26 August 2013).

[7] Northrop Grumman. Space-Based Infrared System (SBIRS). http://www.northropgrumman.com/Capabilites/SBIRS/Pages/default.aspx (accessed 26 August 2013).

[8] U.S. Air Force. Space Based Infrared System Fact Sheet. http://www.af.mil/AboutUs/FactSheets/Display/tabid/224/Article/104549/space-based-infrared-system.aspx (accessed 27 January 2015).

[9] Los Angeles Air Force Base. Infrared Space Systems Directorate. http://www.losangeles.af.mil/library/factsheets/factsheet.asp?id=5514 (accessed 26 August 2013).

[10] National Museum of the U.S. Air Force. Launching Missiles. http://www.nationalmuseum.af.mil/factsheets/factsheet.asp?id=13572 (accessed 26 August 2013).

[11] MacGregor, C.H. and L.H. Livingston (eds.). Air Command and Staff College Space Handbook (11th Revised Edition), Air University, Maxwell Air Force Base, AL (1977).

[12] Humble, R.W., G.N. Henry, and W.J. Larson. Space Technology Series: Space Propulsion Analysis and Design. The McGraw-Hill Companies, Inc., Primis Custom Publishing, New York (1995).

[13] Astronautics and Its Application: 6. Propellants. http://history.nasa.gov/conghand/propelnt.htm (accessed 20 February 2014).

[14] Rocket and Space Technology: Rocket Propellants. http://www.braeunig.us/space/propel.htm (accessed 20 February 2014).

[15] Simmons, F.S., Rocket Exhaust Plume Phenomenology, The Aerospace Press, El Segundo, CA (2000).

[16] Black Hills State University, Signals & Noise: Co-addition. http://www.bhsu.edu/Portals/91/InstrumentalAnalysis/StudyHelp/LectureNotes/Chapter5.pdf (accessed 26 August 2013).

[17] Fermilab Computing Sector. Notes on coaddition, PSF homogenization, and matched filters. http://home.fnal.gov/~neilsen/notebook/PSFhomogenization/PSFhomogenization.html (accessed 26 August 2013).

[18] Air Force Technical Applications Center. A Fifty Year Commemorative History of Long Range Detection: The Creation, Development, and Operation of the United States Atomic Energy Detection System. HQ Air Force Technical Applications Center, Patrick Air Force Base, FL (September 1997).

[19] National Nuclear Security Administration. NNSA Commemorates 50th Anniversary of First Vela Launch. http://nnsa.energy.gov/mediaroom/pressreleases/vela (accessed 20 February 2014).

[20] Peebles, Cutis. High Frontier: The U.S. Air Force and the Military Space Program, Air Force History and Museums Program, Create Space Independent Publishing Platform (May 28, 2012), pp. 41-44.

[21] Turman, B.N., Analysis of Lightning Data from Defense Meteorological Support Program Satellites, J. Geophys. Res., 83(10):5019 (20 October 1978).

[22] Turman, B.N., Detection of Lightning Superbolts, J. Geophys. Res., 82(10):2566 (20 June 1977).

[23] Cooper, P.W. Explosives Engineering, VCH Publishers, Inc., 333 7th Avenue, New York, (1996).

[24] Estimating Equivalency of Explosives through a Thermochemical Approach. https://e-reports-ext.llnl.gov/pdf/241114.pdf (accessed 21 February 2014).

[25] An approach to determining the TNT equivalent of high explosives. http://www.vti.mod.gov.rs/ntp/rad2006/1-06/jere/jere.pdf (accessed 21 February 2014).

[26] Fickett, W. and W.C. Davis., Detonation: Theory and Experiment, Dover Publications, Inc., Mineola, NY (1979).

[27] U.S. Army Materiel Command. AMCP 706-177: Engineering Design Handbook: Explosives Series; Properties of Explosives of Military Interest. HQ U.S. Army Materiel Command, Washington, D.C., (1971). http://archive.org/details/milmanual-amcp-706-177-explosives-data (accessed 26 August 2013).

CHAPTER 14

[1] Smith, S. W., "The Scientist and Engineer's Guide to Digital Signal Processing." http://www.dspguide.com/whatdsp.htm (accessed 6 November 2013).

[2] Kuperman, G.G., Human system interface (HSI) issues in assisted target recognition (ASTR). Proceedings of the IEEE 1997 National Aerospace and Electronics Conference, NAECON 1997. http://ieeexplore.ieee.org/xpl/login.jsp?tp=&arnumber&url=http%3A%2F%2Fieeexplore.org%2Fxpl%2Fabs_all.jsp%3Farnumber%3D617759 (accessed 4 September 2012).

[3] U.S. Geological Survey. Overview of Noise and Artifacts. http://isis.astrogeology.usgs.gov/IsisWorkshop/index.php/Overview_of_Noise_And_Artifacts (accessed 5 September 2012).

[4] Mansurov, N., "Dead vs. Stuck vs. Hot Pixels." http://photographylife.com/dead-vs-stuck-vs-hot-pixels (accessed 7 November 2013).

[5] Fischer, Amber D., T. V. Downes, R. Leathers. Median Spectral-Spatial Bad Identificatiion and Replacement for Hyperspectral SWIR Sensors. Proceedings of SPIE 6565, Algorithms and Technologies for Multispectral, Hyperspectral, and Ultraspectral Imagery XIII, 65651E, May 07, 2007.

[6] Massachusetts Institute of Technology. MITOPENCOURSEWARE. Lecture 6: Order Statistics, Median. http://ocw.mit.edu/courses/electrical-engineering-and-computer-science/6-046j-introduction-to-algorithms-sma-5503-fall-2005/video-lectures/lecture-6-order-statistics-median/ (accessed 12 September 2012).

[7] Hora, J.L., et al., Calibration and performance of the Infrared Array Camera (IRAC). https://www.cfa.harvard.edu/~jhora/jlh/4131-03.pdf (accessed 20 September 2012).

[8] Piccardi, M. Background subtraction techniques: a review. 2004 IEEE International Conference on Systems, Man, and Cybernetics. https://profs.sci.univr.it/~cristanm/teaching/sar_files/lezione4/Piccardi.pdf (accessed 27 September 2012).

[9] Kirk, J.A. and M. Donofrio. Principal Component Background Suppression. Proceedings, 1996 IEEE Aerospace Applications Conference. http://ieeexplore.ieee.org/xpl/login.jsp?tp=&arnumber=496057&url=http%3A%2F%2Fieeexplore.ieee.org%2Fxpl%2abs_all.jsp%3arnumber%3D496057 (accessed 28 September 2012).

[10] Auburn University. Centroids and Center of Mass. http://www.eng.auburn.edu/~marghitu/MECH2110/C_3.pdf (accessed 26 September 2012).

[11] Math Insight. Center of Mass (Centroids). http://mathinsight.org/centers_of_mass_centroids_refresher (accessed 26 September 2012).

[12] National Optical Astronomy Observatory. Table of Bright Infrared Sources. http://www.noao.edu/kpno/bright42.html (accessed 30 September 2012).

[13] High Energy Astrophysics Science Archive Research Center. BSC5P – Bright Star Catalog. http://heasarc.gsfc.nasa.gov/W3browse/star-catalog/bsc5p.html (accessed 30 September 2012).

CHAPTER 15

[1] National Aeronautics and Space Administration. Landsat 7 Science Data Users Handbook. http://landsathandbook.gsfc.nasa.gov/ (accessed 30 August 2013).

[2] National Aeronautics and Space Administration. Landsat Landsat 8 Bands. http://landsat.gsfc.nasa.gov/?page_id=5377 (accessed 22 July 2015).

[3] Pilati, Martin. (personal communication, 24 June 2012).

[4] Satellite Imaging Corp. Satellite Sensors SPOT 5, Ikonos 2, QuickBird, GeoEye 1, and WorldView 2. http://www.satimagingcorp.com/satellite-sensors (accessed 30 August 2013).

[5] United States Geological Survey. Overview of the Resourcesat-1 (IRS-P6). http://calval.cr.usgs.gov/documents/IRSP6.pdf (accessed 30 August 2013).

[6] United States Geological Survey. Indian Remote Sensing Satellites. http://calval.cr.usgs.gov/JACIE_files/JACIE07/Files/111Pucko.pdf (accessed 30 August 2013).

CHAPTER 16

[1] NOAA National Centers for Environmental Information. OLS - Operational Linescan System. http://ngdc.noaa.gov/eog/sensors/ols.html (accessed 10 September 2013).

[2] NOAA. Advanced Very High Resolution Radiometer - AVHRR. http://noaasis.noaa.gov/NOAASIS/ml/avhrr.html (accessed 10 September 2013).

[3] NOAA. GOES Imager Instrument. http://noaasis.noaa.gov/NOAASIS/ml/imager.html (accessed 10 September 2013).

[4] NOAA National Centers for Environmental Information. SSM/T- Atmospheric Temperature Profiler. http://ngdc.noaa.gov/eog/sensors/ssmt.html (accessed 10 September 2013).

[5] eoPortal. NOAA POES Series. https://directory.eoportal.org/web/eoportal/satellite-missions/n/noaa-poes-series-5th-generation (accessed 10 September 2013).

[6] NOAA. GOES Sounder Instrument. http://noaasis.noaa.gov/NOAASIS/ml/sounder.html (accessed 10 September 2013).

[7] Colorado State University. NOAA Technical Report NESDIS 141: The GOES-15 Science Test: Imager and Sounder Radiance and Product Validations. http://rammb.cira.colostate.edu/projects/goes-p/NOAA_Technical_Report_141_GOES-15_Science_Test.pdf (accessed 10 September 2013).

[8] NOAA. GOES Atmospheric Sounders. http://www.orbit.nesdis.noaa.gov/smcd/opdb/goes/soundings/skewt23L/html/skewmap.html (accessed 10 September 2013).

[9] Wang. Fang, Jun Li, Timothy J. Schmit, and Steven A. Ackerman, "Trade-off studies of a hyperspectral infrared sounder on a geostationary satellite," Applied Optics 46 p. 200, 10 January 2007.

[10] ITT Exelis. A Quantum Leap Forward in Meteorological Sensor Capabilities: CrIS - NPP & JPSS. http://www.exelisinc.com/solutions/CrIS/documents/CRIS%20data%20sheet.pdf (accessed 10 September 2013).

[11] NASA Jet Propulsion Lab. Cool Cosmos Infrared World. http://coolcosmos.ipac.caltech.edu/image_galleries (accessed 2 August 2012).

[12] NOAA Office of Satellite and Product Operations: Sea Surface Temperature (SST). http://www.ospo.noaa.gov/Products/ocean/sst.html (accessed 7 August 2014).

[13] ASTER Spectral Library. http://speclib.jpl.nasa.gov (accessed 7 August 2014).

[14] Rencz, Andrew N. (Ed.), "Manual of Remote Sensing, Vol. 3, Remote Sensing for Earth Sciences," John Wiley & Sons, New York, 1999.

[15] Stuart, Donald M, "Sensor Design for Unmanned Aerial Vehicles," Proceedings of Aerospace Conference, Vol. 3, 1997, IEEE.

[16] National Aeronautics and Space Administration. Landsat 7 Science Data Users Handbook. http://landsathandbook.gsfc.nasa.gov/ (accessed 30 August 2013).

[17] Cox, Charles, Stanley Kishner, Richard Whittlesey, and Frederick Gilligan, "Reconnaissance Payloads for Responsive Space (AIAA RS3-2005-5004)," 3rd Responsive Space Conference, 25-28 April 2005.

[18] Applications of the MuSES Infrared Signature Code by Allen R Curran and Teresa G. Gonda. http://oai.dtic.mil/oai/oai?verb=getRecord&metadataPrefix=html&identifier=ADA457152 (accessed 25 February 2014).

[19] Aerodyne Research: SPIRITS. http://www.aerodyne.com/products/spirits (accessed 26 February 2014).

[20] United States Air Force. Fact Sheet: U-2S/TU-2S. http://www.af.mil (accessed 10 September 2013).

CHAPTER 18

[1] Folkman, Mark A., et.al., "Performance characterization and calibration of the TRWIS III hyperspectral imager," SPIE Proceedings Vol. 2819 p. 130, 1996.

[2] Simi, Christopher, Edwin Winter, Mary Williams, and Dave Driscoll, "Compact Airborne Spectral Sensor (COMPASS)," SPIE Proceedings Vol. 4381, p. 129, 2001.

[3] Acker, Andrew, Joel E Pfeiffer, Brian Farm, "Automated subpixel target detection using the LASH hyperspectral sensor," SPIE Proceedings Vol. 5093, p. 75, 2003.

[4] Davis, Curtiss O, et.al., "Calibration, characterization, and first results with the Ocean PHILLS hyperspectral imager," SPIE Proceedings Vol. 3753, pp. 160-168, 1999.

[5] Basedow, R.W., D.C. Carmer, and M.E. Anderson, "HYDICE System, implementation, and performance," SPIE Proceedings Vol. 2480, p. 258, 1995.

[6] Pilati, Martin. (personal communication, 24 June 2012).

[7] Wolboldt, Mark and Martin Pilati, "A Hyperspectral Identification Algorithm for VIS-SWIR Sensors," SPIE 3118 (Imaging Spectroscopy III), p. 271, Oct 1997.

[8] IEEE Aerospace Conference. The EO-1 Hyperion Imaging Spectrometer. http://eo1.gsfc.nasa.gov/new/validationReport/Technology/TRW_EO1%20Papers_Presentations/10.pdf (accessed 12 September 2013).

[9] "Warfighter 1," http://www.vs.afrl.af.mil/vsd-w/warfighter1.html (accessed 12 September 2013).

[10] Lockwood, Ronald B., et.al. "Advanced responsive tactically effective military imaging spectrometer (ARTEMIS): system overview and objectives," SPIE Proceedings Vol. 6661, 2007.

[11] Wilson, Thomas, and Curtiss Davis, "Naval Earth Map Observer (NEMO) satellite," SPIE Proceedings Vol. 3753, pp. 2-11, 1999.

CHAPTER 19

[1] Kelch, David, et.al. "Spectral Phenomena for Detection of Disturbed Earth," The International Symposium of Spectral Sensing Research, 1999.

[2] Kelch, David, et.al. "The Physical Basis for Exploitable Soil Spectral Signatures," The International Symposium of Spectral Sensing Research, 1999.

[3] Hackwell, John A., et.al., "LWIR/MWIR Imaging Hyperspectral Sensor for Airborne and Ground-Based Remote Sensing," SPIE Proceedings Vol. 2819, p. 102, 1996.

[4] The Aerospace Corporation. Remote Infrared Hyperspectral Imaging. http://www.spectir.com/Spanish/assets/Text%20Files/Brochure-Remote_IR_HSI.pdf (accessed 27 September 2013).

[5] Puckrin, E., et.al. "Airborne measurements in the infrared using FTIR-based imaging hyperspectral sensors," SPIE Proceedings Vol. 7324, 2009.

[6] Allard, Jean-Pierre, et.al. "Airborne Measurments in the Longwave Infrared using an Imaging Hyperspectral Sensor," SPIE Proceedings Vol. 7014, 2008.

[7] ITT Exelis. A Quantum Leap Forward in Meteorological Sensor Capabilities: CrIS - NPP & JPSS. http://www.exelisinc.com/solutions/CrIS/documents/CRIS%20data%20sheet.pdf (accessed 10 September 2013).

[8] Bloom, Hal J., "The Cross-track Infrared Sounder (CrIS): A Sensor for Operational Meteorological Remote Sensing," IEEE Geoscience and Remote Sensing Symposium (IGARSS), p. 1341, 2007.

CHAPTER 20

[1] Department of Energy, Nevada Site Office. Nonproliferation Test and Evaluation Complex (NPTEC). http://www.nv.energy.gov/library/FactSheets/DOENV_1062.pdf (accessed 27 September 2013).

[2] Young, S., "Detection and Quantification of Gases in Industrial-Stack Plumes Using Thermal-Infrared Hyperspectral Imaging," Aerospace Corporation Report No. ATR-2002(8407)-1, 2002.

[3] Pilati, Martin. (personal communication, 24 June 2012).

[4] Hammond, Barney, and Mirela Popa, "Overview of the Joint Services Lightweight Standoff Chemical Agent Detector (JSLSCAD), SPIE Proceedings Vol. 5795, pp. 86-95, May 2005.

[5] Cosofret, et.al., "AIRIS Standoff Multispectral Sensor," Chemical and Biological Defense Physical Science and Technology Conference, 17-21 November 2008.

[6] Martinelli, et.al., "AIRIS Wide Area Detector for Integrated Early Warning," 6th Joint Conference on Stand-off Detection for Chemical and Biological Defense, 25-29 October 2004.

[7] Cohn, David B, Jay A Fox, and Cynthia R Swim, "Wavelength Agile CO2 Laser and Chemical Sensor, Proceedings of IRIS Active Systems, Vol 2, 1993.

[8] McDowell, R.S., J.F. Kelly, S.W. Sharp, "Pacific Northwest Laboratory CALIOPE Overview," CALIOPE Interim Technical Review Conference, 27-31 March 1995.

[9] Swim, Cynthia, "Review of active chem-bio sensing," SPIE Proceedings Vol. 5416, pp. 78-185, 2004.

[10] Swim, Cynthia, et.al., "Update on active chem-bio sensing," SPIE Proceedings Vol 5795, pp. 79-85, 2005.

[11] Strawbridge, John, "Biological Standoff Detection System Development," Chem-Bio Quarterly, Jul-Sep 2005.

[12] Suliga, William, et.al., "Short-Range Biological Stand-off Detection System," SPIE Proceedings Vol 3855, p. 72, 1999.

[13] United States Army-Joint Program Executive Office, Chemical and Biological Defense Fact Sheets: M-21 RSCAAL, JSLSCAD, JBTDS, JBPDS, and JBSDS. http://jacks.jpeocbd.army.mil/Default.aspx

CHAPTER 21

[1] Wojciech Matusik, Hanspeter Pfister, Matt Brand, and Leonard McMillan, "A Data-driven Reflectance Model," ACM Transactions on Graphics, 22, p. 759, 2003.

[2] Chenault, David B. (personal communication, August 23, 2013).

[3] Atkinson, G.A. and E.R. Hancock, "Recovery of Surface Orientation from Diffuse Polarization," IEEE Transactions of Image Processing 15, p. 1653, June 2006.

[4] Tyo, J. S., D. L. Goldstein, D. B. Chenault, and J. A. Shaw, "Review of passive imaging polarimetry for remote sensing applications," Applied Optics 45(22) pp. 5453-5469, August 2006.

[5] Slonecker, Terrence, John W. Jones, Susan D. Price, and Dianna Hagan, "Advanced Remote Sensing Research," USGS Fact Sheet 2008-3052, June 2008.

[6] Duggin, Michael J., "Polarimetric Remote Sensing: A Brief Review Emphasizing Feature Discrimination, Shadow Penetration, and the Integral Use of Contrast Stretch," 2002 Optical Polarimetric Sensing and Effects Workshop, Vol. 1, Infrared Information Analysis Center, March 2003.

CHAPTER 22

[1] Joint Electronic Library: Intelligence, Series 2-0 Publications: Joint Publication 2-01.3. http://www.dtic.mil/doctrine/new_pubs/jointpub_intelligence.htm. (accessed 25 February 2014).

[2] Joint Chiefs of Staff. Planner's Handbook for Operational Design, Version 1.0: Joint Staff, J-7 Joint and Coalition Warfighting, Suffolk, Virginia, 1 October 2011. http://www.au.af.mil/au/awc/awcgate/dod/opdesign_hbk.pdf (accessed 28 February 2014).

[3] Central Intelligence Agency. The World Factbook. https://www.cia.gov/library/publications/the-world-factbook/ (accessed 28 February 2014).

[4] Defense Update - International Online Defense Magazine. Accelerating the Kill Chain: Closing the Sensor-to-Shooter Cycle. http://defense-update.com/features/du-1-06/urban-c4i-7.htm (accessed 28 February 2014).

[5] National Air and Space Intelligence Center. http://www.wpafb.af.mil/nasic/ (accessed 22 Jul 2015.

[6] National Ground Intelligence Center. http://www.inscom.army.mil/MSC/NGIC.aspx (accessed 4 February 2014).

[7] Marine Corps Intelligence Activity. http://www.quantico.usmc.mil/activities/?section=MCIA (accessed 4 February 2014).

[8] Office of Naval Intelligence. http://www.oni.navy.mil/ (accessed 4 February 2014).

[9] U.S. Department of Defense: DIA's Missile And Space Intelligence Center Groundbreaking. http://www.defense.gov/advisories/advisory.aspx?advisoryid=1411 (accessed 4 February 2014).

[10] Nuclear Security Systems and Measures for the Detection of Nuclear and Other Radioactive Material out of Regulatory Control. http://www-pub.iaea.org/MTCD/Publications/PDF/Pub1613_web.pdf (accessed 4 February 2014).

[11] U.S. Department of State: Open Skies Treaty. http://www.state.gov/r/pa/prs/ps/2012/03/186738.htm (accessed 2 July 2015).

[12] Higbie, Paul R. and Norman K. Blocker, The Nuclear Detonation Detection System on GPS Satellites, Los Alamos National Laboratory, LA-UR-93-2834, July 1993.

[13] The New York Times. Drug-Sub Culture. http://www.nytimes.com/2009/04/26/magazine/26drugs-t.html?_r=1&pagewanted=print (accessed 20 September 2013).

[14] NBC News. 'Sky's the limit': Drug smugglers buy cargo jets. http://www.msnbc.msn.com/id/40194116/ns/world_news (accessed 20 September 2013).

[15] National Defense: Predators Allow Border Agencies to Reallocate Resources. http://www.nationaldefensemagazine.org/archive/2014/January/pages/PredatorsAllowBorderAgenciestoReallocate Resources.aspx (accessed 4 February 2014).

[16] Kirtland Air Force Base. USAF Fact Sheet: Air Force Maui Optical and Supercomputing Site (AMOS). http://www.kirtland.af.mil/library/factsheets/factsheet.asp?id=16930 (accessed 4 February 2014).

[17] Reed, Sidney G., Richard H. Van Atta, Seymour J. Deitchman, "DARPA Technical Accomplishments, Vol. I," Institute for Defense Analysis, IDA Paper P-2192, AD-A239 925, February 1990.

[18] Price, Stephen, "45 Years of Infrared Astronomy at the Air Force Laboratory," https://www.cfa.harvard.edu/oir/fazio_symposium/pdf/May27_06_price.pdf (accessed 4 February 2014).

[19] Inflated decoy photo. http://www.buzzmuseum.com/wp-content/uploads/2011/03/inflatable-army-truck.jpg (accessed 15 September 2013).

[20] Inflated decoy photo. http://www.buzzmuseum.com/wp-content/uploads/2011/03/inflatable-tank-russia.jpg (accessed 15 September 2013).

[21] Hammond, Barney, and Mirela Popa, "Overview of the Joint Services Lightweight Standoff Chemical Agent Detector (JSLSCAD), SPIE Proceedings Vol. 5795, pp. 86-95, May 2005.

[22] DARPA Strategic Plan: February 2003. https://www.hsdl.org/?view&did=1068 (accessed 18 February 2014).

[23] Defense News. Unearthing secrets - How the US digs up intelligence on underground sites. http://www.c4isrjournal.com/story.php?F=3581781 (accessed 20 September 2013).

[24] Esterbrook, Maj Mark, "'Unearthing' the Truth in Defense of our Nation," NGA Pathfinder, January-February 2005.

[25] Asia Times. Missiles and Madness. http://www.atimes.com/atimes/Korea/HH18Dg02.html (accessed 20 September 2013).

ACOUSTINT (Acoustic Intelligence): Information gathering from sounds emitted or reflected from targets in the atmosphere.

AFRL (Air Force Research Laboratory): An organization of the Air Force wholly dedicated to leading the discovery, development, and integration of warfighting technologies for the Unites States' air, space, and cyberspace forces.

AGI (Advanced Geospatial Intelligence): The technical, geospatial, and intelligence information derived through interpretation or analysis using advanced processing of all data collected by imagery or imagery-related collection systems. Also known as imagery-derived measurement and signature intelligence.

ATI (Advanced Technical Intelligence): Technical intelligence obtained by the use of remote sensors in addition to some of the more conventional means.

BA (Battlespace Awareness): A practice of military philosophy that is used as a valuable asset by joint-component and -force commanders to predict courses of action before employing troops into a prescribed area of operation.

BRDF (Bidirectional Reflectivity Distribution Function): A mathematical description of the amount of radiation reflected into specific directions, relative to its incident direction.

CCD (Charge-Coupled Device): A device for the movement of electrical charge, usually from within the device to an area where the charge can be manipulated, for example conversion into a digital value.

CIA (Central Intelligence Agency): The CIA is an independent US government agency responsible for providing national security intelligence to senior US policy makers.

CMOS (Complementary Metal–Oxide–Semiconductor): A technology for constructing integrated circuits that have high noise immunity and low static power consumption.

COMINT (Communications Intelligence): Intelligence collected from spoken and encoded communications transmitted over airwave, landline, and networked systems.

CYBERINT (Cyber Intelligence): Intelligence collected from networked social media, e-mail, and blogs, and monitoring computer-to-computer exchanges.

DEW (Directed Energy Weapon): A particle beam or laser weapon.

DIA (Defense Intelligence Agency): A Department of Defense combat support agency responsible for providing all-source defense intelligence to prevent strategic surprise and deliver a decision advantage to warfighters, defense planners, and policy makers in support of US military planning and operations and weapon systems acquisition.

DIAL (Differential Absorption Lidar): A two-laser system used to map the concentration of a particular gas type along the line-of-sight.

DMSP (Defense Meteorological Satellite Program): A constellation of low Earth orbiting satellites to monitor meteorological, oceanographic, and solar-terrestrial physics for the US Department of Defense. They provide cloud cover imagery from polar orbits that are sun-synchronous at nominal altitude of 450 nautical miles (830 km).

DOD (Department of Defense): America's largest government agency that provides the military forces needed to deter war and to protect the security of the US.

DOP (Degree of Polarization): A measure of the extent to which an EM wave is linearly polarized.

DSP (Defense Support Program): A constellation of sensors in geosynchronous orbit for early warning of missile launches and nuclear bomb detonation detection.

DSP (Digital Signal Processing): Any means of using electronic computers to process, analyze, and exploit data collected by electro-optical remote sensors.

DTED (Digital Terrain Elevation Data): A worldwide database of terrain elevations maintained by the National Geospatial-Intelligence Agency. Spatial resolution depends on target location and user requirements. Levels 0, 1, and 2 are publicly available, but Levels 3, 4, and 5 are for classified application.

EEI (Essential Element of Information): A detail about a target required to be known by a responsible agency.

ELINT (Electronic Intelligence): Gathering information from the frequency and waveforms of radio signals.

EM (Electromagnetic): The combination of electric and magnetic fields within an electromagnetic wave.

EMP (Electromagnetic Pulse): A short burst of electromagnetic radiation energy from a high energy transmitter or a nuclear detonation.

EO (Electro-Optics): Pertaining to the portion of the electromagnetic spectrum where energy is collected by camera-like remote sensors having collecting optics that form images of targets on a focal plane array, which is then sampled with solid state detectors.

FISINT (Foreign Instrumentation Signals Intelligence): Gathering information from foreign telemetry and remote sensing data streams.

FME (Foreign Materiel Exploitation): The evaluation of foreign ground force systems, related material, and foreign commercial items required for production of scientific and technical intelligence, the assessment of foreign technology, design features, and scientific developments for infusion into US developmental efforts, the support of US systems, and developmental testing/operational testing by providing adversary systems for use in evaluating US systems capabilities.

FPA (Focal Plane Array): A solid state device containing detectors, divided into picture elements (pixels) to convert an electromagnetic image into electronic data.

GEO (Geosynchronous Orbit): A useful satellite orbit that is nearly circular with an altitude of approximately 35,780 km above the Earth, so the satellite travels one complete orbit in one sidereal day, so as to approximately remain over one longitude.

GEOINT (Geospatial Intelligence): The analysis, exploitation, and combination of imagery and geospatial information to describe, assess, and visually depict physical features and geographically referenced activities on the Earth.

GOES (Geostationary Operational Environmental Satellite): A constellation of satellites operated by the National Oceanographic and Atmospheric Administration, supporting weather forecasting, severe storm tracking, and meteorology research.

GPS (Global Positioning System): A system for accurately positioning oneself in three-dimensional near-Earth space using a constellation of precisely orbiting satellites.

HEO (Highly Elliptical Orbit): A satellite in an elliptical orbit making two revolutions around the Earth in one sidereal day, having apogees over two specific longitudes 180° apart.

HDBT (Hardened Deeply Buried Target): Another name for an underground facility.

HSI (Hyperspectral Imaging or Imagery): Information gathering using overlaying images simultaneously collected in hundreds of bands, typically for identifying material types.

HUMINT (Human Intelligence): Intelligence collected by field agents (covert or overt).

IC (Intelligence Community): A confederation of US government information gathering agencies and organizations.

IMINT (Imagery Intelligence): Intelligence gathered from literal pictures collected by remote sensors (cameras).

INT (Intelligence): Any information gathering discipline.

IPB (Intelligence Preparation of the Battlefield): Collected and analyzed information regarding an enemy's order of battle, force geolocations, and suspected engagement tactics.

IPB (Intelligence Preparation of the Battlespace): The analytical methodologies employed by the Services or joint force component commands to reduce uncertainties concerning the enemy, environment, time, and terrain. Intelligence Preparation of the Battlespace supports the individual operations of the joint force component commands.

IR (Infrared): The non-visible portion of the electromagnetic spectrum at wavelengths longer than visible light, but shorter than radio waves; approximately 0.70–100 μm.

I&W (Indications and Warnings): Combination of all possible GEOINT, HUMINT, IMINT, and SIGINT information to anticipate an enemy's engagement strategies and tactics.

JSLSCAD (Joint Service Lightweight Standoff Chemical Agent Detector): A HSI sensor used to detect and identify clouds of chemical agents on the battlefield.

Landsat (Land Satellite): A constellation of Earth-imaging multispectral sensors in low Earth orbit, which began with the launch of Landsat 1 in 1972.

LADAR (Laser Detection And Ranging): A system for locating objects by means of reflected laser light.

Lat (Latitude): The north-south geolocation on the Earth, relative to the equator, measured in degrees.

LASINT (Laser Intelligence): Technical and geolocation intelligence derived from laser systems; a subcategory of electro-optical intelligence.

LEO (Low-Earth Orbit): A satellite not more than approximately 1,000 km above the Earth's surface.

LIDAR (Light Detection and Ranging): A method using coherent visible or infrared laser beams to measure terrain elevation, or to detect gas molecules in the atmosphere.

LITINT (Literature Intelligence): Intelligence collected by analyzing published literature and documents.

Long (Longitude): The east-west geolocation on the Earth relative to an agreed upon Prime Meridian, measured in degrees.

LOS (Line-of-Sight): The direct sight line for information propagation from a target to a remote sensor.

LWIR (Long-Wave Infrared): A portion of the electromagnetic spectrum starting at approximately 8.0 μm and extending to 30.0 or even 100 μm depending on the application.

MASINT (Measurement And Signature Intelligence): Information produced by quantitative and qualitative analysis of physical attributes of targets and events to characterize, locate, and identify targets and events, and derived from specialized, technically derived measurements of physical phenomenon intrinsic to an object or event.

MD (Missile Defense): A system, weapon, or technology involved in the detection, tracking, interception, and destruction of attacking missiles.

MODTRAN: An atmospheric radiative transfer model developed by Spectral Sciences and the Air Force Research Laboratory that serves as a standard atmospheric band model for the remote sensing community.

MSI (Multispectral Imaging or Imagery): Information gathered using overlaying images simultaneously collected in multiple spectral bands (three or more, up to about fifty).

MW (Missile Warning): A protocol to provide long-range warning of a ballistic missile attack over the polar region of the Northern Hemisphere.

MWIR (Mid-Wave Infrared): A portion of the electromagnetic spectrum including approximately 3.5–5.0 μm, although this definition varies dependent upon the application.

NASIC (National Air and Space Intelligence Center): The primary Defense Department producer of foreign aerospace intelligence. NASIC develops its products by analyzing all available data on foreign aerospace forces and weapons systems to determine performance characteristics, capabilities, vulnerabilities and intentions.

NGA (National Geospatial-Intelligence Agency): NGA is the lead federal agency for GEOINT, providing timely, relevant, and accurate geospatial intelligence in support of national security.

NIPF (National Intelligence Priorities Framework): An Intelligence Community (IC) Directive that promulgates responsibilities within the Office of the Director of National Intelligence and IC elements to establish objectives, priorities, and guidance for the IC to ensure timely and effective collection, processing, analysis, and dissemination of national intelligence.

NIR (Near-Visible Infrared): A portion of the electromagnetic spectrum; approximately 0.7–2.0 μm, although sometimes defined as 0.7–1.1 μm; the limit of sensitivity of silicon.

NRO (National Reconnaissance Office): The US Government agency in charge of designing, building, launching, and maintaining America's intelligence satellites.

NSA (National Security Agency): The National Security Agency/Central Security Service (NSA/CSS) leads the US Government in cryptology that encompasses both Signals Intelligence and Information Assurance products and services, and enables Computer Network Operations in order to gain a decision advantage for the Nation and our allies under all circumstances.

ONIR (Overhead Non-imaging Infrared): The former designation for Overhead Persistent Infrared.

OPIR (Overhead Persistent Infrared): A method of collecting information using non-literal image exploitation collected from remote sensors in GEO and HEO orbits.

OSINT (Open Source Intelligence): Intelligence collected from publicly available sources.

OTH (Over the Horizon [Radar]): A radar system that detects objects in motion over the horizon (not in the line of sight) by reflecting electromagnetic waves off the Earth's ionosphere.

PHOTINT (Photographic Intelligence): Intelligence collected from literal pictures taken by hand-held cameras.

PCA (Principal Component Analysis): A multi-variable statistical technique used to suppress the background from a collection.

PI (Polarimetric Imaging): A form of remote sensing that relies on the relative intensity of the polarized components of reflected radiation from natural sources.

PSF (Point Spread Function): The response of an imaging system to a point source or point object. A more general term for the PSF is a system's impulse response; the PSF being the impulse response of a focused optical system.

RADAR (Radio Detection and Ranging): A system for detecting, locating, and identifying objects by means of reflected radio frequency waves.

RCS (Radar Cross Section): The directional reflectivity of a radar target.

RF (Radio Frequency): That portion of the electromagnetic spectrum at wavelengths longer than about one millimeter where energy may be collected using an antenna connected to a tuned receiver.

SAR (Synthetic Aperture Radar): A form of radar with the defining characteristic of using relative motion, between an antenna and its target region, to provide distinctive long-term coherent-signal variations, that are exploited to obtain finer spatial resolution than is possible with conventional beam-scanning means.

SBIRS (Space-Based Infrared System): A follow-on program of early warning sensors to replace the Defense Support Program. The first satellites were launched in the 2000s.

SEBASS (Spatially Enhanced Broadband Array Spectrograph System): An airborne hyperspectral imaging pushbroom scanner designed for nighttime target detection.

SIGINT (Signals Intelligence): Intelligence collected from freely propagating radio frequency electromagnetic radiation sources.

SMO (Support to Military Operations): An umbrella concept including Intelligence Preparation of the Battlefield, Indications and Warnings Situational Awareness/Threat Assessment, Special Operations, targeting support, and deployment and employment of forces.

SONAR (Sound Navigation and Ranging): Locating and characterizing underwater and sea surface targets by emitted or reflected acoustic signals.

SWIR (Shortwave Infrared): A portion of the electromagnetic spectrum including approximately 2.0–3.5 μm; although this definition varies dependent upon the application.

TCPAD (Tasking-Collection-Processing-Analysis-Dissemination): A time and resource management system for the operation of remote sensors, their data analysis, and product preparation and dissemination. Also known as TCPED by some agencies.

TCPED (Tasking-Collection-Processing-Exploitation-Dissemination): A time and resource management system for the operation of remote sensors, their data analysis, and product preparation and dissemination. Also known as TCPAD by some agencies.

TE (Transverse Electric mode): The electric field of a horizontally polarized electromagnetic wave incident upon a surface perpendicularly oriented (transverse) to the plane containing the wave's velocity vector and perpendicular to the surface. Also called the s-wave.

TI (Technical Intelligence): Intelligence derived from the collection, processing, analysis, and exploitation of data and information pertaining to foreign equipment and materiel for the purposes of preventing technological surprise, assessing foreign scientific and technical capabilities, and developing countermeasures designed to neutralize an adversary's technological advantages. Also called TECHINT.

TIR (Thermal Infrared): A portion of the electromagnetic spectrum from about 8.0 through 12.0 or 14.0 μm, sometimes the same as long-wave infrared, and sometimes including the mid-wave infrared.

TM (Transverse Magnetic mode): The magnetic field of a vertically polarized electromagnetic wave incident upon a surface being oriented perpendicular (transverse) to the plane containing the wave's velocity vector and perpendicular to the surface. Also called the p-wave.

UGF (Underground Facility): A hardened facility built underground to withstand enemy attack on high value targets.

Vis (Visible): The portion of the electromagnetic spectrum that can be detected by the human eye, approximately 0.4 μm (blue) through 0.7 μm (red).

Vis-NIR (Visible through Near InfraRed): The portion of the electromagnetic spectrum including both the visible and near infrared, approximately 0.4–1.1 μm (the sensitivity range of silicon).

Symbol	Name	Definition	Value	SI Units	Remarks
		============================= Roman Letters =============================			
A		Area		m^2	Subscript indicates context
A_c		Effective collection area		cm^2	Effective collection area
A_{PIX}		The area a detector sees		m^2	Physical area on the Earth's surface
A_R		Aperture area (receiving area)		m^2	Unobstructed, clear aperture collecting area
$A_\perp$		Area perpendicular to line-of-sight		m^2	Approximation for calculating solid angles
A/D		Analog-to-Digital conversion			Remote sensor data
$Airy$		Point source irradiance distribution			Distribution on Focal Plane Array
B		Blackbody integrated over a bandpass		$W \cdot m^{-2}$	See Stephan-Boltzmann Law for all wavelengths
$\vec{B}$		Magnetic field		$Wb \cdot m^{-2}$	Magnetic field also carries energy
B_λ		Planck function (ideal exitance)		$W \cdot m^{-2} \mu m^{-1}$	When integrated over bandpass = $W \cdot m^{-2}$
BRDF		Bidirectional Reflectivity Distribution Function		sr^{-1}	The amount of light reflected in particular directions
C		Capacitance		F	A quantum well storing electrons under a pixel
c		Speed of light in vacuum	$\approx 3.00 \times 10^8$	$m \cdot s^{-1}$	Remember, this is an approximation
c_1		First radiation constant	$\approx 3.74 \times 10^8$	$W \cdot \mu m^{-4} m^{-2}$	When using wavelength in μm
c_2		Second radiation constant	$\approx 1.44 \times 10^4$	$\mu m \cdot K$	When using wavelength in μm
D		Aperture diameter of collecting optics		m	Area = $\pi D^2 / 4$
D		Detectivity = 1/NEP		W^{-1}	Related to responsivity and quantum efficiency
D^*	D-star	Normalized detectivity		$cm \cdot Hz^{1/2} W^{-1}$	Rarely used
d		Distance, length, or size		m	Use when needed, consider context
d_T		Spectral distance threshold		m	Threshold used in spectral distance calculations
E		Energy (of a photon or quantum system)		J, eV	Usually means total, system, or state energy
$\vec{E}$		Electric field		$V \cdot m^{-1}$	Magnitude is amplitude of an electromagnetic wave
ΔE		Energy difference (between allowed states)		J, eV	For calculating necessary photon energy
$\mathcal{E}$		Irradiance		$W \cdot m^{-2}$	Power received (from any direction)
$\mathcal{E}_\lambda$		Spectral irradiance (received radiation)		$W \cdot m^{-2} \mu m^{-1}$	When integrated over bandpass = $W \cdot m^{-2}$
e		Base for Naperian logarithms (also: exp)	2.71828…		For calculating absorption, scattering, etc.

Symbol	Name	Definition	Value	SI Units	Remarks
F		Radar antenna adjustment factor			For antenna shape, material, and electrical properties
f		Frequency (of a wave)		Hz	Hz = s^{-1}
f		Frame rate		Hz	$f \approx 1/\Delta t_{INT}$ when duty cycle $\approx$ 100%
f		Focal length of a lens or mirror		m	Applies to a single optical element
f		Frequency of oscillation		Hz	Detector output from a Michelson interferometer
f_{eff}		Focal length of lens and mirror system		m	Effective focal length for multiple optical elements
$f/\#$		Aperture stop or f-stop (a ratio)			Ratio of focal length to aperture diameter = f/D
F_{PIX}		Filling factor			Accounts for irradiance on pixel within PSF
FOR		Field of Regard (of a sensor)			Everywhere a sensor could point to and see
FOV		Field of View (of a sensor)		sr	A solid angle—characteristic of sensor
FPA		Focal Plane Array			The de facto modern standard type of detector
FSR		Free Spectral Range		nm, μm, etc	The spacing in λ between two successive reflected or transmitted optical intensity maxima or minima of a diffractive optical element
G		Gain (of an antenna or optical system)			Commonly used in radar
G_N		Newton's gravitational constant	$\approx 6.67 \times 10^{-11}$	N·m^{2}kg^{-2}	For calculating gravitational attraction
g		Acceleration of gravity near the Earth's surface	≈ 9.81	m·s^{-2}	Standard value, but varies with altitude
g_i		Degeneracy			How many ways molecules can occupy one energy state
GSD		Ground Sample Distance		m	Linear dimension of a pixel's IFOV
H, h, or z		Altitude		m	A vertical distance above the Earth's surface
$\hat{H}$		Atmospheric "scale height"		m	Assumes isothermal atmosphere
h		Planck's constant	$\approx 6.63 \times 10^{-34}$	J·s	A fundamental constant of quantum physics
Hα, Hβ		Hydrogen emission lines			Prominent emission lines from the sun
$i(t)$		Detector output from a Michelson inferometer		A	An interferogram
I		Intensity		W·sr^{-1}	Power per unit direction sent from a point source
I_λ		*Spectral* intensity (sent radiation)		W·sr^{-1}μm^{-1}	When integrated over bandpass = W·sr^{-1}

Symbol	Name	Definition	Value	SI Units	Remarks
i		Electrical current		A	Coulombs/second
IFOV		Instantaneous Field of View			Surface area a sensor sees through its FOV
J		Rotational quantum number	$J = 0,1,2,3,\ldots$		Refers to the rotating molecule
ΔJ		Difference in rotational quantum number	$\Delta J = \pm 1$		Rotational transition selection rule
J_1		Bessel function of the first kind (first order)			From the Airy diffraction pattern
k		Extinction coefficient		m^{-1}	Other commonly used symbol: β
k_B		Boltzmann's constant	$\approx 1.38 \times 10^{-23}$	$J \cdot K^{-1}$	A fundamental constant of statistical physics
L or ℓ		Length, size, or distance		m	Context should distinguish from radiance
L		Inductance		H	Used in high-pass filters and tuned circuits
L		Radiance		$W \cdot m^{-2} sr^{-1}$	Power sent from a surface in a direction
L_λ		*Spectral* radiance (sent radiation)		$W \cdot m^{-2} sr^{-1} \mu m^{-1}$	When integrated over band pass $= W \cdot m^{-2} sr^{-1}$
LOS		Line of sight			Also called "boresight"
M		Magnification of an optical system			A ratio of image to object distances
M or m		Mass		kg	Measure of an object's inertia
M		Exitance		$W \cdot m^{-2}$	Power per unit area sent in all directions
M_E		Mass of the Earth	$\approx 5.98 \times 10^{24}$	kg	Used in Kepler's Laws
M_λ		Spectral exitance (sent radiation)		$W \cdot m^{-2} \mu m^{-1}$	When integrated over bandpass $= W \cdot m^{-2}$
m		Order of interference			Integer path difference of interfering light rays
(m, n)		Pixel address on a FPA			The dimensions of a FPA in number of pixels
$\langle m \rangle$		Mean molecular mass of atmosphere	$\approx 4.81 \times 10^{-23}$	kg	Mass per air molecule
N		Number of something			Electrons, atoms, molecules, photons, etc.
η		Noise		Volts or Amperes	Noise sources considered to be uncorrelated
$\tilde{N}$		Digitized output of a photoelectric detector		"LD" or "DN"	End-to-end equation result
$\mathcal{N}$		Column density		m^{-2}	Number of molecules over an area
n		Index of refraction	1 (vacuum)		≈ 1 for air
n		Number density		m^{-3}	Number of particles per unit volume
n		Principal quantum number	$n = 1,2,3\ldots$		Refers to electron energy levels in the atom

Symbol	Name	Definition	Value	SI Units	Remarks
n_r	Particle size distribution			$m^{-3}\mu m^{-1}$	Number density per unit size interval
n_0	Sea level standard number density		$\approx 2.69 \times 10^{25}$	m^{-3}	"Loschmidt's number"
NEP	Noise equivalent power			W	Signal equivalent to noise
NET	Noise equivalent target			W	Signal equivalent to noise
P	Degree of polarization				Depends on angle of incidence
P	Orbital period			minutes, hours	Period of a satellite's orbit
PSF	Point Spread Function				"Blur circle" or spread of energy through a collector
Q	Radiant energy			J	Energy sent, transferred, or collected
Q	Quantity of electrical charge			C	Stored as electrons, each with one quantum of charge
$\{q\}$	Conversion from joules to electron volts		$\approx 1.60 \times 10^{-19}$	$J \cdot eV^{-1}$	Electron volt is a more practical unit for light
q^-	Charge on an electron		$\approx 1.60 \times 10^{-19}$	C	The elementary unit of eletrical charge
R	Range to target, or a distance			m	Line of sight distance
R	Resistance			Ω	Used in Ohm's Law
$\mathcal{R}_e$	Responsivity			$amp \cdot W^{-1}$	Related to detectivity and quantum efficiency
R_E	Radius of the Earth		$\approx 6.73 \times 10^6$	m	Average radius of the Earth
R_M	Meteorological range, or visibility			km	"Standard" $R_M = 23$ km
$\overline{RP}$	Resolving power				Ability to separate two adjacent peaks in a spectrum
R_{ORBIT}	Radius of the Earth's orbit around the Sun		$\approx 1.50 \times 10^{11}$	m	Earth orbit semi-major axis
R_{SUN}	Radius of the Sun		$\approx 6.96 \times 10^8$	m	Average radius of the Sun
r	Reflectance coefficient				Reflection coefficient of electric field at a boundry
r	Radius of a circle, sphere, or orbit			m	Used sparingly as required, consider context
r_A	Radius of Airy disk on FPA			μm	For determining spatial resolution
$r_{1/2}$	Half-power radius of Airy disk			μm	Conventionally used with radar antennas
r_0	Characteristic scattering particle radius			μm	Average of the particle size distribution function
RCS	Radar cross section			m^2	Long wavelength equivalent of scattering
RMS	Root mean square value				Root of the mean of the square
S	Diameter of typical blur circle			m	Usually modeled by a Gaussian or bell-shaped curve
S	Stokes parameter			W	S0, S1, S2, S3
s	Arc length on a circle			m	Approximated by the chord for small angles
Δs	Path length through atmosphere			m	Along line of sight

Symbol	Name	Definition	Value	SI Units	Remarks
SNR		Signal to noise ratio (also "S/N")			Expressed as ratio of voltages, currents, or counts
T		Temperature		K	$T(K) = T(°C) + 273.15$
t		Time		s	Time of day or duration of an event
t		Transmission coefficient			Transmission coefficient of electric field at a boundary
Δt_{INT}		Integration time		s	A detector operating characteristic
U		Etendue		cm² sr	Sensor throughput
V		Voltage		V	An output of an analog photoelectric detector
v		Vibrational quantum number	$v = 0,1,2,3...$		Refers to the vibrating molecule
X_{FOV}, Y_{FOV}		Dimensions of a sensor's IFOV on the ground		m	Dimensions are along track and cross track
x		PSF center separation on FPA		μm	Consideration for determining spatial resolution
x_{FPA}, y_{FPA}		Dimensions of a sensor's FPA		μm	Physical size of FPA
x_{DET}, y_{DET}		Dimensions of a detector		μm	Physical size of detector
Δx		Optical material thickness		m	For calculating optical transmission
Z		Partition function			For calculating number of molecules per energy state
z		Altitude (above sea level or above ground)		m	AGL = above ground level, MSL = mean sea level
z_0		Optical depth		m	Characteristic attenuation length
Δz		Vertical component of path length		m	Used when number density varies vertically only

================================ Greek Letters ================================

Symbol	Name	Definition	Value	SI Units	Remarks
α	alpha	Absorptivity			A fraction of incident light absorbed
α		Interior cone angle (round FOV)		rad	For a sensor having a circular FOV
α		Apex angle		deg	Apex angle of a prism
α_T		Spectral angle threshold			Threshold in spectral angle calculations
β	beta	Extinction coefficient		m⁻¹	Absorption or scattering
Γ	gamma	Path difference		μm	Difference in path traveled
δ	delta	Aspect angle		rad	Angle from event velocity vector to sensor LOS
δ		Angular dispersion			Angular dispersion of a prism
ε	epsilon	Emissivity			A ratio of actual to theoretical emission
η	eta	Quantum efficiency		[electrons per photon]	A detector figure of merit

Symbol	Name	Definition	Value	SI Units	Remarks
θ	theta	An angle		rad	Used as needed, consider context
θ_{MIN}		Minimum angular separation		rad	Rayleigh criterion for spatial resolution
θ_N		Nadir angle		degrees	Angle from directly downward
θ_R		Fixation angle (*receiving* angle)		rad	Measured from sensor boresight
θ_S		Target zenith angle, *sending* angle		rad	Measured from target zenith
θ_x, θ_y		Field of view angles		rad	Rectangular FOV
κ	kappa	Dielectric constant			Figures in quantum well capacitance
λ	lambda	Wavelength		μm	Related to frequency by $\lambda = c/f$
λ_{MAX}		Wavelength of maximum emission		μm	For a blackbody (see Wien's Law)
$d\lambda$		Wavelength increment for integration		μm	Calculus notation—use $\Delta\lambda$ in practice
$\Delta\lambda$		Wavelength interval (bandpass)		μm	$\Delta\lambda = \lambda_2 - \lambda_1$
$\Delta\lambda_{MIN}$		Spectral resolution		μm, mm	Spectral resolution of material
μ	mu	Micro- (prefix)	$\times 10^{-6}$		Common prefix meaning 1/1,000,000
M_E		Kepler's constant for Earth orbits		$N \cdot m^2 kg^{-1}$	$= G_N M_E$
υ		Wavenumber		cm^{-1}	$= 10{,}000/\lambda$ when λ in μm
Π	pi	Product (mathematical operation)			Shorthand notation for multiplication product
π	pi		3.14159...		Ratio of circumference to diameter of a circle
ρ	rho	Reflectivity			A fraction of incident light reflected
$\bar{\rho}$		Average reflectivity			Surface property
ρ_m		Mass density		$kg \cdot m^{-3}$	Mass per unit volume
Σ	sigma	Sum (mathematical operation)			Shorthand notation for addition
σ		Cross section (absorption or scattering)		m^2	Not a real area, but an effective one
σ_m		Mass cross section		$m^2 kg^{-1}$	Used in radiology and high energy physics
σ_r		Particle size standard deviation		$m^2 m^{-1}$	Used in lognormal distribution of particle sizes
σ_{SB}		Stefan-Boltzmann constant	$\approx 5.67 \times 10^{-8}$	$W \cdot m^{-2} K^{-4}$	For calculating total power emitted
τ	tau	Transmission function, in general			Atmospheric or optical
τ_{ATM}		Atmospheric transmission function			Includes absorption *and* scattering (Beer's Law)
τ_{OPT}		Optical transmission function			Includes reflection, transmission, and filters
Φ	phi	Power		W	Power = energy/time

Symbol	Name	Definition	Value	SI Units	Remarks
ϕ		Phase function for reflection or scattering		sr^{-1}	Refers to direction of radiation scattered or sent
ϕ		Work function		eV	Establishes maximum wavelegth for a detector
ϕ, φ		Angle		rad	Used as needed, consider context
Ω	omega	Solid angle		sr	In general $\Omega = A_\perp / R^2$
Ω_{FOV}		Solid angle field of view of entire sensor		sr	Specify shape of FOV
Ω_{PIX}		Solid angle field of view of one pixel		sr	Sum of $\Omega_{PIX} = \Omega_{FOV}$
Ω_R		Solid angle receiving energy *from* target		sr	Subtended by sensor *from* target
$d\Omega$		A direction in 3-D space		sr	Per unit direction

A

Absorption 25-28, 31, 45-46, 61, 119, 124-127, 136, 149-151, 161, 172, 250-252, 339-342, 420, 426-430
Absorption coefficient 124, 172
Absorption cross-section 125, 128, 136-137
Absorptivity 25-27, 61, 136, 328, 334, 340-341
AC-coupled, AC-coupled detector 178
ACOUSTINT (Acoustic Intelligence) 4
Active sensing 131, 426-430
Aerosols 54, 65, 115-118, 131, 133, 294, 419, 430, 438-439, 444, 464
Agriculture 454
Aircraft 100, 102, 145, 149, 183, 222, 235-236, 244-245, 272, 284, 298, 339, 343, 347, 376, 389, 393, 398, 403, 410, 413, 429, 445, 451-455, 458, 461, 463
Aircraft pitch, roll, yaw 244-245
Airy disk, Airy pattern (PSF) 154-157, 168-169, 182, 201, 210, 281
Airy formula (for interference) 201, 377
Airy function (for PSF) 154-156, 168
Albedo 71, 95, 138, 209, 262
Allowed energy states 28, 32-33, 44-45, 124
Allowed transitions (spectral lines) ....
  Atoms 29, 31-32
  Molecules 31-32
Along-range 187
Along-track 186, 188, 248-249, 296
Alpha particle 4, 27, 96-97
Altitude ... 78-79, 92, 100-101, 104-107, 110-118, 121-123, 125, 133, 186-191, 221-236, 238-242, 261-263, 343-347
Amorphous solids 48
Amplitude 18, 33, 64, 155-156, 161, 177, 195-197, 361-363, 366-368, 383-384, 434
Analog to digital conversion 207, 247
Analysis 211-213, 256-263, 264-269, 271-286, 297-316, 328-342, 393-408, 410-417, 420-430, 437-448
Angle of incidence 61-62, 64, 150-151, 351-352, 432, 434, 436-437
Angular momentum 30, 32, 35-36, 38, 40, 226-227
Angular separation 182-183
Antenna 4, 12, 145-146, 156, 160-161, 175, 196, 231, 297, 437, 439
Anti-reflection coatings 151, 153, 172, 214
Aperture 78, 89-92, 134-135, 142-148, 154-157, 182-185, 206, 214, 281, 355, 372
Apogee 227-229, 232-235, 256
Approximations, common 16, 18, 69
Arc length 74-75
Area ....
  Emitting surface 87
  Ground pixel 186-191, 241-247, 288-291, 343-347
  Receiving aperture 351, 359
Argument of perigee 229

ARTEMIS (Advanced Responsive Tactically Effective Military Imaging Spectrometer) 407-423, 430
Artifacts 273-276, 282-283, 291-292, 296, 465
Ascending node 229
Aspect angle 85
Asymmetric molecules 32, 38-40, 49
ATI (Advanced Technical Intelligence) 449-466
Atmosphere 5, 109-118
Atmospheric sounder 322, 325-326, 410, 413
Atmospheric transmission function ... (see Beer's Law)
Atomic energy level transitions 427
Atomic selective radiation 17, 43, 54, 59, 260, 464
Atoms 4, 27-32
Attenuation 5, 119-123
Attenuation coefficient 119-121, 125, 133
Azimuth angle 67, 103, 107, 187, 189, 437, 446

B

Background 43, 46, 90-92, 95-96, 138-140, 157, 177-179, 207-219, 276-285
Band gap (in semiconductors) 163-165, 172
Bandpass 20-22, 87-88, 149-153, 163-164, 193-204
Bathymetry 12, 297, 312-316, 392, 408, 456-457
Beer's Law 118-125, 207-208, 213
Beryllium (mirror) 152, 162
Bessel function 154-155
Beta particle 27, 96
Bias .... see Dark current
Bistatic radar 3
Bit depth 179-180, 207-208, 248, 296
Bits 179-180, 209, 248, 274
Blackbody 16-20, 22-23, 26-27, 46, 49, 80-82, 93-94, 137, 218, 260, 284, 327, 420, 426
Blackbody function (Planck's function) .. 17-19, 87, 340
BLIP (Background Limited Infrared Performance) 217
"Blue spike" 42, 251
Blur circle (see Airy disk) 154-155, 182
Boltzmann distribution 43
Boresight 78-79, 89-91, 186-187, 206-207, 262
Bound states 29
BRDF (Bi-directional Reflectivity Distribution Function) 54, 68, 432-434, 436, 446
Brewster's angle 62, 64
Brightness 29, 32, 42-43, 47-48, 123, 135, 144, 176, 179, 217, 298, 335

C

Calibration 174-176, 202, 213-214, 275, 283-285, 289, 336, 338, 343, 350, 354, 376, 388, 392, 405, 415, 465
Capacitor 113, 163, 166-167, 178, 247
Cassegrain telescope 148-149, 204
Cauchy Series expansion 352
CBRN (Chemical-Biological-Radiological-Nuclear Intelligence) 423-425, 452-453

CCD (Camouflage Concealment and Deception)... 458
CCD (Charge Coupled Device).......... 166, 170, 172, 176, 178, 275
CEM (Constrained Energy Minimization) 399-400, 402, 416, 422-423
CH_4 (Methane) 42, 49, 110, 173, 251, 429
Change detection........................ 297, 309-311, 318, 461
Characteristics, target...... 4-5, 8, 53-60, 86, 88, 90, 202, 207, 213, 254, 464-465
Chemical bond........................ 32-34, 36, 38, 48
Chlorophyll.. 252
Circular aperture 154, 156
Circumference........................ 74, 128-130, 132, 249, 289
Clear aperture 148, 208
Clouds... 115-118, 322-325
Clutter........................... 276-279, 281-282, 422, 424, 464
CMOS (Complementary Metal Oxide Semiconductor) 73, 166, 171-172, 176, 178
CO (Carbon monoxide)...... 34-35, 37, 41-42, 45-46, 49, 110, 260, 267-268, 420, 429
CO_2 (Carbon dioxide) 39-40, 42, 49, 110-111, 251, 260, 267-268, 325, 328, 428-430
COIS (Coastal Ocean Imaging Spectrometer) 407-408
Collection geometry........ 32, 74, 78, 102, 104, 106, 108, 126, 184, 186, 378, 388, 402, 464
Collector............... 144, 148, 152-153, 156, 170, 186, 190, 241, 275, 288, 464
Column density 113, 429
COMET (COMmon Exploitation Tool) 316
COMINT (Communications Intelligence) 3, 102
Conduction band............... 50-51, 161-164, 171-173, 280
Cone angle 76-78, 91
Conservation of ………………..
    Angular momentum...30, 32, 35-36, 38, 40, 226-227
    Exitance 82, 84, 93
    Intensity 86
    Radiance 83-84, 93
    Temperature 17, 82
Constants 17, 113, 161, 178, 275, 284
Continuous mode, detection 215
Continuum radiation...................... 16, 27, 43, 46, 49, 54
Contrast...... 43, 46, 55, 124, 135-137, 185, 411, 446, 464
Conversion (J to eV).. 13
Counter Camouflage Concealment and Deception 458
Cross section......... 54, 76-77, 84, 124-137, 155, 226, 258
Cross-track................. 186, 188, 241, 244-249, 290, 292, 295-296, 322, 326-327, 344, 392, 413, 447
Crystals............ 22, 48, 67, 116, 150, 354, 359, 439-440
Current, electrical....... 18, 25, 51, 160-161, 163-164, 264
Curvature of Earth 104, 113, 121, 187-189, 347
CVF (Continuously Variable Filter) .. 289, 292, 375-376

D

Dark current................................. 173-174, 216, 274, 409
Data processing... 102, 174, 217, 255-256, 271, 273, 349, 388, 393
DC-coupled, DC-coupled detector 176-178
Debris particles 4, 286
Defective detectors 273, 275, 283
Degeneracy 43-44
Degree of polarization 64
Detector(s)................... …141, 159-180, 206-209, 247-249
DEW (Directed Energy Weapon)............................ 3
DIAL (Differential Absorption LIDAR) 428-429
Diatomic molecules............. 32-34, 36, 41, 110, 124, 260
Dielectric constant... 167
Dielectric materials (non-metals) 128, 193, 201
Differential scattering cross-section 131
Diffraction 12-13, 142, 154-155, 355, 357, 359, 361, 363-365, 367-369, 371
Diffraction gratings............ 149, 154, 194, 196, 349, 360
Diffraction-limited optics................................... 155
Diffraction pattern 154, 156, 366-367
Diffuse reflection..................... 53, 69, 431-434, 436-437
Digital to analog conversion..................................... 212
Digital units, DU 207, 219
Dipole moment 32-33, 38-40, 110, 124
Discrete energy levels, atomic and molecular 32, 49-50
Discrimination.. 430
Dispersing elements 59, 149, 201
Dispersion 59, 322, 350-351, 353-356, 359, 368-373, 376, 380, 382, 387, 465
Dissemination 6, 271
Dissociation 111, 132, 250
Distortion............................... 55, 243-244, 246, 291
Distribution .... function 18-22, 27, 65-70, 87-88, 116, 118, 432
DMSP (Defense Meteorological Support Program)....... 252, 322, 324-326
Doppler shift.. 41
Dry aerosols 117-118
DSP (Defense Support Program)......... 85, 254-255, 264
Duality, wave-particle..................................... 12
Dumbbell model.. 34
Dust............................... 7, 37, 68, 115-118, 120, 123, 424
Duty cycle 179, 210, 237, 248, 255-256, 269, 275, 279, 281, 465
Dwell time.. 242, 249, 387
Dye filters... 149
Dynamic events/targets.................................... 213

E

ECI (Earth Centered Inertial coordinates)......... 228-229
Einstein coefficient.. 125
Elastic scattering 129, 426-428
Electric charge 128, 160, 176

Electric field 12, 51, 61-62, 80, 161, 195, 200-201, 360-362, 364-366, 434, 440

Electromagnetic radiation 1, 11-12, 205, 312-313, 437, 464

Electromagnetic spectrum ... 1, 4-5, 9, 14-15, 22, 31, 160, 250, 252, 287, 321

Electromagnetic waves 4, 11-12, 58-59, 124, 159, 161, 195-197, 205, 209, 250, 360-361, 435

Electron orbits, orbitals.. 28
Electron transitions 32
Electron volt (eV) 13
Electrons 27-32, 50, 158-163, 167
Electro-optics.. 3-4, 12, 15, 54, 163
Elementary particles.. 27
ELINT (Electronics Intelligence)....................................... 3
Ellipse (orbit)... 226-229, 278
Emission .. 16-26, 28-31, 32-42, 92-96, 135-140, 256-262, 264-269
Emissive signature 23, 73
Emissivity . 22-25, 86-88, 95, 136-138, 206, 328, 336-337, 340, 412, 420-422
EMP (Electromagnetic Pulse).................................. 3, 264
End-to-end equation 205-209, 211, 213, 283, 336, 351
Energy level transitions 96
Ensembles... 43, 45-47, 92, 228
EO (Electro-Optics) 3-4, 8, 15, 161-164
Ephemeris, ephemerides 228-230
Equilibrium... 16, 100, 268
Etalon 149, 201, 349, 375-378
Etendue 351, 357, 359, 371-374, 378-380, 385-387
Exitance 18-26, 49, 80-85, 87, 93-94, 98, 114, 136, 218
Exploitation..... 6-9, 102, 214, 271-273, 276, 283, 286, 316, 409, 465-466
Explosive event.. 268
Exponential atmosphere 113
Extended source 55-56, 86-87, 90-92, 95-96, 121, 124, 135, 138, 157, 175, 205, 207-208, 351, 355, 371, 378, 385, 464
Extinction (see Attenuation)
Extinction coefficient..... 119-121, 123-124, 126, 136, 149

F

Fabry Perot Etalon................................ 349, 375-376, 378
Fading memory.. 277
False color composite.. 306-308
Fermi-Dirac distribution.. 50
Filling factor 176
Filter wheel.................... 288-290, 292, 326, 375-376, 441
Filter(s).......... 193-204, 214, 288-290, 294-295, 375-380
Finesse 350, 377
Finite bandpass 209
First point of Aries 228

FISINT (Foreign Instrumentation Signals Intelligence) 3
Fixation angle.............................. 78, 80, 90, 206, 208
Flat Earth (approximation)......................... 105, 107, 191
Flick... 87
Fluctuation.............................. 214-215, 217, 273, 276, 422
Fluorescence 427, 430
FME (Foreign Materiel Exploitation) 3
Focal distance (ellipse).. 226
Focal length 55, 142-144, 147-148, 154, 182-183, 186, 189, 205, 208, 241, 246, 290, 374, 378, 385
Fog 7, 111, 115-116, 121, 129, 322
Footprint 185, 188, 241-244, 246, 290, 388
FOR (Field of Regard) 186, 232-234, 238
Fourier analysis................................... 278, 382-383, 385
FOV (Field of View) 77-78, 89-90, 182-191, 207, 238-247
FPA (Focal Plane Array)....................................... 165-171
Frame rate, frame time 179, 210, 242, 248, 279
Fraunhofer diffraction... 364
Free spectral range 350, 392
Frequency................... 4, 12-15, 87, 129, 156, 159-160, 162, 178, 183, 195, 214, 217, 242, 266, 381-382, 384-385, 403, 428, 434
Fresnel formula 67, 150
F-stop 142, 168
FTS (Fourier Transform Spectrometer) 349, 374, 379-380, 382-388, 413
Fully diffuse (Lambertian) reflection 69-70, 137

G

Gain 16, 18, 58, 156-157, 160, 339-340, 370
Gamma ray... 96, 264, 461
Gaps 63, 164, 171, 244-246, 291, 345
Gaseous state 37, 41
Gaussian distribution 44, 155, 283
Generation-recombination noise..................... 172, 217
GEO (Geosynchronous Orbit) 7, 85, 186, 209, 224, 238, 254, 272, 322, 326, 463
Geolocation........ 56-57, 60, 100-108, 160, 286, 425, 465
Geometric optics.. 143
Geospatial Intelligence (GEOINT)........ 3, 100, 209, 286
Glass (material) .. 24, 59-61, 151, 153, 351-353, 355, 368, 380-381
GOES (Geostationary Operational Environmental Satellite).................................... 250, 328-329, 332-333
Graybody emissivity 24-25
Ground pixel.................................. 90, 185-191, 240-245
Ground state ... 28-30, 34-35, 38, 43, 45-46, 50, 427-428
GSD (Ground Sample Distance) 157, 185-186, 189-191, 208, 241, 249, 262, 318, 344, 346-347, 447

H

H2O (Water) 38, 41-42, 49, 110-111, 251, 260-261, 267, 325, 328
Heisenberg's uncertainty principle 46, 280
Hemisphere 69-70, 76, 81, 83, 186, 228, 235, 254, 322, 411, 433, 436, 454
HEO (High Earth Orbit, Highly Elliptical Orbit) .. 9, 224, 230, 232-235, 240, 242, 254-256, 272
HgCdTe (Mercury-Cadmium-Telluride) 164, 166, 254, 291, 295, 392, 407, 413-414, 425
High frequency 4, 15, 178
High pass filter 177-178
Horizontal path 121, 424
HSI (Hyperspectral Imagery) 59, 291, 308, 316, 328, 349-351, 375, 387-389, 391-393, 396-404, 407, 409-410, 412-416, 419-420, 422-424, 431, 433-434, 446, 462
HUMINT (Human Intelligence) 2-3, 102
HYCAS (Hyperspectral Collection and Analysis System) 392
HYDICE (Hyperspectral Digital Imagery Collection Experiment) 392, 404
Hydrogen 28-31, 37, 39, 42-44, 259-260, 264, 429
Hydrometeors 116
Hydrostatic atmosphere model 120, 131
Hyperion 407-408

I

Ideal gas law 112
IFOV (Instantaneous Field of View) 186-190, 241, 243, 281, 284
IMINT (Imagery Intelligence) 3, 55, 102, 165, 170
Inclination 229-233, 235, 240
Index of refraction 12, 59-61, 134, 150-151, 153, 172, 197-198, 352-353, 375-376, 435, 439
Inelastic scattering 129, 426
InSb (Indium Antimonide) 163-164, 172, 291, 295, 392, 413-414
Integration (mathematical/numerical) 20, 94, 119, 177, 214, 269, 281, 286, 387, 465
Integration time 134, 179, 206-207, 209, 211, 216, 218, 236, 242, 247-248, 263, 269, 279, 282-283
Intelligence collection 2, 32-34, 51, 68, 126, 129, 133, 142, 162, 166, 205, 464-466
Intensity 80-86, 88-89, 93, 206-213, 258-259
Interference 12-13, 15, 28, 47, 153, 160, 194-199, 201-202, 360-379, 381, 387
Interference filters 149, 152, 194, 196, 322, 326, 375-376, 378
Interferometers 149, 154, 349, 376-378, 380-382, 385-388, 423
Interferometry 144
Internal noise 217
Ionization 250
IR (Infrared) 1, 3-4, 14-16, 161-165

Irradiance 80-82, 88-92, 206-214
Isotropic 82, 85-86, 88, 93, 285

J

Jacquinot advantage 387
JSLSCAD (Joint Service Lightweight Standoff Chemical Agent Detector) 424-425
Jump, quantum leap 28-29, 31-32, 34-36, 38, 41, 43, 46-47, 50, 124, 126, 163, 464

K

Kelvins 14, 17, 19, 268, 339
Kepler's Laws 226
Kirchhoff's Law 27

L

LADAR (Laser Detection and Ranging) 426
Lambertian . 69-70, 83-86, 90, 93, 95, 137, 431-432, 434
LANDSAT or Landsat (Land Satellite) 173, 230, 235, 251-252, 287, 292-300, 302-303, 305-306, 308-314, 317-318, 322, 334, 338, 388, 408, 461
Laser 3-4, 14, 28, 65, 110, 131, 133, 152, 230, 419, 426-430, 437
LASH (Littoral Airborne Sensor—Hyperspectral) 392-393
Leaf, leaves 437, 455, 462
LEEDR (Laser Environmental Effects Definition and Reference) 133, 464
LEO (Low Earth Orbit) 7, 9, 114, 191, 212, 224, 230-231, 235-236, 238-240
LIDAR (Light Detection and Ranging) 4, 54, 131, 316, 423-424, 426, 428-430, 441
Lifetimes 46, 57, 96, 104-105, 214, 280
Light particle 13
Light wave ... 11-13, 27, 47, 59, 96, 160-161, 193-195, 464
Line radiation (selective radiation) ... 17, 43, 54, 59, 260, 265, 464
Line strength 46, 48
Linear atmosphere 137
Lines, spectral 29, 32, 34, 47, 199, 350, 355, 369, 377, 383, 385
Lognormal distribution 118
Long wavelength cutoff 149, 204
Longitude of ascending node 229
LOS (Line of Sight) 60, 75, 78-79, 92, 100-101, 121-122, 137, 238-242, 343-347
Loschmidt's number 113
Low frequency 4, 15, 217, 384
LWIR (Long-Wave Infrared) 15, 150, 160, 164, 250, 291, 321-343, 354-355, 409-417

M

Magic number 285
Magnetic dipole 33

Magnification 143, 146-148, 263
Major axis 226-229, 235
MASINT (Measurement and Signature
Intelligence) 3-4
Mass density 97, 325
Maximum emission 20
Maxwell's equations 11-12, 435
Mechanical waves 4, 9, 214
Medium frequency (thermal) detectors 161, 173
Metal(s) 24, 50-51, 61, 73, 152-153, 155, 160-163, 166, 275, 284, 305, 328, 368, 434, 439, 444
Meteorological range 121
Metric, metrics 3-4, 7, 9, 56, 58, 60, 73, 75, 99-100, 113, 141, 159, 213, 250, 254, 257, 271, 276, 285-286, 396, 403, 465
Metsats 321-322, 324-326
Michelson interferometer 349, 380-382
Microwave 15, 22, 35-36, 40, 160, 196, 216, 264-265, 325-326, 426, 432, 455, 462-464
Mie scattering 129
Minerals 22, 94, 252, 336-337, 396, 405, 410-411
Minimum separation 50, 183, 350, 373
Minor axis 226-227
Mirror 42, 61, 66, 98, 143-146, 148-149, 152-153, 155, 193, 197, 201, 216, 244-245, 275, 284, 290, 292, 295-296, 317, 322, 326, 349, 357, 372-373, 380-382, 385-388, 428
Misalignment 142, 155, 194
Model 27-29, 33-34, 47, 56, 66, 69-70, 103, 106, 110, 112-113, 115-116, 118, 131-133, 137, 167, 225, 251, 263, 280, 325, 327, 334-335, 339, 347, 375-376, 398
Modes, vibrational 38-39, 42, 48
MODTRAN 94, 126-127, 131-132, 136-139, 207-208, 210, 239, 250, 261, 263, 313, 327, 336-337, 340, 464
Molecules 4, 11, 27, 30-50, 54, 61, 65, 96, 110-119, 123-128, 131, 136, 199, 206, 260-261, 264, 267, 344, 354, 426-429, 437-439, 441
Molniya (HEO) orbit 224, 232-235
Moving target 57
MSI (Multi-Spectral Imagery) 59, 287-288, 290-292, 294, 297-300, 302, 304-306, 308-310, 312, 314-318, 321, 338, 343, 350, 375, 388-389, 393, 397, 413, 415, 431, 433-434, 446
MWIR (Mid-Wave Infrared) 15, 34, 40-42, 49, 126, 164, 209, 250, 286, 291, 312, 326, 328, 336-338, 343, 350, 354, 374-375, 407, 410, 413-417, 443-444, 447-448, 457

N

Nadir 100, 106, 185, 187, 190-191, 228, 238-239, 249, 262, 293, 297, 317-318, 321-322, 338, 343-347, 374, 446-447
Nadir angle 75, 100-101, 103-106, 191, 212, 238-239, 243, 347, 446-448

Nadir viewing 184, 186, 188, 190, 213, 238-239, 321, 343-344, 446-448
NASA (National Aeronautics and Space
Administration) 94, 230, 236, 254, 284, 287, 289, 292, 294, 296, 326, 407-408, 429, 456
Naval Earth Map Observer (NEMO) 407-408
Newton's Universal Law Of Gravitation 224
NIR (Near Infrared) 15, 27, 31, 126, 168-169, 250, 252, 291, 294, 299, 306-308, 318, 322, 326, 334, 350, 375, 407
NOAA (National Oceanic and Atmospheric
Administration) 111, 252, 322-323, 326
Noise 138, 166, 171-179, 205, 209, 213-221, 242, 256, 262-263, 265-266, 271, 273-274, 276-279, 281-282, 351, 389, 395, 413, 465
Non-literal 5, 8, 54-56, 102, 142, 254, 271
Non-selective scattering 129
Normal (to surface) 59, 62, 64, 66, 68, 78-79, 83, 151, 172, 199-202, 435, 437
Number density 111-114, 116, 118, 127, 133, 258
NVIS (Night Vision Imaging Spectrometer) .. 392-393, 407
Nyquist-Shannon criterion 184

O

Ozone 111-112, 133, 326-327, 429
Observable(s) 6, 27-28, 257, 286
Obstruction 22
Ohm's Law 176
One-over-f noise 195, 217
One-over-R-squared law 87
Opaque 24, 26, 49, 60, 126, 144, 172, 268, 275, 330, 360, 368
OPIR (Overhead Persistent Infrared) 3
Optical depth 120-121
Optical materials 150-152, 354
Optical Transfer Function 281
Optical transmission 60, 141, 149, 153, 194, 204, 206-208, 218
Optics 5, 8, 12, 43, 60, 85, 91, 110, 141-143, 154-156, 160, 168, 170, 174-175, 182-183, 186, 190, 201, 204, 208-210, 214, 240-241, 246, 265, 281, 290, 295, 349, 354, 357, 362, 372-374, 378, 385, 388, 392, 464-465
Orbital elements 229-230, 232
Oscillator strength 47-48, 125
OSINT (Open Source Intelligence) 3
OTH (Over-the-Horizon radar) 266

P

Paints and pigments 24, 65-67, 117, 185, 337, 399, 404-406, 410-411, 432, 434-435, 459
Pan sharpening 299
Paraxial approximation 143
Particle size distributions 116, 118
Partition function 43-44

Passive sensing 426
Performance, sensor 250, 317-318, 349-350, 423
Perigee 104, 227-229, 234-235
Persistent events and targets 56-57, 176-177, 256, 263-264, 269, 272, 279, 285
Phase 12, 40, 159, 195-198, 255-256, 264, 360-366, 368, 371, 386, 423
Phase function 67-68, 85, 131
Phasors 195-197, 361-362
Phenomenology 3-5, 8-9, 11, 18, 22, 24, 26, 48, 80, 92, 94, 96, 98-99, 106, 129, 138, 141, 202, 205-207, 209, 218, 250, 252, 262, 268, 283, 406, 446, 465-466
Photodetector 159, 165-166, 171-173, 176-178, 274
Photodiode 162, 164, 264-266
Photoelectric detector 142, 177-178
Photoelectric effect 4, 13, 161-164, 171, 206, 215
Photoemissive 161
Photograph 5-6, 29, 73, 142, 150, 169
Photometry 73, 96, 98-99
Photon 12-17, 161-166, 216
Photon energy 13-14, 28, 80, 124, 138, 161-162, 164
Photon noise 216, 218-219, 262-263, 266, 465
PI (Polarimetric Imagery) 436, 441, 446-447
Pixel 5, 55-56, 69, 86, 91, 169-171, 173-176, 178-180, 183-189
Pixel calibration 174
Pixel field of view 378, 385, 413-414, 425
Planck Function 17-18, 20-23, 43, 94, 415, 420
Planck's constant 13, 17
Plane angle 74-77, 351
Planetary model 27, 29
Plants and vegetation 73, 240, 251-252, 286, 300, 302-303, 306-307,, 310, 444, 454-455, 457-458, 462
Point source 55-56, 80, 85-86, 88-93, 98, 124, 133-134, 138, 154-157, 168-169, 181-185, 190, 205-206, 208-210, 213, 215, 256, 344-345, 350-351, 373, 379, 432, 464
Polarimetry .... See Polarization
Polarization .. 12, 53, 59, 61-62, 64-65, 96, 150, 159-160, 195, 343, 430, 434-444, 448
Polyatomic molecules 41
Population of energy states 45
Precipitation 111, 116
Principal Components 278, 280, 297, 308
Prism 12, 59, 149, 154, 349, 351-359, 372-373, 380, 387-388, 413
Prism spectrometer 354-355, 357-359, 373, 380, 387
Probability of detection 396, 402
Probability of false alarm 402
Processing 1-2, 4, 6-7, 9, 102, 160, 174, 179, 217, 219-220, 239, 248, 255-256, 262, 271-274, 276-277, 297, 305, 308,312, 325, 349, 388-389, 392-393, 400, 404, 436, 454-455, 457, 465-466
Projected area 75, 79, 84, 87, 92

Propagate, propagation 4-5, 8, 12-13, 18, 20, 73, 80, 82, 88, 96, 98, 105, 110-111, 124, 126, 129, 133, 138, 141, 143, 148, 161, 195, 197, 206, 209, 313, 392, 434, 437-439, 464-465
PSF (Point Spread Function) 141-142, 154-157, 160, 168-170, 176, 182-185, 201, 206-208, 210-211, 214, 218-219, 241, 262, 273-274, 281-283, 366, 463, 465
Pushbroom collection 243, 357, 373
Pushbroom scanner... 241-242, 244-245, 290-292, 295, 298, 301, 351-352, 356, 387, 399-400, 404, 427, 455

Q

Quadrupole 33
Quanta 13, 128, 159, 163
Quantized energy 124
Quantum efficiency 171-174, 177, 204, 206-210, 216, 218, 220, 242, 262, 266, 274-275
Quantum mechanics 27-28, 30, 44, 46-48, 125
Quantum number 28-32, 34, 36, 38, 46
Quartz 22-25, 60, 150, 354, 412, 439
Quasi-persistent targets 57-58, 269-270

R

Radar... 2-4, 13, 15, 54, 100, 129, 131, 145-146, 155-156, 160, 240, 316, 402, 406, 426, 435, 437, 453, 463
Radar antenna pattern 154
Radiance 58, 70, 80-97, 114, 134-141, 157, 175, 180, 207-209, 211, 213, 216, 218, 251, 262, 266, 323, 327, 338, 340, 344, 398, 404, 410-411, 414-415, 420-421, 432, 437, 442, 447
Radians 77, 107, 143, 344, 356, 363, 370
Radiant energy 22, 25, 43, 58, 70, 80, 87, 286
Radiation constants 17
Radiative signature 58, 264
Radioactivity 96-97, 452
Radiological (intelligence) 423, 452
Radiometer 73, 88, 337
Radiometric calibration 214, 275, 283
Radiometric quantities 58, 73-74, 80-81, 85, 87-88, 98-99, 336
Radiometry 1, 22, 73-74, 77, 80, 92-93, 96, 98, 138, 141, 206, 344, 464-465
Raman scattering 129, 427-428
Random (polarization) 62, 64, 435-439
Range (to target) ... 73, 100-101, 106, 146, 180, 190, 230, 285
Rayleigh criterion 133, 182-185, 350, 369, 377
Rayleigh scattering 128-129, 131, 426
Rayleigh-Jeans Limit 21
RCS (Radar Cross Section) 54, 155
Readout time 179, 248, 279
Receiving area 90
Recombination 172, 217
"Red spike" 42, 251

Reflected energy 69-70, 73, 433, 436
Reflection... 12-13,
    22, 53-54, 59-62, 64-70, 85, 95, 138-139, 143, 149-153,
    172, 193, 197-198, 200-201, 209, 214, 313, 337, 343,
    359, 368, 412, 431-434, 436-437, 440-441, 447
Reflective signature.. 61, 152
Reflectivity, reflectance 26, 54, 56, 60-61,
    63-65, 67-71, 87, 95, 138, 151, 153, 201-203, 206, 252,
    299-300, 305-306, 323-325, 328, 336, 341, 343, 377,
    393, 399-401, 405, 411-412, 414-415, 432-437, 441,
    447-448, 463
    of ice & water 323-324, 432
    of metals.. 152, 434
    of minerals 250, 334, 424
    of paints & pigments 66-67, 337, 432, 434
    of plants 252
    of roofing materials 337
    of snow & water 337
    of soil backgrounds.. 63
Reflectivity Distribution Function (also see BRDF) ......
    54, 65, 67-70, 432-434, 436, 446
Refraction... 12-13, 59-62,
    98, 101, 105, 134-135, 143, 150-151, 153, 172, 197-198,
    352-353, 375-376, 381, 435, 439
Requirements 6-8, 22, 27, 36,
    54, 58, 124, 161, 183, 185, 194, 214, 228, 235, 237, 240,
    250, 254, 278, 291, 322, 375, 393, 409, 447, 458, 465
Resistance... 28, 275
Resolution, spatial.. 14, 22,
    27, 55, 68, 82, 85-86, 92, 142, 144-145, 169, 181-182,
    184, 208, 214, 230, 235, 246, 250, 289-291, 299, 304,
    317-318, 336-337, 350, 369, 388-389, 425, 463
Resolution, spectral..
    24, 32, 36-37, 42, 46, 214, 250-251, 350-351, 355-358,
    363, 369-370, 372-374, 376-377, 379-380, 384-386,
    388, 413-414, 425, 465
Resolution, temporal... 213-214
Resolving power........... 201, 350-351, 355-356, 359, 369,
    373-374, 377, 379-380, 386-387
Responsivity 171-173, 176, 194, 208, 214
RF (Radio Frequency)......... 3-4, 9, 14-15, 129, 131, 160,
    196, 376
RMS (Root-mean-square) 114, 215, 273
ROC (Receiver Operating Characteristics).............. 402
Rotation......... 32, 34-35, 38, 40-41, 43-44, 48, 228, 231,
    240, 308, 361
Rotational energy...... 34-36, 38, 40-42, 44, 47, 126, 261
Rotational transitions 35-36, 42, 46-47, 49
ROYGBIV 15, 160
Rutherford "planetary model" 27, 29

S

SAM (Spectral Angle Mapper).......................... 399, 416

Sampling 5, 7-8, 43, 55, 57-58, 133, 166-170, 176-179,
    183-184, 186, 209, 214-215, 217, 220, 245-248, 250,
    252, 269, 271, 296, 305, 344-345, 350, 359, 373, 380,
    385, 387, 465
SAR (Synthetic Aperture Radar) 3, 145, 316, 453
SBIRS (Space-Based Infrared System) 85, 254-255
Scale height 113, 115, 120, 122, 125, 178, 258
Scanning sensor.......... 237, 242, 244, 248, 254-255, 291
Scintillation.. 124, 134-135
SEBASS (Spatially Enhanced Broadband Array
Spectrograph System) 413
Selection rules 35-36, 40
Selective radiation 17, 43, 54, 59, 260, 464
Self-radiance (atmosphere) 136-137
Semiconductor 73, 163-164, 166, 172, 275
Sensitivity.... 171, 220, 242, 250, 255-256, 263, 269, 317,
    330, 425, 430
Sensor artifacts.. 273
Shadowing 300, 346
Short wavelength cutoff... 149
Sidelobes... 155
Sidereal time-keeping 232
SIGINT (Signals Intelligence)................................ 3, 160
Signature based detection . 396, 399-402, 406, 408, 416
Signature(s) 3-5, 7, 9, 23-24, 29, 30-31,
    34, 36, 38, 40-42, 46, 48-49, 53-54, 57-59, 61, 63, 73,
    96, 141, 152, 159, 176-178, 213, 242, 254-257, 259-261,
    264, 268-272, 276-279, 281, 283, 285-286, 305, 339,
    396, 399-402, 404, 406, 408, 416, 434, 442, 459-460,
    464-465
Silicon detectors.................................. 288, 291, 295, 392
Sky 56, 76-77, 80, 87, 93, 123, 131-132, 137, 175, 228,
    232, 263, 336, 340-341, 374, 437-440, 447-448,
Slant path 122, 125, 187-188, 343
Slant viewing 121, 123
Small solid angle approximation 77-78
SMF (Spectral Matched Filters)........ 306, 400-402, 416,
    422-423
Smooth surface 61, 65, 432-437, 441, 447
Snell's Law 59, 62, 134, 198-199, 352, 376, 379
SNR, S/R (Signal to Noise Ratio) 173-174, 215, 218-221,
    242, 256, 262-263, 266, 276, 351
Soils & minerals 2, 22, 63, 71, 73, 96, 117, 252, 286, 299,
    302, 322, 336-337, 396, 405, 410-412, 415, 462-463
Solar spectrum 31, 199
Solid angle...... 67, 70, 73, 76-79, 81, 83-84, 87-89, 91-92,
    134, 156, 186-187, 218, 351, 357, 372
Solid angle approximation 78
SONAR (SOund Navigation and Ranging) ... 4, 98, 316
Spatial resolution 14, 22,
    27, 55, 68, 82, 85-86, 92, 142, 144-145, 169, 181-182,
    184, 208, 214, 230, 235, 246, 250, 289-291, 299, 304,
    317-318, 336-337, 350, 369, 388-389, 425, 463
Spatial sampling..... 43, 166, 168-170, 176, 181, 186, 465
Spectral anomaly detection 397, 406

Spectral dispersion 322, 350, 359, 373, 380, 387, 465
Spectral intensity 58, 88, 206, 211-213, 262, 273, 283, 345
Spectral radiance 58, 87-88, 138, 175, 213, 398, 410-411, 415, 420-421
Spectral resolution..
23, 32, 36-37, 42, 46, 214, 250-251, 350-351, 355-358, 363, 369-370, 372-374, 376-377, 379-380, 384-386, 388, 413-414, 425, 465
Spectral sampling 58, 237, 250, 252, 350, 359, 373, 380, 387
Spectrometer ....
23, 88, 153-154, 250, 326, 349-350, 354-355, 357-359, 363, 368-369, 372-376, 378-380, 382, 387-388, 392, 399, 407-408, 413, 423, 425-426, 463
Spectrum (of light) 14
Specular reflection . 59, 61, 64-65, 67-68, 343, 368, 433, 436-437, 447
Spring model 33-34
Standard atmosphere 110, 112, 126-127, 132, 261
Staring sensor 237, 240, 242, 247-248, 255, 269, 271, 288-291, 375-376
State populations 47-48
State vector 281
Steady state.... 16-18, 22, 25-26, 43-46, 82, 86, 115, 264, 268, 339-342
Stefan-Boltzmann constant 22
Steradians... 76-78, 84, 256, 351
Stokes parameters... 441-442
Stray light 216
Sun Synchronous Orbit 230, 293
Support to Military Operations (SMO) 6, 451-452
Suppression........... 219, 276-278, 307-308, 398, 415, 465
Surface (properties) 23, 444
Surface normal..................................... 68, 78-79, 83, 437
Surface temperatures 139, 321, 323-324, 326, 328, 333-338, 343, 410, 420, 462
SWIR (Shortwave Infrared)...
15, 20-21, 34, 41-42, 49, 126, 150, 164, 250, 252, 268, 287, 291, 294, 299, 306-308, 307, 310, 318, 322, 326, 328, 337, 343, 350, 354, 375, 391-392, 404, 407, 409, 413-417, 444, 446-448, 457
Symmetric molecules... 32-33
Synthetic aperture 3, 145-146, 316, 453

T

Target spectral matching..................................... 306, 319
Target zenith angle .. 60, 69-70, 78-79, 83, 122, 125-126, 188-190, 239
TCPED (Tasking-Collection-Processing-Exploitation-Dissemination) 6
Telescope 110, 123, 141, 145, 148-149, 152, 155, 160, 175, 204, 216, 236, 275, 322, 463

Temperature 3, 5, 11, 14-26, 29, 31, 34, 43-48, 50-51, 60, 82, 86, 95, 98, 100, 110-116, 118, 123, 134-136, 139, 155, 173, 176, 194, 202, 260-261, 268, 273, 275, 284, 321, 323-331, 333-343, 355, 409-411, 413-415, 420-422, 425, 434, 455-456, 462, 464-465
Temperature scales 14, 16, 114, 355
Temporal characteristics 4-5, 56-57, 88, 213
Temporal resolution 213-214
Temporal sampling 5, 7, 133, 166, 176, 237, 247-248, 269
Terrain categorization 2 99, 408, 411, 446, 457-458
Thermal detector 161, 173
Thermal imaging.............................. 328, 331-332, 338
Thermal imaging applications 333
Thin film......... 151-153, 193, 197-203, 289, 349, 376, 439
Thin film interference 152, 194, 202, 375, 378-379
Thin lens 142-143
Threshold...... 7-8, 174, 214-215, 253, 256, 277, 301-302, 394-395, 398, 402-403
Time over target.. 57, 240, 253
TIR (Thermal infrared).... 1, 15, 116, 287, 321, 328-334, 336, 338, 342, 391, 409-410, 413, 432, 435, 448
Trace gases 110-111, 116, 133, 136
Trajectory... 56, 226, 254, 277
Transient target................................... 179, 253, 264, 267
Transition (quantum leap) .. 28-29, 31-32, 34-36, 38-39, 41, 46-48, 96, 264, 427-428
Transition probability... 47
Transmission function 60, 122, 175, 204, 206-207
Transparent material 60
Transverse electric (polarization) 62
Transverse magnetic (polarization) 62
Triatomic molecules... 37-42, 44
TRIPS (Tactical Realtime Image Processing Spectrometer).. 392-393, 399
True color map...297-299, 306, 319

U

UAV (Unmanned Aerial Vehicle)..... 222, 389, 425, 455
Ultraspectral... 153
Underground facilities... 461
US Standard Atmosphere Models 110, 112
UV (Ultraviolet).... 15, 18, 31, 37, 111, 133, 160, 162-163, 250, 264-265, 430

V

Vacuum 4, 12, 60, 124, 162, 464
Vegetation 73, 240, 251-252, 286, 300, 302-303, 306, 307, 310, 444, 457-458, 462
Vertical transmission................................. 126, 132, 137
Vibrating bonds 33-34
Vibrational energy................................... 33, 38-41, 44-45

Vibrational quantum number 38
Vibrational transitions 34-36, 42, 47
Vibrotational energy 36, 126, 261
Vibrotational transitions 46, 49
VIS (Visible band) 15
Visibility 121, 251
Vis-Near 373

W

Warfighter (satellite) 407-408
Water vapor 15, 37, 49, 110-112, 115-116, 121, 126-127, 152, 260, 325-327, 354, 422-423, 429
Wave optics 27, 208
Wavenumber 14, 138, 326-327, 382, 384-385
Wedge imaging spectrometer 375
Wet aerosols 116
Whiskbroom scan 244-245, 290, 375, 413
Wien limit 21
Wien's Displacement Law 19-20, 22, 25, 96
Windows (atmospheric) 126, 149, 209, 250, 325-327, 464
Work function 161-163

X

X-ray 15, 31, 123, 160, 264, 335

Y

Young's double slit interference 360-361, 364

Z

Zenith 69, 122, 186, 206-207, 228, 437-439
Zenith angle 60, 69-70, 78-79, 83, 122, 125-126, 188-190, 239, 437-438

BOOKS/TEXTS

Allen, L. and Eberly, J.H., Optical Resonance and Two-Level Atoms, Dover Publications, Inc., New York, 1987.

Banwell, C.N., Fundamentals of Molecular Spectroscopy (Second Edition), McGraw-Hill Book Company (UK) Limited, London, 1972.

Bate, Roger R., Mueller, Donald D., and White, Jerry E., Fundamentals of Astrodynamics, Dover Publications, Inc., 180 Varick Street, New York, NY 10014, 1971.

Berman, Arthur I., The Physical Principals of Astronautics, Fundamentals of Dynamical Astronomy and Space Flight, John Wiley & Sons, Inc., New York, 1961.

Boyd, Robert W., Radiometry and the Detection of Optical Radiation, John Wiley & Sons, New York, 1983.

Bracewell, Ron, The Fourier Transform and Its Applications, McGraw-Hill, New York, NY, 1965.

Buil, Christian, CCD Astronomy: Construction and Use of an Astronomical CCD Camera, Willmann-Bell, Inc., Richmond, VA, 1991.

Condon, E.U. and Shortly, G.H., The Theory of Atomic Spectra, Cambridge University Press, Cambridge, England, 1935.

Cooper, Paul W. Explosives Engineering, VHC Publishers, Inc., 333 7th Avenue, New York, NY 10001, 1996.

Dereniak, Eustance L. and Crowe, Devon G., Optical Radiation Detectors, John Wiley & Sons, New York, 1984.

Ditchburn, R.W., Light, Vol. 1 (Second Edition), John Wiley-Interscience, New York, NY, 1963.

Dunteman, George H., Introduction to Multivariate Statistics, SAGE Publications, 275 South Beverly Drive, Beverly Hills, CA 90212, 1984.

Eisberg, Robert and Resnick, Robert, Quantum Physics of Atoms, Molecules, Solids, Nuclei, and Particles (Second Edition), John Wiley & Sons, New York, 1985.

Fickett, Wildon and Davis, William C., Detonation: Theory and Experiment, Dover Publications, Inc., 31 East 2nd Street, Mineola, NY 11501, 1979.

Fiete, Robert D., Modeling the Imaging Chain of Digital Cameras, SPIE Press, Bellingham, WA, 2010.

-----, Formation of a Digital Image, SPIE Press, Bellingham, WA, 2012.

Gasiorowicz, Stephen, The Structure of Matter: A Survey of Modern Physics, Addison-Wesley Publishing Company, Reading, MA, 1979.

Goody, R.M. and Yung, Y.L., Atmospheric Radiation: Theoretical Basis (Second Edition), Oxford University Press, New York, 1989.

Griffiths, Peter R. and de Haseth, James A., Fourier Transform Infrared Spectrometry (Second Edition), John Wiley & Sons, New York, 2007.

Hecht, Eugene and Zajac, Alfred, Optics, Addison-Wesley Publishing Company, Reading, MA, 1974.

Herzberg, Gerhard, Atomic Spectra and Atomic Structure, Dover Publications, New York, 1944.

Hill, Philip G. and Peterson, Carl R., Mechanics and Thermodynamics of Propulsion, Addison-Wesley Publishing Company, Reading, MA, 1965.

Holder, Bill, Unmanned Air Vehicles, An Illustrated Study of UAVs, Schiffer Publishing Ltd., 4880 Lower Valley Road, Atglen, PA 19310, 2001.

Horowitz, Paul and Hill, Winfield, The Art of Electronics (Second Edition), Cambridge University Press, Cambridge, 1989.

Houghton, John T., The Physics of Atmospheres (Second Edition), Cambridge University Press, Cambridge, 1986.

Hovanessian, S.A., Introduction to Sensor Systems, Artech House, Inc., 685 Canton Street, Norwood, MA 02062, 1988.

Humble, Ronald W., Henry, Gary N., and Larson, Wiley J., Space Propulsion Analysis and Design, The McGraw-Hill Companies, Inc., Primis Custom Publishing, New York, 1995.

Jenkins, Francis A. and White, Harvey E., Fundamentals of Optics (Fourth Edition), McGraw-Hill Book Company, New York, NY, 1976.

Jensen, John R., Remote Sensing of the Environment: An Earth Resource Perspective (Second Edition), Pearson Prentice Hall, Pearson Education, Inc., Upper Saddle River, NJ 07458, 2007.

Keyes, Robert J. (Ed.), Topics in Applied Physics, Vol. 19: Optical And Infrared Detectors (Second Corrected and Updated Edition), Springer-Verlag, Berlin, 1980.

Kitchin, Christopher R., Astrophysical Techniques (Second Edition), Adam Hilger (IOP Publishing Ltd), Bristol, England, 1991.

Klein, Miles V., Optics, John Wiley & Sons, New York, 1970.

Malmstadt, Howard V., Enke, Christie G., and Crouch, Stanley R., Electronic Measurements for Scientists, W. A. Benjamin, Inc, Menlo Park, CA, 1974.

Manly, Bryan F.J., Multivariate Statistical Methods, A Primer, Chapman and Hall/CRC, CRC Press LLC, 2000 N.W. Corporate Blvd., Boca Raton, FL 33431, 2005.

Milman, Andrew S., Mathematical Principles of Remote Sensing, Sleeping Bear Press, 121 South Main Street, P.O. Box 20, Chelsea, MI 48118, 1999.

Mitchell, Allan C.G., and Zemansky, Mark W., Resonance Radiation and Excited Atoms, The Macmillan Company, New York, 1934.

Olsen, Richard C., Remote Sensing from Air and Space, SPIE, Bellingham, WA 98227, 2007.

O'Shea, Donald C., Elements of Modern Optical Design, John Wiley & Sons, New York, 1985.

Petty, Grant W., A First Course in Atmospheric Radiation, Sundog Publishing, 1360 Regent Street, Madison, WI 53715, 2004.

Roy, Archie E., The Foundations of Astrodynamics, The Macmillan Company, New York, 1965.

Rutten, Harrie G.J., and van Venrooij, Martin A.M., Telescope Optics, A Comprehensive Manual for Amateur Astronomers, Willmann-Bell, Inc., P.O. Box 35025, Richmond, VA 23235, 1988.

Saleh, Bahaa E.A. and Teich, Malvin Carl, Fundamentals of Photonics, John Wiley & Sons, New York, 1991.

Schanda, Erwin, Physical Fundamentals of Remote Sensing, Springer-Verlag, Berlin, Heidelberg, 1986.

Sellers, Jerry Jon, Understanding Space: An Introduction to Astronautics (Third Edition), The McGraw-Hill Companies, Inc., New York, 2005.

Simmons, F.S., Rocket Exhaust Plume Phenomenology, The Aerospace Press, El Segundo, CA, 2000.

Slater, Philip N., Remote Sensing: Optics and Optical Systems, Addison-Wesley Publishing Company, Reading, MA, 1980.

Smith, Gregory Hallock, Practical Computer-Aided Lens Design, Willman-Bell, Inc., Richmond, VA, 1998.

Steinfeld, Jeffrey I., Molecules and Radiation, An Introduction to Modern Molecular Spectroscopy (Second Edition), The MIT Press, Cambridge, MA, 1985.

Taylor, Jack H., Radiation Exchange: An Introduction, Academic Press, Inc., 1250 Sixth Avenue, San Diego, CA, 92101, 1990.

Uman, Martin A., Lightning, Dover Publications, Inc., 31 East 2nd Street, Mineola, NY, 1969.

van de Hulst, H. C., Light Scattering by Small Particles, Dover Publications Inc., New York, 1981.

Wertz, James R. and Larson, Wiley J. (Eds.), Space Mission Analysis and Design (Third Edition), Microcosm Press, 401 Coral Circle, El Segundo, CA 90245, 1999.

Wyatt, Clair L., Radiometric System Design, Macmillan Publishing Company, 866 Third Avenue, New York, NY 10022, 1987.

ELECTRONIC MEDIA

Liddiard, Kevin, "Developing the Next Generation of Passive Infrared Security Sensors," SPIE Newsroom.

HANDBOOKS

Accetta, Joseph S., and Schumaker, David L. (Eds), The Infrared and Electro-Optical Systems Handbook (seven volumes), Infrared Information and Analysis (IRIA) Center and SPIE Optical Engineering Press, 1993. (Defense Technical Information Center, DTIC-DF, Cameron Station, Alexandria, Virginia 22304-6145, now located 8725 John J. Kingman Road, Suite 0944, Fort Belvoir, VA 22060-6218).

Augustine, H., et al., Tactical Missile Signatures Measurement Standards Handbook, Environmental Research Institute of Michigan, P.O. Box 134001, Ann Arbor, MI 48113, 1997. (Joint Test Coordination Office, 2001 North Beauregard, Suite 800, Alexandria, VA, 22311.) [Distribution authorized to U.S. Government Agencies and their contractors (Critical Technologies).].

Barter, Nevill J. (Ed.), TRW Space Data (Fourth Edition), TRW Space & Technology Group, Redondo Beach, CA, 1992.

Bergmann, Joan, Bird, Cathrine, and Tyron, Heidi, Atmospheric Slant Path Analysis Model (ASPAM) Quick Reference Users Handbook, AFCCC/UH-96/002, Air Force Combat Climatology Center, 859 Buchanan Street, Scott Air Force Base, IL 62225, 1996.

Engineering Design Handbook: Explosives Series, Properties of Explosives of Military Interest, AMCP 706-177, HQ US Army Materiel Command, Washington, DC, 29 Jan 1971.

Frederick, Richard, IR User's Handbook, FTD-SXO-G-110-90-Vol I, Foreign Technology Division, Air Force Systems Command, United States Air Force, Wright-Patterson Air Force Base, OH 45433, 1990.

Jursa, Adolph S. (Ed.), Handbook of Geophysics and the Space Environment, Air Force Geophysics Laboratory, Air Force Systems Command, United States Air Force, 1985. (ADA 167000, National Technical Information Service, 5285 Port Royal Road, Springfield, VA, 22161.)

MacGregor, Charles H. and Livingston, Lee H. (Eds.), Space Handbook (Eleventh Edition), Air University, Air Command and Staff College, Maxwell Air Force Base, AL, 1977.

Military Standardization Handbook: Optical Design, MIL-HDBK-141, Defense Supply Agency, Washington, DC, 1962.

Radio Corporation of America, Electro-Optical Handbook: A Compendium of Useful Information and Technical Data, Technical Series EOH-10, RCA Commercial Engineering, Harrison, NJ, 1968.

The Photonics Directory™, Book 3: The Photonics Design & Applications Handbook (39th Edition), Laurin Publishing Company, Inc., Berkshire Common, P.O. Box 4949, Pittsfield, MA 01202, 1993.

The Photonics Directory™, Book 4: The Photonics Dictionary (39th Edition), Laurin Publishing Company, Inc., Berkshire Common, P.O. Box 4949, Pittsfield, MA 01202, 1993.

Wolfe, William L. and Zissis, George J. (Eds.), The Infrared Handbook, The Infrared Information and Analysis (IRIA) Center, Environmental Research Institute of Michigan, 1978. (Office of Naval Research, Department of the Navy, Washington, DC).

MONOGRAPHS & PAPERS

Bielecki, Z., "Readout electronics for optical detectors," Opto-Electronics Review, 12(1), 129-137, 2004.

Einstein, A., "On the Quantum Theory of Radiation," Mitteilungen der Physikalischen Gesellschaft Zurich, 18, 1916. (Reprinted in: Holton, Gerald (Ed.), Sources of Quantum Mechanics, Classics of Science, Vol. 5, pp. 63-77, Dover Publications, Inc., New York).

Jellison, Gerard P., Mitchell, Herbert J., and Miller, David P., "Theory, Modeling, and Measurements of Gas Plumes," Proceedings of the SPIE Vol. 5093: Algorithms and Technologies for Multispectral, Hyperspectral, and Ultraspectral Imagery IX, 172 – 183, 2003.

Litwiller, Dave, "CCD vs. CMOS: Facts and Fiction," Photonics Spectra, Laurin Publishing Co., Inc., January 2001.

Lum, Zachary, "The Measure of MASINT," Journal of Electronic Defense, 43 – 48, August 1998.

Mutagi, R.N., "Understanding the sampling process," RF Design, 38 – 48, September 2004.

Nicodemus, Fred E., "Optical Resource Letter on Radiometry," Journal of the Optical Society of America, 59(3), 243-248, March 1969.

Nicodemus, Fred E., "Radiance," American Journal of Physics, 31(5), 368-377, May 1963.

----- (Ed.), Self-Study Manual on Optical Radiation Measurements: Part 1 – Concepts, Chapters 1 to 3, NBS Technical Note 910-1, US Department of Commerce, National Bureau of Standards, US Government Printing Office, Washington, DC, 1976.

----- (Ed.), Self-Study Manual on Optical Radiation Measurements: Part 1 – Concepts, Chapters 4 and 5, NBS Technical Note 910-2, US Department of Commerce, National Bureau of Standards, US Government Printing Office, Washington, DC, 1978.

----- (Ed.), Self-Study Manual on Optical Radiation Measurements: Part 1 – Concepts, Chapter 6, NBS Technical Note 910-3, US Department of Commerce, National Bureau of Standards, US Government Printing Office, Washington, DC, 1977.

----- (Ed.), Self-Study Manual on Optical Radiation Measurements: Part 1 – Concepts, Chapters 7, 8, and 9, NBS Technical Note 910-4, US Department of Commerce, National Bureau of Standards, US Government Printing Office, Washington, DC, 1979.

-----, Richmond, J.C., Hsia, J.J., Ginsberg, I.W., and Limperis, T., Geometrical Considerations and Nomenclature for Reflectance, NBS Monograph 160, US Department of Commerce, National Bureau of Standards, US Government Printing Office, Washington, DC, 1977.

Page, Chester H. and Vigoureux, Paul (Eds.), The International System of Units (SI), NBS Special Publication 330, US Department of Commerce,

National Bureau of Standards, US Government Printing Office, Washington, DC, 1974.

Palmer, James M. Practical Radiometry for Electrical Engineers and Applied Scientists, course notes for S.P.I.E. course "Practical Radiomentry," Los Angeles, CA, 1986.

Taylor, J.H., "Radiation Exchange," *Applied Optics*, 26(4), 619 – 626, 15 February 1987.

Thekaekara, Matthew P. (Ed.), The Solar Constant and the Solar Spectrum Measured from a Research Aircraft, NASA TR-R-351, Goddard Space Flight Center, National Aeronautics and Space Administration, Washington, DC, October 1970.

Thomas, Michael E. and Duncan, Donald D., Propagation in the Atmosphere, course notes for Applied Technology Institute, The Johns Hopkins University, Applied Physics Laboratory, Laurel, MD 20723, 1991.

Turman, B.N., "Detection of Lightning Superbolts," *Journal of Geophysical Research*, 82(18), 2566, June 20, 1977.

-----, "Analysis of Lightning Data from DMSP Satellite," *Journal of Geophysical Research*, 83(10), 5019, October 20, 1978.

Vatsia, Mishri L., Atmospheric Optical Environment, Research and Development Technical Report ECOM-7023, United States Army Electronics Command, Fort Monouth, NJ, 1972.

Welch, Ronald M., Cox, Stephen K., and Davis, John M., Solar Radiation and Clouds, American Meteorological Society, 45 Beacon St., Boston, MA 02108, 1980.

Wolfe, William, "Ruminations on Radiometry," *SPIE's OE Magazine*, pp. 33-36, February 2001.

PAMPHLETS

A Fifty Year Commemorative History of Long Range Detection: The Creation, Development, and Operation of the United States Atomic Energy Detection System, HQ Air Force Technical Applications Center, Patrick Air Force Base, FL, September 1997.

Ballistic and Cruise Missile Threat, NAIC-103100985-00, National Air Intelligence Center, Wright-Patterson Air Force Base, OH 45433, 2000.

Ballistic and Cruise Missile Threat, NAIC-1021-0985-03, National Air & Space Intelligence Center, Wright-Patterson Air Force Base, OH 45433, 2003.

SOFTWARE

ENVITM™ (Environment for Visualizing Images). Developed, maintained, and licensed by ITT Exelis Visual Information Solutions, 1650 Tysons Blvd., Suite 1700, McLean, VA 22102 (http://www.exelisvis.com/).

ERDAS IMAGINETM™. Maintained and licensed by Intergraph Corporation, 19 Interpro Road, Madison, AL 35758 (http://geospatial.intergraph.com/Homepage.aspx).

HydroLight. Developed, maintained, and licensed by Sequoia Scientific, Inc., 2700 Richards Road, Suite 107, Bellevue, WA 98005 (http://www.sequoiasci.com/).

LEEDR (Laser Environmental Effects Definition and Reference). Developed, maintained, and distributed by the Air Force Institute of Technology (AFIT)/ENP Center for Directed Energy, 2950 Hobson Way, Building 640, Wright-Patterson AFB OH 45433-7765 (http://www.afit.edu/en/DE/leedrproducts.cfm). [Distribution authorized to U.S. Government Agencies and their contractors.].

MODTRAN™. Code development and maintenance by Spectral Sciences, Inc., 4 Fourth Avenue, Burlington, MA 01803 (http://www.spectral.com/), and single-user licenses administered by Ontar Corporation, 9 Village Way, North Andover, MA 01845 (http://www.ontar.com/).

Opticks (previously known as COSMEC and COMET). Developed and maintained by the National Air and Space Intelligence Center and Ball Aerospace. Distributed as freeware (http://opticks.org/confluence/display/Welcome+to+Opticks).

STK (System Tool Kit®). Software to model, analyze, and visualize space, defense, and intelligence systems by Analytical Graphics, Inc. (AGI), 220 Valley Creek Blvd, Exton, PA 19341 (http://www.agi.com/).

AUTHOR BIOGRAPHIES

Howard Evans, PhD

Dr. Howard Evans is a Principal Member of the Research Staff at Riverside Research. A 23-year veteran of the US Air Force, Dr. Evans understands the necessity for near real-time, reliable operational intelligence from his days as a combat aircrew member in the Southeast Asian, European, and Korean theaters of operation. During his assignment as Acting Director for Measurement and Signature Intelligence (MASINT) Data Exploitation at the National Air and Space Intelligence Center (NASIC), he assisted in streamlining reporting to the warfighter during Desert Storm. Dr. Evans has been a frequent contributor to the Military Sensing Symposia, notably in the areas of sensor calibration and transient event phenomenology, with major contributions to the theories of monocular passive ranging and asynchronous undersampling signature reconstruction. His teaching experience spans more than thirty years, serving on the physics faculties of the US Air Force Academy, Air Force Institute of Technology (AFIT), and Wright State University. Dr. Evans developed and instructed the Advanced Geospatial Intelligence Infrared/Synthetic Aperture Radar Certificate Program, formerly the MASINT Certificate Program, at AFIT from 2002-2013. He is a principal developer of Advanced Technical Intelligence certification curricula for Dayton area colleges and universities.

James Lange, PhD

Dr. James Lange, a Principal Member of the Research Staff at Riverside Research, has over 45 years of professional experience involving remote sensing techniques, sensors, and data analysis and exploitation. These sensing applications include surveillance, reconnaissance, and targeting from various airborne and satellite platforms using sensors in the ultraviolet, visible, and infrared, utilizing passive and active techniques. His most recent efforts emphasize multispectral and hyperspectral sensing in the visible through thermal infrared, broadband thermal imaging phenomenology and analysis, and polarimetric imaging phenomenology and analysis. Dr. Lange is experienced in mission requirement evaluation, investigations for initial sensor feasibility assessment, sensor design, algorithm evaluation, data analysis, sensor end-to-end performance prediction as well as the preparation and presentation of advocacy and training materials. At AFIT,  he developed seven new courses for three new academic programs, taught undergraduate and graduate level courses for over 18 years, and advised 32 MS theses in the aforementioned areas. Dr. Lange developed and instructed the Advanced Geospatial Intelligence Infrared/Synthetic Aperture Radar certificate program, formerly the MASINT Certificate Program, at AFIT from 2002-2013. Recently, he has developed and taught courses for Dayton area colleges and universities.

James Schmitz, PhD

Dr. James Schmitz is a subject matter expert in MASINT and Geospatial Intelligence (GEOINT) Tasking, Collection, Processing, Exploitation, and Dissemination. He advises and assists the US Government in the development, execution, and transition of cutting-edge GEOINT research and development for wide area surveillance sensors. His thesis and dissertation both focused on the application of "Dual-Surface Magnetic- and Electric-Field Integral Equations for Bodies of Revolution in Electromagnetic Scattering." In addition, Dr. Schmitz concentrated over seven years on electromagnetic scattering theory and radiation modeling techniques at the Air Force Research Laboratory (AFRL). He also supported AFRL, as well as the Defense Advanced Research Projects Agency (DARPA), in the development and evaluation of algorithms for tracking, identification, and automatic target recognition systems using radar and electro-optical sensors. As an Adjunct Instructor at the NGA College, Dr. Schmitz assisted in the development of the Overhead Persistent Infrared 111 course. He instructed the Advanced Geospatial Intelligence Infrared/Synthetic Aperture Radar certificate program at AFIT from 2012-2013. Dr. Schmitz currently has over 25 technical publications.